The Minor Prophets

A COMMENTARY

EXPLANATORY AND PRACTICAL

BY

E. B. PUSEY, D.D.

VOLUME I

HOSEA, JOEL, AMOS, OBADIAH AND JONAH

BAKER BOOK HOUSE
Grand Rapids, Michigan

Library of Congress Catalog Card Number: 55-11418

ISBN: 0-8010-0573-6

First Printing, September 1950
Second Printing, November 1953
Third Printing, August 1956
Fourth Printing, October 1958
Fifth Printing, May 1961
Sixth Printing, February 1963
Seventh Printing, September 1965
Eighth Printing, September 1967
Ninth Printing, April 1970
Tenth Printing, April 1972

PHOTOLITHOPRINTED BY CUSHING - MALLOY, INC.
ANN ARBOR, MICHIGAN, UNITED STATES OF AMERICA
1972

CONTENTS.

3

INTRODUCTORY STATEMENT

ON THE

PRINCIPLES AND OBJECT

OF

THE COMMENTARY.

THE object of the following pages is to evolve some portion of the meaning of the Word of God. In regard to the literal meaning of the sacred text, I have given that which, after a matured study spread over more than thirty years, I believe to be the true, or, in some cases, the more probable only. In so doing, I have purposely avoided all show of learning or embarrassing discussion, which belong to the dictionary or grammar rather than to a commentary on Holy Scripture. Where it seemed to me necessary, on some unestablished point, to set down in some measure, the grounds of the rendering of any word or phrase, I have indicated it very briefly in the lower margin[a]. I hoped, in this way, to make it intelligible to those acquainted with the sacred language, without interrupting the development of the meaning of the text, which presupposes a knowledge of the verbal meaning. Still less have I thought the discussion of different renderings of ancient Versions suited to a commentary of this sort. As soon as

one is satisfied that any given rendering of an ancient version does not correctly represent the Hebrew original, the question how the translators came so to render it, by what misreading or mishearing, or guess, or paraphrase, belongs to a history of that Version, not to the explanation of the sacred original. Still more distracting is a discussion of the various expositions of modern commentators, or an enumeration of names, often of no weight, who adhere to one or the other rendering, or perhaps originated some crotchet of their own. These things, which so often fill modern commentaries, have a show of learning, but embarrass rather than aid a reader of Holy Scripture. I have myself examined carefully every commentator, likely or unlikely to contribute any thing to the understanding of the sacred text; and, if I have been able to gain little from modern German commentaries, (except such as Tholuck, Hengstenberg, Keil, Delitzsch, and Hävernick) it is not that I have not sifted them to the best of the

---

[a] As time went on, and the use and abuse of Hebrew increased, I increased the remarks on the Hebrew in the lower margin, as I hoped might

be useful to those who had some knowledge of Hebrew, without distracting those who had not. 1877.

ability which God gave me. Even Luther said of his adherents, that they were like Solomon's fleet; some brought back gold and silver; but the younger, peacocks and apes. On the other hand, it has been pleasurable to give (at times somewhat condensed) the expositions of Pococke, extracted from the folio, in which, for the most part, they lie entombed amid the heaps of other explanations which his learning brought together. Else it has been my desire to use what learning of this sort I have, in these many years, acquired, to save a student from useless balancing of renderings, which I believe that no one, not under a prejudice, would adopt.

If, in the main, I have adhered to the English Version, it has been from the conviction that our translators were in the right. They had most of the helps for understanding Hebrew, which we have, the same traditional knowledge from the ancient Versions, Jewish commentators or lexicographers or grammarians, (with the exception of the Jewish-Arabic school only,) as well as the study of the Hebrew Scriptures themselves; and they used those aids with more mature and even judgment than has mostly been employed in the subsequent period. Hebrew criticism has now escaped[b], for the most part, from the arbitrariness, which detected a various reading in any variation of a single old Version, or in the error of some small fraction of MSS., which disfigured the commentaries of Lowth, Newcome, and Blayney. But the comparison of the cognate dialects opened for the time an unlimited licence of innovation. Every principle of interpretation, every

rule of language, was violated. The Bible was misinterpreted with a wild recklessness, to which no other book was ever subjected. A subordinate meaning of some half-understood Arabic word was always at hand to remove whatever any one misliked. Now, the manifoldness of this reign of misrule has subsided. But interpretations as arbitrary as any which have perished still hold their sway, or from time to time emerge, and any revisal of the authorized Version of the O. T., until the precarious use of the dialects should be far more settled, would give us chaff for wheat, introducing an indefinite amount of error into the Word of God. In some places, in the following pages, I have put down what I thought an improvement of the Eng. Version; in others, I have marked, by the word, *or*, a rendering which I thought equally or more probable than that which our Translators adopted. Where I have said nothing, it has not been that I have been unaware of any other translation (for I have proved all), but that I thought the received Version most in accordance with the Hebrew, or at least the most probable. For the most part, I have pointed out simple things, which any one would see, who could read the Hebrew text, but which cannot mostly be preserved in a translation without a cumbrousness which would destroy its beauty and impressiveness.

The literal meaning of the words lies, of course, as the basis of any further developement of the whole meaning of each passage of Holy Scripture. Yet any thoughtful reader must have been struck by observing, how independent that meaning is of single words. The general

---

b Ewald re-opened a system of boundless licence which has been copied by his followers; only, instead of drawing from some mistake or paraphrase of an ancient version, such draw from their own imagination. It comes to this, "Had I been the prophet, I would have written so and so." As the pious and original Claudius pictures the commentators on the Gospels in his day,

"There crossed my mind a random thought:
Had I been Christ, so had *I* taught."

It is very piteous, that a mind, with such rare grammatical gifts, which, at 19, laid the foundation of scientific study of Hebrew grammar, should, by over-confidence in self, have become so misled and misleading. 1877.

meaning remains the same, even amid much variation of single words. This is apparent in the passages which the Apostles quote from the LXX, where it is not an exact translation of the Hebrew. The variation arising from any single word does not mostly extend beyond itself.

This is said, that I may not seem to have neglected the letter of Holy Scripture, because I have not set down what is now commonly found in books, which profess to give an explanation of that letter. My wish has been to give the results rather than the process by which they were arrived at; to exhibit the building, not the scaffolding. My ideal has been to explain or develop each word and sentence of Holy Scripture, and, when it should be required, the connection of verses, to leave nothing unexplained, as far as I could explain it; and if any verse should give occasion to enter upon any subject, historical, moral, doctrinal, òr devotional, to explain this, as far as the place required or suggested. Then, if any thoughtful writers with whom I am acquainted, and to whom most English readers have little or no access, have expanded the meaning of any text in a way which I thought would be useful to an English reader, I have translated them, placing them mostly at the end of the comment on each verse, so that the mind might rest upon them, and yet not be sensible of a break or a jar, in passing on to other thoughts in the following verse.

The nature of the subjects thus to be expanded must, of course, vary with the different books of Holy Scripture. The prophets are partly teachers of righteousness and rebukers of unrighteousness; partly they declared things then to come, a nearer and a more distant future, God's judgments on unrighteousness, whether of His own sinful people or of the nations who unrighteously executed God's righteous judgments upon them, and the everlasting righteousness which He willed to bring in through the Coming of Christ. Of these, the nearer future, by its fulfillment of their words, accredited to those who then would hear, the more distant; to us, (with the exception of those more lasting visitations, as on Nineveh and Babylon and God's former people, whose destructions or dispersion have lived on to the present day) the then more distant future, the prophecies as to Christ, which are before us in the Gospels, or of the Church among all nations, whose fulfillment is around us, accredit the earlier. The fulfillments of these prophecies, as they come before us in the several prophets, it lies within the design of the present work, God giving us strength, to vindicate against the unbelief, rife in the present day. Where this can be done without disturbing the interpretation of the Scripture itself, the answers may often be tacitly supplied for those who need them, in the course of that interpretation. Where a fuller discussion may be necessary, it will probably be placed in the Introduction to the several books.

To this employment, which I have had for many years at heart, but from which the various distresses of our times, and the duties which they have involved, have continually withheld me, I hope to consecrate the residue of the years and of the strength which God may give me. "Vitæ summa brevis spem vetat inchoare longam." The wonderful volume of the twelve prophets, "brief in words, mighty in meaning," and, if God continue my life, the Evangelical Prophet, are what I have specially reserved for myself. The New Testament except the Apocalypse, and most of the rest of the Old Testament, have been undertaken by friends whose names will be published, when the arrangement shall finally be completed^c. The Commentary on the Minor

---

^c It is useless to say, *how* these hopes, as to myself, or others have failed. God removed some, by

Prophets is in the course of being printed; the Commentary on S. Matthew is nearly ready for the press. Other portions are begun. But the object of all, who have been engaged in this work, is one and the same, to develop, as God shall enable us, the meaning of Holy Scripture out of Holy Scripture itself; to search in that deep mine and—not bring meanings into it, but—(Christ being our helper, for "the well is deep,") to bring such portions, as they may, of its meaning out of it; to exhibit to our people, truth side by side with the fountain, from which it is drawn; to enable them to see something more of its riches, than a passer-by or a careless reader sees upon its surface.

To this end, it is our purpose to use those more thoughtful writers of all times, who have professedly, or, as far as we know, incidentally developed the meaning of portions or texts of the sacred volume, men who understood Holy Scripture through that same Spirit by Whom it was written, to whom prayer, meditation, and a sanctified life laid open its meaning. For He, Who first gave to man the words of eternal life, still hides their meaning from those who are wise and prudent in their own eyes, and giveth wisdom to the simple. "Lord, to whom shall we go? Thou hast the words of

death, as my friend C. Marriott, that beautiful mind and ripe scholar, James Riddell of Balliol, and when he, at last, had accomplished his 16 years' labor of love for the memory of the Apostolic Bishop Wilson, the revered John Keble. Some thought the plan on too large a scale for them. I myself have only to thank God for enabling me to do the little I could do, praying Him to accept anything which He gave, and to forgive anything amiss for Jesus' sake. 1877.

CHRIST CHURCH,
EASTER, 1860.

eternal life." "The reading of the Scripture is the opening of Heaven." "In the words of God, we learn the Heart of God."

"O Eternal Truth, and True Love, and loving Light, our God and our All, enlighten our darkness by the brightness of Thy light; irradiate our minds by the splendor of holiness, that in Thy Light we may see light, that we, in turn, may enlighten others, and kindle them with the love of Thee. Open Thou our eyes, that we may see wondrous things out of Thy law, Who makest eloquent the minds and tongues of the slow of speech. To Thee, to Thy glory, to the good of Thy Church and people, may we labor, write, live. Thou hast said, Lord, to Thine Apostles and Prophets, their followers and interpreters, 'Ye are the salt of the earth; ye are the light of the world.' Thou hast said it, and, by saying it, hast done it. Grant to us, then, Lord, that we too, like them, may be preachers of heaven, sowers for eternity, that they who read, may, by the knowledge of Thy Scriptures, through the graveness and the weight of Thy promises and threats, despise the ensnaring entanglements of earth, and be kindled with the love of heavenly goods, and the effectual earnest longing for a blessed eternity. This be our one desire, this our prayer, to this may all our reading and writing and all our toil tend, that Thy Holy Name may be hallowed, Thy Holy Will be done, as in heaven, so in earth, Thy Holy kingdom of grace, glory, and endless bliss, where Thou wilt be all things in all, may come to us. Amen."

INTRODUCTION

TO

THE MINOR PROPHETS,

AND CHIEFLY TO

HOSEA.

THE TWELVE PROPHETS, at the head of whom Hosea has been placed, were called of old [a] "the lesser, or minor prophets," by reason of the smaller compass of their prophecies, not as though their prophecies were less important than those of the four greater prophets. Hosea, at least, must have exercised the prophetic office longer than any besides; he must have spoken as much and as often, in the Name of God. A prophecy of Micah and words of Joel are adopted by Isaiah; Jeremiah employs verses of Obadiah to denounce anew the punishment of Edom; a prophecy of Joel is expanded by Ezekiel. The "twelve" were the organs of important prophecy, as to their own people, or foreign nations, or as to Him Whom they looked for, our Lord. Now, since the first five were earlier than Isaiah, and next, in order of time, to the Prophetic Psalms of David, Solomon, Asaph and the sons of Korah, the revelations made to these lesser Prophets even ante-date those given through the four greater. The general out-pouring of the Spirit on all flesh and the Day of the Lord were first spoken of by Joel. Our resurrection in Christ on the 3d day; the inward graces which Christ should bestow on His Church in its perpetual union with Him; the entire victory over death and the grave; and the final conversion of Judah and Israel, were first prophesied by Hosea. When S. James wished to shew that the conversion of the Gentiles had been foretold by a prophet, he quoted a passage of Amos. "The twelve," as they begun, so they closed the cycle of those whom God employed to leave written prophecies. Yet God, Who willed that of all the earlier prophets, who prophesied from the time of Samuel to Elisha, no prophecy should remain, except the few words in the books of Kings, willed also, that little, in comparison, should be preserved, of what these later prophets spake in His Name. Their writings altogether are not equal in compass to those of the one prophet, Isaiah. And so, like the twelve Apostles, they were enrolled in one prophetic band; their writings, both in the Jewish [b] and Christian [c] Church, have been counted as one book; and, like the Apostles, they were called "the twelve [d]."

The earliest of this band followed very closely upon the ministry of Elijah and Elisha. Elisha, in his parting words [e], foretold to Joash the three victories whereby he recovered from Syria the cities of Israel which Hazael had taken from his father Jehoahaz. In the next reign, viz., that of Jeroboam II., there arose the first of that brilliant constellation of prophets, whose light

[a] S. Aug. de Civ. D. xviii. 29. "The Prophet Isaiah is not in the books of the 12 prophets who are therefore called minor, because their discourses are brief in comparison with those who are called 'greater' because they composed considerable volumes."

[b] The Jewish tradition ran, "our fathers made them one book, that they might not perish, for their littleness." Bava Bathra (c. l. f. 14. col. 2.) in Carpzov Intr. iii. p. 72. Josephus must so have counted them, since he counted all the books of the O. T., besides the five books of Moses and the Psalms and books of Solomon, as 13. c. Ap. i. 8. see Cosin. Hist. of the Canon § 25. [c] See Cosin. § 47. sqq.

[d] See Carpzov iii. 270. and Cosin.

[e] 2 K. xiii. 14. sqq. 25.

gleamed over the fall of Israel and Judah, shone in their captivity, and set at last, with the prediction of him, who should precede the rising of the Sun of Righteousness.

In the reign of Jeroboam II., Hosea, Amos, Jonah, prophesied in the kingdom of Israel. Joel was probably called at the same time to prophesy in Judah, and Obadiah to deliver his prophecy as to Edom; Isaiah, a few years later: Micah, we know, began his office in the following reign of Jotham, and then prophesied, together with Isaiah, to and in the reign of Hezekiah.

The order, then, of "the twelve" was probably, for the most part, an order of time. We know that the greater prophets are placed in that order, as also the three last of the twelve, Haggai, Zechariah, and Malachi. Of the five first, Hosea, Amos and Jonah were nearly contemporary; Joel was prior to Amos[f]; and of the four remaining, Micah and Nahum were later than Jonah, whom they succeed in order; Nahum refers to Jonah; Zephaniah quotes Habakkuk. It may be from an old Jewish tradition, that S. Jerome says[g], "know that those prophets, whose time is not prefixed in the title, prophesied under the same kings, as those other prophets, who are placed before them, and who have titles."

Hosea, the first of the twelve, must have prophesied during a period, as long as the ordinary life of man. For he prophesied (the title tells us) while Uzziah king of Judah and Jeroboam II., king of Israel, were both reigning, as also during the reigns of Jotham, Ahaz, and Hezekiah. But Uzziah survived Jeroboam, 26 years. Jotham and Ahaz reigned, each, 16 years. Thus we have already 58 years complete, without counting the years of Jeroboam, during which Hosea prophesied at the beginning of his office, or those of Hezekiah which elapsed before its close. But since the prophecy of Hosea is directed almost exclusively to Israel, it is not probable that the name of Jeroboam would alone have been selected for mention, unless Hosea had prophesied for some time during his reign. The house of Jehu, which sunk after the death of Jeroboam, was yet[h] standing, and in its full strength, when Hosea first prophesied. Its might apparently is contrasted with the comparative weakness of Judah[i]. On the other hand, the office of Hosea probably closed before the end of the 4th year of Hezekiah[k]. For in that year, B. C. 721, the judgment denounced by Hosea upon Samaria was fulfilled, and all his prophecy looks on to this event as yet to

come: the 13th chapter closes with the prophecy of the utter destruction of Samaria; and of the horrible cruelties which would befall her helpless ones. The last chapter alone winds up the long series of denunciations by a prediction of the future conversion of Israel. This chapter, however, is too closely connected with the preceding, to admit of its being a consolation after the captivity had begun. If then we suppose that Hosea prophesied during 2 years only of the reign of Hezekiah, and 10 of those in which the reigns of Jeroboam II. and Uzziah coincided, his ministry will have lasted 70 years. A long and heavy service for a soul full of love like his, mitigated only by his hope of the Coming of Christ, the final conversion of his people, and the victory over the grave! But the length is nothing incredible, since, about this time, Jehoiada "[l]did good in Israel both towards God and towards His House;" until he "was 130 years." The shortest duration of Hosea's office must have been some 65 years. But if God called him quite young to his office, he need but have lived about 95 years, whereas Anna the Prophetess served God in the temple with fasting and prayer night and day, after a widowhood probably of 84 years[m]; and S. John the Evangelist lived probably until 104 years; and S. Polycarp became a martyr, when he was about 104 years old, having served Christ for 86 years[n], and having, when 95, sailed from Asia to Italy. Almost in our own days, we have heard of 100 centenarians, deputed by a religious order who ate no animal food, to bear witness that their rule of life was not unhealthy. Not then the length of Hosea's life, but his endurance, was superhuman. So long did God will that His prophets should toil; so little fruit were they content to leave behind them. For these few chapters alone remain of a labour beyond the ordinary life of man. But they were content to have God for their exceeding great reward.

The time, during which Hosea prophesied, was the darkest period in the history of the kingdom of Israel. Jeroboam II. was almost the last king who ruled in it by the appointment of God. The promise of God to Jehu[o] in reward of his partial obedience, that his "[p]children of the fourth generation should sit on the throne of Israel," expired with Jeroboam's son, who reigned but for 6 months[q] after an anarchy of 11 years. The rest of Hosea's life was passed amid the decline of the kingdom of Israel. Politically all was anarchy or misrule; kings made their way to the throne through the murder of their pre-

[f] See Introd. to Joel.   [g] Præf. in duod. Proph.
[h] Ch. i. 4, 5.   [i] Ch. i. 7.
[k] 2 Kgs xviii. 9.   [l] 2 Chron. xxiv. 15.
[m] So S. Ambrose and others understand the words "a widow of about fourscore and four years;" (S. Luke ii. 37.) and it seems the most natural. If,

according to Jewish law and practice, she was married at 12, her widowhood, after "7 years" began when she was 19, and when she was permitted to see our Lord, she was 103.
[n] Ep. Eccl. Smyrn. in Eus. H. E. iv. 15.
[o] 2 Kgs x. 30.   [p] 2 K. xv. 8.   [q] See Ib. 10, 14, 25, 30.

decessors, and made way for their successors through their own[p]. Shallum slew Zechariah; Menahem slew Shallum; Pekah slew the son of Menahem; Hoshea slew Pekah. The whole kingdom of Israel was a military despotism, and, as in the Roman empire, those in command came to the throne. Baasha, Zimri, Omri, Jehu, Menahem, Pekah, held military office before they became kings[r]. Each usurper seems to have strengthened himself by a foreign alliance. At least, we find Baasha in league with Benhadad, king of Syria[s]; Ahab marrying Jezebel, daughter of a king of Tyre and Zidon[t]; Menahem giving Pul king of Assyria tribute, that he might "confirm the kingdom in his hand[u];" Pekah confederate with Rezin[v]. These alliances brought with them the corruptions of the Phœnician and Syrian idolatry, wherein murder and lust became acts of religion. Jehu also probably sent tribute to the king of Assyria, to secure to himself the throne which God had given him. The fact appears in the cuneiform inscriptions[w]; it falls in with the character of Jehu and his half-belief, using all means, human or divine, to establish his own end. In one and the same spirit, he destroyed the Baal-worshippers, as adherents of Ahab, retained the calf-worship, courted the ascetic Jonadab son of Rechab, spoke of the death of Jehoram as the fulfilment of prophecy, and sought help from the king of Assyria.

These irreligions had the more deadly sway, because they were countenanced by the corrupt worship, which Jeroboam I. had set up as the state religion, over against the worship at Jerusalem. To allow the people to go up to Jerusalem, as the centre of the worship of God, would have risked their

owning the line of David as the kings of God's appointment. To prevent this, Jeroboam set up a great system of rival worship. Himself a refugee in Egypt[x], he had there seen nature (i. e. what are God's workings in nature) worshiped under the form of the calf[y]. He adopted it, in the words in which Aaron had been overborne to sanction it, as the worship of the One True God under a visible form: "These be thy gods, O Israel, which brought thee up out of the land of Egypt[z]." With great human subtlety, he laid hold of Israel's love for idol-worship, and their reverence for their ancestors, and words which even Aaron had used, and sought to replace, by this symbol of God's working. His actual presence over the mercy-seat. Around this he gathered as much of the Mosaic ritual as he could. The Priests and Levites remaining faithful to God[a], he made others priests, not of the line of Aaron[b]. Then, while he gratified the love of idolatry, he decked it out with all the rest of the worship which God had appointed for Himself. He retained the feasts which God had appointed, the three great festivals[c], their solemn assemblies[d], the new moons and sabbaths[e]; and these last feasts were observed even by those, to whose covetousness the rest on the festival was a hindrance[f]. Every kind of sacrifice was retained, the daily sacrifice[g], the burnt-offering[h], the meal-offering[i], the drink-offering[j], thank-offerings[k], peace-offerings[h], free-will offerings[k], sin-offerings[l]. They had hymns and instrumental music[m]. They paid the tithes of the third year[n]; probably they gave the first fruits[o]; they had priests[p] and prophets[q] and temples[r]; the temple at Bethel was the king's chapel, the temple of the state[s]. The worship was maintained by the civil authority[t]. But all this

[r] Nadab was with the army besieging Gibbethon, when Baasha slew him (1 Kgs xv. 27.); Zimri was "captain of half the chariots of Elah son of Baasha" (Ib. xvi. 9.); "all Israel made Omri, the captain of the host, king over Israel in the camp" (Ib. 16.). Jehu seems to have been chief among the captains (2 Kgs ix. 5.). Menahem "went up from Tirzah" (the residence of the kings of Israel until Omri built Samaria) Ib. xvi. 14. Pekah was a captain of Remaliah (Ib. 25.).
[s] 1 Kgs xv. 19. [t] 1 Kgs xvi. 31. [u] 2 Kgs xv. 19.
[v] Is. vii. 1, 9, 16. 2 Chron. xxviii. 5, 6.
[w] Sir H. Rawlinson and Dr. Hincks separately decyphered the name "Jahua (יהוא) son of Khumri," as one of those whose tribute is recorded on the Black obelisk [probably of Shalmanubar,] now in the British Museum. In the same inscription Beth-Khumri i. e. house or city of Omri (ק for ע) occurs for Samaria. Jehu may be so named from his capital, or from supposed or claimed descent from Omri. See Layard Nin. and Bab. p. 613. Rawlins. Herod. i. 465. Dr. Hincks Dublin Univ. Mag. 1853. p. 426. Scripture ascribes to Jehu personal might (גבורה), but in his days Israel lost to Hazael all the country beyond Jordan. The attack of Hazael may have been the cause or the effect of his seeking help of Assyria.
[x] 1 Kgs xi. 40. xii. 2.
[y] Two living bulls, Apis and Mnevis, were wor-

shiped as symbols of Osiris and the sun at Memphis and Heliopolis. Diod. Sic. i. 21. Strabo xvii.
[z] Ex. xxxii. 4. 1 Kgs xii. 28. [a] 2 Chron. xi. 13-15.
[b] 1 Kgs xii. 31. "He made priests out of the lowest of the people," (lit. "the end of the people") should be rendered "from the whole of the people" [indiscriminately] "which were not of the sons of Levi."
[c] Hosea ii. 11. ix. 5. Amos v. 21. Jeroboam transferred, apparently, the feast of tabernacles from the 15th of the seventh month (Lev. xxiii. 34.) to the 15th of the eighth month (1 Kgs xii. 32, 33.)
[d] Amos v. 21. [e] Hosea ii. 11. [f] Amos viii. 5.
[g] Ib. iv. 4. [h] Ib. v. 22. [i] Hosea ix. 4. Amos v. 22.
[j] Hosea ix. 4. [k] Hosea v. 6, vi. 6, perhaps iv. 8.
[l] Amos iv. 5, and of this class generally, Hosea viii. 13.
[m] Amos v. 23. viii. 3. [n] Amos iv. 4.
[o] These were brought to Elisha (2 Kgs iv. 42.) from Baal-Shalisha in the mountainous country of Ephraim, where "the land of Shalisha" was, (1 Sam. ix. 4.) by one probably who could not own the calf-priests. The prophets acted as priests in the kingdom of Israel. 1 Kgs xviii. 36. 2 Kgs iv. 23.) Hence the mention of "altars of the Lord" in Israel also, 1 Kgs xviii. 30. xix. 20.
[p] 1 Kgs xii. 32. Hosea iv. 6, 9. v. 1. vi. 9. x. 5.
[q] Hosea iv. 5. ix. 7, 8.
[r] 1 Kgs xii. 31, 32. Hosea viii. 14.
[s] Amos vii. 13. [t] Hosea v. 11. xiii. 2.

outward shew was rotten at the core. God had forbidden man so to worship Him, nor was it He Who was worshiped at Bethel and Dan, though Jeroboam probably meant it. People, when they alter God's truth, alter more than they think for. Such is the lot of all heresy. Jeroboam probably meant that God should be worshiped under a symbol, and he brought in a worship, which was not, in truth, a worship of God at all. The calf was the symbol, not of the personal God, but of ever-renewed life, His continued vivifying of all which lives, and renewing of what decays. And so what was worshiped was not God, but much what men now call "nature." The calf was a symbol of "nature;" much as men say, "nature does this or that;" "nature makes man so and so;" "nature useth simplicity of means;" "nature provides," &c.; as if "nature were a sort of semi-deity," or creation were its own Creator. As men now profess to own God, and do own Him in the abstract, but talk of "nature," till they forget Him, or because they forget Him, so Jeroboam, who was a shrewd, practical, irreligious man, slipped into a worship of nature, while he thought, doubtless, he was doing honor to the Creator, and professing a belief in Him.

But they were those same workings in creation, which were worshiped by the neighboring heathen, in Baal and Ashtaroth ; only there the name of the Creator was altogether dropped. Yet it was but a step from one to the other. The calf was the immediate and often the sole object of worship. They "sacrificed to the calves[u];" "kissed the calves[v]," in token of worship ; swore by them as living gods[w]. They had literally "[x] changed their Glory [i. e. God] into the similitude of a bull which eateth hay." Calf-worship paved the way for those coarser and more cruel worships of nature, under the names of Baal and Ashtaroth, with all their abominations of consecrated child-sacrifices, and degrading or horrible sensuality. The worship of the calves led to sin. The heathen festival was one of unbridled licentiousness. The account of the calf-festival in the wilderness agrees too well with the heathen descriptions. The very least which can be inferred from the words " Aaron had made them naked to their shame before their enemies[y]," is an extreme relaxedness, on the borders of further sin.

And now in Hosea's time, these idolatries had yielded their full bitter fruits. The course of iniquity had been run. The stream had become darker and darker in its downward flow. Creature worship (as S. Paul points out[z]), was the parent of every sort of abomination ; and religion having become creature-worship, what God gave as the check to sin became its incentive. Every commandment of God was broken, and that, habitually. All was falsehood[a], adultery[b], bloodshedding[c]; deceit to God[d] produced faithlessness to man; excess[e] and luxury[f] were supplied by secret[g] or open robbery[h], oppression[i], false dealing[j], perversion of justice[k], grinding of the poor[l]. Blood was shed like water, until one stream met another[m], and overspread the land with one defiling deluge. Adultery was consecrated as an act of religion[n]. Those who were first in rank were first in excess. People and king vied in debauchery[o], and the sottish king joined and encouraged the freethinkers and blasphemers of his court[p]. The idolatrous priests loved and shared in the sins of the people[q] ; nay, they seem to have set themselves to intercept those on either side of Jordan, who would go to worship at Jerusalem, laying wait to murder them[r]. Corruption had spread throughout the whole land[s] ; even the places once sacred through God's revelations or other mercies to their forefathers, Bethel[t], Gilgal[u], Gilead[v], Mizpah[w], Shechem[x], were especial scenes of corruption or of sin. Every holy memory was effaced by present corruption. Could things be worse ? There was one aggravation more. Remonstrance was useless[y] ; the knowledge of God was wilfully rejected[z] ; the people hated rebuke[a] ; the more they were called, the more they refused[b]; they forbade their prophets to prophesy[c] ; and their false prophets hated God greatly[d]. All attempts to heal all this disease only shewed its incurableness[e].

Such was the condition of the people among whom Hosea had to prophesy for some 70 years. They themselves were not sensible of their decay[f], moral or political. They set themselves, in despite of the Prophet's warning, to prop up their strength by aid of the two heathen nations, Egypt or Assyria. In Assyria they chiefly trusted[g], and Assyria, he had to denounce to them, should carry them captive[h]; stragglers at least,

[u] 1 Kgs xii. 32. [v] Hosea xiii. 2. [w] Amos viii. 4.
[x] Ps. cvi. 20. [y] Ex. xxxii. 25. [z] Rom. i.
[a] Hosea iv. 1. vii. 1, 3.
[b] Ib. iv. 11. v. 3. 4. vii. 4. ix. 10. Amos ii. 7.
[c] Hosea v. 2. vi. 8. [d] Ib. iv. 2. x. 13. xi. 12.
[e] Ib. iv. 11. vii. 5. Amos iv. 1.
[f] Hosea iii. 15. iv. 4-6.
[g] Ib. iv. 2. vii. 1.
[h] Ib. vii. 1. [i] Ib. xii. 7. Amos iii. 9, 10. iv. 1. v. 11.
[j] Hosea xii. 7. Amos viii. 5.
[k] Hosea x. 4. Amos. ii. 6, 7. v. 7, 12. vi. 3, 12.
[l] Amos ii. 7. viii. 6. [m] Hosea iv. 2.

[n] See on iv. 14. [o] Hosea vii. 5. [p] Ib. vii. 5.
[q] Ib. iv. 8, 9. [r] Ib. v. 1. vi. 9. [s] Ib. v. 1.
[t] Hosea iv. 15. x. 5, 8. 15. xii. 4. Amos iii. 14. v. 5.
vii. 10. 13.
[u] Hosea iv. 15. ix. 15. xii. 11. [v] Hosea vi. 8. xii. 11.
[w] v. 1. [x] See on vi. 9. [y] Ib. vi. 6.
[z] Amos v. 10. [a] Hosea xi. 2, add 7.
[c] Amos ii. 12. [d] Hosea ix. 7, 9.
[e] Ib. vii. 1. [f] Ib. vii. 9.
[g] Ib. v. 13. viii. 9, 10. xiv. 3. and with Egypt, vii.
11. xii. 1.
[h] Hosea x. 6. xi. 9. (denying it of Egypt.)

from them fled to Egypt[i], and in Egypt they should be a derision[j], and should find their grave[k]. This captivity he had to foretell as imminent[l], certain[m], irreversible[n]. Once only, in the commencement of his prophecy, does he give any hope, that the temporal punishment might be averted through repentance. This too he follows up by renewing the declaration of God expressed in the name of his daughter, "I will not have mercy[o]." He gives them in God's Name, a distant promise of a spiritual restoration in Christ, and forewarns them that it is distant[p]. But, that they might not look for any temporal restoration, he tells them, on the one hand, in peremptory terms, of their dispersion; on the other, he tells them of their spiritual restoration without any intervening shadows of temporal deliverance. God tells them absolutely, "[q] I will cause the kingdom of the house of Israel to cease;" "I will no more have mercy upon the house of Israel;" "they shall be wanderers among the nations;" "they shall not dwell in the Lord's land;" "Israel is swallowed up; she shall be among the nations like a vessel in which is no pleasure." On the other hand, the promises are markedly spiritual[r]; "Ye are the sons of the living God;" "I will betroth her to Me for ever;" "they shall fear the Lord and His goodness;" "He will raise us up, and we shall live in His sight;" "till He come and rain righteousness upon you." "I will ransom them from the power of the grave, I will redeem them from death." Again, God contrasts[s] with this His sentence on Israel, His future dealings with Judah, and His mercies to her, of which Israel should not partake, while of Judah's spiritual mercies, He says, that Israel should partake by being united with Judah[t].

The ground of this difference was, that Israel's separate existence was bound up with that sin of Jeroboam, which clave to them throughout their history, and which none of their least bad kings ventured to give up. God tried them for two centuries and a half; and not one king was found, who would risk his throne for God. In merciful severity then, the separate kingdom of Israel was to be destroyed, and the separate existence of the ten tribes was to be lost.

This message of woe gives a peculiar character to the prophecies of Hosea. He, like St. Paul, was of the people, whose temporary excision he had to declare. He calls the wretched king of Israel "our king[u];"

and God calls the rebellious people "thy people[v]." Of that people, he was specially the prophet. Judah he mentions incidentally, when he does mention them, not in his warnings only, but in his prophecies of good also. His main commission lay among the ten tribes. Like Elijah and Elisha whom he succeeded, he was raised up out of them, for them. His love could not be tied down to them; and so he could not but warn Judah against sharing Israel's sin. But it is, for the most part, incidentally and parenthetically[w]. He does not speak of them equally, except as to that which was the common sin of both, the seeking to Assyria for help, and unfulfilled promise of amendment[x]. And so, on the other hand, mercies, which belong to all as God's everlasting betrothal of His Church[y], and our redemption from death[z] and the grave, he foretells with special reference to Ephraim, and in one place only expressly includes Judah[a].

The prophecies of Hosea (as he himself collected them) form one whole, so that they cannot be distinctly separated, In one way, as the second chapter is the expansion and application of the first, so the remainder of the book after the third is an expansion and application of the third, The first and third chapters illustrate, summarily, Ephraim's ingratitude and desertion of God and His dealings with her, by likening them to the wife which Hosea was commanded to take, and to her children. The second chapter expands and applies the picture of Israel's unfaithfulness, touched upon in the first, but it dwells more on the side of mercy; the remaining chapters enlarge the picture of the third, although, until the last, they dwell chiefly on the side of judgment. Yet while the remainder of the book is an expansion of the third chapter, the three first chapters, (as every reader has felt) are united together, not by their narrative form only, but by the prominence given to the history of Hosea which furnishes the theme of the book, the shameful unfaithfulness of Israel, and the exceeding tenderness of the love of God, Who, "in wrath, remembers mercy."

The narrative leads us deep into the Prophet's personal sorrows. There is no ground to justify our taking as a parable, what Holy Scripture relates as a fact. There is no instance in which it can be shewn, that Holy Scripture relates that a thing was done, and that, with the names of persons, and yet that God did not intend it to be taken as

[i] Hosea ix. 3.   [j] Hosea vii. 16.
[k] Hosea ix. 6.   [l] i. 4. v. 7.
[m] v. 9. ix. 7.   [n] i. 6. v. 6.
[o] i. 2–4.   [p] iii. 4. 5.
[q] i. 4, 6. ix. 17. ix. 3. viii. 8. and of distant captivity iv. 19 and 16.
[r] i. 10. ii. 19. sqq. iii. 5. vi. 1–3. x. 12. xiii. 14.
[s] i. 7. vi. 11.   [t] i. 11. iii. 5.   [u] vii. 5.

[v] iv. 4. The words, "I have seen a horrible thing in the house of Israel" (vi. 10.), are words of God, not the prophet's own observation.
[w] iv. 15. v. 5, 10. vi. 11. "Judah also;" viii. 14. xi. 12. "Judah yet ruleth;" xii. 2. "with Judah also." [x] v. 13. 14. vi. 4.   [y] ii. 19, 20.
[z] xiii. 14.
[a] i. 11. Judah is included virtually in iii. 5.

literally true[b]. There would then be no test left of what was real, what imaginary; and the histories of Holy Scripture would be left to be a prey to individual caprice, to be explained away as parables, when men mis-liked them. Hosea, then, at God's command, united to himself in marriage, one who, amid the widespread corruption of those times, had fallen manifoldly into fleshly sin. With her he was commanded to live holily, as his wife, as Isaac lived with Rebecca whom he loved. Such an one he took, in obedience to God's command, one Gomer. At some time after she bore the prophet's children, she fell into adultery, and forsook him. Perhaps she fell into the condition of a slave[c]. God anew commanded him to shew mercy to her, to redeem her from her fallen condition, and, without restoring to her the rights of mar-riage[d], to guard and protect her from her sins. Thus, by the love of God and the patient forbearance which He instructed the prophet to shew, a soul was rescued from sin unto death, and was won to God; to the chil-dren of Israel there was set forth continually before their eyes a picture and a prophecy of the punishment upon sin, and of the close union with Himself which He vouchsafes to sinners who repent and return to Him.

"Not only in visions which were seen," says S. Irenæus[e], "and in words which were preached, but in acts also was He [the Word] seen by the Prophets, so as to pre-figure and foreshew things future, through them. For which cause also, the Prophet Hosea took 'a wife of whoredoms,' prophe-sying by his act, that the earth, i. e. the men who are on the earth, shall commit whoredoms, departing from the Lord; and that of such men God will be pleased to take to Himself a Church, to be sanctified by the communication of His Son, as she too was sanctified by the communion of the Prophet. Wherefore Paul also saith, that [f] the unbe-lieving woman is sanctified in her believing husband." "What," asks S. Augustine[g] of the scoffers of his day, "is there opposed to the clemency of truth, what contrary to the Christian faith, that one unchaste, leaving her fornication, should be converted to a chaste marriage? And what so incongruous and alien from the faith of the Prophet, as it would have been, not to believe that all the sins of the unchaste were forgiven, when she was converted and amended? So then, when the Prophet made the unchaste one his wife, a kind provision was made for the woman to amend her life, and the mystery [of the union of Christ Himself with the

Church of Jews and Gentiles] was ex-pressed." "[h] Since the Lord, through the same Scripture, lays clearly open what is figured by this command and deed, and since the Apostolic Epistles attest that this prophecy was fulfilled in the preaching of the New Testament, who would venture to say that it was not commanded and done for that end, for which He who commanded it, explains in the holy Scripture that He com-manded, and that the Prophet did it?"

The names which Hosea, by God's com-mand gave to the children who were born, expressed the temporal punishment, which was to come upon the nation. The prophet himself, in his relation to his restored yet separated wife, was, so long as she lived, one continued, living prophecy of the tenderness of God to sinners. Fretful, wayward, jealous, ungovernable, as are mostly the tempers of those who are recovered from such sins as her's, the Prophet, in his anxious, watchful charge, was a striking picture of the fore-bearing loving-kindness of God to us amid our provocations and infirmities. Nay, the love which the Prophet bare her, grew the more out of his compassion and tenderness for her whom God had commanded him to take as his own. Certain it is, that Holy Scripture first speaks of her as the object of his love, when God commanded him a second time to take charge of her who had be-trayed and abandoned him. God bids him shew active love to her, whom, amid her unfaithfulness, he loved already. *Go yet, love a woman, beloved of her husband, yet an adulteress.* Wonderful picture of God's love for us, for whom He gave His Only-begotten Son, loving us, while alien from Him, and with nothing in us to love!

Such was the tenderness of the Prophet, whom God employed to deliver such a mes-sage of woe; and such the people must have known to be *his* personal tenderness, who had to speak so sternly to them.

The three first prophecies, contained sev-erally in the three first chapters, form each, a brief circle of mercy and judgment. They do not enter into any detail of Israel's sin, but sum up all in the one, which is both centre and circumference of all sin, the all-compre-hending sin, departure from God, choosing the creature rather than the Creator. On this, the first prophecy foretells the entire irrevocable destruction of the kingdom; God's temporary rejection of His people, but their acceptance, together with Judah, in One Head, Christ. The second follows the same outline, rebuke, chastisement, the cessation

---

[b] "The prophet obeys and marries one impure, whose name and her father's name he tells, that what he says might seem not to be a mere fiction, but a true history of facts." Theod. Mops.
[c] See on iii. 2.   [d] See on iii. 3.

[e] iv. 20. 12. p. 374 O. T.   [f] 1 Cor. vii. 14.
[g] c. Faust. xxii. 80. Not only S. Ambrose (Apol. David. ii. 10. p. 726.) Theodoret, S. Cyril Alex., but even Theodore of Mopsuestia understood the his-tory as fact.   [h] S. Aug. ib. 89.

of visible worship, banishment, and then the betrothal for ever. The third speaks of offence against deeper love, and more prolonged punishment. It too ends in the promise of entire restoration; yet only in the latter days, after *many days* of separation, both from idolatry and from the true worship of God, such as is Israel's condition now. The rest is one continuous prophecy, in which the Prophet has probably gathered into one the substance of what he had delivered in the course of his ministry. Here and there, yet very seldom in it[i], the Prophet refers to the image of the earlier chapters. For the most part he exhibits his people to themselves, in their varied ingratitude, folly, and sin. The prophecy has many pauses, which with one exception coincide with our chapters[j]. It rises and falls, and then bursts out in fresh tones of upbraiding[k], and closes mostly in notes of sorrow and of woe[l], for the destruction which is coming. Yet at none of these pauses is there any complete break, such as would constitute what preceded, a separate prophecy; and on the other hand, the structure of the last portion of the book corresponds most with that of the first three chapters, if it is regarded as one whole. For as there, after rebuke and threatened chastisement, each prophecy ended with the promise of future mercy, so here, after finally foreannouncing the miseries at the destruction of Samaria, the Prophet closes his prophecy and his whole book with a description of Israel's future repentance and acceptance, and of his flourishing with manifold grace.

The brief summary, in which the Prophet calls attention to all which he had said, and foretells, who would and who would not understand it, the more marks the prophecy as one whole.

Yet, although these prophecies, as wrought into one by the Prophet, bear a strong impress of unity, there yet seem to be traces, here and there, of the different conditions of the kingdom of Israel, amid which different parts were first uttered. The order, in which they stand, seems, upon the whole, to be an order of time. In the first chapters, the house of Jeroboam is still standing in strength, and Israel appears to have trusted in its own power, as the prophet Amos[m] also, at the same time, describes them. The fourth chapter is addressed to the "house of Israel[n]" only, without any allusion to the king, and accords with that time of convulsive anarchy, which followed the death of Jeroboam II.

The omission of the king is the more remarkable, inasmuch as the "house of the king" *is* included in the corresponding address in ch. v.[o] The "rulers[p]" of Israel also spoken of in the plural; and the bloodshed[q] described seems to be more than individual insulated murders. In this case, the king upbraided in ch. v. would, naturally, be the next king, Zechariah, in whom God's promise to the house of Jehu expired. In the seventh chapter a weak and sottish king is spoken of, whom his princes misled to debauchery, disgusting drunkenness and impiety. But Menahem was a general of fierce determination, energy and barbarity. Debauchery and brutal ferocity are natural associates; but this sottishness here described was rather the fruit of weak compliance with the debauchery of others. "The princes made him sick[r]," it is said. This is not likely to have been the character of successful usurpers, as Menahem, or Pekah, or Hoshea. It is far more likely to have been that of Zechariah, who was placed on the throne for 6 months, "did evil in the sight of the Lord," and then was "slain publicly before the people[s]," no one resisting. Him, as being the last of the line of Jehu, and sanctioned by God, Hosea may the rather have called "our king[t]," owning in him, evil as he was, God's appointment. The words, "they have devoured their judges, all their kings have fallen[u]," had anew their fulfillment in the murder of Zechariah and Shallum (B. C. 772) as soon as the promise to the house of Jehu had expired. The blame of Judah for "[v] multiplying fenced cities," instead of trusting in God, probably relates to the temper in which they were built in the days of Jotham[w], between B. C. 758, and 741. Although Jotham was a religious king, the corruption of the people at this time is especially recorded; "the people did corruptly." Later yet, we have mention of the dreadful battle, when Shalman, or Shalmanezer, took and massacred women and children at Betharbel[x] in the valley of Jezreel, about B. C. 729. Hosea, thus, lived to see the fulfillment of his earlier prophecy, "[y] I will break the bow of Israel in the valley of Jezreel." It has been thought that the question "where is thy king?" relates to the captivity of Hoshea, three years before the destruction of Samaria. This sort of question, however, relates not to the actual place where the king was, but to his ability or inability to help.

It belongs to the mournful solemnity of captivity; ch. xi. that it alone maintained the true religion.

[i] iv. 5. v. 3. 7. ix. 1.
[j] c. v. and vi. alone seems to be one.
[k] See the beginnings of cc. v. vii. viii. ix. x. xi. xii. xiii.
[l] See iv. ult. vii. 16. viii. 14. ix. 17. x. 15. xii. 14. xiii. 16. Chapters vi. and xi. close with the contrast with Judah, ch. vi., declaring that for Judah only was there a harvest reserved on its return from

[m] ii. 14, 16. vi. 13.
[n] Hosea iv. 1.
[o] v. 1.
[p] iv. 18.   [q] iv. 2.
[r] vii. 5.   [s] 2 Kgs xv. 10.
[t] Hosea vii. 5.   [u] vii. 7.   [v] viii. 14.
[v] 2 Chron. xxvii. 2–4.   [x] Hosea x. 14.
[y] Ib. i. 4. see on x. 14.

Hosea's prophecy, that he scarcely speaks to the people in his own person. The ten chapters, which form the centre of the prophecy, are almost wholly one long dirge of woe, in which the prophet rehearses the guilt and the punishment of his people. If the people are addressed, it is, with very few exceptions, God Himself, not the Prophet, Who speaks to them; and God speaks to them as their Judge[a]. Once only does the Prophet use the form, so common in the other Prophets, "[a]saith the Lord." As in the three first chapters, the Prophet, in his relation to his wife, represented that of God to His people, so, in these ten chapters, after the first words of the fourth and fifth chapters, "Hear the word of the Lord, for the Lord hath a controversy with the inhabitants of the land," "Hear ye this, O priests[b]," whenever the prophet uses the first person, he uses it not of himself, but of God. "I" "My[c]" are not Hosea, and the things of Hosea, but God and what belongs to God. God addresses the Prophet himself in the second person[d]. In four verses only of these chapters does the Prophet himself apparently address his own people Israel, in two[e] expostulating with them; in two[f], calling them to repentance. In two other verses he addresses Judah[g], or foretells to him judgment mingled with mercy[h]. The last chapter alone is one of almost unmingled brightness; the Prophet calls to repentance[i], and God in His own Person[j] accepts it, and promises large supply of grace. But this too closes the prophecy with the warning, that righteous as are the ways of God, the transgressors should stumble in them.

It is this same solemn pathos, which has chiefly occasioned the obscurity, complained of in Hosea. The expression of S. Jerome has often been repeated; "[k] Hosea is concise, and speaketh, as it were, in detached sayings." The words of upbraiding, of judgment, of woe, burst out, as it were, one by one, slowly, heavily, condensed, abrupt, from the Prophet's heavy and shrinking soul, as God commanded and constrained him, and put His words, like fire, in the Prophet's mouth. An image of Him Who said, "[l]O Jerusalem, Jerusalem, thou that killest the Prophets and stonest them which are sent unto thee, how often would I have gathered thy children together, even as a hen gathers her chickens under her wings, and ye would

not," he delivers his message, as though each sentence burst with a groan from his soul, and he had anew to take breath, before he uttered each renewed woe. Each verse forms a whole for itself, like one heavy toll in a funeral knell. The Prophet has not been careful about order and symmetry, so that each sentence went home to the soul. And yet the unity of the prophecy is so evident in the main, that we cannot doubt that it is not broken, even when the connection is not apparent on the surface. The great difficulty consequently in Hosea is to ascertain that connection in places where it evidently exists, yet where the Prophet has not explained it. The easiest and simplest sentences[m] are sometimes, in this respect, the most difficult. It is in remarkable contrast with this abruptness in the more mournful parts, that when Hosea has a message of mercy to deliver, his style becomes easy and flowing. Then no sign of present sin or impending misery disturbs his brightness. He lives wholly in the future bliss which he was allowed to foretell. Yet, meanwhile, no prophet had a darker future to declare. The prophets of Judah could mingle with their present denunciations a prospect of an early restoration. The ten tribes, as a whole, had no future. The temporal part of their punishment was irreversible. Hosea lived almost to see its fulfillment. Yet not the less confidently does he foretell the spiritual mercies in store for his people. He promises them as absolutely as if he saw them. It is not matter of hope, but of certainty. And this certainty Hosea announces, in words expressive of the closest union with God; an union shadowed by the closest union which we know, that, whereby a man and his wife are *no more twain, but one flesh.* Here, as filled and overfilled with joy, instead of abrupt sentences, he gladly lingers on his subject, adding in every word something to the fulness of the blessing contained in the preceding[n]. He is, indeed, (if one may venture so to speak) eminently a prophet of the tenderness of the love of God. In foretelling God's judgments, he ventures to picture Him to us, as overcome (so to speak) by mercy, so that He would not execute His full sentence[o]. God's mercies he predicts in the inmost relation of love, that those whom He had rejected, He would own, as "sons of the living God;" that He would betroth them to Himself in righteousness, in judg-

---

[a] Ib. iv. 5, 6, 13, 14. v. 3, 13. vi. 4, 5. viii. 5. ix. 10. xiii. 4, 5, 9, 11. In xi. 8, 9, God speaks to them, in mitigation of His sentence; x. 9, is uncertain, but in x. 10, God speaks.
[a] Hosea xi. 11.
[b] Hosea iv. 1. v. 1.
[c] In fifty-seven verses, iv. 5–9, 12–14. 17. v. 2, 3, 9, 10, 12, 14, 15. vi. 4–7, 10, 11. vii. 1, 2, 12–15. viii. 1, 2, 4, 5, 10, 12, 14. ix. 10, 12, 15, 16. x. 10, 11. xi. 1, 3. 4. 7–9, 12. xii. 9, 10. xiii. 4, 9, 11. There are apparently only ten verses, in which the Prophet speaks of the

Lord in the third person, iv. 10. v. 4, 6, 7. ix. 3, 4. x. 12. xii. 2, 13. xiii. 15. He says, "My God" ix. 8, 17.
[d] iv. 4, 17. viii. 1. [e] ix. 1, 5.
[f] Hosea x. 12; (but followed by a declaration of the fruitlessness of his call 13, 15.) xii. 6.
[g] Hosea iv. 13. [h] See on vi. 11.
[i] Hosea xiv. 1, 3. [j] Ib. xiv. 4, 8.
[k] Osee commaticus est, et quasi per sententias loquitur. Præf. in xii. Proph.
[l] S. Matt. xxiii. 37. [m] e. g. xii. 9, 12, 13.
[n] ii. 14–20. xiv. 1–7. [o] xi. 8, 9.

ment, loving-kindness, mercies, faithfulness, and that, for ever; that He would raise us up on the third day, and that we should live in His sight, ransoming us, Himself, and redeeming us, as our Kinsman, from death and the grave [p].

In this prophecy of the betrothal of the Church to God, he both applies and supplies the teaching of the forty-fifth Psalm and of the Song of Solomon. Moses had been taught to declare to his people that God had, in a special way, made them His people, and was Himself their God. The violation of this relation, by taking other Gods, Moses had also spoken of under the image of married faithlessness. But faithlessness implies the existence of the relation, to which they were bound to be faithful. The whole human family, however, had once belonged to God, and had fallen away from Him. And so Moses speaks of the heathen idolatry also under this name, and warned Israel against sharing their sin. "[q] Lest thou make a covenant with the inhabitants of the land, and they go a whoring after their gods,—and their daughters go a whoring after their gods, and make thy sons go a whoring after their gods." The relation itself of betrothal Moses does not mention; yet it must have been suggested to the mind of Israel by his describing this special sin of choosing other gods, under the title of married faithlessness [r] and of desertion of God [s], and by his attributing to God the title of "Jealous [t]." It was reserved to Hosea, to exhibit at once to Israel under this image, God's tender love for them and their ingratitude, to dwell on their relation to God Whom they forsook [u], and explicitly to foretell to them that new betrothal in Christ which should abide for ever.

The Image, however, presupposes an acquaintance with the language of the Pentateuch; and it has been noticed that Hosea

incidentally asserts that the written Pentateuch was still used in the kingdom of Israel. For God does not say, "I have *given* to him," but "I have *written*," or "I write [v] to him the great" or "manifold [w]" things of the law. The "ten thousand things" which God says that He had written, cannot be the decalogue only, nor would the word "written" be used of an unwritten tradition. God says moreover, "I write," in order to express that the law, although written once for all, still came from the ever-present authority of Him Who wrote it.

The language of Hosea is, for the most part, too concise and broken, to admit of his employing actual sentences of the Pentateuch. This he does sometimes [x], as has been pointed out [y]. On the other hand, his concise allusions would scarcely be understood by those who were not familiar with the history and laws of the Pentateuch [z]. Since then plainly a prophet spoke so as to be understood by the people, this is an evidence of the continual use of the Pentateuch in Israel, after the great schism from Judah. The schools of the Prophets, doubtless, maintained the teaching of the law, as they did the public worship. The people went to Elisha on new-moons and sabbaths, and so to other prophets also [a]. Even after the great massacre of the prophets by Jezebel [b], we have incidental notices of schools of the prophets at Bethel [c], Jericho [d], Gilgal [e], Mount Ephraim [f], Samaria [g], from which other schools were formed [h]. The selection of Gilgal, Bethel, and Samaria, shews that the spots were chosen, in order to confront idolatry and corruption in their chief abodes. The contradiction of men's lives to the law, thus extant and taught among them, could scarcely have been greater than that of Christians now to the Bible which they have in their houses and their hands and their ears, but not in their hearts.

---

[p] See on i. 10. ii. 19. sqq. vi. 2. xiii. 14.
[q] Ex. xxxiv. 15, 16.
[r] Lev. xvii. 7. xx. 5, 6. Num. xiv. 33.
[s] Deut. xxxi. 16.
[t] Ex. xx. 5. xxxiv. 14. Deut. iv. 24. v. 9. vi. 15. Num. xxv. 2.
[u] The language "went a whoring *from* God" &c. occurs in Ps. lxxiii. 27. Hos. i. 2. iv. 12. ix. 1. not in the Pentateuch. In Ezek. xxiii. 5, "when she was Mine."
[v] viii. 12.
[w] lit. "ten thousand" according to the textual reading.

[x] See iii. 1. iv. 8, 10. v. 6, 10, 11, 14. vi. 2, 3. x. 14. xi. 7, 8. xii. 4, 6. xiii. 6, 9. xiv. 2.
[y] Hengstenberg Authentie des Pentateuches, i. 48. sqq. although, naturally, all his instances will not seem to all to have the force of proof.
[z] See i. 10, 11. iii. 2. iv. 4, 8. viii. 6, 11, 13. ix. 3, 10. x. 4, 11. xi. 8, xii. 4–6, 10, 11, 12. xiv. 3, 4.
[a] 2 Kgs iv. 23.   [b] 1 Kgs xviii. 13.   [c] 2 Kgs ii. 3
[d] Ib. 5.   [e] Ib. iv. 38.   [f] Ib. v. 22.
[g] Elisha dwelt in Mount Carmel, 2 Kgs ii. 25. iv. 25. but also at Samaria, 2 Kgs ii. 25. (probably v. 9.) vi. 32. He had a school of "sons of the prophets" with him, vi. 1. ix. 1.   [h] Ib. vi. 1.

HOSEA.

CHAPTER I.

1 Hosea, to shew God's judgment for spiritual whoredom, taketh Gomer, 4 and hath by her Jezreel, 6 Lo-ruhamah, 8 and Lo-ammi. 10 The restoration of Judah and Israel.

THE word of the LORD that came unto Hosea, the son of Beeri, in the days of Uzziah, Jotham, Ahaz, *and* Hezekiah, kings of Judah, and in the days of Jeroboam the son of Joash, king of Israel.

2 The beginning of the word of the LORD by Hosea. And the LORD said to Hosea, ªGo, take

ª So ch. 3. 1.

CHAP. 1., ver. 1. *The word of the Lord, that came unto Hosea.* Hosea, at the very beginning of his prophecy, declares that all this, which he delivered, came, not from his own mind but from God. As S. Paul says, *Paul an Apostle, not of men neither by man, but by Jesus Christ, and God the Father.* He refers all to God, and claims all obedience to Him. That word *came* to him; it existed then before, in the mind of God. It was first God's, then it became the Prophet's, receiving it from God. So it is said, *the word of God came to John*[1].

Hosea, i. e. *Salvation,* or, *the Lord saveth.* The Prophet bare the name of our Lord Jesus, Whom he foretold and of Whom he was a type. *Son of Beeri,* i. e. *my well or welling-forth.* God ordained that the name of his father too should signify truth. From God, as from the Fountain of life, Hosea drew the living waters, which he poured out to the people. *With joy shall ye draw water out of the wells of salvation*[2].

In the days of Uzziah, &c. Hosea, although a Prophet of Israel, marks his prophecy by the names of the kings of Judah, because the kingdom of Judah was the kingdom of the theocracy, the line of David to which the promises of God were made. As Elisha, to whose office he succeeded, turned away from Jehoram[3], saying, *get thee to the prophets of thy father, and to the prophets of thy mother,* and owned Jehoshaphat of Judah only, so, in the title of his prophecy, Hosea at once expresses that the kingdom of Judah alone was legitimate. He adds the name of Jeroboam, partly as the last king of Israel whom, by virtue of His promise to Jehu, God helped; partly to shew that God never left Israel unwarned. Jeroboam I. was warned first by the prophet[4], who by his own untimely death, as well as in his prophecy, was a witness to the strictness of God's judgments, and then by Ahijah[5]; Baasha by Jehu, son of Hanani[6]; Ahab, by Elijah and Micaiah son of Imla; Ahaziah by Elijah[7]; Jehoram by Elisha who exercised his office until the days of Joash[8]. So, in the days of Jeroboam II, God raised up Hosea, Amos and Jonah. "The kings and people of Israel then were without excuse, since God never ceased to send His prophets among them; in no reign did the voice of the prophets fail, warning of the coming wrath of God, until it came." While Jeroboam was recovering to Israel a larger rule than it had ever had since it separated from Judah, annexing to it Damascus[9] which had been lost to Judah even in the days of Solomon, and from which Israel had of late so greatly suffered, Hosea was sent to forewarn it of its destruction. God alone could utter "such a voice of thunder out of the midst of such a cloudless sky." Jeroboam doubtless thought that his house would, through its own strength, survive the period which God had pledged to it. "But temporal prosperity is no proof either of stability or of the favor of God. Where the law of God is observed, there, even amid the pressure of outward calamity, is the assurance of ultimate prosperity. Where God is disobeyed, *there* is the pledge of coming destruction. The seasons when men feel most secure against future chastisement, are often the preludes of the most signal revolutions."

2. *The beginning of the word of the Lord by Hosea* or *in Hosea.* God first revealed Himself and His mysteries to the prophet's soul, by His secret inspiration, and then declared, through him, to others, what He had deposited in him. God enlightened him, and then others through the light in him.

And the Lord said unto Hosea. For this thing was to be done by Hosea alone, because God had commanded it, not by others of their own mind. To Isaiah God first revealed Himself, as sitting in the temple, adored by the Seraphim: to Ezekiel God first appeared, as enthroned above the Cherubim in the Holy of Holies; to Jeremiah God announced that, ere yet he was born, He had sanctified him for this office: to Hosea He enjoined, as the beginning of his prophetic office, an act contrary to man's natu-

---

[1] S. Luke iii. 2.   [2] Isa. xii. 3.   [3] 2 Kgs iii. 13, 14.
[4] 1 Kgs xiii.   [5] Ib. xiv.   [6] Ib. xvi.   [7] 2 Kgs i.   [8] Ib. xiii. 14.   [9] Ib. xiv. 28.

19

unto thee a wife of whoredoms and children of whoredoms: for [b] the land hath committed great

whoredom, *departing* from the LORD.

3 So he went and took Gomer the daughter of

ral feelings, yet one, by which he became an image of the Redeemer, uniting to Himself what was unholy, in order to make it holy.

Go take unto thee. Since Hosea prophesied some eighty years, he must now have been in early youth, holy, pure, as became a prophet of God. Being called thus early, he had doubtless been formed by God as a chosen instrument of His will, and had, like Samuel, from his first childhood, been trained in true piety and holiness. Yet he was to unite unto him, so long as she lived, one greatly defiled, in order to win her thereby to purity and holiness; herein, a little likeness of our Blessed Lord, Who, in the Virgin's womb, to save us, espoused our flesh, in us sinful, in Him All-holy, without motion to sin; and, further, espoused the Church, formed of us who, *whether Jews or Gentiles, were all under sin,* aliens from God and gone away from Him, *serving divers lusts and passions,* [1] *to make it a glorious Church, without spot or wrinkle.*

A wife of whoredoms, i. e. take as a wife, one who up to that time had again and again been guilty of that sin. So *men of bloods*[2] are "men given up to bloodshedding;" and our Lord was *a Man of Sorrows*[3], not occasional only, but manifold and continual, throughout His whole life. She must, then, amid the manifold corruption of Israel, have been repeatedly guilty of that sin, perhaps as an idolatress, thinking of it to be in honour of their foul gods[4]. She was not like those degraded ones, who cease to bear children; still she must have manifoldly sinned. So much the greater was the obedience of the Prophet. Nor could any other woman so shadow forth the manifold defilements of the human race, whose nature our Incarnate Lord vouchsafed to unite in His own Person to the perfect holiness of the Divine Nature.

And children of whoredoms; for they shared the disgrace of their mother, although born in lawful marriage. The sins of parents descend also, in a mysterious way, on their children. Sin is contagious, and, unless the entail is cut off by grace, hereditary. The mother thus far portrays man's revolts, before his union with God; the children, our forsaking of God, after we have been made His children. The forefathers of Israel, God tells them, *served* other *gods, on the other side of the flood*[5], (i. e. in Ur of the Chaldees,

whence God called Abraham) *and in Egypt.* It was out of such defilement, that God took her[6], and He says, *Thou becamest Mine*[7]. Whom He maketh His, He maketh pure; and of her, not such as she was in herself by nature, but as such as He made her, He says[8], *I remember thee, the kindness of thy youth, the love of thine espousals, when thou wentest after Me, in the wilderness.* But she soon fell away; and thenceforth there were among them (as there are now among Christians,) the children of God, *the children of the promise,* and the *children of whoredoms,* or *of the devil.*

For the land, &c. This is the reason why God commands Hosea to do this thing, in order to shadow out their foulness and God's mercy. What no man would dare to do[9], except at God's bidding, God in a manner doth, restoring to union with Himself those who had gone away from Him. *The land,* i. e., Israel, and indirectly, Judah also, and, more widely yet, the whole earth.

Departing from lit. *from after the Lord.* Our whole life should be, [10] *forgetting the things which are behind, to follow after* Him, Whom here we can never fully attain unto, God in His Infinite Perfection, yet so as, with our whole heart, *fully to follow after Him.* To depart from the Creator and to serve the creature, is adultery; as the Psalmist says, [11] *Thou hast destroyed all them, that go a whoring from Thee.* He who seeks any thing out of God, turns from following Him, and takes to him something else as his god, is unfaithful, and spiritually an adulterer and idolater. For he is an adulterer, who becomes another's than God's.

3. *So he went.* He did not demur, nor excuse himself, as did even Moses[12], or Jeremiah[13], or S. Peter[14], and were rebuked for it, although mercifully by the All-Merciful. Hosea, accustomed from childhood to obey God and every indication of the Will of God, did at once, what he was bidden, however repulsive to natural feeling, and became, thereby, the more an image of the obedience of Christ Jesus, and a pattern to us, at once to believe and obey God's commands, however little to our minds.

Gomer, the daughter of Diblaim. Gomer is completion; *Diblaim,* a double lump of figs; which are a figure of sweetness. These names may mean, that "the sweetness of sins is the parent of destruction;" or that Israel,

---

[1] Eph. v. 27   [2] Ps. v. 6.   [3] Isa. liii. 3.
[4] See on iv. 13, 24.   [5] Josh. xxiv. 14.
       [6] Ezek. xxiii. 3, 8.

[7] Ezek. xvi. 8.   [8] Jer. ii. 2.   [9] Ib. iii. 1.
[10] Phil. iii. 13.   [11] Ps. lxxiii. 27.   [12] Ex. iv. 18.
[13] Jer. i. 6.   [14] Acts x. 4.

Before CHRIST cir. 785.	Diblaim; which conceived, and bare him a son.

4 And the LORD said unto him, Call his name

Jezreel; for yet a little *while,* [c]and I will † avenge the blood of Jezreel upon the house of Jehu, [d]and

[c] 2 Kings 10. 11.
† Heb. *visit.*
[d] 2 Kings 15. 10, 12.

---

or mankind had completely forsaken God, and were children of corrupting pleasure.

Holy Scripture relates that all this was done, and tells us the births and names of the children, as real history. As such then, must we receive it. We must not imagine things to be unworthy of God, because they do not commend themselves to us. God does not dispense with the moral law, because the moral law has its source in the Mind of God Himself. To dispense with it would be to contradict Himself. But God, Who is the absolute Lord of all things which He made, may, at His Sovereign Will, dispose of the lives or things which He created. Thus, as Sovereign Judge, He commanded the lives of the Canaanites to be taken away by Israel, as, in His ordinary Providence, He has ordained that the magistrate should not bear the sword in vain, but has made him His *minister, a revenger to execute wrath upon him that doeth evil*[1]. So, again, He, Whose are all things, willed to repay to the Israelites their hard and unjust servitude, by commanding them to *spoil the Egyptians*[2]. He, Who created marriage, commanded to Hosea, *whom* he should marry. The Prophet was not defiled, by taking as his lawful wife, at God's bidding, one defiled, however hard a thing this was. " He who remains good, is not defiled by coming in contact with one evil; but the evil, following his example, is turned into good." But through his simple obedience, he foreshadowed Him, God the Word, Who was called [3]*the Friend of publicans and sinners;* Who warned the Pharisees, that[4] *the publicans and harlots should enter unto the kingdom of God before them;* and who now vouchsafes to espouse, dwell in, and unite Himself with, and so to hallow, our sinful souls. The acts which God enjoined to the Prophets, and which to us seem strange, must have had an impressiveness to the people, in proportion to their strangeness. The life of the Prophet became a sermon to the people. Sight impresses more than words. The Prophet, being in his own person a mirror of obedience, did moreover, by his way of life, reflect to the people some likeness of the future and of things unseen. The expectation of the people was wound up, when they saw their Prophets do things at God's command, which they themselves could not have done. When Ezekiel was bidden to shew no sign of mourning, on the sudden death of [5]*the desire*

of his eyes, his wife; or when he dug through the wall of his house, and carried forth his household stuff in the twilight, with his face covered[6]; the people asked, [7] *Wilt thou not tell us what these things are to us, that thou doest so?* No words could so express a grief beyond all power of grieving, as Ezekiel's mute grief for one who was known to be " *the desire of his eyes,*" yet for whom he was forbidden to shew the natural expressions of grief, or to use the received tokens of mourning. God Himself declares the ground of such acts to have been, that, rebellious as the house of Israel was[8], *with eyes which saw not, and ears which heard not,* they might yet consider such acts as these.

4. *Call his name Jezreel;* i. e. in its first sense here, "God will scatter." The life of the prophet, and his union with one so unworthy of him, were a continued prophecy of God's mercy. The names of the children were a life-long admonition of His intervening judgments. Since Israel refused to hear God's words, He made the prophet's sons, through the mere fact of their presence among them, their going out and coming in, and the names which He gave them, to be preachers to the people. He depicted in them and in their names what was to be, in order that, whenever they saw or heard of them, and those who would take warning, might be saved. If, with their mother's disgrace, these sons inherited and copied their mother's sins, then their names became even more expressive, that, being such as they were, they would be scattered by God, would not be owned by God as His people, or be pitied by Him.

I will avenge the blood of Jezreel upon the house of Jehu. Yet Jehu shed this blood, the blood of the house of Ahab, of Joram and Jezebel and the seventy sons of Ahab, at God's command and in fulfillment of His Will. How was it then sin? Because, if we do what is the Will of God for any end of our own, for any thing except God, we do, in fact, our own will, not God's. It was not lawful for Jehu to depose and slay the king his master, except at the command of God, Who, as the Supreme King, sets up and puts down earthly rulers as He wills. For any other end, and done otherwise than at God's express command, such an act is sin. Jehu was rewarded for the measure in which he fulfilled God's

[1] Rom. xiii. 4.   [2] Ex. iii. 22.   [3] S. Matt. xi. 19.
[4] Ib. xxi. 31.   [5] Ezek. xxiv. 16–18.

[6] Ib. xii. 3–7.   [7] Ib. xxiv. 19. add xii. 10.
[8] Ib. xii. 2.

will cause to cease the kingdom of the house of Israel.

• 2 Kings 15. 29.

5 °And it shall come to pass at that day, that I will break the bow of Israel in the valley of Jezreel.

commands, as Ahab who had *sold himself to work wickedness*, had yet a temporal reward for humbling himself publicly, when rebuked by God for his sin, and so honoring God, amid an apostate people. But Jehu, by cleaving, against the Will of God, to Jeroboam's sin, which served his own political ends, shewed that, in the slaughter of his master, he acted not, as he pretended, out of *zeal*[1] for the Will of God, but served his own will and his own ambition only. By his disobedience to the one command of God, he shewed that he would have equally disobeyed the other, had it been contrary to his own will of interest. He had no principle of obedience. And so the blood, which was shed according to the righteous judgment of God, became sin to *him* who shed it in order to fulfill, not the Will of God, but his own. Thus God said to Baasha[2] *I exalted thee out of the dust, and made thee prince over My people Israel*, which he became by slaying his master, the son of Jeroboam, and all the house of Jeroboam. Yet, because he followed the sins of Jeroboam[3], *the word of the Lord came against Baasha, for all the evil that he did in the sight of the Lord, in being like the house of Jeroboam, and because he killed him.* The two courses of action were inconsistent; to destroy the son and the house of Jeroboam, and to do those things, for which God condemned him to be destroyed. Further yet. Not only was *such* execution of God's judgments itself an offence against Almighty God, but it was sin, whereby he condemned himself, and made his other sins to be sins against the light. In executing the judgment of God against another, he pronounced His judgment against himself, in that he *that judged*, in God's stead, *did the same things*[4]. So awful a thing is it, to be the instrument of God in punishing or reproving others, if we do not, by His grace, keep our own hearts and hands pure from sin.

And will cause to cease the kingdom of the house of Israel. Not the kingdom of the house of Jehu, but all Israel. God had promised that the family of Jehu should sit on the throne to the fourth generation. Jeroboam II., the third of these, was now reigning over Israel, in the fulness of his might. He *restored the coast of Israel from the entering of Hamath*[5], i. e. from the Northern extremity,

near Mount Hermon, where Palestine joins on to Syria, and, which Solomon only in all his glory had won for Israel[6], *unto the sea of the plain*, the Dead sea, regaining all which Hazael had conquered[7], and even subduing Moab also[8], *according to the word of the Lord by Jonah the son of Amittai.* He had recovered to Israel, Damascus, which had been lost to Judah, ever since the close of the reign of Solomon[9]. He was a warlike prince, like that first Jeroboam, who had formed the strength and the sin of the ten tribes. Yet both his house and his kingdom fell with him. The whole history of that kingdom afterwards is little more than that of the murder of one family by another, such as is spoken of in the later chapters of Hosea; and Israel, i. e. the ten tribes, were finally carried captive, fifty years after the death of Zechariah, Jeroboam's son. Of so little account is any seeming prosperity or strength.

5. *I will break the bow of Israel in the valley of Jezreel.* The valley of Jezreel is a beautiful and a broad valley or plain, stretching, from W. to E., from Mount Carmel and the sea to the Jordan, which it reaches through two arms, between the Mountains of Gilboa, little Hermon, and Tabor; and from S. to N. from the Mountains of Ephraim to those of Galilee. Nazareth lay on its Northern side. It is called "[10]the great plain," "[11]the great plain of Esdraelon." There God had signally executed His judgments against the enemies of His people, or on His people, when they became His enemies. There He gave the great victories over the invading hosts of Sisera[12], and of Midian, with the children of the East[13]. There also He ended the life and kingdom of Saul[14], visiting upon him, when his measure of iniquity was full, his years of contumacy, and his persecution of David, whom God had chosen. Jezreel became a royal residence of the house of Ahab[15]. There, in the scenes of Ahab's wickedness and of Jehu's hypocritical zeal; there, where he drave furiously, to avenge, as he alleged, on the house of Ahab, the innocent blood which Ahab had shed in Jezreel, Hosea foretells that the kingdom of Israel should be broken In the same plain, at the battle with Shalmaneser, near Betharbel[16], Hosea lived to see his prophecy fulfilled. The strength of the kingdom was

[1] 2 Kings x. 16. [2] 1 Kings xvi. 2. [3] Ib. xvi. 7. [4] Rom. ii. 1. [5] 2 Kings xiv. 25. [6] 2 Chr. viii. 3, 4. [7] 2 Kings x. 32, 33. [8] See on Am. vi. 14. [9] 1 Kings xi. 24. [10] 1 Macc. xii. 49. [11] Judith i. 8. [12] Jud. iv. 4 sqq. [13] Jud. vi. 33. [14] 1 Sam. xxix. 1. xxxi. 1, 7, 10. [15] 1 Kings xviii. 46. xxi. 1, 2, 3. 2 Kings ix. 10, 25, 30. x. 1, 11. [16] See on x. 14.

Before CHRIST cir. 785.

6 ¶ And she conceived again, and bare a daughter. And God said unto him, Call her name || Lo-ruha-mah : [f]for † I will no more have mercy upon the house of Israel ; || but I will utterly take them away.

|| That is, Not having obtained mercy.
[f]2 Kings 17. 6, 23.
† Heb. I will not add any more to.
|| Or, that I should altogether pardon them.

7 [g]But I will have mercy upon the house of Judah, and will save them by the LORD their God, and [h]will not save them by bow, nor by sword, nor by battle, by horses nor by horsemen.

Before CHRIST cir. 785.

[g]2 Kings 19. 35.
[h]Zech. 4. 6. & 9. 10.

there finally broken ; the sufferings there endured were one last warning before the capture of Samaria [1].

The name of Jezreel blends the sins with the punishment. It resembles, in form and in sound, the name of Israel, and contains a reversal of the promise contained in the name of Israel, in which they trusted. *Yisrael* (as their name was originally pronounced [2]) signifies, *he is a prince with God*; *Yidsreel, God shall scatter.* They who, while they followed the faith, for which their forefather Jacob received from God the name of Israel, had been truly Israel, i. e. "princes with God," should now be *Yidsreel,* "scattered by God."

6. *Call her name Lo-ruhamah.* The name is rendered in St. Paul [3], *not beloved,* in St. Peter [4], *hath not obtained mercy.* Love and mercy are both contained in the full meaning of the intensive form of the Hebrew word, which expresses the deep tender yearnings of the inmost soul over one loved ; as in the words, " [5] *As a father pitieth* [yearneth over] *his own children, so the Lord pitieth* [yearneth over] *them that fear Him.* It is *tender love* in Him Who pitieth ; *mercy,* as shewn to him who needeth mercy. The punishment, foretold under the name of the daughter, *Unpitied,* is a great enlargement of that conveyed under the name of the first son, *God shall scatter.* Judah too was carried captive, and scattered ; but after the 70 years, she was restored. The 10 tribes, it is now foretold, when scattered, should, as a whole, be cut off from the tender mercy of God, scattered by Him, and as a whole, never be restored. Those only were restored, who, when Judah returned from captivity, clave to her, or subsequently, one by one, were united to her.

But I will utterly take them away. Lit., *for,* [6] *taking away, I will take away from them,* or *with regard to them,* viz., everything. He

[1] See on x. 15.
[2] The two names would either be pronounced, *Yisrael, Yidsreel* ; or both, *Israel, Idsreel.*
[3] Romans ix 25.   [4] 1 S. Peter ii. 10.
[5] Ps. ciii. 13.
[6] This mode of speech is often used in Holy Scripture. First, a negative is used ; then, the opposite is said in this emphatic way affirmatively, *Thou shalt not spare him, for killing thou shalt kill him,* Deut. xiii. 8, 9. [9, 10. Heb.] *Thou shalt not*

specifies nothing ; He excepts nothing ; only, with that awful emphasis, He dwells on the taking away, as that which He had determined to do to the utmost. This is the thought, which He wills to dwell on the mind. As a little while after, God says, that He would be nothing to them, so here, where He in fact repeats this one thought, *take away, take away, from them,* the guilty conscience of Israel would at once, supply, "all." When God threatens, the sinful or awakened soul sees instinctively what draws down the lightning of God's wrath, and where it will fall.

7. *I will have mercy on the house of Judah.* For to them the promises were made in David, and of them, according to the flesh, Christ was to come. Israel, moreover, as being founded in rebellion and apostacy, had gone on from bad to worse. All their kings clave to the sin of Jeroboam ; not one did right in the sight of God ; not one repented or hearkened to God. Whereas Judah, having the true Worship of God, and the reading of the law, and the typical sacrifices, through which it looked on to the great Sacrifice for sin, was on the whole, a witness to the truth of God [7].

And will save them by the Lord their God, not by bow, &c. Shortly after this, God did, in the reign of Hezekiah, save them by Himself from Sennacherib, when the Angel of the Lord smote in one night 185,000 in the camp of the Assyrians. "Neither in that night, nor when they were freed from the captivity at Babylon, did they bend bow or draw sword against their enemies or their captors. While they slept, the Angel of the Lord smote the camp of the Assyrians. At the prayers of David and the prophets and holy men, yea, and of the angels [8] too, the Lord stirred up the spirit of Cyrus king of Persia, to set them free *to go up to Jerusalem, and build the temple of the Lord God of Israel* [9].

escape out of his hand ; for, taking, thou shalt be taken. Jer. xxxiv. 3. *We will not hearken unto thee ; for, doing, we will do whatsoever,* &c. Ib. xliv. 17. Add Jer. xlix. 12. Ex. xix. 13. Deut. xx. 17. This uniform usage, doubtless, determined our Translators to prefer the rendering of the text to that in the margin, "That I should altogether pardon them," which would require the two ヽ's to be taken in different senses.

[7] See on xi. 12.   [8] Zech. i. 12.   [9] Ezr. i. 3.

8 ¶ Now when she had weaned Lo-ruhamah, she conceived, and bare a son.

9 Then said *God*, Call his name || Lo-ammi: for ye *are* not my people, and I will not be your *God*.

|| That is, *Not my people*.

But much more, this is the special promise of the Gospel, that God would deliver, not outwardly, but inwardly; not by human wars, but in peace; not by man, but by Himself. *By the Lord their God*, by Himself Who is speaking, or, The Father by the Son, (in like way as it is said, [1] *The Lord rained upon Sodom fire from the Lord.*) They were saved in Christ, the Lord and God of all, not by carnal weapons of warfare, but by the might of Him Who saved them, and shook thrones and dominions, and Who by His own Cross triumpheth over the hosts of the adversaries, and overthroweth the powers of evil, and giveth to those who love Him, to *tread on serpents and scorpions and all the power of the enemy*. They were saved, not for any merits of their own, nor for anything in themselves. But when human means, and man's works, such as he could do of his own free-will, and the power of his understanding, and the natural impulses of his affections, had proved unavailing, then He redeemed them by His Blood, and bestowed on them gifts and graces above nature, and filled them with His Spirit, and gave them *to will and to do of His good pleasure*. But this promise also was, and is, to the true Judah, i. e. to those who, as the name means, *confess* and *praise* God, and who, receiving Christ, Who, as Man, was of the tribe of Judah, became His children, being re-born by His Spirit."

8. *Now when she had weaned, &c.* Eastern women very commonly nursed their children two, or even three [2] years. The weaning then of the child portrays a certain interval of time between these two degrees of chastisement; but after this reprieve, the last and final judgment pictured here was to set in irreversibly.

9. *Call his name Lo-ammi,* i. e. *not My people.* The name of this third child expresses the last final degree of chastisement. As *the scattering by God* did not involve the being wholly *unpitied;* so neither did the being wholly *unpitied* for the time involve the being wholly rejected, so as to be *no more His people.* There were corresponding degrees in the actual history of the kingdom of Israel. God withdrew his protection by degrees. Under Jeroboam, in whose reign was this beginning of Hosea's prophecy, the people was yet outwardly strong. This strength has been thought to be expressed by the sex of the eldest child, that he was a son. On this, followed extreme weakness,

full of mutual massacre and horrible cruelty, first, in a long anarchy, then under Zechariah, Shallum, Menahem, Pekahiah, Pekah, Hosea, within, and through the invasions of Pul, Tiglathpileser, Shalmaneser, kings of Assyria, from without. The sex of the daughter, *Lo Ruhamah, Unpitied,* corresponds with this increasing weakness, and breaking of the spirit. 3. When she was *weaned,* i. e. when the people were deprived of all consolation and all the spiritual food whereby they had hitherto been supported, prophecy, teaching, promises, sacrifices, grace, favour, consolation, it became wholly *Lo-ammi, not My people.* As a distinct part of God's people, it was cast off for ever; and yet it became outwardly strong, as the Jews became powerful, and often were the persecutors of the Christians. The same is seen in individuals. God often first chastens them lightly, then more heavily, and brings them down in their iniquities; but if they still harden themselves, He withdraws both His chastisements and His grace, so that the sinner even prospers in this world, but, remaining finally impenitent, is cast off for ever.

I will not be your God; lit. *I will not be to you,* or, *for you; for you,* by Providence; *to you,* by love. The words say the more through their silence. They do not say what God will not be to those who had been His people. They do not say that He will not be their Defender, Nourisher, Saviour, Deliverer, Father, Hope, Refuge; and so they say that He will be none of these, which are all included in the English, *I will not be your God.* For, as God, He is these, and all things, to us. *I will not be to you.* God, by His love, vouchsafes to give all and to take all. He gives Himself wholly to His own, in order to make them wholly His. He makes an exchange with them. As God the Son, by His Incarnation, took the Manhood into God, so, by His Spirit dwelling in them, He makes men gods, *partakers of the Divine Nature*[3]. They, by His adoption, belong to Him; He, by His promise and gift, belongs to them. He makes them His; He becomes their's. This mutual exchange is so often expressed in Holy Scripture, to shew how God loveth to give Himself to us, and to make us His; and that where the one is, there is the other; nor can the one be without the other. This was the original covenant with Israel: *I will be your God, and you shall be My people*[4];

---

[1] Gen. xix. 24.   [2] 2 Macc. vii. 27.   [3] 2 S. Pet. i. 4.   [4] Lev. xxvi. 12. add Ex. vi. 7.

Before CHRIST cir. 785.

[1] Gen. 32. 12.
Rom. 9. 27, 28.

[k] Rom. 9. 25, 26.
1 Pet. 2. 10.

10 ¶ Yet [1] the number of the children of Israel shall be as the sand of the sea, which cannot be measured or numbered; [k] and it shall come to pass, *that*

‖ in the place where it was said unto them, [1] Ye *are* not my people, *there* it shall ‖ be said unto them, Ye *are* [l] [m] the sons of the living God.

Before CHRIST cir. 785.

‖ Or, *instead of that.*
[l] ch. 2. 23.
[m] John 1. 12.
1 John 3. 1.

---

and as such, it is often repeated in Jeremiah [1] and Ezekiel [2]. Afterwards, this is expressed still more affectionately. *I will be a Father unto you, and ye shall be My sons and daughters* [3]. And in Christ the Son, God saith, *I will be his Father, and he shall be My son* [4]. God, Who saith not this to any out of Christ, nor even to the holy Angels, (as it is written [5], *Unto which of the Angels said He at any time, I will be to him a Father, and he shall be to Me a son?*) saith it to us in Christ. And so, in turn, the Church and each single soul which is His, saith, or rather He saith it in them [6], *My beloved is mine, and I am His*, and more boldly yet, *I am my Beloved's, and my Beloved is mine* [7]. Whence at the Holy Communion we say, "then we dwell in Christ and Christ in us; we are one with Christ, and Christ with us;" and we pray that "we may evermore dwell in Him, and He in us."

10. *Yet* [lit. *and*] *the number of the children of Israel, &c.* Light springeth out of darkness; joy out of sorrow; mercy out of chastisement; life out of death. And so Holy Scripture commonly, upon the threat of punishment, promises blessings to the penitent. "Very nigh to the severest displeasure is the dispersion of sorrows and the promised close of darkness." What God takes away, He replaces with usury; things of time by things eternal; outward goods and gifts and privileges by inward; an earthly kingdom by Heaven. Both St. Peter [8] and St. Paul [9] tell us that this prophecy is already, in Christ, fulfilled in those of Israel, who were the true Israel, or of the Gentiles, to whom the promise was made [10], *In thy Seed shall all the nations be blessed*, and who, whether Jews or Gentiles, believed in Him. The Gentiles were adopted into the Church, which, at the Day of Pentecost, was formed of the Jews, and in which Jews and Gentiles became one in Christ [11]. Yet of the Jews alone, not only did *many tens of thousands in Jerusalem believe* [12], but S. Peter and S. James both write *to the dispersed of the ten tribes* [13]; and the Apostles themselves were Jews. Although, then, those Jews who believed in Christ were few in comparison of those who rejected Him, yet they were, in themselves, many, and,

through those who, in Christ Jesus, were *begotten* by them *through the Gospel* [14], they were numberless. Yet this prophecy, although accomplished in part, will, according to S. Paul [15], be yet more completely fulfilled in the end.

In the place where it was said [or *where it shall be said*, i. e. at the first] *unto them, ye are not My people*, there *it shall*, in after-time, *be said unto them*, ye are *the sons of the living God.* Both the times here spoken of by the Prophet were yet future; for Israel, although they had apostatised from God, had not yet been disowned by God, Who was still sending to them prophets, to reclaim them. They ceased to be owned as God's people, when, being dispersed abroad, they had no share in the sacrifices, no Temple-worship, no prophets, no typical reconciliation for sin. God took no more notice of them than the heathen. The Prophet then speaks of two futures; one, when it shall be said to them, *ye are not My people;* and a yet further future, in which it should be said, *ye are the sons of the living God.* The place of both was to be the same. The place of their rejection, the dispersion, was to be the place of their restoration. And so S. Peter says that this Scripture was fulfilled in them, while still *scattered abroad through Pontus, Galatia, Cappadocia, Asia, and Bithynia.* The place, then, where they shall be called *the sons of the living God*, is, wheresoever they should believe in Christ. Although separated in body, they were united by faith. And so it shall be unto the end. "Nothing now constraineth to go up to Jerusalem, and still to seek for the temple of stones; for neither will they worship God, as aforetime, by sacrifices of sheep or oxen; but their worship will be faith in Christ and in His commandments, and the sanctification in the Spirit, and the regeneration through Holy Baptism, making the glory of sonship their's, who are worthy thereof and are called thereto by the Lord [16]."

It shall be said, ye are the sons of the living God. It was the special sin of Israel, the source of all his other sins, that he had left the *living God*, to serve dead idols. In the times of the Gospel, not only should he own God

---

[1] Jer. xi. 4, 5. xxiv. 7. xxx. 22. xxxi. 1, 33. xxxii. 38.
[2] Ezek. xi. 20. xiv. 11. xxxvi. 28. xxxvii. 23, 27.
[3] 2 Cor. vi. 18. [4] 2 Sam. vii. 14. [5] Heb. i. 5.
[6] Cant. ii. 16. [7] Ib. vi. 3. [8] 1 S. Pet. ii. 10.

[9] Rom. ix. 25, 6. [10] Gen. xxii. 18.
[11] Gal. iii. 28. [12] Acts xxi. 20.
[13] S. James i. 1, 1 S. Pet. i. 1. [14] 1 Cor. iv. 15.
[15] Rom. xi. 25, 6. [16] S. Cyr.

Before
CHRIST
cir. 785.
_____
a Is. 11. 12, 13.
Jer. 3. 18.
Ezek. 34. 23. &
37. 16–24.

11 a Then shall the children of Judah and the children of Israel be gathered together, and appoint themselves one head, and they shall come up out of the land: for great *shall be* the day of Jezreel.

Before
CHRIST
cir. 785.

as his God, but he should have the greatest of all gifts, that the *living God*, the fountain of all life, of the life of nature, of grace, of glory, should be his Father, and as being his Father, should communicate to him that life, which He has and Is. For He Who Is Life, imparts life. God doth not only pour into the souls of His elect, grace and faith, hope and love, or all the manifold gifts of His Spirit, but He, *the living God*, maketh them to be His living sons, by His Spirit dwelling in them, by Whom He adopteth them as His sons, through Whom He giveth them grace. For by His Spirit He adopteth them as sons. [1] *We have received the spirit of adoption of sons, whereby we cry, Abba, Father. And if sons, then heirs; heirs of God and joint-heirs of Christ.* God not only giveth us grace, but adopteth us as sons. He not only accounteth us, but He maketh us sons; He maketh us sons, not outwardly, but inwardly; not by inward grace only, but by His Spirit: not only by the birth from the Spirit, but *in* the Only-Begotten Son; sons of God, because members of Christ, the Son of God; sons of God, by adoption, as Christ is by Nature; but actual sons of God, as Christ is actually and eternally *the* Son of God. God is our Father, not by nature, but by grace; yet He is really our Father, since we are born of Him, *sons of the living God*, born of the Spirit. He giveth us of His Substance, His Nature, although not by nature; not united with us, (as it is, personally, with His Son,) but dwelling in us, and making us *partakers of the Divine Nature.* Sons of the living God must be living by Him and to Him, by His life, yea, through Himself living in them, as our Saviour saith[2], *If any man love Me, he will keep My words, and My Father will love him, and We will come unto him, and make Our abode with him.*

11. *Then shall the children of Judah and the children of Israel be gathered together.* A little image of this union was seen after the captivity in Babylon, when some of the children of Israel, i. e. of the ten tribes, were united to Judah on his return, and the great schism of the two kingdoms came to an end. More fully, both literal Judah and Israel were gathered into one in the one Church of Christ, and all the spiritual Judah and Israel; i. e. as many of the Gentiles as, by following the faith, became the sons of faithful Abraham, and heirs of the promise to him.

And shall make themselves one Head. The act of God is named first, *they shall be gathered;* for without God we can do nothing. Then follows the act of their own consent, *they shall make themselves one Head;* for without us God doth nothing in us. God gathereth, by the call of His grace; they make to themselves one Head, by obeying His call, and submitting themselves to Christ, the one Head of the mystical body, the Church, who are His members. In like way, Ezekiel foretells of Christ, of the seed of David, under the name of David[3]; *I will set up one Shepherd over them, and He shall feed them, even My servant David; and I the Lord will be their God, and My servant David a Prince among them;* and again[4]; *I will make them one nation in the land, upon the mountains of Israel; and one king shall be king to them all; and they shall be no more two nations, neither shall they be divided into two kingdoms any more at all.* But this was not wholly fulfilled, until Christ came; for after the captivity they were under Zorobabel as chief, and Joshua as High-Priest.

And shall come up out of the land. To *come up* or *go up* is a title of dignity; whence, in our time, people are said to go up to the metropolis, or the University; and in Holy Scripture, to "come up," or "go up," out of Egypt[5], or Assyria[6], or Babylon[7], to the land of promise, or from the rest of the land to the place which God chose[8] to place His name there, Shiloh[9], or, afterwards, Jerusalem[10]; and it is foretold that the *mountain of the Lord's house shall be exalted above the hills; and many nations shall come and say, Come, and let us go up to the mountain of the Lord[11].* The land from which they should go up is, primarily and in image, Babylon, whence God restored the two tribes; but, in truth and fully, it is the whole aggregate of lands, the earth, the great *city of confusion,* which Babel designates. Out of which they shall go up, "not with their feet but with their affections," to the *city set upon a hill[12], the heavenly Jerusalem[13]* and Heaven itself, where we are *made to sit together with Christ[14],* and where *our conversation is[15],* that *where* He *is,* there may we *His servants be[16].* They ascend in mind above the earth and the

---

[1] Rom. viii. 15.
[2] S. John xiv. 23.　　[3] Ezek. xxxiv. 23, 24.
[4] Ib. xxxvii. 22.　　[5] Gen. xiii. 1. xlv. 25. &c.
[6] 2 Kgs xvii. 3. xviii. 9, 13. Isa. xxxvi. 1, 10.
[7] 2 Kgs xxiv. 1. Ezr. ii. 1. vii. 6. Neh. vii. 6. xii. 1.

[8] Ex. xxxiv. 24.　　　　[9] 1 Sam. i. 22.
[10] 2 Sam. xix. 34. 1 Kgs xii. 27, 28. Ps. cxxii. 4, &c.
[11] Isa. ii. 2, 3. Mic. iv. 1, 2.　　[12] S. Matt. v. 14.
[13] Heb. xii. 22.　　　　[14] Eph. ii. 6.
[15] Phil. iii. 20.　　　　[16] S. John xii. 26.

Before CHRIST cir. 785.

| That is, *My people.* | That is, *Having obtained mercy.*

SAY ye unto your brethren, ‖ Ammi; and to your sisters, ‖ Ruhamah.

2 Plead with your mother, plead; for ᵃ she is not my wife, neither am I her husband: let her therefore put away her ᵇ whoredoms out of her sight, and her adulteries from between her breasts;

Before CHRIST cir. 785.

ᵃ Isai. 50. 1.

ᵇ Ezek. 16. 25.

things of earth, and the lowness of carnal desires, that so they may, in the end, come up out of the earth, *to meet the Lord in the air, and for ever be with the Lord*[1]. *For great is the day of Jezreel.* God had denounced woe on Israel, under the names of the three children of the prophet, Jezreel, Lo-Ammi, Lo-Ruhamah; and now, under those three names, He promises the reversal of that sentence, in Christ. He begins with the name, under which He had begun to pronounce the woe, the first son, *Jezreel. Jezreel* means *God shall sow,* either for increase, or to scatter. When God threatened, *Jezreel* necessarily meant, *God shall scatter;* here, when God reverses His threatening, it means, *God shall sow.* But the issue of the seed is either single, as in human birth, or manifold, as in the seed-corn. Hence it is used either of Him Who was eminently, *the Seed of Abraham, the Seed of the woman,* or of the manifold harvest, which He, the seed-corn[2], should bring forth, when sown in the earth, by His vicarious Death. It means, then, Christ or His Church. Christ, the Only-Begotten Son of God before all worlds, was, in time, also "conceived by the Holy Ghost, of the Virgin Mary," the Son of God Alone, in a way in which no other man was born of God. Great then should be the day, when "God should sow," or give the increase in mercy, as before He scattered them, in His displeasure. The great Day wherein *God should sow,* was, first, *the day which the Lord hath made*[3], the Incarnation, in which God the Son became Man, *the seed of the woman;* then, it was the Passion, in which, like a seed-corn, He was sown in the earth; then, the Resurrection, when He rose, *the Firstborn among many brethren;* then, all the days in which He *bare much fruit.* It is the one day of salvation, in which, generation after generation, *a new seed* hath been or *shall be born* unto Him, and *shall serve Him*[4]. Even unto the end, every time of any special growth of the Church, every conversion of Heathen tribe or people, is *a day of Jezreel,* a day in which "the Lord soweth." Great, wonderful, glorious, thrice-blessed is the day of Christ; for in it He hath

done great things for us, gathering together under Himself, the Head, those scattered abroad, *without hope and without God in the world;* making "*not* My people" into "My people" and those *not beloved* into His *beloved,* the objects of His tender, yearning compassion, full of His grace and mercy. For so it follows,

II. 1. *Say ye unto your brethren, Ammi,* i. e. *My people, and to your sisters, Ruhamah,* i. e. *beloved or tenderly pitied.* The words form a climax of the love of God. First, the people scattered[5], unpitied[6], and disowned by God[7], is re-born of God; then it is declared to be in continued relation to God, *My people;* then to be the object of his yearning love. The words, *My people,* may be alike filled up, "ye are My people," and "be ye My people." They are words of hope in prophecy, "ye shall be again My people;" they become words of joy in each stage of fulfillment. They are words of mutual joy and gratulation, when obeyed; they are words of encouragement, until obeyed. God is reconciled to us, and willeth that we be reconciled to Him. Among those who already are God's people, they are the voice of the joy of mutual love in the oneness of the Spirit of adoption; *we are His people;* to those without (whether the ten tribes, or the Jews or heretics,) they are the voice of those who know in Whom they have believed, *Be ye also His people.* "Despair of the salvation of none, but, with brotherly love, call them to repentance and salvation."

This verse closes what went before, as God's reversal of His own sentence, and anticipates what is to come[8]. God commands the prophets and all those who love Him, to appeal to those who forget Him, holding out to them the mercy in store for them also, if they will return to Him. He bids them not to despise those yet alien from Him, "but to treat as brethren and sisters, those whom God willeth to introduce into His house, and to call to the riches of His inheritance."

2. *Plead with your mother, plead.* The prophets close the threats of coming judgments with the dawn of after-hopes; and from hopes

[1] 1 Thess. iv. 17.   [2] S. John xii. 24. [3] Ps. cxviii. 24.   [4] Ps. xxii. 30, 31.

[5] Jezreel.   [6] Lo-Ruhamah. [7] Lo-Ammi.   [8] v. 14 sqq.

Before CHRIST cir. 785.
Jer. 13. 22, 26.
Ezek. 16. 37, 39.
Ezek. 16. 4.

3 Lest °I strip her naked, and set her as in the day that she was ᵈborn, and

make her ᵉas a wilderness, and set her like a dry land, and slay her with ᶠthirst.

Before CHRIST cir. 785.
Ezek. 19. 13.
Amos 8. 11, 13.

they go back to God's judgments against sin, pouring in wine and oil into the wounds of sinners. The *mother* is the Church or nation; the *sons*, are its members, one by one. These, when turned to God, must plead with their mother, that she turn also. When involved in her judgments, they must plead with her, and not accuse God. God *had not forgotten to be gracious;* but she "kept not His love, and refused His friendship, and despised the purity of spiritual communion with Him, and would not travail with the fruit of His Will." "[1] The sons differ from the mother, as the inventor of evil from those who imitate it. For as, in good, the soul which, from the Spirit of God, conceiveth the word of truth, is the mother, and whoso profiteth by hearing the word of doctrine from her mouth, is the child, so, in evil, whatsoever soul inventeth evil is the mother, and whoso is deceived by her is the son. So in Israel, the adulterous mother was the Synagogue, and the individuals deceived by her were the sons."

"Ye who believe in Christ, and are both of Jews and Gentiles, say ye to the broken branches and to the former people which is cast off, *My people,* for it is your brother; and *Beloved,* for it is *your sister.* For when [2] the fulness of the Gentiles shall have come in, then shall all Israel be saved. In like way we are bidden not to despair of heretics, but to incite them to repentance, and with brotherly love to long for their salvation [3]."

For she is not My wife. God speaketh of the spiritual union between Himself and His people whom He had chosen, under the terms of the closest human oneness, of husband and wife. She was no longer united to Him by faith and love, nor would He any longer own her. Plead therefore with her earnestly as orphans, who, for her sins, have lost the protection of their Father.

Let her therefore put away her whoredoms. So great is the tender mercy of God. He says, let her but put away her defilements, and she shall again be restored, as if she had never fallen; let her but put away all objects of attachment, which withdrew her from God, and God will again be All to her.

Adulteries, whoredoms. God made the soul for Himself; He betrothed her to Himself through the gift of the Holy Spirit; He united her to Himself. All love, then, out of God, is to take another, instead of God. *Whom have I in heaven but Thee? and there is*

none upon earth that I desire besides Thee. Adultery is to become another's than His, the Only Lord and Husband of the soul. *Whoredom* is to have many other objects of sinful love. Love is one, for One. The soul which has forsaken the One, is drawn hither and thither, has manifold objects of desire, which displace one another, because none satisfies. Hence the prophet speaks of "fornications, adulteries;" because the soul, which will not rest in God, seeks to distract herself from her unrest and unsatisfiedness, by heaping to herself manifold lawless pleasures, out of, and contrary to the Will of, God.

From before her, lit. *from her face.* The face is the seat of modesty, shame, or shamelessness. Hence in Jeremiah God says to Judah, [4] *Thou hadst a harlot's forehead; thou refusedst to be ashamed;* and [5] *they were not at all ashamed, neither will they blush.* The eyes, also, are the [6] *windows, through which death,* i. e. lawless desire, *enters into* the soul, and takes it captive.

From her breasts. These are exposed, adorned, degraded in disorderly love, which they are employed to allure. Beneath too lies the heart, the seat of the affections. It may mean then, that she should no more gaze with pleasure on the objects of her sin, nor allow her heart to dwell on things which she loved sinfully. Whence it is said of the love of Christ, which should keep the soul free from all unruly passions which might offend him, [7] *My Well-beloved shall lie all night betwixt my breasts,* [8] *as a seal upon the heart* beneath.

3. *Lest I strip her naked.* "There is an outward visible nakedness, and an inward, which is invisible. The invisible nakedness is, when the soul within is bared of the glory and the grace of God." The visible nakedness is the privation of God's temporal and visible gifts, the goods of this world, or outward distinction. God's inward gifts the sinful soul or nation despises, while those outward gifts she prizes. And therefore, when the soul parts with the inward ornaments of God's grace, He strips her of the outward, His gifts of nature, of His Providence and of His Protection, if so be, through her outward misery and shame and poverty, she may come to feel that deeper misery and emptiness and disgrace within, which she had had no heart to feel. So, when our first parents lost the robe of innocence, *they knew that they were naked* [9].

[1] Rup.   [2] Rom. xi. 25, 26.
[3] S. Jer.   [4] Jer. iii. 3.

[5] Ib. vi. 15.   [6] Ib. ix. 21.   [7] Cant. i. 13.
[8] Ib. viii. 6.   [9] Gen. iii. 7.

4 And I will not have mercy upon her children;

for they *be* the [g]children of whoredoms.

[g] John 8. 41.

And set her, (lit. "I will *fix* her," so that she shall have no power to free herself, but must remain as a gazing stock,) *as in the day that she was born,* i. e. helpless, defiled, uncleansed, uncared for, unformed, cast out and loathsome. Such she was in Egypt, which is in Holy Scripture spoken of, as her birthplace [1]; for there she first became a people; thence the God of her fathers called her to be His people. There she was naked of the grace and of the love of God, and of the wisdom of the law; indwelt by an evil spirit, as being an idolatress; without God; and under hard bondage, in works of mire and clay, to Pharaoh, the type of Satan, and her little ones a prey. For when a soul casts off the defence of heavenly grace, it is an easy prey to Satan.

And make her as a wilderness, and set her as a dry land, and slay her with thirst. The outward desolation, which God inflicts, is a picture of the inward. Drought and famine are among the four sore judgments, with which God threatened the land, and our Lord forewarned them, [2] *Your house is left unto you desolate;* and Isaiah says, [3] *Whereas thou hast been forsaken and hated, so that no man went through thee.* But the Prophet does not say, *make her a wilderness,* but *make* her *as a wilderness.* The soul of the sinner is solitary and desolate, for it has not the presence of God; unfruitful, bearing briars and thorns only, for it is unbedewed by God's grace, unwatered by the Fountain of living waters; athirst, *not with thirst for water, but of hearing the word of the Lord,* yet also, burning with desire, which the foul streams of this world's pleasure never slake. In contrast with such thirst, Jesus says of the Holy Spirit which He would give to them that believe in Him, *Whosoever drinketh of the water, that I shall give him, shall never thirst; but the water, that I shall give him, shall be in him a well of water, springing up into everlasting life* [4].

"[5] But was not that certain, which God had said, *I will no more have mercy on the house of Israel?* How then does God recall it, saying, ' *Let her put away her fornications, &c. lest I do to her this or that which I have spoken?* ' This is not unlike to that, when sentence had been passed on Nebuchadnezzar, Daniel saying, *This is the decree of the Most High, which is come upon my Lord the king; they shall drive thee from men, and thy dwelling;* the same Daniel says, *Wherefore, O king, let my counsel be acceptable unto thee, and redeem*

thy sins by righteousness, and thine iniquities by shewing mercy on the poor, if it may be a lengthening of thy tranquillity [6]. What should we learn hereby, but that it hangs upon our own will, whether God suspend the judgment or no? For we ought not to impute our own evil to God, or impiously think that fate rules us. In other words, this or that evil comes, not because God foreknew or foreordained it; but, because this evil was to be, or would be done, therefore God both foreknew it, and prefixed His sentence upon it. Why then does God predetermine an irrevocable sentence? Because He foresaw incorrigible malice. Why, again, after pronouncing sentence, doth God counsel amendment? That we may know by experience, that they are incorrigible. Therefore, He waits for them, although they will not return, and with much patience invites them to repentance." Individuals also repented, although the nation was incorrigible.

4. *I will not have mercy upon her children.* God visits the sins of the parents upon the children, until the entailed curse be cut off by repentance. God enforces His own word *lo-ruhamah, Unpitied,* by repeating it here, *lo-arahem,* "I will not pity." Reproaches, which fall upon the mother, are ever felt with especial keenness. Whence Saul called Jonathan, [7] *Thou son of the perverse rebellious woman.* Therefore, the more to arouse them, he says, *for they are the children of whoredoms,* evil children of an evil parent, as S. John Baptist calls the hypocritical Jews, *ye generation of vipers* [8]. "This they were, from their very birth and swaddling-clothes, never touching any work of piety, nor cultivating any grace." As of Christ, and of those who, in Him, are nourished up in deeds of righteousness, it is said, *I was cast upon Thee from the womb; Thou art my God from my mother's belly;* so, contrariwise, of the ungodly it is said, *The wicked are estranged from the womb; they go astray as soon as they be born, speaking lies.* And as they who *live honestly, as in the day and in the light,* are called *children of the day and of the light,* so they who live a defiled life are called *the children of whoredoms.* "[5] To call them *children of whoredoms* is all one with saying, that they too are incorrigible or unchangeable. For of such, Wisdom, after saying, *executing Thy judgments upon them by little and little,* added forthwith, [9] *not being ignorant that they were a naughty generation, and that their malice was bred in them, and that their cogitation would never be changed, for it was a*

---

[1] Ezek. xvi. 4.   [2] S. Matt. xxiii. 38.
[3] Is. lx. 15.   [4] S. John iv. 14. vii. 38, 39.

[5] Rup.   [6] Dan. iv. 24, 25, 27.   [7] 1 Sam. xx. 3
[8] S. Matt. iii. 7.   [9] Wisd. xii. 1

Before
CHRIST
cir. 785.

h Isai. 1. 21.
Jer. 3. 1, 6, 8, 9.
Ezek. 16. 15, 16.
&c.

i ver. 8. 12.
Jer. 44. 17.

5 ʰFor their mother hath played the harlot: she that conceived them hath done shamefully: for she said, I will go after my lovers, ⁱthat give *me* my bread and my water, my wool and my flax, mine oil and my † drink.

6 ¶ Therefore, behold, ᵏI will hedge up thy way with thorns, and † make a wall, that she shall not find her paths.

Before
CHRIST
cir. 785.

† Heb. *drinks.*

k Job 3. 23. & 19. 8.
Lam. 3. 7, 9.
† Heb. *wall a
wall.*

---

cursed seed from the beginning. All this is here expressed briefly by this word, *that they are the children of whoredoms,* meaning that their malice too was inbred, and that they, as much as the Ammorite and Hittite, were *a cursed seed.* Nor yet, in so speaking, did he blame the nature which God created, but he vehemently reproves the abuse of nature, that malice, which cleaves to nature but was no part of it, was by custom changed into nature."

5. *She that conceived them hath done shamefully,* lit. *hath made shameful.* The silence as to *what* she *made shameful* is more emphatic than any words. She *made shameful* every thing which she could *make shameful,* her acts, her children, and herself.

I will go [lit. *let me go, I would go*] *after my lovers.* The Hebrew word *Meahabim* denotes intense passionate love ; the plural form implies that they were sinful loves. Every word aggravates the shamelessness. Amid God's chastisements, she encourages herself, *Come, let me go,* as people harden and embolden, and, as it were, lash themselves into further sin, lest they should shrink back, or stop short in it. *Let me go after.* She waits not, as it were, to be enticed, allured, seduced. She herself, uninvited, unbidden, unsought, contrary to the wont and natural feeling of woman, follows after those by whom she is not drawn, and refuses to follow God Who would draw her [1]. The *lovers* are, whatever a man loves and courts, out of God. They were the idols and false gods, whom the Jews, like the heathen, took to themselves, besides God. But in truth they were devils. Devils she sought ; the will of devils she followed ; their pleasure she fulfilled, abandoning herself to sin, shamefully filled with all wickedness, and travailing with all manner of impurity. These she professed that she loved, and that they, not God, loved her. For whoever receives the gifts of God, except from God and in God's way, receives them from devils. Whoso seeks what God forbids, seeks it from Satan, and holds that Satan, not God, loves him ; since God refuses it, Satan encourages him to possess himself of it. Satan, then, is his *lover.*

That gave me my bread and my water. The

sense of human weakness abides, even when Divine love is gone. The whole history of man's superstitions is an evidence of this, whether they have been the mere instincts of nature, or whether they have attached themselves to religion or irreligion, Jewish or Pagan or Mohammedan, or have been practised by half-Christians. "She is conscious that she hath not these things by her own power, but is beholden to some other for them ; but not remembering Him (as was commanded) Who had *given her power to get wealth,* and *richly all things to enjoy,* she professes them to be the gifts of her lovers." *Bread and water, wool and flax,* express the necessaries of life, *food and clothing ; mine oil and my drink* [Heb. *drinks*], its luxuries. Oil includes also ointments, and so served both for health, food and medicine, for anointing the body, and for perfume. In perfumes and choice drinks, the rich people of Israel were guilty of great profusion ; whence it is said, *He that loveth wine and oil shall not be rich*[2]. For such things alone, the things of the body, did Israel care. Ascribing them to her false gods, she loved those gods, and held that they loved her. In like way, the Jewish women shamelessly told Jeremiah[3], *we will certainly do whatsoever thing goes out of our own mouth, to burn incense unto the queen of heaven, and to pour out drink-offerings unto her, as we have done, we and our fathers, our kings and our princes, in the cities of Judah and in the streets of Jerusalem. For then had we plenty of victuals, and were well, and saw no evil. But since we left off to burn incense to the queen of heaven, and to pour out drink-offerings unto her, we have wanted all things, and have been consumed by the sword and by the famine.*

6. *Therefore,* i. e. because she said, *I will go after my lovers, behold I will hedge up thy ways ;* lit. *behold, I hedging.* It expresses an immediate future, or something which, as being fixed in the mind of God, is as certain as if it were actually taking place. So swift and certain should be her judgments.

Thy way. God had before spoken *of* Israel ; now He turns to her, pronouncing judgment upon her ; then again He turneth away from her, as not deigning to regard her. "If the sinner's way were plain, and the soul

---

[1] See Ezek. xvi. 31–4.   [2] Pr. xxi. 17.   [3] Jer. xliv. 17, 18.

Before
CHRIST
cir. 785.
7 And she shall follow after her lovers, but she shall not overtake them; and she shall seek them, but shall not find *them:*

then shall she say, [1] I will go and return to my[m] first husband; for then[1] *was it* better with me than now.

Before
CHRIST
cir. 785.

ch. 5. 15.
Luke 15. 18.
= Ezek. 16. 8.

---

had still temporal prosperity, after it had turned away from its Creator, scarcely or never could it be recalled, nor would it *hear the* voice *behind it,* warning it. But when adversity befalls it, and tribulation or temporal difficulties overtake it in its course, then it remembers the Lord its God." So it was with Israel in Egypt. When *they sat by the flesh pots, and did eat bread to the full,* amid *the fish, which they did eat freely, the cucumbers and the melons,* they forgat the God of their fathers, and served the idols of Egypt. Then He raised up *a new king,* who *made their lives bitter with hard bondage, in mortar and in brick and in all the service of the field;* then *they groaned by reason of the bondage, and they cried, and their cry came up unto God by reason of their bondage, and God heard their groaning*[1]. So in the book of Judges the ever-recurring history is, they forsook God; He delivered them into the hands of their enemies; they cried unto Him; He sent them a deliverer. A way may be found through a *hedge of thorns,* although with pain and suffering; through a stone *wall* even a strong man cannot burst a way. *Thorns* then may be the pains to the flesh, with which God visits sinful pleasures, so that the soul, if it would break through to them, is held back and torn; the *wall* may mean, that all such sinful joys shall be cut off altogether, as by bereavement, poverty, sickness, failure of plans, &c. In sorrows, we cannot find our idols, which, although so near, vanish from us; but we may find our God, though we are so far from Him, and He so often seems so far from us. "God hedgeth with thorns the ways of the elect, when they find prickles in the things of time, which they desire. They attain not the pleasures of this world which they crave." They cannot *find their paths,* when, in the special love of God, they are hindered from obtaining what they seek amiss. "I escaped not Thy scourges," says St. Augustine, as to his heathen state[2], "for what mortal can? For Thou wert ever with me, mercifully rigorous, and besprinkling with most bitter alloy all my unlawful pleasures, that I might seek pleasure without alloy. But where to find such, I could not discover, save in Thee, O Lord, Who teachest by sorrow, and woundest us, to heal, and killest us, lest we die from Thee."

7. *And she shall follow after.* The words

rendered *follow after* and *seek*[3], are intensive, and express "eager, vehement pursuit," and "diligent search." They express, together, a pursuit, whose minuteness is not hindered by its vehemence, nor its extent and wideness by its exactness. She shall seek far and wide, minutely and carefully, everywhere and in all things, and shall fail in all. For eighteen hundred years the Jews have chased after a phantom, a Christ, triumphing, after the manner of the kings of the earth, and it has ever escaped them. The sinful soul will too often struggle on, in pursuit of what God is withdrawing, and will not give over, until, through God's persevering mercy, the fruitless pursuit exhausts her, and she finds it hopeless. Oh the wilfulness of man, and the unwearied patience of God!

Then shall she say, I will go and return. She encourages herself tremblingly to return to God. The words express a mixture of purpose and wish. Before, she said, "Come, let me go after my lovers;" now, she says, "Come let me go and let me return," as the prodigal in the Gospel, *I will arise and go to my Father.*

To my first husband. "God is the *first Husband* of the soul, which, while yet pure, He, through the love of the Holy Ghost, united with Himself. Him the soul longeth for, when it findeth manifold bitternesses, as thorns, in those delights of time and sense which it coveted. For when the soul begins to be gnawed by the sorrows of the world which she loveth, then she understandeth more fully, how it was better with her, with her former husband. Those whom a perverse will led astray, distress mostly converts." "Mostly, when we cannot obtain in this world what we wish, when we have been wearied with the impossibility of our search of earthly desires, then the thought of God returns to the soul; then, what was before distasteful, becomes pleasant to us; He Whose commands had been bitter to the soul, suddenly in memory grows sweet to her, and the sinful soul determines to be a faithful wife." And God still vouchsafes to be, on her return, the Husband even of the adulterous soul, however far she had strayed from Him.

For then it was better with me than now. It is the voice of the prodigal son in the Gospel, which the Father hears, *How many hired servants of my Father have bread enough and to spare, and I perish with hunger!* "I will

---

[1] Ex. xvi. 3. Nu. xi. 5. Ex. i. 8, 14. ii. 23, 4.

[2] Conf. ii. 4.

בקש. רדף[3].

8 For she did not ⁿ know that °I gave her corn, and † wine, and oil, and multiplied her silver and gold, ‖ which they prepared for Baal.

9 Therefore will I re-

turn, and ᴾtake away my corn in the time thereof, and my wine in the season thereof, and will ‖ recover my wool and my flax given to cover her nakedness.

ⁿ Isa. 1. 3.
° Ezek. 16. 17, 18, 19.
† Heb. *new wine.*
‖ Or, wherewith *they made*
Baal, ch. 8. 4.

ᴾ ver. 3.
‖ Or, *take away.*

serve," Israel would say, "the living and true God, not the pride of men, or of evil spirits; for even in this life it is much sweeter to bear the yoke of the Lord, than to be the servant of men." In regard to the ten tribes, the "then" must mean the time before the apostacy under Jeroboam. God, in these words, softens the severity of His upbraiding and of His sentences of coming woe, by the sweetness of promised mercy. Israel was so impatient of God's threats, that their kings and princes slew those whom He sent unto them. God wins her attention to His accusations by this brief tempering of sweetness.

8. *For she did not know.* The prophet having, in summary[1], related her fall, her chastisement, and her recovery, begins anew, enlarging both on the impending inflictions, and the future mercy. She *did not know,* because she would not; she *would not retain God in her knowledge*[2]. *Knowledge,* in Holy Scripture, is not of the understanding, but of the heart and the will.

That I gave her corn, &c. The *I* is emphatic[3]. *She did not know, that it was I Who gave her.* God gave them the *corn, and wine, and oil,* first, because He gave them the land itself. They held it of Him as their Lord. As He says[4], *The land is Mine, and ye are strangers and sojourners with Me.* He gave them also in the course of His ordinary Providence, wherein He also gave them *the gold and silver,* which they gained by trading. *Silver* He had so multiplied to her in the days of Solomon, that it was *in Jerusalem as stones, nothing accounted of*[5], and *gold,* through the favor which He gave him[6], was in abundance above measure.

Which they prepared for Baal. Rather, as in the E. Margin, *which they made into Baal*[7]. "Of that gold and silver, which God had so multiplied, Israel, revolting from the house of David and Solomon, made, first the calves of gold, and then Baal." Of God's own gifts they made their gods. They took God's gifts as from their gods, and made them into gods to them. *Baal,* Lord, the same as Bel, was an object of idolatry among the Phœnicians and Tyrians. Its worship was brought into Israel by Jezebel, daughter of a king of

Sidon. Jehu destroyed it for a time, because its adherents were adherents of the house of Ahab. The worship was partly cruel, like that of Moloch, partly abominable. It had this aggravation beyond that of the calves, that Jezebel aimed at the extirpation of the worship of God, setting up a rival temple, with its 450 prophets and 400 of the kindred idolatry of Ashtaroth, and slaying all the prophets of God.

It seems to us strange folly. They attributed to gods, who represented the functions of nature, the power to give what God alone gives. How is it different, when men now say, "nature does this, or that," or speak of "the operations of nature," or the laws of "nature," and ignore God Who appoints those laws, and *worketh hitherto*[8] "those operations?" They attributed to planets (as have astrologers at all times) influence over the affairs of men, and worshiped a god, Baal-Gad, or Jupiter, who presided over them. Wherein do those otherwise, who displace God's Providence by fortune or fate or destiny, and say "fortune willed," "fortune denied him," "it was his fate, his destiny," and, even when God most signally interposes, shrink from naming Him, as if to speak of God's Providence were something superstitious? What is this, but to ascribe to Baal, under a new name, the works and gifts of God? And more widely yet. Since "men have as many strange gods as they have sins," what do they, who seek pleasure or gain or greatness or praise in forbidden ways or from forbidden sources, than make their pleasure or gain or ambition their god, and offer their time and understanding and ingenuity and intellect, yea, their whole lives and their whole selves, their souls and bodies, all the gifts of God, in sacrifice to the idol which they have made? Nay, since whosoever believes of God otherwise than He has revealed Himself, does, in fact, believe in another god, not in the One True God, what else does all heresy, but form to itself an idol out of God's choicest gift of nature, man's own mind, and worship, not indeed the works of man's own hands, but the creature of his own understanding?

9. *Therefore I will return.* God is, as it

[1] ver. 5-7.   [2] Rom. i. 28.   [3] אָכִי.
[4] Lev. xxv. 23.   [5] 1 Kgs x. 27, 21.
[6] Ib. ix. 14. x. 10, 14.
[7] See viii. 4. Ezek. xvi. 17-19.   [8] S. John v. 17.

Before CHRIST cir. 785.

10 And now [q] will I discover her † lewdness in the sight of her lovers, and none shall deliver her out of mine hand.

q Ezek. 16. 37. & 23. 29.
† Heb. *folly*, or *villany*.

11 [r] I will also cause all her mirth to cease, her [s] feast days, her new moons, and her sabbaths, and all her solemn feasts.

r Amos 8. 10.
s 1 Kgs 12. 32. Amos 8. 5.

were, absent from men, when He lets them go on in their abuse of His gifts. *His judgments are far above out of their sight.* He *returns* to them, and His Presence is felt in chastisements, as it might have been in mercies. He is not out of sight or out of mind, then. Others render it, *I will turn*, i. e. *I will do other than before; I will turn* from love to displeasure, from pouring out benefits to the infliction of chastisements, from giving abundance of all things to punishing them with the want of all things.

I will take away My corn in the time thereof. God shews us that His gifts come from Him, either by giving them when we almost despair of them, or taking them away, when they are all but our's. It can seem no chance, when He so doeth. The chastisement is severer also, when the good things, long looked-for, are, at the last, taken out of our very hands, and that, when there is no remedy. If in harvest-time there be dearth, what afterwards! "God taketh away all, that they who knew not the Giver through abundance, might know Him through want."

And will recover My wool. God *recovers*, and, as it were, *delivers* the works of His Hands from serving the ungodly. While He leaves His creatures in the possession of the wicked, they are holden, as it were, in captivity, being kept back from their proper uses, and made the handmaidens and instruments and tempters to sin. God made His creatures on earth to serve man, that man, on occasion of them, might glorify Him. It is against the order of nature, to use God's gifts to any other end, short of God's glory; much more, to turn God's gifts against Himself, and make them serve to pride or luxury or sensual sin. It is a bondage, as it were, to them. Whence of them also St. Paul saith [1], *The creature was made subject to vanity, not willingly;* and, *all creation groaneth and travaileth in pain together until now.* Penitents have felt this. They have felt that they deserve no more that the sun should shine on them, or the earth sustain them, or the air support them, or wine refresh them, or food nourish them, since all these are the creatures and servants of the God Whom themselves have offended, and they themselves deserve no more to be served by God's servants, since they have rebelled against their common Master, or to use even rightly what they have abused against the will of their Creator.

My flax, given *to cover her nakedness*, i. e. which God had given to that end. Shame was it, that, covered with the raiment which God had given her to hide her shame, she did deeds of shame. The white linen garments of her Priests also were symbols of that purity, which the Great High Priest should have and give. Now, withdrawing those gifts, He gave them up to the greatest visible shame, such as insolent conquerors, in leading a people into captivity, often inflicted upon them. Thereby, in act, was figured that loss of the robe of righteousness, heavenly grace, wherewith God beautifies the soul, whereof when it is stripped, it is indeed foul.

10. *Her lewdness.* The word originally means *folly*, and so *foulness.* For sin is the only real folly, as holiness is the only true wisdom. But the folly of sin is veiled amid outward prosperity, and men think themselves, and are thought, wise and honorable and in good repute, and are centres of attraction and leaders of society, so long as they prosper; as it is said, [2] *so long as thou doest well unto thyself, men will speak of thee.* But as soon as God withdraws those outward gifts, the mask drops off, and men, being no longer dazzled, despise the sinner, while they go on to hug the sin. God says, *I will discover*, as just before He had said, that His gifts had been given to *cover her.* He would then lay her bare outwardly and inwardly; her folly, foulness, wickedness, and her outward shame; and that, *in the sight of her lovers*, i. e. of those whom she had chosen instead of God, her idols, the heavenly bodies, the false gods, and real devils. Satan must jeer at the wretched folly of the souls whom he deceives.

And none shall deliver her out of My hand. Neither rebel spirits nor rebel men. The evil spirits would prolong the prosperity of the wicked, that so they might sin the more deeply, and might not repent, (which they see men to do amid God's chastisements,) and so might incur the deeper damnation.

11. *I will also cause her mirth to cease, her feast days, &c.* Israel had forsaken the temple of God; despised His priests; received from Jeroboam others whom God had not chosen; altered, at least, one of the festivals; celebrated all, where God had forbidden; and

[1] Rom. viii. 20, 22.

[2] Ps. xlix. 18.

Before
CHRIST
cir. 785.

† Heb. *make des-*
olate.
¹ ver. 5.

ª Ps. 80. 12, 13.
Isai. 5. 5.

12 And I will † destroy her vines and her fig trees, ¹whereof she hath said, These *are* my rewards that my lovers have given me: and ªI will make them a forest, and the beasts of the field shall eat them.

Before
CHRIST
cir. 785.

ˣ Ezek. 23. 40, 42.

13 And I will visit upon her the days of Baalim, wherein she burned incense to them, and she ˣdecked herself with her earrings and her jewels, and she went after her lovers, and forgat me, saith the LORD.

---

worshiped the Creator under the form of a brute creature [1]. Yet they kept the great *feast-days*, whereby they commemorated His mercies to their forefathers; the *new moons*, whereby the first of every month was given to God; *the sabbaths*, whereby they owned God as the Creator of all things; and *all the other solemn feasts*, whereby they thanked God for acts of His special Providence, or for His annual gifts of nature, and condemned themselves for trusting in false gods for those same gifts, and for associating His creatures with Himself. But man, even while he disobeys God, does not like to part with Him altogether, but would serve Him enough to soothe his own conscience, or as far as he can without parting with his sin which he loves better. Jeroboam retained all of God's worship, which he could combine with his own political ends; and even in Ahab's time Israel *halted between two opinions*, and Judah *sware both by the Lord and by Malcham* [2], the true God and the false. All this their worship was vain, because contrary to the Will of God. Yet since God says, *I will take away all her mirth*, they had, what they supposed to be, religious *mirth* in their *feasts*, fulfilling as they thought, the commandment of God, *Thou shalt rejoice in thy feasts* [3]. She could have no real joy, since true joy is *in the Lord* [4]. So, in order that she might not deceive herself any more, God says that He will take away that feigned formal service of Himself, which they blended with the real service of idols, and will remove the hollow outward joy, that, through repentance, they might come to the true joy in Him.

12. *And I will destroy her vines and her fig trees.* Before, God had threatened to take away the fruits in their seasons; now He says, that He will take away all hope for the future; not the fruit only, but the trees which bare it. "The vine is a symbol of joy, the fig of sweetness [5]." It was the plague, which God in former times laid upon those, out of the midst of whom He took them to be His people. *⁶He smote their vines also and*

their *fig trees, and brake the trees of their coasts.* Now that they had become like the heathen, He dealt with them as with the heathen.

Of which she said, these are my rewards; lit. *my hire.* It is the special word, used of the payment to the adulteress, or degraded woman, and so continues the likeness, by which he had set forth the foulness of her desertion of God.

And I will make them a forest. The vines and fig-trees which had aforetime been their wealth, and full of beauty, should, when neglected, run wild, and become the harbour of the wild beasts which should prey upon them. So to the wicked God causes, *that the things which should have been for their wealth should be an occasion of falling* [7]. They contain in themselves the sources of their own decay.

13. *I will visit upon her the days of Baalim,* or *Baals.* When men leave the one true God, they make to themselves many idols. They act, as if they could make up a god piece-meal out of the many attributes of the One God, and create their Creator. His power of production becomes one God; His power of destroying, another; His Providence, a third; and so on, down to the very least acts. So they had many Baals or Lords; a *Baal-berith* [8], *Lord of covenants,* who was to guard the sanctity of oaths; *Baal-zebub* [9], *Lord of flies,* who was to keep off the plague of flies, and *Baal-Peor* [10], who presided over sin. All these their various idolatries, and all the time of their idolatries, God threatens to visit upon them at once. "The days of punishment shall equal the days of the wanderings, in which she burnt incense to Baal." God spares long. But when persevering impenitence draws down His anger, He punishes not for the last sin only, but for all. Even to the penitent, God mostly makes the chastisement bear some proportion to the length and greatness of the sin.

Wherein she burnt incense unto them. Incense was that part of sacrifice, which especially denoted thanksgiving and prayer ascending to God.

And she decked herself with her ear-rings and

---

¹ See Introduction, p. 11.　　² Zeph. i. 5.
³ Deut. xvi. 14.　　⁴ Phil. iv. 4.
⁵ See Jud. ix. 11, 13.

⁶ Ps. cv. 33. See Jer. v. 17.
⁷ Ps. lxix. 22.　　⁸ Jud. viii. 33.
⁹ 2 Kgs. i. 2.　　¹⁰ Num. xxv. 3.

Before CHRIST cir. 785.

ʸ Ezek. 20. 25.

14 ¶ Therefore, behold, I will allure her, and ʸbring her into the wilderness, and speak || †comfortably unto her.

Before CHRIST cir. 785.

|| Or, *friendly.*
† Heb. *to her heart.*

---

her jewels. Christ says to the bride[1], *Thy cheeks are comely with rows of jewels, thy neck with chains of gold.* But what He gave her, she threw away upon another, and *cast her pearls before swine.* She *decked herself,* i. e. made God's ornaments her own, used them not as He gave them, but artificially as an adulteress. And what else is it, to use wit or beauty or any gift of God, for any end out of God? "[2] The ornament of souls which choose to serve idols, is to fulfill those things which seem good to the unclean spirits.—Very beautiful to devils must be the sin-loving soul, which chooses to think and to do whatsoever is sweet to, and loved by them." Sins of the flesh being a part of the worship of Baal, this garish trickery and pains to attract had an immediate offensiveness, besides its belonging to idols. He still pictures her as seeking, not sought by her lovers. *She went after her lovers, and forgat Me.* The original has great emphasis. *She went after her lovers, and Me she forgat, saith the Lord.* She went after vanities, and God, her All, she forgat. Such is the character of all engrossing passion, such is the course of sin, to which the soul gives way, in avarice, ambition, worldliness, sensual sin, godless science. The soul, at last, does not rebel against God; it *forgets* Him. It is taken up with other things, with itself, with the objects of its thoughts, the objects of its affections, and it has no time for God, because it has no love for Him. So God complains of Judah by Jeremiah, *their fathers have forgotten My name for Baal*[3].

14. **Therefore.** The inference is not what we should have expected. Sin and forgetfulness of God are not the natural causes of, and inducements to mercy. But God deals not with us, as we act one to another. Extreme misery and degradation revolt man; man's miseries invite God's mercies. God *therefore* has mercy, not because we deserve it, but because we need it. He *therefore* draws us, because we are so deeply sunken. He prepareth the soul by those harder means, and then the depths of her misery cry to the depths of His compassion, and because chastisement alone would stupify her, not melt her, He changes His wrath into mercy, and speaks to the heart which, for her salvation, He has broken.

I will allure her. The original word is used of one readily enticed, as a simple one,

whether to good or ill. God uses, as it were, Satan's weapons against himself. As Satan had enticed the soul to sin, so would God, by holy enticements and persuasiveness, allure her to Himself. God too hath sweetnesses for the penitent soul, far above all the sweetnesses of present earthly joys; much more, above the bitter sweetnesses of sin.

I Myself (such is the emphasis) *will allure her.* God would shew her something of His Beauty, and make her taste of His Love, and give her some such glimpse of the joy of His good-pleasure, as should thrill her and make her, all her life long, follow after what had, as through the clouds, opened upon her.

And will bring her into the wilderness. God, when He brought Israel out of Egypt, led her apart from the pressure of her hard bondage, the sinful self-indulgences of Egypt and the abominations of their idolatries, into the wilderness, and there, away from the evil examples of the nation from which He drew her and of those whom she was to dispossess, He gave her His law, and taught her His worship, and brought her into covenant with Himself[4]. So in the beginning of the Gospel, Christ allured souls by His goodness in His miracles, and the tenderness of His words, and the sweetness of His preaching and His promises, and the attractiveness of His sufferings, and the mighty manifestations of His Spirit. So is it with each penitent soul. God, by privation or suffering, turns her from her idols, from the turmoil of the world and its distractions, and speaks, Alone to her alone.

And speak to her heart; lit. *on* her heart, making an impression *on* it, soothing it, in words which will dwell in it, and rest there. Thus within, not without, [5]*He putteth His laws in the mind, and writeth them in the heart,* not *with ink,* but *with the Spirit of the living God.* God speaks to the heart, so as to reach it, soften it, comfort it, tranquilize it, and, at the last, assure it. He shall speak to her, not as in Sinai, amid *blackness and darkness and tempest, and the sound of a trumpet, and the voice of words, which voice they that heard intreated that the word should not be spoken to them any more*[6], but *to the heart.* But it is in solitude that He so speaks to the soul and is heard by her, warning, reproving, piercing, penetrating through every fold, until He reaches the very inmost heart and dwells there. And then He infuseth hope of pardon,

---

[1] Cant. i. 10.   [2] S. Cyr.
[3] Jer. xxiii. 27. add Jud. iii. 7. 1 Sam. xii. 9, 10. Jer. ii. 32. iii. 20. xiii. 25. xviii. 15. Ezek. xxii. 12.

xxiii. 35. Isa. xvii. 10. Ps. ix. 17. l. 22. lxxviii. 11. cvi. 13, 21.   [4] See Ezek. xx. 34–36.
[5] Heb. viii. 10. 2 Cor. iii. 3.   [6] Heb. xii. 18, 19.

Before
CHRIST
cir. 785.

z Josh. 7. 26.
Isai. 65. 10.

15 And I will give her vineyards from thence, and *the valley of Achor for a door of hope: and she shall

sing there, as in ᵃthe days of her youth, and ᵇas in the day when she came up out of the land of Egypt.

Before
CHRIST
cir. 785.

ᵃ Jer. 2. 2.
Ezek. 16. 8, 22,
60.
ᵇ Ex. 15. 1.

kindleth love, enlighteneth faith, giveth feelings of child-like trust, lifteth the soul tremblingly to cleave to Him Whose voice she has heard within her. Then His infinite Beauty touches the heart; His Holiness, Truth, Mercy, penetrate the soul; in silence and stillness the soul learns to know itself and God, to repent of its sins, to conquer self, to meditate on God. *Come out¹ from among them and be ye separate, saith the Lord, and touch not the unclean thing, and I will receive you¹.*

"² Search we the Scriptures, and we shall find, that seldom or never hath God spoken in a multitude; but so often as He would have anything known to man, He shewed Himself, not to nations or people, but to individuals, or to very few, and those severed from the common concourse of men, or in the silence of the night, in fields or solitudes, in mountains or vallies. Thus He spake with Noah, Abraham, Isaac, Jacob, Moses, Samuel, David, and all the Prophets. Why is it, God always speaketh in secret, except that He would call us apart? Why speaketh He with a few, except to collect and gather us into one? In this solitude doth God speak to the soul, from the beginning of its conversion to the loneliness of death. Here the soul, which, overspread with darkness, knew neither God nor itself, learns with a pure heart to know God. Here, placed aloft, she sees all earthly things flee away beneath her, yea, herself also passing away in the sweeping tide of all passing things." Here she learns, and so unlearns her sins, sees and hates herself, sees and loves God. Only "³ the solitude of the body availeth not, unless there be the solitude of the heart." And if God so speak to the penitent, much more to souls, who consecrate themselves wholly, cleave wholly to Him, meditate on Him. By His presence "⁴ the soul is renewed, and cleaving, as it were, to Him, feels the sweetness of an inward taste, spiritual understanding, enlightening of faith, increase of hope, feeling of compassion, zeal for righteousness, delight in virtue. She hath in orison familiar converse with God, feeling that she is heard, and mostly answered: speaking face to face with God, and hearing what God speaketh in her, constraining God in prayer and sometimes prevailing."

15. *And I will give her her vineyards from thence.* God's mercies are not only in word,

but in deed. He not only speaks to her heart, but He restores to her what He had taken from her. He promises, not only to reverse His sentence, but that He would make the sorrow itself the source of the joy. He says, I will give her back her vineyards *thence,* i. e. from the wilderness itself; as elsewhere, He says, *The wilderness shall be a fruitful field⁵.* Desolation shall be the means of her restored inheritance and joy in God. Through fire and drought are the new flagons dried and prepared, into which the new wine of the Gospel is poured.

And the valley of Achor [lit. *troubling*] for a *door of hope.* As, at the first taking possession of the promised land, Israel learnt through the transgression and punishment of Achan, to stand in awe of God, and thenceforth all went well with them, when they had wholly freed themselves from the accursed thing, so to them shall "sorrow be turned into joy, and hope dawn there, where there had been despair." "Therefore only had they to endure chastisements, that through them they might attain blessings." It was through the punishment of those who *troubled* the true *Israel,* "the destruction of Jerusalem, that to the Apostles and the rest who believed, the hope of victory over the whole world was opened." "*Hope.*" The word more fully means, a "patient, enduring longing." To each returning soul, *the valley of trouble,* or the lowliness of repentance, becometh a *door of* patient longing, not in itself, but because *God giveth* it to be so; a longing which *reacheth on, awaiteth on,* entering within the veil, and bound fast to the Throne of God. But then only, when none of the *accursed thing⁶* cleaveth to it, when it has no reserves with God, and retains nothing for itself, which God hath condemned.

And she shall sing there, as in the days of her youth. The song is a responsive song, choir answering choir, each stirring up the other to praise, and praise echoing praise, as Israel did after the deliverance at the Red Sea. "⁷ *Then sang Moses and the children of Israel this song unto the Lord. I will sing unto the Lord, for He hath triumphed gloriously. And Miriam the prophetess, the sister of Aaron, took a timbrel, and all the women went out after her. And Miriam answered them, Sing ye to the Lord, for He hath triumphed gloriously. So the Seraphim sing one to another, Holy, holy, holy⁸;* so

¹ 2 Cor. vi. 17.
² Hugo de S. Vict. de Arc. Noe. iv. 4. in Lap.
³ S. Greg. Mor. xxx. 12. Lap.

⁴ Ric. Vict. in Cant. iii. 4. Lap.
⁵ Isa. xxxii. 15.   ⁶ Josh. vii. 11–15.
⁷ Ex. xv. 1, 20, 1.   ⁸ Is. vi. 3.

Before CHRIST cir. 785.

‖ That is, *My husband.*

16 And it shall be at that day, saith the LORD, *that* thou shalt call me ‖ Ishi;

and shalt call me no more ‖ Baali.

17 For [c]I will take

Before CHRIST cir. 785.

‖ That is, *My lord.*

[c] Ex. 23. 13. Josh. 23. 7. Ps. 16. 4. Zech. 13. 2.

S. Paul exhorts Christians *to admonish one another in psalms and hymns and spiritual songs, singing with grace in their hearts to the Lord*[1]; so the Jewish psalmody passed into the Christian Church, and the blessed in heaven, having on the Cross passed the troublesome sea of this world, *sing the new song of Moses and of the Lamb*[2].

She shall sing there. Where? There, where He *allureth* her, where He *leadeth* her, where He *speaketh to her heart,* where He inworketh in her that hope. There, shall she sing, there, give praise and thanks.

As in the days of her youth. Her *youth* is explained, in what follows, to be *the days when she came up out of the land of Egypt,* when she was first born to the knowledge of her God, when the past idolatries had been forgiven and cut off, and she had all the freshness of new life, and had not yet wasted it by rebellion and sin. Then God first called *Israel, My firstborn son. My son, My firstborn*[3]. *She came up* into the land which God chose, out of Egypt, since we *go up* to God and to things above; as, on the other hand, the Prophet says, *Woe to those who go* down *to Egypt*[4], for the aids of this world; and the man who was wounded, the picture of the human race, was *going* down *from Jerusalem to Jericho*[5].

16. *And it shall be—thou shall call Me Ishi* [*my Husband,*] *and shalt call Me no more Baali* [*my Baal, Lord.*] *Baal,* originally Lord, was a title sometimes given to the husband. "The lord of the woman," "her lord," "the heart of her lord," stand for "the husband," "her husband"[6]." God says, "so wholly do I hate the name of idols, that on account of the likeness of the word Baal, *my Lord,* I will not be so called even in a right meaning, lest, while she utter the one, she should think on the other, and calling Me her Husband, think on the idol." Yet, withal, God says that He will put into her mouth the tenderer name of love, *Ishi,* lit. *my Man.* In Christ, the returning soul, which would give herself wholly to God, however far she had wandered, should not call God so much her Lord, as her Husband. "[7]Every soul, although laden with sins, meshed in vices, snared by enticements, a captive in exile, imprisoned in the body, sticking fast in the mud, fixed in the mire, affixed to its earthly members, nailed down by cares, distracted by turmoils, narrowed by fears, prostrated by grief, wandering in errors, tossed by anxieties, restless through suspicions, in fine, a captive *in the land of the enemy, defiled with the dead, accounted with them who go down in the grave*[8],—although she be thus condemned, in state thus desperate, yet she may perceive *that* in herself, whence she may not only respire to hope of pardon and of mercy, but whence she may dare to aspire to the nuptials of the Word, tremble not to enter into alliance with God, be not abashed to take on her the sweet yoke of love with the Lord of Angels. For what may she not safely dare with Him, with Whose image she seeth herself stamped, and glorious with His likeness? To this end God Himself, the Author of our being, willed that the ensign of our Divine nobleness of birth should ever be maintained in the soul, that she may ever have *that* in herself from the Word, whereby she may ever be admonished, either to stand with the Word, or to return to Him, if she have been moved. Moved, not as though removing in space, or walking on foot, but moved (as a spiritual substance is moved) with its affections, yea, its defections, it goes away from itself, as it were, to a worse state, making itself unlike itself and degenerate from itself, through pravity of life and morals; which unlikeness, however, is the fault, not the destruction, of nature. Contrariwise, the return of the soul is its conversion to the Word, to be re-formed by Him, conformed to Him. Wherein? In love. For He saith, *be ye followers of me, as dear children, and walk in love, as Christ also hath loved us.* Such conformity marries the soul to the Word, when she, having a likeness to Him by nature, also maketh herself like to Him in will, loving as she is loved. Wherefore, if she loveth perfectly, she is married. What sweeter than this conformity? What more desirable than this love? For by it, not content with human guidance, thou approachest, by thyself, O soul, confidentially to the Word; to the Word thou constantly cleavest; of the Word thou familiarly enquirest, and consultest as to all things, as capacious in understanding as emboldened in longing. This is contract of marriage, truly spiritual and holy. Contract! I have said too little. It is embrace. For embrace it is, when to will the same and nill the same, maketh of twain, one spirit."

17. *For I will take away the names of Baalim out of her mouth.* It is, then, of grace. He

---

[1] Col. iii. 16.
[2] Rev. xv. 3.
[3] Ex. iv. 22.
[4] Isa. xxxi. 1.
[5] Luke x. 30. See above on i. 11.

[6] Ex. xxi. 22. 2 Sam. xi. 26. Prov. xxxi. 11, &c.
[7] S. Bern. in Cant. Serm. 83. Lap.
[8] Baruch iii. 10, 11.

Before
CHRIST
cir. 785.

away the names of Baalim out of her mouth, and they shall no more be remembered by their name.

18 And in that day will I make a [d]covenant for

[d] Job. 23.
Is. 11. 6-9.
Ezek. 34. 25.

them with the beasts of the field, and with the fowls of heaven, and *with* the creeping things of the ground: and [e]I will break the bow and the sword and the battle out of the earth, and

Before
CHRIST
cir. 785.

[e] Ps. 46. 9.
Isai. 2. 4.
Ezek. 39. 9, 10.
Zech. 9. 10.

does not only promise the ceasing of idolatry, but that it shall be the fruit of His converting grace, the gift of Him from Whom *is both to will and to do. I will take away,* as God saith elsewhere[1], *I will cut off the names of the idols out of the land, and they shall be no more remembered;* and, [2]*the idols He shall utterly abolish.* In like way God foretells of Judah that the fruit of her captivity should be, that her idols should cease, that He would cleanse them from their idols, and renew them by His grace. [3]*In all your dwelling places the cities shall be laid waste, and the high places shall be desolate; that your altars may be laid waste and made desolate, and your idols may be broken and cease, and your images may be cut down, and your works may be abolished.* And, [4]*Then I will sprinkle clean water upon you, and ye shall be clean: from all your filthiness, and from all your idols will I cleanse you. A new heart also will I give you, and a new spirit will I put within you. Neither shall they defile themselves any more with their idols, nor with their detestable things, nor with any of their transgressions.*
And they shall be no more remembered, or, *made mention of.* The names of Baal and the idols, through which Israel sinned, are remembered now, only in the history of their sin.

18. *And in that day.* "[5]Truly and properly is the time of the Incarnation of the Only-Begotten called *the Day,* wherein darkness was dispelled in the world, and the mist dispersed, and bright rays shed into the minds of believers, and the Sun of Righteousness shone upon us, pouring in the light of the true knowledge of God, to those who could open wide the eye of the mind."
And I will make a covenant for them with the beasts of the field, &c. God promises to do away the whole of the former curse. Before, He had said that their vineyards should be laid waste by *the beasts of the field;* now, He would make an entire and lasting peace with them. He, Whose creatures they are, would renew for them in Christ the peace of Paradise, which was broken through Adam's rebellion against God, and would command none to hurt them. The blessings of God do

not correspond only, they go beyond the punishment. The protection is complete. Every kind of evil animal, beast, bird and reptile, is named. So S. Peter *saw all manner of four-footed beasts of the earth, and wild beasts, and creeping things, and fowls of the air.* All were to be slain to their former selves, and pass into the Church. Together the words express, that God would withhold the power of all enemies, visible or invisible; worldly or spiritual. Each also may denote some separate form or character of the enemy. Thus *wild beasts* picture savageness or bloodthirstiness, the ceasing whereof [6]Isaiah prophesies under the same symbols of beasts of prey, as the leopard, lion, wolf, and bear, or of venomous reptiles, as the asp or the basilisk. The *fowls of heaven* denote stealthy enemies, which, unperceived and unawares, take the word of God out of the heart; *creeping things,* such as entice to degrading, debasing sins, love of money or pleasure or appetite, *whose god is their belly, who mind earthly things*[7]. All shall be subdued to Christ or by Him; as He says, *I give you power over serpents and scorpions, and all the power of the enemy:* and *Thou shalt go upon the lion and the adder; the young lion and the adder shalt thou trample under feet*[8].
I will break the bow and the sword and the battle out of the earth. God foretells much more the greatness of what He would do for man, than the little which man receives. The Gospel brings peace within, and, since [9]*wars and fightings come from* evil passions and *lusts,* it brings peace, as far it prevails, without also; *peace,* as the *borders of* the Church[10]; peace in the world, as far as it is won to Christ by the Church; peace to the soul of the believer, so far as he loves God and obeys the Gospel.
And will make them to lie down safely, i. e. in confidence. God gives not outward peace only, but fearlessness. Fearless, the Christian lies down during life, at peace with God, his neighbour, and his own conscience; fearless, because *perfect love casteth out fear*[11]; and fearless in death also, because resting in Jesus, in everlasting, unfailing, unfading peace.

[1] Zech. xiii. 2.   [2] Is. ii. 18.
[3] Ezek. vi. 6.   [4] Ib. xxxvi. 25, 26. xxxvii. 23.
[5] S. Cyr.   [6] c. x.

[7] Phil. iii. 19.   [8] S. Luke x. 19. Ps. xci. 13.
[9] S. James iv. 1.   [10] Ps. cxlvii. 14.
[11] 1 S. John iv. 18.

will make them to [f] lie down safely.

[f] Lev. 26. 5.
Jer. 23. 6.

19 And I will betroth thee unto me for ever; yea,

I will betroth thee unto me in righteousness, and in judgment, and in loving-kindness, and in mercies.

19. *And I will betroth her unto Me for ever.* God does not say here, "I will forgive her;" "I will restore her;" "I will receive her back again;" "I will again shew her love and tenderness." Much as these would have been, He says here much more. He so blots out, forgets, abolishes all memory of the past, that He speaks only of the future, of the new betrothal, as if it were the first espousal of a virgin. Hereafter God would make her wholly His, and become wholly her's, by an union nearer and closer than the closest bond of parent and child, that, whereby *they are no more twain, but one flesh;* and through this oneness, formed by His own indwelling in her, giving her Himself, and taking her into Himself, and so bestowing on her a title to all which is His. And this, *for ever.* The betrothal and union of grace in this life passeth over into the union of glory, of which it is said [1], *Blessed are they who are called to the marriage supper of the Lamb.* He, by His Spirit, shall be with His Church *unto the end of the world,* and so bind her unto Himself that *the gates of hell shall not prevail against her.* The whole Church shall never fail. This *betrothal* implies and involves a new covenant, as God says [2], *Behold the days come, that I will make a new covenant with the house of Israel and the house of Judah, not according to My covenant which I made with their fathers, which My covenant they brake,* and which vanisheth away. To those who had broken His covenant and been unfaithful to Him, it was great tenderness, that He reproached them not with the past; as neither doth He penitents now. But beyond this, in that He speaks of *espousing* her who was already espoused to Him, God shews that He means something new, and beyond that former espousal. What God here promised, He fulfilled, not as God the Father, but in Christ. What God promised of Himself, He only could perform. God said to the Church, *I will betroth thee unto Me.* He Who became the *Bridegroom* [3] of the Church was Christ Jesus; she became the *wife of the Lamb* [4]; to Him the Church was *espoused, as a chaste Virgin* [5]. He then Who fulfilled what God promised that He would Himself fulfill, was Almighty God.

I will betroth thee unto Me in righteousness, or rather, (which is more tender yet and more merciful,) *by, with,* righteousness, &c.

These are the marriage-dowry, the bridal gifts, *with* [6] which He purchaseth and espouseth the bride unto Himself. Righteousness then and Judgment, loving-kindness and mercies, and faithfulness or truth, are attributes of God, wherewith, as by gifts of espousal, He maketh her His own. *Righteousness* is *that* in God, whereby He is Himself righteous and just; *Judgment,* that whereby He puts in act what is right against those who do wrong, and so judges Satan; as when the hour of His Passion was at hand, He said, *when the Comforter is come, He will reprove the world of sin, and of righteousness, and of judgment; of judgment, because the prince of this world is judged* [7]. *Loving-kindness* is that tender affection, wherewith He cherisheth His children, the works of His hands; *Mercies,* His tender yearnings over us [8], wherewith He hath compassion on our weakness; *Faithfulness,* that whereby He *keepeth covenant for ever* [9], and *loveth His own unto the end* [10]. And these qualities, as they are His, whereby He saved us, so doth He impart them to the Church in her measure, and to faithful souls. These are her dowry, her jewels, her treasure, her inheritance. He giveth to her and to each soul, as it can receive it, and in a secondary way, His Righteousness, Judgment, Loving-kindness, Mercies, Faithfulness. His *Righteousness,* contrary to her former unholiness, He poureth into her, and giveth her, with it, grace and love and all the fruits of the Spirit. By His *Judgment,* He giveth her a right judgment in all things, as contrary to her former blindness. *Know ye not,* says the Apostle [11], *that we shall judge angels? how much more, things that pertain to this life? Loving-kindness* is tender love, wherewith we *love one another, as Christ loved us* [12]. *Mercies* are that same love to those who need mercy, whereby we are *merciful, as our Father is merciful* [13]. *Faithfulness* is that constancy, whereby the elect shall *persevere unto the end,* as He saith, *Be thou faithful unto death, and I will give thee a crown of life* [14].

The threefold repetition of the word *betroth* is also, doubtless mysterious, alluding chiefly to the Mystery of the All-Holy Trinity, so often and so manifoldly, in Holy Scripture, foreshadowed by this sacred number. To them is the Church betrothed, by the pronouncing of Whose Names each of her members is, in Holy Baptism, *espoused as a chaste*

[1] Rev. xix. 9.
[2] Jer. xxxi. 31, 32.
[3] S. John iii. 29.
[4] Rev. xxi. 9.
[5] 2 Cor. xi. 2.
[6] As in 2 Sam. iii. 14.

[7] S. John xvi. 8, 11.
[8] See ab. on i. 6.
[9] Ps. cxi. 9.
[10] S. John xiii. 1.
[11] 1 Cor. vi. 3.
[12] S. John xv. 12.
[13] S. Luke vi. 36.
[14] Rev. ii. 10.

Before
CHRIST
cir. 785.

ᵍ Jer. 31, 33, 34.
John 17. 3.

20 I will even betroth thee unto me in faithfulness: and ᵍthou shalt know the LORD.

21 And it shall come to

pass in that day, ʰI will hear, saith the LORD, I will hear the heavens, and they shall hear the earth;

22 And the earth shall

Before
CHRIST
cir. 785.

ʰ Zech. 8. 12.

virgin unto Christ. At three times especially did our Lord espouse the Church unto Himself. "[1] First in His Incarnation, when He willed to unite His own Deity with our humanity," and "in the Virgin's womb, the nature of the woman, our nature, human nature, was joined to the nature of God," and that *for ever.* "He will be for ever the Word and Flesh, i. e. God and Man." Secondly, in His Passion, when He washed her with His Blood, and bought her for His own by His Death. Thirdly, in the Day of Pentecost, when He poured out the Holy Spirit upon her, whereby He dwelleth in her and she in Him. And He Who thus espoused the Church is God; she whom He espoused, an adulteress, and He united her to Himself, making her a pure virgin without spot or blemish. "[2] Human marriage makes those who were virgins to cease to be so; the Divine espousal makes her who was defiled, a pure virgin." *I have espoused you,* says S. Paul to those whom he had won back from all manner of heathen sins[3], *to one Husband, that I may present you a chaste virgin unto Christ.* O the boundless clemency of God! "[4]How can it be possible, that so mighty a King should become a Bridegroom, that the Church should be advanced into a Bride? That alone hath power for this, which is All-powerful; *love, strong as death*[5]. How should it not easily lift her up, which hath already made Him stoop? If He hath not acted as a Spouse, if He hath not loved as a Spouse, been jealous as a Spouse, then hesitate thou to think thyself espoused."

20. *And thou shalt know the Lord.* This knowledge of God follows on God's act of betrothal and of love. *We love God, because God first loved us.* And the true knowledge of God includes the love of God. "To love man, we must know him: to know God, we must love Him." To *acknowledge* God, is not yet to *know* Him. They who love not God, will not even acknowledge Him as He Is, "Supreme Wisdom and Goodness and Power, the Creator and Preserver; the Author of all which is good, the Governor of the world, Redeemer of man, the most bounteous Rewarder of those who serve Him, the most just Retributor of those who persevere in rebellion against Him." They who will not love God, cannot even *know* aright *of* God. But

to *know God*, is something beyond this. It is to know by experience that God is good; and this God makes known to the soul which He loves, while it meditates on Him, reads of Him, speaks of Him, adores Him, obeys Him. "This knowledge cometh from the revelation of God the Father, and in it is true bliss. Whence, when Peter confessed Him to be the Son of Man and Son of God, He said, *Blessed art thou; for flesh and blood hath not revealed it unto thee, but My Father which is in heaven.*" Yea, this knowledge is life eternal, as He said, [6] *This is life eternal, that they might know Thee the only true God, and Jesus Christ Whom Thou hast sent.*

21, 22. *I will hear the heavens, &c.* As all nature is closed, and would refuse her office to those who rebel against her God, so, when He hath withdrawn His curse and is reconciled to man, all shall combine together for man's good, and, by a kind of harmony, all parts thereof join their ministries for the service of those who are at unity with Him. And, as an image of love, all, from lowest to highest, are bound together, each depending on the ministry of that beyond it, and the highest on God. At each link, the chain might have been broken; but God Who knit their services together, and had before withheld the rain, and made the earth barren, and laid waste the trees, now made each to supply the other, and led the thoughts of men through the course of causes and effects up to Himself, Who ever causes all which comes to pass.

The immediate want of His people, was the corn, wine and oil; these needed the fruitfulness of the earth; the earth, by its parched surface and gaping clefts, seemed to crave the rain from heaven; the rain could not fall without the Will of God. So all are pictured as in a state of expectancy, until God gave the word, and His Will ran through the whole course of secondary causes, and accomplished what man prayed Him for. Such is the picture. But, although God's gifts of nature were gladdening tokens of His restored favor, and now too, under the Gospel, we rightly thank Him for the removal of any of His natural chastisements, and look upon it as an earnest of His favor toward us, the Prophet who had just spoken of the highest things, the union of man with God in Christ, does not here speak only of the

[1] Rup.
[3] 2 Cor. xi. 2. see Jer. iii. 1, 2.
[2] S. Jer.
[4] S. Bern. de dedic. Eccl. S. 5. Lap.
[5] Cant. viii. 6.
[6] S. John xvii. 3.

Before
CHRIST
cir. 785.

[1] ch. 1. 4.

[k] Jer. 31. 27.
Zech. 10. 9.
[l] ch. 1. 6.

hear the corn, and the wine, and the oil; [1] and they shall hear Jezreel.

23 And [k] I will sow her unto me in the earth; [l] and will have mercy upon her

Before
CHRIST
cir. 785.

[m] ch. 1. 10.
Zech. 13. 9.
Rom. 9. 26.
1 Pet. 2. 10.

that had not obtained mercy; and I [m] will say to *them which were* not my people, Thou *art* my people; and they shall say, *Thou art* my God.

---

lowest. What God gives, by virtue of an espousal *for ever*, are not gifts in time only. His gifts of nature are, in themselves, pictures of His gifts of grace, and as such the Prophets employ them. So then God promiseth, and this in order, a manifold abundance of all spiritual gifts. Of these, *corn and wine*, as they are the visible parts, so are they often, in the Old Testament, the symbols of His highest gift, the Holy Eucharist; and *oil*, of God's Holy Spirit, through Whom they are sanctified.

God here calls *Israel* by the name of *Jezreel*, repealing, once more in the close of this prophecy, His sentence, conveyed through the names of the three children of the Prophet. The name *Jezreel* combines in one, the memory of the former punishment and the future mercy. God did not altogether do away the temporal part of His sentence. He had said, "I will scatter;" and, although some were brought back with Judah, Israel remained scattered in all lands, in Egypt and Greece and Italy, Asia Minor, and the far East and West. But God turned His chastisement into mercy to those who believed in Him. Now He changes the meaning of the word into, *God shall sow*. Israel, in its dispersion, when converted to God, became everywhere the preacher of Him Whom they had persecuted; and in Him,—the true Seed Whom God sowed in the earth and It *brought forth much fruit*,—converted Israel also bore, *some a hundred-fold; some sixty; some thirty*.

23. *And I will sow her unto Me in the earth.* She whom God sows, is the Church, of whom God speaks as *her*, because she is the Mother of the faithful. After the example of her Lord, and by virtue of His Death, every suffering is to increase her. "The blood of Christians was their harvest-seed [1]." "The Church was not diminished by persecutions, but increased, and the field of the Lord was even clothed with the richer harvest, in that the seeds, which fell singly, arose multiplied [2]."

In the earth. "[3] He does not say *in their own land*, i. e. Judæa, but *the earth*. The whole earth was to be the seed-plot of the Church, where God would sow her to Himself, plant, establish, cause her to increase, and multiply her mightily." As he said [4],

Ask of Me, and I will give Thee the heathen for Thine inheritance, and the utmost parts of the earth for Thy possession. Of this sowing, Jews were the instruments. Of them according to the flesh, Christ came; of them were the Apostles and Evangelists and all writers of Holy Scripture; of them was the Church first formed, into which the Gentiles were received, being, with them, knit into one in Christ.

I will have mercy upon her that had not obtained mercy. This which was true of Israel in its dispersion, was much more true of the Gentiles. These too, the descendants of righteous Noah, God had cast off for the time, that they should be no more His people, when He chose Israel out of them, to make known to them His Being, and His Will, and His laws, and, (although in shadow and in mystery,) Christ Who was to come. So God's mercies again overflow His threatenings. He had threatened to Israel, that he should be *unpitied*, and no more His people; in reversing His sentence, He embraces in the arms of His mercy all who were not His people, and says of them all, that they should be *My people* and *beloved*. At one and the same time, was Israel to be thus multiplied, and *pity* was to be shewn to those *not pitied*, and those who were *not God's people*, were to become *His people*. At one and the same time were those promises fulfilled in Christ; the one through the other; Israel was not multiplied by itself, but through the bringing-in of the Gentiles. Nor was Israel alone, or chiefly, brought into a new relation with God. The same words promised the same mercy to both, Jew and Gentile, that all should be *one in Christ*, all one Jezreel, one Spouse to Himself, one Israel of God, one Beloved; and that all, with one voice of jubilee, should cry unto Him, "my Lord and my God."

And they shall say, Thou art my God, or rather, *shall say, my God.* There seems to be more affectionateness in the brief answer, which sums up the whole relation of the creature to the Creator in that one word, *Elohai, my God.* The prophet declares, as before, that, when God thus anew called them His people, they by His grace would obey His call, and surrender themselves wholly to

---

[1] Tertull. Apol. end. p. 105. Oxf. Tr.
[2] S. Leo. See others quoted Ib. p. 105, 6. note a.

[3] Poc. Not בְּאַרְצָם but בָּאָרֶץ.
[4] Ps. ii. 8.

Before
CHRIST
cir. 785.

CHAPTER III.

1 *By the expiation of an adulteress, 4 is shewed the desolation of Israel before their restoration.*

ᵃ ch. 1. 2.

ᵇ Jer. 3. 20.

THEN said the LORD
unto me, ᵃ Go yet,
love a woman beloved of
her ᵇ friend, yet an adul-

teress, according to the love
of the LORD toward the
children of Israel, who look
to other gods, and love
flagons † of wine.

Before
CHRIST
cir. 785.

† Heb. *of grapes.*

2 So I bought her to me
for fifteen *pieces of* silver,
and *for* an homer of barley,
and an † half homer of barley :

† Heb. *lethech.*

Him. For to say, *my God,* is to own an exclusive relation to God alone. It is to say,
my Beginning and my End, my Hope and my
Salvation, my Whole and only Good, in
Whom Alone I will hope, Whom Alone I
will fear, love, worship, trust in, obey and
serve, with all my heart, mind, soul and
strength ; my God and my All.

III. 1. *Go yet, love a woman, beloved of* her
friend, yet an adulteress. This *woman* is the
same Gomer, whom the Prophet had before
been bidden to *take,* and whom, (it appears
from this verse) had forsaken him, and was
living in adultery with another man. The
*friend*¹ is the husband himself, the Prophet.
The word *friend* expresses, that the husband
of Gomer treated her, not harshly, but mildly
and tenderly so that her faithlessness was
the more aggravated sin. *Friend* or *neighbour* too is the word chosen by our Lord to
express His own love, the love of the good
Samaritan, who, not being akin, became
neighbour to Him who fell among thieves, and had
mercy upon him. Gomer is called *a woman,
ishah,* not, thy wife, *ishteca*², in order to describe the state of separation, in which she
was living. Yet God bids the Prophet to
love her, i. e. shew active love to her, not, as
before, to *take* her ; for she was already and
still his wife, although unfaithful. He is
now bidden to buy her back, with the price
and allowance of food, as of a worthless
slave, and so to keep her apart, on coarse
food, abstaining from her former sins, but
without the privileges of marriage, yet with
the hope of being, in the end, restored to be
altogether his wife. This prophecy is a
sequel to the former, and so relates to Israel,
after the coming of Christ, in which the
former prophecy ends.

*According to the love of the Lord toward the
children of Israel.* The Prophet is directed to
frame his life, so as to depict at once the
ingratitude of Israel or the sinful soul, and
the abiding, persevering, love of God. The
woman, whom God commands him to *love,* he

had loved before her fall ; he was now to love
her after her fall, and amid her fall, in order
to rescue her from abiding in it. His love was
to outlive her's, that he might win her at
last to him. Such, God says, is *the love of
the Lord for Israel.* He loved her, before she
fell ; for the woman was *beloved of her friend,
and* yet *an adulteress.* He loved her after she
fell, and while persevering in her adultery.
For God explains His command to the
Prophet still to love her, by the words, *according to the love of the Lord toward the children of Israel, while they look to other gods,* lit.,
and they are looking. The words express a
contemporary circumstance. God was loving
them and looking upon them ; and they, all
the while, were looking to other gods.

Love flagons of wine ; lit. *of grapes,* or perhaps, more probably, *cakes of grapes,* i. e.
dried raisins. Cakes were used in idolatry³.
The *wine* would betoken the excess common
in idolatry, and the bereavement of understanding : the *cakes* denote the sweetness and
lusciousness, yet still the dryness, of any
gratification out of God, which is preferred to
Him. Israel despised and rejected the true
Vine, Jesus Christ, the source of all the
works of grace and righteousness, and *loved
the dried cakes,* the observances of the law,
which, apart from Him, were dry and worthless.

2. *So I bought her to me for fifteen* pieces *of
silver.* The fifteen shekels were half the
price of a common slave⁴, and so may denote
her worthlessness. The homer and half-homer
of barley, or forty-five bushels, are nearly the
allowance of food for a slave among the Romans, four bushels a month. Barley was the
offering of one accused of adultery, and,
being the food of animals, betokens that she
was *like horse and mule which have no understanding.* The Jews gave dowries for their
wives ; but she was the Prophet's wife already.
It was then perhaps an allowance, whereby
he bought her back from her evil freedom,
not to live as his wife, but to be honestly

---

¹ רֵעַ as in Jer. iii. 20. Cant. v. 16.

² אֵשֶׁת not אִשְׁתֵּךְ.

³ Jer. vii. 18. xliv. 19.

⁴ Ex. xxi. 32.

Before
CHRIST
cir. 785.

3 And I said unto her, Thou shalt *abide for me many days; thou shalt not play the harlot, and thou

*Deut. 21. 13.

shalt not be for *another* man: so *will* I also *be* for thee.

Before
CHRIST
cir. 785.

4 For the children of

---

maintained, until it should be fit, completely to restore her.

3. *Thou shalt abide for me many days;* lit. *thou shalt sit,* solitary and as a widow[1], quiet and sequestered; not going after others, as heretofore, but waiting for him[2]; and *that,* for an undefined, but long season, until he should come and take her to himself.

And thou shalt not be for another *man;* lit. *and thou shalt not be to a man,* i.e. not even to thine own man or husband. She was to remain without following sin, yet without restoration to conjugal rights. Her husband would be her guardian; but as yet, no more. *So will I also be for thee or toward thee.* He does not say " *to* thee," so as to belong to her, but "towards thee;" i.e. he would have regard, respect to her; he would watch over her, be kindly disposed towards her; he, his affections, interests, thoughts, would be directed *towards* her. The word *towards* expresses regard, yet distance also. Just so would God, in those times, withhold all special tokens of His favor, covenant, Providence; yet would he secretly uphold and maintain them as a people, and withhold them from falling wholly from Him into the gulf of irreligion and infidelity.

4. *For the children of Israel shall abide many days.* The condition described is one in which there should be no civil polity, none of the special Temple-service, nor yet the idolatry, which they had hitherto combined with it or substituted for it. *King* and *prince* include both higher and lower governors. Judah had *kings* before the Captivity, and a sort of *prince* in her governors after it. Judah remained still a polity, although without the glory of her kings, until she rejected Christ. Israel ceased to have any civil government at all. *Sacrifice* was the centre of worship before Christ. It was that part of their service, which, above all, fore-shadowed His love, His Atonement and Sacrifice, and the reconciliation of God by His Blood, Whose merits it pleaded. *Images,* were, *contrariwise,* the centre of idolatry, the visible form of the beings, whom they worshipped instead of God. The *Ephod* was the holy garment which the High-priest wore, with the names of the twelve tribes and the Urim and Thummim, over his heart, and by which he enquired of God. The *Teraphim* were idolatrous means of divination. So then, *for many days,* a long, long period, *the children of Israel* should *abide,* in a manner waiting for God, as the

wife waited for her husband, kept apart under His care, yet not acknowledged by Him; not following after idolatries, yet cut off from the sacrificial worship which He had appointed for forgiveness of sins, through faith in the Sacrifice yet to be offered, cut off also from the appointed means of consulting Him and knowing His Will. Into this state the ten tribes were brought upon their Captivity, and (those only excepted who joined the two tribes or have been converted to the Gospel,) they have ever since remained in it. Into that same condition the two tribes were brought, after that, by *killing the Son,* they had *filled up the measure of their father's* sins; and the second temple, where His Presence had hallowed, was destroyed by the Romans. In that condition they have ever since remained; free from idolatry, and in a state of waiting for God, yet looking in vain for a Messias, since they had not and would not receive Him Who came unto them; praying to God; yet without Sacrifice for sin; not owned by God, yet kept distinct and apart by His Providence, for a future yet to be revealed. "No one of their own nation has been able to gather them together or to become their king." Julian the Apostate attempted in vain to rebuild their temple, God interposing by miracles to hinder the effort which challenged His Omnipotence. David's temporal kingdom has perished and his line is lost, because *Shiloh,* the Peace-maker, is come. The typical Priesthood ceased, in presence of the true *Priest after the order of Melchisedek.* The line of Aaron is forgotten, unknown, and cannot be recovered. So hopelessly are their genealogies confused, that they themselves conceive it to be one of the offices of their Messiah to disentangle them. Sacrifice, the centre of their religion, has ceased and become unlawful. Still their characteristic has been to *wait.* Their prayer as to the Christ has been, "may He soon be revealed." Eighteen centuries have flowed by. *Their eyes have failed with looking* for God's promise, whence it is not to be found. Nothing has changed this character, in the mass of the people. Oppressed, released, favoured; despised, or aggrandised; in East or West; hating Christians, loving to blaspheme Christ, forced (as they would remain Jews,) to explain away the prophecies which speak of Him, deprived of the sacrifices which, to their forefathers, spoke of Him and His Atonement;—still, as a mass, they blindly wait for Him, the true

[1] Deut. xxi. 13.

[2] Such is the force of ישב ל Ex. xxiv. 14. Jer iii. 2.

Before CHRIST cir. 785.	Israel shall abide many days [d] without a king, and without a prince, and without a sacrifice, and without [†] an image, and without an [e] ephod, and *without* [f] teraphim :
[d] ch. 10. 3.	
[†] Heb. *a standing,* or, *statue,* or, *pillar,* Isai. 19. 19.	
[e] Exod. 28. 6.	
[f] Judg. 17. 5.	

5 Afterward shall the children of Israel return, and [g] seek the LORD their God, and [h] David their king; and shall fear the LORD and his goodness in the [i] latter days.	Before CHRIST cir. 785.
	[g] Jer. 50. 4, 5. ch. 5. 6.
	[h] Jer. 30. 9. Ezek. 34. 23, 24. & 37. 22, 24.
	[i] Isai. 2. 2.
	Jer. 30. 24. Ezek. 38. 8, 16. . Dan. 2. 28. Mic. 4. 1.

knowledge of Whom, His Offices, His Priesthood, and His Kingdom, they have laid aside. And God has been *towards them.* He has preserved them from mingling with idolaters or Mohammedans. Oppression has not extinguished them, favor has not bribed them. He has kept them from abandoning their mangled worship, or the Scriptures which they understand not, and whose true meaning they believe not ; they have fed on the raisinhusks of a barren ritual and unspiritual legalism since the Holy Spirit they have grieved away. Yet they exist still, a monument to *us,* of God's abiding wrath on sin, as Lot's wife was to them, encrusted, stiff, lifeless, only that we know that *the dead shall hear the voice of the Son of God, and they that hear shall live.*

True it is, that idolatry was not the immediate cause of the final punishment of the two, as it was of the ten, tribes. But the words of the prophecy go beyond the first and immediate occasion of it. The sin, which God condemned by Hosea, was alienation from Himself. He loved them, and they *turned to other gods.* The outward idolatry was but a fruit and a symbol of the inward. The temptation to idolatry was not simply, nor chiefly, to have a visible symbol to worship, but the hope to obtain from the beings so symbolised, or from their worship, what God refused or forbade. It was a rejection of God, choosing His rival. " The adulteress soul is whoever, forsaking the Creator, loveth the creature." The rejection of our Lord was moreover the crowning act of apostacy, which set the seal on all former rejection of God. And when the sinful soul or nation is punished at last, God punishes not only the last act, which draws down the stroke, but all the former accumulated sins, which culminated in it. So then they who "despised the Bridegroom, Who came from heaven to seek the love of His own in faith, and, forsaking Him, gave themselves over to the Scribes and Pharisees who *slew Him, that the inheritance,*

[1] S. John vi. 26. [2] S. Luke xiii. 24.
[3] Ezek. xxxiv. 23, 24. [4] Isa. lv. 4.
[5] Jer. xxiii. 5, 6. [6] Ps. cx. 1.
[7] Jon. Targ. " This is the King Messiah; whether he be from among the living, his name is David, or whether he be from the dead, his name is David." Jerus. Berachoth in Martini Pug. Fid. f. 277. and Schöttg. Horæ Hebr. T. ii. ad loc. So also the mystical books, Zohar, Midrash Shemuel (ap. Schöettg. ii. p. 22.), and Tanchuma, which has, "God said

i. e. God's people, *might be* theirs," having the same principle of sin as the ten tribes, were included in their sentence.

5. *Afterward shall the children of Israel return.* Elsewhere it is said more fully, *return to the Lord.* It expresses more than *turning* or even conversion to God. It is not conversion only, but *reversion* too, a turning *back from* the unbelief and sins, for which they had left God, and a return to Him Whom they had forsaken.

And shall seek the Lord. This word, *seek,* expresses in Hebrew, from its intensive form, a diligent search ; as used with regard to God, it signifies a religious search. It is not such seeking as our Lord speaks of [1], *Ye seek me, not because ye saw the miracles, but becaus ye did eat of the loaves and were filled,* or [2], *many shall seek to enter in and shall not be able,* but that earnest seeking, to which He has promised, *Seek and ye shall find.* Before, she had diligently sought her false gods. Now, in the end she shall as diligently seek God and His grace, as she had heretofore sought her idols and her sins.

And David their King. David himself, after the flesh, this could not be. For he had long since been gathered to his fathers ; nor was he to return to this earth. *David* then must be the Son of David, the same, of Whom God says [3], *I will set up One Shepherd over them, and He shall feed them, even My servant David, and He shall be their Shepherd, and I the Lord will be their God, and My servant David a Prince among them.* The same was to be a *witness, leader, commander to the people* [4] *;* He Who was to be *raised up to David* [5]*,* a *righteous Branch,* and Who was to be *called the Lord our Righteousness;* David's Lord [6] as well as *David's Son.* Whence the older Jews, of every school, Talmudic, mystical, Biblical, grammatical, explained this prophecy, of Christ. Thus their received paraphrase is : " [7] Afterward the children of Israel shall repent, or turn by repentance, and shall seek

to the Israelites ; In this world ye fear for your sins ; but in the world to come [i.e. the time of Christ] when the evil nature shall no longer be, ye shall be amazed at that good which is reserved for you, as it is written, ' Afterwards the children of Israel shall return, &c.'" It is also one of the passages, which, they say, a voice from heaven, *Bath col,* revealed to them, as relating to the Messiah, Schöttg. Ib. p. 141. See also Ibn Ezra and Kimchi in Pococke, p. 139.

CHAPTER IV.

1 *God's judgments against the
sins of the people,* 6 *and of
the priests,* 12 *and against
their idolatry.* 15 *Judah is
exhorted to take warning by
Israel's calamity.*

HEAR the word of the
LORD, ye children
of Israel: for the LORD
hath a [a]controversy with the inhabitants of the land, because *there is* no truth, nor mercy, nor

[a] Isai. 1. 18. & 3. 13, 14. Jer. 25. 31. ch. 12. 2. Mic. 6. 2.

the service of the Lord their God, and shall obey Messiah the Son of David, their King." *And shall fear the Lord ;* lit. *shall fear toward the Lord and toward His goodness.* It is not then a servile fear, not even, as elsewhere, a fear, which makes them shrink back *from* His awful Majesty. It is a fear, the most opposed to this; a fear, whereby "they shall flee to Him for help, from all that is to be feared;" a reverent holy awe, which should even impel them *to* Him; a fear of losing Him, which should make them hasten to Him. "[1]They shall fear, and wonder exceedingly, astonied at the greatness of God's dealing, or of their own joy." Yet they should *hasten tremblingly,* as bearing in memory their past unfaithfulness and ill deserts, and fearing to approach, but for the greater fear of turning away. Nor do they hasten with this reverent awe and awful joy to God only, but *to His Goodness* also. His Goodness draws them, and to it they betake themselves, away from all cause of fear, their sins, themselves, the Evil one. Yet even His Goodness is a source of awe. *His Goodness !* How much it contains. All whereby God is good in Himself, all whereby He is good to us. That whereby He is essentially good, or rather Goodness ; that whereby He is good to us, as His creatures, as yet more as His sinful, ungrateful, redeemed creatures, re-born to bear the Image of His Son. So then His Goodness overflows into beneficence, and condescension, and graciousness and mercy and forgiving love, and joy in imparting Himself, and complacence in the creatures which He has formed, and re-formed, redeemed and sanctified for His glory. Well may His creatures *tremble towards* it, with admiring wonder that all this can be made their's !

This was to take place *in the latter days.* These words, which are adopted in the New Testament, where Apostles say, [2]*in the last days, in these last days,* mean this, the last dispensation of God, in contrast with all which went before, the times of the Gospel[3]. The prophecy has all along been fulfilled during this period to those, whether of the ten or of

the two tribes, who have been converted to Christ, since God ended their temple-worship. It *is* fulfilled in every soul from among them, who now *is converted and lives.* There will be a more full fulfillment, of which S. Paul speaks, when the eyes of all Israel shall be opened to the deceivableness of the last Anti-Christ ; and Enoch and Elias, the two witnesses[4], shall have come to prepare our Lord's second Coming, and shall have been slain, and, by God's converting grace, *all Israel shall be saved*[5].

IV. 1. *Hear the word of the Lord, ye children of Israel.* The Prophet begins here, in a series of pictures as it were, to exhibit the people of Israel to themselves, that they might know that God did not do without cause all this which He denounced against them. Here, at the outset, He summons, the whole people, their prophets and priests, before the judgment-seat of God, where God would condescend, Himself to implead them, and hear, if they had ought in their defence. The title *children of Israel* is, in itself, an appeal to their gratitude and their conscience, as the title "Christian" among us is an appeal to us, by Him Whose Name we bear. Our Lord says, [6]*If ye were Abraham's children, ye would do the works of Abraham ;* and S. Paul [7], *let every one that nameth the name of Christ, depart from iniquity.*

For the Lord hath a controversy. God wills, in all His dealings with us His creatures, to prove even to our own consciences, the righteousness of His judgments, so as to leave us without excuse. Now, through His servants, He shews men their unrighteousness and His justice ; hereafter our Lord, the righteous Judge, will shew it through the book of men's own consciences.

With the inhabitants of the land. God had given *the* land to the children of Israel, on account of the wickedness of those whom He drave out before them. He gave it to them [8]*that they might observe His statutes and keep His laws.* He had promised that His [9]*Eyes* should *always* be *upon it from the beginning of the year unto the end of the year.* This land,

[1] Rup.   [2] Acts ii. 17. Heb. i. 2.
[3] "It is a rule given by Kimchi on Isa. ii. 2. 'Whenever it is said *in the latter days,* it is meant the days of the Messiah.' The same rule is also on that place given by Abarbanel, and backed by

the authority of Moses Ben Nachman, who, on Gen. xlix. 1, gives it as a general rule of all their Doctors." Poc.
[4] Rev. xi. 3.   [5] Rom. xi. 26.   [6] S. John viii. 39.
[7] 2 Tim. ii. 19.   [8] Ps. cv. ult.   [9] Deut. xi. 12.

Before
CHRIST
cir. 780.
b knowledge of God in the land.

b Jer. 4. 22. & 5. 4.
2 By swearing, and lying, and killing, and

stealing, and committing adultery, they break out, and †blood toucheth blood.

Before
CHRIST
cir. 780.

† Heb. bloods.

the scene of those former judgments, given to them on those conditions, [1] the land which God had given to them as their God, they had filled with iniquity.

Because there is no truth, nor mercy. Truth *and mercy* are often spoken of, as to Almighty God. *Truth* takes in all which is right, and to which God has bound Himself; *mercy,* all beyond, which God does out of His boundless love. When God says of Israel, *there is no truth nor mercy,* He says that there is absolutely none of those two great qualities, under which He comprises all His own Goodness. *There is no truth,* none whatever, " no regard for known truth ; no conscience, no sincerity, no uprightness ; no truth of words ; no truth of promises ; no truth in witnessing ; no making good in deeds what they said in words."

Nor mercy. The word has a wide meaning ; it includes all love of one to another, a love issuing in acts. It includes loving-kindness, piety to parents, natural affection, forgiveness, tenderness, beneficence, mercy, goodness. The Prophet, in declaring the absence of this grace, declares the absence of all included under it. Whatever could be comprised under love, whatever feelings are influenced by love, of that there was nothing.

Nor knowledge of God. The union of right knowledge and wrong practice is hideous in itself ; and it must be especially offensive to Almighty God, that His creatures should know Whom they offend, how they offend Him, and yet, amid and against their knowledge, choose that which displeases Him. And, on that ground, perhaps, He has so created us, that when our acts are wrong, our knowledge becomes darkened [2]. The *knowledge of God* is not merely to know some things of God, as that He is the Creator and Preserver of the world and of ourselves. To know things of God is not to know God Himself. We cannot know God in any respect, unless we are so far made like unto Him. *Hereby do we know that we know Him, if we keep His commandments. He that saith, I know Him, and keepeth not His commandments, is a liar and the truth is not in him. Every one that loveth is born of God, and knoweth God. He that loveth not, knoweth not God ; for God is love* [3]. Knowledge of God being the gift of the Holy Ghost, he who hath not grace, cannot

have that knowledge. A certain degree of speculative knowledge of God, a bad man may have, as Balaam had by inspiration, and the Heathen who, *when they knew God, glorified Him not as God.* But even this knowledge is not retained without love. Those who *held the truth in unrighteousness* ended (S. Paul says [4]) by corrupting it. *They did not like to retain God in their knowledge, and so God gave them over to a reprobate,* or undistinguishing *mind,* that they could not. Certainly, the speculative and practical knowledge are bound up together, through the oneness of the relation of the soul to God, whether in its thoughts of Him, or its acts towards Him. Wrong practice corrupts belief, as misbelief corrupts practice. The Prophet then probably denies that there was any true knowledge of God, of any sort, whether of life or faith or understanding or love. Ignorance of God, then, is a great evil, a source of all other evils.

2. *By swearing, and lying ; &c,* lit. *swearing* or *cursing* [5] *, and lying, and killing, and stealing, and committing adultery !* The words in Hebrew are nouns of action. The Hebrew form is very vivid and solemn. It is far more forcible than if he had said, " They swear, lie, kill, and steal." It expresses that these sins were continual, that nothing else (so to speak) was going on ; that it was all one scene of such sins, one course of them, and of nothing besides ; as we say more familiarly, " It was all, swearing, lying, killing, stealing, committing adultery." It is as if the Prophet, seeing with a sight above nature, a vision from God, saw, as in a picture, what was going on, all around, within and without, and summed up in this brief picture, all which he saw. This it was and nothing but this, which met his eyes, wherever he looked, whatever he heard, *swearing, lying, killing, stealing, committing adultery.* The Prophet had before said, that the ten tribes were utterly wanting in all truth, all love, all knowledge of God. But where there are none of these, *there,* in all activity, will be the contrary vices. When the land or the soul is empty of the good, it will be full of the evil. *They break out,* i. e. burst through all bounds, set to restrain them, as a river bursts its banks and overspreads all things or sweeps all before it. *And blood toucheth blood,* lit. *bloods touch bloods* [6]. The

---

[1] See Deut. iv. 1, 40. vi. 21-25. &c.
[2] Rom. i. 21.   [3] 1 S. John ii. 3, 4. iv. 7, 8.
[4] Rom. i. 21, 18, 28.
[5] The word rendered swearing, *aloh,* is derived from the Name of God, *Eloah,* and signifies, using

His name; invoking His name, probably in a *curse,* which the noun *alah* signifies.

[6] "Bloods" is ever, in Holy Scripture, used of blood-shed. On the history, see Introd. p. 5, and below p. 148.

3 Therefore[e] shall the land mourn, and [d]every

[e] Jer. 4. 28. & 12. 4.
Amos 5. 16.
[d] Zeph. 1. 3. 8. 8.

one that dwelleth therein & shall languish, with the beasts of the field, and with the fowls of heaven; yea,

the fishes of the sea also shall be taken away.

4 Yet let no man strive, nor reprove another: for thy people are as [e] they that strive with the priest.

[e] Deut. 17. 12.

blood was poured so continuously and in such torrents, that it flowed on, until stream met stream and formed one wide inundation of blood.

3. *Therefore shall the land mourn.* Dumb inanimate nature seems to rejoice and to be in unison with our sense of joy, when bedewed and fresh through rain and radiant with light; and, again, to mourn, when smitten with drought or blight or disease, or devoured by the creatures which God employs to lay it waste for man's sins. Dumb nature is, as it were, in sympathy with man, cursed in Adam, smitten amid man's offences, its outward show responding to man's inward heart, wasted, parched, desolate, when man himself was marred and wasted by his sins.

With the beasts of the field, lit. "*in* the beasts," &c. God included *the fowl and the cattle and every beast of the field* in His covenant with man. So here, in this sentence of woe, He includes them in the inhabitants of the land, and orders that, since man would not serve God, the creatures made to serve him, should be withdrawn from him. "General iniquity is punished by general desolation."

Yea, the fishes of the sea also. Inland seas or lakes are called by this same name, as the Sea of Tiberias and the Dead Sea. Yet here the Prophet probably alludes to the history of man's creation, when God gave him dominion [1] *over the fish of the sea, and over the fowl of the heaven, and over every living thing (chaiah),* in just the inverse order, in which he here declares that they shall be taken away. There God gives dominion over all, from lowest to highest; here God denounces that He will take away all, down to those which are least affected by any changes. Yet from time to time God has, in chastisement, directed that the shoals of fishes should not come to their usual haunts. This is well known in the history of sea-coasts; and conscience has acknowledged the hand of God and seen the ground of His visitation. Of the fulfillment S. Jerome writes: "Whoso believeth not that this befell the people of Israel, let him survey Illyricum, let him survey the Thraces, Macedonia, the Pannonias, and the whole land which stretches from the Propontis and Bosphorus to the Julian Alps, and he will experience that, together with man, all

the creatures also fail, which afore were nourished by the Creator for the service of man."

4. *Yet let no man strive, nor reprove another,* lit. "*Only man let him not strive, and let not man reprove.*" God had taken the controversy with His people into His own hands; *the Lord,* He said [2], *hath a controversy (rib) with the inhabitants of the land.* Here He forbids man to intermeddle; *man let him not strive.* (He again uses the same word [3].) The people were obstinate and would not hear; warning and reproof, being neglected, only aggravated their guilt: so God bids man to cease to speak in His Name. He Himself alone will implead them, Whose pleading none could evade or contradict. Subordinately, God, teaches us, amid His judgments, not to strive or throw the blame on each other, but each to look to his own sins, not to the sins of others.

For thy people are as they that strive with the priest. God had made it a part of the office of the priest, to *keep knowledge* [4]. He had bidden, that all hard causes should be taken to [5] *the priest who stood to minister there before the Lord their God;* and whoso refused the priest's sentence was to be put to death. The priest was then to judge in God's Name. As speaking in His Name, in His stead, with His authority, taught by Himself, they were called by that Name, in Which they spoke, Elohim [6], God, not in regard to themselves but as representing Him. To *strive* then *with the priest* was the highest contumacy; and such was their whole life and conduct. It was the character of the whole kingdom of *Israel.* For they had thrown off the authority of the family of Aaron, which God had appointed. Their political existence was based upon the rejection of that authority. The national character influences the individual. When the whole polity is formed on disobedience and revolt, individuals will not tolerate interference. As they had rejected the priest, so would and did they reject the prophets. He says not, they *were* priest-strivers, (for they had no lawful priests, against whom to strive,) but they were *like priest-strivers,* persons whose habit it was to strive with those who spoke in God's Name. He says in fact, let not *man* strive with those who strive with God. The uselessness of

[1] Gen. i. 28. [2] iv. 1 ריב [3] ירב [4] Mal. ii. 7. [5] Deut. xvii. 8–12. [6] Ex. xxi. 6. xxii. 8, 9.

5 Therefore shalt thou fall [f]in the day, and the prophet also shall fall with thee in the night, and I will † destroy thy mother.

6 ¶ [g]My people are † destroyed for lack of knowl-

[f]See Jer. 6. 4, 5. & 15. 8.
† Heb. *cut off.*
[g] Isai. 5. 13.
† Heb. *cut off.*

edge: because thou hast rejected knowledge, I will also reject thee, that thou shalt be no priest to me: seeing thou hast forgotten the law of thy God, I will also forget thy children.

such reproof is often repeated. [1] *He that reproveth a scorner getteth to himself shame, and he that rebuketh a wicked man getteth himself a blot. Reprove not a scorner, lest he hate thee.* [2] *Speak not in the ears of a fool, for he will despise the wisdom of thy words.* S. Stephen gives it as a characteristic of the Jews [3], *Ye stiff-necked and uncircumcised in heart and ears, ye do always resist the Holy Ghost; as your fathers did, so do ye.*

5. *Therefore shalt thou fall.* The two parts of the verse fill up each other. "By day and by night shall they fall, people and prophets together." Their calamities should come upon them successively, day and night. They should stumble by day, when there is least fear of stumbling[4]; and night should not by its darkness protect them. Evil should come *at noon-day*[5] upon them, seeing it, but unable to repel it; as Isaiah speaks of it as an aggravation of trouble[6], *thy land strangers devour it in thy presence;* and the false prophets, who saw their visions in the night, should themselves be overwhelmed in the darkness, blinded by moral, perishing in actual, darkness.

And I will destroy thy mother. Individuals are spoken of as the children; the whole nation, as the mother. He denounces then the destruction of all, collectively and individually. They were to be cut off, root and branch. They were to lose their collective existence as a nation; and, lest private persons should flatter themselves with hope of escape, it is said to them, as if one by one, "thou shalt fall."

6. *My people are destroyed for lack of knowledge.* "My people *are*," not, "*is*." This accurately represents the Hebrew[7]. The word "people" speaks of them as a whole; *are*, relates to the individuals of whom that whole is composed. Together, the words express the utter destruction of the whole, one and all. They are destroyed *for lack of knowledge*, lit. "of *the* knowledge," i. e. the only knowledge, which in the creature is real knowledge, that knowledge, of the want of which he had before complained, the knowledge of the Creator. So Isaiah mourns in

the same words[8], *therefore my people are gone into captivity, because they have no knowledge.* They are destroyed for lack of it; for the true knowledge of God is the life of the soul, true life, eternal life, as our Saviour saith, *This is life eternal, that they should know Thee, the only true God, and Jesus Christ Whom Thou has sent.* The source of this lack of knowledge, so fatal to the people, was the wilful rejection of that knowledge by the priest;

Because thou hast rejected knowledge, I will also reject thee, that thou shalt be no priest to Me. God marks the relation between the sin and the punishment, by retorting on them, as it were, their own acts; and that with great emphasis, *I will utterly reject thee*[9]. Those, thus addressed, must have been true priests, scattered up and down in Israel, who, in an irregular way, offered sacrifices for them, and connived at their sins. For God's sentence on them is, *thou shalt be no priest to ME.* But the priests whom Jeroboam consecrated out of other tribes than Levi, were priests not to God, but to the calves. Those then, originally true priests, had probably a precarious livelihood, when the true worship of God was deformed by the mixture of the calf-worship, and the people *halted between two opinions;* and so were tempted by poverty also, to withhold from the people unpalatable truth. They shared, then, in the rejection of God's truth which they dissembled, and made themselves partakers in its suppression. And now, they *despised, were disgusted with*[10] the knowledge of God, as all do in fact despise and dislike it, who prefer ought besides to it. So God repaid their contempt to them, and took away the office, which, by their sinful connivances, they had hoped to retain.

Seeing thou hast forgotten the law of thy God. This seems to have been the sin of the people. For the same persons could not, at least in the same stage of sin, despise and forget. They who despise or *reject*, must have before their mind that which they *reject.* To *reject* is wilful, conscious, deliberate sin, with a high hand; to *forget*, an act of negligence.

[1] Prov. ix. 7, 8.   [2] Ib. xxiii. 9.   [3] Acts vii. 51.
[4] S. John xi. 9, 10.   [5] Jer. xv. 8.   [6] Is. i. 7.
[7] The singular noun, as being a collective, is joined with the plural verb.

[8] מִבְּלִי דָעַת vi. 13. The absence of the article makes no difference
[9] Such is probably the force of the unusual form אֶמְאָסְאָךְ. [10] Such is the first meaning of the word.

Before
C H R I S T
cir. 780.
b ch. 13. 6.
1 Sam. 2. 30.
Mal. 2. 9.
Phil. 3. 19.

7 ᵇAs they were increased, so they sinned against me: ¹ *therefore* will I change their glory into shame.

8 They eat up the sin of my people, and they † set their heart on their iniquity.

Before
C H R I S T
cir. 780.

† Heb. *lift up their soul to their iniquity.*

The rejection of God's law was the act of the understanding and will; forgetfulness of it comes from the neglect to look into it; and this, from the distaste of the natural mind for spiritual things, from being absorbed in things of this world, from inattention to the duties prescribed by it, or shrinking from seeing *that* condemned, which is agreeable to the flesh. The priests knew God's law and *despised* it; the people *forgat* it. In an advanced stage of sin, however, man may come to forget what he once despised; and this is the condition of the hardened sinner. *I will also forget thy children*, lit. *I will forget thy children, I too.* God would mark the more, that His act followed on their's ; they, first; then, He saith, *I too.* He would requite them, and do what it belonged not to His Goodness to do first. Parents who are careless as to themselves, as to their own lives, even as to their own shame, still long that their children should not be as themselves. God tries to touch their hearts, where they are least steeled against Him. He says not, *I will forget thee*, but I will forget those nearest thy heart, *thy children.* God is said to *forget*, when He acts, as if His creatures were no longer in His mind, no more the objects of His Providence and love.

7. *As they were increased, so they sinned against Me.* The *increase* may be, either in actual number or in wealth, power or dignity. The text includes both. In both kinds of increase, the bad abuse God's gifts against Himself, and take occasion of them to offend Him. The more they were increased in number, the more there were to sin, the more they were who sinned. God promised to make Abraham's seed, *as the stars of heaven.* They were to shine in the world through the light of the law, and the glory which God gave them while obeying Him. ¹ *Thy fathers went down into Egypt with threescore and ten persons; and now the Lord thy God hath made thee like the stars of heaven for multitude. Therefore thou shalt love the Lord thy God, and keep His charge, and His statutes, and his judgments and His commandments alway.* God multiplied them, that there might be the more to adore Him. But instead of multiplying subjects, He multiplied apostates. "As many men as Israel had, so many altars did it build to dæmons, in the sacrifices to whom it sinned against Me." "The more sons God gave to Israel, the more enemies He made to Himself; for Israel brought them up in hatred to God, and in the love and worship of idols." "As too among the devout, one provokes another, by word and deed, to good works, so, in the congregation of evil doers, one incites another to sins." Again, worldlings make all God's gifts minister to pride, and so to all the sins, which are the daughters of pride. ²*Jeshurun*, God says, *waxed fat and kicked; then he forsook God which made him, and lightly esteemed the Rock of his salvation.* In this way too, the increase of wealth which God gives to those who forget Him, increases the occasions of ingratitude and sins.

I will turn their glory into shame. Such is the course of sin and chastisement. God bestows on man, gifts, which may be to him matter of praise and glory, if only ordered aright to their highest and only true end, the glory of God; man perverts them to vainglory and thereby to sin ; God turns the gifts, so abused, to shame. He not only gives them shame *instead* of their glory ; He makes the glory itself the means and occasion of their shame. Beauty becomes the occasion of degradation ; pride is proverbially near a fall ; " vaulting ambition overleaps itself, and falls on th'other side ;" riches and abundance of population tempt nations to wars, which become their destruction, or they invite other and stronger nations to prey upon them. *Thou hast indeed smitten Edom*, was the message of Jehoash to Amaziah ³*, and thine heart hath lifted thee up ; glory of this, and tarry at home ; for why shouldest thou meddle to thy hurt, that thou shouldest fall, even thou and Judah with thee ? But Amaziah would not hear.* He lost his own wealth, wasted the treasures in God's house ; and the walls of Jerusalem were broken down.

8. *They eat up the sin of My people.* The priests made a gain of the sins of the people, lived upon them and by them, conniving at or upholding the idolatries of the people, partaking in their idol-sacrifices and idolatrous rites, which, as involving the desertion of God, were *the sin of* the *people*, and the root of all their other sins. This the priests did knowingly. True or false, apostate or irregularly appointed, they knew that there was no truth in the golden calves ; but they withheld the truth, they held it down in unrighteousness, and preached Jeroboam's falsehood, *these be thy gods, O Israel.* The reputation, station, maintenance of the false priests depended upon it. Not being of the line of

---

¹ Deut. x. 22. xi. 1.

² Ib. xxxii. 15.   ³ 2 Kings xiv. 10, 11.

4

Before
CHRIST
cir. 780.

k Isai. 24. 2.
Jer. 5. 31.
† Heb. visit upon
† Heb. cause to
return.
1 Lev. 26. 26.
Mic. 6. 14.
Hag. 1. 6.

9 And there shall be, k like people, like priest: and I will † punish them for their ways, and † reward them their doings.

10 For 1 they shall eat, and not have enough: they shall commit whoredom, and shall not increase: because they have left off to take heed to the LORD.

Before
CHRIST
cir. 780.

Aaron, they could be no priests except to the calves, and so they upheld the sin whereby they lived, and, that they might themselves be accounted priests of God, taught them to worship the calves, as representatives of God.

The word, *sin,* may include indirectly the sin-offerings of the people, as if they loved the sin or encouraged it, in order that they might partake of the outward expiations for it.

And they set their heart on their iniquity, as the source of temporal profit to themselves. "Benefited by the people, they reproved them not in their sinful doings, but charged themselves with their souls, saying, on us be the judgment, as those who said to Pilate, *His blood be upon us."* That which was, above all, *their iniquity,* the source of all the rest, was their departure from God and from His ordained worship. On this they *set their hearts ;* in this they kept them secure by their lies; they feared any misgivings, which might rend the people from them, and restore them to the true worship of God. But what else is it, to extenuate or flatter sin now, to dissemble it, not to see it, not openly to denounce it, lest we lose our popularity, or alienate those who commit it ? What else is it to speak smooth words to the great and wealthy, not to warn them, even in general terms, of the danger of making Mammon their god ; of the peril of riches, of parade, of luxury, of immoral dressing, and, amid boundless extravagance, neglect of the poor ; encouraging the rich, not only in the neglect of Lazarus, but in pampering the dogs, while they neglect him ? What is the praise of some petty dole to the poor, but connivance at the withholding from God His due in them ? "We see now," says an old writer, " 1 how many prelates live on the oblations and revenues of the laity, and yet, whereas they are bound, by words, by prayers, by exemplary life, to turn them away from sin, and to lead them to amendment, they, in various ways, scandalize, corrupt, infect them, by ungodly conversation, flattery, connivance, co-operation, and neglect of due pastoral care. Whence Jeremiah says 2, *My people hath been lost sheep : their shepherds have caused them to go astray.* O how horrible and exceeding great will be their damnation, who shall be tormented for each

of those under their care, who perish through their negligence."

9. *And there shall be like people, like priest.* Priest and people were alike in sin. Yea they are wont, if bad, to foment each other's sin. The bad priest copies the sins which he should reprove, and excuses himself by the frailty of our common nature. The people, acutely enough, detect the worldliness or self-indulgence of the priest, and shelter themselves under his example. Their defence stands good before men ; but what before God ? Alike in sin, priest and people should be alike in punishment. "Neither secular greatness should exempt the laity, nor the dignity of his order, the priest." Both shall be swept away in one common heap, in one disgrace, into one damnation. *They shall bind them in bundles to burn them.*

And I will punish them for their ways, and reward them their doings ; lit. *I will visit upon him his ways, and his doings I will make to return to him.* People and priests are spoken of as one man. None should escape. The judgment comes down *upon* them, overwhelming them. Man's deeds are called his *ways,* because the soul holds on the tenor of its life along them, and those ways lead him on to his last end, heaven or hell. The word rendered *doings* 3 signifies *great doings,* when used of God ; *bold doings,* on the part of man. Those bold presumptuous doings against the law and Will of God, God will bring back to the sinner's bosom.

10. *For they shall eat, and not have enough.* This is almost a proverbial saying of Holy Scripture, and, as such, has manifold applications. In the way of nature, it comes true in those, who, under God's afflictive Hand in famine or siege, *eat* what they have, but *have not enough,* and perish with hunger. It comes true in those, who, through bodily disease, are not nourished by their food. Yet not less true is it of those who, through their own insatiate desires, are never satisfied, but crave the more greedily, the more they have. Their sin of covetousness becomes their torment.

They shall commit whoredom and not increase ; lit. *they have committed whoredom.* The time spoken of is perhaps changed, because God would not speak of their future sin, as certain. There is naturally too a long interval between this sin and its possible fruit,

---

1 Dionys. Carth.   2 l. 6.

3 מַעַלְלֵיהֶם

Before
CHRIST
cir. 780.

■ Isai. 28. 7.
See Eccles. 7.
7.

11 Whoredom and wine and new wine [m] take away the heart.

12 ¶ My people ask

counsel at their [n] stocks, and their staff declareth unto them: for [o] the spirit of whoredoms hath caused

Before
CHRIST
cir. 780.

■ Jer. 2. 27.
Hab. 2. 19.
[o] Isai. 44. 20.
ch. 5. 4.

which may be marked by this change of time. The sin was past, the effect was to be seen hereafter. They used all means, lawful and unlawful, to increase their offspring, but they failed, even because they used forbidden means. God's curse rested upon those means. Single marriage, according to God's law, *they twain shall be one flesh*, yields in a nation larger increase than polygamy. Illicit intercourse God turns to decay. His curse is upon it.

Because they have left off to take heed to the Lord, lit. *to watch, observe, the Lord.* The eye of the soul should be upon God, watching and waiting to know all indications of His Will, all guidings of His Eye. So the Psalmist says[1], *As the eyes of servants look unto the hand of their masters, and as the eyes of a maiden unto the hands of her mistress, even so our eyes wait upon the Lord our God, until He have mercy upon us.* The Angels of God, great and glorious as they are, *do alway behold the Face of the Father*[2], at once filled with His love, and wrapt in contemplation, and reading therein His Will, to do it. The lawless and hopeless ways of Israel sprang from their neglecting to watch and observe God. For as soon as man ceases to watch God, he falls, of himself, into sin. The eye which is not fixed on God, is soon astray amid the vanities and pomps and lusts of the world. So it follows;

11. *Whoredom and wine and new wine take away* (lit. *takes away*) *the heart.* Wine and fleshly sin are pictured as blended in one, to deprive man of his affections and reason and understanding, and to leave him brutish and irrational. In all the relations of life toward God and man, reason and will are guided by the affections. And so, in God's language, the "heart" stands for the "understanding" as well as the "affections," because it directs the understanding, and the understanding, bereft of true affections, and under the rule of passion, becomes senseless. Besides the perversion of the understanding, each of these sins blunts and dulls the fineness of the intellect; much more, both combined. The stupid sottishness of the confirmed voluptuary is a whole, of which each act of sensual sin worked its part. The Heathen saw this clearly, although, without the grace of God, they did not act on what they saw to be true and right. This, the sottishness of Israel,

destroying their understanding, was the ground of their next folly, that they ascribed to *their stock* the office of God. "Corruption of manners and superstition" (it has often been observed) "go hand in hand."

12. *My people ask counsel at* [lit. *on*] *their stocks.* They ask habitually[3]; and that, in dependence *on their stocks.* The word *wood* is used of the idol made of it, to bring before them the senselessness of their doings, in that they asked counsel of the senseless wood. Thus Jeremiah[4] reproaches them for *saying to a stock, my father;* and Habakkuk[5], *Woe unto him that saith to the wood, awake.*

And their staff declareth unto them. Many sorts of this superstition existed among the Arabs and Chaldees. They were different ways of drawing lots, without any dependence upon the true God to direct it. This was a part of their senselessness, of which the Prophet had just said, that their sins took away their hearts. The tenderness of the word, *My people*, aggravates both the stupidity and the ingratitude of Israel. They whom the Living God owned as His own people, they who might have asked of Him, asked of a stock or a staff.

For the spirit of whoredoms. It has been thought of old, that the evil spirits assault mankind in a sort of order and method, different spirits bending all their energies to tempt him to different sins[6]. And this has been founded on the words of Holy Scripture, "a lying spirit," "an unclean spirit," "a spirit of jealousy," and our Lord said of the evil spirit whom the disciples could not cast out[7]; *This kind goeth not out but by prayer and fasting.* Hence it has been thought that "[6]some spirits take delight in uncleanness and defilement of sins; others urge on to blasphemies; others, to anger and fury; others take delight in gloom; others are soothed with vainglory and pride; and that each instills into man's heart that vice in which he takes pleasure himself; yet that all do not urge their own perversenesses at once, but in turn, as opportunity of time or place, or man's own susceptibility, invites them." Or the word, *spirit of whoredoms*, may mean the vehemence with which men were whirled along by their evil passions, whether by their passionate love of idolatry, or by the fleshly sin which was so often bound up with their idolatry.

They have gone a whoring from under their

[1] Ps. cxxiii. 2.   [2] S. Matt. xviii. 10.
[3] The Hebrew tense expresses action which is repeatedly resumed.

[4] ii. 27.   [5] ii. 19.
[6] Cassian Collat. vii. 17.
[7] S. Matt. xvii. 21.

Before
CHRIST
cir. 780. *them* to err, and they have gone a whoring from under their God.

P Isai. 1. 29. & 57.
5, 7.
Ezek. 6. 13. &
20. 28.

13 P They sacrifice upon the tops of the mountains, and burn incense upon the hills, under oaks and poplars and elms, because the shadow thereof *is* good :

q therefore your daughters shall commit whoredom, and your spouses shall com- mit adultery.

Before
CHRIST
cir. 780.

q Amos 7. 17.
Rom. 1. 28.

14 || I will not punish your daughters when they commit w h o r e d o m, nor your spouses when they commit adultery : for them-

|| Or, *Shall I not,
&c.*

God. The words *from under* continue the image of the adulteress wife, by which God had pictured the faithlessness of His people. The wife was spoken of as *under her husband*[1], i. e. under his authority ; she withdrew herself *from under* him, when she withdrew herself *from* his authority, and gave herself to another. So Israel, being wedded to God, estranged herself from Him, withdrew herself from His obedience, cast off all reverence to Him, and prostituted herself to her idols.

13. *They sacrifice upon the tops of the mountains.* The tops of hills or mountains seemed nearer heaven, the air was purer, the place more removed from the world. To worship the Unseen God upon them, was then the suggestion of natural feeling and of simple devotion. God Himself directed the typical sacrifice of Isaac to take place on a mountain; on that same mountain He commanded that the temple should be built; on a mountain, God gave the law; on a mountain was our Saviour transfigured ; on a mountain was He crucified ; from a mountain He ascended into heaven. Mountains and hills have accordingly often been chosen for Christian churches and monasteries. But the same natural feeling, misdirected, made them the places of heathen idolatry and heathen sins. The Heathen probably also chose for their star and planet-worship, mountains or large plains, as being the places whence the heavenly bodies might be seen most widely. Being thus connected with idolatry and sin, God strictly forbade the worship on the high places, and (as is the case with so many of God's commandments) man practised it as diligently[2] as if He had commanded it. God had said[2], *Ye shall utterly destroy all the places, wherein the nations, which ye shall possess, served their gods upon the high mountains, and upon the hills and under every green tree.* But[3] *they set them up images and groves* [rather *images of Ashtaroth*] *in every high hill and under every green tree, and there they burnt incense in all the high places, as did the heathen whom the Lord carried away before them.* The words express, that this which God forbade they did dili-

gently ; *they sacrificed much and diligently ; they burned incense much and diligently*[4] *;* and that, not here and there, but generally, *on the tops of the mountains,* and, as it were, in the open face of heaven. So also Ezekiel complains[5], *They saw every high hill and all the thick trees, and they offered there their sacrifices, and there they presented the provocation of their offering ; there also they made their sweet savor, and poured out there their drink-offerings.*

Under oaks, [*white*] *poplars and elms* [probably the terebinth or turpentine tree] *because the shadow thereof is good.* The darkness of the shadow suited alike the cruel and the profligate deeds which were done in honor of their false gods. In the open face of day, and in secret they carried on their sin.

Therefore their daughters shall commit whoredoms, and their spouses [or more probably, *daughters-in-law*] *shall commit adultery,* or (in the present) *commit adultery.* The fathers and husbands gave themselves to the abominable rites of Baal-peor and Ashtaroth, and so the daughters and daughters-in-law followed their example. This was by the permission of God, Who, since they *glorified not God* as they ought, *gave them up,* abandoned them, *to vile affections.* So, through their own disgrace and bitter griefs, in the persons of those whose honor they most cherished, they should learn how ill they themselves had done, in departing from Him Who is the Father and Husband of every soul. The sins of the fathers descend very often to the children, both in the way of nature, that the children inherit strong temptations to· their parents' sin, and by way of example, that they greedily imitate, often exaggerate, them. Wouldest thou not have children, which thou wouldest wish unborn, reform thyself. The saying may include too sufferings at the hands of the enemy. "What thou dost willingly, that shall your daughters and your daughters-in-law suffer against thine and thy will."

14. *I will not punish your daughters.* God threatens, as the severest woe, that He will not punish their sins with the correction of a Father in this present life, but will leave

---

[1] Num. v. 19, 29. Ezek. xxiii. 5.
[2] Deut. xii. 2.　　[3] 2 Kings xvii. 10, 11.

[4] *yezabbechu,* not *izbechu; yekatteru,* not *yaktiru.*
[5] xx. 28.

Before
C H R I S T
cir. 780.

ᵛ ver. 1, 6.

‖ Or, *be punished.*

selves are separated with whores, and they sacrifice with harlots : therefore the people *that* ᵛ doth not understand shall ‖ fall.

15 ¶ Though thou, Is-

rael, play the harlot, *yet* let not Judah offend ; ˢ and come not ye unto Gilgal, neither go ye up to ᵗ Beth-aven, ᵘ nor swear, The LORD liveth.

Before
C H R I S T
cir. 780.

ˢ ch. 9. 15. & 12. 11.
Amos 4. 4. & 5. 5.
ᵗ 1 Kings 12. 29. ch. 10. 5.
ᵘ Amos 8. 14. Zeph. 1. 5.

the sinners, unheeded, to follow all iniquity. It is the last punishment of persevering sinners, that God leaves them to prosper in their sins and in those things which help them to sin. Hence we are taught to pray[1], *O Lord, correct me, but in judgment, not in Thine anger.* For since God chastiseth those whom He loveth, it follows[2], *if we be without chastisement, whereof all are partakers, then are we bastards, and not sons.* To be chastened severely for lesser sins, is a token of great love of God toward us ; to sin on without punishment is a token of God's extremest displeasure, and a sign of reprobation. [3] "Great is the offence, if, when thou hast sinned, thou art undeserving of the wrath of God."

For themselves are separated with whores. God turns from them as unworthy to be spoken to any more, and speaks of them, They *separate themselves,* from Whom? and with whom? They separate themselves *from* God, and *with* the degraded ones and *with* devils. Yet so do all those who choose wilful sin.

And they sacrifice [*continually,* as before] *with* [*the*] *harlots.* The unhappy women here spoken of were such as were [4] *consecrated* (as their name imports) to their vile gods and goddesses, and to prostitution. This dreadful consecration, yea desecration, whereby they were taught to seek honor in their disgrace, was spread in different forms over Phœnicia, Syria, Phrygia, Assyria, Babylonia. Ashtaroth, (the Greek Astarte) was its chief object. This horrible worship prevailed in Midian, when Israel was entering the promised land, and it suggested the devilish device of Balaam[5] to entangle Israel in sin whereby they might forfeit the favor of God. The like is said to subsist to this day in heathen India. The sin was both the cause and effect of the superstition. Man's corrupt heart gave rise to the worship : and the worship in turn fostered the corruption. He first sanctioned the sin by aid of a degrading worship of nature, and then committed it under plea of that worship. He made his sin a law to him. Women, who never relapsed into the sin, sinned in obedience to the dreadful law[6]. Blinded as they were, individual heathen had the excuse of their hereditary blindness; the

Jews had imperfect grace. The sins of Christians are self-sought, against light and grace. *Therefore the people that doth not understand shall fall.* The word comprises both, *that doth not understand,* and, *that will not understand.* They might have understood, if they *would.* God had revealed Himself to them, and had given them His law, and was still sending to them His prophets, so that they could not but have known and understood God's Will, had they willed. Ignorance, which we might avoid or cure, if we would, is itself a sin. It cannot excuse sin. They shall, he says, *fall,* or *be cast headlong.* Those who blind their eyes, so as not to see or understand God's Will, bring themselves to sudden ruin, which they hide from themselves, until they fall headlong in it.

15. *Let not Judah offend.* The sentence of Israel had been pronounced; she had been declared incorrigible. The Prophet turns from her now to Judah. Israel had abandoned God's worship, rejected or corrupted His priests, given herself to the worship of the calves; no marvel what further excess of riot she run into ! But Judah, who had the law and the temple and the service of God, let not her, (he would say,) involve herself in Israel's sin. If Israel, in wilful blindness, had plunged herself in ruin, let not Judah involve herself in her sin and her ruin. He turns (as elsewhere) incidentally to Judah.

Come ye not unto Gilgal. Gilgal lay between Jericho and the Jordan. There, ten furlongs from the Jordan, first in all the promised land, the people encamped; there Joshua placed the monument of the miraculous passage of the Jordan; there he renewed the circumcision of the people which had been intermitted in the wilderness, and the feast of the passover; thither the people returned, after all the victories by which God gave them possession of the land of promise[7]. There Samuel habitually sacrificed, and there, *before the Lord,* i. e. in His special covenanted Presence, he publicly made Saul king[8]. It was part of the policy of Jeroboam to take hold of all these associations, as a sort of set-off against Jerusalem and the Temple, from which he had separated his people. In op-

[1] Jer. x. 24.   [2] Heb. xii. 8.
[3] S. Jer.   [4] הקרשות
[5] Num. xxv. xxxi. 8, 16.
[6] Herod. i. 199.   It may have been in some such

way, that Gomer, whom the prophet was bidden to marry, had fallen.
[7] Josh. iv. 19, 20. v. 9, 10. ix. 6. x. 6–9. 43. xiv. 6.
[8] 1 Sam. x. 8. xi. 14, 15. xiii. 4–9. xv. 21, 33.

Before
CHRIST
cir. 780.
16 For Israel [x] slideth back as a backsliding heif-

[x] Jer. 3. 6. & 7. 24.
& 8. 5.
Zech. 7. 11.
er: now the LORD will feed them as a lamb in a large place.

17 Ephraim is joined to idols: [y] let him alone.

18 Their drink † is sour: they have committed whoredom continually:

Before
CHRIST
cir. 780.

[y] Matt. 15. 14.
† Heb. is gone.

position to this idolatry, Elisha for a time, established there one of the schools of the Prophets [1].

Neither go ye up to Bethaven. Bethaven, lit. *house of vanity,* was a city East of *Bethel* [2], *the house of God.* But since Jeroboam had set up the worship of the calves at Bethel, Bethel had ceased to be *the house of God,* and had become *a house* or *temple of vanity;* and so the Prophet gave it no more its own name which was associated with the history of the faith of the Patriarchs, but called it what it had become. In Bethel God had twice appeared to Jacob, when he left the land of promise [3] to go to Laban, and when he returned [4]. Thither also the ark of God was for a time in the days of the judges removed from Shiloh [5], near to which on the south [6] Bethel lay. It too Jeroboam profaned by setting up the calf there. To these places then, as being now places of the idolatry of Israel, Judah is forbidden to go, and then to *swear, the Lord liveth.* For to swear by the Lord in a place of idolatry would be to associate the living God with idols [7], which God expressly forbade.

16. *For Israel slideth back, as a backsliding heifer.* The calves which Israel worshiped were pictures of itself. They represented natural, untamed, strength, which, when put to service, started back and shrank from the yoke. "Untractable, petulant, unruly, wanton, it withdrew from the yoke, when it could; if it could not, it drew aside or backward, instead of forward." So is it rare, exceeding rare, for man to walk straight on in God's ways; he jerks, writhes, twists, darts aside hither and thither, hating nothing so much as one straight, even, narrow tenor of his ways.

Now the Lord will feed them as a lamb in a large place. The punishment of Israel was close at hand, *now.* It would not have the straitness of God's commandments; it should have the wideness of a desert. God would withdraw His protecting Providence from them: He would rule them, although unfelt in His mercy. At *large,* they wished to be; at large they should be; but it should be the largeness of *a wilderness where is no way.* There, like a lamb, they should go astray, wandering up and down, unprotected, a prey to wild beasts. Woe is it to that man, whom,

when he withdraws from Christ's easy yoke, God permits to take unhindered the broad road which leadeth to destruction. To Israel, this *wide place* was the wide realms of the Medes, where they were withdrawn from God's worship and deprived of His protection.

17. *Ephraim is joined to idols,* i. e. banded, bound up with them, *associated,* as the word means, with them so as to cleave to them, willing neither to part with, nor to be parted from, them. The *idols* are called by a name, denoting *toils;* with toil they were fashioned, and, when fashioned, they were a toil and grief.

Let him alone, lit. *give him rest,* i. e. from all further expostulations, which he will not hear. It is an abandonment of Israel for the time, as in the prophet Ezekiel [8], *As for you, O house of Israel, thus saith the Lord God, go ye, serve ye every one his idols.* Sinners often long not to be tormented by conscience or by God's warnings. To be left so, is to be abandoned by God, as one whose case is desperate. God will not, while there is hope, leave a man to sleep in sin; for so the numbness of the soul increases, until, like those who fall asleep amid extreme cold of the body, it never awakes.

18. *Their drink is sour,* lit. *turned,* as we say of milk. So Isaiah says [9], *Thy silver is become dross; thy wine is mingled,* i. e. adulterated, *with water;* and our lord speaks of *salt which had lost its savor.* The wine or the salt, when once turned or become insipid, is spoiled, irrecoverably, as we speak of "dead wine." They had lost all their life, and taste of goodness.

Her rulers with shame do love, give ye. Avarice and luxury are continually banded together according to the saying, "covetous of another's, prodigal of his own." Yet it were perhaps more correct to render, *her rulers do love, do love, shame* [10]. They love that which brings shame, which is bound up with shame, and ends in it; and so the Prophet says that they *love* the *shame* itself. They act, as if they were in love with the shame, which, all their lives long, they are unceasingly and, as it were, by system, drawing upon themselves. They chase diligently after all the occasions of sins and sinful pleasures which end in shame; they omit nothing

[1] 2 Kgs. iv. 38.   [2] Josh. vii. 2.   [3] Gen. xxviii. 10, 19.
[4] Ib. xxxv. 1 and 9.   [5] Jud. xx. 26, 7.
[6] Jud. xxi. 19.   [7] Zeph. i. 5.   [8] xx. 39.   [9] i. 22.

[10] אהבו הבו is probably one of the earliest forms of the intensive verb, repeating a part of a verb itself, with its inflection.

Before
CHRIST
cir. 780.

[a] her † rulers *with* shame do love, Give ye.

[a] Mic. 3. 11. & 7. 3.
† Heb. *shields*,
Ps. 47. 9.
[a] Jer. 4. 11, 12. & 51. 1.
[b] Isai. 1. 29.
Jer. 2. 26.

19 [a] The wind hath bound her up in her wings, and [b] they shall be ashamed because of their sacrifices.

CHAPTER V.

1 *God's judgments against the priests, the people, and the*

princes of Israel, for their man-ifold sins, 15 *until they repent.*

Before
CHRIST
cir. 780.

HEAR ye this, O priests; and hearken, ye house of Israel; and give ye ear, O house of the king; for judgment *is* toward you, because [a] ye have been a [a] ch. 6. 9. snare on Mizpah, and a net spread upon Tabor.

---

which brings it, do nothing which can avoid it. What else or what more could they do, if they *loved* the *shame* for its own sake?

19. *The wind hath bound her up in her wings.* When God brought Israel out of Egypt, He *bare them on eagle's wings, and brought them unto Himself*[1]. Now they had abandoned God, and God abandoned them as chaff to the wind. The certainty of Israel's doom is denoted by its being spoken of in the past. It was certain in the Divine judgment. Sudden, resistless, irreversible are God's judgments, when they come. As if "imprisoned in the viewless winds, and" borne "with resistless violence," as it were on the wings of the whirlwind, Israel should be hurried by the mighty wrath of God into captivity in a distant land, bound up so that none should escape, but, when arrived there, dispersed hither and thither, as the chaff before the wind.

And they shall be ashamed because of their sacrifices. They had sacrificed to the calves, to Baal, or to the sun, moon, stars, hoping aid from them rather than from God. When then they should see, in deed, that from those their sacrifices no good came to them, but evil only, they should be healthfully ashamed. So, in fact, in her captivity, did Israel learn to be ashamed of her idols; and so does God, by healthful disappointment, make us ashamed of seeking out of Him, the good things, which He alone hath, and hath in store for them who love Him.

V. 1. *Hear ye this, O ye priests.* God, with the solemn threefold summons, arraigns anew all classes in Israel before Him, not now to repentance but to judgment. Neither the religious privileges of the priests, nor the multitude of the people, nor the civil dignity of the king, should exempt any from God's judgment. The priests are, probably, the true but corrupted priests of God, who had fallen away to the idolatries with which they were surrounded, and, by their apostacy, had strengthened them. The king, here first

mentioned by Hosea, was probably the unhappy Zechariah, a weak, pliant, self-indulgent, drunken scoffer[2], who, after eleven years of anarchy, succeeded his father, only to be murdered.

For judgment is toward you, lit. *the judgment.* The kings and the priests had hitherto been the judges; now they were summoned before Him, Who is *the* Judge of judges, and the King of kings. To teach the law was part of the priest's office; to enforce it, belonged to the king. The guilt of both was enhanced, in that they, being so entrusted with it, had corrupted it. They had the greatest sin, as being the seducers of the people, and therefore have the severest sentence. The Prophet, dropping for the time the mention of the people, pronounces the judgment on the seducers.

Because ye have been a snare on Mizpah. Mizpah, the scene of the solemn covenant of Jacob with Laban, and of his signal protection by God, lay in the mountainous part of Gilead on the East of Jordan. Tabor was the well-known Mountain of the Transfiguration, which rises out of the midst of the plain of Jezreel or Esdraelon, one thousand feet high, in the form of a sugar-loaf. Of Mount Tabor it is related by S. Jerome, that birds were still snared upon it. But something more seems intended than the mere likeness of birds, taken in the snare of a fowler. This was to be seen everywhere; and so, had this been all, there hath no ground to mention these two historical spots. The Prophets has selected places on both sides of Jordan, which were probably centres of corruption, or special scenes of wickedness. Mizpah, being a sacred place in the history of the Patriarch Jacob[3], was probably, like Gilgal and other sacred places, desecrated by idolatry. Tabor was the scene of God's deliverance of Israel by Barak[4]. There, by encouraging idolatries, they became hunters, not pastors, of souls[5]. There is an old Jewish tradition[6], that lyers-in-wait were set in these two places, to intercept and murder

---

[1] Ex. xix. 4. Deut. xxxii. 11.   [2] See Introd. p. 15.
[3] Gen. xxxi. 23–49.   [4] Jud. iv.   [5] Ezek. xiii. 18, 20.

[6] Rashi, Ibn Ezra, Kimchi "out of ancienter Rabbins." Poc.

Before
CHRIST
cir. 780.

b Isai. 29. 15.
| Or, *and, &c.*
† Heb. *a correc-
tion.*
c Amos 3, 2.

2 And the revolters are
b profound to make slaugh-
ter, || though I *have been*
† a rebuker of them all.

3 c I know Ephraim, and
Israel is not hid from me:

for now, O Ephraim, d thou
committest whoredom, *and*
Israel is defiled.

4 † || They will not frame
their doings to turn unto
their God: for e the spirit

Before
CHRIST
cir. 780.

d Ezek. 23. 5. &c.
ch. 4. 17.
† Heb. *They will
not give.*
|| Or, *Their doings
will, not suffer
them.*
e ch. 4. 12.

those Israelites, who would go up to worship
at Jerusalem. And this tradition gains
countenance from the mention of slaughter
in the next verse.

2. *And the revolters are profound to make
slaughter ;* lit. " *They made the slaughter deep,*"
as Isaiah says, " *they deeply corrupted themselves* [1] *;* " and our old writers say " He smote
deep." They willed also doubtless to " make
it deep," hide it so deep, that God should
never know it, as the Psalmist says of the
ungodly, " that *the inward self and heart of the
workers of iniquity is deep,*" whereon it follows,
that God should *suddenly wound them,* as here
the prophet subjoins that God rebuked them.
Actual and profuse murder has been already [2]
mentioned as one of the common sins of
Israel, and it is afterward [3] also charged
upon the priests.

Though I have been a rebuker, lit. *a rebuke,*
as the Psalmist says [4], *I am prayer,* i. e " I am
all prayer." The Psalmist's whole being was
turned into prayer. So here, all the attributes of God, His mercies, love, justice, were
concentrated into one, and that one, *rebuke.*
Rebuke was the one form, in which they were
all seen. It is an aggravation of crime to do it
in the place of judgment or in the presence
of the judge. Israel was immersed in his sin
and heeded not, although God rebuked him
continually by His voice in the law, forbidding
all idolatry, and was now all the while, both
in word and deed, rebuking him.

3. *I know Ephraim.* There is much emphasis on the *I.* It is like our, " *I* have known,"
or " I, I, have known." God had known him
all along, if we may so speak. However deep
they may have laid their plans of blood, however they would or do hide them from man,
and think that no Eye seeth them, and say,
Who seeth me ? and *who knoweth me ? I, to* Whose
Eyes all things are naked and opened [5], have
all along known them, and nothing of them
has been hid from Me. *For,* He adds, even
now, *now* when, under a fair outward shew,
they are veiling the depth of their sin, *now,*
when they think that their way is hid in
darkness, I know their doings, that they are
defiling themselves. Sin never wanted spe-
cious excuse. Now too unbelievers are mostly
fond of precisely those characters in Holy
Scripture, whom God condemns. Jeroboam

doubtless was accounted a patriot, vindicating
his country from oppressive taxation, which
Rehoboam insolently threatened. Jerusalem,
as lying in the Southernmost tribe, was represented, as ill-selected for the place of the
assemblage of the tribes. Bethel, on the
contrary, was hallowed by visions; it had
been the abode, for a time, of the ark. It lay
in the tribe of Ephraim, which they might
think to have been unjustly deprived of its
privilege. Dan was a provision for the
Northern tribes. Such was the exterior.
God says in answer, *I know Ephraim.* [6] *Known
unto God are all his works from the beginning of
the world.* Although (in some way unknown to
us) not interfering with our free-will, known
unto God are our thoughts and words and
deeds, before they are framed, while they are
framed, while they are being spoken and
done ; known to Him is all which we do, and
all which, under any circumstances, we should
do. This he knows with a knowledge, before
the things were. " [7] All His creatures, corporeal or spiritual, He doth not therefore
know, because they are ; but they therefore
are, because He knoweth them. For He was
not ignorant, what He was about to create ;
nor did He know them, after He had created
them, in any other way than before. For no
accession to His knowledge came from them ;
but, they existing when and as was meet,
that knowledge remained as it was." How
strange then to think of hiding from God a
secret sin, when He knew, before He created
thee, that He created thee liable to this very
temptation, and to be assisted amidst it with
just that grace which thou art resisting !
God had known Israel, but it was not with the
knowledge of love, of which He says, *The
Lord knoweth the way of the righteous* [8], and [9],
if any man love God, the same is known of Him,
but with the knowledge of condemnation,
whereby He, the Searcher of hearts, knows
the sin which He judges.

4. *They will not frame their doings, &c.* They
were possessed by an evil spirit, impelling
and driving them to sin ; *the spirit of whoredoms is in the midst of them,* i. e. in their very
inward self, their centre, so to speak ; in their
souls, where reside the will, the reason, the
judgment; and so long as they did not, by
the strength of God, dislodge him, they

[1] xxxi. 6.　　　[2] iv. 2.　　　[3] vi. 9.
[4] Ps. cix. 4.　　　[5] Heb. iv. 13.

[6] Acts xv. 18.　　　　　　[7] S. Aug.
[8] Ps. i. 6.　　　　　　　[9] 1 Cor. viii. 3.

Before
CHRIST
cir. 780.
of whoredoms *is* in the midst of them, and they have not known the LORD.

f ch. 7. 10.

5 And f the pride of Is-

rael doth testify to his face: therefore shall Israel and Ephraim fall in their iniquity; Judah also shall fall with them.

Before
CHRIST
cir. 780.

---

would and could not frame their acts, so as to repent and turn to God. For a mightier impulse mastered them and drove them into sin, as the evil spirit drove the swine into the deep.

The rendering of the margin, although less agreeable to the Hebrew, also gives a striking sense. *Their doings will not suffer them to turn unto their God.* Not so much that their habits of sin had got an absolute mastery over them, so as to render repentance impossible; but rather, that it was impossible that they should turn inwardly, while they did not turn outwardly. Their evil doings, so long as they persevered in doing them, took away all heart, whereby to turn to God with a solid conversion.

And yet He was *their God ;* this made their sin the more grievous. He, Whom they would not turn to, still owned them, was still ready to receive them as *their God.* For the Prophet continues, *and they have not known the Lord.* Him, *their God,* they knew not. For the spirit which possessed them hindered them from thought, from memory, from conception of spiritual things. They did not turn to God, 1) because the evil spirit held them, and so long as they allowed his hold, they were filled with carnal thoughts which kept them back from God. 2) They did not know God ; so that, not knowing how good and how great a good He is in Himself, and how good to us, they had not even the desire to turn to Him, for love of Himself, yea even for love of themselves. They saw not, that they lost a loving God.

5. *And the pride of Israel.* Pride was from the first the leading sin of Ephraim. Together with Manasseh, (with whom they made, in some respects, one whole, as *the children of Joseph* [1],) they were nearly equal in number to Judah. When numbered in the wilderness, Judah had 74,600 fighting men, Ephraim and Manasseh together 72,700. They speak of themselves as *a great people, forasmuch as the Lord has blessed me hitherto* [2]. God having chosen, out of them, the leader under whom He brought Israel into the land of promise, they resented, in the following time of the Judges, any deliverance of the land, in which they were not called to take a part. They

chode with Gideon [3], and suffered very severely for insolence [4] to Jephthah and the Gileadites. When Gideon, who had refused to be king, was dead, Abimelech, his son by a concubine out of Ephraim, induced the Ephraimites to make Him king over Israel, as being *their bone and their flesh* [5]. Lying in the midst of the tribes to the North of Judah, they appear, in antagonism to Judah, to have gathered round them the other tribes, and to have taken, with them, the name of Israel, in contrast with Judah [6]. Shiloh, where the ark was, until taken by the Philistines, belonged to them. Samuel, the last judge, was raised up out of them [7]. Their political dignity was not aggrieved, when God gave Saul, out of *little Benjamin,* as king over His people. They could afford to own a king out of the least tribe. Their present political eminence was endangered, when God chose David out of their great rival, the tribe of Judah ; their hope for the future was cut off by His promise to the posterity of David. They accordingly upheld, for seven years [8], the house of Saul, knowing that they were acting against the Will of God [9]. Their religious importance was aggrieved by the removal of the ark to Zion, instead of its being restored to Shiloh [10]. Absalom won them by flattery [11]; and the rebellion against David was a struggle of Israel [12] against Judah. When Absalom was dead, they had scarcely aided in bringing David back, when they fell away again, because their advice had not been first had in bringing him back [13]. Rehoboam was already king over Judah [14], when he came to Shechem to be made king over Israel [15]. Then the ten tribes sent for Jeroboam of Ephraim [16], to make him their spokesman, and, in the end, their king. The rival worship of Bethel provided, not only for the indolence, but for the pride of his tribe. He made a state-worship at Bethel, over-against the worship ordained by God at Jerusalem. Just before the time of Hosea, the political strength of Ephraim was so much superior to that of Judah, that Jehoash, in his pride, compared himself to the cedar of Lebanon, Amaziah king of Judah to the thistle [17]. Isaiah speaks of "jealousy [18]" or "envy," as the characteristic sin of Israel, which perpetuated that

---

[1] Josh. xvi 4. xvii. 14.   [2] Josh. xvii. 14.
[3] Jud. viii. 1 sqq.   [4] Ib. xii. 1 sqq.
[5] Ib. viii. 31. ix. 1–3, 22.
[6] 2 Sam. ii. 9, 10. iii. 17.   [7] 1 Sam. i. 1.
[8] 2 Sam. v. 5.   [9] Ib. iii. 9.   [10] Ps. lxxviii. 60, 67–69.

[11] 2 Sam. xv. 2, 5, 10, 12, 13.
[12] xvi. 15. xvii. 15. xviii. 6.
[13] Ib. xix. 41–3. xx. 1, 2.
[14] 1 Kgs xi. 43.
[15] 1 Kgs xii. 1.   [16] 1 Kgs xi. 26.
[17] 2 Kgs xiv. 9.   [18] xi. 13.

Before
CHRIST
cir. 780.

e Prov. 1. 28.
Isai. 1. 15.
Jer. 11. 11. Ezek. 8. 18. Mic. 3. 4. John 7. 34.

6 e They shall go with their flocks and with their herds to seek the LORD; but they shall not find *him;* he hath withdrawn himself from them.

Before
CHRIST
cir. 780.

division, which, he foretold, should be healed in Christ. Yet although such was the power and pride of Israel, God foretold that he should first go into captivity, and so it was. This pride, as it was the origin of the schism of the ten tribes, so it was the means of its continuance. In whatever degree any one of the kings of Israel was better than the rest, still *he departed not from the sins of Jeroboam, who made Israel to sin.* The giving up of any other sin only shewed, how deeply rooted this sin was, which even then they would not give up. As is the way of unregenerate man, they would not give themselves up without reserve to God, to do *all* His will. They could not give up *this* sin of Jeroboam, without endangering their separate existence as *Israel,* and owning the superiority of Judah. From this complete self-surrender to God, their pride shrank and held them back.

The pride, which Israel thus shewed in refusing to turn to God, and in preferring their sin to *their God,* itself, he says, witnessed against them, and condemned them. In the presence of God, there needeth no other witness against the sinner than his own conscience. It *shall witness to his face,* " openly, publicly, themselves and all others seeing, acknowledging, and approving the just judgment of God and the recompense of their sin." Pride and carnal sin are here remarkably united.

"[1] The Prophet having said, *the spirit of fornication is in the midst of them,* assigns as its ground, *the pride of Israel will testify to his face,* i. e. the sin which, through pride of mind, lurked in secret, bore open witness through sin of the flesh. Wherefore the cleanness of chastity is to be preserved by guarding humility. For if the spirit is piously humbled before God, the flesh is not raised unlawfully above the spirit. For the spirit holds the dominion over the flesh, committed to it, if it acknowledges the claims of lawful servitude to the Lord. For if, through pride, it despises its Author, it justly incurs a contest with its subject, the flesh."

Therefore shall Israel and Ephraim fall in [or *by*] *their iniquity.* Ephraim, the chief of the ten tribes, is distinguished from the whole, of which it was a part, because it was the rival of Judah, the royal tribe, out of which Jeroboam had sprung, who had formed the kingdom of Israel by the schism from Judah. All Israel, even its royal tribe, where was Samaria, its capital and strength, should fall, their iniquity being the stumbling-block, on which they should fall.

Judah also shall fall with them. "Judah also, being partaker with them in their idolatry and their wickedness, shall partake with them in the like punishment. Sin shall have the like effect in both." Literally, he saith, *Judah hath fallen,* denoting, as do other prophets, the certainty of the future event, by speaking of it, as having taken place already ; as it had, in the Mind of God.

6. *They shall go with their flocks.* "They had let slip the day of grace, wherein God had called them to repentance, and promised to be found of them and to accept them. When then the decree was gone forth and judgment determined against them, all their outward shew of worship and late repentance shall not prevail to gain admittance for them to Him. He will not be found of them, hear them, nor accept them. They stopped their ears obstinately against Him calling on them, and proffering mercy in the day of mercy : He will now stop His ear against them, crying for it in the Day of judgment." Repenting thus late, (as is the case with most who repent, or think that they repent, at the close of life) they did not repent out of the love of God, but out of slavish fear, on account of the calamity which was coming upon them. But the main truth, contained in this and other passages of Holy Scripture which speak of a time when it is too late to turn to God, is this: that "[2] it shall be too late to knock when the door shall be shut, and too late to cry for mercy when it is the time of justice." God waits long for sinners; He threatens long before He strikes; He strikes and pierces in lesser degrees, and with increasing severity, before the final blow comes. In this life, He places man in a new state of trial, even after His first judgments have fallen on the sinner. But the general rule of His dealings is this; that, when the time of each judgment is actually come, then, as to *that* judgment, it is too late to pray. It is *not* too late for other mercy, or for final forgiveness, so long as man's state of probation lasts; but it is too late as to this one. And thus, each judgment in time is a picture of the Eternal Judgment, when the day of mercy is past for ever, to those who have finally, in this life, hardened themselves against it. But temporal mercies correspond with temporal judgments; eternal mercy with

1 S. Greg.

2 Commination Service.

Before
CHRIST
cir. 780.

h Isai. 48. 8.
Jer. 3. 20. & 5.
11.
ch. 6. 7.
Mal. 2. 11.

7 They have ^h dealt treacherously against the LORD: for they have begotten strange children:

now shall ⁱ a month devour them with their portions.

8 ^k Blow ye the cornet in Gibeah, *and* the trumpet

Before
CHRIST
cir. 780.

i Zech. 11. 8.
k ch. 8. 1.
Joel 2. 1.

---

eternal judgment. In time, it may be too late to turn away temporal judgments; it is not too late, while God continues grace, to flee from eternal; and the desire not to lose God, is a proof to the soul that it is not forsaken by God, by Whom alone the longing for Himself is kept alive or re-awakened in His creature.

They shall not find Him. This befell the Jews in the time of Josiah. Josiah himself[1] *turned to the Lord with all his heart and with all his soul and with all his might, according to all the law of Moses.* He put away idolatry thoroughly; and the people so far followed his example. He held such a Passover, as had not been held since the time of the judges. *Notwithstanding the Lord turned not from the fierceness of His great wrath, wherewith His anger was kindled against Judah because of all the provocations that Manasseh had provoked Him withal. And the Lord said, I will remove Judah out of My sight, as I have removed Israel, and will cast off this city Jerusalem, which I have chosen, and the house of which I said, My name shall be there.*

The Prophet describes the people, as complying with God's commands; *they shall go,* i. e. to the place which God had chosen and commanded, *with their flocks and their herds,* i. e. with the most costly sacrifices, *the flocks* supplying the sheep and goats prescribed by the law; the *herds* supplying the bullocks, calves and heifers offered. They seem to have come, so far, sincerely. Yet perhaps it is not without further meaning, that the Prophet speaks of those outward sacrifices only, not of the heart; and the reformation under Josiah may therefore have failed, because the people were too ingrained with sin under Manasseh, and returned outwardly only under Josiah, as they fell back again after his death. And so God speaketh here, as He does by David[2], *I will take no bullock out of thine house, nor he-goat out of thy fold. Thinkest thou, that I will eat bulls' flesh, or drink the blood of goats?* and by Isaiah[3], *To what purpose is the multitude of your sacrifices unto Me? I am full of the burnt offerings of rams, and the fat of fed beasts.*

He hath withdrawn Himself from them. Perhaps he would say, that God, as it were, *freed Himself* from them, as He saith in Isaiah[4], *I am weary to bear them,* the union of sacrifices and of sin.

7. *They have dealt treacherously;* lit. *have cloaked,* and so, acted deceitfully. The word is used of treachery of friend towards his friend, of the husband to his wife, or the wife to her husband[5]. *Surely as a wife treacherously departeth from her husband, so have ye dealt treacherously with Me, O house of Israel, saith the Lord.* God, even in His upbraiding, speaks very tenderly to them, as having been in the closest, dearest relation to Himself.

For they have begotten strange children. God had made it a ground of the future blessing of Abraham[6], *I know him, that he will command his children and his household after him, and they shall keep the way of the Lord, to do justice and judgment.* But these, contrariwise, themselves being idolaters and estranged from God, had children, who fell away like themselves, strangers to God, and looked upon as strangers by Him. The children too of the forbidden marriages with the heathen were, by their birth, *strange* or foreign children, even before they became so in act; and they became so the more in act, because they were so by birth. The next generation then growing up more estranged from God than themselves, what hope of amendment was there?

Now shall a month devour. The word *now* denotes the nearness and suddenness of God's judgments; the term *month,* their rapidity. A *month* is not only a brief time, but is almost visibly passing away; the moon, which measures it, is never at one stay, waxing till it is full, then waning till it disappears. Night by night bears witness to the month's decay. The iniquity was full; the harvest was ripe; *now,* suddenly, rapidly, completely, the end should come. One month should *devour them with their portions.* God willed to be the Portion of His people; He had said[7], *the Lord's portion is His people; Jacob is the lot of His inheritance.* To Himself He had given the title[8], *the portion of Jacob.* Israel had chosen to himself *other portions* out of God; for these, he had forsaken his God; therefore he should be consumed with them. "All that they had, all that they possessed, enjoyed, trusted in, all, at once, shall that short space, suddenly and certainly to come, devour, deprive and bereave them of; none of them shall remain with them or profit them in the Day of wrath."

8. *Blow ye the cornet in Gibeah.* The evil

---

[1] 2 Kgs xxiii. 25–27.   [2] Ps. 1. 9, 13.
[3] i. 11.   [4] i. 14.

[5] Jer. iii. 20.   [6] Gen. xviii. 19.
[7] Deut. xxxii. 9.   [8] Jer. x. 16.

Before
CHRIST
cir. 780.

1 Isai. 10. 30.
m Josh. 7. 2.
ch. 4. 15.
n Judg. 5. 14.

in Rama: [1] cry aloud *at* [m] Bethaven, [n] after thee, O Benjamin.

9 Ephraim shall be desolate in the day of rebuke: among the tribes of Israel have I made known that which shall surely be.

10 The princes of Judah

were like them that [o] remove the bound: *therefore* I will pour out my wrath upon them like water.

11 Ephraim *is* [p] oppressed *and* broken in judgment, because he willingly walked after [q] the commandment.

Before
CHRIST
cir. 780.

o Deut. 19. 14. &
27. 17.

p Deut. 28. 33.

q 1 Kgs. 12. 28.
Mic. 2. 16.

day and destruction, denounced, is now vividly pictured, as actually come. All is in confusion, hurry, alarm, because the enemy was in the midst of them. The *cornet*, an instrument made of horn, was to be blown as the alarm, when the enemy was at hand. The *trumpet* was especially used for the worship of God. *Gibeah* and *Ramah* were cities of Benjamin, on the borders of Ephraim, where the enemy, who had possessed himself of Israel, would burst in upon Judah. From *Beth-aven* or Bethel, the seat of Ephraim's idolatry, on the border of Benjamin, was to break forth the outcry of destruction, *after thee, O Benjamin;* the enemy is upon thee, just behind thee, pursuing thee. God had promised His people, if they would serve Him [1], *I will make all thine enemies turn their backs unto thee,* and had threatened the contrary, if they should *walk contrary to Him.* Now that threat was to be fulfilled to the uttermost. The ten tribes are spoken of, as already in possession of the enemy, and he was *upon Benjamin* fleeing before them.

9. *Ephraim shall be desolate.* It shall not be lightly rebuked, nor even more grievously chastened; it shall not simply be wasted by famine, pestilence, and the sword; it *shall be* not simply desolate, but *a desolation,* one waste, *in the day of rebuke,* when God brings home to it its sin and punishment. Ephraim was not taken away for a time; it was never restored.

I have made known that which shall surely be. [*2] Doubt not that this which I say shall come upon thee, for it is a sure saying which I have made known;" lit. one *well-grounded,* as it was, in the mind, the justice, the holiness, the truth of God. All God's threatenings or promises are grounded in past experience. So it may also be, as though God said, "Whatever I have hitherto promised or threatened to Israel, has come to pass. In all I have proved Myself true. Let no one then flatter himself, as though this were uncertain; for in this, as in the rest, I shall be found to be God, faithful and true."

10. *The princes of Judah were like them that*

remove the bound. All avaricious encroachment on the paternal inheritance of others, was strictly forbidden by God in the law, under the penalty of His curse. [3] *Cursed is he that removeth his neighbor's landmark. The princes of Judah,* i. e. those who were the king's counsellors and chief in the civil polity, had committed sin, *like* to this. Since the prophet had just pronounced the desolation of Israel, perhaps that sin was, that instead of taking warning from the threatened destruction, and turning to God, they thought only how the removal of Ephraim would benefit them, by the enlargement of their borders. They might hope also to increase their private estates out of the desolate lands of Ephraim, their brother. The unregenerate heart, instead of being awed by God's judgment on others, looks out to see, what advantages it may gain from them. Times of calamity are also times of greediness. Israel had been a continual sore to Judah. The princes of Judah rejoiced in the prospect of their removal, instead of mourning their sin and fearing for themselves. More widely yet, the words may mean, that the *princes of Judah* "burst all bounds, set to them by the law of God, to which nothing was to be added, from which nothing was to be diminished," transferring to idols or devils, to sun, moon and stars, or to the beings supposed to preside over them, the love, honor, and worship, due to God Alone.

I will pour out My wrath like water. So long as those bounds were not broken through, the Justice of God, although manifoldly provoked, was yet stayed. When Judah should break them, they would, as it were, make a way for the chastisement of God, which should burst in like a flood upon them, overspreading the whole land, yet bringing, not renewed life, but death. Like a flood, it overwhelmed the land; but it was a flood, not of water, but of the wrath of God. They had burst the bounds which divided them from Israel, and had let in upon themselves its chastisements.

11. *Ephraim is oppressed and broken in judg-*

1 Ex. xxiii. 27.   2 Rup.   3 Deut. xxvii. 17.

Before CHRIST cir. 780.

r Prov. 12. 4.
| Or, *a worm.*

12 Therefore *will* I be unto Ephraim as a moth, and to the house of Judah r as || rottenness.

13 When Ephraim saw his sickness, and Judah *saw*

his *wound, then went Ephraim t to the Assyrian, u and sent || to king Jareb : yet could he not heal you, nor cure you of your wound.

Before CHRIST cir. 780.

* Jer. 30. 12.
t 2 Kings 15. 19. ch. 7. 11. & 12. 1.
u ch. 10. 6.
|| Or, *to the king of Jareb;* or, *to the king that should plead.*

ment, lit. *crushed in judgment.* Holy Scripture, elsewhere also, combines these same two words, rendered *oppressed* and *crushed*[1], in speaking of man's oppression by man. Ephraim preferred man's commands and laws to God's; they obeyed man and set God at nought; therefore they should suffer at man's hands, who, while he equally neglected God's will, enforced his own. The *commandment,* which *Ephraim willingly went after,* was doubtless that of Jeroboam[2]; *It is too much for you to go up to Jerusalem; behold thy gods, O Israel, which brought you out of the land of Egypt; and Jeroboam ordained a feast unto the children of Israel.* Through this *commandment,* Jeroboam earned the dreadful title, *who made Israel to sin.* And Israel *went willingly after it,* for it is said; *This thing became a sin; and the people went to worship before the one, even unto Dan:* i. e. while they readily accepted Jeroboam's plea. *It is too much for you to go up to Jerusalem,* they *went willingly* to the Northernmost point of Palestine, *even to Dan.* For this sin, God judged them justly, even through the unjust judgment of man. God mostly punishes, through their own choice, those who choose against His. The Jews said, *we have no king but Cæsar,* and Cæsar destroyed them.

12. *Therefore I will be unto Ephraim a moth,* lit. *and I as a moth.* This form of speaking expresses what God was doing, while Ephraim was *willingly following* sin. *And I* was all the while *as a moth.* The moth in a garment, and the decay in wood, corrode and prey upon the substance, in which they lie hid, slowly, imperceptibly, but, at the last, effectually. Such were God's first judgments on Israel and Judah; such are they now commonly upon sinners. He tried, and now too tries at first, gentle measures and mild chastisements, uneasy indeed and troublesome and painful, yet slow in their working; each stage of loss and decay, a little beyond that which preceded it; but leaving long respite and time for repentance, before they finally wear out and destroy the impenitent. The two images, which He uses, may describe different kinds of decay, both slow, yet the one slower than the other, as Judah was, in

[1] Deut. xxviii. 33. 1 Sam. xii. 3, 4. Is. lviii. 6 Am. iv. 1. עשק and its derivatives are scarcely used of anything else.

fact, destroyed more slowly than Ephraim. For the *rottenness,* or caries in wood, preys more slowly upon wood, which is hard, than the moth on the wool. So God visits the soul with different distresses, bodily or spiritual. He impairs, little by little, health of body, or fineness of understanding; or He withdraws grace or spiritual strength; or allows lukewarmness and distaste for the things of God to creep over the soul. These are the gnawing of the moth, overlooked by the sinner, if he persevere in carelessness as to his conscience, yet in the end, bringing entire decay of health, of understanding, of heart, of mind, unless God interfere by the mightier mercy of some heavy chastisement, to awaken him. "[3] A moth does mischief, and makes no sound. So the minds of the wicked, in that they neglect to take account of their losses, lose their soundness, as it were, without knowing it. For they lose innocency from the heart, truth from the lips, continency from the flesh, and, as time holds on, life from their age." To Israel and Judah the moth and rottenness denoted the slow decay, by which they were gradually weakened, until they were carried away captive.

13. *When Ephraim saw his sickness,* lit. *And Ephraim saw,* i. e. perceived it. God proceeds to tell them, how they acted when they felt those lighter afflictions, the decline and wasting of their power. The *sickness* may further mean the gradual inward decay; the *wound,* blows received from without.

And sent to king Jareb, or, as in the E. M. *a king who should plead,* or, *an avenging king.* The *hostile king* is, probably, the same Assyrian Monarch, whom both Israel and Judah courted, who was the destruction of Israel and who weakened Judah. Ahaz king of Judah did send to Tiglath-Pileser king of Assyria to come and save him[4], when *the Lord brought Judah low; and Tiglath-Pileser king of Assyria came unto him and distressed him, but strengthened him not.* He who held his throne from God sent to a heathen king[5], *I am thy servant and thy son; come up and save me out of the hand of the king of Syria, and out of the hand of the king of Israel, which rise up against me.* He emptied his own treasures,

[2] 1 Kgs xii. 28, 32, 33.
[3] S. Greg. on Job iv. 19.
[4] 2 Chr. xxviii. 19, 20.
[5] 2 Kings xvi. 7, 8.

Before
CHRIST
cir. 780.

x Lam. 3. 10.
ch. 13. 7, 8.
y Ps. 50. 22.

14 For ˣI *will be* unto Ephraim as a lion, and as a young lion to the house of Judah : ʸI, *even* I, will tear and go away; I will take away, and none shall rescue *him.*

15 ¶ I will go *and* return to my place,
† till ᶻthey acknowledge their offence, and seek my face: ᵃin their affliction they will seek me early.

Before
CHRIST
cir. 780.

† Heb. *till they be guilty.*
ᶻ Lev. 26. 40, 41.
Jer. 29, 12, 13.
Ezek. 6. 9.
& 20. 43.
& 36. 31.
ᵃ Ps. 78. 34.

and pillaged the house of God, in order to buy the help of the Assyrian, and he taught him an evil lesson against himself, of his wealth and his weakness. God had said that, if they were faithful [1], *five shall chase an hundred, and an hundred put ten thousand to flight.* He had pronounced him *cursed, who trusted in man, and made flesh his arm, and whose heart departed from the Lord* [2]. But Judah sought man's help, not only apart from God, but against God. God was bringing them down, and they, by man's aid, would lift themselves up. *The king* became an *avenger,* for "[3] whoso, when God is angry, striveth to gain man as his helper, findeth him God's avenger, who leadeth into captivity God's deserters, as though he were sworn to avenge God."

14. *For I* will be *unto Ephraim as a lion.* He who would thus strengthen himself by outward help against God's chastisements, challenges, as it were, the Almighty to a trial of strength. So then God, unwilling to abandon him to himself, changes His dealings, and "[4] He Who had heretofore, in His judgments, seemed but as a tender moth or a weak worm," now shews forth His resistless power, imaged by His creatures in whom the quality of power is most seen. It may again be, that the fiercer animal (lit. *the roaring*) is associated with the name of Ephraim; that of the younger lion, fierce and eager for prey, yet not full-grown, with that of Judah.

I, I will tear. It is a fearful thing, to fall into the Hands of the Living God [5]. *The Assyrian was* but *the rod of God's anger, and the staff,* He says, *in thine hand is His indignation* [6]. Whatever is done, is done or overruled by God, Who gives to the evil his power to do, in an evil way, what He Himself overrules to the end of His wisdom or justice. God, Himself would tear them asunder, by giving the Assyrians power to carry them away. And since it was God Who did it, there was no hope of escape. He Who was faithful to his word would do it. There is great emphasis on the *I, I.* God and not man ; He, the author of all good, would Himself be the Cause of their evil. What hope then is there, when He, Who is Mercy, becomes the Avenger ?

15. *I will go* and *return to My place.* As the wild beast, when he has taken his prey, returns to his covert, so God, when He had fulfilled His Will, would, for the time, withdraw all tokens of his Presence. God, Who is wholly everywhere, is said to dwell *there,* relatively to us, where He manifests Himself, as of old, in the Tabernacle, the Temple, Zion, Jerusalem. He is said to *go and return,* when He withdraws all tokens of His Presence, His help, care, and Providence. This is worse than any affliction on God's part, "[4] a state like theirs who, in the lowest part of hell, are *delivered into chains of darkness,* shut out from His Presence, and so from all hope of comfort ; and this must needs be their condition, so long as He shall be absent from them ; and so perpetually, except there be a way for obtaining again His favorable Presence."

Till they acknowledge their offence. "[4] He Who *hath no pleasure in the death of the wicked, but that the wicked turn from his way and live,* withdraws Himself from them, not to cast them off altogether, but that they might know and acknowledge their folly and wickedness, and, seeing there is no comfort out of Him, prefer His Presence to those vain things." which they had preferred to Him. To say, that God would hide His Face from them, *till they should acknowledge their offence,* holds out in itself a gleam of hope, that hereafter they would turn to Him, and would find Him.

And seek My Face. The first step in repentance is confession of sin ; the second, turning to God. For to own sin without turning to God is the despair of Judas.

In their affliction they shall seek Me early. God does not only leave them hopes, that He would shew forth his Presence, when they sought him, but He promises that they shall seek Him, i. e. He would give them His grace whereby alone they could seek Him, and that grace should be effectual. Of itself affliction drives to despair and more obdurate rebellion and final impenitence. Through the grace of God, "evil brings forth good ; fear, love ; chastisement, repentance." *They shall seek Me early,* originally, *in the morning,* i. e. with all diligence and earnestness, as a

CHAPTER VI.

1 *An exhortation to repentance.*

4 *A complaint of their unto-wardness and iniquity.*

COME, and let us return unto the LORD: for ªhe hath torn, and ᵇhe will heal us; he hath smitten, and he will bind us up.

2 °After two days will he revive us: in the third day he will raise us up, and we shall live in his sight.

ᶜ1 Cor. 15. 4.

man riseth early to do what he is very much set upon. So these shall "shake off the sleep of sin and the torpor of listlessness, when the light of repentance shall shine upon them."

This was fulfilled in the two tribes, toward the end of the seventy years, when many doubtless, together with Daniel[1], *set their face unto the Lord God to seek by prayer and supplication with fasting and sackcloth and ashes;* and again in, those [2]*who waited for redemption in Jerusalem,* when our Lord came; and it will be fulfillment in all at the end of the world. "The first flash of thought on the power and goodness of the true Deliverer, is like the morning streaks of a new day. At the sight of that light, Israel shall arise early to seek his God; he shall rise quickly like the Prodigal, out of his wanderings and his indigence."

VI. 1. *Come and let us return unto the Lord.* These words depend closely on the foregoing. They are words put into their mouth by God Himself, with which or with the like, they should exhort one another to return to God. Before, when God smote them, they had gone to Assyria; now they should turn to Him, owning, not only that Hè Who *tore* has the power and the will to *heal* them, but that He tore, *in order to* heal them; He smote them, *in order to* bind them up. This closeness of connection is expressed in the last words; lit. *smite He and He will bind us up.* "He smiteth the putrefaction of the misdeed; He healeth the pain of the wound. Physicians do this; they cut; they smite; they heal; they arm themselves in order to strike; they carry steel, and come to cure."

They are not content to return singly or to be saved alone. Each encourageth another to repentance, as before to evil. The dry bones, scattered on the face of the earth, re-unite. There is a general movement among those *who sat in darkness and the shadow of death,* to return together to Him, Who is the Source of life.

2. *After two days will He revive us* or *quicken us, give us life, in the third day He will raise us up.* The Resurrection of Christ, and our res-urrection in Him and in His Resurrection, could not be more plainly foretold. The Prophet expressly mentions *two days,* after which life should be given, and a *third day, on* which the resurrection should take place. What else can this be than the two days in which the Body of Christ lay in the tomb, and the third day, on which He rose again, as [3]*the Resurrection and the life,* [4]*the first fruits of them that slept,* the source and earnest and pledge of our resurrection and of life eternal? The Apostle, in speaking of our resurrection in Christ, uses these self-same words of the Prophet; [5]*God, Who is rich in mercy, for His great love wherewith He loved us—hath quickened us together with Christ, and hath raised us up and made us to sit together in heavenly places in Christ Jesus.* The Apostle, like the Pro-phet, speaks of that which took place in Christ our Head, as having already taken place in us, His members. "If we unhesi-tatingly believe in our heart," says a father[6], "what we profess with our mouth, *we* were crucified in Christ, *we* died, *we* were buried, *we* also were raised again on that very third day. Whence the Apostle saith[7], *If ye rose again with Christ, seek those things which are above, where Christ sitteth at the right hand of God.*" As Christ died for us, so He also rose for us. "Our old man was nailed to the wood, in the flesh of our Head, and the new man was formed in that same Head, rising glorious from the tomb." What Christ, our Head, did, He did, not for Himself, but for His redeemed, that the benefits of His Life, Death, Resurrection, Ascension, might re-dound to all. He did it for them; they par-took of what He did. In no other way, could our participation of Christ be foretold. It was not the Prophet's object here, nor was it so direct a comfort to Israel, to speak of Christ's Resurrection in itself. He took a nearer way to their hearts. He told them, "all we who turn to the Lord, putting our whole trust in Him, and committing ourselves wholly to Him, to be healed of our wounds and to have our griefs bound up, shall re-ceive life from Him, shall be raised up by Him." They could not understand *then,* how He would do this. The *after two days* and, *in the third day,* remained a mystery, to be ex-plained by the event. But the promise itself was not the less distinct, nor the less full of hope, nor did it less fulfill all cravings for

---

[1] Dan. ix. 2, 3.
[2] S. Luke ii. 25, 38.

[3] S. John xi. 25.   [4] 1 Cor. xv. 20.   [5] Eph. ii. 4–6.
[6] S. Leo.   [7] Col. iii. 1.

Before
CHRIST
cir. 780.

d Is. 54. 13.
e 2 Sam. 23. 4.

3 [d] Then shall we know, *if* we follow on to know the LORD: his going forth is prepared [e] as the morning;

and [f] he shall come unto us [g] as the rain, as the latter *and* former rain unto the earth.

Before
CHRIST
cir. 780.

f Ps. 72. 6.
g Job 29. 23.

life eternal and the sight of God, because they did not understand, *how shall these things be.* Faith is unconcerned about the "*how.*" Faith believes what God says, because He says it, and leaves Him to fulfill it, "how" He wills and knows. The words of the promise which faith had to believe, were plain. The life of which the Prophet spoke, could only be life from death, whether of the body or the soul or both. For God is said to *give life,* only in contrast with such death. Whence the Jews too have ever looked and do look, that this should be fulfilled in the Christ, though they know not that it has been fulfilled in Him. They too explain it; "[1] He will quicken us in the days of consolation which shall come; in the day of the quickening of the dead; He will raise us up, and we shall live before Him."

In shadow, the prophecy was never fulfilled to Israel at all. The ten tribes were never restored; they never, as a whole, received any favor from God, after He gave them up to captivity. And unto the two tribes, (of whom, apart from the ten, no mention is made here) what a mere shadow was the restoration from Babylon, that it should be spoken of as the gift of life or of resurrection, whereby we should live before Him! The strictest explanation is the truest. The *two days* and *the third day* have nothing in history to correspond with them, except that in which they were fulfilled, when Christ, "rising on the third day from the grave, raised with Him the whole human race [2]."

And we shall live in His sight, lit. *before His Face.* In the face, we see the will, and mind, the love, the pleasure or displeasure of a human being whom we love. In the holy or loving face of man, there may be read fresh depths of devotion or of love. The face is turned away in sorrowful displeasure; it is turned full upon the face it loves. Hence it is so very expressive an image of the relation of the soul to God, and the Psalmists so often pray, Lord *lift up the light of Thy countenance upon us; make Thy Face to shine upon Thy servant; God bless us, and cause His Face to shine upon us; cast me not away from Thy Presence* or *Face; look Thou upon me and be merciful unto me; look upon the Face of thine anointed; how long wilt Thou hide Thy Face*

from me? hide not Thy Face from Thy servant [3]; or they profess, *Thy Face, Lord, will I seek* [4]; or they declare that the bliss of eternity is in the *Face of God* [5].

God had just said, that He would withdraw His Presence, until they should *seek His Face;* now He says, they should *live before His Face.* To Abraham He had said [6], *Walk before Me,* lit. *before My Face, and be thou perfect.* Bliss from the Creator, and duty from the creature, answer to one another. We *live in His sight,* in the way of duty, when we refer ourselves and our whole being, our courses of action, our thoughts, our love, to Him, remembering that we are ever in His Presence, and ever seeking to please Him. We *live in His sight,* in the bliss of His Presence, when we enjoy the sense of His favor, and know that His Eye rests on us in love, that He cares for us, guides us, guards us; and have some sweetness in contemplating Him. Much more fully shall we live in His sight, when, in Him, we shall be partakers of His Eternal Life and Bliss, and shall behold Him *face to face,* and *see Him as He is,* and the sight of Him shall be our bliss, *and in His light we shall see light* [7].

3. *Then shall we know, if we follow on to know the Lord;* rather, *Then shall we know, shall follow on to know the Lord,* i. e. we shall not only know Him, but we shall grow continually in that knowledge. Then, in Israel, God says, *there was no knowledge* of Him; His *people* was *destroyed for lack of* it [8]. In Christ He promises, that they should have that inward knowledge of Him, ever growing, because the grace, through which it is given, ever grows, and *the depth of the riches of His wisdom and knowledge is unsearchable, passing knowledge.* We *follow on,* confessing that it is He who maketh us to follow Him, and draweth us to Him. We know, in order to follow; we follow, in order to know. Light prepares the way for love. Love opens the mind for new love. The gifts of God are interwoven. They multiply and reproduce each other, until we come to the perfect state of eternity. For here *we know in part* only; then *shall we know, even as we are known. We shall follow on.* Whither shall we *follow on?* To the fountains of the water of life, as another Prophet saith; *For He that hath*

[1] Targ.
[2] S. Jer. so Tertull. adv. Jud. c. 13. Orig. Hom. 5. in Exod. S. Cypr. Test. ii. 25. S. Cyr. Jer. Cat. xiv. 14. S. Greg. Nyss. de cogn. Dei. S. Aug. de Civ. D. xviii. 28. Ruf. de exp. Symb. S. Cyr. Al. in S. Joh. L. ii. S. Greg. in Ezek. Hom. 20.

[3] Ps. iv. 6; xxxi. 16 (from Num. vi. 25.); lxvii. 1. lxxx. 7. cxix. 135; li. 11; cxix. 132; lxxxiv. 9; xiii. 1. lxix, 17. &c.
[4] Ps. xxvii. 8. See xxiv. 6. cv. 4.
[5] Ps. xi. 7. xvi. 11. xvii. 15.
[6] Gen. xvii. 1.   [7] Ps. xxxvi. 9.   [8] ch. iv. 1, 6.

4 ¶ ʰ O Ephraim, what shall I do unto thee? O Judah, what shall I do unto thee? for your

|| goodness *is* ¹as a morning cloud, and as the early dew it goeth away.

mercy upon them shall lead them, even by the springs of water shall He guide them ¹. And in the Revelations we read, that *the Lamb Who is in the midst of the throne shall feed them, and shall lead them unto living fountains of waters* ². The bliss of eternity is fixed; the nearness of each to the throne of God, the *mansion* in which he shall dwell, admits of no change; but, through eternity, it may be, that we shall *follow on to know* more of God, as more shall be revealed to us of that which is infinite, the Infinity of His Wisdom and His Love.

His going forth, i. e. the going forth of God, *is prepared,* firm, fixed, certain, established, (so the word means) *as the morning.* Before, God had said, He would withdraw Himself from them; now, contrariwise, He says, that He would *go forth.* He had said, *in their affliction they shall seek Me early* or *in the morning;* now, *He shall go forth as the morning.* "³They shall seek for Him, as they that long for the morning; and He will come to them as the morning," full of joy and comfort, of light and warmth and glorious radiance, which shall diffuse over the whole compass of the world, so that *nothing shall be hid from its light* and *heat.* He Who should so go forth, is the same as He Who was to *revive them* and *raise them up,* i. e. Christ. Of Him it is said most strictly, that He *went forth,* when from the Bosom of the Father He came among us; as of Him holy Zacharias saith, (in the like language,) *The Dayspring from on high hath visited us, to give light to them that sit in darkness and in the shadow of death, to guide our feet into the way of peace.* Christ goeth forth continually from the Father, by an eternal, continual, generation. In time, He *came forth* from the Father in His Incarnation; He *came forth* to us from the Virgin's womb; He *came forth,* from the grave in His Resurrection. His *coming forth, as the morning,* images the secrecy of His Birth, the light and glow of love which He diffuseth throughout the whole new creation of His redeemed. "⁴As the dawn is seen by all and cannot be hid, and appeareth, that it may be seen, yea, that it may illuminate, so His going forth, whereby He proceeded from His own invisible to our visible condition, became known to all," tempered to our eyes, dissipating our darkness, awakening our nature as from a grave, unveiling to man the works of God, making His ways plain before his face, that he should no longer *walk in darkness, but have the light of life.*

He shall come unto us as the rain, as the latter and *former rain unto the earth.* So of Christ it is foretold ⁵, *He shall come down like rain upon the mown grass, as showers that water the earth.* Palestine was especially dependent upon rain, on account of the cultivation of the sides of the hills in terraces, which were parched and dry, when the rains were withheld. The *former,* or autumnal *rain,* fell in October, at the seed-time; the *latter* or spring *rain,* in March and April, and filled the ears before harvest. Both together stand as the beginning and the end. If either were withheld, the harvest failed. Wonderful likeness of Him Who is the Beginning and the End of our spiritual life; from Whom we receive it, by Whom it is preserved unto the end; through Whom the soul, enriched by Him, hath abundance of all spiritual blessings, graces, and consolations, and yieldeth all manner of fruit, each after its kind, to the praise of Him Who hath given it life and fruitfulness.

4. *O Ephraim, what shall I do unto thee?* It is common with the prophets, first to set forth the fullness of the riches of God's mercies in Christ, and then to turn to their own generation, and upbraid them for the sins which withheld the mercies of God from *them,* and were hurrying them to their destruction. In like way Isaiah ⁶, having prophesied that the Gospel should go forth from Zion, turns to upbraid the avarice, idolatry, and pride, through which the judgment of God should come upon them.

The promises of God were to those who should turn with true repentance, and seek Him early and earnestly. Whatever of good there was, either in Ephraim or Judah, was but a mere empty shew, which held out hope, only to disappoint it. God, Who *willeth not that any should perish, but that all should come to repentance,* appeals to His whole people, *What shall I do unto thee?* He had shewn them abundance of mercies; He had reproved them by His prophets; He had chastened them; and all in vain. As he says in Isaiah ⁷, *What could have been done more to My vineyard, that I have not done in it?* Here He asks them Himself, what He could do to convert and to save them, which He had not done. He would take them on their own terms, and whatever they would prescribe to His Almightiness and Wisdom, as means for their conversion, *that* He would use, so that they would but turn to Him. "What means

¹ Is. xlix. 10.　² Rev. vii. 17.　³ Poc.　⁴ Rup.

⁵ Ps. lxxii. 6.　⁶ ch. ii.　⁷ ch. v.

Before
CHRIST
cir. 780.

k Jer. 1. 10 & 5.
14.
l Jer. 23. 29.
Heb. 4. 12.
‖ Or, *that thy judgments might be, &c.*

5 Therefore have I hewed *them* ᵏ by the prophets; I have slain them by ˡ the words of my mouth: ‖ and

thy judgments *are as* the light *that* goeth forth.

6 For I desired ᵐ mercy, and ⁿ not sacrifice; and

Before
CHRIST
cir. 780.

ᵐ 1 Sam. 15. 22.
Eccles. 5. 1.
Mic. 6. 8.
Matt. 9. 23. &
12. 7.   ⁿ Ps. 50. 8, 9. Prov. 21. 3.   Is. 1. 11.

shall I use to save thee, who wilt not be saved?" It has been a bold saying, to describe the *love of Christ which passeth knowledge,* "Christ so loveth souls, that He would rather be crucified again, than allow any one (as far as in Him lies) to be damned."

For your goodness is as a morning cloud. Mercy or *loving-kindness,* (which the E. M. suggests as the first meaning of the word) stands for all virtue and goodness toward God or man. For love to God or man is one indivisible virtue, issuing from one principle of grace. Whence it is said [1], *love is the fulfilling of the law. He that loveth another hath fulfilled the law.* And [2], *Beloved, let us love one another; for love is of God, and every one that loveth is born of God, and knoweth God.* Of this their goodness, he says the character was, that it never lasted. The *morning cloud* is full of brilliancy with the rays of the rising sun, yet quickly disappears through the heat of that sun, which gave it its rich hues. The *morning dew* glitters in that same sun, yet vanishes almost as soon as it appears. Generated by the cold of the night, it appears with the dawn; yet appears, only to disappear. So it was with the whole Jewish people; so it ever is with the most hopeless class of sinners; ever beginning anew, ever relapsing; ever making a shew of leaves, good feelings, good aspirations, but yielding no fruit. "There was nothing of sound, sincere, real, lasting goodness in them;" no reality, but all shew; quickly assumed, quickly disused.

5. *Therefore have I hewed* them *by the prophets.* Since they despised God's gentler warnings and measures, He used severer. *He hewed* them, He says, as men hew stones out of the quarry, and with hard blows and sharp instruments overcome the hardness of the stone which they have to work. Their piety and goodness were light and unsubstantial as a summer cloud; their stony hearts were harder than the material stone. The stone takes the shape which man would give it; God hews man in vain; he will not receive the image of God, for which and in which he was framed.

God, elsewhere also, likens the force and vehemence of His word to [3] *a hammer which breaketh the rocks in pieces;* [4] *a sword which pierceth even to the dividing asunder of soul and spirit.* He " [5] continually hammered, beat

upon, disquieted them, and so vexed them (as they thought) even unto death, not allowing them to rest in their sins, not suffering them to enjoy themselves in them, but forcing them (as it were) to part with things which they loved as their lives, and would as soon part with their souls as with them."

And thy judgments are as *the light* that *goeth forth.* The *judgments* here are the acts of justice executed upon a man; the "judgment upon him," as we say. God had done all which could be done, to lay aside the severity of His own judgments. All had failed. Then His judgments, when they came, would be manifestly just; their justice clear as *the light which goeth forth* out of the darkness of night, or out of the thick clouds. God's past loving-kindness, His pains, (so to speak,) His solicitations, the drawings of His grace, the tender mercies of His austere chastisements, will, in the Day of judgment, stand out clear as the light, and leave the sinner confounded, without excuse. In this life, also, God's final *judgments are as a light which goeth forth,* enlightening, not the sinner who perishes, but others, heretofore in the darkness of ignorance, on whom they burst with a sudden blaze of light, and who reverence them, owning that *the judgments of the Lord are true and righteous altogether* [6].

And so, since they would not be reformed, what should have been for their wealth, was for their destruction. *I slew them by the words of My mouth.* God spake yet more terribly to them. He slew them in word, that He might not slay them in deed; He threatened them with death; since they repented not, it came. The stone, which will not take the form which should have been imparted to it, is destroyed by the strokes which should have moulded it. By a like image Jeremiah compared the Jews to ore which is consumed in the fire which should refine it, since there was no good in it. [7] *They are brass and iron; they* are *all corrupted; the bellows are burned, the lead is consumed of the fire; the founder melteth in vain; for the wicked are not plucked away. Reprobate silver shall* men *call them, because the Lord hath rejected them.*

6. *For I desired mercy and not sacrifice.* God had said before, that they should *seek* Him *with their flocks and herds, and not find*

[1] Rom. xiii. 10, 8.   [2] 1 S. John iv. 7.
[3] Jer. xxiii. 29.   [4] Heb. iv. 12.   [5] from Poc.

[6] Ps. xix. 9.
[7] Jer. vi. 28-30.

the °knowledge of God || more than burnt offerings.

° Jer. 22. 16. John 17. 3.

Him. So here He anticipates their excuses with the same answer wherewith He met those of Saul, when he would compensate for disobedience by burnt offerings. The answer is, that all which they did to win His favor, or turn aside His wrath, was of no avail, while they wilfully withheld what He required of them. Their mercy and goodness were but a brief, passing, shew; in vain He had tried to awaken them by His Prophets; therefore judgment was coming upon them; for, to turn it aside, they had offered Him what He desired not, sacrifices without love, and had not offered Him, what He did desire, love of man out of love for God. God had Himself, after the fall, enjoined sacrifice, to foreshew and plead to Himself the meritorious Sacrifice of Christ. *He* had not contrasted *mercy* and *sacrifice*, Who enjoined them both. When then they were contrasted, it was through man's severing what God united. If we were to say, "Charity is better than Church-going," we should be understood to mean that it is better than such Church-going as is severed from charity. For, if they were united, they would not be contrasted. The soul is of more value than the body. But it is not contrasted, unless they come in competition with one another, and their interests (although they cannot in trust *be*,) *seem* to be separated. In itself, *Sacrifice* represented all the direct duties to God, all the duties of the first table. For Sacrifice owned Him as the One God, to Whom, as His creatures, we owe and offer all; as His guilty creatures, it owned that we owed to Him our lives also. *Mercy* represented all duties of the second table. In saying then, *I will have mercy and not sacrifice,* he says, in effect, the same as S. John [1], *If a man say, I love God, and hateth his brother, he is a liar; for he that loveth not his brother, whom he hath seen, how can he love God Whom he hath not seen?* As the love, which a man pretended to have for God, was not real love, if a man loved not his brother, so *sacrifice* was not an offering, to God at all, while man withheld from God that offering, which God most required of him, the oblation of man's own self. They were, rather, offerings to satisfy and bribe a man's own conscience. Yet the Jews were profuse in making these sacrifices, which cost them little, hoping thereby to secure to themselves impunity in the wrongful gains, oppressions, and unmercifulnesses which they would not part with. It is with this contrast, that God so often rejects the sacrifices of the Jews, [2] *To what*

purpose is the multitude of your oblations unto Me? Bring no more vain oblations unto Me; new moons and sabbaths, the calling of assemblies, I cannot away with; iniquity and the solemn meeting. [3] *I spake not to your fathers, nor commanded them, in the day that I brought them out of the land of Egypt, concerning burnt-offerings or sacrifices; but this thing commanded I them, saying, Obey My voice, and I will be your God, and ye shall be My people.* And the Psalmist; [4] *I will not reprove thee for thy sacrifices or thy burnt-offerings, to have been continually before Me. Offer unto God thanksgiving, &c.* But *unto the wicked God saith, What hast thou to do, to declare My statutes, &c.*

But, further, the prophet adds, *and the knowledge of God more than burnt-offerings.* The two parts of the verse fill out one another, and the latter explains the former. *The knowledge of God* is, as before, no inactive head-knowledge, but that knowledge, of which S. John speaks, [5] *Hereby we do know that we know Him, if we keep His commandments.* It is a knowledge, such as they alone can have, who love God and do His Will. God says then, that He prefers the inward, loving, knowledge of Himself, and lovingkindness toward man, above the outward means of acceptableness with Himself, which He had appointed. He does not lower those His own appointments; but only when, emptied of the spirit of devotion, they were lifeless bodies, unensouled by His grace.

Yet the words of God go beyond the immediate occasion and bearing, in which they were first spoken. And so these words, [6] *I will have mercy and not sacrifice,* are a sort of sacred proverb, contrasting *mercy,* which overflows the bounds of strict justice, with *sacrifice,* which represents that stern justice. Thus, when the Pharisees murmured at our Lord for eating with Publicans and sinners, He bade them, *Go and learn what that meaneth. I will have mercy and not sacrifice.* He bade them learn that deeper meaning of the words, that God valued mercy for the souls for which Christ died, above that outward propriety, that He, the All-Holy, should not feast familiarly with those who profaned God's law and themselves. Again, when they found fault with the hungry disciples for breaking the sabbath by rubbing the ears of corn, He, in the same way, tells them, that they did not know the real meaning of that saying. [7] *If ye had known what this meaneth, I will have mercy and not sacrifice, ye would not have condemned the guiltless.* For as, before, they were envious as to mercy to the souls of sinners,

[1] 1 S. John iv. 20.
[2] Is. i. 11–3.

[3] Jer. vii. 22, 3.   [4] Ps. l. 8. 14. 16.
[5] Eph. ii. 3.   [6] S. Matt. ix. 13.   [7] Ib. xii. 7.

Before CHRIST cir. 780.

7 But they ‖ like men [p] have transgressed the covenant: there [q] have they dealt treacherously against me.

8 [r] Gilead *is* a city of

‖ Or, *like Adam.* Job 31. 33.
p ch. 8. 1. q ch. 5. 7.
r ch. 12. 11.

so now they were reckless as to others' bodily needs. Without that love then, which shews itself in acts of mercy to the souls and bodies of men, all sacrifice is useless.

Mercy is also more comprehensive than *sacrifice.* For sacrifice was referred to God only, as its end; *mercy,* or love of man for the love of God, obeys God Who commands it; imitates God, "Whose property it is always to have mercy;" seeks God Who rewards it; promotes the glory of God, through the thanksgiving to God, from those whom it benefits. "Mercy leads man up to God, for mercy brought down God to man; mercy humbled God, exalts man." Mercy takes Christ as its pattern, Who, from His Holy Incarnation to His Precious Death on the Cross, *bare our griefs, and carried our sorrows* [1]. Yet neither does mercy itself avail without true knowledge of God. For as mercy or love is the soul of all our acts, so true knowledge of God and faith in God are the source and soul of love. "Vain were it to boast that we have the other members, if faith, the head, were cut off [2]."

7. *But they like men,* or (better as in the E. M.) *like Adam, have transgressed the covenant.* As Adam our first parent, in Paradise, not out of any pressure, but wantonly, through self-will and pride, broke the covenant of God, eating the forbidden fruit, and then defended himself in his sin against God, casting the blame upon the woman: so these, in the good land which God had given them, *that they should* therein *keep His covenant and observe His laws* [3], wantonly and petulantly broke that covenant; and then obstinately defended their sin. Wherefore, as Adam was cast out of Paradise, so shall these be cast out of the land of promise.

There have they dealt treacherously against Me. There! He does not say, *where.* But Israel and every sinner in Israel knew full well, where. *There,* to Israel, was not only Bethel or Dan, or Gilgal, or Mizpah, or Gilead, or any or all of the places, which God had hallowed by His mercies, and they had defiled. It was every high hill, each idol-chapel, each field-altar, which they had multiplied to their idols. To the sinners of Israel, it was every spot of the Lord's land which they had defiled by their sin. God points out to the conscience of sinners the place and time, the very spot where they offended Him. Wheresoever and whensoever they broke God's commands, *there they dealt treacherously against* God Himself. There is much emphasis upon the *against Me.* The sinner, while breaking the laws of God, contrives to forget God. God recalls him to himself, and says, *there,* where and when thou didst those and those things, thou didst deal falsely with, and against, *Me.* The sinner's conscience and memory fills up the word *there.* It sees the whole landscape of its sins around; each black dark spot stands out before it, and it cries with David, *there,* in this and this and this, *against Thee, Thee only, have I sinned, and done this evil in Thy sight* [4].

8. *Gilead is a city of them that work iniquity.* If we regard "Gilead," (as it elsewhere is,) as the country beyond Jordan, where the two tribes and a half dwelt, this will mean that the whole land was banded in one, as one city of evil-doers. It had an unity, but of evil. As the whole world has been pictured as divided between "the city of God" and the city of the devil, consisting respectively of the children of God and the children of the devil; so the whole of Gilead may be represented as one city, whose inhabitants had one occupation in common, to work evil. Some think that there was a city so called, although not mentioned elsewhere in Holy Scripture, near that Mount Gilead, dear to the memory of Israel, because God there protected their forefather Jacob. Some think that it was Ramoth in Gilead [5], which God appointed as "a city of refuge," and which, consequently, became a city of Levites and priests [6]. Here, where God had preserved the life of their forefather, and, in him, had preserved them; here, where He had commanded the innocent shedder of blood to be saved; here, where He had appointed those to dwell, whom He had hallowed to Himself, all was turned to the exact contrary. It, which God had hallowed, was become *a city of workers of iniquity,* i. e. of men, whose habits and wont was to work iniquity. It, where God had appointed life to be preserved, was *polluted* or *tracked with blood.* Everywhere it was marked and stained with the bloody footsteps of those, who (as David said) *put* innocent *blood in their shoes which were on their feet* [7], staining their shoes with blood which they shed, so that, wherever they went, they left marks and signs of it." *Tracked with blood* it was, through the sins of its inhabitants; *tracked with blood* it was again, when it first was taken

[1] Is. liii. 4. [2] S. Jer. [3] Ps. cv. 44. [4] Ib. li. 4.
[5] Deut. iv. 43. Jos. xx. 8. S. Jerome instances Ramoth and the deeds there, but does not identify Gilead with it, since he supposes the prophet to speak of "the Province itself."
[6] Jos. xxi. 38. [7] 1 Kgs ii. 5.

Before CHRIST cir. 780, them that work iniquity, and is ‖ polluted with

‖ Or, *cunning for* blood.
blood.
ª Jer. 11. 9.
Ezek. 22. 25.
† Heb. *with* one
shoulder, or, *to Shechem.*

9 And as troops of robbers wait for a man, *so* ª the company of priests murder in the way † by consent:

for they commit ‖ lewdness.

10 I have seen ᵗ an horrible thing in the house of Israel: there *is* ᵘ the whoredom of Ephraim; Israel is defiled.

11 Also, O Judah, ˣ he

Before CHRIST cir. 780.

‖ Or, *enormity.*
ᵗ Jer. 5. 30.
ᵘ ch. 4. 12, 13, 17.

ˣ Jer. 51. 33.
Joel 3. 13.
Rev. 14. 15.

---

captive¹, and "*it,* which had swum with the innocent blood of others, swam with the guilty blood of its own people." It is a special sin, and especially avenged of God, when what God had hallowed, is made the scene of sin.

9. *And as troops of robbers wait for a man, so the company of priests murder in the way by consent;* or (more probably) *in the way to Shechem*². Shechem too was a "city of refuge³," and so also a city of Levites and priests⁴. It was an important city. For there Joshua assembled all Israel for his last address to them, and made a covenant with them⁵. There, Rehoboam came to be accepted by Israel as their king⁶, and was rejected by them. There Jeroboam after the schism, for a time, made his residence⁷. The priests were banded together; their counsel was one; they formed one company; but they were bound together as a band of robbers, not to save men's lives but to destroy them. Whereas the way to the cities of refuge was, by God's law, to be *prepared*⁸, clear, open, without let or hindrance to the guiltless fugitive, to save his life, the priests, the guardians of God's law, obstructed the way, to rob and destroy. They, whom God appointed to teach the truth that men might live, were banded together against His law.

Shechem, besides that it was a city of refuge, was also hallowed by the memory of histories of the patriarchs who walked with God. There, was Jacob's well⁹; there Joseph's bones were buried¹⁰; and the memory of the patriarch Jacob was cherished there, even to the time of our Lord⁹. Lying in a narrow valley between Mount Ebal and Gerizim, it was a witness, as it were, of the blessing and curse pronounced from them, and had, in the times of Joshua, an ancient sanctuary of God¹¹. It was a halting-place for the pilgrims of the northern tribes, in their way to the feasts at Jerusalem; so that these murders by the priests coincide with the tradition of the Jews, that they who would go

up to Jerusalem were murdered in the way. *For they commit lewdness,* lit. *For they have done deliberate sin*¹². The word literally means *a thing thought of,* especially an evil, and so, deliberate, contrived, bethought-of, wickedness. They did deliberate wickedness, gave themselves to do it, and did nothing else.

10. *I have seen a horrible thing,* lit. *what would make one shudder.* God had seen it; therefore man could not deny it. In the sight of God, and amid the sense of His Presence, all excuses fail.

In the house of Israel. "¹³ For what more horrible, more amazing than that this happened, not in any ordinary nation but *in the house of Israel,* in the people of God, in the portion of the Lord, as Moses said, *the Lord's portion is His people, Jacob is the lot of His inheritance?* In another nation, idolatry was error. In Israel, which had the knowledge of the one true God and had received the law, it was horror." *There is the whoredom of Ephraim,* widespread, over the whole land, wherever the house of Ephraim was, through the whole kingdom of the ten tribes, *there* was its spiritual adultery and defilement.

11. *Also, O Judah, He hath set a harvest for thee, when I returned* (rather, *when I return*) *the captivity of My people.*

The *harvest* may be either for good or for bad. If the harvest is spoken of, as bestowed upon the people, then, as being of chief moment for preserving the life of the body, it is a symbol of all manner of good, temporal or spiritual, bestowed by God. If the people is spoken of, as themselves being the harvest which is ripe and ready to be cut down, then it is a symbol of their being ripe in sin, ready for punishment, to be cut off by God's judgments. In this sense, it is said of Babylon¹⁴, *Yet a little while, and the time of her harvest shall come;* and of the heathen, ¹⁵ *put ye in the sickle, for their harvest is ripe, for their wickedness is great;* and of the whole earth, ¹⁶ *the harvest of the earth is ripe.* Here God must be

---

¹ 2 Kgs xv. 29.
² This translation accounts for the grammatical form שִׁכְמָה "*towards* Shechem;" (as in Gen. xxvii. 14. &c.). The consent of many in doing a thing is indeed expressed by saying "they did it with *one* shoulder," (Zeph. iii. 9.) Yet the word *one* (which is not used here,) is essential to the figure, which is, that many did the act, as if they were one.

³ Joh. xx. 7.
⁴ Ib. xxi. 21.
⁵ Ib. xxiv. 1. 25.
⁶ 1 Kgs xii. 1.
⁷ Ib. 25.
⁸ Deut. xix. 3.
⁹ S. Joh. iv. 5, 6.
¹⁰ Josh. xxiv. 32.
¹¹ Ib. 26.
¹² It is used of sins of the flesh in Lev. xix. 29. xx. 14. Job xxxi. 11. and especially in Ezek.
¹³ Rup.
¹⁴ Jer. li. 33.
¹⁵ Joel iii. 13.
¹⁶ Rev. xiv. 15.

Before
CHRIST
cir. 780.

ʸ Ps. 126. 1.

hath set an harvest for thee, ʸwhen I returned

Before
CHRIST
cir. 780.

the captivity of my people.

speaking of a *harvest*, which he willed hereafter to give *to* Judah. For the time of the harvest was to be, when He should *return the captivity of His people*, restoring them out of their captivity, a time of His favor and of manifold blessings. *A harvest then God appointed for Judah.* But when? Not at that time, not for a long, long period, not for any time during the life of man, but at the end of the captivity of 70 years. God promises relief, but after suffering. Yet He casts a ray of light, even while threatening the intermediate darkness. He foreshews to them a future harvest, even while their coming lot was captivity and privation. Now Judah, His people, was entangled in the sins of Ephraim, and, like them, was to be punished. Suffering and chastisement were the condition of healing and restoration. But whereas the destruction of the kingdom of Israel was final, and they were no more to be restored as a whole, God Who loveth mercy, conveys the threat of impending punishment under the promise of future mercy. He had rich mercies in store for Judah, yet not until after the captivity, when He should again own them as *My people*. Meantime, there was withdrawal of the favor of God, distress, and want.

The distinction between Judah and Israel lay in the promise of God to David. ¹ *The Lord hath sworn in truth to David, He will not turn from it ; of the fruit of thy body . will I set upon thy throne.* It lay in the counsels of God, but it was executed through those who knew not of those counsels. The ten tribes were carried away by the Assyrians into Media ; Judah, by Nebuchadnezzar, into Babylon. The Babylonian empire, which, under Nebuchadnezzar, was the terror of Asia, was but a continuation of the Assyrian, being founded by a revolted Assyrian general². The seat of empire was removed, the policy was unchanged. In man's sight there was no hope that Babylon would give back her captives, any more than Assyria, or than the grave would give back her dead. To restore the Jews, was to reverse the human policy, which had removed them ; it was to re-create an enemy ; strong in his natural position, lying between themselves and Egypt, who could strengthen, if he willed, their great rival. The mixed multitude of Babylonians and others, whom the king of Assyria had settled in Samaria, in their letter to a successor of Cyrus, appealed to these fears,

and induced the impostor Smerdis to interrupt the restoration of Jerusalem. They say ; ³ *We have sent and certified the king, that search may be made in the book of the records of thy fathers. So shalt thou find in the book of the records, and know that this city is a rebellious city, and hurtful unto kings and provinces, and that they have moved sedition within the same of old time ; for which cause was this city destroyed.* The king did find in his records, that Judah had been of old powerful, and had refused the yoke of Babylon. ⁴ *I commanded, and search hath been made, and it is found that this city of old time hath made insurrection against kings, and that rebellion and sedition hath been made therein. There have been mighty kings over Jerusalem, which have ruled over all countries beyond the river, and toll, tribute, and custom, hath been given to them.* Conquerors do not think of restoring their slaves, nor of reversing their policy, even when there is no constraining motive to persevere in it. What is done, remains. This policy of transplanting nations, when once begun, was adopted, as a regular part of Assyrian, Babylonian, and Persian policy⁵. Yet no case is known, in which the people once removed were permitted to return, save the Jews. But God first foretold, that Cyrus should restore His people and build His temple ; then, through men's wills He ordered the overthrow of empires. Cyrus overcame the league against him, and destroyed first the Lydian, then the Babylonian, empire. God then brought to his knowledge the prophecy concerning him, given by Isaiah 178 years before, and disposed his heart to do, what Isaiah had foretold that he should do. *Cyrus made his proclamation throughout all his kingdom.* The terms were ample. ⁶ *Who is there among you of all His people?* His God be with him, and let him go up to Jerusalem, which is in Judah, and build the house of the Lord God of Israel (He is the God) which is in Jerusalem.* The proclamation must have reached *the cities of the Medes*, where the ten tribes were. But they only, *whose spirit God had raised*, returned to their land. Israel remained, of his own free will, behind ; and fulfilled unwittingly the prophecy that they should be *wanderers among the nations*, while in Judah *the Lord brought again the captivity of His people*, and gave them *the harvest* which He had appointed for them. A Psalmist of that day speaks of the strangeness of the deliverance to them. ⁷ *When the Lord turned again the*

---

¹ Ps. cxxxii. 11.
² Nabopolassar. See Abyden. in Eus. Chron. Arm. i. p. 54.

³ Ezra iv. 14, 15.   ⁴ Ib. 19, 20.
⁵ See instances in Rawlinson Herod. T. ii. p. 564.
⁶ Ezra i. 3.   ⁷ Ps. cxxvi. 1, 5.

Before
CHRIST
cir. 780.

CHAPTER VII.

1 *A reproof of manifold sins.* 11 *God's wrath against them for their hypocrisy.*

WHEN I would have healed Israel, then the iniquity of Ephraim was

discovered, and the † wickedness of Samaria: for [a] they commit falsehood; and the thief cometh in, *and* the troop of robbers † spoileth without.

Before
CHRIST
cir. 780.

† Heb. *evils.*
[a] ch. 5. 1. & 6. 10.

† Heb. *strippeth.*

---

captivity of Zion, we were like them that dream. And primarily of that *bringing back the captivity of His people,* he uses Hosea's image of the *harvest. They which sow in tears shall reap in joy.* To the eye of the politician, it was an overthrow of empires and convulsion of the world, the herald of further convulsions, by which the new-established empire was in its turn overthrown. In the real, the religious, history of mankind, of far greater moment were those fifty thousand souls, to whom, with Zorobabel of the line of David, Cyrus gave leave to return. In them he fulfilled prophecy, and prepared for that further fulfillment, after his own empire had been long dissolved, and when, from the line of Zorobabel, was that Birth which was promised in Bethlehem of Judah.

VII. 1. *When I would have healed Israel.* God begins anew by appealing to Israel, that all which He had done to heal them, had but served to make their sin more evident, and *that,* from highest to lowest, as to all manners and ways of sin. When the flash of God's light on the sinner's conscience enlightens it not, it only discloses its darkness. The name *Israel* includes the whole people; the names, Ephraim and Samaria, probably are meant to designate the chief among them, Ephraim having been their royal tribe, and being the chief tribe among them; Samaria being their royal city. The sins, which Hosea denounces in this chapter, are chiefly the sins of the great, which, from them, had spread among the people. Whatever healing methods God had used, whether through the teaching of the prophets or through His own fatherly chastisements, they "[1] would not hearken nor be amended, but ran on still more obstinately in their evil courses. The disease prevailed against the remedy, and was irritated by it, so that the remedy served only to *lay open* the extent of its malignity, and to shew that there was worse in it, than did at first appear." So. S. Paul says of all human nature. [2] *When the commandment came, sin revived.* Apart from grace, the knowledge of good only enhances evil. "[3] So, when God, made Man, present and visible, willed to *heal Israel,* then that iniquity of the Jews and wickedness of the Scribes and Pharisees was discovered, whereof this iniquity of Ephraim and wickedness of Sa-

maria was a type. For an evil spirit goaded them to mock, persecute, blaspheme the Teacher of repentance Who, together with the word of preaching, did works, such as none other man did. For Christ pleased them not, a Teacher of repentance, persuading to poverty, a Pattern of humility, a Guide to meekness, a Monitor to mourn for sins, a Proclaimer of righteousness, a Requirer of mercy, a Praiser of purity of heart, a Rewarder of peace, a Consoler of those who suffered persecution for righteousness' sake. Why did they reject, hate, persecute, Him Who taught thus? Because they loved all contrary thereto, and wished for a Messiah, who should exalt them in this world, and disturb the peace of nations, until he should by war subdue to their empire all the rest of the world, build for them on earth a Jerusalem of gold and gems, and fulfil their covetousness in all things of this sort. This their mind His once briefly expressed; "[4] *How can ye believe which receive honor one of another, and seek not the honor which cometh from God only?* They persecuted Him then Who willed to heal them, as madmen strike the physician offering them medicine, nor did they cease, until they required Him their King to be crucified. Thus was *the iniquity of Ephraim and wickedness of Samaria discovered,* yet filled up by them; and so they filled up the measure of their fathers, and discovered and testified, that they were of the same mind with their fathers.—In all these things they *committed falsehood,* lying against their King Whom they denied, and accused as seditious."

For they [i. e. all of them] *commit falsehood.* Falsehood was the whole habit and tissue of their lives. "[5] They dealt falsely in all their doings both with God and man, being hypocritical and false in all their words and doings, given to fraud and deceit, from the highest to the lowest." Night and day; in silence and in open violence; *within,* where all seemed guarded and secure, and *without,* in open defiance of law and public justice; these deeds of wrong went on in an unceasing round. In the night, *the thief cometh in,* breaking into men's houses and pillaging secretly; *a troop of robbers spoileth without,* spreading their ravages far and wide, and desolating without resistance. It was all one state of anarchy, violence, and disorganization.

---

[1] Poc.   [2] Rom. vii. 9.   [3] Rup.   [4] S. John v. 24.   [5] Poc.

Before
CHRIST
cir. 780.

† Heb. *say not
to.*
ᵇ Jer. 17. 1.
ᵉ Ps. 9. 16.
Prov. 5. 22.

2 And they † consider not in their hearts *that I* ᵇ remember all their wickedness: now ᵉ their own

doings have beset them about; they are ᵈ before my face.

3 They make the king

Before
CHRIST
cir. 780.

ᵈ Ps. 90. 8.

2. *And they consider not in their hearts,* lit. (as in the E. M.) *they say not to their hearts.* The conscience is God's voice to the heart from within; man's knowledge of the law of God, and his memory of it, is man's voice, reminding his heart and rebellious affections to abide in their obedience to God. God speaks through the heart, when by His secret inspirations He recalls it to its duty. Man speaks to his own heart, when he checks its sinful or passionate impulses by the rule of God's law, *Thou shalt not.* " At first, men feel the deformity of certain sorts of wickedness. When accustomed to them, men think that God is indifferent to what no longer shocks themselves." *They say not to their heart* any more, that *God remembers them.*

I remember all their wickedness. This was the root of *all their wickedness,* want of thought. They would not stop to say to themselves, that God not only saw, but *remembered their wickedness,* and not only this, but that He remembered it *all.* Many will acknowledge that God *sees* them. He sees all things, and so them also. This is a part of His natural attribute of omniscience. It costs them nothing to own it. But what God *remembers, that* He will repay. This belongs to God's attributes, as the moral Governor of the world; and this, man would gladly forget. But in vain. God does *remember,* and remembers in order to punish. *Now,* at the very moment when man would not recall this to his own heart, *their own doings have beset them about; they are before my face.* Unless or until man repent, God sees man continually, encompassed by all his past evil deeds; they surround him, accompany him, whithersoever he goeth; they attend him, like a band of followers; they lie down with him, they await him at his awakening; they live with him, but they do not die with him; they encircle him, that he should in no wise escape them, until he come attended by them, as witnesses against him, at the judgment-seat of God. ¹ *His own iniquities shall take the wicked himself, and he shall be holden with the cords of his sins.* God *remembers all their wickedness.* Then He will requite *all;* not the last sins only, but all. So when Moses interceded for his people after the sin of the calf, God says to him, ² *go lead the people unto the place, of which I have spoken unto thee; behold My Angel shall go before thee; nevertheless, in the day when I visit, I will visit their sin upon*

them; and of the sins of Israel and their enemies; ³ *Is not this laid up in store with Me,* and *sealed up among My treasures? to Me* belongeth *vengeance and recompense; their foot shall slide in* due *time.* The sins, forgotten by man, are remembered by God, and are requited all together in the end. A slight image of the Day of Judgment, *the Day of wrath and revelation of the righteous judgment of God, against* which the hard and impenitent heart *treasures up unto* itself *wrath!*

They are before My face. All things, past, present, and to come, are present before God. He sees all things which have been, or which are, or which shall be, or which could be, although He shall never will that they should be, in one eternal, unvarying, present. To what end then for man to cherish an idle hope, that God will not *remember,* what He is ever seeing? In vain wouldest thou think, that the manifold ways of man are too small, too intricate, too countless, to be remembered by God. God says, *They are before My Face.*

3. *They make the king glad with their wickedness.* Wicked sovereigns and a wicked people are a curse to each other, each encouraging the other in sin. Their king, being wicked, had pleasure in their wickedness; and they, seeing him to be pleased by it, set themselves the more, to do what was evil, and to amuse him with accounts of their sins. Sin is in itself so shameful, that even the great cannot, by themselves, sustain themselves in it, without others to flatter them. A good and serious man is a reproach to them. And so, the sinful great corrupt others, both as aiding them in their debaucheries, and in order not to be reproached by their virtues, and because the sinner has a corrupt pleasure and excitement in hearing of tales of sin, as the good joy to hear of good. Whence S. Paul says, ⁴ *who, knowing the judgment of God that they which commit such things are worthy of death, not only do the same, but have pleasure in them that do them.*

But whereas, they all, kings, princes, and people, thus agreed and conspired in sin, and the sin of the great is the most destructive, the prophet here upbraids the people most for this common sin, apparently because they were free from the greater temptations of the great, and so their sin was the more wilful. "An unhappy complaisance was the ruling character of Israel. It preferred its kings to God. Conscience was versatile, ac-

---

¹ Prov. v. 22.   ² Ex. xxxii. 34.   ³ Deut. xxxii. 34. 5.   ⁴ Rom. i. 32.

Before
CHRIST
cir. 780.

• Rom. 1. 32.

f Jer. 9. 2.

‖ Or, *the raiser
will cease.*
‖ Or, *from
waking.*

glad with their wickedness, and the princes ᵉ with their lies.

4 ᶠThey *are* all adulterers, as an oven heated by the baker, ‖ who ceaseth ‖ from raising after he hath kneaded the dough, until it be leavened.

5 In the day of our king the princes have made *him* sick ‖ with bottles of wine; he stretched out his hand with scorners.

6 For they have ‖ made ready their heart like an oven, whiles they lie in wait: their baker sleepeth

Before
CHRIST
cir. 780.

‖ Or, *with heat
through wine.*

‖ Or, *applied.*

---

commodating. Whatever was authorized by those in power, was approved." Ahab added the worship of Baal to that of the calves; Jehu confined himself to the sin of Jeroboam. The people acquiesced in the legalized sin. Much as if now, marriages, which by God's law are incest, or remarriages of the divorced, which our Lord pronounces adultery, were to be held allowable, because man's law ceases to annex any penalty to them.

4. *They* are *all adulterers.* The Prophet continues to picture the corruption of all kinds and degrees of men. *All of them,* king, princes, people; all were given to adultery, both spiritual, in departing from God, and actual, (for both sorts of sins went together,) in defiling themselves and others. *All of them* were, (so the word[1] means,) habitual *adulterers.* One only pause there was in their sin, the preparation to complete it. He likens their hearts, inflamed with lawless lusts, to the heat of *an oven* which *the baker* had already *heated.* The unusual construction "burning *from* the baker[2]" instead of "heated *by* the baker" may have been chosen, in order to express, how the fire continued to burn of itself, as it were, (although at first kindled by the baker,) and was ever ready to burn whatever was brought to it, and even now was all red-hot, burning on continually; and Satan, who had stirred it, gave it just this respite, *from the time when he had kneaded the dough*[3], until the leaven, which he had put into it, had fully worked, and the whole was ready for the operation of the fire.

The world is full of such men now, ever on fire, and pausing only from sin, until the flatteries, whereby they seduce the unstable, have worked and penetrated the whole mind, and victim after victim is gradually leavened and prepared for sin.

5. *In the day of our king, the princes have made* him *sick with bottles of wine* [or, *with heat from wine.*] Their holydays, like those of so many Englishmen now, were days of excess. *The day of* their *king* was probably some civil festival; his birthday, or his coronation-day.

The Prophet owns the king, in that he calls him *our king ;* he does not blame them for keeping the day, but for the way in which they kept it. Their festival they turned into an irreligious and anti-religious carousal; making themselves like *the brutes which perish,* and tempting their king first to forget his royal dignity, and then to blaspheme the majesty of God.

He stretched out his hand with scorners, as it is said[4], *Wine is a mocker* (or *scoffer*). Drunkenness, by taking off all power of self-restraint, brings out the evil which is in the man. The *scorner* or *scoffer* is one who *neither fears God nor regards man*[5], but makes a jest of all things, true and good, human or divine. Such were these corrupt princes of the king of Israel; with these *he stretched out the hand,* in token of his good fellowship with them, and that he was one with them. He withdrew his hand or his society from good and sober men, and *stretched it out,* not to punish these, but to join with them, as men in drink reach out their hands to any whom they meet, in token of their sottish would-be friendliness. With these the king drank, jested, played the buffoon, praised his idols, scoffed at God. The flattery of the bad is a man's worst foe.

6. *For they have made ready their heart like an oven.* He gives the reason of their bursting out into open mischief; it was ever stored up within. They *made ready,* (lit. *brought near*) *their heart.* Their heart was ever brought nigh to sin, even while the occasion was removed at a distance from it. "The *oven* is their heart ; the fuel, their corrupt affections, and inclinations, and evil concupiscence, with which it is filled ; *their baker,* their own evil will and imagination, which stirs up whatever is evil in them." The Prophet then pictures how, while they seem for a while to rest from sin, it is but *whilst they lie in wait;* still, all the while, they made and kept their hearts ready, full of fire for sin and passion; any breathing-time from actual sin was no real rest; the heart was still all on fire; *in the*

---

[1] מְנָאֲפִים   [2] בֹעֵרָה מֵאֹפֶה
[3] The E. V. *who ceaseth from raising,* and the E. M. *the raiser will cease,* mean the same thing.

[4] Prov. xx. 1. The word is the same, לִיץ or
לוּץ.

[5] S. Luke xviii. 4.

Before
CHRIST
cir. 780.

Fulfilled 772.
all the night; in the morning it burneth as a flaming
fire.

7 They are all hot as an
oven, and have devoured

their judges; [g] all their kings
[h] are fallen: [i] *there is* none
among them that calleth
unto me.

8 Ephraim, he [k] h a t h

Before
CHRIST
cir. 780.

g ch. 8. 4.
h 2 Kgs 15, 10,
14, 25, 30.
i Is. 64. 7.
k Ps. 106. 35.

morning, right early, as soon as the occasion
came, it burst forth.

The same truth is seen where the tempter
is without. Such, whether Satan or his
agents, having lodged the evil thought or
desire in the soul, often feign themselves
asleep, as it were, "letting the fire and the
fuel which they had inserted, work together,"
that so the fire pent-in might kindle more
thoroughly and fatally, and, the heart being
filled and penetrated with it, might burst
out of itself, as soon as the occasion should
come.

7. *They are all hot as an oven, and have
devoured their judges.* Plans of sin, sooner or
later, through God's overruling Providence,
bound back upon their authors. The wisdom
of God's justice and of His government shews
itself the more, in that, without any apparent
agency of His own, the sin is guided by Him,
through all the intricate mazes of human
passion, malice, and cunning, back to the
sinner's bosom. Jeroboam, and the kings
who followed him, had corrupted the people,
in order to establish their own kingdom.
They had heated and inflamed the people,
and had done their work completely, for the
Prophet says, *They are all hot as an oven;*
none had escaped the contagion; and they,
thus heated, burst forth and, like the furnace
of Nebchadnezzar, devoured not only what
was cast into it, but those who kindled it.
The heathen observed, that the "artificers of
death perished by their own art."

Probably the Prophet is describing a scene
of revelry, debauchery, and scoffing, which
preceded the murder of the unhappy Zechariah; and so fills up the brief history of the
Book of Kings. He describes a profligate
court and a debauched king; and him doubtless, Zechariah [1]; those around him, delighting him with their wickedness; all of them
habitual adulterers; but one secret agent
stirring them up, firing them with sin, and
resting only, until the evil leaven had worked
through and through. Then follows the revel,
and the ground why they intoxicated the king,
viz. their lying-in-wait. "*For*," he adds, "they
prepared their hearts like a furnace, *when
they lie in wait.*" The mention of dates, of
facts, and of the connection of these together;
"the day of our king;" his behavior: their

lying in wait; the secret working of one
individual; the bursting out of the fire in
the morning; the falling of their kings;
looks, as if he were relating an actual history.
We know that Zechariah, of whom he is
speaking, was slain through conspiracy publicly in the open face of day, "before all the
people," no one heeding, no one resisting.
Hosea seems to supply the moral aspect of
the history, how Zechariah fell into this
general contempt; how, in him, all which
was good in the house of Jehu expired.

All their kings are fallen. The kingdom of
Israel, having been set up in sin, was,
throughout its whole course, unstable and
unsettled. Jeroboam's house ended in his
son; that of Baasha, who killed Jeroboam's
son, Nadab, ended in his own son, Elah;
Omri's ended in his son's son, God having
delayed the punishment on Ahab's sins for one
generation, on account of his partial repentance; then followed Jehu's, to whose house
God, for his obedience in some things, continued the kingdom to *the fourth generation.*
With these two exceptions, in the houses of
Omri and Jehu, the kings of Israel either
left no sons, or left them to be slain. Nadab,
Elah, Zimri, Tibni, Jehoram, Zechariah,
Shallum, Pekahiah, Pekah, were put to death
by those who succeeded them. Of all the
kings of Israel, Jeroboam, Baasha, Omri,
Menahem, alone, in addition to Jehu and the
three next of his house, died natural
deaths. So was it written by God's hand on
the house of Israel, *all their kings have fallen.*
The captivity was the tenth change after
they had deserted the house of David. Yet
such was the stupidity and obstinacy both of
kings and people, that, amid all these chastisements, none, either people or king, turned
to God and prayed Him to deliver them.
Not even distress, amid which almost all
betake themselves to God, awakened any
sense of religion in them. *There is none among
them, that calleth unto Me.*

8. *Ephraim, he hath mixed himself among the
people;* i. e. with the heathen; he *mixed* or
mingled himself among or with them, so as to
corrupt himself [2], as it is said [3], *they were mingled among the heathen and learned their works.*
God had forbidden all intermarriage with the
heathen [4], lest His people should corrupt

[1] See Introd. p. 5.

[2] The word בלל is used not of mingling only, but
of a mingling which involved confusion, (as in the

origin of the name *Babel*, Gen xi. 7,) or contamina-
tion, (as in תבל.)

[3] Ps. cvi. 35   [4] Ex. xxxiv. 12-16.

Before
CHRIST
cir. 780.

[1] ch. 8. 7.

† Heb.
sprinkled.

mixed himself among the people; Ephraim is a cake not turned.

9 [1]Strangers have devoured his strength, and he knoweth *it* not: yea, gray hairs are † here and

there upon him, yet he knoweth not.

10 And the [m] pride of Israel testifieth to his face: and [n] they do not return to the Lord their God, nor seek him for all this.

Before
CHRIST
cir. 780.

[m] ch. 5. 5.

[n] Is. 9. 13.

themselves: they thought themselves wiser than He, intermarried, and were corrupted. Such are the ways of those who put themselves amid occasions of sin.

Ephraim is (lit. *is become*) *a cake* (lit. *on the coals*) *not turned.* The Prophet continues the image.[1] *Ephraim had been mingled,* steeped, kneaded up into one, as it were, *with the heathen,* their ways, their idolatries, their vices. God would amend them, and they, withholding themselves from His discipline, and not yielding themselves wholly to it, were but spoiled. The sort of cake, to which Ephraim is here likened, *uggah* [2], lit. *circular,* was a thin pancake, to which a scorching heat was applied on one side; sometimes by means of hot charcoal heaped upon it; sometimes, (it is thought,) the fire was within the earthen jar, around which the thin dough was fitted. If it remained long *unturned,* it was burnt on the one side; while it continued unbaked, doughy, reeking, on the other; the fire spoiling, not penetrating it through. Such were the people; such are too many so-called Christians; they united in themselves hypocrisy and ungodliness, outward performance and inward lukewarmness; the one overdone, but without any wholesome effect on the other. The one was scorched and black; the other, steamed, damp, and lukewarm; the whole worthless, spoiled irremediably, fit only to be cast away. The fire of God's judgment, with which the people should have been amended, made but an outward impression upon them, and reached not within, nor to any thorough change, so that they were the more hopelessly spoiled through the means which God used for their amendment.

9. *Strangers have devoured his strength, and he knoweth* it *not.* Like Samson, when, for sensual pleasure, he had betrayed the source of his strength and God had departed from him, Israel knew not how or wherein his alliances with the heathen had impaired his strength. He thought his losses at the hand of the enemy, passing wounds, which time would heal; he thought not of them, as tokens of God's separation from him, that his time of trial was coming to its close, his strength

decaying, his end at hand. Israel was not only incorrigible, but *past feeling* [3], as the Apostle says of the heathen. The marks of wasting and decay were visible to sight and touch; yet he himself perceived not what all saw except himself. Israel had sought to strangers for help, and it *had turned to his decay.* Pul and Tiglath-pileser had *devoured his strength,* despoiling him of his wealth and treasure, the flower of his men, and the produce of his land, draining him of his riches, and hardly oppressing him through the tribute imposed upon him. But "like men quite stupified, they, though thus continually gnawed upon, yet suffered themselves willingly to be devoured, and seemed insensible of it." Yet not only so, but the present evils were the forerunners of worse. Grey hairs, themselves the effects of declining age and tokens of decay, are the forerunners of death. "[4] Thy grey hairs are thy passing-bell," says the proverb.

The Prophet repeats, after each clause, *he knoweth not.* He knoweth nothing; he knoweth not the tokens of decay in himself, but hides them from himself; he knoweth not God, Who is the Author of them; he knoweth not the cause of them, his sins; he knoweth not the end and object of them, his conversion; he knoweth not, what, since he knoweth not any of these things, will be the issue of them, his destruction. Men hide from themselves the tokens of decay, whether of body or soul. And so death, whether of body or soul or both, comes upon them unawares. "[5] Looking on the surface, he imagines that all things are right with him, not feeling the secret worm which gnaws within. The outward garb remains; the rules of fasting are observed; the stated times of prayer are kept; but the heart is far from Me, saith the Lord. Consider diligently what thou lovest, what thou fearest, whereat thou rejoicest or art saddened, and thou will find, under the habit of religion, a worldly mind; under the rags of conversion, a heart of perversion."

10. *And the pride of Israel testifieth to his face.* His pride convicted him. All the afflictions of

---

[1] The word, *hath mingled,* includes also doubtless the meaning of *kneaded up with,* בלול ב, as in Lev. ii. 4, 5. &c.

[2] עֻנָה.

[3] Eph. iv. 19.
[4] lit. "Thy grey hairs are the proclaimer of thy death," an Arabic proverb.
[5] S. Bern. Serm. 2. in cap. jej. § 2, 3.

Before
CHRIST
cir. 780.
o ch. 11. 11.
p See 2 Kings
15. 19. & 17. 4.
ch. 5. 13. & 9.
3. & 12. 1.

11. ¶ °Ephraim also is like a silly dove without heart : ᵖ they call to Egypt, they go to Assyria.

12 When they shall go, ᑫI will spread my net upon them ; I will bring them down as the fowls of the

Before
CHRIST
cir. 780.

q Ezek. 12. 13.

God humbled him not ; yea, they but brought out his pride, which "¹ kept him from acknowledging and repenting of the sins which had brought those evils upon him, and from *turning to God and seeking to Him* for remedy." Men complain of their "fortune" or "fate" or "stars," and go on the more obstinately, to build up what God destroys, to prop up by human means or human aid what, by God's Providence, is failing ; they venture more desperately, in order to recover past losses, until the crash at last becomes hopeless and final.

Nor seek Him for all this. God had exhausted all the treasures of His severity, as, before, of His love. He Himself marvels at His incorrigible and contumacious servant, as He says in Isaiah ², *Why should ye be stricken any more? Ye will revolt more and more.* How is this ? It follows, because they have *no heart.*

11. *Ephraim is* [*become*] *like a silly dove.* "There is nothing more simple than a dove," says the Eastern proverb. Simplicity is good or bad, not in itself, but according to some other qualities of the soul, good or evil, with which it is united, to which it opens the mind, and which lead it to good or mislead it to evil. The word ³ describes one, easily persuaded, open, and so, one who takes God's word simply, obeys His Will, without refinement or subtlety or explaining it away ; in which way it is said ⁴, *The Lord preserveth the simple ;* or, on the other hand, one who lets himself easily be led to evil, as the heathen said of youth, that they were "like wax to be bent to evil." In this way, it is said ⁵, *How long, ye simple ones, will ye love simplicity?* Our Lord uses this likeness of the dove, for good⁶, *be wise as serpents, simple,* or *harmless as doves.* Hosea speaks of simplicity without wisdom ; for he adds, *a silly dove without understanding,* (lit. *without a heart,*) whereby they should love God's Will, and so should understand it. Ephraim *became,* he says, like a silly dove. Neglecting God's calls, unmoved by calamity or sufferings, and not *seeking* to God *for all this* which He has done to recall them, they grew in folly. Man is ever *growing in wisdom* or in folly, in grace or in gracelessness. This new stage of folly lay in their flying to Assyria, to help them, in fact, against God ; as it follows,

They call to Egypt. Instead of *calling to* God Who could and would help, they *called to Egypt* who could not, and *went to Assyria* who

would not. So God complains by Isaiah ⁷, *To Me, thou hast not called, O Jacob.* This was their folly ; they called not to God, Who had delivered them out of Egypt, but, alternately, to their two powerful neighbors, of whom Egypt was a delusive promiser, not failing only, but piercing, those who leant on it ; Assyria was a powerful oppressor. Yet what else is almost the whole history of Christian states ? The "balance of power," which has been the pride of the later policy of Europe, which has been idolized as a god, to which statesmen have looked, as a deliverance out of all their troubles ; as if it were a sort of Divine Providence, regulating the affairs of men, and dispensing with the interference of God ; what is it but the self-same wisdom, which balanced Egypt against Assyria ?

12. *When they go,* (lit. *according as* they go, in all circumstances of time or place or manner, when whithersoever or howsoever they shall go,) *I will spread My net upon them,* so as to surround and envelop them on all sides and hold them down. The *dove* soaring aloft, with speed like the storm-wind ⁸, is a picture of freedom, independence, impetuous, unhindered, following on its own course ; weak and timid, it trusts in the skillfulness with which it guides its flight, to escape pursuit ; the *net,* with its thin slight meshes, betokens how weak instruments become all-sufficient in the hands of the Almighty ; the same dove, brought down from its almost viewless height, fluttering weakly, helplessly and hopelessly, under those same meshes, is a picture of that same self-dependent spirit humiliated, overwhelmed by inevitable evils, against which it impotently struggles, from which it seems to see its escape, but by which it is held as fast, as if it lay motionless in iron.

As their congregation hath heard. Manifoldly had the message of reward on obedience, and of punishment on disobedience, come to Israel. It was spread throughout the law ; it fills the book of Deuteronomy ; it was concentrated in the blessing and the curse on mount Ebal and Gerizim ; it was put into their mouths in the song of Moses ; it was inculcated by all the prophets who had already prophesied to them, and now it was being enforced on that generation by Hosea himself. Other kingdoms have fallen ; but their fall, apart from Scripture, has not been the subject of prophecy. Their ruin has come

¹Poc.   ²i. 5.   ³פתה.   ⁴Ps. cxvi. 6.   ⁵Prov. i. 22.

⁶S. Matt. x. 16.   ⁷Isai. xliii. 22.   ⁸Ps. lv. 6-8.

Before CHRIST cir. 780.

heaven; I will chastise them, ^r as their congrega-

r Lev. 26. 14, &c.
Deut. 28. 15,
&c. 2 Kings 17.
13; 18.

† Heb. spoil.

tion hath heard.

13 Woe unto them! for they have fled from me: † destruction unto them! because they have transgressed against me: though

^s I have redeemed them, yet they have spoken lies against me.

14 ^t And they have not cried unto me with their heart, when they howled upon their beds: they assemble themselves for corn

Before CHRIST cir. 780.

s Mic. 6. 4.
t Job 35. 9, 10.
Ps. 78. 36.
Jer. 3. 10.
Zech. 7. 5.

---

mostly unexpected, either by themselves or others. 13. *Woe unto them, for they have fled from Me.* The threatening rises in severity, as did the measure of their sin. Whereas ¹ *Salvation belonged to God* alone, and they only ² *abide under His shadow*, who make Him their *refuge, woe* must needs come on them, who leave Him. ³ *They forsake their own mercy.* Woe they draw upon themselves, who forget God; how much more then they, who wilfully and with a high hand transgress against Him! *Destruction unto them, for they have transgressed against Me.* To be separated from God is the source of all evils; it is the "pain of loss" of God's Presence, in hell; but *destruction* is more than this; it is everlasting death.

And I have redeemed them and they have spoken lies against Me. The *I* and *they* are both emphatic in Hebrew; ⁴ "*I* redeemed;" "*they* spoke lies." Such is man's requital of His God. Oft as He redeemed, so often did they traduce Him. Such was the history of the passage through the wilderness; such, of the period under the Judges; such had it been recently, when God delivered Israel by the hand of Jereboam II ⁵. The word, *I have redeemed*, denotes "habitual oft-renewed deliverance," "that He was their constant Redeemer, from Whom they had found help, did still find it, and might yet look to find it, if they did not, by their ill behavior, stop the course of His favor towards them ⁶." God's mercy overflowed their ingratitude. *They* had spoken lies against Him, often as He had delivered them; *He* was still their abiding Redeemer. *I do redeem them.*

They have spoken lies against Me. Men *speak lies* against God, in their hearts, their words, their deeds, whenever they harbor thoughts, speak words, or act, so as to deny that God is what He is, or as to imply that He is not what He has declared Himself to be. Whoever seeks anything out of God or against His Will; whoever seeks from man, or from idols, or from fortune, or from his own powers, what God alone bestows; whoever

¹ Ps. iii. 8. ² Ib. xci. 1, 2.
³ Jon. ii. 8.
⁴ ואנכי אפדם והמה דברו.
⁵ 2 Kings xiv. 25-27. ⁶ Poc.

acts as if God was not a good God, ready to receive the penitent, or a just God Who will avenge the holiness of His laws and *not clear the guilty*, does in fact, *speak lies against God*. People, day by day, *speak lies against* God, against His Wisdom, His Providence, His Justice, His Goodness, His Omniscience, when they are thinking of nothing less. Jeroboam spake *lies against God*, when he said, *these be thy gods, O Israel, which brought thee out of the land of Egypt*, whereas God had so often enforced upon them ⁷, *the Lord redeemed you out of the house of bondmen, from the hand of Pharaoh king of Egypt;* ⁸ *the Lord thy God brought thee out thence with a mighty hand and stretched out arm.* Israel *spake lies against God*, when he said ⁹, *these are my rewards which my lovers have given me,* or when, *they returned not to Him* but *called on Egypt*, as though God would not help them, Who said that He would, or as though Egypt could help them, of whom God said that it should not. Sometimes, they *spoke out lies* boldly, telling God's true prophets that He had not sent them, or forbidding them to speak in His Name; sometimes covertly, as when they turned to God, not sincerely but feignedly; but always perversely. And when God the Son came on earth to *redeem them*, then still more, they spoke lies against Him, all His life long, saying, *He deceiveth the people*, and all their other blasphemies, and "¹⁰ when He forgave them the sin of His death, saying, *Father, forgive them for they know not what they do*, they persevered in *speaking lies* against Him, and bribed the soldiers to speak lies against Him," and themselves do so to this day.

14. *And they have not cried unto Me with their heart, when they howled upon their beds*, or, in the present time, *they cry not unto Me when they howl.* They did *cry*, and, it may be, they *cried* even *unto God.* At least, the prophet does not deny that they cried to God at all; only, he says, that they did *not cry to Him with their heart.* Their cries were wrung from them by their temporal distresses, and ended in them, not in God. There was no sincerity in their hearts, no change in their doings.

⁷ Ex. xx. 2. Lev. xix. 36. xxiii. 43. Num. xv. 41. Deut. v. 6, 15.
⁸ Deut. vii. 8; add. xiii. 5. xv. 15. xxiv. 18.
⁹ ch. ii. 12. ¹⁰ Rup.

Before
CHRIST
cir. 780.

‖ Or, *chastened*.

ᵘ ch. 11. 7.

and wine, *and* they rebel against me.

15 Though I ‖ h a v e bound *a n d* strengthened their arms, yet do they imagine mischief against me.

16 ᵘ They return, *but* not

Before
CHRIST
cir. 780.

ˣ Ps. 78. 57.

ʸ Ps. 73. 9.

ᶻ ch. 9. 3, 6.

to the most High : ˣ they are like a deceitful bow : their princes shall fall by the sword for the ʸ rage of their tongue : this *shall be* their derision ᶻ in the land of Egypt.

Their *cry* was a mere *howling*. The secret complaint of the heart is a loud cry in the ears of God. The impetuous *cry* of impatient and unconverted suffering is a mere brutish *howling*. Their heart was set wholly on their earthly wants ; it did not thank God for giving them good things, nor cry to Him truly when He withheld them.

But, it may be, that the Prophet means also to contrast the acts of the ungodly, private and public, amid distress, with those of the godly. The godly man implores God in public and in private. The prayer on the *bed*, expresses the private prayer of the soul to God, when, the world being shut out, it is alone with Him. In place of this, there was the *howling*, as men toss fretfully and angrily on their beds, roar for pain ; but, instead of complaining *to* God, complain *of* Him, and are angry, not with themselves, but with God. In place of the public prayer and humiliation, there was a mere tumultuous assembly, in which they clamored *for corn and wine*, and *rebelled against* God. *They assemble themselves ;* (lit. *they* ¹ *gather themselves tumultuously together*). *They rebel against Me ;* (lit. *they turn aside against Me*). They did not only (as it is expressed elsewhere) "turn aside *from* God." *They turn aside against Me* ², He says, flying, as it were, in the very face of God. This *tumultuous assembly* was either some stormy civil debate, how to obtain the corn and wine which God withheld, or a tumultuous clamoring to their idols and false gods, like that of the priests of Baal, when arrayed against Elijah on Mount Carmel ; whereby they removed the further from God's law, and rebelled with a high hand against Him.

" ³ What is to *cry to the Lord*, but to long for the Lord ? But if any one multiply prayers, crying and weeping as he may, yet not with any intent to gain God Himself, but to obtain some earthly or passing thing, he cannot truly be said to *cry unto the Lord*, i. e. so to cry that his cry should come to the hearing of the Lord. This is a cry like Esau's, who sought no other fruit from his father's blessing, save to be rich and

powerful in this world. When then He saith, *They cried not to Me in their heart*, &c., He means, they were not devoted to Me, their heart was not right with Me ; they sought not Myself, but things of Mine. They howled, desiring only things for the belly, and seeking not to have Me. Thus they belong not to *the generation of those who seek the Lord, who seek the face of the God of Jacob* ⁴, but to the generation of Esau."

15. *Though I have bound*, rather, (as in the E. M.) *And I have chastened* ⁵, *I have strengthened their arms, and they imagine mischief against Me*. God had tried all ways with them, but it was all one. He chastened them in love, and in love He strengthened them ; He brought the enemy upon them, (as aforetime in the days of the Judges,) and He gave them strength to repel the enemy ; as He raised up judges of old, and lately had fulfilled His promise which He had made to Joash through Elisha. But it was all in vain. Whatever God did, Israel was still the same. All only issued in further evil. The Prophet sums up in four words all God's varied methods for their recovery, and then sets over against them the one result, fresh rebellion on the part of His creatures and His people.

They imagine or *devise mischief against Me*. The order in the Hebrew is emphatic, *and against Me they devise evil ;* i. e. *against Me*, Who had thus tried all the resources and methods of Divine wisdom to reclaim them, *they devise evil*. These are words of great condescension. For the creature can neither hurt nor profit the Creator. But since God vouchsafed to be their King, He deigned to look upon their rebellions, as so many efforts to injure Him. All God's creatures are made for His glory, and on earth, chiefly man ; and among men, chiefly those whom He had chosen as His people. In that, then, they set themselves to diminish that glory, giving to idols ⁶, they, as far as in them lay, *devised evil against* Him. Man would dethrone God, if he could.

16. *They return*, but *not to the most High.*

---

¹ גּוּר, when used of assembling, is always used of tumultuous assembling, as in Ps. lvi. 7. lix. 4. cxl. 3. Is. liv. 15.
² This is in two words in Hebrew, בִּי יָסוּרוּ.
³ Rup.   ⁴ Ps. xxiv. 6.

⁵ The two words *asar*, אָסַר, *bound*, and *issar*, יָסַר, *chastened*, differ but by a letter in the Hebrew. Yet one is never put for the other. The Heb. Comm., whom the E. V. followed, did but guess from the context.   ⁶ See Is. xli. 8.

Before
CHRIST
cir. 760.

CHAPTER VIII.

1, 12 *Destruction is threatened for their impiety,* 5 *and idolatry.*

ª ch. 5. 8.
† Heb. *the roof of thy mouth.*

SET ª the trumpet to † thy mouth. *He shall come*

ᵇ as an eagle against the house of the LORD, because ᶜthey have transgressed my covenant, and trespassed against my law.

Before
CHRIST
cir. 760.

ᵇ Deut. 28. 49.
Jer. 4. 13.
Hab. 1. 8.
ᶜ ch. 6. 7.

God exhorts by Jeremiah [1], *If thou wilt return, O Israel, saith the Lord, return unto Me.* They changed, whenever they did change, with a feigned, hypocritical conversion, but not to God, nor acknowledging His Majesty. Man, until truly converted, *turns* to and fro, unstably, hither and thither, changing from one evil to another, from the sins of youth to the sins of age, from the sins of prosperity to the sin of adversity ; but he remains himself unchanged. *He turns, not to the most High.* The Prophet says this in three, as it were, broken words, *They turn,* [2] *not most High.* The hearer readily filled up the broken sentence, which fell, drop by drop, from the Prophet's choked heart.

They are like a deceitful bow, which, "howsoever the archer directs it, will not carry the arrow right home to the mark," but to other objects clean contrary to his will. "[3] God had, as it were, bent Israel, as His own bow, against the tyranny of the devil and the deceit of idolatry. For Israel alone in the whole world cast aside the worship of idols, and was attached to the true and natural Lord of all things. But they turned themselves to the contrary. For, being bound to this, they fought against God for the glory of idols. They became then as a warped bow, shooting their arrows contrariwise." In like way doth every sinner act, using against God, in the service of Satan, God's gifts of nature or of outward means, talents, or wealth, or strength, or beauty, or power of speech. God gave all for His own glory ; and man turns all aside to do honor and service to Satan.

Their princes shall fall by the sword for the rage of their tongue. The word, rendered [4] *rage,* is everywhere else used of the wrath of God ; here, of the *wrath* and *foaming* of man against God. Jeremiah relates how, the nearer their destruction came upon Judah, the more madly the politicians and false prophets cantradicted what God revealed. Their tongue was *a sharp sword.* They sharpened their tongue like a sword ; and the sword pierced their own bosom. The phrensy of their speech not only drew down God's anger, but was the instrument of their destruction. They misled the people ; taught them to trust in Egypt, not in God ; persuaded them to believe themselves, and to

disbelieve God ; to believe, that the enemy should depart from them and not carry them away captive. They worked up the people to their will, and so they secured their own destruction. The princes of Judah were especially judged and put to death by Nebuchadnezzar [5]. The like probably took place in Israel. In any case, those chief in power are chief objects of destruction. Still more did these words come true before the final destruction of Jerusalem by the Romans. They were maddened by their own curse, *the rage of their tongue* against their Redeemer, *His blood be on us and on our children.* Phrensy became their characteristic. It was the amazement of the Romans, and their own destruction.

This shall be their derision in the land of Egypt. *This,* i. e. all this, their boasting of Egypt, their failure, their destruction, shall become their *derision.* In Egypt had they trusted ; to Egypt had they gone for succor ; in Egypt should they be derided. Such is the way of man. The world derides those who trusted in it, sued it, courted it, served it, preferred it to their God. Such are the wages, which it gives. So Isaiah prophesied of Judah [6], *the strength of Pharaoh shall be your shame, and the trust in the shadow of Egypt your confusion. They were all ashamed of a people that could not profit them, nor be an help nor profit, but a shame and also a reproach.* VIII. 1. *The trumpet to thy mouth!* So God bids the prophet Isaiah [7], *Cry aloud, spare not, lift up thy voice like a trumpet.* The prophets, as watchmen, were set by God to give notice of His coming judgments [8]. As the sound of a war-trumpet would startle a sleeping people, so would God have the Prophet's warning burst upon their sleep of sin. The ministers of the Church are called to be "watchmen [9]" "They too are forbidden to keep a cowardly silence, when *the house of the Lord* is imperilled by the breach of the covenant or violation of the law. If fear of the wicked or false respect for the great silences the voice of those whose office it is to *cry aloud,* how shall such cowardice be excused ?"

He shall come *as an eagle against the house of the Lord.* The words "he shall come" are inserted for clearness. The Prophet beholds the enemy speeding with the swiftness of an eagle, as it darts down upon its prey. The

[1] ch. iv. 1.   יָשׁוּבוּ לֹא עַל [2]
[3] S. Cyr.   זַעַם. [4]   [5] Jer. lii. 10.   [6] xxx. 3, 5.

[7] ch. lviii. 1.   [8] Ezek. xxxiii. 3, Am. iii. 6.
[9] Service for Ordering Priests.

Before
CHRIST
cir. 760.

d Ps. 78. 34.
ch. 5. 15.
e Tit. 1. 16.

2 ^dIsrael shall cry unto me, My God, ^ewe know thee.

3 Israel hath cast off the

thing that is good: the enemy shall pursue him.

4 ^fThey have set up kings, but not by me: they

Before
CHRIST
cir. 760.

f 2 Kings 15. 13,
17, 25.
Shallum,
Menahem,
Pekahiah.

house of the Lord is, most strictly, the Temple, as being *the place which God had chosen to place His name there.* Next, it is used, of the kingdom of Judah and Jerusalem, among whom the Temple was; whence God says[1], *I have forsaken My house, I have left Mine heritage; I have given the dearly-beloved of My soul into the hands of her enemies,* and [2], *What hath My beloved to do in Mine house, seeing she hath wrought lewdness with many?* Yet the title of *God's house* is older than the Temple; for God Himself uses it of His whole people, saying of Moses[3], *My servant Moses is not so, who is faithful in all Mine house.* And even the ten tribes, separated as they were from the Temple-worship, and apostates from the true faith of God, were not, as yet, counted by Him as wholly excluded from *the house of God.* For God, below, threatens that removal, as something still to come; *for the wickedness of their doings I will drive them out of My house*[4]. The eagle, then coming down *against* or *upon* the house of the Lord, is primarily Shalmaneser, who came down and carried off the ten tribes. Yet since Hosea, in these prophecies, includes Judah, also, *the house of the Lord* is most probably to be taken in its fullest sense, as including the whole people of God, among whom He dwelt, and the Temple where His Name was placed. The *eagle* includes then Nebuchadnezzar also, whom other prophets so call[5]; and (since, all through, the principle of sin is the same and the punishment the same) it includes the Roman eagle, the ensign of their armies.

Because they have transgressed My covenant. "God, Whose justice is always unquestionable, useth to make clear to men its reasonableness." Israel had broken the covenant which God had made with their fathers, that He would be to them a God, and they to Him a people. The *covenant* they had broken chiefly by idolatry and apostacy; the *law*, by sins against their neighbor. In both ways they had rejected God; therefore God rejected them.

2. *Israel shall cry unto Me, My God, we know Thee.* Or, according to the order in the Hebrew, *To Me shall they cry, we know Thee, Israel,* i. e. we, *Israel,* Thy people, *know Thee.* It is the same plea which our Lord says that He shall reject in the Day of Judgment[6]. *Many shall say unto Me, in that Day, Lord, Lord, have we not prophesied in Thy Name, and*

in Thy Name cast out devils, and in Thy Name done many wonderful works. In like way, when our Lord came in the flesh, they said of God the Father, *He is our God.* But our Lord appealed to their own consciences[7]; *It is My Father Who honoreth Me, of Whom ye say, He is our God, but ye have not known Him.* So Isaiah, when speaking of his own times, prophesied of those of our Lord also[8]; *This people draweth nigh unto Me, with their mouth and honoreth Me with their lips; but their heart is far from Me.* "God says, that they shall urge this as a proof, that they know God, and as an argument to move God to have respect unto them, viz. that they are the seed of Jacob, who was called Israel, because he prevailed with God, and they were called by his name." As though they said, "*we,* Thy *Israel, know thee.*" It was all hypocrisy, the cry of mere fear, not of love; whence God, using their own name of Israel which they had pleaded, answers the plea, declaring what *Israel* had become.

3. *Israel has cast off the* thing that is *good*, or (since the word means "to cast off with abhorrence") *Israel hath cast off and abhorred Good*, both "Him who is Good" and "that which is good." The word *tob* includes both. They rejected good in rejecting God, "[9] Who is simply, supremely, wholly, universally good, and good to all, the Author and Fountain of all good, so that there is nothing simply good but God; nothing worthy of that title, except in respect of its relation to Him Who is *good and doing good*[10]. So then whatsoever any man hath or enjoys of good, is from his relation to Him, his nearness to Him, his congruity with Him. [11] *The drawing near to God is good to me.* All that any man hath of good, is from his being near to God, and his being, as far as human condition is capable of, like unto Him. So that they who are far from Him, and put Him far from them, necessarily *cast off* all that is *good.*"

The enemy shall pursue him. "Forsaking God, and forsaken by Him, they must needs be laid open to all evils." *The enemy,* i. e. the Assyrian, *shall pursue him.* This is according to the curse, denounced against them in the law, if they should forsake the Lord, and break His covenant, and *not hearken to His voice to observe to do His commandments*[12].

4. *They have set up kings, but not by ME.*

1 Jer. xii. 7.   2 Ib. xi. 15.
3 Num. xii. 7.   4 ch. ix. 15.
5 Ezek. xvii. 3, 12. Jer. xlviii. 40. Hab. i. 8.

6 S. Matt. vii. 22.   7 S. John viii. 54.
8 S. Matt. xv. 8. Is. xxix. 13. 9 Poc. 10 Ps. cxix. 68.
11 Ps. lxxiii. 28.   12 Deut. xxviii. 15–25.

Before
CHRIST
cir. 760.
have made princes, and I knew *it* not: [5] of their

[ε] ch. 2. 8. & 13. 2. silver and their gold

have they made them idols, that they may be cut off.
Before
CHRIST
cir. 760.

God Himself foretold to Jeroboam by Ahijah the prophet, that He would *rend the kingdom out of the hands of Solomon, and give ten tribes* to him, *and* would *take* him, *and* he *should reign according to all that* his *soul desired and* should *be king over Israel*[1]; and, after the ten tribes had made Jeroboam king, God said by Shemaiah the prophet to Rehoboam and the two tribes[2], *Ye shall not go up, nor fight against your brethren the children of Israel; return every man to his house; for this thing is from Me.*

Yet although here, as everywhere, man's self-will was overruled by God's Will, and fulfilled it, it was not the less self-will, both in the ten tribes and in Jeroboam. It was so in the ten tribes. For they cast off Rehoboam, simply of their own mind, because he would not lessen the taxes, as they prescribed. If he would have consented to their demands, they would have remained his subjects[3]. *They set up kings, but not by* or *through* God, Whom they never consulted, nor asked His Will about the rules of the kingdom, or about its relation to the kingdom of Judah, or the house of David. They referred these matters no more to God, than if there had been no God, or than if He interfered not in the affairs of man. It was self-will in Jeroboam himself, for he received the kingdom (which Ahijah told him, he *desired*) not from God, not inquiring of him, how he should undertake it, nor anointed by Him, nor in any way acknowledging Him, but from the people. And as soon as he had received it, he set up rebellion against God, in order to establish his kingdom, which he founded in sin, whereby he made Israel to sin.

In like way, the Apostle says[4], *against Thy holy Child Jesus, Whom Thou hast anointed, both Herod and Pontius Pilate, with the Gentiles and the people of Israel, were gathered together, for to do whatsoever Thy hand and Thy counsel determined before to be done.* Yet not the less did they sin in this Deicide; and the Blood of Jesus has ever since, as they imprecated on themselves, been on the Jews and on their children, as many as did not repent.

As was the beginning of the kingdom of Israel, such was its course. *They made kings, but not from God.* Such were all their kings, except Jehu and his house. During 253 years, for which the kingdom of Israel lasted, eighteen kings reigned over it, out of ten different families, and no family came to a close, save by a violent death. The like self-will and independence closed the existence of the Jewish people. The Roman Emperor being afar off, the Scribes and Pharisees hoped, under him, without any great control, to maintain their own authority over the people. They themselves, by their *God forbid !* [5] owned that our Lord truly saw their thoughts and purpose, *This is the heir; come let us kill Him, that the inheritance may be ours.* They willed to reign without Christ, feared the Heathen Emperor less than the holiness of Jesus, and in the words, *We have no king but Cæsar,* they deposed God, and shut themselves out from His kingdom.

And I knew it not. "As far as in them lay, they did it without His knowledge.[6]" They did not take Him into their counsels, nor desire His cognizance of it, or His approbation of it. If they could, they would have had Him ignorant of it, knowing it to be against His Will. And so in His turn, God knew it not, owned it not, as He shall say to the ungodly, *I know you not*[7].

Of their silver and their gold have they made them idols. God had multiplied them, (as He said before[8]) and they ungratefully abused to the dishonor of the Giver, what He gave them to be used to His glory.

That they may be cut off, lit. *that he may be cut off.* The whole people is spoken of as one man, "one and all," as we say. It is a fearful description of obstinate sin, that their very object in it seemed to be their own destruction. They acted with one will as one man, who had, in all he did, this one end,— to perish. "[9] As if on set purpose they would provoke destruction, and obstinately run themselves into it, although forewarned thereof." Holy Scripture speaks of that, as men's end, at which all their acts aim. [10] *They see not, nor know, that they may be ashamed;* i. e. they blind themselves, as though their whole object were, what they will bring upon themselves, their own shame. [11] *They prophesy a lie in My Name, that I might drive you out, and that ye might perish, ye, and the prophets that prophesy unto you.* This was the ultimate end of those false prophecies. The false prophets of Judah filled them with false hopes; the real and true end of those prophecies, that in which they ended, was the ruin of those who uttered, and of those who listened to them. We ourselves say almost proverbially, "he goes the way to ruin himself;" not that such is the man's own object, but that he obstinately chooses a course of conduct, which,

---

[1] 1 Kings xi. 31, 37.   [2] xii. 22-4.   [3] Ib. 4
[4] Acts iv. 27, 8.   [5] S. Luke xx. 16.

[6] S. John viii. 54.   [7] S. Matt. xxv. 12.
[8] ch. ii. 8.   [9] Poc.   [10] Is. xliv. 9.   [11] Jer. xxvii. 15.

6

Before
CHRIST
cir. 760.

h Jer. 13. 27.

5 ¶ Thy calf, O Sama-
ria, hath cast *thee* off; mine
anger is kindled against
them : [h] how long *will it be*

ere they attain to inno-
cency?

6 For from Israel *was*
it also: the workman made

Before
CHRIST
cir. 760.

others see, must end in utter ruin. So a man
chooses destruction or hell, if he chooses
those things which, according to God's known
law and word, end in it. Man hides from his
own eyes the distant future, and fixes them
on the nearer objects which he has at heart.
God lifts the veil, and discovers to him the
further end, at which he is driving, which he
is, in fact, compassing, and which is in truth
the end ; for his own fleeting objects perish in
the using ; this and this alone abides.

5. *Thy calf, O Samaria, hath cast thee off.*
Israel had cast off God, his good. In turn,
the Prophet says, the *calf*, which he had
chosen to be his god instead of the Lord his
God, *has cast* him *off.* He repeats the word,
by which he had described Israel's sin,
[1] *Israel hath cast off and abhorred good*, in order
to shew the connection of his sin and its punishment. " *Thy* calf," whom thou madest
for thyself, whom thou worshipest, whom
thou lovest, of whom thou saidst [2], *Behold
thy gods, O Israel, which brought thee up out of
the land of Egypt ; thy* calf, in whom thou didst
trust instead of thy God, it has requited thee
the dishonor thou didst put on thy God ; it
hath *cast thee off* as a thing *abhorred.* So it is
with all men's idols, which they make to
themselves, instead of God. First or last,
they all fail a man, and leave him poor indeed. Beauty fades ; wealth fails ; honor is
transferred to another ; nothing abides, save
God. Whence our own great poet of nature
makes a fallen favorite say, " had I but
serv'd my God with half the zeal I served my
king, He would not in mine age have left me
naked to mine enemies."

Mine anger is kindled against them. Our
passions are but some distorted likeness of
what exists in God without passion ; our
anger, of His displeasure against sin. And
so God speaks to us after the manner of men,
and pictures His Divine displeasure under
the likeness of our human passions of anger
and fury, in order to bring home to us, what
we wish to hide from ourselves, the severe
and awful side of His Being, His Infinite
Holiness, and the truth, that He will indeed
avenge. He tells us, that He will surely
punish ; as men, who are extremely incensed,
execute their displeasure if they can.

*How long will it be ere they attain to inno-
cency?* lit. *how long will they not be able innocency?* So again it is said, *him that hath an
high look and a proud heart, I cannot* [3] ; we
supply, *suffer. New moons and Sabbaths I*

cannot [4]; our version adds, *away with,* i. e.
endure. So here probably. As they had with
abhorrence cast off God their good, so God
says, *they cannot endure innocency* ; but He
speaks as wondering and aggrieved at their
hardness of heart and their obdurate holding
out against the goodness, which He desired
for them. *How long will they not be able to
endure innocency ?* " What madness this, that
when I give them place for repentence, they
will not endure to return to health of soul ! "

6. *For.* This verse may assign the reasons
of God's displeasure, *mine anger is kindled* ; or
of Israel's impenitency, *How long will it be?*
This indeed is only going a little further
back ; for Israel's incorrigibleness was the
ground of God's displeasure. And they were
incorrigible ; because they had themselves
devised it ; *for from Israel was it also.* Those
are especially incorrigible, who do not fall
into error through ignorance, but who
through malice devise it out of their own
heart. Such persons act and speak, not as
seduced by others, but seducing themselves,
and condemned by their own judgment.
Such were Israel and Jeroboam his king, who
were not induced or seduced by others to
deem the golden calf to be God, but devised
it, of malicious intent, knowing that it was
not God. Hence Israel could be cured of the
worship of Baal, for this was brought from
without by Jezebel ; and *Jehu destroyed Baal
out of Israel.* But of the sin of the calf they
could not be healed. In this sin all the kings
of Israel were impenitent.

From Israel was it also. Their boast, that
they were of Israel, aggravated their sin.
They said to God, *we, Israel, know thee.* So
then their offence, too, their brutishness also,
was from those who boasted themselves of
bearing the name of their forefather, Israel,
who were the chosen people of God, so distinguished by His favor. The name of Israel,
suggesting their near relation to God, and the
great things which He had done for them,
and their solemn covenant with Him to be
His people as He was their God, should, in
itself, have made them ashamed of such
brutishness. So S. Paul appealeth to us by
our name of Christians [5], *Let every one who
nameth the Name of Christ depart from iniquity.*

The workman made it, therefore it is not God.
The workman was rather a god to his idol,
than it to him ; for *he* made it ; *it* was a thing
made. To say that it was made, was to deny
that it was God. Hence the prophets so often

[1] ver. 3. זָנַח.   [2] 1 Kings xii. 28–31.   [3] Ps. ci. 5.   [4] Is. i. 13.   [5] 2 Tim. ii. 19.

Before
CHRIST
cir. 760.

it; therefore it *is* not God: but the calf of Samaria shall be broken in pieces.

[1] Prov. 22. 8. ch. 10, 12, 13.

7 For [1] they have sown the wind, and they shall reap the whirlwind: it hath

no || stalk: the bud shall yield no meal: if so be it yield, [k] the strangers shall swallow it up.

8 [1] Israel is swallowed up: now shall they be

Before
CHRIST
cir. 760.

|| Or, *standing corn.*
[k] ch. 7. 9.
[1] 2 Kgs. 17. 6.

---

urge this special proof of the vanity of idols. No creature can be God. Nor can there be anything, between God and a creature. " [1] Every substance which is not God is a creature; and that which is not a creature, is God." God Himself could not make a creature who should be God. The Arian heresy, which imagined that God the Son could be a creature and yet an object of our worship, or that there could be a secondary god, was folly [2] as well as blasphemy. They did not conceive what God is. They had low, debased notions of the Godhead. They knew not that the Creator must be removed as infinitely above His most exalted creature, as above the lowest.

Nor do the prophets need any subtleties (such as the heathen alleged) that their idol might be indwelt by some influence. Since God dwelt not in it, any such influence could only come from a creature, and that, an evil one.

The calf of Samaria shall be broken in pieces. The calves were set up at Bethel and at Dan, but they were the sort of tutelar deity of the ten tribes; therefore they are called *the calf of Samaria.* They represented one and the same thing; whence they are called as one, *the calf,* not "calves." A thing of nought it was in its origin, for it had its form and shape from man; a thing of nought it should be in its end, for it should be *broken in pieces,* or become *chips, fragments,* for fire [3].

7. *For they have sown the wind, and they shall reap the whirlwind. They shall reap,* not merely as *they have sown,* but with an awful increase. They sowed folly and vanity, and shall reap, not merely emptiness and disappointment, but sudden, irresistible destruction [4]. *They sowed the wind,* and, as one seed bringeth forth many, so the wind, " penn'd up," as it were, in this destructive tillage, should "burst forth again, reinforced in strength, in mightier store and with greater violence." Thus they *reaped the whirlwind,* yea, (as the word means) *a mighty whirlwind* [5]. But the whirlwind which they reap doth not belong to *them;* rather they belong to it,

[1] S. Aug. de Trin. i. 6.

[2] See S. Athanas. against Arians, p. 3. n. f. 10. u. 191. d. 301.c. 411. b. 423. m. Oxf. Tr.

[3] Some derive the word שְׁבָבִים from an Arabic root, *kindled,* others from a Talmudic word, *fragment.* The word is the same as the Arabic *Shebab,* "that whereby fire is kindled," fuel for fire. The

blown away by it, like chaff, the sport and mockery of its restless violence.

It hath no stalk. If their design should for the time seem to prosper, all should be but empty shew, disappointing the more, the more it should seem to promise. He speaks of three stages of progress. First, the seed should not send forth the corn with the ear; *it hath no stalk* or *standing corn;* even if it advanced thus far, still the ear should yield no meat; or should it perchance yield this, the enemy should devour it. Since the yielding fruit denotes doing works, the fruit of God's grace, the absence of the *standing corn* represents the absence of good works altogether; the absence of the *meal,* that nothing is brought to ripeness; the *devouring* by *the enemy,* that what would otherwise be good, is, through faulty intentions or want of purity of purpose, given to Satan and the world, not to God. " [6] When hypocrites make a shew of good works, they gratify therewith the longings of the evil spirits. For they who do not seek to please God therewith, minister not to the Lord of the field, but to *strangers.* The hypocrite then, like a fruitful but neglected "ear," cannot retain his fruit, because the "ear" of good works lieth on the ground. And yet he is fed by this very folly, because for his good works he is honored by all, eminent above the rest; men's minds are subject to him; he is raised to high places; nurtured by favors. But *then* will he understand that he has done foolishly, when, for the delight of praise, he shall receive the sentence of the rebuke of God."

8. *Israel is swallowed up.* Not only shall all which they have, be swallowed up by the enemy, but themselves also; and this, not at any distant time, but *now. Now,* at a time all but present, *they shall be among the Gentiles, as a vessel wherein is no pleasure,* or, quite strictly, *Now they have become, among the Gentiles.* He speaks of what should certainly be, as though it already were. *A vessel wherein is no pleasure,* is what S. Paul calls [7] *a vessel to dishonor,* as opposed to *vessels to honor* or honorable uses. It is then some vessel put to vile uses,

Talm. word may be no original word, but formed from the Heb. in the sense which those writers conceived it to have in this place.

[4] Hosea expressed this in four words; רוּחַ יִזְרָעוּ וְסוּפָתָה יִקְצֹרוּ.

[5] The form סוּפָתָה is intensive of סוּפָה.
[6] S. Greg. Mor. viii. 71.   [7] 2 Tim. ii. 20.

Before
CHRIST
cir. 760.

m Jer. 22. 28. &
48. 38.
n 2 Kgs. 15. 19.

among the Gentiles ᵐ as a vessel wherein is no pleasure.

9 For ⁿ they are gone

up to Assyria, ° a wild ass alone by himself: Ephraim ᵖ hath hired † lovers.

Before
CHRIST
cir. 760.

° Jer. 2. 24.
cir. 771.
ᵖ Isai. 30. 6.
Ezek. 16. 33, 34.
† Heb. loves.

such as people turn away from with disgust. Such has been the history of the ten tribes ever since: *swallowed up*, not destroyed; *among* the nations, yet not of them; despised and mingled among them, yet not united with them; having an existence, yet among that large whole, *the nations*, in whom their national existence has been at once preserved and lost; everywhere had in dishonor; the Heathen and the Mohammedan have alike despised, outraged, insulted them; avenging upon them, unconsciously, the dishonor which they did to God. The Jews were treated by the Romans of old as offensive to the smell, and are so by the Mohammedans of North Africa still. "Never," says a writer of the fifth century [1], "has Israel been put to any honorable office, so as, after losing the marks of freedom and power, at least to have the rank of honorable servitude; but, like a vessel made for dishonorable offices, so they have been filled with revolting contumelies." "The most despised of those in servitude" was the title given by the Roman historian to the Jews, while yet in their own land. Wealth, otherwise so coveted, for the most part has not exempted them from dishonor, but exposed them to outrage. Individuals have risen to eminence in philosophy, medicine, finance; but the race has not gained through the credit of its members; rather, these have, for the most part, risen to reputation for intellect, amid the wreck of their own faith. When Hosea wrote this, two centuries had passed, since the fame of Solomon's wisdom (which still is venerated in the East) spread far and wide; Israel was hated and envied by its neighbors, not despised; no token of contempt yet attached to them; yet Hosea foretold that it should shortly be; and, for two thousand years, it has, in the main, been the characteristic of their nation.

9. *For they are gone up to Assyria.* The ground of this their captivity is that wherein they placed their hope of safety. They shall be presently swallowed up; *for* they went to Asshur. The Holy Land being then honored by the special presence of God, all nations are said to *go up* to it. Now, since Israel forgetting God, their strength and their glory, went to the Assyrian for help, he is said to *go up* thither, whither he went as a suppliant.

A wild ass alone by himself. "As *the ox* which *knoweth its owner, and the ass its Master's crib*, represents each believer, of Jew or Gentile; Israel, who would not know Him, is called the *wild ass*." The *pere*, or *wild ass* of the East, is " [2] heady, unruly, undisciplinable [3], obstinate, running with swiftness far outstripping the swiftest horse [4], whither his lust, hunger, thirst, draw him without rule or direction, hardly to be turned aside from his intended course." Although often found in bands, one often breaks away by himself, exposing itself for a prey to lions, whence it is said, *the wild ass is the lion's prey in the wilderness* [5]. Wild as the Arab was, a "wild ass's colt by himself [6]," is to him a proverb for one " [7] singular, obstinate, pertinacious in his purpose." Such is man by nature [8]; such, it was foretold to Abraham, Ishmael would be [9]; such Israel again became; "stubborn, heady, selfwilled, refusing to be ruled by God's law and His counsel, in which he might find safety, and, of his own mind, running to the Assyrian," there to perish.

Ephraim hath hired lovers or *loves.* The plural, in itself, shews that they were sinful loves, since God had said, *a man shall cleave unto his wife and they twain shall be one flesh.* These sinful *loves* or *lovers* she was not tempted by, but she herself invited them [10]. It is a special and unwonted sin, when woman, forsaking the modesty which God gives her as a defence, becomes the temptress. "Like such a bad woman, luring others to love her, they, forsaking God, to Whom, as by covenant of marriage, they ought to have cleaved, and on Him alone to have depended, sought to make friends of the Assyrian, to help them in their rebellions against Him, and so put themselves to that charge (as sinners usually do) in the service of sin, which in God's service they need not to have been at."

And yet that which God pictures under colors so offensive, what was it in human eyes? The *hire* was presents of gold to powerful nations, whose aid, humanly speaking, Israel needed. But wherever it abandoned its trust in God, it adopted their idols. "Whoever has recourse to human means, without consulting God, or consulting whether He will, or will not bless them, is guilty of unfaithfulness which often leads to many

[1] Orosius App. Ruf. p. 439. Lap.   [2] Poc.
[3] Pallas. Reisen iii. p. 511.
[4] See Ker Porter, Travels, i. p. 459. Its Hebrew names פֶּרֶא and perhaps עָרוֹד are from swiftness.

[5] Ecclus. xiii. 19.
[6] The root in Arabic is the same as that here, בֶּרֶךְ Poc.   [7] See in Poc.   [8] Job xi. 12.
[9] Gen. xvi. 12.   [10] See Ezek. xvi. 33, 4.

Before
CHRIST
cir. 760.
q Ezek. 16. 37.
· ch. 10. 10.
Or, *begin.*
Or, *in a little
white,* as Hag.
2. 6.
r Isai. 10. 8.
Ezek. 26. 7.
Dan. 2. 37.

10 Yea, though t h e y have hired among the nations, now P will I gather them, and they shall || sorrow || a little for the burden of r the king of princes.

11 Because Ephraim hath made ˢ many altars to sin, altars shall be unto him to sin.

12 I have written to him ᵗ the great things of my

Before
CHRIST
cir. 760.

s ch. 12. 11.

t Deut. 4. 6, 8.
Ps. 119. 18.
& 147. 19, 20.

others. He becomes accustomed to the tone of mind of those whose protection he seeks, comes insensibly to approve even their errors, loses purity of heart and conscience, sacrifices his light and talents to the service of the powers, under whose shadow he wishes to live under repose."

10. *Yea, though they have hired,* or better, *because* or *when they hire among the heathen, now will I gather them ;* i. e. I will gather the nations together. The sin of Israel should bring its own punishment. He sent presents to the king of Assyria, in order to strengthen himself against the will of God ; " he thought himself secured by his league made with them; but he should find himself much deceived in his policy;" he had *hired among them* only ; *now,* ere long, very speedily, God Himself would *gather them,* i. e. those very nations, not in part, but altogether ; not for the help of Israel, but for its destruction. As though a man would let out some water from a deep lake ponded up, the water, as it oozed out, loosened more and more the barriers which withheld it, until, at length, all gave way, and the water of the lake was poured out in one wide wild waste, desolating all, over which it swept. It may be, that Assyria would not have known of, or noticed Israel, had not Israel first invited him.

And they shall sorrow a little for the burden of the king of princes. So great shall be the burden of the captivity hereafter, that they shall then sorrow but little for any burdens put upon them now, and which they now feel so heavy. *The king of princes* is the king of Assyria, who said ¹, *Are not my princes altogether kings?* The burden of which they complained will then be the thousand talents of silver which Menahem gave to Pul, king of Assyria, to support him in his usurpation, and in order to pay which, he *exacted the money of Israel, even of all the mighty men of wealth, of each man fifty shekels of silver* ². If we adopt the E. M., *begin,* we must render, *and they shall begin to be minished through the burden of the king of the princes,* i. e. they shall be gradually reduced and brought low through the exactions of the Assyrians, until in the end they shall be carried away. This

describes the gradual decay of Israel, first through the exactions of Pul, then through the captivity of Gilead by Tiglathpileser.

11. *Because Ephraim hath made many altars to sin, altars shall indeed be unto him to sin,* i. e. they shall be proved to him to be so, by the punishment which they shall draw upon him. The prophet had first shewn them their folly in forsaking God for the help of man; now he shews them the folly of attempting to "secure themselves by their great shew and pretences of religion and devotion in a false way." God had appointed one altar at Jerusalem. There He willed the sacrifices to be offered, which He would accept. To multiply altars, much more to set up altars against the one altar, was to multiply sin. Hosea charges Israel elsewhere with this multiplying of altars, as a grievous sin. *According to the multitude of his fruit, he hath increased altars. Their altars are as heaps in the furrows of the field* ³. They pretended doubtless, that they did it for a religious end, that they might thereon offer sacrifices for the expiation of their sins and appeasing of God. They endeavored to unite their own selfwill and the outward service of God. Therein they might deceive themselves ; but they could not deceive God. He calls their act by its true name. To make altars at their own pleasure and to offer sacrifices upon them, under any pretence whatever, was to sin. So then, as many altars as they reared, so often did they repeat their sin ; and this sin should be their only fruit. They should be, but only for sin. So God says of the two calves, *This thing became a sin* ⁴, and of the indiscriminate consecration of Priests (not of the family of Aaron), *This thing became sin unto the house of Jeroboam, even to cut it off and to destroy it from the face of the earth* ⁵.

12. *I have written to him the great things of My law,* lit. *I write.* Their sin then had no excuse of ignorance. God had written their duties for them in the ten commandments with His own Hand ; He had written them of old and *manifoldly* ⁶, often repeated and in divers manners. He wrote those manifold things *to them* [or *for them*] by Moses, not for that time only, but that they might be con-

¹ Is. x. 8.   ² 2 Kgs xv. 19, 20.   ³ x. 1. xii. 11.
⁴ 1 Kgs xii. 30.   ⁵ Ib. xiii. 33, 34.
⁶ The E. V. translates the Kri, or marginal correction. The meaning is much the same, but the

reading of the text, although often more difficult, is almost always right. Here, רבי, "ten thousand things," as we say, "a thousand times," manifoldly, i. e. again and again.

Before
CHRIST
cir. 760.
u Jer. 7. 21.
Zech. 7. 6.
‖ Or, *In the
sacrifices of
mine offerings,
they,* &c.
x Jer. 14. 10, 12. c. 5. 6. & 9. 4. Amos 5. 22.

law, *but* they were counted as a strange thing.

13 u‖ They sacrifice flesh *for* the sacrifices of mine offerings, and eat *it;* x*but*

the LORD accepteth them not; y now will he remember their iniquity, and visit their sins: z they shall return to Egypt.

Before
CHRIST
cir. 760.

y ch. 9. 9.
Amos 8, 7.
z Deut. 28. 68.
ch. 9, 3, 6. &
11. 5.

tinually before their eyes, as if He were still writing. He had written to them since, in their histories, in the Psalms. His words were still sounding in their ears through the teaching of the prophets. God did not only give His law or revelation once for all, and so leave it. By His providence and by His ministers He continually renewed the knowledge of it, so that those who ignored it, should have no excuse. This ever-renewed agency of God He expresses by the word, *I write,* what in substance was long ago written. What God then wrote, were *the great things of His law* (as the converted Jews, on the day of Pentecost speak of *the great* or *wonderful things of God*[1]) or *the manifold things of His law,* as the Apostle speaks of *the manifold wisdom of God*[2], and says, that [3] *God at sundry times and in divers manners spake in time past unto the fathers by the prophets.*

They were counted as a strange thing by them. These *great,* or *manifold things of God's law,* which ought to have been continually before their eyes, in their mind and in their mouth[4], they, although God had written them for them, *counted as a strange thing,* a thing quite foreign and alien to them, with which they had no concern. Perhaps this was their excuse to themselves, that it was *foreign to them.* As Christians say now, that one is not to take God's law so precisely; that the Gospel is not so strict as the law; that men, before the grace of the Gospel, had to be stricter than *with* it; that *the liberty of the Gospel* is freedom, not from sin, but from duty; that such and such things belonged to the early Christians, while they were surrounded by heathen, or to the first times of the Gospel, or to the days when it was persecuted; that riches were dangerous, when people could scarcely have them, not now, when every one has them; that "vice lost half its evil, by losing all its grossness[5];" that the world was perilous, when it was the Christian's open foe, not now, when it would be friends with us, and have us friends with it; that, *love not the world* was a precept for times when the world hated us, not now, when it is all around us, and steals our hearts. So Jeroboam and Israel too doubtless said, that those prohibitions of idolatry

were necessary, when the heathen were still in the land, or while their forefathers were just fresh out of Egypt; that it was, after all, God, Who was worshiped under the calves; that state-policy required it; that Jeroboam was appointed by God, and must needs carry out that appointment, as he best could. With these or the like reasons, he must doubtless have excused himself, as though God's law were good, but *foreign to them.* God counts such excuses, not as a plea, but as a sin.

13. *They sacrifice flesh* for *the sacrifices of Mine offerings, and eat* it; but *the Lord accepteth them not.* As they rejected God's law, so God rejected their *sacrifices,* which were not offered according to His law. They, doubtless, thought much of their sacrifices; and this the prophet perhaps expresses by an intensive form[6]; *the sacrifices of My gifts, gifts,* as though they thought, that they were ever giving. God accounted such sacrifices, not being hallowed by the end for which He instituted them, as mere *flesh.* They *offered flesh* and *ate* it. Such was the beginning, and such the only end. *He* would *not accept them.* Nay, contrariwise, *now,* now while they were offering the sacrifices, God would shew in deed that He *remembered* the sins, for which they were intended to atone. God seems to man to forget his sins, when He forbears to punish them; to *remember* them, when He punishes.

They shall return to Egypt. God had commanded them to return no more to Egypt[7] of their own mind. But He had threatened that, on their disobedience, *the Lord would bring them back to Egypt by the way, whereof He spake unto them, Thou shalt see it no more again*[8]. Hosea also foretells to them, that they (i. e. many of them) should go to Egypt and perish there[9]. Thence also, as from Assyria, they were to be restored[10]. Most probably then, Hosea means to threaten an actual return to Egypt, as we are told, that some of the two tribes did go there for refuge, against the express command of God[11]. The main part of the ten tribes were taken to Assyria, yet as they were, even under Hosea, conspiring with Egypt[12], such as could, (it is likely) took refuge there. Else, as future

---

[1] τὰ μεγαλεῖα τοῦ θεοῦ Acts ii. 11.   [2] Eph. iii. 10.
[3] Heb. i. 1.   [4] Deut. vi. 7-9.
[5] Burke on the French Revolution.
[6] הַבְהִיבֵי is an intensive form from יָהַב *gave.* See

above on iv. 18. The word occurs here only, and was probably made by Hosea.
[7] Deut. xvii. 16.   [8] Ib xxviii. 68.   [9] ch. ix. 3, 6.
[10] ch. xii. 11.   [11] Jer. xlii. xliii.   [12] 2 Kgs xvii. 4.

Before
C H R I S T
cir. 760.

a Deut. 32. 18.
b Isai. 29. 23.
Eph. 2. 10.
c 1 Kgs. 12. 31.

d Jer. 17. 27.
Amos 2. 5.

14 ᵃ For Israel hath forgotten ᵇ his Maker, and ᶜ buildeth temples; and Judah hath multiplied fenced cities; but ᵈ I will send a fire upon his cities, and it shall devour the palaces thereof.

CHAPTER IX.

The distress and captivity of Israel for their sins and idolatry.

REJOICE not, O Israel, for joy, as *other* people; for thou ᵃhast gone a whoring from thy God, thou hast loved a ᵇreward ‖ upon every cornfloor.

Before
C H R I S T
cir. 760.

ᵃ ch. 4. 12. & 5.
4, 7.
ᵇ Jer. 44. 17.
ch. 2. 12.
‖ Or, *in, &c.*

deliverance, temporal or spiritual, is foretold under the image of the deliverance out of Egypt, so, contrariwise, the threat, *they shall return to Egypt,* may be, in figure, a cancelling of the covenant, whereby God had promised, that *His* people should not return : a threat of renewed bondage, *like* the Egyptian; an abandonment of them to the state, from which God once had freed them and had made them His people.

14. *For Israel hath forgotten his Maker.* God was his Maker, not only as the Creator of all things, but as the Author of his existence as a people, as He saith¹, *hath He not made thee, and established thee?*

And buildeth temples; as for the two calves, at Bethel and at Dan. Since God had commanded to build one temple only, that at Jerusalem, to *build* temples was in itself sin. The sin charged on Ephraim is idolatry; that of Judah is self-confidence²; whence Isaiah blames them, that they were busy in repairing the breaches of the city, and cutting off the supplies of water from the enemy; *but ye have not looked unto the Maker thereof, neither had respect unto Him, that fashioned it long ago*³. Jeremiah also says⁴, *that they shall impoverish* [or, *crush*] *the fenced cities, wherein thou trustedst, with the sword.*

But I will send a fire upon his cities. In the letter, the words relate to Judah; but in substance, the whole relates to both. Both had forgotten God; both had offended Him. In the doom of others, each sinner may read his own. Of the cities of Judah, Isaiah says, *your country is desolate, your cities are burned with fire*⁵ and *in the fourteenth year of Hezekiah,* (some twelve years probably after the death of Hosea) *Sennacherib came up against all the cities of Judah and took them*⁶; and of Jerusalem it is related, that Nebuchadnezzar⁷ *burnt the house of the Lord, and the king's house, and all the houses of Jerusalem, and every great man's house he burnt with fire.* Man set them on fire; God brought it to pass; and, in order to teach us that He doeth all things, giving all good, overruling all evil, saith that He was the doer of it.

IX. 1. *Rejoice not, O Israel, for joy, as* other *people.* lit. *rejoice not to exultation,* so as to bound and leap for joy⁸. The prophet seems to come across the people in the midst of their festivity and mirth, and arrests them by abruptly stopping it, telling them, that they had no cause for joy. Hosea witnessed days of Israel's prosperity under Jeroboam II; the land had peace under Menahem after the departure of Pul; Pekah was even strong, so as, in his alliance with Rezin, to be an object of terror to Judah⁹, until Tiglath-Pileser came against him. At some of these times, Israel seems to have given himself to exuberant mirth, whether at harvest-time, or on any other ground, enjoying the present, secure for the future. On this rejoicing Hosea breaks in with his stern, *rejoice not.* "¹⁰ *In His Presence is fulness of joy,*" true, solid, lasting joy." How then could Israel joy, *who had gone a whoring from his God?* Other nations might joy; for they had no imminent judgment to fear. Their sins had been sins of ignorance; none had sinned like Israel. They had not even ¹¹*changed their gods, which were no gods. If other people* did not thank God for His gifts, and thanked their idols, they had not been taught otherwise. Israel had been taught, and so his sin was sin against light. Whence God says by Amos¹², *You only have I known of all the families of the earth; therefore I will punish you for all your iniquities.* "¹³ It was ever the sin of Israel to wish to joy as other nations. So they said to Samuel, *make us a king to judge us, like all the nations.* And when Samuel told the people the word of God, they have rejected Me that I should not reign over them, they still said, Nay, but we will have a king over us, that we may be like all the nations*¹⁴. This was the joy of the nations, to have another king than God, and with this joy Israel wished to exult, when it asked for Saul as king; when it followed Jeroboam; when it *denied* Christ *before the presence of Pilate, saying, we have no king but Cæsar.* But the people who received the law, and professed the worship of God, might not exult as other people who had not

¹ Deut. xxxii. 6.   ² See Introd. p. 5.
³ ch. xxii. 11.   ⁴ ch. v. 17.   ⁵ ch. i. 7.
⁶ 2 Kgs xviii. 13.   ⁷ Ib. xxv. 8, 9.

⁸ as in Job iii. 22.   ⁹ Is. vii.   ¹⁰ Ps. xvi. 11.
¹¹ Jer. ii. 11.   ¹² iii. 2.   ¹³ Rup.
¹⁴ 1 Sam. viii. 5, 10, 7, 19, 20.

Before
CHRIST
cir. 760.

• ch. 2. 9, 12.
| Or, *winefat.*

2 °The floor and the
|| winepress shall not feed
them, and the new wine
shall fail in her.

3 They shall not dwell

in ᵈthe LORD's land; °but
Ephraim shall return to
Egypt, and ᶠthey shall
eat unclean *things* ᵍin
Assyria.

Before
CHRIST
cir. 760.
ᵈLev. 25. 23.
Jer. 2. 7. & 16.
18.
° ch. 8. 13, &
11. 5. Not in
Egypt itself,
but into another bondage as bad as that. ᶠEzek. 4.
13. Dan. 1. 8. ᵍ2 Kgs. 17. 6. ch. 11. 11.

the knowledge of God, that, like them, it
should, after forsaking God, be allowed to
enjoy temporal prosperity, like theirs. He
says, *rejoice not like the nations,* viz. for it is not
allowed thee. Why? *for thou hast gone a
whoring from thy God.* The punishment of
the adulteress, who departs by unfaithfulness
from her husband, is other than that of the
harlot, who had never plighted her faith,
nor had ever been bound by the bond of
marriage. Thou obtainedst God for thy
Husband, and didst forsake Him for another,
yea, for many others, in the desert, in
Samaria, even in Jerusalem, for the golden
calves, for Baal, and the other monstrous
gods, and lastly, when, denying Christ, thou
didst prefer Barabbas. *Rejoice not* then, with
the *joy* of the *nations;* for the curses of the
law, written against thee, allow thee not.
¹ *Cursed shalt thou be in the city, cursed in the
field; cursed thy basket and thy store; cursed
shall be the fruit of thy body, and the fruit of thy
land; the increase of thy kine and the flocks of
thy sheep; cursed thou in thy coming in, and
cursed thou in thy going out.* Other nations
enjoyed the fruit of their own labors; thou
tookest the labors of others as a hire, *to observe
His laws* ²."
Thou hast loved a reward [lit. *the hire* ³ of a
harlot] *on every corn-floor.* Israel had no
heart, except for temporal prosperity. This
he loved, wheresoever he found it; and so,
on every corn-floor, whereon the fruits of the
earth were gathered for the threshing, he
received it from his idols, as the *hire,* for
which he praised them " for the good things
which he had received from a better Giver."
" ⁴ Perverse love! Thou oughtest to *love* God
to use His rewards. *Thou* lovedst *the reward,*
despisedst God. So then thou *wentest a whoring from thy God,* because thou didst turn
away the love, wherewith thou oughtest to
love God, to love the hire: and this not
sparingly, nor any how, but *on every barn-
floor,* with avarice so boundless and so deep,
that all the barn-floors could not satisfy
thee." The first-fruits, and the free-will-
offering, they retained, turned them away
from the service of God, and offered them to
their idols.

¹ Deut. xxviii. 16–19.   ² Ps. cv. 45.
³ ii. 12. viii. 9. Ezek. xxi. 31, 34. Mic. i. 7.
⁴ Rup.   ⁵ vii. 13.
⁶ The fact that Greek or Latin poets use the same
language without any moral reference, is no reason

2. *The floor and winepress shall not feed them.*
God turneth away wholly from the adulterous people, and telleth others, how justly
they shall be dealt with for this. " Because
she loved My reward, and despised Myself,
the reward itself shall be taken away from
her." When the blessings of God have been
abused to sin, He, in mercy and judgment,
takes them away. He cut them off, in order
to shew that He alone, Who now withheld
them, had before given them. When they
thought themselves most secure, when the
corn was stored on the floor, and the grapes
were in the press, then God would deprive
them of them.
And the new wine shall fail in her, or *shall
fail her,* lit. *shall lie to her.* It may be, he
would say, that as Israel had lied to his God,
and had *spoken lies against Him* ⁵, so, in
requital, the fruits of the earth should disappoint her, and holding out hopes which never
came to pass, should, as it were, lie to her,
and in the bitterness of her disappointment,
represent to her her own failure to her
God. The prophet teaches through the workings of nature, and gives, as it were, a tongue
to them ⁶.
3. *They shall not dwell in the Lord's land.
The earth is the Lord's and the fulness thereof.*
Yet He had chosen the land of Canaan, there
to place His people; there, above others, to
work His miracles; there to reveal Himself;
there to send His Son to take our flesh. He
had put Israel in possession of it, to hold it
under Him on condition of obedience. Contrariwise, God had denounced to them again
and again; ⁷ *if thine heart turn away, so that
thou wilt not hear, but shalt be drawn away, ye
shall not prolong your days upon the land,
whither thou passest over Jordan to possess it.*
The fifth commandment, ⁸ *the first commandment with promise,* still implies the same condition, *that thy days may be long in the land
which the Lord thy God giveth thee.* God
makes the express reserve that the land is
His. *The land shall not be sold for ever; for
the land is Mine; for ye are strangers and
sojourners with Me* ⁹. It was then an aggravation of their sin, that they had sinned in
God's land. It was to sin in His special
why there should be none such in a prophet's.
They spoke the language of earthly disappointment; *he* declares the judgment of God.
⁷ Deut. xxx. 17, 18.   ⁸ Eph. v. 2.
⁹ Lev. xxv. 23.

Before
CHRIST
cir. 760.

h ch. 3. 4.
i Jer. 6. 20.
ch. 8. 13.
k Deut. 26. 14.

4 [h] They shall not offer wine *offerings* to the LORD, [i] neither shall they be pleasing unto him: [k] their sacri-

fices *shall be* unto them as the bread of mourners; all that eat thereof shall be polluted: for their bread

Before
CHRIST
cir. 760.

Presence. To offer its first-fruits to idols, was to disown God as its Lord, and to own His adversary. In removing them, then, from His land, God removed them from occasions of sin.

But Ephraim shall return to Egypt. He had broken the covenant, whereon God had promised, that they should not return there [1]. They had recourse to Egypt against the Will of God. Against their own will, they should be sent back there, in banishment and distress, as of old, and in separation from their God.

And they shall eat unclean things in Assyria. So in Ezekiel, [2] *The children of Israel shall eat their defiled bread among the Gentiles, whither I will drive them.* Not to eat things common or unclean was one of the marks which God had given them, whereby he distinguished them as His people. While God owned them as His people, He would protect them against such necessity. The histories of Daniel, of Eleazar and the Maccabees [3], shew how sorely pious Jews felt the compulsion to eat things unclean. Yet this doubtless Israel had done in his own land, if not in other ways, at least in eating things offered to idols. Now then, through necessity or constraint, they were to be forced, for their sustenance, to eat things unclean, such as were, to them, all things killed with the blood in them, i. e. as almost all things are killed now. They who had wilfully transgressed God's law, should now be forced to live in the habitual breach of that law, in a matter which placed them on a level with the heathen. People, who have no scruple about breaking God's moral law, feel keenly the removal of any distinction, which places them above others. They had been as heathen; they should be in the condition of heathen.

4. *They shall not offer wine-offerings to the Lord.* The *wine* or *drink-offering* was annexed to all their burnt-offerings, and so to all their public sacrifices. The burnt-offering (and with it the meal and the wine-offering,) was *the* daily morning and evening sacrifice [4], and the sacrifice of the Sabbath [5]. It was offered, together with the sin-offering, on the first of the month, the Passover, the feast of the first-fruits, of trumpets, of tabernacles, and the Day of Atonement, besides

the special sacrifices of that day [6]. It entered also into private life [7]. The drink-offering accompanied also the peace-offering [8]. As the burnt-offering, on which the offerer laid his hand [9], and which was wholly consumed by the sacred fire which at first fell from heaven, expressed the entire self-devotion of the offerer, that he owed himself wholly to his God; and as the peace-offering was the expression of thankfulness, which was at peace with God; so the outpouring of the wine betokened the joy, which accompanies that entire self-oblation, that thankfulness in self-oblation of a soul accepted by God. In denying, then, that Israel should *offer wine-offerings,* the prophet says, that all the joy of their service of God, nay all their public service should cease. As he had before said, that they should be *for many days without sacrifice* [10], so now, he says, in fact, that they should live without the prescribed means of pleading to God the Atonement to come. Whence he adds,

Neither shall they be pleasing to the Lord; for they should no longer have the means prescribed for reconciliation with God [11], Such is the state of Israel now. God appointed one way of reconciliation with Himself, the Sacrifice of Christ. Sacrifice pictured this, and pleaded it to Him, from the fall until Christ Himself *appeared, once in the end of the world, to put away sin by the sacrifice of Himself* [12]. Soon after, when time had been given to the Jews to learn to acknowledge Him, all bloody sacrifices ceased. Since then the Jews have lived without that means of reconciliation, which God appointed. It availed, not in itself, but as being appointed by God to foreshadow and plead that one sacrifice. So He Who, by our poverty and void, awakens in us the longing for Himself, would through the anomalous condition, to which He has, by the orderings of His Divine Providence, brought His former people, call forth in them that sense of need, which would bring them to Christ. In their half-obedience, they remain under the ceremonial law which He gave them, although He called them, and still calls them, to exchange the shadow for the substance in Christ. But in that they cannot fulfill the requirements of the law, even in its outward form, the law, which

---

[1] See ab. on viii. 13.   [2] iv. 13.
[3] Dan. i. 8. 2 Macc. vi. vii.
[4] Ex. xxix. 38–41. Nu. xxviii. 3–8.   [5] Ib. 9.
[6] Ib. 11, 15, 16, 19, 22, 26, 7, 30. xxix. 11, 1. 2, 5, 7, 8,
12–38.   [7] Lev. i. Nu. xv. 3, 10.
[8] Nu. xv. 8, 10.   [9] Lev. i. 4.   [10] iii. 4.

[11] The word עֲרַב *shall be pleasing* is most naturally understood of the persons of whom it had just been said, *they shall not offer,* not of the *wine:* for this is the object, not the subject; and is in the singular, not the plural.
[12] Heb. ix. 26.

Before
CHRIST
cir. 760.
[1] for their soul shall not
come into the house of the
LORD.

[1] Lev. 17. 11.

5 What will ye do in
[m] ch. 2. 11. [m] the solemn day, and in
the day of the feast of the
LORD?

6 For, lo, they are gone

because of † destruction :   Before
CHRIST
cir. 760.
[n] Egypt shall gather them
up, Memphis shall bury   † Heb. spoil.
[n] ch. 7. 16.
them : || † the pleasant   ver. 3.
|| Or, their silver
places for their silver, [o] net-   shall be desired,
the nettle, &c.
tles shall possess them :   † Heb. the desire.
thorns *shall be* in their   [o] Is. 5, 6. & 32.
13. & 34. 13.
ch. 10. 8.
tabernacles.

---

they acknowledge, bears witness to them,
that they are not living according to the
mind of God.

Their sacrifices shall be *unto them as the
bread of mourners.* He had said that they
should not sacrifice to God, when no longer
in the Lord's land. He adds that, if they
should attempt it, their sacrifices, so far from
being a means of acceptance, should be defiled,
and a source of defilement to them. *All*
which was *in* the same *tent* or house with a
dead body, was *unclean for seven days* [1]. The
bread, which they ate then, was defiled. If
*one unclean by a dead body touched bread or
pottage or any meat, it* was *unclean* [2]. In offering the tithes, a man was commanded to declare, *I have not eaten of it in my mourning* [3].
So would God impress on the soul the
awfulness of death, and man's sinfulness, of
which death is the punishment. He does
not say, that they would offer sacrifices, but
that their sacrifices, if offered as God did not
command, would defile, not atone. It is in
human nature, to neglect to serve God, when
He wills it, and then to attempt to serve
Him when He forbids it. Thus Israel,
affrighted by the report of the spies [4], would
not go up to the promised land, when God
commanded it. When God had sentenced
them, not to go up, but to die in the wilderness, *then* they attempted it. Sacrifice,
according to God's law, could only be offered
in the promised land. In their captivity,
then, it would be a fresh sin.

For their bread for their soul, or *is for their
soul,* i. e. *for themselves ;* it is for whatever use
they can make of it for this life's needs,
to support life. Nothing of it would be
admitted *into the house of the Lord,* as offered
to Him or accepted by Him.

5. *What will ye do in the solemn day?* Man
is content to remain far from God, so that
God do not shew him, that He has withdrawn Himself from him. Man would
fain have the power of drawing near to
God in time of calamity, or when he himself likes. He would fain have God
at his command, as it were, not be at

the command of God. God cuts off this
hope altogether. He singles out the great
festivals, which commemorated His great
doings for His people, as though they had
no more share in those mercies. The more
solemn the day, the more total man's exclusion, the more manifest God's withdrawal.
To one shut out from His service, the days
of deepest religious joy became the days of
deepest sorrow. Mirth is turned into heaviness. To be deprived of the ordinary daily
sacrifice was a source of continual sorrow ;
how much more, *in the days of their gladness* [5],
in which they were bidden to rejoice before
the Lord, and "in which they seemed to
have a nearer and more familiar access to
God." True, that having separated themselves from the Temple, they had no right to
celebrate these feasts, which were to be held
in the place *which God had chosen to place His
name there.* Man, however, clings to the
shadow of God's service, when he has parted
with the substance. And so God foretold
them before [6], that He would *make all their
mirth to cease.*

6. *For lo, they are gone because of destruction.*
They had fled, for fear of destruction, to
destruction. For fear of the destruction
from Assyria, they were fled away and gone
to Egypt, hoping, doubtless, to find there
some temporary refuge, until the Assyrian
invasion should have swept by. But, as
befalls those who flee from God, they fell
into more certain destruction.

*Egypt shall gather them up, Memphis shall
bury them.* They had fled singly, in making
their escape from the Assyrian. Egypt shall
receive them, and shall gather them together,
but only to one common burial, so that none
should escape. So Jeremiah says [7], *They shall
not be gathered nor buried ;* and Ezekiel [8], *Thou
shalt not be brought together, nor gathered.*
Memphis is the Greek name for the Egyptian
Mamphta, whence the Hebrew *Moph* [9]; or *Man-
uph,* whence the Hebrew *Noph* [10]. It was at
this time the capital of Egypt, whose idols
God threatens [11]. Its name, "the dwelling of
Phta," the Greek Vulcan, marked it, as a

[1] Nu. xix. 14.   [2] Hagg. ii. 12,13.
[3] Deut. xxvi. 15.   [4] Nu. xiv.
[5] Num. x. 10.   [6] ch. ii. 11.

[7] viii. 2.   [8] xxix. 5.   [9] here.
[10] Is. xix. 13. Jer. ii. 16. xliv. 1. xlvi. 14. Ezek. xxx.
13 sqq.   [11] Ezek. l. c.

7 The days of visitation
are come, the days of recom-
pence are come; Israel
shall know *it*: the prophet

is a fool, [p] the † spiritual
man *is* mad, for the multitude of thine iniquity, and
the great hatred.

Before
CHRIST
cir. 760.

[p] Ezek. 13. 3,
&c.
Mic. 2. 11.
Zeph. 3. 4.

† Heb. *man of the spirit*.

---

seat of idolatry; and in it was the celebrated court of Apis[1], the original of Jeroboam's calf. There in the home of the idol for whom they forsook their God, they should be gathered to burial. It was reputed to be the burial-place of Osiris, and hence was a favorite burial-place of the Egyptians. It once embraced a circuit of almost 19 miles[2], with magnificent buildings; it declined after the building of Alexandria; its very ruins gradually perished, after Cairo rose in its neighborhood.

The pleasant places *for their silver, nettles shall possess them.* The E. M. gives the same sense in different words; *their silver shall be desired;* (as Obadiah saith[3], *his hidden* treasures *were searched out) nettles shall inherit them.* In either way, it is a picture of utter desolation. The long rank grass or the nettle, waving amid man's habitations, looks all the sadder, as betokening that man once was there, and is gone. The desolate house looks like the grave of the departed. According to either rendering, the silver which they once had treasured, was gone. As they had *inherited* and *driven* out (the word is one) the nations, whose land God had given them, so now nettles and thorns should *inherit them.* These should be the only tenants of their treasure-houses and their dwellings.

7. *The days of visitation are come.* The false prophets had continually hood-winked the people, promising them that those days would never come. *They had put far away the evil day*[4]. Now it was not at hand only. In God's purpose, those *days* were *come,* irresistible, inevitable, inextricable; days in which God would visit, what in His long-suffering, He seemed to overlook, and would *recompense* each *according to his works.*

Israel shall know it. Israel would not know by believing it; now it should *know,* by feeling it.

The prophet is *a fool, the spiritual man* is *mad.* The true Prophet gives to the false the title which they claimed for themselves, *the prophet* and *the man of the spirit.* Only the event shewed what spirit was in them, not the spirit of God but a lying spirit. The men of the world called the true prophets, *mad,* lit. maddened, *driven mad*[5], as Festus thought

of S. Paul[6]; *Thou art beside thyself; much learning doth make thee mad.* Jehu's captains called by the same name the young prophet whom Elisha sent to anoint him. *Wherefore came this mad fellow unto thee*[7]? Shemaiah, the false prophet, who deposed God's priest, set false priests to *be officers in the house of the Lord,* to have an oversight as to *every man who is mad and maketh himself a prophet,* calling Jeremiah both a false prophet and a *madman*[8]. The event was the test. Of our Lord Himself, the Jews blasphemed, *He hath a devil and is mad*[9]. And long afterward, "madness," "phrensy" were among the names which the heathen gave to the faith in Christ[10]. As S. Paul says, that *Christ crucified* was *to the Greeks* and to *them that perish, foolishness,* and that *the things of the Spirit of God, are foolishness to the natural man, neither can he know* them, *because they are spiritually discerned*[11]. The man of the world and the Christian judge of the same things by clean contrary rules, use them for quite contrary ends. The slave of pleasure counts him mad, who foregoes it; the wealthy trader counts him mad, who gives away profusely. In these days, profusion for the love of Christ has been counted a ground for depriving a man of the care of his property. One or the other *is* mad. And worldlings must count the Christian mad; else they must own themselves to be so most fearfully. In the Day of Judgment, Wisdom says[12], *They, repenting and groaning for anguish of spirit, shall say within themselves, This was he whom we had sometimes in derision and a proverb of reproach. We fools counted his life madness, and his end to be without honor. How is he numbered among the children of God, and his lot is among the saints!*

For the multitude of thine iniquity and the great hatred. The words stand at the close of the verse, as the reason of all which had gone before. Their *manifold iniquity* and their *great hatred* of God were the ground why the *days of visitation* and *recompense* should *come.* They were the ground also, why God allowed such prophets to delude them. The words, *the great hatred,* stand quite undefined, so that they may signify alike the hatred of Ephraim against God and good men and His true prophets, or God's hatred of them. Yet it,

---

[1] Herod. ii. 153.   [2] Diod. Sic. i. 51.
[3] ver. 6.   [4] Am. vi. 3.
[5] The form מְשֻׁגָּע in passive. It is used of one driven to distraction through distress, (Deut. xxviii. 34,) and of loss of reason, 1 Sam. xxi. 16.

[6] Acts xxvi. 24.   [7] 2 Kings ix. 11.
[8] Jer. xxix. 25, 6. The word is the same.
[9] S. John x. 20.
[10] See Tertul. Apol. 1. p. 4. and on de Test. An. p. 136. not. s. t. Oxf. Tr.
[11] 1 Cor. i. 18, 23. ii. 14.   [12] Wisd. v. 3–6.

Before
CHRIST
cir. 760.

q Jer. 6. 17. &
31. 6.
Ezek. 3. 17. & 33. 7.

8 The ^q watchman of
Ephraim *was* with my God:
but the prophet *is* a snare

of a fowler in all his ways
and hatred || in the house
of his God.

Before
CHRIST
cir. 760.

|| Or, *against*.

most likely, means, *their* great hatred, since
of them the Prophet uses it again in the next
verse. The sinner first neglects God; then,
as the will of God is brought before him, he
wilfully disobeys Him; then, when, he finds
God's Will irreconcilably at variance with
his own, or when God chastens him, he hates
Him, and (the Prophet speaks out plainly)
hates Him *greatly*.

8. *The watchman of Ephraim* was *with my
God.* These words may well contrast the
office of the true prophet with the false. For
Israel had had many true prophets, and such
was Hosea himself now. The true prophet
was at all times *with God.* He was *with God,*
as holpen by God, *watching* or looking out and
on into the future by the help of God. He
was *with God,* as walking with God in a constant sense of His Presence, and in continual
communion with Him. He was *with God,* as
associated by God with Himself, in teaching,
warning, correcting, exhorting His people,
as the Apostle says [1], *we then as workers together*
with *Him.*

It might also be rendered in nearly the
same sense, *Ephraim was a watchman with my
God,* and this. is more according to the
Hebrew words [2]. As though the whole people of Israel had an office from God, "[3] and
God addressed it as a whole, 'I made thee, as
it were, a watchman and prophet of God to
the neighboring nations, that through My
Providence concerning thee, and thy living
according to the law, they too might receive
the knowledge of Me. But thou hast acted
altogether contrary to this, for thou hast
become a snare to them.' "

Yet perhaps, if so construed, it would
rather mean, " Ephraim is a watchman,
beside my God," as it is said, ⁴ *There is none
upon earth, that I desire with Thee,* i. e. beside
Thee. In God the Psalmist had all, and
desired to have nothing *with,* i. e. beside God.
Ephraim was not content with God's revelations, but would himself be *a seer, an espier*
of future events, the Prophet says with indignation, *together with my God.* God, in fact,
sufficed Ephraim **not.** Ahab hated God's
prophet, because *he did not speak good concerning him but evil*[5]. And so the kings of Israel
had court-prophets of their own, an establishment, as it would seem, of four hundred and
fifty prophets of Baal, and four hundred
prophets of Ashtaroth[6], which was filled up

again by new impostors[7], when after the
miracle of Mount Carmel, Elijah, according
to the law[8], put to death the prophets of
Baal. These false prophets, as well as those
of Judah in her evil days, flattered the kings
who supported them, misled them, encouraged them in disbelieving the threatenings
of God, and so led to their destruction. By
these means, the bad priests maintained their
hold over the people. They were the Anti-
Christs of the Old Testament, disputing the
authority of God, in Whose Name they
prophesied. Ephraim encouraged their sins,
as God says of Judah by Jeremiah, *My people
love to have it so*[9]. It willed to be deceived,
and was so.

" On searching diligently ancient histories,"
says S. Jerome, " I could not find that any
divided the Church, or seduced people from
the house of the Lord, except those who
have been set by God as priests and prophets,
i. e. watchmen. These then are turned into
a snare, setting a stumbling-block everywhere, so that whosoever entereth on their
ways, falls, and cannot stand in Christ, and
is led away by various errors and crooked
paths to a precipice." "No one," says
another great father[10], "doth wider injury
than one who acteth perversely, while he
hath a name or an order of holiness." "God
endureth no greater prejudice from any than
from priests, when He seeth those whom He
has set for the correction of others, give
from themselves examples of perverseness,
when *we* sin, who ought to restrain sin.—
What shall become of the flock, when the
pastors become wolves?"

The false *prophet* is *the snare of a fowler in*
(lit. *upon*) *all his ways;* i. e. whatever Ephraim
would do, wherever the people, as a whole or
any of them, would go, there the false
prophet beset them, endeavoring to make each
and everything a means of holding them
back from their God. This they did, *being
hatred in the house of his God.* As one says[11].
I am (all) *prayer,* because he was so given up
to prayer that he seemed turned into prayer;
his whole soul was concentrated in prayer;
so of these it is said, *they were hatred.* They
hated so intensely, that their whole soul was
turned into hatred; they were as we say,
hatred personified; hatred was embodied in
them, and they ensouled with hate. They
were also the source of hatred against God

[1] 2 Cor. vi. 1.
[2] צֹפֶה not being in construction with Ephraim.
[3] Theod.   ⁴ Ps. lxxiii. 25.
[5] 1 Kgs. xxii. 8, 18.   ⁶ Ib. xviii. 19.

[7] 2 Kgs. iii. 13. x. 19.   ⁸ Deut. xiii. 5. xvii. 5.
[9] v. 31.   [10] S. Greg. Past. i. 2; in Evang. Hom.
xvii. 14.
[11] Ps. cix. 4.

Before
CHRIST
cir. 760.

r Isai. 31. 6.
ch. 10. 9.
s Judg. 19. 22.
t ch. 8. 13.

9 ʳThey have deeply corrupted *themselves,* as in the days of ˢGibeah: ᵗthere-*fore* he will remember their iniquity, he will visit their sins.

10 I found Israel like grapes in the wilderness; I saw your fathers as ᵘthe first-ripe in the fig tree ˣat her first time: *but* they went to ʸBaal-peor, and ᶻseparated themselves ᵃun-to *that* shame; ᵇand *their* abominations were accord-ing as they loved.

Before
CHRIST
cir. 760.

u Isai. 28. 4.
Mic. 7. 1.
x See chap.
2. 15.
y Num. 25. 3.
Ps. 106. 28.
z ch. 4. 14.
a Jer. 11. 13.
See Judg. 6.
32.
b Ps. 81. 12.
Ezek. 20. 8.
Amos 4. 5.

and man. And this each false prophet was *in the house of his God!* for God was still his God, although not owned by him as God. God is the sinner's God to avenge, if he will not allow Him to be his God, to convert and pardon.

9. *They have deeply corrupted* themselves; lit. *they have gone deep, they are corrupted.* They have deeply immersed themselves in wicked-ness; have gone to the greatest depth they could, in it; they are sunk in it, so that they could hardly be extricated from it; and this, of their own deliberate intent; they contrived it deeply, hiding themselves, as they hoped, from God.

As in the days of Gibeah, when Benjamin espoused the cause of *the children of Belial* who had wrought such horrible brutishness in Gibeah towards the concubine of the Levite. This they maintained with such obstinacy, that, through God's judgment, the whole tribe perished, except six hundred men. Deeply they must have already cor-rupted themselves, who supported such guilt. Such corruption and such obstinacy was their's still.

Therefore he will remember their iniquity. God seemed for a time, as if He overlooked the guilt of Benjamin in the days of Gibeah; for at first He allowed them to be even vic-torious over Israel, yet in the end, they were punished, almost to extermination, and Gibeah was destroyed. So now, although He bore long with Ephraim, He would, in the end shew that He remembered all by visit-ing all.

10. *I found Israel like grapes in the wilder-ness.* God is not said to find anything, as though He had lost it, or knew not where it was, or came suddenly upon it, not expecting it. *They* were lost, as relates to Him, when they were found by Him. As our Lord says of the returned prodigal, *This my son was lost and is found* [1]. He *found* them and made them pleasant in His own sight, " as grapes which a man finds unexpectedly, in *a great terrible*

wilderness of fiery serpents and drought [2]," where commonly nothing pleasant or refreshing grows; or *as the first ripe in the fig-tree at her fresh time,* whose sweetness passed into a proverb, both from its own freshness and from the long abstinence [3]. God gave to Israel both richness and pleasantness in His own sight; but Israel, from the first, cor-rupted God's good gifts in them. This gen-eration only did as their fathers. So S. Stephen, setting forth to the Jews how their fathers had rebelled against Moses, and per-secuted the prophets, sums up; *as your fathers did, so do ye* [4]. Each generation was filling up the measure of their fathers, until it was full; as the whole world is doing now [5].

But *they went to Baal-Peor. They,* the word is emphatic; these same persons to whom God shewed such love, to whom He gave such gifts, *went.* They left God Who called them, and *went* to the idol, which could not call them. Baal-Peor, as his name probably implies, was "the filthiest and foulest of the heathen gods." It appears from the history of the daughters of Midian, that his worship consisted in deeds of shame [6].

And separated themselves unto that *shame,* i. e. to Baal-Peor, whose name of *Baal, Lord,* he turns into *Bosheth, shame* [7]. Holy Scrip-ture gives disgraceful names to the idols, (as *abominations, nothings, dungy things, vanities, uncleanness* [8],) in order to make men ashamed of them. *To this shame they separated them-selves* from God, in ordér to unite themselves with it. The Nazarite *separated himself from* certain earthly enjoyments, and consecrated himself, for a time or altogether, to *God* [9]; these *separated themselves from* God, and united, devoted, consecrated themselves *to shame.* " They made themselves, as it were," Nazarites to shame." Shame was the object of their worship and their God, *and* their *abominations were according as they loved,* i. e. they had as many *abominations* or abominable idols, *as* they had *loves.* They multiplied

---

[1] S. Luke xv. 32. [2] Deut. viii. 15.
[3] See Is. xxviii. 4. [4] Acts vii. 51. [5] Rev. xiv. 15.
[6] Num. xxv. [7] as in 2 Sam. xi. 21.

[8] שׁקוצים, אלילים, גלולים, הבלים all common names of idols; (also, אָוֶן,) נִדָּה 2 Chr. xxix. 5.
[9] הִנָּזֵר לְ Num. vi. 2, 5, 6. מִן Ib. 3. See on Am. ii. 11.

Before
CHRIST
cir. 760.

11 *As for* Ephraim, their glory shall fly away like a bird, from the birth, and

from the womb, and from the conception.

Before
CHRIST
cir. 760.

12 ᶜ Though they bring

ᶜ Job 27. 14.

abominations, *after their heart's desire;* their abominations were manifold, because their passions were so; and their love being corrupted, they loved nothing but abominations. Yet it seems simpler and truer to render it, *and they became abominations, like their loves;* as the Psalmist says, [1] *They that make them are like unto them.* "[2] The object which the will desires and loves, transfuses its own goodness or badness into it." Man first makes his god like his own corrupt self, or to some corruption in himself, and then, worshiping this ideal of his own, he becomes the more corrupt through copying that corruption. He makes his god *in his* own *image and likeness,* the essence and concentration of his own bad passions, and then conforms himself to the likeness, not of God, but of what was most evil in himself. Thus the Heathen made gods of lust, cruelty, thirst for war; and the worship of corrupt gods reacted on themselves. They forgot that they were *the work of their own hands,* the conception of their own minds, and professed to "do gladly [3]" "what so great gods" had done. And more widely, says a father [4], "what a man's love is, that he is. Lovest thou earth? thou art earth. Lovest thou God? What shall I say? thou shalt be god." "[5] Naught else maketh good or evil actions, save good or evil affections." Love has a transforming power over the soul, which the intellect has not. "He who serveth an abomination is himself an abomination [6]," is a thoughtful Jewish saying. "The intellect brings home to the soul the knowledge on which it worketh, impresses it on itself, incorporates it with itself. Love is an impulse whereby he who loves is borne forth towards that which he loves, is united with it, and is transformed into it." Thus in explaining the words, *Let Him kiss me with the kisses of* His *Mouth* [7], the fathers say, "[8] Then the Word of God kisseth us, when He enlighteneth our heart with the Spirit of Divine knowledge, and the soul cleaveth to Him and His Spirit is transfused into him."

11. As for *Ephraim, their glory shall fly away, like a bird.* Ephraim had parted with God, his true Glory. In turn, God would quickly take from him all created glory, all which he counted glory, or in which he gloried. When man parts with the substance, his true honor, God takes away the shadow, lest he should content himself therewith,

and not see his shame, and, boasting himself to be something, abide in his nothingness and poverty and shame to which he had reduced himself. *Fruitfulness,* and consequent strength, had been God's especial promise to Ephraim. His name, Ephraim, contained in itself the promise of his future fruitfulness [9]. With this Jacob had blessed him. He was to be greater than Manasseh, his elder brother, *and his seed shall become a multitude of nations* [10]. Moses had assigned to him *tens of thousands* [11], while to Manasseh he had promised *thousands* only. On this blessing Ephraim had presumed, and had made it to feed his pride; so now God, in his justice and mercy, would withdraw it from him. It should *make* itself *wings, and fly away* [12], with the swiftness of a bird, and *like a bird,* not to return again to the place, whence it has been scared.

From the birth. Their children were to perish at every stage in which they received life. This sentence pursued them back to the very beginning of life. First, when their parents should have joy in *their birth,* they were to come into the world only to go out of it; then, their mother's womb was to be itself their grave; then, stricken with barrenness, the womb itself was to refuse to conceive them.

"[13] The glory of Ephraim passes away, from the birth, the womb, the conception, when the mind which before was, for glory, half-deified, receives, through the just judgment of God, ill report for good report, misery for glory, hatred for favor, contempt for reverence, loss for gain, famine for abundance. Act is the *birth;* intention the *womb;* thought the *conception. The glory of Ephraim* then *flies away from the birth, the womb, the conception,* when, in those who before did outwardly live nobly, and gloried in themselves for the outward propriety of their life, the acts are disgraced, the intention corrupted, the thoughts defiled."

12. *Though they bring up children.* God had threatened to deprive them of children, in every stage before or at their birth. Now, beyond this, he tells them, as to those who should escape this sentence, he would bereave them of them, or make them childless.

That there shall not be a man left; lit. *from man.* The brief word may be filled up, as the E. V. has done, (by an idiom not infrequent) 1) "*from there being a man;*" or

---

[1] Ps. cxv. 8.   [2] Lap. from Aq.   [3] Ter. Eun.
[4] S. Aug. in Ep. S. Joh. Tr. ii.
[5] S. Aug. Ep. 155. ad Macedon. § 13. amores, mores; amours, mœurs.

[6] Kimchi, MS. in Poc.   [7] Cant. i. 2.
[8] S. Ambr. de Isaac. c. 3. Lap.   [9] Gen. xli. 52.
[10] Ib. xlviii. 19.   [11] Deut. xxxiii. 17.
[12] Prov. xxiii. 5.   [13] Julian. Tolet. in Nah. Lap.

Before
CHRIST
cir. 760.
d Deut. 28.41,
62.
e Deut. 31. 17.
2 Kgs. 17. 18.
ch. 5. 6.
f See 1 Sam. 28.
15, 16.

up their children, yet ^d will
I bereave them, *that there
shall* not *be* a man *left:*
yea, ^e woe also to them when
I ^f depart from them!

13 Ephraim, ^g as I saw
Tyrus, *is* planted in a
pleasant place: ^h but Ephraim shall bring forth his
children to the murderer.

Before
CHRIST
cir. 760.

g See Ezek. 26,
& 27, & 28.
h ver. 16.
ch. 13. 16.

2) *from* among *men;* as Samuel said to
Agag[1], *as thy sword has made women childless,
so shall thy mother be childless among women;*
or 3) *from* becoming *men,* i. e. from reaching
man's estate. The Prophet, in any case,
does not mean absolute excision, for he says,
they shall be wanderers among the nations, and
had foretold, that they should abide, as they
now are, and be converted in the end. But
since their pride was in their numbers, he
says, that these should be reduced in every
stage from conception to ripened manhood.
So God had forewarned Israel in the law[2],
*If thou wilt not observe to do all the words of
this law,—ye shall be left few in number, whereas
ye were as the stars of heaven for multitude.* A
sentence, felt the more by Ephraim, as being
the head of the most powerful division of the
people, and himself the largest portion of it.
Yea, [lit. *for*] *woe also unto them, when I
depart from them.* This is, at once, the ground
and the completion of their misery, its
beginning and its end. God's departure was
the source of all evil to them; as He foretold them[3], *I will forsake them, and I will hide
My face from them, and they shall be devoured,
and many evils and troubles shall befall them, so
that they shall say in that day, Are not these
evils come upon us, because our God is not among
us?* But His departure was itself above all.
For the Prophet says *also; for woe also unto
them.* This was the last step in the scale of
misery. Beyond the loss of the children,
whom they hoped or longed for, beyond the
loss of their present might, and all their hope
to come, there is a further undefined, unlimited, evil, *woe to them also,* when God should
withdraw, not His care and Providence only,
but Himself also from them; *when I depart
from them.* They had *departed* and turned
away, from or *against* God[4]. It had been
their characteristic[5]. Now God Himself
would requite them, as they had requited
Him. He would depart from them. This
is the last state of privation, which forms the
"punishment of loss" in Hell. When the
soul has lost God, what has it?

13. *Ephraim, as I saw Tyrus, is planted in a
pleasant place;* or (better) *as I saw* (her)

towards Tyre, or *as I saw as to Tyre.* Ephraim
stretched out, in her dependent tribes, *towards*
or *to* Tyre itself. Like to Tyrus she was, "in
her riches, her glory, her pleasantness, her
strength, her pride," and in the end,
her fall. The picture is that of a fair
tree, not chance-sown, but *planted* carefully by hand in a pleasant place[6]. Beauty
and strength were blended in her. On
the tribe of Joseph especially, Moses had
pronounced the blessing[7]; *Blessed of the Lord
be his land, for the precious things of heaven, for
the dew, and for the deep which coucheth beneath,
and for the precious fruits brought forth by the
sun, and for the precious things put forth by the
moons (i. e. month by month) and for the chief
things of the ancient mountains, and for the
precious things of the lasting hills and for the
precious things of the earth and the fulness thereof,
and for the good pleasure of Him who dwelt in
the bush.* Beautiful are the mountains of
Ephraim, and the rich valleys or plains which
break them. And chief in beauty and in
strength was the valley, whose central hill its
capital, Samaria, crowned; *the crown of pride*
to the *drunkards of Ephraim, whose glorious
beauty is a fading flower which is on the head of
the fat valleys of them that are overcome with
wine*[8]. The blessing of Moses pointed perhaps to the time when Shiloh was the tabernacle of Him, Who once dwelt and revealed
Himself in the Bush. Now that it had exchanged its God for the calves, the blessings
which it still retained, stood but in the more
awful contrast with its future.

*But Ephraim shall bring forth his children to
the murderer;* lit. *and Ephraim is to bring forth
&c.* i. e. proud though her wealth, and high
her state, pleasantly situated and firmly
rooted, one thing lay before her, one destiny,
she *was to bring forth children* only *for the
murderer.* Childlessness in God's Providence
is the appropriate and frequent punishment
of sins of the flesh. Pride too brought Pen-
innah, the adversary of Hannah, low, even as
to that which was the ground of her pride,
her children. [9] *The barren hath born seven, and
she that hath many children is waxed feeble.* So as
to the soul, "pride deprives of grace."

[1] 1 Sam. xv. 33. מנשים, as here מאדם. add Prov.
xxx. 14. [2] Deut. xxviii. 58, 62. [3] Ib. xxxi. 17.
[4] See on vii. 13.
[5] Hos. iv. 16. The word in each place, is virtually
the same, סור, written here שור, and סיר.
[6] שתל is always used of *planting* with choice of

situation. See Ezek. xvii. 8, 22, 23. xix. 10 and in a
bad soil, of set purpose, Ib. 13. See Jer. xvii. 8. Ps. i.
3. and in a figure, *They who are planted in the house
of the Lord,* Ps. xcii. 14.
[7] Deut. xxxiii. 13–16. [8] Is. xxviii. 1.
[9] 1 Sam. ii. 5.

Before
CHRIST
cir. 760.

1 Luke 23. 29.
† Heb. that
casteth the
fruit.

k ch. 4. 15.
& 12. 11.
1 ch. 1. 6.

14 Give them, O LORD:
what wilt thou give? give
them[1] a † miscarrying
womb and dry breasts.

15 All their wickedness
[k] *is* in Gilgal: for there I
hated them: [1] for the wick-

edness of their doings I will
drive them out of mine
house, I will love them no
more: [m] all their princes
are revolters.

16 Ephraim is smitten,
their root is dried up, they

Before
CHRIST
cir. 760.

m Is. 1. 23.

---

14. *Give them a miscarrying womb.* The
Prophet prays for Israel, and debates with
himself what he can ask for, amid this their
determined wickedness, and God's judgments.
Since *Ephraim was to bring forth children to the
murderer,* then it was mercy to ask for them,
that they might have no children. Since such
are the evils which await their children,
grant them, O Lord, as a blessing, the sorrows
of barrenness. What God had before pronounced as a punishment, should, as compared
to other evils, be a mercy, and an object of
prayer. So our Lord pronounces as to the
destruction of Jerusalem[1]. *Behold the days
are coming, in which they shall say, Blessed are the
barren, and the wombs that never bare, and the paps
that never gave suck.* "O unhappy fruitfulness
and fruitful unhappiness, compared with
which, barrenness, which among them was
accounted a curse, became blessedness."

15. *All their wickedness is in Gilgal.* *Gilgal,*
having been the scene of so many of God's
mercies, had been, on that very ground,
chosen as a popular scene for idol-worship[2].
And doubtless, Ephraim still deceived himself, and thought that his idolatrous worship,
in a place once so hallowed, would still be
acceptable with God. "There, where God of
old was propitious, He would be so still, and
whatever they did, should, even for the
place's sake, be accepted; the hallowed place
would necessarily sanctify it." In answer to
such thoughts, God says, *all their wickedness,*
the very chief and sum, the head from which
the rest flowed, their desertion of God Himself, whatever they hoped or imagined, *all
their wickedness is* there.

For there I hated them. "*There,* in the very
place where heretofore I shewed such great
tokens of love to, and by My gracious presence with, them, *even there I have hated them*
and now hate them." "He saith not, there
was I angry, or displeased with them, but in
a word betokening the greatest indignation,
I hated them. Great must needs be that
wickedness which provoked the Father of
mercies to so great displeasure as to say, that
He *hated them;* and severe must needs be
those judgments which are as effects of hatred
and utter aversation of them, in Him."

For the wickedness of their doings. The sin

of Israel was no common sin, not a sin of ignorance, but against the full light. Each word
betokens evil. The word *doings* expresses *great
bold doings.* It was *the wickedness of their wicked
works,* a deeper depth of wickedness in their
wickedness, an essence of wickedness, for
which, God saith, *I will drive them out of My
house,* i. e. as before, out of His whole land[3].

I will love them no more. So He saith, in the
beginning[4]; *I will have no more mercy upon
the house of Israel, but I will utterly take them
away.* "[5] This was a national judgment, and
so involved the whole of them, as to their
outward condition, which they enjoyed as
members of that nation, and making up one
body politic. It did not respect the spiritual
condition of single persons, and their relation,
in this respect, to God." As individuals,
they were, "not cut off from God's favor and
tokens of His love, nor from the power of
becoming members of Christ, whenever any
of them should come to Him. It only struck
them for ever out of that *house of the Lord*
from which they were then driven," or from
hopes that that kingdom should be restored,
which God said, He would cause to cease.

All their princes are revolters. Their case then
was utterly hopeless. No one of their kings
*departed from the sin of Jeroboam who made
Israel to sin.* The political power which
should protect goodness, became the fountain
of corruption. "[6] None is there, to rebuke
them that offend, to recall those that err; no
one who, by his own goodness, and virtue,
pacifying God, can turn away His wrath, as
there was in the time of Moses." "[7] Askest
thou, why God cast them out of His house,
why they were not received in the Church or
the house of God? He saith to them, because
they *are all revolters, departers,* i. e. because,
before they were cast out visibly in the body,
they departed in mind, were far away in
heart, and therefore were cast out in the
body also, and lost, what alone they loved, the
temporal advantages of the house of God."

16. *Ephraim is smitten.* The Prophet, under
the image of a tree, repeats the same sentence
of God upon Israel. The word *smitten* is used
of the smiting of the tree from above, especially by the visitation of God, as by *blasting*
and *mildew*[8]. Yet such smiting, although it

---

1 S. Luke xxiii. 29.   2 ab. iv. 15.   3 See ab. viii. 1.   4 i. 6.   5 Poc.   6 S. Cyr.   7 Rup.   8 Am. iv. 9.

Before
CHRIST
cir. 760.

shall bear no fruit: yea, [n]though they bring forth, yet will I slay *even* † the beloved *fruit* of their womb.

[n] ver. 13.
† Heb. *the desires.*
Ezek. 24. 21.

17 My God will cast them away, because they did not hearken unto him: and they shall be [o]wanderers among the nations.

Before
CHRIST
cir. 760.

[o] Deut. 28. 64, 65.

---

falls heavily for the time, leaves hope for the future. He adds then, *their root is* also *withered, so that they should bear no fruit;* or if, perchance, while the root was still drying up and not quite dead, any fruit be yet found, *yet will I slay,* God says, *the beloved,* fruit *of their womb,* the desired fruit of their bodies, that which their souls longed for. "[1]So long as they have children, and multiply the fruit of the womb, they think that they bear fruit, they deem not that *their root is dried,* or that they have been severed by the axe of excision, and *rooted out of the land of the living;* but, in the anguish at the *slaying* of those they most loved, they shall say, better had it been to have had no children."

17. *My God hath cast them away. My God* (he saith) as if God were *his* God only who clave to him, not their's who had, by their disobedience, departed from Him. *My God.* "He had then authority from Him," Whom he owned and Who owned *him,* and Who bade him so speak, as though God were *his* God, and no longer their's. God *casts them away,* lit. *despises them,* and so rejects them as an object of aversion to Him, *because they did not hearken to him.* "God never forsakes unless He be first forsaken." When they would not hearken, neither doing what God commanded, nor abstaining from what He forbade, God at last rejected them, as worthless, wanting altogether to that end for which He created them.

And they shall be wanderers among the nations. This was the sentence of Cain[2]; a *fugitive and a vagabond shalt thou be in the earth.* So God had forewarned them[3]. *The Lord shall scatter thee among all people, from the one end of the earth even unto the other end of the earth—and among these nations shalt thou find no ease, neither shall the sole of thy foot have rest.* The words of the Prophet imply an abiding condition. He does not say, *they shall wander,* but, *they shall be wanderers*[4]. Such was to be

their lot; such has been their lot ever since; and such was not the ordinary lot of those large populations whom Eastern conquerors transported from their own land. Those conquerors took away with them into their own land, portions of the people whom they conquered, for two ends. When a people often rebelled, they were placed where they could rebel no more, among tribes more powerful than they, and obedient to the rule of the conqueror. Or they were carried off, as slaves to work in bricks, like Israel in Egypt[5]. Their workmen, smiths, artificers, were especially taken to labor on those gigantic works, the palaces and temples of Nineveh or Babylon. But, for both these purposes, the transported population had a settled abode allotted to it, whether in the capital or the provinces. Sometimes new cities or villages were built for the settlers[6]. Israel at first was so located. Perhaps on account of the frequent rebellions of their kings, the ten tribes were placed amid a wild, warlike, population, *in the cities of the Medes*[7]. When the interior of Asia was less known, people thought that they were still to be found there. The Jews fabled, that the ten tribes lay behind some mighty and fabulous river, Sambatyon[8], or were fenced in by mountains[9]. Christians thought that they might be found in some yet unexplored part of Asia. Undeceived as to this, they still asked whether the Afghans, or the Yezides, or the natives of North America were the ten tribes, or whether they were the Nestorians of Kurdistan. So natural did it seem, that they, like other nations so transported, should remain as a body, near or at the places, where they had been located by their conquerors. The Prophet says otherwise. He says their abiding condition shall be, *they shall be wanderers among the nations,* wanderers among them, but no part of them. Before the final dispersion of the Jews at the destruction of Jerusalem,

---

[1] Rup.　[2] Gen. iv. 12. The word נוד or נדד occurs in both.　[3] Deut. xxviii. 64, 5.
[4] Not נדד, but יהיו נדדים בגוים.
[5] This appears both from the sculptures of Nineveh in which multitudes of workmen, of countenance and form distinct from the Assyrians, are represented as working in chains, and from the inscriptions of the kings. "I [Sennacherib] carried off into captivity a great number of workmen. All the young active men of Chaldæa and Aramea, Manna, &c. who had refused to submit to my government, I carried them all away, to make bricks for me." (Bellino Cylinder in Fox Talbot's Assyr. Texts. p. 9.) "I carried them off as slaves, and compelled

them to make bricks for me." (Cyl. of Esarhad. Ib. p. 17.) "By the labor of foreign slaves, my captives, who lifted up their hands in the name of the great gods, my lords, I built thirty temples in Assyria and in—" (Ib. p. 16.)
[6] "A city I built. City of Esarhaddon I called it. Men who were—, natives of the land of [Caramania?] and of the sea of the rising sun, in that city I caused to dwell. I appointed my secretaries to be magistrates over them." (Cyl. of Esarh. Ib. p. 11. et al.)
[7] 2 Kings xvii. 6.　[8] Jon. in Ex. xxxiv. 14.
[9] Peritsol Orchot Olam. c. 4. 9. quoted by Basnage, Hist. d. Juifs. vi. 3. 3.

Before
CHRIST
cir. 740.

CHAPTER X.

*Israel is reproved and threatened
for their impiety and idolatry.*

ª Nah. 2. 2.
I Or, *a vine
emptying the
fruit which it
giveth.*

ISRAEL *is* ª|| an empty
vine, he bringeth forth
fruit unto himself: accord-

ing to the multitude of his
fruit ᵇ he hath increased
the altars; according to
the goodness of his land
ᶜ they have made goodly
† images.

Before
CHRIST
cir. 740.

ᵇ ch. 8. 11.
& 12. 11.

ᶜ ch. 8. 4.
† Heb. *statues,
or, standing
images.*

"the Jewish race," Josephus says [1], "was in great numbers through the whole world, interspersed with the nations." Those assembled at the day of Pentecost had come from all parts of Asia Minor but also from Parthia, Media, Persia, Mesopotamia, Arabia, Egypt, maritime Lybia, Crete, and Italy [2]. Wherever the Apostles went, in Asia or Greece, they found Jews, in numbers sufficient to raise persecution against them. S. James writes to those whom, with a word corresponding to that of Hosea, he calls, "the dispersion." *James—to the twelve in the dispersion* [3]. The Jews, scoffing, asked, whether our Lord would go to *the dispersion among the Greeks* [4]. They speak of it, as a body, over against themselves, to whom they supposed that He meant to go, to teach them, when He said, *Ye shall seek Me and shall not find Me.* The Jews of Egypt were probably the descendants of those who went thither, after the murder of Gedaliah. The Jews of the North, as well as those of China, India, Russia, were probably descendants of the ten tribes. From one end of Asia to the other and onward through the Crimea, Greece and Italy, the Jews by their presence, bare witness to the fulfillment of the prophecy. Not like the wandering Indian tribe, who spread over Europe, living apart in their native wildness, but settled, among the inhabitants of each city, they were still distinct, although with no polity of their own; a distinct, settled, yet foreign and subordinate race. "[5] Still remains unreversed this irrevocable sentence, as to their temporal state and face of an earthly kingdom, that they remain still *wanderers* or dispersed among other nations, and have never been restored, nor are in likelihood of ever being restored to their own land, so as to call it their own. If ever any of them hath returned thither, it hath been but as strangers, and all, as to any propriety that they should challenge in it, to hear the ruins and waste heaps of their ancient cities to echo in their ears the Prophet's words, *[6] Arise ye and depart, for this is not your rest;* your ancestors polluted it, and ye shall never return as a people thither, to inhabit it, as in your former condition."

"Meanwhile Ephraim here is an example,

not only to particular persons, that as they will avoid personal judgments, so they take care faithfully to serve God and hearken unto Him; but to nations and kingdoms also, that as they will prevent national judgments, so they take care that God be truly served, and the true religion maintained in purity and sincerity among them. Ephraim, or Israel, held their land by as good and firm tenure as any people in the world can theirs, having it settled on them by immediate gift from Him Who is the Lord of the whole earth, Who promised it to their forefathers, Abraham and his seed for ever [7], called therefore the land which the Lord sware unto them [8]; and which He had promised them [9], the land of Promise [10]. Who could have greater right to a place, better and firmer right, than they had to the Lord's land, by *His* promise which never fails, and *His* oath Who will not repent, confirmed to them? Certainly, if they had observed conditions and kept covenant with Him, all the people in the world could never have driven them out, or dispossessed them of it. But, seeing they revolted and brake His covenant, and did not hearken to Him, He would not suffer them longer to dwell in it, but drave and cast them out of it, so that they could never recover it again, but continue to this day *wandering among the nations,* having no settled place of their own, nowhere where they can be called a people, or are for such owned. If God so dealt with Israel on their disobedience and departing from His service, to whom He had so particularly engaged himself to make good to them the firm possession of that land; how shall any presume on any right or title to any other, or think to preserve it to themselves by any force or strength of their own, if they revolt from Him, and cast off thankful obedience to Him? The Apostle cautioneth and teacheth us so to argue, *if God spared not the natural branches, take heed lest He also spare not thee,* and therefore warneth, *be not high-minded,* and presumptuous, *but fear* [11]."

X. 1. *Israel is an empty vine,* or, in the same sense, *a luxuriant vine;* lit. *one which poureth out,* poureth itself out into leaves, abundant in switches, (as most old versions explain it,) luxuriant in leaves, emptying itself in them,

[1] de B. J. vii. 33.   [2] Acts ii. 9–11.
[3] ἐν τῇ διασπορᾷ. S. James i. 1.
[4] διασποράν. S. John vii. 35.   [5] Poc.

[6] Mic. ii. 10.   [7] Gen. xiii. 14. 15. Deut. xxxiv. 4.
[8] Num. xiv.   [9] Deut. ix. 28.
[10] Heb. xi. 9.   [11] Rom. xi. 20, 21.

Before CHRIST cir. 740. 2 || Their heart is [d] divided; now shall they be found faulty: he shall

I Or, *He hath divided their heart.* [d] 1 Kgs. 18. 21. Matt. 6. 24.

† break down their altars, he shall spoil their images. Before CHRIST cir. 740.

† Heb. *behead.*

---

and empty of fruit; like the fig-tree, which our Lord cursed. For the more a fruit tree putteth out its strength in leaves and branches, the less and the worst fruit it beareth. "[1] The juices which it ought to transmute into wine, it disperseth in the ambitious idle shew of leaves and branches." The sap in the vine is an emblem of His Holy Spirit, through Whom alone we can bear fruit. *His grace which was in me,* says St. Paul, *was not in vain.* It is in vain to us, when we waste the stirrings of God's Spirit in feelings, aspirations, longings, transports, "which bloom their hour and fade [2]." Like the leaves, these feelings aid in maturing fruit; when there are leaves only, the tree is barren and *nigh unto cursing, whose end is to be burned* [3].

It bringeth forth fruit for itself, lit. setteth *fruit to,* or *on itself.* Luxuriant in leaves, its fruit becomes worthless, and is from itself to itself. It is uncultured; (for Israel refused culture,) pouring itself out, as it willed, in what it willed. It had a rich shew of leaves, a shew also of fruit, but not for the Lord of the vineyard, since they came to no size or ripeness. Yet to the superficial glance, it was rich, prosperous, healthy, abundant in all things, as was the outward state of Israel under Jehoash and Jeroboam II.

According to the multitude of his fruit, or more strictly, *as his fruit was multiplied, he multiplied altars; as his land was made good, they made goodly their images.* The more of outward prosperity God bestowed upon them, the more they abused His gifts, referring them to their idols; the more God lavished His mercies on them, the more profuse they were in adoring their idols. The superabundance of God's goodness became the occasion of the superabundance of their wickedness. They rivalled and competed with, and outdid the goodness of God, so that He could bestow upon them no good, which they did not turn to evil. Men think this strange. Strange it is, as is all perversion of God's goodness; yet so it is now. Men's sins are either the abuse of what God gives, or rebellion, because He withholds. In the sins of prosperity, wealth, health, strength, powers of mind, wit, men sin in a way in which they could not sin, unless God continually supplied them with those gifts which they turn to sin. The more God gives, the more opportunity and ability they have to sin, and the more they

sin. They are *evil,* not only in despite of God's goodness, but *because* He is *good.*

2. *Their heart is divided* between God and their idols, in that they would not wholly part with either, as Elijah upbraided them [4], *How long halt ye between the two opinions?* When the heathen, by whom the king of Assyria replaced them, had been taught by one of the priests whom the king sent back, in order to avert God's judgments, they still propagated this division. Like Jeroboam, [5] *they became fearers of the Lord,* His worshipers, *and made to themselves out of their whole number* (i.e. indiscriminately) *priests of the high places. They were fearers of the Lord, and they were servers of their gods, according to the manner of the nations whom they carried away from thence.—These nations were fearers of the Lord, and they were servers of their idols, both their children and their children's children. As did their fathers, so do they unto this day.* This divided allegiance was their hereditary worship. These heathen, as taught by one of the priests of Israel, added the service of God to that of their idols, as Israel had added the service of the idols to that of God. But God rejecteth such half service; whence he adds, *now,* in a brief time, all but come, *they shall be found faulty,* lit. *they shall be guilty,* shall be convicted of guilt and shall bear it. They thought to *serve at once God and Mammon;* but, in truth, they served their idols only, whom they would not part with for God. God Himself then would turn away all their worship, bad and, as they thought, good. *He,* from Whom their heart was divided, He Himself, by His mighty power which no man can gain-say, *shall break down their altars,* lit. shall *behead* them. As they out of His gifts multiplied their altars and slew their sacrifices upon them against His will, so now should the altars themselves, be demolished; and *the images* which they had decked with the gold which He had given, should, on account of that very gold, tempt the spoiler, through whom God would spoil them.

He shall break down. He Himself [6]. The word is emphatic. "[7] God willeth not that, when the merited vengeance of God is inflicted through man, it should be ascribed to man. Yea, if any one ascribeth to himself what, by permission of God, he hath power to do against the people of God, he draweth down on him the displeasure of God, and, at

[1] S. Jer.   [2] Lyra Apost. N. 67.   [3] Heb. vi. 8.
[4] 1 Kings xviii. 21.
[5] 2 Kgs. xvii. 32, 33, 41. The form הָיוּ יְרֵאִים אֶת

expresses that they were habitual worshippers of God.
[6] הוּא.   [7] Rup.

Before
CHRIST
cir. 740.

e ch. 3. 4. & 11. 5.
Mic. 4. 9. ver. 7.

f See Deut.
29. 18.
Amos 5. 7.
& 6. 12.
Acts 8. 23.
Heb. 12. 15.

3 e For now they shall
say, We have no king, be-
cause we feared not the
LORD; what then should a
king do to us?

4 They have spoken
words, swearing falsely in
making a covenant: thus
judgment springeth up f as

hemlock in the furrows of
the field.

5 The inhabitants of Sa-
maria shall fear because of
g the calves of h Beth-aven:
for the people thereof shall
mourn over it, and ‖ the
priests thereof that rejoiced
on it, i for the glory thereof,

Before
CHRIST
cir. 740.

g 1 Kgs. 12.
28. 29.
ch. 8. 5, 6.
h ch. 4. 15.
‖ Or, Chemarim,
2 Kgs. 23. 5.
Zeph. 1. 4.
i 1 Sam. 4.
21. 22.
ch. 9. 11.

times, on that very ground, can hurt the
less [1]." The prophet then says very earnestly, *He Himself shall break*, meaning us to
understand, not the lofty hand of the enemy,
but that the Lord Himself did all these
things.

3. *For now they shall say, we have no king.*
These are the words of despair, not of repentance; of men terrified by the consciousness of guilt, but not coming forth out of its
darkness; describing their condition, not
confessing the iniquity which brought it on
them. In sin, all Israel had asked for a
king, when the Lord was their king; in sin,
Ephraim had made Jeroboam king; in sin,
their subsequent kings were made, without
the counsel and advice of God; and now as
the close of all, they reflect how fruitless it
all was. They had a king, and yet, as it
were, they had no king, since, God being
angry with them, he had no strength to deliver them. And now, without love, the
memory of their evil deeds crushes them beyond hope of remedy. They groan for their
losses, their sufferings, their fears, but do not
repent. Such is the remorse of the damned.
All which they had is lost; and what availed
it now, since, when they had it, they feared
not God?

4. *They have spoken words.* The words
which they spoke were eminently *words;*
they were mere *words,* which had no substance; *swearing falsely in making a covenant,*
lit. *swearing falsely, making a covenant, and
judgment springeth up as hemlock in the furrows of the field.* "[2] There is no truth in
words, no sanctity in oaths, no faithfulness
in keeping covenants, no justice in giving
judgments." Such is the result of all their
oaths and covenants, that *judgment springeth
up,* yea, flourisheth; but, what judgment?
Judgment, bitter and poisonous as hemlock,
flourishes, as hemlock would flourish on
ground broken up and prepared for it. They
break up the ground, make the *furrows.* They
will not have any chance self-sown seed;
they prepare the soil for harvest, full, abundant, regular, cleared of all besides. And

what harvest? Not any wholesome plant,
but poison. They cultivate injustice and
wickedness, as if these were to be the fruits
to be rendered to God from His own land.
So Amos says [3], *Ye have turned judgment into
gall* or *wormwood,* and Habakkuk, *Judgment
went forth perverted* [4].

5. *The inhabitants of Samaria shall fear because of* [i. e. *for*] *the calves of Beth-aven.* He
calls them in this place *cow-calves* [5], perhaps
to denote their weakness and helplessness.
So far from their idol being able to help *them,*
they shall be anxious and troubled for their
idols, lest these should be taken captive from
them. The *Bethel* (*House of God*) of the
Patriarch Jacob, was now turned into *Beth-
aven, the house of vanity.* This, from its old
sacred memories, was a more celebrated place
of the calf-worship than Dan. Hosea then
gives to the calf of Bethel its precedence,
and ranks both idols under its one name, as
calves of the house of vanity.

For the people thereof shall mourn over it.
They had set up the idols, instead of God;
so God calls them no longer His people, but
the people of the calf whom they had chosen
for their god; as Moab was called [6] *the people
of Chemosh,* its idol. They had joyed in it,
not in God; now they, *its people* and its priests,
should *mourn over it,* when unable to help
itself, much less, them. Both their joy and
their sorrow shewed that they were without
excuse, that they had *gone willingly after the*
king's *commandment,* serving it of their own
free-will out of love, not out of fear of the
king, and, neither out of love or fear, serving
God purely.

*For the glory thereof, because it is departed
from it.* The true glory of Israel was God;
the Glory of God is in Himself. *The glory
of the calves,* for whom Ephraim had exchanged their God, was something quite outward to them, the gold of which they were
made, and the rich offerings made to them.
Both together became an occasion of their
being carried captive. They mourned, not
because they had offended God by their sin,
but for the loss of that dumb idol, whose

[1] See Deut. xxxii. 26, 7. Is. x. 5 sqq.　　[2] Osorius.　　　[3] vi. 12. v. 7.　[4] i. 4.　[5] עֶגְלוֹת.　[6] Num. xxi. 29.

Before
CHRIST
cir. 740.
because it is departed from it.

6 It shall be also carried unto Assyria *for* a present to [k] king Jareb: Ephraim shall receive

[k] ch. 5. 13.

shame, and Israel shall be ashamed [1] of his own counsel.

7 [m] *As for* Samaria, her king is cut off as the foam upon † the water.

Before
CHRIST
cir. 740.

[1] ch. 11. 6.

[m] ver. 3, 15.

† Heb. *the face of the water.*

worship had been their sin, and which had brought these heavy woes upon them. Impenitent even under chastisement! The Prophet does not mention any grief for "the despoiling of their country, the burning of their cities, the slaughter of their people, their shame [1]." One only thing he names as moving them. Even then their one chief anxiety was, not that God was departed from them, but that their calf in which they had set their *glory*, whereupon they so franticly relied, on which they had lavished their substance, their national distinction and disgrace, was gone. Without the grace of God men mourn, not their sins, but their idols.

6. *It shall be also carried;* [i. e. *Itself* [2] *also shall be carried.*] Not Israel only shall be carried into captivity, but its god also. The victory over a nation was accounted of old a victory over its gods, as indeed it shewed their impotence. Hence the excuse made by the captains of Benhadad, that the *gods of Israel* were *gods of the hills, and not gods of the valleys* [3], and God's vindication of His own Almightiness, which was thus denied. Hence also the boast of Sennacherib by Rabshakeh, [4] *have any of the gods of the nations delivered at all his land out of the hand of the king of Assyria? Where are the gods of Hamath and of Arpad? where are the gods of Sepharvaim, Hena, and Ivah? have they delivered Samaria out of mine hand? Who are they among all the gods of the countries,* [5] *that have delivered their country out of mine hand, that the Lord should deliver Jerusalem out of mine hand?* When God then, for the sin of His people, gave them into the hand of their enemies, He vindicated His own glory, first by avenging any insult offered to His worship, as in the capture of the ark by the Philistines, or Belshazzar's insolent and drunken abuse of the vessels of the temple; or by vindicating His servants, as in the case of Daniel and the three children, or by chastening pride, as in Nebuchadnezzar, and explaining and pointing His chastisement through His servant Daniel, or by prophecy, as of Cyrus by Isaiah and Daniel. To His own people, His chastisements were the vindication of His glory which they had dishonored, and the close of

the long strife between the true prophets and the false. The captivity of the calf ended its worship, and was its final disgrace. The destruction of the temple and the captivity of its vessels and of God's people ended, not the worship, but the idolatries of Judah, and extended among their captors, and their captors' captors, the Medes and Persians, the knowledge of the One true God.

Unto Assyria, for a present to king Jareb or *to a hostile* or *strifeful* [6] *king.* Perhaps the name *Jareb* designates the Assyrian by that which was a characteristic of their empire, love of *strife.* The history of their kings, as given by themselves in the newly-found inscriptions, is one warfare. To that same king, to whom they sent for aid in their weakness, from whom they hoped for help, and whom God named as what He knew and willed him to be to them, *hostile, strifeful,* and *an avenger,* should the object of their idolatry be carried in triumph [7]. They had trusted in the calf and in the Assyrians. The Assyrian, to whom they looked as the protector of their liberties, was to carry away their other trust, their god [1].

Ephraim shall receive shame. This shall be all his gain; this his purchase; this he had obtained for himself by his pride and wilfulness and idolatry and ambition and wars; this is the end of all, as it is of all pursuits apart from God; this he *shall receive* from the Giver of all good, *shame. And Israel shall be ashamed of his own counsel.* Ephraim's special *counsel* was that which Jeroboam *took* with the most worldly-wise of his people, a counsel which admirably served their immediate end, the establishment of a kingdom, separate from that of Judah. It was acutely devised; it seemed to answer its end for 230 years, so that Israel, until the latter part of the reign of Pekah, was strong, Judah, in comparison, weak. But it was *the sin wherewith he made Israel to sin,* and for which God scattered him among the heathen. His wisdom became his destruction and his shame. The policy which was to establish his family and his kingdom, destroyed his own family in the next generation, and ultimately, his people, not by its failure, but by its success.

7. *Her king is cut off like foam* (or, more

---

[1] from Osor.　　[2] The *itself,* אתו, is emphatic.
[3] 1 Kgs. xx. 23, 28.
[4] 2 Kgs. xviii. 33-35. add. xix. 10-13.
[5] Num. xxi. 29.　　　　　　[6] See ab. v. 13.

[7] יובל is used of solemn stately processions, as of a royal bride, Ps. xlv. 15, 16; or a burial, Job x. 19. xxi. 30, 32. and so of the lengthened train of presents, Ps. lxviii. 30.

Before
CHRIST
cir. 740.
n ch. 4. 15.
o Deut. 9. 21.
1 Kgs. 12. 30.
p ch. 9. 6.

8 [n] The high places also of Aven, [o] the sin of Israel, shall be destroyed: [p] the thorn and the thistle shall

come up on their altars; [q] and they shall say to the mountains, Cover us; and to the hills, Fall on us.

Before
CHRIST
cir. 740.
q Is. 2. 19.
Luke 33. 30.
Rev. 6. 16.
& 9. 6.

probably, [1] *a straw) on the* [lit. *face of the*] *water.* A bubble, or one of those little shreds which float in countless numbers on the surface of the water, give the same image of lightness, emptiness, worthlessness, a thing too light to sink, but driven impetuously, and unresistingly, hither and thither, at the impulse of the torrent which hurries it along. Such was the king, whom Israel had set in the highest place, in whom it had trusted, instead of God. So easily was Hoshea, their last king, swept away by the flood, which broke in on Ephraim, from Assyria. Piety is the only solidity; apart from piety all is emptiness.

8. *The high places of Aven,* i. e. of vanity or iniquity. He had before called *Bethel, house of God,* by the name of *Bethaven, house of vanity;* now he calls it *Aven, vanity* or *iniquity,* as being the concentration of those qualities. Bethel was situated on a *hill,* the *mount of Bethel,* and, from different sides, people were said to *go up* [2] to it. *The high place* often means the shrine, or *the house of the high places.* Jeroboam had built such at Bethel [3]; many such already existed in his time, so that, *whoever would, he consecrated* as their *priests* [4]. The high-place or shrine, is accordingly said to be *built* [5], *broken down and burnt* [6]. At times, they were tents, and so said to be *woven* [7], *made* of *garments* of *divers colors* [8]. The calf then, probably, became a centre of idolatry; many such *idol-shrines* were formed around it, on its mount, until Bethel became a metropolis of idolatry. This was *the sin of Israel,* as being the source of all its sins.

The thorn and the thistle shall come up upon their altars. This pictures, not only the desolation of the place, as before [9], but the forced cessation of idolatry. Fire destroys, down to the root, all vegetable life which it has once touched. The thorn, once blackened by fire, puts out no fresh shoot. But now, these idol fires having been put out for ever, from amid the crevices of the broken altars, *thorn and thistle* [10] should grow freely as in a fallow soil. Where the victims aforetime *went up* [11], or were offered, now the wild briars and thistles alone should *go up,* and wave freely in undis-

puted possession. Ephraim had *multiplied altars,* as God multiplied their *goods;* now their altars should be but monuments of the defeat of idolatry. They remained, but only as the grave-stones of the idols, once worshiped there.

They shall say to the mountains, cover us. Samaria and Bethel, the seats of the idolatry and of the kingdom of Israel, themselves both on heights, had both, near them, mountains higher than themselves. Such was to Bethel, the mountain on the East, where Abraham built an altar to the Lord [12]; Samaria was encircled by them. Both were probably scenes of their idolatries; from both, the miseries of the dwellers of Bethel and Samaria could be seen. Samaria especially was in the centre of a sort of amphitheatre; itself, the spectacle. No help should those high places now bring to them in their need. The high hills round Samaria, when the tide of war had filled the valley around it, hemmed them in, the more hopelessly. There was no way, either to break through or to escape. The narrow passes, which might have been held, as flood gates against the enemy, would then be held against them. One only service could it seem, that their mountains could then render, to destroy them. So should they be freed from evils worse than the death of the body, and escape the gaze of men upon their misery. "They shall wish rather to die, than to see what will bring death." "They shall say to the mountains on which they worshiped idols, fall on us, and anticipate the cruelty of the Assyrians and the extreme misery of captivity." Nature abhors annihilation; man shrinks from the violent marring of his outward form; he clings, however debased, to the form which God gave him. What misery, then, when men long for, what their inmost being shrinks from !

The words of the Prophet become a sort of proverbial saying for misery, which longs for death rather than life. The destruction of Samaria was the type of the destruction of Jerusalem by the Romans, and of every other final excision, when the measure of iniquity was filled, and there was neither

[1] From the use of קצפה "shredding," Joel i. 7. and the Arab.
[2] Josh. xvi. 1. 1 Sam. xiii. 2. ab. iv. 13. Gen. xxxv. 1. Judg. i. 22. 1 Sam. x. 3. 2 Kgs. ii. 23.
[3] 1 Kgs. xii. 31. [4] Ib. xiii. 32, 33. [5] Ib. xi. 7.
[6] 2 Kgs. xxiii. 15. [7] Ib.7.
[8] Ezek. xvi. 16. [9] ch. ix. 6.
[10] These same two plants are named together in the cursing of the ground for Adam's sin (Gen. iii.

18.) and there alone does the word, translated *this-tle,* occur. Hosea, probably, was using the words of Genesis, in that, as a sort of proverb, he joins these two, out of sixteen names of the class of plant which occur in the Old Testament.

[11] עלה (whence עלה *whole burnt offering,* lit. that which *goeth up*) is also a sacrificial term.
[12] Gen. xii. 8.

Before CHRIST cir. 740.

9 ʳO Israel, thou hast sinned from the days of Gibeah: there they stood: ˢthe battle in Gibeah against the children of iniquity did not overtake them.

10 ʰIt *is* in my desire that I should chastise them; and ᵘthe people shall be gathered against them, ‖ when they shall bind themselves in their two furrows.

Before CHRIST cir. 740.

ᵘ Jer. 16. 16.
Ezek. 23. 46.
47. ch. 8. 10.
‖ Or, *when I shall bind them for their two transgressions,* or, *in their two habitations.*

hope nor remedy. This was the characteristic of the destruction of Samaria. They had been God's people; they were to be so no more. This was the characteristic of the destruction of Jerusalem, not by the Babylonians, after which it was restored, but by the Romans, when they had rejected Christ, and prayed, *His Blood be on us and on our children.* So will it be in the end of the world. Hence our Lord uses the words[1], to forewarn of the miseries of the destruction of Jerusalem, when the Jews hid themselves in caves for fear of the Romans[2]; and S. John uses them to picture man's despair at the end of the world[3]. "I dread" says S. Bernard[4], "the gnawing worm, and the living death. I dread to fall into the hands of a living death, and a dying life. This is *the second death,* which never out-killeth, yet which ever killeth. How would they long to die once, that they may not die for ever! *They who say to the mountains, fall on us, and to the hills, cover us,* what do they will, but, by the aid of death, either to escape or to end death? *They shall seek death, but shall not find it, and shall desire to die, and death shall flee from them,* saith S. John[5]."

9. *O Israel, thou hast sinned from the days of Gibeah.* There must have been great sin, on both sides, of Israel as well as Benjamin, when Israel punished the atrocity of Gibeah, since God caused Israel so to be smitten before Benjamin. Such sin had continued ever since, so that, although God, in His long-suffering, had hitherto spared them, "it was not of late only that they had deserved those judgments, although now at last only, God inflicted them." *There* in Gibeah, *they stood.* Although smitten twice at Gibeah, and heavily chastened, *there* they were avengers of the sacredness of God's law, and, in the end, *they stood; chastened but not killed.* But *now,* none of the ten tribes took the side of God. Neither zeal for God, nor the greatness of the guilt, nor fear of judgment, nor the peril of utter ruin, induced any to set themselves against sin so great. The sin devised by one, diffused among the many, was burnt and branded into them, so that they never parted with it[6]. *The battle in Gibeah*

against the children of iniquity did not overtake them, i. e. it did not overtake them then, but it shall overtake them now. Or if we render, (as is more probable,) *shall not overtake them,* it will mean, not a battle like that in Gibeah, terrible as that was, *shall* now *overtake them;* but one far worse. For, although the tribe of Benjamin was then reduced to six hundred men, yet the tribe still survived and flourished again; now the kingdom of the ten tribes, and the name of Ephraim, should be utterly blotted out.

10. *It is in My desire that I should chastise them.* God *doth not afflict willingly, nor grieve the children of men*[7]. Grievous then must be the cause of punishment, when God not only chastens men, but, so to speak, longs to chasten them, when He chastens them without any let or hindrance from His mercy. Yet so God had said[8]; *It shall come to pass, that as the Lord rejoiced over you to do you good and to multiply you, so the Lord will rejoice over you to destroy you and to bring you to nought.* God willed to enforce His justice, with no reserve whatever from His mercy. His whole mind, so to speak, is to punish them. God is "without passions." Yet, in order to impress on us the truth, that one day there will, to some, be *judgment without mercy*[9], He speaks as one, whose longing could not be satisfied, until the punishment were executed. So He says[10], *I will ease Me of Mine adversaries;* [11] *Mine anger shall be accomplished and I will cause My fury to rest upon them, and I will be comforted.*

And the people shall be gathered against him. "As all the other tribes were gathered against Benjamin at Gibeah to destroy it, so, although that war did not overtake them, now *against him,* i. e. against Ephraim or the ten tribes, *shall be gathered* divers *peoples* and nations, to destroy them." The number gathered against them shall be as overwhelming, as that of all the tribes of Israel against the one small tribe of Benjamin. "[6]As of old, they ought to have bound themselves to extinguish this apostacy in its birth, as they bound themselves to avenge the horrible wickedness at Gibeah. But since they bound themselves not against sin, but to it, God says

[1] S. Luke xxiii. 30.   [2] Jos. de B. J. vi. 9.
[3] Rev. vi. 16.   [4] De consid. v. 12.   [5] Rev. ix. 6.

[6] Osor.   [7] Lam. iii. 33.   [8] Deut. xxviii. 63.
[9] S. James ii. 13.   [10] Is. i. 24.   [11] Ezek. v. 13.

Before
CHRIST
cir. 740.

x Jer. 50. 11.
Mic. 4. 13.

11 And Ephraim *is as*
ˣ an heifer *that is* taught,
and loveth to tread out *the
corn;* but I passed over

upon † her fair neck: I will
make Ephraim to ride;
J u d a h shall plow, *and*
Jacob shall break his clods.

Before
CHRIST
cir. 740.

† Heb. *the beauty
of her neck.*

that He would gather Heathen nations
against them, to punish their obstinate rebellion against Himself. They who will
neither be drawn by piety, nor corrected by
moderate chastisements, must needs be visited
by sharper punishments, that some, who will
not strive to the uttermost against the mercy
of God, may be saved."

*When they shall bind themselves in their two
furrows.* They *bind themselves* and Satan *binds
them* to their sin. In harmony and unity in
nothing else, they will bind themselves, and
plough like two oxen together, adding furrow to furrow, joining on line to line of sin.
They who had thrown off the light and easy
yoke of God, who were ever like a restive,
untamed, heifer, starting aside from the yoke,
would *bind* and band themselves steadily in
their own ways of sin, cultivating sin, and in
that sin should destruction overtake them.
Men who are unsteady and uneven in every
thing besides, will be steadfast in pursuing
sin ; they who will submit to no constraint,
human or Divine, will, in their slavery to
their passions, submit to anything. No
slavery is so heavy as that which is self-
imposed.

This translation has followed an old Jewish
tradition, expressed by the vowels of the
text,[1] and old Jewish authorities. With
other vowels, it may be rendered, lit. *in their
binding to their two transgressions,* which gives
the same sense, "because they bound themselves to their two transgressions," or, passively, *when they are bound, on account of their
two transgressions.* The *two transgressions,*
may designate the two calves, *the sin of Israel,* or the twofold guilt of fornication, spiritual, and in the body ; the breach of both
tables of God's law ; or as Jeremiah says[2],
*My people hath committed two evils; they have
forsaken Me, the Fountain of living waters, and
hewed them out cisterns, broken cisterns, which
can hold no water.* "[3] This could not be said
of any other nation, which knew not God.
For if any such worshiped false gods, they
committed only one transgression ; but this
nation, in which God was known, by declining to idolatry, is truly blamed as guilty of
two transgressions; they left the true God,
and for, or against, Him they worshiped other
gods. For he hath twofold guilt, who, knowing

good, rather chooseth evil; but *he* single, who,
knowing no good, taketh evil for good.
That nation then, both when, after seeing
many wonderful works of God, it made and
worshiped one calf in the wilderness; and
when, forsaking the house of David and the
temple of the Lord, it made itself two calves ;
yea, and so often as it worshiped those gods
of the heathen; and yet more, when it asked
that Barabbas should be released but that
Christ should be crucified, committed two
transgressions, rejecting the good, electing
the evil; [4] *setting sweet for bitter, and bitter
for sweet ; setting darkness as light, and light
as darkness."*

11. *Ephraim is an heifer that is taught and
that loveth to tread out the corn.* The object of
the metaphor in these three verses seems to
be, to picture, under operations of husbandry,
what God willed and trained His people to
do, how they took as much pains in evil, as
He willed them to do for good. One thing
only they did *which* He willed, but not because He willed it,—what pleased themselves.
Corn was threshed in the East chiefly by
means of oxen, who were either driven round
and round, so as to trample it out with their
feet, or drew a cylinder armed with iron, or
harrow-shaped planks, set with sharp stones
which at the same time cut up the straw for
provender. The treading out the corn was
an easy and luxurious service, since God had
forbidden to *muzzle the ox*[5], while doing it.
It pictures then the sweet gentle ways by
which God wins us to His service. Israel
would serve thus far; for she liked the service, *she was accustomed* to it, and *she loved it,*
but she would do no more. *She waxed fat
and kicked.*[6]

"[7] The heifer when accustomed to the
labor of treading out the corn, mostly,
even unconstrained, returns to the same
labor. So the mind of the ungodly, devoted
to the slaveries of this world, and accustomed
to the fatigues of temporal things, even if it
may have leisure for itself, hastens to subject itself to earthly toils, and, inured to its
miserable conversation, seeks the renewal of
toil, and will not, though it may, cease from
the yoke of this world's slavery. This yoke
our Lord would remove from the necks of
His disciples, saying[8], *Take heed, lest at any*

[1] in that they have pointed עֲוֹנוֹתָם not עֲוֹנֹתָם
iniquities. Another rendering *before their two eyes,*
is altogether wrong. 1. It would, at least, be,
עֵינֵיהֶם. not עֵינֹתָם which means *their fountains.*
2. There is probably no such reading as עֵי־נֹתָם,

the merely indicating a reading עֲינֹתָם without ו.
Hiller. Arc. Cethib. p. 233.

[2] ii. 13.   [3] Rup.   [4] Is. v. 20.
[5] Deut. xxv. 4.   [6] Ib. xxxii. 15.
[7] S. Greg. Mor. xx. 16. Rib.   [8] S. Luke xxi. 34.

Before
CHRIST
cir. 740.
ʸ Prov. 11. 18.

12 ʸ Sow to yourselves in righteousness, reap in mercy; ᶻ break up your fallow ground: for it

Before
CHRIST
cir. 740.
ᶻ Jer. 4. 3.

time *your hearts be overcharged with cares of this life, and that Day come upon you unawares.* And again, *Come unto Me, all ye who labor and are heavy laden, and I will refresh you. Take My yoke upon you.*" " ¹ Some, in order to appear somewhat in this world, overload themselves with earthly toils, and although, amid their labors, they feel their strength fail, yet, overcome by love of earthly things, they delight in their fatigue. To these it is said by the Prophet, *Ephraim is a heifer taught and loving to tread out the corn.* They ask that they may be oppressed ; in rest, they deem that they have lighted unto a great peril."

And I passed over her fair neck, handling her gently and tenderly, as men put the yoke gently on a young untamed animal, and inure it softly to take the yoke upon it. Yet " ² to *pass over,* especially when it is said of God, always signifies inflictions and troubles." To pass over sins, is to remit them ; to pass over the sinner, is to punish him. *I will make Ephraim to ride* or *I will make it,* i. e. the yoke, to *ride* on *Ephraim's* neck, as the same word is used for " ³ place the hand on the bow ;" or, perhaps better, *I will set a rider on Ephraim,* who should tame and subdue him. Since he would not submit himself freely to the easy yoke of God, God would set a ruler upon him, who should be his master. Thus, the Psalmist complains, ⁴ *Thou hast made men to ride on our head,* directing us at their pleasure.

" ⁵ The *beauty of the neck* designates those who sin and take pleasure in their sins. That passing over or ascending, said both in the past and the future, *I passed, I will make to ride,* signifies that what He purposes is most certain. It expresses that same vengeance as, ⁶ *Ye are a stiffnecked people ; I will come up into the midst of thee in a moment, and consume thee.* The *beauty* of the *neck* here is the same as the ornament there, when the Lord says, *therefore now put off thy ornaments from thee, that I may know what to do unto thee.* As long as the sinner goes adorned, i. e. is proud in his sins, as long as he stiffens his fair neck, self-complacent, taking pleasure in the ills which he has done, God, in a measure, knows not what to do to him; mercy knows not how, apart from the severity of judgment, to approach him ; and so after the sentence of the judge, *thou art a stiffnecked people, &c.* He gives the counsel *put off thine ornaments &c.*

i. e. humble thyself in penitence, that I may have mercy upon thee."

Judah shall plow, Jacob shall break his clods. In the Will of God, Judah and Israel were to unite in His service, Judah first, Jacob, after him, breaking the clods, which would hinder the seed from shooting up. Judah being mentioned in the same incidental way, as elsewhere by Hosea, it may be, that he would speak of what should follow on Ephraim's chastisement. " ⁷ When they shall see this, the two tribes shall no longer employ themselves in treading out the corn, but shall plow. To *tread out the corn* is to " act " in hope of present gain ; to *plow,* is to labor in that, which has no instant fruit, but promiseth it hereafter, i. e. the fulfillment of God's commands." *Jacob* will then be the remnant of the ten tribes, who, at Hezekiah's invitation, out of Ephraim, Manasseh, Issachar, Asher, and Zebulun, joined in celebrating the passover at Jerusalem, and subsequently in destroying idolatry ⁸. Hosea had already foretold that Judah and Israel shall be *gathered together,* under *one Head* ⁹. Here, again, he unites them in one, preparing His way first in themselves, then, in others. Judah is placed first ; for to him was the promise in his forefather, the Patriarch, and then in David. Ephraim was to be partaker of his blessings, by being united to him. The image of the heifer has been dropped. He had spoken of them as husbandmen ; as such he addresses them.

12. *Sow to yourselves in righteousness, reap in mercy ;* lit. *in the proportion of mercy,* not in proportion to what you have sown, nor what justice would give, but beyond all deserts, *in the proportion of mercy ;* i. e. " according to the capacity and fullness of the mercy of God ; what becometh the mercy of God, which is boundless," which overlooketh man's failings, and giveth an infinite reward for poor imperfect labor. As our Lord says ¹⁰, *Give, and it shall be given unto you ; good measure, pressed down, and shaken together and running over, shall men give into your bosom.* " ¹¹ If the earth giveth thee larger fruits than it has received, how much more shall the requiting of mercy repay thee manifold more than thou gavest !" Sowing and reaping always stand over against each other, as labor and reward. ¹² *He that soweth sparingly shall reap also sparingly ; and he which soweth bountifully shall reap also bountifully.* And, ¹³ *whatsoever*

---

¹ S. Greg. in Ezek. Hom. x. Ib.
² S. Jer. See Job ix. 11. xiii. 13. Ps. lxxxviii. 17.
Heb. Is. xxviii. 18.
³ הרכב 2 Kings xiii. 16. twice.   ⁴ Ps. lxvi. 12.

⁵ Rup.   ⁶ Ex. xxxiii. 5.   ⁷ Rib.
⁸ 2 Chron. xxx. xxxi.   ⁹ i. 11.   ¹⁰ S. Luke vi. 38.
¹¹ S. Ambr. de Naboth, § 7. Rib.
¹² 2 Cor. ix. 6.   ¹³ Gal. vi. 7, 8, 9.

is time to seek the LORD, till he come, and

rain righteousness upon you.

a man soweth, that shall he also reap. For he that soweth to the flesh, shall of the flesh reap corruption ; but he that soweth to the Spirit shall of the Spirit reap life everlasting. In due season we shall reap, if we faint not. We are bidden to sow to ourselves, for, [1] *our goodness reacheth not to God ;* our's is the gain, if we love God, the Fountain of all good. This reward, *according to mercy,* is in both worlds. It is in this world also. For "grace well used draws more grace." God giveth *grace upon grace* [2] ; so that each good deed, the fruit of grace, is the seed-corn of larger grace. "If thou humble thyself, it stimulates thee to humble thyself more. If thou prayest, thou longest to pray more. If thou givest alms, thou wishest to give more." It is in the world to come. For, says a holy man [3], "our works do not pass away as it seems, but each thing done in time, is sown as the seed of eternity. The simple will be amazed, when from this slight seed he shall see the copious harvest arise, good or evil, according as the seed was." "Thou seekest two sheaves, rest and glory. They shall reap glory and rest, who have sown toil and self-abasement [4]."

Break up your fallow ground. This is not the order of husbandry. The ground was already plowed, harrowed, sown. Now he bids her anew, *Break up your fallow ground.* The Church breaks up her own fallow ground, when she stirs up anew the decaying piety of her own members; she breaks up fallow ground, when, by preaching the Gospel of Christ, she brings new people into His fold. And for us too, one sowing sufficeth not. It must be no surface-sowing. And "the soil of our hearts must ever be anew cleansed ; for no one in this mortal life is so perfect, in piety, that noxious desires will not spring up again in the heart, as tares in the well-tilled field."

For it is time to seek the Lord, until He come and rain righteousness upon you, or better, *until He shall come and teach you righteousness.* To *rain righteousness* is the same image as Solomon uses of Christ ; [5] *He shall come down like rain upon the mown grass, as showers that water the earth,* and Isaiah, [6] *drop down ye heavens from above and let the skies pour down righteousness.* It expresses in picture-language how He, Who is *our Righteousness,* came down from heaven, to give life to us, who were dried and parched up and withered, when the whole face of our mortal nature was as dead.

Yet there is nothing to indicate that the Prophet is here using imagery. The Hebrew word is used very rarely in the meaning, to *rain ;* in that of teaching, continually, and that, in exactly the same idiom as here [7]. One office of our Lord was to teach. Nicodemus owned Him, *as a teacher sent from* God [8]. The Samaritans looked to the Messiah, as one who should *teach all things* [9]. The prophets foretold that He should *teach us His ways* [10], that He should be *a witness unto the people* [11].

The Prophet bids them *seek diligently* [12], and perseveringly, "not leaving off or desisting," if they should not at once find, but continuing the search, quite *up to* [13] the time when they should find. His words imply the need of perseverance and patience, which should stop short of nothing but God's own time for finding. The Prophet, as is the way of the prophets, goes on to Christ, who was ever in the prophets' hearts and hopes. The words could only be understood improperly of God the Father. God does not *come,* Who is everywhere. He ever was among His people, nor did He will to be among them otherwise than heretofore. No coming of God, *as* God, was looked for, to *teach righteousness.* Rather, the time was coming, when He would be less visibly among them than before. Among the ten tribes, as a distinct people, He would shortly be no more, either by prophecy, or in worship, or by any perceptible token of His Providence. From Judah also He was about, although at a later period, to withdraw the kingdom of David, and the Urim and Thummim, and the Shechinah, or visible Presence. Soon after the Captivity, prophecy itself was to cease. But "the coming of Christ the Patriarchs and holy men all along desired to see : Abraham saw it and was glad [14]. Jacob longed for it [15]. The law and the Prophets directed to it, so that there were always in Israel such as waited for it, as appears by the example of old Simeon and Joseph of Arimathæa, and those many prophets and righteous men whom our Saviour speaks of [16]. *He that should come* seems to have been a known title for Him ; since John Baptist sent two of his disciples, to say unto Him, *Art thou He that shall come, or do we look for another* [17] *?*"

The Prophet saith then, "Now is the time to seek the Lord, and prepare for the coming

[1] Ps. xvi. 2.　　　　[2] S. John i. 16.
[3] S. Bern. de Conv. c. 8. Lap.
[4] Id. Serm. de S. Bened. § ii. Ib.
[5] Ps. lxxii. 6.　　　　[6] xlv. 8.
[7] with accusat. of that which is taught and dat. of the person, Deut. xxxiii. 10.
[8] S. John iii. 2.　[9] Ib. iv. 25.　[10] Is. ii. 3.
[11] Ib. lv. 4.　　　　　　[12] שרד.
[13] This is the force of עד.
[14] S. John viii. 56.　　[15] Gen. xlix. 18.
[16] S. Luke ii. 25.　S. Mark xv. 43.　S. Matt. xiii. 17.
[17] S. Matt. xi. 3.

13 [a] Ye have p l o w e d wickedness, ye have reaped

[a] Job 4. 8. Prov. 22. 8. ch. 8. 7. Gal. 6. 7, 8.

of Christ; for He, when He cometh, will teach you, yea, will give you true righteousness, whereby ye shall be righteous before God, and heirs of His kingdom." [1] So God speaketh through Isaiah, *keep ye judgment and do justice, for My salvation is near to come, and my righteousness to be revealed.* In both places, men are warned, *to prepare the way* to receive Christ, which was the office assigned to the law. As S. Paul saith, *Whereunto was the law? It was added because of transgressions.* It was given to restrain the passions of men by fear of punishment, lest they should so defile themselves by sin, as to despise the mercy and office of Christ. It was given to prepare our souls by love of righteousness and mercy to receive Christ, that he might enrich them with the Divine wealth of righteousness." " [2] If Israel of old were so to order their ways in expectation of Him, and that they might be prepared for His coming; and if their neglecting to do this made them liable to such heavy judgments, how much severer judgments shall they be worthy of, who, after His Coming and raining upon them the plentiful showers of heavenly doctrine, and abundant measure of His grace and gifts of His Holy Spirit, do, for want of breaking up the fallow ground of their hearts, suffer His holy word to be lost on them. The fearful doom of such unfruitful Christians is set down by S. Paul [3]."

The present is ever the time to seek the Lord. [4] *Behold now is the accepted time; behold now is the Day of Salvation.* As Hosea says, *it is time to seek the Lord till He come,* so S. Paul saith, [5] *unto them that look for Him, shall he appear the second time, without sin, unto salvation.*

13. *Ye have plowed wickedness.* They not only did not that which God commanded, but they did the exact contrary. They cultivated wickedness. They broke up their fallow ground, yet to sow, not wheat, but tares. They did not leave it even to grow of itself, although even thus, on the natural soil of the human heart, it yields a plenteous harvest; but they bestowed their labor on it, plowed it, sowed, and as they sowed, so they reaped, an abundant increase of it. "They brought their ill doings to a harvest, and laid up as in provision the fruits thereof." Iniquity and the results of iniquity, were the gain of all their labor. Of all their toil, they shall have no fruits, except the

iniquity; ye have eaten the fruit of lies: because thou

iniquity itself. " [6] By the plowing, sowing, eating the fruits, he marks the obstinacy of incorrigible sinners, who begin ill, go on to worse, and in the worst come to an end. Then too, when the corrupted soul labors with the purpose of a deed of sin, and resolves in its inmost thoughts, how it may bring the ungodly will into effect in deed, it is like one plowing or sowing. But when, having completed the work of iniquity, it exults that it has done ill, it is like one reaping. When further it has broken out so far as, in pride of heart to defend its sins against the law of God prohibiting them, and goes on unconcerned in impenitence, he is like one who, after harvest, eats the fruits stored up."

Ye have eaten the fruit of lies. They had been full of *lies* [7]; they had *lied* against God by hypocrisy [8] and idolatry; they had *spoken lies against Him* [9]; by denying that He gave them what He bestowed upon them, and ascribing it to their idols [10]. All iniquity is a lie. Such then should be *the fruit* which they tasted, on which they fed. It should not profit, nor satisfy them. It should not merely be empty, as in the case of those who are said to *feed on ashes* [11], but hurtful. As Isaiah saith [12], *they conceive mischief and bring forth iniquity. They hatch cockatrice' eggs, and weave the spider's web; he that eateth of their eggs dieth, and that which is crushed, breaketh out into a viper.* " Gain deceives, lust deceives, gluttony deceives; they yield no true delight; they satisfy not, they disgust; and they end in misery of body and soul." " Bodily delights," says a father [13], "when absent, kindle a vehement longing; when had and eaten, they satiate and disgust the eater. Spiritual delights are distasteful, when unknown; when possessed, they are longed for; and the more those who hunger after them feed upon them, the more they are hungered for. Bodily delights please, untasted; when tasted, they displease; spiritual, when untasted, are held cheap; when experienced, they please. In bodily delights, appetite generates satiety; satiety, disgust. In spiritual, appetite produceth satiety; satiety appetite. For spiritual delights increase longing in the soul, while they satisfy. For the more their sweetness is perceived, so much the more is *that* known which is loved more eagerly. Unpossessed, they cannot be loved, because their sweetness is unknown."

Because thou didst trust in thy way. Thy way, i. e. not God's. They forsook God's

[1] Osor.   [2] Poc.   [3] Heb. vi. 4–8.   [4] 2 Cor. vi. 2.
[5] Heb. ix. 28.   [6] Rup.
[7] ch. iv. 1, 2. vii. 3.   [8] v. 7. vi. 7. vii. 16. x. 4.

[9] vii. 13.   [10] ii. 5, 12.   [11] Is. xliv. 20.
[12] Ib. lix. 4, 5.
[13] S. Greg. in Evang. Hom. 36. init. L.

Before
CHRIST
cir. 740. didst trust in thy way, in the multitude of thy mighty men.

b ch. 13. 16. 14 b Therefore shall a

tumult arise among thy people, and all thy fortresses shall be spoiled, as Shalman spoiled c Betharbel in the Before
CHRIST
cir. 740.

c 2 Kgs. 18. 34.
& 19. 13.

way, followed " ways of wickedness and mis-belief." While displeasing God, they trusted in the worship of the calves and in the help of Egypt and Assyria, *making flesh their arm, and departing from the living God.* So long as a man mistrusts his ways of sin, there is hope of his conversion amid any depths of sin. When he *trusts in his ways,* all entrance is closed against the grace of God. He is as one dead; he not only justifies himself, but is self-justified. There is nothing in him, neither love nor fear, which can be awakened

14. *Therefore shall a tumult arise among thy people,* lit. *peoples.* Such was the immediate fruit of departing from God and trusting in men and idols. They trusted in their own might, and the multitude of their people. That might should, through intestine division and anarchy, become their destruction. As in the dislocated state of the Roman empire under the first emperors, so in Israel, the successive usurpers arose out of their armies, [1] *the multitude of their mighty ones,* in whom they trusted. The *confused noise* [2] *of war* should first *arise in* the midst of their own *peoples.* They are spoken of not as one, but as many ; *peoples* [3], not, as God willed them to be, one people, for they had no principle of oneness or stability, who had no legitimate succession, either of kings or of priests; who had *made kings, but not through* God. Each successor had the same right as his predecessor, the right of might, and furnished an example and precedent and sanction to the murderer of himself or of his son.

All thy fortresses shall be spoiled, lit. *the whole of thy fortresses shall be wasted.* He speaks of the whole as one. Their fenced cities, which cut off all approach [4], should be one waste [5].

[1] See Introd. p. 2.   [2] as in Am. ii. 2.
[3] עַמֶּיךָ plural. The corruption in some MSS. עַמֶּךְ (sing.) and the rendering of the old Versions (as of our own) in the singular, (with the same general sense,) illustrate the peculiarity of the idiom for which they substituted an easier, and nearly equivalent, phrase.
[4] The Etymology of מִבְצָר, as of *Bozrah.*
[5] expressed by the union of כֹּל with the genitive plur. and the sing. verb, which is very rare. Is. lxiv. 7. Nah. iii. 7. Prov. xvi. 2. have been cited as the only instances.
[6] 2 Kings xvii. 3.
[7] *Eser* occurs in *Esarhaddon,* Tiglath pil*eser* and, probably, is the same as *ezzar* and *ezer* in Nebuchad-nezzar, and Sharezer. It probably signifies " help." A much stronger omission occurs probably in the name of the parricide Sharezer, 2 Kings xix. 37. whose whole name was Nergal Sharezer. Merodach Baladan is probably the Mardocempal of Ptol. Rawl.

They had forsaken God, their *fortress and deliverer,* and so He gave up their fortresses to the enemy, so that all and each of them were laid waste. The confusion, begun among themselves, prepared for destruction by the enemy. Of this he gives one awful type.

As Shalman spoiled (or *wasted*) *Beth-Arbel in the day of battle. Shalman* is, no doubt, *Shalmaneser king of Assyria,* who came up against Hoshea, early in his reign, *and he became a servant to him and brought him a present* [6]. *Shalman* being the characteristic part of the name [7], the Prophet probably omitted the rest, on the ground of the rhythm. *Beth-Arbel* is a city, which the Greeks, retaining, in like way, only the latter and characteristic half of the name, called Arbela [8]. Of the several cities called Arbela, that celebrated in Grecian history, was part of the Assyrian empire. Two others, one " [9] in the mountain-district of Pella " and so on the East side of Jordan, the other between Sepphoris and Tiberias [10], (and so in Naphthali) must, together with the countries in which they lay, have fallen into the hands of the Assyrians in the reign of *Tiglath-pileser,* who *took—Gilead and Galilee, all the land of Naphtali* [11], in the reign of Pekah. The whole country, East of Jordan, being now in the hands of Shalmaneser, his natural approach to Samaria was over the Jordan, through the valley or plain of Jezreel. Here was the chief wealth of Israel, and the fittest field for the Assyrian horse. Over the Jordan then, whence Israel itself came when obedient to God, whence came the earlier instruments of God's chastisements, came doubtless the host of Shalmaneser, along the "great plain" of Esdraelon. " In that plain " also

Herod. i. p. 502. *Chedorlaomer* (Gen. xiv. 1. 9.) is very probably the same as the *kudurmapula* of the Babylonian bricks, *mapula* being omitted, and *laomer,* i. e. *el-omer* " the ravager" being equivalent to the meaning of *abda Mactu* of the bricks, "waster of the West." See Rawl. Herod. i. 436.
[8] as Beth Aven, (although on other grounds,) was called Aven (ver. 8.) Both Baal Meon is called more commonly Baal Meon, but also Beth Meon and now *Maein* or *Myun; Gilgal* is probably called *Beth Haggilgal,* Neh. xii. 29 ; *Diblathaim* (afterward *Diblatai*) is *Beth Diblathaim,* Jer. xlviii. 22; the people of *Bethear* are called by Josephus (Ant. vi. 2. 2.) *Corræi; Ophrah* is probably Bethle *aphrah,* Mic. i. 10; *Beth Millo,* 2 Kings xii. 21. *Millo; Beth Nimra,* now *Nemrin; Beth Eden,* now *Eden; Beth Azmaveth, Azmaveth; Beth-eked-harohim,* 2 Kings x. 12. *Beth-eked,* 14 in Eus. *Baithakath; Beeshterah,* (for *Beth Ashtarah*) *Ashtaroth.* See all these in Ges. Lex. v. בֵּית pp. 193-6.
[9] Eus. Onom. s. v.
[10] Jos. B. J. i. 16. 2. Vit. 37. 66.   [11] 2 Kings xv. 29.

CHAPTER XI.

Before CHRIST cir. 740.

d ch. 13. 16.

† Heb. *the evil of your evil.*

e ver. 7.

day of battle: ^d the mother was dashed in pieces upon her children.

15 So shall Bethel do unto you because of † your g r e a t wickedness: in a morning ^e shall the king of Israel utterly be cut off.

CHAPTER XI.

1 *The ingratitude of Israel unto God for his benefits.* 5 *His judgment.* 8 *God's mercy toward them.*

WHEN ^a Israel *was* a child, then I loved him, and ^b called my ^c son out of Egypt.

Before CHRIST cir. 740.

a ch. 2. 15.

b Matt. 2. 15.
c Ex. 4. 22, 23.

lay an *Arbela*, "nine miles from Legion [1]." Legion itself was at the Western extremity of the plain, as Scythopolis or Bethshean lay at the East [2]. It was about fifteen miles West of Nazareth [3], and ten miles from Jezreel [4]. Beth-Arbel must accordingly have lain somewhere in the middle of the valley of Jezreel. Near this Arbela, then, Israel must have sustained a decisive defeat from Shalmaneser. For the Prophet does not say only, that he *spoiled Beth-Arbel*, but that he did this *in a day of battle.* Here Hosea, probably in the last years of his life, saw the fulfillment of his own earlier prophecy; and God *brake the bow of Israel in the valley of Jezreel* [5].

The mother was dashed to pieces on the children. It was an aggravation of this barbarity, that, first the infants were dashed against the stones before their mother's eyes, then the mothers themselves were dashed upon them. Syrians [6], Assyrians [7], Medes [8], Babylonians [9], used this barbarity. India has borne witness to us of late, how heathen nature remains the same.

It may be that, in the name *Betharbel*, the Prophet alludes to the name *Bethel* [10]. As *Betharbel*, i. e. *the house*, or it may be the idolatrous *temple of Arbel*, rescued it not, but was rather the cause of its destruction, so shall Bethel. The holy places of Israel, the memorials of the free love of God to their forefathers, were pledges to *them*, the children of those forefathers, that, so long as they continued in the faith of their fathers, God the Unchangeable, would continue those same mercies to them. When they *turned* Bethel, *the house of God*, into Bethaven, *house of vanity*, then it became, like Betharbel, lit. *house of ambush of God*, the scene and occasion of their desolation.

15. *So shall Bethel do unto you.* God was the Judge, Who condemned them so to suffer from the enemy. The Assyrian was the instrument of the wrath of God. But, in order to point out the moral government of God, the Prophet says, neither that God did it, nor that the Assyrian did it, but Bethel,

once *the house of God*, now the place where they dishonored God, *because of your great wickedness*, lit. *the wickedness of your wickedness.* In their wickedness itself, there was an essence of wickedness, malice within malice.

In a morning shall the king of Israel be cut off. Hoshea was cut off finally, leaving neither root nor branch. His kingdom perished; he left no memorial. Like the morning, he seemed to dawn on the troubles of his people: he sinned against God: and *in a morning*, the kingdom, in *the multitude of* whose *mighty men* he trusted, *was cut off* for ever.

XI. 1. *When Israel was a child, then I loved him.* God loved Israel, as He Himself formed it, ere it corrupted itself. He loved it for the sake of the fathers, Abraham, Isaac, and Jacob, as he saith [11], *Jacob have I loved, but Esau have I hated.* Then, when it was weak, helpless, oppressed by the Egyptians, afflicted, destitute, God loved him, cared for him, delivered him from oppression, and called him out of Egypt. " [10] When did He love Israel? When, by His guidance, Israel regained freedom, his enemies were destroyed, he was fed with *food from heaven*, he heard the voice of God, and received the law from Him. He was unformed in Egypt; then he was informed by the rules of the law, so as to be matured there. He was a child in that vast waste. For he was nourished, not by solid food, but by milk, i. e. by the rudiments of piety and righteousness, that he might gradually attain the strength of a man. So that law was a schoolmaster, to retain Israel as a child, by the discipline of a child, until the time should come when all, who despised not the heavenly gifts, should receive the Spirit of adoption. The Prophet then, in order to shew the exceeding guilt of Israel," says, " *When Israel was a child*, (in the wilderness, for then he was born when he bound himself to conform to the Divine law, and was not yet matured) *I loved him*, i. e. I gave him the law, priesthood, judgments, precepts, instructions; I loaded him with most ample

1 Eus. l. c.
2 Eus. (v. Ἰεσραὴλ) assigns these, as the two extremities. 3 Reland, p. 873. 4 Itin. Hieros. p. 586.

5 ch. i. 5. 6 2 Kgs. viii. 12. 7 here and xiii. ult.
8 Is. xiii. 16. 9 Ps. cxxxvii. 8, 9.
10 Osor. 11 Mal. i. 2.

Before
CHRIST
cir. 740.
d 2 Kgs 17.
16. ch. 2. 13.
& 13. 2.

2 *As* they called them, so they went from them: ^dthey sacrificed unto Baalim, and burned incense to graven images.

Before
CHRIST
cir. 740.

benefits; I preferred him to all nations, expending on him, as on My chief heritage and peculiar possession, much watchful care and pains."

I called My son out of Egypt, as He said to Pharaoh [1], *Israel is My son, even My firstborn ; let My son go, that he may serve Me.* God chose him out of all nations, to be His peculiar people. Yet also God chose him, not for himself, but because He willed that Christ, His only Son, should *after the flesh* be born of him, and for, and in, the Son, God called His people, *My son.* "[2] The people of Israel was called a son, as regards the elect, yet only for the sake of Him, the Only-Begotten Son, Begotten, not adopted, Who, *after the flesh,* was to be born of that people, that, through His Passion, He might bring many sons to glory, disdaining not to have them as brethren and co-heirs. For, had He not come, Who was to come, the Well Beloved Son of God, Israel too could never, any more than the other nations, have been called the son of so great a Father, as the Apostle, himself of that people, saith [3], *For we were, by nature, children of wrath, even as others.*"

Since, however, these words relate to literal Israel, the people whom God brought out by Moses, how were they fulfilled in the infant Jesus, when He was brought back out of Egypt, as S. Matthew teaches us, they were [4]?

Because Israel himself was a type of Christ, and for the sake of Him Who was to be born of the seed of Israel, did God call Israel, *My son;* for His sake only did He deliver him. The two deliverances, of the whole Jewish people, and of Christ the Head, occupied the same position in God's dispensations. He rescued Israel, whom He called His son, in its childish and infantine condition, at the very commencement of its being, as a people. His true Son by Nature, Christ our Lord, He brought up in His Infancy, when He began to shew forth His mercies to us in Him. Both had, by His appointment, taken refuge in Egypt; both were, by His miraculous call, to Moses in the bush, to Joseph in the dream, recalled from it. S. Matthew apparently quotes these words, not to prove anything, but in order to point out the relation of God's former dealings with the latter, the beginning and the close, what relates to the body, and what relates to the Head. He tells us that the former deliverance had its completion in Christ, that in His deliverance

was the full solid completion of that of Israel; and that then indeed it might, in its completest fullness, be said, *Out of Egypt have I called My Son.*

When Israel was brought out of Egypt, the figure took place; when Christ was called, the reality was fulfilled. The act itself, on the part of God, was prophetic. When He delivered Israel, and called him His firstborn, He willed, in the course of time, to bring up from Egypt His Only-Begotten Son. The words are prophetic, because the event which they speak of, was prophetic. "They speak of Israel as one collective body, and, as it were, one person, called by God *My son,* viz. by adoption, still in the years of innocency, and beloved by God, called of God out of Egypt by Moses, as Jesus, His true Son, was by the Angel." The following verses are not prophetic, because in them the Prophet no longer speaks of Israel as one, but as composed of the many sinful individuals in it. Israel was a prophetic people, in regard to this dispensation of God towards him; not in regard to his rebellions and sins.

2. *As they called them, so they went from them.* The Prophet changes his tone, no longer speaking of that one first call of God to Israel as a whole, whereby He brought out Israel as one man, His one son; which one call he obeyed. Here he speaks of God's manifold calls to the people, throughout their whole history, which they as often disobeyed, and not disobeyed only, but went contrariwise. *They called them.* Whether God employed Moses, or the judges, or priests, or kings, or prophets, to call them, it was all one. Whenever or by whomsoever they were called, they turned away in the opposite direction, to serve their idols. They proportioned and fitted, as it were, their disobedience to God's long-suffering. "[5] Then chiefly they threw off obedience, despised their admonitions, and worked themselves up the more franticly to a zeal for the sin which they had begun." *They,* God's messengers, *called; so,* in like manner, *they went away from them. They sacrificed unto Baalim,* i. e. their many Baals, in which they cherished idolatry, cruelty, and fleshly sin. So "[6] when Christ came and called them manifoldly, as in the great day of the feast, *If any man thirst, let him come unto Me and drink,* the more diligently He called them, the more diligently they went away from Him, and returned to their idols,

[1] Ex. iv. 22, 3.   [2] Rup.   [3] Eph. ii. 3.   [4] ii. 15.   [5] Osor.   [6] Rib.

Before
CHRIST
cir. 740.

• Deut. 1. 31. &
32. 10, 11, 12.
Is. 46. 3.
f Ex. 15. 26.

3 [e]I taught Ephraim also to go, taking them by their arms; but they knew not that [f]I healed them.

4 I drew them with cords

of a man, with bands of love: and [g]I was to them as they that † take off the yoke on their jaws, and [h]I laid meat unto them.

Before
CHRIST
cir. 740.

[g] Lev. 26. 13.
† Heb. *lift up.*
[h] Ps. 78. 25.
ch. 2. 8.

to the love and possession of riches and houses and pleasures, for whose sake they despised the truth."

3. *I taught Ephraim also to go,* lit. *and I set Ephraim on his feet;* i. e. while they were rebelling, I was helping and supporting them, as a nurse doth her child, teaching it to go with little steps, step by step, "accustoming it to go by little and little without weariness;" and not only so, but *taking them by their arms;* or it may be equally translated, *He took them in His arms,* i. e. God not only gently *taught* them *to walk,* but when they were wearied, *He took them up in His arms,* as a nurse doth a child when tired with its little attempts to walk. Such was the love and tender care of God, guiding and upholding Israel in His ways which He taught him, guarding him from weariness, or, if wearied, taking him in the arms of His mercy and refreshing him. So Moses says[1], *In the wilderness thou hast seen, how that the Lord thy God bare thee, as a man doth bear his son, in all the way that ye went, until ye came unto this place;* and he expostulates with God, [2] *Have I conceived all this people? have I begotten them, that Thou shouldest say unto me, Carry them in thy bosom, as a nursing father beareth his sucking child, unto the land which Thou swarest unto their fathers?* "[3] Briefly yet magnificently doth this place hint at the wondrous patience of God, whereof Paul too speaks, [4] *for forty years suffered He their manners in the wilderness.* For as a nursing father beareth patiently with a child, who hath not yet come to years of discretion, and, although at times he be moved to strike it in return, yet mostly he sootheth its childish follies with blandishments, and, ungrateful though it be, carries it in his arms, so the Lord God, Whose are these words, patiently bore with the unformed people, ignorant of the spiritual mysteries of the kingdom of heaven, and although He slew the bodies of many of them in the wilderness, yet the rest He soothed with many and great miracles, *leading them about,* and *instructing them,* (as Moses says) *keeping them as the apple of His eye* [5]."

But they knew not that I healed them. They laid it not to heart, and therefore what they knew with their understanding was worse than ignorance. "[6]I Who was a Father, became a nurse, and Myself carried My little

one in My arms, that he should not be hurt in the wilderness, or scared by heat or darkness. By day I was a cloud; by night, a column of fire, that I might by My light illumine, and heal those whom I had protected. And when they had sinned and had made the calf, I gave them place for repentance, and they knew not that I healed them, so as, for forty years, to close the wound of idolatry, and restore them to their former health."

"[7] The Son of God carried us in His arms to the Father, when He went forth carrying His Cross, and on the wood of the Cross stretched out His arms for our redemption. Those too doth Christ carry daily in His arms, whom He continually entreateth, comforteth, preserveth, so gently, that with much alacrity and without any grievous hindrance they perform every work of God, and with heart enlarged run, rather than walk, the way of God's commandments. Yet do these need great caution, that they be clothed with great circumspection and humility, and despise not others. Else Christ would say of them, *They knew not that I healed them.*"

4. *I drew them with the cords of a man.* "[8]Wanton heifers such as was Israel, are drawn with ropes; but although Ephraim struggled against Me, I would not draw him as a beast, but I drew him as *a man,* (not a servant, but a son) *with cords* of love." "Love is the magnet of love." "[9]The first and chief commandment of the law, is not of fear, but of love, because He willeth those whom He commandeth, to be sons rather than servants." "[10]Our Lord saith, *No man cometh unto Me, except the Father Who hath sent Me, draw him.* He did not say, lead *him,* but *draw him.* This violence is done to the heart, not to the body. Why marvel? Believe and thou comest; love and thou art drawn. Think it not a rough and uneasy violence: it is sweet, alluring; the sweetness draws thee. Is not a hungry sheep drawn, when the grass is shewn it? It is not, I ween, driven on in body, but is bound tight by longing. So do thou too come to Christ. Do not conceive of long journeyings. When thou believest, then thou comest. For to Him Who is everywhere, men come by loving, not by travelling." So the Bride saith, [11]*draw me and I will run after Thee.* "How sweet," says S. Augustine, when converted [12], "did it at once

[1] Deut. i. 31.   [2] Num. xi. 12.   [3] Rup.   [4] Acts xiii. 18.
[5] Deut. xxxii. 10.   [6] S. Jer.   [7] Dion.   [8] Lap.

[9] Rib.   [10] S. Aug. Serm. 81. on N. T. § 2. Oxf. Tr.
[11] Cant. i. 4.   [12] Conf. ix. 1.

Before
CHRIST
cir. 740.
5 ¶ [1] He shall not re-
turn into the land of Egypt,
but the Assyrian shall be
his king, [k] because they refused to return.

[1] See ch. 8. 13.
& 9. 3.
[k] 2 Kgs. 17. 13,
14.

6 And the sword shall
abide on his cities, and
shall consume his branches,
and devour *them*, [1] because
of their own counsels.

Before
CHRIST
cir. 740.

cir. 728.
They became
tributaries to
Salmanasser.
[1] ch. 10. 6.

become to me, to want the sweetnesses of
those toys; and what I feared to be parted
from, was now a joy to part with. For Thou
didst cast them forth from me, Thou true and
highest Sweetness. Thou castedst them forth,
and for them enteredst in Thyself, sweeter
than all pleasure, though not to flesh and
blood; brighter than all light, but more hidden than all depths; higher than all honor,
but not to the high in their own conceits."

"[1] Christ *drew* us also *with the cords of a man*,
when for us He became Man, our flesh, our
Brother, in order that by teaching, suffering,
dying for us, He might in a wondrous way
bind and draw us to Himself and to God;
that He might redeem the earthly Adam,
might transform and make him heavenly;"
"[2] giving us ineffable tokens of His love. For
He giveth Himself to us for our Food; He
giveth us sacraments; by Baptism and
repentance He conformeth us anew to original righteousness. Hence He saith [3], *I, if I
be lifted up from the earth, shall draw all men
unto me;* and Paul [4], *I live by the faith of the
Son of God, Who loved me and gave Himself
for me.* This most loving drawing, our dullness and weakness needeth, who ever, without grace, grovel amidst vile and earthly
things."

"All the methods and parts of God's government are twined together, as so many
twisted cords of love from Him, so ordered,
that they ought to draw man with all his
heart to love Him again." "[5] Man, the
image of the Mind of God, is impelled to zeal
for the service of God, not by fear, but by
love. No band is mightier, nor constrains
more firmly all the feelings of the mind. For
it holdeth not the body enchained, while the
mind revolteth and longeth to break away,
but it so bindeth to itself the mind and will,
that it should will, long for, compass, nought
beside, save how, even amid threats of death,
to obey the commands of God. Bands there
are, but bands so gentle and so passing sweet,
that we must account them perfect freedom
and the highest dignity."

And I was to them as they that take off (lit.
*that lift up) the yoke on their jaws, and I laid
meat unto them.* Thus explained, the words
carry on the description of God's goodness,
that He allowed not the yoke of slavery to
weigh heavy upon them, as He saith [6], *I am*

the Lord your God, Which brought you out of
the land of Egypt, that ye should not be their
bondmen, and I have broken the bands of your
yoke, and made you go upright; and God appealeth to them [7], Wherein have I wearied
thee ? testify against Me.

But the words seem more naturally to
mean, *I was to them,* in their sight, I was regarded by them, *as they that lift up the yoke on
their jaws,* i. e. *that raise the yoke,* (not being
already upon them) to place it *over their jaws.*
"For plainly the yoke never rests on the
jaws, but only passed over them, either when
put on the neck, or taken off." This, God
seemed to them to be doing, ever placing
some new yoke or constraint upon them. *And
I*, God adds, all the while *was placing meat
before them;* i. e. while God was taking all
manner of care of them, and providing for
them *all things richly to enjoy,* He was
regarded by them as one who, instead of *laying food before them,* was *lifting the yoke over
their jaws.* God did them all good, and they
thought it all hardship.

5. *He shall not return to Egypt.* Some had
probably returned already to Egypt; the rest
were looking to Egypt for help, and rebelling
against the Assyrian, (whose servant their
king Hoshea had become), and making alliance with So king of Egypt. The Prophet
tells them, as a whole, that they shall not
return to Egypt to which they looked, but
should have the Assyrian for their king,
whom they would not. *They refused to return*
to God, Who lovingly called them; therefore,
what they desired, they should not have;
and what they feared, that they should have.
They would not have God for their king;
therefore *the Assyrian* should *be their king,* and
a worse captivity than that of Egypt should
befall them. For, from *that* they were delivered; from this, now hanging over them,
never should they be restored.

6. *And the sword shall abide on his cities,* lit.
shall light, shall whirl down upon. It shall
come with violence upon them as a thing
whirled with force, and then it shall alight
and abide, to their destruction; as Jeremiah
says [8], *a whirlwind of the Lord is gone forth in
fury, a grievous whirlwind; it shall fall grievously* [lit. *whirl down] on the head of the wicked.*
As God said to David, after the murder of
Uriah [9], *Now therefore the sword shall never de-*

[1] Rup. Lap.   [2] Dion.   [3] S. John xii. 32.
[4] Gal. ii. 20.   [5] Osor.

[6] Lev. xxvi. 13.   [7] Mic. vi. 3.
[8] Jer. xxiii. 19.   [9] 2 Sam. xii. 10.

Before CHRIST cir. 740.	

7 And my people are bent to ^mbacksliding from me: ⁿthough they called them to the most High, † none at all would exalt him.

Before CHRIST cir. 740.
^m Jer. 3. 6, &c.
& 8. 5.
ch. 4. 16.
ⁿ ch. 7. 16.
† Heb. together they exalted not.

8 ^oHow shall I give thee up, Ephraim? how shall I deliver thee, Israel? How shall I make thee as ^pAdmah? how shall I set thee as Zeboim? ^qmine heart is

Before CHRIST cir. 740.
^o Jer. 9. 7.
ch. 6. 4.
^p Gen. 14. 8.
& 19. 24, 25.
Deut. 29. 23.
Amos 4. 11.
^q Deut. 32. 36.
Is. 63. 15.
Jer. 31. 20.

part from thy house, so as to Israel, whose kings were inaugurated by bloodshed. By God's appointment, "blood will have blood." Their own sword first came down and rested upon them; then the sword of the Assyrian. So after they *had killed the Holy One and the Just,* the sword of the Zealots came down and rested upon them, before the destruction by the Romans.

And shall consume his branches, i. e. his mighty men. It is all one, whether the mighty men are so called, by metaphor, from the *branches* of a tree, or from the *bars* of a city, made out of those branches. Their mighty men, so far from escaping for their might, should be the first to perish.

And devour them, *because of their own counsels.* Their counsels, wise after this world's wisdom, were without God, against the counsels of God. Their destruction then should come from their own wisdom, as it is said[1], *Let them fall by their own counsels,* and Job saith[2], *He taketh the wise in their own craftiness, and the counsel of the cunning is carried headlong,* i. e. it is the clean contrary of what they intend or plan; they purpose, as they think, warily; an unseen power whirls their scheme on and precipitates it. *And his own counsel shall cast him down*[3]; and above; [4] *Israel shall be ashamed through his own counsels.* Hoshea's conspiracy with So, which was to have been his support against Assyria, brought Assyria against him, and his people into captivity.

7. *And My people are bent to backsliding from Me,* lit. *are hung to it!* as we say, " a man's whole being *hangs* on a thing." A thing *hung* to or *on* another, sways to and fro within certain limits, but its relation to that on which it is hung, remains immovable. Its power of motion is restrained within those limits. So Israel, so the sinner, however he veer to and fro in the details and circumstances of his sin, is fixed and immovable in his adherence to his sin itself. Whatever else Israel did, on one thing his whole being, as a nation, depended, on *backsliding* or aversion[5] from God. The political existence of Israel, as a separate kingdom, depended on his worship of the calves, *the sin wherewith* Jeroboam *made Israel to sin.* This was the ground of their[6] *refusing*

to return, that, through habitual sin, they were no longer in their own power: they were fixed in evil.

Though they called them to the most High, lit. *called him.* As one man, the prophets called Israel; as one man, Israel refused to return; *none at all would exalt* Him, lit. *together he exalteth* Him *not.*

8. *How shall I give thee up, Ephraim?* "[7]God is infinitely just and infinitely merciful. The two attributes are so united in Him, yea, so one in Him Who is always One, and in Whose counsels *there is no variableness, nor shadow of turning,* that the one doth not ever thwart the proceeding of the other. Yet, in order to shew that our ills are from our own ill-deserts, not from any pleasure of His in inflicting ill, and that what mercy He sheweth, is from His own goodness, not from any in us, God is represented in this empassioned expression as in doubt, and (so to say) divided betwixt justice and mercy, the one pleading against the other. At the last, God so determines, that both should have their share in the issue, and that Israel should be both justly punished and mercifully spared and relieved."

God pronounces on the evil deserts of Israel, even while He mitigates His sentence. The depth of the sinner's guilt reflects the more vividly the depth of God's mercy. In saying, *how shall I make thee as Admah?* how *shall I set thee as Zeboim?* He says, in fact, that they were, for their sins, worthy to be utterly destroyed, with no trace, no memorial, save that eternal desolation like the five *cities of the plain,* of which were Sodom and Gomorrah, which God[8] *hath set forth for an example, suffering the vengeance of eternal fire.* Such was their desert. But God says, with inexpressible tenderness, *Mine heart is turned within Me* lit. *upon Me* or *against Me,* so as to be a burden to Him; as we say of the heart, that it is "heavy." God deigneth to speak as if His love was heavy, or a weight upon Him, while He thought of the punishment which their sins deserved.

My heart is turned. "[9]As soon as I had spoken evil against thee, mercy prevailed, tenderness touched Me; and the tenderness of the Father overcame the austerity of the Judge."

[1] Ps. v. 10.   [2] v. 13.   [3] Ib. xviii. 7.   [4] ch. x. 6.
[5] The Rabbins observe that מְשׁוּבָה is used in an

evil sense of *aversion* from God, תְּשׁוּבָה of conversion to Him.   [6] ver. 5.   [7] Poc.   [8] S. Jude 7.   [9] Rup.

Before
C H R I S T
cir. 740.
turned within me, my re-
pentings are kindled to-
gether.

9 I will not execute the
fierceness of mine anger, I

will not return to destroy
Ephraim : [r] for I am God,
and not man ; the Holy One
in the midst of thee : and
I will not enter into the city.

Before
C H R I S T
cir. 740.

[r] Num. 23. 19.
Is. 55. 8, 9.
Mal. 3. 6.

My repentings are kindled together, or *My
strong compassions* [1] *are kindled,* i. e. with the
heat and glow of love ; as the disciples say [2],
Did not our hearts burn within us? and as it is
said of Joseph *his bowels did yearn* [3] (lit. *were
hot) towards his brother;* and of the true mother
before Solomon, *her bowels yearned* [4] (E. M.
were hot) upon her son.

Admah and *Zeboim* were cities in the same
plain with Sodom and Gomorrah, and each
had their petty king [5]. In the history of the
destruction of Sodom and Gomorrah, they
are not named, but are included in the general title *those cities and all the plain* [6]. The
more then would Hosea's hearers think of that
place in Moses where he does mention them,
and where he threatens them with the like
end ; [7] *when the stranger shall see,* that *the whole
land thereof* is *brimstone and salt and burning,
that it is not sown, nor beareth, nor any grass
groweth therein, like the overthrow of Sodom and
Gomorrah, Admah and Zeboim, which the Lord
overthrew in His anger and His wrath.* Such
was the end, at which all their sins aimed ;
such the end, which God had held out
to them ; but His *strong compassions were
kindled.*

9. *I will not execute the fierceness of Mine
anger.* It is the voice of *mercy, rejoicing
over judgment.* Mercy prevails in God over
the rigor of His justice, that though He will
not suffer them to go utterly unpunished, yet
He will abate of it, and not utterly consume
them.

I will not return to destroy Ephraim. God
saith that He will not, as it were, glean
Ephraim, going over it again, as man doth,
in order to leave nothing over. As it is in
Jeremiah [8], *They shall thoroughly glean the
remnant of Israel, as a vine. Turn back thine
hand, as a grapegatherer into the baskets;* and, *If
grapegatherers come to thee, would they not leave
some gleaning-grapes? but I have made Esau
bare* [9].

For I am *God and not man,* " [10] not swayed
by human passions, but so tempering His
wrath, as, in the midst of it, to remember
mercy ; so punishing the iniquity of the sinful children, as at once to make good His
gracious promises which He made to their
forefathers." " [11] Man punishes, to destroy ;
God smites, to amend."

The Holy One in the midst of thee. The
holiness of God is at once a ground why He
punishes iniquity, and yet does not punish to
the full extent of the sin. Truth and faithfulness are part of the holiness of God. He,
the Holy One Who was *in the midst* of them,
by virtue of His covenant with their fathers,
would keep the covenant which He had
made, and for their father's sakes would not
wholly cut them off. Yet the holiness of
God hath another aspect too, in virtue of
which the unholy cannot profit by the
promises of the All-Holy. "I will not," paraphrases S. Cyril, "use unmingled wrath. I
will not *give* over Ephraim, wicked as he has
become, to entire destruction. Why? Do
they not deserve it? Yes, He saith, but *I
am God and not man,* i. e. Good, and not suffering the motions of anger to overcome Me.
For that is a human passion. Why then
dost Thou yet punish, seeing Thou art God,
not overcome with anger, but rather following Thine essential gentleness? I punish, He
saith, because I am not only Good, as God,
but Holy also, hating iniquity, rejecting the
polluted, turning away from God-haters, converting the sinner, purifying the impure, that
he may again be joined to Me. We, then, if
we prize the being with God, must, with all
our might, fly from sin, and remember what
He said, *Be ye holy, for I am holy.*"

And I will not enter the city. God, Who is
everywhere, speaks of Himself, as present to
us, when He shews that presence in acts of
judgment or of mercy. He visited His
people in Egypt, to deliver them ; He visited
Sodom and Gomorrah as a Judge, making
known to us that He took cognizance of their
extreme wickedness. God says, that He
would *not enter the city,* as He did *the cities of
the plain,* when He overthrew them, because
He willed to save them. As a Judge, He
acts as though He looked away from their
sin, lest, seeing their city to be full of wickedness, He should be compelled to punish it.
" [12] I will not smite indiscriminately, as man
doth, who when wroth, bursts into an offending city, and destroys all. In this sense, the
Apostle says [13], *Hath God cast away His people?
God forbid! For I also am an Israelite, of the
seed of Abraham, of the tribe of Benjamin. God
hath not cast away His people, whom He foreknew.*

---

[1] The word נחומי is an intensive.
[2] S. Luke xxiv. 32.   [3] Gen. xliii. 30.
[4] 1 Kings iii. 26. The word is the same in all
three places נכמרו.

[5] Gen. xiv. 2.   [6] Ib. xix. 25.
[7] Deut. xxix. 22, 3.   [8] vi. 9.
[9] Ib. xlix. 9, 10.   [10] Poc.   [11] S. Jer.
[12] Rup.   [13] Rom. xi. 1, 2, 4, 5.

Before
CHRIST
cir. 740.

a Is. 31. 4.
Joel 3. 16.
Amos 1. 2.

t Zech. 8. 7.

10 They shall walk after the LORD: a he shall roar like a lion: when he shall roar, then the children s h a l l tremble t from the west.

11 They shall tremble as a bird out of Egypt, u and as a dove out of the land of Assyria: x and I will place them in their houses, saith the LORD.

Before
CHRIST
cir. 740.

u Is. 60. 8.
ch. 7. 11.
x Ezek. 28. 25,
26. & 37. 21, 25.

What saith the answer of God to Elias! I have reserved to Myself seven thousand men, who have not bowed the knee to Baal. Even so then, at this present time also, there is a remnant according to the election of grace. God then was wroth, not with His people, but with unbelief. For He was not angered in such wise, as not to receive the remnant of His people, if they were converted. No Jew is therefore repelled, because the Jewish nation denied Christ; but whoso, whether Jew or Gentile, denieth Christ, he himself, in his own person, repels himself."

10. *They shall walk after the Lord.* Not only would God not destroy them all, but a remnant of them should *walk after the Lord*, i. e. they shall believe in Christ. The Jews of old understood this of Christ. One of them saith [1], "this pointeth to the time of their redemption." And another [2], "Although I will withdraw from the midst of them My Divine Presence for their iniquity, and remove them out of their own land, yet shall there be a long time in which they shall seek after the Lord and find Him." This is what Hosea has said before [3], that they should *abide many days without a king and without a prince, and without a sacrifice;—afterward shall the children of Israel return and seek the Lord their God, and David their king.* " [4] Whereas now they *fled from God*, and *walked after other gods after the imagination of their evil hearts, after their own devices* [5], then He promises, they shall *walk after* God *the Lord*, following the will, the mind, the commandments, the example of Almighty God. As God says of David, He *kept My commandments, and walked after Me with all his heart* [6]; and Micah foretells that *many nations shall say, we will walk in His paths* [7]." They shall *follow after* Him, Whose Infinite perfections none can reach; yet they shall *follow after*, never standing still, but reaching on to that which is unattainable; by His grace, attaining the more by imitating what is inimitable, and stopping short of no perfection, until, in His Presence, they be perfected in Him.

He shall roar like a lion. Christ is called *the Lion of the tribe of Judah* [8]. His *roaring* is His loud call to repentance, by Himself and by His Apostles. The voice of God to sin-

ners, although full of love, must be full of awe too. He calls them, not only to flee to His mercy, but to *flee from the wrath to come.* He shall call to them with a voice of Majesty and command.

When He shall roar, the children shall tremble from the West, i. e. they shall come in haste and fear to God. " [9] *His word is powerful, sharper than any two-edged sword, piercing even to the dividing asunder of soul and spirit, and of the joints and marrow.* Whence those whose hearts were pricked at the preaching of St. Peter, said to him with trembling [10], *Men and brethren what shall we do?* So did the preaching of judgment to come terrify the world, that from all places some did come out of the captivity of the world and did fly to Christ [11]." He says, *from the West;* for *from the West* have most come in to the Gospel. Yet the Jews were then about to be carried to the East, not to the West; and of the West the prophets had no human knowledge. But the ten tribes, although carried to the East into Assyria, did not all remain there, since before the final dispersion, we find Jews in Italy, Greece, Asia Minor; whither those who had been restored to their own land, would not have anew exiled themselves. In these, whenever they were converted, this prophecy was fulfilled.

11. *They shall tremble as a bird out of Egypt.* The West denoted Europe; Egypt and Assyria stand, each for all the lands behind them, and so for Africa and Asia; all together comprise the three quarters of the world, whence converts have chiefly come to Christ. These are likened to birds, chiefly for the swiftness with which they shall then haste to the call of God, who now turned away the more, the more they were called. The dove, especially, was a bird of Palestine, proverbial for the swiftness of its flight, easily affrighted, and flying the more rapidly, the more it was frightened, and returning to its cot from any distance whither it might be carried; whence Isaiah also says of the converts [12], *Who are these that fly as a cloud, and as the doves to their windows?* "The Hebrews," says S. Jerome, " refer this to the coming of the Christ, Who, they hope, will come; we shew that it hath taken place already. For both from Egypt and Assyria, i. e.

1 Tanchum, in Poc.   2 Kimchi.
3 Hos. iii. 4, 5.   4 Poc.
5 Hos. vii. 13.   Jer. vii. 9. iii. 17. xviii. 12.

6 1 Kings xiv. 8.   7 iv. 2.   8 Rev. v. 5.
9 Heb. iv. 12.   10 Acts ii. 37.
11 Poc.   12 Is. lx. 8.

Before CHRIST cir. 740.

ʲ ch. 12. 1.

12 ʲ Ephraim compasseth me about with lies, and the house of Israel with deceit: but Judah yet ruleth with God, and

is faithful ‖ with the saints.

Before CHRIST cir. 740.

‖ Or, *with the most holy.*

CHAPTER XII.

1 *A reproof of Ephraim, Judah, and Jacob.* 3 *By former favors*

from East and West, from North and South, have they come, and daily do they come, who sit down with Abraham, Isaac and Jacob."

And I will place them in their houses. Their houses may be their own particular Churches, in the one Church or *House of God*[1]. In this house, God says, that He will make them to dwell, not again to be removed from it, nor shaken in it, but in a secure dwelling-place here until they be fitted to be removed to everlasting habitations. "[2] *In their houses,* i. e. in the mansions prepared for them. For from the beginning of the world, when He created our first parents, and blessed them and said, *Increase and multiply and replenish the earth,* He prepared for them everlasting *houses* or mansions. Whereof He said, just before His Death, *In My father's house are many mansions,* and in the last Day, He will say, *Come ye blessed of My Father, inherit the kingdom prepared for you from the foundation of the world.*

12. *Ephraim compasseth Me about with lies.* Having spoken of future repentance, conversion, restoration, he turns back to those around him, and declares why they can have no share in that restoration. Nothing about them was true. If ever they approached God, it was *with lies.* "[3] God, being infinite, cannot really be *compassed about.*" The Prophet so speaks, to describe the "great multitude of those who thus lied to God, and the multitude and manifoldness of their lies. Wherever God looked, in all parts of their kingdom, in all their doings, all which He could see was lying to Himself." All was, as it were, one throng of lies, heaped on one another, jostling with one another. Such is the world now. "Their sin was especially a lie, because they sinned, not through ignorance, but through malice." Their chief lie was the setting up of the worship of the calves, with a worldly end, yet with pretence of religion towards God; denying Him, the One true God, in that they joined idols with Him, yet professing to serve Him. And so all their worship of God, their repentance, their prayers, their sacrifices were all one lie. For one lie underlay all, penetrated all, corrupted all. All half-belief is unbelief; all half-repentance is unrepentance, all half-worship is unworship; and, in that each and all give themselves out for that Divine whole, whereof they are but the coun-

terfeit, each and all are *lies,* wherewith men, on all sides, encompass God. From these wrong thoughts of God all their other deceits flowed, while yet, "they deceived, not Him but themselves, in that they thought that they could deceive Him, Who cannot be deceived." When Christ came, the house of Israel surrounded Him with lies, the scribes and lawyers, the Pharisees and Sadducees and Herodians, vying with one another, *how they might entangle Him in His talk*[4].

But Judah yet ruleth with God. Ephraim had cast off the rule of God, the kings and priests whom He had appointed, so that his whole kingdom and polity was without God and against Him. In contrast with this, Judah, amid all His sins, was outwardly faithful. He adhered to the line of kings, from whom was to spring the Christ, David's Son but David's Lord. He worshiped with the priests whom God had appointed to offer the typical sacrifices, until *He* should come, *the High Priest forever, after the order of Melchisedek,* Who should end those sacrifices by the Sacrifice of Himself. Thus far Judah *ruled with God*; he was on the side of God, maintained the worship of God, was upheld by God. So Abijah said to Jeroboam[5], *The Lord is our God, and we have not forsaken Him, and the priests which minister unto the Lord are the sons of Aaron, and the Levites wait upon their business. For we keep the charge of the Lord our God, but ye have forsaken Him, and behold God is with us for our Captain, &c.*

And is faithful with the saints; or [better perhaps, with the E. M.] *with the All-Holy.* The same plural is used of God elsewhere[6]; and its use, like that of the ordinary name of God, is founded on the mystery of the Trinity. It does not teach it, but neither can it be accounted for in any other way. This faithfulness of Judah was outward only, (as the upbraiding of the Prophet to Judah testifies,) yet did it much favor inward holiness. *The body without the soul is dead;* yet the life, even when seeming to be dying out, might be brought back, when the body was there; not, when it too was dissolved. Hence Judah had many good kings, Israel none. Yet, in that he says, *yet ruleth with God,* he shews that a time was coming when Judah too would be, not *with God* but against Him, and also would be cast off.

XII. 1. *Ephraim feedeth on wind, and fol-*

---

[1] 1 Tim. iii. 15.   [2] Rup.   [3] Poc.

[4] S. Matt. xxii. 15.   [5] 2 Chron. xiii. 10–12.

[6] קדושים Josh. xxiv. 19. and in Prov. xxx. 3. where our translators too render it *the holy.*

Before
CHRIST
cir. 725.

ᵃ ch. 8. 7.

ᵇ 2 Kgs. 17. 4.
ch. 5. 13. & 7.
11.

he exhorteth to repentance. 7
Ephraim's sins provoke God.

EPHRAIM ᵃfeedeth on wind, and followeth after the east wind: he daily increaseth lies and desolation; ᵇand they do make a covenant with the

Assyrians, and ᶜoil is carried into Egypt.

2 ᵈThe LORD hath also a controversy with Judah, and will †punish Jacob according to his ways; according to his doings will he recompense him.

Before
CHRIST
cir. 725.

ᶜ Is. 30. 6.
& 57. 9.
ᵈ ch. 4. 1.
Mic. 6. 2.
† Heb. *visit upon.*

loweth after the east wind. The East wind in Palestine, coming from Arabia and the far East, over large tracts of sandy waste, is parching, scorching, destructive to vegetation, oppressive to man, violent and destructive on the sea ¹, and, by land also, having the force of the whirlwind. ² *The East wind carrieth him away and he departeth, and as a whirlwind hurleth him out of his place.* In leaving God and following idols, Ephraim *fed on* what is unsatisfying, and chased after what is destructive. If a hungry man were to *feed on wind,* it would be light food. If a man could overtake the East wind, it were his destruction. Israel "³ *fed on wind,* when he sought by gifts to win one who could aid him no more than the wind; *he chased the East wind,* when, in place of the gain which he sought, he received from the patron whom he had adopted, no slight loss." Israel sought for the scorching wind, when it could betake itself under the shadow of God. " ⁴ The scorching wind is the burning of calamities, and the consuming fire of affliction."

He increaseth lies and desolation. Unrepented sins and their punishment are, in God's government, linked together; so that to multiply sin is, in fact, to multiply desolation. Sin and punishment are bound together, as cause and effect. Man overlooks what he does not see. Yet not the less does he ⁵ *treasure up wrath against the Day of wrath and revelation of the righteous Judgment of God.* "³ *Lying* will signify false speaking, false dealing, false belief, false opinions, false worship, false pretences for color thereof, false hopes, or relying on things that will deceive. In all these kinds, was Ephraim at that time guilty, adding one sort of lying to another."

They do make a covenant with the Assyrians and oil is carried into Egypt. Oil was a chief product of Palestine, whence it is called ⁶ *a land of oil olive;* and *oil* with balm was among its chief exports to Tyre ⁷. It may also include precious ointments, of which it was the basis. As an export of great value, it stands for all other presents, which Hoshea

sent to So, King of Egypt. Ephraim, threatened by God, looked first to the Assyrian, then to Egypt, to strengthen itself. Having dealt falsely with God, he dealt falsely with man. First, he *made covenant with* Shalmaneser, king of *Assyria;* then, finding the tribute, the price of his help, burdensome to him, he broke that covenant, by sending to Egypt. Seeking to make friends out of God, Ephraim made the more powerful, the Assyrian, the more his enemy, by seeking the friendship of Egypt ; and God executed His judgments through those, by whose help they had hoped to escape them.

2. *The Lord hath also a controversy with Judah, and will punish Jacob.* The guilt of Judah was not open apostasy, nor had he filled up the measure of his sins. Of him, then, God saith only, that He *had a controversy with* him, as our Lord says to the *Angel of the Church of Pergamos* ᵇ, *I have a few things against thee. Repent, or else I will come unto thee quickly, and fight against thee with the sword of My mouth.* Of Ephraim, whose sin was complete, He says, that the Lord *is to punish.* God had set His mind, as we say, on punishing him ; He had (so to speak) set Himself to do it ⁹. Jacob, like Israel, is here the name for the chief part of Israel, i. e. the ten tribes. Our Lord uses the same gradation in speaking of different degrees of evil-speaking ¹⁰ ; *Whosoever of you is angry without a cause, shall be in danger of the judgment ; and whosoever shall say to his brother, Raca, shall be in danger of the council ; but whosoever shall say, Thou fool, shall be in danger of hell-fire.* " ¹¹ The justice of God falls more severely on those who degenerate from a holy parent, than on those who have no incitement to good from the piety of their home." To amplify this, " ¹² The Prophet explains what good things Jacob received, to shew both the mercy of God to Jacob, and the hardness of Ephraim towards God. While Jacob was yet in his mother's womb, he took his brother by the heel, not by any strength of his own, but by the mercy of God, Who knows and loves those whom he hath predestinated."

¹ Ps. xlviii. 7.   ² Job xxvii. 21. See Jer. xviii. 17.
³ Poc.   ⁴ S. Cyr.
⁵ Rom. ii. 5.   ⁶ Deut. viii. 8.

⁷ Ezek. xxvii. 17.   See ab. ii. 8.
⁸ Rev. ii. 12, 16.   ⁹ The force of ל.
¹⁰ S. Matt. v. 22.   ¹¹ Osor.   ¹² S. Jer.

Before
CHRIST
cir. 725.

*Gen. 25. 26.
† Heb. *was a
prince*, or,
behaved himself † *'had power with God :
princely.* *Gen. 32, 24, &c.

3 ¶ He took his brother
*by the heel in the womb,
and by his strength he
*'had power with God :

4 Yea, he had power
over the angel, and pre-
vailed: he wept, and made
supplication unto him : he

Before
CHRIST
cir. 725.

---

3. *He took his brother by the heel in the womb.*
Whether or no the act of Jacob was beyond
the strength, ordinarily given to infants in
the womb, the meaning of the act was beyond
man's wisdom to declare. Whence the Jews
paraphrased, "[1] Was it not predicted of your
father Jacob, before he was born, that he
should become greater than his brother?"
Yet this was not fulfilled until more than
500 years afterwards, nor completely until
the time of David. These gifts were promised
to Jacob out of the free mercy of God, antecedent to all deserts. But Jacob, thus
chosen without desert, shewed forth the power
of faith; *By his strength he had power with God.*
"[2] The strength by which he did this, was
God's strength, as well as that by which God
contended with him ; yet it is well called *his*,
as being by God given to him. Yet *he had
power with God,* God so ordering it, that the
strength which was in Jacob, should put
itself forth with greater force, than that in
the assumed body, whereby He so dealt with
Jacob. God, as it were, bore the office of two
persons, shewing in Jacob more strength than
He put forth in the Angel." "By virtue of
that faith in Jacob, it is related that God
could not prevail against him. He could not
because He would not overthrow his faith
and constancy. By the touch in the hollow
of his thigh, He but added strength to his
faith, shewing him Who it was Who wrestled
with him, and that He willed to bless him."
For thereon Jacob said those words which
have become a proverb of earnest supplica-
tion [3], *I will not let thee go, except thou bless me,*
and, *I have seen God, face to face, and my life
is preserved.* "[4] He was strengthened by the
blessing of Him Whom he overcame."
4. *He wept and made supplication unto Him.*
Jacob's weeping is not mentioned by Moses.
Hosea then knew more than Moses related.
He could not have gathered it out of Moses;
for Moses relates the words of earnest supplication; yet the tone is that of one, by force of
earnest energy, wresting, as it were, the blessing from God, not of one weeping. Yet Hosea adds this, in harmony with Moses. For
"vehement desires and earnest petitions frequently issue in tears." "[5] To implore
means to ask with tears." "Jacob, learning,
that God Himself thus deigned to deal with
him, might well out of amazement and wonder,

out of awful respect to Him, and in earnest
desire of a blessing, pour out his supplication
with tears." Herein he became an image of
Him, *Who, in the days of His flesh, offered up
prayers and supplications, with strong crying and
tears unto Him that was able to save Him from
death, and was heard in that He feared* [6].
"[7] This which he saith, *he prevailed,* sub-
joining, *he wept and made supplication,*
describes the strength of penitents ; for in
truth they are strong by weeping earnestly
and praying perseveringly for the forgiveness of sins, according to that, *From the days
of John the kingdom of heaven suffereth violence,
and the violent take it by force.* Whosoever
so imitates the Patriarch Jacob, who wrestled
with the Angel, and, as a conqueror, extorted
a blessing from him, he, of whatever nation
he be, is truly Jacob, and deserveth to be
called Israel." "[8] Yea, herein is the uncon-
querable might of the righteous, this his
wondrous wrestling, herein his glorious victories, in glowing longings, assiduous prayers,
joyous weeping. Girt with the might of holy
orison, they strive with God, they wrestle
with His judgment, and will not be overcome,
until they obtain from His goodness all they
desire, and extort it, as it were, by force,
from His hands."
He found him in *Bethel.* This may mean
either that "God found Jacob," or that
"Jacob found God;" which are indeed one
and the same thing, since we find God, when
He has first found us. God *found,* i. e. made
Himself known to Jacob twice in this place;
first, when he was going toward Haran,
when he saw the vision of the ladder and
the angels of God ascending and descending,
and the Lord stood above it and said, I am *the
Lord God of Abraham and the God of Isaac;* and
Jacob first called the place *Bethel;* secondly,
on his return, when God spake with him,
giving him the name of Israel. Both revelations of God to Jacob are probably included
in the words, *He found him in Bethel,* since,
on both occasions, God did *find him,* and come
to him, and he *found* God. In Bethel, where
God *found* Jacob, Israel deserted Him, setting up the worship of the calves; yea, he
deserted God the more there, because of God's
mercy to his forefather, desecrating to false
worship the place which had been consecrated by the revelation of the true God; and

[1] Jon.   [2] Poc.   [3] Gen. xxxii. 26, 30.   [4] S. Jer.
[5] Implorare est fletu rogare. Imploro is formed
from ploro, which relation is retained in the French

Implorer, pleurer, pleurs. So we have *cry* (i. e.
weep) and *cry on him,* [R. Glouc.] *cry unto.*
[6] Heb. v. 7.   [7] Rup.   [8] Osor.

found him *in* ᵉ Beth-el,
and there he spake with
us ;

5 Even the LORD God
of hosts; the LORD *is* his
ʰ memorial.

---

choosing it the rather, because it had been
so consecrated.

And there He spake with us. For what He
said to Jacob, He said not to Jacob only, nor
for Jacob's sake alone, but, in him, He spake
to all his posterity, both the children of his
body and the children of his faith. Thus it is
said [1], *There did we rejoice in Him*, i. e. we, their
posterity, rejoiced in God there, where He so
delivered our forefathers, and, [2] *Levi also,
who receiveth tithes, paid tithes in Abraham, for
he was yet in the loins of his father, when Melchizedek met him.* And S. Paul saith, that what
was said to Abraham, *therefore it was imputed to
him for righteousness, was not written for his sake
alone, but for us also, to whom it shall be imputed,
if we believe on Him that raised up Jesus our
Lord from the dead* [3]. There He spake with
us, how, in our needs, we should seek and
find Him. In loneliness, apart from distractions, in faith, rising in proportion to our
fears, in persevering prayer, in earnestness,
which "clings so fast to God, that if God
would cast us into Hell, He should, (as one
said) Himself go with us, so should Hell not
be Hell to us," God is sought and found.

5. *Even the Lord God of Hosts, the Lord* is
His memorial. The word, here as elsewhere,
translated and written LORD, is the special
and, so to say, the proper Name of God, that
which He gave to Himself, and which declares His Being. God Himself authoritatively explained its meaning. When Moses
inquired of Him, what he should say to
Israel, when they should ask him, *what is the
Name* of the God of their fathers, Who, he was
to tell them, had sent him to them [4], *God
said*, I AM THAT I AM ; *thus shalt thou say,
I AM (EHYeH) hath sent me unto you; and
God said again unto Moses, Thus shalt thou say
unto the children of Israel; The* LORD [lit HÉ
IS, YeHeVeH [5],] *the God of your fathers, the
God of Abraham, the God of Isaac, and the
God of Jacob, hath sent me unto you ; This is
My Name for ever, and this is My memorial
unto all generations.* I AM, expresses Self-
existence ; He Who Alone IS. I AM THAT

[1] Ps. lxvi. 6.   [2] Heb. vii. 9, 10.
[3] Rom. iv, 23, 4.   [4] Ex. iii. 13-15.
[5] יְהוָֹה "HE IS," from an old verb הוה "*is*," which
exists in Chaldee and Syriac, and which in Hebrew
became הָיָה, as חוה "lives" (whence the name of
Eve חַוָּה) became היה. The old form remained in
poetic language in the Imperative (Gen. xxvii. 19.
Job xxxvii. 6. Is. xvi. 4.) and in the Participle, Eccl.
ii. 22. Neh. vi. 6. The root הוה must have been
almost out of use in the time of Moses, since the
word is explained in Exodus by the use of the verb
היה, not by הוה. The vowels, by which the consonants are to be pronounced, must remain uncertain. It might be pronounced *Yihveh* (like יְהְיֶה)

I AM, expresses His Unchangeableness, the
necessary attribute of the Self-existent, Who,
since HE IS, ever IS all which He IS.
"To Be," says S. Augustine [6], "is a name of
unchangeableness. For all things which are
changed, cease to be what they were, and
begin to be what they were not. True Being,
pure Being, genuine Being, no one hath, save
He Who changeth not. He hath Being to
Whom it is said, *Thou shalt change them and
they shall be changed, but Thou art the Same.*
What is, I AM THAT I AM, but, I am
Eternal? What is, I AM THAT I AM,
save, I cannot be changed? No creature, no
heaven, no earth, no angel, *nor Power, nor
Throne, nor Dominion, nor Principality.* This
then being the name of eternity, it is somewhat more, than He vouchsafed to him **a**
name of mercy, *I am the God of Abraham, the
God of Isaac, the God of Jacob. That,* He is
in Himself, *this,* to us. If he willed only to
be That which he is in Himself, what should
we be? Since Moses understood, when it
was said to him, I AM THAT I AM, HE
Who IS hath sent me unto you, he believed
that this was much to men, he saw that this
was far removed from men. For whoso hath
understood, as he ought, That which IS, and
which truly IS, and, in whatever degree,
hath even transiently, as by a lightning flash,
been irradiated by the light of the One True
Essence, sees himself far below, in the utmost
farness of removal and unlikeness." This,
the Self-existent, the Unchangeable, was the
meaning of God's ancient Name, by which
He was known to the Patriarchs, although
they had not in act seen His unchangeableness ; for theirs was a life of faith, hoping
for what they saw not. The word, HE IS,
when used of Him by His creatures, expresses
the same which He says of Himself, I AM.
This He willed to be *His memorial forever.*
This the way in which He willed that we
should believe in Him and think of Him as
HE Who IS, the Self-existing, the Self-Same.

The way of pronouncing that Name is
lost [7]. The belief has continued, wherever
or *Yeheveh* (after the analogy of יְהֶמֶה) or less
probably, *Yehveh* like יְהְנֶה. Another pronunciation,
Yahaveh or *Yahveh*, might seem to be favored by
Theodoret's statement, that the Samaritans pronounced it IABE (Quest. 15. in Exod.); but on the
other hand the Samaritans, like the Galileans, had
probably a broader pronunciation than the Jews.
[6] Serm. 7. §7.
[7] The popular pronunciation *Jehovah*, is altogether
a mistake. When a word in the text is not read by
the Jews, (and this ceased to be read before the
vowels were written) the vowels belong, not to the
word itself, but to another, which is to be substituted
for it. Those placed under this word, יְהוָֹה, vary.

Before
CHRIST
cir. 725.
l ch. 14. 1. Mic. 6. 8.

6 l Therefore turn thou to thy God: keep mercy and judgment, and k wait on thy God continually.

Before
CHRIST
cir. 725.
k Ps. 37. 7.

the LORD is named. For by the Lord we mean the Unchangeable God. That belief is contradicted, whenever people use the name Jehovah, to speak of God, as though the belief in Him under the Old Testament differed from that of the New. Perhaps God allowed it to be lost, that people might not make so familiar with it, as they do with the word Jehovah, or use it irreverently and anti-Christianly, as some now employ other ways of pronouncing it. The Jews, even before the time of our Lord, ceased ordinarily to pronounce it. In the translations of the Old Testament, and in the Apocrypha, the words, "the Lord," were substituted for it. Jewish tradition states, that in later times the Name was pronounced in the Temple only, by the priests, on pronouncing the blessing commanded by God in the law[1]. On the great Day of atonement, it was said that the High Priest pronounced it ten times[2], and that when the people heard it, they fell on their faces, saying, "Blessed be the glorious name of His kingdom for ever and ever[3]." They say, however, that in the time of Simeon the Just [i. e. Jaddua[4].] who died about B. C. 322, the High Priests themselves disused it, for fear of its being pronounced by some irreverent person[5].

Our Lord Himself sanctioned the disuse of it, (as did the inspired Apostles yet more frequently,) since, in quoting places of the Old Testament in which it occurs, He uses instead of it the Name, the Lord[6]. It stands, throughout the Old Testament, as the Name which speaks of God in relation to His people, that He ever IS ; and, since He ever IS, then He IS unchangeably to us, all which He ever was, The Same, yesterday and to-day and for ever[7].

He then Who appeared to Jacob, and Who, in Jacob, spake to all the posterity of Jacob, was God ; whether it was (as almost all the early fathers thought[8],) God the Son, Who thus appeared in human form to the Patriarchs, Moses, Joshua, and in the time of the Judges, under the name of the

Angel of the Lord, or whether it was the Father. God Almighty thus accustomed man to see the form of Man, and to know and believe that it was God. He it was, the Prophet explains, the Lord, i. e. the Self-existent, the Unchangeable, Who was, and is and is to come[9], Who Alone Is, and from Whom are all things, "[10] the Fullness of Being, both of His own, and of all His creatures, the boundless Ocean of all which is, of wisdom, of glory, of love, of all good."

The Lord of Hosts, i. e. of all things visible and invisible, of the angels and heavenly spirits, and of all things animate and inanimate, which, in the history of the Creation, are called the host of heaven and earth[11], the one host of God. This was the way in which He willed to be had in mind, thought of, remembered. On the one hand then, as relates to Ephraim's sin, not by the calves, nor by any other created thing, did He will to be represented to men's minds or thoughts. On the other hand, as relates to God's mercies, since He, who revealed Himself to Jacob, was the unchangeable God, Israel had no cause to fear, if he returned to the faith of Jacob, whom God there accepted. Whence it follows ;

6. Therefore turn thou to thy God [lit. And thou, thou shalt turn so as to lean on thy God[12].] And thou unlike, he would say, as thou art to thy great forefather, now at least, turn to thy God; hope in Him, as Jacob hoped; and thou too shalt be accepted. God was the Same. They then had only to turn to Him in truth, and they too would find Him, such as Jacob their father had found Him, and then trust in him continually. Mercy and judgment include all our duty to our neighbor, love and justice. The Prophet selects the duties of the second table, as Micah also places them first[13], What doth the Lord require of thee, but to do justly and love mercy, and walk humbly with thy God ? and our Lord chooses those same commandments, in answer to the rich young man, who asked him, What shall I do, in order to enter into life[14] ? For men

They direct mostly, that the word Adonai, LORD, is to be read for it. But if this has just occurred, other vowels are placed, directing that it should be read Elohim, God. The placing of the vowels under the word are an indication, not that they are to be used with the word, but that they are not to be used with it. The vowels of a textual reading, when there is also a marginal reading, are always to be supplied by conjecture. It is better to own ignorance, how this name of God is pronounced, than to use the name Jehovah, which is certainly wrong, or any other which can only be conjectural. The subject is fully discussed in the disputations, edited by Reland, Decas Exercit. de nom. Jeh., esp. those of Drusius, Amama and Buxtorf.

[1] Num. vi. 24–26. see Massecheth Sota in Amama, l. c. p. 173.
[2] Massecheth Yoma, f. 39. p. 2. ib. p. 177.
[3] Lib. prec. 356. 2 Drus. Ib. p. 51.
[4] Drus. Tetr. c. 10. ib. 59.
[5] Maim. Yad Chazaka, c. 14. ⅔ 10. Ib. 174. Drus. p. 59.
[6] S. Matt. iv. 7. from Deut. vi. 16, and S. Matt. xxii. 44. from Ps. cx. 1. [7] Heb. xiii. 8.
[8] See Bp. Bull, Def. Fid. Nic. i. 1. 3–8. 12. ii. 4, 5. Tertullian de Præscr. ⅔ 13. p. 447. note. Oxf. Tr. [p. 463. ed. 2.] S. Athan. de Conc. Arim. p. 120 note q. Orat. l. c. Arian. pp. 235. 418. note h. Oxf. Tr.
[9] Rev. i. 4, 8.   [10] Lap.   [11] Gen. ii. 1.
[12] באלהיך תשוב.   [13] vi. 8.   [14] S. Matt. xix. 17.

Before
CHRIST
cir. 725.

|| Or, Ca-
naan: See
Ezek. 16. 3.
1 Prov. 11. 1.
Amos 8. 5.
|| Or, deceive.

7 ¶ *He is* || a merchant, [1] the balances of deceit *are* in his hand: he loveth to || oppress.

8 And Ephraim said,

Before
CHRIST
cir. 725.

m Zech. 11. 5.
Rev. 3. 17.
|| Or, *all my
labors suffice
me not:* he
shall have
† Heb. *which.*

m Yet I am become rich, I have found me out substance: || *in* all my labors they shall find none iniquity in me † that *were* sin. *punishment of iniquity in whom is sin.*

---

cannot deceive themselves so easily about their duties to their neighbor, as about their duty to God. It was in love to his neighbor that the rich young man failed.

Thou shalt turn, i. e. it is commonly said, thou oughtest to turn ; as our's has it, *turn.* But it may also include the promise that, at one time, *Israel shall turn to the Lord,* as S. Paul says, *so shall all Israel be saved.*

And wait on thy God continually. If they did so, they should not wait in vain. " [1] This word, *continually,* hath no small weight in it, shewing with what circumstances or properties their waiting or hope on God ought to be attended ; that it ought to be on Him alone, on Him always, without doubting, fainting, failing, intermission or ceasing, in all occasions and conditions which may befall them, without exception of time, even in their adversity." "Turn to *thy* God," he saith, " wait on *thy* God," as the great ground of repentance and of trust. *God had avouched them for His peculiar people* [2], and they had *avouched Him for* their only *God.* He then was still their God, ready to receive them, if they would return to Him.

7. He is *a merchant,* or, indignantly, *a merchant in whose hands are the balances of deceit !* How could they love *mercy and justice,* whose trade was *deceit,* who weighed out deceit with their goods? False in their dealings, in their weights and measures, and, by taking advantage of the necessities of others, oppressive also. Deceit is the sin of weakness, oppression is the abuse of power. Wealth does not give the power to use naked violence, but wealthy covetousness manifoldly grinds the poor. When for instance, wages are paid in necessaries priced exorbitantly, or when artizans are required to buy at a loss at their masters' shops, what is it but the union of deceit and oppression? The trading world is full of oppression, scarcely veiled by deceit. *He loveth to oppress.* Deceit and oppression have, each, a devilish attractiveness to those practiced in them ; deceit, as exercising cleverness, cunning, skill in overreaching, outwitting ; oppression, as indulging self-will, caprice, love of power, insolence, and the like vices. The word *merchant,* as the Prophet spoke it, was *Canaan* [3] ; merchants being so called, because the Canaanites or Phœnicians were the then great mer-

chant-people, as astrologers were called Chaldeans. The Phœnicians were, in Homer's time, infamous for their griping in traffic. They are called "gnawers [4]" and "moneylovers [5]." To call Israel, *Canaan,* was to deny to him any title to the name of Israel, "reversing the blessing of Jacob, so that, as it had been said of Jacob, *Thy name shall be called no more Jacob, but Israel,* he would in fact say, ' Thy name shall be called no more Israel, but *Canaan* ' ; as being, through their deeds, heirs, not to the blessings of Israel but to the curse of Canaan." So Ezekiel saith [6], *Thy father was an Amorite, and thy mother a Hittite.*

8. *And Ephraim said, Yet am I become rich,* lit. *I am simply rich.* As if he said, " the only result of all this, with which the Prophets charge me, is that *I am become rich :* and since God thus prospers me, it is a sure proof that he is not displeased with me, that *no iniquity* can be *found in me ;*" the ordinary practical argument of men, as long as God withholds His punishments, that their ways cannot be so displeasing to Him. With the men of this world, with its politicians, in trade, it is the one decisive argument : " I was in the right, for I succeeded." " It was a good speculation, for he gained thousands." " It was good policy ; for, see its fruits." An answer, at which the heathen laughed, " the people hisses me, but I, I, safe at home, applaud myself, when the coin jingles in my chest [7]." The heathen ridiculed it ; Christians enact it. But in truth, the fact that God does not punish, is often the evidence of His extremest displeasure.

They shall find none iniquity in me, that were sin. The merchants of Ephraim continue their protest ; " In all the toil of my hands, all my buying and selling, my bargains, contracts, they can bring no iniquity home to me," and then, in a tone of simple innocence, they add, *that* were *sin,* as though they *could* not do, what to do were sin. None suspect themselves less, than those intent on gain. The evil customs of other traders, the habits of trade, the seeming necessity for some frauds, the conventional nature of others, the minuteness of others, with their frequent repetition, blind the soul, until it sees no sin, while, with every smallest sale, "they sell their own souls into the bargain [8]."

1 Poc.   2 Deut. xxvi. 17, 18.   3 כנען.
4 Philostratus in Grot.

5 Od. xiv. 283. xv. 413.   6 xvi. 3.
7 Hor. Sat. i. 1. 66.   8 South's Sermons.

Before
CHRIST
cir. 725.
ᵃ ch. 13. 4.
ᵒ Lev. 23. 42, 43.
Neh. 8. 17. Zech. 14. 16.

9 And ⁿI *that am* the LORD thy God from the land of Egypt ᵒwill yet

make thee to dwell in tabernacles, as in the days of the solemn feast.

Before
CHRIST
cir. 725.

9. *And I, the Lord thy God from the land of Egypt.* God, in few words, comprises whole centuries of blessings, all, from the going out of Egypt to that very day, all the miracles in Egypt, in the wilderness, under Joshua, the Judges; one stream of benefits it had been, which God had poured out upon them from first to last. The penitent sees in one glance, how God had been *his* God, from his birth till that hour, and how he had all along offended God.

Will yet make thee to dwell in tabernacles. The feast of tabernacles was the yearly remembrance of God's miraculous guidance and support of Israel through the wilderness. It was the link, which bound on their deliverance from Egypt to the close of their pilgrim-life and their entrance into their rest. The passage of the Red Sea, like Baptism, was the beginning of God's promises. By it Israel was saved from Egypt and from bondage, and was born to be a people of God. Yet, being the beginning, it was plainly not the completion; nor could they themselves complete it. Enemies, more powerful than they, had to be dispossessed; *the great and terrible wilderness, the fiery serpents and scorpions, and the land of exceeding drought, where was no water* [1], had to be surmounted; no food was there, no water, for so vast a multitude. It was a time of the visible Presence of God. He promised [2]; *I send an Angel before thee to keep thee in the way and to bring thee into the place which I have prepared.* He brought them *forth water out of the rock of flint, and fed them with Manna which,* He says, *thy fathers knew not* [3]. *Thy raiment,* He appeals to them, *waxed not old, nor did thy foot swell these forty years* [4]; *thy shoe is not waxen old upon thy foot; ye have not eaten bread, neither have ye drunk wine or strong drink, that ye may know that I am the Lord your God* [5]. It was a long trial-time, in which they were taught entire dependence upon God; a time of sifting, in which God proved His faithfulness to those who persevered. Standing there between the beginning and the end of the accomplishment of God's promise to Abraham and to them, it was a type of His whole guidance of His people at all times. It was a pledge that God would held His own, if often *by a way which they knew not* [6], yet to rest, with Him. The yearly commemoration of it was not only a thanksgiv-

ing for God's past mercies; it was a confession also of their present relation to God, that *here we have no continuing city* [7]; that they still needed the guidance and support of God; and that their trust was not in themselves, nor in man, but in Him. This they themselves saw. "[8] When they said, 'Leave a fixed habitation, and dwell in a chance abode,' they meant, that the command to dwell in tabernacles was given, to teach us, that no man must rely on the height or strength of his house, or on its good arrangements though it abound in all good; nor may he rely on the help of any man, not though he were lord and king of the whole earth, but must trust in Him by Whose word the worlds were made. For with Him alone is power and faithfulness, so that, whereinsoever any man may place his trust, he shall receive no consolation from it, since in God alone is refuge and trust, as it is said, *Whoso putteth his trust in the Lord, mercy embraceth him on every side,* and *I will say unto the Lord, my Refuge and my Fortress, my God, in Him will I trust.*"

The feast of Tabernacles was also a yearly thanksgiving for the mercies with which God had *crowned the year.* The joy must have been even the greater, since it followed, by five days only, after the mournful day of Atonement, its rigid fast from evening to evening, and its confession of sin. Joy is greater when ushered in by sorrow; sorrow for sin is the condition of joy in God. The Feast of Tabernacles was, as far it could be, a sort of Easter after Lent. At the time when Israel rejoiced in the good gifts of the year, God bade them express, in act, their fleeting condition in this life. It must have been a striking confession of the slight tenure of all earthly things, when their kings and great men, their rich men and those who lived at ease, had all, at the command of God, to leave their ceiled houses, and dwell for seven days in rude booths, constructed for the season, pervious in some measure to the sun and wind, with no fixed foundation, to be removed when the festival was passed. "Because," says a Jewish writer [9], "at the time of the gathering of the increase from the field, man wishes to go from the field to his house to make a fixed abode there, the law was anxious, lest on account of this fixed abode, his heart should be lifted up at hav-

[1] Deut. viii. 15.
[2] Ex. xxiii. 20.
[3] Deut. viii. 15, 16.
[4] Ib. 4.
[5] Ib. xxix. 5, 6.
[6] Is. xlii. 16.
[7] Heb. xiii. 14. comp. xi. 9, 10.

[8] Menorat Hammaor, f. 39, col. 2 in Dachs Succa, pp. 527, 8.
[9] R. Sal. Ephr. Keli Yakar in Lev. l. c. in Dachs, p. 546.

Before
CHRIST
cir. 725.

P 2 Kgs. 17. 13.

10 [p] I have also spoken by the prophets, and I have multiplied visions, and used

similitudes, † by the ministry of the prophets.

11 [q] *Is there* iniquity *in*

Before
CHRIST
cir. 725.

† Heb. *by the hand.*
q ch. 5. 1. & 6. 8.

ing found a sort of palace, and he should *wax fat and kick.* Therefore it is written, *all that are Israelites born shall dwell in booths.* Whoso begins to think himself a citizen in this world, and not a foreigner, him God biddeth, leaving his ordinary dwelling, to remove into a temporary lodging, in order that, leaving these thoughts, he may learn to acknowledge that he is only a stranger in this world and not a citizen, in that he dwells as in a stranger's hut, and so should not attribute too much to the shadow of his beams, but *dwell under the shadow of the Almighty."* Every year, the law was publicly read in the feast. Ephraim was living clean contrary to all this. He boasted in his wealth, justified himself on the ground of it, ascribed it and his deliverance from Egypt to his idols. He would not keep the feast, as alone God willed it to be kept. While he existed in his separate kingdom, it could not be. Their political existence had to be broken, that they might be restored.

God then conveys the notice of the impending punishment in words which promised the future mercy. He did not, *then, make* them *to dwell in tabernacles.* For all their service of Him was out of their own mind, contrary to His Will, displeasing to Him. This, then, "I will *yet* make thee dwell in tabernacles," implies a distant mercy, beyond and distinct from their present condition. Looking on beyond the time of the Captivity, He says that they shall yet have a time of joy, *as in the days of the solemn feast.* God would give them a new deliverance, but out of a new captivity.

The feast of Tabernacles typifies this our pilgrim-state, the life of simple faith in God, for which God provides; poor in this world's goods, but rich in God. The Church militant dwells, as it were, in tabernacles; hereafter, we hope to be *received into everlasting habitations,* in the Church triumphant.

10. *I have also spoken by the prophets,* lit. *upon the prophets,* the revelation coming down from heaven upon them. Somewhat like this, is what Ezekiel says, *the hand of the Lord was strong upon me*[1]. God declares, in what way He had been their God *from the land of Egypt.* Their ignorance of Him was without excuse; for He had ever taught them, although they ever sought the false prophets, and persecuted the true. He taught them continually and in divers ways, if so be any impression might be made upon them.

He taught them, either in plain words, or in the *visions* which He *multiplied* to the prophets; or in the *similitudes* or parables, which He taught through their ministry. In the *vision,* God is understood to have represented the things to come, as a picture, to the prophet's mind, "[2] whether the picture were presented to his bodily eyes, or impressed on his imagination, and that, either in a dream, or without a dream." The *similitude,* which God says that He repeatedly, continually, used[3], seems to have been the parable, as when God compared His people to a vine, Himself to the Lord of the vineyard, or when He directed His prophets to do acts which should shadow forth some truth, as in the marriage of Hosea himself. God had said to Aaron, that He would thus make Himself known by the prophets. [4] *If there be a prophet among you, I, the Lord, will make Myself known unto him in a vision, and will speak unto him in a dream. My servant Moses is not so, who is faithful in all My house. With him will I speak mouth to mouth, even apparently, and not in dark speeches.* The dark *speech* in Moses answers to the *similitude* of Hosea; the *vision* and *dream* in Moses are comprehended in *visions,* as used by Hosea. The prophet Joel also says[5], *your old men shall dream dreams, your young men shall see visions.* So little ground then have they, who speak of the visions of Daniel and Zechariah, as if they belonged to a later age. "[6] I have instructed," God saith, "men of God, to form thee to piety, enlightening their minds with manifold knowledge of the things of God. And because the light of Divine wisdom could not otherwise shine on men placed here below in the prison-house of the body, I had them taught through figures and corporeal images, that, through them, they might rise to the incorporeal, and receive some knowledge of Divine and heavenly things. And thou, how didst thou require me? How didst thou shew thy teachableness? It follows;"

11. Is there *iniquity* in *Gilead?* The Prophet asks the question, in order to answer it the more peremptorily. He raises the doubt, in order to crush it the more impressively. Is there *iniquity* in *Gilead?* Alas, there was nothing else. *Surely they are vanity,* or, strictly, *they have become merely vanity.* As he said before, *they become abominations like their love.* "For such as men make their idols, or conceive their God to

1 iii. 14, etc.   2 Poc.
3 Such is the force of the Heb. אֲדַמֶּה.

4 Num. xii. 6–8.
5 ii. 28.   6 Osor.

Before CHRIST cir. 725.	

Before CHRIST cir. 725.

r ch. 4. 15. & 9. 15.
Amos 4. 4. & 5. 5.
s ch. 8. 11. & 10. 1.
t Gen. 28. 5. Deut. 26. 5.
u Gen. 29. 20, 28.

Gilead? surely they are vanity: they sacrifice bul-locks in r Gilgal: yea, s their altars *are* as heaps in the furrows of the fields.

12 And Jacob t fled into the country of Syria, and Israel u served for a wife, and for a wife he kept *sheep.*

13 x And by a prophet the LORD brought Israel out of Egypt, and by a prophet was he preserved.

14 y Ephraim provoked *him* to anger † most bit-terly: therefore shall he leave his † blood upon him, z and his a reproach shall his Lord return unto him.

Before CHRIST cir. 725.

x Ex. 12. 50, 51. & 13. 3.
Ps. 77. 20.
Is. 63. 11.
Mic. 6. 4.
y 2 Kgs. 17. 11–18.
† Heb. *with bitternesses.*
† Heb. *bloods.* See Ezek. 18.
13. & 24. 7, 8.
z Dan. 11. 18.
a Deut. 28. 37.

be, such they become themselves. As then he who worships God with a pure heart, is made like unto God, so they who worship stocks and stones, or who make passions and lusts their idols, lose the mind of men and become *like the beasts which perish." In Gil-gal they have sacrificed oxen. Gilead* represents all the country on its side, the East of Jor-dan; *Gilgal,* all on its side, the West of Jor-dan. In both, God had signally shewn forth His mercies; in both, they dishonored God, sacrificing to idols, and offering His crea-tures, as a gift to devils.

Yea, their altars are *as heaps in the furrows of the field.* Their altars are like the heaps of stones, from which men clear the ploughed land, in order to fit it for cultivation, as nu-merous, as profuse, as worthless, as desolate. *Their* altars they were, not God's. They did, (as sinners do,) in the service of devils, what, had they done it to God, would have been accepted, rewarded, service. Full often they sacrificed oxen[1]; they threw great state into their religion; they omitted nothing which should shed around it an empty shew of worship. They multiplied their altars, their sins, their ruins; many altars over against His one altar; "[2] rude heaps of stones, in His sight; and such they should become, no one stone being left in order upon another." In contrast with their sins and ingratitude, the Prophet exhibits two pictures, the one, of the virtues of the Patriarch whose name they bore, from whom was the beginning of their race; the other, of God's love to them, in that beginning of their national existence, when God brought those who had been a body of slaves in Egypt, to be His own people.

12. *And Jacob fled into the country of Syria.* Jacob chose poverty and servitude rather than marry an idolatress of Canaan. He knew not whence, except from God's bounty and Providence, he should have *bread to eat,* or *raiment to put on*[3]*; with his staff* alone he

passed over *Jordan*[4]. His voluntary poverty, bearing even unjust losses[5], and *repaying the things which he never took,* reproved their dis-honest traffic; his trustfulness in God, their mistrust; his devotedness to God, their alienation from Him, and their devotion to idols. And as the conduct was opposite, so was the result. Ill-gotten riches end in pov-erty; stable wealth is gained, not by the cu-pidity of man, but by the good pleasure of God. Jacob, having *become two bands,* trust-ing in God and enriched by God, returned from Syria to the land promised to him by God; Israel, distrusting God and enriching himself, was to return out of the land which the Lord his God had given him, to Assyria, amid the loss of all things.

13. *By a Prophet was he preserved* or *kept.* Jacob *kept sheep* out of love of God, sooner than unite himself with one, alien from God; his posterity *was kept* like a sheep by God, as the Psalmist said[6], *He led His people like sheep by the hand of Moses and Aaron.* They were *kept* from all evil and want and danger, by the direct power of God; *kept* from all the might of Pharaoh in Egypt and the Red Sea, "[2] not through any power of their own, but by the ministry of a single prophet; *kept, in that great and terrible wilderness*[7], wherein were *fiery serpents and scorpions and drought, where* was *no water,* but what God brought out of the rock of flint; no bread, but what he sent them from heaven." All this, God did for them *by a single Prophet; they* had many Prophets, early and late, calling upon them in the name of God, but they would not hearken unto them."

14. *Ephraim provoked* the Lord *most bitterly,* lit. *with bitternesses,* i. e. with most heinous sins, such as are most grievously displeasing to God, and were a most bitter requital of all His goodness. Wherefore *He shall leave* [or, *cast*] *his blood* [lit. *bloods*] *upon him.* The plural *bloods*[8] expresses the manifoldness of

[1] The force of זֶבַח. [2] Poc. [3] Gen. xxviii. 20.
[4] Ib. xxxii. 10. [5] Ib. xxxi. 39.
[6] Ps. lxxvii. 20. [7] Deut. viii. 15.
[8] דְּמִים. When David said to the Amalekite, *Thy*

bloods be upon thy head, 2 Sam. i. 16. it was the blood-guiltiness in slaying Saul, which he had imputed to himself. When the spies said, *his blood* [sing.] *be upon his head,* (Josh. ii. 19.) they meant, let him-self and no other be guilty of the loss of his life.

CHAPTER XIII.

1 *Ephraim's glory, by reason of
idolatry, vanisheth.* 5 *God's
anger for their unkindness.* 9
A promise of God's mercy. 15
A judgment for rebellion.

WHEN Ephraim spake
trembling, he exalted
h i m s e l f in Israel; but
ᵃ when he offended in Baal,
he died.

ᵃ Kgs. 17. 16, 18.
ch. 11. 2.

the bloodshed. It is not used in Holy Scripture of mere guilt. Ephraim had shed blood profusely, so that it ran like water in the land [1]. He had sinned with a high hand against God, in destroying man made in the image of God. Amid that bloodshed, had been the blood not of the innocent only, but of those whom God sent to rebuke them for their idolatry, their rapine, their bloodshed. *Jezebel cut off the prophets of the Lord* [2], as far as in her lay, with a complete excision. Ephraim thought his sins past; they were out of his sight; he thought that they were out of God's also; but they were laid up with God; and God, the Prophet says, would *cast* them down *upon him*, so that they would crush him.
And his reproach shall his Lord return unto him. For the blood which he had shed, should his own blood be shed; for the reproaches which he had in divers ways cast against God or brought upon Him, he should inherit reproach. Those who rebel against God, bring reproach on Him by their sins, reproach Him by their excuses for their sins, reproach Him in those whom He sends to recall them from their sins, reproach Him for chastening them for their sins. All who sin against the knowledge of God, bring reproach upon Him by acting sinfully against that knowledge. So Nathan says to David [3], *Thou hast given much occasion to the enemies of God to blaspheme.* The reproachful words of the enemies of God are but the echo of the opprobrious deeds of His unfaithful servants. The reproach is therefore, in an especial manner, *their reproach* who caused it. All Israel's idolatries had this aggravation. Their worship of the calves or of Baal or of any other gods of the nations, was a triumph of the false gods over God. Then, all sin must find some plea for itself, by impugning the wisdom or goodness of God who forbad it. Jeroboam, and Ephraim by adhering to Jeroboam's sin, reproached God, as though the going up to Jerusalem was a hard service. *It is too much for you to go up to Jerusalem; Behold thy gods, O Israel, which brought thee up out of the land of Egypt.* "[4] It was an open injury and reproach to God, to attribute to dead lifeless things those great and wonderful things done by Him for them." All the reproach, which they, in these ways, brought,

or cast upon God, he says, *his Lord shall return* or *restore* to them. Their's it was; He would give it back to them, as He says [5], *Them that honor Me, I will honor; and they that despise Me, shall be lightly esteemed.* Truly shame and reproach have been for centuries the portion of God's unfaithful people. To those who are lost, He gives back their reproach, in that they *rise to reproaches* [6] *and everlasting abhorrence* [7]. It is an aggravation of this misery, that He Who shall *give back to him* his reproach, had been *his God.* Since *his God* was against him, who could be for him? "For whither should we go for refuge, save to Him? If we find wrath with Him, with whom should we find ruth?" Ephraim did not, the sinner will not, allow God to be *his God* in worship and service and love: but whether he willed or no, God would remain his Lord. He was, and might still have been their Lord for good; they would not have Him so, and so they should find Him still their Lord, as an Avenger, returning their own evil to them.

XIII. I. *When Ephraim spake trembling,* i. e. probably "there was trembling." "[8] Ephraim was once very awful, so as, while he spake, the rest of the tribes were ready to tremble." The prophet contrasts two conditions of Ephraim, of prosperity, and destruction. His prosperity he owed to the undeserved mercy of God, Who blessed him for Joseph's sake; his destruction, to his own sin. There is no period recorded, *when Ephraim spake tremblingly,* i. e. in humility. Pride was his characteristic, almost as soon as he had a separate existence as a tribe [9]. Under Joshua, it could not be called out, for Ephraim gained honor, when Joshua, one of themselves, became the captain of the Lord's people. Under the Judges, their pride appeared. Yet God tried them, by giving them their hearts' desire. They longed to be exalted, and He satisfied them, if so be they would thus serve Him. They had the chief power, and were a *terror* to Judah. *He exalted himself,* (or perhaps *he was exalted,*) *in Israel; but when he offended in Baal he died;* lit. *and he offended in Baal and died.* He abused the goodness of God; his sin followed as a consequence of God's goodness to him. God raised him, and he offended. The alliance with a king of Tyre

[1] See ab. iv. 2. v. 2.
[3] 2 Sam. xii. 14.
[5] 1 Sam. ii. 30.
[2] 1 Kings xviii. 4.
[4] S. Cyr.
[6] Dan. xii. 2.
[7] The word is the same as in Is. lxvi. 24.
[8] Bp. Hall.
[9] See on v. 5.

Before
CHRIST
cir. 725.

† Heb. *they
add to sin.*
ᵇ ch. 2. 8. & 8. 4.

2 And now † they sin
more and more, and ᵇ have
made them molten images
of their silver, *and* idols
according to their own understanding, all of it the
work of the craftsmen :
they say of them, Let ‖ the
men that sacrifice ᶜ kiss the
calves.

Before
CHRIST
cir. 725.

‖ Or, *the sacri-
ficers of men.*
ᶜ 1 Kgs. 19. 18.

and Sidon, which brought in the worship of
Baal, was a part of the worldly policy of the
kings of Israel [1]. *As if it had been a light
thing for him to walk in the sins of Jeroboam the
son of Nebat, he took to wife the daughter of
Ethbaal, king of the Zidonians, and went and
served Baal and worshiped him.* The twenty-
two years of Ahab's reign established the
worship. The prophets of Baal became 450 ;
the prophets of the kindred idolatry of
Ashtoreth, or Astarte, became 400 ; Baal had
his one central temple, large and magnificent [2], a rival of that of God. The prophet
Elijah thought the apostacy almost universal ; God revealed to him that He had
reserved to Himself *seven thousand in Israel.*
Yet these were *all the knees which had not
bowed to Baal, and every mouth which had not
kissed him* [3].
And died. Death is the penalty of sin.
Ephraim *died* spiritually. For sin takes
away the life of grace, and separates from
God, the true life of the soul, the source of
all life. He " died more truly, than he who
is dead and at rest." Of this death, our
Lord says [4], *Let the dead bury their dead ;* and
S. Paul [5], *She who liveth in pleasure is dead
while she liveth.* He *died* also as a nation and
kingdom, being sentenced by God to cease to
be.
2. *And now they sin more and more.* Sin
draws on sin. This seems to be a third stage in
sin. First, under Jeroboam, was the worship
of the calves. Then, under Ahab, the worship of Baal. Thirdly, the multiplying of
other idols [6], penetrating and pervading the
private life, even of their less wealthy people.
The calves were of gold ; now they *made
them molten images of their silver,* perhaps
plated with silver. In Egypt, the mother of
idolatry, it was common to gild idols, made
of wood, stone, and bronze. The idolatry,
then, had become more habitual, daily, universal. These idols were made of *their silver ;*
they themselves had had them *molten* out of
it. Avaricious as they were [7], they lavished
their silver, to make them their gods. *According to their own understanding,* they had had
them formed. They employed ingenuity
and invention to multiply their idols. They
despised the wisdom and commands of God
Who forbad it. The rules for making and
coloring the idols were as minute as those,

which God gave for His own worship.
Idolatry had its own vast system, making
the visible world its god and picturing its
operations, over against the worship of God
its Creator. But it was all, *their own understanding.* The conception of the idol lay in
its maker's mind. It was his own creation.
He devised, what his idol should represent ;
how it should represent what his mind
imagined ; he debated with himself, rejected,
chose, changed his choice, modified what he
had fixed upon ; all *according to his own
understanding.* Their own understanding
devised it ; the labor of the craftsmen completed it.
All of it the work of the craftsmen. What man
could do for it, he did. But man could not
breathe into his idols the breath of life ;
there was then no spirit, nor life, nor any
effluence from any higher nature, nor any
deity residing in them. From first to last
it was *all* man's *work ;* and man's own wisdom was its condemnation. The thing
made must be inferior to its maker. God
made man, inferior to Himself, but lord of
the earth, and all things therein ; man
made his idol of the things of earth, which
God gave him. It too then was inferior to
its maker, man. He then worshiped in it,
the conception of his own mind, the work of
his own hands.
They say of them. Strictly, *Of them,* (i. e.
of these things, such things, as these,) *they,*
say, *Let the men that sacrifice kiss the calves.*
The prophet gives the substance or the
words of Jeroboam's edict, when he said, *It
is too much for you to go up to Jerusalem, behold
thy gods, O Israel.* "Whoever would sacrifice,
let him do homage to the calves." He would
have calf-worship to be the only worship of
God. Error, if it is strong enough, ever per-
secutes the truth, unless it can corrupt it.
Idol-worship was striving to extirpate the
worship of God, which condemned it. Under
Ahab and Jezebel, it seemed to have succeeded. Elijah complains to God in His
own immediate presence ; *the children of Israel
have forsaken Thy covenant, thrown down Thine
altars, and slain Thy Prophets with the sword ;
and I, even I, only am left, and they seek my life,
to take it away* [8]. Kissing was an act of
homage in the East, done upon the hand or
the foot, the knees or shoulder. It was a

---

[1] 1 Kings xvi. 31. see Introd. p. 2.
[2] 2 Kings x. 21, 22, 25.   [3] 1 Kings xix. 18.
[4] S. Matt. viii. 22.

[5] 1 Tim. v. 6.
[6] See 2 Kings xvii. 9, 10.   [7] Above xii. 7, 8.
[8] 1 Kings xix. 10, 14.

Before
CHRIST
cir. 725.

d ch. 6. 4.

e Dan. 2. 35.

3 Therefore they shall be ^das the morning cloud, and as the early dew that passeth away, ^eas the chaff *that* is driven with t h e whirlwind out of the floor, and as the smoke out of the chimney.

4 Yet ^fI *am* the LORD thy God from the land of

Before
CHRIST
cir. 725.

f Is. 43. 11.
ch. 12. 9.

token of Divine honor, whether to an idol[1] or to God[2]. It was performed, either by actually kissing the image, or when the object could not be approached, (as the moon) kissing the hand[3], and so sending, as it were, the kiss to it. In the Psalm, it stands as a symbol of worship, to be shewn towards *the Incarnate Son,* when God should make Him *King upon* His *holy hill of Sion.*

3. *Therefore they shall be as the morning cloud.* There is often a fair show of prosperity, out of God; but it is short-lived. "The third generation," says the heathen proverb, "never enjoys the ill-gotten gain." The highest prosperity of an ungodly state is often the next to its fall. Israel never so flourished, as under Jeroboam II. Bright and glistening with light is *the early dew ;* in an hour it is gone, as if it had never been. Glowing and gilded by the sun is *the morning cloud ;* while you admire its beauty, its hues have vanished. *The chaff* lay in one heap *on the floor* with the wheat. Its owner casts the mingled chaff and wheat against the strong wind; in a moment, it *is driven by the wind out of the floor.* While every grain falls to the ground, the chaff, light, dry, worthless, unsubstantial, is hurried along, unresisting, the sport of the viewless wind, and itself is soon seen no more. The *smoke,* one, seemingly solid, full, lofty, column, ascendeth, swelleth, welleth, vanisheth[4]. In form, it is as solid, when about to be dispersed and seen no more, as when it first issued *out of the chimney.* "[5] It is raised aloft, and by that very uplifting swells into a vast globe; but the larger that globe is, the emptier; for from that unsolid, unbased, inflated greatness it vanisheth in air, so that its very greatness injures it. For the more it is uplifted, extended, diffused on all sides into a larger compass, so much the poorer it becometh, and faileth, and disappeareth." Such was the prosperity of Ephraim, a mere show, to vanish for ever. In the image of *the chaff,* the Prophet substitutes the *whirlwind* for the wind by which the Easterns used to winnow, in order to picture the violence with which they should be whirled away from their own land.

While these four emblems, in common, picture what is fleeting, two, the *early dew*

and the *morning cloud,* are emblems of what is in itself good, but passing[6] ; the two others, the chaff and the smoke, are emblems of what is worthless. The dew and the cloud were temporary mercies on the part of God which should cease from them, "good in themselves, but to their evil, soon to pass away." If the dew have not, in its brief space, refreshed the vegetation, no trace of it is left. It gives way to the burning sun. If grace have not done its work in the soul, its day is gone. Such dew were the many prophets vouchsafed to Israel ; such was Hosea himself, most brilliant, but soon to pass away. The chaff was the people itself, to be carried out of the Lord's land ; the smoke, "its pride and its errors, whose disappearance was to leave the air pure for the household of God." "[7] So it is written[8] ; *As the smoke is driven away, so shalt thou drive* them *away ;* as *wax melteth before the fire, so shall the ungodly perish before the presence of God ;* and in Proverbs[9] ; *As the whirlwind passeth, so is the wicked no* more ; *but the righteous is an everlasting foundation.* Who although they live and flourish, as to the life of the body ; yet spiritually they die, yea, and are brought to nothing ; for by sin man became a nothing. Virtue makes man upright and stable ; vice, empty and unstable. Whence Isaiah says[10], *the wicked are like the troubled sea, which cannot rest ;* and Job[11] ; *If iniquity be in thy hand, put it far away ; then shalt thou be steadfast.*"

4. *Yet,* [lit. *and] I* am *the Lord thy God from the land of Egypt.* God was still the same God Who had sheltered them with His providence, ever since He had delivered them from Egypt. He had the same power and will to help them. Therefore *their* duty was the same, and their destruction arose, not from any change in Him, but from themselves. " God is the God of the ungodly, by creation and general Providence."

And thou shalt [i. e. oughtest to] *know no God but Me, for* [lit. *and]* there is *not a Saviour but ME.* " To be God and Lord and Saviour are incommunicable properties of God. Wherefore God often claimed these titles to Himself, from the time He revealed Himself to Israel. In the song of Moses, which they were commanded to rehearse, He says[12], *See now that I, I am He, and there is no*

[1] 1 Kings xix. 18 and here.
[3] Job xxxi. 26, 27.
[5] Id. in Ps. xxxvi. S. ii. § 12.

[2] Ps. ii. 12.
[4] S. Aug.
[6] Rup.

[7] Dion.
[9] Prov. x. 25.
[11] xi. 14, 15.

[8] Ps. lxviii. 2.
[10] Is. lvii 20..
[12] Deut. xxxii. 39.

Before
CHRIST
cir. 725.

g Is. 43. 11.
& 45. 21.
h Deut. 2. 7.
& 32. 10.
i Deut. 8. 15.
& 32. 10.
† Heb. *droughts.*

Egypt, and thou shalt know no god but me: for g *there is* no saviour beside me.

5 ¶ h I did know thee in the wilderness, i in the land of † great drought.

Before
CHRIST
cir. 725.

k Deut. 8. 12.
14. & 32. 15.

l ch. 8. 14.

6 k According to their pasture, so were they filled; they were filled, and their heart was exalted; therefore l have they forgotten me.

God with Me: I kill, and I make alive; I wound, and I heal; neither is there any that can deliver out of My hand. Isaiah repeats this same [1], *Is there a God besides Me? yea there is no God;* and [2] *There is no God else besides Me, a just God and a Saviour; there is none else. Look unto Me and be ye saved; for I am God and there is none else;* and [3], *I am the Lord, that is My Name; and My glory will I not give to another; neither My praise to graven images.* " [4] That God and Saviour is Christ; God, because He created; Saviour, because, being made Man, He saved. Whence He willed to be called Jesus, i. e. Saviour. Truly *beside* Him, *there is no Saviour; neither is there salvation in any other; for there is none other name under heaven, given among men, whereby we must be saved* [5]." " It is not enough to recognize in God this quality of a Saviour. It must not be shared with *any other.* Whoso associates with God any power whatever to decide on man's salvation makes an idol, and introduces a new God."

5. *I did know thee in the wilderness.* " God so knew them, as to deserve to be known by them. By *knowing* them, He shewed how He ought to be acknowledged by them." *As we love God, because He first loved us,* so we come to know and own God, having first been owned and known of Him. God shewed His knowledge of them, by knowing and providing for their wants; He knew them *in the wilderness, in the land of great drought,* where the land yielded neither food nor water. He supplied them with the *bread from heaven* and with *water from the flinty rock.* He knew and owned them all by His Providence; He knew in approbation and love, and fed in body and soul those who, having been known by Him, knew and owned Him. " [4] No slight thing is it, that He, Who knoweth all things and men, should, by grace, know us with that knowledge according to which He says to that one true Israelite, Moses [6], *thou hast found grace in My sight, and I know thee by name.* This we read to have been said to that one; but what He says to one, He says to all, whom now, before or since that time, He has chosen, being foreknown and predestinate; for He wrote the names of all in the book of life. All these elect are *known*

in the wilderness, in the land of loneliness, in the wilderness of this world, where no one ever saw God, in the solitude of the heart and the secret of hidden knowledge, where God alone, beholding the soul tried by temptations, exercises and proves it, and accounting it, when *running lawfully,* worthy of His knowledge, professes that He *knew it.* To those so known, or named, He Himself saith in the Gospel, *rejoice, because your names are written in heaven* [7]."

6. *According to their pasture, so were they filled.* " [4] He implies that their way of being *filled* was neither good nor praiseworthy, in that he says, *they were filled according to their pastures.* What or of what kind were these *their pastures?* What they longed for, what they murmured for, and spoke evil of God. For instance, when they said, *who will give us flesh to eat? We remember the flesh which we did eat in Egypt freely. Our soul is dried up, because our eyes see nothing but this manna* [8]. Since they desired such things in such wise, and, desiring, were filled with them to loathing, well are they called ' *their* pastures.' For they sought God, not for Himself, but for them. They who follow God for Himself, things of this sort are not called *their* pastures, but the word of God is their pasture, according to that [9], *Man shall not live by bread alone, but by every word, which proceedeth out of the mouth of God.* These words, *according to their pastures,* convey strong blame. It is as if he said, ' in their eating and drinking, they received their whole reward for leaving the land of Egypt and receiving for a time the law of God.' It is sin, to follow God for such *pastures.* Blaming such in the Gospel, Jesus saith [10], *Verily, verily, I say unto you, ye seek Me, not because ye saw the miracles, but because ye did eat of the loaves and were filled. Labor not for the meat which perisheth, but for that which endureth unto everlasting life.* In like way, let all think themselves blamed, who attend the altar of Christ, not for the love of the sacraments which they celebrate, but only to *live of the altar.* This fullness is like that of which the Psalmist says [11], *The Lord gave them their desire and sent leanness withal into their bones.* For such fullness of the belly generates elation of spirit; such satiety produces forgetfulness of God." It is

[1] xliv. 8.   [2] xlv. 21, 2.   [3] xlii. 8.   [4] Rup.
[5] Acts iv. 12.   [6] Ex. xxxiii. 17.   [7] S. Luke x. 20.

[8] Num. xi. 4–6.   [9] Deut. viii. 3.
[10] S. John vi. 26, 27.   [11] Ps. cvi. 15.

Before
CHRIST
cir. 725.

m Lam. 3. 10.
ch. 5 14.
n Jer. 5. 6.

7 Therefore [m] I will be unto them as a lion: as [n] a leopard by the way will I observe them :

8 I will meet them [o] as a bear that is bereaved of her whelps, and will rend the caul of their heart, and

Before
CHRIST
cir. 725.

o 2 Sam. 17. 8.
Prov. 17. 12.

more difficult to bear prosperity than adversity. They who, in the waste howling wilderness, had been retained in a certain degree of duty, forgat God altogether in the good land which He had given them. Whence it follows;

They were filled, and their heart was exalted; therefore have they forgotten Me. For they owned not that they had all from Him, therefore they were puffed up with pride, and forgot Him in and by reason of His gifts. This was the aggravation of their sin, with which Hosea often reproaches them[1]. They abused God's gifts, (as Christians do now) against Himself, and did the more evil, the more good God was to them. God had forewarned them of this peril[2], *When thou shalt have eaten and be full, beware lest thou forget the Lord which brought thee forth out of the land of Egypt, from the house of bondage.* He pictured it to them with the song of Moses[3]; *Jeshurun waxed fat and kicked; thou art waxen fat; thou art grown thick; thou art covered with fatness; then he forsook God which made him;— thou hast forgotten God that formed thee.* They acted (as in one way or other do most Christians now,) as though God had commanded what He foretold of their evil deeds, or what He warned them against. [4] *As their fathers did, so did they.* [5] *They walked in the statutes of the heathen, whom the Lord cast out from before the children of Israel, and of the kings of Israel which they made. They wrought wicked things to provoke the Lord to anger. And the Lord testified against Israel and against Judah by all the prophets and by all the seers, saying, turn ye from your evil ways. And they hearkened not, and hardened their necks, like to the neck of their fathers, that did not believe in the Lord their God.* [6] "*The words are true also of those rich and ungrateful, whom God hath filled with spiritual or temporal goods. But they, being in honor, and having no understanding, abuse the gifts of God, and, becoming unworthy of the benefits which they have received, have their hearts uplifted and swollen with pride, despising others, *glorying as though they had not received,* and not obeying the commands of God. Of such the Lord saith in Isaiah, *I have nourished and brought up children and they have rebelled against Me.*"

7. *I will be unto them as a lion.* They had waxen fat, were full; yet it was, to become

themselves a prey. Their wealth which they were proud of, which they abused, allured their enemies. To cut off all hopes of God's mercy, He says that He will be to them, as those creatures of His, which never spare. The fierceness of the lion, and the swiftness of the leopard, together portray a speedy inexorable chastisement. But what a contrast! He Who bare Israel in the wilderness like a Father, Who bare them on eagle's wings, Who drew them with the cords of a man, with bands of love, He, the God of mercy and of love, their Father, Protector, Defender, Avenger, He it is Who will be their Destroyer.

8. *As a bear bereaved* of her whelps. The Syrian bear is fiercer than the brown bears to which we are accustomed. It attacks flocks[7], and even oxen[8]. The fierceness of the she-bear, *bereaved of her whelps,* became a proverb[9]. "[10] They who have written on the nature of wild beasts, say that none is more savage than the she-bear, when she has lost her whelps or lacks food." It blends wonderfully most touching love and fierceness. It tenderly protects its wounded whelps, reckless of its life, so that it may bring them off, and it turns fiercely on their destroyer. Its love for them becomes fury against their injurer. Much more shall God avenge those who destroy His sons and daughters, leading and enticing them into sin and destruction of body and soul.

Rend the caul of [what encloses] *their heart,* i. e. the pericardium. They had closed their hearts against God. Their punishment is pictured by the rending open of the closed heart, by the lion which is said to go instinctively straight to the heart, tears it out, and sucks the blood[11]. Fearful will it be in the Day of Judgment, when the sinner's heart is laid open, with all the foul, cruel, malicious, defiled, thoughts which it harbored and concealed, against the Will of God. *It is a fearful thing to fall into the hands of the living God*[12].

And there will I devour them. There, where they sinned, shall they be punished. *The wild beast shall tear them.* What God does, He does mostly through instruments, and what His instruments do, they do fulfilling His Will through their own blind will or appetite. Hitherto, He had spoken, as being

1 ii. 5. iv. 7. x. 1.
2 Deut. vi. 11, 12, add viii. 11, &c.
3 Ib. xxxii. 15, 18.   4 Acts vii, 51.
5 2 Kings xvii. 8, 11, 13, 14.   6 Rib.

7 1 Sam. xvii. 34.   8 Plin. viii. 54.
9 2 Sam. xvii. 8, Prov. xvii. 12. and here.
10 S Jer.   11 See in Boch. iii. 2. pp. 740, 1.
12 Heb. x. 31.

Before CHRIST cir. 725.

† Heb. *the beast of the field.*
p Prov. 6. 32.
ch. 14. 1.
Mal. 1. 9.
q ver. 4.
† Heb. *in thy help.*

there will I devour them like a lion : † the wild beast shall tear them.

9 ¶ O Israel, p thou hast destroyed thyself ; q but in me † *is* thine help.

10 || I will be thy king : r where *is any other* that may save thee in all thy cities? and thy judges of whom s thou saidst, Give me a king and princes ?

Before CHRIST cir. 725.

|| Rather, *Where is thy king?* King Hoshea being then in prison.
s 1 Sam. 8. 5, 19.
2 Kgs. 17. 4.
r Deut. 32. 38.
ch. 10. 3.
ver. 4.

Himself their Punisher, although laying aside, as it were, all His tenderness ; now, lest the thought, that still it was He, the God of love Who punished, should give them hope, He says, *the wild beast shall devour them.* He gives them up, as it were, out of His own hands to the destroyer.

9. *O Israel, thou hast destroyed thyself, but in Me* is *thy help.* This is one of the concise sayings of Hosea, which is capable of many shades of meaning. The five words, one by one, are lit. *Israel, thy destruction, for or that, in* or *against Me, in* or *against thy help.* Something must be supplied any way; the simplest seems ; *O Israel, thy destruction* is, *that* thou hast been, hast rebelled *against Me, against thy help* [1]. Yet, in whatever way the words are filled up, the general sense is the same, that God alone is our help, we are the sources of our own destruction ; and *that,* in separating ourselves from God, or rebelling against Him Who is our help until we depart from Him, Who Alone could be, and Who if we return, will be, our help. The sum of the meaning is, all our destruction is from ourselves ; all our salvation is from God. "[2] Perdition, reprobation, obduration, damnation, are not, properly and in themselves, from God, dooming to perdition, reprobating, obdurating, damning, but from man sinning, and obduring or hardening himself in sin to the end of life. Contrariwise, predestination, calling, grace, are not from the foreseen merits of the predestinate, but from God, predestinating, calling, and, by His grace, forecoming the predestinate. Wherefore although the cause or ground, why they are predestinated, does not lie in the predestinate, yet in the not-predestinated does lie the ground or cause why they are not predestinated."

"This saying then, *O Israel, thou hast destroyed thyself, but in Me* is *thy help,* may be thus unfolded ;

Thy captivity, Israel, is from thee ; thy redemption from Me.

Thy perishing is from thee ; thy salvation from Me.

Thy death from thee ; thy life from Me.

Thy evil from thee ; thy good from Me.

Thy reprobation from thee ; thy predestination from Me, Who ever stand at the door of thy heart and in mercy knock.

Thy dereliction from thee ; thy calling from Me.

Thy misery from thee ; thy bliss from Me.

Thy damnation from thee, thy salvation and beatifying from Me."

For "[3] many good things doeth God in man, which man doeth not, but none doeth man, which God endueth not man to do." "[4] The first cause of the defect of grace is from us ; but the first cause of the gift of grace is from God." "[5] Rightly is God called, not the Father of judgments or of vengence, but the *Father of mercies,* because from Himself is the cause and origin of His mercy, from us the cause of His judging or avenging."

"Blessed the soul which comprehendeth this, not with the understanding only, but with the heart. Nothing can destroy us before God, but sin, the only real evil ; and sin is wholly from us, God can have no part in it. But every aid to withdraw us from sin, or to hinder us from falling into it, comes from God alone, the sole Source of our salvation. The soul then must ever bless God, in its ills and its good ; in its ills, by confessing that itself is the only cause of its suffering ; in its good, owning that, when altogether unworthy of it, God prevented it by His grace, and preserves it each instant by His Almighty goodness."

"[6] No power, then, of the enemy could harm thee, unless, by thy sins, thou calledst forth the anger of God against thee to thy destruction. Ascribe it to thyself, not to the enemy. So let each sinful city or sinful soul say, which by its guilt draws on it the vengeance of God."

This truth, that in Him alone is help, He confirms by what follows :

10. *I will be* [lit. *I would be*] *thy King ; Where* is any other that &c. Better, [7] *Where now is thy king, that he may save thee in all thy cities ; and thy judges, of whom thou saidst, give me a king and princes.*

As Israel was under Samuel, such it remained. *Then* it mistrusted God, and looked

---

1 Rashi. 2 Lap. from Theologians on 1 p. q. 23.
3 S. Aug. c. 2 Epp. Pet. ii. 21. Ib.
4 Aq. 1. 2. q. 112. a. 3. ad. 2 Ib.
5 S. Bern. Serm. 8 in Nat. Dom. Ib. 6 Lap.

[7] אֵפוֹא, which our Version renders *where?* never occurs alone as an interrogative, but always as subjoined to אַיֵּה, with which אֵי is identical and identified by great Jewish authorities, as Abulvalid.

Before
C H R I S T
cir. 725.

t 1 Sam. 8. 7.
& 10. 19. & 15.
22, 23. & 16. 1. ch. 10. 3.

11 ᵗI gave thee a king in mine anger, and took *him* away in my wrath.

12 ᵘThe iniquity of Ephraim *is* bound up; his sin *is* hid.

Before
C H R I S T
cir. 725.

ᵘ Deut. 32. 34.
Job 14. 17.

to man for help, saying¹, *Nay, but we will have a king over us, that we also may be like other nations, and that our king may judge us, and go out before us, and fight our battles.* In choosing man they rejected God. The like they did, when they chose Jeroboam. In order to rid themselves of the temporary pressure of Rehoboam's taxes, they demanded anew *king and princes*. First they rejected God as their king; then they rejected the king whom God appointed, and Him in His appointment. *In all thy cities.* It was then to be one universal need of help. They had chosen a king *to fight their battles*, and had rejected God. Now was the test, whether their choice had been good or evil. One cry for help went up from *all their cities*. God would have heard it; could man?

"² This question is like that other³, *Where are their gods, their rock in whom they trusted, which did eat the fat of their sacrifices, and drink the wine of their drink offerings?* As there, when no answer could be made, He adds, *See now that I, I am He, and that there is no god with Me,* so here He subjoins;"

11. *I gave thee a king in Mine anger.* "⁴God, when He is asked for ought amiss, sheweth displeasure, when He giveth, hath mercy, when He giveth not." "The devil was heard," [in asking to enter into the swine] "the Apostle was not heard," [when he prayed that the messenger of Satan might depart from him.] "⁵ God heard him whom He purposed to condemn; and He heard not him whom He willed to heal." "⁶ God, when propitious, denieth what we love, when we love amiss; when wroth, He giveth to the lover, what he loveth amiss. The Apostle saith plainly, *God gave them over to their own hearts' desire.* He gave them then what they loved, but, in giving, condemned them." God did appoint Jeroboam, although not in the way in which Israel took him. Jeroboam and Israel took, as from themselves, what God appointed; and, so taking it, marred God's gift. Taking it to themselves from themselves, they maintained it for themselves by human policy and sin. As was the beginning, such was the whole course of their kings. The beginning was rebellion; murder, intestine commotion, anarchy, was the oft-repeated issue. God was against them and their kings; but he let them have their way.

In His displeasure with them He allowed them their choice; in displeasure with their evil kings He took them away. Some He smote in their own persons, some in their posterity. So often as He gave them, so often He removed them⁷, until, in Hoshea, He took them away for ever. This too explains, how what God *gave in anger*, could be *taken away* also *in anger*. The civil authority was not a thing wrong in itself, the ceasing whereof must be a mercy. Israel was in a worse condition through its separate monarchy; but, apart from the calf-worship, it was not sin. The changing of one king for another did not mend it. Individual kings were taken away in anger against themselves; their removal brought fresh misery and bloodshed. Nations and Churches and individuals may put themselves in an evil position, and God may have allowed it in His anger, and yet, it may be their wisdom and humility to remain in it, until God change it, lest He should *take* it away, not in forgiveness, but in *anger*. "⁸ David they neither asked for, nor did the Lord give him in His anger; but the Lord first chose him in mercy, gave him in grace, in His supreme good-pleasure He strengthened and preserved him." "⁹ Let no one who suffereth from a wicked ruler, accuse *him* from whom he suffereth; for it was from his own ill deserts, that he became subject to such a ruler. Let him accuse then his own deeds, rather than the injustice of the ruler; for it is written, *I gave thee a king in Mine anger.* Why then disdain to have as rulers, those whose rule we receive from the anger of God?" "¹⁰ When a reprobate people is allowed to have a reprobate pastor, that pastor is given, neither for his own sake, nor for that of the people; inasmuch as he so governeth, and they so obey, that neither the teacher nor the taught are found meet to attain to eternal bliss. Of whom the Lord saith by Hosea, *I gave thee a king in Mine anger.* For in the anger of God is a king given, when the bad have a worse appointed as their ruler. Such a pastor is then given, when he undertakes the rule of such a people, both being condemned alike to everlasting punishment."

12. *The iniquity of Ephraim* is bound up (as in a bag or purse, and so, *treasured up*), as Job saith, using the same word, ¹¹ *My trans-*

1 1 Sam. viii. 19.
2 Rup.   3 Deut. xxxii. 37-9.
4 Sent. 252. ap. S. Aug. Apo. T. x. p. 239 Lap.
5 Id. in Ps. lxxxv. §9.
6 Id. in Ps. xxvi. §7.

7 The words אקח, את, ליתן, express this oft-renewed dealing of God.
8 Rup.   9 S. Greg. in Job L. xxv. c. 20. Rib.
10 Id. in 1 Reg. ix. T. iii. pp. 215, 16. Ib.
11 Job xiv. 17. בצרור as here צרור.

Before
C H R I S T
cir. 725.

x Is. 13. 8.
Jer. 30. 6.
y Prov. 22. 3.

13 ^x The sorrows of a travailing woman shall come upon him: he is ^y an un-

wise son; for he should not ^z stay† long in *the place of the* breaking forth of children.

Before
C H R I S T
cir. 725.

z 2 Kgs 19. 3.
† Heb. *a time.*

gression is sealed up in a bag, and Thou sewest up mine iniquity. His sin is hid, i. e. as people lay up hidden treasure, to be brought out in its season. What Job feared for himself, was to be the portion of Ephraim. All his sins should be counted, laid by, heaped up. No one of them should escape His Eye Who sees all things as they pass, and with Whom, when past, they are present still. One by one, sins enter into the treasure-house of wrath; silently they are stored up, until the measure is full; to be brought out and un-folded in the Great Day. Ephraim thought, as do all sinners, that because God does not punish at once, He never will. They think, either that God will bear with them always, because He bears with them so long; or that He does not see, does not regard it, is not so precise about His laws being broken. ¹ *Be-cause sentence against an evil work is not executed speedily, therefore the heart of the sons of men is fully set in them to do evil.* But God had fore-warned them ²; *Is not this laid up in store with Me, and sealed up among My treasures? To Me belongeth vengeance and recompense; their foot shall slide in due time:* and ³, *These things hast thou done, and I kept silence; and thou thought-est wickedly that I was altogether such an one as thyself; I will reprove thee, and set them in order before thine eyes.* Unrepented sin is an ever-growing store of the wrath of God, hid out of sight in the depths of the Divine judg-ments, but of which nothing will be lost, nothing missing. Man treasures it up, lays it up in store for himself, as the Apostle saith ⁴; *Despisest thou the riches of His good-ness and forbearance and long-suffering, not knowing that the goodness of God leadeth thee to repentance; but after thy hardness and impeni-tent heart treasurest up unto thyself wrath against the Day of wrath and revelation of the righteous judgment of God, Who will render to every man according to his deeds?* " ⁵ *Sin is hidden,* when it is laid open by no voice of confession; yea, when it is covered with a shield of proud self-defence. Then iniquity is bound up, so that it cannot be loosed or forgiven. Con-trariwise a holy man saith ⁶, *I acknowledged my sin unto Thee, and my iniquity have I not hid. I said, I will confess my transgressions unto the Lord; and Thou forgavest the iniquity of my sin.* But these hide their sin in the sight of men, and since they cannot hide it in the sight of God, they defend it with im-penitent hearts, but *the pangs of a travailing woman,* he saith, *shall come upon him.* For as

a woman can conceal her conception for a time, but, at last, the travail-pangs be-traying her, she discloses what was con-cealed, so these can dissemble and conceal for a time their sin, but in their time all the hidden things of their hearts shall, with anguish, be revealed, according to that ⁷, *There is nothing covered, that shall not be revealed, and hid, that shall not be known.*"

13. *The sorrows of a travailing woman are come upon him.* The travail-pangs are vío-lent, sudden, irresistible. A moment before they come, all is seemingly perfect health; they come, increase in vehemence, and, if they accomplish not that for which they are sent, end in death, both to the mother and the child. Such are God's chastisements. If they end not in the repentance of the sinner, they continue on in his destruction. But never is man more secure, than just before the last and final throe comes upon him. "The false security of Israel, when Samaria was on the point of falling into the hands of its enemies, was a picture of that of the Synagogue, when greater evils were coming upon it. Never did the Jews less think that the axe was laid to the root of the trees." This blind pre-sumption is ever found in a people whom God casts off. At the end of the world, amid the awful signs, the fore-runners of the Day of Judgment, people will be able to reassure themselves, and say ⁸, *Peace and safety; then sudden destruction cometh upon them as travail upon a woman with child, and they shall not escape.*

The prophet first compares Israel to the mother, in regard to the sufferings which are a picture of the sudden overwhelming visita-tions of God; then to the child, on whose staying or not staying in the womb, the wel-fare of both depends.

He is an unwise son, for he should not stay long. Senseless would be the child, which, if it had the power, lingered, hesitated, whether to come forth or no. While it lingers, at one time all but coming forth, then returning, the mother's strength is wasted, and both perish. Wonderful picture of the vacillating sinner, acted upon by the grace of God, but resisting it; at one time all but ready to pour out before his God the hidden burthen which oppresses him, at the next, withholding it; impelled by his sufferings, yet presenting a passive resistance; almost constrained at times by some mightier pang, yet still with-held; until, at the last, the impulses become

1 Eccl. viii. 11.   2 Deut. xxxii. 34, 5.
3 Ps. l. 21.   4 Rom. ii. 4–6.

5 Rup.   6 Ps. xxxii. 5.
7 S. Matt. x. 26.   8 1 Thess. v. 3.

Before
CHRIST
cir. 725.

a Is. 25. 8.
Ezek. 37. 12.
† Heb. *the hand.*
b 1 Cor. 15.
54, 55.

14 a I will ransom them from † the power of the grave; I will redeem them from death: b O death, I will be thy plagues; O grave, I will be thy destruction: c repentance shall be hid from mine eyes.

Before
CHRIST
cir. 725.

c Jer. 15. 6.
Rom. 11. 29.

weaker, the pangs less felt, and he perishes with his unrepented sin. "[1] He had said, that the unwise cannot bring forth, that the wise can. He had mentioned *children*, i. e. such as are not still-born; who come forth perfect into the world. These, God saith, shall by His help be redeemed from everlasting destruction, and, at the same time, having predicted the destruction of that nation, He gives the deepest comfort to those who will to retain firm faith in Him, not allowing them to be utterly cast down."

14. *I will ransom them from the power of the grave ;* lit. *from the hand,* i. e. the grasp *of the grave,* or *of hell.* God, by His prophets, mingles promises of mercy in the midst of His threats of punishment. His mercy overflows the bounds of the occasion upon which He makes it known. He had sentenced Ephraim to temporal destruction. This was unchangeable. He points to that which turns all temporal loss into gain, their eternal redemption. The words are the fullest which could have been chosen. The word rendered *ransom,* signifies, rescued them by the payment of a price, the word rendered *redeem,* relates to one, who, as the nearest of kin, had the right to acquire anything as his own, by paying that price. Both words, in their exactest sense, describe what Jesus did, buying us *with a price,* a full and dear price, *not of corruptible things, as of silver and gold, but with His precious blood* [2] ; and that, becoming our near kinsman, by His Incarnation, *for which cause He is not ashamed to call us brethren* [3], and *little children* [4]. This was never done by God at any other time, than when, out of love for our lost world, [5] *He gave His Only Begotten Son, that whosoever believeth in Him should not perish but have everlasting life;* and He *came to give His life a ransom for many* [6]. Then only was man really delivered from the *grasp* of the *grave ;* so that *the first death* should only be a freedom from corruption, an earnest, and, to fallen man, a necessary condition of immortality ; and *the second death* should have *no power over* them [7]. Thenceforward "[8] death, the parent of sorrow, ministers to joy ; death, our dishonor, is employed to our glory ; the *gate of hell* is the portal to the kingdom of heaven ; the *pit of destruction* is the entrance to salvation; and that to man, a sinner." At no other time, "[9] were men freed from death and the grave, so as to make any distinction between them and others subject to mortality." The words refuse to be tied down to a temporal deliverance. A little longer continuance in Canaan is not a redemption from the power of the grave ; nor was Ephraim so delivered. Words of God "[10] cannot mean so little, while they express so much." Then and then alone were they, in their literal meaning, fulfilled when God the Son *took* our flesh [11], *that, through death, He might destroy him that had the power of death, that is the devil; and deliver them who, through fear of death, were all their lifetime subject to bondage.*

The Jews have a tradition wrapped up in their way, that this was to be accomplished in Christ. "[12] I went with the angel Kippod, and Messiah son of David went with me, until I came to the gates of hell. When the prisoners of hell saw the light of the Messiah, they wished to receive him, saying, this is he who will bring us out of this darkness, as it is written, *I will redeem them from the hand of hell.*"

"[13] Not without reason is the vouchsafed mercy thus once and again outspoken to us, *I will ransom them from the power of the grave ; I will redeem them from death.* It is said in regard to that twofold death whereby we all died in Adam, of the body and of the soul." *O death, I will be thy plagues ; O grave, I will be thy destruction.* So full is God's word, that the sense remains the same, amid much difference of rendering. Christ was the death of death, when He became subject to it ; the destruction of the grave when He lay in the tomb. Yet to render it in the form of a question is most agreeable to the language [14]. *O death, where are thy plagues? O grave, where is thy destruction?* It is a burst of triumph at the promised redemption, then fulfilled to us in earnest and in hope, when *Christ,* being *risen from the dead, became the First-fruits of them that slept*[15], and we rose in Him. But the Apostle teaches us, that then it shall be altogether fulfilled, when, at the last Day, *this corruptible*

1 Osor.   2 1 Pet. i. 18, 19.   3 Heb. ii. 11.
4 S. John xiii. 33.   5 S. John iii. 16.
6 S. Matt. xx. 28. add 1 Tim. ii. 6.
7 Rev. xx. 6.   8 S. Bern. Serm. 26 in Cant. Lap.
9 Poc.   10 Davison on Prophecy.
11 Heb. ii. 14, 15.
12 Bereshith Rabba, in Martin. Pug. Fid. f. 005, 6.

13 Rup.
14 יְהִי is most naturally taken in the sense in which Hosea had just used it, as equivalent to אֱהִי. As a verb, it would mean, *I would be,* which would not agree with the absolute declaration just before, *I will ransom, I will redeem.*
15 1 Cor. xv 20.

Before
CHRIST
cir. 725.

15 ¶ Though [d] he be fruitful among his brethren, [e] an east wind shall come, the wind of the LORD shall come up from the wilderness, and his

[d] See Gen. 41.
52. & 48. 19.
[e] Jer. 4. 11.
Ezek. 17. 10.
& 19. 12.
ch. 4. 19.

spring shall become dry and his fountain shall be dried up: he shall spoil the treasure of all † pleasant vessels.

16 ‖ Samaria shall be-

Before
CHRIST
cir. 725.
† Heb. vessels of desire.
Nah. 2. 9.
‖ Fulfilled,
cir. 721.
2 Kgs 17. 6.

shall have put on *incorruption, and this mortal shall have put on immortality*[1]. *Then shall death and hell deliver up the dead which* shall be *in them, and themselves* be *cast into the lake of fire*[2]. "Then shall there be no sting of death; sorrow and sighing shall flee away; fear and anxiety shall depart; tears shall be no more, and in place thereof shall be boundless pleasure, everlasting joy, praise of the glory of God in most sweet harmony." But now too, through death, the good man "ceases to die, and begins to live;" he "[3] dies wholly to the world, that he may live perfectly with God; the soul returns to the Author of its being, and is hidden in the hidden Presence of God."

Death and hell had no power to resist, and God says that He will not alter His sentence; *Repentance shall be hid from Mine eyes;* as the Apostle says[4], *the gifts and calling of God are without repentance.*

15. *Though* [lit. *when*] *he* [*shall*] *be fruitful among his brethren.* Fruitfulness was God's promise to Ephraim, and was expressed in his name. It was fulfilled, abused, and, in the height of its fulfillment, was taken away. Ephraim is pictured as a fair and fruitful tree. An *East wind,* so desolating in the East, and that, no chance wind, but *the wind of the Lord,* a wind, sent by God and endued by God with the power to destroy, *shall come up from the wilderness,* parching, scorching, fiery, from the burning sands of "Arabia the desert," from which it came, *and shall dry up the fountain* of his being. Deep were the roots of this fair and flourishing tree, great its vigor, ample and perpetual the fountain of its waters, over which it grew and by which it was sustained. He calls it "*his* spring, *his* fountain," as though this source of its life were made over to it, and made its own. It *was planted by the water side;* but it was not of God's planting. *The East wind from the Lord* should dry up the deepest well-spring of its waters, and the tree should wither. Such are ungodly greatness and prosperity. While they are fairest in show, their life-fountains are drying up.

He shall spoil the treasure of all pleasant vessels. He, emphatically[5], the enemy whom the Prophet had ever in his mind, as the

instrument of God's chastisement on His people, and who was represented by the East wind; the Assyrian, who came from the East, to whom, as to the East wind, the whole country between lay open, for the whirlwinds of his armies to sweep over in one straight course from the seat of his dominion.

16. *Samaria shall become desolate,* or *shall bear her iniquity.* Her iniquity should now find her out, and rest upon her. Of this, "desolation" was, in God's judgments, the consequence. Samaria, "the nursery of idolatry and rebellion against God," the chief in pride should be chief in punishment. *For she hath rebelled against her God.* It aggravated her sin, that He *against* Whom *she rebelled,* was *her* own God. He Who had chosen her to be His, and made Himself her God; Who had shewed Himself *her God* in the abundance of His loving-kindness, from the deliverance out of Egypt to that day. This her desolation, it is again said, should be complete. Hope remains, if the men of a generation are cut off; yet not only should these fall by the sword; those already born were to be dashed in pieces; those as yet unborn were to be sought out for destruction, even in their mother's womb. Such atrocities were common then. Elisha foretold to Hazael that he would perpetrate both cruelties[6], Shalmaneser dashed the young children in pieces[7], as did the conqueror of No-Ammon[8], and the Babylonians[9] afterward. The children of Ammon ripped up the women with child in Gilead[10], and the usurper Menahem in Tiphsah and its coasts[11]. Isaiah prophesies that Babylon should undergo, in its turn, the same as to its children[12], and the Psalmist pronounces God's blessing on its destroyer who should so requite him[9].

Such was to be the end of the pride, the ambition, the able policy, the wars, the oppressions, the luxury, the self-enjoyment, and, in all, the rebellion of Samaria against *her God.* She has stood the more in opposition to God, the nearer she might have been to Him, and *bare her iniquity.* As a city of God's people, it was never restored. The spot, in its heathen colonists, with which Assyrian policy repeopled it[13], was still the abode of a mingled religion. Corruption clung, by inheritance,

[1] 1 Cor. xv. 54.   [2] Rev. xx. 13, 14.
[3] de dign. Div. Am. fin. ap. S. Bern. ii. 274.
[4] Rom. xi. 29.   [5] הוא   [6] 2 Kings viii. 12.
[7] Above x. 14.   [8] Nah. iii. 10.   [9] Ps. cxxxvii. 9.
[10] Am. i. 13.   [11] 2 Kings xv. 16.
[12] xiii. 16.   [13] 2 Kings xvii. 24.

CHAPTER XIV.

Before CHRIST cir. 725.

[f 2 Kgs 18. 12.
g 2 Kgs 8. 12, & 15. 16.
Is. 13. 16.
ch. 10. 14, 15.
Amos 1. 13.
Nah. 3. 10.]

come desolate; [f] for she hath rebelled against her God: [g] they shall fall by the sword: their infants shall be dashed in pieces, and their women with child shall be ripped up.

1. *An exhortation to repentance.*
4. *A promise of God's blessing.*

Before CHRIST cir. 725.

O ISRAEL, [a] return unto the LORD thy God; [b] for thou hast fallen by thine iniquity.

[a ch. 12. 6.
Joel 2. 13.
b ch. 13. 9.]

---

to its site. This too was destroyed by John Hyrcanus. "He effaced the marks that it had ever been a city [1]." It was rebuilt by the Romans, after Pompey had taken Jerusalem [2]. Herod reinclosed a circuit of two miles and a half of the ancient site; fortified it strongly, as a check on the Jews; repeopled it, partly with some who had served in his wars, partly with the people around; gave them lands, revived their idolatry by replacing their poor temple by one remarkable for size and beauty, in an area of a furlong and a half; and called the place Sebaste in honor of his heathen patron, Augustus [3]. A coin of Nero, struck there, bears the figure (it is thought) of its old idol, Ashtaroth [4]. S. Jerome says, that S. John the Baptist was buried there [5]. The heathen, who were encouraged in such desecrations by Julian the Apostate [6], opened the tomb, burned the bones, and scattered the dust [7]. The city became a Christian see, and its Bishops were present at the four first General Councils [8]. It is now but a poor village, connected with the strongly-fortified town of Herod by its heathen name Sebastieh, a long avenue of broken pillars, and the tomb of the great Forerunner [9]. Of the ancient capital of Ephraim, not even a ruin speaks.

The Prophet closes this portion of his prophecy, as other prophets so often do, with the opposite end of the righteous and the wicked. He had spoken of the victory over death, the irrevocable purpose of God for good to his own; then he speaks of utter final destruction. Then when the mercy of God shall be shewn to the uttermost, and the victory over sin and death shall be accomplished, then shall all the pomp of the world, its riches, joys, luxuries, elegance, glory, dignity, perish, and not a wreck be left behind of all which once dazzled the eyes of men, for which they forsook their God, and sold themselves to evil and the evil one.

XIV. 1. *O Israel, return [now, quite] unto the Lord your God.* The heavy and scarcely interrupted tide of denunciation is now past. Billow upon billow have rolled over Ephraim; and the last wave discharged itself in the overwhelming, indiscriminating destruction of the seat of its strength. As a nation, it was to cease to be. Its separate existence was a curse, not a blessing; the offspring of rivalry, matured by apostacy; the parent, in its turn, of jealousy, hatred, and mutual vexation.

But while the kingdom was past and gone, the children still remained heirs of the promises made to their fathers. As then, before, Hosea declared that Israel, after having long remained solitary, should in the end *seek the Lord and David their king* [10], so now, after these manifold denunciations of their temporal destruction, God not only invites them to repentance, but foretells that they should be wholly converted.

Every word is full of mercy. God calls them by the name of acceptance, which He had given to their forefather, Jacob; *O Israel.* He deigns to beseech them to return; *return now*; and that not "towards" but *quite up to* [11] Himself, the Unchangeable God, Whose mercies and promises were as immutable as His Being. To Himself, the Unchangeable, God invites them to return; and that, as being still their God. They had cast off their God; God had *not cast off His people Whom He foreknew* [12].

"[13] He entreats them not only to turn back and look toward the Lord with a partial and imperfect repentance, but not to leave off till they were come quite home to Him by a total and sincere repentance and amendment." He bids them *return quite to* Himself, the Unchangeable God, and their God. "Great is repentance," is a Jewish saying [14], "which maketh men to reach quite up to the Throne of glory."

For thou hast fallen by thine iniquity. "This is the first ray of Divine light on the sinner. God begins by discovering to him the abyss into which he has fallen," and the way by which he fell. Their own iniquity it was, on which they had stumbled and so had fallen, powerless to rise, except through *His* call, Whose *voice is with power* [15], and "Who giveth what He commandeth." "[16] Ascribe

1 Jos. Ant. 13. 10. 3.
2 Ib. 14. 4. 4. and 5. 3.   3 Ib. 15. 8. 5.
4 Vaillant, Num. Imp. p. 370 in Reland, Pal. p. 981.
5 On Hos. i. 5. Obad. init. Mic. i. 6. Onom. v. Semeron.
6 Misopog. p. 95.   7 Theod. H. E. iii. 7.

8 See in Reland, p. 983.
9 Stanley, Palestine, p. 245.   10 iii. 5.
11 Not אֶל but עַד.   12 Rom. xi. 2.
13 Poc.   14 Yoma, c. 8. in Poc.
15 Ps. xxix. 4.   16 Osor.

2 Take with you words, and turn to the LORD : say unto him, Take away all

iniquity, and ‖ receive *us* graciously : so will we render the °calves of our lips.

not thy calamity," He would say, "to thine own weakness, to civil dissension, to the disuse of military discipline, to want of wisdom in thy rulers, to the ambition and cruelty of the enemy, to reverse of fortune. These things had not gone against thee, hadst not thou gone to war with the law of thy God. Thou inflictest the deadly wound on thyself; thou destroyedst thyself. Not as fools vaunt, by fate, or fortune of war, but *by thine iniquity hast thou fallen.* Thy remedy then is in thine own hand. *Return to thy God.*"

"[1] In these words, *by thine iniquity*, he briefly conveys, that each is to ascribe to himself the iniquity of all sin, of whatsoever he has been guilty, not defending himself, as Adam did, in whom we all, Jews and Gentiles, have sinned and fallen, as the Apostle says [2], *For we were by nature the children of wrath, even as others.* By adding actual, to that original, sin, Israel and every other nation falleth. He would say then, O Israel, be thou first converted, for thou hast need of conversion; *for thou hast fallen;* and confess this very thing, that *thou hast fallen by thine iniquity;* for such confession is the beginning of conversion."

But wherewith should he return?

2. *Take with you words.* He bids them not bring costly offerings, that they might regain His favor; not whole burnt offerings of bullocks, goats or rams; with which, and with which alone, they had before gone to seek Him [3]; not the silver and gold which they had lavished on their idols; but what seems the cheapest of all, which any may have, without cost to their substance; *words;* worthless, as mere words; precious when from the heart; words of confession and prayer, blending humility, repentance, confession, entreaty and praise of God. God seems to assign to them a form, with which they should approach Him. But with these words, they were also to turn inwardly *and turn unto the Lord*, with your whole heart, and not your lips alone. "After ye shall be converted, confess before Him."

Take away all iniquity [lit. and pleadingly, *Thou will take away all iniquity.*] They had *fallen by their iniquities;* before they can rise again, the stumbling-blocks must be taken out of their way. They then, unable themselves to do it, must turn to God, with Whom alone

is power and mercy to do it, and say to Him, *Take away all iniquity,* acknowledging that they had manifold iniquities, and praying Him to forgive all, *take away all. All iniquity!* "not only then the past, but what we fear for the future. Cleanse us from the past, keep us from the future. Give us righteousness, and preserve it to the end."

And receive us graciously, [lit. *and receive good* [4].] When God has forgiven and taken away iniquity, He has removed all hindrance to the influx of His grace. There is no vacuum in His spiritual, any more than in His natural, creation. When God's good Spirit is chased away, the evil spirits enter the house, which is *empty, swept, and garnished* [5] for them. When God has forgiven and taken away man's evil, He pours into him grace and all good. When then Israel and, in him, the penitent soul, is taught to say, *receive good,* it can mean only, the good which Thou Thyself hast given; as David says, *of Thine own we have given Thee* [6]. As God is said to " crown in us His own gifts;" ("His own gifts," but " in us [7];") so these pray to God to receive from them His own good, which they had from Him. For even the good, which God giveth to be in us, *He* accepteth in condescension and forgiving mercy, *Who crowneth thee in mercy and lovingkindness* [8]. " They pray God to accept their service, forgiving their imperfection, and mercifully considering their frailty. For since *our righteousnesses are filthy rags,* we ought ever humbly to entreat God, not to despise our dutifulness, for the imperfections, wanderings, and negligences mingled therewith. For exceedingly imperfect is it, especially if we consider the majesty of the Divine Nature, which should be served, were it possible, with infinite reverence." They plead to God, then, to accept what, although from Him they have it, yet through their imperfection, were, but for His goodness, unworthy of His acceptance. Still, since the glory of God is the end of all creation, by asking Him to accept it, they plead to Him, that this is the end for which He made and remade them, and placed the good in them, that it might redound to His glory. As, on the other hand, the Psalmist says [9], *What profit is there in my blood, if I go down into the pit,* as though

---

[1] Rup. [2] Eph. ii. 3. [3] See ab. v. 6.
[4] The rendering, *And receive* us *graciously*, overlooks the contrast of the two clauses. Israel is bidden to pray God, to *take away,* and to *receive.* On the two verbs, there follow two nouns, which stand naturally as the object of each; עָוֹן וְקַח טוֹב
תִּשָּׂא. No one would have doubted that קַח טוֹב

means, *receive good,* as just before, קְחוּ דברים
means, *take words,* but for the seeming difficulty, " what good had they?"
[5] S. Matt. xii. 44.
[6] 1 Chr. xxix. 14. [7] S. Aug.
[8] Ps. ciii. 4. [9] xxx. 9.

Before CHRIST cir. 725.

d Jer. 31. 18, &c. ch. 5. 13. & 12. 1.
e Deut. 17. 16. Ps. 33. 17. Is. 30. 2, 16. & 31. 1. f ch. 2. 17. ver. 8.

3 ^d Asshur shall not save us; ^e we will not ride upon horses; ^f neither will we say any more to the

work of our hands, *Ye are our gods:* ^g for in thee the fatherless findeth mercy.

Before CHRIST cir. 725.

g Ps. 10. 14. & 68. 5.

his own perishing were a loss to God, his Creator, since thus there were one creature the less to praise Him. "[1] *Take from us all iniquity,* leave in us no weakness, none of our former decay, lest the evil root should send forth a new growth of evil; *and receive good;* for unless Thou take away our evil, we can have no good to offer Thee, according to that [2], *depart from evil, and do good."*
So *will we render the calves of our lips,* lit. *and we would fain repay, calves, our lips;* i. e. when God shall have *forgiven us all our iniquity,* and received at our hands what, through His gift, we have to offer, the *good* which through His good Spirit we can do, then would we *offer* a perpetual thank-offering, *our lips.* This should be the substitute for the thank-offerings of the law. As the Psalmist says [3], *I will praise the Name of God with a song, and magnify Him with thanksgiving. This also shall please the Lord, better than a bullock that hath horns and hoofs.* They are to bind themselves to perpetual thanksgiving. As the morning and evening sacrifice were continual, so was their new offering to be continual. But more. The material sacrifice, *the bullock,* was offered, consumed, and passed away. Their *lips* were offered, and remained; a perpetual thank-offering, even a *living sacrifice,* living on like the mercies for which they thanked; giving forth their "endless song" for never-ending mercies.
This too looks on to the Gospel, in which, here on earth, our unending thanksgiving is beginning, in which also it was the purpose of God to restore those of Ephraim who would return to Him. "[4] Here we see law extinguished, the Gospel established. For we see other rites, other gifts. So then the priesthood is also changed. For three sorts of sacrifices were of old ordained by the law, with great state. Some signified the expiation of sin; some expressed the ardor of piety; some, thanksgiving. To those ancient signs and images, the truth of the Gospel, without figure, corresponds. Prayer to God, *to take away all iniquity,* contains a confession of sin, and expresses our faith, that we place our whole hope of recovering our lost purity and of obtaining salvation in the mercy of Christ. *Receive good.* What other good can we offer, than detestation of our past sin, with burning desire of holiness? This is the burnt offering. Lastly, *we will repay the*

calves of our lips, is the promise of that solemn vow, most acceptable to God, whereby we bind ourselves to keep in continual remembrance all the benefits of God, and to render ceaseless praise to the Lord Who has bestowed on us such priceless gifts. For *the calves of the lips* are orisons well-pleasing unto God. Of which David says [5], *Then shalt Thou be pleased with the sacrifices of righteousness, with burnt offerings and whole burnt offerings; then shall they offer bullocks upon Thine altar."*
3. *Asshur shall not save us.* After prayer for pardon and for acceptance of themselves, and thanksgiving for acceptance, comes the promise not to fall back into their former sins. Trust in man, in their own strength, in their idols, had been their besetting sins. Now, one by one, they disavow them.
First, they disclaim trust in man, and making [6] *flesh their arm.* Their disclaimer of the help of the Assyrian, to whom they had so often betaken themselves against the will of God, contains, at once, that best earnest of true repentance, the renewal of the confession of past sins, and the promise to rely no more on any princes of this world, of whom he was then chief. The horse, in like way, is the symbol of any warlike strength of their own. As the Psalmist says [7], *Some put their trust in chariots and some in horses, but we will remember the name of the Lord our God;* and [8], *a horse is a vain thing for safety, neither shall he deliver any by his great strength;* and Solomon [9], *The horse is prepared for the day of battle, but salvation is of the Lord.* War was almost the only end for which the horse was used among the Jews. If otherwise, it was a matter of great and royal pomp. It was part of a standing army. Their kings were especially forbidden to *multiply horses* [10] *to* themselves. Solomon, indeed, in his prosperity, broke this, as well as other commands of God. The pious king Hezekiah, although possessed at one time of large treasure, so kept that command as to furnish matter of mockery to Rabshakeh, the blaspheming envoy of Assyria, that he had neither horses nor horsemen [11]. The horses being procured from Egypt [12], the commerce gave fresh occasion for idolatry.
Neither will we say any more to the work of our hands, ye are our gods. This is the third disavowal. Since it was folly and sin to trust

[1] S. Jer. [2] Ps. xxxvii. 27. [3] lxix. 30, 1. [4] Osor. [5] Ps. li. ult. [6] Jer. xvii. 5. [7] Ps. xx. 7.

[8] Ps. xxxiii. 17. [9] Prov. xxi. 31. [10] Deut. xvii. 16. [11] 2 Kings xviii. 23. [12] 1 Kings x. 28.

Before CHRIST cir. 725.

h Jer. 5. 6. & 14. 7.
ch. 11. 7.   i Eph. 1. 6.

4 ¶ I will heal [h] their backsliding, I will l o v e them [i] freely: for m i n e

anger is turned away from him.

5 I will be as [k] the dew

Before CHRIST cir. 725.

k Job 29. 19.
Prov. 19. 12.

in the creatures which God had made, apart from God, how much more, to trust in things which they themselves had made, instead of God, and offensive to God!

For in Thee [or, *O Thou, in Whom*] *the fatherless findeth mercy.* He is indeed fatherless who hath not God for his Father. They confess then, that they were and deserved to be thus *fatherless* and helpless, a prey to every oppressor; but they appeal to God by the title which He had taken, *the Father of the fatherless*[1], that He would have mercy on them, who had no help but in Him. "[2] We promise this, they say, hoping in the help of Thy mercy, since it belongeth to Thee and is for Thy Glory to have mercy on the people which believeth in Thee, and to stretch forth Thine Hand, that they may be able to leave their wonted ills and amend their former ways."

4. *I will heal their backsliding.* God, in answer, promises to *heal* that wound of their souls, whence every other evil came, their fickleness and unsteadfastness. Hitherto, this had been the characteristic of Israel. [3] *Within a while they forgat His works, and would not abide His counsels.* [4] *They forgat what He had done. Their heart was not whole with Him; neither continued they steadfast in His covenant. They turned back and tempted God. They kept not His testimonies, but turned back and fell away like their forefathers, starting aside like a broken bow.* Steadfastness to the end is the special gift of the Gospel. *Lo, I am with you alway, even unto the end of the world. The gates of hell shall not prevail against it*[5]. And to individuals, Jesus, *having loved His own, loved them unto the end*[6]. In healing that disease of unsteadfastness, God healed all besides. This He did to all, wheresover or howsoever dispersed, who receive1 the Gospel; this He doth still; and this He will do completely in the end, when *all Israel shall be saved.*

I will love them freely; i.e. as the word means, *impelled*[7] thereto by Himself alone, and so, (as used of God) moved by His own Essential Bountifulness, the exceeding greatness of His Goodness, largely, bountifully. God *loves* us *freely* in loving us against our deserts, because He *is love;* He *loves* us *freely* in that He freely became Man, and, having become Man freely shed His Blood for the remission of our sins, freely forgave our sins;

He *loves* us *freely*, in *giving us grace, according to the good pleasure of His will*[8], to become pleasing to Him, and causing all good in us; He *loves* us *freely*, in rewarding infinitely the good which we have from *Him*. "[9] More manifestly here speaketh the Person of the Saviour Himself, promising His own Coming to the salvation of penitents, with sweetly sounding promise, with sweetness full of grace."

For Mine anger is turned away from him. As He says [10], *In My wrath I smote thee; but in My favor have I had mercy on thee.* He doth not withhold only, or suspend His anger, but He taketh it away wholly. So the Psalmist saith [11], *Thou hast forgiven the iniquity of Thy people; Thou hast covered all their sin; Thou hast taken away all Thy wrath; Thou hast turned from the fierceness of Thine anger.*

5. *I will be as the dew unto Israel.* Before, He had said [12], *his spring shall become dry and his fountain shall be dried up.* Now again He enlarges the blessing; their supply shall be unfailing, for it shall be from God; yea, God Himself shall be that blessing; *I will be the dew;* descending on the mown grass [13], to quicken and refresh it; descending, Himself, into the dried and parched and sere hearts of men, as He saith, *We will come unto him and make Our abode in him* [14]. The grace of God, like the dew, is not given once for all, but is, day by day, waited for, and, day by day, renewed. Yet doth it not pass away, like the fitful goodness [15] of God's former people, but turns into the growth and spiritual substance of those on whom it descends.

He shall grow as the lily. No one image can exhibit the manifold grace of God in those who are His own, or the fruits of that grace. So the Prophet adds one image to another, each supplying a distinct likeness of a distinct grace or excellence. The *lily* is the emblem of the beauty and purity of the soul in grace; the *cedar* of Lebanon, of its strength and deep-rootedness, its immovableness and uprightness; the evergreen *olive tree* which "remaineth in its beauty both winter and summer," of the unvarying presence of Divine Grace, continually, supplying an ever-sustained freshness, and issuing in fruit; and the fragrance of the aromatic plants with which the lower parts of Mount Lebanon are decked, of its loveliness and sweetness; as a native explains this [16], "he takes a sec-

1 Ps. lxviii. 5.
2 Rup.
4 Ps. lxxviii. 12, 37, 42, 57, 58.
5 S. Matt. xxviii. 20. xvi. 18.

3 Ps. cvi. 13.

6 S. John xiii. 1.   7 נרבה.   8 Eph. i. 5.
9 Rup.   10 Is. lx. 10.   11 lxxxv. 2, 3.
12 xiii. 15.   13 Ps. lxxii. 6.   14 S. John xiv. 23.
15 Above vi. 4.   16 R. Tanchum, in Poc.

‖ Or, *blossom.*
† Heb. *strike.*
† Heb. *shall go.*

[1] Ps. 52. 8. &
128. 3.

unto Israel : he shall ‖ grow as the lily, and † cast forth his roots as Lebanon.

6 His branches † shall spread, and [1] his beauty shall be as the olive tree,

and [m] his smell as Lebanon.

7 [n] They that dwell under his shadow shall return ; they shall revive *as* the corn, and ‖ grow as the

[m] Gen. 27. 27.
Cant. 4. 11.
[n] Ps. 91. 1.

‖ Or, *blossom.*

---

ond comparison from Mount Lebanon for the abundance of aromatic things and odoriferous flowers." Such are the myrtles and lavender and the odoriferous reed ; from which " [1] as you enter the valley " [between Lebanon and Anti-lebanon] "straightway the scent meets you." All these natural things are established and well-known symbols of things spiritual. The lily, so called in Hebrew from its dazzling whiteness, is, in the Canticles [2], the emblem of souls in which Christ takes delight. The lily multiplies exceedingly [3] ; yet hath it a weak root and soon fadeth. The Prophet, then, uniteth with these, plants of unfading green, and deep root. The seed which *had no root,* our Lord says, *withered away* [4], as contrariwise, St. Paul speaks of those, who are *rooted and grounded in love* [5], and of being *rooted and built up in Christ* [6]. The wide-spreading branches are an emblem of the gradual growth and enlargement of the Church, as our Lord says [7], *It becometh a tree, so that the birds of the air come and lodge in the branches thereof.* The symmetry of the tree and its outstretched arms express, at once, grace and protection. Of the *olive* the Psalmist says [8], *I am like a green olive tree in the house of God ;* and Jeremiah says [9], *The Lord called thy name a green olive tree, fair and of goodly fruit ;* and of "fragrance" the spouse says in the Canticles [10], *because of the savor of Thy good ointments, Thy name is as ointment poured forth ;* and the Apostle says [11], *thanks be to God, which maketh manifest the savor of His knowledge by us in every place.* Deeds of charity also are *an odor of good smell* [12] ; the prayers of the saints also are *sweet odors* [13]. All these are the fruits of the Spirit of God Who says, *I will be as the dew unto Israel.* Such reunion of qualities, being beyond nature, suggests the more, that that, wherein they are all combined, the future Israel, the Church, shall flourish with graces beyond nature, in their manifoldness, completeness, unfadingness.

7. *They that dwell under his shadow,* i. e. the shadow of the restored Israel, who had just been described under the image of a magnificent tree uniting in itself all perfections. " [14] They that are under the shadow of the Church are together under the shadow of

Christ the Head thereof, and also of God the Father." The Jews, of old, explained it [15], "they shall dwell under the shadow of their Messias." These, he says, *shall return,* i. e. they shall turn to be quite other than they had been, even back to Him, to Whom they belonged, Whose creatures they were, God. *They shall revive as the corn.* The words may be differently rendered, in the same general meaning. The simple words, *They shall revive* [lit. *give life* to, or *preserve in life,*] *corn,* have been filled up differently. Some of old, (whence ours has been taken) understood it, *they shall revive* themselves, [16] and so, *shall live,* and that either *as corn,* (as it is said, *shall grow as the vine*) ; or *by corn* [17] which is also very natural, since "bread is the staff of life," and our spiritual Bread is the support of our spiritual life. Or lastly, (of which the grammar is easier, yet the idiom less natural) it has been rendered *they shall give life to corn,* make corn to live, by cultivating it. In all ways the sense is perfect. If we render, *shall revive as corn,* it means, being, as it were, dead, they shall not only live again with renewed life, but shall even increase. Corn first dies in its outward form, and so is multiplied ; the fruit-bearing branches of the vine are pruned and cut, and so they bear richer fruit. So through suffering, chastisement, or the heavy hand of God or man, the Church, being purified, yields more abundant fruits of grace. Or if rendered, *shall make corn to grow,* since the Prophet, all around, is under figures of God's workings in nature, speaking of His workings of grace, then it is the same image, as when our Lord speaks of those *who receive the seed in an honest and true heart and bring forth fruit, some an hundredfold, some sixty, some thirty* [18]. Or if we were to render, *shall produce life through wheat,* what were this, but that seed-corn, which, for us and for our salvation, was sown in the earth, and died, and *brought forth much fruit ;* the Bread of life, of which our Lord says [19], *I am the Bread of life, Whoso eateth of this bread shall live for ever, and the bread which I will give is My Flesh, which I will give for the life of the world ?*

The scent thereof shall be *as the wine of Lebanon.* The grapes of Lebanon have been of the size of plums ; its wine has been spoken

---

[1] Theophr. Hist. Plant. x. 7. [2] Cant. ii. 1. 2.
[3] Plin. in Poc. . [4] S. Matt. xiii. 6.
[5] Eph. iii. 17. [6] Col. ii. 7. [7] S. Matt. xiii. 32.
[8] Ps. lii. 8. [9] xi. 16. [10] i. 3.

[11] 2 Cor. ii. 14. [12] Phil. iv. 18. [13] Rev. v. 8.
[14] Poc. [15] Jon. [16] Kimchi.
[17] As the old versions, LXX. Vulg. Syr.
[18] S. Matt. xiii. 23. [19] S. John vi. 48, 51.

Before
CHRIST
cir. 725. vine: the ‖ scent thereof *shall be* as the wine of Leba-

‖ Or, *memorial.* non.

8 Ephraim *shall s a y,*

[o] ver. 3.   [o] What have I to do any

more with idols? [p] I have heard *him,* and observed him: I *am* like a green fir tree. [q] From me is thy fruit found.

Before
CHRIST
cir. 725.

[p] Jer. 31. 18.

[q] Jam. 1. 17.

of as the best in the East or even in the world [1]. Formerly Israel was as a luxuriant, but empty, vine, bringing forth no fruit to God [2]. God [3] *looked that it should bring forth grapes, and it brought forth wild grapes.* Now its glory and luxuriance should not hinder its bearing fruit, and *that,* the noblest of its kind. Rich and fragrant is the odor of graces, the inspiration of the Spirit of God, and not fleeting, but abiding.

8. *Ephraim* shall say, *what have I to do any more with idols?* So Isaiah foretells [4], *The idols He shall utterly abolish.* Aforetime Ephraim said obstinately, in the midst of God's chastisements [5]; *I will go after my lovers, who give me my bread and my water, my wool and my flax, mine oil and my drink.* Now she shall renounce them wholly and for ever. This is entire conversion, to part wholly with everything which would dispute the allegiance with God, to cease to look to any created thing or being, for what is the gift of the Creator alone. So the Apostle says [6], *what concord hath Christ with Belial?* This verse exhibits in few, vivid, words, converted Ephraim speaking with God, and God answering; Ephraim renouncing his sins, and God accepting him; Ephraim glorying in God's goodness, and God reminding him that he holds all from Himself.

I have heard and observed him. God answers the profession and accepts it. *I,* (emphatic) *I Myself have heard* and *have answered,* as He says [7], *Before they call I will answer.* Whereas God, before, had hid His face from them, or had *observed* [8] them, only as the object of His displeasure, and as ripe for destruction, now He reverses this, and *observes* them, in order to forecome the wishes of their hearts before they are expressed, to watch over them and survey and provide for all their needs. To this, Ephraim exulting in God's goodness, answers, *I am like a green fir tree,* i. e. evergreen, ever-fresh. The *berosh,* (as S. Jerome, living in Palestine, thought) one of the large genus of the *pine* or *fir,* or (as others trans-

lated) the *cypress* [9], was a tall stately tree [10]; in whose branches the stork could make its nest [11]; its wood precious enough to be employed in the temple [12]; fine enough to be used in all sorts of musical instruments [13]; strong and pliant enough to be used for spears [14]. It was part of the glory of Lebanon [15]. A Greek historian says that Lebanon "[16] was full of cedars and pines and cypresses, of wonderful beauty and size." A modern traveller says, of "the cypress groves of Lebanon;" "[17] Each tree is in itself a study for the landscape painter—some, on account of their enormous stems and branches. —Would you see trees in all their splendor and beauty, then enter these wild groves, that have never been touched by the pruning knife of art." This tree, in its majestic beauty, tenacity of life, and undying verdure, winter and summer, through the perpetual supply of sap, pictures the continual life of the soul through the unbroken supply of the grace of God. Created beauty must, at best, be but a faint image of the beauty of the soul in grace; for this is from the indwelling of God the Holy Ghost.

From Me is thy fruit found. Neither the pine nor the cypress bear any fruit, useful for food. It is probable then that here too the Prophet fills out one image by another and says that restored Israel, the Church of God, or the soul in grace, should not only have beauty and majesty, but what is not, in the way of nature, found united therewith, fruitfulness also. *From Me is thy fruit found;* as our Lord says [18], *I am the vine, ye are the branches.* Human nature, by itself, can as little bear fruit well-pleasing to God, as the pine or cypress can bear fruit for human use. As it were a miracle in nature, were these trees to bring forth such fruit, so, for man to bring forth fruits of grace, is a miracle of grace. The presence of works of grace attests the immediate working of God the Holy Ghost, as much as any miracle in nature.

[1] See in Œdmann, ii. 193. Germ. and Maronites in Lap.
[2] x. 1.   [3] Is. v. 2.   [4] ii. 18.   [5] ch. ii. 5.
[6] 2 Cor. vi. 15.   [7] Is. lxv. 24.   [8] xiii. 7.
[9] S. Jerome uniformly renders abies. The LXX. and Syr. vary, rendering both cypress and pine. The Syriac *berutho* (doubtless the same tree and used sometimes for it in the Peshito) is said by Bar Bahlul to be the Arabic *Abuhul;* and this Ibn Baithar describes as "a large tree with leaves like the tamarisk." He identifies it also with the βράθυ of Dioscorides, who mentions a second sort, "with

leaves like the cypress, more prickly than the other." Pliny (xxv. 11) says that some called this "the Cretan cypress." The bratum is commonly called the "Juniperus Sabina," which, however, is not known to be a tall tree, although some of the Juniper tribe are.
[10] Is. lv. 13.   [11] Ps. civ. 17.
[12] 1 Kings v. 22, 24. [8. 10. Eng.] vi. 15, 34.
[13] 2 Sam. vi. 5.   [14] Nah. ii. 3.
[15] Is. xxxvii. 24. lx. 13.   [16] Diod. Sic. xix. 58.
[17] Van de Velde Syr. and Pal. ii. 475.
[18] S. John xv. 5.

Before
CHRIST
cir. 725.
9 [r] Who *is* wise, and he shall understand these

[r] Ps. 107. 43. Jer. 9. 12. Dan. 12. 10. John 8. 47. & 18. 37.

things? prudent, and he shall know them? for [s] the

Before
CHRIST
cir. 725.

[s] Prov. 10. 29. Luke 2. 34. 2 Cor. 2. 16. 1 Pet. 2. 7, 8.

---

9. *Who is wise and he shall understand these things?* The Prophet says this, not of the words in which he had spoken, but of the substance. He does not mean that his style was obscure, or that he had delivered the message of God in a way difficult to be understood. This would have been to fail of his object. Nor does he mean that human acuteness is the key to the things of God. He means that those only of a certain character, those *wise*, through God, unto God, will understand the things of God. So the Psalmist, having related some of God's varied chastenings, mercies and judgments, sums up [1], *Whoso is wise and will observe these things, even they shall understand the loving kindness of the Lord.* So Asaph says that God's dealings with the good and bad in this life were *too hard* for him to *understand, until* he *went into the sanctuary of God;* then *understood* he *their end* [2]. In like way Daniel, at the close of his prophecy, sums up the account of a sifting-time [3], *Many shall be purified and made white and tried, and the wicked shall do wickedly; and none of the wicked shall understand, but the wise shall understand.* As these say that the wise alone understand the actual dealings of God with man, so Hosea says, that the wise alone would understand what he had set forth of the mercy and severity of God, of His love for man, His desire to pardon, His unwillingness that any should perish, His longing for our repentance, His store of mercies in Christ, His gifts of grace and His free eternal love, and yet His rejection of all half-service and His final rejection of the impenitent. *Who is wise?* "[4] The word *who* is always taken, not for what is impossible, but for what is difficult." So Isaiah saith [5], *Who hath believed our report, and to whom is the Arm of the Lord revealed?* Few are wise with *the wisdom which is from above;* few understand, because few wish to understand, or seek wisdom from Him *Who giveth to all men liberally, and upbraideth not* [6]. The question implies also, that God longs that men should *understand* to their salvation. He inquires for them, calls to them that they would meditate on His mercies and judgments. As S. Paul says [7], *Behold the goodness and severity of God; on them which fell, severity; but toward thee, goodness, if thou continue in His goodness. O the depth of the riches both of the wisdom and knowledge of God! how unsearchable are His judgments, and His ways past finding out.* Unsearchable to intellect and theory; intelligible to faith and for acting on.

And he shall understand, (i. e. *that he may understand* [8]) *these* things. The worldly-wise of that generation, too, doubtless, thought themselves too wise to need to understand them; as the wise after this world counted the Cross of Christ foolishness.

Prudent. Properly "gifted with understanding," the form of the word expressing, that he was *endowed with* this *understanding* [9], as a gift from God. *And He shall know them.* While the wise of this world disbelieve, jeer, scoff at them, in the name of human reason, he who has not the natural quickness of man only, but who is endued with the true wisdom, shall *know* them. So our Lord says [10], *If any man will do His will, he shall know of the doctrine whether it is of God.* The word, *wise,* may specially mean him who contemplates these truths and understands them in themselves, yet plainly so as to act upon them; and the word *endued with prudence,* may specially describe such as are gifted with readiness to apply that knowledge to practice, in judgment, discrimination, act [11]. By uniting both, the Prophet joins contemplative and practical wisdom, and intensifies the expression of God's desire that we should be endowed with them.

For the ways of the Lord are right. If in the word, *ways,* the figure is still preserved [12], the Prophet speaks of the *ways,* as "direct and straight;" without a figure, as "just and upright."

The ways of the Lord are, what we, by a like figure, call "the course of His Providence;" of which Scripture says [13], *His ways are judgment;* [14] *God, His ways are perfect;* [15] *the Lord is righteous in all His ways, and holy in all His works;* [16] *Thy way is in the sea, and Thy paths in the great waters, and Thy footsteps are not known;* [17] *lo, these are parts of His ways, but how little a portion is heard of Him, and the thunder of His power who can understand?* [18] *Who hath enjoined Him His way, and who can say, Thou hast wrought iniquity?* These *ways* of God include His ordering for us, in His eternal wisdom, that course of life, which leads most directly to Himself. They include, then, all God's commandments, pre-

---

[1] Ps. cvii. 43.   [2] Ib. lxxiii. 16, 17.   [3] Dan. xii. 10.
[4] S. Jer. on Eccl. iii. 21.   [5] liii. 1.
[6] S. James i. 5.   [7] Rom. xi. 22, 33.
[8] The force of the abbreviated form, יָבִן.
[9] נָבוֹן, the passive of the יָבִן which had just preceded.   [10] S. John vii. 17.

[11] As in their degree, the heathen too distinguish σοφία and φρόνησις.
[12] יָשָׁר is both used of physical and moral straightness.
[13] Deut. xxxii. 4. Dan. iv. 37.   [14] Ps. xviii. 30.
[15] Ib. cxlv. 17.   [16] Ib. lxxvii. 19.
[17] Job xxvi. 14.   [18] Ib. xxxvi. 23.

ways of the LORD *are* right, and the just shall walk in || them : but the transgressors shall fall therein.

cepts, counsels, His whole moral law, as well as His separate purpose for each of us. In the one way, they are God's ways toward us ; in the other they are God's ways for us. *The just shall walk in them.* God reveals His ways to us, not that we may know them only, but that we may do them. "The end of moral science is not knowledge, but practice," said the Heathen philosopher[1]. But the life of grace is a life of progress. The word, *way*, implies not continuance only, but advance. He does not say, "they shall *stand* in God's ways," but *they shall walk in them*. They shall go on in them "upright, safe, and secure, in *great peace* and with *nothing whereat to stumble*[2]. In God's ways there is no stumbling block, and they who walk in them, are free from those of which other ways are full. Whereas, out of God's ways, all paths are tangled, uneven, slippery, devious, full of snares and pitfalls, God maketh His *way straight*, a royal highway, smooth, even, direct unto Himself. *But* [*and*] *the transgressors shall fall therein*, lit. *shall stumble thereon*[3]. *Transgressors*, i. e. those who rebel against the law of God, *stumble* in divers manners, not *in*, but *at*[4] the ways of God. They stumble at God Himself, at His All-Holy Being, Three and One; they stumble at His attributes; they stumble at His Providence, they stumble at His acts; they stumble at His interference with them; they stumble at His requirements. They rebel against His commandments, as requiring what they like not; at His prohibitions, as refusing what they like. They stumble at His Wisdom, in ordering His own creation ; at His Holiness, in punishing sin; but most of all, they stumble at His Goodness and condescension. They have a greater quarrel with His condescension than with all His other attributes. They have stumbled, and still stumble at God the Son, becoming Man, and taking our flesh in the Virgin's womb ; they stumble at the humility of the Crucifixion; they stumble at His placing His Manhood at the Right Hand of God; they stumble at the simplicity, power and condescension, which He uses in the Sacraments; they stumble at His giving us His Flesh to eat ; they stumble at His forgiving sins freely, and again and again ; they stumble at His making us members of Himself, without waiting for our own wills ; they stumble at His condescension in using our own acts, to the attainment of our degree of everlasting glory. Every attribute, or gift, or revelation of God,

which is full of comfort to the believer, becomes in turn an occasion of stumbling to the rebellious. *The things which should have been for his wealth, become to him an occasion of falling*[5]. "They cannot attemper their own wishes and ways to the Divine law, because, obeying what they themselves affect, *the law of their members*, they stumble at that other law, which leadeth unto life[6]." With this the Prophet sums up all the teaching of the seventy years of his ministry. This is the end of all which he had said of the severity and mercy of God, of the Coming of Christ, and of our resurrection in Him. This is to us the end of all ; this is thy choice, Christian soul, to walk in God's ways, or to stumble at them. As in the days when Christ came in the Flesh, so it is now ; so it will be to the end. So holy Simeon prophesied, "[7] *This Child is set for the fall and rising again of many in Israel ;* and our Lord said of Himself, [8]*For judgment I am come into this world, that they which see not might see, and that they which see might be made blind.* And S. Peter[9]; *Unto you which believe* He is *precious ; but unto them which be disobedient, the stone which the builders disallowed, the same is made the head of the corner, and a stone of stumbling and rock of offence, to them which stumble at the word, being disobedient. Christ crucified* was *unto the Jews a stumbling block, and unto the Greeks foolishness, but unto them which are called, both Jews and Greeks, Christ the Power of God, and the Wisdom of God*[10]. *The commandment, which* was ordained *to life*, Paul, when yet unregenerate, *found* to be *unto death*[11]. "[12]Pray we then the Eternal Wisdom, that we may be truly wise and understanding, and receive not in vain those many good things which Christ has brought to the race of man. Let us cleave to Him by that *faith, which worketh by love* ; let us seek the Good, seek the Just, *seek the Lord while He may be found, and call upon Him while He is near.* Whatever God doeth toward ourselves or others, let us account right ; *for the ways of the Lord are right,* and *that* cannot be unjust, which pleaseth the Just. Whatever He teacheth, whatever He commandeth, let us believe without discussion, and embrace most firmly for *that* cannot be false, which the Truth hath taught. Let us walk in His ways ;" for Christ Himself is *the Way* unto Himself, *the Life.* "[13] Look up to heaven ; look down to Hell; live for Eternity." "[14] Weigh a thousand, yea thousands of years against eternity what dost thou, weighing a finite, how vast soever, against Infinity ?"

[1] Aristot. Eth. i. 3.   [2] Poc.   [3] Ps. cxix. 165.
[4] As in Nah. iii. 3. Prov. iv. 19.   [5] Ps. lxix. 22.
[6] from Sanct.   [7] S. Luke ii. 34.

[8] S. John ix. 39.   [9] 1 Ep. ii. 7, 8.   [10] 1 Cor. i. 23, 24.
[11] Rom. vii. 10.   [12] Rib.   [13] Lap.
[14] S. Aug. in Ps. xxxvi. L.

INTRODUCTION

TO

THE PROPHET

JOEL.

THE Prophet Joel relates nothing of himself. He gives no hints as to himself, except the one fact which was necessary to authenticate his prophecy, that the word of the Lord came to him, and that the book to which that statement is prefixed is that "word of the Lord." *The word of the Lord, which came to Joel, son of Pethuel.* Like Hosea, he distinguished himself from others of the same name, by the mention of the name of his unknown father. But his whole book bears evidence, that he was a prophet of Jerusalem. He was living in the centre of the public worship of God: he speaks to the priests as though present, *Come ye, lie all night in sackcloth*[a]; he was, where the *solemn assembly*[b], which he bids them *proclaim*, would be held; *the house of the Lord*[c], from which *meat-offering and drink-offering were cut off*, was before his eyes. Whether for alarm[d], or for prayer[e], he bids, *blow ye the trumpet in Zion. The city*[f], which he sees the enemy approaching to beleaguer and enter, is Jerusalem. He addresses the *children of Zion*[g]; he reproaches Tyre, Zidon, and Philistia, with selling to the Greeks *the children of Zion and Jerusalem*[h]. God promises by him to *bring back the captivity of Judah and Jerusalem*[i]. Of Israel, in its separated existence, he takes no more notice, than if it were not. They may be included in the three places in which he uses the name; *Ye shall know that I am in the midst of Israel; I will plead for My people and My heritage, Israel; the Lord will be the strength of Israel*[k]; but, (as the context shews) only as included, together with Judah, in the one people of God. The prom-

ises to Judah, Jerusalem, Zion, with which he closes his book, being simply prophetic, must, so far, remain the same, whomsoever he addressed. He foretells that those blessings were to issue from Zion, and that the Church was to be founded there. Yet the absence of any direct promise of the extension of those blessings to the ten tribes, (such as occur in Hosea and Amos) implies that he had no office in regard to them.

Although a prophet of Jerusalem, and calling, in the name of God, to a solemn and strict fast and supplication, he was no priest. He mentions the priests as a class to which he did not belong[l], *the priests, the Lord's ministers; ye priests; ye ministers of the altar; ye ministers of my God; let the priests, the ministers of the Lord, weep between the porch and the altar*, the place where they officiated. He calls upon them to proclaim the fast, which he enjoined in the Name of God. *Sanctify ye a fast, call a solemn assembly*[m], he says to those, whom he had just called to mourn, *ye priests, ye ministers of the altar.* As entrusted with a revelation from God, he had an authority superior to that of the priests. While using this, he interfered not with their own special office.

Joel must have completed his prophecy in its present form, before Amos collected his prophecies into one whole. For Amos takes as the key-note of his prophecy, words with which Joel almost closes his; *The Lord shall roar from Zion, and utter His voice from Jerusalem*[n]. Nor only so, but Amos inserts at the end of his own prophecy some of Joel's closing words of promise. Amos thus identi-

[a] i. 13, 14.   [b] ii. 15–17.   [c] i. 9.   [d] ii. 1.
[e] ii. 15.   [f] ii. 9.   [g] ii. 23.   [h] iii. 4, 6.

[i] iii. 1.   [k] ii. 27, iii. 2, 16.   [l] i. 9, 13, ii. 17.
[m] i. 14.   [n] Joel iii. 16.

143

fied his own prophecy with that of Joel. In the threatening with which he opens it, he retains each word of Joel, in the self-same order, although the words admit equally of several different collocations, each of which would have had an emphasis of its own [o]. The symbolic blessing, which Amos takes from Joel at the close of his prophecy *the mountains shall drop with new wine* [p], is found in these two prophets alone; and the language is the bolder and more peculiar, because the word *drop* [q] is used of dropping from above, not of flowing down. It seems as if the picture were, that the mountains of Judæa, *the mountains*, instead of mist or vapor, should *distill* that which is the symbol of joy, *wine which maketh glad the heart of man* [r]. The ground why Amos, in this marked way, joined on his own book of prophecy to the book of Joel, must remain uncertain, since he did not explain it. It may have been, that, being called in an unusual way to the Prophetic office, he would in this way identify himself with the rest of those whom God called to it. A prophet, out of Judah but for Israel, Amos identified himself with the one prophet of Judah, whose prophecy was committed to writing. Certainly those first words of Amos, *The Lord shall roar from Zion, and utter His voice from Jerusalem*, pointed out to the ten tribes, that Zion and Jerusalem were the place *which God had chosen to place His Name there*, the visible centre of His government, whence proceeded His judgments and His revelation. Others have supposed that bad men thought that the evil which Joel had foretold would not come, and that the good may have looked anxiously for the fulfillment of God's promises; and that on that ground, Amos renewed, by way of allusion, both God's threats and promises, thereby impressing on men's minds, what Habakkuk says in plain terms [s], *The vision is for the* [t] *appointed time, and it hasteth to the end* [u]: *though it tarry, wait for it; for it will come, it will not tarry, or be behindhand* [v].

However this may have been, such marked renewal of threatenings and promises of Joel by Amos, attests two things; 1) that Joel's prophecy must, at the time when Amos wrote, have become part of Holy Scripture, and its authority must have been acknowledged; 2) that its authority must have been acknowledged by, and it must have been in circulation among, those to whom Amos prophesied; otherwise he would not have prefixed

to his book those words of Joel. For the whole force of the words, as employed by Amos, depends upon their being recognized by his hearers, as a renewal of the prophecy of Joel. Certainly bad men jeered at Amos, as though his threatenings would not be fulfilled [w].

Since, then, Amos prophesied during the time, when Azariah and Jeroboam II. reigned together, the book of Joel must have been at that time written, and known in Israel also. Beyond this, the brief, although full, prophecy of Joel affords no clue as to its own date. Yet probably it was not far removed from that of Amos. For Amos, as well as Joel, speaks of the sin of Tyre and Zidon and of the Philistines in selling the children of Judah into captivity [x]. And since Amos speaks of this, as the crowning sin of both, it is perhaps likely that some signal instance of it had taken place, to which both prophets refer. To this, the fact that both prophets speak of the scourge of locusts and drought [y], (if this were so) would not add any further evidence. For Joel was prophesying to Judah; Amos, to Israel. The prophecy of Joel may indeed subordinately, although very subordinately at the most, *include* real locusts; and such locusts, if he meant to include them, could have been no local plague, and so could hardly have passed over Israel. But Amos does not speak of the ravages of the locusts, by which, in addition to drought, mildew, pestilence, God had, when he prophesied, recently chastened Israel, as distinguished above others which God had sent upon this land. There is nothing therefore to identify the locusts spoken of by Amos with those which Joel speaks of as an image of the terrible, successive, judgments of God. Rather Amos enumerates, one after the other, God's ordinary plagues in those countries, and says that all had failed in the object for which God sent them, the turning of His people to Himself.

Nor, again, does anything in Joel's own prophecy suggest any particular date, beyond what is already assigned through the relation which the book of Amos bears to his book. On the contrary, in correspondence, perhaps, with the wide extent of his prophecy, Joel says next to nothing of what was temporary or local. He mentions, incidentally, in one place the *drunkards* [z] of his people; yet in this case too, he speaks of the sin as especially affected and touched by the chastisement, not

º ‏ויהוה מציון ישאג ומירושלם יתן קולו‎ Amos, since he opens his prophecy with these words, omits the ‏ן‎ (and that alone,) with which Joel joins them on with what preceded.

p Joel iv. 18. ‏עסיס ההרים יטפו‎ Am. ix. 13. ‏והטיפו ההרים עסיס‎.

q ‏נטף חטיף‎, are used of "the heavens," Jud. v. 4, Ps. lxviii. 9; of "the fingers trickling," Cant. v.

5, 13; "the lips dropping honey," Cant. iv. 11, Prov. v. 3; then of speech.

r Ps. civ. 15.   s Hab. ii. 3.   t ‏למועד‎.

u lit. *breatheth*, as we say "panteth," ‏יפח‎.

v ‏אחר‎.   w v. 18, vi. 3, ix. 10.

x Jo. iii. 4–6. Am. i. 6, 9.

y "drought," Joel i. 17, 20, Am. iv. 7, 8; "locusts," Am. iv. 9.   z i. 5.

of the chastisement, as brought upon the sinner or upon the sinful people by that sin. Beyond this one case, the Prophet names neither sins nor sinners among his own people. He foretells chastisement, and exhorts to repentance as the means of averting it, but does not specify any sins. His prophecy is one declaration of the displeasure of God against all sin, and of His judgments consequent thereon, one promise of pardon upon earnest repentance; and so, perhaps, what is individual has, for the most part been purposely suppressed.

The notices in the book of Joel, which have been employed to fix more precisely the date of the Prophet, relate 1) to the proclamation of the solemn assembly, which, it is supposed, would be enjoined thus authoritatively in a time when that injunction would be obeyed; 2) to the mention of certain nations, and the supposed omission of certain other nations, as enemies of Judah. Both arguments have been overstated and misstated.

1) The call to public humiliation implies, so far, times in which the king would not interfere to prevent it. But ordinarily, in Judah, even bad and irreligious kings did not interfere with extraordinary fasts in times of public distress. Jehoiakim did not; the king, who hesitated not to cut in shreds the roll of Jeremiah's prophecies when three or four columns or chapters[a] had been read before him, and burnt it on the hearth by which he was sitting. The fast-day, upon which that roll had been read in the ears of all the people, was an extraordinary *fast before the Lord, proclaimed to all the people in Jerusalem, and to all the people that came from the cities of Judah unto Jerusalem*[b]. This fasting day was not their annual fast, the day of Atonement. For the day of Atonement was in the seventh month; this, Jeremiah tells us, *was in the ninth month*[c]. When such a king as Jehoiakim tolerated the appointment of an extraordinary fast, not for Jerusalem only, but for *all the people who came from the cities of Judah*, we may well think that no king of ordinary impiety would, in a time of such distress as Joel foretells, have interfered to hinder it. There were, at most, after Athaliah's death, two periods only of decided antagonism to God. The first was at the close of the reign of Joash, after the death of Jehoiada, when Joash with the princes gave himself to the idolatry of Ashtaroth and put to death Zechariah, the son of Jehoiada, upon whom *the Spirit of God came*. and he foretold their destruction; *Because ye have forsaken the Lord, He had also forsaken you*[d]. The period after the murder of Zechariah was very short. *As*

the year came round, the Syrians came against them; and *when they departed, his own servants slew him*[e]. The only space, left uncertain, is the length of time, during which the idolatry lasted, before the murder of Zechariah. The second period, that in which Amaziah fell away to the idolatry of the Edomites, silenced the prophet of God, and was abandoned by him to his destruction[f], was also brief, lasting probably some sixteen years.

2) The argument from the Prophet's mention of some enemies of God's people[g] and the supposed omission of other later enemies, rests partly on a wrong conception of prophecy, partly on wrong interpretation of the Prophet. On the assumption that the Prophets did not speak of nations, as instruments of God's chastisements on His people, until they had risen above the political horizon of Judah, it has been inferred that Joel lived before the time when Assyria became an object of dread, because, mentioning other enemies of God's people, he does not mention Assyria. The assumption, which originated in unbelief, is untrue in fact. Balaam prophesied the captivity through Assyria[h], when Israel was entering on the promised land; he foretold also the destruction of Assyria or the great empire of the East through a power who should come from Europe[i]. The prophet Ahijah foretold to Jeroboam I. that the Lord would *root up Israel out of the good land which He gave to their fathers, and* would *scatter them beyond the river*[k]. Neither in temporal nor spiritual prophecy can we discern the rules, by which, *at sundry times and in divers manners*, God revealed Himself *through the Prophets*, so that we should be able to reduce to one strict method *the manifold wisdom* of God, and infer the age of a prophet from the tenor of the prophecy which God put into his mouth.

It is plain, moreover, from the text of Joel himself, that God had revealed to him, that other more formidable enemies than had yet invaded Judah would hereafter come against it, and that those enemies whom he speaks of, he mentions only, as specimens of hatred against God's people and of its punishment. There can really be no question, that by *the Northern*[1] army, he means the Assyrian. God foretells also by him the capture of Jerusalem, and the punishment of those who *scattered Israel, My heritage, among the heathen, and divided My land*[m]. Such words can only be understood of an entire removal of Judah, whereby others could come and take possession of his land. In connection with these great powers occurs the mention of Tyre Sidon and Philistia, petty yet vexatious enemies, contrasted with the more powerful.

[a] Jer. xxxvi. 23.   [b] Ib. 9.   [c] Ib.
[d] 2 Chron. xxiv. 17–21.   [e] Ib. 23, 25.
[f] Ib. xxv. 14–16, 23.

[g] Tyre, Zidon, Philistia, iii. 4; Egypt and Edom, iii. 19.   [h] Nu. xxiv. 22.   [i] Ib. 24.   [k] 1 Kgs xiv. 15. [l] ii. 20.   [m] iii. 2.

10

The very formula with which that mention is introduced, shews that they are named only incidentally and as instances of a class. *And also* [n], *what are ye to Me, O Tyre, and Zidon, and all the coasts of Philistia ?* The mighty nations were to come as lions, to lay waste; these, like jackals, made their own petty merchants gain. The mighty divided the land; these were plunderers and men-stealers. In both together, he declares that nothing, either great or small, should escape the righteous judgments of God. Neither shall might save the mighty, nor shall the petty malice of the lesser enemies of God be too small to be requited. But not only is there no proof that Joel means to enumerate all the nations who had hitherto infested Judah, but there is proof that he did not.

One only has been found to place Joel so early as the reign of Jehoshaphat. But in his reign, after the death of Ahab, (B. C. 897,) *Moab and Ammon and with them others, a great multitude* [o], invaded Judah. Since then it is tacitly admitted, that the absence of the mention of Moab and Ammon does not imply that Joel prophesied before their invasion (B. C. 897,) neither is the non-mention of the invasion of the Syrians any argument that he lived before the end of the reign of Jehoash (B. C. 840). Further, not the mere invasion of Judah, but the motives of the invasion or cruelty evinced in it, drew down the judgments of God. The invasion of Hazael was directed not against Judah, but *against Gath* [p]. But *a small company of men* [p] went up against Jerusalem; *and the Lord delivered a very great company into their hand, because they had forsaken the Lord God of their fathers. They executed,* we are told, *judgment against Joash.* Nor does it appear, that they, like the Assyrians, exceeded the commission for which God employed them. [r] *They destroyed all the princes of the people from among the people,* the princes who had seduced Joash to idolatry and were the authors of the murder of Zechariah. [s] *They conspired against him, and stoned him (Zechariah) with stones at the commandment of the king.* Amos mentions, as the last ground of God's sentence against Damascus, not this incursion, but the cruelty of Hazael to Gilead [t]. The religious aspect of the single invasion of Judah by this band of Syrians was very different from the perpetual hostility of the Philistines, or the malicious cupidity of the Phœnicians.

Still less intelligible is the assertion, that Joel would not have foretold any punishment

of Edom, had he lived after the time when Amaziah smote 20,000 of them *in the valley of salt, and took Selah* [u], or Petra B. C. 838. For Amos confessedly prophesied in the reign of Azariah, the son of Amaziah. Azariah recovered Elath also from Edom [v]; yet Amos, in his time, foretells the utter destruction of Bozra and Teman [w]. The victory of Amaziah did not humble Edom. They remained the same embittered foe. In the time of Ahaz, they again invaded Judah and *smote* it and *carried away a captivity* [x]. Prophecy does not regard these little variations of conquest or defeat. They do not exhaust its meaning. It pronounces God's judgment against the abiding character of the nation; and while that continues unchanged, the sentence remains. Its fulfillment seems often to linger, but in the end, it does not fail nor remain behind God's appointed time. Egypt and Edom moreover, in Joel, stand also as symbols of nations or people like themselves. They stand for the people themselves, but they represent also others of the same character, as long as the struggle between "the city of God" and "the city of the devil [y]" shall last, i. e. to the end of time.

There being then no internal indication of the date of Joel, we cannot do better than acquiesce in the tradition, by which his book is placed next to that of Hosea, and regard Joel as the prophet of Judah, during the earlier part of Hosea's office toward Israel, and rather earlier than Isaiah. At least, Isaiah, although he too was called to the prophetic office in the days of Uzziah, appears to have embodied in his prophecy, words of Joel, as well of Micah, bearing witness to the unity of prophecy, and, amid the richness and fullness of his own prophetic store, purposely borrowing from those, of whose ministry God did not will that such large fruit should remain. The remarkable words [z], *Near is the Day of the Lord, like destruction from the Almighty shall it come,* Isaiah inserted, word for word [a], from Joel [b], including the remarkable alliteration, ceshod mishshaddai, "like *a mighty* destruction from the *Almighty*."

The prophecy of Joel is altogether one. It extends from his own day to the end of time. He gives the key to it in a saying, which he casts into the form of a proverb, that judgment shall follow after judgment [c]. Then he describes that first desolation, as if present, and calls to repentance [d]; yet withal he says expressly, that the day of the Lord is not come, but is at hand [e]. This he repeats at the beginning of the second chapter [f], in

---

[n] וְגַם iv. 4 Heb.; iii. 4 Eng.

[o] 2 Chron. xx. 1, 2. [p] 2 Kgs xii. 17.

[q] 2 Chron. xxiv. 24. [r] Ib. 23; add 17, 18.

[s] Ib. 21. [t] i. 3. [u] 2 Kgs xiv. 7. 2 Chron. xxv. 11.

[v] 2 Kgs xiv. 22. 2 Chron. xxvi. 2. [w] i. 12.

[x] 2 Chron. xxviii. 17.

[y] See S. Aug. de Civ. Dei. i. 1. [z] Isaiah xiii. 6.

[a] קָרוֹב יוֹם יְהוָה כְּשֹׁד מִשַּׁדַּי יָבוֹא Isaiah has omitted the "and" only. Other correspondences, as the use of בָּרַךְ Is. lxv. 8. Jo. ii. 14, and that between Is. xiii. 10 and Jo. ii. 31, which is an agreement in substance not of words, have no force of proof. [b] Joel i. 15. [c] i. 4.

[d] i. 5 sqq. [e] i. 15. [f] ii. 1.

which he describes the coming judgment more fully, speaks of it, as coming [g], and, when, he has pictured it as just ready to break upon them, and God, as giving the command to the great camp assembled to fulfill His word [h], he calls them, in God's name, yet more earnestly to repentance [i], and promises, upon that repentance, plenary forgiveness and the restoration of everything which God had withdrawn from them [k]. These promises culminate in the first Coming of Christ, the outpouring of the Spirit upon all flesh, and the enlarged gift of prophecy at the same time among the sons and daughters of Judah [l]. Upon these mercies to His own people, follow the judgments upon His and their enemies, reaching on to the second Coming of our Lord.

An attempt has been made to sever the prophecy into two discourses, of which the first is to end at c. ii. 17, the second is to comprise the remainder of the book [m]. That scheme severs what is closely united, God's call to prayer and His promise that He will answer it. According to this severance of the prophecy, the first portion is to contain the exhortation on the part of God, without any promise; the second is to contain an historical relation that God answered, without saying what He answered. The notion was grounded on unbelief, that God absolutely foretold, that He would, beyond the way of nature, bring, what He would, upon repentance, as certainly remove. It is rested on a mere error in grammar [n]. The grammatical form was probably chosen, in order to express how instantaneously God would hearken to real repentance, *that the Lord is jealous for His land.* The words of prayer should not yet have escaped their lips, when God answered. As He says, [o] *And it shall be, before they shall call, I will answer; while they are yet speaking, I will hear.* Man has to make up his mind on a petition; with God, hearing and answering are one.

The judgments upon God's people, described in the two first chapters of Joel, cannot be limited to a season of drought and a visitation of locusts, whether one or more. i) The prophet includes all which he foretells, in one statement, which, both from its form and its preternatural character, has the appearance of a proverbial saying [p]. It does

stand, as a summary. For he draws the attention of all to *this* [q]; *Hear this, ye old men, and give ear, all ye inhabitants of the land. Hath this been in your days?* &c. He appeals to the aged, whether they had heard the like, and bids all transmit it to their posterity [r]. The summary is given in a very measured form, in three divisions, each consisting of four words, and the four words standing, in each, in the same order [s]. The first and third words of the four are the same in each; and the fourth of the first and second four become the second of the second and third four, respectively. Next to Hebrew, its force can best be seen in Latin;

Residuum	erucæ	comedit	locusta;
Residuumque	locustæ	comedit	bruchus;
Residuumque	bruchi	comedit	exesor.

The structure of the words resembles God's words to Elijah [t], whose measured rhythm and precise order of words may again be best, because most concisely, exhibited in Latin; Each division contains five words in the same order; and here, the first, second, and fourth words of each five remain the same, and the Proper name which is the fifth in the first five becomes the third in the second five [u].

Profugum	gladii	Hazaelis	occidet	Jehu;
Profugumque	gladii	Jehu	occidet	Elisha.

In this case, we see that the form is proverbial, because the slaying by Elisha is different in kind from the slaying by Jehu and Hazael, and is the same of which God speaks by Hosea [v], *I hewed them by the Prophets; I slew them by the words of my mouth.* But so also is it with regard to the locust. Except by miracle, what the Prophet here describes, would not happen. He foretells, not only that a scourge should come, unknown in degree and number, before or afterward, in Palestine, but that four sorts of locusts should come successively, the latter destroying what the former left. Now this is not God's ordinary way in bringing this scourge. In His ordinary Providence different sorts of locusts do not succeed one another. Nor would it be any increase of the infliction, anything to record or forewarn of. At times, by a very rare chastisement, God has brought successive flights of the same insect from the same common birthplace; and generally, where the female locusts deposit their eggs and die,

---

[g] ii. 2-10.   [h] ii. 11.   [i] ii. 12-17.
[k] ii. 18-27.   [l] ii. 28, 29.   [m] Ewald, p. 65.
[n] Forms, like וַיַּעַן וַיְקַם are only used of the past, when a past has been already expressed or implied, as, in English, we may use a present in vivid description, in which the mind, as it were, accompanies and sees the action, although past. The past having once been expressed, we might say "and he goes" &c. without ambiguity. But the form being relative, it must be understood of the same time, as that which has preceded. Here the time, which has preceded, is future. So also then is the word. The same form is used of the future,

---

[Hos.] viii. 10, Am. ix. 5, Is. ix. 5, 10, 13. Hæv. Einl. ii. 232.

[o] Isa. lxv. 24.   [p] i. 4.   [q] i. 2.   [r] i. 3.

יתר הגזם אכל האארבה
ויתר הארבה אכל הילק
ויתר הילק אכל החסיל

[t] 1 Kgs. xix. 17.

הנמלט מחרב חזאל ימית יהוא [u]
והנמלט מחרב יהוא ימית אלישע   [v] vi. 5.

unless a moist winter or man's forethought destroy the eggs, the brood which issues from them in the next spring, being as voracious as the full grown locusts, but crawling through the land, does, in that immediate neighborhood, destroy the produce of the second year, more fatally than the parent had that of the preceding. This however is, at most, the ravage of two stages of the same insect, not four successive scourges, the three last destroying what the former had spared. What the Prophet predicted, if taken literally, was altogether out of the order of nature, and yet its literal fulfillment has not the character of a miracle; for it adds nothing to the intensity of what is predicted. The form of his prediction is proverbial; and this coincides with the other indications that the Prophet did not intend to speak of mere locusts.

1) In order to bring down this summary of the Prophet to the level of an ordinary event in God's ordinary Providence, a theory has been invented, that he is not here speaking of different sorts of locusts, but of the same locust in different stages of its growth, from the time when it leaves the egg, until it attains its full development and its wings. According to the inventor of this theory [w], the first, the *gazam* (the *palmer-worm* of our version) was to be the migratory locust, which visits Palestine (it was said) chiefly in Autumn; the second, *arbeh*, (the ordinary name of the locust) was to stand for the young locust, as it first creeps out of the shell; the *yelek* (translated *cankerworm*) was to be the locust, in what was supposed to be the third stage of development; the *chasil* (translated *caterpillar*) was to be the full-grown locust. According to this form of the theory, the *gazam* was to be the same as the *chasil*, the first as the last; and two of the most special names of the locust, *gazam* and *chasil*, were, without any distinction, to be ascribed to the full-grown locust, of one and the same species. For, according to the theory, the *gazam* was to be the full-grown locust which arrived by flight and deposited its eggs; the *arbeh*, *yelek*, *chasil*, were to be three chief stages of development of the locusts which left those eggs. So that the *chasil*, although not the same individual, was to be exactly the same insect as the *gazam*, and at the same stage of existence, the full-grown locust, the gryllus migratorius with wings. But while these two, more special,

names were appropriated to the self-same species of locust, in the same, its full-grown stage (which in itself is unlikely, when they are thus distinguished from each other) one of the two names which remained to describe (as was supposed) the earlier, (so to speak) infantine or childish [x] stages of its development, *arbeh*, is the most general name of locust. This was much as if, when we wished to speak of a "colt" as such, we were to call it "horse," or were to use the word "cow" to designate a "calf." For, according to this theory, Joel, wishing to mark that he was speaking of the pupa, just emerged from the egg, called it "arbeh," the most common name of the locust tribe.

This theory then was tacitly modified [y]. In the second form of the theory, which is more likely to be introduced among us, *gazam* was to be the locust in its first stage; *arbeh* was to be the second, instead of the first; *yelek* was to be the last but one; *chasil* was, as before, to be the full-grown locust. This theory escaped one difficulty, that of making the *gazam* and *chasil* full-grown locusts of the same species. It added another. The three moultings which it assumes to be represented by the *arbeh*, *yelek*, and *gazam*, correspond neither with the actual moults of the locust, nor with those which strike the eye. Some observers have noticed four moultings of the locust, after it had left the egg [z]. Some write, as if there were yet more [a]. But of marked changes which the eye of the observer can discern, there are two only, that by which it passes from the larva state into the pupa, and that by which it passes from the pupa to the full-grown locust. The *three* names, arbitrarily adapted to the natural history of the locust, correspond neither with the *four* actual, nor with the *two* noticeable changes.

But even these terms larva and pupa, if taken in their popular sense, would give a wrong idea of the moults of the locust. The changes with which we are familiar under these names, take place in the locust, before it leaves the egg [b]. " [c] The pupæ are equally capable of eating and moving with the larvæ, which they resemble except in having rudiments of wings or of wings and elytra:" having in fact "complete wings, only folded up longitudinally and transversely, and inclosed in membranous cases." "The pupæ of the orthoptera" [to which the locust belongs] "resemble the perfect insect, both as to shape and the organs for taking their food,

---

[w] Credner on Joel i. 4. p. 102. followed by Scholz only.

[x] The expression of Van der Hœven, Handbook of Zoology i. 273, to convey the idea of growth, rather than of change.

[y] Gesenius (Thesaur. p. 1257. v. אַרְבֶּה) tacitly corrects Credner. Maurer, Ewald, Umbreit, follow Gesenius; yet Ewald thinks that the *gazam, yelek, chasil*, need not belong to the proper locust tribe *arbeh*, (which is in fact an abandonment of the theory).

[a] Thomson, The Land and the book, ii. p. 104. Rœsel Insecten Belustigungen T. ii. Heuschrecken 7. 8. pp. 69, 70. Van der Hœven. i. 4.

[a] "Après plusieurs mues." Nouveau Dict. d'hist. natur. 1817. viii. 446. The Encyclopédie Méthodique v. Criquet (Ib. p. 706) says that the number was not ascertained.

[b] Owen Invertebrata Lect. 18.pp. 424, 435, 6.

[c] See Spence and Kirby, Introd. to Entomol. iii. 240, 1. Van der Hœven, i. p. 273.

except in not having their wings and elytra fully developed."

These changes regard only its outward form, not its habits. Its voracity begins almost as soon as it has left the egg. The first change takes place "a few days [d]" after they are first in motion. "They fast, *for a short time* [d]," before each change. But the creature continues, throughout, the same living, devouring, thing [e]. From the first, "creeping and jumping in the same general direction, they begin their destructive march [d]." The change, when it is made, takes place "in seven or eight minutes" by the creature disengaging itself from its former outward skin [f]. All the changes are often completed in six weeks. In the Ukraine, six weeks after it has left the egg, it has wings and flies away [g]. In the warmer climate of Palestine, the change would be yet more rapid. "They attain their natural size," Niebuhr says of those in Mosul [h], "with astonishing rapidity." "Tis three weeks," says Le Bruyn [i], "before they can use their wings."

But 2) the Prophet is not writing on "natural history," nor noticing distinctions observable only on minute inspection. He is foretelling God's judgments. But, as all relate, who have described the ravages of locusts, there are not three, four or five, but two stages only, in which its ravages are at all distinct, the unwinged and the winged state.

3) Probably, only in a country which was the birthplace of locusts, and where consequently they would, in all the stages of their existence, be, year by year, before the eyes of the people, would those stages be marked by different names. Arabia was one such birthplace, and the Arabs, living a wild life of nature, have invented, probably beyond any other nation, words with very special physical meanings. The Arabs, who have above fifty names for different locusts, or locusts under different circumstances, as they distinguished the sexes of the locust by different names, so they did three of its ages. "[j] When it came forth out of its egg, it was called *doba;* when its wings appeared and

grew, it was called *ghaugha;* and this, when they jostled one another; and when their colors appeared, the males becoming yellow, the females black, then they were called *jerad.*" This is no scientific description; for the wings of the locust are not visible, until after the last moult. But in the language of other countries, where this plague was not domestic, these different stages of the existence of the locust are not marked by a special name. The Syrians added an epithet "the flying," "the creeping," but designated by the "creeping" the *chasil* as well as the *yelek* [k], which last the Chaldees render by (*parecha*) "the flying." In Joel where they had to designate the four kinds of locusts together, they were obliged, like our own version, in one case to substitute the name of another destructive insect; in another, they use the name of a different kind of locust, the *tsartsuro,* or *tsartsero,* the Syrian and Arabic way of pronouncing the Hebrew *tselatsal* [l]. In Greek the Βροῦχος and ʾΑττέλαβος have been thought to be two stages of the unwinged, and so, unperfected, locusts. But S. Cyril [m] and Theodoret [m] speak of the Βροῦχος as having wings; Aristotle [n] and Plutarch [o] speak of the eggs of the Αττέλαβος.

4) The Prophet is speaking of successive ravagers, each devouring what the former left. If the theory of these writers was correct, the order in which he names them, would be the order of their development. But in the order of their development, they never destroy what they left in their former stages. From the time when they begin to move, they march right onward "creeping and jumping, all in the same general direction [p]." This march never stops. They creep on, eating as they creep, in the same tract of country, not in the same spot. You could not say of creatures (were we afflicted with such,) who crawled for six weeks, devouring, over two counties of England, that in their later stage they devoured what in their former they left. We should speak of the plague "spreading" over two counties. We could not use the Prophet's description, for it would not be true. This mere march, however destructive in its course, does not correspond

---

[d] Thomson, l. c. "*No sooner were any of them hatched,* than they immediately collected themselves together, each of them forming a compact body of several hundred yards in square, which, marching afterwards directly forward, climbed over trees, walls and houses, eat up every plant in their way, *and let nothing escape them.*" Shaw, Travels p. 257.

[e] "This is a character of the whole of the hemoptera and orthoptera. The development is attended with no loss of activity or diminution of voracity." Owen, p. 423. "The whole life of the orthopterous insect from the exclusion [from the egg] to flight, may be called an active nymphhood." Ib. 436.

[f] Shaw, Ib. He is speaking of the last and chief change to the winged state.

[g] About mid-April " they hatch and leap all about,

being six weeks before they can fly," de Beauplan, Ukraine, in Churchill's Voyages i. 600.

[h] Descr. de l' Arab. p. 149.   [i] Travels, p. 179.

[j] Demiri, quoted by Bochart. iv. 1.

[k] In Joel i. 2, ii. 25, the Syriac renders the *arbeh, kamtso porecho* (the flying locust), and the *yelek, kamtso dsochelo,* (the creeping locust). In 1 Kgs viii. 37 and 2 Chron. vi. 28, it renders *chasil* by *dsochelo, creeping.* In Ps. lxxviii. 46, it renders *chasil* by *kamtso, locust,* and *arbeh,* by *dsochelo, creeper.* In Ps. cv. 34, it renders *arbeh,* by *kamtso* only [as also in 2 Chron. vi.] and *yelek* again by *dsochelo.*

[l] צלצל Deut. xxviii. 42.

[m] on Nah. iii. 16, quoted by Bochart, iii. 262.

[n] Hist. Anim. v. 29. Ib.   [o] de Isid. ib.

[p] Thomson, l. c.

with the Prophet's words. The Prophet then must mean something else. When the locust becomes winged it flies away, to ravage other countries. So far from destroying what, in its former condition, it left, its ravages in that country are at an end. Had it been ever so true, that these four names, *gazam, arbeh, yelek, chasil*, designated four stages of being of the one locust, of which stages *gazam* was the first, *chasil* the last, then to suit this theory, it should have been said, that *gazam*, the young locust, devoured what the *chasil*, by the hypothesis the full-grown locust, left, not the reverse, as it stands in the Prophet. For the young, when hatched, do destroy in the same place which their parents visited, when they deposited their eggs; but the grown locust does not devastate the country which he wasted before he had wings. So then, in truth, had the Prophet meant this, he would have spoken of two creatures, not of four; and of those two he would have spoken in a different order from that of this hypothesis.

5) Palestine not being an ordinary breeding place of the locusts, the locust arrives there by flight. Accordingly, on this ground also, the first mentioned would be the winged, not the crawling, locust. 6) The use of these names of the locust, elsewhere in Holy Scripture, contradicts the theory, that they designate different stages of growth, of the same creature. a) The *arbeh* is itself one of the four kinds of locust, allowed to be eaten, having subordinate species. *q The locust* (arbeh) *after his kind, and the bald locust* (sol'am *the devourer*) *after his kind, and the beetle* (chargol, lit. *the springer*) *after his kind, and the grasshopper* (chagab, perhaps, *the overshadower*) *after his kind*. It is to the last degree unlikely, that the name *arbeh*, which is the generic name of the most common sort of the *winged* locust, should be given to one imperfect, unwinged, stage of one species of locust.

b) The creeping, unwinged, insect, which has just come forth from the ground, would more probably be called by yet another name for "locust," *gob, gobai*, "the creeper," than by that of *gazam*. But though such is probably the etymology of *gob*, probably it too is winged [r].

c) Some of these creatures here mentioned by Joel are named together in Holy Scripture as distinct and winged. The *arbeh* and *chasil*, are mentioned together [s]; as are also the *arbeh* and the *yelek* [t]. The *arbeh*, the *yelek*, and the *chasil*, are all together mentioned in regard to the plague of Egypt [u], and all consequently, as winged, since they were brought by the wind. The prophet Nahum also speaks of the *yelek*, a *spoiling and fleeing away* [v]. According to the theory, the *yelek*, as well as the *arbeh*, ought to be unwinged.

Nor, again, can it be said, that the names are merely poetic names of the locust. It is true that *arbeh*, the common name of the locust, is taken from its number; the rest, *gazam, yelek, chasil*, are descriptive of the voracity of that tribe. But both the *arbeh* and the *chasil* occur together in the historical and so in prose books. We know of ninety sorts of locusts [w], and they are distinguished from one another by some epithet. It would plainly be gratuitous to assume that the Hebrew names, although epithets, describe only the genus in its largest sense, and are not names of species. If moreover these names were used of the same identical race, not of different species in it, the saying would the more have the character of a proverb. We could not say, for instance, "what the horse left, the steed devoured," except in some proverbial meaning.

This furnishes a certain probability that the Prophet means something more under the locust, than the creature itself, although this in itself too is a great scourge of God.

ii. In the course of the description itself, the Prophet gives hints, that he means, under the locust, a judgment far greater, an enemy far mightier, than the locust. These hints have been put together most fully, and supported in detail by Hengstenberg [x], so that here they are but re-arranged.

1) Joel calls the scourge, whom he describes, *the Northern* or Northman. But whereas the Assyrian invaders of Palestine did pour into it from the North, the locust, almost always, by a sort of law of their being, make their inroads there from their birth-place in the south [y].

2) The Prophet directs the priests to pray, *O Lord give not Thine heritage to reproach, that the heathen should rule over them* [z]. But there is plainly no connection between the desolation caused by locusts, and the people being given over to a heathen conqueror.

3) The Prophet speaks of, or alludes to, the agent, as one responsible. It is not likely that, of an irrational scourge of God, the Prophet would have assigned as a ground of its destruction, *he hath magnified to do* [a]; words used of human pride which exceeds the measure appointed to it by God. On the other hand, when God says, *a nation is come up upon My land* [b] *then will the Lord be jealous for His land* [c], the words belong rather to a heathen invader of God's land, who

---

q Lev. xi. 22.   r Nah. iii. 17.
s 1 Kings viii. 37, 2 Chr. vi. 28, Ps. lxxviii. 46.
t Nah. iii. 16, 17, Ps. cv. 34.   u Ps. l. c.   v iii. 16.
w Encyclopédie Méthodique Hist. Nat. Insectes, T.

vi. v. Criquet pp. 209–33.   x Christol. iii. 352–58. ed. 2.
y See on ii. 20, p. 123.   z ii 17.
a See on ii. 20, p. 124.   b i. 6.
c ii. 18.

disputed with His people the possession of the land which He had given them, than to an insect, which was simply carried, without volition of its own, by the wind. With this, falls in the use of the title *people, goi* [d], used often of heathen, not (as is *'am* [e]) of irrational creatures.

4) After the summary which mentions simply different kinds of locusts, the prophet speaks of *fire, flame, drought* [f], which shew that he means something beyond that plague.

5) The imagery, even where it has some correspondence with what is known of locusts, goes beyond any mere plague of locusts. a) People are terrified at their approach; but Joel says not *people*, but *peoples* [g], nations. It was a scourge then, like those great conquering Empires, whom God made *the hammer of the whole earth* [h]. b) The locusts darken the air as they come; but the darkening of the sun and moon, the withdrawing of the shining of the stars [i] (which together are incompatible) are far beyond this, and are symbols elsewhere of the trembling of all things before the revelation of the wrath of God. [k] c) Locusts enter towns and are troublesome to their inhabitants [l]; but the fields are the scenes of their desolation, in towns they are destroyed [m]. These in Joel are represented as taking *the city*, Jerusalem [l], symbols of countless hosts, but as mere locusts, harmless.

6) The effects of the scourge are such as do not result from mere locusts. a) The quantity used for *the meat-offering and drink-offering* [n] was so small, that even a famine could not occasion their disuse. They were continued even in the last dreadful siege of Jerusalem. Not materials for sacrifice, but sacrificers were wanting [o]. b) God says, *I will restore the years which the locust hath eaten* [p]. But the locust, being a passing scourge, did not destroy the fruits of several *years*, only of that one year. c) The *beasts of the field* are bidden to rejoice, *because the tree beareth her fruit* [q]. This must be metaphor, for the trees are not food for cattle. d) The scourge is spoken of as greater than any which they or their fathers knew of, and as one to be ever remembered [r]; but Israel had many worse scourges than any plague of locusts, however severe. God had taught them by David, It is better to fall into the hands of God, than into the hands of men.

7) The destruction of this scourge of God is described in a way, taken doubtless in its details from the destruction of locusts, yet, as a whole, physically impossible in a literal sense [s].

8) The Day of the Lord, of which he speaks,

is identical with the scourge which he describes, but is far beyond any plague of locusts. It includes the captivity of Judah [t], the division of their land [u], its possession by strangers, since it is promised that these are *no more to pass through her* [v]. It is a day of utter destruction, such as the Almighty alone can inflict. *It shall come like a mighty destruction from the Almighty* [w].

Attempts have been made to meet some of these arguments; but these attempts for the most part only illustrate the strength of the arguments, which they try to remove.

I. 1) *Northern* has been taken in its natural sense, and it has been asserted, contrary to the fact, that locusts did come from the North into Palestine [x]; or it has been said [y], that the locusts were first driven from their birthplace in Arabia Deserta through Palestine *to* the North, and then brought back again into Palestine *from* the North; or that *Northern* meant that part of the whole body of locusts which occupied the Northern parts of Palestine [z], Judea lying to the extreme south.

But an incidental flight of locusts, which should have entered Palestine from the North, (which they are not recorded to have done) would not have been called "*the* Northern." The object of such a name would be to describe the locale of those spoken of, not a mere accident or anomaly. Still less, if this ever happened, (of which there is no proof) would a swarm of locusts be so called, which had first come from the South. The regularity, with which the winds blow in Palestine, makes such a bringing back of the locusts altogether improbable. The South wind blows chiefly in March; the East wind in Summer, the North wind mostly about the Autumnal equinox. But neither would a body so blown to and fro, be the fearful scourge predicted by the Prophet, nor would it have been called *the Northern*. The i of the word *tsephoni*, like our *ern* in *Northern*, designates that which is spoken of, as coming incidentally from the North, but as having an habitual relation to the North. A flight of locusts driven back, contrary to continual experience, from the North, would not have been designated as *the Northern*, any more than a Lowlander who passes some time in the Highlands would be called a Highlander, or a Highlander, passing into the South, would be called a "Southron." With regard to the third explanation, Joel was especially a prophet of Judah. The supposition that, in predicting the destruction of the locusts, he spoke of the Northern not of the Southern portion of them,

[d] i. 6. [e] עַם, [f] i. 19, 20. [g] ii. 6.
[h] Jer. l. 23. [i] ii. 10. [k] Is. xiii. 10.
[l] See on ii. 9, p. 117. [n] i. 9.
[m] Niebuhr, Descr. de l' Arabie, p. 149.
[o] Hengst. from Jos. B. J. 6, 2, 1. [p] ii. 25.

[q] ii. 22. [r] i. 2, 3, ii. 2. [s] See on ii. 20.
[t] iii. 1. [u] iii. 2. [v] iii. 17. [w] i. 15.
[x] Aben Ezra, Kimchi, followed by Lightfoot, Chron. V. T. i. 94. Cast. Scholz. [y] Credner.
[z] Bochart (Hieroz. P. ii. L. iv. c. 5.), Lively.

implies that he promised on the part of God, as the reward of the humiliation of Judah, that God would remove this scourge from the separated kingdom of the ten tribes, without any promise as to that part which immediately concerned themselves. Manifestly also, *the Northern* does not, by itself, express the Northern part of a whole.

It is almost incredible that some have understood by *the Northern*, those driven toward the North, and so those actually in the South [a]; and *I will remove far from you the Northern*, "I will remove far from *you* who are in the South, the locusts who have come to you from the South, whom I will drive to the North."

2) Instances have been brought *from other lands*, to which locusts have come from the North. This answer wholly misstates the point at issue. The question is not as to the direction which locusts take, *in other countries*, whither God sends them, but as to the quarter from which they enter Judea. The direction which they take, varies in different countries, but is on one and the same principle. It is said by one observer, that they have power to fly against the wind [b]. Yet this probably is said only of light airs, when they are circling round in preparation for their flight. For the most part, they are carried by the prevailing wind, sometimes, if God so wills, to their own destruction, but, mostly, to other counties as a scourge. "When they can fly, they go," relates Beauplan [c] of those bred in the Ukraine, "wherever the wind carries them. If the North-east wind prevails, when they first take flight, it carries them all into the Black Sea; but if the wind blows from any other quarter, they go into some other country, to do mischief." Lichtenstein writes [d], "They never deviate from the straight line, so long as the same wind blows." Niebuhr says, "[e] I saw in Cairo a yet more terrible cloud of locusts, which came by a South-west wind and so from the desert of Libya." "[f] In the night of Nov. 10, 1762, a great cloud passed over Jidda with a West wind, consequently over the Arabian gulf which is very broad here." Of two flights in India which Forbes witnessed, he relates [g], "Each of these flights were brought by an East wind; they took a Westerly direction, and, without settling in the country, probably perished in the gulf of Cambay." Dr. Thomson who had spent 25 years in the Holy Land, says in illustration of

David's words, [h] *I am tossed up and down like the locust*, "[i] This refers to the flying locust. I have had frequent opportunities to notice, how these squadrons are tossed up and down, and whirled round and round by the evervarying currents of the mountain winds." Morier says, "[k] The South-east wind constantly brought with it innumerable flights of locusts," but also "[l] a fresh wind from the South-west which had brought them, so completely drove them forward that not a vestige of them was to be seen two hours afterward." These were different kinds of locusts, the first "at Bushire," having "legs and body of a light yellow and wings spotted brown [1]; " the second at Shiraz (which "the Persians said came from the Germesir,") being "larger and red."

The breeding country for the locust in South-western Asia, is the great desert of Arabia reaching to the Persian gulf. From this, at God's command, *the East wind brought the locust* [m] to Egypt. They are often carried by a West or South-west wind into Persia. "I have often in spring," relates Joseph de S. Angelo [n], "seen the sun darkened by very thick clouds (so to say) of locusts, which cross the sea from the deserts of Arabia far into Persia." In Western Arabia, Burckhard [o] writes, "the locusts are known to come invariably from the East," i. e. from the same deserts. The South wind carries them to the different countries Northward. This is so general, that Hasselquist wrote; "[p] The locusts appear to be directed—in a direct meridian line by keeping nearly from South to North, turning very little either to the East or West. They come from the deserts of Arabia, take their course on through Palestine, Syria, Carmania, Natolia, go sometimes through Bithynia. They never turn from their course, for example, to the West, wherefore Egypt is not visited by them, though so near their usual tract. Neither do they turn to the East, for I never heard that Mesopotamia or the confines of the Euphrates are ravaged by them." And Volney reports, as the common observation of the natives [q]; "The inhabitants, of Syria remarked that the locusts only came after overmild winters, and that they always came from the deserts of Arabia." Whence S. Jerome, himself an inhabitant of Palestine, regarded this mention of the North as an indication that the prophet intended us to understand under the name of locusts, the

---

[a] Jun. Trem. Justi.

[b] "They fly high and quick, even against the wind, or in circles; but often so low, that one, riding through them, can see nothing before him, and is often hit in the face." Schlatter, Bruchstucke aus einigen Reisen nach d. sudl. Russland, p. 320.

[c] Description of Ukraine in Churchill's voyages, i. 600.

[d] Travels in S. Africa, c. xlvi. p. 251.

[e] Descr. de l' Arabie, p. 148.

[f] Ib. p. 149. Of the other flights, which Niebuhr mentions, he does not specify whether they came with or without wind. Ib.

[g] ii. 273, 4.   [h] Ps. cix. 23.

[i] The Land and the Book, T. ii. 106.

[k] 2d Journey, p. 43.   [l] Ib. 98.   [m] Ex. x. 13.

[n] Gazoph. Pers. v. Locusta, quoted by Ludolf Comm. in Hist. Æth. pp. 175, 6.

[o] Notes, ii. 90.   [p] Travels, pp. 446, 7.

[q] Voyages en Syrie, i. 277, 8.

great Conquerors who did invade Palestine from the North. "[r] According to the letter, the South wind, rather than the North, hath been wont to bring the flocks of locusts, i. e. they come not from the cold but from the heat. But since he was speaking of the Assyrians, under the image of locusts, therefore he inserted the mention of the North, that we may understand, not the actual locust, which hath been wont to come from the South, but under the locust, the Assyrians and Chaldees."

On the same ground, that the locusts came to Palestine from the South, they were brought from Tartary, (the breeding-place of the locust thence called the Tartarian locust) by an East or South-east wind to the Ukraine. "[s] They generally come [to the Ukraine] from toward Tartary, which happens in a dry spring; for Tartary and the countries East of it, as Circassia, Bazza and Mingrelia, are seldom free from them. The vermin being driven by an East or South-east wind come into the Ukraine." To the coasts of Barbary or to Italy for the same reason they come from the South; to Upper Egypt from Arabia; and to Nubia from the North[t], viz. from Upper Egypt. "In the summer of 1778," Chenier says of Mauritania[u], there "were seen, coming from the South, clouds of locusts which darkened the sun. Strabo states, that, "[v] the strong S. W. or W. winds of the vernal equinox drive them together into the country of Acridophagi." To the Cape of Good Hope they come from the North, whence alone they could come [w]; to Senegal they come with the wind from the East[x]. "They infest Italy," Pliny says[y], "chiefly from Africa;" whence of course, they come to Spain also[z]. Shaw writes of those in Barbary[a]; "Their first appearance was toward the latter end of March, the wind having been for some time Southerly." "As the direction of the marches and flight of them both," [i. e. both of the young brood and their parents, their "marches" before they had wings, and their "flight" afterward] "was always to the Northward, it is probable that they perished in the sea."

All this, however, illustrates the one rule of their flight, that they come with the wind from their birthplace to other lands. On the same ground that they come to Italy or Barbary from the South, to the Ukraine or Arabia Felix from the East, to Persia from the South or South-west, to Nubia or to the Cape, or Constantinople sometimes, from the North,

they came to Judea from the South. The word "Northern" describes the habitual character of the army here spoken of. Such was the character of the Assyrian or Chaldean conquerors, who are described oftentimes, in Holy Scripture, as coming "out of the North," and such was not the character of the locusts, who, if described by the quarter from which they habitually came, must have been called "the Southern."

3) The third mode of removing the evidence of the word "Northern," has been to explain its meaning. But in no living, nor indeed in any well-known language, would any one have recourse to certain or uncertain etymology, in order to displace the received meaning of a word. Our "North" originally meant "narrowed, contracted;" the Latin "Septentrionalis" is so called from the constellation of the Great Bear; yet no one in his right mind, if he understood not how anything was, by an English author, called "Northern," would have recourse to the original meaning of the word and say "Northern" might signify "hemmed in," or that "septentrionalis" or septentrionel meant "belonging to the seven plowers," or whatever other etymology might be given to septentrio. No more should they, because they did not or would not understand the use of the word tsephoni, have had recourse to etymologies. Tsaphon[b] as uniformly signifies the North, as our word "North" itself. Tsephoni signifies Northern, the i having the same office as our ending ern in Northern. The word Tsaphan originally signified hid; then, laid up; and, it may be, that the North was called tsaphon, as the hidden, "shrouded in darkness." But to infer from that etymology, that tsephoni here may signify the hider[c], "that which obscures the rays of the sun," is, apart from its grammatical incorrectness, much the same argument as if we were to say that Northern meant, that which "narrows, contracts, hems in," or "is fast bound."

Equally capricious and arbitrary is the coining of a new Hebrew word to substitute for the word tsephoni; as one[d], first reading it tsipponi, supposes it to mean captain, or main army, because in Arabic or Aramaic, tsaphpha means, "set things in a row," "set an army in array," of which root there is no trace in Hebrew. Stranger yet is it to identify the well-known Hebrew word Tsaphon with the Greek τύφων, and tsephoni with τυφωνικός; and because Typhon was, in Egyptian mythology, a principle of evil, to infer that tsephoni

[r] in Joel ii. 20.　　　[s] Beauplan, Ib. i. 599.
[t] Burckhardt, Notes, ii. 89, 90.
[u] Sur les Maures, iii. 495.　　　[v] xvi. 4. 12. Kr.
[w] Sparrmann, p. 366.　[x] Adansson, Voyage, p. 88.
[y] Hist. Nat. xi. 35. Liv. xlii. 10.
[z] Asso y del Rio, von der Heuschrecken, ed. Tychsen.

[a] Nat. Hist. of Algiers and Tunis. Travels, pp. 256, 8.　　　[b] אִצְפֹּן

[c] Justi, Maurer, adopted by Gesenius sub. v. Maurer, in his commentary of 1838, suggested two yet more improbable etymologies.
[d] Ewald. "Van Cölln and Meier would also alter the text." Hengst.

meant a *destroyer*[e]. Another[f], who would give to *tsephoni* the meaning of "Barbarian," admits in fact the prophetic character of the title; since the Jews had as yet, in the time of Joel, no external foe on their North border; no one, except Israel, as yet invaded them from the North. Not until the Assyrian swept over them, was *the Northern* any special enemy of Judah. Until the time of Ahaz, Syria was the enemy, not of Judah, but of Israel.

This varied straining to get rid of the plain meaning of the word *the Northern*, illustrates the more the importance of the term as one of the keys of the prophecy.

One and the same wind could not drive the same body of locusts, to perish in three different, and two of them opposite, directions. Yet it is clear that the Prophet speaks of them as one and the same. The locusts are spoken of as one great army, (as God had before called them[g],) with front and rear. The resource has been to say that the van and rear were two different bodies of locusts, destroyed at different times, or to say that it is only Hebrew parallelism. In Hebrew parallelism, each portion of the verse adds something to the other. It does not unite things incompatible. Nor is it here the question of two but of three directions, whither this enemy was to be swept away and perish.

But Joel speaks of them first as one whole. *I will drive him into a land barren and desolate*, the wastes South of Judah, and then of the front and rear, as driven into the two seas, which bound Judah on the East and West. The two Hebrew words, *panaiv vesopho*[h], *his front and his rear*, can no more mean two bodies, having no relation to one another and to the whole, than our English words could, when used of an army.

II. Equally unsuccessful are the attempts to get rid of the proofs, that the invader here described is a moral agent. In regard to the words assigned as the ground of his destruction, *for he hath magnified to do*, 1) it has been denied, contrary to the Hebrew idiom and the context, that they do relate to moral agency, whereas, in regard to creatures, the idiom is used of nothing else, nor in any other sense could this be the ground why God destroyed them. Yet, that this their pride was the cause of their destruction, is marked by the word *for*. 2 (Strange to say) one has been found who thought that the Prophet spoke of the locusts as moral agents. 3)

Others have applied the words to God, again contrary to the context. For God speaks in this same verse of Himself in the first person, of the enemy whom He sentences to destruction, in the third. "And *I* will remove far off from you the Northern army, and *I* will drive *him* into a land barren and desolate, *his* face towards the Eastern sea, and *his* rear towards the Western sea, and *his* stink shall come up, and *his* ill savor shall come up, because *he* hath magnified to do." Joel does not use rapid transitions. And rapid transitions, when used, are never without meaning. A sacred writer who has been speaking of God, does often, in holy fervor, turn suddenly to address God; or, having upbraided a sinful people, he turns away from them, and speaks, not *to* them any more but *of* them. But it is unexampled in Holy Scripture, that in words in the mouth of God, God should speak of Himself first in the first person, then in the third.

III. Instead of "*that the heathen should rule over them*," they render, "*That the heathen should jest at them*," But besides this place, the phrase occurs fifty times in the Hebrew Bible, and in every case means indisputably "rule over[i]." It is plainly contrary to all rules of language, to take an idiom in the fifty-first case, in a sense wholly different from that which it has in the other fifty. The noun also signifying "proverb," is derived from a root entirely distinct from the verb to *rule;* the verb which Ezekiel perhaps formed (as verbs are formed in Hebrew) from the noun, is never used except in connection, direct or implied, with that noun[k]. The idiom "became a proverb," "make a proverb of," is always expressed, not by the verb, but by the noun with some other verb, as "became, give, set, place[l]." It is even said[m], *I will make him desolate to a proverb*, or *shall take up a parable against him*[n], but in no one of these idioms is the verb used.

IV. The word "jealousy" is used twenty times in the Old Testament, of that attribute in God, whereby He does not endure the love of His creatures to be transferred from Him, or divided with Him. Besides this place, it is used by the Prophets fifteen times, of God's love for His people, as shewn against the Heathen who oppressed them. In all the thirty-five cases it is used of an attribute of Almighty God toward His rational creatures. And it is a violation of the uniform usage of Holy Scripture in a matter which relates to the attributes of Almighty

---

[e] Hitzig on Joel ii. 20.
[f] Umbreit on Joel, Ib.
[g] ii. 11.   פניו וספוֹ[h].   מָשַׁל בּ׳ [i].
[k] The phrase is מָשָׁל מָשַׁל in 6 of the places in Ezekiel. In the 7th, Ezek. xvi. 44, a proverb is spoken of. It is used by no other of the sacred writers. In this sense it corresponds with the Arab. *mathala*, Syr. *methal*. Mashal, *rule*, occurs in

Phœnician only, and, (as Ges. pointed out) in the Greek βασιλεύς.
[l] הָיָה Deut. xxviii. 1 Kgs. ix. 7. Ps. lxix. 12. נָתַן 2 Chr. vii. 20. Jer. xxiv. 9. הָצִין Job xvii. 6. שִׂים Ps. xliv. 15.
[m] הֲשִׁמֹּתִי Ezek. xiv. 8, combining the two, "I will make him a desolation and a proverb."
[n] יִשָּׂא מָשָׁל Mich. ii. 4. Hab. ii. 6.

God and His relation to the creatures which He has made, to extend it to His irrational creation. It is to force on Holy Scripture an unauthorized statement as to Almighty God.

Of these hints that the prophecy extends beyond any mere locusts, five are given in the space of four verses at the close of that part of the prophecy, and seem to be condensed there, as a key to the whole. Joel began his prophecy by a sort of sacred enigma or proverb, which waited its explanation. At the close of the description of God's judgments on His people, which he so opened, he concentrates traits which should indicate its fullest meaning. He does not exclude suffering by locusts, fire, drought, famine, or any other of God's natural visitations. But he indicates that the scourge, which he was chiefly foretelling, was man. Three of these hints combine to shew that Joel was speaking of Heathen scourges of God's people and Church. The mention *of the Northern* fixes the prophecy to enemies, of whom Joel had no human knowledge, but by whom Judah was carried away captive, and who themselves were soon afterward destroyed, while Judah was restored. Not until after Joel and all his generation were fallen asleep, did a king of Assyria come up against Israel, nor was the North a quarter whence men would then apprehend danger. Pul came up against Menahem, king of Israel, at the close of the reign of Uzziah. The reign of Jotham was victorious. Not until invited by his son Ahaz, did Tiglath-pileser meddle with the affairs of Judah. In yet another reign, that of Hezekiah, was the first invasion of Judah. Sennacherib, first the scourge of God, in his second invasion blasphemed God, and his army perished in one night, smitten by the Angel of God.

It seems then probable, that what Joel describes was presented to him in the form of a vision, the title which he gives to his prophecy. There, as far as we can imagine what was exhibited by God to His prophets, he saw before him the land wasted and desolate; pastures and trees burned up by fire; the channels of the rivers dried up, the barns broken down as useless, and withal, the locusts, such as he describes them in the second chapter, advancing, overspreading the land, desolating all as they advanced, marching in the wonderful order in which the locust presses on, indomitable, unbroken, unhindered; assaulting the city Jerusalem, mounting the walls, possessing themselves of it, entering its houses, as victorious. But withal he knew, by that same inspiration which spread this scene before his eyes, that not mere locusts were intended, and was inspired to intermingle in his description expressions which forewarned his people of invaders yet more formidable.

It may be added, that S. John, in the Revelation, not only uses the symbol of locusts as a type of enemies of God's Church and people, whether actual persecutors or spiritual foes or both, but, in three successive verses of his description, he takes from Joel three traits of the picture. *The shapes of the locusts were like unto horses prepared unto battle; their teeth were as the teeth of lions; the sound of their wings was as the sound of chariots of many horses running to battle* [o]. It seems probable, that as S. John takes up anew the prophecies of the Old Testament, and embodies in his prophecy their language, pointing on to a fulfillment of it in the Christian Church, he does, by adopting the symbol of the locusts, in part in Joel's own words, express that he himself understood the Prophet to speak of enemies, beyond the mere irrational scourge.

The chief characteristic of the Prophet's style is perhaps its simple vividness. Every thing is set before our eyes, as though we ourselves saw it. This is alike the character of the description of the desolation in the first chapter; the advance of the locusts in the second; or that more awful gathering in the valley of Jehoshaphat, described in the third. The Prophet adds detail to detail; each, clear, brief, distinct, a picture in itself, yet adding to the effect of the whole. We can, without an effort, bring the whole of each picture before our eyes. Sometimes he uses the very briefest form of words, two words, in his own language, sufficing for each feature in his picture. One verse consists almost of five such pairs of words [p]. Then, again, the discourse flows on in a soft and gentle cadence, like one of those longer sweeps of an Æolian harp. This blending of energy and softness is perhaps one secret, why the diction also of this Prophet has been at all times so winning and so touching. Deep and full, he pours out the tide of his words, with an unbroken smoothness, carries all along with him, yea, like those rivers of the new world, bears back the bitter, restless billows which oppose him, a pure strong stream amid the endless heavings and tossings of the world.

Poetic as Joel's language is, he does not much use distinct imagery. For his whole picture is one image. They are God's chastenings through inanimate nature, picturing the worse chastenings through man. So much had he, probably, in prophetic vision, the symbol spread before his eyes, that he likens it in one place to that which it represents, the men of war of the invading army. But

o Rev. ix. 7–9. Joel ii. 4. i. 6. ii. 5.
p i. 10. In one of them *For*, is added. Other pairs of words in Hebrew occur i. 11, 12, 14, 17. ii. 9, 15, 16.

this too adds to the formidableness of the picture.

Full of sorrow himself, he summons all with him to repentance, priests and people, old and young, bride and bridegroom. Yet his very call, *let the bridegroom go forth out of his chamber, and the bride out of her closet*, shews how tenderly he felt for those, whom he called from the solaces of mutual affection to fasting and weeping and girding with sackcloth. Yet more tender is the summons to all Israel[q], *Lament like a virgin girded with sackcloth for the husband of her youth.* The tenderness of his soul is evinced by his lingering over the desolation which he foresees. It is like one, counting over, one by one, the losses he endures in the privations of others. Nature to him "seemed to mourn ;" he had a feeling of sympathy with the brute cattle which in his ears mourn so grievously ; and, if none else would mourn for their own sins, he himself would mourn to Him Who is full of compassion and mercy. He announces to the poor cattle the removal of the woe, *Fear not, fear ye not*[r]. Few passages in Scripture itself are more touching, than when, having represented God as marshalling His creatures for the destruction of His people, and just ready to give the word, having expressed the great terribleness of the Day of the Lord, and asked *who can abide it?* he suddenly turns, *And now too*[s], and calls to repentance.

Amid a wonderful beauty of language, he employs words not found elsewhere in Holy Scripture. In one verse, he has three such words[t]. The degree to which the prophecies of Joel reappear in the later prophets has been exaggerated. The subjects of the prophecy recur ; not, for the most part, the form in which they were delivered. The subjects could not but recur. For the truths, when once revealed, became a part of the hopes and fears of the Jewish Church ; and the Prophets, as preachers and teachers of their people, could not but repeat them. But it was no mere repetition. Even those truths which, in one of their bearings, or, again, in outline were fully declared, admitted of subordinate enlargement, or of the revelation of other accessory truths, which filled up or determined or limited that first outline. And as far as anything was added or determined by any later prophet, such additions constituted a fresh revelation by him. It is so in the case of the wonderful image, in which, taking occasion of the fact of nature, that there was a fountain under the temple[u], which carried off the blood of the sacrifices, and, carrying it off, was intermingled with that blood, the image of the All-atoning Blood,

Joel speaks of *a fountain flowing forth from the House of the Lord and watering the valley of Shittim*, whither by nature its waters could not flow. He first describes the holiness to be bestowed upon Mount Zion ; then, how from the Temple, the centre of worship and of revelation, the place of the shadow of the Atonement, the stream should gush forth, which, pouring on beyond the bounds of the land of Judah, should carry fertility to a barren and thirsty land. (For in such lands the shittah grows.) To this picture Zechariah[v] adds the permanence of the life-giving stream and its perennial flow, *in summer and in winter shall it be.* Ezekiel, in his full and wonderful expansion of the image[w], adds the ideas of the gradual increase of those waters of life, their exceeding depth, the healing of all which could be healed, the abiding desolation where those waters did not reach ; and trees, as in the garden of Eden, yielding food and health. He in a manner anticipates our Lord's prophecy, *ye shall be fishers of men.* S. John takes up the image[x], yet as an emblem of such fullness of bliss and glory, that, amid some things, which can scarcely be understood except of this life, it seems rather to belong to life eternal.

Indeed, as to the great imagery of Joel, it is much more adopted and enforced in the New Testament than in the Old. The image of the locust is taken up in the Revelation ; that of the "pouring out of the Spirit" (for this too is an image, how largely God would bestow Himself in the times of the Gospel) is adopted in the Old Testament by Ezekiel[y], yet as to the Jews only ; in the New by St. Peter and St. Paul[z]. Of those condensed images, under which Joel speaks of the wickedness of the whole earth ripened for destruction, the harvest and the wine-treading, that of the harvest is employed by Jeremiah[a] as to Babylon, that of the wine-press is enlarged by Isaiah[b]. The harvest is so employed by our Lord[c] as to explain the imagery of Joel ; and in that great embodiment of Old Testament prophecy, the Revelation[d], St. John expands the image of the wine-press in the same largeness of meaning as it is used by Joel.

The largeness of all these declarations remains peculiar to Joel. To this unknown Prophet, whom in his writings we cannot but love, but of whose history, condition, rank, parentage, birth-place, nothing is known, nothing beyond his name, save the name of an unknown father, of whom moreover God has allowed nothing to remain save these few chapters,—to him God reserved the prerogative, first to declare the out-pouring

q i. 8.   r ii. 21, 22.   s ii. 12.
t i. 16.   u See on iii. 18.
v xiv. 8.   w xlvii. 1–12.
x Rev. xxii. 1–5.   y xxxix. 29.
a "On the Gentiles also is *poured out* (ἐκκέχυται)

the gift of the Holy Ghost," Acts x. 45 ; "the love of God is poured out (ἐκκέχυται) in our hearts by the Holy Ghost Who hath been given to us," Rom. v. 5.
a Ii. 33.   b lxiii. 1–6.
c S. Matt. xiii. 39.   d xiv. 18–20.

of the Holy Ghost upon all flesh, the perpetual abiding of the Church, the final struggle of good and evil, the last rebellion against God, and the Day of Judgment. *The Day of the Lord, the great and terrible day,* the belief in which now forms part of the faith of all Jews and Christians, was a title first revealed to this unknown Prophet.

The primæval prophecy on Adam's expulsion from Paradise, had been renewed to Abraham, Jacob, Moses, David, Solomon. In Abraham's seed were all nations of the earth to be blessed[e]; the obedience[f] of the nations was to be rendered to Shiloh the Peacemaker[g]; the nations were to rejoice with the people of God[h]; God's anointed king was from Mount Zion to have the heathen for his inheritance[i]; David's Son and David's Lord was to be a king and priest forever after the order of Melchizedek[k]; the peoples were to be willing in the Day of His power. All nations were to serve him[l]. This had been prophesied before. It was part of the body of belief in the time of Joel. But to Joel it was first foreshewn that the Gentiles too should be filled with the Spirit of God. To him was first declared that great paradox, or mystery, of faith, which, after his time, prophet after prophet insisted upon, that while deliverance should be in Mount Zion, while sons and daughters, young and old, should prophesy in Zion, and the stream of God's grace should issue to the barren world from the Temple of the Lord, those in her who

[e] Gen. xxii. 18.
[f] Such must be the meaning of יקחה in the other place in which it occurs, Prov. xxx. 17, as it is of the corresponding Arabic root. Onkelos so understood it.

should be delivered should be a remnant only[m].

Marvelous faith, alike in those who uttered it and those who received it; marvelous, disinterested faith! The true worship of God was, by the revolt of the ten tribes, limited to the two tribes, the territory of the largest of which was but some 50 miles long, and not 30 miles broad; Benjamin added but 12 miles to the length of the whole. It was but 12 miles from Jerusalem on its Southern Border to Bethel on its Northern. They had made no impression beyond their own boundaries. Edom, their "brother", was their bitterest enemy, wise in the wisdom of the world[n], but worshiping false gods[o]. Nay they themselves still borrowed the idolatries of their neighbors[p]. Beset as Judah was by constant wars without, deserted by Israel, the immediate band of worshipers of the one God within its narrow borders thinned by those who fell away from Him, Joel foretold, not as uncertainly, not as anticipation, or hope, or longing, but absolutely and distinctly, that God would *pour out* His *Spirit upon all flesh;* and that the healing stream should issue forth from Jerusalem. Eight centuries rolled on, and it was not accomplished. *He* died, of Whom it was said, *we trusted that it had been He Who should have redeemed Israel*[q]; and it was fulfilled. Had it failed, justly would the Hebrew Prophets have been called fanatics. The words were too distinct to be explained away. It could not fail; for God had said it.

[g] Gen. xlix. 10.
[i] Ps. ii.
[l] Ps. lxxii. 11.
[n] Obad. 8. Jer. xlix. 7.
[p] Ib.

[h] Deut. xxxii. 43.
[k] Ps. cx.
[m] ii. 32.
[o] Chr. xxv. 14, 20.
[q] S. Luke xxiv. 21.

JOEL.

CHAPTER I.

1 *Joel, declaring sundry judg-*
ments of God, exhorteth to ob-
serve them, 8 and to mourn. 14
He prescribeth a fast for com-
plaint.

THE word of the LORD
that came to Joel the
son of Pethuel.

2 Hear this, ye old men,
and give ear, all ye inhab-

itants of the land. ᵃ Hath
this been in your days, or
even in the days of your
fathers?

3 ᵇ Tell ye your children
of it, and *let* your children
tell their children, and
their children another generation.

4 ᶜ † That which the
palmerworm hath left hath

ᵃch. 2, 2.

ᵇPs. 78. 4.

ᶜDeut. 28. 38.
ch. 2. 25.
†Heb. *The*
residue of the
palmerworm.

CHAP. I. Ver. I. *The word of the Lord that*
came to Joel. Joel, like Hosea, mentions the
name of his father only, and then is silent
about his extraction, his tribe, his family.
He leaves even the time when he lived, to be
guessed at. He would be known only, as the
instrument of God. *The word of the Lord came*
to him [1], and he willed simply to be the voice
which uttered it. He was " content to live
under the eyes of God, and, as to men, to be
known only in what concerned their salvation." But *this* he declares absolutely, that
the Word of God came to him; in order that
we may give faith to his prophecy, being well
assured that what he predicted, would come
to pass. So the Saviour Himself says, " *My*
words shall not pass away [2]. For truth admits of
nothing false, and what God saith, will certainly be. For *He confirmeth the word of His*
servant, and performeth the counsel of His mes-
sengers [3]. The Prophet claimeth belief then,
as speaking not out of his own heart, but out
of the mouth of the Lord speaking in the
Spirit." *Joel* signifies, *The Lord is God.* It
owns that God Who had revealed Himself, is
alone the God. The Prophet's name itself,
embodied the truth, which, after the miraculous answer to Elijah's prayer, all the people
confessed, *The Lord He is the God, The Lord*
He is the God. *Pethuel* signifies, " persuaded
of God." The addition of his father's name
distinguished the Prophet from others of that
name, as the son of Samuel, of king Uzziah,
and others.

2. *Hear this, ye old men.* By reason of their
age they had known and heard much; they
had heard from their fathers, and their
father's fathers, much which they had not
known themselves. Among the people of the
East, memories of past times were handed
down from generation to generation, for
periods, which to us would seem incredible.
Israel was commanded, so to transmit the

vivid memories of the miracles of God. The
Prophet appeals *to the old men, to hear,* and,
(lest, anything should seem to have escaped
them) to the whole people of the land, to
give their whole attention to *this* thing, which
he was about to tell them, and then, review-
ing all the evils which each had ever heard
to have been inflicted by God upon their
forefathers, to say whether *this* thing had
happened in their days or in the days of their
fathers.

3. *Tell ye your children of it.* In the order
of God's goodness, generation was to declare
to generation the wonders of His love. [4] *He*
established a testimony in Jacob, and appointed
a law in Israel, which He commanded our fathers
that they should make them known to their chil-
dren, that the generation to come might know
them, the children which should be born, who should
arise and declare them to their children that they
might—not forget the works of God. This tradition of thankful memories God, as the
Psalmist says, enforced in the law [5]; *Take heed*
to thyself, lest thou forget the things which thine
eyes have seen, but teach them thy sons and thy sons'
sons. This was the end of the memorial acts
of the ritual, that their sons might inquire
the meaning of them, the fathers tell them
God's wonders [6]. Now contrariwise, they are,
generation to generation, to tell *concerning it,*
this message of unheard-of woe and judgment.
The memory of God's deeds of love should
have stirred them to gratitude; now He
transmits to them memories of woe, that they
might entreat God against them, and break
off the sins which entail them.

4. *That which the palmerworm hath left, hath*
the locust eaten. The creatures here spoken of
are different kinds of locusts, so named
from their number or voracity. We, who
are free from this scourge of God, know them
only by the generic name of locusts. But the
law mentions several sorts of locusts, each

---

[1] See on Hos. i. 1.
xliv. 26.

[2] S. Matt. xxiv. 35.
[4] Ps. lxxviii. 5–7.

[5] Deut. iv. 9. add vi. 6, 7. xi. 19.
[6] Ib. vi. 20–24.

the locust eaten; and that which the locust hath left hath the c a n k e r w o r m eaten; and that which the cankerworm hath left hath the caterpillar eaten.

after its kind, which might be eaten [1]. In fact, above eighty different kinds of locusts have been observed [2], some of which are twice as large as that which is the ordinary scourge of God [3]. Slight as they are in themselves, they are mighty in God's Hand; beautiful and gorgeous as they are, floating in the sun's rays [4], they are a scourge, including other plagues, famine, and often, pestilence. Of the four kinds, here named by the Prophet, that rendered *locust* is so called from its multitude, (whence Jeremiah says [5], *they are more numerous than the locust;*) and is, probably, the creature which desolates whole regions of Asia and Africa. The rest are named from their voracity, the "gnawer," "licker," "consumer," but they are, beyond doubt, distinct kinds of that destroyer. And this is the characteristic of the Prophet's threatening, that he foretells a succession of destroyers, each more fatal than the preceding; and that, not according to the order of nature. For in all the observations which have been made of the locusts, even when successive flights have desolated the same land, they have always been successive clouds of the same creature.

Over and above the fact, then, that locusts are a heavy chastisement from God, these words of Joel form a sort of sacred proverb. They are the epitome of his whole prophecy. It is *this* which he had called the old men to hear, and to say whether they had known anything like *this*; that scourge came after scourge, judgment after judgment, until man yielded or perished. The visitation of locusts was one of the punishments threatened in the law, *Thou shall carry much seed out into the field, and shalt gather but little in; for the locust shall consume it* [6]. It was one of God's ordinary punishments for sin, in that country, like famine, or pestilence, or blight, or mildew, or murrain, or (in this) potato disease. Solomon, accordingly, at the dedication of the Temple mentions the locust among the other plagues, which he then solemnly entreated God to remove, when individuals or the whole people should spread forth their hands in penitence towards that house [7]. But the characteristic of *this* prophecy is the successiveness of the judgments, each in itself, desolating, and the later following quick upon the earlier, and completing their destructiveness. The judgments of God are linked together by an invisible chain, each drawing on the other; yet, at each link of the lengthening chain, allowing space and time for repentance to break it through. So in the plagues of Egypt, God, *executing His judgments upon them by little and little, gave them time for repentance* [8]; yet, when Pharaoh hardened his heart, each followed on the other, until he perished in the Red Sea. In like way God said [9], *him that escapeth the sword of Hazael shall Jehu slay; and him that escapeth from the sword of Jehu shall Elisha slay.* So, in the Revelation, the *trumpets* are sounded [10], and *the vials of the wrath of God are poured out upon the earth,* one after the other [11]. Actual locusts were very likely one of the scourges intended by the Prophet. They certainly were not the whole; but pictured others fiercer, more desolating, more overwhelming. The proverbial dress gained and fixed men's attention on the truth, which, if it had been presented to the people nakedly, they might have turned from. Yet as, in God's wisdom, what is said generally, is often fulfilled specially, so here there were four great invaders which in succession wasted Judah; the Assyrian, Chaldæan, Macedonian and Roman.

Morally, also, four chief passions desolate successively the human heart. " [12] For what is designated by the *palmerworm,* which creeps with all its body on the ground, except it be lust, which so pollutes the heart which it possesses, that it cannot rise up to the love of heavenly purity? What is expressed by the *locust,* which flies by leaps, except vain glory which exalts itself with empty presumptions? What is typified by the *cankerworm,* almost the whole of whose body is gathered into its belly, except gluttony in eating? What but anger is indicated by mildew, which burns as

---

[1] Lev. xi. 22. אַרְבֶּה [the ordinary name] חָרְגֹּל "hopper," סָלְעָם "devourer," (these two occur in that place of Lev. only) and חָנָב so called, it is thought, from veiling the sun in its flight.

[2] Dict. de l' Hist. Natur. v. Criquet.

[3] "The Gryllus Tartaricus is almost twice as large as the ordinary locust" [gryllus gregarius.] Clarke, Travels, i. 437. Beauplan speaks of those which, for several years, he observed in the Ukraine, as being "as thick as a man's finger and twice as long." Churchill, i. 600.

[4] "The gryllus Migratorius has red legs, and its inferior wings have a lively red color, which gives a bright fiery appearance to the animals when fluttering in the sun's rays." Clarke, i. 438. Schlatter has much the same description, Bruchstucke aus einigen Reisen nach dem sudlichen Russland, A.D. 1820–28. p. 326. in Ersch, Encycl. v. Heuschrecken-züge, p. 315. Those mentioned by Fr. Alvarez as the great scourge of Æthiopia were different. They had yellow under-wings, which also reflected the sun's rays, c. 32.

[5] xlvi. 23. רַבּוּ מֵאַרְבֶּה. See Jud. vi. 5. vii. 12. Ps. cv. 34. Nah. iii. 15. It is a proverb in Arabic also.

[6] Deut. xxviii. 38.

[7] 1 Kings viii. 37, 8.

[8] Wisd. xii. 10.

[9] 1 Kings xix. 17.

[10] Rev. viii. ix. xi. 15.

[11] Ib. xvi.

[12] S. Greg. Mor. xxxiii. 65. p. 614. Oxf. Tr.

Before
C H R I S T
cir. 800.

5 Awake, ye drunkards,
and weep; and howl, all
ye drinkers of wine, be-
cause of the new wine;
^d for it is cut off from your
mouth.

d Is. 32. 10.

6 For ^e a nation is come
up upon my land, strong,
and without n u m b e r,
^f whose teeth are the teeth
of a lion, and he hath the
cheek teeth of a great lion.

Before
C H R I S T
cir. 800.

e So Prov. 30.
25, 26, 27.
ch. 2. 2. 11, 25.
f Rev. 9. 8.

---

it touches? What *the palmerworm* then *hath
left the locust hath eaten,* because, when the sin
of lust has retired from the mind, vain glory
often succeeds. For since it is not now subdued
by the love of the flesh, it boasts of itself, as if
it were holy through its chastity. And *that
which the locust hath left, the cankerworm hath
eaten,* because when vain glory, which came,
as it were, from holiness, is resisted, either the
appetite, or some ambitious desires are indulged
in too immoderately. For the mind which
knows not God, is led the more fiercely to
any object of ambition, in proportion as it is
not restrained by any love of human praise.
That which the cankerworm hath left, the mildew
consumes, because when the gluttony of the
belly is restrained by abstinence, the impatience of anger holds fiercer sway, which, like
mildew, eats up the harvest by burning it,
because the flame of impatience withers the
fruit of virtue. When then some vices
succeed to others, one plague devours the
field of the mind, while another leaves it."

5. *Awake, ye drunkards, and weep.* All sin
stupefies the sinner. All intoxicate the mind,
bribe and pervert the judgment, dull the
conscience, blind the soul and make it insensible to its own ills. All the passions, anger,
vain glory, ambition, avarice and the rest are
a spiritual drunkenness, inebriating the soul,
as strong drink doth the body. "¹ They are
called drunkards, who, confused with the love
of this world, feel not the ills which they
suffer. What then is meant by, *Awake, ye
drunkards and weep,* but, 'shake off' the sleep
of your insensibility, and oppose by watchful
lamentations the many plagues of sins, which
succeed one to the other in the devastation of
your hearts?'" God arouse those who will
be aroused, by withdrawing from them the
pleasures wherein they offended Him. Awake,
the Prophet cries, from the sottish slumber
of your drunkenness; awake to weep and
howl, at least when your feverish enjoyments
are dashed from your lips. Weeping for
things temporal may awaken to the fear of
losing things eternal.

6. *For a nation is come up upon my land.*
He calls this scourge of God *a nation,* giving
them the title most used in Holy Scripture,
of heathen nations. The like term, *people,*

folk, is used of the *ants* and the *conies*², for
the wisdom with which God teaches them to
act. Here it is used, in order to -include at
once, the irrational invader, guided by a
Reason above its own, and the heathen conqueror. This enemy, he says, is *come up* (for
the land as being God's land, was exalted in
dignity, above other lands,) *upon My land,*
i. e. *the Lord's land*³, hitherto owned and
protected as God's land, *a land which,* Moses
said to them⁴, *the Lord thy God careth for ; the
eyes of the Lord thy God are always upon it,
from the beginning of the year even unto the end
of the year.* Now it was to be bared of God's
protection, and to be trampled upon by a
heathen foe.

Strong and without number. The figure is
still from the locust, whose numbers are
wholly countless by man. Travellers sometimes use likenesses to express their number,
as clouds darkening the sun⁵ or discharging
flakes of snow⁶; some grave writers give
it up, as hopeless. "⁷ Their multitude is
incredible, whereby they cover the earth
and fill the air; they take away the brightness of the sun. I say again, the thing is
incredible to one who has not seen them."
"It would not be a thing to be believed, if
one had not seen it." "On another day, it
was beyond belief: they occupied a space of
eight leagues [about 24 English miles]. I
do not mention the multitude of those without wings, because it is incredible." "⁸ When
we were in the Seignory of Abrigima, in a
place called Aquate, there came such a
multitude of locusts, as cannot be said.
They began to arrive one day about terce
[nine] and till night they cease not to
arrive; and when they arrived, they
bestowed themselves. On the next day
at the hour of prime they began to depart,
and at midday there was not one, and
there remained not a leaf on the trees.
At this instant others began to come, and
stayed like the others to the next day at the
same hour; and these left not a stick with
its bark, nor a green herb, and thus did they
five days one after another ; and the people
said that they were the sons, who went to
seek their fathers, and they took the road
towards the others which had no wings.

1 S. Greg. Mor. xxxiii. 66.
2 Prov. xxx. 25, 6.
3 Hos. ix. 3.
4 Deut. xi. 12.
5 See on ii. 10.

6 Clarke's Travels, l. c. p. 437. Beauplan, Ukraine,
in Churchill, i. 599. Lichtenstein, c. 46.
7 Fr. Alvarez do Preste Joan, das Indias, c. 32.
8 Ib. c. 33.

Before CHRIST cir. 800.

g Is. 5. 6.
† Heb. laid my fig tree for a barking.

7 He hath ^g laid my vine waste, and † barked my fig tree: he hath made

it clean bare, and cast it away; the branches thereof are made white.

Before CHRIST cir. 800.

After they were gone, we knew the breadth which they had occupied, and saw the destruction which they had made, it exceeded three leagues [nine miles] wherein there remained no bark on the trees." Another writes of South Africa[1]; "Of the innumerable multitudes of the incomplete insect or larva of the locusts, which at this time infested this part of Africa, no adequate idea could be conceived without having witnessed them. For the space of ten miles on each side of the Sea-Cow river, and eighty or ninety miles in length, an area of 16, or 1800 square miles, the whole surface might literally be said to be covered with them. The water of the river was scarcely visible on account of the dead carcasses which floated on the surface, drowned in the attempt to come at the weeds which grew in it." "[2] The present year is the third of their continuance, and their increase has far exceeded that of a geometrical progression whose whole ratio is a million." A writer of reputation says of a "column of locusts" in India; "[3] It extended, we were informed, 500 miles, and so compact was it when on the wing, that, like an eclipse, it completely hid the sun; so that no shadow was cast by any object, and some lofty tombs, not more than 200 yards distant, were rendered quite invisible." In one single neighborhood, even in Germany, it was once calculated that near 17,000,000 of their eggs were collected and destroyed [4]. Even Volney writes of those in Syria[5], "the quantity of these insects is a thing incredible to any one who has not seen it himself; the ground is covered with them for several leagues." "The steppes," says Clarke[6], an incredulous traveler, "were entirely covered by their bodies, and their numbers falling resembled flakes of snow,

carried obliquely by the wind, and spreading thick mists over the sun. Myriads fell over the carriage, the horses, the drivers. The Tartars told us, that persons had been suffocated by a fall of locusts on the *steppes*. It was now the season, they added, in which they began to diminish." "[7] It was incredible, that their breadth was eight leagues."

Strong. The locust is remarkable for its long flights. "Its strength of limbs is amazing; when pressed down by the hand on the table, it has almost power to move the fingers [8]".

Whose teeth are *the teeth of a lion.* The teeth of the locust are said to be "harder than stone." "[9] They appear to be created for a scourge; since to strength incredible for so small a creature, they add saw-like teeth admirably calculated to *eat up all the herbs in the land.*" Some near the Senegal, are described as "[10] quite brown, of the thickness and length of a finger, and armed with two jaws, toothed like a saw, and very powerful." The Prophet ascribes to them the sharp or prominent eye-teeth of the lion and lioness, combining strength with number. The ideal of this scourge of God is completed by blending numbers, in which creatures so small only could exist together, with the strength of the fiercest. "[11] Weak and short-lived is man, yet when God is angered against a sinful people, what mighty power does He allow to man against it!" "And what more cruel than those who endeavor to slay souls, turning them from the Infinite and Eternal Good, and so dragging them to the everlasting torments of Hell?"

7. *He hath laid my vine waste, and barked my fig tree.* This describes an extremity of desolation. The locusts at first attack all

[1] Barrow, S. Africa, p. 257.   [2] Ib. 258.
[3] Major Moor in Kirby on Entomology, Letter vi.
[4] 16,690,905. They were collected near Droschen. Half a peck was found to contain 39,272. Ersch, Heuschreckenzüge, p. 314. Beauplan says (Ib.) "wheresoever they come, in less than 2 hours they crop all they can, which causes great scarcity of provisions; and if the locusts remain there in Autumn when they die, after laying at least 300 eggs apiece, which hatch next spring, if it be dry, then the country is 300 times worse pestered."
[5] Voyage en Syrie, i. 277.
[6] Travels, c. 18. i. 437. "At Vienna they were half an hour's journey in breadth, but, after 3 hours, though they seemed to fly fast, one could not yet see the end of the column." Philosophical Transactions, T. 46. p. 36. "In Cyprus, in going in a chaise 4 or 5 miles, the locusts lay swarming above a foot deep in several parts of the high road, and thousands were destroyed by the wheels of the carriage driving over them." Russell, Nat. Hist. of Aleppo, ii. 229. "I have seen them at night when they sit to rest them, that the roads were 4 inches

thick of them one upon another, so that the horses would not trample over them, but as they were put on with much lashing—the wheels of our carts and the feet of our horses bruising those creatures, there came from them such a stink, as not only offended the nose but the brain." Beauplan, 599, 600. "This place stands on a high hill, whence large tracts and many places could be seen all yellow with locusts." Fr. Alvarez, c. 32. "The face of the country is covered with them for many miles." Forbes, ii. 273. "In Senegal, they come almost every three years, and when they have covered the ground, they gnaw almost every thing, and are in such numbers as to shadow the heaven for xii. [Italian] miles. If they came every year, all would be consumed and desert. I have seen them sometimes fly in a troop over the sea; their number was almost infinite." Aluise da cà da Mosto, Navig. c. 13. "The locusts cover the ground, so that it can scarcely be seen." Le Bruyn, Lev. 252.
[7] Alvarez, c. 32.   [8] Clarke, i. 438.
[9] Morier, 2d. Journey, p. 99.
[10] Adansson, Voyage au Sénégal, p. 88.   [11] Rup.

which is green and succulent; when this has been consumed, then they attack the bark of trees. "[1] When they have devoured all other vegetables, they attack the trees, consuming first the leaves, then the bark." "[2] A day or two after one of these bodies were in motion, others were already hatched to glean after them, gnawing off the young branches and the very bark of such trees as had escaped before with the loss only of their fruit and foliage." "[3] They carried desolation wherever they passed. After having consumed herbage, fruit, leaves of trees, they attacked even their young shoots and their bark. Even the reeds, wherewith the huts were thatched, though quite dry, were not spared." "[4] Every thing in the country was devoured; the bark of figs, pomegranates, and oranges, bitter hard and corrosive, escaped not their voracity." The effects of this wasting last on for many years[5].

He hath made it clean bare. "[6] It is sufficient, if these terrible columns stop half an hour on a spot, for everything growing on it, vines, olive trees, and corn, to be entirely destroyed. After they have passed, nothing remains but the large branches, and the roots which, being under ground, have escaped their voracity." "[7] After eating up the corn, they fell upon the vines, the pulse, the willows and even the hemp, notwithstanding its great bitterness." "[8] They are particularly injurious to the palm trees; these they strip of every leaf and green particle, the trees remaining like skeletons with bare branches." "[9] The bushes were eaten quite bare, though the animals could not have been long on the spot.—They sat by hundreds on a bush gnawing the rind and the woody fibres."

The branches thereof are made white. "[10] The country did not seem to be burnt, but to be much covered with snow, through the whiteness of the trees and the dryness of the herbs. It pleased God that the fresh crops were already gathered in."

The *vine* is the well-known symbol of God's people[11]; the fig too, by reason of its sweetness, is an emblem of His Church and of each soul in her, bringing forth the fruit of grace[12]. When then God says, *he hath laid My vine waste,* He suggests to us, that He is not speaking chiefly of the visible tree, but of that which it represents. The locusts, accordingly, are not chiefly the insects, which bark the actual trees, but every enemy which wastes the heritage of God, which He calls by those names. His vineyard, the Jewish people, was outwardly and repeatedly desolated by the Chaldæans, Antiochus Epiphanes, and afterward by the Romans. The vineyard, which the Jews had, was, (as Jesus foretold,) *let out to other husbandmen* when they had killed Him; and, thenceforth, is the Christian Church, and, subordinately each soul in her. "[13] Heathen and heretical Emperors and heresiarchs wasted often the Church of Christ. Anti-Christ shall waste it. They who have wasted her are countless. For the Psalmist says, *They who hate me without a cause are more than the hairs of my head*[14]."

"[15] The nation which cometh up against the soul, are the princes of this world and of darkness and spiritual wickedness in high places, whose *teeth* are the teeth of a lion, of whom the Apostle Peter saith, *Our adversary the devil, as a roaring lion, walketh about seeking whom he may devour*[16]. If we give way to this nation, so that they should come up in us, forthwith they will make our vineyard where we were wont to make *wine to gladden the heart of man*[17], a desert, and bark or break our fig tree, that we should no more have in us those most sweet gifts of the Holy Spirit. Nor is it enough for that nation to destroy the vineyard and break the fig tree, unless it also destroy whatever there is of life in it, so that, its whole freshness being consumed, the switches remain white and dead, and that be fulfilled in us, *If they do these things in a green tree, what shall be done in the dry?*[18]" "[19] The Church, at least a part of it, is turned into a desert, deprived of spiritual goods, when the faithful are led, by consent to sin, to forsake God. *The fig tree is barked,* when the soul which once abounded with sweetest goods and fruits of the Holy Ghost, hath those goods lessened or cut off. Such are they who, having *begun in the Spirit*[20], are perfected by the flesh."

"[21] By spirits lying in wait, the vineyard of God is made a desert, when the soul, replenished with fruits, is wasted with longing for the praise of men. That *people barks the fig tree* of God, in that, carrying away the misguided soul to a thirst for applause, in proportion as it draws her on to ostentation, it strips her of the covering of humility. *Making it clean bare, it despoils it,* in that, so long as it lies hidden in its goodness, it is, as it

---

[1] Jackson's Travels to Morocco ap. Kirby.
[2] Shaw's Travels, p. 257. [3] Adansson, Ib.
[4] Chénier, Recherches Historiques sur les Maures, iii. 496. "They destroyed the leaves and bark of the olive." Dr. Freer, in Russell's Aleppo, p. 230.
[5] "The wine of Algiers, before the locusts in 1723 wasted the vineyards, was, in flavor not inferior to the best Hermitage. Since that time the wine has much degenerated and has not yet (1732) recovered its usual qualities." Shaw, p. 227.
[6] Constitutionnel, May, 1841, of locusts in Spain in that year. K.

[7] Phil. Trans. 1686. T. xvi. p. 148.
[8] Burckhardt, Notes, ii. 90.
[9] Lichtenstein, Trav. in S. Afr. c. 46. p. 251.
[10] Fr. Alvarez, c. 33.
[11] Ps. lxxx. 8, 14. Cant. ii. 13, 15. Hos. x. 1. Is. v. 1-7. xxvii. 2.
[12] Hos. ix. 10.   S. Matt. xxi. 19.   S. Luke xiii. 6, 7.
[13] Rib.   [14] Ps. lxix. 4.   [15] S. Jer.
[16] 1 S. Pet. v. 8.   [17] Ps. civ. 15.
[18] S. Luke xxiii. 31.   [19] Dion.
[20] Gal. iii. 3.
[21] S. Greg. on Job L viii. § 82.

Before
CHRIST
cir. 800.

h Is. 22. 12.
i Prov. 2. 17. Jer.
3. 4.
k ver. 13.
ch. 2. 14.

8 ¶ h Lament like a vir-
gin girded with sackcloth
for i the husband of her
youth.

9 k The meat offering

and the drink offering is
cut off from the house
of the LORD; the priests,
the LORD's ministers,
mourn.

Before
CHRIST
cir. 800.

were, clothed with a covering of its own, which protects it. But when the mind longs that which it has done should be seen by others, it is as though *the fig tree despoiled* had lost the bark that covered it. And so, as it follows, *The branches thereof are made white;* in that his works, displayed to the eyes of men, have a bright shew; a name for sanctity is gotten, when good actions are published. But as, upon the bark being removed, the branches of the fig tree wither, so observe that the deeds of the arrogant, paraded before human eyes, wither through the very act of seeking to please. Therefore the mind which is betrayed through boastfulness is rightly called a fig tree barked, in that it is at once fair to the eye, as being seen, and within a little of withering, as being bared of the covering of the bark. Within, then, must our deeds be laid up, if we look to a reward of our deeds from Him Who seeth within."

8. *Lament like a virgin.* The Prophet addresses the congregation of Israel, as one espoused to God [l]; "*Lament thou,* daughter of Zion," or the like. He bids her lament, with the bitterest of sorrows, as one who, in her virgin years, was just knit into one with the husband of her youth, and then at once was, by God's judgment, on the very day of her espousal, ere yet she ceased to be a virgin, parted by death. The mourning which God commands is not one of conventional or becoming mourning, but that of one who has put away all joy from her, and takes the rough garment of penitence, girding the haircloth upon her, enveloping and embracing, and therewith, wearing the whole frame. The haircloth was a coarse, rough, formless, garment, girt close round the waist, afflictive to the flesh, while it expressed the sorrow of the soul. God regarded as a virgin, the people which He had made holy to Himself [2]; He so regards the soul which He has regenerated and sanctified. The people, by their idolatry, lost Him Who was a Husband to them; the soul, by inordinate affections, is parted from its God. "[3]God Almighty was the Husband of the Synagogue, having espoused it to Himself in the Patriarchs and at the giving of the law. So long as she did not, through idolatry and other heavy sins, depart from God, she was a spouse in the in-

tegrity of mind, in knowledge, in love and worship of the true God." "[4]The Church is a Virgin; Christ her Husband. By prevailing sins, the order, condition, splendor, worship of the Church, are, through negligence, concupiscence, avarice, irreverence, worsened, deformed, obscured." "The soul is a virgin by its creation in nature; a virgin by privilege of grace; a virgin also by hope of glory. Inordinate desire maketh the soul a harlot; manly penitence restoreth to her chastity; wise innocence, virginity. For the soul recovereth a sort of chastity, when through thirst for righteousness, she undertakes the pain and fear of penitence; still she is not as yet raised to the eminence of innocence.—In the first state she is exposed to concupiscence; in the second, she doth works of repentance; in the third, bewailing her Husband, she is filled with the longing for righteousness; in the fourth, she is gladdened by virgin embraces and the kiss of Wisdom. For Christ is the Husband of her youth, the Betrother of her virginity. But since she parted from Him to evil concupiscence, she is monished to return to Him by sorrow and the works and garb of repentance." "[5]So should every Christian weep who has lost Baptismal grace, or has fallen back after repentance, and, deprived of the pure embrace of the Heavenly Bridegroom, *embraced* instead these earthly things which are as *dunghills* [6], *having been brought up in scarlet,* and *being in honor, had no understanding* [7]. Whence it is written [8], *let tears run down like a river day and night; give thyself no rest.* Such was he who said [9]; *rivers of waters run down mine eyes, because they keep not Thy law.*"

9. *The meat offering and the drink offering is cut off.* The meat offering and drink offering were part of every sacrifice. If the materials for these, the corn and wine, ceased, through locusts or drought or the wastings of war, the sacrifice must become mangled and imperfect. The priests were to mourn for the defects of the sacrifice; they lost also their own subsistence, since the altar was, to them, in place of all other inheritance. The meat and drink offerings were emblems of the materials of the Holy Eucharist, by which Malachi foretold that, when God had rejected the offering of the Jews, there should be a *pure offering*

---

[1] The Hebrew אל is feminine.   [2] Jer. ii. 2.
[3] Rup.   [4] Huge de S. Vict.   [5] Dion.

[6] Lam. iv. 5.   [7] Ps. xlix. 12, 20.
[9] Lam. ii. 18.   [9] Ps. cxix. 136.

Before
C H R I S T
cir. 800.

[1] Jer. 12. 11. &
14. 2.
[m] Is. 24. 7.
ver. 12.
‖ Or, *ashamed.*
[n] Jer. 14. 3, 4.

10 The field is wasted, [1] the land mourneth; for the corn is wasted: [m] the new wine is ‖ dried up, the oil languisheth.

11 [n] Be ye ashamed, O ye husbandmen; howl, O ye vinedressers, for the wheat and for the barley; because the harvest of the field is perished.

12 [o] The vine is dried up, and the fig tree languisheth; the pomegranate tree, the palm tree also, and the apple tree, *even* all

[o] ver. 10.

---

among the heathen[1]. When then Holy Communions become rare, the meat and drink offering are literally cut off from the house of the Lord, and those who are indeed priests, the ministers of the Lord, should mourn. Joel foretells that, however love should wax cold, there should ever be such. He forsees and foretells at once, the failure, and the grief of the priests. Nor, is it an idle regret which he foretells, but a mourning unto their God. " [2] Both meat offering and drink offering hath perished from the house of God, not in actual substance but as to reverence, because, amid the prevailing iniquity there is scarcely found in the Church, who should duly celebrate, or receive the Sacraments."

10. *The field is wasted, the land mourneth.* As, when God pours out His blessings of nature, all nature seems to smile and be glad, and as the Psalmist says, *to shout for joy and sing*[3], so when He withholds them, it seems to mourn, and, by its mourning, to reproach the insensibility of man. Oil is the emblem of the abundant graces and gifts of the Holy Spirit, and of the light and devotion of soul given by Him, and of spiritual gladness, and overflowing, all-mantling charity.

11. *Be ye ashamed, O ye husbandmen.* The Prophet dwells on and expands the description of the troubles which he had foretold, setting before their eyes the picture of one universal desolation. For the details of sorrow most touch the heart, and he wished to move them to repentance. He pictures them to themselves; some standing aghast and ashamed of the fruitlessness of their toil, others giving way to bursts of sorrow, and all things around waste and dried. Nothing was exempt. Wheat and barley, wide-spread as they were (and the barley in those countries, " more fertile[4]" than the wheat,) perished utterly. The rich juice of the vine, the luscious sweetness of the fig the succulence of the ever-green pomegranate, the majesty of the palm tree, the fragrance of the Eastern apple, exempted them not. All, fruitbearing or barren, were dried up; for joy itself, and every source of joy was dried up from the sons of men.

All these suggest a spiritual meaning. For we know of a spiritual *harvest*, souls born to God, and a spiritual *vineyard*, the Church of God; and spiritual *husbandmen* and *vinedressers*, those whom God sends. The trees, with their various fruits were emblems of the faithful, adorned with the various gifts and graces of the Spirit. All well-nigh were dried up. Wasted without, in act and deed, the sap of the Spirit ceased within; the true laborers, those who were jealous for the vineyard of the Lord of hosts were ashamed and grieved. " [5] *Husbandmen* and *vinedressers*, are priests and preachers; *husbandmen* as instructors in morals, *vinedressers* for that joy in things eternal, which they infuse into the minds of the hearers. *Husbandmen*, as instructing the soul to deeds of righteousness; *vinedressers*, as exciting the minds of hearers to the love of wisdom. Or, *husbandmen*, in that by their doctrine they uproot earthly deeds and desires; *vinedressers*, as holding forth spiritual gifts." "The vine is the richness of divine knowledge; the fig the sweetness of contemplation and the joyousness in things eternal." The pomegranate, with its manifold grains contained under its one bark, may designate the variety and harmony of graces, disposed in their beautiful order. "The palm, rising above the world." " [6] Well is the life of the righteous likened to *a palm*, in that the palm below is rough to the touch, and in a manner enveloped in dry bark, but above it is adorned with fruit, fair even to the eye; below it is compressed by the enfoldings of its bark; above, it is spread out in amplitude of beautiful greenness. For so is the life of the elect, despised below, beauti.ul above. Down below, it is, as it were, enfolded in many barks, in that it is straitened by innumerable afflictions. But on high it is expanded into a foliage, as it were, of beautiful greenness by the amplitude of the rewarding."

Because joy is withered away. " [5] There are four sorts of joy, a joy in iniquity, a joy in vanity, a joy of charity, a joy of felicity. Of the first we read, *Who rejoice to do evil,* and *delight in the forwardness of the wicked*[7]. Of

---

[1] i. 11.
[3] Ps. lxv. 13.
[2] Hugo de S. V. A. D. 1120.
[4] S. Jer.

[5] Hugo de S. V.
[6] S. Greg. on Job L. xix. § 49.
[7] Prov. ii. 14.

Before
CHRIST
cir. 800.

p Is. 24. 11.
Jer. 48. 33.
See Ps. 4. 7.
Is. 9. 3.
q Jer. 4. 8.
ver. 8.

r ver. 9.

the trees of the field, are withered: because P joy is withered away from the sons of men.

13 q Gird yourselves, and lament, ye priests: howl, ye ministers of the altar: come, lie all night in sackcloth, ye ministers of my God: for r the meat

offering and the drink offering is withholden from the house of your God.

14 ¶ s Sanctify ye a fast, call t a || solemn assembly, gather the elders and u all the inhabitants of the land into the house of the LORD your God, and cry unto the LORD.

Before
CHRIST
cir. 800.

s 2 Chr. 20. 3, 4.
ch. 2. 15, 16.
t Lev. 23. 36.
|| Or, day of
restraint.
u 2 Chr. 20. 13.

---

the second, *They take the timbrel and harp, and rejoice at the sound of the organ*[1]. Of the third, *Let the saints be joyful in glory*[2]. Of the fourth, *Blessed are they that dwell in Thy house; they will be still praising Thee*[3]. The joy of charity and the joy of felicity *wither from the sons of men*, when the virtues aforesaid failing, there being neither knowledge of the truth nor love of virtue, no reward succeedeth, either in this life or that to come."

Having thus pictured the coming woe, he calls all to repentance and mourning, and those first, who were to call others. God Himself appointed these afflictive means, and here He "gives to the priest a model for penitence and a way of entreating mercy."
"[4] He invites the priests first to repentance through whose negligence chiefly the practice of holiness, the strictness of discipline, the form of doctrine, the whole aspect of the Church was sunk in irreverence. Whence the people also perished, hurrying along the various haunts of sin. Whence Jeremiah says, *The kings of the earth and all the inhabitants of the world would not have believed that the adversary and the enemy should have entered into the gates of Jerusalem. For the sins of her Prophets and the iniquities of her priests that have shed the blood of the just in the midst of her, they have wandered as blind men in the streets, they have polluted themselves with blood*[5].

13. *Gird yourselves*, i. e. with haircloth, as is elsewhere expressed[6]. The outward affliction is an expression of the inward grief, and itself excites to further grief. This their garment of affliction and penitence, they were not to put off day and night. Their wonted duty was, to *offer up sacrifice for their own sins and the sins of the people*[7], and to entreat God for them. This their office the Prophet calls them to discharge day and night; to *come* into the court of the Temple, and there, where God shewed Himself in majesty and mercy, *lie all night* prostrate before God, not at ease, but in sackcloth. He calls to them

in the Name of his God, *Ye ministers of my God;* of Him, to Whom, whosoever forsook Him, he himself was faithful. "[8]The Prophets called the God of all, their own God, being united to Him by singular love and reverential obedience, so that they could say, *God is the strength of my heart and my portion for ever*[9]." He calls Him, further, *their God,* (*your God*) in order to remind them of His special favor to them, and their duty to Him Who allowed them to call Him *their God.*

14. *Sanctify ye a fast.* He does not say only, "proclaim," or "appoint a fast," but *sanctify it.* Hallow the act of abstinence, seasoning it with devotion and with acts meet for repentance. For fasting is not accepted by God, unless done in charity and obedience to His commands. "[10]*Sanctify* it, i. e. make it an offering to God, and as it were a sacrifice, a holy and blameless fast." "[11]To sanctify a fast is to exhibit abstinence of the flesh, meet toward God, with other good. Let anger cease, strife be lulled. For in vain is the flesh worn, if the mind is not held in from evil passions, inasmuch as the Lord saith by the Prophet[12], *Lo! in the day of your fast you find your pleasures.* The fast which the Lord approveth, is that which lifteth up to Him hands full of almsdeeds, which is passed with brotherly love, which is seasoned by piety. What thou subtractest from thyself, bestow on another, that thy needy neighbor's flesh may be recruited by means of that which thou deniest to thine own."

Call a solemn assembly. Fasting without devotion is an image of famine. At other times *the solemn assembly* was for festival-joy. Such was the last day of the feast of the Passover[13] and of Tabernacles[14]. No servile work was to be done thereon. It was *then* to be consecrated to thanksgiving, but now to sorrow and supplication. "[8]The Prophet commands that all should be called and gathered into the Temple, that so the prayer

[1] Job xxi. 12.   [2] Ps. cxlix. 5.
[3] Ib. lxxxiv. 4.   [4] Hugo de S. V.
[5] Lam. iv. 13, 14.   [6] Is. xxii. 12. Jer. iv. 8. vi. 26.
[7] Heb. vii. 27.   [8] Dion.   [9] Ps. lxxiii. 26.

[10] S. Cyr.   [11] S. Greg. in Ev. Hom. 16.
[12] Is. lviii. 3.   [13] Deut. xvi. 8.
[14] Lev. xxiii. 36. Num. xxix. 35. 2 Chr. vii. 9.
Neh. viii. 18.

Before
CHRIST
cir. 800.

x Jer. 30. 7.
y Is. 13. 6, 9.
ch. 2. 1.

15 x Alas for the day!
for y the day of the
LORD is at hand, and

as a destruction from
the Almighty shall it
come.

Before
CHRIST
cir. 800.

might be the rather heard, the more they were who offered it. Wherefore the Apostle besought his disciples to pray for him, that so what was asked might be obtained the more readily through the intercession of many."

Gather the elders. Age was, by God's appointment[1], had in great reverence among the Hebrews. When first God sent Moses and Aaron to His people in Egypt, He bade them collect the elders of the people[2] to declare to them their own mission from God; through them He conveyed the ordinance of the Passover to the whole congregation[3]; in their presence was the first miracle of bringing water from the rock performed[4]; then He commanded Moses to choose seventy of them, to appear before Him before He gave the law[5]; then to bear Moses' own burden in hearing the causes of the people, bestowing His spirit upon them[6]. The elders of each city were clothed with judicial authority[7]. In the expiation of an uncertain murder, the elders of the city represented the whole city[8]; in the offerings for the congregation, the elders of the congregation represented the whole[9]. So then, here also, they are summoned, chief of all, that "the authority and example of their grey hairs might move the young to repentance." "[10]Their age, near to death and ripened in grace, makes them more apt for the fear and worship of God." All however, *priests, elders,* and the *inhabitants,* or *people of the land*[11], were to form one band, and were, with one heart and voice, to cry unto God; and that *in the house of God.* For so Solomon had prayed, that God would *in Heaven His dwelling place, hear whatever prayer and supplication* might there be *made by any man or by all His people Israel*[12]; and God had promised in turn,[13] *I have hallowed this house which thou hast built, to put My name there for ever, and Mine eyes and Mine heart shall be there perpetually.* God has given to united prayer a power over Himself, and "prayer overcometh God[14]." The Prophet calls God *your God,* shewing how ready He was to hear; but he adds, *cry unto the Lord;* for it is not a listless prayer, but a loud earnest *cry,* which reacheth to the throne of God.

15. *Alas for the day! for the Day of the Lord is at hand.* The judgment of God, then, which they were to deprecate, was still to come. "[15]All times and all days are God's. Yet they are said to be our days, in which God leaves us to our own freedom, to do as we will," and which we may use to repent and turn to Him. "Whence Christ saith[16], *O Jerusalem—if thou hadst known in this thy day the things which belong unto thy peace.* That time, on the contrary, is said to be God's Day, in which He doth any new, rare, or special thing, such as is the Day of Judgment or vengeance." All judgment in time is an image of the Judgment for eternity. "The Day of the Lord" is, then, each "day of vengeance in which God doth to man according to His will and just judgment, inflicting the punishment which he deserves, as man did to Him in his day, manifoldly dishonoring Him, according to his own perverse will." That Day *is at hand;* suddenly to come. Speed then must be used to prevent it. Prevented it may be by speedy repentance before it comes; but when it does come, there will be no avoiding it; for

As a destruction from the Almighty shall it come. The name *the Almighty* or *God Almighty* is but seldom used in Holy Scripture. God revealed Himself by this Name to Abraham, when renewing to him the promise which was beyond nature, that he should be a father of many nations, when he and Sarah were *old and well stricken in age.* He said, *I am God Almighty; walk before Me and be thou perfect*[17]. God Almighty uses it again of Himself in renewing the blessing to Jacob[18]; and Isaac and Jacob use it in blessing in His Name[19]. It is not used as a mere name of God, but always in reference to His might, as in the book of Job which treats chiefly of His power[20]. In His days of judgment God manifests Himself as the All-mighty and All-just. Hence in the New Testament, it occurs almost exclusively in the Revelations, which reveal His judgments to come[21]. Here the words form a sort of terrible proverb, whence they are adopted from Joel by the prophet Isaiah[22]. The word *destruction, shod,* is formed from the same root as *Almighty,*

[1] Lev. xix. 32.
[2] Ex. iii. 16. iv. 29. comp. Deut. xxxi. 28.
[3] Ex. xii. 3. 21.   [4] Ex. xvii. 5. add. xviii. 12.
[5] Ib. xxiv. 1. 9.   [6] Num. xi. 16 sqq.
[7] Deut. xix. 12. xxii. 15. xxv. 7.   [8] Ib. xxi. 3–6.
[9] Lev. iv. 15. ix. 1.   [10] S. Jer.   [11] Jer. i. 18.
[12] 1 Kings viii. 39.   [13] Ib. ix. 3.
[14] Tert. de orat. § 29. p. 321. O. T.
[15] Dion.   [16] S. Luke xix. 42.
[17] Gen. xvii. 1–6. 16–21. xviii. 10–14. Rom. iv. 17–21.

[18] Gen. xxxv. 11.
[19] Gen. xxviii. 3. xliii. 14. xlviii. 3. xlix. 25.
[20] In the book of Job, it occurs 31 times; else it is used twice by the heathen Ruth, i. 20, 1; twice by Balaam, Num. xxiv. 4, 16; twice by Ezekiel of God revealing Himself in Majesty, i. 24. x. 5: and twice in the Psalms, of God putting forth His might, lxviii. 15. or protecting, xci. 1.
[21] Eight times, else only in 2 Cor. vi. 18, referring to the O. T.   [22] xiii. 6.

Before
CHRIST
cir. 800.

16 Is not the meat cut off before our eyes, *yea,* [z] joy and gladness from the house of our God?

17 The [†] seed is rotten under their clods, the garners are laid desolate, the barns are broken down; for the corn is withered.

[a] See Deut. 12.
6, 7. & 16,
11, 14, 15.

[†] Heb. *grains.*

18 How do [a] the beasts groan! the herds of cattle are perplexed, because they have no pasture; yea, the flocks of sheep are made desolate.

19 O LORD, [b] to thee will I cry: for [c] the fire hath devoured the || pas-

Before
CHRIST
cir. 800.

[a] Hos. 4. 3.

[b] Ps. 50. 15.
[c] Jer. 9. 10.
ch. 2. 3.
|| Or, *habitations.*

Shaddai[1]. *It shall come as might from the Mighty.* Only, the word *might* is always used of "might" put forth to destroy, a *mighty destruction.* He says then, in fact, that that Day shall come, like might put forth by the Almighty Himself, to destroy His enemies, irresistible, inevitable, unendurable, overwhelming the sinner.

16. *Is not the meat cut off before our eyes?* The Prophet exhibits the immediate judgment, as if it were already fulfilled in act. He sets it in detail before their eyes. "When the fruits of the earth were now ripe, the corn now calling for the reaper, and the grapes fully ripe and desiring to be pressed out, they were taken away, when set before their eyes for them to enjoy." *Yea, joy and gladness from the house of our God.* The joy in the abundance of the harvest was expressed in one universal thanksgiving to God, by fathers of families, sons, daughters, menservants, maidservants, with the priest and Levite. All this was to be cut off together. The courts of God's house were to be desolate and silent, or joy and gladness were to be turned into sorrow and wailing. "[2] So it befell those who rejected and insulted Christ. *The Bread of life Which came down from Heaven and gave life to the world*[3], *the corn of wheat, which fell into the ground and died, and brought forth much fruit*[4], that spiritual *wine* which knoweth how to *gladden the heart of man,* was already in a manner before their eyes. But when they ceased not to insult Him in unbelief, He, as it were, disappeared from their eyes, and they lost all spiritual sustenance. All share in all good is gone from them. *Joy and gladness* have also gone *from the House* which they had. For they are given up to desolation, and *abide without king or prince or sacrifice*[5]. Again, the Lord said[6], *Man shall not live by bread alone, but by every word which cometh forth out of the Mouth of God.* The word of God then is food. This hath been taken away from the Jews; for they understood not the writings of Moses, but *to this day the veil is upon their heart*[7].

For they hate the oracles of Christ. All spiritual food is perished, not in itself but to *them.* To them, it is as though it were not. But the Lord Himself imparts to those who believe in Him a right to all exuberance of joy in the good things from above. For it is written[8], *The Lord will not suffer the soul of the righteous to famish; but He thrusts away the desire of the wicked.*"

17. *The seed is rotten under the clods.* Not only was all to be cut off for the present, but, with it, all hope for the future. The scattered seed, as it lay, each under its clod known to God, was dried up, and so decayed. The garners lay desolate, nay, were allowed to go to ruin, in hopelessness of any future harvest.

18. *How do the beasts groan!* There is something very pitiable in the cry of the brute creation, even because they are innocent, yet bear man's guilt. Their groaning seems to the Prophet to be beyond expression. *How* vehemently *do they groan! The herds of cattle are perplexed,* as though, like man, they were endued with reason, to debate where to find their food. *Yea,* not these only, but *the flocks of sheep,* which might find pasture where the herds could not, these too shall *bear the punishment of guilt.* They suffered by the guilt of man; and yet so stupid was man, that he was not so sensible of his own sin for which they suffered, as they of its effect. The beasts cried to God, but even their cries did not awaken His own people. The Prophet cries for them;

19. *O Lord, to Thee will I cry.* This is the only hope left, and contains all hopes. From the Lord was the infliction; in Him is the healing. The Prophet appeals to God by His own Name, the faithful Fulfiller of His promises, Him Who Is, and Who had promised to hear all who call upon Him. Let others call to their idols, if they would, or remain stupid and forgetful, the Prophet would cry unto God, and that earnestly.

For the fire hath devoured the pastures. The gnawing of locusts leaves things, as though

---

[1] שָׁדַי, שָׁדַי, This last is from an old root, שׁוּד i. q. שׁוּד.   [2] S. Cyr.   [3] S. John vi. 48, 51.

[4] Ib. xii. 24.   [5] Hos. iii. 4.
[6] S. Matt. iv. 4.   [7] 2 Cor. iii. 15.   [8] Prov. x. 3.

Before
CHRIST
cir. 800.

tures of the wilderness, and
the flame hath burned all
the trees of the field.

20 The beasts of the
field [d] cry also unto thee:
for [e] the rivers of waters
are dried up, and the fire
hath devoured the pastures
of the wilderness.

[d] Job 38. 41.
Ps. 104. 21.
& 145. 15.
[e] 1 Kings 17. 7.
& 18. 5.

CHAPTER II.

1 *He sheweth unto Zion the ter-*
ribleness of God's judgment.
12 *He exhorteth to repentance,*
15 *prescribeth a fast,* 18 *prom-*
iseth a blessing thereon. 21
He comforteth Zion with pres-
ent, 28 *and future blessings.*

[a] BLOW ye the || trumpet
in Zion, and [b] sound
an alarm in my holy moun-

Before
CHRIST
cir. 800.

[a] Jer. 4. 5.
ver. 15.
|| Or, *cornet.*
[b] Num. 10. 5, 9.

scorched by fire[1]; the sun and the East
wind scorch up all green things, as though it
had been the actual contact of fire. Spontaneous combustion frequently follows. The
Chaldees wasted all before them with fire and
sword. All these and the like calamities are
included under *the fire,* whose desolating is
without remedy. What has been scorched
by fire never recovers. "[2] The famine," it
is said of Mosul, "was generally caused by
fire spreading in dry weather over pastures,
grass lands, and corn lands, many miles in
extent. It burnt night and day often for a
week and sometimes embraced the whole
horizon."

20. *The beasts of the field cry also unto Thee.*
"[3] There is an order in these distresses. First
he points out the insensate things wasted ;
then those afflicted, which have sense only ;
then those endowed with reason ; so that to
the order of calamity there may be consorted
an order of pity, sparing first the creature,
then the things sentient, then things rational.
The Creator spares the creature; the Or-
dainer, things sentient ; the Saviour, the
rational." Irrational creatures joined with
the Prophet in his cry. The beasts of the
field cry to God, though they know it not;
it is a cry to God, Who compassionates all
which suffers. God makes them, in act, a
picture of dependence upon His Providence,
"seeking to It for a removal of their sufferings, and supply of their wants." So He
saith [4], *the young lions roar after their prey, and*
seek their meat from God, and [5], *He giveth to the*
beast his food and to the young ravens that cry,
and [6], *Who provideth for the raven his food?*
when his young ones cry unto God. If the
people would not take instruction from him,
he "bids them learn from the beasts of the field
how to behave amid these calamities, that
they should cry aloud to God to remove them."

II. 1. The Prophet begins anew in this
chapter, first delineating in greater detail the
judgments of God ; then calling to repentance. The image reaches its height in the
capture of Jerusalem by the Babylonians,
itself an image only of worse judgments, first
on the Jews by the Romans; then on particular Churches; then of the infliction through
Anti-Christ; lastly on the whole world.
"[3] The Prophet sets before them the greatness of the coming woe, of the approaching
captivity, of the destruction imminent, in
order to move the people to terror at the
judgment of God, to compunction, to love of
obedience. This he does from the manifoldness of the destruction, the quality of the
enemy, the nature of the victory, the weight
of the misery, the ease of the triumph, the
eagerness for ill, the fear of the besieged
princes, the sluggishness of the besieged
people. He exhorts all in common to prostrate themselves at the feet of the Divine
judgment, if so be God would look down
from His dwelling place, turn the storm into
a calm, and at length out of the shipwreck
of captivity bring them back to the haven of
consolation." "[7] It is no mere prediction.
Everything stands before them, as in actual
experience, and before their eyes." Things
future affect men less; so he makes them, as
it were, present to their souls. "[7] He will
not let them vacillate about repentance, but
bids them, laying aside all listlessness, set
themselves courageously to ward off the peril,
by running to God, and effacing the charges
against them from their old sins by ever-
renewed amendment."

Blow ye the trumpet. The trumpet was
wont to sound in Zion, only for religious uses;
to call together the congregations for holy
meetings, to usher in the beginnings of their
months and their solemn days with festival

---

[1] See on ii. 3.   [2] Ainsworth, ii. 127. "The whole
of the mountain is thickly covered with dry grass
which readily takes fire, and the slightest breath
of air instantly spreads the conflagration far over
the country. The Arabs who inhabit the valley of
the Jordan invariably put to death any person who
is known to have been even the innocent cause of
firing the grass, and they have made it a public law
among themselves, that even in the height of intes-

tine warfare, no one shall attempt to set his enemy's
harvest on fire. One evening at Tabaria, I saw a
large fire on the opposite side of the lake, which
spread with great velocity for two days, till its
progress was checked by the Wady Feik." Burckhardt, Travels in Syria, pp. 331, 2. See also Thomson, i. 529.

[3] Hugo de S. V.   [4] Ps. civ. 21.   [5] Ps. cxlvii. 9.
[6] Job xxxviii. 41.   [7] S. Cyr.

Before
CHRIST
cir. 800.
ᵉch. 1. 15.
Obad. 15.
Zeph. 1. 14, 15.

tain: let all the inhabitants of the land tremble:
for ᶜ the day of the LORD

cometh, for *it is* nigh at
hand;

Before
CHRIST
cir. 800.

2 ᵈ A day of darkness ᵈ Amos 5. 18, 20.

gladness. Now in Zion itself, the stronghold of the kingdom, the Holy City, the place which God chose to put His Name there, which He had promised to establish, the trumpet was to be used, only for sounds of alarm and fear. Alarm could not penetrate there, without having pervaded the whole land. With it, the whole human hope of Judah was gone. *Sound an alarm in My holy mountain.* He repeats the warning in varied expressions, in order the more to impress men's hearts and to stir them to repentance. Even *the holy mountain* of God was to echo with alarms; the holiness, once bestowed upon it, was to be no security against the judgments of God; yea, in it rather were those judgments to begin. So St. Peter saith [1], *The time is come, that judgment must begin at the house of God.* The alarm being blown in Zion, terror was to spread to all the inhabitants of the land, who were, in fear, to repent. The Church of Christ is foretold in prophecy under the names of *Zion* and of the *holy mountain.* It is the *stone cut out without hands, which became a great mountain, and filled the whole earth* [2]. Of it, it is said [3], *Come ye and let us go up to the mountain of the Lord, to the house of the God of Jacob!* And St. Paul says, *ye are come unto mount Zion and unto the city of the living God* [4]. The words then are a rule for all times. The judgments predicted by Joel represent all judgments unto the end; the conduct, prescribed on their approach, is a pattern to the Church at all times. "[5] In this mountain we must wail, considering the failure of the faithful, in which, *iniquity abounding, charity waxeth cold.* For now (A. D. 1450) the state of the Church is so sunken, and you may see so great misery in her from the most evil conversation of many, that one who burns with zeal for God, and truly loveth his brethren, must say with Jeremiah [6], *Let mine eyes run down with tears night and day, and let them not cease, for the virgin daughter of my people is broken with a great breach.*"

Let all the inhabitants of the land tremble. "[5] We should be troubled when we hear the words of God, rebuking, threatening, avenging, as Jeremiah saith [7], *my heart within me is broken, all my bones shake, because of the Lord and because of the words of His holiness.* Good is the trouble which shaketh carnal peace, vain security, and the rest of bodily delight, when

men, weighing their sins, are shaken with fear and trembling, and repent."

For the Day of the Lord is at hand. The *Day of the Lord* is any day in which He avengeth sin, any day of Judgment, in the course of His Providence or at the end; the day of Jerusalem from the Chaldees or Romans, the day of Anti-Christ, the day of general or particular judgment, of which St. James says [8], *The coming of the Lord draweth nigh. Behold the Judge standeth before the door.* "[9] Well is that called *the day of the Lord,* in that, by the Divine appointment, it avengeth the wrongs done to the Lord through the disobedience of His people."

2. *A day of darkness and of gloominess.* "[5] A day full of *miseries;* wherefore he accumulates so many names of terrors. There was inner darkness in the heart, and the darkness of tribulation without. They hid themselves in dark places. There was the cloud between God and them; so that they were not protected nor heard by Him, of which Jeremiah saith [10], *Thou hast covered Thyself with a cloud, that our prayers should not pass through.* There was the whirlwind of tempest within and without, taking away all rest, tranquillity and peace. Whence Jeremiah hath [11], *A whirlwind of the Lord is gone forth in fury, it shall fall grievously upon the head of the wicked. The anger of the Lord shall not return, until He have executed it.*" [12] *The Day of the Lord too shall come as a thief in the night. Clouds and darkness are round about Him* [13].

A day of clouds and of thick darkness. The locusts are but the faint shadow of the coming evils, yet as the first harbingers of God's successive judgments, the imagery, even in this picture is probably taken from them. At least there is nothing in which writers, of every character, are so agreed, as in speaking of locusts as clouds darkening the sun. "[14] These creatures do not come in legions, but in whole clouds, 5 or 6 leagues in length and 2 or 3 in breadth. All the air is full and darkened when they fly. Though the sun shine ever so bright, it is no brighter than when most clouded." "[15] In Senegal we have seen a vast multitude of locusts shadowing the air; for they come almost every three years, and darken the sky." "[16] About 8 o'clock there arose above us a thick cloud, which darkened the air, depriving us of the

[1] 1 Pet. iv. 17.   [2] Dan. ii. 34, 5.   [3] Is. ii. 3.
[4] Heb. xii. 22.   [5] Dion.   [6] xiv. 17.
[7] xxiii. 9.   [8] v. 8, 9.   [9] Hugo de S. V.
[10] Lam. iii. 44.   [11] xxiii. 19.   [12] 1 Thess. v. 2.

[13] Ps. xcvii. 2.
[14] Beauplan, Ukraine, l. c. p. 599.
[15] Aluise, da cà da Mosto Navig. c. 13.
[16] Adansson, Voyage au Sénégal, p. 87, 8,

and of gloominess, a day of clouds and of thick || darkness, as the morning spread upon the mountains:

rays of the sun. Every one was astonished at so sudden a change in the air, which is so seldom clouded at this season ; but we soon saw that it was owing to a cloud of locusts. It was about 20 or 30 toises from the ground [120–180 feet] and covered several leagues of the country, when it discharged a shower of locusts, who fed there while they rested, and then resumed their flight. This cloud was brought by a pretty strong wind, it was all the morning passing the neighborhood, and the same wind, it was thought, precipitated it in the sea." "[1] They take off from the place the light of day, and a sort of eclipse is formed." "[2] In the middle of April their numbers were so vastly increased, that in the heat of the day they formed themselves into large bodies, appeared like a succession of clouds and darkened the sun." "[3] On looking up we perceived an immense cloud, here and there semi-transparent, in other parts quite black, that spread itself all over the sky, and at intervals shadowed the sun." The most unimaginative writers have said the same; "[4] When they first appear, a thick dark cloud is seen very high in the air, which, as it passes, obscures the sun. Their swarms were so astonishing in all the steppes over which we passed in this part of our journey [the Crimea,] that the whole face of nature might have been described as concealed by a living veil." "[5] When these clouds of locusts take their flight to surmount some obstacle, or traverse more rapidly a desert soil, one may say, to the letter, that the heaven is darkened by them."

As the morning spread upon the mountains. Some have thought this too to allude to the appearance which the inhabitants of Abyssinia too well knew, as preceding the coming of the locusts[6]. A sombre yellow light is cast on the ground, from the reflection, it was thought, of their yellow wings. But that appearance itself seems to be peculiar to that country, or perhaps to certain flights of locusts. The image naturally describes, the suddenness, universality of the darkness, when men looked for light. As the mountain-tops first catch the gladdening rays of the sun, ere yet it riseth on the plains, and the light spreads from height to height, until the whole earth is arrayed in light, so wide

and universal shall the outspreading be, but it shall be of darkness, not of light ; the light itself shall be turned into darkness.

A great people and a strong. The imagery throughout these verses is taken from the flight and inroad of locusts. The allegory is so complete, that the Prophet compares them to those things which are, in part, intended under them, warriors, horses and instruments of war ; and this, the more, because neither locusts, nor armies are exclusively intended. The object of the allegory is to describe the order and course of the Divine judgments ; how they are terrific, irresistible, universal, overwhelming, penetrating everywhere, overspreading all things, excluded by nothing. The locusts are the more striking symbol of this, through their minuteness and their number. They are little miniatures of a well-ordered army, unhindered by what would be physical obstacles to larger creatures, moving in order inimitable even by man, and, from their number, desolating to the uttermost. "What more countless or mightier than the locusts," asks S. Jerome, who had seen their inroads, "which human industry cannot resist?" "It is a thing invincible," says S. Cyril, "their invasion is altogether irresistible, and suffices utterly to destroy all in the fields." Yet each of these creatures is small, so that they would be powerless and contemptible, except in the Hands of Him, Who brings them in numbers which can be wielded only by the Creator. Wonderful image of the judgments of God, Who marshals and combines in one, causes each unavailing in itself, but working together the full completion of His inscrutable Will.

There hath not been ever the like. The courses of sin and of punishment are ever recommencing anew in some part of the world and of the Church. The whole order of each, sin and punishment, will culminate once only, in the Day of Judgment. Then only will these words have their complete fulfillment. The Day of Judgment alone is that Day of terror and of woe, such as never has been before, and shall never be again. For there will be no new day or time of terror. Eternal punishment will only be the continuation of the sentence adjudged *then.* But, in time and in the course of

[1] Nieuhoff, China, p. 377.   [2] Shaw, p. 256.
[3] Morier, Second Journey, p. 98.
[4] Clarke, i. c. 18. p. 437.
[5] Volney, i. 277. "While I was at Sale in Morocco, after midday the sun was darkened, we knew not why, until we saw very many kinds of locusts, exceeding great." R. Anania of Fez, in Lud. Comm. p. 176. "The wagons passed directly through them, before which they rose up in a cloud which darkened the air on each side." Barrow, S. Afr. i.

242. "A. D. 1668, there were, in the whole country of Cyprus, such numbers of locusts, that when they flew, they were like a dark cloud, through which the rays of the sun could scarcely penetrate." Le Bruyn, Lev. c. 72. "The swarm had exactly the appearance of a vast snow-cloud hanging on the slope of a mountain from which the snow was falling in very large flakes." Lichtenstein, c. 46. "The air at a distance had the appearance of smoke." Forskäl, p. 8.   [6] See on ver. 6.

Before
CHRIST
cir. 800.

* ch. 1. 6.
ver. 5, 11, 25.
f Ex. 10. 14.

e a great people and a strong; f there hath not been ever the like, neither shall be any more after it,

even to the years † of many generations.

Before
CHRIST
cir. 800.

† Heb. *of gener-
ation and gen-
eration.*
g ch. 1. 19, 20.

3 g A fire devoureth before them; and behind

God's Providential government, the sins of each soul or people or Church draw down visitations, which are God's final judgments there. Such to the Jewish people, before the Captivity, was the destruction of the Temple, the taking of Jerusalem by Nebuchadnezzar, and that Captivity itself. The Jewish polity was never again restored as before. Such, to the new polity after the Captivity, was the destruction by the Romans. Eighteen hundred years have seen nothing like it. The Vandals and then the Mohammedans swept over the Churches of North Africa, each destructive in its own way. Twelve centuries have witnessed one unbroken desolation of the Church in Africa. In Constantinople, and Asia Minor, Palestine, Persia, Churches of the Redeemer became the mosques of the false prophet. Centuries have flowed by, *yet we see not our signs, neither is there any among us, that knoweth how long*[1]. Wealthy, busy, restless, intellectual, degraded, London, sender forth of missionaries, but, save in China, the largest heathen city in the world; converter of the isles of the sea, but thyself unconverted; fullest of riches and of misery, of civilization and of savage life, of refinements and debasement; heart, whose pulses are felt in every continent, but thyself diseased and feeble, wilt thou, in this thy day, anticipate by thy conversion the Day of the Lord, or will It come upon thee, *as hath never been the like, nor shall be, for the years of many generations?* Shalt thou win thy lost ones to Christ, or be thyself the birthplace or abode of Anti-Christ? *O Lord God, Thou knowest.*

Yet the words have fulfillments short of the end. Even of successive chastisements upon the same people, each may have some aggravation peculiar to itself, so that of each, in turn, it may be said, in *that* respect, that no former visitation had been like it, none afterwards should resemble it. Thus the Chaldæans were chief in fierceness, Antiochus Epiphanes in his madness against God, the Romans in the completeness of the desolation. The fourth beast which Daniel saw *was*[2] *dreadful and terrible and strong exceedingly, and it was diverse from all the beasts that were before it.* The persecutions of the Roman Emperors were in extent and cruelty far beyond any

before them. They shall be as nothing, in comparison to the deceivableness and oppression of Anti-Christ. The Prophet, however, does not say that there should be absolutely *none like it*, but only not *for the years of many generations.* The words *unto generation and generation* elsewhere mean *for ever;* here the word "years" may limit them to length of time. God, after some signal visitation, leaves a soul or a people to the silent workings of His grace or of His Providence. The marked interpositions of His Providence, are like His extraordinary miracles, rare; else, like the ordinary miracles of His daily operations, they would cease to be interpositions.

3. *A fire devoureth before them, &c.* Travelers, of different nations and characters, and in different lands, some unacquainted with the Bible words, have agreed to describe under this image the ravages of locusts. " [3] They scorch many things with their touch." " [4] Whatever of herb or leaf they gnaw, is, as it were, scorched by fire." " [5] Wherever they come, the ground seems burned, as it were with fire." " [6] Wherever they pass, they burn and spoil everything, and that irremediably." " [7] I have myself observed that the places where they had browsed were as scorched, as if the fire had passed there." " [8] They covered a square mile so completely, that it appeared, at a little distance, to have been burned and strewn over with brown ashes. Not a shrub, nor a blade of grass was visible." " [9] A few months afterwards, a much larger army alighted and gave the whole country the appearance of having been burned." "Wherever they settled, it looks as if fire had devoured and burnt up everything." " [10] It is better to have to do with the Tartars, than with these little destructive animals; you would think that fire follows their track," are the descriptions of their ravages in Italy, Æthiopia, the Levant, India, S. Africa. The locust, itself the image of God's judgments, is described as an enemy, invading, as they say, "with fire and sword," "breathing fire," wasting all, as he advances, and leaving behind him the blackness of ashes, and burning villages. " [11] Whatsoever he seizeth on, he shall consume as a devouring flame and shall leave nothing whole behind him."

[1] Ps. lxxiv. 9. [2] Dan. vii. 7–19. [3] Plin. xi. 35. [4] Lud. Hist. Æth. i. 13. [5] Alvarez, c. 32. [6] Villamont, Voyage, p. 226. [7] Le Bruyn, Lev. c. 72. [8] Barrow, S. Afr. i. 242. "According to all accounts,

wherever the swarms of locusts arrive, the vegetables are sometimes entirely consumed and destroyed, appearing as if they had been burnt up by fire." Sparrman, i. 367. [9] Forbes, ii. 274. [10] Volney, i. 177. [11] S. Jer.

Before CHRIST cir. 800.

b Gen. 2. 8. & 13.
10. Is. 51. 3.
i Zech. 7. 14.

them a flame burneth: the land *is* as [h] the garden of Eden before them, [i] and

behind them a desolate wilderness; yea, and nothing shall escape them.

Before CHRIST cir. 800.

The land is as the garden of Eden before them. In outward beauty the land was like that Paradise of God, where He placed our first parents; as were Sodom and Gomorrah, before God overthrew them [1]. It was like a garden enclosed and protected from all inroad of evil. They sinned, and like our first parents forfeited its bliss. *A fruitful land God maketh barren, for the wickedness of them that dwell therein* [2]. Ezekiel foretells the removal of the punishment, in connection with the Gospel-promise of [3] *a new heart and a new spirit. They shall say, This land that was desolate is become like the garden of Eden.*

And behind them a desolate wilderness. The desolation caused by the locust is even more inconceivable to us, than their numbers. We have seen fields blighted; we have known of crops, of most moment to man's support, devoured; and in one year we heard of terrific famine, as its result. We do not readily set before our eyes a whole tract, embracing in extent several of our counties, in which not the one or other crop was smitten, but every green thing was gone. Yet such was the scourge of locusts, the image of other and worse scourges in the treasure-house of God's displeasure. A Syrian writer relates [4], "A. D. 1004, a large swarm of locusts appeared in the land of Mosul and Bagdad, and it was very grievous in Shiraz. It left no herb nor even leaf on the trees, and even gnawed the pieces of linen which the fullers were bleaching; of each piece the fuller gave a scrap to its owner: and there was a famine, and a cor [about two quarters] of wheat was sold in Bagdad for 120 gold dinars, [about £54]:" and again [5], "when it [the locust of A. D. 784,] had consumed the whole tract of Edessa and Sarug, it passed to the W. and for three years after this heavy chastisement there was a famine in the land." "[6] We traveled five days through lands wholly despoiled; and for the canes of maize, as large as the largest canes used to prop vines, it cannot be said how they were broken and trampled, as if asses had trampled them; and all this from the locusts. The wheat, barley, tafos [7], were as if they had never been sown; the trees without a single leaf; the tender wood all eaten; there was no memory of herb of any sort. If we had not been advised to take mules laden with barley and

provisions for ourselves, we should have perished of hunger, we and our mules. This land was all covered with locusts without wings, and they said that they were the seed of those who had all gone, who had destroyed the land." "[8] Everywhere, where their legions march, verdure disappears from the country, like a curtain which is folded up; trees and plants stripped of leaves, and reduced to their branches and stalks, substitute, in the twinkling of an eye, the dreary spectacle of winter for the rich scenes of spring." "Happily this plague is not very often repeated; for there is none which brings so surely famine and the diseases which follow it." "[9] Desolation and famine mark their progress; all the expectations of the husbandman vanish; his fields, which the rising sun beheld covered with luxuriance, are before evening a desert; the produce of his garden and orchard are alike destroyed; for where these destructive swarms alight, not a leaf is left upon the trees, a blade of grass in the pastures, nor an ear of corn in the field." "[10] In 1654 a great multitude of locusts came from the N. W. to the Islands Tayyovvan and Formosa, which consumed all that grew in the fields, so that above eight thousand men perished by famine." "[11] They come sometimes in such prodigious swarms, that they darken the sky as they pass by and devour all in those parts where they settle, so that the inhabitants are often obliged to change their habitations for want of sustenance, as it has happened frequently in China and the Isle of Tajowak." "[12] The lands, ravaged throughout the West, produced no harvest. The year 1780 was still more wretched. A dry winter produced a new race of locusts which ravaged what had escaped the inclemency of the season. The husbandman reaped not what he had sown, and was reduced to have neither nourishment, seed, nor cattle. The people experienced all the horrors of famine. You might see them wandering over the country to devour the roots; and, seeking in the bowels of the earth for means to lengthen their days, perhaps they rather abridged them. A countless number died of misery and bad nourishment. I have seen countrymen on the roads and in the streets dead of starvation, whom others were laying across asses, to

1 Gen. xiii. 10.   2 Ps. cvii. 34.
3 Ezek. xxxvi. 26, 35.
4 Barhebr. Chron. Syr. p. 214.   5 Ib. p. 134.
6 Alvarez, c. 33.
7 One of the best Æthiopian grains.

8 Volney, i. 277.
9 Forbes, c. 22. ii. 273.
10 Nieuhoff, 2d. Emb. to China, p. 29.
11 Nieuhoff, Voyage in Churchill, ii. 359.
12 Chénier, iii. 496–8.

Before
CHRIST
cir. 800.

k Rev. 9. 7.

4 k The appearance of them *is* as the appearance of horses; and as horsemen, so shall they run.

5 ¹ Like the noise of chariots on the tops of mountains shall they leap, like the noise of a flame

Before
CHRIST
cir. 800.

1 Rev. 9. 9.

go bury them. Fathers sold their children. A husband, in concert with his wife, went to marry her in some other province as if she were his sister, and went to redeem her, when better off. I have seen women and children run after the camels, seek in their dung for some grain of indigested barley and devour it with avidity."

Yea, and nothing shall escape them; or (which the words also include) *none shall escape him,* lit. *and also there shall be no escaping as to him* or *from him.* The word ¹, being used elsewhere of the *persons* who escape, suggests, in itself, that we should not linger by the type of the locusts only, but think of enemies more terrible, who destroy not harvests only, but men, bodies or souls also. Yet the picture of devastation is complete. No creature of God so destroys the whole face of nature, as does the locust. A traveler in the Crimea uses unconsciously the words of the Prophet ²; "On whatever spot they fall, the whole vegetable produce disappears. Nothing escapes them, from the leaves of the forest to the herbs on the plain. Fields, vineyards, gardens, pastures, everything is laid waste; and sometimes the only appearance left is a disgusting superficies caused by their putrefying bodies, the stench of which is sufficient to breed a pestilence." Another in S. Africa says ³, "When they make their appearance, not a single field of corn remains unconsumed by them. This year the whole of the Sneuwberg will not, I suppose, produce a single bushel." "⁴They had [for a space 80 or 90 miles in length] devoured every green herb and every blade of grass; and had it not been for the reeds on which our cattle entirely subsisted while we skirted the banks of the river, the journey must have been discontinued, at least in the line that had been proposed." "⁵ Not a shrub nor blade of grass was visible." The rapidity with which they complete the destruction is also observed ⁶. "In two hours, they destroyed all the herbs around Rama."

All this which is a strong, but true, image of the locusts is a shadow of God's other judgments. It is often said of God ⁷, *A fire goeth before Him and burneth up His enemies on every side.* ⁸ *The Lord will come with fire; by fire will the Lord plead with all flesh.* This is

said of the Judgment-day, as in S. Paul ⁹, *The Lord Jesus shall be revealed from heaven with His mighty angels, in flaming fire taking vengeance on them that know not God, and that obey not the Gospel of our Lord Jesus Christ.* That awful lurid stream of fire shall burn up *the earth and all the works that are therein* ¹⁰. All this whole circuit of the globe shall be enveloped in one burning deluge of fire; all gold and jewels, gardens, fields, pictures, books; "the cloud-capt towers and gorgeous palaces, shall dissolve, and leave not a rack behind." The good shall be removed beyond its reach; for they shall be *caught up to meet the Lord in the air* ¹¹. But all which is in the earth and those who are of the earth shall be swept away by it. It shall go before the army of the Lord, the Angels whom ¹² *the Son of man shall send forth, to gather out of His kingdom all things that shall offend and them that do iniquity.* It *shall burn after them.* For it shall burn on during the Day of Judgment until it have consumed all for which it is sent. *The land will be a garden of Eden before it.* For they will, our Lord says, be eating, drinking, buying, selling, planting, building, marrying and giving in marriage ¹³; the world will be *glorifying itself and living deliciously,* full of riches and delights, when it *shall be utterly burned with fire,* and *in one hour so great riches shall come to nought* ¹⁴. *And after it a desolate wilderness,* for there shall be none left. *And none shall escape.* For our Lord says ¹⁵, *they shall gather all things that offend; the angels shall come forth and sever the wicked from among the just, and shall cast them into the furnace of fire.*

4. *The appearance of them* is *as the appearance of horses.* "If you carefully consider the head of the locust," says Theodoret, a Bishop in Syria, "you will find it exceedingly like that of a horse." Whence the Arabs, of old ¹⁶ and to this day ¹⁷, say; "In the locust, slight as it is, the nature of ten of the larger animals, the face of a horse, the eyes of an elephant, the neck of a bull, the horns of a deer, the chest of a lion, the belly of a scorpion, the wings of an eagle, the thighs of a camel, the feet of an ostrich, the tail of a serpent."

5. *Like the noise of chariots on the tops of the mountains shall they leap.* The amazing noise

¹ פליטה as "captivity" for "captives."
² Clarke, i. 428, 9.   ³ Barrow, i. 248, 9.   ⁴ Ib. 257.
⁵ Ib. 242.   ⁶ Le Bruyn, c. 46.   ⁷ Ps. xcvii. 3.
⁸ Is. lxvi. 15, 16.   ⁹ 2 Thess. i. 7, 8.
¹⁰ 2 Pet. iii. 10.   ¹¹ 1 Thess. iv. 17 .
¹² S. Matt. xiii. 41.   ¹³ S. Luke xvii. 27, 8, 30.

¹⁴ Rev. xviii. 7, 8, 17.   ¹⁵ S. Matt. xiii. 41, 49, 50.
¹⁶ Demiri in Bochart, ii. iv. 4.
¹⁷ The Arabs remarked to Niebuhr, the likeness to the horse, the lion, the camel, the serpent, the scorpion; and foremost that of the head to the horse's. Descr. de l' Arabie, p. 153.

Before CHRIST cir. 800.

m ver. 2.

of fire that devoureth the stubble, ^m as a strong people set in battle array.

Before CHRIST cir. 800.
n Jer. 8. 21.
Lam. 4. 8.
Nah. 2. 10.
† Heb. *pot.*

6 Before their face the people shall be much pained: ⁿ all faces shall gather † blackness.

---

of the flight of locusts is likened by those who have heard them, to all sorts of deep sharp rushing sounds. One says[1], "their noise may be heard six miles off." Others, "[2] within a hundred paces I heard the rushing noise occasioned by the flight of so many millions of insects. When I was in the midst of them, it was as loud as the dashing of the waters occasioned by the mill-wheel." "[3] While passing over our heads, their sound was as of a great cataract." "[4] We heard a noise as of the rushing of a great wind at a distance." "[5] In flying they make a rushing rustling noise, as when a strong wind blows through trees." "[6] They cause a noise, like the rushing of a torrent." To add another vivid description[7], "When a swarm is advancing, it seems as though brown clouds were rising from the horizon, which, as they approach, spread more and more. They cast a veil over the sun and a shadow on the earth. Soon you see little dots, and observe a whizzing and life. Nearer yet, and the sun is darkened; you hear a roaring and rushing like gushing water. On a sudden you find yourself surrounded with locusts."

Like the noise of a flame of fire that devoureth the stubble. The sharp noise caused by these myriads of insects, while feeding, has also been noticed. "[8] You hear afar the noise which they make in browsing on the herbs and trees, as of an army which is foraging without restraint." "[9] When they alight upon the ground to feed, the plains are all covered, and they make a murmuring noise as they eat, when in two hours they devour all close to the ground." "[10] The noise which they make in devouring, ever announces their approach at some distance." "[11] They say, that not without a noise is their descent on the fields effected, and that there is a certain sharp sound, as they chew the corn, as when the wind strongly fanneth a flame."

Their noise, Joel says, is *like the noise of chariots.* Whence St. John says [12], *the sound of their wings was as the sound of many horses rushing to battle.* Their sound should be like

the sound of war-chariots, bounding in their speed; but their inroad should be, where chariots could not go and man's foot could rarely reach, *on the tops of the mountains* [13]. A mountain range is, next to the sea, the strongest natural protection. Mountains have been a limit to the mightiest powers. The Caucasus of old held in the Persian power; on the one side, all was enslaved; on the other, all was fearlessly free [14]. Of late it enabled a few mountaineers to hold at bay the power of Russia. The pass of Thermopylæ, until betrayed, enabled a handful of men to check the invasion of nearly two millions. The mountain-ridges of Spain were, from times before our Lord, the last home and rallying-place of the conquered or the birth-place of deliverance [15]. God had assigned to His people a spot, central hereafter for the conversion of the world, yet where, meantime, they lay enveloped and sheltered *amid the mountains* which *His Right-Hand purchased* [16]. The Syrians owned that *their God was the God of the hills* [17]; and the people confessed [18], *as the hills are round about Jerusalem, so the Lord is round about His people.* Their protection was a symbol of His. But His protection withdrawn, nothing should be a hindrance to those whom He should send as a scourge. The Prophet combines purposely things incompatible, the terrible heavy bounding of the scythed chariot, and the light speed with which these countless hosts should in their flight bound over the tops of the mountains, where God had made no path for man. Countless in number, boundless in might, are the instruments of God. The strongest national defences give no security. Where then is safety, save in fleeing from God displeased to God appeased?

6. *Before their face the people shall be much pained.* The locust being such a scourge of God, good reason have men to be terrified at their approach; and those are most terrified who have most felt the affliction. In Abyssinia, some province of which was desolated every year, one relates [19], "When the locusts travel, the people know of it a day before, not

---

[1] Remigius, ad loc. "as they relate," he adds, "into whose country they have been often wont to come."
[2] Lichtenstein, c. 46. [3] Forskål, p. 81.
[4] Morier, 2d Journey, p. 98.
[5] Nieuhoff, 2d. Emb. p. 29.
[6] Forbes, ii. 273.
[7] Schlatter. Pliny says (probably of some smaller sort which reached Italy,) "they fly with such clashing of wings, that they are believed to be other large winged creatures." xi. 35.

[8] Volney, i. 177. [9] Beauplan, i. 599.
[10] Chénier, iii. 82. [11] S. Cyr. [12] Rev. ix. 9.
[13] It should be read, *Like the noise of chariots, on* or *over the tops of mountains shall they leap.*
[14] Herod. iii. 97.
[15] See Alison's Hist. of Europe, c. 53. beg.
[16] Ps. lxxviii. 54. [17] 1 Kings xx. 23.
[18] Ps. cxxv. 2.
[19] Fr. Alvarez, c. 32. "In this part and in the whole seignory of Prester John, there is a very great plague of locusts, which destroy every fresh

7 They shall run like mighty men; they shall

climb the wall like men of war; and they shall march

because they see them, but they see the sun yellow and the ground yellow, through the shadow which they cast on it(their wings being yellow) and forthwith the people become as dead, saying, 'we are lost, for the Ambadas (so they call them) are coming.' I will say what I have seen three times; the first was at Barva. During three years that we were in this land, we often heard them say, 'such a realm, such a land, is destroyed by locusts:' and when it was so, we saw this sign, the sun was yellow, and the shadow on the earth the same, and the whole people became as dead." "The Captain of the place called Coiberia came to me with men, Clerks, and Brothers [Monks] to ask me, for the love God, to help them, that they were all lost through the locusts." "[1] There were men, women, children, sitting among these locusts, [the young brood] as stupefied. I said to them 'why do you stay there, dying? Why do you not kill these animals, and avenge you of the evil which their parents have done you? and at least when dead, they will do you no more evil.' They answered, that they had no courage to resist a plague which God gave them for their sins. We found the roads full of men, women, and children, (some of these on foot, some in arms) their bundles of clothes on their heads, removing to some land where they might find provisions. It was pitiful to see them." Burkhardt relates of S. Arabia, "[2] The Bedouins who occupy the peninsula of Sinai are frequently driven to despair by the multitudes of locusts, which constitute a land-plague. They remain there generally for forty or fifty days, and then disappear for the rest of the year." Pliny describes their approach, "[3] they overshadow the sun, the nations looking up with anxiety, lest they should cover their lands. For their strength suffices, and as if it were too little to have passed seas, they traverse immense tracts, and overspread them with a cloud, fatal to the harvest."

All faces shall gather blackness. Others, of high-authority, have rendered, shall *withdraw* [their] *beauty* [4]. But the word signifies to *collect together*, in order that what is so collected should be present, not absent [5]; and so is very different from another saying, *the stars shall withdraw their shining* [6]. He expresses

how the faces contract a livid color from anxiety and fear, as Jeremiah says of the Nazarites [7], *Their visage is darker than blackness.* "[8] The faces are clothed with lurid hue of coming death; hence they not only grow pale, but are blackened." A slight fear drives the fresh hue from the cheek: the livid hue comes only with the deepest terror. So Isaiah says [9]; *they look amazed one to the other; faces of flame are their faces.*

7. *They shall run like mighty men.* They are on God's message, and they linger not, *but rejoice to run their course* [10]. "The height of walls cannot hinder the charge of the mighty; they enter not by the gates but over the walls [11]," as of a city taken by assault. Men can mount a wall few at a time; the locusts scale much more steadily, more compactly, more determinately, and irresistibly. The picture unites the countless multitude, condensed march, and entire security of the locust with the might of warriors.

They shall march every one on his ways. There is something awful and majestic in the well-ordered flight of the winged locusts, or their march while yet unwinged. "This," says S. Jerome, "we have seen lately in this province [Palestine]. For when the hosts of locusts came, and filled the air between heaven and earth, they flew, by the disposal of God ordaining, in such order, as to hold each his place, like the minute pieces of mosaic, fixed in the pavement by the artist's hands, so as not to incline to one another a hair's breadth." "You may see the locust," says Theodoret, "like enemies, both mounting the walls, and marching on the roads, and not allowing itself to be dispersed by any violence, but making the assault by a sort of concert." "It is said," says S. Cyril, "that they go in rank, and fly as in array, and are not severed from each other, but attend one on the other, like sisters, nature infusing into them this mutual love." "[12] They seemed to be impelled by one common instinct, and moved in one body, which had the appearance of being organized by a leader." "[13] There is something frightful in the appearance of these locusts proceeding in divisions, some of which are a league in length and 200 paces in breadth." "[14] They continued their journey, as if a signal had been actually given

green thing most grievously. Their multitude is past belief, they cover the ground and fill the air; they take away the brightness from the sun. I say again, it would not be a thing to be believed, if one had not seen it. They are not general in all the realms every year; for if they were, the land would be desert, according to the destruction which they make; but in one year they are in one part; in another year, in another;—sometimes in 2 or 3 parts of these provinces."

[1] Ib. c. 33.   [2] Burckhardt, Notes, ii. 91.
[3] N. H. xi. 35.
[4] Abulwalid, Aben Ezra, see Poc.
[5] Jos. Kimchi, Ib.
[6] אסף (ii. 10, iii. 15.) The *their* had also needed to be expressed.
[7] Lam. iv. 8. see Margin.   [8] Oros.
[9] xiii. 8.   [10] Ps. xix. 5.   [11] S. Jer.
[12] Morier, p. 98.   [13] Constitutionnel, 1841.
[14] Philos. Trans. xlvi. 9. p. 31.

every one on his ways, and they shall not break their ranks :

8 Neither shall one thrust another; they shall walk every one in his path:

them to march." So, of the young brood it is related; "¹ In June, their young broods begin gradually to make their appearance; no sooner were any of them hatched than they immediately collected themselves together, each of them forming a compact body of several hundred yards square, which, marching afterward directly forward, climbed over trees, walls and houses, ate up every plant in their way, *and let nothing escape them.*' "² They seemed to march in regular battalions, crawling over everything that lay in their passage, in one straight front." So the judgments of God hold on their course, each going straight to that person for whom God in the awful wisdom of His justice ordains it. No one judgment or chastisement comes by chance. Each is directed and adapted, weighed and measured, by Infinite Wisdom, and reaches just that soul, for which God appointed it, and no other, and strikes upon it with just that force which God ordains it. As we look on, God's judgments are like a heavy sleet of arrows; yet as each arrow, shot truly, found the mark at which it was aimed, so, and much more, does each lesser or greater judgment, sent by God, reach the heart for which He sends it and pierces it just as deeply as He wills.

8. When *they fall upon the sword* [lit. *among the darts*] *they shall not be wounded.* It may be that the Prophet would describe how the locust seems armed as in a suit of armor. As one says, "³ Their form was wondrous; they had a sort of gorget round their neck like a lancer, and a helm on their head, such as soldiers wear." But, more, he exhibits their indomitableness and impenetrableness, how nothing checks, nothing retards, nothing makes any impression upon them. "⁴ They do not suffer themselves to be impeded by any obstacles, but fly boldly on, and are drowned in the sea when they come to it." "⁵ When on a march during the day, it is utterly impossible to turn the direction of a troop, which is generally with the wind." "⁶ The guard of the Red Town attempted to stop their irruption into Transylvania by firing at them; and indeed when the balls

and shot swept through the swarm, they gave way and divided; but having filled up their ranks in a moment, they proceeded on their journey." And in like way of the young swarms; "⁷ The inhabitants, to stop their progress, made trenches all over their fields and gardens and filled them with water; or else, placing in a row great quantities of heath, stubble, and such like combustible matter, they set them on fire on the approach of the locusts. But all this was to no purpose, for the trenches were quickly filled up, and the fires put out by infinite swarms, succeeding one another; whilst the front seemed regardless of danger, and the van pressed on so close, that a retreat was impossible." "⁸ Like waves, they roll over one another on and on, and let themselves be stopped by nothing. Russians and Germans try many means with more or less success against them, when they come from the waste against the cornlands. Bundles of straw are laid in rows and set on fire before them; they march in thick heaps into the fire, but this is often put out thro' the great mass of the animals and those advancing from behind march away over the corpses of their companions, and continue the march." "⁹ Their number was astounding; the whole face of the mountain was black with them. On they came like a living deluge. We dug trenches, and kindled fires, and beat and burned to death heaps upon heaps, but the effort was utterly useless. Wave after wave rolled up the mountain side, and poured over rocks, walls, ditches and hedges, those behind covering up and bridging over the masses already killed. After a long and fatiguing contest, I descended the mountain to examine the *depth* of the column, but I could not see to the end of it." " It was perfectly appalling to watch this animated river, as it flowed *up* the road and ascended the hill." " Both in ancient and modern times, armies have been marched against them ¹⁰; but in vain, unless they destroyed them, before they were full-grown.

Since the very smallest of God's judgments are thus irreversible, since creatures so small

¹ Shaw, p. 237.
² Morier, p. 100.
³ Nieuhoff, 2d. Emb. p. 29.
⁴ Sparrman, Cape of G. Hope, i. 366.
⁵ Barrow. p. 258.   ⁶ Phil. Trans.
⁷ Shaw, l. c. p. 257.   ⁸ Schlatter.
⁹ Thomson, The Land and the Book, ii. 103.
¹⁰ " The inhabitants of Asia, as well as Europe, sometimes take the field against locusts with all the dreadful apparatus of war. The Bashaw of Tripoli in Syria, some years ago, raised 4000 soldiers against these insects, and ordered those to be hanged

who refused to go." Hasselq. p. 447. " In Cyrenaica, there is a law to wage war with them thrice in the year; first crushing the eggs, then the young, then when full grown; whoso neglects this, lies under the penalty of a deserter. At Lemnos too a certain measure is filled, which each is to bring of these creatures killed, to the magistrates. In Syria too, they are compelled, under military command, to kill them." Plin. xi. 35. " The marches cannot be stopped; only quite early, during the dew, when the locust can neither fly nor hop, they must be killed in masses." Ersch, 34.

Before
CHRIST
cir. 800.

| Or, *dart.*

and *when* they fall upon the ‖ sword, they shall not be wounded.

9 They shall run to and fro in the city; they shall

run upon the wall, they shall climb up upon the houses; they shall º enter in at the windows ᴾ like a thief.

Before
CHRIST
cir. 800.

º Jer. 9. 21.

ᴾ John 10. 1.

cannot be turned aside, since we cannot turn away the face of one of the least of our Master's servants, since they are each as a *man of might*[1] (so he calls them, it is the force of the word rendered *each*) what of the greater? what of the whole?

9. *They shall run to and fro in the city.* "*The* city" is questionless Jerusalem. So to the Romans, "the city" meant Rome; to the Athenians, Athens; among ourselves, "town" or "the city" are idiomatic names for the whole of London or "the city of London." In Wales "town" is, with the country-people, the neighboring town with which alone they are familiar. There is no ambiguity in the living language. In Guernsey, one who should call Port St. Pierre by any other name than "the town," would betray himself to be a stranger. In Hosea, and Amos, prophets for Israel, *the city* is Samaria[2]. In Solomon[3] and the prophets of Judah[4], *the city* is Jerusalem; and that the more, because it was not only the capital, but the centre of the worship of the One True God. Hence it is called *the city of God*[5], *the city of the Lord*[6], then *the city of the Great King*[7], *the holy city*[8]; and God calls it *the city I have chosen out of all the tribes of Israel*[9], *the city of righteousness*[10]. So our Lord spake[11], *go ye into the city*, and perhaps,[12] *tarry ye in the city*. So do His Evangelists[13], and so does Josephus[14].

All around corresponds with this. Joel had described their approach; they had come over "the tops of *the* mountains," those which protected Jerusalem; and now he describes them scaling "*the* wall," "mounting *the* houses," "entering *the* windows," "running to and fro in *the* city." Here the description has reached its height. The city is given over to those who assault it. There remaineth nothing more, save the shaking of the heaven and the earth.

They shall enter in at the windows. So in that first great judgment, in which God employed the locust, He said, [15] *They shall cover the face of the earth, that one cannot be able*

to see *the earth ; and they shall fill thy houses, and the houses of all thy servants, and the houses of all the Egyptians.* "[16] For nothing denies a way to the locusts, inasmuch as they penetrate fields, cornlands, trees, cities, houses, yea, the retirement of the bed-chambers." "Not that they who are victors, have the fear which thieves have, but as thieves are wont to enter through windows, and plunder secretly, so shall these, if the doors be closed, to cut short delay, burst with all boldness through the windows." "[17] We have seen this done, not by enemies only, but often by locusts also. For not only flying, but creeping up the walls also, they enter the houses through the openings for light." "[18] A.D. 784, there came the flying locust, and wasted the corn and left its offspring; and this came forth and crawled, and scaled walls and entered houses by windows and doors; and if it entered the house on the S. side, it went out on the N.; together with herbs and trees it devoured also woolen clothing, and men's dresses." Modern travelers relate the same. "[19] They entered the inmost recesses of the houses, were found in every corner, stuck to our clothes and infested our food." "[20] They overwhelm the province of Nedjd sometimes to such a degree, that having destroyed the harvest, they penetrate by thousands into the private dwellings, and devour whatsoever they can find, even the leather of the water-vessels." "[21] In June 1646, at Novogorod it was prodigious to behold them, because they were hatched there that spring, and being as yet scarce able to fly, the ground was all covered, and the air so full of them, that I could not eat in my chamber without a candle, all the houses being full of them, even the stables, barns, chambers, garrets, and cellars. I caused cannon-powder and sulphur to be burnt, to expel them, but all to no purpose. For when the door was opened, an infinite number came in, and the others went fluttering about; and it was a troublesome thing when a man went abroad, to be hit on the face by

[1] נבר.   [2] Hos. xi. 9. Am. iii. 6.
[3] Ps. lxxii. 16. Prov. i. 21. viii. 3.
[4] Mic. vi. 9. Lam. i. 1, &c. Ezek. vii. 23. xxxiii. 21.
[5] Ps. xlvi. 4. xlviii. 1, 8. lxxxvii. 3.
[6] Ps. ci. 8. Is. lx. 14.   [7] Ps. xlviii. 2. S. Matt. v. 35.
[8] Is. xlviii. 2. lii. 1. Neh. xi. 1, 18. Dan. ix. 24.
[9] 1 Kings xi. 32.   [10] Is. i. 26.
[11] S. Matt. xxvi. 18. S. Mark xiv. 13. S. Luke xxii. 10.
[12] S. Luke xxiv. 49. Important MSS. omit "Jerusalem."

[13] S. Matt. xxi. 17, 18. xxviii. 11. S. Mark xi. 1, 19. S. Luke xix. 41. Acts vii. 58. S. John xix. 20.
[14] Ant. x. 31, no mention of Jerusalem having immediately preceded. He calls Manasseh's mother πολίτις, "a citizen," i. e. of Jerusalem.
[15] Ex. x. 5, 6.
[16] S. Jerome, ad loc.
[17] Theod. ad loc.   [18] Barh. Chron. Syr. p. 134.
[19] Morier, p. 100.
[20] Burckhardt, Notes, ii. 90.
[21] Beauplan, p. 599.

Before
CHRIST
cir. 800.

q Ps. 18. 7.
r Is. 13. 10.
Ezek. 32. 7.
ver. 31.
ch. 3. 15. Matt. 24. 29.

10 q The earth shall quake before them; the heavens shall tremble: r the sun and the moon

shall be dark, and the stars shall withdraw their shining:

11 s And the Lord shall

Before
CHRIST
cir. 800.

s Jer. 25. 30.
ch. 3. 16.
Amos 1 2.

those creatures, on the nose, eyes, or cheeks, so that there was no opening one's mouth, but some would get in. Yet all this was nothing ; for when we were to eat, they gave us no respite ; and when we went to cut a piece of meat, we cut a locust with it, and when a man opened his mouth to put in a morsel, he was sure to chew one of them." The Eastern windows, not being glazed but having at most a lattice-work[1], presented no obstacle to this continuous inroad. All was one stream of infesting, harassing foes.

As the windows are to the house, so are the senses and especially the sight to the soul. As the strongest walls and battlements and towers avail not to keep out an enemy, if there be an opening or chink through which he can make his way, so, in vain is the protection of God's Providence or His Grace[2], if the soul leaves the senses unguarded to admit unchallenged sights, sounds, touches, which may take the soul prisoner. "[3] Death, says Jeremiah[4], entereth through the window. Thy window is thy eye. If thou seest, to lust, death hath entered in ; if thou hearest enticing words, death hath entered in : if softness gain possession of thy senses, death has made his way in." The arrow of sin is shot through them. "[5] When the tongue of one introduces the virus of perdition, and the ears of others gladly drink it in, death enters in ; while with itching ears and mouth men minister eagerly to one another the deadly draught of detraction, death enters in at the windows." "[6] Eve had not touched the forbidden tree, except she had first looked on it heedlessly. With what control must we in this dying life restrain our sight, when the mother of the living came to death through the eyes ! The mind of the Prophet, which had been often lifted up to see hidden mysteries, seeing heedlessly another's wife, was darkened," and fell. "To keep purity of heart, thou must guard the outward senses." An enemy is easily kept out by the barred door or window, who, having entered in unawares, can only by strong effort and grace be forced out. "It is easier," said the heathen philosopher[7], "to forbid the beginnings of feelings than to control their might."

Like a thief, i. e. they should come unawares, so as to take men by surprise, that there should be no guarding against them. As this is the close of this wonderful description, it may be that he would, in the end, describe the suddenness and inevitableness of God's judgments when they do come, and of the final judgment. It is remarkable that our Lord, and His Apostles from Him adopt this image of the Prophet, in speaking of the coming of the Day of Judgment and His own. *Behold I come as a thief. This know, that if the goodman of the house had known what hour the thief would come, he would have watched. Be ye therefore ready also ; for the Son of man cometh at an hour when ye think not. Yourselves know perfectly that the Day of the Lord so cometh as a thief in the night. Ye are not in darkness, that that Day should overtake you as a thief*[8].

10. *The earth shall quake before them.* "Not," says S. Jerome, "as though locusts or enemies had power to move the heavens or to shake the earth ; but because, to those under trouble, for their exceeding terror, the heaven seems to fall and the earth to reel. But indeed, for the multitude of the locusts which cover the heavens, sun and moon shall be turned into darkness, and the stars shall withdraw their shining, while the cloud of locusts interrupts the light, and allows it not to reach the earth." Yet the mention of moon and stars rather suggests that something more is meant than the locusts, who, not flying by night except when they cross the sea, do not obscure either. Rather, as the next verse speaks of God's immediate, sensible, Presence, this verse seems to pass from the image of the locusts to the full reality, and to say that heaven and earth should shake at the judgments of God, before He appeareth. Our Lord gives the same description of the forerunners of the Day of Judgment[9] ; *there shall be signs in the sun and in the moon and in the stars ; and upon the earth distress of nations with perplexity ; the sea and the waves roaring, men's hearts failing them for fear and for looking after those things which are coming on the earth ; for the powers of heaven shall be shaken.*

11. *And the Lord shall utter His voice.* The Prophet had described at length the coming

[1] S. Jerome, in Ezek. xli. 16. אַרְבֶּה and הרכים are both derived from "twisting" and so reticulating.
[2] from Lap. on Jer.   [3] S. Ambr. de fug Sæc. § 3
[4] ix. 21.   [5] S. Bern. in Cant. S. 24.

[6] from S. Greg. on Job L. xxi. § 4.
[7] Senec. Ep. 96. L.
[8] Rev. xvi. 15. (add iii. 3.) S. Matt. xxiv. 43, 44. S. Luke xii. 39. 1 Thess. v. 2. 2 Pet. iii. 10.
[9] S. Luke xxi. 25, 6.

Before
CHRIST
cir. 800.

t ver. 25.
u Jer. 50. 34.
Rev. 18. 8.

utter his voice before [t] his army : for his camp is very great : [u] for he is strong that executeth his word :

for the [x] day of the LORD is great and very terrible; and [y] who can abide it?

Before
CHRIST
cir. 800.

x Jer. 30. 7.
Amos 5. 18.
Zeph. 1. 15.
y Num. 24. 23.
Mal. 3. 2.

of God's judgments, as a mighty army. But lest amid the judgments, men should, (as they often do) forget the Judge, he represents God, as commanding this His army, gathering, ordering, marshalling, directing them, giving them the word, when and upon whom they should pour themselves. Their presence was a token of His. They should neither anticipate that command, nor linger. But as an army awaits the command to move, and then, the word being given, rolls on instantly, so God's judgments await the precise moment of His Will, and then fall. The voice of the Lord is elsewhere used for the thunder; because in it He seems to speak in majesty and terror to the guilty soul. But here the voice refers, not to us, but to the army, which He is imaged as marshalling; as Isaiah, referring perhaps to this place, says The Lord of hosts mustereth the host of the battle [1]. God had spoken, and His people had not obeyed; now He speaks not to them any more, but to their enemies. He calls the Medes and Persians, My sanctified ones, My mighty ones [2], when they were to exercise His judgments on Babylon ; and our Lord calls the Romans His armies. He sent forth His armies and destroyed those murderers and burned up their city [3]. Then follow as threefold ground of terror. For His camp is very great. All the instruments wherewith God punishes sin, are pictured as His one camp, each going, as He commands, Who bringeth forth the host of heaven by number : He calleth them all by names, by the greatness of His might, for that He is strong in power; not one faileth [4]. For he is strong, that executeth His word, or, for it (His camp) is strong, executing His word. Weak though His instruments be in themselves, they are mighty when they do His commands, for He empowers them, as S. Paul saith, I can do all things through Christ instrengthening me [5]. For the Day of the Lord is great, great, on account of the great things done in it. As those are called evil days, an evil time, in which evil comes ; as it is called an acceptable time ; in which we may be accepted ; so the Day of God's judgment is great and very terrible, on account of the great and terrible acts of His justice done in it. Who can abide it ? The answer is implied in the question. "No one, unless God enable him."

This is the close of the threatened woe. The close, so much beyond any passing

scourge of any created destroyer, locusts or armies, suggests the more what has been said already, that the Prophet is speaking of the whole aggregate of God's judgments unto the Day of Judgment.

"[6] The Lord saith, that He will send an Angel with the sound of a trumpet, and the Apostle declares that the resurrection of the dead shall take place amid the sound of a trumpet. In the Revelation of John too, we read that the seven Angels received seven trumpets, and as they sounded in order, that was done which Scripture describes. The priests and teachers accordingly are here bidden to lift up their voice like a trumpet in Zion, that is, the Church, that so all the inhabitants of the earth may be troubled or confounded, and this confusion may draw them to Salvation. By the Day of the Lord, understand the Day of judgment, or the day when each departeth out of the body. For what will be to all in the Day of judgment, this is fulfilled in each in the day of death. It is a day of darkness and gloominess, a day of clouds and of thick darkness, because everything will be full of punishment and torment. The great and strong people of the angels will come, to render to each according to his works; and as the rising morn first seizes the mountains, so judgment shall begin with the great and mighty, so that mighty men shall be mightily tormented [7]. There hath not been ever the like, neither shall be any more after it. For all evils, contained in ancient histories and which have happened to men, by inundation of the sea, or overflow of rivers, or by pestilence, disease, famine, wild beasts, ravages of enemies, cannot be compared to the Day of judgment. A fire devoureth, or consumeth before this people, to consume in us hay, wood, stubble. Whence it is said of God [8], thy God is a consuming fire. And after him a flame burneth, so as to leave nothing unpunished. Whomsoever this people toucheth not, nor findeth in him what is to be burned, shall be likened to the garden of God, and the paradise of pleasure, i. e. of Eden. If it burn any, it will reduce this (as it were) wilderness to dust and ashes, nor can any escape its fury. For they shall run to and fro to torture those over whom they shall receive power, like horsemen flying hither and thither. Their sound shall be terrible, as chariots hurrying along level places, and

1 Is. xiii. 4.   2 Ib. 3.
3 S. Matt. xxii. 7.   4 Is. xl. 26.

5 Phil. iv. 13.   6 S. Jer.
7 Wisd. vi. 6.   8 Deut. iv. 24.

Before CHRIST cir. 800.

ᵃ Jer. 4. 1.
Hos. 12. 6.
& 14. 1.

12 ¶ Therefore also now, saith the LORD, ᵃ turn ye *even* to me with all your heart, and with fasting, and with weeping, and with mourning :

Before CHRIST cir. 800.

upon the tops of the mountains they *shall leap, longing to torment all who are lofty and set on high in the Church. And since before them there is a devouring fire,* they will destroy everything, *as the fire devoureth the stubble.* They shall come to punish, *as a strong people in battle array.* Such will be the fear, of all, such the conscience of sinners, that none shall shine or have any brightness of joy, but his face shall be turned into darkness. They shall not turn aside, in fulfilling the office enjoined them, but each shall carry on the punishments on sinners entrusted to him.— At the presence of that people, *the earth shall quake* and *the heavens tremble.* For *heaven and earth shall pass away, but the word of the Lord shall endure for ever.* The sun and moon also shall not endure to see the punishments of the miserable, and shall remove and, for bright light, shall be shrouded in terrible darkness. *The stars also shall withdraw their shining,* in that the holy also shall not without fear behold the presence of the Lord. Amid all this, *The Lord shall utter His voice before His army.* For as the Babylonians, in punishing Jerusalem, are called the army of God, so the evil angels (of whom it is written [1], *He cast upon them the fierceness of His anger, wrath, and indignation, and trouble, by sending evil angels among them*) are called the army of God and His camp, in that they do the Will of God."

The Day of the Lord, is great and terrible, of which it is written elsewhere [2], *to what end do ye desire the Day of the Lord? it is darkness and not light and very terrible,* and few or none *can abide it,* but will furnish some ground of severity against himself.

12. *Therefore* [*And*] *now also.* All this being so, one way of escape there is, true repentance. As if God said [3], "All this I have therefore spoken, in order to terrify you by My threats. Wherefore *turn unto Me with all your hearts,* and shew the penitence of your minds *by fasting and weeping and mourning,* that, fasting now, ye may *be filled* hereafter ; *weeping now,* ye may *laugh* hereafter ; *mourning now,* ye may hereafter be *comforted* [4]. And since it is your wont to *rend your garments* in sorrow, I command you to rend, not them but your hearts which are full of sin, which, like bladders, unless they be opened, will burst of themselves. And when ye have done this, return unto the Lord your God, whom your former sins alienated from you ;

and despair not of pardon for the greatness of your guilt, for mighty mercy will blot out mighty sins."

" [5] The strict Judge cannot be overcome, for He is Omnipotent; cannot be deceived, for He is Wisdom ; cannot be corrupted, for He is Justice; cannot be sustained, for He is Eternal ; cannot be avoided, for He is everywhere. Yet He can be entreated, because He is Mercy ; He can be appeased, because He is Goodness; He can cleanse, because He is the Fountain of grace; He can satisfy, because He is the Bread of life ; He can soothe, because He is the Unction from above; He can beautify, because He is Fullness; He can beatify because He is Bliss. Turned from Him, then, and fearing His Justice, turn ye to Him, and flee to His Mercy. Flee from Himself to Himself, from the rigor of Justice to the Bosom of Mercy. The Lord Who is to be feared saith it. He Who is Truth enjoins what is just, profitable, good, *turn ye to Me,* &c."

Turn ye even to Me, i. e. so as to return *quite to* [6] God, not halting, not turning half way, not in some things only, but from all the lusts and pleasures to which they had turned from God. " [7] *Turn quite to Me,* He saith, *with all your heart,* with your whole mind, whole soul, whole spirit, whole affections. For I am the Creator and Lord of the heart and mind, and therefore will, that that whole should be given, yea, given back, to Me, and endure not that any part of it be secretly stolen from Me to be given to idols, lusts or appetites." " It often happens with some people," says S. Gregory [8], " that they stoutly gird themselves up to encounter some vices, but neglect to overcome others, and while they never rouse themselves up against these, they are re-establishing against themselves, even those which they had subdued." Others, " in resolve, aim at right courses, but are ever doubling back to their wonted evil ones, and being, as it were, drawn out without themselves, they return back to themselves in a round, desiring good ways, but never forsaking evil ways." In contrast to these half conversions, he bids us turn to God with our whole inmost soul, so that all our affections should be fixed on God, and all within us, by a strong union, cleave to Him ; for " in whatever degree our affections are scattered among created things, so far is the conversion of the heart to God impaired."

[1] Ps. lxxviii. 49.   [2] from Am. v. 18.   [3] S. Jer.
[4] S. Luke vi. 21. S. Matt. v. 4.   [5] Hugo de S. V.

[6] The force of שׁוּב. See on Hos. xiv. 2.   [7] Lap.
[8] on Job vii. § 35. 34. p. 390. O. T.

13 And *rend your heart and not ᵇ your gar-

ᵃ Ps. 34. 18. & 51. 17.   ᵇ Gen. 37. 34. 2 Sam. 1. 11.
                              Job. 1. 20.

ments, and turn unto the LORD your God: for he is

"Look diligently," says S. Bernard[1], "what thou lovest, what thou fearest, wherein thou rejoicest or art saddened, and under the rags of conversion thou wilt find a heart perverted. The whole heart is in these four affections; and of these I think we must understand that saying, *turn to the Lord with all thy heart.* Let then thy love be converted to Him, so that thou love nothing whatever save Himself, or at least for Him. Let thy fear also be converted unto Him; for all fear is perverted, whereby thou fearest anything besides Him or not for Him. So too let thy joy and sorrow equally be converted unto Him. This will be, if thou only grieve or joy according to Him." "[2] There is a conversion with the whole heart, and another with a part. The conversion with the whole heart God seeketh, for it suffices to salvation. That which is partial he rejecteth, for it is feigned and far from salvation. In the heart, there are three powers, reason, will, memory; reason, of things future; will, of things present; memory, of things past. For reason seeks things to come; the will loves things present; memory retains things past. Reason illumines; will loves; memory retains. When then the reason seeks that Highest Good and finds, the will receives and loves, the memory anxiously keeps and closely embraces, then the soul turns with the whole heart to God. But when the reason slumbers and neglects to seek heavenly things, or the will is tepid and cares not to love them, or the memory is torpid and is careless to retain them, then the soul acts false, falling first into the vice of ignorance, secondly into the guilt of negligence, thirdly into the sin of malice. In each, the soul acts false; else ignorance would be expelled by the light of reason, and negligence be excluded by zeal of will, and malice be quenched by diligence of memory [of Divine things]. Reason then seeking begetteth knowledge; will embracing produceth love; memory holding fast, edification. The first produceth the light of knowledge, the second, the love of righteousness; the third preserveth the treasure of grace. This is that conversion of heart, which God requireth; this is that, which sufficeth to salvation."

And with fasting. "[3] In their returning to Him, it is required in the first place, that it be with the heart in the inward man, yet so that the outward man is not left unconcerned, but hath his part also, in performance of

such things whereby he may express, how the inward man is really affected; and so by the concurrence of both is true conversion made up. *With fasting*, which shall make for the humbling of the heart, which pampering of the flesh is apt to puff up and make insensible of its own condition, and forgetful of God and His service, as Jeshurun who, being *waxed fat, kicked, and forsook the God which made him and lightly esteemed the God of his salvation*[4]. To waiting then on God's service and prayer, it is usually joined in Scripture, as almost a necessary accompaniment, called for by God, and by holy men practised."

And with weeping and with mourning; i. e. by *beating*[5] on the breast, (as the word originally denoted,) *as the publican smote upon his breast*[6], and *all the people that came together to that sight* [of Jesus on the Cross], *beholding the things which were done, smote their breasts*[7]. "[8] These also, in themselves signs of grief, stir up in the heart more grief, and so have their effects on the person himself, for the increase of his repentance, as well as for shewing it." It also stirs up in others like passions, and provokes them also to repentance." "[9] These things, done purely and holily, are not conversion itself, but are excellent signs of conversion." "[10] We ought *to turn in fasting*, whereby vices are repressed, and the mind is raised. We ought to *turn in weeping*, out of longing for our home, out of displeasure at our faults, out of love to the sufferings of Christ, and for the manifold transgressions and errors of the world." "What avails it," says S. Gregory[11], "to confess iniquities, if the affliction of penitence·follow not the confession of the lips? For three things are to be considered in every true penitent, conversion of the mind, confession of the mouth, and revenge for the sin. This third sort is as a necessary medicine, that so the imposthume of guilt, pricked by confession, be purified by conversion, and healed by the medicine of affliction. The sign of true conversion is not in the confession of the mouth, but in the affliction of penitence. For then do we see that a sinner is well converted, when by a worthy austerity of affliction he strives to efface what in speech he confesses. Wherefore John Baptist, rebuking the ill-converted Jews who flock to him says, *O generation of vipers—bring forth therefore fruits worthy of repentance.*"

13. *And rend your hearts and not your garments,* i. e. *not your garments* only[12]. The

---

[1] Serm. 2. de Quadr. Lap.   [2] Hugo de S. V.   [3] Poc.
[4] Deut. xxxii. 15.   [5] כָּפַד   [6] S. Luke xviii. 13.
[7] Ib. xxiii. 48.   [8] Poc.   [9] Mont. ap. Poc.   [10] Dion.

[11] in 1 Reg. L. vi. c. 2. § 33. See Tertullian Note K. Oxf. Tr.
[12] See on Hos. vi. 6.

Before
CHRIST
cir. 800.

[c] gracious and merciful, slow to anger, and of great

kindness, and repenteth him of the evil.

Before
CHRIST
cir. 800.

[c] Ex. 34. 6. Ps. 86. 5, 15. Jonah 4. 2.

rending of the clothes was an expression of extraordinary uncontrollable emotion, chiefly of grief, of terror, or of horror. At least, in Holy Scripture it is not mentioned as a part of ordinary mourning, but only upon some sudden overpowering grief, whether public or private [1]. It was not used on occasion of death, unless there were something very grievous about its circumstances. At times it was used as an outward expression, one of deep grief, as when the leper was commanded to keep his clothes rent [2], or when David, to express his abhorrence at the murder of Abner, commanded *all the people with him, rend your clothes;* Ahab used it, with fasting and haircloth, on God's sentence by Elijah and obtained a mitigation of the temporal punishment of his sin; Jeremiah marvels that neither *the king,* Jehoiakim, *nor any of his servants, rent their garments* [3], on reading the roll containing the woes which God had by him pronounced against Judah. The holy garments of the priests were on no occasion to be rent [4]; (probably because the wholeness was a symbol of perfection, whence care was to be taken that the ephod should not accidentally be rent [5]) so that the act of Caiaphas was the greater hypocrisy [6]. He used it probably to impress his own blasphemous accusation on the people, as for a good end, the Apostles Paul and Barnabas rent their [7] clothes, when they heard that, after the cure of the impotent man, the priest of Jupiter with the people would have done sacrifice unto them. Since then apostles used this act, Joel plainly doth not forbid the use of such outward behavior, by which their repentance might be expressed, but only requires that it be done not in outward shew only, but accompanied with the inward affections. "[8] The Jews are bidden then to rend their hearts rather than their garments, and to set the truth of repentance in what is inward, rather than in what is outward." But since the rending of the garments was the outward sign of very vehement grief, it was no commonplace superficial sorrow, which the Prophet enjoined, but one which should pierce and rend the inmost soul, and empty it of its sins and its love for sin. [9] Any very grieving thing is said to cut one's heart, to "cut him to the heart." A truly penitent

heart is called *a broken and a contrite heart.* Such a penitent rends and "rips up by a narrow search the recesses of the heart, to discover the abominations thereof," and pours out before God "the diseased and perilous stuff" pent up and festering there, " expels the evil thoughts lodged in it, and opens it in all things to the reception of Divine grace. This rending is no other than the spiritual circumcision to which Moses exhorts. Whence of the Jews, not thus rent in heart, it is written in Jeremiah [10], *All the nations are uncircumcised, and all the house of Israel are uncircumcised in heart.* This *rending* then is the casting out of the sins and passions."

And turn unto the Lord your God. God owns Himself as still *their* God, although they had turned and were gone from Him in sin and were alienated from Him. To Him, the true, Unchangeable God, if they returned, they would find Him still *their God. Return, ye backsliding children, I will heal your backsliding,* God saith by Jeremiah [11]; *Behold,* Israel answers, *we come unto Thee, for Thou art the Lord our God.*

For He is *very gracious and very merciful.* Both these words are intensive [12]. All the words, *very gracious, very merciful, slow to anger, and of great kindness,* are the same and in the same order as in that revelation to Moses, when, on the renewal of the two tables of the law, *the Lord descended in the cloud and proclaimed the name of the Lord* [13]. The words are frequently repeated, shewing how deeply that revelation sunk in the pious minds of Israel. They are, in part, pleaded to God by Moses himself [14]; David, at one time, pleaded them all to God [15]; elsewhere he repeats them of God, as in this place [16]. Nehemiah, in praising God for His forgiving mercies, prefixes the title, *God of pardons* [17], and adds, *and Thou forsakedst them not;* as Joel, for the special object here, adds, *and repenteth Him of the evil.* A Psalmist, and Hezekiah in his message to Isaiah, and Nehemiah in the course of that same prayer, repeat the two words of intense mercy, *very gracious and very merciful* [18], which are used of God only, except once by that same Psalmist [19], with the express object of shewing how the good man conformeth himself to God. The word *very gracious* ex-

[1] The instances are; Gen. xxxvii. 29, 34. xliv. 13. Num. xiv. 6. Josh. vii. 6. Jud. xi. 35. 1 Sam. iv. 12, 25. 2 Sam. i. 2, 11. iii. 31. xiii. 19, 31. xv. 32. 1 Kings xxi. 27. 2 Kings v. 7, 8. vi. 30. xi. 14. xviii. 37. xix. 1. xxii. 11, 19. Ezr. ix. 3, 5. Esth. iv. 1. Job i. 20. ii. 12. Jer. xli. 5.
[2] Lev. xiii. 45. The word is not, as here, קרע, but פרם, used only in Leviticus.
[3] Jer. xxxvi. 24.   [4] Lev. x. 6. xxi. 10.

[5] Ex. xxviii. 32. xxxix. 23.
[6] S. Matt. xxvi. 65. S. Mark xiv. 63.   [7] Acts xiv. 14.
[8] Dion.   [9] Poc. and Dion.   [10] ix. 26.
[11] iii. 22.   [12] רחום חנון.   [13] Ex. xxxiv. 5, 6.
[14] Num. xiv. 18.   [15] Ps. lxxxvi. 15.
[16] Ps. ciii. 8. cxlv. 8.   [17] Neh. ix. 17.
[18] Ps. cxi. 4. 2 Chr. xxx. 9. Neh. ix. 31.
[19] Ps. cxii. 4.

Before
CHRIST
cir. 800.
14 [d] Who knoweth *if he will return and repent,* and leave [e] *a blessing behind him ; even [f] a meat offering and a drink offer-*

[d] Josh. 14. 12.
2 Sam. 12. 22.
2 Kings 19. 4.
Amos 5. 15.
Jonah 3. 9.
Zeph. 2. 3.
[e] Is. 65. 8.   [f] Hag. 2. 19. ch. 1. 9. 13.

ing unto the LORD your God?

15 ¶ [g] Blow the trumpet in Zion, [h] sanctify a fast, call a solemn assembly :

Before
CHRIST
cir. 800.

[g] Num. 10. 3.
ver. 1.
[h] ch. 1. 14.

---

presses God's free love, whereby He sheweth Himself good to us ; *very merciful* expresses the tender yearning of His love over our miseries[1] ; *great kindness,* expresses God's tender love, as love. He first says, that God is *slow to anger* or *long-suffering,* enduring long the wickedness and rebellion of man, and waiting patiently for the conversion and repentance of sinners. Then he adds, that God is *abundant in kindness,* having manifold resources and expedients of His tender love, whereby to win them to repentance. Lastly He is *repentant of the evil.* The evil which He foretells, and at last inflicts, is (so to speak) against His Will, Who *willeth not that any should perish,* and, therefore, on the first tokens of repentance He *repenteth Him of the evil,* and doeth it not.

The words rendered, *of great kindness,* are better rendered elsewhere, *abundant, plenteous in goodness, mercy*[2]. Although the mercy of God is in itself one and simple, yet it is called *abundant* on account of its divers effects. For God knoweth how in a thousand ways to succor His own. Whence the Psalmist prays, *According to the multitude of Thy mercies, turn Thou unto me*[3]. *According to the multitude of Thy tender mercies, do away mine offences*[4].

14. *Who knoweth if He will return.* God has promised forgiveness of sins and of eternal punishment to those who turn to Him with their whole heart. Of this, then, there could be no doubt. But He has not promised either to individuals or to Churches, that He will remit the temporal punishment which He had threatened. He forgave David the sin. Nathan says, *The Lord also hath put away thy sin.* But he said at the same time, *the sword shall never depart from thy house*[5] ; and the temporal punishment of his sin pursued him, even on the bed of death. David thought that the temporal punishment of his sin, in the death of the child, might be remitted to him. He used the same form of words as Joel[6], *I said, who can tell whether God will be gracious unto me, that the child may live ?* But the child died. The king of Nineveh used the like words[7], *Who can tell if God will return and repent and turn away from His fierce anger, that we perish not ?* And he was heard. God retained or remitted the temporal punish-

ment, as He saw good for each. This of the Prophet Joel is of a mixed character. The *blessing* which they crave, he explains to be *the meat offering and the drink offering,* which had been *cut off or withholden from the house of their God.* For "[8] if He gave them wherewith to serve Him," after withdrawing it, it was clear that "He would accept of them and be pleased with their service." Yet this does not imply that He would restore all to them. A Jewish writer[9] notes that after the Captivity, "the service of sacrifices alone returned to them," but that "prophecy, [soon after], the ark, the Urim and Thummim, and the other things [the fire from heaven] were wanting there." As a pattern, however, to all times, God teaches them to ask first what belongs to His kingdom and His righteousness, and to leave the rest to Him. So long as the means of serving Him were left, there was hope of all. Where the Sacrament of the Body and Blood of Christ (whereof *the meat offering and the drink offering* were symbols) remains, there are "[10] the pledges of His love," the earnest of all other blessing.

He says, *leave a blessing behind Him,* speaking of God as one estranged, who had been long absent and who returns, giving tokens of His forgiveness and renewed good-pleasure. God often visits the penitent soul and, by some sweetness with which the soul is bathed, leaves a token of His renewed Presence. God is said to repent, not as though He varied in Himself, but because He deals variously with us, as we receive His inspirations and follow His drawings, or no.

15. Before, he had, in these same words[11], called to repentance, because the Day of the Lord was coming, was nigh, *a day of darkness,* &c. Now[12], because God is *gracious and merciful, slow to anger and plenteous in goodness,* he agains exhorts, *Blow ye the trumpet;* only the call is more detailed, that every sex and age should form one band of suppliants to the mercy of God. "[13] Most full abolition of sins is then obtained, when one prayer and one confession issueth from the whole Church. For since the Lord promiseth to the pious agreement of two or three, that He will grant whatever is so asked, what shall be denied to a people of many thousands, fulfilling together one observance, and supplicating in

---

[1] See on Hos. ii. 19.
[2] Ex. xxxiv. 6. Ps. lxxxvi. 15. ciii. 8.
[3] Ps. xxv. 7, 16.   [4] Ps. li. 1.   [5] 2 Sam. xii. 13, 10.

[6] Ib. 22.   [7] Jon. iii. 9.   [8] Poc.   [9] Abarb. in Poc.
[10] Communion Service.   [11] ii. 1. i. 14.   [12] S. Jer.
[13] S. Leo Serm. 3 de jej. 7 mens. ⅔ 3. Lap.

Before
CHRIST
cir. 800.

1 Ex. 19. 10, 22.
k ch. l. 14.
l 2 Chr. 20. 13.

m 1 Cor. 7. 5.

16 Gather the people,
¹ sanctify the congregation,
ᵏ assemble the elders,
ˡ gather the children, and
those that suck the breasts:
ᵐ let the bridegroom go
forth of his chamber, and
the bride out of her closet.

17 Let the priests, the
ministers of the LORD,
weep ⁿ between the porch
and the altar, and let them
say, ° Spare thy people, O
LORD, and give not thine
heritage to reproach, that
the heathen should ‖ rule

Before
CHRIST
cir. 800.

n Ezek. 8. 16.
Matt. 23. 35.

o Ex. 32. 11, 12.
Deut. 9. 26–29.

‖ Or, use a
byword against
them.

harmony through One Spirit?" "We come together," says Tertullian¹ of Christian worship, "in a meeting and congregation as before God, as though we would in one body sue Him by our prayers. This violence is pleasing to God."

16. *Sanctify the congregation.* "²Do what in you lies, by monishing, exhorting, threatening, giving the example of a holy life, that the whole people present itself holy before its God," "³lest your prayers be hindered, and a little leaven corrupt the whole lump."

Assemble the elders. "⁴The judgment concerned all; all then were to join in seeking mercy from God. None were on any pretence to be exempted; not the oldest, whose strength was decayed, or the youngest, who might seem not yet of strength." The old also are commonly freer from sin and more given to prayer.

Gather the children. "⁴He Who feedeth the young ravens when they cry, will not neglect the cry of poor children. He assigns as a reason, why it were fitting to spare Nineveh, the ⁵*six-score thousand persons that could not discern between their right hand and their left.*" The sight of them who were involved in their parents' punishment could not but move the parents to greater earnestness. So when Moab and Ammon⁶, *a great multitude, came against Jehoshaphat, he proclaimed a fast throughout all Judah, and Judah gathered themselves together to ask help of the Lord; even out of all the cities of Judah, they came to seek the Lord. And all Judah was standing before the Lord, their little ones also, their wives, and their children.* So it is described in the book of Judith, how "⁷with great vehemency did they humble their souls, both they and their wives and their children—and every man and woman and the little children—fell before the temple, and cast ashes upon their heads and spread out their sackcloth before the Face of the Lord."

Let the bridegroom go forth. He says not even, the married, or the newly married, he who had taken a new wife, but he uses the special terms of the marriage-day, *bridegroom*

and *bride.* The new-married man was, during a year, exempted from going out to war, or from any duties which might *press upon him*⁸. But nothing was to be free from this common affliction of sorrow. Even the just newly married, although it were the very day of the bridal, were to leave the marriage-chamber and join in the common austerity of repentance. It was mockery of God to spend in delights time consecrated by Him to sorrow. He says⁹, *In that day did the Lord God of hosts call to weeping, and to mourning, and to baldness, and to girding with sackcloth. And behold joy and gladness—surely this iniquity shall not be purged from you till ye die, saith the Lord God of Hosts.* Whence, in times of fasting or prayer, the Apostle suggests the giving up of pure pleasures¹⁰, *that ye may give yourselves to fasting and prayer.*

"³He then who, by chastisement in food and by fasting and alms, says that he is doing acts of repentance, in vain doth he promise this in words, unless he *go forth out of his chamber* and fulfill a holy and pure fast by a chaste penitence."

17. *Let the priests, the ministers of the Lord, weep between the porch and the altar.* The porch in this, Solomon's temple, was in fact a tower, in front of the Holy of Holies, of the same breadth with the Temple, viz. 20 cubits, and its depth half its breadth, viz. 10 cubits¹¹, and its height 120 cubits, the whole *overlaid within with pure gold*¹². The brazen altar for burnt offerings stood in front of it¹³. The altar was of brass, twenty cubits square; and so, equal in breadth to the Temple itself, and ten cubits high¹⁴. The space then *between the porch and the altar* was inclosed on those two sides¹⁵; it became an inner part of the court of the priests. Through it the priests or the high priest passed, whenever they went to sprinkle the blood, typifying the Atonement, before the veil of the tabernacle, or for any other office of the tabernacle. It seems to have been a place of prayer for the priests. It is spoken of as an aggravation of the sins of those 25 idolatrous priests, that here, where they ought to worship God, they turned

1 Apol. c. 39. p. 80. Oxf. Tr. 2 Lap. 3 S. Jer.
4 Poc. 5 Jon. iv. 11. 6 2 Chr. xx. 1–4, 13.
7 iv. 9–11. 8 Deut. xxiv. 5. 9 Is. xxii. 12–14.

10 1 Cor. vii. 5. 11 1 Kings vi. 3.
12 2 Chr. iii. 4. 13 Ib. viii. 12.
14 Ib. iv. 1. 15 Ib. vii. 7.

Before CHRIST cir. 800.

p Ps. 42. 10. & 79. 10. & 115. 2. Mic. 7. 10.
q Zech. 1. 14. & 8. 2.
r Deut. 32. 36. Is. 60. 10.

over them: p wherefore
should they say among the
people, Where *is* their God?
18 ¶ Then will the
LORD q be jealous for his
land, r and pity his people.
19 Yea, the LORD will
answer and say unto his
people, Behold, I will send
you s corn, and wine, and
oil, and ye shall be satisfied
therewith: and I will no
more make you a reproach
among the heathen:

Before CHRIST cir. 800.

s See ch. 1. 10. Mal. 3. 10, 11, 12.

their backs toward the Temple of the Lord, to worship the sun[1]. Here, in the exercise of his office, Zechariah was standing[2], when the Spirit of God came upon him and he rebuked the people and they stoned him. Here the priests, with their faces toward the Holy of Holies and the Temple which He had filled with His Glory, were to *weep*. Tears are a gift of God. In holier times, so did the priests weep at the Holy Eucharist in thought of the Passion and Precious Death of our Lord Jesus, which we then plead to God, that they bore with them, as part of their dress, linen wherewith to dry their tears[3].

And let them say. A form of prayer is provided for them. From this the words, *spare us, good Lord, spare thy people*, enter into the litanies of the Christian Church.

And give not thine heritage to reproach. The enmity of the heathen against the Jews was an enmity against God. God had avouched them as His people and His property. Their land was an heritage from God. God, in that He had separated them from the heathen, and revealed Himself to them, had made them His especial heritage. Moses[4], then Joshua[5], the Psalmists[6], plead with God, that His own power or will to save His people would be called in question, if he should destroy them, or give them up. God, on the other hand, tells them, that not for any deserts of theirs, but for His own Name's sake, He delivered them, lest the Heathen should be the more confirmed in their errors as to Himself[7], It is part of true penitence to plead to God to pardon us, not for anything in ourselves, (for we have nothing of our own but our sins) but because we are the work of His hands, created in His image, the price of the Blood of Jesus, called by His Name.

That the heathen should rule over them. This, and not the rendering in the margin, *use a byword against them*, is the uniform meaning of the Hebrew phrase. It is not to be supposed that the Prophet Joel would use it in a sense contrary to the uniform usage of all the writers before him. Nor is there any instance of any other usage of the idiom in any later writer[8]. "The enigma which was closed," says St. Jerome, "is now opened. For who that people is, manifold and strong, described above under the name of the *palmerworm, the locust, the canker-worm* and the *catterpillar*, is now explained more clearly, *lest the heathen rule over them.* For the heritage of the Lord is given to reproach, when they serve their enemies, and the nations say, *Where is their God*, Whom they boasted to be their Sovereign and their Protector?" Such is the reproach ever made against God's people, when He does not visibly protect them, which the Psalmist says was as a sword in his bones[9]; his *tears* were his *meat day and night* while they said it. The Chief priests and scribes and elders fulfilled a prophecy by venturing so to blaspheme our Lord[10], *He trusted in God; let Him deliver Him now, if He will have Him.*

18. *Then will the Lord be jealous for His land.* Upon repentance, all is changed. Before, God seemed set upon their destruction. It was His great army which was ready to destroy them; He was at its head, giving the word. Now He is full of tender love for them, which resents injury done to them, as done to Himself. The word might more strictly perhaps be rendered, *And the Lord is jealous*[11]. He would shew how instantaneous the mercy and love of God for His people is, restrained while they are impenitent, flowing forth upon the first tokens of repentance. The word, *jealous for*, when used of God, jealous for My holy Name[12], jealous for Jerusalem[13], is used, when God resents evil which had been actually inflicted.

19. *I will send you corn, &c.* This is the beginning of the reversal of the threatened judgments. It is clear from this, and still

1 Ezek. viii. 16.
2 2 Chr. xxiv. 20, 1. S. Matt. xxiii. 35.
3 Amalar. de Eccl. Off. iii. 22.
4 Ex. xxxii. 12. Num. xiv. 13–16. Deut. ix. 28, 9.
5 Josh. vii. 9.
6 Ps. lxxiv. lxxix. cxv.
7 Ezek. xx. 5. xxxvi. 21–3.
8 See Introd. to Joel, p. 102.
9 Ps. xlii. 3, 10; add Ps. lxxix. 10. cxv. 2. Mic. vii. 16.
10 S. Matt. xxvii. 43, from Ps. xxii. 8.
11 It is not an absolute past. For the ו *conversive* only denotes a past, by connecting the word with some former past, as we could say in vivid description of the past, "then he goes." But here no past has preceded, except the prophetic past mixed with the future, in the description of the inroad of this scourge.
12 Ezek. xxxix. 25.
13 Zech. i. 14. viii. 2.

Before
CHRIST
cir. 800.
t See Ex. 10. 19.
u Jer. 1. 14.

20 But [t] I will remove far off from you [u] the northern *army*, and will

drive him into a land barren and desolate, with his face [x] toward the east sea,

Before
CHRIST
cir. 800.
x Ezek. 47. 18.
Zech. 14. 8

more from what follows, that the chastisements actually came, so that the repentance described, was the consequence, not of the exhortations to repentance, but of the chastisement. What was removed was the chastisement which had burst upon them, not when it was ready to burst. What was given, was what before had been taken away. So it ever was with the Jews; so it is mostly with the portions of the Christian Church or with individuals now. Seldom do they take warning of coming woe; when it has begun to burst, or has burst, then they repent and God gives them back upon repentance what He had withdrawn or a portion of it. So the Prophet seems here to exhibit to us a law and a course of God's judgments and mercies upon man's sin. He takes away both temporal and spiritual blessings symbolized here by the corn and wine and oil; upon repentance He restores them. "[1] Over and against the wasting of the land, he sets its richness; against hunger, fullness; against reproach, unperiled glory; against the cruelty and incursion of enemies, their destruction and putrefaction; against barrenness of fruits and aridity of trees, their fresh shoots and richness; against the hunger of the word and thirst for doctrine, he brings in the fountain of life, and the Teacher of righteousness; against sadness, joy; against confusion, solace; against reproaches, glory; against death, life; against ashes, a crown." "O fruitful and manly penitence! O noble maiden, most faithful intercessor for sins! A plank after shipwreck! Refuge of the poor, help of the miserable, hope of exiles, cherisher of the weak, light of the blind, solace of the fatherless, scourge of the petulant, axe of vices, garner of virtues. Thou who alone bindest the Judge, pleadest with the Creator, conquerest the Almighty. While overcome, thou overcomest; while tortured, thou torturest; while wounding, thou healest; while healthfully succumbing, thou triumphest gloriously. Thou alone, while others keep silence, mountest boldly the throne of grace. David thou leadest by the hand and reconcilest; Peter thou restorest; Paul thou enlightenest; the Publican, taken from the receipt of custom, thou boldly insertest in the choir of the Apostles; Mary, from a harlot, thou bearest aloft and joinest to Christ; the robber nailed to the cross, yet fresh from blood, thou introducest into Paradise. What

more? At thy disposal is the court of heaven."

And I will no more make you a reproach. All the promises of God are conditional. They presuppose man's faithfulness. God's pardon is complete. He will not, He says, for these offences, or for any like offences, give them over to the heathen. So after the Captivity He no more made them a reproach unto the heathen, until they finally apostatized, and leaving their Redeemer, owned no king but Cæsar. They first gave themselves up; they chose Cæsar rather than Christ, and to be servants of Cæsar, rather than that *He* should not be crucified; and so God left them in *his* hands, whom they had chosen.

20. *And I will remove far off from you the northern* army. God speaks of the human agent under the figure of the locusts, which perish in the sea; yet so as to shew at once, that He did not intend the locust itself, nor to describe the mode in which He should overthrow the human oppressor. He is not speaking of the locust itself, for the Northern is no name for the locust which infested Palestine, since it came from the South; nor would the destruction of the locust be in two opposite seas, since they are uniformly driven by the wind into the sea, upon whose waves they alight and perish, but the wind would not carry them into two opposite seas; nor would the locust perish in a *barren and desolate land*, but would fly further; nor would it be said of the locust that he was destroyed, *Because he had done great things* [2]. But He represents to us, how this enemy should be driven quite out of the bounds of His people, so that he should not vex them more, but perish. The imagery is from the Holy Land. The *East sea* is the Dead Sea, once the fertile *vale of Siddim* [3], "[4] in which sea were formerly Sodom and Gomorrah, Admah and Zeboim, until God overthrew them." This, in the Pentateuch, is called *the salt sea* [5], or *the sea of the plain*, or *desert* [6], explained in Deuteronomy and Joshua to be *the salt sea* [7]; Ezekiel calls it *the East sea* [8], and in Numbers it is said of it [9], *your south border shall be the salt sea eastward. The utmost*, or rather, *the hinder sea* [10] (i. e. that which is behind one who is looking toward the East whose Hebrew name [11] is from "fronting" you) is the Mediterranean, "on whose shores are Gaza and Ascalon, Azotus and Joppa and Cæsarea." The *land barren and desolate*, lying

[1] Hugo de S. Victor.
[2] See Introduction to Joel, p. 153.
[3] Gen. xiv. 3.   [4] S. Jer.
[5] Gen. Ib. Num. xxxiv. 3, 12.

[6] Deut. iii. 17. iv. 49. Josh. iii. 16. xii. 3. xv. 25. xviii. 19, also in 2 Kings xiv. 25.
[7] Deut. iii. Josh. iii. xii.   [8] xlvii. 18.
[9] xxxiv. 3.   [10] Deut. xi. 24. xxxiv. 2.   [11] קָדִים.

Before
CHRIST
cir. 800.

y Deut. 11. 24.

and his hinder party
y toward the utmost sea,
and his stink shall come up,

and his ill savor shall
come up, because † he hath
done great things.

Before
CHRIST
cir. 800.

† Heb. *he hath
magnified to do.*

between, is the desert of Arabia, the southern
boundary of the Holy Land. The picture
then seems to be, that the *Northern* foes
filled the whole of Judæa, in numbers like
the locust, and that God drove them violently
forth, all along the bounds of the Holy Land,
into the desert, the Dead Sea, the Mediterranean. S. Jerome relates a mercy of God in
his own time which illustrates the image;
but he writes so much in the language of
Holy Scripture, that perhaps he only means
that the locusts were driven into the sea, not
into both seas. "In our times too we have
seen hosts of locusts cover Judæa, which
afterward, by the mercy of the Lord, when
the priests and people, *between the porch and
the altar*, i. e. between the place of the Cross
and the Resurrection prayed the Lord and
said, *spare Thy people*, a wind arising, were
carried headlong *into the Eastern sea, and the
utmost sea.*" Alvarez relates how, priests and
people joining in litanies to God, He delivered them from an exceeding plague of locusts, which covered 24 English miles, as He
delivered Egypt of old at the prayer of
Moses. "[1] When we knew of this plague
being so near, most of the Clerks of the place
came to me, that I should tell them some
remedy against it. I answered them, that I
knew of no remedy except to commend themselves to God, and to pray Him to drive the
plague out of the land. I went to the Embassador and told him that to me it seemed
good that we should make a procession with
the people of the land and that it might
please our Lord God to hear us; it seemed
good to the Embassador; and, in the morning of the next day, we collected the people
of the place and all the Clergy; and we took
our Altar-stone, and those of the place theirs,
and our Cross and theirs, singing our litany,
we went forth from the Church, all the Portuguese and the greater part of the people of
the place. I said to them that they should
not keep silence, but should, as we, cry aloud
saying in their tongue Zio marinos, i. e. in
our's, Lord Jesus Christ, have mercy on us.
And with this cry and litany, we went
through an open wheat-country for the space
of one third of a league.—It pleased our Lord
to hear the sinners, and while we were turning to the place, because their [the locusts']
road was toward the sea whence they had
come, there were so many after us, that it
seemed no otherwise than that they sought
to break our ribs and heads with blows of

stones, such were the blows they dealt us.
At this time a great thunderstorm arose from
toward the sea, which came in their face with
rain and hail, which lasted three good hours;
the river and brooks filled greatly ; and when
they had ceased to drive, it was matter of
amazement, that the dead locusts on the bank
of the great river measured two cubits high;
and so for the rivulets, there was a great
multitude of dead on their banks. On the
next day in the morning there was not in the
whole land even one live locust."
And his stink shall come up. The image is
still from the locust. It, being such a fearful scourge of God, every individual full of
activity and life repeated countlessly in the
innumerable host, is, at God's will and in
His time, cast by His word into the sea, and
when thrown up by the waves on the shore,
becomes in a few hours one undistinguishable, putrefying, heaving mass. Such does
human malice and ambition and pride become, as soon as God casts aside the sinful
instrument of His chastisement. Just now,
a world to conquer could not satisfy it; superior to man, independent, it deems, of God.
He takes away its breath, it is a putrid carcase. Such was Sennacherib's army; *in the
evening inspiring terror; before the morning, he
is not*. *They were all dead corpses* [3].
The likeness stops here. For the punishment is at an end. The wicked and the persecutors of God's people are cut off, the
severance has taken place. On the one side,
there is the putrefying mass; on the other,
the jubilee of thanksgiving. The gulf is
fixed between them. The offensive smell of
the corruption ascends; as Isaiah closes his
prophecy, *the carcases* of the wicked, the perpetual prey of *the worm* and *the fire, shall be an
abhorring* to all *flesh*. The righteous behold
it, but it reaches them not, to hurt them. In
actual life, the putrid exhalations at times
have, among those on the sea-shore, produced
a pestilence, a second visitation of God, more
destructive than the first. This, however,
has been but seldom. Yet what must have
been the mass of decay of creatures so slight,
which could produce a wide-wasting pestilence ! What an image of the numbers of
those who perish, and of the fetidness of sin !
S. Augustine, in answer to the heathen who
imputed all the calamities of the later Roman
Empire to the displeasure of the gods, because the world had become Christian, says [4],
"They themselves have recorded that the

[1] c. 32.   [2] Is. xvii. 14.   [3] Ib. xxxvii. 36.
[4] de Civ. Dei. iii. 71. fin. He is referring, doubtless, to Julius Obsequens, a heathen writer, (de

prodig. c. xc.) "Immense armies of locusts in
Africa, which, cast by the wind into the sea, and
thrown up by the waves, through the intolerable

Before
CHRIST
cir. 800.

21 ¶ Fear not, O land; be glad and rejoice: for the LORD will do great things.

Before
CHRIST
cir. 800.

multitude of locusts was, even in Africa, a sort of prodigy, while it was a Roman province. They say that, after the locusts had consumed the fruits and leaves of trees, they were cast into the sea, in a vast incalculable cloud, which having died and being cast back on the shores, and the air being infected thereby, such a pestilence arose, that in the realm of Masinissa alone 800,000 men perished, and many more in the lands on the coasts. Then at Utica, out of 30,000 men in the prime of life who were there, they assert that 10 only remained." S. Jerome says of the locusts of Palestine [1]; " when the shores of both seas were filled with heaps of dead locusts which the waters had cast up, their stench and putrefaction was so noxious as to corrupt the air, so that a pestilence was produced among both beasts and men." Modern writers say [2], "The locusts not only produce a famine, but in districts near the sea where they had been drowned, they have occasioned a pestilence from the putrid effluvia of the immense numbers blown upon the coast or thrown up by the tides." "[3] We observed, in May and June, a number of these insects coming from the S. directing their course to the Northern shore; they darken the sky like a thick cloud, but scarcely have they quitted the shore before they who, a moment before, ravaged and ruined the country, cover the surface of the sea with their dead bodies, to the great distress of the Franks near the harbor, on account of the stench from such a number of dead insects, driven by the winds close to the very houses." "[4] All the full-grown insects were driven into the sea by a tempestuous N. W. wind, and were afterward cast upon the beach, where, it is said, they formed a bank of 3 or 4 feet high, extending—a distance of near 50 English miles. It is asserted that when this mass became putrid and the wind was S. E. the stench was sensibly felt in several parts of Sneuwberg. The column passed the houses of two of our party, who asserted that it continued without any interruption for more than a month." "[5] The South and East winds drive the clouds of locusts with violence into the Mediterranean,

and drown them in such quantities that when their dead are cast on the shore, they infect the air to a great distance." Wonderful image of the instantaneous, ease, completeness, of the destruction of God's enemies ; a mass of active life exchanged, in a moment, into a mass of death.

Because he hath done great things ; lit. (as in the E. M.) *because he hath magnified to do,* i. e. as used of man, *hath done proudly.* To do greatly [6], or to magnify Himself [7], when used of God, is to display His essential greatness, in goodness to His people, or in vengeance on their enemies. Man's great deeds are mostly deeds of great ambition, great violence, great pride, great iniquity; and so of him, the words *he magnified himself* [8], *he did greatly* [9], mean, he did ambitiously, proudly, and so offended God. In like way *great doings,* when used of God, are His great works of good [10] ; of man, his great works of evil [11]. "[12] Man has great deserts, but evil." To *speak great things* [13], is to speak proud things : *greatness of heart* [14] is pride of heart. He is speaking then of man who was God's instrument in chastening His people ; since of irrational, irresponsible creatures, a term which involves moral fault, would not have been used, nor would a moral fault have been set down as the ground why God destroyed them. The destruction of Sennacherib or Holofernes have been assigned as the fulfillment of this prophecy. They were part of its fulfillment, and of the great law of God which it declares, that instruments, which He employs, and who exceed or accomplish for their own ends, the office which He assigns them, He casts away and destroys.

21. *Fear not, O land.* Before, they were bidden to tremble [15], now they are bidden, *fear not;* before, *to turn in weeping, fasting and mourning ;* now, to *bound for joy and rejoice ;* before, *the land mourned ;* now, *the land* is bidden to *rejoice.* The enemy had *done great things ;* now the cause of joy is that God had *done great things ;* the Almightiness of God overwhelming and sweeping over the might put forth to destroy. It is better rendered, *the Lord hath*

smell produced a grievous pestilence to the cattle ; and of man it is related that 800,000 perished through this plague." Orosius says, " In Numidia, 800,000 perished ; on the sea coast, especially that near Carthage and Utica, it is said that more than 200,000 perished. In Utica itself, 30,000 soldiers, placed as a guard for all Africa, were destroyed. At Utica in one day, at one gate, more than 1500 of their corpses were carried out." (v. 11.)

[1] ad. loc.   [2] Forbes, i. 373.   [3] Hasselquist, p. 445.
[4] Barrow, S. Afr. p. 239.   [5] Volney, i. 278.
[6] ii. 21. Ps. cxxvi. 2, 3. 1 Sam. xii. 24.

[7] Ezek. xxxviii. 23.   [8] Is. x. 15. Dan. xi. 36, 37.
[9] Lam. i. 9. Zeph. ii. 8. Dan. viii. 4, 8, 11, 25.
[10] עֲלִילוֹת Ps. ix. 12. lxxvii. 13. lxxviii. 11. ciii. 7.
Is. xii. 4 ; מֵעֲלִים Ps. lxxvii. 12. lxxviii. 7.
[11] עֲלִילוֹת Ps. cxli. 4. 1 Sam. ii. 3. Ezek. xiv. 22.
23. xx. 43. xxi. 29. Zeph. iii. 11; מֵעֲלִים Jer. iv. 18.
xi. 18. xxi. 14, see Hos. xii. 2.
[12] S. Aug.   [13] Ps. xii. 3. Dan. vii. 8, 11, 20.
[14] Is. ix. 9. x. 12.   [15] ii. 1.

Before
CHRIST
cir. 800.

[a]ch. 1. 18, 20.
[a]Zech. 8. 12.
See ch. 1. 19.

22 Be not afraid, [x]ye beasts of the field : for [a]the pastures of the wilderness do spring, for the tree beareth her fruit, the fig tree

and the vine do yield their strength.

23 Be glad then, ye children of Zion, and [b]rejoice in the LORD your

Before
CHRIST
cir. 800.

[b]Is. 41. 16.
& 61. 10.
Hab. 3. 18.
Zech. 10. 7.

---

done great things. If Joel includes herein God's great doings yet to come, he speaks of them as, in the purpose of God, already in being; or he may, in this verse, presuppose that this new order of God's mercies has begun, in the destruction of the Heathen foe.

22. The reversal of the whole former sentence is continued up to man. The beasts of the field *groaned, were perplexed, cried unto God;* now they are bidden, *be not afraid;* before, *the pastures of the wilderness* were *devoured by fire;* now, they *spring* with fresh tender life; before, *the fig tree* was *withered, the vine languished;* now, they should *yield their strength, put out their full* vigor. For God was reconciled to His people; and all things served them, serving Him.

23. *Be glad then and rejoice in the Lord your God.* All things had been restored for their sakes; they were to rejoice, not chiefly in these things, but in God; nor only in God, but in the Lord their God. *For He hath given you the former rain moderately.* The word rendered *moderately* should be rendered *unto righteousness;* the word often as it occurs never having any sense but that of *righteousness;* whether of God or man. The other word *moreh,* rendered *the former rain,* confessedly has that meaning in the latter part of the verse, although *yoreh* is the distinctive term for *latter rain*[1]. *Moreh* mostly signifies a *teacher*[2], which is connected with the other ordinary meanings of the root, *torah, law, &c.* The older translators then agreed in rendering, *of righteousness,* or, *unto righteousness*[3], in which case the question as to *moreh,* is only, whether it is to be taken literally of a *teacher,* or figuratively of spiritual blessings, as we say, "the dew of His grace." Even a Jew paraphrases, "[4]But ye, O children of Zion, above all other nations, be glad and rejoice in the Lord your God. For in Him ye shall have perfect joy, in the time of your captivity. For He will give you an *instructor to righteousness;* and He is the king Messias, which shall teach them the way in which they shall walk, and the doings which they shall do." The grounds for so rendering the word are; 1) such is almost its uniform meaning. 2) The righteousness spoken

of is most naturally understood of righteousness in man; it is a condition which is the result and object of God's gifts, not the Righteousness of God. But "He hath given you the early rain unto righteousness," i. e. that ye may be righteous, is an unwonted expression. 3) There is a great emphasis on the word [5], which is not used in the later part of the verse, where rain, (whether actual, or symbolical of spiritual blessings) is spoken of. 4) The following words, *and He maketh the rain to descend for you,* according to the established Hebrew idiom [6], relates to a separate action, later, in order of time or of thought, than the former. But if the former word *moreh* signified *early rain,* both would mean one and the same thing. We should not say, "He giveth you the former rain to righteousness, and then He maketh the rain, the former rain and the latter rain to descend;" nor doth the Hebrew.

It seems then most probable, that the Prophet prefixes to all the other promises, that first all-containing promise of the Coming of Christ. Such is the wont of the Prophets, to go on from past judgments and deliverances, to Him Who is the centre of all this cycle of God's dispensations, the Son manifest in the Flesh. He had been promised as a Teacher when that intermediate dispensation of Israel began, the Prophet like unto Moses. His Coming old Jacob looked to, *I have longed for Thy salvation, O Lord.* Him, well known and longed for by the righteous of old, Joel speaks of as the subject of rejoicing, as Zechariah did afterward, *Rejoice greatly, daughter of Zion; behold thy King cometh unto thee.* So Joel here, *Exult and joy in the Lord thy God; for He giveth,* or *will give thee, the Teacher unto righteousness,* i. e. the result and object of Whose Coming is righteousness; or, as Daniel says, *to bring in everlasting righteousness;* and Isaiah, *By His knowledge,* i. e. by the knowledge of Him, *shall My righteous Servant justify many,* i. e. make many righteous. How His coming should issue in righteousness, is not here said. It is presupposed. But Joel speaks of His Coming, as a gift, *He shall give you;* as Isaiah says, *unto us a Son is given;* and that, as *the Teacher,* as Isaiah says[7], *I have given Him a witness to the peoples,*

---

[1] Deut. xi. 14. Jer. v. 24.

[2] 2 Kings xvii. 28. Job xxxvi. 22. Prov. v. 13. Is. ix. 15. xxx. 20. (twice) Hab. ii. 18.

[3] Jon. "has restored to you your instructor (or instructors) in righteousness;" Vulg. "teacher of

righteousness;" LXX. "the foods unto righteousness;" followed by Syr. and Arab.

[4] Abarb. in Poc. so also Jon. and, (following him,) Rashi, R. Japhet.

[5] את המורה.   [6] The ו conv.   [7] Is. lv. 4.

Before CHRIST cir. 800.

|| Or, *a teacher of righteousness.*
† Heb. *according to righteousness.*

God, for he hath given you || the former rain † moderately, and he [c] will cause

[c] Lev. 26. 4. Deut. 11. 14. & 28. 12.

to come down for you [d] the rain, the former rain and the latter rain in the first *month.*

Before CHRIST cir. 800.

[d] Jam. 5. 7.

a Prince and a Commander unto the people; and that, *for righteousness.*

" It is the wont of the holy prophets," says S. Cyril, " on occasion of good things promised to a part or a few, to introduce what is more general or universal. And these are the things of Christ. To this then the discourse again proceeds. For when was ground given to the earth to rejoice? When did the Lord do mighty things, but when the Word, being God, became Man, that, flooding all below with the goods from above, He might be found to those who believe in Him, as a river of peace, a torrent of pleasure, as the former and latter rain, and the giver of all spiritual fruitfulness? "

The early rain and the latter rain. "[1] He multiplies words, expresssive of the richness of the fruits of the earth, that so we may understand how wondrous is the plenteousness of spiritual goods." Being about to speak of the large gift of God the Holy Ghost as an *out-pouring,* he says here that "[2] the largeness of the spiritual gifts thereafter should be as abundant as the riches temporal blessings" hitherto, when God disposed all things to bring about the fruitfulness which He had promised. *The early and latter rain,* coming respectively at the seed-time and the harvest, represent the beginning and the completion; and so, by the analogy of earthly and spiritual sowing, growth and ripeness, they represent [3] preventing and perfecting grace; the inspiration of good purposes and the gift of final perseverance, which brings the just to glory consummated; *the principles of the doctrine of Christ* and *the going on unto perfection* [4].

In the first month. This would belong only to the latter rain, which falls about the first month, Nisan, or our April, *the former rain* falling about 6 months earlier, at their seed time [5]. Or, since this meaning is uncertain [6], it may be, *at the first* [7], i. e. as soon as ever it is needed, or in contrast to the more extensive gifts afterward; or, *as at first* [8], i. e. all shall, upon their penitence, be restored as at first. These lesser variations leave the sense of the whole same, and all are supported by good authorities. It is still a reversal of the former sentence, that, whereas

afore the rivers of water were dried up, now the rains should come, each in its season. *In the first month,* and *at the beginning,* express the same thought, the one with the other without a figure. For no one then needed to be told that the latter rain, if it fell, should fall *in the first month,* which was its appointed season for falling. If then the words had this meaning, there must have been this emphasis in it, that God would give them good gifts punctually, instantly, at man's first and earliest needs, at the first moment when it would be good for him to have them. *As at the beginning,* would express the same which he goes on to say, that God would bestow the same largeness of gifts as He did, before they forfeited His blessings by forsaking Him. So He says [9], *I will restore thy judges as at the first, and thy counsellors as at the beginning ;* and [10], *She shall sing there us in the days of her youth, and as in the day when she come up out of the land of Egypt ;* and [11], *then shall the offering of Judah and Jerusalem be pleasant unto the Lord, as in the days of old and as in the former years.* Likeness does not necessarily imply equality [12], as in the words [13], *The Lord thy God will raise up unto thee a Prophet like unto me ;* and [14] *that they may be one, even as We are One.* The good things of the Old Testament had a likeness to those of the New, else *the law* would not have been even *the shadow of good things to come* [15]; they had not equality, else they would have been the very things themselves. "[16] Christ is the whole delight of the soul, from Whom and through Whom there cometh to those who love Him, all fullness of good and supply of heavenly gifts, represented in *the early and latter rain,* and *the full floor of wheat,* and *the fats overflowing with wine and oil.* It is true also as to the fullness of the mysteries. For the living water of Holy Baptism is given us as in rain ; and as in corn, the Bread of Life, and as in wine the Blood." Before, *the barns were broken down,* since there was nothing to store therein. As other parts of the natural and spiritual husbandry correspond, and our Lord Himself compares His gracious trials of those who bear fruit, with the pruning of the vine [17]; it may be that the *vat* wherein the grape or the olive, through pressure, yield

[1] Rib. [2] Lap. [3] Dion. Castr. Lap. [4] Heb. vi. 1. [5] See on Hos. vi. 3. [6] In the known cases, where, *in the first,* בראשון, stands for *in the first month,* (Gen. viii. 13. Num. ix. 5. Ezek. xxix. 17. xlv. 18, 21) this is marked in the sentence itself.

[7] S. Jer. R. Tanchum, in Poc. [8] Abarb. R. Tanch. LXX. Syr. Vulg. [9] Is. i. 26. Rib. [10] Hos. ii. 15. [11] Mal. iii. 4. [12] Rib. [13] Deut. xviii. 15. [14] S. John xvii. 22. [15] Heb. x. 1. [16] S. Cyr. [17] S. John xv. 2.

Before
CHRIST
cir. 800.

24 And the floors shall be full of wheat, and the fats shall overflow with wine and oil.

25 And I will restore to you the years [e]that the locust hath eaten, the cankerworm, and the cater-

Before
CHRIST
cir. 800.

[e] ch. 1. 4.

their rich juice, is a symbol of the *tribulations,* through which we *must enter the kingdom of God*[1]. "[2]The holy mind, placed as if in a winefat, is pressed, refined, drawn out pure. It is pressed by calamity; refined from iniquity, purified from vanity. Hence are elicited the groans of pure confession; hence stream the tears of anxious compunction; hence flow the sighs of pleasurable devotion; hence melt the longings of sweetest love; hence are drawn the drops of purest contemplation. Wheat is the perfecting of righteousness; wine, the clearness of spiritual understanding; oil, the sweetness of a most pure conscience."

25. *And I will restore to you the years that the locust hath eaten.* The order in which these destroyers are named not being the same as before, it is plain that the stress is not on the order, but on the successiveness of the inroads, scourge after scourge. It is plain too that they did not come in the same year, or two years, but year after year; for he says, not *year,* but in the plural, *years.* The locusts, although not the whole plague, intended, are not excluded. "[3]As the power of God was shewn in the plagues of Egypt by small animals, such as the cyniphes, gnats so small as scarce to be seen, so also now," in creatures so small "is shown the power of God and weakness of man. If a creature so small is stronger than man, *why are earth and ashes proud?*" The locusts, small as they are, are in God's hands *a great army,* (and from this place probably, Mohammed[4] taught his followers so to call them) and mighty empires are but "[5]the forces of God and messengers of His Providence for the punishing of" His people " by them, " *the rod of His* Anger; and when they have done their commission and are cast away by Him, they are as the vilest worms.

"[3]Since then after repentance God promises such richness, what will Novatus say, who denies repentance or that sinners can be re-formed into their former state, if they but do works meet for repentance? For God in such wise receives penitents, as to call them His people, and to say, that they *shall never be confounded,* and to promise, that He will dwell in the midst of them, and that they shall have no other God, but shall, with their whole mind, trust in Him Who abides in them forever."

Through repentance all which had been lost by sin, is restored. In itself deadly sin is an irreparable evil. It deprives the soul of grace, of its hope of glory; it forfeits heaven, it merits hell. God, through Christ, restores the sinner, blots out sin, and does away with its eternal consequences. He replaces the sinner where he was before he fell. So God says by Ezekiel[6]; *If the wicked will turn from all the sins which he hath committed and keep all My statutes, and do that which is lawful and right, he shall surely live, he shall not die; all his transgressions that he hath committed shall not be mentioned unto him;* and[7], *as for the wickedness of the wicked, he shall not fall thereby in the day that he turneth from his wickedness.* God forgives that wickedness, as though it had never been. If it had never been, man would have all the grace, which he had before his fall. So then also, after he has been forgiven, none of his former grace, no store of future glory, will be taken from him. The time which the sinner lost, in which he might have gained increase of grace and glory, is lost for ever. But all which he had gained before, returns. All his lost love returns through penitence; all his past attainments, which were before accepted by God, are accepted still for the same glory. "Former works which were deadened by sins following, revive through repentance[8]." The penitent begins anew God's service, but he is not at the beginning of that service, nor of his preparation for life eternal. If the grace which he had before, and the glory corresponding to that grace, and to his former attainments through that grace, were lost to him, then, although eternally blessed, he would be punished eternally for forgiven sin, which, God has promised, should *not be remembered.* God has also promised to reward all which is *done in the body*[9]. What is evil, is effaced by the Blood of Jesus. What, through His Grace, was good, and done for love of Himself, He rewards, whether it was before any one fell, or after his restoration. Else He would not, as He says He will, reward all. And who would not believe, that, after David's great fall and great repentance, God still rewarded all that great early simple faith and patience, which He gave him? Whence writers of old say, "[10]It is pious to believe that the recovered grace of God which destroys a man's former evils, also reintegrates

[1] Acts xiv. 22.   [2] Hugo de S. V.   [3] S. Jer.
[4] Mohammed probably had it from the apostate Jew who helped him in composing the Coran.

[5] Abarb. in Poc.   [6] xviii. 21, 22.   [7] Ib. xxxiii. 12.
[8] Gloss in Ep. ad Heb.   [9] 2 Cor. v. 10.
[10] de ver. et fals. pœnit. c. 14.

Before
CHRIST
cir. 800.
pillar, and the palmer-worm, *my great army which I sent among you.

f ver. 11.

26 And ye shall *eat in plenty, and be satisfied, and praise the name of the LORD your God, that hath dealt wondrously with you:

g Lev. 26. 5.
Ps. 22. 16.
See Lev. 26. 26.
Mic. 6. 14.

and my people shall never be ashamed.

Before
CHRIST
cir. 800.

27 h And ye shall know that I am ¹ in the midst of Israel, and that k I am the LORD your God, and none else: and my people shall never be ashamed.

h ch. 3. 17.
i Lev. 26. 11, 12.
Ezek. 37, 26,
27, 28.
k Is. 45. 5, 21, 22.
Ezek. 39. 22, 23.
¹ Is. 44. 3.
Ezek. 39. 29.
Acts 2. 17.

28 ¶ ¹ And it shall come

---

his good, and that God, when He hath destroyed in a man what is not His, loves the good which He implanted even in the sinner." " ¹ God is pleased alike with the virtue of the just, and the meet repentance of sinners, which restored to their former estate David and Peter." " Penitence is an excellent thing which recalleth to perfection every defect." " ² God letteth His sun arise on sinners, nor doth He less than before, give them, most large gifts of life and salvation." Whence, since the cankerworm, &c. are images of spiritual enemies, this place has been paraphrased; " ³ I will not allow the richness of spiritual things to perish, which ye lost through the passions of the mind." Nay, since none can recover without the grace of God and using that grace, the penitent, who really rises again by the grace of God, rises with larger grace than before, since he has both the former grace, and; in addition, this new grace, whereby he rises.

26. *And ye shall eat in plenty and be satisfied.* It is of the punishment of God, when men eat and are *not* satisfied ⁴; it is man's sin, that they are satisfied, and do not to praise God, but the more forget Him ⁵. And so God's blessings become a curse to him. God promises to restore His gifts, and to give grace withal, that they should own and thank Him.

Who hath dealt wondrously with you. " First, wonderfully He afflicted and chastened them, and then gave them wonderful abundance of all things, and very great and miraculous consolation after vehement tribulation, so that they might truly say, *This is the change of the Right Hand of the Most High.*"

And My people shall never be ashamed. " ⁶ So that they persevere in His service. Although he incur temporal confusion, yet this shall not last for ever, but the people of the predestinate, penitent, and patient in adversity, will be saved for ever."

27. *And ye shall know that I am in the midst of Israel.* God had foretold their rebellions,

His forsaking them, *the troubles* which should *find* them, and that *they* should say ⁷, *Are not these evils come upon us, because our God is not among us?* It had been the mockery of the Heathen in their distress ⁸, *Where is their God?* " Now, by the fulfillment of His promises and by all God's benefits, they should know that He was among them by special grace as His own peculiar people." Still more was this to be fulfilled to Christians, in whose heart He dwells by love and grace, and of whom He says, *Where two or three are gathered together in My name, there will I be in the midst of them.* In the highest sense, *God was in the midst of them,* in that " ⁹ God the Son, equal to God the Father as touching His Godhead, did, in the truth of human nature, take our flesh. This to see and know, is glory and bliss ineffable. Therefore He repeats, and by repeating, confirms, what he had said, *And My people shall never be ashamed.* Yea, glorious, magnified, honored, shall be the people, to whom such a Son was promised, and of whom He was born. Glorious to them is that which the Apostle saith, that *He took not on Him the nature of Angels, but He took the seed of Abraham,* and this glory shall be eternal."

28. *And it shall come to pass afterward.* After the punishment of the Jews through the Heathen, and their deliverance; after the Coming of the Teacher of righteousness, was to follow the outpouring of the Spirit of God.

I will pour out My Spirit on all flesh. " ⁹ This which He says, *on all flesh,* admits of no exception of nations or persons. For before Jesus was glorified, He had poured His Spirit only on the sons of Zion, and out of that nation only were there Prophets and wise men. But after He was glorified by His Resurrection and Ascension, He made no difference of Jews and Gentiles, but willed that remission of sins should be preached to all alike."

All flesh is the name of all mankind. So

¹ Gloss on Lev. vii. init.
² S. Aug. Ep. 153, ad Macedon. § 7.
³ Gloss hic. The above passages are quoted by Medina, de pœnit. q. 8. who uses these arguments.

⁴ See Hos. iv. 10.
⁵ Hos. xiii. 6.
⁷ Deut. xxxi. 17.
⁸ ii. 17.

⁶ Dion.

⁹ Rup.

Before
CHRIST
cir. 800.
m Zech. 12. 10.
John 7. 39.
n Is. 54. 13.
o Acts 21. 9.

to pass afterward, *that I* [m] will pour out my spirit upon all flesh; [n] and your sons and [o] your daughters shall prophesy, your old men shall dream dreams, your young men shall see visions:

Before
CHRIST
cir. 800.

in the time of the flood, it is said *all flesh had corrupted his way: the end of all flesh is come before Me.* Moses asks, *who of all flesh hath heard the voice of the Lord God, as we have, and lived?* So in Job; *in Whose Hand is the breath of all flesh of man. If He set His heart upon man, if He gather to Himself his spirit and his breath, all flesh shall perish together.* And David; *Thou that hearest prayer, to Thee shall all flesh come; let all flesh bless His Holy Name for ever and ever* [1]. In like way speak Isaiah, Jeremiah, Ezekiel, Zechariah [2]. The words *all flesh* are in the Pentateuch, and in one place in Daniel, used, in a yet wider sense, of everything which has life [3]; but, in no one case, in any narrower sense. It does not include every individual in the race, but it includes the whole race, and individuals throughout it, in every nation, sex, condition, *Jew or Gentile, Greek or Barbarian,* i. e. educated or uneducated, rich or poor, bond or free, male or female. As *all* were to be *one in Christ Jesus* [4], so on all was to be poured the Holy Spirit, the Bond Who was to bind all in one. He names our nature from that which is the lowest in it, *the flesh,* with the same condescension with which it is said, *The Word was made flesh* [5], whence we speak of the *Incarnation* of our Blessed Lord, i. e. "His taking on Him our Flesh." He humbled Himself to take our flesh; He came, as our Physician, to heal our flesh, the seat of our concupiscence. So also God the Holy Ghost vouchsafes to dwell in our flesh, to sanctify it and to heal it. He, Whom God saith He will pour out on all flesh, is the Spirit of God, and God. He does not say that He will pour out graces, or gifts, ordinary or extraordinary, influences, communications, or the like. He says, *I will pour out My Spirit;* as S. Paul says, *know ye not that ye are the temple of God, and the Spirit of God dwelleth in you* [6]? *Ye are not in the flesh but in the Spirit, if so be that the Spirit of God dwell in you. Now if any man have not the Spirit of Christ, he is none of His* [7]. It is said indeed, *on the Gentiles also was poured out the gift of the Holy Ghost,* but the gift of the Holy Ghost was the Holy Ghost Himself, as it had been just said, *the Holy Ghost fell on all them that heard the word* [8]. It is said, *the love of God is shed abroad in our hearts by the*

Holy Ghost, which is given us [9]; but the *Holy Ghost* is first *given,* and He poureth out into the soul the *love of God.* As God the Word, when He took human nature, came into it personally, so that *the fullness of the Godhead dwelt bodily in it* [10]; so, really, although not personally, "doth the Holy Spirit, and so the whole Trinity, enter into our mind by sanctification, and dwelleth in it as in His throne." No created being, no Angel, nor Archangel could dwell in the soul. "[11] God Alone can be poured out into the soul, so as to possess it, enlighten it, teach, kindle, bend, move it as He wills," sanctify, satiate, fill it. And "as God is really present with the blessed, when He sheweth to them His Essence by the beatific vision and light of glory, and communicates it to them, to enjoy and possess; so He, the Same, is also in the holy soul, and thus diffuseth it in His grace, love, and other divine gifts." At the moment of justification, "the Holy Ghost and so the whole Holy Trinity entereth the soul at His temple, sanctifying and as it were dedicating and consecrating it to Himself, and at the same moment of time, although in the order of nature subsequently, He communicates to it His love and grace. Such is the meaning of, *We will come unto him, and make Our abode with him.* This is the highest union of God with the holy soul; and greater than this can none be given to any creature, for by it we become *partakers of the divine Nature,* as S. Peter [12] saith. See here, O Christian, the dignity of the holiness whereunto thou art called and with all zeal follow after, preserve, enlarge it."

This His Spirit, God says, *I will pour,* i.e. give largely, as though He would empty out Him Who is Infinite, so that there should be no measure of His giving, save our capacity of receiving. So He says of converted Israel [13], *I have poured out My Spirit upon the house of Israel,* and [14], *I will pour out upon the house of David and upon the inhabitants of Jerusalem the Spirit of grace and supplication.*

And your sons and your daughters shall prophesy. This cannot limit what he has said, that God would pour out His Spirit upon all flesh. He gives instances of that out-pouring, in those miraculous gifts, which were at the first to be the tokens and evidence of His

[1] Gen. vi. 12, 13. Deut. v. 26. Job xii. 10. xxxiv. 14, 15. Ps. lxv. 2. cxlv. 21.
[2] Is. xl. 5, 6. xlix. 26. lxvi. 16, 23, 24. Jer. xxv. 31. xxxii. 27. xlv. 5. Ezek. xx. 48. xxi. 4, 5. Zech. ii. 13.
[3] Gen. vi. 17, 19. vii. 15, 16, 21. viii. 17. ix. 11, 15, 16, 17.

Lev. xvii. 14. Num. xviii. 15. Dan. iv. 12; probably Ps. cxxxvi. 25.
[4] Gal. iii. 28. [5] S. Aug. Ep. 140. c. 4. Lap.
[6] 1 Cor. iii. 16. [7] Rom. viii. 9, 10. [8] Acts x. 44, 45.
[9] Rom. v. 5. [10] Col. ii. 9. [11] Lap. [12] 2 S. Pet. i. 4.
[13] Ezek. xxxix. 29. [14] Zech. xii. 10.

29 And also upon [p] the servants and upon the

[p] 1 Cor. 12. 13. Gal. 3. 28. Col. 3. 11.

handmaids in those days will I pour out my spirit.

inward Presence. These gifts were at the first bestowed on the Jews only. The highest were reserved altogether for them. Jews only were employed as Apostles and Evangelists; Jews only wrote, by inspiration of God, *the oracles of God*, as the source of the faith of the whole world. "[1] The Apostles were sons of Israel; the Mother of our Lord Jesus Christ, and the other women who abode at the same time and prayed with the Apostles, were daughters. S. Luke mentions, *All these were persevering with one accord in prayer with the women and Mary the Mother of Jesus, and His brethren.* These sons and daughters of the Sons of Zion, having received the Spirit, prophesied, i. e. in divers tongues they spoke of the heavenly mysteries." In the narrower sense of "[2] foretelling the future, the Apostles, the Blessed Virgin [3], Zacharias [4] and Anna [5], Elizabeth [6], the virgin daughters of Philip [7], Agabus [8], S. John in the Apocalypse," Simeon [9], and S. Paul also oftentimes [10] prophesied. At Antioch, there were certain *prophets* [11]; and [12] *the Holy Ghost in every city witnessed, saying, that bonds and afflictions awaited him* in Jerusalem. "But it is superfluous," adds Theodoret [13] after giving some instances, "to set myself to prove the truth of the prophecy. For down to our times also hath this gift been preserved, and there are among the saints, men who have the eye of the mind clear, who foreknow and foretell many of the things which are about to be." So the death of Julian the Apostate, who fell, as it seemed, by a chance wound in war with the Persians was foreseen and foretold [14]; and S. Cyprian foretold the day of his own martyrdom and the close of Decian persecution, which ended through the death of the Emperor in a rash advance over a morass, when victory was gained [15]. The stream of prophecy has been traced down through more than four centuries from the Birth of the Redeemer. One of the Bishops of the Council of Nice was gifted with a prophetic spirit [16].

Your old men shall dream dreams, and your young men shall see visions. "[8] God often attempers Himself and His oracles to the condition of men, and appears to each, as suits his state." It may then be, that to old men, while sleeping by reason of age, He appeared most commonly in dreams; to young men,

while watching, in visions. But it is so common in Hebrew, that each part of the verse should be filled up from the other, that perhaps the Prophet only means, that their old and young should have dreams and see visions, and both from God. Nor are these the highest of God's revelations; as He says, that to the prophet He would *make* Himself *known in a vision* and would *speak in a dream*, but to Moses *mouth to mouth; even apparently, and not in dark speeches; and the similitude of the Lord shall he behold* [17].

The Apostles also saw waking visions, as S. Peter at Joppa [18]; (and that so frequently, that when the Angel delivered him, he thought that it was one of his accustomed visions [19],) and S. Paul after his conversion, and calling him to Macedonia; and the Lord appeared unto him in vision at Corinth, revealing to him the conversions which should be worked there, and at Jerusalem foretelling to him the witness he should bear to Him at Rome. In the ship, the Angel of the Lord foretold to him his own safety, and that God had given him all who sailed with him [20]. Ananias [21] and Cornelius [22] also received revelations through visions. But all these were only revelations of single truths or facts. Of a higher sort seems to be that revelation, whereby our Lord revealed to S. Paul Himself and His Gospel which S. Paul was to preach, and *the wisdom of God*, and the glories of the world to come, and the conversion of the Gentiles; and when he was *caught up to the third heaven, and abundance of revelations* were vouchsafed to him [23].

29. *And also upon the servants.* God tells beforehand that he would be no respecter of persons. He had said, that He would endow every age and sex. He adds here, and every condition, even that of slaves, both male and female. He does not add here, that they shall prophesy. Under the law, God had provided for slaves, that, even if aliens, they should by circumcision be enrolled in His family and people; that they should have the rest and the devotion of the sabbath; and share the joy of their great festivals, going up with their masters and mistresses to the place which God appointed. They were included in one common ordinance of joy; *Ye shall rejoice before the Lord your God, ye and your sons and your daughters, and* [lit.]

[1] Rup. [2] Lap. [3] S. Luke i. 48.
[4] Ib. 67 sqq. [5] Ib. ii. 36, 38.
[6] Ib. i. 42-45. [7] Acts xxi. 9.
[8] Ib. xi. 28. xxi. 10, 11. [9] S. Luke ii. 27-35.
[10] Acts xx. 29, 30. 2 Thess. ii. 3-12. 2 Tim. iii. 1, 4.
1 Tim. iv. 1.
[11] Acts xiii. 1. [12] Ib. xx. 23. [13] ad loc.
[14] Theodoret H. E. iii. 18, 19.

[15] See Pref. to S. Cyprian's Epistles and Ep. xi. p. 27. note k. Oxf. Tr.
[16] S. Greg. Naz. Orat. 18. in fun. patr. § 12.
[17] Num. xii. 6, 8. [18] Acts x. 10 sqq. xi. 5 sqq.
[19] Ib. xii. 9.
[20] Acts ix. 12. xvi. 6, 7, 9. xviii. 9. xix. 21. xxiii. 11. xxvii. 24. [21] Ib. ix. 10. [22] Ib. x. 3.
[23] Gal. i. 12, 16. 1 Cor. ii. 7. Eph. iii. 3. 2 Cor. xii. 1-7.

Before
CHRIST
cir. 800.

30 And [q] I will shew wonders in the heavens

[q] Matt. 24. 29. Mark 13. 24. Luke 21. 11, 25.

and in the earth, blood, and fire, and pillars of smoke.

Before
CHRIST
cir. 800.

your men slaves and your women slaves, and the Levite which is within your gates [1]. In the times before the Gospel, they doubtless fell under the contempt in which the Pharisees held all the less educated class; *These people who knoweth not the law* (i. e. according to the explanation of their schools) *is cursed.* Whence it was a saying of theirs, " [2] Prophecy doth not reside except on one wise and mighty and rich." As then elsewhere it was given as a mark of the Gospel, *the poor have the Gospel preached unto them,* so here. It was not what the Jews of his day expected; for he says, *And on the servants too.* But he tells beforehand, what was against the pride both of his own times and of the time of its fulfillment, that [3] *God chose the foolish things of the world to confound the wise, and God hath chosen the weak things of the world to confound the things which are mighty ; and base things of the world and things which are despised hath God chosen, and things which are not, to bring to naught things that are, that no flesh should glory in His presence.* The prophetic word circles round to that wherewith it began, the all-containing promise of the large out-pouring of the Spirit of God ; and that, upon those whom the carnal Jews at all times would least expect to receive it. It began with including the heathen; *I will pour out My Spirit on all flesh;* it instances individual gifts; and then it ends by resting on the slaves ; *and on these too in those days will I pour out My Spirit.* The order of the words is significant. He begins, *I will pour out My Spirit upon all flesh,* and then, in order to leave the mind resting on these same great words, he inverts the order, and ends, *and upon the servants and upon the handmaidens I will pour out My Spirit.* It leaves the thoughts resting on the great words, *I will pour out My Spirit.*

The Church at Rome, whose *faith was spoken of throughout the whole world* [4], was, as far as it consisted of converted Jews, made up of slaves, who had been set free by their masters. For such were most of the Roman Jews, " [5] who occupied that large section of Rome beyond the Tiber." Most of these, Philo says, " having been made freemen, were Roman citizens. For having been brought as captives to Italy, set free by their purchasers, without being compelled to change any of

[1] Gen. xvii. 23, 27. Ex. xx. 10. Deut. xii. 12, 18. xvi. 11, 14.　　[2] Moreh Nebochim, ii. 32. in Poc.
[3] 1 Cor. i. 27–30.　　　　　[4] Rom. i. 8.
[5] Philo leg. ad Caium, p. 1014. ed. Paris.
[6] Dion.　　　　　　　[7] Ps. cxvi. 16.
[8] Gen. xxvi. 24. Num. xii. 7, 8. Josh. i. 2. 2 Kings xxi. 8. Job i. 8. ii. 3. xlii. 7, 8. 2 Sam. vii. 5. &c. Is. xx. 3.

their country's rites, they had their synagogues and assembled in them, especially on the sabbath."

S. Peter, in declaring that these words began to be fulfilled in the Day of Pentecost, quotes them with two lesser differences. *I will pour out of My Spirit,* and *upon My servants and My handmaidens.* The words declare something in addition, but do not alter the meaning, and so S. Peter quotes them as they lay in the Greek, which probably was the language known by most of the mixed multitude, to whom he spake on the day of Pentecost. The words, *I will pour out My Spirit,* express the largeness and the fullness of the gift of Him, " [6] Who is Very God, Unchangeable and Infinite, Who is given or poured out, not by change of place but by the largeness of His Presence." The words, *I will pour out of My Spirit,* express in part, that He Who is Infinite cannot be contained by us who are finite ; in part, they indicate, that there should be a distribution of gifts, although *worked by One and the Same Spirit,* as the Prophet also implies in what follows. Again, the words, *the servants and the handmaidens,* mark the outward condition; the words *My servants and My handmaidens,* declare that there should be no difference between *bond and free.* The servants and handmaidens should have that highest title of honor, that they should be the servants of God. For what more can the creature desire? The Psalmist says to God [7], *Lo I am Thy servant and the son of Thine handmaid ;* and God gives it as a title of honor to Abraham and Moses and Job and David and Isaiah [8], and Abraham and David call themselves the servants of God [9], and S. Paul, S. Peter, and S. Jude, *servants of Jesus Christ* [10], and S. James, *the servant of God* [11]; and the blessed Virgin, *the handmaid of the Lord* [12]; yea, and our Lord Himself, in His Human Nature is spoken of in prophecy as [13] *the Servant of the Lord.*

30. *And I will shew wonders.* Each revelation of God prepares the way for another, until that last revelation of His love and of His wrath in the Great Day. In delivering His people from Egypt, *the Lord shewed signs and wonders, great and sore, upon Egypt* [14]. Here, in allusion to it, He says, in the same words [15], of the new revelation, *I will shew,* or *give, wonders,* or *wondrous signs,* (as the word

[9] Gen. xix. 19. Ps. lxxxvi. 2, 4.
[10] Rom. i. 1. Gal. i. 10. 2 S. Pet. i. 1. S. Jude 1.
[11] S. Jam. i. 1, also Tit. i. 1.
[12] S. Luke i. 38, 48.
[13] Is. xlii. 1. xlix.6. lii. 13. Zech. lii. 8. Ezek. xxxiv. 23, 4. xxxvii. 24, 5.　　　　[14] Deut. vi. 22.
[15] ‏ונתתי מופתים‎ Deut. ‏ויתן יי אותת ומפתים‎ Joel.

Before CHRIST cir. 800.

31 [r] The sun shall be turned into darkness, and the moon into

[r] Is. 13. 9, 10. ch. 3. 1, 15. ver. 10. Matt. 24. 29. Mark. 13. 24. Luke 21. 25. Rev. 6. 12.

blood, [s] before the great and the terrible day of the LORD come.

Before CHRIST cir. 800.

[s] Mal. 4. 5.

includes both) wonders beyond the course and order of nature, and portending other dispensations of God, of joy to His faithful, terror to His enemies. As when Israel came out of Egypt, [1] *the pillar of the cloud was a cloud and darkness to the camp of the Egyptians*, but *gave light by night* to the *camp of Israel*, so all God's workings are light and darkness at once, according as men are, who see them or to whom they come. These wonders in heaven and earth " began in" the First Coming and " Passion of Christ, grew in the destruction of Jerusalem, but shall be perfectly fulfilled toward the end of the world, before the final Judgment, and the destruction of the Universe." At the birth of Christ, there was *the star* which appeared unto the wise men, and *the multitude of the heavenly host*, whom the shepherds saw. At His Atoning Death, *the sun was darkened*, there was the three hours' darkness over the whole land; and on earth *the veil of the temple was rent in twain from the top to the bottom, and the earth did quake, and the rocks rent, and the graves were opened* [2]: and the Blood and water issued from the Saviour's side. After His Resurrection, there was the vision of Angels, terrible to the soldiers who watched the sepulchre, comforting to the women who sought to honor Jesus. His Resurrection was a sign on earth, His Ascension in earth and heaven. But our Lord speaks of signs both in earth and heaven, as well before the destruction of Jerusalem, as before His second Coming.

With regard to the details, it seems probable that this is an instance of what we may call an inverted parallelism, that having mentioned generally that God would give *signs in* 1) *heaven and* 2) *earth*, the Prophet first instances the *signs in earth*, and then those *in heaven*. A very intellectual Jewish expositor [3] has suggested this, and certainly it is frequent enough to be, in conciser forms, one of the idioms of the sacred language. In such case, *the blood and fire and pillars of smoke*, will be *signs in earth; the turning of the sun into darkness and the moon into blood* will be *signs in heaven*. When fortelling the destruction of Jerusalem, the Day of vengeance, which fell with such accumulated horror on the devoted city, and has for these 1800 years dispersed the people of Israel to the four winds, our Lord mentions first the signs

[1] Ex. xiv. 19, 20. [2] S. Luke xxiii. 44, 5. S. Matt. xxvii. 45, 51, 52. [3] Aben Ezra. [4] S. Luke xxi. 10, 11.

on earth, then those in heaven. *Nation shall arise against nation, and kingdom against kingdom, and great earthquakes shall be in divers places, and famines, and pestilences; and fearful sights and great signs shall there be from heaven* [4]. Before the Day of Judgment our Lord also speaks of both [5]; 1) *there shall be signs in the sun and in the moon and in the stars;* 2) *and upon the earth distress of nations with perplexity; the sea and the waves roaring; men's hearts failing them for fear and for looking after those things which are coming on the earth; for the powers of heaven shall be shaken.*

The Jewish historian relates signs both in heaven and in earth, before the destruction of Jerusalem [6]. " A star stood like a sword over Jerusalem;" " a light which, when the people were assembled at the Passover at 9 at night, shone so brightly around the altar and the temple, that it seemed like bright day, and this for half an hour; the Eastern door of the temple, which 20 men scarcely shut at eventide, stayed with iron-bound bars and very deep bolts let down into the threshold of one solid stone, was seen at 6 o'clock at night to open of its own accord; chariots and armed troops were seen along the whole country, coursing through the clouds, encircling the cities; at the feast of Pentecost, the priests entering the temple by night, as their wont was for worship, first perceived a great movement and sound, and then a multitudinous voice, ' Let us depart hence.' " These signs were authenticated by the multitude or character of those who witnessed them.

31. *Before the great and terrible Day of the Lord come.* " [7] The days of our life are our days wherein we do what we please; *that* will be the *Day of the Lord*, when He, our Judge, shall require the account of all our doings. It will be *great*, because it is the horizon of time and eternity; the last day of time, the beginning of eternity. It will put an end to the world, guilt, deserts, good or evil. It will be *great*, because in it great things will be done. Christ with all His Angels will come down and sit on His Throne; all who have ever lived or shall live, shall be placed before Him to be judged; all thoughts, words, and deeds shall be weighed most exactly; on all a sentence will be passed, absolute, irrevocable throughout eternity; the saints shall be assigned to

[5] Ib. 25, 26. [6] Jos. de bell. Jud. vi. 5. 3; also in Euseb. H. E. iii. 8. [7] Lap.

Before
CHRIST
cir. 800.

t Rom. 10. 13.

32 And it shall come to pass, *that* t *whosoever shall* call on the name of the LORD *shall be delivered:*

Before
CHRIST
cir. 800.

heaven, the ungodly to hell; a great gulf shall be placed between, which shall sever them for ever, so that the ungodly shall never see the godly nor heaven nor God; but shall be shut up in a prison for ever, and shall burn as long as heaven shall be heaven, or God shall be God." "¹ That day shall be great to the faithful, terrible to the unbelieving; great to those who said, *Truly this is the Son of God;* terrible to those who said, *His blood be upon us and upon our children.*" "² When then thou art hurried to any sin, think on that terrible and unendurable judgment-seat of Christ, where the Judge sits on His lofty Throne, and all creation shall stand in awe at His glorious Appearing and we shall be brought, one by one, to give account of what we have done in life. Then by him who hath done much evil in life, there will stand terrible angels.—*There* will be the deep gulf, the impassable darkness, the lightless fire, retaining in darkness the power to burn, but reft of its rays. *There* is the empoisoned and ravenous worm insatiably devouring and never satisfied, inflicting by its gnawing pangs unbearable. There that sharpest punishment of all, that shame and everlasting reproach. Fear these things; and, instructed by this fear, hold in thy soul as with a bridle from the lust of evil."

32. *Whosoever shall call upon the name of the Lord.* To call upon *the name of the Lord,* is to worship Him, as HE IS, depending *upon* Him. *The name of the Lord,* expresses His True Being, That which He IS. Hence so often in Holy Scripture, men are said to *call on the Name of the Lord,* to bless the Name of the Lord, to praise the Name of the Lord, to sing praises to His Name, to make mention of His Name, to tell of His Name, to know His Name ³; but it is very rarely said *I will praise the Name of God* ⁴. For the Name rendered *the Lord,* expresses that HE IS, and that He Alone IS, the Self-Same, the Unchangeable; the name rendered *God* is not the special Name of God. Hence as soon as men were multiplied and the corrupt race of Cain increased, men *began,* after the birth of Enos, the son of Seth, *to call upon the Name of the Lord* ⁵, i. e. in public worship. Abraham's worship, in the presence of the idolatries of Canaan, is spoken of, under the same words, *he called upon the Name of the Lord* ⁶. Elijah says to the prophets of Baal, *call ye on the name of your gods,*

and I will call on the Name of the Lord ⁷. Naaman the Heathen says of Elisha ⁸, *I thought that he would come out to me, and stand and call on the Name of the Lord his God.* Asaph and Jeremiah pray God ⁹; *Pour out Thy wrath upon the heathen that have not known Thee, and upon the kingdoms* [*families* Jer.] *which have not called upon Thy Name;* and Zephaniah foretells the conversion of the Heathen ¹⁰, *that they may all call upon the Name of the Lord, to serve Him with one consent.*

To *call* then *upon the Name of the Lord* implies right faith, to call upon Him as He IS; right trust in Him, leaning upon Him; right devotion, calling upon Him as He has appointed; right life, ourselves who call upon Him being, or becoming by His Grace, what He wills. They *call* not *upon the Lord,* but upon some idol of their own imagining, who call upon Him, as other than He has revealed Himself, or remaining themselves other than those whom He has declared that He will hear. For such deny the very primary attribute of God, His truth. *Their* God is not a God of truth. But whosoever shall in true faith and hope and charity have in this life worshiped God, *shall be delivered,* i. e. out of the midst of all the horrors of that Day, and the horrible damnation of the ungodly. The *deliverance* is by way of *escape* (for such is the meaning of the word ¹¹,) *he shall be made to escape, slip through* (as it were) perils as imminent as they shall be terrible. Our Lord uses the like word of the same Day ¹², *Watch ye therefore and pray always, that ye may be accounted worthy to escape all these things that shall come to pass, and to stand before the Son of man.* Those who so call upon Him in truth shall be heard in that day, as He says ¹³, *Ask and it shall be given you; Whatsoever ye shall ask the Father in My Name, He will give it you.*

"¹⁴ That calling on God whereon salvation depends, is not in words only, but in heart and in deed. For what the heart believeth, the mouth confesseth, the hand in deed fulfilleth, The Apostle saith ¹⁵, *No man can say that Jesus is the Lord, but by the Holy Ghost;* yet this very *saying* must be weighed not by words, but by the affections. Whence we read of Samuel, *And Samuel among those who call upon His Name,* and of Moses and Aaron ¹⁶, *These called upon the Lord, and He heard them.*

For in Mount Zion—shall be deliverance. Re-

---

¹ Hugo de S. V.　² S. Basil in Ps. xxxiii. § 8. Lap.

³ אודה, אזכירה, אכפרה שמך, יודעי שמך,
קרא בשם יי. ברך, הלל את שם יי. אזמרה

⁴ Ps. lxix. 31. Heb.　　⁵ Gen. iv. 26.
⁶ Ib. xii. 8. xiii. 4. xxi. 33. xxvi. 25.

⁷ 1 Kings xviii. 24.　　⁸ 2 Kings v. 11.
⁹ Ps. lxxix. 6. Jer. x. 25.　　¹⁰ iii. 9.
¹¹ ימלט　　　　　¹² S. Luke xxi. 36.
¹³ S. Matt. vii. 7. S. John xvi. 23.
¹⁴ Hugo de S. V. partly from S. Jer.
¹⁵ 1 Cor. xii. 3.　　　¹⁶ Ps xcix. 6.

Before
CHRIST
cir. 800.
u Is. 46. 13.
& 59. 20.
Obad. 17. Rom. 11. 26.

for ^u in mount Zion and in Jerusalem shall be deliverance, as the LORD

hath said, and in ^x the remnant whom the LORD shall call.

Before
CHRIST
cir. 800.
x Is. 11. 11, 16.
Jer. 31. 7.
Mic. 4. 7. & 5. 3, 7, 8. Rom. 9. 27. & 11. 5, 7.

pentance and remission of sins were to be preached *in the Name* of Jesus, *in all nations, beginning at Jerusalem* [1]. *There* was, under the Old Testament, the centre of the worship of God; *there* was the Church founded; thence it spread over the whole world. The place [2], *whither the tribes went up, the tribes of the Lord, unto the testimony of Israel, to give thanks unto the Name of the Lord,* where God had set His Name, where alone sacrifice could lawfully be offered, stands, as elsewhere, for the whole Church. Of that Church, we are in Baptism all made members, when we are made members of Christ, children of God, and heirs of heaven. Of that Church all remain members, who do not, by viciousness of life, or rejecting the truth of God, cast themselves out of it. They then are members of the *soul* of the Church, who, not being members of the visible Communion and society, know not, that in not becoming members of it, they are rejecting the command of Christ, to Whom by faith and love and in obedience they cleave. And *they*, being members of the *body* or visible communion of the Church, are not members of the *soul* of the Church, who, amid outward profession of the faith, do, in heart or deeds, deny Him Whom in words they confess. The deliverance promised in that Day, is to those who, being in the body of the Church, shall by true faith in Christ and fervent love to Him belong to the soul of the Church also, or who, although not in the body of the Church shall not, through their own fault, have ceased to be in the body, and shall belong to its soul, in that through faith and love they cleave to Christ its Head.

As the Lord hath said, by the Prophet Joel himself. This which he had said, is not man's word, but God's; and what God had said, shall certainly be. They then who have feared and loved God in this their day, shall not need to fear Him in that Day, for He is the Unchangeable God; as our Blessed Saviour says [3]; *Heaven and earth shall pass away, but My words shall not pass away.* God had said of both Jews and Gentiles, united in one [4]; *Rejoice, O ye nations, with His people, for He will avenge the blood of His servants, and will render vengeance to His adversaries, and will be merciful to His land and unto His people.*

And in the remnant. While foretelling His mercies in Christ, God foretells also, that [5] *few they be that find* them. It is evermore *a remnant, a residue, a body which escapes;* and so here, the mercies should be fulfilled, literally, *in the fugitives,* in those who flee from the wrath to come. All prophecy echoes the words of Joel; all history exemplifies them. Isaiah, Micah, Zephaniah, Jeremiah, Ezekiel, Zechariah, all foretell with one voice, that a remnant, and a remnant only, shall be left. In those earlier dispensations of God, in the flood, the destruction of Sodom and Gomorrah; in His dealings with Israel himself at the entrance into the promised land, the return from the Captivity, the first preaching of the Gospel, the destruction of Jerusalem, *a remnant* only was saved. It is said in tones of compassion and mercy, that *a remnant should be saved. The remnant should return, the remnant of Jacob, to the Mighty God* [6]. *The Lord of hosts shall be for a crown of glory to the residue of His people* [7]. *The Lord shall set His Hand to recover the remnant of His people which shall be left* [8]. *I will gather the remnant of My flock out of all countries whither I have driven them* [9]. *Publish ye, praise ye, and say, O Lord, save Thy people, the remnant of Israel* [10]. *Yet I will leave a remnant, that ye may have some that escape the sword among the nations* [11]. *Therein shall be left a remnant which shall be brought forth* [12]. *I will surely gather the remnant of Israel* [13]. *Who is a God like Thee, that pardoneth iniquity, and passeth by the transgression of the remnant of His heritage* [14]? *The remnant of Israel shall not do iniquity* [15]. *The residue of the people shall not be cut off from the city* [16]. It is then a summary of the declarations of the Prophets, when S. Paul says [17], *Even so, at this present time also, there is a remnant according to the election of grace. Israel hath not obtained that which he seeketh for; but the election hath obtained it, and the rest were blinded.* And so the Prophet says here;

Whom the Lord shall call. He had said before, *whosoever shall call upon the Name of the Lord shall be delivered.* Here he says, that they who should *so call on God,* shall themselves have been first *called by God.* So S. Paul [18], *to them that are sanctified in Christ Jesus, called to be Saints, with all that in every place call upon the Name of Jesus Christ our Lord.* It is all of grace. God must first call by His

[1] S. Luke xxiv. 47.
[2] Ps. cxxii. 4.
[3] S. Mark xiii. 31.
[4] Deut. xxxii. 43.
[5] S. Matt. vii. 14.
[6] Is. x. 20; add 21, 22. vi. 9–13, &c.
[7] Ib. xxviii. 5.
[8] Ib. xi, 11, add 16.

[9] Jer. xxiii. 3.
[10] Ib, xxxi. 7.
[11] Ezek. vi. 8.
[12] Ib. xiv. 22.
[13] Mic. ii. 12; add iv. 7. v. 3, 7, 8.
[14] Ib. vii. 18.
[15] Zeph. iii. 13. add ii. 9.
[16] Zech. xiv. 2.
[17] Rom. xi. 5, 7.
[18] 1 Cor. i. 2.

Before
C H R I S T
cir. 800.

CHAPTER III.

1 *God's judgments against the
enemies of his people.* 9 *God
will be known in his judgment.*
18 *His blessing upon the
Church.*

ᵃ Jer. 30. 3.
Ezek. 38. 14.

FOR, behold, ᵃ in those
days, and in that time,
when I shall bring again

the captivity of Judah and
Jerusalem,

Before
C H R I S T
cir. 800.

2 ᵇ I will also gather all ᵇ Zech. 14. 2, 3, 4.
nations and will bring them
down into ᶜ the valley ᶜ 2 Chr. 20. 26.
Jehoshaphat, and ᵈ will ᵈ Isai. 66. 16.
plead with them there for
my people and *for* my her-

ver. 12.
Ezek. 38. 22.

---

grace; then we obey His call, and call upon
Him; and He has said [1], *call upon Me in the
day of trouble, and I will deliver thee, and thou
shalt glorify Me.* God accounts our salvation
His own glory.

III. 1. *For, behold.* The Prophet by the
word, *for*, shews that he is about to explain
in detail, what he had before spoken of, in
sum. By the word, *behold*, he stirs up our
minds for something great, which he is to set
before our eyes, and which we should not be
prepared to expect or believe, unless he
solemnly told us, *Behold.* As the detail, then,
of what goes before, the prophecy contains
all times of future judgment on those who
should oppose God, oppress His Church and
people, and sin against Him in them and all
times of His blessing upon His own people,
until the Last Day. And this it gives in
imagery, partly describing nearer events of
the same sort, as in the punishments of Tyre
and Sidon, such as they endured from the
kings of Assyria, from Nebuchadnezzar, from
Alexander; partly using these, His earlier
judgments, as representatives of the like
punishments against the like sins unto the
end.

In those days and in that time. The whole
period of which the Prophet had been speaking, was the time from which God called His
people to repentance, to the Day of Judgment. The last division of that time was
from the beginning of the Gospel unto that
Day. He fixes the occasion of which he
speaks by the words, *when I shall bring again
the captivity of Judah and Jerusalem.* This
form was used, before there was any general
dispersion of the nation. For all captivity
of single members of the Jewish people
had this sore calamity, that it severed them
from the public worship of God, and exposed
them to idolatry. So David complains, *they
have driven me out this day from abiding in the
inheritance of the Lord, saying, go serve other
gods* [2]. The restoration then of single members, or of smaller bodies of captives, was, at
that time, an unspeakable mercy. It was the
restoration of those shut out from the worship of God; and so was an image of *the de-*

liverance from the bondage of corruption into the
glorious liberty of the sons of God [3], or of any
return of those who had gone astray, *to the
Shepherd and Bishop of their souls* [4]. The
grievous captivity of the Jews, now, is to
Satan, whose servants they made themselves,
when they said, *we have no king but Cæsar;
His Blood be upon us and upon our children.*
Their blessed deliverance will be *from the
power of Satan unto God* [5]. It is certain from
S. Paul [6], that there shall be a complete conversion of the Jews, before the end of the
world, as indeed has always been believed.
This shall probably be shortly before the end
of the world, and God would here say, " when
I shall have brought to an end *the captivity of
Judah and Jerusalem,* i. e. of that people *to
whom were the promises* [7], and shall have
delivered them from the bondage of sin and
from blindness to light and freedom in Christ,
then will I gather all nations to judgment."

2. *I will gather all nations and bring them
down to the valley of Jehoshaphat.* It may be
that the imagery is furnished by that great
deliverance which God gave to Jehoshaphat,
when *Ammon and Moab and Edom come against
him, to cast God's people out of* His *possession,*
which He *gave* them *to inherit* [8], and Jehoshaphat appealed to God, *O our God, wilt Thou
not judge them?* and God said, *the battle is not
your's but God's,* and God turned their swords
everyone against the other, *and none escaped.
And on the fourth day they assembled themselves
in the valley of Berachah* (blessing); *for there
they blessed the Lord* [9]. So, in the end, He shall
destroy Anti-Christ, not by human aid, but
by the breath of His mouth, and then the end
shall come and He shall sit on the throne of
His glory to judge all nations. Then shall
none escape of those gathered against Judah
and Jerusalem, but shall be judged of their
own consciences, as those former enemies of
His people fell by their own swords.

That valley, however, is nowhere called *the
valley of Jehoshaphat.* It continued to be *called
the valley of Berachah,* the writer adds, *to this
day.* And it is so called still. Caphar Barucha,
"the village of blessing," was still known in
that neighborhood in the time of S. Jerome [10];

[1] Ps. l. 15.   [2] 1 Sam. xxvi. 19.   [3] Rom. viii. 21
[4] 1 S. Pet. ii. 25.   [5] Acts xxvi. 18.   [6] Rom. xi. 26.

[7] Ib. ix. 4.   [8] 2 Chr. xx. 11.   [9] Ib. 24, 26.
[10] Ep. 108. ad Eustoch. ℥ 11.

itage Israel, whom they have scattered among the

nations, and parted my land.

it had been known in that of Josephus[1]. S. W. of Bethlehem and E. of Tekoa are still 3 or 4 acres of ruins[2], bearing the name Bereikut[3], and a valley below them, still bearing silent witness to God's ancient mercies, in its but slightly disguised name, "the valley of Bereikut" (Berachah). The only valley called the *valley of Jehoshaphat*[4], is the valley of Kedron, lying between Jerusalem and the Mount of Olives, encircling the city on the East. There Asa, Hezekiah, and Josiah cast the idols, which they had burned[5]. The valley was the common burying-place for the inhabitants of Jerusalem[6]. *There* was the garden whither Jesus oftentimes resorted with His disciples; *there* was His Agony and Bloody Sweat; there Judas betrayed Him; thence He was dragged by the rude officers of the High Priest. The Temple, the token of God's presence among them, the pledge of His accepting their sacrifices which could only be offered there, overhung it on the one side. There, under the rock on which that temple stood, they dragged Jesus, *as a lamb to the slaughter*[7]. On the other side, it was overhung by the Mount of *Olives*, whence *He beheld the city and wept over it*, because it *knew not in that its day, the things which belong to its peace;* whence, after His precious Death and Resurrection, Jesus ascended into Heaven. There the Angels foretold His return[8], *This same Jesus which is taken up from you into heaven shall so come in like manner as ye have seen Him go into heaven.* It has been a current opinion, that our Lord should descend to judgment, not only in like manner, and in the like Form of Man, but in the same place, over this valley of Jehoshaphat. Certainly, if so it be, it were appropriate, that He should appear in His Majesty, where, for us, He bore the extremest shame; that He should judge *there*, where for us, He submitted to be judged. "He sheweth," says S. Hilary[9], "that the Angels bringing them together, the assemblage shall be in the place of His Passion; and meetly will His Coming in glory be looked for *there*, where He won for us the glory of eternity by the sufferings of His humility in the Body." But since the Apostle says, *we shall meet the Lord in the air*, then, not *in* the valley of Jehoshaphat, but *over* it, in the clouds, would His throne be. "[10] Uniting, as it were, Mount Calvary and Olivet, the spot would be well suited to that judgment wherein the saints shall partake of the glory

of the Ascension of Christ and the fruit of His Blood and Passion, and Christ shall take deserved vengeance of His persecutors and of all who would not be cleansed by His Blood."

God saith, *I will gather all nations*, of the gathering together of the nations against Him under Anti-Christ, because He overrules all things, and while they, in *their* purpose, are gathering themselves against His people and elect, He, in His purpose secret to them, is gathering them to sudden destruction and judgment, *and will bring them down;* for their pride shall be brought down, and themselves laid low. Even Jewish writers have seen a mystery in the word, and said, that it hinteth "the depth of God's judgments," that God "would descend with them into the depth of judgment[11]," "a most exact judgment even of the most hidden things."

His very Presence there would say to the wicked, "[12] In this place did I endure grief for you; here, at Gethsemane, I poured out for you that sweat of water and Blood; here was I betrayed and taken, bound as a robber, dragged over Cedron into the city; hard by this valley, in the house of Caiaphas and then of Pilate, I was for you judged and condemned to death, crowned with thorns, buffeted, mocked and spat upon; here, led through the whole city, bearing the Cross, I was at length crucified for you on Mount Calvary; here, stripped, suspended between heaven and earth, with hands, feet, and My whole frame distended, I offered Myself for you as a Sacrifice to God the Father. Behold the Hands which ye pierced; the Feet which ye perforated; the Sacred prints which ye anew imprinted on My Body. Ye have despised My toils, griefs, sufferings; ye have counted the Blood of My covenant an unholy thing; ye have chosen to follow your own concupiscences rather than Me, My doctrine and law; ye have preferred momentary pleasures, riches, honors, to the eternal salvation which I promised; ye have despised Me, threatening the fires of hell. Now ye see Whom ye have despised; now ye see that My threats and promises were not vain, but true; now ye see that vain and fallacious were your loves, riches, and dignities; now ye see that ye were fools and senseless in the love of them; but too late. *Depart, ye cursed, into everlasting fire, prepared for the devil and his*

---

[1] Jos. Ant. ix. 1. 3. [2] Robins. Pal. iii. 275.
[3] in Seetzen's map (Ritter, Erdk. xv. 635), Wolcott, Excurs. to Hebron, p. 43.
[4] Euseb. Onom. κοιλὰς 'Ιωσαφάτ.
[5] 1 Kings xv. 13. 2 Chr. xxx. 14. 2 Kings xxiii. 6, 12.
[6] Williams, H. C. ii. 523. Thomson, The Land, &c.
ii. 481. Josephus places the death of Athaliah in that valley. Ant. ix. 7. 3.
[7] Is. liii. 7. [8] Acts i. 11. [9] in S. Matt. c. 25.
[10] Suarez, in 3. p. q. 59. art. 6. disp. 53. sect. 3.
[11] Rashi and Abarbanel in Poc.
[12] abridged from Lap.

Before
CHRIST
cir. 800.
* Obad. 11.
Nah. 3. 10.

3 And they have ° cast lots for my people; and have given a boy for an harlot, and sold a girl for wine, that they might drink.

Before
CHRIST
cir. 800.

angels. But ye who believed, hoped, loved, worshiped Me, your Redeemer, who obeyed My whole law; who lived a Christian life worthy of Me ; who lived soberly, godly and righteously in this world, looking for the blessed hope and this My glorious Coming, *Come ye blessed of My Father, inherit the kingdom of heaven prepared for you from the foundation of the World.—And these shall go into everlasting fire ; but the righteous into life eternal.* Blessed he whoso continually thinketh or foreseeth, provideth for these things."

And will plead with them there. Woe to him, against whom God pleadeth! He saith not, "judgeth" but *pleadeth,* making Himself a party, the Accuser as well as the Judge, "[1] Solemn is it indeed when Almighty God saith, *I will plead. He that hath ears to hear let him hear.* For terrible is it. Wherefore also that *Day of the Lord* is called *great and terrible.* For what more terrible than, at such a time, the pleading of God with man? For He says, *I will plead,* as though He had never yet pleaded with man, great and terrible as have been His judgments since that first destruction of the world by water. Past are those judgments on Sodom and Gomorrah, on Pharaoh and his hosts, on the whole people in the wilderness from twenty years old and upward, the mighty oppressions of the enemies into whose hands He gave them in the land of promise ; past were the four Empires ; but now, in the time of Anti-Christ, *there shall be tribulation, such as there had not been from the beginning of the world.* But all these are little, compared with that *great and terrible Day ;* and so He says, *I will plead,* as though all before had not been, to *plead.*"

God maketh Himself in such wise a party, as not to condemn those unconvicted ; yet the *pleading* has a separate awfulness of its own. God impleads, so as to allow Himself to be impleaded and answered ; but there is no answer. He will set forth what He had done, and how we have requited Him. And we are without excuse. Our memories witness against us ; our knowledge acknowledges His justice ; our conscience convicts us ; our reason condemns us ; all unite in pronouncing ourselves ungrateful, and God holy and just. For a sinner to see himself is to condemn himself ; and in the Day of Judgment, God will bring before each sinner his whole self.

For My people. "[1] God's people are the one true Israel, *princes with God,* the whole multitude of the elect, foreordained to eternal life." Of these, the former people of Israel, once chosen of God, was a type. As St. Paul says[2], *They are not all Israel which are of Israel ;* and again[3], *As many as walk according to this rule* of the Apostle's teaching, *peace be on them and mercy, and upon the Israel of God,* i. e. not among the Galatians only, but in the whole Church throughout the world. Since the whole people and Church of God is one, He lays down one law, which shall be fulfilled to the end ; that those who, for their own ends, even although therein the instruments of God, shall in any way injure the people of God, shall be themselves punished by God. God makes Himself one with His people. *He that toucheth you, toucheth the apple of My eye*[4]. So our Lord said, [5] *Saul, Saul, why persecutest thou Me?* and in the Day of Judgment He will say[6], *I was an hungered and ye gave me no meat. Forasmuch as ye did it not unto one of the least of these My brethern, ye did it not to Me.* "[7] By calling them *My heritage,* He shews that He will not on any terms part with them or suffer them to be lost, but will vindicate them to Himself for ever."

Whom they have scattered among the nations. Such was the offence of the Assyrians and Babylonians, the first *army,* which God sent against His people. And for it, Nineveh and Babylon perished. "[8] Yet he does not speak of that ancient people, or of its enemies only, but of all the elect both in that people and in the Church of the Gentiles, and of all persecutors of the elect. For that people were a figure of the Church, and its enemies were a type of those who persecute the Saints." The dispersion of God's former people by the heathen was renewed in those who persecuted Christ's disciples *from city to city,* banished them, and confiscated their goods. Banishment to mines or islands were the slightest punishments of the early Christians[9].

3. *And they have cast lots.* They treated God's people as of no account, and delighted in shewing their contempt toward them. They chose no one above another, as though all alike were worthless. *They cast lots,* it is said elsewhere[10], *upon their honorable men,* as a special indignity, above captivity or slavery. A *girl* they sold for an evening's revelry, and a *boy* they exchanged for a night's debauch.

[1] from Rup.   [2] Rom. ix. 6.
[3] Gal. vi. 16.   [4] Zech. ii. 8.   [5] Acts ix. 4.
[6] S. Matt. xxv. 34, 35.   [7] Poc.   [8] Rib.

[9] See Tertull. Apol. c. 12. p. 30. Oxf. Tr. S. Cypr. Ep. x. 1. xi. 1. xx. 3. xxii. xxxi. xxxvii. 2. 3. xxxix. 1. lxxvi. 2. p. 304. n. y.   [10] Nah. iii. 10.

Before
CHRIST
cir. 800.

f Amos 1. 6, 9.

g Ezek. 25. 15,
16, 17.

4 Yea, and what have
ye to do with me, [f] O Tyre,
and Zidon, and all the
coasts of Palestine? [g] will
ye render me a recom-
pense? and if ye recom-
pense me, swiftly *and* speed-

ily will I return your recompense upon your own head;
5 Because ye have taken
my silver and my gold, and
have carried into your temples my goodly † pleasant
things:

Before
CHRIST
cir. 800.

† Heb. *desirable:*
Dan. 11. 38.

---

4. *Yea, and what have ye to do with Me?* lit. *and also, what are ye to Me?* The words, *And also,* shew that this is something additional to the deeds of those before spoken of. Those, instanced before, were great oppressors, such as dispersed the former people of God and *divided their land.* In addition to these, God condemns here another class, those who, without having power to destroy, harass and vex His heritage. The words, *what are ye to Me?* are like that other phrase [1], *what is there to thee and me?* i. e. what have we in common? These words, *what are ye to Me?* also declare, that those nations had no part in God. God accounts them as aliens, *what are ye to Me?* Nothing. But the words convey, besides, that they would, unprovoked, have to do with God, harassing His people without cause. They obtruded themselves, as it were, upon God and His judgments; they challenged God; they thrust themselves in, to their destruction, where they had no great temptation to meddle, nothing, but inbred malice, to impel them. This was, especially, the character of the relations of Tyre and Zidon and Philistia with Israel. They were allotted to Israel by Joshua, but were not assailed [2]. On the contrary, *the Zidonians* are counted among those who *oppressed* Israel, and *out of* whose *hand* God *delivered* him, when he *cried* to God [3]. The Philistines were the unwearied assailants of Israel in the days of the Judges, and Saul, and David [4]; during 40 years Israel was given into the hands of the Philistines, until God delivered them by Samuel at Mizpeh. When David was king of all Israel, the Philistines still acted on the offensive, and lost Gath and her towns to David in an offensive war [5]. To Jehoshaphat some of them voluntarily paid tribute [6]; but in the reign of Jehoram his son, they, with some Arabians, marauded in Judah, plundering the king's house and slaying all his sons, save the youngest [7]. This is the last event before the time of Joel. They stand among

the most inveterate and unprovoked enemies of God's people, and probably as enemies of God also hating the claim of Judah that their God was the One God.

Will ye render Me a recompense? Men never want pleas for themselves. The Philistines, although the aggressors, had been signally defeated by David. Men forget their own wrong-doings and remember their sufferings. It may be then, that the Philistines thought that they had been aggrieved when their assaults were defeated, and looked upon their own fresh aggressions as a requital. If moreover, as is probable, they heard that the signal victories won over them were ascribed by Israel to God, and themselves also suspected, that these *mighty Gods* [8] were the cause of their defeat, they doubtless turned their hatred against God. Men, when they submit not to God chastening them, hate Him. This belief that they were retaliating against God, (not, of course, knowing Him as God,) fully corresponds with the strong words, "will ye render Me *a recompense* [9]?" Julian's dying blasphemy, "Galilean, thou hast conquered," corresponds with the efforts of his life against the gospel, and implies a secret consciousness that He Whose religion he was straining to overthrow *might* be, What he denied Him to be, God. The phrase [10] *swiftly,* lit. *lightly, and speedily,* denotes the union of easiness with speed. The recompense is returned *upon* their head, coming down upon them from God.

5. *Ye have taken My silver and My gold.* Not the silver and gold of the temple, (as some have thought.) At least, up to the Prophet's time, they had not done this. For the inroad of the Philistines in the reign of Jehoram was, apparently, a mere marauding expedition, in which they slew and plundered, but are not said to have besieged or taken any city, much less Jerusalem. God calls the *silver and gold* which He, through His Providence, had bestowed on Judah, *My* gold and silver; as He said by Hosea [11],

---

[1] Josh. xxii. 24, &c. S. Matt. viii. 29, &c.
[2] Zidon, Josh. xix. 28. xiii. 6. see Judg. i. 31. iii. 3. Tyre, Josh. xix. 29. the Philistines, Josh. xiii. 2, 3. xv. 45-7. xix. 43. see Jud. iii. 3.
[3] Judg. x. 12.
[4] Ib. xiii. 1. 1 Sam. iv. xiii. xvii. xxiii. 1. xxx. xxxi.
[5] 2 Sam. v. 17-end. viii. 1. 1 Chr. xviii. 1. 2 Sam. xxi. 18. xxiii. 9-16.

[6] 2 Chr. xvii. 11.   [7] 2 Chr. xxi. 16, 17. xxii. 1.
[8] 1 Sam. iv. 7, 8.

[9] גמל, rendered *recompense,* is used, although rarely, of one who "begins good or evil," but, as united with the word שלם *repay, make good,* it can only denote *required.*
[10] It recurs Is. v. 26.   [11] ii. 8.

6 The children also of || Judah and the children of

She knew not that I multiplied her silver and gold, whereof she made Baal ; and by Haggai[1], *The silver is Mine, and the gold is Mine, saith the Lord of Hosts.* For they were His people, and what they had, they held of Him ; and the Philistines too so accounted it, and dedicated a part of it to their idols, as they had the ark formerly, accounting the victory over God's people to be the triumph of their idols over God.

6. *The children also,* lit. *And the sons of Judah and the sons of Jerusalem have ye sold to the sons of the Greeks.* This sin of the Tyrians was probably old and inveterate. The Tyrians, as they were the great carriers of the world's traffic, so they were slave-dealers, and, in the earliest times, men-stealers. The Greek ante-historic tradition exhibits them, as trading and selling women, from both Greece[2] and Egypt[3]. As their trade became more fixed, they themselves stole no more, but, like Christian nations, sold those whom others stole or made captive. Ezekiel speaks of their trade in *the souls of men*[4] with *Greece* on the one side, and *Tubal and Mesech* near the Black Sea on the other. The beautiful youth of Greece of both sexes were sold even into Persia[5]. In regard to the Moschi and Tibareni, it remains uncertain, whether they sold those whom they took in war (and, like the tribes of Africa in modern times, warred the more, because they had a market for their prisoners,) or whether, like the modern Circassians, they sold their daughters. Ezekiel however says, *men,* so that he cannot mean, exclusively, women. From the times of the Judges, Israel was exposed in part both to the violence and fraud of Tyre and Sidon. The tribe of Asher seems to have lived in the open country among fortified towns of the Zidonians. For whereas of Benjamin, Manasseh, Ephraim, Zabulon, it is said that the old inhabitants of the land *dwelt among them*[6], of Asher it is said, that they *dwelt among the Canaanites, the inhabitants of the land*[7], as though these were the more numerous. And not only so, but since they did *not drive out the inhabitants* of seven cities, *Accho, Zidon, Ahlab, Achzib, Helbah, Aphek, Rehob,* they must have been liable to incursions from them. The Zidonians were among those who *oppressed Israel*[8]. Sisera's army came from their territory, (for Jabin was king of Hazor,) and Deborah

speaks of *a damsel or two,* as the expected prey of each man in the whole multitude of his host. An old proverb, mentioned B. C. 427, implies that the Phœnicians sent circumcised slaves into the fields to reap their harvest[9]. But there were no other circumcised there besides Israel.

But the Phœnician slave-trade was also probably, even in the time of the Judges, exercised against Israel. In Joel and Amos, the Philistines and Tyrians appear as combined in the traffic. In Amos, the Philistines are the robbers of men ; the Phœnicians are the receivers and the sellers[10]. Heathen nations retain for centuries the same inherited character, the same natural nobleness, or, still more, the same natural vices. The Phœnicians, at the date of the Judges, are known as dishonest traders, and that, in slaves. The Philistines were then also inveterate oppressors. On one occasion *the captivity of the land* coincided with the great victory of the Philistines, when Eli died and the ark of God was taken. For these two dates are given in the same place as the close of the idolatry of Micah's graven image. It endured *unto the captivity of the land*[11] and, *and all the time that the house of God was at Shiloh,* whence the ark was removed, never to return, in that battle when it was taken. But *the captivity of the land* is not merely a subdual, whereby the inhabitants would remain tributary or even enslaved, yet still remain. A captivity implies a removal of the inhabitants ; and such a removal could not have been the direct act of the Philistines. For dwelling themselves in the land only, they had no means of removing the inhabitants from it, except by selling them ; and the only nation, who could export them in such numbers as would be expressed by the words *a captivity of the land,* were the Zidonians. Probably such acts were expressly prohibited by the *brotherly covenant*[12] or treaty between Solomon and Hiram King of Tyre. For Amos says that Tyre forgot that treaty, when she sold wholesale the captive Israelites whom the Philistines had carried off. Soon after Joel, Obadiah speaks of a captivity at *Sepharad,* or *Sardis*[13], the capital of the Lydian empire. The Tyrian merchants were *the* connecting link between Palestine and the coasts of Asia-minor. The Israelites must have been sold thither as slaves, and that by

---

[1] ii. 8.
[2] Herod. i. 1. Eurip. Helen. 190. Movers quotes these and the following authorities Phœnic. Alterthum. c. 4. p. 71.
[3] Herod. ii. 54.   [4] xxvii. 13.
[5] Bochart Phaleg. iii. 3. p. 154.
[6] Judg. i. 21, 27, 29, 30.
[7] Ib. 31, 2.

[8] Judg. v. 30. see iv. 3, 7, 13, 15, 16.
[9] "Cuckoo; ye circumcised, to field." The Cuckoo's note was, in Phœnicia, the signal for harvest, (Aristoph. Av. 505-7,) and those sent out, with a term of contempt, to gather it, were "circumcised."
[10] Am. i. 6, 9.   [11] Judg. xviii. 30, 31.
[12] See on Am. i. 9.   [13] See on Ob. 20.

Jerusalem have ye sold unto † the Grecians, that

† Heb*. *the sons of the Grecians.*

ye might remove them far from their border.

the Phœnicians. In yet later times the Tyrian merchants followed, like vultures, on the rear of armies to make a prey of the living, as the vultures of the dead. They hung on the march of Alexander as far as India[1]. In the wars of the Maccabees, at Nicanor's proclamation, a thousand[2] merchants gathered to the camp of Gorgias[3] *with silver and gold, very much, to buy the children of Israel as slaves,* and with chains[4] wherewith to secure them. They assembled in the rear of the Roman armies, "[5] seeking wealth amid the clash of arms, and slaughter, and fleeing poverty through peril." Reckless of human life, the slave-merchants commonly, in their wholesale purchase of captives, abandoned the children as difficult of transport, whence the Spartan king was praised for providing for them[6].

The temptation to Tyrian covetousness was aggravated by the ease with which they could possess themselves of the Jews, the facility of transport, and, as it seems, their value. It is mentioned as the inducement to slave-piracy among the Cilicians. "The export of the slaves especially invited to misdeeds, being most gainful; for they were easily taken, and the market was not so very far off and was most wealthy[7].

The Jewish slaves appear also to have been valued, until those times after the taking of Jerusalem, when they had become demoralized, and there was a plethora of them, as God had predicted[8]. The post occupied by the *little maid* who *waited on Naaman's wife*[9], was that of a favorite slave, as Greek tradition represented Grecian maidens to have been an object of coveting to the wife of the Persian Monarch[10]. The *damsel or two* for the wives of each man in Jabin's host appear as a valuable part of the spoil. The wholesale price at which Nicanor set the Jews his expected prisoners, and at which he hoped to sell some 180,000[11], shews the extent of the then traffic and their relative value. £2. 14s. 9d. as the average price of each of ninety slaves *in* Judea, implies a retail-price at the place of sale, above the then ordinary price of man. This wholesale price for what was expected to be a mixed multitude of nearly

200,000, (for "[12] Nicanor undertook to make so much money of the captive Jews as should defray the tribute of 2000 talents which the king was to pay to the Romans,") was nearly 5 times as much as that at which Carthaginian soldiers were sold at the close of the first Punic war[13]. It was two-thirds of the retail price of a good slave at Athens[14], or of that at which, about B. C. 340, the law of Greece prescribed that captives should be redeemed[15]; or of that, (which was nearly the same) at which the Mosaic law commanded compensation to be made for a slave accidentally killed[16]. The facility of transport increased the value. For, although Pontus supplied both the best and the most of the Roman slaves[17], yet in the war with Mithridates, amid a great abundance of all things, slaves were sold at 3s. 3d.[18] The special favors also shewn to the Jewish captives at Rome and Alexandria shew the estimation in which they were held. At Rome, in the reign of Augustus, "[19] the large section of Rome beyond the Tiber was possessed and inhabited by Jews, most of them Roman citizens, having been brought as captives into Italy and made freedmen by their owners." On whatever ground Ptolemy Philadelphus redeemed 100,000 Jews whom his father had taken and sold[20], the fact can hardly be without foundation, or his enrolling them in his armies, or his employing them in public offices or about his own person.

Joel lived before the historic times of Greece. But there are early traces of slave-trade carried on by Greeks[21]. According to Theopompus, the Chians, first among the Greeks, acquired barbarian slaves in the way of trade[22]. The Ionian migration had filled the islands and part of the coasts of Asia Minor with Greek traders about two centuries before Joel, B. C. 1069[23]. Greeks inhabited both the coasts and islands between Tyre and Sardis, whither we know them to have been carried. Cyprus and Crete, both inhabited by Greeks and both in near intercourse with Phœnicia, were close at hand.

The demand for slaves must have been enormous. For wives were but seldom allowed them; and Athens, Ægina, Corinth alone had in the days of their prosperity

1 Arr. Exped. vi. 22. 8.   2 2 Macc. viii. 34.
3 1 Macc. iii. 41.
4 Jos. Ant. xii. 7. 3. and 1 Macc. see Eng. Marg.
5 S. Jer. on Ezek. xxvii. 16.
6 Xenoph. Agesil. i. 21.
7 Strabo xiv. 5. 2.
8 Deut. xxviii. 68. Glycas says that Adrian sold 4 Jews for a modius [two gallons] of barley. Ann. iii. p. 448. M.
9 2 Kgs v. 2.   10 Herod. iii. 134.
11 Ninety being offered for a talent, this would be the number whose sale would bring in 2000 talents.

12 2 Macc. viii. 10.
13 18 Denarii, i. e. 11s. 3d. Liv. xxi. 41. Boeckh Econ. of Ath. i. 92.
14 Boeckh i. 94.   15 Aristot. Eth. v. 7. 1.
16 Ex. xxi. 30.   17 Polyb. iv. 38.
18 Plutarch Lucull. ⅔ 14.
19 Philo Leg. ad Caium Opp. ii. 568.
20 Jos. Ant. xii. 2. and 4.
21 Movers quotes instances from Samos, Lesbos, Ephesus, Miletus, p. 81.
22 In Athenæus vi. 88. p. 574. Mov.
23 Eus. Chron. ii. 304-18.

Before
C H R I S T
cir. 800.

h Isal. 43. 5, 6. &
49. 12.
Jer. 23. 8.

7 Behold, [h] I will raise
them out of the place
& whither ye have sold them,
and will return your rec-

ompense upon your own
head:

8 And I will sell your
sons and your daughters

Before
C H R I S T
cir. 800.

1,330,000 slaves[1]. At the great slave-mart at Delos, 10,000 were brought, sold, removed in a single day[2].

That ye might remove them far from their border. The Philistines hoped thus to weaken the Jews, by selling their fighting men afar, whence they could no more return. There was doubtless also in this removal an anti-religious malice, in that the Jews clung to their land, as *the Lord's land*, the land given by Him to their fathers; so that they, at once, weakened their rivals, aggravated and enjoyed their distress, and seemed again to triumph over God. Tyre and Sidon took no active share in making the Jews prisoners, yet, partaking in the profit and aiding in the disposal of the captives, they became, according to that true proverb " the receiver is as bad as the thief," equally guilty of the sin, in the sight of God.

7. *Behold I will raise them.* If this promise relates to the same individuals who had been sold, it must have been fulfilled silently; as indeed the return of captives to their own land, unless brought about by some historical event, belongs not to history, but to private life. The Prophet, however, is probably predicting God's dealings with the nations, not with those individuals. The enslaving of these Hebrews in the time of Joram was but one instance out of a whole system of covetous misdeeds. The Philistines carried away captives from them again in the time of Ahaz[3], and yet again subsequently[4]; and still more at the capture of Jerusalem[5].

8. *I will sell your sons.* God Himself would reverse the injustice of men. The sons of Zion should be restored, the sons of the Phœnicians and of the Philistines sold into distant captivity. Tyre was taken by Nebuchadnezzar, and then by Alexander, who sold " more than 13,000 " of the inhabitants into slavery[6]; Sidon was taken and destroyed by

Artaxerxes Ochus, and it is said, above 40,000 of its inhabitants perished in the flames[7]. The like befell the Philistines[8]. The Sabæans are probably instanced, as being the remotest nation in the opposite direction, a nation, probably, the partner of Tyre's traffic in *men*, as well as in their other merchandise, and who (as is the way of unregenerate nature) would as soon trade *in* Tyrians, as *with* Tyrians. The Sabæans were like the Phœnicians, a wealthy merchant people, and, of old, united with them in the trade of the world, the Sabæans sending forth their fleets across the Indian Ocean, as the Tyrians along the Mediterranean. Three fathers of distinct races bore the name Sheba; one, a descendant of Ham, the other two, descended from Shem. The Hamite Sheba was the son of Raamah, the son of Cush[9], and doubtless dwelt of old in the country on the Persian gulf called by the name Raamah[10]. Traces of the name Sheba occur there, and some even after our era[11]. The Shemite Sabæans, were, some descendants of Sheba, the tenth son of Joktan[12]; the others from Sheba, the son of Abraham and Keturah[13]. The Sabæans, descended from Joktan, dwelt in the S. W. extremity of Arabia, extending from the Red Sea to the Sea[14] of Babel-mandeb. The country is still called " ard-es-Seba[15]," " land of Saba ; " and Saba is often mentioned by Arabic writers[16]. To the Greeks and Latins they were known by the name of one division of the race (Himyar) Homeritæ[17]. Their descendants still speak an Arabic, acknowledged by the learned Arabs to be a distinct language from that which, through Mohammed, prevailed and was diffused[18]; a " species[19] " of Arabic which they attribute " to the times of (the Prophet) Hud [perhaps Eber] and those before him." It belonged to them as descendants of Joktan. Sabæans are mentioned, distinct from both

[1] Athens, 400,000. (Ctesicles in Athen. vi. 103,) Corinth, 460,000. (Timæus ib.) Ægina, 470,000. (Aristot. ib.)   [2] Strabo xiv. 5. 2.
[3] 2 Chr. xxviii. 18.   [4] Ezek. xvi. 27, 57.
[5] Ib. xxv. 15.
[6] Diod. Sic. xvii. 46. Arrian says 30,000. ii. 24.
[7] Diod. xvi. 45.   [8] See on Zeph. ii. 4–7.
[9] Gen. x. 7.
[10] Regma, Steph. Byz. sub v. רעמה is pronounced 'Ρέγμα by the LXX. " Regma," Vulg.
[11] In the names " The promontory of 'Ασαβώ, or 'Ασαβῶν " in Ptolemy vi. 7, and Marcian Heracl. p. 16. " The black mountains called 'Ασαβῶν," Ptol. Ib. " a very great mountain, called Σαβώ," at the entrance of the Persian gulf. (Arrian. Peripl. p. 20) Batrasaves or Batrasabbes a city in Pliny, (vi. 28. 32.) Sabis, a river in Carmania on the opposite side of

the Persian gulf. (Mela iii. 8.) Dionysius Perieg. also places the Sabæ next to the Pasargadæ, v. 1069. see Bochart, iv. 7.
[12] Gen. x. 28.   [13] Ib. xxv. 3.   [14] Plin. vi. 28, 32.
[15] Cruttenden in Journ. Geogr. Soc. 1838. viii. 268.
[16] See De Sacy below.
[17] Philostg. ii. 6. iii. 4. (Arr.) Peripl. p. 13. Marcian 13. Plin. vi. 28. 32.
[18] Authorities referred to by Soiuthi, quoted by Fresnel Lettre iv. in Journal Asiatique T. v. p. 512. Fresnal says that the grammatical forms most resemble Æthiopic, although it is richer than Arabic both in consonants and vowels, and has more Hebrew roots than ordinary Arabic. Ib. 533, sqq. De Sacy observed that the difference was one of language, (not of dialect only.) Acad. d. Inscr. T. 48. p. 509. note.   [19] Soiuthi Ib.

Before
CHRIST
cir. 800.

into the hand of the chil-dren of Judah, and they

[1] Ezek. 23. 42.   shall sell them to the [1]Sa-

[k] Jer. 6. 20.   beans, to a people [k]far off: for the LORD hath spoken *it*.

9 ¶ [1]Proclaim ye this among the Gentiles; † Pre-pare war, wake up the mighty men, let all the men of war draw near; let them come up:

Before
CHRIST
cir. 800.

[1] See Isaiah
8, 9, 10.
Jer. 46. 3, 4.
Ezek. 38. 7.
† Heb.
Sanctify.

---

of these, as "[1]dwelling in Arabia Felix, next beyond Syria, which they frequently in-vaded, before it belonged to the Romans." These Sabæans probably are those spoken of as marauders by Job[2]; and may have been descendants of Keturah. Those best known to the Greeks and Romans were, naturally, those in the South Western corner of Ara-bia. The account of their riches and luxu-ries is detailed, and, although from different authorities[3], consistent; else, almost fabu-lous. One metropolis is said to have had 65 temples[4], private individuals had more than kingly magnificence[5]. Arabic historians expanded into fable the extent and preroga-tives[6] of their Paradise lands, before the breaking of the artificial dike, made for the irrigation of their country[7]. They traded with India, availing themselves doubtless of the Monsoon, and perhaps brought thence their gold, if not also the best and most costly frankincense[8]. The Sheba of the Prophet appears to have been the wealthy Sheba near the Red Sea. Indeed, in absence of evidence to the contrary, it is natural to un-derstand the name of those best known. Sol-omon unites it with Seba[9], (the Æthiopian Sabæ.) The known frankincense-districts are on the S. W. corner of Arabia[10]. The tree has diminished, perhaps has degenerated through the neglect consequent on Moham-medan oppression, diminished consumption, change of the line of commerce; but it still survives in those districts[11]; a relic of what is passed away. Ezekiel indeed unites *the merchants of Sheba and Raamah*[12], as trading with Tyre. *The merchants of Sheba and Raamah, they were thy merchants; with the chief of all spices and with all precious stones and gold they occupied in thy fairs.* It may be that he joins them together as kindred tribes; yet it is as probable that he unites the two

great channels of merchandise, East and West, Raamah on the Persian Gulf, and Sheba near the Red Sea. Having just men-tioned the produce of Northern Arabia as poured into Tyre, he would, in this case, enumerate North, East, and West of Arabia as combined to enrich her. Agatharcides unites the Sabæans of S. W. Arabia with the Gerrhæans, who were certainly on the Per-sian Gulf[13]. "No people," he says[5], "is apparently richer than the Sabæans and Gerrhæans, who dispense forth everything worth speaking of from Asia and Europe. These made the Syria of Ptolemy full of gold. These supplied the industry of the Phœnicians with profitable imports, not to mention countless other proofs of wealth." Their caravans went to Elymais, Carmania; Charræ was their emporium; they returned to Gabala and Phœnicia[14]. Wealth is the parent of luxury and effeminacy. At the time of our Lord's Coming, the softness and effeminacy of the Sabæans became prover-bial. The "soft Sabæans" is their charac-teristic in the Roman poets[15]. Commerce, navigation, goldmines, being then carried on by means of slaves, and wealth and luxury at that time always demanding domestic slaves, the Sabæans had need of slaves for both. They too had distant colonies[16], whither the Tyrians could be transported, as far from Phœnicia, as the shores of the Ægean are from Palestine. The great law of Divine Justice[17], *as I have done, so God hath requited me,* was again fulfilled. It is a sacred pro-verb of God's overruling Providence, written in the history of the world and in men's consciences.

9. *Proclaim ye this among the Gentiles.* God having before said that He would *gather all nations,* now, by a solemn irony, bids them prepare, if, by any means, they can fight

---

[1] Strabo, xvi. 4. 21.   [2] Job i. 15. Bochart iv. 9.
[3] Agatharcides (p. 61,) Strabo from Metrodorus and Eratosthenes, (xvi. 4. 19.) Diodorus "from memoirs in the Alexandrian library or eye wit-nesses." iii. 38. 47. The account of their natural productions is exaggerated, yet with a mixture of truth, e. g. as to a very venomous sort of serpent.
[4] Thomna. Plin. vi. 28. 32. Movers, p. 300.
[5] Geogr. Vet. Scriptt. Min. T. i. p. 64, 5. Oxon.
[6] See Kazvini, the Turkish Jehan-numa from older writers, Masudi, in de Sacy Mem. de l'Acad. d. Inscr. T. 48. p. 506, note 629.
[7] De Sac. Ib.
[8] see Ritter's Diss. Erdk. xii. 356–372. Strabo however (quoted there p. 364) says, that most

cassia came from India; "the best frankincense is that near Persia.
[9] Ps. lxxii. 10.
[10] Theophr. Hist. Plant. ix. 4. Agatharc. p. 61–4, 5. Eratosthenes in Strabo xvi. 4. 4.
[11] Capt. Haines in Geogr. Soc. ix. 154. Wellsted. Travels in Arabia. Survey in Bombay Geogr. Soc. 1839. p. 55. quoted Ritter, Erdk. xii. 259, 60.
[12] xxvii. 22.
[13] Ptol. vi. 7. Strabo, xvi. 3. 3.
[14] Juba in Plin. H. N. xii. 18. n. 40.
[15] Virg. Geogr. i. 57. also Metrodorus in Strabo xvi. 4. 19. See other authorities in Smith, Dict. of Geogr. Art. Saba, p. 862.
[16] Agatharc. p. 64.   [17] Judg, i. 7.

Before
CHRIST
cir. 800.
_____
m See Is. 2. 4.
Mic. 4. 3.
‖ Or *scythes*.

10 ᵐBeat your plow-
shares into swords,
and your ‖pruning-

hooks into spears: ⁿlet
the weak say, I *am*
strong.

Before
CHRIST
cir. 800.
_____
n Zech. 12. 8.

against Him. So in Isaiah [1]; *Associate yourselves,
O ye people, and ye shall be broken in pieces ; and
give ear, all ye of far countries ; gird yourselves,
and ye shall be broken in pieces ; gird yourselves,
and ye shall be broken in pieces ; take counsel
together, and it shall come to nought ; speak the
word, and it shall not stand ; for God is with us.*

Prepare, lit. *hallow, war.* To *hallow war* was
to make it holy, either in appearance or in
truth, as the prophet bade them, *sanctify a
fast,* i. e. keep it holily. So God calls the
Medes, whom He employed against Babylon [2],
My sanctified ones, and bids [3], *sanctify the nations
against her ;* and the enemies of Judah encourage themselves [4], *sanctify ye war against her ;*
and Micah says, that whosoever bribed not the
false prophets, *they sanctify war against him* [5],
i. e. proclaim war against him in the Name of
God. The enemies of God, of His people,
of His truth, declare war against all, in the
Name of God. The Jews would have stoned
our Lord for blasphemy, and, at the last,
they condemned Him as guilty of it. [6] *He hath
spoken blasphemy. What further need have we of
witnesses ? behold, now ye have heard His blasphemy.* And He foretold to His disciples [7],
*Whosoever killeth you, will think he doeth God
service.* St. Stephen was persecuted for speaking [8] *blasphemous words against Moses and
against God, this holy place and the law.* St.
Paul was persecuted for [9] *persuading men to
worship God contrary to the law and polluting this
holy place.* Anti-Christ shall set himself up
as God, [10] *so that he, as God, sitteth in the
temple of God, shewing himself that he is God.*
Heretics and unbelievers declaim against the
Gospel, as though it, and not themselves,
were opposed to the holiness and Majesty and
love of God. The Gnostics of old spake
against the Creator in the Name of God.
Arians affected reverence for the glory of
God [11], being, on their own mis-belief, idolaters or polytheists [12]. The Apollinarians
charged the Church with ascribing to our
Lord a sinful soul, as though the soul must
needs be such [13], and themselves held the
Godhead to have been united to a soulless, and
so a brute, nature. Manichæans accused her
of making God the author of evil, and themselves, as do Pantheists now, invented a god
who sinned [14]. Novatians and Donatists accused

the Church of laxity. Pelagians charged
her with denying the perfectibility of man's
nature, themselves denying the grace whereby
it is perfected. Mohammed arrayed the truth
of the Unity of God against His Being in
Three Persons, and fought against the truth as
Idolatry. Some now array "Theism," i. e.
truths as to God which they have stolen from
Holy Scripture, against the belief in God as
He has revealed Himself. Indeed, no imposture ever long held its ground against truth,
unless it masked itself under some truth of
God which it perverted, and so *hallowed* its
war against God in the Name of God.

Wake up the mighty men ; arouse them, as if
their former state had been a state of sleep;
arouse all their dormant powers, all within
them, that they may put forth all their
strength, if so be they may prevail against
God.

Let all the men of war draw near, as if to
contend, and close, as it were, with God and
His people [15], as, on the other hand, God says [16],
*I will come near to you to judgment. Let them
come up* into His very Presence. Even while
calling them to fulfill this their vain purpose
of striving with God, the Prophet keeps in
mind, into Whose Presence they are summoned, and so calls them to *come up,* as to a
place of dignity.

10. *Beat your ploughshares into swords.* Peace
had been already promised, as a blessing of
the gospel. *In His days,* foretold Solomon [17],
*shall the righteous flourish, and abundance of
peace, so long as the moon endureth.* And
another [18], *He maketh thy borders peace.* Peace
within with God flows forth in peace with
man. *Righteousness and peace kissed each
other* [19]. Where there is not rest in God, all
is unrest. And so, all which was needful for
life, the means of subsistence, care of health,
were to be forgotten for war.

Let the weak say, I am strong. It is one last
gathering of the powers of the world against
their Maker ; the closing scene of man's
rebellion against God. It is their one universal gathering. None, however seemingly unfit,
was to be spared from this conflict ; no one
was to remain behind. The husbandman was
to forge for war the instruments of his peaceful toil ; the sick was to forget his weakness and

[1] viii. 9, 10. see also Ezek. xxxviii. 7-end.
[2] Is. xiii. 3.   [3] Jer. li. 27.   [4] Ib. vi. 4.
[5] Mic. iii. 5.   [6] S. Matt. xxvi. 65.
[7] S. John xvi. 2.   [8] Acts vi. 11, 13.
[9] Ib. xviii. 13. xxi. 28. xxiv. 6.   [10] 2 Thess. ii. 4.
[11] See Arius Thalia in S. Ath. Counc. of Arim. § 15.
p. 94. Oxf. Tr. S. Ath. ag. Ar. i. 28. p. 221. and the full
note f.

[12] Ib. p. 191. n. d. p. 206. 301. c. 310. h. 411. b. 423.
m. n.
[13] See in S. Ath. p. 221. n. f. O. T.
[14] See S. Aug. Conf. Note at the end.
[15] See 1 Sam. xvii. 41. 2 Sam. x. 13.
[16] Mal. iii. 5. see Is. xli. 1. l. 8.
[17] Ps. lxxii. 7.
[18] Ib. cxlvii. 14.   [19] Ib. lxxxv. 10.

Before
CHRIST
cir. 800.

o ver. 2.

‖ Or, *the
LORD shall
bring down.*
p Ps. 103. 20.
Isa. 13. 3.

11 °Assemble your-
selves, and come, all ye
heathen, and gather your-
selves together round
about: thither ‖ cause ᵖ thy
mighty ones to come down,
O LORD.

12 Let the heathen be

wakened, ᑫand come up to
the valley of Jehoshaphat:
for there will I sit to ʳjudge
all the heathen round
about.

13 ˢ Put ye in the sickle,
for ᵗthe harvest is ripe:
come, get you down; for

Before
CHRIST
cir. 800.

q ver. 2.
Ps. 96. 13.
& 98. 9. &
110. 6.
Is. 2. 4. & 3. 13.
Mic. 4. 3.
s Matt. 13. 39.
Rev. 14. 15,
18.
t Jer. 51. 33.
Hos. 6. 11.

to put on a strength which he had not, and
that to the uttermost. But as weakness is, in
and through God, strength, so all strength out
of God is weakness. Man may say, *I am
strong ;* but, against God, he remains weak as,
it is said, that *weak man* [1] *from the earth may
no more oppress.*

11. Once more all the enemies of God are
summoned together. *Assemble yourselves* [2],
(Others in the same sense render, *Haste ye,*)
and come, all ye heathen, round about, lit. *from
round about,* i. e. from every side, so as to
compass and hem in the people of God, and
then, when the net had been, as it were,
drawn closer and closer round them, and no
way of escape is left, the Prophet prays God
to send His aid ; *thither cause Thy mighty ones
to come down, O Lord.* Against *the mighty ones*
of the earth, or *the weak* who *say* they are
mighty, (the same word is used throughout,)
there *come down the mighty ones of God.* The
mighty ones of God, whom He is prayed to
cause to come down, i. e. from heaven, can be
no other than the mighty angels, of whom it
is said, they *are mighty in strength* [3] (still the
same word,) to whom God gives *charge over* [4]
His own, *to keep them in all their ways,* and
one of whom, in this place, slew [5] *one hundred
and fourscore and five thousand* of the Assyrians. So our Lord saith [6], *The Son of man
shall send forth His Angels, and they shall gather
out of His kingdom all things that offend, and
them that do iniquity.*

12. *Let the heathen be awakened.* This emphatic repetition of the word, *awaken,* seems
intended to hint at the great awakening, to
Judgment [7], when they *who sleep in the dust of
the earth shall awake, being awakened* from the
sleep of death. Another word is used of
awakening [8]. On the destruction of Anti-
Christ it is thought that the general Judgment will follow, and *all who are in the graves
shall hear the voice of the Son of Man and shall
come forth* [9]: They are bidden to *come up* into the
valley of Jehoshaphat, "[10] for to come into the

Presence of the most High God, may well be
called *a coming up.*" *For there will I sit to
judge all the heathen round about,* (again lit.
from round about,) *from every side,* all nations
from all the four quarters of the world. The
words are the same as before. There *all nations from every side* were summoned to come,
as they thought, to destroy God's people and
heritage. Here the real end is assigned, for
which they were brought together ; for God
would sit to judge them. In their own blind
will and passion they came to destroy ; in
God's secret overruling Providence, they were
dragged along by their passions,—to be judged
and to be destroyed. So our Lord says [11],
*When the Son of Man shall come in His Glory,
and all the Holy Angels with Him, then shall He
sit on the throne of His Glory and before Him
shall be gathered all nations.* Our Lord, in that
He uses words of Joel, seems to intend to
direct our minds to the Prophet's meaning.
What follows are nearly His own words ;

13. *Put ye in the sickle, for the harvest is ripe.*
So Jesus saith, *let both grow together until the
harvest, and in the time of the harvest I will say
to the reapers, Gather ye together the tares and
bind them in bundles to burn them ;* and this He
explains [12], *The harvest is the end of the world ;
and the reapers are the Angels.* He then Who
saith, *put ye in the sickle, for the harvest is ripe,*
is the Son of Man, Who, before He became
the Son of Man, was, as He is now, the Son
of God, and spake this and the other things
by the Prohets ; they to whom He speaketh
are His reapers, the Angels ; and the ripeness
of the harvest is the maturity of all things
here, good and evil, to be brought to their
last end.

In itself, the harvest, as well as the vintage,
might describe the end of this world, as to
both the good and the bad, in that the wheat
is severed from the chaff and the tares, and
the treading of the winepress separates the
wine which is stored up from the husks
which are cast away. Yet nothing is said,

---

[1] Ps. x. 18. אנוֹשׁ.
[2] The word עוּשׁ occurs here only. The E. V.
follows the chief authorities.
[3] Ps. ciii. 20.   [4] Ib. xci. 11.   [5] 2 Kings xix. 35.
[6] S. Matt. xiii. 41.
[7] This same word is used Job xiv. 12. Even

[8] הקִיץ, also Job Ib. Ps. xvii. 15. Is. xxvi. 19. Dan.
xii. 2.
[9] S. John v. 27-9.   [10] Poc.
[11] S. Matt. xxv. 31, 2.   [12] Ib. xiii. 30, 39.

Abarbanel understands this of the Resurrection;
see in Poc. on ver. 11.

Before
CHRIST
cir. 800.
u Is. 63. 3.
Lam. 1 15.
Rev. 14. 19, 20.
x ver. 2.
‖ Or, con-
cision, or,
threshing.
y ch. 2. 1.

the ^upress is full, the fats overflow; for their wicked-ness *is* great.

14 Multitudes, multi-tudes, in ^xthe valley of ‖ decision : for ^y the day of

the LORD *is* near in the valley of decision.

15 The ^zsun and the moon shall be darkened, and the stars shall with-draw their shining.

Before
CHRIST
cir. 800.

z ch. 2. 10, 31.

---

here of storing up aught, either the wheat or the wine, but only of the ripeness of the har-vest, and that *the fats overflow, because their wickedness is great.* The harvest is sometimes, although more rarely, used of destruction[1]; the treading of the winepress is always used as an image of God's anger[2]; the vintage of destruction[3]; the plucking off the grapes, of the rending away of single lives or souls[4]. It seems probable then, that the ripeness of the harvests and the fullness of the vats are alike used of the ripeness for destruction, that "[5]they were ripe in their sins, fit for a harvest, and as full of wickedness as ripe grapes, which fill and overflow the vats, through the abundance of the juice with which they swell." Their ripeness in iniquity calls, as it were, for the sickle of the reaper, the trampling of the presser.

For great is their wickedness. The whole world is flooded and overflowed by it, so that it can no longer contain it, but, as it were, cries to God to end it. The long suffering of God no longer availed, but would rather increase their wickedness and their damna-tion. So also, in that first Judgment of the whole world by water, when *all flesh had cor-rupted his way upon the earth, God said, the end of all flesh is before Me*[6]; and when the hun-dred and twenty years of the preaching of Noah were ended without fruit, *the flood came.* So Sodom was *then* destroyed, when not ten righteous could be found in it; and the seven nations of Canaan were spared above four hundred years, because the *iniquity of the Amorites was not yet full*[7]; and our Lord says[8], *fill ye up the measure of your fathers,—that upon you may come all the righteous blood shed upon the earth.* So "[9]God condemneth each of the damned, when he hath filled up the measure of his iniquity."

14. The prophet continues, as in amaze-ment at the great throng assembling upon one another, *multitudes, multitudes, in the val-*

ley *of decision,* as though, whichever way he looked, there were yet more of these *tumultuous masses,* so that there was nothing beside them. It was one living, surging, boiling, sea : throngs upon throngs, mere throngs[10]! The word rendered *multitudes* suggests, besides, the thought of the hum and din[11] of these masses thronging onward, blindly, to their own destruction. They all *tumultuously rage together, and imagine a vain thing, against the Lord and against His Christ*[12]; but the place whither they are gathered, (although they know it not,) is *the valley of decision,* i. e. of "sharp, severe judgment." The valley is the same as that before called *the valley of Jehoshaphat;* but whereas that name only signifies *God judgeth,* this further name denotes the strictness of God's judgment. The word signifies "cut," then "decided;" then is used of severe punishment, or destruc-tion decided and decreed[13], by God.

For the Day of the Lord is near in the valley of decision. Their gathering against God shall be a token of His coming to judge them. They come to fulfill their own ends; but His shall be fulfilled on them. They are left to bring about their own doom; and being abandoned by Him, rush on the more blindly because it is at hand. When their last sin is committed, their last defiance of God spoken or acted against Him, it is come. At all times, indeed, *the Lord is at hand*[14]. It may be, that we are told, that the whole future revealed to us *must shortly come to pass*[15], in order to show that all time is a mere nothing, a moment, a dream, when it is gone. Yet here it is said, relatively, not to us, but to the things foretold, that it *is near* to come.

15. *The sun and the moon shall be darkened.* This may be, either that they shall be out-shone by the brightness of the glory of Christ, or that they themselves shall under-go a change, whereof the darkness at the Crucifixion was an image. An ancient

---

[1] Is. xvii. 5. Jer. li. 33.
[2] Lam. i. 15. Is. lxiii. 3. Rev. xix. 15.
[3] Is. xvii. 6. Judg. viii. 2. Mic. vii. 1.
[4] Ps. lxxx. 12.   [5] Poc.   [6] Gen. vi. 12, 13.
[7] Gen. xv. 16.   [8] S. Matt. xxiii. 32, 35.   [9] Dion.
[10] As Gen. xiv. 10, *pits, pits,* i. e. *full of pits,* nothing but *pits;* 2 Kings iii. 16, *ditches, ditches,* i. e. *full of ditches.* By another idiom, it has been taken to mean that the *multitudes* were of two sorts ; whence Abarbanel explains it, "a multitude of living, and a multitude of dead," in Poc. Others, the good and the bad.

[11] The word המה (whence המון) is identical with our *hum;* then, "noise," and, among others, "the hum of a multitude ;" then, a multitude even apart from that noise. It is used of the throng of a large army, Judg. iv. 7, Dan. xi. 11, 12, 13; of whole peoples, Ezek. xxxii. 12, 16, 18, 20, 22, 26.
[12] Ps. ii. 1, 2.
[13] *destruction determined,* Is. x. 22; *destruction, and that determined,* Is. x. 23, xxviii. 22, Dan. ix. 27; *that which is decreed of desolations,* i. e. *the desolations decreed,* Ib. 26.
[14] Phil. iv. 5.   [15] Rev. i. 1.

Before CHRIST cir. 800.	16 The LORD also shall [a] roar out of Zion, and utter his voice from Jerusalem; and [b] the heavens and the earth shall shake: [c] but the LORD *will be* the †hope of	his people, and the strength of the children of Israel. 17 So [d] shall ye k n o w that I *am* the LORD your God dwelling in Zion, [e] my holy mountain: then shall	Before CHRIST cir. 800.
[a] Jer. 25. 30. ch. 2. 11. Amos 1. 2. [b] Hag. 2. 6. [c] Is. 51. 5, 6. † Heb. *place of repair.* or, *harbor.*			[d] ch. 2. 27. [e] Dan. 11. 45. Obad. 16. Zech. 8. 3.

writer says[1]; "As in the dispensation of the Cross the sun failing, there was darkness over all the earth, so when *the sign of the Son of man* appeareth in heaven in the Day of Judgment, the light of the sun and moon and stars shall fail, consumed, as it were by the great might of that sign." And as the failure of the light of the sun at our Lord's Passion betokened the shame of nature at the great sin of man, so, at the Day of Judgment, it sets before us the awfulness of God's judgments, as though "[2] it dared not behold the severity of Him Who judgeth and returneth every man's work upon his own head;" as though "[3] every creature, in the sufferings of others, feared the judgment on itself."

16. *The Lord shall roar out of Zion.* As in the destruction of Sennacherib, when he was now close upon his prey, and *shook his hand against the mount of the daughter of Zion, the hill of Jerusalem, the Lord of hosts lopped the bough with terror, and the high ones of stature were hewn down, and the haughty* were *humbled*[4], so at the end. It is foretold of Anti-Christ, that his destruction shall be sudden[5], *Then shall that Wicked one be revealed, whom the Lord shall consume with the spirit of His mouth, and shall destroy with the brightness of His Coming.* And Isaiah saith of our Lord[6], *He shall smite the earth with the rod of His mouth, and with the breath of His lips shall He slay the wicked.* When the multitudes of God's enemies were thronged together, then would He speak with His Voice of terror. The terrible voice of God's warnings is compared to the roaring of a lion[7]. *The lion hath roared, who will not fear? the Lord hath spoken, who can but prophesy?* Much more, when those words of awe are fulfilled. Our Lord then, *The Lion of the tribe of Judah*[8], Who is here entitled by the incommunicable Name of God, I AM, shall utter His awful Voice, as it is said[9]; *The Lord Himself shall descend from heaven with a shout, with the voice of the Archangel and with the Trump of God;* and He Himself says, [10] *The hour is coming, in the which all that are in the graves shall hear His voice and shall come forth, they that have done good unto the*

Resurrection of life, and they that have done evil unto the resurrection of damnation.

And shall utter His voice from Jerusalem, i. e. either from His Throne aloft *in the air* above the holy city, or from the heavenly Jerusalem, out of the midst of the tens of thousands of His holy angels[11], and saints[12], who shall *come with Him.* So terrible shall that voice be, that *the heavens and the earth shall shake,* as it is said[13], *the heavens shall pass away with a great noise, and the elements shall melt with fervent heat, the earth also and the works that are therein shall be burned up;* and "[14] heaven shall open for the coming of the saints," and *hell shall be moved at the coming*[15] of the evil. "[16] Nor shall it be a slight shaking of the earth at His Coming, but such that all the dead shall be roused, as it were from their sleep, yea, the very elect shall fear and tremble, but, even in their fear and trembling, shall retain a strong hope. This is what he saith forthwith, *The Lord will be the hope* (or *place of refuge*) *of His people, and the strength* (or *strong hold*) *of the children of Israel,* i. e. of the true Israel, the whole people of the elect of God. All these He will then by that His Majesty at once wonderfully terrify and strengthen, because they ever hoped in God, not in themselves, and ever trusted in the strength of the Lord, never presumed on their own. Whereas contrariwise the false Israelites hope in themselves, while, *going about to establish their own righteousness, they submitted themselves not to the righteousness of God*[17]. The true Israel shall trust much more than ever before; yet none can trust then, who in life, had not trusted in Him Alone.

17. God Himself wondrously joins on His own words to those of the Prophet, and speaks to His own people; *so* (lit. *and*) *ye shall know,* by experience, by sight, face to face, what ye now believe, *that I am the Lord your God, dwelling in Zion, My holy mountain.* So He saith in the second Psalm[18], *Then shall he speak unto them* (the enemies of His Christ) *in His wrath, and vex them in His sore displeasure; And I have set My king on My holy hill of Zion;* and[19], *Behold the tabernacle of*

---

[1] Orig. Tr. 30. in S. Matt.
[2] S. Jer.
[3] Hugo de S. V.
[4] Is. x. 32, 3.
[5] 2 Thess. ii. 8.
[6] Is. xi. 4.
[7] Am. iii. 8.
[8] Rev. v. 5.
[9] 1 Thess. iv. 16.
[10] S. John v. 28, 29.

[11] S. Matt. xvi. 27. xxv 31. S. Mark viii. 38. 2 Thess. i. 7.
[12] Zech. xiv. 5. Jude 14.
[13] 2 Pet. iii. 10.
[14] Lyr. Lap.
[15] Is. xiv. 9.
[16] Rup.
[17] Rom. x. 3.
[18] Ps. ii. 5, 6.
[19] Rev. xxi. 3.

Before
CHRIST
cir. 800.
† Heb. holi-
ness.
f Is. 35. 8 & 52. 1. Nah. 1. 15. Zech. 14. 21. Rev. 21. 27.

Jerusalem be †holy, and there shall no ᶠstrangers pass through her any more.

18 ¶ And it shall come to pass in that day,ᵇthat the mountains shall ᵍ drop

Before
CHRIST
cir. 800.
g Amos 9. 13.

God is with men, and He will dwell with them, and they shall be His people, and God Himself shall be with them, their God, dwelling with them and in them, by an unvarying, blissful, hallowing Presence, never withdrawn, never hidden, never shadowed, but ever shining upon them. *Your God,* your own, as much as if possessed by none besides, filling all with gladness, yet fully possessed by each, as though there were none besides, so that each may say, *Thou art my Portion, O Lord*[1]; my *Lord, and my God*[2], as He saith, *I am thy exceeding great Reward*[3].

And Jerusalem shall be holy, lit. *holiness* as John saith[4], *He carried me away in the Spirit to a great and high mountain, and shewed me that great city, the holy Jerusalem, descending out of heaven from God, having the glory of God.*

And there shall no stranger pass through her any more. Without, says S. John[5], *are dogs and sorcerers, and whoremongers, and murderers, and idolaters, and whosoever loveth and maketh a lie.* None alien from her shall pass through her, so as to have dominion over her, defile or oppress her.

This special promise is often repeated. [6] *It shall be called the way of holiness, the unclean shall not pass over it.* [7] *Henceforth there shall no more come into thee the uncircumcised and the unclean.* [8] *The wicked shall no more pass through thee.*[9] *In that day there shall be no more the Canaanite in the house of the Lord of hosts.* [10] *And there shall in no wise enter into it any thing that defileth.* These promises are, in their degree and in the image and beginning, made good to the Church here, to be fully fulfilled when it shall be[11] *a glorious Church, not having spot or wrinkle or any such thing, but holy and without blemish.* Here they do not pass through her, so as to overcome; *the gates of hell shall not prevail against her.* However near, as hypocrites, they come to her, they feel in themselves that *are not of her*[12]. There they shall be severed from her for ever. "[13]Heretics came, armed with fantastic reasons and deceitful arguments; but they could not pass through her, repelled by the truth of the word, overcome by reason, cast down by the testimonies of Scripture and by the glow of faith." They fell backward to the ground before her. They [14] *go out from her, because they are not of her.* They

who are not of her can mingle with her, touch her sacraments, but their power and virtue they partake not. They are inwardly repelled.

18. *And it shall come to pass in that Day.* After the destruction of Anti-Christ, there will, it seems, still be a period of probation, in which the grace of God will abound and extend more and more widely. The Prophet Zechariah, who continues on the image, of the *living waters going out from Jerusalem*[15], places this gift after God had gathered all nations against Jerusalem, and had visibly and miraculously overthrown them[16]. But in that the blessings which he speaks of, are regenerating, they belong to time; the fullness of the blessing is completed only in eternity; the dawn is on earth, the everlasting brightness is in heaven. But though the prophecy belongs eminently to one time, the imagery describes the fulness of spiritual blessings which God at all times diffuses in and through the Church; and these blessings, he says, shall continue on in her for ever; her enemies shall be cut off for ever. It may be, that Joel would mark a fresh beginning and summary by his words, *It shall be in that Day.* The prophets do often begin, again and again, their descriptions. Union with God, which is their theme, is one. Every gift of God to His elect, except the beatific vision, is begun in time, union with Himself, indwelling, His Spirit flowing forth from Him into His creatures, His love, knowledge of Him, although here through a glass darkly.

The promise cannot relate to exuberance of temporal blessings, even as tokens of God's favor. For he says, *a fountain shall come forth of the house of the Lord, and shall water the valley of Shittim.* But *the valley of Shittim* is on the other side Jordan, beyond the Dead Sea, so that by nature the waters could not flow thither. The valley of Shittim or acacia trees is a dry valley; for in such the Easten Acacia, i. e. the sant or sandal wood grows. "It is," says S. Jerome[17], "a tree which grows in the desert, like a white thorn in color and leaves, not in size. For they are of such size, that very large planks[18], are cut out of them. The wood is very strong, and of incredible lightness and beauty. They do not grow in cultivated places, or in the Roman soil, save only in the desert of

1 Ps. cxix. 57. Lam. iii. 24.
2 S. John xx. 28.
3 Gen. xv. 1.
4 Rev. xxi. 10, 11.
5 Ib. xxii. 15.
6 Is. xxxv. 8.
7 Ib. lii. 1.
8 Nah. i. 15.
9 Zech. end.
10 Rev. xxi. 27.
11 Eph. v. 27.
12 1 S. John ii. 19.
13 Hugo Vict.
14 1 S. John ii. 19.
15 Zech. xiv. 8.
16 Ib. 2-4.
17 on Is. xli. 19.
18 12 els long. Theophr. plant. iv. 3.

Before CHRIST cir. 800.

b Is. 30. 25.

down new wine, and the hills shall flow with milk, [h] and all the rivers of Judah

Before CHRIST cir. 800.

† Heb. go.

shall † flow with waters, and [i] a fountain shall come forth of the house of the

i Ps. 46. 4. Ezek. 47. 1. Zech. 14. 8. Rev. 22. 1.

Arabia." It does not decay [1]; and when old becomes like ebony [2]. Of it the Ark of God was made, its staves, the table of Shewbread, the tabernacle and its pillars, the altar for burnt offerings, and of incense [3]. The valley is about six miles from Livias [4], seven and a half beyond the Dead Sea [5]. It was the last station of Israel, before entering the land of promise [6], whence Joshua sent out the spies [7]; where God turned the curse of Balaam into a blessing [8]; and he prophesied of the Star which should arise out of Israel, even Christ [9]; where Israel sinned in Baal Peor, and Phineas turned aside His displeasure [10].

The existence of a large supply of water under the Temple is beyond all question. While the Temple was still standing, mention is made of a "[11] fountain of ever-flowing water under the temple," as well as pools and cisterns for preserving rain-water. One evidently well acquainted with the localities says [12], " The pavement has slopes at befitting places, for the sake of a flush of water which takes place in order to cleanse away the blood from the victims. For on festivals many myriads of animals are sacrificed. But of water there is an unfailing supply, a copious and natural fountain within gushing over, and there being moreover wonderful underground-receptacles in a circuit of five furlongs, in the substructure of the temple, and each of these having numerous pipes, the several streams inter-communicating, and all these closed up below and on the sides.—There are also many mouths toward the base, invisible to all except those to whom the service of the temple belongs. So that the manifold blood of the sacrifices being brought together are cleansed by the gush [of water down] the slope." This same writer relates that, more than half a mile from the city, he was told to stoop down and heard the sound of gushing waters underground. The natural fountain, then, beneath the temple was doubtless augmented by waters brought from a distance, as required for the " divers wash-

ings" both of the priests and other things, and to carry off the blood of the victims. Pools near the temple are mentioned by writers of the third and fourth century [13] ; and Omar, on the surrender of Jerusalem, A. D. 634, was guided to the site of the ancient temple (whereon he built his Mosk) by the stream of water which issued through a water-channel from it [14]. Whencesoever this water was derived, whether from a perennial spring beneath the temple itself, or whether brought thither from some unfailing source without, it afforded Jerusalem an abundant supply of water. Much as Jerusalem suffered in sieges by famine, and its besiegers by thirst, thirst was never any part of the sufferings of those within [15]. The superfluous water was and still is carried off underground, to what is now " the fountain of the Virgin [16]," and thence again, through the rock, to the pool of Siloam [17]. Thence it carried fertility to the gardens of Siloam, in Joel's time doubtless *the king's gardens* [18], still " [19] a verdant spot, refreshing to the eye in the heat of summer, while all around is parched and dun." The blood of the victims flowed into the same brook Kidron, and was a known source of fertility, before the land was given to desolation. The waters of Kidron, as well as all the waters of Palestine, must have been more abundant formerly. Isaiah speaks of it as *flowing softly* [20] ; Josephus [21], of the "abundant fountain ;" an official report [22], of the "fountain gushing forth with abundance of water." Still its fertilizing powers formed but one little oasis, where all around was arid. It fertilized those gardens five miles from the city, but the mid-space was waterless [23], thirsty, mournful [24]. Lower down, the rivulet threaded its way to the Dead Sea, through a narrow ravine which became more and more wild, where St. Saba planted his monastery. "A howling wilderness, stern desolation, stupendous perpendicular cliffs, terrific chasms, oppressive solitude" are the terms by which one endeavors to characterize "the heart of this stern desert of Judæa [25]."

[1] Jos. Ant. iii. 6.   [2] Vell. Pat. ii. 56.
[3] Ex. lxxv. 5, 10, 13, 23, 28. xxvi. 15, 26, 32, 37. xxvii. 1, 6. xxx. 1. xxxv. 7, 24. xxxvi. 20, 31, 36. xxxvii. 1, 4, 10, 15, 25, 28. xxxviii. 1, 6. Deut. x. 3.
[4] S. Jer.   [5] Josh. Ant. v. 1. 1.
[6] Num. xxxiii. 49.   [7] Jos. ii. 1.
[8] Num. xxiii. xxiv. Mic. vi. 5.
[9] Num. xxiv. 17.
[10] Ib. xxv. 1, 7, 11.
[11] fons perennis aquæ. Tac. Hist. v. 12.
[12] Aristeas in App. ad Joseph. ed. Hav. p. 112.
[13] The Bourdeaux Pilgrim and Philostorg. ap. Phot. vii. 14. Itin. Hieros. p. 152. quoted in Williams'

full account of the waters of the Holy City and their connection. Holy City, ii. 466 sqq.
[14] Williams, H. C. i. 216. Arabic authorities.
[15] Williams, H. C. ii. 453, 4.
[16] Ib. 468. Robinson i. 344.
[17] Robinson i. 231, 2. 338, 9.
[18] 2 Kgs xxv. 4. Jer. xxxix. 4. lii. 7. Neh. iii. 15. Williams ii. 477.
[19] Williams ii. 456.   [20] viii. 6.   [21] B. J. v. 4. 1.
[22] in Eus. Præp. Ev. ix. 36. Williams ii. 464.
[23] Timochares in Eus. ix. 35 Williams ii. 478.
[24] Strabo xvi. c. 2. § 36. 40. p. 761, 3. W. ii. 453.
[25] Thomson ii. 435. 431.

Before
CHRIST
cir. 800.
ᵏ Num. 25. 1.
¹ Is. 19. 1, &c.

LORD, and shall water ᵏthe valley of Shittim.

19 ¹Egypt shall be a

desolation, and ᵐEdom shall be a desolate wilderness, for the violence against Egypt.

Before
CHRIST
cir. 800.
ᵐ Jer. 49. 17.
Ezek. 25. 12, 13. Amos 1. 11. Obad. 10.

Such continues to be its character, in the remaining half of its course, until it is lost in the Dead Sea, and is transmuted into its saltness. Its valley bears the name of desolation, Wady en Nar¹, "valley of fire." No human path lies along it. The Kidron flows along "²a deep and almost impenetrable ravine," "in a narrow channel between perpendicular walls of rock, as if worn away by the rushing waters between those desolate chalky hills." That little oasis of verdure was fit emblem of the Jewish people, itself bedewed by the stream which issued from the Temple of God, but, like Gideon's fleece, leaving all around dry. It made no sensible impression out of, or beyond itself. Hereafter, the stream³, the Siloah, whose streamlets, i. e. the artificial fertilizing divisions⁴, made glad the city of God, should make the wildest, driest spots of our mortality like the garden of the Lord. Desolation should become bright and gay; the parched earth should shoot up fresh with life; what was by nature barren and unfruitful should bring forth good fruit; places heretofore stained by sin should be purified; nature should be renewed by grace; and that, beyond the borders of the promised land, in that world which they had left, when Joshua brought them in thither. This, which it needs many words to explain, was vivid to those to whom Joel spoke. They had that spot of emerald green before their eyes, over which the stream which they then knew to issue from the Temple trickled in transparent brightness, conducted by those channels formed by man's diligence. The eyes of the citizens of Jerusalem must have rested with pleasure on it amid the parched surface around. Fresher than the gladliest freshness of nature, brighter than its most kindled glow, is the renewing freshness of grace; and this, issuing from mount Zion, was to be the portion not of Judæa only, but of the world. The vision of Ezekiel⁴, which is a comment on the prophecy of Joel, clearly belongs primarily to this life. For in this life only is there need for healing; in this life only is there a desert land to be made fruitful; death to be changed into life; death and life, the healed and unhealed, side by side; life, where the stream of God's grace reacheth, and death and barrenness, where it reacheth not. The fishers who spread their nests amid the fish, exceeding many, are an emblem which waited for and received its explanation from the parables of our Lord.

In the Revelation, above all, the peace, glory, holiness, vision of God, can only be fulfilled in the sight of God. Yet here too the increase of the Church, and the healing of the nations⁵, belong to time and to a state of probation, not of full fruition. But then neither can those other symbols relate to earthly things.

The mountains shall drop down new wine, lit. *trodden* out. What is ordinarily obtained by toil, shall be poured forth spontaneously. *And the hills shall flow with milk*, lit. *flow milk*, as though they themselves, of their own accord, gushed forth into the good gifts which they yield. *Wine* ever new, and ever renewing, sweet and gladdening the heart; *milk*, the emblem of the spiritual food of childlike souls, of purest knowledge, holy devotion, angelic purity, heavenly pleasure. And these shall never cease. These gifts are spoken of, as the spontaneous, perpetual flow of the mountains and hills; and as the fountain gushes forth from the hill or mountain-side in one ceaseless flow, day and night, streaming out from the hidden recesses to which the waters are supplied by God from His treasure-house of the rain, so day and night, in sorrow or in joy, in prosperity or adversity, God pours out, in the Church and in the souls of His elect, the riches of His grace. *All the rivers*, lit. channels⁶, *of Judah shall flow with water*. Every *channel*, however narrow and easily drying up, shall *flow with water*, gushing forth unto everlasting life; the love of God shall stream through every heart; each shall be full according to its capacity, and none the less full, because a larger tide pours through others. How much more, "⁷ in those everlasting hills of heaven, *the heavenly Jerusalem*, resting on the eternity and Godhead of the Holy Trinity, shall that long promise be fulfilled of the land flowing with milk and honey, where God, through the beatific vision of Himself, shall pour into the blessed *the torrent of pleasure*, the unutterable sweetness of joy and gladness unspeakable in Himself; and *all the rivers of Judah*, i. e. all the powers, capacities, senses, speech of the saints who *confess* God, shall flow with a perennial stream of joy, thanksgiving, and jubilee, as of all pleasure and bliss."

19. *Egypt shall be a desolation. Egypt* and *Edom* represent each a different class of enemies of the people of God, and both together exhibit the lot of all. Egypt was the powerful oppressor, who kept Israel long time in

---

¹ Robinson i. 531.　² Ps. xlvi. 4.　³ פלגיו.
⁴ Ezek. xlvii. 1–12.

⁵ Rev. xxi. 24–26. xxii. 21.
⁶ אפיק.　　　⁷ from Lap.

the children of Judah, because they have shed innocent blood in their land.

hard bondage, and tried, by the murder of their male children, to extirpate them. Edom was, by birth, the nearest allied to them, but had, from the time of their approach to the promised land, been hostile to them, and shewed a malicious joy in all their calamities[1]. *Their land*, in which Egypt and Edom shed the *innocent blood of the children of Judah*, may either be Edom, Egypt, or Judæa. If the land was Judæa, the sin is aggravated by its being God's land, the possession of which they were disputing with God. If it was Egypt and Edom, then it was probably the blood of those who took refuge there, or, as to Edom, of prisoners delivered up to them[2].

This is the first prophecy of the humiliation of Egypt. Hosea had threatened, that Egypt should be the grave of those of Israel who should flee there[3]. He speaks of it as the vain trust, and a real evil to Israel[4]; of its own future he says nothing. Brief as Joel's words are, they express distinctly an abiding condition of Egypt. They are expanded by Ezekiel[5]; particular chastisements are foretold by Isaiah[6], Jeremiah[7], Ezekiel[8], Zechariah[9]. But the three words of Joel[10], *Egypt shall become desolation*, are more comprehensive than any prophecy, except those by Ezekiel. They foretell that abiding condition, not only by the force of the words, but by the contrast with an abiding condition of bliss. The words say, not only "it shall be desolated," as by a passing scourge sweeping over it, but "it shall itself *pass over into* that state;" it shall become what it had not been[11]; and this, in contrast with the abiding condition of God's people. The contrast is like that of the Psalmist[12], *He turneth a fruitful land into barrenness for the wickedness of them that dwell therein. He turneth the wilderness into a standing water, and dry ground into water-springs*. Judah should overflow with blessing, and the streams of God's grace should pass beyond its bounds, and carry fruitfulness to what now was dry and barren. But what should reject His grace should be itself rejected.

Yet when Joel thus threatened Egypt, there were no human symptoms of its decay; the instruments of its successive overthrows were as yet wild hordes, (as the Chaldees, Persians, and Macedonians,) to be consolidated thereafter into powerful empires, or (as Rome) had not the beginnings of being. The "[13] continuous monumental history of Egypt" went back seven centuries before this, to about 1520, B. C. They had had a line of conquerors among their kings, who subdued much of Asia, and disputed with Assyria the country which lay between them[14]. Even after the time of Joel, they had great conquerors, as Tirhaka; Psammetichus won Ashdod back from Assyria[15], Neco was probably successful against it, as well as against Syria and king Josiah; for he took Cadytis on his return[16] from his expedition against Carchemish[17]; Pharaoh Hophra, or Apries, until he fell by his pride[18], renewed for a time the prosperity of Psammetichus[19]; the reign of Amasis, even after Nebuchadnezzar's conquest, was said to be "the most prosperous time which Egypt ever saw[20];" it was still a period of foreign conquest[21], and its cities could be magnified into 20,000. The Persian invasion was drawn upon it by an alliance with Lydia, whither Amasis sent 120,000 men[22]; its, at times, successful struggles against the gigantic armies of its Persian conquerors[23] betoken great inherent strength; yet it sank for ever, a perpetual desolation. "Rent, twenty-three centuries ago, from her natural proprietors," says an unbelieving writer[24], "she has seen Persians, Macedonians, Romans, Greeks, Arabs, Georgians, and at length, the race of Tartars, distinguished by the name of Ottoman Turks, establish themselves in her bosom." "The system of oppression is methodical;" "an universal air of misery is manifest in all which the traveler meets." "[25] Mud-walled cottages are now the only habitations, where the ruins of temples and palaces abound. The desert covers many extensive regions, which once raised Egypt among the chief of the kingdoms." The desolation of Egypt is the stranger, because exceeding misrule alone could have effected it.

Egypt, in its largest dimensions, has been calculated to contain 123,527 square miles or 79,057,339 acres, and to be three fourths of

---

[1] Ob. 10–14. Ez. xxv. 12. xxxv. 15. xxxvi. 5. Lam. iv. 22. Ps. cxxxvii. 7. See on Am. i. 11.
[2] See on Amos i. 9.
[3] ix. 6.
[4] vii. 11, 12, 16. viii. 13. ix. 3. xi. 5.
[5] xxix. 9–12. 15.
[6] xix. xx.
[7] xlvi.
[8] xxix.–xxxii.
[9] x. 11.
[10] מצרים לשממה תהיה.
[11] Such is the force of היה ל.
[12] Ps. cvii. 33–5.
[13] Sir G. Wilkinson Hist. Notice of Eg. in Rawl. Herod. ii. 354.

[14] See Ib. pp. 356–377.
[15] Herod. ii. 157.
[16] Ib. 159.
[17] 2 Kgs xxiii. 29.
[18] Ezek. xxix. 3.
[19] Herod. ii. 161 and p. 248. n. 8. Rawl.
[20] Her. ii. 177.
[21] Ib. 182.
[22] Cyrop. vi. 2. 10. vii. 1. 30–45.
[23] Sir G. Wilkinson in note in Rawl. Herod. ii. p. 393.
[24] Volney Voyage c. 6. also c. 12. 18. quoted by Keith.
[25] Keith on Prophecy, Egypt. p. 500–3.

the size of France[1]. The mountains which hem in Upper Egypt, diverge at Cairo, parting, the one range, due East, the other N. W. The mountains on the West sink into the plains; those on the East retain their height as far as Suez. About 10 miles below Cairo, the Nile parted, inclosing within the outside of its seven branches, that triangle of wondrous fertility, the Delta. A network of canals, formed by the stupendous industry of the ancient Egyptians, inclosed this triangle in another yet larger, whose base, along the coast, was 235 miles, in direct distance about 181. East of the Eastern-most branch of the Nile, lay the *land of Goshen*, formerly, at least for cattle, *the good of the land*[2], a part, at least, of the present esh-Sharkiyyeh, second in size of the provinces of Egypt, but which, A. D. 1375, yielded the highest revenue of the state[3]. On the Western side of the Nile, and about a degree South of the apex of the Delta, a stupendous work, the artificial lake of Mœris[4], inclosing within masonry $64\frac{3}{4}$ square miles of water, received the superfluous waters of the river, and thus at once prevented the injury incidental on any too great rise of the Nile, and supplied water during six months for the irrigation of 1724 square miles, or 1,103,375, acres[5]. The Nile which, when it overflowed, spread like a sea over Egypt[6], encircling its cities like islands, carried with it a fertilizing power, attested by all, but which, unless so attested, would seem fabulous. Beneath a glowing heat, greater than its latitude will account for, the earth, supplied with continual moisture and an ever renewed alluvial deposit which supersedes all need of "dressing" the soil, yields, within the year, three harvests of varied produce[7]. This system of canalising Egypt must have been of very early antiquity. That giant conception of the water system of lake Mœris is supposed to have been the work of Ammenemhes, perhaps about 1673, B. C.[8]. But such a giant plan presupposes the existence of an artificial system of irrigation which it expanded. In the time of Moses, we hear incidentally of *the streams* of Egypt, *the canals*[9] (that is, those used for irrigation), and *the ponds*[10], the receptacles of the water which was left when the Nile retired. Besides these, an artificial mode of irrigation *by the*

foot[11] is mentioned, now no longer distinctly known, but used, like the present plans of the water-wheel and the lever[12], to irrigate the lands for the later harvests. This system of irrigation had, in the time of Joel, lasted probably for above 1000 years. The Egyptians ascribed the first turning of the Nile to their first king, Menes[13], of fabulous antiquity. But while it lasted in any degree, Egypt could not become barren except by miracle. Even now it recovers, whenever water is applied. "Wherever there is water, there is fertility." "[14] The productive powers of the soil of Egypt are incalculable. Wherever water is scattered, there springs up a rapid and beautiful vegetation. The seed is sown and watered, and scarcely any other care is requisite for the ordinary fruits of the earth. Even in spots adjacent to the desert and which seem to be taken possession of by the sands, irrigation brings rapidly forth a variety of green herbs and plants." For its first crop, there needed but to cast the seed, and have it trodden in by cattle[15].

Nothing then could desolate Egypt, except man's abiding negligence or oppression. No passing storm or inroad could annihilate a fertility, which poured in upon it in ever-renewing richness. For 1000 years, the Nile had brought to Egypt unabated richness. The Nile overflows still, but in vain amid depopulation, and grinding, uniform, oppression. Not the country is exhausted, but man.

" If " says Mengin[16], " it is true that there is no country richer than Egypt in its territorial productions, still there is perhaps no one whose inhabitants are more miserable. It is owing solely to the fertility of its soil and the sobriety of its cultivators, that it retains the population which it still has." The marked diminution of the population had begun before the Birth of our Lord. " Of old," says Diodorus[17], " it far exceeded in denseness of population all the known countries in the world, and in our days too it seems to be inferior to no other. For in ancient times it had more than 18,000 considerable villages and towns, as you may see registered in the sacred lists. In the time of Ptolemy Lagus more than 30,000 were counted, a number which has continued until now. But the

---

[1] Descript. de l' Egypte (Col. Jacotin) Etat Moderne. T. ii. P. ii. p. 571. ed. fol.
[2] Gen. xlvii. 6. 11.
[3] Etat de l' Eg. from the Arabic. De Sac. Abdal. p. 595.
[4] This is the interesting discovery of M. Linant de Bellefonds, Mémoire sur le lac de Mœris. 1843.
[5] 967,948 feddans. The feddan, an Arabic acre (i. q. פֵד) varied at different times. M. Linant counts it at 4200 mètres 83 centimètres carrés, $1\frac{1}{20}$ Eng. Acre. Col. Jacotin estimates it at 5929 mètres carrés, a little under $1\frac{1}{2}$ Eng. Acre, 1. 42577. (Descr. de l' Eg. Ib. 573.) Mr. Lane states it at $1\frac{1}{10}$ Eng. Acre a little before 1836, "more at an

earlier period," (i. 158) less than an acre now (ii. 371).
[6] Herod. ii. 97.   [7] Lane Egypt ii. 26.
[8] Lepsius Kœnigsbuch d. alten Ægypt. Synopt. Tafeln p. 5.
[9] אֲרִים, the Egyptian word *ior*, "ditch" or "river."
[10] Ex. vii. 19 viii. 1.   [11] Deut. xi. 40.
[12] Sackiyeh and shadoof. See Lane ii. 24.
[13] Herod. ii. 4. 99.
[14] Bowring Report on Egypt. 1840. p. 12.
[15] Herod. ii. 14. and Sir G. Wilk. Rawl. Herod. ii. 18.
[16] Hist. de l' Eg. ii. 342.
[17] i. 31. He wrote, in part, 20 B. C. i. 44.

whole people are said of old to have been about seven millions, and in our days not less than three[1]." A modern estimate supposes that Egypt, if cultivated to the utmost, would, in plentiful years, support eight millions[2]. It is difficult to calculate a population where different ranks wish to conceal it. It has been guessed however that, two centuries ago, it was four millions; that, at the beginning of this century, it was two millions and a half; and that, in 1845, it was 1,800,000[3]. The great diminution then had begun 1900 years ago. Temporary causes, plague, smallpox, conscription, have, in this last century, again halved the population; but down to that time, it had sunk to no lower level than it had already reached at least 18 centuries before. The land still, for its fruitfulness, continues to supply more than its inhabitants consume; it yields over and above cotton[4], for strangers to employ. Yet its brilliant patches of vegetation are but indications how great the powers implanted in it. In vain " the rising Nile overflows (as it is thought) a larger proportion of the soil[5]" than heretofore; in vain has the rich alluvial deposit encroached upon the gradual slope of the desert; in vain, in Upper Egypt has a third been added since about the time of the Exodus. Egypt is stricken. Canals and even arms of the Nile, were allowed to choke up. Of the seven branches of the Nile, two only, at first artificial, remain[6]. " The others have either entirely disappeared or are dry in summer." The great Eastern arm, the Pelusian, is nearly effaced "[7] buried almost wholly beneath the sands of the desert." "[8] The land at the mouth of the canal which represents it, is a sand waste or a marsh." "[9] There is now no trace of vegetation in the whole Pelusian plain. Only one slight isolated rise has some thickets on it, and some shafts of columns lie on the sand." "[10] In the midst of a plain the most fertile, they want the barest necessaries of life." The sand of the desert, which was checked by the river and by the reeds on its banks, has swept over lands no longer fertilized. "[11] The sea has not been less destructive. It has broken down the dykes, wherewith man's labor held it in, and has carried barrenness over the productive lands, which it converted into lakes and marshes." A glance at the map of Egypt will shew

how widely the sea has burst in, where land once was. On the East, the salt lake Menzaleh, (itself from W. N. W. to S. S. E. about 50 miles long, and above 10 miles from N. to S.) absorbs two more of the ancient arms of the Nile, the Tanitic and the Mendesian[12]. The Tanitic branch is marked by a deeper channel below the shallow waters of the lake[13]. The lake of Burlos "[14] occupies from E. to W. more than half the basis of the Delta." Further Westward are a succession of lakes, Edkou, Madyeh (above 12½ miles) Mareotis (37½ miles). "[15] The ancient Delta has lost more than half its surface, of. which one-fifth is covered with the waters of the lakes Mareotis, Madyeh, Edkou, Bourlos, and Menzaleh, sad effects of the carelessness of the rulers or rather spoilers of this unhappy country." Even when the lake Mareotis was, before the English invasion in 1801, allowed nearly to dry up, it was but an unhealthy lagoon; and the Mareotic district, once famous for its wine and its olives and papyrus[16], had become a desert. So far from being a source of fertility, these lakes from time to time, at the low Nile, inundate the country with salt water, and are "surrounded by low and barren plains[17]."

The ancient populousness and capabilities of the Western province are attested by its ruins. "[18] The ruins which the French found everywhere in the military reconnaissances of this part of Egypt attest the truth of the historical accounts of the ancient population of the Province, now deserted;" "[19] so deserted, that you can scarce tell the numbers of ruined cities frequented only by wandering Arabs."

According to a calculation lower than others, ⅓ of the land formerly tilled in Egypt has been thrown out of cultivation, i. e. not less than 1,763,895 acres or $2755\frac{7}{10}$ square miles[20]. And this is not of yesterday. Towards the end of the 14th century, the extent of the land taxed was 3,034,179 feddans[21], i. e. 4,377,836⅝ acres or 6840⅓ square miles. The list of lands taxed by the Egyptian government in 1824 yields but a sum of 1,956,340 feddans[22], or 2,822,171 acres or 4409 square miles. Yet even this does not represent the land actually cultivated. Some even of the taxed land is left wholly, some partially, uncultivated[23]. In an official

---

[1] Only one late MS. omits the word τριακοσίων, making the sense, that the number was still no less than seven millions. It has no weight against the greater authority of MSS.
[2] Lane's Egypt i. 27.
[3] Sir G. Wilkinson Modern Egypt i. 257. M. Jomard (Descr. de l' Eg. ii. 2. p. 364.) sets it at 2,422,200.
[4] 100,000 bales of a cwt. each in one year. Lane i. 28.   [5] Wilkinson Anc. Eg. i. 218, 9.
[6] Wilkinson mod. Eg. i. 403.
[7] Malus sur l'état anc. et mod. des Provinces Orient. de la Basse Eg. Descr. Eg. ii. p. 305.
[8] Ritter Erdk. i. 824. 6.   [9] Ib. 827.
[10] Malus Ib. p. 310.

[11] Col. Jacotin in Descr. de l' Eg. M. ii. p. 576.
[12] Andréossy in Descr. Eg. M. i. pp. 261 sqq.
[13] Ib. § 4.   [14] Ritter i. 821.   [15] Le Père Ib. ii. 1. 471.
[16] Athen. i. 60. pp. 76, 7. Dind. Strab. xvii. 1, 14, 15. Ritter i. 871.
[17] Le Père Ib. ii. 2. 482.   [18] Id. ib. ii. p. 10.   [19] Ib. 7.
[20] 474. 24 square leagues. Col. Jacotin ii. 2. p. 577.
[21] from the Arabic list published by De Sacy at the end of his Abdallatif, p. 597–704.
[22] Mengin Hist. de l' Eg. i. 343.
[23] Sir G. Wilkinson, says, " The land N. and S. of the canal, particularly round Menzaleh, is little productive, and in parts perfectly barren. The increase of nitre in the soil seems to doom to

report[1], 2,000,000 feddans are stated to be cultivated, when the overflow of the Nile is the most favorable, i. e. ⅘ only of the estimated cultivable amount. The French, who surveyed Egypt minutely, with a view to future improvement, calculated that above 1,000,000 feddans (1,012,887) might be proximately restored by the restoration of the system of irrigation, and nearly 1,000,000 more (942,810) by the drainage of its lakes, ponds and marshes, i. e. nearly as much again as is actually cultivated. One of the French surveyors sums up his account of the present state of Egypt[2]; "without canals and their dykes, Egypt, ceasing to be vivified throughout, is only a corpse which the mass of the waters of its river inundates to superfluity, and destroys through fullness. Instead of those ancient cultivated and fertile plains, one only finds, here and there, canals filled up or cut in two, whose numerous ramifications, crossing each other in every direction, exhibit only some scarcely distinguishable traces of a system of irrigation; instead of those villages and populous cities, one sees only masses of bare and arid ruins, remnants of ancient habitations reduced to ashes; lastly, one finds only lagoons, miry and pestilential, or sterile sands which extend themselves, and unceasingly invade a land which the industry of man had gained from the desert and the sea."

Yet this is wholly unnatural. In the Prophet's time, it was contrary to all experience. Egypt is alike prolific in its people and in the productions of the earth. The Egyptian race is still accounted very prolific[3]. So general is this, that the ancients thought that the waters of the Nile must have some power of fecundity[4]. Yet with these powers implanted in nature unimpaired, the population is diminished, the land half-desert. No one doubts that man's abiding misgovernment is the cause of Egypt's desolation. Under their native princes, they were happy and prosperous[5]. Alexander, some of the Ptolemies, the Romans, saw, at least, the value of Egypt. The great conception of its Greek conqueror, Alexandria, has been a source of prosperity to strangers for above 2000 years. Prosperity has hovered around Egypt. Minds, the most different, are at one in thinking that, with a good government, internal prosperity and its far-

famed richness of production might at once be restored. Conquerors of varied nations, Persians, Macedonians, Romans, Greeks, Arabs, Georgians, Tartars, or Turks have tried their hands upon Egypt. Strange that selfishness or powerlessness for good should have rested upon all; strange that no one should have developed its inherent powers! Strange contrast. One long prosperity, and one long adversity. One scarcely broken day, and one troubled night. And that doom foretold in the midday of its prosperity, by those three words, *Egypt shall be a desolation.*

Edom shall be a desolate wilderness. Edom, long unknown, its ancient capital, its rock-dwellings, have been, within these last forty years, anew revealed. The desolation has been so described to us, that we have seen it, as it were, with our own eyes. The land is almost the more hopelessly desolate, because it was once, artificially, highly cultivated. Once it had *the fatness of the earth and the dew of heaven from above*[6]: it had [7]cornfields and *vineyards* in abundance, and *wells* of water; its vegetation, its trees, and its vineyards, attracted the dew by which they were supported. "Petra," says Strabo[8], "lies in a spot precipitous and abrupt without, but within possessed of abundant fountains for watering and horticulture." The terrace-cultivation, through which each shower which falls is stored to the uttermost, clothing with fertility the mountain-sides, leaves those steep sides the more bare, when disused. "We saw," says a traveler[9], "many ruined terraces, the evidences and remains of a flourishing agriculture, which, in the prosperous days of Edom and Petra, clothed many of these now sterile mountains with fertility and beauty.—Fields of wheat and some agricultural villages still exist in the eastern portion of Edom; but, with very slight exceptions, the country is blighted with cheerless desolation and hopeless sterility. The hill-sides and mountains, once covered with earth and clothed with vineyards, are now bare rocks. The soil no longer supported by terraces and sheltered by trees, has been swept away by the rains. The various contrivances for irrigation, which even now might restore fertility to many considerable tracts, have all disappeared. Sand from the desert, and the debris of the soft rock of the

---

destruction even that which is still deserving of cultivation. Some land scarcely repays the labor of tilling, and some has been found so unproductive that, *though rated for taxation and annually paying firdeh,* it has been left uncultivated." Mod. Eg. i. 441, 2. Again, of the province of Behnesa; "The land for the most part lies fallow, for three months before the inundation, partly from the indolence of the people, and partly from the want of hands to cultivate." ii. 30.

[1] "When the Nile rises from 23 to 24 coudées, 2,000,000 feddans are cultivated. But often the Nile does not rise above 19 coudées, and the inundation

is not permanent enough to produce the effect desired. Egypt is calculated to have 3,500,000 feddans of cultivable land, if cultivation were pushed to its greatest extent." Bowring Report p. 13.

[2] Le Père Mémoire sur les lacs et les deserts de la basse Egypte in Descr. de l' Eg. Mod. ii. 1. p. 481.

[3] Bowring p. 5. Lane i. 195.

[4] Aristotle and Aristobulus in Strabo xv. 1. § 22. Plin. vii. 3. and others.

[5] Wilkinson Anc. Eg. c. 3. end.

[6] Gen. xxvii. 39.

[7] Nu. xx. 17.   [8] xvi. 4. 21.

[9] Olin T. ii. pp. 15, 55. Keith p. 308.

Before
CHRIST
cir. 800.
20 But Judah shall || dwell [n]for ever, and Je-

|| Or, *abide.* [n] Amos 9. 15.

rusalem from generation to generation.

Before
CHRIST
cir. 800.

mountains, cover the valleys which formerly smiled with plenty." Now "[1] the springs have been dried up to such an extent, as to render the renewal of the general fertility of Edom [well nigh] impossible. In places along the course of the stream, reeds and shrubs grow luxuriantly, oleanders and wild figs abound, and give proof that a little cultivation would again cover the rock, and fill the cliffs with the numberless gardens which once adorned them. The traces of former fertility are innumerable; every spot capable of sustaining vegetable life was carefully watered and cultivated. There are numerous grooves in the rocks to carry rainwater to the little clefts in which even now figs are found. Every spot capable of being so protected has been walled up, however small the space gained, or however difficult the means of securing it. The ancient inhabitants seem to have left no accessible place untouched. They have exhibited equal art and industry in eliciting from the grand walls of their marvelous capital whatever the combination of climate, irrigation and botanical skill could foster in the, scanty soil afforded them. The hanging gardens must have had a wondrous effect among the noble buildings of the town when it was in all its glory." This desolation began soon after the captivity of Judah and Edom's malicious joy in it. For Malachi appeals to Judah, that whereas God had restored him, He had[2] *laid the mountains and the heritage* of Esau *waste for the jackals of the wilderness.*

Yet Edom was the centre of the intercourse of nations. Occupying, as it did in its narrowest dimensions, the mountains between the S. end of the Dead Sea and the Ælanitic gulf, it lay on the direct line between Egypt and Babylonia. A known route lay from Heroopolis to Petra its capital, and thence to Babylon[3]. Elath and Ezion-geber discharged through its vally, the Arabah, the wealth which they received by sea from India or Africa. Petra was the natural halting-place of the caravans. "The Nabatæans," says Pliny[4], "inclose Petra, in a valley of rather more than two miles in extent, surrounded by inaccessible mountains, through which a stream flows. Here the two roads meet of those who go to Palmyra of Syria, and of those who come from Gaza." Eastward again, he says[5], "they went from Petra to Fora, and thence to Charax" on the banks of

the Tigris, near the Persian gulf. Yet further the wealth of Arabia Felix poured by a land-route through Petra. "[6]To Petra and Palestine, Gerræns and Minæans and all the neighboring Arabs brought down from the upper country the frankincense, it is said, and all other fragrant merchandise." Even after the foundation of Alexandria had diverted much of the stream of commerce from Leuce Come, the Ælanitic gulf, and Petra to Myos Hormus[7] on the Egyptian side of the Red Sea, the Romans still connected Elath and Petra with Jerusalem by a great road, of which portions are still extant[8], and guarded the intercourse by military stations[9]. Of these routes, that from Arabia Felix and from Egypt to Babylonia had probably been used for above 1000 years before the time of Joel. Elath and Eziongeber were well-known towns at the time of the Exodus[10]. The intercourse was itself complex and manifold. The land exports of Arabia Felix and the commerce of Elath necessarily passed through Edom, and thence radiated to Egypt, Palestine, Syria. The withdrawal of the commerce of Egypt would not alone have destroyed that of Petra, while Tyre, Jerusalem, Damascus still received merchandise through her. To them she was the natural channel; the pilgrim-route from Damascus to Mecca lies still by Petra. In Joel's time, not the slightest shadow was cast on her future. Then Babylon destroyed her for a time; but she recovered. The Babylonian and Persian Empires perished; Alexander rose and fell; Rome, the master alike of Alexandria and Petra, meant Petra still to survive. No human eye could even then tell that it would be finally desolate; much less could any human knowledge have foreseen it in that of Joel. But God said by him, *Edom shall be a desolate wilderness,* and it is so!

As, however, Egypt and Edom are only instances of the enemies of God's people and Church, so their desolation is only one instance of a great principle of God's Government, that[11] *the triumphing of the wicked* is *short, and the joy of the ungodly for a moment;* that, after their short-lived office of fulfilling God's judgment on His people, the judgment rolls round on themselves, *and they that hate the righteous shall be desolate*[12].

20. *Judah shall dwell for ever.* Not earthly Judah, nor earthly Jerusalem; for these must come to an end, together with the earth itself, of

[1] Lord C. Hamilton Journal in Keith Ib. Idumæa pp. 338, 9. see also Count Portalis, Ib. p. 332.
[2] Mal. i. 3.
[3] Strabo xvi. 4. 2.
[4] vi. 28.　　　　　　　　　　　　　　[5] Ib.

[6] Agatharcides p. 57 in Geogr. Min. ed. Oxen, quoted in Vincent's Periplus ii. 262.
[7] Strab. xvi. 4. 24.　　　[8] Robins. Pal. ii. 161.
[9] Reland p. 230.　　　　　[10] Deut. ii. 8.
[11] Job xx. 5.　　　　　　　[12] Ps. xxxiv. 21.

Before
CHRIST
cir. 800.
21 For I will °cleanse their blood *that* I have not

° Is. 4. 4.

cleansed : P ‖ for the LORD dwelleth in Zion.

Before
CHRIST
cir. 800.

P Ezek. 48. 35. ver. 17. Rev. 21. 3.
‖ Or, *even I the Lord that dwelleth in Zion.*

whose end the Prophets well knew. It is then the one people of God, the true Judah, the people who praise God, the Israel, which is indeed Israel. Egypt and Edom and all the enemies of God should come to an end; but His people shall never come to an end. *The gates of hell shall not prevail against her.* The enemy shall not destroy her; time shall not consume her; she shall never decay. The people of God shall abide before Him and through Him here, and shall dwell with Him for ever.

21. *For I will cleanse her blood that I have not cleansed.* The word rendered *cleansed* [1] is not used of natural cleansing, nor is the image taken from the cleansing of the body. The word signifies only to pronounce innocent, or to free from guilt. Nor is *blood* used of sinfulness generally, but only of the actual guilt of shedding blood. The whole then cannot be an image taken from the cleansing of physical defilement, like the words in the prophet Ezekiel [2], *then washed I thee with water; yea, I thoroughly washed away thy blood from thee.* Nor again can it mean the forgiveness of sins generally, but only the pronouncing innocent the blood which had been shed. This, the only meaning of the words, fall in with the mention of the *innocent blood,* for shedding which, Egypt and Edom had been condemned. The words are the same. There it was said, *because they have shed innocent blood; dam naki;* here, *I will pronounce innocent their blood, nikkethi damam. How,* it is not said. But the sentence on Egypt and Edom explains how God would do it, by punishing those who shed it. For in that He punishes the shedding of it, He declared the *blood* innocent, whose shedding He punished. So in the Revelation is said [3], *I saw under the altar the souls of them that were slain for the word of God, and for the testimony which they held, and they cried with a loud voice, saying, How long, O Lord, holy and true, dost Thou not judge and avenge our blood on them that dwell on the earth?* " [4] Then, at the last judgment, when the truth in all things shall be made manifest, He shall declare the blood of His people, who clave to Him and His truth, which shed their enemies thought they had shed justly and deservedly as the blood of guilty persons, to have indeed been innocent, by absolving them from eternal destruction to which He shall then adjudge their enemies for shedding of it."

For [lit. *and*] *the Lord dwelleth in Zion.* He closes with the promise of God's abiding dwelling. He speaks, not simply of a future, but of an ever-abiding present. He Who IS, the unchangeable God, " [4] the Lord, infinite in power and of eternal Being, Who gives necessary being to all His purposes and promises," dwelleth now in [5] *Mount Zion, the city of the living God, the heavenly Jerusalem,* now by grace and the presence of His Holy Spirit, hereafter in glory. Both of the Church militant on earth and that triumphant in heaven, it is truly to be said, that the Lord dwelleth in them, and that, perpetually. Of the Church on earth will be verified what our Saviour Christ saith [6], *lo I am with you always, even unto the end of the world;* and of its members S. Paul saith, that *they* are *of the household of God, an holy temple in the Lord, in Whom they are builded together for an habitation of God through the Spirit* [7]. Of the Church triumphant, there is no doubt, that *He* doth and will there dwell, and manifest His glorious Presence for ever, *in* Whose *Presence is the fullness of joy, and at His Right Hand* there are *pleasures for evermore* [8]. It is an eternal dwelling of the Eternal, varied as to the way and degree of His Presence by our condition, now imperfect, there perfected in Him; but He Himself dwelleth on for ever. He, the Unchangeable, dwelleth unchangeably; the Eternal, eternally.

" [9] *Glorious things are spoken of thee, thou city of God* [10]. Jerusalem, our mother, we thy children now groan and weep in this valley of tears, hanging between hope and fear, and, amid toil and conflicts, *lifting up our eyes* to thee and greeting thee from far. Truly *glorious things are spoken of thee.* But whatever can be said, since it is said to men and in the words of men, is too little for the *good things* in thee, which *neither eye hath seen, nor ear heard, nor hath entered into the heart of man* [11]. Great to us seem the things which we suffer; but one of thy most illustrious citizens, placed amid those sufferings, who knew something of thee, hesitated not to say [12], *Our light affliction, which is but for a moment, worketh out for us a far more exceeding and eternal weight of glory.* We will then *rejoice in hope,* and *by the waters of Babylon,* even while *we sit and weep,* we will *remember thee, O Zion. If I forget thee, O Jerusalem, may my right hand forget* her cunning. *Let my tongue cleave to the roof of my mouth, I do*

[1] נקיתי.　　[2] xvi. 9.　　[3] vi. 10. 11.　　[4] Poc.
[5] Heb. xii. 22. add Gal. iv. 26. Rev. iii. 12. xiv. 1. xxi. 2. 10.

[6] S. Matt. xxviii. 20.　　　[7] Eph. ii. 19, 21, 2.
[8] Ps. xvi. 12.　　[9] Rib.　　[10] Ps. lxxxvii. 3.
[11] 1 Cor. ii. 9.　　　　[12] 2 Cor. iv. 17.

not remember thee, if I prefer not Jerusalem above my chief joy [1]. O blessed longed-for day, when we shall enter into the city of the saints, *whose light is the Lamb,* where *the King is seen in His beauty,* where *all tears are wiped off from the eyes* of the saints, *and there shall be no more death neither sorrow nor pain; for the former things have passed away* [2]. *How amiable are Thy tabernacles, O Lord of Hosts! My soul longeth, yea fainteth for the courts of the Lord; my heart and my flesh crieth out for the living God* [3]. *When shall I come and appear before God* [4]? when shall I see that Father, Whom I ever long for and never see, to Whom out of this exile, I cry out, *Our Father, which art in Heaven?* O true Father, [5], *Father of our Lord Jesus Christ,* [6] *Father of mercies and God of all comfort!* When shall I see *the Word,*

Who *was in the beginning with God,* and Who *is God* [7]? When may I kiss His sacred Feet, pierced for me, put my mouth to His sacred Side, sit at His Feet, never to depart from them? O Face, more Glorious than the sun! Blessed is he, who beholdeth Thee, who hath never ceased to say [8], *I shall see Him, but not now; I shall behold Him, but not nigh.* When will the day come, when, cleansed from the defilement of my sins, I shall, [9] *with unveiled face, behold the glory of the Lord,* and see the sanctifying Spirit, the Author of all good, through Whose sanctifying we are cleansed, that [10] *we may be like Him, and see Him as He is?* [11] *Blessed are all they that dwell in Thy house, O Lord, they shall ever praise Thee;* for ever shall they behold Thee and love Thee."

[1] Ps. cxxxvii.
[2] Rev. xxi. 23. Is. xxxiii. 17. Rev. xxi. 4.
[3] Ps. lxxxiv. 1, 2. [4] Ps. xlii. 2. [5] Rom. xv. 6. &c.

[6] 2 Cor. i. 3.
[8] Nu. xxiv. 17.
[10] 1 Joh. iii. 2.
[7] S. Joh. i. 1.
[9] 2 Cor. iii. 18.
[11] Ps. lxxxiv. 4.

INTRODUCTION

TO

THE PROPHET

AMOS.

"[a] He *Who made*, one by one, *the hearts of men*, and *understandeth all their works*, knowing the hardness and contrariousness of the heart of Israel, reasoneth with them not through one Prophet only, but, employing as His ministers many, and those, wondrous men, both monisheth them and foretelleth the things to come, evidencing through the harmony of many the truthfulness of their predictions."

As the contradiction of false teachers gave occasion to S. Paul to speak of himself, so the persecution of the priest of Bethel has brought out such knowledge as we have of the life of Amos, before God called him to be a prophet. *I*, he says [b], *was no prophet, neither was I a prophet's son.* He had not received any of the training in those schools of the prophets which had been founded by Samuel, and through which, amid the general apostasy and corruption, both religious knowledge and religious life were maintained in the remnant of Israel. He was a herdsman, whether (as this word would naturally mean [c]) *a cowherd* or (less obviously) *a shepherd.* He was *among the herdsmen of Tekoah; among* them, and, outwardly, as they, in nothing distinguished from them. The sheep which he tended (for he also kept sheep) may have been his own. There is nothing to prove or to disprove it. But any how he was not like the king of Moab, "a sheep-master [d]," as the Jews, following out their principle, that "[e] prophecy was only bestowed by God on the rich and noble," wish to make him. Like David, he was following the sheep [f], as their shepherd. But his employment as *a gatherer* (or, more probably, *a cultivator) of sycamore fruit*, the rather designates him, as one living by a rural employment for hire. The word, probably, designates the artificial means by which the sycamore fruit was ripened, irritating, scraping, puncturing, wounding it [g]. Amos does not say that these were his food, but that one of his employments was to do a gardener's office in maturing them. A sort of gardener then he was, and a shepherd among other shepherds. The sheep which he fed were also probably a matter of trade. The breed of sheep and goats, *nakad*, from keeping which his peculiar name of shepherd, *noked*, was derived, is still known by the same name in Arabia; a race, small, thin, short-legged, ugly, and stunted. It furnished a proverb, "viler than a nakad;" yet the wool of the sheep was accounted the very best. The goats were found especially in Bahrein. Among the Arabs also, the shepherd of these sheep was known by a name derived from them. They were called "nakad;" their shepherd "nokkad [h]."

The prophet's birthplace, Tekoah, was a town which, in the time of Josephus and of S. Jerome, had dwindled into a "village [i],"

---

[a] Theod. [b] vii. 14. [c] בקר being used always of the "ox" or "herd," in contrast with the "flocks" of sheep or goats, and the name being derived from "ploughing."

[d] The term נוקד is used of the king of Moab 2 K. iii. 4. [e] See on Joel ii. 29.

[f] vii. 15. *He took me* מאחרי הצאן.

[g] κνιζων. LXX. vellicans, S. Jer. See Theophr. iv. 2. Dioscor. L. i. Plin. xiii. 7. in Bochart ii. 39. p. 384. The Hebrew word בולם (from בלם "a fig" or sycamore in Arab. and Æthiop. signifies only "employed about figs" or sycamores.

[h] See Arabic authorities in Bochart L. ii. c. 34. pp. 442, 3. and Freytag Lexicon. [i] Josephi Vit. § 75.

"a little village[j]," on a high hill, twelve miles from Jerusalem, "which," S. Jerome adds, "we see daily." "It lay," S. Jerome says[k], "six miles southward from holy Bethlehem where the Saviour of the world was born, and beyond it is no village save some rude huts and movable tents. Such is the wide waste of the desert which stretcheth to the Red Sea, and the bounds of the Persians, Ethiopians, and Indians. And no grain whatever being grown upon this dry and sandy soil, it is all full of shepherds, in order, by the multitude of the flocks, to make amends for the barrenness of the land." From Tekoah Joab brought the *wise woman*[l] to intercede for Absalom; Rehoboam built it[m]; i. e. whereas it had been before (what it afterward again became) a village, and so was not mentioned in the book of Joshua, he made it a fortified town toward his South-Eastern border. The neighboring wilderness was called after it[n]. Besides its sycamores, its oil was the best in Judah[o]. War and desolation have extirpated both from this as well as from other parts of Palestine[p]. Its present remains are Christian, "[q]ruins of 4 or 5 acres." It, as well as so many other places near the Dead Sea, is identified by the old name, slightly varied in pronunciation, Theku'a, as also by its distance from Jerusalem[r]. In the sixth century we hear of a chapel in memory of the holy Amos at Tekoa[s], where the separated monks of the lesser laura of S. Saba communicated on the Lord's day. The wide prospect from Tekoa embraced both the dead and the living, God's mercies and His judgments. To the South-East "[t] the view is bounded only by the level mountains of Moab, with frequent bursts of the Dead Sea, seen through openings among the rugged and desolate mountains which intervene." On the North, the Mount of Olives is visible, at that time dear to sight, as overhanging the place, which God had *chosen to place His Name there.* Tekoah, however, although the birthplace, was not the abode of the prophet. He was *among the herdsmen from Tekoah*[u], their employment, as shepherds, leading them away *from Tekoah*. In the wilds of the desert while he was following his sheep, God saw him and revealed Himself to him, as he had to Jacob and to Moses, and said to him, *Go prophesy unto My people Israel.* And as the Apostle left their nets and their father, and Matthew the receipt of custom, and followed Jesus, so Amos left his sheep and his cultivation of syca-

mores, and appeared suddenly in his shepherd's dress at the royal but idolatrous[v] sanctuary, the temple of the state, to denounce the idolatry sanctioned by the state, to foretell the extinction of the Royal family, and the captivity of the people. This, like Hosea, he had to do in the reign of the mightiest of the sovereigns of Israel, in the midst of her unclouded prosperity. Bethel was but twelve miles Northward from Jerusalem[w], as Tekoah was twelve miles toward the South-East. Six or seven hours would suffice to transport the shepherd from his sheep and the wilderness to that fountain of Israel's corruption, the high places of Bethel, and to confront the inspired peasant with the priests and the prophets of the state-idolatry. There doubtless he said[x], *the sanctuaries of Israel shall be laid waste ;* and there, like the former *man of God*, while standing over against *the altar*, he renewed the prophecy against it, and prophesied that in its destruction it should involve its idolatrous worshipers[y]. Yet although he did deliver a part of his prophecy at Bethel, still, like his great predecessors Elijah and Elisha, doubtless he did not confine his ministry there. His summons to the luxurious ladies of Samaria, whose expenses were supported by the oppressions of the poor[z], was questionless delivered in Samaria itself. The call to the heathen to look down into Samaria from the heights which girt in the valley out of which it rose[a], thence to behold its din and its oppressions, to listen to the sound of its revelries and the wailings of its oppressed, and so to judge between God and His people, would also be most effectively given within Samaria. The consciences of the guilty inhabitants to whom he preached, would people the heights around them, their wall of safety, as they deemed, between them and the world, with heathen witnesses of their sins, and heathen avengers. The Prophet could only know by inspiration the coming destruction of the house of Jeroboam and the captivity of Israel. The sins which he rebuked, he probably knew from being among them. As S. Paul's *spirit was stirred in him* at Athens, *when he saw the city wholly given to idolatry*[b], so that of Amos must have been stirred in its depths by that grievous contrast of luxury and penury side by side, which he describes in such vividness of detail. The sins which he rebukes are those of the outward prosperity especially of a capital, the extreme luxury[c], revelries[d], debauchery[e], of the rich, who sup-

[j] S. Jer. on Jerem. vi. 1.
[k] Præf. ad. Amos.   [l] 1 Sam. xiv. 2.
[m] 2 C. xi. 6.
[n] 2 C. xx. 20, 1 Macc. ix. 33.
[o] Menachot viii. 3. in Reland p. 1029.
[p] See Keith land of Israel c. 3. 4. 5. Stanley Palestine p. 120. Robinson i. 552.
[q] Robinson i. 486.   [r] Ritter Erdk. xv. p. 629.

[s] Vita S. Sabæ in Cotelre. Ecc. Græc. Mon. iii. p. 272.
[t] Rob. Ib.   [u] מתקוע.
[v] iii. 13.   [w] Euseb. sub. v.   [x] vii. 9.
[y] ix. 1.   [a] iv. 1.   [z] See on iii. 9.
[b] Acts xvii. 16.
[c] iii. 12, 15, iv. 1. v. 11. vi. 4–6.
[d] ii. 8. iii. 9.   [e] ii. 7.

ported their own reckless expenditure by oppression of the poor [f], extortion [g], hard bargains with their necessities [h], perversion of justice [i], with bribing [k], false measures [l], a griping, hard-fisted, and probably usurious sale of corn [m]. In grappling with sin, Amos deals more with the details and circumstances of it than Hosea. Hosea touches the centre of the offence; Amos shews the hideousness of it in the details into which it branches out. As he is everywhere graphic, so here he points out the events of daily life in which the sin shewed itself, as the vile price or, it may be, the article of luxury, *the pair of sandals* [n], for which the poor was sold, or *the refuse of wheat* (he invents the word) which they sold, at high prices and with short measure to the poor [o].

According to the title which Amos prefixes to his prophecy, his office fell within the 25 years, during which Uzziah and Jeroboam II. were contemporary, B.C. 809-784. This falls in with the opinion already expressed [p], that the bloodshed mentioned by Hosea in the list of their sins, was rather blood shed politically in their revolutions after the death of Jeroboam II., than individual murder. For Amos, while upbraiding Israel with the sins incidental to political prosperity and wealth, (such as was the time of Jeroboam II.) does not mention bloodshed.

It has been thought that the mention of the earthquake, two years before which Amos began his prophecy, furnishes us with a more definite date. That earthquake must have been a terrible visitation, since it was remembered after the captivity, two centuries and a half afterward. *Ye shall flee,* says Zechariah [q], as of a thing which his hearers well knew by report, *as ye fled before the earthquake in the days of Uzziah king of Judah.* Josephus connects the earthquake with Uzziah's act of pride in offering the incense, for which God smote him with leprosy. He relates it as a fact. "[r] Meanwhile a great earthquake shook the ground, and, the temple parting, a bright ray of the sun shone forth, and fell upon the king's face, so that forthwith the leprosy came over him. And before the city, at the place called Eroge, the Western half of the hill was broken off and rolled half a mile to the mountain Eastward, and there stayed, blocking up the ways and the king's gardens." This account of Josephus, however, is altogether unhistorical. Not to argue from the improbability, that such an event as the rending of the temple itself should not have been mentioned, Josephus has confused Zechariah's description of

an event yet future with the *past* earthquake under Uzziah. Nor can the date be reconciled with the history. For when Uzziah was stricken with leprosy [s], *Jotham, his son, was over the king's house, judging the people of the land.* But Jotham was only twenty-five years at his father's death, *when he himself began to reign* [t]. And Uzziah survived Jeroboam 26 years. Jotham then, who judged for his father after his leprosy, was not born when Jeroboam died. Uzziah then must have been stricken with leprosy some years after Jeroboam's death; and consequently, after the earthquake also, since Amos, who prophesied *in the* days of Jeroboam, prophesied *two years before the earthquake.*

An ancient Hebrew interpretation [u] of the prophecy of Isaiah [v], *within threescore and five years shall Ephraim be broken that it be no more a people,* assumed that Isaiah was foretelling the commencement of the captivity under Tiglath-Pileser or Sargon, and since the period of Isaiah's own prophecy to that captivity was not 65 years, supposed that Isaiah counted from a prophecy of Amos [w], *Israel shall surely be led captive out of his own land.* This prophecy of Amos they placed in the 25th year of Uzziah. Then his remaining 27 years, Jotham's 16, Ahaz 16, and the six first of Hezekiah would have made up the 65. This calculation was not necessarily connected with the error as to the supposed connection of the earthquake and the leprosy of Uzziah. But it is plain from the words of Isaiah, *in yet* [x] *threescore and five years,* that he is dating from the time when he uttered the prophecy; and so the prophecy relates, not to the imperfect captivity which ended the *kingdom* of Israel, but to that more complete deportation under Esarhaddon [y], when the ten tribes ceased to be *any more a people* (Ahaz 14, Hezekieh 29, Manasseh 22, in all 65). Neither then does this fix the date of Amos.

Nor does the comparison, which Amos bids Israel make between his own borders, and those of Calneh, Hamath and Gath, determine the date of the prophecy. Since Uzziah brake down the walls of Gath [z], and Hamath was recovered by Jeroboam II. to Israel [a], it is probable that the point of comparison lay between the present disasters of these nations, and those with which Amos threatened Israel, and which the rich men of Israel practically did not believe. For it follows [b], *ye that put far away the evil day.* It is probable then that Calne (the very ancient city [c] which subsequently became Ctesiphon,) on the other side of the Euphrates, had lately

[f] ii. 7. 8. iii. 9. iv. 1. v. 11. vi. 3. viii. 4-6.　[g] iii. 10.
[h] ii. 8.　[i] ii. 7. v. 7, 12.　[k] ii. 6. v. 12.
[l] viii. 5.　[m] viii. 5. 6.　[n] ii. 6. viii. 6.　[o] viii. 6.
[p] See Introd. to Hos. p. 15.
[q] xiv. 5.　[r] Ant. ix. 10.
[s] 2 C. xxvi. 21.　[t] Ib. xxvii. 1.

[u] in Euseb. & S. Jer. ad. loc. found also in Rashi, Aben Ezra, Abarbenel.
[v] vii. 8.　[w] vii. 11. 17.　[x] בְּעוֹד.
[y] Ezr. iv. 2. 2 Chr. xxxiii. 11. 2 Kgs xvii. 24.
[z] 2 Chr. xxvi. 6.　[a] 2 Kgs xiv. 28.
[b] Am. vi. 3.　[c] Gen. x. 10.

15

suffered from Assyria, as Gath and Hamath from Judah and Israel. But we know none of these dates. Isaiah speaks of the Assyrian as boasting that *Calno* was *as Carchemish* [d], *Hamath as Arpad, Samaria as Damascus.* But this relates to times long subsequent, when Hamath, Damascus, and Samaria, had fallen into the hands of Assyria. Our present knowledge of Assyrian history gives us no clue to the event, which was well known to those to whom Amos spoke.

Although, however, the precise time of the prophetic office of Amos cannot thus be fixed, it must have fallen within the reign of Jeroboam, to whom Amaziah, the priest of Bethel, accused him [e]. For this whole prophecy implies that Israel was in a state of prosperity, ease, and security, whereas it fell into a state of anarchy immediately upon Jeroboam's death. The mention of *the entering in of Hamath* [f] as belonging to Israel implies that this prophecy was after Jeroboam had recovered it to Israel [g]; and the ease, pride, luxury, which he upbraids, evince that the foreign oppressions [h] had for some time ceased. This agrees with the title of the prophecy, but does not limit it further. Since he prophesied while Uzziah and Jeroboam II. reigned together, his prophetic office must have fallen between B.C. 809 and B.C. 784, in the last 25 years of the reign of Jeroboam II. His office, then, began probably after that of Hosea, and closed long before its close. He is, in a manner then, both later and earlier than Hosea, later than the earliest period of Hosea's prophetic office, and long earlier than the latest.

Within this period, there is nothing to limit the office of Amos to a very short time. The message of Amaziah, the priest of Bethel, implies that Amos' words of woe had shaken Israel through and through. [i] *Amos hath conspired against thee in the midst of the house of Israel; the land is not able to bear all his words.* It may be that God sent him to the midst of some great festival at Bethel, as, at Jeroboam's dedication-feast, He sent the prophet who afterward disobeyed Him, to foretell the desecration of the Altar, which Jeroboam was consecrating, in God's Name, against God. In this case, Amos might, at once, like Elijah, have been confronted with a great concourse of the idol-worshipers. Yet the words of Amaziah seem, in their obvious meaning, to imply that Amos had had a more pervading influence than would be produced by the delivery of God's message in one place. He says of *the land,* i. e. of all the ten tribes generally, it *is not able to bear all his words.* The accusation also of a *conspiracy* probably implies, that some had

not been shaken only, but had been converted by the words of Amos, and were known by their adherence to him and his belief.

Amos seems also to speak of the prohibition to God's prophets to prophesy, as something habitual, beyond the one opposition of Amaziah, which he rebuked on the spot. *I raised up of your sons for prophets; but ye commanded the prophets, saying, Prophesy not* [k]. Nor, strictly speaking, was Amos a *son* of Ephraim. The series of images in the 3d chapter seem to be an answer to an objection, why did he prophesy among them? People, he would say, were not, in the things of nature, surprised that the effect followed the cause. God's command was the cause; his prophesying, the effect [l]. Then *they put away from them the evil day* [m], forgetting future evil in present luxury; or they professed that God was with them; "the LORD, the God of hosts, shall be with you, *as ye have spoken* [n];" or trusting in their half-service of God and His imagined Presence among them, they jeered at Amos's prophecies of ill, and professed to desire the Day of the Lord, with which he threatened them; they said that evil should not reach them; *Woe unto you that desire the Day of the Lord! to what end is it to you* [o]? *All the sinners of My people shall die by the sword, which say, the evil shall not overtake nor prevent us* [p]. They shewed also in deed that they hated those who publicly reproved them [q]; and Amos, like Hosea, declares that they are hardened, so that wisdom itself must leave them to themselves [r]. All this implies a continued intercourse between the prophet and the people, so that his office was not discharged in a few sermons, so to say, or inspired declarations of God's purpose, but must have been that of a Pastor among them during a course of years. His present book, like Hosea's, is a summary of his prophecies.

That book, as he himself subsequently gathered into one his prophetic teaching, is one well-ordered whole. He himself, in the title, states that it had been spoken before it was written. For in that he says, these are *the words* which in prophetic vision he *saw, two years before the earthquake,* this portion of his prophecies must have preceded his writings by those two years at least. That terrible earthquake was probably the occasion of his collecting those prophecies. But that earthquake doubtless was no mere note of time. Had he intended a date only, he would probably have named, as other prophets do, the year of the king of Judah. He himself mentions earthquakes [s], as one of the warnings of God's displeasure. This more destructive earthquake was probably the first great token of God's displeasure during the

d Is. x. 9.　　　e vii. 10. 11.　　　f vi. 14.
g 2 Kgs xiv. 25.　　h Ib. 26.　　　i vii. 10.

k ii. 11, 12.　　l iii. 3-8.　　m vi. 3.　　n v. 14.
o v. 18.　　p ix. 10.　　q v. 10.　　r v. 13.　　s iv. 11.

prosperous reign of Jeroboam II., the first herald of those heavier judgments which Amos had predicted, and which brake upon Israel, wave after wave, until the last carried him away captive. For two years, Israel had been forewarned; now *the beginning of sorrows*[t] had set in.

Amos, at the beginning of his book, (as has been already noticed) joins on his book with the book of the prophet Joel. Joel had foretold, as instances of God's judgments on sin, how He would recompense the wrongs, which Tyre, Zidon, Philistia and Edom had done to Judah, and that He would make Egypt desolate. Amos, omitting Egypt, adds Damascus, Ammon and Moab, and Judah itself. It may be, that he selects seven nations in all, as a sort of whole (as that number is so often used), or that he includes all the special enemies of the Theocracy, the nations who hated Israel and Judah, *because* they were the people of God, and God's people itself, as far as it too was alienated from its God. Certainly, the sins denounced are sins against the Theocracy or government of God[v]. It may be, that Amos would exhibit to them the truth, that *God is no respecter of persons;* that He, the Judge of the whole earth, punishes every sinful nation; and that he would, by this declaration of God's judgments, prepare them for the truth, from which sinful man so shrinks;—that God punishes most, where He had most shewn His light and love[w]. The thunder-cloud of God's judgments, having passed over all the nations round about, Syria and Philistia, Tyre, Edom, Ammon, Moab, and even discharged the fire from heaven on Judah and Jerusalem, settles at last on Israel. The summary which closes this circle of judgments on Israel, is fuller in regard to *their* sins, since they were the chief objects of his mission. In that summary he gathers in one the sins with which he elsewhere upbraids them, and sets before them their ingratitude and their endeavors to extinguish the light which God gave them.

Our chapters follow a natural division, in that each, like those of Hosea, ends in woe. The 3d, 4th, and 5th are distinguished by the three-fold summons, *Hear ye this word.* In each, he sets before them some of their sins, and in each pronounces God's sentence upon them. *Therefore thus saith the Lord God; Therefore thus will I do unto thee, O Israel; Therefore the Lord, the God of hosts, the Lord, saith thus*[x]. On this follows a two-fold woe, *Woe unto you that desire*[y]*; Woe to them that are at ease*[z]*;* both which sections alike end in renewed sentences of God's judg-

ment; the first, of the final captivity of Israel *beyond Damascus;* the second, of their nearer afflictions through the first invasion of Tiglath-pileser[a]. In the 7th chapter he begins a series of visions. In the two first, God forgives, at the intercession of the prophet[b]. The 3d vision God interprets, that He would forgive no more[c]. On this followed the prohibition from Amaziah to prophesy, and God's sentence against him. In the 8th chapter, Amos resumes (as though nothing had intervened), the series of visions, upon which Amaziah had broken in. He resumes them exactly where he had been stopped. Amaziah broke in, when he declared that God would not *pass by* the house of Israel *any more,* but would desolate the idol-sanctuaries of Israel and bring a sword against the house of Jeroboam. The vision in which Amos resumes, renews the words[d], *I will not again pass by them any more,* and foretells that the songs of the idol-temple should be turned into howlings. The last chapter he heads with a vision, that not only should the idol-altar and temple be destroyed, but that it should be the destruction of its worshipers[e]. Each of these visions Amos makes a theme which he expands, both ending in woe; the first, with the utter destruction of the idolaters of Israel[f]; the 2d, with that of the sinful *kingdom* of Israel[g]. With this he unites the promise to the *house* of Israel, that, *sifted* as they should be *among the nations, not one grain should fall to the earth*[h]. To this he, like Hosea, adds a closing promise, the first in his whole book, that God would raise the fallen tabernacle of David, convert the heathen, and therewith restore the captivity of Israel, amid promises, which had already, in Joel, symbolized spiritual blessings[i].

Amos, like Hosea, was a prophet for Israel. After the 2d chapter in which he includes Judah in the circle of God's visitations, because he had *despised the law of the Lord*[k], Amos only notices him incidentally. He there foretells that Jerusalem should (as it was) be burned with fire. Judah also must be included in the words, "[l]against the *whole* family which God brought up out of the land of Egypt," and *woe* is pronounced against those who are *at ease in Zion*[m]. Else, *Israel, the house of Israel, the virgin of Israel, the sanctuaries of Israel, Jacob, the house of Jacob,* and (in the same sense) *the high places of Isaac, the house of Isaac; the house of Joseph, the remnant of Joseph, the affliction of Joseph, the mountain,* or *the mountains of Samaria, Samaria* itself, *Bethel*[n], occur interchangeably as the object of his prophecy. Amaziah's

[t] S. Matt. xxiv. 8.
[v] See below in the Commentary.
[w] iii. 2.   [x] iii. 11. iv. 12. v. 16. as before, ii. 14.
[y] v. 18.   [z] vi. 1.   [a] See on vi. 14.   [b] vii. 3, 6.

[c] Ib. 8.   [d] viii. 2.   [e] ix. 1.   [f] viii. 14.   [g] ix. 8.
[h] Ib. 9.   [i] Ib. 13.   [k] ii. 4, 5.   [l] iii. 1.   [m] vi. 1.
[n] iii. 9, 12, 13, 14. iv. 1, 4, 5, 12. v. 1, 4, 6, 15, 25. vi. 1, 6, 8, 14. vii. 2, 5, 8, 9, 16, 17. viii. 2, 14. ix. 7, 8, 9.

taunt, that his words, as being directed against Israel and Bethel, would be acceptable in the kingdom of Judah, implies the same; and Amos himself declares that this was his commission, *go, prophesy unto My people Israel.* In speaking of the idolatry of Beersheba, he uses the word, *pass not over to Beersheba*[o], adding the idolatries of Judah to their own. The word, *pass not over*, could only be used by one prophesying in Israel. It must have been then the more impressive to the faithful in Israel, that he closed his prophecy by the promise, not to them primarily, but to the house of David, and to Israel through its restoration. Amos, like Hosea, foretells the utter destruction of *the kingdom* of Israel, even while pronouncing that God would not utterly destroy *the house* of Jacob[p], but would save the elect in it.

The opposition of Amaziah stands out, as one signal instance of the manifold cry, *Prophesy not*, with which men sought to drown the Voice of God. Jeroboam left the complaint unheeded. His great victories had been foretold to him by the Prophet Jonah; and he would not interfere with the Prophet of God, although he predicted, not as Amaziah distorted his words, that *Jeroboam* should *die by the sword*, but that *the house of Jeroboam*[p] should so perish. But his book is all comprised within the reign of Jeroboam and the kingdom of Israel. He was called by God to be a prophet there; nor is there any, the slightest, trace of his having exercised his office in Judah, or having retired thither in life.

A somewhat late tradition places Amos among the many prophets, whom, our Lord says, His people slew. The tradition bore, "that after he had been often beaten (the writer uses the same word[r] which occurs in Heb. xi. 35) by Amaziah the priest of Bethel, the son of that priest, Osee, broke his temples with a stake. He was carried half-dead to his own land, and, after some days, died of the wound, and was buried with his fathers." But the anonymous Greek writer who relates it, (although it is in itself probable) has not, in other cases, trustworthy information, and S. Jerome and S. Cyril of Alexandria knew nothing of it. S. Jerome[s] relates only that the tomb of Amos was still shewn at Tekoa, his birthplace.

The influence of the shepherd-life of Amos appears most in the sublimest part of his prophecy, his descriptions of the mighty workings of Almighty God[t]. With those awful and sudden changes in nature, whereby what to the idolaters was an object of worship, was suddenly overcast, and *the day made dark with night*, his shepherd-life had

made him familiar. The starry heavens had often witnessed the silent intercourse of his soul with God. In the calf, the idolaters of Ephraim worshiped "nature." Amos then delights in exhibiting to them *his* God, Whom they too believed that they worshiped, as the Creator of "nature," wielding and changing it at His Will. All nature too should be obedient to its Maker in the punishment of the ungodly[v], nor should any thing hide from Him[w]. The shepherd-life would also make the Prophet familiar with the perils from wild beasts which we know of as facts in David's youth. The images drawn from them were probably reminiscences of what he had seen or met with[x]. But Amos lived, a shepherd in a barren and for the most part treeless wild, not as a husbandman. His was not a country of corn, nor of cedars and oaks; so that images from stately trees[y], a heavy-laden wain[z], or the sifting of corn[a], were not the direct results of his life amid sights of nature. The diseases of corn, locusts, drought, which, the Prophet says, God had sent among them, were inflictions which would be felt in the corn-countries of Israel, rather than in the wilderness of Tekoah. The insensibility for which he upbraids Israel was, of course, their hardness of heart amid their own sufferings[b]; the judgments, with which he threatens them in God's Name[c], can have no bearing on his shepherd-life in his own land.

Even S. Jerome, while laying down a true principle, inadvertently gives as an instance of the images resulting from that shepherd-life, the opening words of his book, which are in part words of the Prophet Joel. "It is natural," he says, "that all who exercise an art, should speak in terms of their art, and that each should bring likenesses from that wherein he hath spent his life.—Why say this? In order to shew, that Amos the Prophet too, who was a shepherd among shepherds, and that, not in cultivated places, or amid vineyards, or woods, or green meadows, but in the wide waste of the desert, where were witnessed the fierceness of lions and the destruction of cattle, used the language of his art, and called the awful and terrible Voice of the Lord, the roaring of lions, and compared the overthrow of the cities of Israel to the lonely places of shepherds or the drought of mountains."

The truth may be, that the religious life of Amos, amid scenes of nature, accustomed him, as well as David, to express his thoughts in words taken from the great picture-book of nature, which, as being also written by the Hand of God, so wonderfully expresses the things of God. When his Prophet's life

o v. 5.   p ix. 8–10.   q vii. 9.
r τυμπανίσας, Auct. de vit. Proph. ap. S. Epiph. ii. 145.   s de loc. Hebr. T. iii. 206. ed. Vall.

t iv. 13. v. 8. ix. 5, 6.   v viii. 8.   w ix. 2, 3, 5.
x iii. 4, 5, 12. v. 19.   y ii. 9.   z ii. 13.
a ix. 9.   b iv. 7–9.   c vii. 1–3.

brought him among other scenes of cultivated nature, his soul, so practiced in reading the relations of the physical to the moral world, took the language of his parables alike from what he saw, or from what he remembered. He was what we should call "a child of nature," endued with power and wisdom by his God. Still more mistaken has it been, to attribute to the Prophet any inferiority even of outward style, in consequence of his shepherd-life. Even a heathen has said, "words readily follow thought;" much more, when thoughts and words are poured into the soul together by God the Holy Ghost. On the contrary, scarcely any Prophet is more glowing in his style, or combines more wonderfully the natural and moral world, the Omnipotence and Omniscience of God[d]. Visions, if related, are most effectively related in prose. Their efficacy depends, in part, on their simplicity. Their meaning might be overlaid and hidden by ornament of words. Thus much of the book of Amos, then, is naturally in prose. The poetry, so to speak, of the visions of Amos or of Zechariah is in the thoughts, not in the words. Amos has also chosen the form of prose for his upbraidings of the wealthy sinners of Israel. Yet, in the midst of this, what more poetic than the summons to the heathen enemies of Israel, to people the heights about Samaria, and behold its sins[e]? What more graphic than that picture of utter despair which dared not name the Name of God?[f] What bolder than the summons to Israel to come, if they willed, at once to sin and to atone for their sin[g]? What more striking in power than the sudden turn[h], "You only have I known: *therefore* I will punish you for all your iniquities? or the sudden summons[i], "because I will do *this* unto thee," (the silence, what the *this* is, is more thrilling than words) "prepare to meet thy God, O Israel?" Or what more pathetic than the close of the picture of the luxurious rich, when, having said, how they heaped luxuries one on another, he ends with what they did *not* do[k]; *they are not grieved for the afflictions of Joseph?*

S. Augustine selects Amos, as an instance of unadorned eloquence. Having given instances from S. Paul, he says[l], "These things, when they are taught by professors, are accounted great, bought at a great price, sold amid great boasting. I fear these discussions of mine may savor of the like boasting. But I have to do with men of a spurious learning, who think meanly of our writers, not because they have not, but because they make no shew of the eloquence which these prize too highly.—

"I see that I must say something of the eloquence of the prophets. And this I will do, chiefly out of the book of that prophet, who says that he was a shepherd or a cowherd, and was taken thence by God and sent to prophesy to His people.

"When then this peasant, or peasant-prophet, reproved the ungodly, proud, luxurious, and therefore most careless of brotherly love, he cries aloud, *Woe to them that are at ease in Zion*, &c. Would they who, as being learned and eloquent, despise our prophets as unlearned and ignorant of elocution, had they had aught of this sort to say, or had they to speak against such, would they, as many of them as would fain not be senseless, wish to speak otherwise? For what would any sober ear desire more than is there said? First, the inveighing itself, with what a crash is it hurled as it were, to awaken their stupefied senses!"

Then, having analysed these verses, he says, "How beautiful this is, and how it affects those who, reading, understand, there is no use in saying to one who does not himself feel it. More illustrations of the rules of rhetoric may be found in this one place, which I have selected. But a good hearer will not be so much instructed by a diligent discussion of them, as he will be kindled by their glowing reading. For these things were not composed by human industry, but were poured forth in eloquent wisdom from the Divine mind, wisdom not aiming at eloquence, but eloquence not departing from wisdom." "For if, as some most eloquent and acute men could see and tell, those things which are learned as by an art of rhetoric, would not be observed and noted and reduced to this system, unless they were first found in the genius of orators, what wonder if they be found in those also, whom *He* sends, Who creates genius? Wherefore we may well confess that our canonical writers and teachers are not wise only but eloquent, with that eloquence which beseems their character."

S. Jerome, in applying to Amos words which S. Paul spake of himself[m], *rude in speech but not in knowledge*, doubtless was thinking mostly of the latter words; for he adds, "For the same Spirit Who spake through all the Prophets, spake in him." Bp. Lowth says happily[n], "Jerome calls Amos, *rude in speech but not in knowledge*, implying of him what Paul modestly professed as to himself, on whose authority many have spoken of this Prophet, as though he were altogether rude, ineloquent, unadorned. Far otherwise! Let any fair judge read his writings, thinking not who wrote them, but what he wrote, he will think that our shepherd was *in no wise behind the very chiefest* Prophets; in the loftiness of his thoughts and the mag-

---

[d] iv. 13. [e] iii. 9. [f] vi. 9, 10. [g] iv. 4. [h] iii. 2. [i] iv. 12. [k] vi. 6. [l] De doctr. Christ. iv. 7. n. 15–21.

[m] 2 Cor. xi. 6.
[n] de S. Poesi Hebr. Præl. xxi.

nificence of his spirit, nearly equal to the highest, and in the splendor of his diction and the elegance of the composition scarcely inferior to any. For the same Divine Spirit moved by His Inspiration Isaiah and Daniel in the court, David and Amos by the sheepfold; ever choosing fitting interpreters of His Will and sometimes perfecting praise out of the mouth of babes. Of some He useth the eloquence; others He maketh eloquent."

It has indeed been noticed that in regularity of structure he has an elegance peculiar to himself. The strophaic form, into which he has cast the heavy prophecies of the two first chapters adds much to their solemnity; the recurring " burden " of the fourth[o], *Yet have ye not returned unto Me, saith the Lord*, gives it a deep pathos of its own. Indeed no other prophet has bound his prophecies into one, with so much care as to their outward form, as this inspired shepherd. Amos (to use human terms) was not so much the poet as the sacred orator. One of those energetic turns which have been already instanced, would suffice to stamp the human orator. Far more, they have shaken through and through souls steeped in sin from the Prophet's time until now. It has been said of human eloquence, " he lightened, thundered, he commingled Greece." The shepherd has shaken not one country, but the world; not by a passing earthquake, but by the awe of God which, with electric force, streamed through his words.

Some variation of dialect, or some influence of his shepherd-life on his pronunciation, has been imagined in Amos. But it relates to five words only. In three, his orthography differs by a single letter from that found elsewhere in Hebrew. In two cases, the variation consists in the use of a different sibilant[p]; the 3d in the use of a weaker guttural[q].

Besides these, he uses a softer sound of the name Isaac[r], which also occurs in Jeremiah and a Psalm; and in another word, he, in common with two Psalms, employs a root with a guttural[s], instead of that common in Hebrew which has a strong sibilant. In four of these cases, Amos uses the softer form; in the 5th, we only know that the two sibilants were pronounced differently once, but cannot guess what the distinction was. The two sibilants are interchanged in several Hebrew words, and on no rule, that we can discover[t]. In another of the sibilants, the change made by Amos is just the reverse of that of the Ephraimites who had only the pronunciation of s for sh; "sibboleth" for "shibboleth." But the Ephraimites could not pronounce the sh at all; the variation in Amos is limited to a single word. The like variations to these instances in Amos are also found in other words in the Bible. On the whole, we may *suspect* the existence of a softer pronunciation in the South of Judæa, where Amos lived; but the only safe inference is, the extreme care with which the words have been handed down to us, just as the Prophet spoke and wrote them.

It has been noticed already that Amos and Hosea together shew, that all the Mosaic festivals and sacrifices, priests, prophets, a temple, were retained in Israel, only distorted to calf-worship[u]. Even the third-year's tithes they had not ventured to get rid of[v]. Amos supplies some yet more minute traits of ritual; that they had the same rules in regard to leaven[w]; that their altar too had horns (as prescribed in the law), on which the blood of the sacrifices was to be sprinkled[x], they had the altar-bowls[y] whence the blood of the victim was sprinkled[z], such as the princes of the congregation offered in the time of Moses[a], and *their* rich men, at times at least, plundered to drink

---

[o] iv. 6, 8, 9, 10, 11.

[p] a) בושׁכבם for what would elsewhere be בוסכבם v. 10. (the actual form does not occur elsewhere). b) מסרף for משׁרף vi. 10.

[q] מתאב for מתעב vi. 8. The use of the common word פתאם, from פתע, and אורות probably from אור i. q. עוּד, are instances of the like change within the language itself, from its earliest times. Isaiah probably uses אנם (xix. 10) for ענם (Job xxx. 25). (נאל for נעל is used by Isaiah (lix. 3, lxiii. 3,) Zephaniah (iii. 1) and Jeremiah (Lam iv. 14) as well as after the captivity by Malachi (i. 7, 12) Ezra (ii. 62) Nehemiah (vii. 64).

[r] שׂחק for יצחק, Am. vii. 9, 16. The verb, צחק, from which יצחק is formed, occurs twice only out of the Pentateuch (Jud. xvi. 25, Ez. xxiii. 32). The form which Amos and Jeremiah (xxxiii. 26) use, (as also Ps. cv. 9) is from the verb, as it was subsequently written, שׂחק.

[s] מעיק from a root עוק i. q. צוק whence עקה Ps. lv. 4. מועקה Ps. lxvi. 11.

[t] בעשׂ occurs four times in Job for בעס, but contrariwise הסיג (Job xxiv. 2) for השׂיג in Hos. ix. 12 for סור; פרשׁ in Mic. iii. 4, Lam. iv. 4 for פרם; שׂבך and שׂבך passim; סרר and שׂדרה 3ce in Kings; שׂון 2 S. i. 22. and שׂיג 1 K. xviii. 27, for סון; שׂבך Ex. xxxiii. 22; else סבך Ex. xl. 3, xxv. 20 &c. סעפם 1 K. xviii. 21 and שׂעפים Job iv. 13, xx. 2; סער and שׂער; ספה and שׂפח Is. iii. 17, v. 7.

[u] Introd. to Hosea, p. 2.   [v] Ib.   [w] iv. 5.

[x] iii. 14. See Ex. xxvii. 2. xxix. 12. Lev. iv. 25.

[y] vi. 6.

[z] מזרק is only used of such a bowl; and its meaning "a vessel for *sprinkling*," agrees herewith. Its employment by the rich, when it had once been desecrated to idolatry, is nothing strange; far less, than the use of chalices to adorn the side-boards of rich English, when Church-plate had been plundered in England or Spain.   [a] Nu. vii. 13 sqq.

wine from. They had also true Nazarites, raised up among them, as well as true prophets; and they felt the weight of the influence of these Religious against them, since they tried by fraud or violence to make them break their vow [b]. Amos, while upbraiding their rich men for breaking the law between man and man, presupposes that the law of Moses was, in this respect also, acknowledged among them. For in his words, "they turn aside the way of the meek [c]," "they turn aside the poor in the gate [e]," "they take a ransom [d]" (from the rich for their misdeeds), he retains the peculiar term of the Pentateuch; as also in that, "on clothes laid to pledge [e] they lie down by every altar;" "who make the Ephah small [f]." "Balances of deceit [g]" are the contrary of what are enjoined in the law, "balances of right [h]." In upbraiding them for a special impurity, forbidden in principle by the law [i], he uses the sanction often repeated in the law, " [k] to profane My Holy Name." In the punishments which he mentions, he uses terms in which God threatens those punishments. The two remarkable words, rendered "blasting and mildew [l]," occur only in Deuteronomy, and in Solomon's prayer founded upon it [m], and in Haggai [n] where he is referring to Amos. In the words, " [o] as God overthrew Sodom and Gomorrah," the peculiar term and form of Deuteronomy, as well as the threat, are retained. The threat, "Ye have built houses of hewn stone, and ye shall not dwell therein; ye have planted pleasant vineyards, but ye shall not drink the wine thereof;" but blends and enlarges those in Deuteronomy [p]. The remarkable term describing their unrepentance is taken from the same [q]. So also the image of "gall and wormwood [r]," two bitter plants, into which they turned judgment and righteousness. There are other verbal reminiscences of the Pentateuch, interwoven with the words of Amos, which presuppose that it was in the memory of both the Prophet and his hearers in Israel [s]. Indeed, after that long slavery of four hundred years in Egypt, the traditions of the spots, hallowed by God's intercourse with the Patriarchs, probably even their relations to "Edom [t] their brother," must have been lost.

The book of Genesis did not embody popular existing traditions of this sort, but must have revived them. The idolatry of Beersheba [u], as well as that of Gilead, alluded to by Hosea, as also Jeroboam's choice of Bethel itself for the calf-worship [u], imply on the part of the idolaters a knowledge and belief of the history, which they must have learned from the Pentateuch. Doubtless it had been a part of Jeroboam's policy to set up, over-against the exclusive claim for the temple at Jerusalem, rival places of traditional holiness from the mercies of God to their forefathers, much as Mohammed availed himself of the memory of Abraham, to found his claim for an interest in Jerusalem. But these traditions too must have been received by the people not derived from them. They were not brought with them from Egypt. The people, enslaved, degraded, sensualized, idolatry-loving, had no hearts to cherish the memories of the pure religion of their great forefathers, who worshiped the un-imaged Self-existing God.

As Amos employed the language of the Pentateuch and cited the book of Joel, so it seems more probable, that in the burden of his first prophecies, " [v] I will send a fire upon——and it shall devour the palaces of——" he took the well-known words of Hosea [w], and, by their use, gave an unity to their prophecies, than that Hosea, who uses no language except that of the Pentateuch, should, in the one place where he employs this form, have limited the "burden" of Amos to the one case of Judah. Besides, in Hosea, the words, declaring the destruction of the cities and palaces of Judah, stand in immediate connection with Judah's wrong temper in building them whereas in Amos they are insulated. Beside this, the language of the two prophets does not bear upon each other, except that both have the term " [x] balances of deceit," which was originally formed in contrast with what God had enjoined in the law, "balances of right," and which stands first in the Proverbs of Solomon [y].

Of later prophets, Jeremiah renewed against Damascus the prophecy of Amos in his own words; only, the memory of Hazael having been obliterated perhaps in the destruction under Tiglath-Pileser, Jeremiah

---

[b] ii. 12. [c] ii. 7. v. 12. הטו. See Ex. xxiii. 6. Deut. xvi. 19. xxiv. 17. xxvii. 19.

[d] v. 12. לקחי כפר; Nu. xxxv. 31. לא תקחו כפר.

[e] ii. 8. על בגדים חבלים. See Ex. xxii. 26, 7.

[f] viii. 5. See Deut. xxv. 14. 15. [g] Am. Ib. [h] Lev. xix. 36. [i] Deut. xxiii. 1.

[k] להלל את שם קדשי ii. 7. Lev. xx. 3.

[l] ירקון, שדפון. iv. 9. Deut. xxviii. 22.

[m] 1 K. viii. 37. [n] ii. 17.
[o] iv. 11. Deut. xxix. 23. כמהפכת סדם ועמרה.

[p] v. 11. Deut. xxviii. 30, 39. לא שבתם עד iv. 6, 8, 9, 10. See Deut. iv. 29.

[r] vi. 12, from Deut. xxix. 18. לענה occurs alone, in the same image, Am. v. 7 and ראש in Hos. x. 4. They are used together as an image of the bitter draught of affliction (Jer. ix. 15, xxiii. 15, Lam. iii. 19, and לענה Lam. iii. 15) and of the bitter end of sin, Prov. v. 4. Not elsewhere.

[s] See ii. 2, 10, 11. iii. 2. vi. 1. vii. 16. ix. 8, 12.
[t] i. 11.

[u] v. 8. The above instances are selected from Hengstenberg, Auth. d. Pent. i. 83-104.

[v] i. 4, 7, 10, 12, ii. 2, 5. It is slightly varied in i. 14.
[w] Hos. vii. 14. [x] Hos. xii. 8. [7 Eng.] Am. viii. 5.
[y] Prov. xi. 1. xx. 23.

calls it not after Hazael, but by its own name and that of Benhadad [z]. The words of Amos had once been fulfilled, and its people had been transported to Kir. Probably fugitives had again repeopled it, and Jeremiah intended to point out, that the sentence pronounced through Amos was not yet exhausted. On the like ground probably, when upbraiding Ammon for the like sins and for that for which Amos had denounced woe upon it, its endeavor to displace Israel [a], Jeremiah used the words of Amos, *their king shall go into captivity,—and his princes together* [b]. In like way Haggai upbraids the Jews of his day for their impenitence under God's chastisements, in words varied in no essential from those of Amos [c]. The words of Amos, so repeated to the Jews upon their restoration, sounded, as it were, from the desolate heritage of Israel, *Sin no more, lest a worse thing happen unto thee.*

Other reminiscences of the words of Amos are only a part of the harmony of Scripture [d], the prophets in this way too indicating their unity with one another, that they use the words, the one of the other.

The might of his teaching at the time, the state-priest Amaziah impressed on Jeroboam. Contemptuous toward Amos himself, Amaziah admitted the truth to Jeroboam. *The land is not able to bear all his words.* Doubtless, as the Jews were mad against S. Stephen, *not being able to resist the wisdom and Spirit by which he spake* [e], so God accompanied with power His servant's words to His people. They had already seen God's words fulfilled against the houses of Jeroboam I., of Baasha, of Ahab. That same doom was now renewed against *the house of Jeroboam*, and with it the prophecy of the dispersion of the ten tribes [f], which Hosea contemporaneously foretold [g]. The two prophets of Israel confirmed one another, but also left themselves no escape. They staked the whole reputation of their prophecy on this definite issue. We know it to have been fulfilled on the house of Jeroboam; yet the house of Jeroboam was firmer than any before or after it. We know of the unwonted captivity of the ten tribes. Had they not been carried captive, prophecy would have come to shame; and such in proportion is its victory. Each step was an

instalment, a pledge, of what followed. The death of Zechariah, Jeroboam's son, was the first step in the fulfillment of the whole; then probably, in the invasion of Pul against Menahem [h], followed the doom of Amaziah. God is not anxious to vindicate His word. He does not, as to Shebna [i], or Amaziah, or the false prophets Ahab, Zedekiah [j] or Shemaiah [k], or Pashur [l] or other false prophets [m]. At times, as in the case of Hananiah [n], Scripture records the individual fulfillment of God's judgments. Mostly, it passes by unnoticed the execution of God's sentence. The sentence of the criminal, unless reprieved, in itself implies the execution [o]. The fact impressed those who witnessed it; the record of the judgment suffices for us.

Then followed, under Tiglath-pileser, the fulfillment of the prophecy as to Damascus [p], and Gilead [q]. Under Sargon was fulfilled the prophecy on the ten tribes [r]. That on Judah [s] yet waited 133 years, and then was fulfilled by Nebuchadnezzar. A few years later, and he executed God's judgments foretold by Amos on their enemies, Moab, Ammon, Edom, Tyre [t]. [u] Kings of Egypt, Assyria, and the Macedonian Alexander fulfilled in succession the prophecy as to Philistia. So various were the human wills, so multitudinous the events, which were to bring about the simple words of the shepherd-prophet. Amos foretells the events; he does say, why the judgments should come; he does not foretell "when," or "through whom:" but the events themselves he foretells absolutely, and they came. Like Joel, he foretells the conversion of the Heathen and anticipates so far the prophecies of Isaiah, that God would work this through the restoration of the house of David, when fallen. Strange comment on human greatness, that the royal line was not to be employed in the salvation of the world, until it was fallen! The Royal Palace had to become the hut of Nazareth, ere the Redeemer of the world could be born, Whose glory and kingdom were not of this world, Who came, to take from us nothing but our nature, that He might sanctify it, our misery, that He might bear it for us. Yet flesh and blood could not foresee it ere it came, as flesh and blood could not believe it, when He came.

---

[z] Jer. xlix. 27.   [a] Am. i. 13. Jer. xlix. 1.
[b] Am. i. 15. Jer. xlix. 3. Jeremiah retains the idiom הלך בגולה, only adding "his priests," before the words "and his princes." He retains also the characteristic word תרועה Am. i. 14, and for באש תצתנה,הצתי אש Am. iv. 9. Hagg. ii. 19.
[d] Such are, the use of the words of Amos ii. 14 in Jer. xlvi. 6; the use of the idiom of Amos, *I take up a lamentation* נשא עליכם קינה (v. 1.) three times by Ezekiel, xxvii. 2, xxviii. 12, xxxii. 2; the use of the image, *a brand plucked out of the burning*, Am. iv. 11, Zech. iii. 2.   [e] Acts vi. 10.   [f] v. 27. vii. 8, 9, 17.

[g] Hos. i. 6. ix. 17.   [h] 2 Kgs xv. 19.
[i] Is. xxii. 17, 18.   [j] Jer. xxix. 20–22.   [k] Ib. 32.
[l] Ib. xx. 6.   [m] Ib. xiv. 15.   [n] Ib. xxviii. 17.
[o] A recent writer "on the interpretation of Scripture" (Essays and Reviews, p. 343.) ventures to give this (Amos vii. 10–17) as one of three instances in proof that "the failure of prophecy is never admitted *in spite of Scripture and of history.*" Certainly, no Christian thinks that God's word can have failed. But unless the execution of God's sentence on one of the many calf-priests of Bethel is necessarily matter of history, it has rather to be shewn why it should be mentioned, than why it was omitted.   [p] i. 5.   [q] vi. 14.
[r] v. 27. vii. 8, 9, 17. ix. 8.   [s] ii. 5.   [t] i. 9. ii. 3.   [u] i. 6–8.

AMOS.

CHAPTER I.

1 *Amos sheweth God's judgment upon Syria,* 6 *upon the Philistines,* 9 *upon Tyrus,* 11 *upon Edom,* 13 *upon Ammon.*

THE words of Amos, [a] who was among the herdmen of [b] Tekoa, which he saw concerning Israel

[e] in the days of Uzziah king of Judah, and in the days of [d] Jeroboam the son of Joash king of Israel, two years before the [e] earthquake.

2 And he said, The LORD will [f] roar from Zion, and utter his voice from

[a] ch. 7. 14.

[b] 2 Sam. 14. 2.
2 Chr. 20. 20.

[e] Hos. i. 1.
[d] ch. 7. 10.

[e] Zech. 14. 5.

[f] Jer. 25. 30.
Joel 3. 16.

CHAP. I. ver. 1. *The words of Amos, who was among the herdmen.* "Amos begins by setting forth his own nothingness, and withal the great grace of his Teacher and Instructor, the Holy Spirit, referring all to His glory." He, like David, Peter, Paul, Matthew, was one of *the weak things of the world, whom God chose to confound the mighty.* He was himself a herdsman only *among herdsmen;* but the words which he spake were not his own. They were words which he saw, not with eyes of flesh, but "with that vision wherewith words can be seen, the seer's vision in the mind." They were *words concerning,* or rather *upon Israel,* heavy words coming upon the heavy transgressions of Israel. The Hebrew word *saw*[1] is not of mere sight, but of a vision given by God. Amos only says that they were *his* words, in order immediately to add, that they came to him from God, that he himself was but the human organ through which God spake.

Two years before the earthquake. This earthquake must plainly have been one of the greatest, since it was vividly in men's memories in the time of Zechariah, and Amos speaks of it as "*the* earthquake." The earthquakes of the East, like that of Lisbon, destroy whole cities. In one, a little before the birth of our Lord, "[2] some ten thousand were buried under the ruined houses." This terrific earthquake (for as such Zechariah describes it) was one of the preludes of that displeasure of God, which Amos foretold. A warning of two years, and time for repentance, were given, *before the earthquake* should come, the token and beginning of a further shaking of both kingdoms, unless they should repent. In effect, it was the first flash of the lightning which consumed them.

2. *The Lord will roar.* Amos joins on his prophecy to the end of Joel's, in order at once

in its very opening to attest the oneness of their mission, and to prepare men's minds to see, that his own prophecy was an expansion of those words, declaring the nearer and coming judgments of God. Those nearer judgments, however, of which he spake, were but the preludes of the judgments of the Great Day which Joel foretold, and of that last terrible voice of Christ, *the Lion of the tribe of Judah,* of Whom Jacob prophesies; *He couched, He lay down as a lion, and as a young lion; who shall raise Him up*[3]? God is said to *utter His* awful *voice from Zion and Jerusalem,* because there He had set His Name, there He was present in His Church. It was, as it were, His own place, which He had hallowed by tokens of His Presence, although *the heaven and the heaven of heavens cannot contain Him.* In the outset of his prophecy, Amos warned Israel, that there, not among themselves in their separated state, God dwelt. Jeremiah, in using these same words toward Judah, speaks not of Jerusalem, but of heaven; [4] *The Lord shall roar from on high, and utter His voice from His holy habitation.* The prophecy is to the ten tribes or to the heathen: God speaks out of the Church. He uttereth His Voice out of Jerusalem, as He saith, [5] *Out of Zion shall go forth the law, and the word of the Lord from Jerusalem,* "where was the Temple and the worship of God, to shew that God was not in the cities of Israel, i. e. in Dan and Bethel, where were the golden calves, nor in the royal cities of Samaria and Jezreel, but in the true religion which was then in Zion and Jerusalem."

And the habitations of the shepherds shall mourn. Perhaps, with a feeling for the home which he had loved and left, the Prophet's first thought amid the desolation which he predicts, was toward his own shepherd-haunts. The well-known Mount Carmel[6]

[1] חֹזֶה, whence חֹזֶה *seer,* חִזֹּון, חִזְיֹון, vision.

[2] Jos. Ant. xv. 5. 2.   [3] Gen. xlix. 9.
[4] Jer. xxv. 30.   [5] Is. ii. 3.
[6] The mention of the *head of Carmel* marks out that the Mount Carmel is meant (see ix. 3, 1 Kgs xviii. 42) not the town Carmel (now Kurmul) in the

south of Judah, lying around the head and sides of a valley of some width and depth. The whole plain around it is high, and it seems probable that a district was called by its name (1 Sam. xxv. 2, 7, 2 Chr. xxvi. 10), but the hill of Main is only 200 feet above the plain. Robinson, i. 433.

Before
CHRIST
cir. 787.

g 1 Sam. 25.2.
Is. 33. 9.

Jerusalem; and the habitations of the shepherds shall mourn, and the top of [g] Carmel shall wither.

3 Thus saith the LORD; For three transgressions of [h] Damascus, || and for four, I will not || turn away

|| Or, *yea, for four.* || Or, *convert it,* or, *let it be quiet: and so ver.* 6, &c.

Before
CHRIST
cir. 787.

h Is. 8. 4. & 17. 1.
Jer. 49. 23.
Zech. 9. 1.

was far in the opposite direction in the tribe of Asher. Its name is derived from its richness and fertility, perhaps "a land of vine and olive yards [1]." In S. Jerome's time, it was "[2] thickly studded with olives, shrubs and vineyards." "Its very summit of glad pastures." It is one of the most striking natural features of Palestine. It ends a line of hills, eighteen miles long, by a long bold headland reaching out far into the Mediterranean, and forming the South side of the Bay of Acco or Acre. Rising 1200 feet above the sea [3], it stands out "like some guardian of its native strand ;" yet withal, it was rich with every variety of beauty, flower, fruit, and tree. It is almost always called "*the Carmel,*" "the rich garden-ground." From its neighborhood to the sea, heavy dews nightly supply it with an ever-renewed freshness, so that in mid-summer it is green and flowery [4]. Travelers describe it, as "[5] quite green, its top covered with firs and oaks, lower down with olives and laurels, and everywhere excellently watered." "There is not a flower," says Van de Velde [6], "that I have seen in Galilee or on the plains along the coasts, that I do not find here again on Carmel. It is still the same fragrant lovely mountain as of old." "[5] Its varied world of flowers attracts such a number of the rarer varicolored insects that a collector might for a whole year be richly employed." "It is a natural garden and repository of herbs." Its pastures were rich, so as to equal those of Bashan [7]. "It gives rise to a number of crystal streams, the largest of which gushes from the spring of Elijah." It had abundant supplies in itself. If it too became a desert, what else would be spared ? [8] *If they do these things in a green tree, what shall be done in the dry ?* All, high and low, shall be stricken in one common desolation ; all the whole land, from *the pastures of the shepherds* in the South to Mount Carmel in the North. And this, as soon as God had spoken. *He spake, and it was made.* So now, contrariwise, He uttereth His Voice, and Carmel hath languished. Its glory hath passed away, as in the twinkling of an eye. God hath spoken the word, and it is gone. What depended on God's gifts, abides ;

what depended on man, is gone. There remains a wild beauty still ; but it is the beauty of natural luxuriance. "All," says one who explored its depths [9], "lies waste ; all is a wilderness. The utmost fertility is here lost for man, useless to man. The vineyards of Carmel, where are they now ? Behold the long rows of stones on the ground, the remains of the walls ; they will tell you that here, where now with difficulty you force your way through the thick entangled copse, lay, in days of old, those incomparable vineyards to which Carmel owes its name."

3. The order of God's threatenings seems to have been addressed to gain the hearing of the people. The punishment is first denounced upon their enemies, and that, for their sins, directly or indirectly, against themselves, and God in them. Then, as to those enemies themselves, the order is not of place or time, but of their relation to God's people. It begins with their most oppressive enemy, Syria ; then Philistia, the old and ceaseless, although less powerful, enemy ; then Tyre, not an oppressor, as these, yet violating a relation which they had not, the bonds of a former friendship and covenant ; malicious also and hardhearted through covetousness. Then Edom, Ammon, Moab, who burst the bonds of blood also. Lastly, and nearest of all, it falls on Judah, who had the true worship of the true God among them, but despised it. Every infliction on those like ourselves finds an echo in our own consciences. Israel heard and readily believed God's judgments upon others. It was not tempted to set itself against believing them. How then could it refuse to believe of itself, what it believed of others like itself ? "Change but the name, the tale is told of thee [10]," was a heathen saying which has almost passed into a proverb. The course of the prophecy convicted *them,* as the things written in Holy Scripture *for our ensamples* convict Christians. *If they* who [11] *sinned without law, perished without law,* how much more should they who *have sinned in the law, be judged by the law.* God's judgments rolled round like a thunder-cloud, passing from land to land, giving warning of their ap-

---

[1] כרם lit. "a rich and fertile land" (as in Arabic) is used of the olive-*garden* Jud. xv. 7, as well as of the more ordinary vineyard. כרמל is probably a collective from it.
[2] in Jer. iv. 26.

[3] Schubert in Ritter, xvi. 721.   Porter says 1750. (Handb. 371).
[4] Thomson, The Land, &c. ii. 231.
[5] O. v. Richter.   [6] i. 317, 8.
[7] Jer. l. 19. Nah. i. 4.   [8] S. Luke xxiii. 31.
[9] Van de Velde, i. 318.   [10] Horace.   [11] Rom. ii. 12.

Before
CHRIST
cir. 787.

the punishment thereof; [1] because they have threshed

[1] 2 Kings 10. 33 & 13. 7.

Gilead with threshing in-
struments of iron :

Before
CHRIST
cir. 787.

proach, at last to gather and centre on Israel itself, except it repent. In the visitations of others, it was to read its own ; and that, the more, the nearer God was to them. *Israel* is placed the last, because on it the destruction was to fall to the uttermost, and rest there.

For three transgressions and for four. These words express, not four transgressions added to the three, but an additional transgression beyond the former, the last sin, whereby the measure of sin, which before was full, overflows, and God's wrath comes. So in other places, where the like form of words occurs, the added number is one beyond, and mostly relates to something greater than all the rest. So, [1] *He shall deliver thee in six troubles ; yea, in seven there shall no evil touch thee.* The word, *yea*, denotes, that the seventh is some heavier trouble, beyond all the rest, which would seem likely to break endurance. Again [2], *give a portion to seven, and also to eight. Seven* is used as a symbol of a whole, since *on the seventh day God rested from all which He had made*, and therefore the number seven entered so largely into the whole Jewish riual. All time was measured by seven. The rule then is; "give without bounds; when that whole is fulfilled, still give." Again in that series of sayings in the book of Proverbs [3], the fourth is, in each, something greater than the three preceding. *There are three things that are never satisfied ; yea, four things say not,* it is *enough* [4]. The other things cannot be satisfied ; the fourth, fire, grows fiercer by being fed. Again [5], *There be three things which go well ; yea, four are comely in going.* The moral majesty of a king is obviously greater than the rest. So [6] *the handmaid which displaceth her mistress* is more intolerable and overbearing than the others. The art and concealment of man in approaching a maiden is of a subtler kind than things in nature which leave no trace of themselves, the eagle in the air, the serpent on the rock, the ship in its pathway through the waves [7]. Again [8], *Sowing discord among brethren,* has an especial hatefulness, as not only being sin, but causing widewasting sin, and destroying in others the chief grace, love. Soul-murder is worse than bodily murder, and requires more devilish art.

These things, Job says [9], *worketh God twice and thrice with man, to bring back his soul from*

the pit. The last grace of God, whether sealing up the former graces of those who use them, or vouchsafed to those who have wasted them, is the crowning act of His love or forbearance.

In heathen poetry also, as a trace of a mystery which they had forgotten, three is a sacred whole; whence "thrice and fourfold blessed" stands among them for something exceeding even a full and perfect blessing, a super-abundance of blessings.

The fourth trangression of these Heathen nations is alone mentioned. For the Prophet had no mission to *them ;* he only declares to Israel the ground of the visitation which was to come upon them. The three transgressions stand for a whole sum of sin, which had not yet brought down extreme punishment ; the fourth was the crowning sin, after which God would no longer spare. But although the fourth drew down His judgment, God, at the last, punishes not the last sin only, but all which went before. In that the Prophet says, not, *for the fourth,* but *for three transgressions and for four,* he expresses at once, that God did not punish until the last sin, by which *the iniquity* of the sinful nation became *full* [10], and that, *then,* He punished for all, for the whole mass of sin described by the three, and for the fourth also. God is long-suffering and ready to forgive; but when the sinner finally becomes a *vessel of wrath* [11], He punishes all the earlier sins, which, for the time, He passed by. Sin adds to sin, out of which it grows ; it does not overshadow the former sins, it does not obliterate them, but increases the mass of guilt, which God punishes. When the Jews slew the Son, there [12] *came on* them *all the righteous bloodshed upon the earth, from the blood of righteous Abel unto the blood of Zacharias, son of Barachias.* All the blood of all the prophets and servants of God under the Old Testament came upon that generation. So each individual sinner, who dies impenitent, will be punished for all which, in his whole life, he did or became, contrary to the law of God. Deeper sins bring deeper damnation at the last. So St. Paul speaks [13] of those who *treasure up to* themselves *wrath against the Day of wrath and revelation of the righteous judgment of God.* As good men, by the grace of God, do, through each act done by aid of that grace, gain an addition to their everlasting reward, so the wicked, by each added sin, add to their damnation.

Of Damascus. Damascus was one of the

[1] Job v. 19.   [2] Eccl. xi. 2.   [3] xxx.   [4] Ib. 15, 16.
[5] Ib. 29-31.   [6] Ib. 21-23.   [7] Ib. 18, 19.
[8] Ib. vi. 16-19.   [9] xxxiii. 29.

[10] Gen. xv. 16.   [11] Rom. ix. 22.
[12] S. Matt. xxiii. 35, 6. S. Luke xi. 50, 1.
[13] Rom. ii. 5.

oldest cities in the world, and one of the links of its intercourse. It lay in the midst of its plain, a high table-land [1] of rich cultivation, whose breadth, from Anti-libanus Eastward, was about half a degree. On the W. and N. its plain lay sheltered under the range of Anti-libanus; on the East, it was protected by the great desert which intervened between its oasis-territory and the Euphrates. Immediately, it was bounded by the three lakes which receive the surplus of the waters which enrich it. The Barada [the "cold"] having joined the Fijeh, (the traditional Pharpar[2], a name which well designates its tumultuous course)[3], runs on the N. of, and through the city, and then chiefly into the central of the three lakes, the Bahret-el-kibliyeh, [the "South" lake;] thence, it is supposed, but in part also directly, into the Bahret-esh-Shurkiyeh [the "East" lake[4]]. The 'Awaj [the "crooked"] (perhaps the old Amana, "the never-failing," in contrast with the streams which are exhausted in irrigation) runs near the old South boundary of Damascus[5], separating it probably from the Northern possessions of Israel beyond Jordan, Bashan (in its widest sense), and Jetur or Ituræa. The area has been calculated at 236 square geographical miles[6]. This space rather became the centre of its dominions, than measured their extent. But it supported a population far beyond what that space would maintain in Europe. Taught by the face of creation around them, where the course of every tiny rivulet, as it burst from the rocks, was marked by a rich luxuriance [7], the Damascenes of old availed themselves of the continual supply from the snows of Hermon or the heights of Anti-libanus, with a systematic diligence [8], of which, in our Northern clime, as we have no need, so we have no idea. "Without the Barada," says Porter[9], "the city could not exist, and the plain would be a parched desert; but now aqueducts intersect every quarter, and fountains sparkle in almost every dwelling, while innumerable canals extend their ramifications over the vast plain, clothing it with verdure and beauty.

Five of these canals are led off from the river at different elevations, before it enters the plain. They are carried along the precipitous banks of the ravine, being in some places tunnelled in the solid rock. The two on the Northern side water Salahiyeh at the foot of the hills about a mile from the city, and then irrigate the higher portions of the plain to the distance of nearly twenty miles. Of the three on the S. side, one is led to the populous village Daraya, five miles distant; the other two supply the city, its suburbs, and gardens." The like use was made of every fountain in every larger or lesser plain. Of old it was said, "[10] the Chrysorrhoas [the Barada] "is nearly expended in artificial channels." "[11] Damascus is fertile through drinking up the Chrysorrhoas by irrigation." Fourteen names of its canals are still given[12]; and while it has been common to select 7 or 8 chief canals, the whole have been counted up even to 70[13]. No art or labor was thought too great. The waters of the Fijeh were carried by a great aqueduct tunnelled through the side of the perpendicular cliff[14]. Yet this was as nothing. Its whole plain was intersected with canals, and tunnelled below. "[15] The waters of the river were spread over the surface of the soil in the fields and gardens; underneath, other canals were tunnelled to collect the superfluous water which percolates the soil, or from little fountains and springs below. The stream thus collected is led off to a lower level, where it comes to the surface. "[16] The whole plain is filled with these singular aqueducts, some of them running for 2 or 3 miles underground. Where the water of one is diffusing life and verdure over the surface, another branch is collecting a new supply." "In former days these extended over the whole plain to the lakes, thus irrigating the fields and gardens in every part of it."

Damascus then was, of old, famed for its beauty. Its white buildings, embedded in the deep green of its engirdling orchards, were like diamonds encircled by emeralds. They reach nearly to Anti-libanus [17] West-

[1] "2200 feet above the sea." Porter, Five years in Dam. i. 26.

[2] G. Williams. Ibn. Haukal says, "the river of Damascus rises under a Christian church, called al-Fijat. It unites with the river, called Barada." in Abulf. Tab. Syr. p. 15. The Fijeh is "pure, sweet and limpid" (Rob. ii. 476); the Barada is undrinkable, producing goitre. (G. Will. in Smith Geogr. Dict. v. Damascus.)

[3] Unsteady and in part headlong motion, is the central meaning of the Arabic "pharphara;" "parting asunder, and so flight," of the Arabic "pharra." On the bursting forth of the Fijeh, see Porter, Five years, i. 260.

[4] Ib. 375–82. Journ. of Sacr. Lit. 1853. July. Oct.

[5] Five years i. 26. 318. 321. 389. ii. 13, 247, 8.

[6] Ib. 27.

[7] "Nothing can be conceived more dreary than the ravines near Damascus, except when streams

flow through them, which are always fringed with green." Ld. Lindsay, Holy Land, p. 330. See Porter, Five years, i. 324. 280.

[8] "Every stream that descended from the hills (in the upper valley of the Barada) was made available to the irrigation of long slips of green which marked its course." Ib. p. 332. See Porter, Five years, i. 21, 277, 8, 9, 321. 358. 375. ii. 276. 306, 7, and accounts of canals i. 23, 372. 376. 321. 393. ii. 14. 16. 247. (at Lebweh ii. 322.) and aqueducts i. 329. in Hauran ii. 29. 77.   [9] Ib. 27, 8.

[10] Strabo xvi. 2. 16.   [11] Plin. v. 18. 16.

[12] Wilson, Lands of the Bible, ii. 325. note.

[13] Hajji Chalifa, See Ritter's Diss. Erdk. xvii p. 1303 sqq.

[14] Ib. 257.

[15] Five years, i. 394, 5. See further i. 159, 162. 371. ii. 11. [54. 205. of Hauran] 248, 9. 358.

[16] Porter, Handbook, p. 497.   [17] Five years, i. 27.

ward, "[1] and extend on both sides of the Barada some miles Eastward. They cover an area at last 25 [or 30] miles in circuit, and make the environs an earthly Paradise." Whence the Arabs said[2], "If there is a garden of Eden on earth, it is Damascus; and if in Heaven, Damascus is like it on earth." But this its beauty was also its strength. "The river," says William of Tyre[3], "having abundant water, supplies orchards on both banks, thick-set with fruit-trees, and flows Eastward by the city wall. On the W. and N. the city was far and wide fenced by orchards, like thick dense woods, which stretched four or five miles toward Libanus. These orchards are a most exceeding defence; for from the density of the trees and the narrowness of the ways, it seemed difficult and almost impossible to approach the city on that side." Even to this day it is said[4], "The true defence of Damascus consists in its gardens, which, forming a forest of fruit-trees and a labyrinth of hedges, walls and ditches, for more than 7 leagues in circumference, would present no small impediment to a Mussulman enemy."

The advantage of its site doubtless occasioned its early choice. It lay on the best route from the interior of Asia to the Mediterranean, to Tyre, and even to Egypt. Chedorlaomer and the four kings with him, doubtless, came that way, since the first whom they smote was at Ashteroth Karnaim[5] in Jaulan or Gaulonitis, and thence they swept on Southward, along the west side of Jordan, smiting, as they went, first the *Zuzim*, (probably the same as the Zamzummim[6]) in Ammonitis; then *the Emim in the plain of Kiriathaim* in Moab[7], then *the Horites in Mount Seir unto Elparan* (probably Elath on the Gulf called from it.) They returned that way, since Abraham overtook them at Hobah near Damascus[8]. Damascus was already the chief city, through its relation to which alone Hobah was known. It was on the route by which Abraham himself came at God's command from Haran (Charræ of the Greeks) whether over Tiphsach ("the passage," Thapsacus) or any more Northern passage over the Euphrates. The fact that his chief and confidential servant whom he entrusted to seek a wife for Isaac, and who was, at one time, his heir, was a Damascene[9], implies some intimate connection of Abraham with Damascus. At the time of our era, the name of Abraham was still held in honor in the country of Damascus[10]; a village was

named from him "Abraham's dwelling;" and a native historian Nicolas[11] said, that he reigned in Damascus on his way from the country beyond Babylon to Canaan. The name of his servant "Eliezer" "my God is help," implies that at this time too the servant was a worshiper of the One God. The name Damascus probably betokened the strenuous[12], energetic character of its founder. Like the other names connected with Aram in the Old Testament[13], it is, in conformity with the common descent from Aram, Aramaic. It was no part of the territory assigned to Israel, nor was it molested by them. Judging, probably, of David's defensive conquests by its own policy, it joined the other Syrians who attacked David, was subdued, garrisoned, and became tributary[14]. It was at that time probably a subordinate power, whether on the ground of the personal eminence of Hadadezer king of Zobah, or any other. Certainly Hadadezer stands out conspicuously; the Damascenes are mentioned only subordinately. Consistently with this, the first mention of the kingdom of Damascus in Scripture is the dynasty of Rezon son of Eliada's, a fugitive servant of Hadadezer, who formed a marauding band, then settled and reigned in Damascus[15]. Before this, Scripture speaks of the people only of Damascus, not of their kings. Its native historian admits that the Damascenes were, in the time of David, and continued to be, the aggressors, while he veils over their repeated defeats, and represents their kings, as having reigned successively from father to son, for ten generations, a thing unknown probably in any monarchy. "[16]A native, Adad, having gained great power, became king of Damascus and the rest of Syria, except Phœnicia. He, having carried war against David, king of Judæa, and disputed with him in many battles, and that finally at the Euphrates where he was defeated, had the character of a most eminent king for prowess and valor. After his death, his descendants reigned for ten generations, each receiving from his father the name [Hadad] together with the kingdom, like the Ptolemies of Egypt. The third, having gained the greatest power of all, seeking to repair the defeat of his grandfather, warring against the Jews, wasted what is now called Samaritis." They could not brook a defeat, which they had brought upon themselves. Rezon renewed, throughout the later part of Solomon's reign, the aggression of Hadad. On the schism of the

---

[1] Porter, Five years, i. 29, add pp. 152, 3.
[2] in R. Pethakiah in Journ. As. 1831. viii. 388, and Ibn Batuta in Ritter, xvii. 1346, with much more.
[3] xvii. 3.   [4] Ali Bey travels, ii. 282.
[5] Gen. xiv. 5, 6.   [6] Deut. ii. 20.   [7] Ib. 9, 11.
[8] Gen. xiv. 15.   [9] Gen. xv. 2, 3.
[10] Jos. Ant. i. 7, 2.   [11] L. iv. ap. Jos. ibid.
[12] Dimashko, Damshako, "swift, ready, strenuous." Arab.

[13] as Aram Naharaim, Aram Beth Rehob, Aram Maachah, Padan Aram, Hamath, Tadmor, Tiphsach, &c. The Arabic form of the name Mabug [Hierapolis], Manbej, is probably the original; so that Hitzig is wrong as to the three which he assumed to be proofs of a non-Semitic origin of the cities on this line of traffic. (quoted by Ritter, xvii. 1337.)
[14] 2 Sam. viii. 5, 6.   [15] 1 Kgs xi. 23, 24.
[16] Nicolaus, Damasc. Hist. iv. in Jos. Ant. vii. 2. 2.

ten tribes, the hostility of Damascus was concentrated against Israel who lay next to them. Abijam was in league with the father of Benhadad[1]. Benhadad at once broke his league with Baasha at the request of Asa in his later mistrustful days[2], and turned against Baasha[3]. From Omri also Benhadad I. took cities and extorted *streets*, probably a Damascus-quarter, in Samaria itself[4]. Benhadad II. had *thirty-two* vassal *kings*[5], (dependent kings like those of Canaan, each of his own city and little territory,) and led them against Samaria, intending to plunder it[6], and, on occasion of the plundering, probably to make it his own or to destroy it. By God's help they were twice defeated; the second time, when they directly challenged the power of God[7], so signally that, had not Ahab been flattered by the appeal to his mercy[8], Syria would no more have been in a condition to oppress Israel. Benhadad promised to restore the cities which his father had taken from Israel, and to make an Israel-quarter in Damascus[9]. If this promise was fulfilled, Ramoth-Gilead must have been lost to Syria at an earlier period, since, three years afterward, Ahab perished in an attempt, by aid of Jehoshaphat, against the counsels of God, to recover it[10]. Ramoth-Gilead being thus in the hands of Syria, all North of it, half of Dan and Manasseh beyond Jordan, must also have been conquered by Syria. Except the one great siege of Samaria, which brought it to extremities and which God dissipated by a panic which He infused into the Syrian army[11], Benhadad and Hazael encouraged only marauding expeditions against Israel during the 14 years of Ahaziah and Jehoram. Benhadad was, according to Assyrian inscriptions defeated thrice, Hazael twice, by Shalmanubar king of Assyria[12]. Benhadad appears to have acted on the offensive, in alliance with the kings of the Hittites, the Hamathites and Phœnicians[12]; Hazael was attacked alone, driven to take refuge in Anti-libanus, and probably became tributary[13]. Assyrian chronicles relate only Assyrian victories. The brief notice, that through Naaman[14] *the Lord gave deliverance to Syria,* probably refers to some signal check which Assyria received through him. For there was no other enemy, from whom Syria had to be *delivered.* Subsequently to that retreat from Samaria, he even lost Ramoth[15] to Jehoram after a battle before it[16], in which Jehoram was wounded. It is a probable conjecture[17] that Jehu, by his political submission to Assyria, drew on himself the

calamities which Elisha foretold. Hazael probably became the instrument of God in chastening Israel, while he was avenging Jehu's submission to a power whom he dreaded and from whom he had suffered. Israel, having lost the help of Judah, became the easier prey. Hazael not only took from Israel all East of Jordan[18], but made the whole open country unsafe for the Israelites to dwell in. Not until God *gave Israel a saviour,* could they *dwell in their tents as beforetime*[19]. Hazael extended his conquests to Gath[20], intending probably to open a connecting line with Egypt. *With a small company of men* he defeated a large army of Judah[21]. Joash king of Judah bought him off, when advancing against Jerusalem, with everything of gold, consecrated or civil, in the temple or in his own treasures[22]. Jehoash recovered from Benhadad III. the cities this side Jordan[23]; Jeroboam II., all their lost territories and even Damascus and Hamath[24]. Yet after this, it was to recover its power under Rezin, to become formidable to Judah, and, through its aggressions on Judah, to bring destruction on itself. At this time, Damascus was probably, like ourselves, a rich, commercial, as well as warlike, but not as yet a manufacturing[25] nation. Its wealth, as a great emporium of transit-commerce, (as it is now) furnished it with sinews for war. The *white wool*[26], in which it traded with Tyre, implies the possession of a large outlying tract in the desert, where the sheep yield the whitest wool. It had then doubtless, beside the population of its plain, large nomadic hordes dependent upon it.

I will not turn away the punishment *thereof;* lit. *I will not turn it back.* What was this, which God would not turn back? Amos does not express it. Silence is often more emphatic than words. Not naming it, he leaves it the rather to be conceived of by the mind, as something which had been of old coming upon them to overwhelm them, which God had long stayed back, but which, since He would now stay it no longer, would burst in, with the more terrific and overwhelming might, because it had been restrained before. Sin and punishment are by a great law of God bound together. God's mercy holds back the punishment long, allowing only some slight tokens of His displeasure to shew themselves, that the sinful soul or people may not be unwarned. When He no longer withholds it, the law of His moral government holds its course. "Seldom[27]," said heathen experience, "hath punishment with linger-

---

[1] 1 Kgs xv. 19.
[2] 1 Chr. xvi. 2-7.
[3] Ib. and 1 Kgs xv. 20.
[4] 1 Kgs xx. 34.
[5] Ib. 1, 24.
[6] Ib. 6, 7.
[7] Ib. 22-25, 28.
[8] Ib. 31, 32.
[9] Ib. 34.
[10] 1 Kgs xxii.
[11] 2 Kgs vii. 6.
[12] See Rawl. Herod. i. 464.
[13] Ib. Dr. Hincks, Dubl. Univ. Mag. Oct. 1853, pp. 422, 5, 6.

[14] 2 Kgs v. 1.
[15] Ib. ix. 14, 15.
[16] Ib. viii. 29.
[17] Rawl. Herod. i. p. 465.
[18] 2 Kgs x. 32, 33.
[19] Ib. xiii. 5.
[20] Ib. xii. 17.
[21] 2 Chr. xxiv. 23, 24.
[22] 2 Kgs xii. 18.
[23] Ib. xiii. 25.
[24] Ib. xiv. 28.
[25] See on iii. 12.
[26] Ezek. xxvii. 18.
[27] Horace.

Before
CHRIST
cir. 787.
4 [k] But I will send a fire into the house of Hazael,

[k] Jer. 17. 27. & 49. 27. ver. 7. 10. 12. ch. 2. 2. 5.

which shall devour the palaces of Benhadad.

Before
CHRIST
cir. 787.

ing foot parted with the miscreant, advancing before."

Because they have threshed Gilead with threshing instruments of iron. The instrument, St. Jerome relates here, was "a sort of wain, rolling on iron wheels beneath, set with teeth ; so that it both threshed out the grain and bruised the straw and cut it in pieces, as food for the cattle, for lack of hay." A similar instrument, called by nearly the same name [1], is still in use in Syria and Egypt. Elisha had foretold to Hazael his cruelty to Israel [2]; *Their strong holds thou wilt set on fire, and their young men wilt thou slay with the sword, and wilt dash their children, and rip up their women with child.* Hazael, like others gradually steeped in sin, thought it impossible, but did it. In the days of Jehu [3], *Hazael smote them in all the coasts of Israel from Jordan Eastward; all the land of Gilead, the Gadites and the Reubenites and the Manassites, from Arorer which is by the river Arnon, even Gilead and Bashan;* in those of Jehoahaz, Jehu's son [4], *he oppressed them, neither did he leave of the people to Jehoahaz but fifty horsemen and ten chariots, and ten thousand footmen; for the king of Syria had destroyed them, and had made them like the dust by threshing.* The death here spoken of, although more ghastly, was probably not more severe than many others; not nearly so severe as some which have been used by Christian Judicatures. It is mentioned in the Proverbs, as a capital punishment [5]; and is alluded to as such by Isaiah [6]. David had had, for some cause unexplained by Holy Scripture, to inflict it on the Ammonites [7]. Probably not the punishment in itself alone, but the attempt so to extirpate the people of God brought down this judgment on Damascus.

Theodoret supposes the horrible aggravation, that it was thus that the women with child were destroyed with their children, "casting the aforesaid women, as into a sort of threshing-floor, they savagely threshed them out like ears of corn with saw-armed wheels."

Gilead is here doubtless to be taken in its widest sense, including all the possessions of Israel, E. of Jordan, as, in the account of Hazael's conquests, *all the land of Gilead* [3] is explained to mean, all which was ever given to the two tribes and a half, and to include Gilead proper, as distinct from Basan. In like way Joshua relates [8], that *the children of*

[1] Nauraj, probably a corruption from the Heb. מורג. The חרוץ and the מורג חרוץ are plainly the same. See the last woodcut in Thomson, The Land, ii. 315, and Wilkinson, ii. 190.

Reuben and the children of Gad and the half tribe of Manasseh returned to go into the country of Gilead, to the land of their possessions. Throughout that whole beautiful tract, including 2½ degrees of latitude, Hazael had carried on his war of extermination into every peaceful village and home, sparing neither the living nor the unborn.

4. *And I will send a fire on the house of Hazael.* The *fire* is probably at once material fire, whereby cities are burned in war, since he adds, *it shall devour the palaces of Benhadad,* and also stands as a symbol of all other severity in war as in the ancient proverb [9], *a fire is gone out from Heshbon, a flame from the city of Sihon; it hath consumed Ar of Moab, the lords of the high places of Arnon;* and again of the displeasure of Almighty God, as when He says [10], *a fire is kindled in Mine anger, and it shall burn unto the lowest hell.* For the fire destroys not the natural buildings only, but *the house of Hazael,* i. e. his whole family. In these prophecies, a sevenfold vengeance by fire is denounced against the seven people, an image of the eternal fire into which all iniquity shall be cast.

The palaces of Benhadad. Hazael, having murdered Benhadad his master and ascended his throne, called his son after his murdered master, probably in order to connect his own house with the ancient dynasty. Benhadad, i. e. *son* or worshiper of the idol *Hadad,* or "the sun," had been the name of two of the kings of the old dynasty. Benhadad III. was at this time reigning. The prophet foretells the entire destruction of the dynasty founded in blood. The prophecy *may* have had a fulfillment in the destruction of the house of Hazael, with whose family Rezin, the king of Syria in the time of Ahaz, stands in no known relation. Defeats, such as those of Benhadad III. by Jeroboam II. who took Damascus itself, are often the close of an usurping dynasty. Having no claim to regard except success, failure vitiates its only title. The name Hazael, "whom God looked upon," implies a sort of owning of the One God, like Tab-el, "God is good," El-iada', "whom God knoweth," even amid the idolatry in the names, Tab-Rimmon, "good is Rimmon ;" Hadad-ezer, "Hadad is help ;" and Hadad, or Benhadad. Bad men abuse every creature, or ordinance, or appointment of God. It may be then that, as Sennacherib boasted [11], *am I now come up without the Lord against this land*

[2] 2 Kgs viii. 12. [3] Ib. x. 32, 3. [4] Ib. xiii. 7.
[5] xx. 26. [6] xxviii. 28.
[7] 2 Sam. xii. 31. 1 Chr. xx. 3. [8] Josh. xxii. 9.
[9] Nu. xxi. 28. [10] Deut. xxxii. 22.
[11] Is. xxxvi. 10.

Before
C H R I S T
cir. 787.
5 I will break also the
[1] bar of Damascus, and cut

[1] Jer. 51. 30. Lam. 2. 9.

off the inhabitant f r o m
||the plain of Aven, and

Before
C H R I S T
cir. 787.

|| Or, *Bikath-aven*.

to destroy it? the Lord said unto me, Go up against this land and destroy it; so Hazael made use of the prophecy of Elisha, to give himself out as the scourge of God, and thought of himself as one "on whom God looked." Knowledge of futurity is an awful gift. As "Omniscience alone can wield Omnipotence," so superhuman knowledge needs superhuman gifts of wisdom and holiness. Hazael seemingly hardened himself in sin by aid of the knowledge which should have been his warning. Probably he came to Elisha, with the intent to murder his master already formed, in case he should not die a natural death; and Elisha read him to himself. But he very probably justified himself to himself in what he had already purposed to do, on the ground that Elisha had foretold to him that he should be king over Syria[1], and, in his massacres of God's people, gave himself out as being, what he was, the instrument of God. "Scourges of God" have known themselves to be what they were, although they themselves were not the less sinful, in sinfully accomplishing the Will of God[2]. We have heard of a Christian Emperor, who has often spoken of his "mission," although his "mission" has already cost the shedding of much Christian blood.

5. *I will also break the bar of Damascus.* In the East, every city was fortified; the gates of the stronger cities were cased in iron, that they might not be set on fire by the enemy; they were fastened within with bars of brass[3] or iron[4]. They were flanked with towers, and built over, so that what was naturally the weakest point and the readiest access to an enemy became the strongest defence. In Hauran the huge doors and gates of a single stone 9 and 10 feet high[5], and 1½ foot thick[6], are still extant, and "[6] the place for the ponderous bars," proportioned to such gates, "may yet be seen." The walls were

loosened with the battering-ram, or scaled by mounds: the strong gate was seldom attacked; but, when a breach was made, was thrown open from within. The *breaking of the bar* laid open the city to the enemy, to go in and come out at his will. The whole strength of the kingdom of Damascus lay in the capital. It was itself the seat of empire and was the empire itself. God says then, that He Himself would shiver all their means of resistance, whatever could hinder the inroad of the enemy.

And cut off the inhabitant from the plain of Aven; lit. from the vale of vanity, the *Bik'ah* being a broad vale between hills[7]. Here it is doubtless the rich and beautiful valley, still called el-bukâa by the Arabs, La Boquea by William of Tyre[8], lying between Lebanon and Anti-libanus, the old Cœle-Syria in its narrowest sense. It is, on high ground, the continuation of that long deep valley which, along the Jordan, the Dead sea, and the Arabah, reaches to the Red Sea. Its extreme length, from its Southern close at Kal'at-esh-shakîf to Hums (Emesa) has been counted at 7 days journey[9]; it narrows toward its Southern extremity, expands at its Northern, yet it cannot any how be said to lose its character of a valley until 10 miles N. of Riblah[10]. Midway, on its highest elevation about 3800 feet above the sea[11], was Baalbek, or Heliopolis, whither the Egyptian worship is said to have been brought of old times from their "city of the sun[12]." Baalbek, as the ruins still attest, was full of the worship of the sun. But the whole of that beautiful range, "[13] a magnificent vista," it has been said, "carpeted with verdure and beauty," "[14] a gem lying deep in its valley of mountains," was a citadel of idolatry. The name Baal-Hermon connects Mount Hermon itself, the snow-capt height which so towers over its S. E. extremity, with the worship of

[1] 2 Kgs viii. 13.
[2] See on Hos. i. 4.   [3] 1 Kgs iv. 13.
[4] Ps. cvii. 16. Is. xlv. 2; comp. Is. xlviii. 14. Jer. li. 30.
[5] Burckhardt's Syria, 90. quoted in Five years, ii. 201.   [6] Five years, ii. 196.
[7] Etymologically, it would mean "cleft." It does mean a valley, as contrasted with hills, Deut. viii. 7. xi. 11. Is. xl. 4. xli. 18. lxiii. 14. Ezek. iii. 22, 3. It is used of the "valley of the Chebar," in contrast with the *hill* of *Tel*-Abib. As united with proper names, it answers to our "vale," a broad valley between hills; as "the vale of Megiddo," "of Jericho," "of Mizpeh," "under Hermon," (Jos. xi. 8, 3.) probably the upper part of the valley of the Jordan above the lake Merom (v. 7.), along the course of the river Hasbany; the "vale of Lebanon" being probably the Southern part of the great Bik'ah, where Baal-gad lay under Hermon (Ib. xi. 17), and east of Lebanon (Ib. xiii. 5). So also probably the "vale of Dura." (Dan. iii. 1.) A long valley, though broad, if seen from a height, looks like a cleft. In Arabic, the original force of the root is altogether lost. In nouns, we have, in different forms, the varying meanings assigned, bekâ, "a plateau;" bak'a, "low ground, where water stagnates;" baki'a, "a plain." See Freytag Lex. Burckhardt mentions "a broad valley called El Bekka [Bek'a] N. and N. E. of Ssafout [near Amman] at the foot of the mountain on which it stands." Syria, 362.
[8] xviii. 17.
[9] Berggren, Guide Franc. Arab. p. 458. in Ritter, xvii. 154.
[10] The "end of the central ridge of Anti-lebanon." Porter, Handb. p. 578.
[11] See V. de Velde, Memoir, p. 175.
[12] (Lucian) de Syria Dea § 5. Macr. Sat. i. 23. Robins. iii. 518.
[13] Robins. iii. 493.   [14] Ib. 504.

Before
C H R I S T
cir. 787.

| Or. Beth-eden.
m Fulfilled,
2 Kings 16. 9.

him that holdeth the scep-
t r e from || the house of
Eden : and [m] the people of

Syria shall go into cap-
tivity [n] unto Kir, saith the
LORD.

Baal or the sun, and that, from the time of the Judges[1]. The name Baal-gad connects *the valley of Lebanon,* i. e. most probably the S. end of the great valley, with the same worship, anterior to Joshua[2]. The name Baalbek is probably an abbreviation of the old name, Baal-bik'ah[3], "Baal of the valley," in contrast with the neighboring Baal-hermon. "[4]The whole of Hermon was girded with temples." "[5] Some eight or ten of them cluster round it," and, which is more remarkable, one is built "[6] to catch the first beams of the sun rising over Hermon;" and temples on its opposite sides face toward it, as a sort of centre[7]. In S. Jerome's time, the Heathen still reverenced a celebrated temple on its summit[8]. On the crest of its central peak, 3000 feet above the glen below, in winter inaccessible, beholding far asunder the rising and the setting sun on the Eastern desert and in the Western sea, are still seen the foundations of a circular wall or ring of large stones, a rude temple, within which another of Grecian art was subsequently built[9]. "On three other peaks of the Anti-libanus range are ruins of great antiquity[10]." "[11] The Bukâa and its borders are full of the like buildings." "Lebanon, Anti-lebanon and the valleys between are thronged with ancient temples[12]." Some indeed were Grecian, but others Syro-Phœnician. The Grecian temples were probably the revival of Syro-Phœnician. The "[13] massive substructions of Baalbek are conjectured to have been those of an earlier temple." The new name *Heliopolis* only substituted the name of the object of worship (the *sun*) for its title Lord. The Heathen emperors would not have lavished so much

and such wondrous cost and gorgeous art on a temple in Cœle-Syria, had not its Pagan celebrity recommended it to their superstition or their policy. On the W. side of Lebanon at Afca, (Apheca) was the temple of Venus at the source of the river Adonis[14], a centre of the most hateful Syrian idolatry, "[15] a school of misdoing for all profligates." At Heliopolis too, men "[16] shamelessly gave their wives and daughters to shame." The outburst of Heathenism there in the reign of Julian the Apostate[17] shows how deeply rooted was its idolatry. Probably then, Amos pronounces the sentence of the people of that whole beautiful vale, as *valley of vanity* or *iniquity*[18], being wholly given to that worst idolatry which degraded Syria. Here, as the seat of idolatry, the chief judgments of God were to fall. Its inhabitants were to be *cut off,* i. e. utterly destroyed ; on the rest, captivity is the only sentence pronounced. The Assyrian monarchs not unfrequently put to death those who despised their religion[19], and so may herein have executed blindly the sentence of God.

From the house of Eden, a Proper, but significant, name, " Beth-Eden," i. e. " house of pleasure." The name, like the Eden of Assyria[20], is, in distinction from man's first home, pronounced ĕden, not ēden[21]. Two places near, and one in, the Bik'ah have, from similarity of name, been thought to be this " house of delight." 1. Most beautiful now for situation and climate, is what is probably mispronounced Ehden ; a Maronite Village " [22] of 4 or 500 families, on the side of a rich highly-cultivated valley " near Beshirrai on the road from Tripolis to the Cedars. Its climate is described as a ten

---

[1] Jud. iii. 3. [2] Jos. xi. 17. xii. 7. xiii. 5.

[3] The older Eastern names often re-appear, when the Greek names, which their conquerors gave, passed away with themselves. This is not a revival of the old name, but a continuance of it. During the reign of their conquerors, we hear from *them* the names which they gave. When they are gone, we hear from the Easterns the old Eastern name which lived on among them. The name Baalbek re-appears in the tenth century in Mohammedan writers (Rob. iii. 524.) But in none but Pagan times would a pagan name have been given to it.

[4] Robins. iii. 432.

[5] Porter, Handb. 451.

[6] Porter, 452. Stonehenge is said to be built so that the first rays of the sun on the longest day fell through the entrance on the altar.

[7] Ib. 457. Rob. iii. 417, 8.

[8] Euseb. Onom. v. 'Αερμὼν. " It is said that on its summit there is a celebrated temple, which is the object of reverence to the Heathen towards Paneas and Libanus." S. Jerome. S. Hilary also mentions the reverence to Hermon, (or, as he says, worship of it,) up to his day, in Ps. 133. Reland, 323.

[9] Porter, 454.

[10] Ib. and p. 451. "At Kula't Bustra, 1000 feet above" the road, "is a groupe of ruined temples, simple in form, and rude in style." Add Rob. iii. 414, 5.

[11] Rob. iii. 438. [12] Ib. 417.

[13] Ib. 520. [14] Rob. iii. 606.

[15] Eus. Vit. Const. iii. 55. Ib.

[16] Ib. iii. 58.

[17] Soz. v. 10. Theod. H. E. iii. 7. Rob. iii. 52.

[18] It has been conjectured, that, with the worship of the sun, the Egyptian name for Heliopolis, On, (Light) may have been brought from Egypt, and that, as Ezekiel calls the Heliopolis of Egypt, *Aven,* vanity, for "On," (xxx. 17) and Hosea calls "Bethel," "Bethaven," (iv. 15, x. 5) so Amos *may* have called this "the valley of vanity " "for the valley of On." But this is mere conjecture. There is no trace of the name "On" in the whole tract. Baalbek must have been an ancient name.

[19] See authorities in Rawl. Herod. i. 495.

[20] 2 Kgs xix. 12. Is. xxxvii. 12. Ezek. xxvii. 23.

[21] עֶדֶן not עֵדֶן.

[22] Irby and Mangles, Travels in Syria, p. 64.

months spring[1]; "the hills are terraced up to their summits;" and every place full of the richest, most beautiful, vegetation; "grain is poured out into the lap of man, and wine into his cup without measure." "The slopes of the valleys, one mass of verdure, are yet more productive than the hills; the springs of Lebanon gushing down, fresh, cool and melodious in every direction[2]." The wealthier families of Tripoli still resort there for summer, "the climate being tempered by the proximity of the snow-mountains, the most luxuriant vegetation favored by the soft airs from the sea[3]." It is still counted "[4]the Paradise of Lebanon." 2. Beit-el-Janne, lit. "house of Paradise," is an Arabic translation of Beth-Eden. It "lies under the root of Libanus, [Hermon] gushing forth clear water, whence," says William of Tyre[5], "it is called 'house of pleasure.'" It lies in a narrow valley, where it widens a little, about ¾ of an hour from the plain of Damascus[6], and about 27 miles[7] from that city on the way from Banias. "[8]Numerous rock-tombs, above and around, bear testimony to the antiquity of the site." It gives its name to the Jennani (Paradise-river), one of two streams which form the second great river near Damascus, the Awadj. 3. The third, the Paradisus of the Greeks, one of the three towns of Laodicene[9], agrees only accidentally with the Scripture name, since their Paradisus signifies not an earthly Paradise, but a hunting-park. For this the site is well suited; but in that country so abounding in water, and of soil so rich that the earth seems ready, on even slight pains of man, to don itself in luxuriant beauty, what probably is the site[10] of the old Paradisus, is hopelessly barren[11]. Beth-eden may have been the residence of one of the subordinate kings under the king of Damascus, who was to be involved in the ruin of his suzerain; or it may have been a summer-residence of the king of Damascus himself, where, in the midst of his trust in his false gods, and in a Paradise, as it were, of delight, God would cut him off altogether. Neither wealth nor any of a man's idols protect against God. As Adam, for sin, was expelled

from Paradise, so the rulers of Damascus from the place of their pleasure and their sin.

And the people of Syria shall go into captivity. Syria or Aram perhaps already included, under the rule of Damascus, all the little kingdoms on this side of the Euphrates, into which it had been formerly sub-divided. At least, it is spoken of as a whole, without any of the additions which occur in the earlier history, Aram-beth-rehob, Aram-zobah, Aram-Maachah. Before its captivity Damascus is spoken of as *the head of Syria*[12].

Into Kir. Kir has been identified 1) with the part of Iberia near the river Kur[13] which unites with the Araxes, not far from the Caspian, to the North of Armenia; 2) a city called by the Greeks Kourēna[14] or Kourna on the river Mardus[15] in Southern Media; 3) a city, Karine[16], the modern Kerend[17]. The first is the most likely, as the most known; the Kur is part probably of the present name Kurgistan, our "Georgia." Armenia at least which lay on the South of the River Kur, is frequently mentioned in the cuneiform inscriptions, as a country where the kings of Assyria warred and conquered[18]. The two parricide sons of Sennacherib are as likely to have fled[19] to a distant portion of their father's empire, as beyond it. Their flight thither may have been the ground of Esarhaddon's war against it[20]. It has at all times afforded a shelter to those expelled from others' lands[21]. The domestic, though late, traditions of the Armenians count as their first inhabitants some who had fled out of Mesopotamia to escape the yoke of Bel, king of Babylon[22]. Whatever be the value of particular traditions, its mountain-valleys form a natural refuge to fugitives. On occasion of some such oppression, as that from which Asshur fled before Nimrod[23], Aram may have been the first of those who took shelter in the mountains of Armenia and Georgia, and thence spread themselves, where we afterward find them, in the lowlands of Mesopotamia. The name Aram however is in no way connected with Armenia, which is itself no indigenous name of that country, but was probably formed by the Greeks, from a name which

---

[1] Ritter, Erdk. xvii. 650. from Roth, Reise in v. Schubert, iii. 306. I. and M. ib. "It seemed as though the spring never left this country." De la Roque.
[2] Lord Lindsay, Holy Land, p. 355 more fully.
[3] Ritter, ib.
[4] Wilson, Lands of the Bible, p. 394.
[5] xxi. 10, in Gesta Dei per Francos, pp. 1002, 3. He calls it Bedegene.
[6] Burckhardt, Syria, pp. 45–7.
[7] See Burckhardt, corrected in Five years, i. 313.
[8] Porter, Handb. p. 449.
[9] Ptol. v. 15. 20.
[10] A monument at its site "near the source of the Orontes" (Strabo xvi. 2. 19.) has hunting-scenes on its four sides. G. Williams, in Smith's Geogr. Dict. v. Orontes.

[11] "A more dreary and barren situation could scarcely be imagined. There is no stream or fountain within miles of it, and the inhabitants were wholly dependent upon wells and cisterns for supply of water." Porter, Handb. p. 577.
[12] Is. vii. 8.   [13] Dion. L. 36. Boch. Phal. iv. 32.
[14] Ptol. vi. 2.   [15] Boch. Phal. iv. 32.
[16] Vitr. on Is. xxii. 6.
[17] Ritt. Erdk. ix. 359. 391.
[18] See in Rawl. Herod. i. 464. 470. 473. 475. 481. 484.
[19] Is. xxxvii. 38.
[20] The subdual of Armenia by Esarhaddon is mentioned in the cuneiform Inscr., Rawl. Herod. i. 481.
[21] See Ritter, x. 584 sqq.
[22] Moses Choren i. 9. 1b.
[23] Gen. x. 11. See Introd. to Nahum.

they heard[1]. The name Aram, "lofty," obviously describes some quality of the son of Shem, as of others who bore the name [2]. Contrariwise, Canaan, (whether or no anticipating his future degraded character as partaking in the sin of Ham) may signify "crouching." But neither has Aram any meaning of "highland," nor Canaan of "lowland," as has of late been imagined [3].

From Kir the forefathers of the Syrians had, of their own will, been brought by the good all-disposing Providence of God; to Kir should the Syrians, against their will, be carried back. Aram of Damascus had been led to a land which, for its fertility and beauty, has been and is still praised as a sort of Paradise. Now, softened as they were by luxury, they were to be transported back to the austere though healthy climate, whence they had come. They had abused the might given to them by God, in the endeavor to uproot Israel; now they were themselves to be utterly uprooted. The captivity which Amos foretells is complete; a captivity by which (as the word means [4]) the land should be *bared* of its inhabitants. Such a captivity he foretells of no other, except the ten tribes. He foretells it absolutely of these two nations alone [5], of the king and princes of Ammon [6], not of Tyre, or the cities of Philistia, or Edom, or Ammon, or Moab. The punishment did not reach Syria in those days, but in those of Rezin who also oppressed Judah. The sin not being cut off, the punishment too was handed down. Tiglath-pileser carried them away, about fifty years after this, and *slew Rezin* [7]. In regard to these two nations, Amos foretells the captivity absolutely. Yet at this time, there was no human likelihood, no ground, except of a Divine knowledge, to predict it of these two nations especially. They went into captivity too long after this for human foresight to predict it; yet long enough before the captivity of Judah for the fulfillment to have impressed Judah if they would. The transportation of whole populations, which subsequently became part of the standing policy of the Persian and of the later Assyrian Empires, was not, as far as we know, any part of Eastern policy at the time of the prophet. Sesostris, the Egyptian conqueror, some centuries before Amos, is related to have brought together "[8] many men," "a crowd," from the nations whom he had subdued, and to have employed them on his buildings and canals. Even this account has received no support from the Egyptian monuments, and the deeds ascribed by the Greeks to Sesostris have been supposed [9] to be a blending of those of two monarchs of the xix. Dynasty, Sethos I. and Raamses II., interwoven with those of Ousartesen III. (Dynasty xii.) and Tothmosis III. (Dyn. xviii). But the carrying away of any number of prisoners from fields of battle is something altogether different from the political removal of a nation. It had in it nothing systematic or designed. It was but the employment of those whom war had thrown into their hands, as slaves. The Egyptian monarchs availed themselves of this resource, to spare the labor of their native subjects in their great works of utility or of vanity. But the prisoners so employed were but a slave population, analogous to those who, in other nations, labored in the mines or in agriculture. They employed in the like way the Israelites, whom they had

---

[1] Xen. An. iv. 5. Armenia is probably i. q. הר מני har-minni, "mountain of Minni" (i. q. Minyas) a name of one portion of Armenia (Jer. li. 27). Aram has only the *m* in common with Minni.

[2] A son of Kemuel, Gen. xxii. 21; and son of Shemer, 1 Chr. vii. 34.

[3] The theory that Aram means "highland," Canaan "lowland," 1) ignores that, in the Bible, they are the names of men, not of lands. 2) It is contrary to the facts, as they appear in Holy Scripture. The borders of Canaan extended from Zidon Southwards to Gaza, and thence to the S. of the Dead Sea (Gen. x. 19) and, according to their own coins, included Laodicea ad Libanum (Ges. Thes. s. v.). Damascus (2400 feet above the sea), the highest place in Aram, was lower than Jerusalem (2610) or Bethlehem (2704) or Ramah (2800) or Hebron (3029) (See V. de Velde Memoir, p. 176–80), and the common names of Aram, "plain of Aram," "field of Aram," (Padan Aram, Sedeh Aram,) "Aram between the two rivers," (Aram Naharaim) all agree in describing a flat country. Aram Naharaim or Mesopotamia is only about 435 Eng. feet above the sea (408 Fr. feet Ritter, viii. 16) i. e. ⅙ of the height of Jerusalem. Heights are spoken of once in connection with Aram (*from Aram, from the mountains of the East* Nu. xxiii. 7) and Mesopotamia is bounded on the N. by Mt. Masius, but it is itself a plain. 3) The root from which the word Canaan is derived has in no case the sense of physical depression. Its very varied Arabic meanings centre in that of "contracted;" thence "bowed," bowed towards, "i. e. was submissive," "was *bent* upon a thing." In Hebrew it is used of wares "compressed," "packed together;" of bowing down an enemy, or one's self in submission. 4) For the real lowland of Canaan, that near the coast (from Joppa to Gaza) there is specific term, שפלה, "the low," which occurs in the first detailed descriptions of Canaan in Joshua, is the received Hebrew word, thence passed into Greek, ἡ Σεφηλά 1 Macc. xii. 38, of which Eusebius says "and it is yet called Sephēla. This is the whole low country, N. and W. around Eleutheropolis." (Onom. See Reland, p. 307, add 372) whence the Carthaginians carried it to Spain, (Seville) with many other names (See Movers, Phœnic. iii. 640, 1.). It is used also of that same part of Palestine by Arabic authors.

The idea then that Canaan is used for lowland, as contrasted with Aram, highland, is contrary to the fact (in that Aram mostly was low, Canaan, high), contrary to the meaning of the word (which is never used in this sense, for which another word is employed), contrary to the simple sense of Scripture, where the names are originally those of the fathers of the races who lived in those countries.

[4] גלה.

[5] See below as to Israel, or its rich men. v. 5, 27. vi. 7. vii. 11, 17.

[6] i. 15.

[7] 2 Kgs xvi. 9.

[8] Herod. ii. 107, 8.

[9] Brugsch, Hist. de l' Eg. c. 8. p. 153.

Before
CHRIST
cir. 787.
°2 Chr. 28. 18.
Is. 14. 29.
Jer. 47. 4, 5. 6 ¶ Thus saith the Lord; For three transgressions of °Gaza, and Ezek. 25. 15. Zeph. 2. 4.

for four, I will not turn away *the punishment* thereof; because they ‖ carried with *an entire captivity*, 2 Chron. 21. 16, 17. Joel 3. 6.

received peacefully. Their earlier works were carried on by native labor[1]. After Tothmosis III., in whose reign is the first representation of prisoners employed in forced labor[2], they could, during their greatness, spare their subjects. They imported labor, not by slave trade, but through war. Nubia was incorporated with Egypt[3], and Nubian prisoners were, of course, employed, not in their own country but in the North of Egypt; Asiatic prisoners in Nubia[4]. But they were prisoners made in a campaign, not a population; a foreign element in Egyptian soil, not an interchange of subject-populations. Doubtless, the *mixed multitude*[5], which *went up with* Israel from Egypt, were in part these Asiatic captives, who had been subjected to the same hard bondage. The object and extent of those forced transportations by the later Assyrians, Babylonians, and Persians were altogether different. Here the intention was to remove the people from their original seat, or at most to leave those only who, from their fewness or poverty, would be in no condition to rebel. The cuneiform inscriptions have brought before us, to a great extent, the records of the Assyrian conquests, as given by their kings. But whereas the later inscriptions of Sargon, Sennacherib, Esarhaddon, mention repeatedly the deportation of populations, the earlier annals of Asshurdanipal or Asshurakhbal relate the carrying off of soldiers only as prisoners, and women as captives[6]. They mention also receiving slaves as tributes, the number of oxen and sheep, the goods and possessions and the gods of the people which they carry off[7]. Else the king relates, how he crucified or impaled or put to death[6] men at arms or the people generally, but in no one of his expeditions does he mention any deportation. Often as modern writers *assume*, that the transportation of nations was part of the hereditary policy of the Monarchs of Asia, no instances before this period have been found. It appears to have been a later policy, first adopted by Tiglath-pileser towards Damascus and East and North Palestine, but

foretold by the Prophet long before it was adopted. It was the result probably of experience, that they could not keep these nations in dependence upon themselves while they left them in their old abodes. As far as our knowledge reaches, the prophet foretold the removal of these people, at a time when no instance of any such removal had occurred.

6. *Gaza* was the Southernmost city of the Philistines, as it was indeed of Canaan[8] of old, the last inhabited place at the beginning of the desert, on the way from Phœnicia to Egypt[9]. Its situation was wonderfully chosen, so that, often as a Gaza has been destroyed, a new city has, if even after long intervals, risen up again in the same immediate neighborhood[10]. The fragments of the earlier city became materials for the later. It was first Canaanite[8]; then Philistine; then, at least after Alexander, Edomite[11]; after Alexander Janneus, Greek[12]; conquered by Abubekr the first Khalif, it became Arabian; it was desolated in their civil wars, until the Crusaders rebuilt its fort[13]; then again, Mohammedan. In the earliest times, before the destruction of Sodom and Gomorrah, Gaza was the S. angle of the border of the Canaanites, whence it turned to the S. of the Dead Sea. Even then it was known by its name of strength, 'Azzah "the strong," like our "Fort." For a time, it stood as an island-fort, while the gigantic race of the Avvim wandered, wilder probably than the modern Bedaween, *up to* its very gates. For since it is said[14], *the Avvim dwelt in open villages*[15] *as far as Gaza*, plainly they did not dwell in Gaza itself, a fortified town. The description assigns the bound of their habitations, up to the furthest town on the S. E., Gaza. They prowled around it, infested it doubtless, but did not conquer it, and were themselves expelled by the Caphtorim[14]. The fortress of the prince of Gaza is mentioned in the great expedition of Tothmosis III.[16], as the conquest of Ashkelon was counted worthy of mention in the monuments of Raamses II[17]. It was strengthened

---

[1] See Ib. p. 35, 51, 2, 68, 9. The first mention which we have as yet of numerous captives is in the victory in Mesopotamia by Tothmosis I. (Ib. 90.)
[2] See in Brugsch, p. 106.   [3] Ib.·pp. 8, 9.
[4] Ib. p. 154.   [5] Ex. xii. 38.
[6] Fox Talbot, Assyrian texts translated, p. 22, 24, &c.
[7] So also the Egyptian inscriptions, in remarkable conformity with the account given by the priests to Germanicus, "There were read also the tributes imposed on the nations, the weight of silver and gold, the number of arms and horses, and gifts to

the temples, ivory and incense, and what quantity of corn and all utensils each nation paid, on a scale not less magnificent than is now prescribed by the violence of the Parthians or the power of the Romans." Tac. Ann. ii. 60.
[8] Gen. x. 19.   [9] Arr. ii. 27.
[10] See further on Zeph. ii. 4.
[11] Alexander repeopled it from its own neighborhood.   [12] Jos. Ant. xvii. 11. 4.
[13] Will. Tyre. xvii. 12.   [14] Deut. ii. 23.
[15] םיִרֵצֲה.
[16] Brugsch, Hist. de l' Eg. p. 96.   [17] Ib. p. 146.

Before
CHRIST
cir. 787. away captive the whole captivity, [p] to deliver *them* up to Edom:

[p] ver. 9.

7 [q] But I will send a fire on the wall of Gaza, which shall devour the palaces thereof: Before
CHRIST
cir. 787. [q] Jer. 47. 1.

doubtless by giving refuge to the Anakim, who, after Joshua had expelled them *from Hebron* and neighboring cities, *and the mountains of Judah and Israel, remained in Gaza, in Gath, and in Ashdod* [1]. Its situation, as the first station for land-commerce to and from Egypt, whether toward Tyre and Sidon, or Damascus and the upper Euphrates, or towards Petra, probably aggrandized it early. Even when the tide of commerce has been diverted into other channels, its situation has been a source of great profit. A fertile spot, touching upon a track through a desert, it became a mart for caravans, even those which passed, on the pilgrim-route to Mekka, uniting traffic with their religion Where the five cities are named together as unconquered, Gaza is mentioned first, then Ashdod [2]. Samson, after he had betrayed his strength, was *brought down to Gaza* [3], probably as being their strongest fortress, although the furthest from *the valley of Sorek* [4], where he was ensnared. There too was the vast temple of Dagon, which became the burying-place of so many of his worshipers. In Solomon's reign it was subject to Israel [5]. After the Philistine inroad in the time of Ahaz [6], and their capture of towns of Judah in the south and the low country, Shephelah [7], Hezekiah drove them back as far as Gaza [8], without apparently taking it. Its prince was defeated by Sargon [9], whose victory over Philistia Isaiah foretold [10]. Sennacherib gave to its king, together with those of Ascalon and Ekron [11], "fortified and other towns which" he "had spoiled," avowedly to weaken Judah; "so as to make his (Hezekiah's) country small;" probably also as a reward for hostility to Judah. Greek authors speak of it, as "a very large city of Syria [12]," "a great city [13]." Like other cities of old, it was, for fear of pirates, built at some distance from the sea (Arrian says "2½ miles"), but had a port called, like that of Ascalon [14], Maiuma [15], which itself too in Christian times became a place of importance [16].

Because they carried away the whole captivity ; lit. *a complete captivity ;* complete, but for evil ; a captivity in which none were spared, none left behind ; old or young, woman or child ; but a whole population (whatever its

extent) was swept away. Such an inroad of the Philistines is related in the 'time of Jehoram [17].

To deliver them up to Edom ; lit. *to shut them up to Edom,* in the power of Edom, their bitter enemy, so that they should not be able to escape, nor be restored. The hands, even if not the land, of Edom were already dyed in the blood of Jacob [18] *their brother.* "Any whither but there," probably would cry the crowd of helpless captives. It was like driving the shrinking flock of sheep to the butcher's shambles, reeking with the gore of their companions. Yet therefore were they driven there to the slaughter. Open markets there were for Jewish slaves in abundance. "Sell us, only not to slaughter." "Spare the greyheaded ;" "spare my child," would go up in the ears of those, who, though enemies, understood their speech. But no! Such was the compact of Tyre and Philistia and Edom against the people of God. Not one was to be spared ; it was to be a *complete captivity ;* and that, to Edom. The bond was fulfilled. *Whoso stoppeth his ears at the cry of the poor, he too shall cry and shall not be heard* [19]. Joel mentions the like sin of the Philistines and Phœnicians, and foretold its punishment [20]. That in the reign of Jehoram is the last which Scripture mentions, but was not therefore, of necessity or probably, the last. Holy Scripture probably relates only the more notable of those border-raids. Unrepented sin is commonly renewed. Those strong Philistine fortresses must have given frequent, abundant opportunity for such inroads ; as now too it is said in Arabia, "the harvest is to the stronger;" and while small protected patches of soil in Lebanon, Hauran, &c. are cultivated, the open fertile country often lies uncultivated [21], since it would be cultivated only for the marauder. Amos renews the sentence of Joel, forewarning them that, though it seemed to tarry, it would come.

7. *But* lit. *and.* Thus had Gaza done, *and* thus would God do ; *I will send a fire upon Gaza.* The sentence on Gaza stands out, probably in that it was first in power and in sin. It was the merchant-city of the five ; the caravans parted from it or passed

[1] Josh. xi. 21-23.   [2] Josh. xiii. 3.   [3] Jud. xvi. 21.
[4] Ib. 4.   Its situation was marked in S. Jerome's time, by a "village" named from it "Capharsorech," village of Sorech, "N. of Eleutheropolis near Saraa [Zorah Jud. xiii. 2.] whence Samson was." de loc. Hebr.   [5] 1 K. iv. 21.   [6] 2 Chr. xxviii. 18.
[7] See ab. p. 160. note 25.   [8] 2 Kgs xviii. 8.
[9] Rawl. Her ʿ 473. from Cuneif. Inscr.
[10] xiv. 29.

[11] Cuneif. Inscr. in Layard, Nin. & B. p. 144.
[12] Plut. Alex. 25.
[13] Arr. l. c.   Mela (i. 11) calls it "large and well fortified."   [14] See Reland, p. 590, note 2.
[15] lit. "Place on the sea" (in Egyptian), Quatremère in Ritt. xvi. 60.
[16] Soz. v. 3.   [17] 2 Chr. xxi. 16.   [18] Joel iii. 19.
[19] Pr. xxi. 13.   [20] iii. 4. 6.
[21] See e. g. Five years in Damasc. ii. 175.

Before
CHRIST
cir. 787.
Zeph. 2. 4. Zech. 9. 5, 6.

8 And I will cut off the inhabitant *from Ashdod,

and him that holdeth the sceptre from Ashkelon, and

Before
CHRIST
cir. 787.

through it ; and so this sale of the Jewish captives was ultimately effected through them. First in sin, first in punishment. Gaza was strong by nature and by art. "The access to it also," Arrian notices [1], "lay through deep sand." We do not hear of its being taken, except in the first times of Israel under the special protection of God [2], or by great conquerors. All Philistia, probably, submitted to David ; we hear of no special conquest of its towns [3]. Its siege cost Alexander 2 months [4], with all the aid of the engines with which he had taken Tyre, and the experience which he had there gained. The Egyptian accounts state, that when besieged by Tothmosis III. it capitulated [5]. Thenceforth, it had submitted neither to Egypt nor Assyria. Yet Amos declared absolutely, that Gaza should be destroyed by fire, and it was so. Sennacherib first, then, after Jeremiah had foretold anew the destruction of Gaza, Ashkelon, and the Philistines, Pharaoh Necho *smote Gaza* [6]. Yet who, with human foresight only, would undertake to pronounce the destruction of a city so strong?

8. *And I will cut off the inhabitant from Ashdod.* Ashdod, as well as Ekron, have their names from their strength ; Ashdod, "the mighty," like Valentia ; Ekron, "the firm-rooted." The title of Ashdod implied that it was powerful to inflict as to resist. It may have meant, "the waster." It too was eminent in its idolatry. The ark, when taken, was first placed in its Dagon-temple [7] ; and, perhaps, in consequence, its lord is placed first of the five, in recounting the trespass-offerings which they sent to the Lord [8]. Ashdod (Azotus in the N. T. now a village, Esdud or Shdood [9],) lay 34 or 36 miles from Gaza [10], on the great route from Egypt Northward, on that which now too is most used even to Jerusalem. Ashkelon lay to the left of the road, near the sea, rather more than half-way. Ekron (Akir, now a village of 50 mud-houses [11],) lay a little to

the right of the road North-ward from Gaza to Lydda (in the same latitude as Jamnia, Jabneel) on the road from Ramleh to Beit Jibrin (Eleutheropolis). Ekron, the furthest from the sea, lay only 15 miles from it. They were then a succession of fortresses, strong from their situation, which could molest any army, which should come along their coast. Transversely, in regard to Judah, they enclosed a space parallel to most of Judah and Benjamin. Ekron, which by God's gift was the Northern line of Judah [12], is about the same latitude as Ramah in Benjamin ; Gaza, the same as Carmel (Kurmul). From Gaza lay a straight road to Jerusalem ; but Ashkelon too, Ashdod, and Ekron lay near the heads of valleys, which ran up to the hill-country near Jerusalem [13]. This system of rich valleys, in which, either by artificial irrigation or natural absorption, the streams which ran from the mountains of Judah westward fertilised the corn-fields of Philistia, afforded equally a ready approach to Philistine marauders into the very heart of Judah. The Crusaders had to crown with castles the heights in a distant circle around Ashkelon [14], in order to restrain the incursions of the Mohammedans. On such occasions doubtless, the same man-stealing was often practised on lesser scales, which here, on a larger scale, draws down the sentence of God. Gath, much further inland, probably formed a centre to which these maritime towns converged, and united their system of inroads on Judah.

These five cities of Philistia had each its own petty king (Seren, our "axle"). But all formed one whole ; all debated and acted together on any great occasion ; as in the plot against Samson [15], the sacrifice to Dagon in triumph over him, where they perished [16] ; the inflictions on account of the ark [17] ; the great attack on Israel [18], which God defeated at Mizpeh ; the battle when Saul fell, and the dismissal of David [19]. The cities divided their idolatry also, in a manner, between

[1] l. c. [2] Jud. i. 1, 2, 18. [3] 2 Sam. viii. 1.
[4] Jos. Ant. xi. 8, 4. Arrian's description of the siege implies a longer time.
[5] "He entered this place by combat, by force, and by convention," Karnac Inscr. in Brugsch, p. 96, after Birch.
[6] Jer. xlvii. 1. [7] 1 Sam. v. 1-7. [8] Ib. vi. 17.
[9] Kinnear, Kairo, &c. p. 214. Ali bey, "Zedoud." Travels, ii. 208. Ritt. xvi. 90.
[10] Reland, p. 608. from Itin. Anton. and Hieros. and Diod. Sic.
[11] Porter, Handb. 275.
[12] Josh. xv. 11.
[13] Ashkelon, at the head of Wadi Simsim which joins on to the Wady el Hasy and drains all the country round Beit Jibrin and Tel-es-Safieh (Rob. ii. 48, 9) which reaches on beyond Ajjar (Ritt. xvi.

68) near Yarmuth. Ashdod, at the head of the valley called from it, meeting the valley of Ashkelon at Beit Jibrin. (Ritt. 91.) Ekron near the Wady-es-Surrar, the trunk of the system of valleys in N. Philistia, reaching on into the mountains of Judah, and ramifying greatly. (Ritt. 102, 3.)
[14] viz. Blanche Garde, Tel-es-Safieh. (Robinson, ii. 31, 32.) South of this, Beit-Jibrin (Eleutheropolis) on the road from Gaza; (Rob. ii. 28, 9. This was fortified by the Turks probably to restrain Bedaween incursions, as late as A. D. 1551. Robins. Ib. 25.) Castellum Arnaldi at Beit Nube on the Ramleh road to Jerusalem, (Ritter, xvi. 92, 3) and Ibelin (Jamnia, or Yebna) on the North. (Rob. Ib. 66. note 5.) [15] Jud. xvi. 5, 8, 18. [16] Ib. 23, 27, 30.
[17] 1 Sam. v. 8, 11. vi. 4, 12, 1C, 18. [18] Ib. vii. 7.
[19] Ib. xxxi. 2, 6, 7. 1 Chr. xii. 19.

I will ᵃturn mine hand ‖ against Ekron: and ᵗthe

ᵃ Ps. 81. 14.   ᵗ Jer. 47. 4. Ezek. 25. 16.

them, Ashdod being the chief seat of the worship of Dagon[1], Ashkelon, of the corresponding worship of Derceto[2] the fish-goddess, the symbol of the passive principle in re-production. Ekron was the seat of the worship of Baalzebub and his oracle, whence he is called "*the* god of Ekron[3]." Gaza, even after it had become an abode of Greek idolatry and had seven temples of Greek gods, still retained its worship of its god Marna ("our Lord") as the chief[4]. It too was probably "nature[5]," and to its worship they were devoted. All these cities were as one; all formed one state; all were one in their sin; all were to be one in their punishment. So then for greater vividness, one part of the common infliction is related of each, while in fact, according to the wont of Prophetic diction, what is said of each is said of all. King and people were to be cut off from all; all were to be consumed with fire in war; on all God would, as it were, *turn* (lit. *bring back*) *His Hand*, visiting them anew, and bringing again the same punishment upon them: In truth these destructions came upon them, again and again, through Sargon, Hezekiah, Pharaoh, Nebuchadnezzar, Alexander, the Maccabees.

Ashdod. Uzziah about this time *brake down its walls and built cities about*[6] it, to protect his people from its inroads. It recovered, and was subsequently besieged and taken by Tartan, the Assyrian General under Sargon[7] (about B. C. 716). Somewhat later, it sustained the longest siege in man's knowlege, for 29 years, from Psammetichus[8] king of Egypt (about B. C. 635). Whence, probably Jeremiah, while he speaks of Ashkelon, Gaza, Ekron, mentions *the remnant of Ashdod*[9] only. Yet, after the captivity, it seems to have been the first Philistine city, so that the Philistines were called Ashdodites[10], and their dialect Ashdodite[11]. They were still hostile to the Jews[10]. The war, in which Judas Maccabæus spoiled Ashdod and other Philistine cities[12], was a defensive war against a war of extermination. "The nations round about[13]," it is said at the beginning of the account of that year's campaign, "thought to destroy the generation of

Jacob that was among them, and thereupon they began to slay and destroy the people." Jonathan, the brother of Judas, "set fire to Azotus and the cities round about it[14]," after a battle under its walls, to which his enemies had challenged him. The temple of Dagon in it was a sort of citadel[15].

Ashkelon is mentioned as a place of strength, when by the great conqueror, Raamses II. Its resolute defence and capture are represented, with its name as a city of Canaanites, on a monument of Karnac[16]. Its name most naturally signifies "hanging." This suits very well with the site of its present ruins, which "hang" on the side of the theatre or arc of hills, whose base is the sea. This, however, probably was not its ancient site. [17] Its name occurs in the wars of the Maccabees, but rather as submitting readily[18]. Perhaps the inhabitants had been changed in the intervening period. Antipater, the Edomite father of Herod, courted, we are told[19], "the Arabs and the Ascalonites and the Gazites." "Toward the Jews their neighbors, the inhabitants of the Holy Land," Philo says[20] to the Roman emperor, "the Ascalonites have an irreconcilable aversion, which will come to no terms." This abiding hatred[21] burst out at the beginning of the war with the Romans, in which Jerusalem perished. The Ascalonites massacred 2500 Jews dwelling among them[22]. The Jews "fired Ascalon and utterly destroyed Gaza[23]."

Ekron was apparently not important enough in itself to have any separate history. We hear of it only as given by Alexander Balas "with the borders thereof in possession[24]" to Jonathan the Maccabee. The valley of Surâr gave the Ekronites a readier entrance into the centre of Judæa, than Ascalon or Ashdod had. In S. Jerome's time, it had sunk to "a very large village."

The residue of the Philistines shall perish. This has been thought to mean *the rest*[25], i. e. Gath, (not mentioned by name any more as having ceased to be of any account[26]) and the towns, dependent on those chief cities[27]. The common (and, with a proper name, universal[28]) meaning of the idiom is, *the rem-*

[1] See p. 162.   [2] Herod. i. 105 Diod. ii. 4.
[3] 2 Kgs i. 2, 3, 16.
[4] Vit. S. Porph. Gaz. c. 9 (in Act. Sanct. v. 655.)
Rel. p. 793. See also S. Jer. in Is. 17. Ep. ad Læt.
[5] See Movers, Phœn. i. pp. 662, 3.
[6] 2 Chr. xxvi. 6.   [7] Is. xx. 1.
[8] Herod. ii. 157.   [9] Jer. xxv. 20.   [10] Neh. iv. 7.
[11] Ib. xiii. 24.   [12] 1 Macc. v. 68.   [13] Ib. 1, 2.
[14] Ib. x. 82, 4.   [15] Ib. 83.
[16] Brugsch, Hist. de l 'Eg. p. 146.
[17] See on Zeph. ii. 4.   [18] 1 Macc. x. 86. xi. 60.
[19] Jos. Ant. xiv. 1. 3.
[20] Leg. ad Cai. p. 1021. Rel. p. 587.

[21] Jos. B. S. iii. 2. 2.   [22] Ib. ii. 18. 5.
[23] Ib. 1. This occurred first, unless the account
be a summary.   [24] 1 Macc. x. 89.
[25] as in Jer. xxxix. 3. Neh. vii. 72.
[26] See on Am. vi. 3.   [27] So S. Jer. Theod.
[28] as, "the remnant of Judah," Jer. xl. 15. xlii. 15.
xliv. 28; "the remnant of Jerusalem," Jer. xxiv. 8;
"the remnant of Israel," Is. xlvi. 3. Jer. vi. 9. xxxi.
7. Ez. ix. 8. Mic. ii. 12; "of Jacob," Mic. v. 6, 7, (7, 8
Eng.); "the remnant of the house of Judah," Zeph.
ii. 7; "the remnant of Mine inheritance," 2 K. xxi.
14; "of My flock," Jer. xxiii. 3; "the remnant
which is left," Is. xxxvii. 4; "go forth a remnant,"

Before
C H R I S T
cir. 787.
remnant of the Philistines shall perish, saith the Lord GOD.

u Is. 23. 1.
Jer. 47. 4.
Ezek. 26, &
27, & 28.
Joel 3. 4. 5.
9 ¶ Thus saith the LORD; For three transgressions of u Tyrus, and for four, I will not turn

away *the punishment there*of ; x because they delivered up the whole captivity to Edom, and remembered not † the brotherly covenant ;

Before
C H R I S T
cir. 787.

x ver. 6.
† Heb. *the
covenant of
brethren,*
2 Sam. 5. 11.
1 Kings 5. 1.
&. 9. 11–14.

10 y But I will send a y ver. 4, 7, &c.

nant, those who remain over after a first destruction. The words then, like those just before, *I will bring again my hand against Ekron,* foretell a renewal of those first judgments. The political strength which should survive one desolation should be destroyed in those which should succeed it. In tacit contrast with the promises of mercy to the remnant of Judah[1], Amos foretells that judgment after judgment should fall upon Philistia, until the Philistines ceased to be any more a people; as they did.

9. The last crowning sin, for which judgment is pronounced on Tyre, is the same as that of Philistia, and probably was enacted in concert with it. In Tyre, there was this aggravation, that it was a violation of a previous treaty and friendship. It was not a covenant only, nor previous friendliness only; but a specific covenant, founded on friendship which they forgat and brake. If they retained the memory of Hiram's intercourse with David and Solomon, it was a sin against light too. After David had expelled the Jebusites from Jerusalem[2], *Hiram King of Tyre sent messengers to David, and cedar trees and carpenters and masons; and they built David a house.* The Philistines contrariwise invaded him[3]. This recognition of him by Hiram was to David a proof[4], *that the Lord had established him king over Israel, and that He had exalted his kingdom for His people, Israel's sake.* Hiram seems, then, to have recognized something super-human in the exaltation of David. *Hiram was ever a lover of David*[5]. This friendship he continued to Solomon, and recognized his God as *the* God. Scripture embodies the letter of Hiram[6]; *Because the Lord hath loved his people, He hath made thee king over them. Blessed be the Lord God of Israel, that made heaven and earth, who hath given to David a wise son—that he might build an house for the Lord.* He must have known then the value which the pious Israelites attached to the going up to that

temple. A later treaty, offered by Demetrius Nicator to Jonathan, makes detailed provision that the Jews should have " † the feasts and sabbaths and new moons and the solemn days and the three days before the feast and the three days after the feast, as days of immunity and freedom." The three days before the feast were given, that they might go up to the feast. Other treaties guarantee to the Jews religious privileges[8]. A treaty between Solomon and Hiram, which should not secure any religious privileges needed by Jews in Hiram's dominion, is inconceivable. But Jews were living among the Zidonians[9]. The treaty also, made between Hiram and Solomon, was subsequent to the arrangement by which Hiram was to supply cedars to Solomon, and Solomon to furnish the corn of which Hiram stood in need[10]. *The Lord gave Solomon wisdom, as He promised him*[11]; and, as a fruit of that wisdom, *there was peace between Hiram and Solomon; and they two made a covenant*[12]. The terms of that covenant are not there mentioned; but a covenant involves conditions. It was not a mere covenant; but a distinct *covenant,* sanctioned by religious rites and by sacrifice[12]. This *brotherly covenant* Tyre *remembered not,* when they delivered up to Edom *a complete captivity,* all the Jews who came into their hands. It seems then, that that covenant had an especial provision against selling them away from their own land. This same provision other people made[13] for love of their country or their homes; the Jews, for love of their religion. This covenant Tyre remembered not, but brake. They knew doubtless why Edom sought to possess the Israelites; but the covetousness of Tyre fed the cruelty of Edom, and God punished the broken appeal to Himself.

10. *I will send a fire upon the wall of Tyre.* Tyre had long ere this become tributary to Assyria. Asshur-dan-ipal (about B. C.

Ib. 32; "of Moab," Is. xv. 9; "of Philistia," Is. xiv. 30; and in Amos himself, "the remnant of Joseph," v. 15; "the remnant of Edom," ix. 12.
·1 See ab. on Joel ii. 32.
2 Sam. v. 11.   3 Ib. 17.   4 Ib. 12.   5 1 Kgs v. 1.
6 2 Chr. ii. 11. *Hiram answered in writing, which he sent to Solomon.* 7 1 Macc. x. 34. Jos. Ant. xiii. 2, 3.
8 1 Macc. xi. 34. Jos. Ant. xiii. 4, 9. renewed to Simon, 1 Macc. xiii. 35–40.
9 See on Joel iii. 6.

10 1 Kgs v. 7–11.   11 Ib. 12.   12 יכרתו ברית.
13 Strabo xii. 3, 4. "This too is said, that the Milesians who first founded Heraclea constrained the Mariandyni, who possessed it before, to act as serfs, and to be liable eyen to be sold by them, *but not beyond their borders (for they covenanted as to this),* in likeway as the so-called Mnoan-union became serfs to the Cretans, and the Penestæ to the Thessalians." quoted by Movers, Phœn. ii. 1. pp. 313, 4. who so interprets Amos.

Before
C H R I S T
cir. 787.
fire on the wall of Tyrus, which shall devour t h e palaces thereof.

11 ¶ Thus saith t h e Lord : For three trans-gressions of ᶻ Edom, and

Before
C H R I S T
cir. 787.

ᶻ Is. 21. 11. & 34. 5.
Jer. 49. 8. &c.
Ezek. 25. 12, 13, 14. & 35. 2, &c. Joel 3. 19. Obad.
1, &c. Mal. 1. 4.

930,) records his " [1] taking tribute from the kings of all the chief Phœnician cities as Tyre, Sidon, Biblus and Aradus." His son Shalmanubar records his taking tribute from them in his 21st year [2] about 880, B.C.), as did Ivalush III. [3], and after this time Tiglath-pileser II. [4], the same who took Damascus and carried off its people, as also the East and North of Israel. The Phœnicians had aided Benhadad, in his unsuccessful war or rebellion against Shalmanubar [5], but their city had received no hurt. There was nothing, in the time of Amos, to indicate any change of policy in the Assyrian conquerors. They had been content hitherto with tribute from their distant dependencies; they had spared them, even when in arms against them. Yet Amos says absolutely in the name of God, *I will send a fire upon the wall of Tyre*, and the fire did fall, first from Shalamaneser or Sargon his successor, and then from Nebuchadnezzar. The Tyrians (as is men's wont) inserted in their annals their successes, or the successful resistance which they made for a time. They relate that " [6] Elulæus, king of Tyre, reduced the Kittiæans (Cypriotes) who had revolted. The king of Assyria invaded all Phœnicia, and returned, having made peace with all. Sidon and Ace and old Tyre, and many other cities revolted from the Tyrians, and sur-rendered to the king of Assyria. Tyre then not obeying, the king returned against them, the Phœnicians manning 60 ships for him." These, he says, were dispersed, 500 prisoners taken; the honor of Tyre intensi-fied. " The king of Assyria, removing, set. guards at the river and aqueducts, to hinder the Tyrians from drawing water. This they endured for 5 years, drinking from the wells sunk." The Tyrian annalist does not relate the sequel. He does not venture to say that the Assyrian King gave up the siege, but, having made the most of their resistance, breaks off the account. The Assyrian in-scriptions say, that Sargon took Tyre [7], and received tribute from Cyprus, where a monu-ment has been found, bearing the name of Sargon [8]. It is not probable that a monarch, who took Samaria and Ashdod, received trib-ute from Egypt, the "Chief of Saba," and

"Queen of the Arabs," overran Hamath, Tubal, Cilicia, Armenia, reduced Media, should have returned baffled, because Tyre stood out a blockade for 5 years. Since Sar-gon wrested from Tyre its newly-recovered Cyprus, its insular situation would not have protected itself. Nebuchadnezzar took it after a thirteen years' siege [9].

11. *Edom.* God had impressed on Israel its relation of brotherhood to Edom. Moses expressed it to Edom himself [10], and, after the suspicious refusal of Edom to allow Israel to march on the highway through his territory, he speaks as kindly of him [11], as before ; *And when we passed by from our brethren, the children of Esau.* It was the unkindness of worldly politics, and was forgiven. The religious love of the Egyptian and the Edomite was, on distinct grounds, made part of the law. [12] *Thou shalt not abhor an Edomite; for he is thy brother : thou shalt not abhor an Egyptian; be-cause thou wast a stranger in his land.* The grandchild of an Egyptian or of an Edomite was religiously to become as an Israelite [13]. Not a foot of Edomite territory was Israel to appropriate, however provoked. It was God's gift to Edom, as much as Canaan to Israel. [14] *They shall be afraid of you, and ye shall take exceeding heed to yourselves.* Quarrel not with them, for I will give you of their land, no, not so much as the treading of the sole of the foot; for I have given Mount Seir unto Esau for a posses-sion. From this time until that of Saul, there is no mention of Edom; only that the Maonites and the Amalekites, who oppressed Israel [15], were kindred tribes with Edom. The increasing strength of Israel in the early days of Saul seems to have occasioned a conspiracy against him, such as Asaph after-ward complains of [16] ; *They have said, come and let us cut them off from* being *a nation, that the name of Israel may be no more in remembrance. For they have consulted together with one consent, they are confederate against Thee ; the taberna-cles of Edom and the Ishmaelites ; of Moab and the Hagarenes ; Gebal and Ammon and Amalek ; the Philistines with the inhabitants of Tyre ; Assur also is joined with them ; they have been an arm to the children of Lot.* Such a combi-nation began probably in the time of Saul. [17] *He fought against all his enemies on every side ;*

[1] Rawl. Herod. T. i. Ess. vii. § 11. from Cuneiform Inscr.
[2] Rawl. Ib. § 14. p. 463.   [3] Rawl. Ib. § 19. p. 467.
[4] Rawl. § 22. p. 470.   [5] Rawl. § 15. p. 464.
[6] Menander in Jos. Ant.ix. 14. 2.
[7] Rawl, § 24. p. 474.
[8] "The statue of Sargon, now in the Berlin Mu-

seum, brought from Idalium, commemorates the Cyprian expedition " Rawl. Ib.
[9] Ezek. xxvi. 7-12, see on Is. xxiii.
[10] Nu. xx. 14. *thus saith thy brother Israel.*
[11] Deut. ii. 8.   [12] Ib. xxiii. 7.   [13] Ib. 8.
[14] Ib. ii. 4, 5.   [15] Jud. vi. 3. x. 12.
[16] Ps. lxxxiii. 4–8.   [17] 1 Sam. xiv. 47.

for four, I will not turn away *the punishment* there- of; because he did pursue
ᵃh i s brother ᵇwith t h e

ᵃ Gen. 27. 41. Deut. 23. 7. Mal. 1. 2.　ᵇ 2 Chr. 28. 17.

against Moab, and against the children of Ammon, and against the king of Edom, and against the Philistines. They were *his enemies,* and that, round about, encircling Israel, as hunters did their prey. *Edom,* on the S. and S. E.; *Moab* and *Ammon* on the East; the Syrians of *Zobah* on the N.; the Philistines on the W. enclosed him as in a net, and he repulsed them one by one. *Whichever way he turned, he worsted* [1] them. It follows [2], *he delivered Israel out of the hands of them that spoiled them.* The aggression was from Edom, and that in combination with old oppressors of Israel, not from Saul [3]. The wars of Saul and of David were defensive wars. Israel was recovering from a state of depression, not oppressing. *The valley of salt* [4], where David defeated the Edomites, was also doubtless within the borders of Judah, since *the city of salt* was [5]; and the valley of salt was probably near the remarkable "mountain of salt," $5\frac{3}{5}$ miles long, near the end of the Dead Sea [6], which, as being Canaanite, belonged to Israel. It was also far north of Kadesh, which was *the utmost boundary* of Edom [7]. From that Psalm too of mingled thanksgiving and prayer which David composed after the victory, *in the valley of salt* [8], it appears that, even after that victory, David's army had not yet entered Edom. [9] *Who will bring me into the strong city? who will lead me into Edom?* That same Psalm speaks of grievous suffering before, *in* which God had *cast them off* and *scattered* them; *made the earth tremble and cleft it;* so that *it reeled* [10]. Joab too had *returned* from the war in the North against the Syrians of Mesopotamia, to meet the Edomites. Whether in alliance with the Syrians, or taking advantage of the absence of the main army there, the Edomites had inflicted some heavy blow on Israel; a battle in which Abishai slew 18,000 men [11] had been indecisive. The Edomites were repulsed by the rapid countermarch of Joab. The victory, according to the Psalm, was still incomplete [12]. David put *garrisons in Edom* [13], to restrain them from further outbreaks. Joab avenged the wrong of the Edomites, conformably to his character [14]; but the fact that *the captain of the host* had *to go up to bury the slain* [15], shews the extent of the deadly blow, which he so fearfully avenged.

[1] יָרֵשׁ.　[2] ver. 48.
[3] as has often been carelessly assumed.
[4] 2 Sam. viii. 13.　[5] Josh. xv. 62.
[6] Robinson, ii. 108, 9.　[7] Nu. xx. 16.
[8] Ps. lx. title.　[9] Ib. 9.　[10] Ib. 1–3, 10.
[11] 1 Chr. xviii. 12.　[12] Ib. 1, 5, 9–12.
[13] 2 Sam. viii. 14.　[14] 1 Kgs xi. 16.
[15] Ib. 15. It should be rendered, not, *after he had slain,* but, *and he slew, &c.*

The store set by the king of Egypt on Hadad, the Edomite prince who fled to him [16], shews how gladly Egypt employed Edom as an enemy to Israel. It has been said that he rebelled and failed [17]. Else it remained under a dependent king appointed by Judah, for $1\frac{1}{2}$ century [18]. One attempt against Judah is recorded [19], when those of Mount Seir combined with Moab and Ammon against Jehoshaphat after his defeat at Ramothgilead. They had penetrated beyond Engedi [20], on the road which Arab marauders take now [21], toward the wilderness of Tekoa, when God set them against one another, and they fell by each other's hands [22]. But Jehoshaphat's prayer at this time evinces that Israel's had been a defensive warfare. Otherwise, he could not have appealed to God [23], *the children of Ammon and Moab and mount Seir, whom Thou wouldest not let Israel invade when they came out of the land of Egypt, but they turned from them, and destroyed them not, behold, they reward us, to come to cast us out of Thy possession, which Thou hast given us to inherit.* Judah held Edom by aid of garrisons, as a wild beast is held in a cage, that they might not injure them, but had taken no land from them, nor expelled them. Edom sought to cast Israel out of God's land. Revolts cannot be without bloodshed; and so it is perhaps the more probable, that the words of Joel [24], *for the violence against the children of Judah, because they have shed innocent blood in their land,* relate to a massacre of the Jews, when Esau revolted from Jehoram [25]. We have seen, in the Indian Massacres, how every living being of the ruling power may, on such occasions, be sought out for destruction. Edom gained its independence, and Jehoram, who sought to recover his authority, escaped with his life by cutting through the Edomite army by night [26]. Yet in Amaziah's time they were still on the offensive, since the battle wherein he defeated them, was again *in the valley of salt* [27]. Azariah, in whose reign Amos prophesied, regained Elath from them, the port for the Indian trade [28]. Of the origin of that war, we know nothing; only the brief words as to the Edomite invasion against Ahaz [29], *and yet again had the Edomites come, and smitten in Judah, and carried captive a captivity,* attest previous and, it may be,

[16] 1 Kgs xi. 14–20.　[17] Jos. Ant. viii. 7. 6.
[18] 1 Kgs xxii. 47.　2 Kgs iii. 9 sqq.
[19] 2 Chr. xx. 10.
[20] Ib. 2, 16, 20.
[21] Rob. i. 508.　[22] ver. 22–24.
[23] Ib. 10, 11.　[24] iii. 19.
[25] 2 Kgs viii. 20–22.　[26] Ib. 21.
[27] Ib. xiv. 7. 2 Chr. xxv. 11, 14.
[28] 2 Chr. xxvi. 2.　[29] Ib. xxviii. 17.

sword, and † did cast off all pity, ᶜ and his anger

† Heb. *corrupted his compassions.*   ᶜ Ezek. 35. 5.

did tear perpetually, and he kept his wrath for ever:

---

habitual invasions. For no *one* such invasion had been named. It may probably mean, "they did *yet again,* what they had been in the habit of doing." But in matter of history, the prophets, in declaring the grounds of God's judgments, supply much which it was not the object of the historical books to relate. *They* are histories of God's dealings with His people, His chastisements of them or of His sinful instruments in chastising them. Rarely, except when His supremacy was directly challenged, do they record the ground of the chastisements of heathen nations. Hence, to those who look on the surface only, the wars of the neighboring nations against Israel look but like the alternations of peace and war, victory and defeat, in modern times. The Prophets draw up the veil, and shew us the secret grounds of man's misdeeds and God's judgments. *Because he did pursue his brother.* The characteristic sin of Edom, and its punishment are one main subject of the prophecy of Obadiah, inveterate malice contrary to the law of kindred. Eleven hundred years had passed since the birth of their forefathers, Jacob and Esau. But, with God, eleven hundred years had not worn out kindred. He Who willed to knit together all creation, men and angels, in one in Christ [1], and, as a means of union [2], *made of one blood all nations of men for to dwell on all the face of the earth,* used all sorts of ways to impress this idea of brotherhood. *We* forget relationship mostly in the third generation, often sooner; and we think it strange when a nation long retains the memories of those relationships [3]. God, in His law, stamped on His people's minds those wider meanings. To slay a man was to slay a *brother* [4]. Even the outcast Canaan was a *brother* [5] to Shem and Ham. Lot speaks to the men of Sodom amidst their iniquities, *my brethren* [6]; Jacob so salutes those unknown to him [7]. The descendants of Ishmael and Isaac were to be brethren; so were those of Esau and Jacob [8]. The brotherhood of blood was not to wear out, and there was to be a brotherhood of love also [9]. Every Israelite was a brother [10]; each tribe was a brother to every other [11]; the force of the appeal was remembered, even when passion ran high [12]. It enters habitually into the Divine legislation. *Thou shall open thy hand wide unto thy brother* [13]; *if thy brother, a*

Hebrew, sell himself to thee [14]; *thou shalt not see thy brother's ox or his sheep go astray and hide thyself from them* [15]; *if thy brother be waxen poor, then shalt thou relieve him,* though *a stranger and a sojourner, that he may live with thee* [16]. In that same law, Edom's relationship as a brother was acknowledged. It was an abiding law that Israel was not to take Edom's land, nor to refuse to admit him into the congregation of the Lord. Edom too remembered the relation, but to hate him. The nations around Israel seem to have been little at war with one another, bound together by common hatred against God's people. Of their wars indeed we should not hear; for they had no religious interest. They would be but the natural results of the passions of unregenerate nature. Feuds there doubtless were and forays, but no attempts at permanent conquest or subdual. Their towns remain in their own possession [17]. Tyre does not invade Philistia; nor Philistia, Tyre or Edom. But all combine against Israel. The words, *did pursue his brother with the sword,* express more than is mentioned in the historical books. To *pursue* is more than to fight. They followed after, in order to destroy a remnant, *and cast off all pity,* lit. and more strongly, *corrupted his compassions, tendernesses.* Edom did violence to his natural feelings, as Ezekiel, using the same word, says of Tyre, *corrupting* [18] *his wisdom,* i. e. perverting it from the end for which God gave it, and so destroying it. Edom "steeled himself," as we say, "against his better feelings," "his better nature," "deadened" them. But so they do not live again. Man is not master of the life and death of his feelings, any more than of his natural existence. He can destroy; he cannot re-create. And he does, so far, *corrupt,* decay, do to death, his own feelings, whenever, in any signal instance, he acts against them. Edom was not simply unfeeling. He destroyed all *his tender yearnings* [19] over suffering, such as God has put into every human heart, until it destroys them. Ordinary anger is satisfied and slaked by its indulgence; malice is fomented and fed and invigorated by it. Edom ever, as occasion came, gratified his anger; *his anger did tear continually ;* yet, though raging as some wild ravening animal, without control, *he kept his wrath for ever,* not within bounds, but to let it loose anew. He retained it when he ought

---

[1] Eph. i. 10.   [2] Acts xvii. 26.   [3] as the Scotch.
[4] Gen. ix. 5.   [5] Ib. 25.   [6] Ib. xix. 7.
[7] Ib. xxix. 4.   [8] Ib. xvi. 12. xxv. 18.
[9] Ib. xxvii. 29, 37.
[10] Ex. ii. 11. iv. 18; the king and his people, Deut. xvii. 20. 1 Chr. xxviii. 2.

[11] Deut. x. 9. xviii. 2. Jud. xx. 23, 28.
[12] 2 Sam. ii. 26.   [13] Deut. xv. 11.   [14] Ib. 12.
[15] Ib. xxii. 1-4.
[16] Lev. xxv. 35-39. add Lev. xxiv. 7, 10, 14.   [17] On Moab and Edom see on ii. 1.
[18] Ez. xxviii. 17.   [19] שַׁחַת רַחֲמָיו.

| Before CHRIST cir. 787. | 12 But [d] I will send a fire upon Teman, which shall devour the palaces of Bozrah. | 13 ¶ Thus saith the LORD; For three transgressions of [e] the children of Ammon, and for four, I | Before CHRIST cir. 787. |

[d] Obad. 9, 10.

[e] Jer. 49. 1, 2. Ezek, 25. 2. Zeph. 2. 9.

to have parted with it, and let it loose when he ought to have restrained it. "What is best, when spoiled, becomes the worst," is proverbial truth. "[1] As no love wellnigh is more faithful than that of brothers, so no hatred, when it hath once begun, is more unjust, no odium fiercer. Equality stirs up and inflames the mind; the shame of giving way and the love of preeminence is the more inflamed, in that the memory of infancy and whatever else would seem to gender good will, when once they are turned aside from the right path, produce hatred and contempt." They were proverbial sayings of Heathenism, "fierce are the wars of brethren[2]," and "they who have loved exceedingly, they too hate exceedingly[2]." "[3] The Antiochi, the Seleuci, the Gryphi, the Cyziceni, when they learnt not to be all but brothers, but craved the purple and diadems, overwhelmed themselves and Asia too with many calamities."

12. *But* [*And I,* in My turn and as a consequence of these sins] *will send a fire upon Teman.* "Teman," say Eusebius and S. Jerome[4], "was a country of the princes of Edom, which had its name from Teman son of Eliphaz, son of Esau[5]. But even to this day there is a village, called Teman, about 5 (Eusebius says 15) miles from Petra, where also is a Roman garrison, from which place was Eliphaz, king of the Themanites." It is, however, probably the district which is meant, of which Bozra was then the capital. For Amos when speaking of cities, uses some word to express this, as *the palaces of Benhadad, the wall of Gaza, of Tyrus, of Rabbah;* here he simply uses the name Teman, as he does those of Moab and Judah. Amos does not mention Petra, or Selah; for Amaziah had taken it, and called it Joktheel, "which God subdued," which name it for some time retained[6].

Bozrah (lit. which cuts off approach) is mentioned, as early as Genesis[7], as the seat of one of the elective kings who, in times before Moses, reigned over Edom. It lay

then doubtless in Idumea itself, and is quite distinct from the Bozrah of Hauran or Auranitis, from which S. Jerome also distinguishes it[4]. "There is another Bosor also, a city of Esau, in the mountains of Idumea, of which Isaiah speaks." There is yet a small village of the like name (Busaira "the little Bozrah") which "appears," it is said[8], "to have been in ancient times a considerable city, if we may judge from the ruins which surround the village." It has now "some 50 houses, and stands on an elevation, on the summit of which a small castle has been built." The name however, "little Bozrah," indicates the existence of a "great Bozrah," with which its name is contrasted, and is not likely to have been the place itself[9]. Probably the name was a common one, "the strong place" of its neighborhood[10]. The Bozrah of Edom is either that little village, or is wholly blotted out.

13. *Ammon.* Those who receive their existence under circumstances, in any way like those of the first forefathers of Moab and Ammon, are known to be under physical as well as intellectual and moral disadvantages. Apart from the worst horrors, on the one side reason was stupefied, on the other it was active in sin. He who imprinted His laws on nature, has annexed the penalty to the infraction of those laws. It is known also how, even under the Gospel, the main character of a nation remains unchanged. The basis of natural character, upon which grace has to act, remains, under certain limits, the same. Still more in the unchanging East. Slave-dealers know of certain hereditary good or evil qualities in non-Christian nations in whom they traffic. What marvel then that Ammon and Moab retained the stamp of their origin, in a sensual or passionate nature? Their choice of their idols grew out of this original character and aggravated it. They chose them gods like themselves, and worsened themselves by copying these idols of their sinful nature. The chief god of the fierce Ammon was Milchom or Molech, the

[1] F. Petrarch. Dial. ii. 45. Bas. 1554. Lap.
[2] in Arist. Pol. vii. 7. Lap.
[3] Plut. de frat. amore. 1b.
[4] de locis Hebr.
[5] Gen. xxxvi. 11, 15.
[6] 2 Kgs xiv. 7.   [7] xxxvi. 33.
[8] Burckhardt, Syria, 407.
[9] as has been assumed since Robinson, ii. 167.
[10] i. "Bezer in the wilderness" or "plain" in Reuben opposite to Jericho, one of the cities of refuge. (Deut. iv. 43. Josh. xx. 8.) ii. Bosor, a "strong and great city" of Gilead. (1 Macc. v. 26,

36. Ant. xii. 8. 4.) iii. Besara, on the confines of Ptolemais, 2½ miles from Geba (Jos. Vit. § 24.) iv. Bozrah of Moab, (Jer. xlviii. 24.) The Bostra which the Romans rebuilt, 24 miles from Edrei, which became the Metropolis of Arabia, and, in Arabic times of Hauran, (see the description of the remains, Porter, Five years, ii. 140 sqq.) lay too far North to be any of these. It is probably a corruption of בְעַשְׁתְּרֹה, "house of Ashtoreth" in Manasseh (Jos. xxi. 27. see Reland, v. Bostra p. 666.); and Bosorra (distinct from Bosor, 1 Macc.v. 26, 28,) may be another corruption of the name.

Before
CHRIST
cir. 787.
‖ Or, *divided the
mountains.*
ᶠ Hos. 13. 16.

will not turn away *the
punishment* thereof; be-
cause they have ‖ ᶠripped

up the women with child
of Gilead, ᵍthat they might
enlarge their border :

Before
CHRIST
cir. 787.

ᵍ Jer. 49. 1.

principle of destruction, who was appeased
with sacrifices of living children, given to the
fire to devour. Moab, beside its idol Chemosh, had the degrading worship of Baal
Peor ¹, re-productiveness the counterpart of
destruction. And, so, in fierce or degrading
rites, they worshiped the power which belongs to God, to create, or to destroy. Moab
was the seducer of Israel at Shittim ¹. Ammon, it has been noticed, shewed at different
times a peculiar wanton ferocity ². Such was
the proposal of Nahash to the men of Jabesh-
Gilead, when offering to surrender ³, *that I
may thrust out all your right eyes and lay it* for
a reproach unto all Israel. Such was the insult
to David's messengers of peace, and the hir-
ing of the Syrians in an aggressive war
against David ⁴. Such, again, was this war
of extermination against the Gileadites. On
Israel's side, the relation to Moab and Ammon had been altogether friendly. God recalled to Israel the memory of their common
descent, and forbade them to war against
either. He speaks of them by the name of
kindness, *the children of Lot,* the companion
and friend of Abraham. ⁵ *I will not give thee
of their land* for *a possession, because I have
given it unto the children of Lot* for *a possession.*
Akin by descent, their history had been
alike. Each had driven out a giant tribe ;
Moab, the Emim ; Ammon, the Zamzummim⁶.
They had thus possessed themselves of the
tract from the Arnon, not quite half way
down the Dead Sea on its East side, to the
Jabbok, about half way between the Dead
Sea and the Sea of Galilee ⁷. Both had been
expelled by the Amorites, and had been
driven, Moab, behind the Arnon, Ammon,
behind the *strong border* ⁸ of the upper part of
the Jabbok, what is now the Nahr Amman,
"the river of Ammon," Eastward. The
whole of what became the inheritance of the
2½ tribes, was in the hands of the Amorites,
and threatened very nearly their remaining
possessions; since, at Aroer *that is before Rab-*

bah ⁹, the Amorites were already over
against the capital of Ammon ; at the Arnon
they were but 2½ hours ¹⁰ from Ar-Moab, the
remaining capital of Moab. Israel then, in
destroying the Amorites, had been at once
avenging and rescuing Moab and Ammon;
and it is so far a token of friendliness at this
time, that, after the victory at Edrei, the
great *iron bedstead* of Og was placed *in Rabbah of the children of Ammon* ¹¹. Envy, jealousy, and fear, united them to *hire Balaam to
curse* Israel ¹², although the king of Moab was
the chief actor in this ¹³, as he was in the
seduction of Israel to idolatry ¹⁴. Probably
Moab was then, and continued to be, the more
influential or the more powerful, since in
their first invasion of Israel, the Ammonites
came as the allies of Eglon king of Moab.
*He gathered unto him the children of Ammon
and Amalek* ¹⁵. *And* they *served Eglon.* Yet
Ammon's subsequent oppression must have
been yet more grievous, since God reminds
Israel of His delivering them from the Am-
monites¹⁶, not from Moab. There we find
Ammon under a king, and in league with the
Philistines¹⁷, *crushing and crushing* ¹⁸ *for* 18
years all the children of Israel in Gilead. The
Ammonites carried a wide invasion across
the Jordan against Judah, Benjamin and
Ephraim ¹⁹, until they were subdued by
Jephthah. Moab is not named; but the king
of Ammon claims as *my land* ²⁰, the whole
which Moab and Ammon had lost to the
Amorites, and they to Israel, *from Arnon unto
Jabbok and unto Jordan* ²⁰. The range also of
Jephthah's victories included probably all
that same country from the Arnon to the
neighborhood of Rabbah of Ammon²¹.
The Ammonites, subdued then, were again
on the offensive in the fierce siege of Jabesh-
Gilead and against Saul ²². Yet it seems
that they had already taken from Israel
what they had lost to the Amorites; for
Jabesh-Gilead was beyond the Jabbok ²³ ;
and *Mizpeh of Moab,* whither David went

---

¹ Nu. xxv. 1–3.
² Grote in Smith, Bibl. Dict. v. Ammon.
³ 1 Sam. xi. 1–3.   ⁴ 2 Sam. x. 1–6.
⁵ Deut. ii. 9, 19.   ⁶ Ib. 10, 11, 20. 1.
⁷ Nu. xxi. 23–30. Of this, Moab had the part from
the Arnon to the N. of the Dead Sea, including *the
plains of Moab* (עֲרְבוֹת מוֹאָב) i. e. the part of the
valley of the Jordan on the E. side, opposite to
Jericho, the subsequent possession of Reuben.
Gilead, to the S. and E. of the Jabbok, had belonged
to Ammon, whence it is said that Moses gave to
the 2½ tribes the land *unto the border of the children
of Ammon,* (Jos. xiii. 10.) i. e. Westward, and yet
half the land of the children of Ammon, (Ib. 25.) i. e.
what they had lost to the Amorites.
⁸ Nu. xxi. 24.   ⁹ Jos. xiii. 25.

¹⁰ Porter, Handb. 302.   ¹¹ Deut. iii. 11.
¹² Ib. xxiii. 4. ¹³ Nu. xxii.–xxiv. ¹⁴ Ib. xxv. 1–3.
¹⁵ Jud. iii, 13.   ¹⁶ Ib. x. 11.   ¹⁷ Ib. 7.
¹⁸ וְיִרְעֲצוּ וַיְרֹצֲצוּ. Ib. 8. The two alliterate and
equivalent words are joined us intensive.
¹⁹ Ib. 9.   ²⁰ Ib. xi. 13.
²¹ Ib. 33. *He smote them from Aroer to Minnith,*
(Minnith was "4 miles from Heshbon on the way to
Philadelphia," i. e. Rabbah) *twenty cities and unto
Abel-keramim* "7 (Eus. 6.) miles from Rabbah." S.
Jer. If Aroer is here the best known, that by the
Arnon, the account describes one line from the
Arnon to a little beyond Heshbon and then to a place
near the Jabbok.   ²² See above on ver. 11.
²³ "6 miles from Pella on a hill towards Gerasa"
(Jerash). S. Jer. de loc. Hebr. Both places were

Before
CHRIST
cir. 787.

14 But I will kindle a fire in the wall of [h] Rab-

[h] Deut. 3. 11. 2 Sam. 12. 26. Jer. 49. 2. Ezek. 25. 5.

bah, and it shall devour the palaces thereof, [i] with

Before
CHRIST
cir. 787.

[i] ch. 2. 2.

to seek the king of Moab [1], was probably no other than the Ramoth-Mizpeh [2] of Gad, the Mizpeh [3] whence Jephthah went over to fight the Ammonites. With Hanan, king of Ammon, David sought to remain at peace, on account of some kindness, interested as it probably was, which his father Nahash had shewn him, when persecuted by Saul [4]. It was only after repeated attempts to bring an overwhelming force of the Syrians against David, that Rabbah was besieged and taken, and that awful punishment inflicted. The severity of the punishment inflicted on Moab and Ammon, in that two-thirds of the fighting men of Moab were put to death [5], and fighting men of *the cities of Ammon* [6] were destroyed by a ghastly death, so different from David's treatment of the Philistines or the various Syrians, implies some extreme hostility on their part, from which there was no safety except in their destruction. Moab and Ammon were still united against Jehoshaphat [7], and with Nebuchadnezzar against Jehoiakim [8], whom they had before sought to stir up against the king of Babylon [9]. Both profited for a time by the distresses of Israel, *magnifying* themselves *against her border* [10], and taking possession of her cities [11], after the 2½ tribes has been carried away by Tiglath-pileser. Both united in insulting Judah, and (as it appears from Ezekiel [12]) out of jealousy against its religious distinction. When some of the scattered Jews were reunited under Gedaliah, after the destruction of Jerusalem by Nebuchadnezzar, it was a king of Ammon, Baalis, who instigated Johanan to murder him [13]. When Jerusalem was to be rebuilt after the return from the captivity, Ammonites and Moabites [14], *Sanballat the Horonite* (i. e. out of Horonaim, which Moab had taken to itself [15],) *and Tobiah the servant, the Ammonite*, were chief in the opposition to it. They helped on the persecution by Antiochus [16]. Their anti-religious character, which shewed itself in the hatred of Israel and the hire of Balaam, was the ground of the exclusion of both from admission *into the congregation of the Lord forever* [17]. The seduction of Solomon by his Ammonite and Moabite wives illustrates the infectiousness of their

idolatry. While he made private chapels *for all his strange wives, to burn incense and sacrifice to their gods* [19], the most stately idolatry was that of Chemosh and Molech, the abomination of Moab and Ammon [19]. For Ashtoreth alone, besides these, did Solomon build high-places in sight of the temple of God, on a lower part of the Mount of Olives [20].

They have ripped up the women with child in Gilead. Since Elisha prophesied that Hazael would be guilty of this same atrocity, and since Gilead was the scene of his chief atrocities [21], probably Syria and Ammon were, as of old, united against Israel in a war of extermination. It was a conspiracy to displace God's people from the land which He had given them, and themselves to re-place them. The plan was effective; it was, Amos says, executed. They expelled and *inherited Gad* [22]. Gilead was desolated for the sins for which Hosea rebuked it; "blood had blood." It had been *tracked with blood* [23]; now life was sought out for destruction, even in the mother's womb. But, in the end, Israel, whose extermination Ammon devised and in part effected, survived. Ammon perished and left no memorial.

That they might enlarge their border. It was a horror, then, exercised, not incidentally here and there, or upon a few, or in sudden stress of passion, but upon system and in cold blood. We have seen lately, in the massacres near Lebanon, where male children were murdered on system, how methodically such savageness goes to work. A massacre, here and there, would not have *enlarged their border*. They must have carried on these horrors then, throughout all the lands which they wished to possess, making place for themselves by annihilating Israel, that there might be none to rise up and thrust them from their conquests, and claim their old inheritance. Such was the fruit of habitually indulged covetousness. Yet who beforehand would have thought it possible?

14. *I will kindle a fire in the wall of Rabbah.* Rabbah, lit. *the great*, called by Moses [24] *Rabbah of the children of Ammon*, and by later Greeks, *Rabathammana* [25], was a strong city

---

beyond the Jabbok. The name Jabesh, "dry," still survives in the valley *Yabes*, (the Arabic pronunciation) which, with its brook, ends in the Jordan 7 or 8 geogr. miles N. of the Jabbok.

[1] 1 Sam. xxii. 3.   [2] Josh. xiii. 26.   [3] Jud. xi. 29.
[4] 2 Sam. x. 2.   [5] Ib, viii. 2.   [6] Ib. xii. 31.
[7] 2 Chr. xx.   [8] 2 Kgs xxiv. 2.   [9] Jer. xxvii. 3.
[10] Zeph. ii. 8.
[11] On Ammon see below. When Isaiah prophesied, Moab was in possession of all the cities of Reuben, Is. xv. xvi.
[12] Ez. xxv. 2-8.   [13] Jer. xl. 11-14. xli. 10.

[14] Neh. ii. 10, 19. iv. 1-3.
[15] Is. xv. 5. Jer. xlviii. 3, 5, 34.
[16] 1 Macc. v. 6.   [17] Deut. xxiii. 3.
[18] 1 Kgs xi. 8.
[19] Solomon's worship of Ashtoreth as well as of Milcom is mentioned 1 Kgs xi. 5. The high places of Chemosh and Molech are alone mentioned there, ver. 7; that of Ashtoreth is mentioned in the account of its defilement by Josiah.
[20] Kgs xxiii. 13.   [21] Ab. 3.   [22] Jer. xlix. 1.
[23] See on Hos. vi. 8. p. 42.   [24] Deut. iii. 11.
[25] Polyb. v. 71. 4. Steph. Byz.

shouting in the day of battle, with a tempest in the day of the whirlwind:

15 And [k] their king shall go into captivity, he and his princes together, saith the LORD.

[k] Jer. 49. 3.

---

with a yet stronger citadel. Ruins still exist, some of which probably date back to these times. The lower city "[1] lay in a valley bordered on both sides by barren hills of flint," at ½ an hour from its entrance. It lay on a stream, still called by its name Moyet or Nahr Ammân, "waters" or "river of Ammon," which ultimately falls into the Zurka (the Jabbok.) "[2] On the top of the highest of the Northern hills," where at the divergence of two valleys it abuts upon the ruins of the town, "stands the castle of Ammon, a very extensive rectangular building," following the shape of the hill and wholly occupying its crest. "Its walls are thick, and denote a remote antiquity; large blocks of stone are piled up without cement, and still hold together as well as if they had been recently placed; the greater part of the wall is entire. Within the castle are several deep cisterns." There are remains of foundations of a wall of the lower city at its Eastern extremity [3]. This lower city, as lying on a river in a waterless district, was called the *city of waters* [4], which Joab had taken when he sent to David to come and besiege the Upper City. In later times, that Upper City was resolutely defended against Antiochus the Great, and taken, not by force but by thirst [5]. On a conspicuous place on this castle-hill, stood a large temple, some of its broken columns 3½ feet in diameter [6], probably the Grecian successor of the temple of its idol Milchom. Rabbah, the capital of Ammon, cannot have escaped, when Nebuchadnezzar, "[7] in the 5th year of his reign, led an army against Cœle-Syria, and, having possessed himself of it, warred against the Ammonites and Moabites, and having made all these nations subject to him, invaded Egypt, to subdue it." Afterward, it was tossed to and fro in the desolating wars between Syria and Egypt. Ptolemy II. called it from his own surname Philadelphia [8], and so probably had had to restore it. It brought upon itself the attack of Antiochus III. and its own capture, by its old habit of marauding

against the Arabs in alliance with him. At the time of our Lord, it, with "Samaria, Galilee and Jericho," is said by a heathen [9] to be "inhabited by a mingled race of Egyptians, Arabians and Phœnicians." It had probably already been given over to *the children of the East*, the Arabs, as Ezekiel had foretold [10]. In early Christian times Milchom was still worshiped there under its Greek name of Hercules [11]. Trajan recovered it to the Roman empire [12], and in the 4th century it, with Bostra [13], was still accounted a "vast town most secured by strong walls," as a frontier fortress "to repel the incursions of neighboring nations." It was counted to belong to Arabia [14]. An Arabic writer says that it perished before the times of Mohammed, and covered a large tract with its ruins [15]. It became a station of pilgrims to Mecca, and then, till now, as Ezekiel foretold [16], *a stable for camels* and *a couching place for flocks.*

I will kindle a fire in the wall. It may be that the prophet means to speak of some conflagration from within, in that he says not, as elsewhere [17], *I will send a fire upon*, but, *I will kindle a fire in*. But *the shouting* is the battle-cry [18] of the victorious enemy, the cheer of exultation, anticipating its capture. That onslaught was to be resistless [19], sweeping, like a whirlwind, all before it. The fortress and walls of Rabbah were to yield before the onset of the enemy, as the tents of their caravans were whirled flat on the ground before the eddying of the whirlwinds from the desert, burying all beneath them.

15. *And their king.* The king was commonly, in those nations, the centre of their energy. When *he and his princes* were *gone into captivity*, there was no one to make head against the conqueror, and renew revolts. Hence, as a first step in the subdual, the reigning head and those who shared his counsels were removed. Ammon then, savage as it was in act, was no ill-organized horde. On the contrary, barren and waste as all that country now is, it must once have been

---

[1] Burckhardt, Syria, 358, 8.
[2] Ib. 359, 60. and see plan p. 357.
[3] Buckingham, Trav. Ritter, xv. 1150.
[4] 2 Sam. xii. 27.
[5] Polyb. l. c. A prisoner shewed how the access of the garrison to the water might be cut off.
[6] Burckhardt, 360.
[7] Jos. Ant. x. 9. 7.
[8] S. Jer. in Ezek. xxv.
[9] Strabo, xvi. 2. 34. Ritt. 1156.   [10] xxv. 4.
[11] Coins from Trajan to Commodus, see authorities, Ritt. 1157.

[12] Amm. xiv. 8. 13.   [13] "and Gerasa," Ib.
[14] S. Epiph. Synops. L. ii. adv. Hær. p. 397. Anaceph. p. 145. Reland, 612.
[15] Abulfeda, (who, at Hamath, must have known it, as lying on the pilgrim-road to Mecca) Tab. Syr. p. 91.
[16] Ezek. xxv. 5. See Lord Lindsay. 278–82. Porter, Handb. 304, 5. Lord C. Hamilton's Journal in Keith on Prophecy, 270, 1.
[17] i. 4, 7, 10, 12. ii. 2, 5.
[18] Job xxxix. 25. Jer. xx. 16. Zeph. i. 16, &c.
[19] The etymol. of סוּפָה.

Before
CHRIST
cir. 787.

CHAPTER II.

1 *God's wrath against Moab, 4 upon Judah, 6 and upon Israel. 9 God complaineth of their unthankfulness.*

T HUS saith the LORD: For three transgressions of [a] Moab, and for four, I will not turn away

Before
CHRIST
cir. 787.
[a] Is. 15, & 16.
Jer. 48.
Ezek. 25. 8.
Zeph. 2. 8.

highly cultivated by a settled and laborious people. The abundance of its ruins attests the industry and habits of the population. "The whole of the country," says Burckhardt [1], "must have been extremely well cultivated, to have afforded subsistence to the inhabitants of so many towns." "The low hills are, for the most part, crowned with ruins." Of the "[2] thirty ruined or deserted places, which including Ammân," have been even lately "counted East of Assalt" (the village which probably represents Ramoth-Gilead, "about 16 miles West of Philadelphia [3]" i. e. Ammân,) several are in Ammonitis. Little as the country has been explored, ruins of large and important towns have been found S.S.E. and S. of Ammân [4]. Two hours S.E. of Ammân, Buckingham relates [5], "an elevation opened a new view before us, in the same direction. On a little lower level, was a still more extensive track of cultivated plain than that even which we had already passed—Throughout its whole extent were seen ruined towns in every direction, both before, behind, and on each side of us; generally seated on small eminences; all at a short distance from each other; and all, as far as we had yet seen, bearing evident marks of former opulency and consideration. There was not a tree in sight as far as the eye could reach; but my guide, who had been over every part of it, assured me that the whole of the plain was covered with the finest soil, and capable of being made the most productive corn land in the world—For a space of more than thirty miles there did not appear to me a single interruption of hill, rock or wood, to impede immediate tillage. The great plain of Esdraelon, so justly celebrated for its extent and fertility, is inferior in both to this plain of Belkah. Like Esdraelon, it appears to have been once the seat of an active and numerous population; but in the former the monuments of the dead only remain, while here the habitations of the living are equally mingled with the tombs of the departed, all thickly strewn over every part of the soil from which they drew their sustenance." Nor does the crown, of a

talent of gold weight, with precious stones [6], belong to an uncivilized people. Such hordes too depend on the will and guidance of their single Skeikh or head. This was a hereditary kingdom [7]. The kings of Ammon had their constitutional advisers. These were they who gave the evil and destructive counsel to insult the ambassadors of David. Evil kings have evermore evil counsellors. It is ever the curse of such kings to have their own evil, reflected, anticipated, fomented, enacted by bad advisers around them. [8] *Hand in hand the wicked shall not be unpunished.* They link together, but to drag one another into a common destruction. Together they had counselled against God; *king and princes together,* they should *go into captivity.*

There is also doubtless, in the word Malcham, a subordinate allusion to the god whom they worshipped under the title Molech or Malchom. Certainly Jeremiah *seems* so to have understood it. For, having said of Moab, [9] *Chemosh shall go into captivity, his priests and his princes together,* he says as to Ammon, *in* the self-same formula and almost in the words of Amos; [10] *Malcham shall go into captivity, his priests and his princes together.* Zephaniah [11] also speaks of the idol under the same name Malcham, "their king." Yet since Ammon had kings before this time, and just before their subdual by Nebuchadnezzar, and king Baalis [12] was a murderer, it is hardly likely that Jeremiah too should not have included him in the sentence of his people, of whose sins he was a mainspring. Probably, then, Amos and Jeremiah foretell, in a comprehensive way, the powerlessness of all their stays, human and idolatrous. All in which they trusted should not only fail them, but should be carried captive from them.

II. 1. *Moab.* The relation of Moab to Israel is only accidentally different from that of Ammon. One spirit actuated both, venting itself in one and the same way, as occasion served, and mostly together [13]. Beside those more formal invasions, the history of Elisha mentions one probably of many in-

---

[1] Syria, 357. (See also Porter, Hdb. 307.)
[2] Keith, c. 6. end 274. Of the 30 in Dr. Smith's list (Robinson App. iii. 168. ed. i.) several are clearly W. of Ammon, in Gilead, several are not in the maps; some are clearly in Ammonitis.
[3] Eus. Onom. Our copies of S. Jerome have by mistake, East. "6 hours" Porter, 307. See 309. and Ritter, xv. 1136–8.   [4] Buckingham, p. 83–96.
[5] Ib. 85.   [6] 2 Sam. xii. 30.   [7] Ib. x. 1.
[8] Pr. xi. 21.   [9] xlviii. 7.

[10] xlix. 3. מַלְכָּם בְּגוֹלָה יֵלֵךְ כֹּהֲנָיו וְשָׂרָיו יַחְדָּיו.
Am. הֵלֵךְ מַלְכָּם בַּגּוֹלָה הוּא וְשָׂרָיו יַחְדָּו. They use the same idiom and words, including the word הֵלֵךְ, not יֵצֵא which Jeremiah has xxix. 16. xlviii.
[7]. S. Jerome here renders Chemosh, and so did the Greek copies which Theodoret used. Aq. Sym. and Syr.
[11] i. 5.   [12] Jer. xl. 14.   [13] See on i. 13.

the punishment thereof;
because he [b]burned the
bones of the king of Edom
into lime:

roads of *bands of the Moabites.* It seems as
though, when *the year entered in,* and with it
the harvest, *the bands of the Moabites entered
in*[1] too, like *the Midianites and Amalekites and
the children of the East*[2] in the time of
Gideon, or their successors the Bedaweens,
now. This their continual hostility is related in the few words of a parenthesis.
There was no occasion to relate at length an
uniform hostility, which was as regular as
the seasons of the year, and the year's produce, and the temptation to the cupidity
of Moab, when Israel was weakened by
Hazael.

*Because he burned the bones of the king of
Edom.* The deed here condemned, is unknown. Doubtless it was connected with
that same hatred of Edom, which the king of
Moab shewed, when besieged by Israel.
Men are often more enraged against a friend
or ally who has made terms with one whom
they hate or fear, than with the enemy himself. Certainly, *when the king of Moab saw
that the battle was too sore for him*[3], his fury
was directed personally against the king of
Edom. He *took with him* 700 chosen men *to
cut through to the king of Edom, and they could
not.* Escape was not their object. They
sought not *to cut through* the Edomite contingent into the desert, but *to the king of Edom.*
Then *he took his eldest son,* i. e. probably the
eldest son of the king of Edom[4] whom he
captured, *and offered him up as a burnt offering on the wall.* Such is the simplest structure
of the words ; *He strove to cut through to the
king of Edom, and they could not, and he took
his eldest son, &c, and there was great indignation against Israel.* That *indignation* too
on the part of Edom (for there was no
other to be indignant *against Israel*) is best
accounted for, if this expedition, undertaken
because Moab had rebelled against Israel,
had occasioned the sacrifice of the son of the
king of Edom, who took part in it only as a
tributary of Judah. Edom would have had
no special occasion to be indignant with
Israel, if on occasion of an ordinary siege,
the king of Moab had, in a shocking way,
performed the national idolatry of child-
sacrifice. That hatred the king of Moab
carried beyond the grave, hatred which the
heathen too held to be unnatural in its im-

placableness 'and unsatiableness. The soul
being, after death, beyond man's reach, the
hatred, vented upon his remains, is a sort of
impotent grasping at eternal vengeance. It
wreaks on what it knows to be insensible, the
hatred with which it would pursue, if it
could, the living being who is beyond it.
Its impotence evinces its fierceness, since,
having no power to wreak any real revenge,
it has no object but to shew its hatred.
Hatred, which death cannot extinguish, is
the beginning of the eternal hate in hell.
With this hatred Moab hated the king of
Edom, seemingly because he had been,
though probably against this will, on the
side of the people of God. It was then sin
against the love of God, and directed against
God Himself. The single instance, which
we know, of any feud between Moab and
Edom was, when Edom was engaged in a
constrained service of God. At least there
are no indications of any conquest of each
other. The Bozrah of Moab, being in the
Mishor, *the plain*[5], is certainly distinct from
the Bozrah of Edom, which Jeremiah speaks
of at the same time, as belonging to Edom[6].
Each kingdom, Edom and Moab, had its
own strong city, Bozrah, at one and the same
time. And if "the rock," which Isaiah
speaks of as the strong hold of Moab[7], was
indeed the Petra of Edom, (and the mere
name, in that country of rock-fortresses is not
strong, yet is the only, proof,) they won it
from Judah who had taken it from Edom,
and in whose hands it remained in the
time of Amos[8], not from Edom itself. Or,
again, the tribute *may* have been only sent
through Petra, as the great centre of
commerce. Edom's half-service gained it
no good, but evil; Moab's malice was its
destruction.

The proverb, " speak good only of the
dead," shews what reverence human nature
dictates, not to condemn those who have
been before their Judge, unless He have
already openly condemned them. " Death,"
says S. Athanasius[9] in relating the death of
Arius on his perjury, " is the common end
of all men, and we ought not to insult the
dead, though he be an enemy ; for it is
uncertain whether the same event may not
happen to ourselves before evening."

---

[1] 2 Kgs xiii. 20. lit. *And the bands of Moab were
wont to come in,* (the force of יָבֹאוּ) as *the year came
in* (בָּא). ² Jud. vi. 3, 4, 11. ³ 2 Kgs iii. 26, 7.
[4] Josephus understands it of the king of Moab's
own son ; but then he misses the force of every
expression. He supposes that the king of Moab
tried to cut his way to escape only, and explains
the great indignation against Israel, of the com-

passion of Israel himself (Ant. ix. 3, 2.) Theodoret
supposes that the Moabites took the king of Edom
[i. e. the heir apparent] prisoner, and so sacrificed
him.
[5] Jer. xlviii. 21, 24. ⁶ Ib. xlix. 13. ⁷ Is. xvi. 1.
⁸ 2 Kgs xiv. 7. See ab. on i. 12.
[9] ad. Ep. Æg. § 19, in S. Ath. Hist. Tracts, p. 147.
Oxf. Tr.

17

Before
CHRIST
cir. 787.

e Jer. 48. 41.
d ch. 1. 14.

2 But I will send a fire upon Moab, and it shall devour the palaces of °Kirioth: and Moab shall die with tumult, ^dwith shout-

ing, *and* with the sound of the trumpet:

3 And I will cut off °the judge from the midst thereof, and will slay all

Before
CHRIST
cir. 787.

e Num. 24. 17.
Jer. 48. 7.

---

2. *It shall devour the palaces of Kerioth;* lit. *the cities,* i. e. a collection of cities. It may have received a plural form upon some enlargement, as Jerusalem received a dual form, as a double city. The name is, in different forms, very common [1]. In the plain or high downs of Moab itself, there were both Kiriathaim, "double city" and Kerioth [2]; in Naphthali, a Kiriathaim [3], or Kartan [4]; in Judah, the Kerioth [5] whence the wretched Judas has his name Iscariot [6]; in Zebulon, Kartah [7] also, which reappears as the Numidian Cirta. Moab had also a Kiriath-huzoth [8], "city of streets," within the Arnon [9]. This alone was within the proper border of Moab, such as the Amorites had left it. Kerioth and Kiriathaim were in the plain country which Israel had won from the Amorites, and its possession would imply an aggression of Moab. Jeroboam II. had probably at this time brought Moab to a temporary submission [10]; but Israel only required fealty and tribute of Moab; Moab appears even before the captivity of the 2½ tribes,to have invaded the possessions of Israel. Kerioth was probably a new capital, beyond the Arnon, now adorned with *palaces* and enlarged, as "Paris, Prague, Cracow [11]," London, are composed of different towns. In S. Jerome's time, it had probably ceased to be [12].

Shall die with tumult. Jeremiah, when prophesying the destruction of Moab, designates it by this same name *sons of tumult* [13]. *A flame shall devour the corner of Moab and the crown of the sons of tumult.* And probably herein he explains the original prophecy of Balaam [14], *shall smite the corners of Moab, and destroy all the children of tumult* [15]. As they had done, so should it be done to them; tumults they caused, *in tumult* they should perish.

After the subdual of Moab by Nebuchad-

nezzar, it disappears as a nation, unless indeed Daniel in his Prophecy [16], *Edom and Moab and the chief of the children of Ammon shall escape out of his hand* [Antiochus Epiphanes,] means the nations themselves, and not such as should be like them. Else the inter-marriage with Moabitish women [17] is mentioned only as that with women of other heathen nations which had ceased to be. The old name, Moabitis, is still mentioned; but the Arabs had possessed themselves of it, and bore the old name. Alexander Jannæus "subdued [18]," we are told, "of the Arabians, the Moabites and Gileadites," and then, again, when in difficulty, made it over with its fortified places, to the king of the Arabians [19]. Among the cities which Alexander took from the king of the Arabians [20], are cities throughout Moab, both in that part in which they had succeeded to Israel, and their proper territory S. of the Arnon [21].

3. *And I will cut off the judge.* The title *judge* (shophet) is nowhere used absolutely of a king. Holy Scripture speaks in several places of *all the judges of the earth* [22]. Hosea [23], under *judges,* includes *kings and princes,* as *judging the people.* The word *judge* is always used as one invested with the highest, but not regal authority, as of all the judges from the death of Joshua to Samuel. In like way it (Sufetes) is the title of the chief magistrates of Carthage [24], with much the same authority as the Roman Consuls [25]. The Phœnician histories, although they would not own that Nebuchadnezzar conquered Tyre, still own that, after his thirteen years' siege [26], Baal reigned 10 years, and after him *judges* were set up, one for two months, a second for ten, a third, a high-priest, for three, two more for six, and between these one reigned for a year. After his death, they sent for Merbal from Babylon, who reigned for four years, and on

---

[1] Besides the following, there is a Kuryetein, about half-way between Damascus and Palmyra (See Five years, i. 252 sqq. ii. 358.) and a Kureiyeh "in a broad valley at the S. W. base of the Jebel Hauran," near the Roman Bostra with "remains of remote antiquity." Ib. ii. 191. 8. add Burckhardt, Syria, 103, 4.
[2] Jer. xlviii. 23, 24.   [3] 1 Chr. vi. 76. (61. Heb.)
[4] Josh. xxi. 32.   [5] Josh. xv. 25.   [6] קריות א׳ ש׳.
[7] Josh. xxi. 34.   [8] Nu. xxii. 39.
[9] Balak met Balaam at *a city of Moab in the border of Arnon,* and then returned apparently to Kiriath-Huzoth.
[10] See on vi. 14.   [11] Lap.
[12] Kiriathaim was according to S. Jerome in his time "a Christian village called Coraiatha, 10 miles W. of Medaba, near Baare" [perhaps the valley so

called, near Machærus, Jos. B. J. vii. 6. 3. Ritter, xv. 582.] Of Kerioth he only says, "in the country of Moab, as Jeremiah writes." The present Korriath lies under the Jebel Attarus, S. W. of Medeba, by the streamlet el Wal. Ritter, Ib. and map in Robinson.   [13] xlviii. 45.   [14] Nu. xxiv. 17.
[15] שת i. q. שאון.   [16] xi. 41.   [17] Ezr. ix. 1.
[18] Jos. Ant. xiii. 13. 5.   [19] Ib. 14. 2.
[20] xiv. 1. 1. comp. xiii. 15, 4.
[21] Medaba and Livias N. of the Arnon; Agalla [Eglaim] "8 miles S. of it" (Eus.); Zoar, near the South of the Dead Sea; Oronæ [Horonaim] on Edom's boundary. Is. xv. 5.
[22] Job ix. 24. Ps. ii. 10. cxlviii. 11. Pr. viii. 16. Is. xl. 23.
[23] xiii. 10.
[24] Liv. xxviii. 37. Phœnic. Inscr. in Ges. Lex.
[25] Liv. xxx. 7.   [26] Jos. c. Ap. i. 21.

Before
CHRIST
cir. 787.

the princes thereof with him, saith the LORD.

4 ¶ Thus saith the LORD; For three transgressions of Judah, and for [f]four, I will not turn away *the punishment* thereof; [r]be-

[f] Lev. 26. 14,
15. Neh. 1. 7.
Dan. 9. 11.

cause they have despised the law of the LORD, and have not kept his commandments, and [g]their lies caused them to err, [h]after the which their fathers have walked :

Before
CHRIST
cir. 787.

[g] Is. 28, 15.
Jer. 16. 19, 20.
Rom. 1. 25.

[h] Ezek. 20, 13,
16, 18, 24, 30.

his death, they sent for Hiram his brother who reigned for twenty. The judges then exercised the supreme authority, the king's sons having been carried away captive. Probably, then, when Jeroboam II. recovered the old territory of Israel, Moab lost its kings. It agrees with this, that Amos says, *the princes thereof*, lit. *her princes*, the princes of Moab, not as of Ammon, *his princes*, i. e. the princes of the king.

4. *For three transgressions of Judah, &c.* "[1] Here too there is no difference of Jew and Gentile. The word of God, a just judge, spareth no man's person. If sin joins in one, the sentence of the Judge disjoins not in punishment." [2] *As many as have sinned without law, shall also perish without law, and as many as have sinned in the law, shall be judged by the law.* "[3] Those other nations, Damascus and the rest, he upbraids not for having *cast away the law of God,* and *despised His commandments ;* for they had not the written law, but that of nature only. So then of them he says, that *they corrupted all their compassions*— and the like. But Judah, who, at that time, had the worship of God and the temple and its rites, and had received the law and commandments and judgments and precepts and testimonies, is rebuked and convicted by the Lord, for that it had *cast aside His law and not kept His commandments ;* wherefore it should be punished as it deserved. And since they rejected and despised these, then, in course, *their lies deceived* them, i. e. their idols ;" *lies* on their part who made them and worshiped them for the true God, and *lies* and lying to them, as deceiving their hopes. For *an idol is nothing in the world* [4], as neither are all the vanities in the world whereof men make idols, but they deceive by a vain shew, as though they were something. "[3]They would not have been deceived by their idols, unless they had first *rejected the law of the Lord and not done His commandments.*" They had sinned with a high hand, *despising* and so rejecting the law of God ; and so He despised and rejected them, leaving them to be deceived by the lies which they themselves had chosen. So it ever is with man. Man must either [5] *love* God's *law* and *hate and abhor lies,* or he will despise God's

law and cleave to lies. He first in act *despises* God's law, (and whoso does not keep it, despises it,) and then he must needs be deceived by some idol of his own, which becomes his God. He first chooses wilfully his own *lie,* i. e. whatever he chooses out of God, and then his own *lie* deceives him. So, morally, liars at last believe themselves. So, whatever false maxim any one has adopted against his conscience, whether in belief or practice, to justify what he wills against the Will of God, or to explain away what God reveals and he mislikes, stifling and lying to his conscience, in the end deceives his conscience, and at the last, a man believes that to be true, which, before he had lied to his conscience, he knew to be false. The Prophet uses a bold word in speaking of man's dealings with his God, *despises.* Man carries on the serpent's first fraud, *Hath God indeed said ?* Man would not willingly own, that he is directly at variance with the Mind of God. Man, in his powerlessness, at war with Omnipotence, and, in his limited knowledge, with Omniscience ! It were too silly, as well as too terrible. So he smoothes it over to himself, *lying* to himself. " God's word must not be taken so precisely ;" " God cannot have meant ;" " the Author of nature would not have created us so, if He had meant ; " and all the other excuses, by which he would evade owning to himself that he is directly rejecting the Mind of God and trampling it under foot. Scripture draws off the veil. Judah had the law of God, and did not keep it ; then, he *despised* it. On the one side was God's Will, His Eternal Wisdom, His counsel for man for good ; on the other, what debasements ! On the one side were God's awful threats, on the other, His exceeding promises. Yet man chose whatever he willed, lying to himself, and acting as though God had never threatened or promised or spoken. This ignoring of God's known Will and law and revelation is to despise them, as effectually as to *curse God to His face* [6]. This rejection of God was hereditary. Their lies were those *after which their fathers walked,* in Egypt and from Egypt onwards, in the wilderness [7], "[3] making the image of the calf of Egypt and worshiping Baalpeor and Ashtoreth and Baalim." Evil

---

[1] Rup.   [2] Rom. ii. 12.   [3] S. Jer.   [4] 1 Cor. viii. 4.   [5] Ps. cxix. 163.   [6] Job. ii. 5.   [7] See on v. 25, 6.

5 [1] But I will send a fire upon Judah, and it shall devour the palaces of Jerusalem.

6 ¶ Thus saith the LORD; For three trans-

gressions of Israel, and for four, I will not turn away the punishment thereof; because [k] they sold the righteous for silver, and the poor for a pair of shoes;

acquires a sort of authority by time. Men become inured to evils, to which they have been used. False maxims, undisputed, are thought indisputable. They are in possession; and "possession" is held a good title. The popular error of one generation becomes the axiom of the next. The descent *of the image of the great goddess Diana from Jupiter*, or of the Coran, becomes a *thing* which *cannot be spoken against*[1]. The *lies after which the fathers walked* deceive the children. The children canonize the errors of their fathers." Human opinion is as dogmatic as revelation. The second generation of error demands as implicit submission as God's truth. The transmission of error against Himself, God says, aggravates its evil, does not excuse it. "[10] Judah is the Church. In her the Prophet reproves whosoever, worshiping his own vices and sins, cometh to have that as a god by which he is overcome; as St. Peter saith[2], *Whereby a man is overcome, of the same is he brought in bondage.* The covetous worshipeth mammon; the glutton, his belly[3]; the impure, Baalpeor; she who, *living in pleasure, is dead while she liveth*[4], the pleasure in which she liveth." Of such idols the world is full. Every fair form, every idle imagination, everything which gratifies self-love, passion, pride, vanity, intellect, sense, each the most refined or the most debased, is such a *lie*, so soon as man loves and regards it more than his God.

5. *I will send a fire upon Judah.* All know now, how Jerusalem, its temple, and its palaces perished by fire, first by Nebuchadnezzar, then by the Romans. Yet some two centuries passed, before that first destruction came. The ungodly Jews flattered themselves that it would never come. So we know that a *fiery stream*[5] will issue and come forth from Him; *a fire* that *consumeth to destruction*[6] all who, whether or no they are in the body of the Church, are not of the heavenly Jerusalem; dead members in the body which belongs to the Living Head. And it will not the less come, because it is not regarded. Rather, the very condition of all God's judg-

ments is, to be disregarded and to come, and then most to come, when they are most disregarded.

6. 7. *For three transgressions of Israel, and for four.* In Israel, on whom the Divine sentence henceforth rests, the Prophet numbers four classes of sins, running into one another, as all sins do, since all grievous sins contain many in one, yet in some degree distinct. 1) Perversion of justice; 2) oppression of the poor; 3) uncleanness; 4) luxury with idolatry.

They sold the righteous for silver. It is clear from the opposite statement, *that we may buy the poor for silver and the needy for a pair of shoes*, that the Prophet is not speaking of judicial iniquity, but of actual buying and selling. The law allowed a Hebrew who was poor to sell himself[7], and a Hebrew to buy him until the year of release; yet this too with the express reserve, that the purchaser was forbidden to *serve himself with him with the service of a slave, but as a hired servant and a sojourner shall he be with thee*[8]. The thief who could not repay what he stole, was to be *sold for his theft*[9]. But the law gave no power to sell an insolvent debtor. It grew up in practice. The sons and daughters of the debtor[10], or *his wife and children*[11], nay even the sons of a deceased debtor[12], were sold. Nehemiah rebuked this sharply. In that case, the hardness was aggravated by the fact that the distress had been fomented by usury. But the aggravation did not constitute the sin. It seems to be this merciless selling by the creditor, which Amos rebukes. The *righteous* is probably one who, without any blame, became insolvent. The *pair of shoes*, i.e. sandals, express the trivial price, or the luxury for which he was sold. They had him sold *for the sake of*[13] *a pair of sandals*, i.e. in order to procure them. Trivial in themselves, as being a mere sole, the sandals of the Hebrew women were, at times, costly and beautiful[14]. Such a sale expressed contempt for man, made in the image of God, that he was sold either for some worthless price, or for some needless adornment.

1 Acts xix. 35, 6.　　　　　2 2 Pet. ii. 19.
3 Phil. iii. 19.　4 1 Tim. v. 6.　5 Dan. vii. 10.
6 Job xxxi. 12.
7 In Lev. xxv. 39. Deut. xv. 12. נִמְכַּר should be rendered, according to the first sense of the conjugation, *sell himself*, not, *be sold*.

8 Lev. xxv. 39, 40.　　　　　Ex. xxii. 2, 3.
10 Neh. v. 5.
11 S. Matt. xviii. 25.
12 2 Kgs iv. 1.
13 בֵעֲבוּר
14 Cant. vii. 1. Ez. xvi. 10. Judith xvi. 9.

Before CHRIST cir. 787.	7 That pant after the dust of the earth on the head of the poor, and [1]turn aside the way of the meek:	[m]and a man and his father will go in unto the *same* [||]maid, [n]to profane my holy name:	Before CHRIST cir. 787.

[1] Is. 10. 2. ch. 5. 12.

[m] Ezek. 22. 11. [||] Or, *young woman.* [n] Lev. 20. 3. Ezek. 36. 20. Rom. 2. 24.

7. *That pant after the dust of the earth;* lit. *the panters!* with indignation. Not content with having rent from him the little hereditary property which belonged to each Israelite, these creditors grudged him even the *dust,* which, as a mourner, he strewed on his head [1], since it too was *earth.* Covetousness, when it has nothing to feed it, craves for what is absurd or impossible. What was Naboth's vineyard to a king of Israel with his *ivory palace?* What was Mordecai's refusal to bow to one in honor like Haman? What a trivial gain to a millionaire? The sarcasm of the Prophet was the more piercing, because it was so true. Men covet things in proportion, not to their worth, but to their worthlessness. No one covets what he much needs. Covetousness is the sin, mostly not of those who have not, but of those who have. It grows with its gains, is the less satisfied, the more it has to satisfy it, and attests its own unreasonableness, by the uselessness of the things it craves for.

And turn aside the way of the meek. So Solomon said [2], *A wicked man taketh a bribe out of the bosom, to pervert the ways of judgment.* God had laid down the equality of man, made in His own image, and had forbidden to favor either poor [3] or rich [4]. Amos calls these by different names, which entitled them to human sympathy; *poor, depressed, lowly; poor,* in their absolute condition; *depressed* [5], as having been brought low; *lowly,* as having the special grace of their state, the wonderful meekness and lowliness of the godly poor. But all these qualities are so many incentives to injury to the ungodly. They hate the godly, as a reproach to them; because [6] *he is clean contrary to their doings, his life is not like other men's; his ways are of another fashion.* Wolves destroy, not wolves, but sheep. Bad men circumvent, not the bad, but the good. Besides the easiness of the gain, there is a devilish fascinating pleasure to the bad, to overreach the simple and meek, because they are such. They love also to *turn aside the way of the meek,* by "[7]turning them from what is truly right and good;" or from the truth; or again to thwart them in all their ways and endeavors, by open injustice or by perverting justice. Every act of wrong prepares the way for the crowning act; and

so *the turning aside the way of the meek* foreshadowed and prepared for the unjust judgment of Him Who was *the Meek and Lowly* One [8]; the selling the righteous for a trifling sum prepared for the selling [9] *the Holy One and the Just* for the *thirty pieces of silver.* "[10]Contrariwise, whoso is truly wise, cordially venerates the humble and abject, the poor and simple, and prefers them in his own heart to himself, knowing that God has [11] *chosen the poor, and the weak things of the world, and things despised, and things which are not;* and that Christ hath likened Himself to such, saying in the Psalm, [12] *I am poor and sorrowful.*"

The same damsel. This is not expressly forbidden by the law, except in the case of marriage, the father being forbidden to marry his son's widow, and the son to take his father's widow to wife [13]. Abominations, unless they had become known to Israel in Egypt, were not expressly forbidden, but were included in the one large prohibition, which, as our Lord explains, forbade every offence, bearing upon it. Israel must have so understood the law, since Amos could upbraid them with this, which is not forbidden by the letter of the law, as a wilful insult to the Majesty of God. Reverence was due from the son to the father, example from the father to the son. But now the father was an example of evil to the son; and the son sinned in a way which had no temptation except its irreverence. Men, sated with ordinary sin seek incitement to sin, in its very horrors. Probably this sin was committed in connection with their idolworship [14]. The sin of marrying the father's widow was fornication not so much as named among the Gentiles [15]; it was unknown, as seemingly legalizing what was so unnatural. Oppression of the poor, wronging the righteous, perverting the way of the meek, laid the soul open for any abomination.

To profane My Holy Name, i. e. as called upon them, as the people of God. God had said, *ye shall keep My commandments and do them* [16]. *I am the Lord, and ye shall not defile My Holy Name. For I will be sanctified among the children of Israel. I am the Lord Who sanctify you.* The sins of God's people are a reproach upon Himself. They bring Him,

[1] Job ii. 12.
[2] Pr. xvii. 23. להטות ארחות with the same image as here דרך יטו.
[3] Ex. xxiii. 3.   [4] Ib. 6.   [5] דל
[6] Wisd. ii. 12, 15.   [7] S. Cyr.

[8] S. Matt. xi. 29.   [9] Acts iii. 14.
[10] Dion.   [11] i Cor. i. 27, 8.
[12] Ps. lxix, 29.   [13] Lev. xviii. 8, 15.
[14] See on Hosea iv. 14.   [15] 1 Cor v. 1.
[16] Levit. xxii. 31, 32. add Ib. xx. 3. xviii. 21. xxi. 6.

Before
CHRIST
cir. 787.
º Ex. 22. 26.
P Ezek. 23. 41.
1 Cor. 8. 10 & 10. 21.

8 And they lay *them-selves* down upon clothes º laid to pledge P by every

altar, and they drink the wine of || the condemned *in* the house of their god.

Before
CHRIST
cir. 787.
|| Or, *such as have fined*, or *mulcted.*

so to say, in contact with sin. They defeat the object of His creation and revelation. He created man in His Image, to bear His likeness, to have one will with Himself. In effect, through sin, He has created rebels, deformed, unlike. So long as He bears with them, it seems as if He were indifferent to them. Those to whom He has not revealed Himself, must needs think that He takes no account of what He permits unnoticed. Israel, whom God had separated from the Heathen, did, by *mingling with the Heathen and learning their works* [1], all which in them lay, to *profane* His *Holy Name.* They acted as if they had no other purpose than to defile it [2]. Had such been their object, they could not have done it more effectually, they could not have done otherwise. In deliberate sin men act, at last, in defiance of God, in set purpose to dishonor Him. The Name of God has ever since been blasphemed, on account of the sins of the Jews, as though it were impossible that God should have chosen for His own, a people so *laden with iniquities* [3]. Nathan's words to David [4], *Thou hast given great occasion to the enemies of the Lord to blaspheme*, have been fulfilled till this day. How much more, Christians, who not only are called "the people of God," but bear the name of Christ incorporated in their own. Yet have we not known Mohammedans flee from our Christian capital, in horror at its sins? "He lives like a Christian," is a proverb of the Polish Jews, drawn from the debased state of morals in Socinian Poland. The religion of Christ has no such enemies as Christians. "[5] As the devout by honoring God, shew that He is Holy, Great, Most High, Who is obeyed in holiness, fear and reverence, so the ungodly, by dishonoring God, exhibit God as far as in them lies, as if He were not Holy. For they act so as if evil were well-pleasing to Him, and induce others to dishonor Him. Wherefore the Apostle saith; *the name of God is blasphemed among the Gentiles through you* [6]; and by

Ezekiel the Lord saith oftentimes, *Ye have profaned My Holy Name. And I will sanctify My great Name which was profaned among the heathen, which ye have profaned in the midst of them* [7]. The devout then are said to *magnify*, sanctify, *exalt God;* the unrighteous to *profane* [8], *despise*, God."

8. *They lay* themselves *down.* They condensed sin. By a sort of economy in the toil of sinning, they blended many sins in one; idolatry, sensuality, cruelty, and, in all, the express breach of God's commandments. The *clothes* here are doubtless the same as the *raiment* in the law, the large enfolding cloak, which by day was wrapped over the long loose shirt [9], the poor man's only dress besides, and by night was his only bedding [10]. God had expressly commanded [11], *If the man be poor, thou shalt not sleep with his pledge;* in any case *thou shalt deliver him the pledge again, when the sun goeth down, that he may sleep in his own raiment, and bless thee; and it shall be righteousness to thee before the Lord thy God.* Here the *garments laid to pledge* are treated as the entire property of the creditors. They stretch [12] their listless length along upon them in their idol-feasts *by every altar.* Ezekiel speaks of a *stately bed*, upon which they *sat, and a table prepared before it* [13]. Isaiah; *Upon a lofty and high mountain hast thou set up thy bed; even thither wentest thou up to offer sacrifice;—thou hast enlarged thy bed; thou hast loved their bed; thou providedst room* [14]. In luxury and state then, and withal in a shameless publicity, they *lay on the garments* of the despoiled *by every altar.* The multiplication of altars [15] was, in itself, sin. By each of these multiplied places of sin, they committed fresh sins of luxury and hard-heartedness, (perhaps, from the character of the worship of nature, yet grosser sins,) *and drink the wine of the condemned*, or (as the E. M. more exactly) *the amerced*, those whom, unjustly, persons in any petty judicial authority had amerced, expending in revelry and debauchery in the idol's temple what they had unjustly

[1] Ps. cvi. 35.   [2] See on Hos. viii. 4.   [3] Is. i. 4.
[4] 2 Sam. xii. 14.   [5] Dion.
[6] Rom. ii. 24.   [7] Ezek. xxxvi. 23.
[8] Ib. xiii. 19.
[9] בְּגָד χιτών. as well as שִׂמְלָה, is used of the outside cloak, Gen. xxxix. 12, 13, 15. It is the more generic name, like our "clothes," except that it is chiefly used of large raiment and even of the outside covering, in which the ark, the table of shew-bread, &c. were covered in the journeys in the wilderness (E. V. cloth) Nu. iv. 6, 11, 13; and of the bed-coverings of the great. 1 Sam. xix. 13. 1 Kgs. i. 1. It is used also of state robes, 1 Kgs. xxii. 10. 2 Chr. xviii. 9. It is the word commonly used in the

plural of "rending the clothes;" שִׂמְלָה being used Gen. xxxvii. 34. xliv. 13. Josh. vii. 6 and כְּרִי 1 Sam. iv. 12; else בְּגָדִים, whether of kings or others. It is the word used of "washing the clothes," except in Ex. xix. 10, 14. where שִׂמְלֹת is used.
[10] Ex. xxii. 26. 7.   [11] Deut. xxiv. 12, 13.
[12] נָטָה, יְטוּ is not used elsewhere of stretching out the person, but it is used intrans. of "turning aside," Is. xxx. 11. Job xxiii. 11. Ps. cxxv. 5; and כָּם (like κλίνη, κλισία from κλίνω) is a place where one reclines at full length, bed, sofa, litter, or bier.
[13] xxiii. 41.   [14] lvii. 7, 8.
[15] Hos. viii. 11. x. 1. xii. 11.

Before CHRIST cir. 787.

q Num. 21. 24.
Deut. 2. 31.
Josh. 24. 8.
r Num. 13. 28, 32, 33.

9 ¶ Yet destroyed I the q Amorite before them, r whose height was like the height of the cedars, and

he was strong as the oaks; yet I s destroyed his fruit from above, and his roots from beneath.

Before CHRIST cir. 787.

s Is. 5. 24.
Mal. 4. 1.

extorted from the oppressed. There is no mask too transparent to serve to hide from himself one who does not wish to see himself. Nothing serves so well as religion for that self-deceit, and the less there is of it, or the more one-sided it is, the better it serves. For the narrower it is, the less risk of impinging on the awful reality of God's truth; and half a truth as to God is mostly, a lie which its half-truth makes plausible. So this dreadful assemblage of cruelty, avarice, malice, mockery of justice, unnatural debauchery, hard-heartedness, was doubtless smoothed over to the conscience of the ten tribes by that most hideous ingredient of all, that *the house of their god* was the place of their ill-purchased revelry. Men do not serve their idols for nothing; this costly service at Bethel was not for nought. They did all these things; but they did something for "the Deity" or "Nature" or "Ashtoreth;" and so "the Deity" was to be at peace with them. Amos, with wonderful irony, marks the ghastly mixture of sin and worship, *they drank the wine of the amerced*—where? *in the house of their God*, condemning in five words [1] their luxury, oppression, perversion of justice, cruelty, profaneness, unreal service and real apostacy. What hard-heartedness to the wilfully-forgotten poor is compensated by a little Church-going!

9. *Yet [and I] I* (Emphatic) *destroyed*. Such were *their* doings; such their worship of *their* God. And what had *God* done? what was it, which they thus required?

The Amorite. These, as one of the mightiest of the Canaanite tribes, stand in Moses for all. Moses, in rehearsing to them the goodness of God and their backsliding, reminds them, how he had said [2], *Ye have come to the mountain of the Amorites, which the Lord your God giveth you;* and that they, using this same word, said [3], *Because the Lord hateth us, He hath brought us forth out of the land of Egypt, to give us into the hand of the Amorite to destroy us.* The aged Joshua, in rehearsing God's great deeds for Israel, places first by

itself the destruction of the Amorite before them, with the use of this same idiom, [4] *I brought you into the land of the Amorites which dwelt on the other side of Jordan—and I destroyed them before you.* The Amorites were descended from the 4th son of Canaan [5]. At the invasion of Chedorlaomer, a portion of them [6] dwelt at Hazezon-Tamar or Engedi, half way on the W. side of the Dead Sea, and at Hebron near it [7]. Their corruption had not yet reached its height, and the return of Israel was delayed to the four hundredth year, *because the iniquity of the Amorite was not yet full* [8]. When Israel returned, the Amorites, (together with the Hittites and the Jebusites) held the hill country [9], Jerusalem, Hebron, Gibeon [10], and, on the skirts of the mountains Westward [11], Jarmuth, Lachish, and Eglon [12]. They dwelt on the side of the Jordan Westward [13], besides the two kingdoms which they had formed East of Jordan, reaching to Mount Hermon [14] and Bashan up to the territory of Damascus. Afterward a small remnant remained only in the portion of Dan, and in the outskirts of Judah, from the South of the Dead Sea, Maaleh Akrabbim (Scorpion-pass) and Petra [15]. Those near Idumea were probably absorbed in Edom; and the remnant in Dan, after becoming tributary to Ephraim [15], lost their national existence perhaps among the Philistines, since we have thenceforth only the single notice in the days of Samuel after the defeat of the Philistines, *there was peace between Israel and the Amorites* [16].

Whose height was like the height of the cedars. The giant sons of Anak were among the Amorites at *Hebron* [17] (called for a time Kiriath Arba [18] from their giant father) *Debir, Anab, and the mountains of Judah and Israel* [19]. *The valley of Rephaim* [20], S. W. of Jerusalem, connects this giant race with the Amorites, as does the fact that Og, king of the Amorites in Basan, was *of the remnant of the Rephaim* [21]. Basan and Argob were, in Moses' time, still called *the land of Rephaim* [22]. The Rephaim, with the Perizzites, dwelt still in woody mountains near Ephraim; whence,

[1] ויין עגושים ישתו בית אלהיהם.
[2] Deut. i. 20.   [3] Ib. 27.
[4] Josh. xxiv. 8. אל ארץ האמרי-ואשמידם מפניכם
Josh. ואנכי השמדתי את האמרי מפניכם Am. Moses has the same idiom of God's act on behalf of Ammon and Edom. Deut. ii. 21, 22.
[5] Gen. x. 16.
[6] האמרי הישב "those Amorites who dwelt."
[7] Ib. xiv. 7, 13. comp. xiii. 18. 2 Chr. xx. 2.

[8] Ib. xv. 16.
[9] Nu. xiii. 29. Deut. i. 7. 44.   [10] 2 Sam. xxi. 2.
[11] Jarmuth, 10 miles N. of Eleutheropolis (Beth Jabrin); Eglon, 10 miles West; and Lachish, 7 miles S. Eus. S. Jer.
[12] Josh. x. 3, 5.   [13] Ib. v. 1.   [14] Deut. iii. 8.
[15] Jud. i. 35, 6.   [16] 1 Sam. vii. 14. [17] Nu. xiii. 22.
[18] Josh. xiv. 15. xv. 13, 14.   [19] Ib. xi. 21.
[20] 2 Sam. v. 18.   [21] Deut. iii. 11. Josh. xii. 4. xiii. 12.
[22] Deut. iii. 13.

Before
CHRIST
cir. 787.
ᵗ Ex. 12. 51.
Mic. 6. 4.
ᵘ Deut. 2. 7. & 8. 2.

10 Also ᵗ I brought you up from the land of Egypt, and ᵘ led you forty years through the wilderness, to possess the land of the Amorite.

Before
CHRIST
cir. 787.

on the complaint that the lot of the sons of Joseph was too narrow, Joshua bade his tribe to expel them [1]. The Rephaim are mentioned between the Perizzites and the Amorites [2], in God's first promise of the land to Abraham's seed, and perhaps some inter-mixture of race gave the giant stature to the Amorites. It is clear from Amos that the report of the spies, *all the people that we saw in it were men of stature* [3], was no exaggeration, nor did Joshua and Caleb deny *this*. The name of the Amorite [4], is probably connected with "commanding," describing some quality of their forefather, which descended to his race. *Whose height was like the height of cedars.* Giant height is sometimes a cause of weakness. Amos, in a degree like Hosea [5], combines distinct images to make up the idea of stateliness and strength. The cedar is the ideal of Eastern trees for height [6], stretching forth its arms as for protection. " [7] It groweth to an exceeding height, and with increasing time ever riseth higher." The oak has its Hebrew name from strength [8]. The more majestic the tall strength of the Amorite, the more manifest that Israel [9] *gat not the land in possession by their own sword*, who had counted themselves, in sight of the Amorite, *as grasshoppers* [10]. God, Who gave him that strength, took it away, as we say, "root and branch," leaving him no shew above, no hope of re-covered life below [11]. Having compared each Amorite to a majestic tree, he compares the

excision of the whole nation to the cutting down of that one tree [12], so swift, so entire, so irrecoverable. Yet the destruction of the Am-orite, a mercy to Israel in the purpose of God, was a warning to Israel when it became as they. God's terrors are mercies to the re-pentant; God's mercies are terrors to the impenitent. [13] *Ye shall keep My statutes and My judgments and shall not commit* any *of these abominations*, was the tenure upon which they held the Lord's land, *that the land spue not you out also, when ye defile it, as it spued out the na-tions that were before you.*

10. *Also I* (lit. *And I, I,* emphatic; thus and thus did ye to Me; and thus and thus, with all the mercy from the first, did *I* to you,) *I brought you up from the land of Egypt.* It is this language in which God, in the law, reminded them of that great benefit, as a motive to obedience [14]; *I brought thee forth out of the land of Egypt, out of the house of bondage;* only there, since God has not as yet *brought them up* into the land which He promised them, but they were yet in the wilderness, He says, *brought them forth;* here, *brought them up* [15], as to a place of dignity, His own land.

And led you forty years through the wilder-ness. These are the very words of the law [16], and reminded them of so many benefits dur-ing the course of those *forty years,* which the law rehearsed; the daily supply of manna, the water from the rock, the deliverance from the serpents and other perils, the manifold forgivenesses. To be *led forty years through*

---

[1] Josh. xvii. 15, 18.   [2] Gen. xv. 20, 1.   [3] Nu. xiii. 32.
[4] The idea of physical height does not exist in the root *amar* in any Semitic language. In the only word alleged in Hebrew, it has been inferred from the context, rather than from any knowledge as to the word itself, that אָמִיר (which occurs in Is. xvii. 6, 9. only) signifies *uppermost branch.* The Vulg. however, Chald. and Saadia render it "branch" only, in which case אָכִיר would be equivalent to the Syriac 'Amiro. The LXX. alone has μετεώρου. Even if אָכִיר have the meaning "uppermost," this would probably be by way of metaphor from the Arabic *Emir* (from which Aben Ezra derives it) as we speak of "a commanding height," and so would not imply that the idea of physical elevation ever existed in the root. 2) If the word had had the meaning of height, it would describe the high stature of the forefather of the tribe and the tribe itself, as Rephaim from Rapha' (tall), Enakim from Anek (long-necked). We use the word "heights," but we should not infer that "high" meant "a dweller on heights," a "moun-taineer." 3) This meaning, which writers of late have, one after the other, ascribed to אָכִיר, would obviously have been expressed by the word הָרָרִי, as derived from the common Hebrew word for mountain, הָר. (Perhaps this does exist 2 Sam. xxiii. 11. 33.) 4) The word (even if it had the meaning,) would not be characteristic of the Amorites, since the Jebusites and the Hittites and

the Rephaim equally dwelt in the mountains: and the Amorites did not dwell in the mountains only. The apparent object of this unlikely inference from imagined etymology is to find a meaning for the names of the Canaanite nations, expressive of some local circumstance. But as to the names of the sons of Canaan as also that of Canaan himself, the attempt obviously fails as to all enumerated in Gen. x. 15-18. The Perizzites, who are perhaps persons "living in the open country," are not there mentioned.
[5] See ab. p. 90.
[6] Is. ii. 13. Ezek. xvii. 22. xxxi. 3.   1 Kgs iv. 33. 2 Kgs xiv. 9.
[7] Comm. in Is. ii. 13. ap. S. Basil. Opp.
[8] אַלּוֹן from אָלַל i. q. אוּל as the Latin, "robur."
[9] Ps. xliv. 3.   [10] Nu. xiii. 33.
[11] See Hos. ix. 16. Job xviii. 16. Ezek. xvii. 9.
[12] Dion.   [13] Lev. xviii. 26, 38.
[14] Ex. xx. 2. Deut. v. 6. vi. 12.
[15] In the Pentateuch, הוֹצֵאתִיךָ מֵאֶרֶץ מִצְרַיִם; here, הֶעֱלֵיתִי אֶתְכֶם מֵאֶרֶץ מִצְרַיִם.
[16] Deut. xxix. 4. [5 Eng.] only slightly transposing the בַּמִּדְבָּר. In Deut. וָאוֹלֵךְ אֶתְכֶם אַרְבָּעִים שָׁנָה; here, וָאוֹלֵךְ אֶתְכֶם בַּמִּדְבָּר אַרְבָּעִים שָׁנָה.

11 And I raised up of your sons for prophets, and

the wilderness, alone, had been no kindness, but a punishment. It was a blending of both. The abiding in the wilderness was punishment or austere mercy, keeping them back from the land which they had shewn themselves unqualified to enter: God's *leading* them was, His condescending mercy. The words, taken from the law, must have re-awakened in the souls of Israelites the memory of mercies which they did not mention, how that same book relates [1] *He found him in a desert land, and in the waste howling wilderness; He led him about; He instructed him; He kept him as the apple of His eye. The Lord alone did lead him.* [2] *In the wilderness, where thou hast seen how that the Lord thy God bare thee, as a man doth bear his son, in all the way that ye went until ye came to this place;* or that minute tender care, mentioned in the same place [3], *your clothes are not waxen old upon you, and thy shoe is not waxen old upon thy foot.* But unless Israel had known the law well, the words would only have been very distantly suggestive of mercy, that it must have been well with them even in the wilderness, since God led them. They had then the law in their memories, in Israel also [4], but distorted it or neglected it.

11. *And I raised up of your sons for Prophets.* Amos turns from outward mercies to inward, from past to present, from miracles of power to miracles of grace. God's past mercies live on in those of to-day; the mercies of to-day are the assurance to us that we have a share in the past; His miracles of grace are a token that the miracles of His power are not our condemnation. God had, from the time of Moses, *raised up* prophets. Eldad and Medad [5] were images of those, whom God would raise up beyond the bounds of His promise. The divine Samuel was an Ephrathite [6]; Ahijah the Shilonite, i. e. of Shiloh in Ephraim, lived on to old age [7] in the kingdom of the ten tribes after their schism, the witness against the apostacy of Jeroboam [8], yet acknowledged by the king whose rise and of the destruction of whose house he prophesied [7]. Jehu, son of Hanani, was the prophet of both kingdoms [9]; Micaiah, son of Imlah, was well known to Ahab, as *prophesying evil concerning him* [10] continually;

unknown to Jehoshaphat [11]. That wondrous pair, marvelous for superhuman sanctity and power among the marvelous miracles of God, Elijah and Elisha, were both *sons* of Israel, whom God *raised up; Elijah the Tishbite* [12], born doubtless at Thisbe, a village of Naphthali [13], and one of the sojourners [14] in Gilead; Elisha of Abelmeholah [15], on the West side of the valley of the Jordan [16]. And even now He had raised up to them of their own *sons*, Hosea and Jonah. Their presence was the presence of God among them, Who, out of the ordinary way of His Providence, *raised* them *up* and filled them with His Spirit; and where the Presence of God is, if there is fear, yet there is also hope.

And of your young men for Nazarites. The Nazarite was a fruit of the grace of God in its moral and religious workings, superhuman in holiness and self-denial, as the Prophets were of that same grace, conferring superhuman wisdom and knowledge also. Of both, God says, *I raised up*, teaching that both alike, holiness of life and superhuman wisdom, were His own special gift to each individual, His own creation. God surveyed His people, called, and *raised up*, by His grace, out of the crowd, those souls which responded to His call. The life of the Nazarites was a continual protest against the self-indulgence and worldliness of the people. It was a life above nature. Unless any prophet like Samuel [17], was also a Nazarite, they had no special office except to live that life. Their life taught. Nay, it taught in one way the more, because they had no special gifts of wisdom or knowledge, nothing to distinguish them from ordinary men, except extraordinary grace. They were an evidence, what all might do and be, if they used the grace of God. The power of the grace of God shews itself the more wondrously in those who have nought beside. The essence of the Nazarite life, as expressed by its name [18], was "separation," separation from things of the world, with a view to God. The separation was not, necessarily, for more than a limited time. In such case, it answered to the strictness of the Christian Lent. It was a considerable discipline for a time. In those simpler days, when luxury

[1] Deut. xxxii. 10, 12. [2] Ib. i. 31.
[3] Deut. xxix. 4. [5. Eng.] only slightly transposing the במדבר. In Deut. ואולך אתכם ארבעים שנה; here, במדבר; ואולך אתכם במדבר ארבעים שנה.
[4] See Introd. to Amos p. 152. [5] Nu. xi. 26–9.
[6] 1 Sam. i. 1. [7] 1 Kgs xiv. 2, 4.
[8] Ib. 7–14. xv. 29.
[9] Ib. xvi. 1, 7, 12. 2 Chr. xix. 2. xx. 34.

[10] 1 Kgs xxii. 8, 18. [11] Ib. 7. [12] Ib. xvii. 1.
[13] Tob. i. 2. See Reland, 1035. Eus. and S. Jer. mention the village Thisbe.
[14] מתושב. [15] 1 Kgs xix. 16.
[16] See 1 Kgs iv. 12. Eus. S. Jer. say, "it is now a village, in the valley of the Jordan, 10 miles South of Scythopolis [Bethshean] and is now called Bethmaela [our copies of Jerome have Bethaula]. There is also [a little village S. Jer.]. Abelmeon, on the way from Neapolis [Nablus] to Scythopolis."
[17] 1 Sam. i. 11. [18] נזיר.

of your young men f o r
[x] Nazarites. *Is it* not even

thus, O ye children of Israel? saith the Lord.

had not been so busy [1], the absolute prohibition of anything fermented [2], whether
from the grape or any other substance [3], or
vinegar made of either, or any liquor or refreshing food or drink, made in any way
from the grape, fresh or dry, its husks or its
kernels, while it cut off every evasion, involved the giving up not only every drink,
in any way exciting or stimulating, but very
much also, which was refreshing. Water,
which in the East has seldom the freshness
of ours, was their only drink. This, which
to individuals may be an easy rule, would
not be so in the main. Those only think an
undeviating rule slight, who have never
tried one, nor set themselves on system to
conquer self-will. Such a rule would not be
acted upon, except for God. The long
never-shorn hair was probably intended to
involve the neglect of personal appearance.
Yet this was the body only of the vow; its
soul was the dedication to God. The Nazarite not only *separated himself from* [4] those
earthly things; he *separated himself* to the
Lord [5]: he *consecrated to the Lord the days of
his separation* [6]: *all the days of his separation
he was holy to the Lord* [7]: *the separation of his
God was upon his head* [8]. The vow was a
great and singular thing. *When man or
woman shall vow a special vow of a Nazarite* [9].
The ritual of the Nazarite likened him to
the priest. Giving him no priestly office, it
yet even intensified some of the rules of the
priesthood. The priest was to abstain from
wine and strong drink, only *when he went
into the tabernacle of the congregations, that he
might put difference between holy and unholy,
and teach Israel the statutes* of the Lord [10]: the
Nazarite, so long as he remained such. The
priest might defile himself for certain very
near dead [11]; the high priest alone and the
Nazarite, *neither for father nor mother* [12]: and
that for the kindred reason; the high priest,
*because the crown of the anointing oil of his God
was upon him;* the Nazarite, *because the consecration of his God* was *upon his head!* His

consecrated hair was called by the self-same
name [13] as the mitre of the priest. It appears
to have been woven into *seven locks* [14], itself a
number of consecration. If his consecration
came to an end, that hair was mingled with
the sacrifice [15], and on *his* hands alone, besides
the priest's at his consecration, was part of
the offering laid [16]. All Israel was, in God's
purpose, *a kingdom of priests* [17]; and, among
them, the Nazarite was brought yet nearer,
not to the priest's office, but to his character.
This must have diffused itself indefinitely
through the outward and inward life. Further strictness probably lay in the spirit of
the vow. The outward appearance of the
Nazarites appears to have been changed by
their abstemiousness [18]. *Her Nazarites were
purer than snow; they were whiter than milk.*
Their countenance had that transparent [19]
purity, which sometimes results from a pure
abstemious life; as S. Athanasius is said to
have been "bloodless." S. John Baptist, the
counterpart of Elijah, ate only of the food of
the wilderness, *locusts and wild honey;* his
clothing was the hair cloth [20]. Of S. James
the Just it is related with reference to the
Nazarite vow; "[21] He was holy from his
mother's womb; wine and strong drink he
drank not, nor ate any living thing; the
razor came not up upon his head; he
anointed him not with oil, and he used not a
bath." Nazarites there had been in the most
disorganized times of Israel. The histories
of Samson and Samuel stand over against
one another, as Nazarites who, the one forfeited, the other persevered in, his vocation.
Elijah's ascetic character is as if he had been
one of them, or deepened the lines of their
rule. Ahaziah's ungodly messengers described him contemptuously as *a man,
lord of hair,* as though he had nothing but
his prophet's broad mantle of hair, and *the
leathern girdle about his loins* [22]. The Rechabites, although Kenites by origin [23], had been
enrolled in the people of God, and had received a rule from their father, uniting with

---

[1] Coffee, though invented for vigils, was adopted
as a compensation for Mohammed's prohibition of
wine. See the history in de Sacy, Chrest. Arab. T.
i. p. 412. ed. 2.

[2] Nu. vi. 3, 4.

[3] The *strong drink* (שֵׁכָר) was the more comprehensive, because it was undefined. S. Jerome
enumerates, as prohibited under it, "every inebriating drink, whether made of barley, or juice of
apples, or when honey is decocted into a sweet barbarian drink, or liquor is expressed from the date,
or when water is colored and thickened by boiled
fruit." (Ep. ad Nepotian.) Accordingly beer, cider,
mead (οἰνόμελι) or "dibs," datewine, and any other
fermented liquor, of whatever, (like our British
wines,) it might be made, was forbidden.

[4] Nu. vi. 3.   [5] Ib. 2, 5, 6.   [6] Ib. 12.
[7] Ib. 8.   [8] Ib. 7.
[9] Ib. 2. כִּי יַפְלִא לִנְדֹּר נֶדֶר נָזִיר. In Lev. xxvii.
2. the E. V. renders the same word and form,
יַפְלִא נֶדֶר *make a singular vow.*
[10] Lev. x. 9–11.   [11] Lev. xxi. 1–3.
[12] Ib. 11, 12. Nu. vi. 7.   [13] נֵזֶר Nu. vi. 19.
[14] Jud. xvi. 13.   [15] Nu. vi. 18.   [16] Ib. 19.
[17] Ex. xix. 6.   [18] Lam. iv. 7.
[19] The LXX. render זַךְ Ex. xxx. 34 by διαφανής.
[20] S. Luke i. 15. vii. 33. S. Matt. iii. 4.
[21] Hegesippus in Eus. H. E. ii. 23.
[22] 2 Kgs. i. 8. The mention of the girdle shews
that the *hair* was the "garment of hair," (Zech.
xiii. 4. Heb. xi. 37) not the Nazarite's hair.
[23] 1 Chr. ii. 55.

12 But ye gave the Nazarites wine to drink;

the abstinence of the Nazarites, a mode of life which kept them aloof from the corruptions of cities[1]. The rules of their Nomadic life were consecrated to God, for He says[2], *There shall not be cut off from Jonadab, the son of Rechab, a man standing before Me for ever*, i. e. as the servant of God. God uses as to them the term which marks the service of the Levites[3], Priests[4], and Prophets[5]. Jonadab, the author of their rule, was plainly an ascetic, through whose presence Jehu hoped to cast a religious character over his ambitious execution of God's command[6]. But the value which the artful, though impetuous[7], bloodstained, captain attached to the presence of the ascetic shews the weight which they had with the people. Strange sight it must have been, the energetic warrior in his coat of mail, and the ascetic, as energetic, in his hair-cloth. Deeper far the contrast within. But the more marvelous the contrast, the more it attests the influence which the unworldly ascetic had over the world. Like the garb of the prophets, their appearance was a standing rebuke to a life of sense. Like the patriarchs, it professed that they were *strangers and pilgrims upon the earth*. They who sought nothing of the world or of time, were a witness to the belief in their eternal home. The Nazarites must now have been a numerous body, since Amos speaks of them, as a known class, like the prophets, of whose numbers we hear incidentally[8]. Yet the memory of these, who, amid the general corruption, were, each in his own sphere, centres of pure faith and life, is embalmed in these few words only. So little reason is there to think that God's commands were neglected by all, because their observance is not related. Amos appeals publicly to the people that the fact was so, that God had raised up Nazarites as well as prophets among them. He had His *little flock*[9], His *seven thousand*[10], who escaped the eye even of Elijah. The gift of the Nazarites was a special favor to Israel, as a memorial what the grace of God could do for man, what man could do, with the grace of God. His *raising up Nazarites*,

out of their young men, men in their first bloom of unmarried[11], virgin[12], life, their picked "very chosen men[13]," such as furnished the prime of their warriors[14], strengthened that teaching. Even now, one devoted to God in his youth is a witness for God, leaven of the world around him. But the Nazarite had also to bear an outward mark for good, to be singular. His appearance bespoke that he had chosen God. His vow was not only a living up to the law; it lay beyond the law, the free-will offering of those whom God called. At an age, when so many do things unlawful, to gratify passion, these abstained even from things lawful. "Canst thou not do what these youths and these maidens can? or can they either in themselves, and not rather in the Lord their God?" was St. Augustine's upbraiding of himself[15], on the eve of his conversion, in thought of those who were living a devoted virgin life.

Is it not even thus? It were enough that God, the Truth, said it. But He condemns not, without giving space for excuse or defense. So he describes the Day of Judgment[16]. *The books were opened,—and the dead were judged out of those things which were written in the books, according to their works*[17]. Now, in the time of grace, the question asks, what, written under the picture of Christ crucified, once converted a sinner; "This have I done for thee: What doest thou for Me?" What did they? What had they done? What would they do?

12. *But ye gave the Nazarites wine to drink;* lit. *and*, (this, on their part, was the consequence of what God did for them) *ye caused the Nazarites to drink wine*. God appointed; Israel strove to undo His appointment. God *raised up Nazarites*, as a testimony to them; they sought to make His servants break their vow, in order to rid themselves of that testimony. Their pains to destroy it, is a strong proof of its power. The world is mad against true religion, because it feels itself condemned by it. Men set themselves against religion and the religious, the Church or the Priesthood, only when and because they feel their power

---

[1] Jer. xxxv. 7, 9.   [2] Ib. 19.   [3] Deut. x. 8.
[4] Jud. xx. 28.   [5] 1 Kgs xvii. 1.
[6] 2 Kgs x. 15, 16, 23. Jehonadab, beforehand, was present to observe if there were any worshipers of God, in Baal's temple; his influence was not with the Baal-worshipers, but with the vacillating people.
[7] Ib. ix. 20.
[8] See Introduction to Hosea, p. 6. Obadiah saved the lives of *an hundred prophets*. 1 Kgs xviii. 4.
[9] S. Luke xii. 32.   [10] 1 Kgs xix. 18.
[11] Ruth iii. 10. (in ii. 9. where there was no emphasis, נערים is used) Is. lxii. 5.
[12] Hence joined with בתולה "virgin," Deut.

xxxii. 25. 2 Chr. xxxvi. 17. Jer. li. 22. and in the plur. Ps. lxxviii. 63. cxlviii. 12. Is. xxiii. 4. Jer. xxxi. 13. Lam. i. 18. ii. 21. Zech. ix. 17. and by Amos himself, viii. 13.
[13] בחור is, by its form, intensive, not "chosen" only, but "greatly chosen." It is nowhere used without emphasis.
[14] Hence in the idiom "shall slay their young men with the sword," &c. 2 Kgs. viii. 12. Jer. xi. 22. xv. 8. xviii. 21. &c. Ezek. xxx. 17, and in the remaining place in Amos iv. 10.
[15] Conf. viii. 27. p. 152. Oxf. Tr.
[16] S. Matt. xxv. 24–30. 41–5. xxii. 11.
[17] Rev. xx. 12.

phets,ʸsaying,Prophesy not.

ʸ Is. 30. 10. Jer. 11. 21. ch. 7. 12, 13.
Mic. 2. 6.

on God's side against them. What men
despise, they do not oppose. "They kill us,
they do not despise us," were true words of a
French priest, as to the "reign of reason" in
the first French revolution. Had the men
in power not respected the Nazarites, or felt
that the people respected them, they would
not have attempted to corrupt or to force
them to break their vow. The word, *cause*
them *to drink*, does not express whether they
used constraint or seduction. Israel's consciences supplied it. Yet since they *persecuted the prophets* and put them to death, it
seems likely that Amos means that they
used violence, either by forcing the wine into
their mouths, as the swine-flesh was forced
into the mouth of Eleazar[1], and, in the
Decian persecution an infant was made to eat
of the idol oblation[2], or by threat of death.

*And commanded the prophets, saying, Pro-
phesy not.* God had commanded the prophets
to prophesy. Israel issued and laid upon
them his commands against the commands of
God. The more God reveals His Will, the
directer and more determinate the opposition
of those who will not yield. God's perseverance in trying to win them irritates them;
they oppose grace, and are angered at not
being let alone. This large statement of
Amos means much more than the prohibition
of Amaziah to himself[3]. Jeroboam I. was
prevented only by miracle[4] from seizing the
prophet who denounced the altar at Bethel.
Ahab, during the famine foretold by Elijah,
sought him everywhere to destroy him[5], and
Jezebel, after the miracle at Carmel and the
death of her prophets, swore by her gods to
do so[6]. Ahab's last act was to imprison
Micaiah[7], the son of Imlah, for prophesying
his death, when adjured by himself to speak
truly. Ahaziah, his son, undeterred by the
fire from heaven which destroyed two captains, each with his fifty, sent yet a 3d to
take Elijah, when he prophesied that the king
would not recover from his sickness[8]. Jehoram, his 2d son, swore by God to destroy
Elisha[9], laying the evils of the siege to the
Prophet, as the Romans did the evils of their
decaying empire to the Christian. Micah
and Isaiah, a little later, speak of such oppo-

sition, in Judah, as habitual[10]; much more
in Israel, where the opposition to God's law
was more fundamental, and where God's
prophet's had been all but exterminated.
Even Asa, in his degenerate days, imprisoned
Hanani for prophesying that he would *have
wars*[11]; Joash slew Zechariah son of Jehoiada[12]; Amaziah silenced the prophet who
rebuked him[13], *Art thou made of the king's
counsel? forbear. Why shouldest thou be smitten?* Jehoiakim sent even into Egypt to
fetch Uriah and slew him[14]. Jeremiah's life
was one continuous encounter with false accusations[15], contradictions by false prophets[16],
hatred[17], mockery[18], persecution[19], imprisonment[20], attempts to destroy him[21]. The
complaint was, as here, *wherefore dost thou
prophesy*[22]? What, when our Lord gives it
as the characteristic of Jerusalem[23], that she
was "the slayer of the prophets, the stoner
of those sent unto her?" They would not
have slain the prophets, if they could have
silenced them. Men are loth to go to extremities with God; they will make an armis-
tice with Him; their awe of holiness makes
them inwardly shrink from laying hands on
it. Like the wolf in the fable, they must
have a plea against it; and that plea against
those who have the truth is obstinacy[24]. If
the Christians would have abstained from
converting the world, they would not have
been persecuted. The Chief-priests at first
sought simply to silence the Apostles[25]; then
they enforced their command with scourges[26];
then persecuted them and the Christians to
death[27]. Direct contumacy to God's known
voice and silencing His messenger, is a last
stage of obduracy and malice, which leaves
God no further avenue to the soul or the
people. His means of grace are exhausted
when the soul or people not only deaden His
voice within, but obstruct it without. One
who, through vehemence of his passions, refuses to hear, is within the reach of the grace
of God, afterward. He who stifles God's
word to others has mostly hardened his heart
deliberately and maliciously in unlove to
man, as well as contempt of God. Hence God
speaks, as though this brought the day of
grace to a close.

[1] 2 Macc. vi. 18.
[2] S. Cyprian on the lapsed § 16. p. 169. Oxf. Tr.
[3] vii. 13.   [4] 1 Kgs xiii. 4.   [5] Ib. xviii. 10–12.
[6] Ib. xix. 2, 3.
[7] Ib. xxii. 26, 7.   [8] 2 Kgs i. 9–13.
[9] Ib. vi. 31.   [10] Mic. ii. 6. Is. xxx. 10, 11.
[11] 2 Chr. xvi. 7, 10.   [12] Ib. xxiv. 20, 1.
[13] Ib. xxv. 15, 16.   [14] Jer. xxvi. 20–3.
[15] Ib. xx. 10. xxxvii. 13. xxxviii. 4.
[16] Ib. xxiii. 17 sqq. xxvii. 9, 10, 14–16. xxviii. xxix.
[17] Ib. xv. 10.
[18] Ib. xvii. 15. xx. 7, 8. xxiii. 33.

[19] Ib. xvii. 18.
[20] Ib. xx. 2. xxxii. 3. xxxiii. 1. xxxvii. 15–21.
xxxviii. 6–13.
[21] Ib. xi. 18–21 xviii. 18, 20–23. xxvi. 8 sqq. xxxvi.
26.
[22] Ib. xxxii. 3.
[23] S. Matt. xxiii. 37. ἡ ἀποκτείνουσα τοὺς προφήτας
καὶ λιθοβολοῦσα.
[24] See on Tert. de spect. 1. p. 189. n. f. Oxf. Tr.
[25] Acts iv. 18, 21.
[26] Ib. v. 40.
[27] Ib. vii. 57–9. viii. 1–4. ix. 1, 2. xii. 1–3. xxii. 4, 5.

Before
CHRIST
cir. 787.

x Is. 1. 14.
|| Or, *I will press
your place, as
a cart full of
sheaves presseth.*
a Jer. 9. 23.
ch. 9. 1, &c.

b Ps. 33. 16.

† Heb. *his soul,*
or, *life.*

13 ˣ B e h o l d , || I am pressed under you, as a cart is pressed *that is* full of sheaves. 14 ᵃ Therefore the flight shall perish from the swift, and the strong shall not strengthen his force, ᵇ neither shall the mighty deliver † himself :
15 N e i t h e r shall he stand that handleth t h e bow ; and *he that is* swift of foot shall not deliver himself : ᶜ neither shall he that rideth the horse deliver himself. 16 And *he that is* † courageous among the mighty shall flee away naked in that day, saith the LORD.

Before
CHRIST
cir. 787.

c Ps. 33. 17.

† Heb. *strong of
his heart.*

---

13. *Behold, I am pressed under you.* God bore His people, as the wain bears the sheaves. *Ye yourselves have seen,* He said to them by Moses [1], how *I bare you on eagle's wings, and brought you unto Myself.* [2] *Thou hast seen how the Lord thy God bare thee, as a man doth bear his son, in all the way that ye went, until ye came into this place.* And by Isaiah [3], *He bare them and carried them all the days of old;* and [4], *which are born by Me from the belly, which are carried from the womb.* Now, He speaks of Himself as wearied by them, as by Isaiah [5], *thou hast wearied Me with thine iniquities;* and by Malachi [6], *ye have wearied the Lord: yet ye say, wherewith have we wearied Him?* His long-suffering was, as it were, worn out by them. He was straitened under them, as the wain groans under the sheaves with which it is over-full. The words are literally, *Behold I, I* [emphatic *I,* your God, of Whom it would seem impossible] *straiten myself* [i. e. of My own Will allow Myself to be straitened] *under you* [7], *as the wain full for itself,* i. e. as full as ever it can contain, is *straitened, groans,* as we say. God says, (the word in Hebrew is half active) that He allows Himself to be straitened, as in Isaiah He says, *I am weary to bear,* lit., " I let Myself be wearied." *We* are simply passive under weariness or oppressiveness: God endures us, out of His own free condescension in enduring us. But it follows, that when He shall cease to endure our many and grievous sins, He will cast them and the sinner forth from Him.

1 Ex. xix. 4.   2 Deut. i. 31.   3 lxiii. 9.
4 xlvi. 3.   5 xliii. 24.   6 ii. 17.
7 The E. M. gives as a choice, the rendering, " I will press your place, as a cart full of sheaves presseth." But 1) תחת never occurs as the first object of a verb. In Job xxxvi. 20. xl. 12. it stands absolutely, as with the intrans. verb, Hab. iii. 7. 2) Nor is the object pressed down omitted, as if " press down under you," could stand for " press *you* down." 3) Nor is the slight track made by a two-wheeled cart (such as is used in the East and in many mountainous countries) likely to be an image of the utter crushing of a people.   8 vi. 13.
9 So מנוס probably means in the same idiom, Job xi. 20. Ps. cxlii. 5. Jer. xxv. 35.

14-16. Israel relied, against God, on his own strength. *Have we not,* they said [8], *taken to us horns by our own strength?* Amos tells them then, that every means of strength, resistance, flight, swiftness of foot, of horse, place of refuge, should fail them. Three times he repeats, as a sort of dirge, *he shall not deliver himself.*

Therefore the flight (probably *place of flight* [9],) *shall perish.* They had despised God, as their *place of refuge* [10], so *the place of refuge should perish from the swift,* as though it were not. He should flee amain, but there would be *no place to flee unto.* God alone *renews strength;* therefore *the strong* man should not *strengthen his force* or *might,* should not be able to gather or " collect his strength [11]," as we say. Fear should disable him. *The handler of the bow* [12], and who by habit is a skilled archer, although himself out of the immediate reach of the enemy, and able, unharmed, to annoy him and protect the fugitives, *shall not stand* [13]. Panic should overtake him. The *mighty* man, the *fleet of foot* should *not deliver,* yea, the *horseman* should not *deliver himself;* yea, he who, *among the mighty,* was *strongest of his heart,* firm-souled among those of mightiest prowess, *shall flee away naked,* i. e. bared of all, armor [14] or dress, which might encumber his flight *in that day,* which the Lord made a day of terror, His own day.

Saith the Lord. Probably lit. *the secret utterance* [15] *of the Lord.* Amos, more than Hosea, uses this special authentication of his words [16], which is so common in Isaiah, Jeremiah,

10 מנוס is so used as to God, 2 Sam. xxii. 3. Ps. lix. 17. Jer. xvi. 19.
11 So Prov. xxiv. 5.
12 As in Jer. xlvi. 9. תפש מגן.
13 As in Jer. xlvi. 21. Nah. ii. 8.
14 As Livy speaks of persons "unarmed and naked," iii. 23; or S. Peter is said to be " naked," before he had girt on his upper garment, (ἐπενδύτης) S. Joh. xxi. 7; and Virgil directs his husbandmen to " plough and sow naked," Georg. i. 229. i. e. unencumbered with the upper dress.
15 From the Arab.
16 At the end of the sentence, here and iii. 13, 15. iv. 3, 5, 6, 8, 9, 10, 11. ix. 8. 12; in the middle, iii. 10. vi. 8, 14, viii. 3, 9, 11. ix. 7, 13.

Before
CHRIST
cir. 787.

CHAPTER III.

1 *The necessity of God's judgment against Israel.* 9 *The
publication of it, with the causes
thereof.*

HEAR this word that the
LORD hath spoken

against you, O children of
Israel, against the whole
family which I brought up
from the land of Egypt,
saying,

2 [a]You only have I

Before
CHRIST
cir. 787.

[a]Deut. 7. 6.
& 10, 15.
Ps. 147. 19, 20.

Ezekiel, and Zechariah. He claims a knowledge, which those around him had not, and
ratifies it by the express appeal to the direct,
though secret, revelation of God; what those
who were not of God, would deny; what they
who were of God, would believe.

III. 1. Amos, like Hosea, rebukes Israel
directly, Judah indirectly. He had warned
each nation separately. Now, ere he concentrates himself on Israel, he sums up what he
had before said to Judah and in the Person of
God. "Ye have been alike in My gifts to
you, alike in your waste of them and your
sins; alike ye shall be in your punishment."
What was said to Israel was said also to Judah: what was directed first to the former
people, belongs to us, the later. What Jesus
said to the Apostles, He said also to the
Church, and to single souls, [1] *What I say unto
you, I say unto all, Watch.*

1. *Hear ye this word.* With that solemn
threefold call, so frequent in the Old Testament, he summons them thrice [2], as in the
Name of the Holy Trinity, to hear God's
words. "[3] The Prophet, at the outset
of the chapter, rouses the hearers to
anxious consideration. For the words of the
most High God are to be heard, not with a
superficial, unawed, wandering mind, but
with reverence, fear, and love."

That the Lord hath spoken against (and upon [4])
you, (coming down *from heaven* [5], both *upon*
and *against* them) *the whole family which I
brought up from the land of Egypt.* To Abraham God had said [6], *in thee shall all the families of the earth be blessed.* So now, in withdrawing that blessing from them. He takes
it away from them, family by family [7]. He
includes them, one and all, and Judah also,
since all had been *brought out of Egypt.*

2. *You only have I known of all the families
of the earth; therefore I will punish you for all
your iniquities.* Such is the one law of God.
The nearer any is brought unto God, the
worse is his fall, and, his trial over, the more
heavily is he punished. Nearness to God is
a priceless, but an awful gift. The intensest
blessing becomes, by the abuse of free will,
the most dreadful woe. For the nearer God
places any one to His own light, the more

malignant is the choice of darkness instead of
light. The more clearly any one knows the
relation to God, in which God has placed
him, the more terrible is his rejection of God.
The more God reveals to any, what He IS,
His essential perfections, His holiness and
love, the more utter, fearful malignity it is,
to have been brought face to face with God,
and to have in deed said to Him, "On Thy
terms I will have none of Thee." The angels
who sinned against fullest light, had no redemption or repentance; but became devils.
[8] *He took not on Him the nature of angels.*
[9] *The angels which kept not their first estate, but
left their own habitations, He hath reserved in
everlasting chains under darkness unto the judgment of the great Day.* Of the former people,
when their first day of grace was past, Daniel
says [10]; *under the whole heaven hath not been
done, as hath been done upon Jerusalem. Begin,*
God saith in Ezekiel [11], *at My sanctuary.
Then they began at the ancient men which* were
before the house. So our Lord lays down the
rule of judgment and punishment hereafter [12]:
*the servant which knew his Lord's will, and pre-
pared not himself, neither did according to His
will, shall be beaten with many stripes. But he
that knew not, and did commit things worthy of
stripes, shall be beaten with few stripes. For
unto whomsoever much has been given, of him shall
much be required, and to whom men have committed much, of him they will ask the more.* The
time is come, says S. Peter [13], *that judgment
must begin at the house of God.*

You only I have known. Such care had God
had of Israel, so had He known them, and
made Himself known to them, as if He had,
in comparison, disregarded all besides, as He
remained unknown by them. Knowledge,
among men, is mutual, and so it seemed as if
God knew not those, of whom He was not
known. Knowledge, with God, is love, and
so He seemed not to have known those, to
whom, although *He left not Himself without witness* [14], He had shown no such love [15]. Whence
our Lord shall say to the wicked [16], *I never
knew you;* and contrariwise, He says [17], *I am
the good Shepherd and know My sheep, and am
known of Mine.* "[18] Myriads of cities and
lands are there under the whole heaven, and

---

[1] S. Mark xiii. 37.   [2] iii. 1. iv. 1. v. 1.   [3] Dion.

[4] עֲלֵיכֶם.   [5] Heb. xii. 25.   [6] Gen. xii. 3.

[7] Zech. xii. 12.   [8] Heb. ii. 16.   [9] S. Jude 6.

[10] ix. 12.   [11] ix. 6.   [12] S. Luke xii. 47, 8.
[13] 1 Ep. iv. 17.   [14] Acts xiv. 17.
[15] See on Hos. xiii. 5. p. 83.   [16] S. Matt. vii. 23.
[17] S. John x. 14. see 2 Tim. ii. 19.   [18] S. Cyr.

known of all the families of the earth : ᵇ therefore I

will †punish you for all your iniquities.

in them countless multitudes; but you alone have I chosen out of all, made Myself known and visible among you by many miracles, chosen you out of a bitter unbearable bondage, trained you by My law to be well-pleasing to Me, fenced you with protection, brought you into the land promised to your fathers, enlightened you with prophecies."

"[1] Not, I deem, as though in the time of Israel and of the Old Testament, there were not, in the whole world, some good men and predestinated; but because God did not then choose any nation or whole people, save the children of Israel. For it was meet that that people, of which God willed to be Incarnate, should be distinguished by some special grace."

Therefore I will punish you. "[2] To depise God and to neglect the Lord's Will procureth destruction to those who have known Him or been known of Him, and been spiritually made His own." " I made you My own people, friends, sons. As a Father, I cherished, protected, exalted, you. Ye would not have Me as a Father, ye shall have Me as a Judge." "[3] As Israel has, in its elect, been glorious above all, so, in the reprobate, has it been made viler than all, both before God and before men." How much more Christians, and, among Christians, priests! It has of old been believed, that the deepest damnation will be that of ungodly priests.

Yet since almost all punishment in this life is remedial, the saying admits another meaning that God would leave no sin unchastened in those whom He had made His own. Both are true meanings, fulfilled at different times. God chastens in proportion to His love, in the Day of grace. He punishes, in proportion to the grace and love despised and trampled upon without repentance in eternity. Here, "[4] the most merciful Physician, cutting away the cancrous flesh, spareth not, that He may spare; He pitieth not, that He may be the more pity. For *whom the Lord loveth He chasteneth, and scourgeth every son whom He receiveth.*" Hence the prayer [5] " Burn, cut, here; and spare forever." Contrariwise, "[6] we should esteem any sinner the more miserable, when we see him left in his sin, unscourged. Whence it is said [7], *The turning away of the simple shall slay them, and the prosperity of fools shall destroy them.* For whoso turneth away from God and is *prosperous,* is the nearer to perdition, the more he is removed from the severity of discipline."

"[8] This is the terrible, this the extreme case, when we are no longer chastened for sins, when we are no more corrected for offending. For when we have exceeded the measure of sinning, God, in displeasure, turneth away from us His displeasure." "[9] When you see a sinner, affluent, powerful, enjoying health, with wife and circle of children, and that saying is fulfilled, [10] *They are not in trouble as other men, neither are they plagued like other men,* in him is the threat of the Prophet fulfilled, *I will not visit.*"

3. Sacred parables or enigmas must have many meanings. They are cast on the mind, to quicken it and rouse it by their very mystery. They are taken from objects which in different lights, represent different things, and so suggest them. This series of brief parables have, all of them, this in common, that each thing spoken of is alternately cause and effect, and where the one is found, *there* must be the other. From the effect you can certainly infer the cause, without which it could not be, and from the cause you may be sure of the effect. Then, further, all the images are of terror and peril to the objects spoken of. The Prophet impresses upon their minds both aspects of these things; "evil will not befall, unless it has been prepared;" "signs of evil will not shew themselves, unless the evil be at hand." The bird will not fall without the snare; if the snare rises and so shews itself, the bird is as good as taken. As surely then (the Prophet would say) as the roaring of the lion, the rising of the snare, the alarm of the trumpet, betokens imminent peril, so surely does the warning Voice of God. *The lion hath roared; who will not fear?* Again, as surely as these are the effects of their causes, so surely is all infliction sent by Him Who Alone has power over all things, and is the cause of all. *Shall there be evil in a city, and the Lord hath not done* it? Again, as these tokens are given before the evil comes, and the God of nature and of grace has made it a law in nature, that what is fearful should give signs of coming evil, so has He made it a law of His own dealings, not to inflict evil, without having fore-announced it. *Surely the Lord God will do nothing, but He revealeth His secret unto His servants the prophets.* As nothing else is by chance, nor happens without cause, much less the acts of God. The lion or young lion when they roar, the bird when it falls to the ground, the snare when it rises, the trumpet's

1 Dion.   2 S. Cyr.   3 Rup.
4 S. Jerome in Ezek. vii. Sanct. in Hos. iv. 14.
5 Ap. S. Aug. Bp. Andrewes, Prayers.

6 S. Greg. in Ezek. L. i. Hom. xii. 18.
7 Pr. i. 32.   8 Orig. Hom. viii. 5. in Ex. xx. S.
9 S. Jer. in Hos. iv. 14. S.   10 Ps. lxxiii. 5.

Before
C H R I S T
cir. 787.

3 Can two walk together, except they be agreed?

4 Will a lion roar in the forest, when he hath no prey? will a young lion † cry out of his den, if he have taken nothing?

5 Can a bird fall in a

† Heb.
give forth
his voice.

snare upon the earth, where no gin *is* for him? shall *one* take up a snare from the earth, and have taken nothing at all?

6 Shall a trumpet be blown in the city, and the people || not be afraid?

Before
C H R I S T
cir. 787.

|| Or, *not run together?*

sound, all have their cause and ground: shall not then much more the acts and works of God? Shall evil happen in the city, and have no ground in the Cause of all causes, God in His righteous judgments? As there is fear, whenever there are tokens and causes of fear, so fear ye now and watch, lest the fear overtake you and it be too late. The first words then,

3. *Can [Will] two walk together, except they be agreed?* are at once a general rule for all which follows, and have different bearings according to those its several aspects. And, before all these, it is an appeal at once to the conscience which feels itself parted from its God; "so neither will God be with thee, unless thou art agreed and of one mind with God. Think not to have God with thee, unless thou art with God;" as He saith[1], *I will not go up in the midst of thee, for thou art a stiff-necked people, lest I consume thee in the way;* and [2], *if ye walk contrary unto Me, then will I also walk contrary unto you, and will punish you yet seven times for your sins.* And on the other hand[3], *They shall walk with Me in white, for they are worthy.* "[4] God cannot be agreed with the sinner who justifies himself. "[5] God Who rebuketh, and Israel who is rebuked, are two. God saith, We are not agreed, in that Israel, when rebuked, heareth not Me, God, rebuking. Herein we are not agreed, that I rebuke, Israel justifieth himself. Lo, for so many years since Jeroboam made the golden calves, have I sent Prophets, and none agreeth, for no one king departed from the sin of Jeroboam. So then I came Myself, God made Man, rebuking and reproving: but[6] *ye are they which justify yourselves before men,* and, being sick, ye say to the Physician, we need Thee not." "[7] So long as thou confessest not thy sins, thou art in a manner litigating with God. For what displeaseth Him, thou praisest. Be at one with God. Let what displeaseth Him, displease thee. Thy past evil life displeaseth Him. If it please thee, thou art disjoined from Him; if it displease thee, by confessing thy sins, thou art joined to Him." So He awakens

and prepares the soul for the following words of awe.

In connection with what follows, the words are also the Prophet's defence of his Mission. Israel *said to the Prophets, prophesy not*[8], or, *The Lord our God hath not sent thee*[9], because, while it disobeyed God, the Prophets must *speak concerning it not good, but evil.* Amos prepares the way for his answer; ye yourselves admit, that *two will* not *walk together, unless they be agreed.* The seen and the unseen, the words of the Prophets and the dealings of God, would not meet together, unless the Prophets were of one mind with God, unless God had admitted them into His counsels, and *were agreed* with them, so that their words should precede His deeds, His deeds confirm His words by them.

Then, further, each question by itself suggests its own thought. Amos had already, in repeating Joel's words, spoken of God's Voice, under the image of a lion roaring[10]. Hosea had likened Israel to *a silly dove without heart*[11]; on the other hand, he had likened God's loud call to repentance to the roaring of the lion, the conversion of Israel to the return of the dove to its home[12]. As the roaring of the lion causeth terror, for he sendeth forth his terrible roar when he is about to spring on his prey[13], so God threatens by His Prophets, only when He is about to punish. Yet the lion's roar is a warning to escape. God's threatening is a warning to betake them to repentance, and so to escape from all fear, by fleeing from their sins. If the season is neglected, wilt thou rescue the prey from the lion's grasp, or thyself from the wrath of God?

Again, the bird taken in the snare is the image of those drawn down from heaven, where *our conversation is*[14] and the soul may rise free toward its God, "[15] drawn up by the Spirit to high and heavenly things." Such souls being allured by the things of earth, are entangled and taken by Satan; as, on the other hand, *the soul, escaped as a bird out of the snare of the fowler*[16], is a soul, set free by Christ and restored to Heaven.

[1] Ex. xxxiii. 3.   [2] Lev. xxvi. 23, 4.
[3] Rev. iii. 4.   [4] Lap.   [5] Rup.
[6] S. Luke xvi. 15.   [7] S. Aug. in Ps. lxxv. Lap.
[8] See ab. on ii. 12.   [9] Jer. xliii. 2.

[10] i. 2. Hos. xi. 10 (add v. 14. vi. 1. xiii. 7.) Jer. xxv. 30.
[11] vii. 11.   [12] xi. 10, 11.   [13] Boch. Hieroz. i. iii. 2.
[14] Phil. iii. 20.   [15] Art. xvii.   [16] Ps. cxxiv. 7.

Before CHRIST cir. 787.
c Is. 45. 7.
‖ Or, and shall not the LORD do somewhat.

c shall there be evil in a city, ‖ and the LORD hath not done it ?

7 Surely the Lord GOD

will do nothing, but d he revealeth his secret unto his servants the prophets.

8 e The lion hath roared,

Before CHRIST cir. 787.
d Gen. 6. 13. & 18. 17.
Ps. 25. 14.
John 15. 15.
e ch. 1. 2.

In the last likeness, the Prophet comes nearer to the people themselves, and the trumpet is, at once, the well-known token of alarm among men, and of the loud voice of God, wakening them to repentance[1] and still oftener, warning them of the approach of judgment[2], or summoning man before Him[3]. " [4] God's Voice will not always be *a still small voice*, or whispered only among the Angels, or heard as from the ground. It will be heard terribly in the whole world." " [5] Whatever is said in Holy Scripture is a trumpet threatening, and with loud voice sinking into the hearts of believers. If we are righteous, we are called by the trumpet of Christ to bliss. If we are sinners, we know that we are to suffer torment." *Is there evil in the city and the Lord hath not done it?* Evil is of two sorts, evil of sin, and evil of punishment. There is no other; for evil of nature, or evil of fortune, are evils, by God's Providence, punishing the evil of sin. " [6] Evil, which is sin, the Lord hath not done; evil, which is punishment for sin, the Lord bringeth." The Providence of God governing and controlling all things, man doth ill which he wills, so as to suffer ill which he wills not. Only, evil which is by God's Providence the punishment of sin is in this life remedial, and through final impenitence alone becomes purely judicial. " [7] Refer not, the Prophet would say, the ills which ye suffer and will suffer, to any other causes, as men are wont to do. God, in His displeasure, sends them upon you. And that ye may know this the more certainly, whatever He shall send He will first reveal to the Prophets and by them ye shall be forewarned. See then that ye despise not my words, or the words of the other prophets. Men ascribe their sufferings to fortune, accident, any cause, rather than the displeasure of God. The intemperate will think anything the cause of their illness rather than their intemperance. Men love the things of the world and cannot and will not be persuaded that so many evils are brought on them by the things which they love. So then God explains through the prophets the punishment which He purposes to bring on men."

7. *Surely the Lord God will do* [*For the Lord GOD doeth*] *nothing, but He revealeth His*

secret unto His servants the prophets. So our Lord saith[8], *And now I have told you before it come to pass, that, when it is come to pass, ye may believe.* While it is yet a *secret* counsel within Himself, He admitteth to it His servants the prophets. The same word signifies " secret [9] " and " secret counsel with a friend." So " [10] God revealed to Noah that He would bring the deluge, and to Abraham and Lot, that He would destroy the cities of the plain, and to Joseph the 7 years' famine in Egypt, and to Moses its plagues, and to Moses and Joshua all the chastisements of His people, and to Jonah the destruction of Nineveh, that they who heard of the coming punishment, might either avoid it by repentance, or, if they should despise it, might be more justly punished. And so now the Lord is about to reveal through Amos, His servant and prophet, what He willeth to do to the 10 tribes, that forsaking their idols and turning to Him, they might be freed from the impending peril; which is of the great mercy of God. He foretelleth evil to come, that He may not be compelled to inflict it. For He Who forewarneth, willeth not to punish sinners."

" [11] So He inflicted not on Egypt any plagues by the hand of Moses, but He first forewarned Pharaoh and the Egyptians by him; nor the sufferings by the Ammonites, Midianites and Philistines, related in the book of Judges, but He foremonished Israel by Joshua ; [12] nor did He inflict on the Jews that destruction by Titus and the Romans, but He foremonished them by Christ[13] and the Apostles. So neither will He bring that last destruction on the world, without having first sent the Prophets and Angels, who, sounding with the seven trumpets, shall proclaim it throughout the world[14]."

8. *The Lion hath roared : who will not fear? The Lord God hath spoken : who can but prophesy?* i. e. there is cause for you to fear, when the Lord *roareth from Zion ;* but if ye fear not, God's prophets dare not but fear. So S. Paul saith [15], *necessity is laid upon me ; yea, woe is unto me if I preach not the Gospel! For if I do this thing willingly, I have a reward ; but if against my will, a dispensation of the Gospel is committed unto me ;* and SS. Peter and John[16], *whether it be right in the sight of*

---

[1] Is. lviii. 1. Joel ii. 15.
[2] Is. xviii. 3. Jer. iv. 5. vi. 1. Ez. xxxiii. 2-6. Hos. v. 8. viii. 1. Rev. viii.
[3] 1 Cor. xv. 52. 1 Thess. iv. 16.
[4] Rup.
[5] S. Jer.
[6] S. Aug. c. Adim. 26.
[7] Rib.

[8] S. John xiv. 29. comp. Ib. xiii. 19.
[9] סוֹד, used here.
[10] S. Jer.
[11] Lap.
[12] Jos. xxiii. 12–16. xxiv. 19, 20.
[13] S. Luke xix. 42–44.
[14] Rev. viii. 2.
[15] 1 Cor. ix. 16, 17.
[16] Acts iv. 19, 20.

18

Before
CHRIST
cir. 787.
f Acts 4. 20.
& 5. 20, 29.
1 Cor. 9. 16. who will not fear? the Lord GOD hath spoken, f who can but prophesy?

9 ¶ Publish in the palaces at Ashdod, and in the palaces in the land of Egypt, and say, Assemble yourselves upon the moun- Before
CHRIST
cir. 787.

God to hearken unto you more than unto God, judge ye! For we cannot but speak the things which we have seen and heard. Moses was not excused, though slow of speech; nor Isaiah, though of polluted lips; nor Jeremiah, because he was a child; but God said [1], Say not, I am a child; for thou shalt go to all that I shall send thee, and whatsoever I command thee, thou shalt speak. And Ezekiel was bidden [2], be not rebellious, like that rebellious house. And when Jeremiah would keep silence, he saith [3], His Word was in mine heart as a burning fire, shut up in my bones, and I was weary with forbearing and I could not stay.

9. Publish [ye, they are the words of God, commissioning His prophets,] in [on] the palaces of Ashdod, [i. e. on the flat roofs of their high buidings, whence all can hear] and in [on] the palaces in the land of Egypt. " [4] Since ye disbelieve, I will manifest to Ashdodites and Egyptians the transgressions of which ye are guilty." Amos had already pronounced God's sentence on the palaces of Ashdod and all Philistia, for their sins against Himself in His people [5]. Israel now, or a little later, courted Egypt [6]. To friend then and to foe, to those whom they dreaded and those whom they courted, God would lay open their sins. Contempt and contumely from an enemy aggravate suffering: man does not help whom he despiseth. They were all ashamed of a people who could not profit them, saith Isaiah [7] subsequently, of Egypt in regard to Judah. From those palaces, already doomed to destruction for their sins, the summons was to go, to visit Samaria, and see her sins, amid grace which those people had not. As our Lord says [8], It shall be more tolerable for Sodom and Gomorrah in the Day of Judgment, than for that city. Shame toward man survives shame toward God. What men are not ashamed to do, they are, apart from any consequences, ashamed to confess that they have done. Nay, to avoid a little passing shame, they rush upon everlasting shame. So God employs all inferior motives, shame, fear, hope of things present, if by any means He can win men, not to offend Him.

Assemble yourselves upon the mountains of Samaria, i. e. those surrounding it. Samaria was chosen with much human wisdom for the strong capital of a small people. Imbedded in mountains, and out of any of the usual routes [9], it lay, a mountain-fastness in a rich valley. Armies might surge to and fro in the valley of Jezreel, and be unconscious of its existence. The way from that great valley to Samaria lay, every way, through deep and often narrowing valleys [10], down which the armies of Samaria might readily pour, but which, like Thermopylæ, might be held by a handful of men against a large host. The broad vale near the hill of Dothan [11], along which the blinded Syrian army followed Elisha to Samaria, contracts into "a narrow valley [12]," before it reaches Samaria. The author of the book of Judith, who knew well the country, speaks of "the passages of the hill-country" near Dothaim, "by" which "there was an entrance into Judæa, and it was easy to stop them that would come up, because the passage was strait for two men at the most [13]." " [14] A series of long winding ravines open from the mountains to the plain; these were the passes so often defended by the 'horns of Joseph, the ten thousands of Ephraim, and the thousands of Manasseh' against the invaders from the North." Within these lay " [15] the wide rocky rampart" which fenced in Samaria from the N. " [16] The fine round swelling hill of Samaria, now cultivated to the top, [about 1100 feet above the sea [17], and 300 from its own valley [18],] stands alone in the midst of a great basin of some two hours [or 5 miles] in diameter surrounded by higher mountains on every side." " [19] The view from its summit presents a splendid panorama of the fertile basin and the mountains around, teeming with large villages, and includes not less than 25 degrees of the Mediterranean." Such a place, out of reach, in those days, from the neighboring heights,

---

[1] Jer. i. 7.   [2] ii. 8.   [3] xx. 9.   [4] Theod.
[5] See on i. 6–8.   [6] Hos. vii. 11. xii. 1.   [7] xxx. 5.
[8] S. Matt. x. 15.
[9] Even the route from Beisan [Beth-shean] and Zerin [Jezreel] to Ramleh and Egypt lay N. of Samaria, passing through the valley of Yabud to Ferasin and Zeita. (Rob. iii. 122–4.)
[10] Maundrell "passed through narrow valleys for four hours," before he reached Caphar Arab, taking the road to the left of Arab (Arrabeh) and Rama and "over Selee." pp. 77, 8. "The way from Sanur to Jenin ran uniformly through a narrow wadi ("a sort of defile," Wilson, Lands, &c. ii. 84.), opening

into the plain of Esdraelon." (V. de Velde i. 367. Rob. ii. 314.)
[11] "A huge hill, covered over with ruins." V. de Velde, i. 364.   [12] Ib. 370.
[13] iv. 7. This was probably a proverbial expression.
[14] Porter, Hdb. 350. "Almost all travelers are compelled to draw conclusions from the well-known descent from Sebaste through Sanur to Jenin. But the general nature of the ground cannot be doubted." Stanley, Pal. 246.
[15] V. de V. 373.   [16] Rob. ii. 304.
[17] Poole, in V. de Velde, Memoir, 178.
[18] Porter, 344.   [19] Rob. ii. 307.

tains of Samaria, and be-
hold the great tumults in the
midst thereof, and the ‖ oppressed in the midst thereof.

10 For they ᵍ know not
to do right, saith the LORD,
who store up violence and
‖ robbery in their palaces.

was well-nigh impregnable, except by famine.
But its inhabitants must have had handed
down to them the memory, how those heights
had once been peopled, while their valleys
were thronged with *all the hosts*[1] of Benhadad, his chariots and his horsemen; and
the mountains, in which they had trusted to
shut out the enemy, were the prison-walls
of their famished people. From those
heights, "[2] the Syrians could plainly distinguish the famishing inhabitants of the city.
The adjacent circle of hills were so densely
occupied, that not a man could push through
to bring provisions to the beleaguered city."
The city, being built on the summit and terraced sides of the hill, unfenced and uncon-
cealed by walls which, except at its base,
were unneeded, lay open, unsheltered in
every part from the gaze of the besiegers.
The surrounding hills were one large amphitheatre, whence to behold the tragedy of
Israel[3], and enemies were invited to be the
spectators. They could see its famine-
stricken inhabitants totter along those open
terraces. Sin had brought this chastisement
upon them. God had forgiven them then.
When God Who had, by His Prophet,
foretold their relief then[4], now by His Prophet called anew those enemies of Samaria
to those same heights to behold her sins,
what could this mean but that He summoned
them to avenge what He summoned them to
behold ? It was no figure of speech. God
avenges, as He comforts, not in word, but in
deed. The triumph of those enemies David
had especially deprecated[5], *Tell it not in
Gath, publish it not in the streets of Askelon;
lest the daughters of the Philistines rejoice, lest
the daughters of the uncircumised triumph.* To
these Israel was to be a gazing-stock. They
were like *the woman set in the midst*[6], amid
one encircling sea of accusing insulting faces,
with none to pity, none to intercede, none to
shew mercy to them *who had shewed no mercy.*
Faint image of the shame of that Day, when
not men's deeds only, but [7] *the secrets of all
hearts shall be revealed,* and [8] *they shall begin to
say to the mountains, Fall on us, and to the hills,
Cover us ;* and of that *shame* there will be no
end ; for it is *everlasting*[9].

And behold the great tumults, i. e. the alarms,
restlessness, disorders and confusion of a people intent on gain; turning all law upside

down, the tumultuous noise of the oppressors
and oppressed. It is the word which Solomon uses [10], *Better is little with the fear of the
Lord, than great treasure and tumult therewith,*
the tumults and restlessness of continual
gaining. And the *oppressed,* or better (as in
the E. M.) *the oppressions* [11], the manifold ever-
repeated acts by which men were crushed
and trampled on.

In the midst thereof, admitted within her,
domiciled, reigning there in her very centre,
and never departing out of her, as the
Psalmist says [12], *Wickedness is in the midst
thereof; deceit and guile depart not from her
streets.* Aforetime, God spared His people,
that His *Name* [13] *should not be polluted before
the heathen, among whom they were, in whose
sight I made Myself known unto them in bringing them forth out of the land of Egypt.* Now He
summons those same heathen as witnesses
that Israel was justly condemned. These
sins, being sins against the moral law, the
Heathen would condemn. Men condemn in
others, what they do themselves. But so
they would see that God hated sin, for which
He spared not His own people, and could the
less triumph over God, when they saw the
people whom God had established and protected, given up to the king of Assyria.

10. *For* [and] *they know not to do right.*
They *have not known* [14], they have lost all
sense and knowledge, how *to do right* (lit.
what is *straight-forward* [15]) because they had
so long ceased to do it. It is part of the
miserable blindness of sin, that, while the
soul acquires a quick insight into evil, it becomes, at last, not paralyzed only to *do* good,
but unable to perceive it. So Jeremiah
says [16], *they are wise to do evil, but to do good
they have no knowledge.'* Whence of the
Christian S. Paul says, *I would have you wise
unto that which is good, and simple concerning
evil* [17]. People, step by step, lose the power
of understanding either good or evil, the love
of the world or the love of God. Either becomes "a strange language" to ears accustomed to the *songs of Zion* or the din of the
world. When our Lord and God came to
His own, they said, [18] *we know that God spake
unto Moses :* as for *this man we know not whence
He is.* And this blindness was wrought by
covetousness which *blindeth the eyes* even of
the wise [19], as he adds;

our *oppressions,* is a passive, made active by its use
as an abstract.

[1] 2 Kings vi. 24. [2] V. de Velde, i. 377. [3] Mont.
[4] 2 Kgs vii. 1, 2. [5] 2 Sam. i. 20.
[6] S. John viii. 3. [7] Rom. ii. 16.
[8] S. Luke xxiii. 30. [9] Dan. xii. 2. [10] Prog. xv. 16.
[11] As in Job xxxv. 9. Eccl. iv. 1. The word, like

[12] Ps. lv. 11. [13] Ezek. xx. 9. [14] לֹא יָדְעוּ.
[15] נְכֹחָה. [16] iv. 22. [17] Rom. xvi. 19.
[18] S. John ix. 29. [19] Ex. xxiii. 8.

Before
C H R I S T
cir. 787.

[h] 2 Kings 17.
3, 6. & 18. 9, 10,
11.

11 Therefore thus saith the Lord God; [h] An adversary *there shall be* even round about the land; and

he shall bring down thy strength from thee, and thy palaces shall be spoiled.

Before
C H R I S T
cir. 787.

Who store [lit. with indignation, *the storers* [1]] *with violence and robbery.* They could not understand what was right, while they habitually did what was wrong. They *stored up*, as they deemed, the gains and fruits; the robbery and injustice they saw not, because they turned away from seeing. But what is stored up, is not what wastes away, but what abides. Who doubts it? Then, what they treasured, were not the perishing things of earth, but, in truth, the sins themselves, as *a* [2] *treasure of wrath against the Day of wrath and revelation of the righteous judgment of God.* Strange treasure, to be so diligently accumulated, guarded, multiplied! Yet it is, in fact, all which remains. [3] *So* is *he that layeth up treasure for himself and is not rich towards God.* He adds, as an aggravation, *in their palaces.* Deformed as in all oppression, yet *to oppress the poor, to increase his riches* [4], has an unnatural hideousness of its own. What was wrung from the poor, laid up *in palaces!* Yet what else is it to cheapen luxuries at the cost of the wages of the poor?

11. *Therefore thus saith the Lord God.* There was no human redress. The oppressor was mighty, but mightier the Avenger of the poor. Man would not help; therefore God would. *An adversary* there shall be, *even round about the land;* lit. *An enemy, and around the land!* The Prophets speaks, as seeing him. The abruptness tells how suddenly that enemy should come, and *hem* [5] in the whole land on all sides. What an unity in their destruction! He sees one *enemy, and* him everywhere, all *around*, encircling, encompassing, as with a net, their whole land, narrowing in, as he advanced, until it closed around and upon them. The corruption was universal, so should be the requital.

And he shall bring down thy strength from (i. e. *away from*) *thee.* The word *bring down* implies a loftiness of pride which was to be brought low, as in Obadiah [6], *thence will I bring thee down;* and in Isaiah [7], *I will bring down their strength to the earth.* But further, their strength was not only, as in former oppressions, to be *brought down*, but *forth from thee.* *Thy palaces shall be spoiled;* those palaces, in which they had heaped up the spoils of the oppressed. Man's sins are, in God's Providence, the means of their punishment. [8] *Woe to thee that spoilest and* [i. e. whereas]

thou wert *not spoiled, and dealest treacherously, and they dealt not treacherously with thee! when thou perfectest spoiling, thou shalt be spoiled; when thou accomplishest dealing treacherously, they shall deal treacherously with thee.* Their spoiling should invite the spoiler, their oppressions should attract the oppressor, and they, with all which they held to be their strength, should go *forth* into captivity.

" [9] *The Lord will be justified in His sayings*, and in His works, when He executeth judgment on *us and shall be cleared*, even by the most unjust judges, *when He is judged* [10]. He cites the Ashdodites and Egyptians as judges, who were witnesses of His benefits to this people, that they might see how justly He punished them. And now the hardened Jews themselves, Turks and all Hagarenes, might be called to behold at once our iniquities, and *the mercies of the Lord, that we are not consumed* [11]. If these were gathered on the mountains of Samaria, and surveyed from aloft our sins, who worship Mammon and Vain-glory and Venus for God, doubtless the Name of God would through us be blasphemed among the heathen. ' Imagine yourselves withdrawn for a while to the summit of some lofty mountain,' says the blessed martyr Cyprian [12], 'view thence the face of things, as they lie beneath you, yourself free from contact of earth, cast your eyes hither and thither, and mark the turmoils of this billowy world. You too, recalled to self-remembrance, will pity the world; and, made more thankful to God, will congratulate yourself with deeper joy that you have escaped it. See thou the ways obstructed by bandits, the seas infested by pirates, war diffused everywhere by the camp's bloodstained fierceness: a world reeking with mutual slaughter; and homicide, a crime in individuals, called virtue when wrought by nations. Not innocence but the scale of its ferocity gains impunity for guilt. Turn thy eyes to the cities, thou wilt see a peopled concourse more melancholy than any solitude.' This and much more which he says of the life of the Gentiles, how it fits in with our's, any can judge. What greater madness than that men, called to heavenly thrones, should cling to trifles of earth? immortal man glued to passing, perishable things! men, redeemed by the Blood of Jesus Christ, for lucre wrong their brethren, redeemed by the same Price,

[1] הָאֹצְרִים, as before (ii. 7) הַשָׁאֲפִים.
[2] Rom. ii. 5.   [3] S. Luke xii. 21.
[4] Pr. xxii. 16.   [5] צַר.   [6] ver. 4.

[7] Is. lxiii. 6.   [8] Ib. xxxiii. 1.
[9] Rib.   [10] Ps. li. 4.   [11] Lam. iii. 22.
[12] ad Don. Treatises, p. 5. Oxf. Tr.

Before CHRIST cir. 787.

† Heb. delivereth.

12 Thus saith the LORD; as the shepherd † taketh out of the mouth of the lion two legs, or a piece of an ear; so shall the chil-

dren of Israel be taken out that dwell in Samaria in the corner of a bed, and ‖ in Damascus *in* a couch.

Before CHRIST cir. 787.

‖ Or, on the bed's feet.

the same Blood! No marvel then, that the Church is afflicted, and encompassed by unseen enemies, and her strength drawn down from her spoiled houses."

"Samaria is also every soul, which willeth to please man by whom it thinketh it may be holpen, rather than God, and, boasting itself to be Israel, yet worshipeth the golden calves, i. e. gold, silver, honors, and pleasures. Let men alien from the light of the Gospel survey *its tumults*, with what ardor of mind riches, pleasures are sought, how ambition is served, how restless and disturbed the soul is in catching at nothings, how forgetful of God the Creator and of heavenly things and of itself, how minded, as if it were to perish with the body! What tumults, when ambition bids one thing, lust another, avarice another, wrath another, and, like strong winds on the sea, strong, unbridled passions strive together! They *know not to do right*, bad ends spoiling acts in themselves good. They *treasure up violence*, whereas they ought to treasure up grace and charity against that Day when God shall judge the secrets of men. And when they ascribe to themselves any benefits of the Divine mercy, and any works pleasing to God, which they may have done or do, what else do they than *store up robbery?* So then the powers of the soul are *spoiled*, when truths as to right action, once known and understood by the soul, fade and are obscure, when the memory retaineth nothing useful, when the will is spoiled of virtues and yields to vicious affections."

¹ The uniform meaning of הִצִּיל with מִן, as also of the Niphal.
² The LXX. Aq. Symm. Theod. Syr. Ch. S. Jer. retain "Damascus" as a proper name. Of late, it has become a fashion to render it, "and in the damask of a couch." But 1) the fact that Ezekiel (xxvii. 18) speaks of *wine* and *white wool*, (the raw material) as the exports of Damascus to Tyre, seems a decisive proof, that the manufactures, for which Damascus has in modern times been so celebrated, did not exist there then. 2) It does not appear that the manufacture, which in modern European language is called from the city, "damask" or the like, is so called in Arabic. There has been a two-fold error in comparing an Arabic word. *a)* The word which, though foreign, had been naturalized in Arabia before Mohammed, was "Dimakso." This occurs in old poets [Amrulkeis v. 10. Ham. pp. 265, 6, 556.] Scholiasts or Lexica mention corruptions of this; "midakso," "dikamso," "dimkâso," but no trace of these has yet been observed in the actual language. The alleged forms, Dimssâko, Dimssako, Dimasko, (which alone would have corresponded with the Hebrew word) have no existence, except in error. See Freyt. Lex. Arab. ii. 57. The word "dimakso" is probably, from its different forms, a corrupted and foreign word. But the corruption

12. *As the shepherd taketh* [rather, *rescueth*¹] *out of the mouth of the lion two legs* [properly, the shank, the lower part of the leg below the knee, which in animals is dry, and bone only and worthless] *or a piece* [the tip] *of an ear, so* [i. e. so few and weak, so bared and spoiled, a mere remnant,] *shall the children of Israel be taken out* [rather, *rescued*¹] *that now dwell at ease in Samaria in the corner of a bed, and in Damascus*², *in a couch*, or rather *in Damascus, a couch.* Now, that soft, rounded, oblong, hill of Samaria, was one large luxurious couch, in which its rich and great rested securely, propped and cushioned up on both sides, *in*, what is still the place of dignity, *the corner of a bed*, or "Divan," i. e. the inner corner where the two sides meet. Damascus also, which Jeroboam had won for Israel, was a canopied couch to them, in which they stayed themselves. It is an image of listless ease and security, like that of those whom the false prophetesses lulled into careless stupidity as to their souls; *sewing pillows to all armholes*, or *wrists*³, whereon to lean in a dull inertness. In vain! Of all those who then dwelt at ease and in luxury, the Good Shepherd Himself should rescue from *the lion*, (the enemy, in the first instance the Assyrian,) a small remnant, in the sight of the enemy and of man of little account, but precious in the sight of God. The enemy would leave them perhaps, as not worth removing, just as, when the lion has devoured the fat and the strong, the shepherd may recover from him some slight

has no near relation to the name of the city, Dimashko. It would have been strange that Arabs, speaking the same, and Hebrews, a kindred dialect, should have corrupted the name, as Europeans have not. Nor does any native Scholiast connect Dimakso with the city Damascus. *b)* The meaning of this word Dimakso, was not "manufactured," but "raw silk." Freyt. from Kam. Dj. It is silk "thread," which can be "twisted." Amrulk. "raw white silk or what is like it in whiteness and softness." Abulala in Tebriz. Scholl. ad. Ham. p. 566. The garment made of it was called, in the passive participle, "modamkaso," i. e., made of "dimakso." The punctuation of the Hebrew word is certainly varied here, דְּמֶשֶׂק, for what is elsewhere and in Amos himself (i. 3, 5. v. 27.) דַּרְמֶשֶׂק. Yet there are two other variations in pronouncing the name, דַּרְמֶשֶׂק 1 Chr. xviii. 5. דּוּמֶשֶׂק 2 Kgs. xvi. 10. It may have been pointed so by those who, like Aben Ezra, guessed from the context, that בְּרִמְשֶׂק was i. q. בְּפָאַת. On the other hand, very old and very accurate MSS. have here too the usual punctuation. See De Rossi. ³ Ezek. xiii. 18.

13 Hear ye, and testify in the house of Jacob, saith the Lord GOD, the God of hosts,

14 That in the day that I shall || visit the transgressions of Israel upon him I will also visit the

piece of skin or extremity of the bones. Amos then, as well as Joel [1], preaches that same solemn sentence, so repeated throughout the prophets, *a remnant* only *shall be saved*. So doubtless it was in the captivity of the ten tribes, as in the rest. So it was in Judah, when certain *of the poor of the land* only were *left for vinedressers and for husbandmen* [2]. In the Gospel, *not many wise men after the flesh, not many mighty, not many noble were called* [3], but *God chose the poor of this world, rich in faith* [4]: and the Good Shepherd rescued from the mouth of the lion those whom man despised, yet who *had ears to hear*. After the destruction of Jerusalem by the Romans, a poor remnant only escaped. "[5] The spirit of prophecy foresaw both captivities, the end whereof was to confirm the faith, not in one place only but in all the earth, and so a slight remnant was *rescued from the mouth of the lion*, i. e. from the slaughter of the destroyers, and permitted to live, that through them, as a witness and monument, the justice of God might be known from age to age, and the truth of the Scriptures might be everywhere borne about by them, still witnessing to Christ the Son of God, Who is known by the law and the prophets. Hapless remnants, so *taken out for the good of others, not their own!*" As these remnants of the animal shew what it was which the lion destroyed, yet are of no further profit, so are they now a memorial of what they once were, what grace through their sins they have lost.

"[6] Many souls will perish, because they trust in their own strength, and no more call on God to have mercy on them than if they could rise of themselves and enter the way of salvation without God. They trust in the power of their friends, or the friendship of princes, or the doctrines of philosophers, and repose in them as in a couch of Damascus. But Christ the Good Shepherd will rescue out of the mouth of *the lion*, who *goeth about seeking whom he may devour*, what is last and of least esteem in this world, who have any thing whereby the Good Shepherd can hold them. The *legs* signify the desire to go to hear the Word of God ; the extremity of the ear, that obedience was not wholly lost. For if any begin even in part to obey the word of God which he hath heard, God, of

His fatherly mercy, will help him and lead him on to perfect obedience. The legs also denote desire [7], whereby, as by certain steps, the soul approacheth to God or departeth from Him. Yet if a soul would be saved, desires suffice not ; but if to these obedience to the heavenly commands be added, it shall be rescued from the mouth of the lion."

13. *Hear ye and testify ye in* [rather *unto* or *against* [8]] *the house of Israel;* first *hear* yourselves, then *testify*, i. e. solemnly *protest*, in the Name of God ; and *bear witness unto* and *against* them, so that the solemn words may sink into them. It is of little avail to *testify*, unless we first *hear ;* nor can man *bear witness* to what the both not know ; nor will words make an *impression*, i. e. leave a trace of themselves, be stamped in or on men's souls, unless the soul which utters them have first hearkened unto them.

Saith the Lord God of hosts. "So [9] thundereth, as it were, the authority of the Holy Spirit, through the mouth of the shepherd. Foretelling and protesting the destruction of the altar of Bethel, he sets his God against the god whom Israel had chosen as theirs and worshiped there, *the Lord God of hosts*, against [10] *the similitude of a calf that eateth hay*. Not I, a shepherd, but so speaketh my God against your god."

14. *In the day that I shall visit the transgression of Israel upon him, I will also visit* [*upon*] *the altars of Bethel.* Israel then hoped that its false worship of "nature" would avail it. God says, contrariwise, that when He should punish, all their false worship, so far from helping them, should itself be the manifest object of His displeasure. Again God attests, at once, His long-suffering and His final retribution. Still had He foreborne to punish, *being slow to anger and of great goodness ;* but when that day, fixed by the divine Wisdom, should come, wherein He should vindicate His own holiness, by enduring the sin no longer, then He would *visit their transgressions*, i. e. all of them, old and new, forgotten by man or remembered, *upon them.* Scripture speaks of "visiting offences upon" because, in God's Providence, the sin returns upon a man's own head. It is not only the cause of his being punished, but it becomes part of his punishment. The memory of a man's sins will be part of his eternal suffering.

[1] See on Joel ii. 32. p. 199.
[2] 2 Kgs xxv. 12. Jer. lii. 16.
[3] 1 Cor. i. 26.
[5] Rup.
[7] S. Greg. on Job L. vi. n. 25.
[4] S. Jam. ii. 5.
[6] Rib.

[8] As in Deut. viii. 19, *I testify against you this day that ye shall utterly perish;* Ps. l. 7, *hear, O Israel, and I will testify against thee ; I am God, thy God.* Comp. Ps. lxxxi. 8. *I will testify unto thee.*
[9] From Rup.
[10] Ps. cvi. 20.

Before
CHRIST
cir. 787.
altars of Beth-el: and the
horns of the altar shall be
cut off, and fall to the
ground.

ⁱ Jer. 36. 22.

15 And I will smite ⁱ the

winter house with ᵏ the summer house; and ˡ the houses
of ivory shall perish, and
the great houses shall have
an end, saith the LORD.

Before
CHRIST
cir. 787.

ᵏ Judg. 3. 20.
ˡˡ 1 Kings 22. 39.

Even in this life, "remorse," as distinct from
repentance, is the "gnawing" of a man's
own conscience for the folly of his sin. Then
also God would visit upon the false worship. It is thought that God visits less
speedily even grave sins against Himself, (so that man does not appeal falsely
to Him and make Him, in a way, a partner
of his offence,) than sins against His own
creature, man. It may be that, All-Merciful
as He is, He bears the rather with sins, involving corruption of the truth as to Himself,
so long as they are done in ignorance, on account of the *ignorant worship*[1] of Himself, or
the fragments of truth which they contain, until the evil in them have its full
sway in moral guilt[2]. "[3] Wonderful is the
patience of God in enduring all those crimes
and injuries which appertain directly to
Himself; wonderful His waiting for repentance. But the deeds of guilt which violate
human society, faith, and justice, hasten
judgment and punishment, and, as it were,
with a most effectual cry call upon the Divine
Mind to punish, as it is written, [4] *The voice of
thy brother's blood crieth unto Me from the
ground, And now cursed art thou, &c.* If then
upon that very grave guilt against God Himself there be accumulated these other sins,
this so increases the load, that God speedily
casts it off. However long then Israel had,
with impunity, given itself to that vain, alien
worship, this evinced the patience, not the
approval, of God. Now, when they are to be
punished for the fourth transgression, they
will be punished for the first, second and
third, and so, most grievously; when brought
to punishment for their other sins, they
should suffer for their other guilt of impiety
and superstition."

And the horns of the altar. This was *the* one
great *altar*[5] for burnt offerings, set up by
Jeroboam, in imitation of that of God at
Jerusalem, whose doom was pronounced in
the act of its would-be consecration. He had
copied faithfully its outward form. At each
corner, where the two sides met in one, rose
the *horn*, or pillar, a cubit high[6], there to
sacrifice victims[7], there to place the blood
of atonement[8]. So far from atoning, they
themselves were *the* unatoned *sin* of Jeroboam

whereby [9] he *drave Israel from following the
Lord, and made them sin a great sin.* These
were to be *cut off*, hewn down, with violence.
A century and a half had passed, since the
man of God had pronounced its sentence.
They still stood. The day was not yet come;
Josiah was still unborn; yet Amos, as peremptorily, renews the sentence. In rejecting
these, whereon the atonement was made, God
pronounced them out of covenant with Himself. Heresy makes itself as like as it can to
the truth, but is thereby the more deceiving,
not the less deadly. Amos mentions *the
altars of Bethel*, as well as *the altar*. Jeroboam
made but *one altar*, keeping as close as he
could to the Divine ritual. But false worship and heresy ever hold their course, de-
veloping themselves. They never stand still
where they began, but *spread, like a cancer* [10].
It is a test of heresy, like leprosy, that *it
spreads abroad* [11], preying on what at first
seemed sound. The oneness of the Altar had
relation to the Unity of God. In Samaria,
they worshiped, they *knew not what* [12], not
God, but some portion of His manifold operations. The many altars, forbidden as they
were, were more in harmony with the religion of Jeroboam, even because they were
against God's law. Heresy develops, becoming more consistent, by having less of
truth.

15. *And I will smite the winter house with
the summer house.* Upon idolatry, there follow luxury and pride. "So wealthy were
they," says S. Jerome, "as to possess two
sorts of houses, *the winter house* being turned
to the South, *the summer house* to the North,
so that, according to the variety of the seasons, they might temper to them the heat
and cold." Yet of these luxuries, (so much
more natural in the East where summer-heat
is so intense, and there is so little provision
against cold) the only instance expressly recorded, besides this place, is *the winter house* [13]
of Jehoiakim. In Greece [14] and Rome [15], the
end was attained, as with us, by North and
South rooms in the same house. These,
which Amos rebukes, were like our town and
country houses, separate residences, since
they were to be destroyed, one on the other.
Ivory houses were houses, pannelled, or inlaid,

---

[1] Acts xvii. 23. 30. xiv. 16.   [2] Rom. i.   [3] Mont.
[4] Gen. iv. 10, 11.   [5] 1 Kgs xii. 32, 3. xiii. 1-5.
[6] The size under the second temple.
[7] Ps. cxviii. 27.   [8] Ex. xxix. 12.
[9] 2 Kgs xvii. 21.   [10] 2 Tim. ii. 17.   [11] Lev. xiii.

[12] S. John. iv. 22.
[13] Jer. xxxvi. 22. Eglon, king of Moab, had only
"a cool upper room," עלית המקרה. Jud. iii. 24.
[14] Xen. Mem. iii. 8. 9.   [15] Pall. de re rust. i. 8.

Before
CHRIST
cir. 787.

CHAPTER IV.

1 *He reproveth Israel for oppression, 4 for idolatry, 6 and for their incorrigibleness.*

ª Ps. 22. 12.
Ezek. 39. 18.

HEAR this word, ye ª kine of Bashan, that

Before
CHRIST
cir. 787.

are in the mountain of Samaria, which oppress the poor, which crush the needy, which say to their masters, Bring, and let us drink.

---

with ivory. Such a palace Ahab built[1]. Even Solomon *in all his glory* had but an ivory throne[2] Else *ivory palaces* [3] are only mentioned, as part of the symbolical glory of the King of glory, the Christ. He adds, *and the great* [or *many*] [4] *houses shall have an end, saith the Lord.* So prosperous were they in outward shew, when Amos foretold their destruction. The desolation should be wide as well as mighty. All besides should pass away, and the Lord Alone abide in that Day. "[5] What then shall we, if we would be right-minded, learn hence? How utterly nothing will all earthly brightness avail, all wealth, glory, or ought besides of luxury, if the love of God be wanting, and righteousness be not prized by us! For *treasures of wickedness profit nothing; but righteousness delivereth from death* [6]."

IV. 1. *Hear ye this, ye kine of Bashan.* The pastures of Bashan were very rich, and it had its name probably from its richness of soil [7]. The Batanea of later times was a province only of the kingdom of Bashan, which, with half of Gilead, was given to the half tribe of Manasseh. For the Bashan of Og included Golan [8], (the capital of the subsequent Gaulonitis, now Jaulân) Beeshterah [9] (or Ashtaroth [10],) very probably Bostra [11], and Elrei [12], in Hauran or Auranitis; the one on its S. border, the other perhaps on its Northern boundary towards Trachonitis [13]. Its Eastern extremity at Salkah [14], (Sulkhad [15]) is the Southern point of Batanea (now Bathaniyyeh); Argob, or Trachonitis [16], (the Lejah) was its N. Eastern fence. Westward it reached to Mount Hermon [17]. It included the subsequent divisions, Gaulonitis, Auranitis, Batanea, and Trachonitis. Of these the mountain range on the N. W. of Jaulân is still "[18] everywhere clothed with oak-forests." The Ard-el-Bathanyeh, "[19] the country of Batanea or Bashan, is not surpassed in that land for the beauty of its scenery, the rich-

ness of its pastures, and the extent of its oak-forests." "The Arabs of the desert still pasture their flocks on the luxuriant herbage of the Jaulân [20]." Its pastures are spoken of by Micah [21] and Jeremiah [22]. The animals fed there were among the strongest and fattest [23]. Hence the male animals became a proverb for the mighty on the earth [24], the bulls furnished a type for fierce, unfeeling, enemies [25]. Amos however speaks of *kine;* not, as David, of *bulls.* He upbraids them not for fierceness, but for a more delicate and wanton unfeelingness, the fruit of luxury, fullness of bread, a life of sense, which destroy all tenderness, dull the mind, "banker out the wits," deaden the spiritual sense.

The female name, *kine,* may equally brand the luxury and effeminacy of the rich men, or the cruelty of the rich women, of Samaria. He addresses these *kine* in both sexes, both male and female [26]. The reproachful name was then probably intended to shame both; men, who laid aside their manliness in the delicacy of luxury; or ladies, who put off the tenderness of womanhood by oppression. The character of the oppression was the same in both cases. It was wrought, not directly by those who revelled in its fruits, but through the seduction of one who had authority over them. To the ladies of Samaria, *their lord* was their husband, as the husband is so called; to the nobles of Samaria, he was their king, who supplied their extravagances and debaucheries by grants, extorted from the poor.

Which oppress, lit. *the oppressing!* The word expresses that they habitually oppressed and crushed the poor. They did it not directly; perhaps they did not know that it was done; they sought only, that their own thirst for luxury and self-indulgence should be gratified, and knew not, (as those at ease often know not now,) that their luxuries are continually watered by the tears of the poor, tears shed, almost unknown except by the

---

[1] 1 Kgs xxii. 39.   [2] Ib. x. 18.   [3] Ps. xlv. 8.
[4] As the same words בתים רבים are translated, Is. v. 9.
[5] S. Cyr.   [6] Pr. x. 2.
[7] In Arab. "a soft smooth soil." On the richness of the Ard-el-Bathanyeh, see Five years, ii. 52, 7, 8, 60, 71, 82, 146, 9 ; on Jaulân, Port. Hdb. 461, 4.
[8] Deut. iv. 43   [9] Josh. xxi. 27.   [10] 1 Chr. vi. 71.
[11] See ab. on i. 12.   [12] Deut. i. 4.
[13] Five years, ii. 220-3.
[14] Deut. iii. 10. Jos. xiii. 11,
[15] Five years, ii. 184-8. "Szalkhat" Burckh. Syr. 99.

[16] Five years, ii. 268-72, 240-3.
[17] Deut. iii. 8. Josh. xii. 5. xiii. 11. 1 Chr. v. 23.
[18] Five years, ii. 259.
[19] Ib. 267; add. 57, 8, 67, 133.
[20] Porter, Hdb. 460, 2. On the Jebel Hauran, see Burckh. Syr. 309.
[21] vii. 14.   [22] Jer. l. 19.
[23] Deut. xxxii. 14.
[24] Ez. xxxix. 18.   [25] Ps. xxii. 12.
[26] "Hear *ye, your* Lord, upon *you,* they shall take *you,*" are masculine; "*that* oppress, *that* crush, *that* say, *your* posterity, *ye* shall go out, *each* before *her,* and *ye* shall be cast forth," feminine.

Before
CHRIST
cir. 787.

b Ps. 89. 35.

c Jer. 16. 16.
Hab. 1. 15.

2 ᵇ The Lord GOD hath
sworn by his holiness, that
lo, the days shall come
upon you, that he will
take you away ᶜ with

hooks, and your posterity
with fishhooks.

3 And ᵈ ye shall go out
at the breaches, every *cow*
at that which is before her;

Before
CHRIST
cir. 787.

d Ezek. 12. 5, 12.

Maker of both. But He counts wilful ignorance no excuse. "He who doth through another, doth it himself," said the heathen proverb. God says, they did *oppress*, were *continually oppressing* [1], *those in low estate* [2], and *crushing the poor* (a word is used expressing the vehemence with which they *crushed* [3] them.) They *crushed* them, only through the continual demand of pleasures of sense, reckless how they were procured; *bring and let us drink.* They invite their husband or lord to joint self-indulgence.

2. *The Lord God hath sworn by His holiness.* They had sinned to profane His *Holy Name* [4]. God swears by that holiness which they had profaned in themselves on whom it was called, and which they had caused to be profaned by others. He pledges His own holiness, that He will avenge their unholiness. "⁵ In swearing *by His holiness*, God sware by Himself. For He is the supreme uncreated Justice and Holiness. This justice each, in his degree, should imitate and maintain on earth, and these had sacrilegiously violated and overthrown."

Days shall come [lit. *are among*] *upon you.* God's Day and eternity are ever coming. He reminds them of their continual approach. He says not only that they *will* certainly come, but they *are* ever *coming.* They are holding on their steady course. Each day which passes, they advance a day closer upon the sinner. Men put out of their minds what *will come ;* they *put far the evil day.* Therefore God so often in His notices of woe to come [6], brings to mind, that those *days are* ever *coming* [6]; they are not a thing which shall be only; in God's purpose, they already *are;* and with one uniform steady noiseless tread *are coming upon* the sinner. Those *days* shall come upon *you*, heavily charged with the displeasure of God, crushing you, as ye have crushed the poor. They come doubtless, too, unexpectedly upon them, as our Lords says, *and so that day come upon you unawares.*

He [i. e. *one*] *will take you away.* In the

midst of their security, they should on a sudden be taken away violently from the abode of their luxury, as the fish, when hooked [7], is lifted out of the water. The image pictures [8] their utter helplessness, the contempt in which they would be had, the ease with which they would be lifted out of the flood of pleasures in which they had immersed themselves. People can be reckless, at last, about themselves, so that their *posterity* escape, and they themselves survive in their offspring. Amos foretells, then, that these also should be swept away.

3. *Ye shall go out through the breaches.* Samaria, the place of their ease and confidence, being broken through, they should go forth one by one, *each straight before her*, looking neither to the right nor to the left, as a herd of cows go one after the other through a gap in a fence. Help and hope have vanished, and they hurry pell-mell after one another, reckless and desperate, as the animals whose life of sense they had chosen.

And ye shall cast them *into the palace*, or, better, (since nothing has been named which they could cast) *cast yourselves* [9]. The word may describe the headlong motion of the animal, and the desperate gestures of the hopeless. They should cast themselves from palace to palace, from the palace of their luxuries to the palace of their enemies, from a self-chosen life of sensuousness to be concubines in the harem. If the rulers are still included, it was reserved for the rich and noble to become eunuchs in the palace of their Assyrian or Babylonian conquerors, as Isaiah foretold to Hezekiah [10]. It is another instance of that great law of God [11], *wherewithal a man sinneth, by the same shall he be tormented.* They had lived in luxury and wantonness; in luxury and wantonness they should live, but amid the jealousies of an Eastern harem, and at the caprice of their sensual conquerors.

The word however rendered, *to the palace* [12], occurring only here, is obscure. The other

¹ The force of the participles הַרֹצְצוֹת הָעֹשְׁקוֹת.
² דָּלִים.   ³ רָצַץ.   ⁴ See on ii. 7.
⁵ From Lap. who applies it to princes and judges.
⁶ 1 Sam. ii. 31. Is. xxxix. 6. Jer. vii. 32. ix. 25. xvii. 14. xix. 6. xxiii. 5, 7. xxx. 3. xxxi. 27–31, 38. xxxiii. 14. xlviii. 12. xlix. 2. li. 47, 52. [Ges.] Am. viii. 11.
⁷ The fem. צִנּוֹת. סִירוֹת, were probably used to distinguish the artificial hook from the actual thorns, צְנִים. סִירִים.
⁸ See Hab. i. 15. Ezek. xxix. 4, 5.
⁹ הִשְׁלַכְתֶּנָה is rendered actively by the rigid

Aquila, and so pointed in all collated MSS. but one. It is rendered passively by the LXX; impersonally, by Jon. "they shall carry you captive;" both as paraphrases. The Hiphil is used of a person's own actions, in regard to certain qualities, their acting on themselves.
¹⁰ Is. xxxix. 7.   ¹¹ Wisd. xi. 16.
¹² הָרַרְמוֹנָה. Kimchi accounts הָרְמוֹן to be only a stronger pronunciation of אַרְמוֹן. It is some objection to this, that Amos five times wrote the word in its ordinary way. Yet there is abundant

Before CHRIST cir. 787. and || ye shall cast *them* into the palace, saith the LORD.

|| *Or, ye shall cast away the things of the palace.*

4 ¶ °Come to Beth-el and transgress; at ᶠGilgal multiply transgression; and ᵍbring your sacrifices

° Ezek. 20. 39.
ᶠ Hos. 4. 15. & 12. 11. ch. 5. 5.
ᵍ Num. 28. 3, 4.

every morning, ʰ*and* your tithes after † three years :

Before CHRIST cir. 787.

5 ¹And † offer a sacrifice of thanksgiving with leaven, and proclaim *and* publish ᵏ the free offerings : ¹for †this liketh you, O

ʰ Deut. 14. 28.
† Heb. *three years of days.*
ⁱ Lev. 7. 13. & 23. 17.
† Heb. *offer by burning.*
ᵏ Lev. 22. 18, 21.
Deut. 12. 6.
¹ Ps. 81. 12.
† Heb. *so ye love.*

---

most probable conjecture is, that it is a name of a country, *the mountains of Monah,* i. e. perhaps Armenia. This would describe accurately enough the country to which they were to be carried; *beyond Damascus; the cities of the Medes.* The main sense is the same. They should be cast forth from the scene of their pleasures and oppression, to be themselves oppressed. The whole image is one, which an inspired prophet alone could use. The reproof was not from man, but from God, unveiling their sins to them in their true hideousness. Man thinks nothing of being more degraded than the brutes, so that he can hide from himself, that he is so.

4 *Come to Gilgal and transgress.* Having foretold their captivity, the prophet tries irony. But his irony is in bidding them go on to do, what they were doing earnestly, what they were set upon doing, and would not be withdrawn from. As Micaiah in irony, until adjured in the name of God, joined Ahab's court-priests, bidding him *go to Ramoth-Gilead*[1], where he was to perish; or Elijah said to the priests of Baal[2], *Cry aloud, for he is a god;* or our Lord[3], *Fill ye up then the measure of your fathers;* so Amos bids them do all they did, in their divided service of God, but tells them that to multiply all such service was to multiply transgression. Yet they were diligent in their way. Their offerings were daily, as at Jerusalem; the tithes of the third year[4] for the poor was paid, as God had ordained[5]. They were punctual in these parts of the ritual, and thought much of their punctuality. So well did they count themselves to stand with God, that there is no mention of sin offering or trespass offering. Their sacrifices were *sacrifices of thanksgiving* and *free will offerings,* as if out of exuberance of devotion, such as David said that Zion would *offer,* when God had been *favorable and*

analogy for the change of ה and א. Most of the old Versions regard the word as a proper Name, simple or compound; "the mountains of Armenia," Ch. Syr. Symm.; "the hill of Romman or Remman," LXX.; Armon i. e. Armenia, S. Jer. as if כונה i. q. מני. "The hill Mona," Theod. in S. Jerome. To that also the article is an objection. Another Greek rendering, "to a lofty mountain," is obviously a conjecture.

gracious unto her[6]. These things they did; they *proclaimed* and *published* them, like the hypocrites whom our Lord reproves, *sounding a trumpet before them*[7], when they did alms; proclaiming these private offerings, as God bade proclaim the solemn assemblies. *For so ye love.* They did it, because they liked it, and it cost them nothing, for which they cared. It was more than most Christians will sacrifice, two fifteenths of their yearly income, if they gave the yearly tithes, which were to be shared with the poor also. But they would not sacrifice what God, above all, required, the fundamental breach of God's law, on which their kingdom rested, *the sin which Jeroboam made Israel to sin.* They did what they liked; they were pleased with it, and they had that pleasure for their only reward, as it is of all which is not done for God.

But amid this boastful service, all was self-will. In little or great, the calf-worship at Bethel, or the use of leaven in the sacrifice, they did as they willed. The Prophet seems to have joined purposely the fundamental change, by which Jeroboam substituted the worship of nature for its God, and a minute alteration of the ritual, to shew that one and the same temper, self-will, reigned in all, dictated all they did. The use of leaven in the things sacrificed was forbidden, out of a symbolic reason, i. e. not in itself, but as representing something else. The Eastern leaven, like that used in France, consisting of what is sour, had the idea of decay and corruption connected with it. Hence it was unfit to be offered to God. For whatever was the object of any sacrifice, whether of atonement or thanksgiving, perfection in its kind was essential to the idea of offering. Hence it was expressly forbidden[8]. *No meat offering, which ye shall bring unto the Lord, shall be made with leaven; for ye shall burn no leaven in an offering of the Lord made by fire.* At other

[1] 1 Kings xxii. 15.   [2] Ib. xviii. 27.
[3] S. Matt. xxiii. 32.
[4] So E. V. rightly, according to the idiomatic use of ימים, "days," for one circle of days, i. e. a year. Lev. xxv. 29. Jud. xvii. 10. 1 Sam. xxvii. 7. &c. To "bring tithes every three years," would be too strong an irony, as being a contradiction.
[5] Deut. xiv. 28. xxvi. 12.   [6] Ps. li. 18, 19.
[7] S. Matt. vi. 2.   [8] Lev. ii. 11; add. vi. 17.

ye children of Israel, saith the Lord GOD.

6 ¶ And I also have

teeth in all your cities, and want of bread in all your

---

times it is expressly commanded, that *unleavened bread* should be used. In two cases only, in which the offering was not to be burned, were offerings to be made of leavened bread, 1) the two loaves of first-fruits at Pentecost[1], and 2) an offering with which the thank offering was accompanied, and which was to be the priest's[2]. The special meat offering of the thank offering was to be without leaven[3]. To *offer a sacrifice of thanksgiving with leaven* was a direct infringement of God's appointment. It proceeded from the same frame of mind, as the breach of the greatest. Self-will was their only rule. What they willed, they kept; and what they willed, they brake. Amos bids them then go on, as they did in their wilfulness, breaking God's commands of set purpose, and keeping them by accident.

"[4] This is a most grave mode of speaking, whereby He now saith, 'Come and do so and so, and He Himself Who saith this, hateth those same deeds of their's. He so speaketh, not as willing, but as abandoning; not as inviting, but as expelling; not in exhortation, but in indignation. He subjoins then, (as the case required,) *for so ye loved.* As if He said, 'I therefore say, *come to Bethel* where is your god, your calf, because *so ye loved,* and hitherto ye have come. I therefore say, *transgress,* because ye do transgress, and ye will to transgress. I say, *come to Gilgal,* where were idols[5] long before Jeroboam's calves, because ye come and ye will to come. I say, *multiply transgressions,* because ye do multiply it, and yet will to multiply it. I say, *bring your sacrifices,* because ye offer them and ye will to offer them, to whom ye ought not.—I say, *offer a sacrifice of thanksgiving with leaven,* because ye so do, and ye will do it, leavened as ye are with *the old leaven of malice and wickedness,* against the whole authority of the holy and spiritual law, which forbiddeth to offer in sacrifice anything leavened. This pleaseth your gods, that ye be leavened, and without [6] *the unleavened bread of sincerity and truth.* To them then *sacrifice the sacrifice of thanksgiving with leaven,* because to Me ye, being sinners, cannot offer a seemly sacrifice of praise. And so doing, *proclaim and publish the free offerings,* for so ye do, and so ye will to do, honoring the sacrifices which ye offer to your calves with the same names, whereby the authority of the law nameth those which are offered unto Me; *burnt offerings,* and *peace offerings;* and *proclaim* them[7] *with the*

sound of trumpet and harp, with timbrel and dancing, with strings and organ, upon the well tuned cymbals and the loud cymbals, that so ye may be thought to have sung louder and stronger than the tribe of Judah or the house of David in the temple of the Lord, because ye are more.' All these things are said, not with the intention of one willing, but with the indignation of One forsaking, as in many other instances. As that which the same Lord said to His betrayer[8]; *what thou doest, do quickly.* And in the Revelations[9] we read, *He that is unjust, let him be unjust still; and he that is filthy, let him be filthy still.* These things, and the rest of the like sort, are not the words of one commanding, or, of His own Will, conceding, but permitting and forsaking. *For He was not ignorant, (Wisdom saith[10]) that they were a naughty generation, and their malice was inbred, and that their cogitation never would be changed.*"

Proclaim and publish the free offerings. "[11] Account much of what ye offer to God, and think that ye do great things, as though ye honored God condignly, and were under no obligation to offer such gifts. The whole is said in irony. For some there are, who appreciate magnificently the gifts and services which they offer to God, and think they have attained to great perfection, as though they made an adequate return to the Divine benefits, not weighing the infinite dignity of the Divine Majesty, the incomparable greatness of the Divine benefits, the frailty of their own condition and the imperfection of their service. Against whom is that which the Saviour saith[12], *When ye shall have done all those things which are commanded you, say, We are unprofitable servants, we have done that which was our duty to do.* Hence David saith[13] *all things come of Thee, and of Thine own have we given Thee.*"

6. *And I, I too[14] have given you.* Such had been their gifts to God, worthless, because destitute of that which alone God requires of His creatures, a loving, simple, single-hearted, loyal obedience. So then God had but one gift which He could bestow, one only out of the rich storehouse of His mercies, since all besides were evil,—chastisement. Yet this too is a great gift of God, a pledge of *His* love, Who willed not that they should perish; an earnest of greater favors, had they used it. It is a great gift of God, that He should care for us, so as to chasten us. The chastisements too were no ordinary chastisements, but

---

[1] Lev. xxiii. 17. [2] Ib. vii. 13, 14. [3] Ib. 12. [4] Rup. [5] Jud. iii. 19 E. M. [6] 1 Cor. v. 8. [7] Ps. cl.

[8] S. John xiii. 27. [9] xxii. 11. [10] xii. 10. [11] Dion. [12] S. Luke xvii. 10. [13] 1 Chr. xix. 14. [14] גַם אֲנִי emphatic.

Before CHRIST cir. 787.

places: ^m yet have ye not returned unto me, saith the LORD.

7 And also I have withholden the rain from you,

m Is. 26. 11.
Jer. 5. 3.
ver. 8, 9.
Hag. 2. 17.

when *there were* yet three months to the harvest: and I caused it to rain upon one city, and caused it not to rain upon another city:

Before CHRIST cir. 787.

those which God forewarned in the law, that He would send, and, if they repented, He would, amid the chastisements, forgive. This famine God had sent everywhere, *in all their cities*, and *in all their places*, great and small. Israel thought that its calves, i. e. nature, gave them these things. *She did not know*, God saith, *that I gave her corn and wine and oil;* but said, *These* are *my rewards that my lovers have given me* [1]. In the powers and operations of "nature," they forgat the God and Author of nature. It was then the direct corrective of this delusion, that God withheld those powers and functions of nature. So might Israel learn, if it would, the vanity of its worship, from its fruitlessness. Some such great famines in the time of Elijah and Elisha [2] Scripture records; but it relates them, only when God visibly interposed to bring, or to remove, or to mitigate them. Amos here speaks of other famines, which God sent, as He foretold in the law, but which produced no genuine fruits of repentance.

And ye returned not unto Me. He says not, that they "*returned not* at all," but that they *returned not wholly, quite back to God* [3]. Nay, the emphatic saying, *ye did not return quite to Me*, so as to reach Me, implies that they did, after a fashion, return. Israel's worship was a half, halting [4], worship. But a half-worship is no worship; a half-repentance is no repentance; repentance for one sin or one set of sins is no repentance, unless the soul repent of all which it can recall wherein it displeased its God. God does not half-forgive; so neither must man half-repent. Yet of its one fundamental sin, the worship of nature for God, Israel would not repent. And so, whatever they did was not that entire repentance, upon which God, in the law, had promised forgiveness; repentance which stopped short of nothing but God.

7. *And I, I too* [5] *have withholden the rain.* S. Jerome, dwelling in Palestine, says, that "this rain, when *three months yet remained until harvest*, was the *latter* rain, of the very greatest necessity for the fields of Palestine and the thirsty ground, lest, when the blade is swelling into the crop, and gendering the wheat, it should dry up through lack of moisture. The time intended is the spring, at

the end of April, whence, to the wheat-harvest, there remain three months, May, June, July." "God withheld the rain that they might endure, not only lack of bread, but burning thirst and penury of drink also. For in these places, where we now live, all the water, except small fountains, is of cisterns; and if the wrath of God should withhold the rain, there is greater peril of thirst than of hunger, such as Scripture relates to have endured for three years and six months in the days of the prophet Elijah. And lest they should think that this had befallen their cities and people, by a law of nature, or the influence of the stars, or the variety of the seasons, He says, that He rained upon one city and its fields, and from another withheld the rain."

This was a second visitation of God. First, a general famine, *in all their cities;* secondly, a discriminating visitation. "Nature" possesses no discrimination or power over her supplies. Seeming waste is one of the mysteries of God in nature, [6] *to cause it to rain on the earth* where *no man* is; on *the wilderness wherein* there *is no man*. Ordinarily too, God [7] *maketh His sun to rise on the evil and on the good, and sendeth rain on the just and on the unjust*. But God does not enslave Himself, (as men would have it) to His own laws. Amos appeals to them, that God had dealt with them, not according to His ordinary laws; that not only God had given to one city the rain which He had withheld from another, but that He had made the same difference as to smaller *pieces* of ground, the inherited *portions* of individuals [8]. Some such variations have been observed in Palestine now [9]. But this would have been no indication of God's Providence, had not the consciences of men responded to the Prophet's appeal, and recognized that the rain had been given or withholden according to the penitence or impenitence, the deeper or more mitigated idolatry, the greater or less sinfulness of the people. We have, then, in these few words a law of God's dealing with Israel. God, in His word, reveals to us the meaning of His daily variations in the workings of nature; yet, hardly even in such instances, as men can scarcely elude, do they think of God

---

[1] Hos. ii. 8, 12.
[2] 1 Kgs xvii. xviii. 2 Kgs viii. 1–6.
[3] צוב; see on Joel ii. 12, and Introd. to Am. p. 152.
[4] 1 Kgs xviii. 21.
[5] וגם אנכי.
[6] Job xxxviii. 26.
[7] S. Matt. v. 45.

[8] Such is the common force of חלקה, "the portion of ground, belonging to one." Deut. xxxiii. 21. Ruth ii. 3. iv. 3. 2 Sam. xiv. 30, 1. 2 Kgs ix 21, 25.
[9] Thomson, The Land, ii. 66.

Before CHRIST cir. 787.

one piece was rained upon, and the piece whereupon it rained not withered.

8 So two *or* three cities wandered unto one city, to drink water : but they were not satisfied : [n] yet have ye not returned unto me saith the LORD.

9 [o] I have smitten you with blasting and mildew : || when your gardens and

your vineyards and your fig trees and your olive trees increased, [p] the palmerworm devoured *them :* yet have ye not returned unto me, saith the LORD.

10 I have sent among you the pestilence || [q] after the manner of Egypt: your young men have I slain with the sword, † and have taken away your

[n] ver. 6, 10, 11.

[o] Deut. 28. 22. Hag. 2. 17.
|| Or, *the multitude of your gardens, &c. did* the palmerworm, &c.

[p] Joel 1. 4. & 2. 25.

|| Or, *in the way.* [q] Ex. 9. 3, 6.
& 12. 29. Deut. 28. 27, 60.
† Heb. *with the captivity of your horses,* [z] Kings 13. 7.

---

the Creator, rather than of "nature," His creation.

8. *Two or three cities wandered into one city.* Those then who were punished, were more than those who were reprieved. The word *wandered* lit. *trembled,* expresses the unsteady reeling gate of those exhausted, in quest of food[1]. They staggered through weakness, and uncertain, amid the general drought, whither to betake themselves. This was done, not in punishment but to heal. God paused, in order to give them opportunity to repent ; in deed, His long-suffering only shewed to themselves and to others, that they would not ; *and ye returned not unto Me; saith the Lord.*

9. *I have smitten you with blasting;* lit. *an exceeding scorching,* such as the hot East wind produced, and *an exceeding mildew,* a blight, in which the ears turn untimely a pale yellow, and have no grain. Both words are doubly intensive. They stand together in the prophecy of Moses[2], among the other scourges of disobedience ; and the mention of these would awaken, in those who would hear, the memory of a long train of other warnings and other judgments.

When your gardens—increased ; better, as E. M. *the multitude*[3] *of your gardens.* The garden of the East united the orchard[4], herb[5], and flower garden. It comprised what was necessary for use as well as what was fragrant. It furnished part of their support[6]. Its trees[7], as well as the garden[8] generally, being mostly watered artificially, it was beyond the reach of ordinary drought. The

tree, *planted by the channels of waters*[9], was an image of abiding freshness and fertility. Yet neither would these escape God's sentence. On these He sent the locusts, which, in a few hours, leaves all, flower, herb or tree, as dead[10].

10. *I have sent among you the pestilence after the manner of Egypt;* i. e. after the way in which God had dealt with Egypt[11]. God had twice promised, when the memory of the plagues which He sent on Egypt was still fresh[12], *if thou wilt diligently hearken to the voice of the Lord thy God,—I will put none of the diseases upon thee which I have brought upon the Egyptians.* Contrariwise, God had forewarned them in that same prophecy of Moses, that, if they disobeyed Him[13], *He will bring upon thee all the diseases of Egypt which thou was afraid of, and they shall cleave unto thee.* Egypt was, at times, subject to great visitations of the plague[14] ; it is said to be its birthplace[15]. Palestine was, by nature, healthy. Hence, and on account of the terribleness of the scourge, God so often speaks of it, as of His own special sending. He had threatened in the law ;[16] *I will send a pestilence upon you*[17]; *the Lord thy God will make the pestilence cleave unto you.* Jeremiah says to the false prophet Hananiah[18] ; *The prophets that have been before me and before thee of old prophesied both against many countries and against great kingdoms, of war and of evil and of pestilence.* Amos bears witness that those visitations came. Jeremiah[19] and Ezekiel[20] prophesied them anew, together with the sword and with famine. Israel, having sinned like Egypt, was to be punished like Egypt.

[1] Ps. lix. 15. cix. 10; of one blind, Lam. v. 14.
[2] Deut. xxviii. 22. [3] הרבות (here, and Pr. xxv. 7.) is i. q. ארבה. The word and the construction are probably the same as in Eccl. i. 16.
[4] Job viii. 16. Cant. iv. 13, 14. vi. 11.
[5] Deut. xi. 10. Cant. iv. 14. vi. 2.
[6] Am. iv. 14. Jer. xxix. 5, 28. [7] Eccl. ii. 6.
[8] Cant. iv. 15. Ecclus. xxiv. 30.
[9] Ps. i. 3. Jer. xvii. 8; add Is. lviii. 11. Jer. xxxi. 12, contrariwise Is. i. 30.
[10] See on Joel i. 7. p. 106.
[11] דרך "way" with the gen. is either act. "the

way of a man," i. e. his way of acting, dealing, &c. or pass. "the way in which he is dealt with or it fares with him," as in Isa. x. 24. Gen. xxxi. 35.
[12] Ex. xv. 26. Deut. vii. 15.
[13] Deut. xxviii. 60, add 27.
[14] "A violent plague used formerly to occur about once in 10 or 12 years. It was always less frequent at Cairo than at Alexandria." Sir G. Wilk. Hdb. Eg. p. 7. [15] Prosp. Alp. rer. Æg. i. 19. Win.
[16] Lev. xxvi. 25. [17] Deut. xxviii. 21.
[18] xxviii. 8. [19] xiv. 12. xxix. 17, 18. xxxiv. 17.
[20] v. 12, vi. 11, &c.

Before
CHRIST
cir. 787.

ʳ ver. 6.

horses; and I have made the stink of your camps to come up unto your nostrils: ʳ yet have ye not returned unto me, saith the LORD.

11 I have overthrown

Before
CHRIST
cir. 787.

ˢ Gen. 19. 24, 25.
Is. 13. 19.
Jer. 49. 18.
ᵗ Zech. 3. 2.
Jude 23.
ᵘ ver. 6.

some of you, as God over-threw ˢ Sodom and Gomorrah, ᵗ and ye were as a firebrand plucked out of the burning: ᵘ yet have ye not returned unto me, saith the LORD.

And have taken away your horses; lit. as E. M. *with the captivity of your horses.* After famine, drought, locust, pestilence, followed that worst scourge of all, that through man. The possessions of the plain of Jezreel, so well fitted for cavalry, probably induced Israel to break in this respect the law of Moses. Hazael *left to Jehoahaz but fifty horsemen and ten chariots and ten thousand footmen; for the king of Syria had destroyed them, and had made them like the dust by threshing.* Their armies, instead of being a defence, lay unburied on the ground, a fresh source of pestilence.

11. *I have overthrown* some *of you.* The earthquake is probably reserved to the last, as being the rarest, and so the most special, visitation. Frequent as earthquakes have been on the borders of Palestine, the greater part of Palestine was not on the line, which was especially shaken by them. The line, chiefly visited by earthquakes, was along the coast of the Mediterranean or parallel to it, chiefly from Tyre to Antioch and Aleppo. Here were the great historical earthquakes, which were the scourges of Tyre, Sidon, Beirut, Botrys, Tripolis, Laodicea on the sea; which shattered Litho-prosopon, prostrated Baalbek and Hamath, and so often afflicted Antioch and Aleppo [1], while Damascus was

mostly spared [2]. Eastward it may have reached to Safed, Tiberias, and the Hauran. Ar-Moab perished by an earthquake in the childhood of S. Jerome [3]. But, at least, the evidence of earthquakes, except perhaps in the ruins of the Hauran [4], is slighter. Earthquakes there have been (although fewer) at Jerusalem. Yet on the whole, it seems truer to say that the skirts of Palestine were subject to destructive earthquakes, than to affirm this of central Palestine [5]. The earthquake must have been the more terrible, because unwonted. One or more terrible earthquakes, overthrowing cities, must have been sent, before that, on occasion of which Amos collected his prophecies. For his prophecies were uttered *two years before* that *earthquake;* and this earthquake had preceded his prophecy. *I overthrew,* God says, *among you, as God overthrew Sodom and Gomorrah.* He uses the word, especially used by Moses and the prophets of that dread overthrow of Sodom and Gomorrah, when they were turned, as it were, upside down. The earthquake is at all times the more mysterious, because unseen, unannounced, unlooked for, instantaneous, complete. The ground under a man's feet seems no longer secure: his shelter is his destruction; men's houses become their graves. Whole cities

---

[1] See authorities in Ritter, Erdk. xvi. 731. xvii. 37. 119. 225. 249. 334–6. 365. 437. 599. 600, 7. 836. 925. 1034. 1155–7. 64. 74, 5. 83, 8. 1206. 1504. 1654, 68. 1711, 35, 44. 52, 6. The terrible earthquake of 1837 which reached the interior of Palestine from Tyre to Bethlehem and Hebron, and northward to Beirut, Cyprus and Damascus (auth. in Ritter, xv. 254, 335. xvi. 210, 28. 647. xvii. 334, 5. 365, 406.) was, from its extent, exceptional. 250,000 perished at Antioch in one earthquake which destroyed Beirut, Biblos with all its inhabitants, and Sidon in part. Ritt. xvii. 437, 8. [2] Ritter, xvii. 1315. [3] S. Jer. on Is. xv.
[4] The Hauran, besides being basaltic, has on the East a very remarkable volcanic country, occupying 2 degrees of latitude (32–34) and 1¼ longitude, "surpassed perhaps in extent, but scarcely in intensity by any like formation in the world." See Wetzstein, [its discoverer] Reisebericht des Hauran, p. 6–20, and woodcuts of extinct volcanoes.
[5] Baronius, Pagi, Fleuri, Tillemont, the Univ. Hist. (Mod.) only mention the following earthquakes as afflicting Palestine.   i. an earthquake on Julian's attempt to rebuild the temple, A. D. 363. (from Ruf. H. E. i. 38, 9.) ii. a shock only, A. D. 394. (from S. Jer. c. Vigil.) iii. "strong shocks," A. D. 633. (from Elmacin p. 19.) iv. a severe one "in Palestine and Syria" (locality undefined) A. D. 658, from Theophanes; [A. D. 650. Theoph. i. 531.] v. "in Palestine round the Jordan and throughout Syria," A. D. 746.

(Bar. i. Pag. ii.) also from Theoph. "many thousands, yea, countless. perished; Churches and monasteries fell in; and chiefly in the desert of the Holy City." (Theoph. A. 738. i. 651. ed. Class. Paul. Diac. L. xxii. Bibl. Patr. xii. 311.) vi. "no slight one," A. D. 756. (Bar. xv.) from the same. [A. D. 748. i. 662 Class.] vii. a severe earthquake at Ramleh and its vicinity, A. D. 1066. radiating along the coast Southwards, from Renaud. Hist. Patr. Al. 433. Von Raumer (Palest. 91. ed. 4) quotes Vitriaco, who speaks chiefly of the sea-coast, and specifies Tyre (in Gesta Dei p. 1097.); a shock A. D. 1105, another A. 1114, destructive in Cilicia and Antioch (Ib. 419, 424, 610.) frequent shocks at Nablus, A. 1120. (Ib, 824.) The list of earthquakes given by Von Hoff in his Chronik der Erdbeben vom. J. 3460 vor bis 1759 unserer Zeitrechnung in his Gesch. d. Veränd. d. Erdöberfl. (T. iv. 122–430.) (as extracted for me) adds, at most, one only affecting Palestine (in common with Syria), A. D. 1182, but does not name the authority. (That of 1353, 4, is not related to have affected Palestine.) Cedrenus also only adds one A. D. 532, 3, "pervading the whole world and lasting 40 days." He mentions Arabia, Palestine, Mesopotamia, Antioch as suffering by it. (i. 674 ed. Bekk.) Abulfaraj (Hist. Dyn.) adds none. The list in Berryat, Collection Académique T. vi. pp. 488–675, adds one, A. D. 650, "in Syria, Persia, especially in Judæa; but without naming any authority."

Before
CHRIST
cir. 787.
12 Therefore thus will I do unto thee, O Israel: ^x prepare

^x See Ezek. 13.
5. & 22. 30.
Luke 14. 31, 32.
and because I will do this unto thee,

to meet thy God, O Israel.

Before
CHRIST
cir. 787.

13 For, lo, he that formeth the mountains,

must have been utterly overthrown, for He compares the overthrow wrought *among* them, to the overthrow of *the cities of the plain.* Other visitations have heralds sent before them. War, pestilence, famine, seldom break in at once. The earthquake at once, buries, it may be, thousands or tens of thousands, each stiffened (if it were so) in that his last deed of evil; each household with its own form of misery; each in its separate vault, dead, dying, crushed, imprisoned; the remnant indeed "surviving," for most whom they loved were gone. So he says; *And ye,* who escaped, *were as a firebrand, plucked out of the burning.* Once it had been green, fresh, fragrant, with leaf or flower; now scorched, charred, blackened, all but consumed. In itself, it was fit for nothing, but to be cast back into the fire whence it had been rescued. Man would so deal with it. A re-creation alone could restore it. Slight emblem of a soul, whose freshness sin had withered, then God's severe judgment had half-consumed; in itself, meet only for the everlasting fire, from which yet God withdraws it.

12. *Therefore thus will I do unto thee.* God says more by His silence. He had enumerated successive scourges. Now, with His hand uplifted to strike, He mentions none, but says, *thus.* "[1] So men too, loth to name evils, which they fear and detest, say, *God do so to me, and more also.* God using the language of men," "[2] having said, *thus will I do unto thee,* is silent as to what He will do; that so, Israel hanging in suspense, as having before him each sort of punishment (which are the more terrible, because he imagines them one by one), may indeed repent, that God inflict not what He threatens."

Prepare to meet thy God, in judgment, face to face, final to them. All the judgments which had been sent hitherto were but heralds, forerunners of the judgment to come. He Himself was not in them. In them, He passed no sentence upon Israel. They were medicinal, corrective; they were not His final sentence. Now, having tried all ways of recovering them in vain, God summons them before His tribunal. But although the judgment of the ten tribes, as a whole, was final, to individuals there was place for repentance. God never, in this life, bids people or individuals *prepare to meet Him,* without a purpose of good to those who do prepare to receive His sentence aright. He

saith not then, "come and hear your doom," but *prepare to meet thy God.* It has hope in it, to be bidden to *prepare;* yet more, that He Whom they were to prepare to meet, was *their God.* It must have recurred full often to the mind of the ten tribes during their unrestored captivity of above seven centuries before the Coming of our Lord; a period as long as the whole existence of Rome from its foundation to its decay; as long as our history from our king Stephen until now. Full oft must they have thought, "we have not met Him yet," and the thought must have dawned upon them; "It is because He willed to *do thus* with us, that He bid us *prepare to meet* Him. He met us not, when He did it. It was then something further on; it is in the Messiah that we are to meet and to see Him." "[2] *Prepare to meet thy God,* receiving with all eagerness the Lord coming unto thee." So then, is this further sense which lay in the words, "[1] he (as did Hosea at the end) exhorts the ten tribes, after they had been led captive by the Assyrians, not to despond, but to *prepare to meet their God,* i. e. to acknowledge and receive Christ their God, when the Gospel should be preached to them by the Apostles." "[1] God punisheth, not in cruelty, but in love. He warns then those whom He strikes, to understand what He means by these punishments, not thinking themselves abandoned by God, but, even when they seem most cast away and reprobate, rousing themselves, in the hope of God's mercy through Christ, to call upon God, and *prepare to meet their God.* For no one's salvation is so desperate, no one is so stained with every kind of sin, but that God cometh to him by holy inspirations, to bring back the wanderer to Himself. Thou therefore, O Israel, whoever thou art, who didst once serve God, and now servest vilest pleasures, when thou feelest God coming to thee, *prepare to meet* Him. Open the door of thy heart to that most kind and benevolent Guest, and, when thou hearest His Voice, deafen not thyself: flee not, like Adam. For He seeketh thee, not to judge, but to save thee."

13. *For lo, He that formeth the mountains.* Their God whom they worshiped was but nature. Amos tells them, Who *their God* is, Whom they were to prepare to meet. He describes Him as the Creator of that, which to man seems most solid, to go furthest back in times past. Before the everlasting moun-

¹ Rib.

² S. Jer.

and createth the || wind,
ʸ and declareth unto man
what is his thought, ᶻ that
maketh the morning dark-
ness, ª and treadeth upon
the high places of the
earth, ᵇ The LORD, The
God of hosts, is his name.

CHAPTER V.

1 *A lamentation for Israel.* 4
An exhortation to repentance.

tains were, God IS; for He made them.
Yet God is not a Creator in the past alone.
He is a continual Worker. *And formeth the
wind,* that finest subtlest creature, alone invisible in this visible world; the most immaterial of things material; the breath of our
life, the image of man's created immaterial
spirit, or even of God's uncreated presence,
the mildest and the most terrific of the
agents around us. But the thought of God,
as a Creator or Preserver without, affects
man but little. To man, a sinner, far more
impressive than all majesty of Creative
power, is the thought that God knows his
inmost soul. So he adds; *and declareth unto
man what is his thought,* i. e. his meditation,
before he puts it into words. God knows
our thoughts more truly than we ourselves.
We disguise them to ourselves, know not
our own hearts, wish not to know them.
God reveals us to ourselves. As He says[1],
*The heart is deceitful above all things;—who
can know it? I, the Lord, search the heart; I
try the reins, even to give every man according to
his ways and according to the fruit of his doings.*
Man's own conscience tells him that God's
knowledge of his inmost self is no idle knowledge. [2] *If our heart condemn us, God is greater
than our heart and knoweth all things.*
*That maketh the morning darkness. If the
light* become *darkness, how great that darkness!*
From the knowledge of man's heart, the
Prophet goes on to retribution. Morning is
the symbol of all which is beautiful, cheering,
radiant, joyous to man; darkness effaces all
these. Their God, he tells them, can do all
this. He can quench in gloom all the magnificent beauty of His own creation and make
all which gladdened the eyes of man, " one
universal blot." *And treadeth upon the high
places of the earth.* He *treadeth* them, to tread
them under. He humbleth all which exalteth itself. "God walketh, when He
worketh. He is without all, within all, con-
taineth all, worketh all in all. Hence it is

[1] Jer. xvii. 9, 10.
[3] Ps. civ. 3.
[2] 1 S. John iii. 20.
[4] Job ix. 8.

21 *God rejecteth their hypocritical service.*

HEAR ye this word
which I ª take up
against you, *even* a lamentation, O house of Israel.
2 The virgin of Israel
is fallen; she shall no
more rise: she is forsaken
upon her land; *there is*
none to raise her up.

said, *He walketh on the wings of the wind*[3]; *He
walketh on the heights of the sea*[4]; *He walketh on
the circuit of Heaven*[5].
Such was He, Who made Himself *their
God,* The Author of all, the Upholder of all,
the Subduer of all which exalted itself, Who
stood in a special relation to man's thoughts,
and Who punished. At His command stand
all the hosts of heaven. Would they have
Him for them, or against them? Would they
be at peace with Him, before they met Him,
face to face?
V. 1. In order to impress Israel the more,
Amos begins this his third appeal by a *dirge*
over its destruction, mourning over those who
were full of joy, and thought themselves safe
and enviable. As if a living man, in the
midst of his pride and luxury and buoyant
recklessness of heart, could see his own funeral procession, and hear, as it were, over
himself the " earth to earth, ashes to ashes,
dust to dust." It would give solemn thoughts,
even though he should impatiently put them
from him. So must it to Israel, when after
the tide of victories of Jeroboam II.,
Amos said, *Hear this word which I am lifting
up,* as a heavy weight, to cast it down *against*
or *upon you,* a funeral *dirge,* O house of Israel.
Human greatness is so unstable, human
strength so fleeting, that the prophet of decay
finds a response in man's own conscience, however he may silence or resent it. He would
not resent it, unless he felt its force.
" [6] Amos, an Israelite, mourneth over
Israel, as Samuel over Saul[7], or as Isaiah
says[8], *I will weep bitterly; labor not to comfort
me, because of the spoiling of the daughter of my
people;* images of Him Who wept over Jerusalem." " So are they bewailed, who know
not why they are bewailed, the more miserable, because they know not their own
misery."
2. *She hath fallen, she shall rise no more, the
virgin of Israel; she hath been dashed down
upon her land, there is* none *to raise her up.*

[5] Ib. xxii. 14.
[7] 1 Sam. xv. 35.
[6] from Dion.
[8] Is. xxii. 4.

Before
CHRIST
cir. 787.

3 For thus saith the Lord GOD; The city that went out *by* a thousand shall leave an hundred, and that which went forth *by* an hundred shall leave ten, to the house of Israel.

4 ¶ For thus saith the LORD unto the house of Israel, [b] Seek ye me, [c] and ye shall live:

5 But seek not [d] Beth-el,

Before
CHRIST
cir. 787.

b 2 Chr. 15. 2.
  Jer. 29. 13.
  ver. 6.
c Is. 55. 3.
d ch. 4. 4.

Such is the dirge, a dirge like that of David over Saul and Jonathan, over what once was lovely and mighty, but which had perished. He speaks of all as past, and that, irremediably. Israel is one of the things which had been, and which would never again be. He calls her tenderly, *the virgin of Israel*, not as having retained her purity or her fealty to God; still less, with human boastfulness, as though she had as yet been unsubdued by man. For she had been faithless to God, and had been many times conquered by man. Nor does it even seem that God so calls her, because He once espoused her to Himself. For Isaiah so calls Babylon. But Scripture seems to speak of cities, as women, because in women tenderness is most seen; they are most tenderly guarded; they, when pure, are most lovely; they, when corrupted, are most debased. Hence "[1] God says on the one hand, [2] *I remember thee, the love of thine espousals;* on the other [3], *Hear, thou harlot, the word of the Lord.* When He claims her faithfulness He calls her, betrothed." Again, "[1] when He willeth to signify that a city or nation has been as tenderly loved and anxiously guarded, whether by Himself or by others, He calleth it *virgin*, or when He would indicate its beauty and lovely array. Isaiah saith [4], *come down and sit in the dust, virgin daughter of Babylon*, i.e. thou who livedest before in all delicacies, like a virgin under the shelter of her home. For it follows, *for thou shalt no more be called tender and delicate.*" More pitiable, for their tenderness and delicacy, is the distress of women. And so he pictures her as already fallen, *dashed* (the word imitates the sound [5]) to the earth *upon her own ground*. An army may be lost, and the nation recover. She was *dashed down upon her own ground*. In the abode of her strength, in the midst of her resources, in her innermost retreat, she should fall. In herself, she fell powerless. And he adds, she has *no one to raise her up;* none to have ruth upon her; image of the judgment on a lost soul, when the terrible sentence is spoken and none can intercede! *She shall not rise again.* As she fell, she did not again rise. The Prophet beholds beyond the eighty-five years which separated the prosperity under Jeroboam II. from her captivity. As a people, he says, she should be restored no more; nor was she.

3. *The city that went out* by a *thousand*, (i. e. probably that sent out a thousand fighting men, as the word *went out* is often used for, *went out* [6] to fight,) *shall have* lit. *shall retain, an hundred.* She was to be decimated. Only, the tenth alone was to be reserved alive; the nine-tenths were to be destroyed. And this, alike in larger places and in the small. The city *that went forth an hundred shall retain ten.* Smaller places escape for their obscurity, the larger from their strength and situation. One common doom was to befall all. Out of all that multitude, one tithe alone was to be preserved, "[1] dedicated to God," that remnant which God always promised to reserve.

4. *Seek ye Me and ye shall live;* lit. seek *Me and live.* Wonderful conciseness of the word of God, which, in two words [7], comprises the whole of the creature's duty and his hopes, his time and his eternity. The Prophet uses the two imperatives, inoneing both, man's duty and his reward. He does not speak of them, as cause and effect, but as one. Where the one is, there is the other. To seek God is to live. For to seek God is to find Him, and God is Life and the source of life. Forgiveness, grace, life, enter the soul at once. But the seeking is diligent seeking [8]. "[9] It is not to seek God anyhow, but as it is right and meet that He should be sought, longed for, prayed for, Who is so great a Good, constantly, fervently, yea, to our power, the more constantly and fervently, as an Infinite Good is more to be longed for, more loved than all created good." The object of the search is God Himself. *Seek Me*, i. e. seek God for Himself, not for anything out of Him, not for His gifts, not for anything to be loved with Him. This is not to seek Him purely. All is found in Him, but by seeking Him first, and then loving Him in all, and all in Him. *And ye shall live*, first by the life of the body, escaping the enemy; then by the life of grace now, and the life of glory hereafter, as in that of the Psalmist [10], *your heart shall live who seek God.*

5. *But* [And] *seek not Bethel.* Israel pretended to seek God in Bethel. Amos sets the two seekings, as incompatible. The god, worshiped at Bethel, was not the One God.

---

1 from Rib.   2 Jer. ii. 2.   3 Ezek. xvi. 35.
4 Is. xlvii. 1.   5 נטשה.

6 See in Ges. Thes. v. יצא.   7 דרשוני וחיו.
8 דרש.   9 Dion.   10 Ps. lxix. 32.

Before
CHRIST
cir. 787.

• ch. 8. 14.

f Hos. 4. 15.
& 10. 8.

nor enter into Gilgal, and pass not to e Beersheba : for Gilgal shall surely go into captivity, and f Beth-el shall come to nought.

Before
CHRIST
cir. 787.

g ver. 4.

6 g Seek the LORD, and ye shall live ; lest he break out like fire in the house of Joseph, and devour it, and there be none to quench it in Beth-el.

To seek God there was to lose Him. " Seek not God," he would say, "and a phantom, which will lead from God."

And pass not to Beersheba. Jeroboam I. pretended that it was too much for Israel to go up to Jerusalem. And yet Israel thought it not too much to go to the extremest point of Judah toward Idumæa[1], perhaps, four times as far South of Jerusalem, as Jerusalem lay from Bethel. For Beersheba is thought to have lain some thirty miles South of Hebron[2], which is twenty-two miles South of Jerusalem[3] ; while Bethel is but twelve to the North. So much pains will men take in self-willed service, and yet not see that it takes away the excuse for neglecting the true. At Beersheba, Abraham[4] called upon the name of the Lord, the everlasting God. There God revealed Himself to Isaac and Jacob[5]. There, because He had so revealed Himself, Judah made a place of idolatry, which Israel, seeking nought besides from Judah, sought. Beersheba was still a town[6] or large village[7] in the time of S. Jerome. Now all is swept away, except "[8] some foundations of ruins," spread over ¾ of a mile, "with scarcely one stone upon another[9]." The wells alone remain[10], with the ancient names.

Gilgal shall surely go into captivity. The verbal allusions in the Prophets are sometimes artificial ; sometimes, they develop the meaning of the word itself, as when Zephaniah says[11], Ekron [probably the firm-rooting] shall be uprooted ; sometimes, as here, the words are connected, although not the same. In all cases, the likeness of sound was calculated to fix them in men's memories. It would be so, if one with authority could say, "Paris périra[12]," " Paris shall perish," or " London is undone." Still more would the words, Hag-gilgal galo yigleh, because the name Gilgal still retained its first meaning, the great rolling[13], and the word joined with it had a kindred meaning[14]. Originally it probably means, " swept clear away." God

first rolled away the reproach of Egypt[15] from His people there. Then, when it made itself like the heathen, it should itself be rolled clear away[16]. Gilgal was originally in Benjamin, but Israel had probably annexed it to itself, as it had Bethel and Jericho[17], both of which had been assigned by Joshua to Benjamin[18].

And Bethel shall come to nought. Hosea had called Bethel, God's house, by the name of Bethaven[19], Vanity-house. Amos, in allusion to this probably, drops the first half of the name, and says that it shall not merely be house of vanity, but Aven, vanity itself. " By sin the soul, which was the house or temple of God, becomes the temple of vanity and of devils."

6. Seek ye the Lord and ye shall live ; lit. seek the Lord and live ; being united to Him, the Fountain of life. He reimpresses on them the one simple need of the creature, seek God, the one true God as He revealed Himself, not as worldly men, or the politicians of Jeroboam's court, or the calf-priests, fabled of Him. Seek Him. For in Him is all ; without Him, nothing.

Lest He break out like fire in Bethel. Formerly the Spirit of God came vehemently down[20] upon Samson[21] and Saul[22] and David[23], to fit them as instruments for God ; as did the Evil spirit, when God departed from Saul[24]. So now, unless they repented, God Himself would suddenly shew His powerful Presence among them, but, as He had revealed Himself to be[25], the Lord thy God is a consuming Fire. And devour it, lit. and it [the fire] shall devour, and there be none to quench it in [better, for] Bethel. Bethel, the centre of their idol-hopes, so far from aiding them then, shall not be able to help itself, nor shall there be any to help it. The fire of God kindles around it, and there is none to quench it for her[26].

"[27] The whole place treateth of mercy and justice. The whole ground of men's punish-

[1] Jos. Ant. 8. 13. 7.
[2] Robinson, i. 206. Eus. and S. Jer. have twenty.
[3] Euseb. S. Jer. v. Arbo.   [4] Gen. xxi. 33.
[5] Ib. xxvi. 23, 4. xlvi. 1.
[6] S. Jer. Qu. ad Gen. xxii. 30.   [7] de loc. Hebr.
[8] Van de Velde, ii. 127.   [9] Robinson, i. 204.
[10] There are now seven wells, 2 large and separate from the other 5. But Moses speaks of one well only, dug by Abraham and reopened by Isaac. Gen. xxi. 30. xxvi. 18, 32, 3.
[11] ii. 4.   [12] instanced by Mercier here.

[13] The article is prefixed to proper names, which are still in a degree appellatives.
[14] גלה and גלל both from a biliteral root, גל.
[15] Josh. v. 9.   [16] See גלגלתיך Jer. li. 25.
[17] 1 Kgs x7i. 34.
[18] Josh. xviii. 21, 22.   [19] iv. 15. x. 5.
[20] The same word is used In all these places.
[21] Jud. xiv. 6, 19. xv. 14.   [22] 1 Sam. x. 6. xi. 6.
[23] Ib. xvi. 13.   [24] Ib. xviii. 10.   [25] Deut. iv. 24.
[26] as in Jer. iv. 4.   [27] Mont.

Before
CHRIST
cir. 787.

b ch. 6. 12.

7 Ye who [h] turn judgment to wormwood, and leave off righteousness in the earth,

8 *Seek him* that maketh

Before
CHRIST
cir. 787.

i Job 9. 9.
& 38. 31.
k Ps. 104. 20.
l Job 38. 34.
ch. 9. 6.

the [i] seven stars and Orion, and turneth the shadow of death into the morning, [k] and maketh the day dark with night: that [l] calleth

---

ment, calamities, condemnation is ascribed to their own fault and negligence, who neglect the deliverance often promised and offered them by God, and [1] *love darkness rather than light, because their deeds are evil.* Whoever is not saved, the whole blame lies in their own will and negligence and malice. God, Who [2] *willeth not that any should perish, but that all should come to repentance,* Himself unsought, seeks, entreats, ceases not to monish, exhort, set before them their guilt, that they may cease to prepare such evil for themselves. But they neither give Him entrance, nor hear His entreaties, nor admit the warnings of the Divine mercy, which if they neglect, they must needs be made over to His justice. The goodness of God is wanting to no one, save those who are wanting to themselves. Wherefore, having often besought them before, He invites them yet again to salvation, putting forth that His Name, so full of mysteries of mercy ; *Seek the Lord and live,"* seek Him Who IS, the Unchangeable. He Who had willed their salvation, still willed it, for He *changes not* [3]. "He adds threatenings, that those whom He calls to life, He might either allure by promises, or scare from death through fear of the impending evil."

7. *Ye who turn.* Those whom he calls to seek God, were men filled with all injustice, who turned the sweetness of justice into the bitterness of wormwood [4]. Moses had used *gall* and *wormwood* as a proverb [5] ; *lest there be among you a root that beareth gall and wormwood ; the Lord will not spare him, but then the anger of the Lord and His jealousy shall smoke against that man, and all the curses that are written in this book shall lie upon him.* The word of Amos would remind them of the word of Moses.

And leave off righteousness in the earth; better, *and set righteousness to rest on the ground* [6]. They dethroned righteousness, the representative and vice-gerent of God, and made it rest on the ground. The *little horn,* Daniel says [7], should *cast truth to the ground.* These seem to have blended outrage with insult, as when *the Lord our Righteousness* [8] took our flesh, they *put on Him the scarlet robe, and the crown of thorns* upon His Head, *and bowed the knee before Him, and mocked Him,* and then *crucified Him.* They "deposed" her, "set

[1] S. John iii. 19.   [2] 2 S. Pet. iii. 9.
[3] Mal. iii. 6.   [4] S. Jer.
[5] Deut. xxix. 18, 20.
[6] הַצִּיג is used of casting forth, Nu. xix. 9 ; cast-

her down," it may be, with a mock make-believe deference, as men now-a-days, in civil terms, depose God, ignoring Him and His right over them. They set her on the ground and so left her, the image of God. This they did, not in one way only, but in all the ways in which they could. He does not limit it to the *righteousness* shewn in doing justice. It includes all transactions between man and man, in which right enters, all buying and selling, all equity, all giving to another his due. All the bands of society were dissolved, and *righteousness* was placed on the ground, to be trampled on by all in all things.

8. Seek Him *that maketh the seven stars.* Misbelief effaces the thought of God as He Is. It retains the name God, but means something quite different from the One True God. So men spoke of "the Deity," as a sort of First Cause of all things, and did not perceive that they only meant to own that this fair harmony of things created was not (at least as it now exists,) self-existent, and that they had lost sight of the Personal God Who had made known to them His Will, Whom they were to believe in, obey, fear, love. "The Deity" was no object of fear or love. It was but a bold confession that they did not mean to be Atheists, or that they meant intellectually to admire the creation. Such confessions, even when not consciously Atheistic, become at least the parents of Atheism or Panotheism, and slide insensibly into either. For a First Cause, who is conceived of as no more, is an abstraction, not God. God *is* the Cause of all causes. All things *are,* and have their relations to each other, as cause and effect, because He so created them. A "Great First Cause," who is only thought of as a Cause, is a mere fiction of a man's imagining, an attempt to appear to account for the mysteries of being, without owning that, since our being is from God, we are responsible creatures whom He created for Himself, and who are to yield to Him an account of the use of our being which He gave us. In like way, Israel had probably so mixed up the thought of God with Nature, that it had lost sight of God, as distinct from the creation. And so Amos, after appealing to their consciences, sets forth God to them as the Creator, Disposer

ing violently to the ground, Is. xxviii. 2 ; casting into a furnace, Ez. xxii. 20. Yet ordinarily it has the simple meaning "placed, made to rest."
[7] viii. 12.   [8] Jer. xxiii. 6.

Before
CHRIST
cir. 787.

m ch. 4. 13.

for the waters of the sea, and poureth them out upon the face of the earth: [m] The LORD *is* his name :

Before
CHRIST
cir. 787.

† Heb. *spoil.*

9 That strengtheneth the † spoiled against the strong, so that the spoiled shall come against the fortress.

---

of all things, and the Just God, who redresseth man's violence and injustice. The *seven stars,* lit. *the heap,* are the striking cluster of stars, called by Greeks and Latins the Pleiades[1], which consist of seven larger stars, and in all of above forty. Orion[2], a constellation in one line with the Pleiades, was conceived by the Arabs and Syrians also, as a gigantic figure. The Chaldee also renders, the "violent" or "the rebel." The Hebrew title *Cesil, fool,* adds the idea of an irreligious man, which is also the meaning of Nimrod, *rebel,* lit. "let us rebel." Job, in that he speaks of *the bands of Orion*[3], pictures him as "bound," the "belt" being the *band.* This falls in with the later tradition, that Nimrod, who, as the founder of Babel, was the first rebel against God[4], was represented by the easterns in their grouping of the stars, as a giant chained[5], the same constellation which we call Orion.

And turneth the shadow of death into the morning. This is no mere alternation of night and day, no "kindling" of "each day out of night." The *shadow of death* is strictly the darkness of death, or of the grave[6]. It is used of darkness intense as the darkness of the grave[7], of gloom[8], or moral benightening[9] which seems to cast *the shadow of death* over the soul, of distress which is as the forerunner of death[10], or of things, hidden as the grave, which God alone can bring to light[11]. The word is united with darkness, physical, moral, mental, but always as intensifying it, beyond any mere darkness. Amos first sets forth the power of God, then His goodness. Out of every extremity of ill, God can, will, does, deliver. He Who said, *let there be light and there was light,* at once changeth any depth of darkness into light, the death-darkness of sin into the dawn of grace, the hopeless night of ignorance into *the day-star from on high,* the night of the grave into the eternal morn of the Resurrection which knoweth no setting. But then on impenitence the contrary follows ;

And maketh the day dark with night ; lit. *and*

darkeneth day into night. As God withdraws *the shadow of death,* so that there should be no trace of it left, but all is filled with His light, so, again, when His light is abused or neglected, He so withdraws it, as at times, to leave no trace or gleam of it. Conscience becomes benighted, so as to sin undoubtingly : faith is darkened, so that the soul no more even suspects the truth. Hell has no light.

That calleth for the waters of the sea. This can be no other than a memory of the flood, *when the waters prevailed over the earth*[12]. The Prophet speaks of nothing partial. He speaks of *sea* and *earth,* each, as a whole, standing against the other. *God calleth the waters of the sea and poureth them over the face of the earth.* They seem ever threatening the land, but for Him[13] *which hath placed the sand for the bound of the sea, that it cannot pass it.* Now God calls them, and *pours them over the face,* i. e. the whole surface. The flood, He promised, should not again be. But it is the image of that universal destruction, which shall end man's thousands of years of rebellion against God. The words then of Amos, in their simplest sense, speak of a future universal judgment of the inhabitants of the earth, like, in extent, to that former judgment, when God *brought in the flood upon the world of the ungodly*[14].

The words have been thought also to describe that daily marvel of God's Providence, how, from the salt briny sea, which could bring but barrenness, He, by the heat of the Sun, draws up the moisture, and discharges it anew in life-giving showers on the surface of the earth. God's daily care of us, in the workings of His creatures, is a witness[15] of His relation to us as our Father; it is an earnest also of our relation, and so of our accountableness, to Him.

The Lord is His name. He, the One Self-existent Unchangeable God, who revealed Himself to their forefathers, and forbade them to worship Him under any form of their own device.

9. *That strengtheneth the spoiled,* (lit. *spoil*

---

[1] כִּימָה (i. q. Arab. koumah, "heap,") is rendered πλειάδα by Symm. Theod. here; by the LXX. Aq. and S. Jer. in Job xxxviii. 31; by the LXX. also Job ix. 9 (the two names Ἀρκτοῦρον and πλειάδα, being transposed). The Syr. and Ch. retain the Hebrew word, which the Arab. Transl. in Job renders "Thorayya," "little multitude," the Arabic name of the Pleiades.

[2] Aquila and S. Jerome here, S. Jer. in Job ix. 9, the LXX. in Is. xiii. 10 and Job xxxviii. 31, render, "Orion." The Ch. in Job has כְּסִילָא; its plural here; in Isaiah, the Heb. word. The Syr. here and

in Job has "jaboro" (the Heb. נָבִיר. Mighty, Gen. x. 8). The Arab. in Job, the same.
[3] xxxviii. 31.
[4] Gen. x. 9, 10. xi. 4-9. Josephus (Arch. i. 4. 2.) does but develop Genesis.
[5] Chron. Pasch. p. 36.
[6] Job iii. 5. x. 21, 22. xxxiv. 22 xxxviii. 17. Ps. xxiii. 4. Jer. xiii. 16.　　　[7] Job xxviii. 3.
[8] Ib. xxiv. 17.　　　[9] Is. ix. 2. (1 Heb.)
[10] Job xvi. 16. Ps. xliv. 19. cvii. 10, 14. Jer. ii. 6. xiii. 16.　　[11] Job xii. 22.　　[12] Gen. vii. 24.
[13] Jer. v. 22.　　[14] 2 S. Pet. il. 5.　　[15] Acts xiv. 17.

10 ⁿ They hate him that rebuketh in the gate, and they º abhor him that speaketh uprightly.
11 Forasmuch therefore as your treading is upon

E. M.) probably *That maketh devastation to smile on the strong*[1]. The *smile*, in anger, attests both the extremity of anger, and the consciousness of the ease, wherewith the offence can be punished. They were strong in their own strength ; strong, as they deemed, in their *fortress ;* "[2]strong with an evil strength, like one phrensied against his physician." But their strength would be weakness. *Desolation*, when God willed, would *smile at* all which they accounted *might*, and would *come against the fortress*, which, as they deemed, *cut off*[3] all approach.

10. *They hate him that rebuketh. The gate* is the well-known place of concourse, where just or, in Israel now, unjust judgment was given[4], where all was done which was to be done publicly[5]. Samaria had a large area[6] by its chief gate, where two kings could hold court, and the 400 false prophets and the people, in great numbers, could gather[7], and a market could be held[8]. Josiah brake down an idol-shrine, which was in one of the gates of Jerusalem[9]. The prophets seized the opportunity of finding the people together, and preached to them there. So it was even in the days of Solomon[10]. *Wisdom crieth without ; she uttereth her voice in the streets ; she crieth in the chief place of concourse, in the openings of the gates, in the city she uttereth her words, How long, ye simple ones, will ye love simplicity ?* &c., and again[11], *She standeth in the top of high places, by the way, in the meeting of the paths. She crieth at the gates, at the entry of the city, at the coming in at the doors ; Unto you, O men, I call,* &c. Jeremiah mentions two occasions, upon which God bade him reprove the king and people in the gates of Jerusalem[12]. There doubtless Amos and Hosea *reproved* them, and, for reproving, were *hated*. As Isaiah says[13], *they lay a snare for him that reproveth in the gate.* They sinned publicly, and therefore they were to be rebuked publicly. They sinned *in the gate* by injustice and oppression, and therefore were to be *rebuked before all, that others also might fear*[14]. *And they abhor him that speaketh uprightly,* lit. *perfectly.* The prophets spoke *perfectly,* "[15]for they spoke the all-perfect word of God, of which David says[16], *The law of the Lord is perfect, converting the soul."* "Carnal

eyes hate the light of truth, which they cast aside for execrable lies, closing to themselves the fountain of the Divine mercy[15]." "[2]This is the sin which hath no remission ; this is the sin of the strong and mighty, who sin not out of ignorance or weakness, but with impenitent heart proudly defend their sin, and *hate him that rebuketh and abhor him who* dareth to *speak perfectly,* i. e. not things which please them, but resisting their evil." This, like all other good of God and evil of man, met most in and against Christ. "[2]Who is he who *rebuked in the gate* or who *spake perfectly ?* David rebuked them, and spake much perfectly, and so they hated him and said[17], *what portion have we in David, or what inheritance have we in the son of Jesse ?* Him also who spake these very words, and the other prophets they hated and abhorred. But as the rest, so this too, is truly and indubitably fulfilled in Christ, rebuking justly and speaking perfectly. He Himself saith in a Psalm[18], *They that sat in the gate spake against Me,* wherefore, when He had said[19], *he that hateth Me hateth My Father also,* and, *now they have both seen and hated both Me and My Father,* He subjoined, *that the word might be fulfilled that is written in their law, they hated Me without a cause.* Above all then, we understand Christ, Whom they hated, *rebuking in the gate,* i. e. openly and in public ; as He said[20], *I spake openly to the world, and in secret have I said nothing.* He alone spake perfectly, *Who did no sin, neither was guile found in His mouth*[21]. In wisdom also and doctrine, He alone spake perfectly, perfectly and so wonderfully, that *the officers of the chief priests and Pharisees* who were *sent to take Him,* said, *Never man spake like this Man*[22]." "[23]It is a great sin to hate him who rebuketh, especially if he rebuke thee, not out of dislike, but out of love, if he doth it *between thee and him alone*[24], if, *taking with* him a brother, if afterward, in the presence of the Church, accuse thee ; that it may be evident that he does not blame thee out of any love of detraction, but out of zeal for thine amendment."

11. *Forasmuch therefore,* (since they rejected reproof, he pronounces the sentence of God upon them,) *as your treading is upon the poor.*

[1] The E. V. has followed a conjecture of Jon. and Kimchi, founded on the context of Job ix. 27, x. 20. Aquila, ὁ μειδιῶν, and S. Jerome, *subridens,* agree with the Arabic use, which suits all the places in Heb. " smiled, was gladdened, was cheered." Others here, "made to dawn," from the Arab. ᵈThe force of סבד.
[2] Rup. ᵈThe force of יצר.
[4] Deut. xxv. 7. Job v. 4. xxxi. 21. 2 Sam. xv. 2. Pr. xxii. 22. Is. xxix. 21. [5] Ruth iv. 1, 11. [6] גרן.

[7] 1 Kgs xxii. 10. 2 Chr. xviii. 9.
[8] 2 Kgs vii. 1.
[10] Pr. i. 20–22.
[12] xvii. 19. xix. 2.
[13] xxix. 21.
[16] Ps. xix. 7. [17] 1 Kgs xii. 16.
[19] S. John xv. 23–25.
[21] 1 S. Pet. ii. 22.
[23] S. Jer.

[9] Ib. xxiii. 8.
[11] Ib. viii. 2–4.

[14] 1 Tim. v. 20.

[15] Lyr.
[18] lxix. 12.
[20] Ib. xviii. 20.

[22] S. John vii. 45, 6.
[24] S. Matt. xviii. 15–17.

Before
CHRIST
cir. 787.

P Deut. 28. 30,
38, 39.
Mic. 6. 15.
Zeph. 1. 13.
Hag. 1. 6.
† Heb. vineyards
of desire.

the poor, and ye take from him burdens of wheat: P ye have built houses of hewn stone, but ye shall not dwell in them; ye have planted † pleasant vine-

yards, but ye shall not drink wine of them.

12 For I know your manifold transgressions and your mighty sins: q they afflict the just, they

Before
CHRIST
cir. 787.

q ch. 2. 6.

This expresses more habitual trampling on the poor, than if he had said, *ye tread upon the poor.* They were ever trampling on those who were already of low and depressed condition. *And ye take from him burdens of wheat, presents of wheat.* The word always signifies presents, voluntary [1], or involuntary [2], what was *carried,* offered to any one. They received *wheat* from the poor, cleansed [3], winnowed, and *sold the refuse* [4], requiring what it was wrong to receive, and selling what at the least it was disgraceful not to give. God had expressly forbidden to [5] *lend food for interest.* It may be that, in order to evade the law, the interest was called *a present.*

Ye have built houses of hewn stone. The houses of Israel were, perhaps most commonly, built of brick [6] dried in the sun only. As least, houses built of hewn stone, like most of our's, are proverbially contrasted with them, as the more solid with the more ordinary building. [7] *The white bricks are fallen down, and we will build with hewn stones.* And Ezekiel is bidden to dig through the wall of his house [8]. Houses of stone there were, as appears from the directions as to the unhealthy accretions, called the leprosy of the house [9]. It may be, however, that their houses of *hewn stone,* had a smoothed surface, like our "ashlar." Anyhow, the sin of luxury is not simply measured by the things themselves, but by their relation to ourselves and our condition also; and wrong is not estimated by the extent of the gain and loss of the two parties only, but by the injury inflicted. These men, who built houses, luxurious for them, had wrung from the poor their living, as those do, who beat down the wages of the poor. Therefore they were not to take possession of what was their own; as Ahab, who by murder possessed himself of Naboth's vineyard, forfeited his throne and his life. God, in the law, consulted for the feeling which desires to enter into the fruit of a man's toil. When they should go to war they were to proclaim, [10] *what man is there*

that hath built a new house, and hath not dedicated it? let him go and return to his house, lest he die in the battle, and another man dedicate it. And what man is he that hath planted a vineyard and hath not eaten of it? let him go. and return unto his house, lest he die in the battle and another man eat of it.* Now God reversed all this, and withdrew the tender love, whereby He had provided it. The words, from their proverbial character, express a principle of God's judgments, that wrong dealing, whereby a man would secure himself or enlarge his inheritance, destroys both. Who poorer than our Lord, bared of all upon the Cross, of Whom it had been written, [11] *They persecuted the poor helpless man, that they might slay him who was vexed at the heart,* and of whom the Jews said [12], *Come let us kill Him, that the inheritance may be our's?* They killed Him, they said [13], *lest the Romans take away our place and nation.* The vineyard was taken from them; their *place* destroyed, their *nation* dispersed.

12. *For I know;* lit. *I have known.* They thought that God did not know, because He did not avenge; as the Psalmist says, [14] *Thy judgments are far above out of his sight.* Men who do not act with the thought of God, cease to know Him, and forget that He knows them. *Your manifold transgressions;* lit. *many* are *your transgressions and mighty your sins.* Their deeds, they knew, were mighty, strong, vigorous, decided. God says, that their *sins* were so, not many and great only, but *mighty, strong,* "[15] issuing not out of ignorance and infirmity, but out of proud strength:" "[16] *strong* in the oppression of the poor and in provoking God," and bringing down His wrath. So Asaph says of the prosperous [17]; *Pride encompasseth them, as a chain; they are corrupt, they speak oppression wickedly; they speak from on high.*

They afflict the just, lit. *afflicters of the just,* i. e. such as habitually afflicted him; whose habit and quality it was to afflict him. Our version mostly renders the word *enemies.* Originally, it signifies *afflicting, persecuting* enemies. Yet it is used also of the enemies of

[1] of the "mess" sent, Gen. xliii. 34, 2 Sam. xi. 8; of the gifts of one superior in rank, Esth. ii. 18, Jer. xl. 5.
[2] of a contribution appointed by Divine law, 2 Chr. xxiv. 6-9, Ez. xx. 40. The masc. משׂא is used, of tribute, 2 Chr. xvii. 11
[3] Such is בַּר as distinct from חטה, the name of the grain, "wheat."

[4] Am. viii. 6.
[5] Lev. xxv. 37. Deut. xxiii. 19.
[7] Is. ix. 10.
[9] Lev. xiv. 34-48.
[10] Deut. xx. 5, 6.
[12] S. Matt. xxi. 38.
[13] S. John xi. 48.
[15] Rup.   [16] Hug.

[6] לבנים.
[8] xii. 5, 7.

[11] Ps. cix. 15.

[14] Ps. x. 5.
[17] Ps. lxxiii. 6, 8.

take ‖ a bribe, and they
ʳ turn aside the poor in the
gate *from their right.*

13 Therefore ˢ the pru-
dent shall keep silence in

that time: for it *is* an evil
time.

14 Seek good, and not
evil, that ye may live: and
so the LORD, the God of

‖ Or, *a ransom.*
ʳ Is. 29. 21.
ch. 2. 7.
ˢ ch. 6. 10.

God, perhaps such as persecute Him in His
people, or in His Son when in the flesh.
The unjust hate the just, as is said in the
book of Wisdom[1]; *The ungodly said, There-*
fore let us lie in wait for the righteous, because
he is not for our turn, and is clean contrary to
our doings: he upbraideth us with our offending
the law. He professeth to have the knowledge of
God, and he calleth himself the child of the Lord.
He was made to reprove our thoughts. He is
grievous unto us even to behold ; for his life is not
as other men's, his ways are of another fashion.
So when the Truth and Righteousness came
into the world, the Scribes and Pharisees hated
Him because He reproved them, *denied*[2] and
crucified *the Holy one and the Just, and desired*
a murderer to be granted unto them, haters and
enemies of the Just, and preferring to Him the
unjust.

That take a bribe, lit. *a ransom.* It may be
that, contrary to the law, which forbade, in
these same words[3], *to take any ransom for the*
life of a murderer,'they took some ransom to
set free rich murderers, and so, (as we have
seen for many years to be the effect of unjust
acquittals,) blood was shed with impunity,
and was shed the more, because it was disregarded. The word, however, is used in one
place apparently of any bribe, through which
a man connives at injustice[4].

13. *Therefore the prudent shall keep silence in*
that time. The *time* may be either the time
of the obduracy of the wicked, or that of the
common punishment. For a time may be
called *evil,* whether evil is done, or is suffered
in it, as Jacob says[5], *Few and evil have the*
days of the years of my life been. Of the first,
he would perhaps say, that the oppressed poor
would, if wise, be silent, not complaining or
accusing; for, injustice having the mastery,
complaint would only bring on them fresh
sufferings. And again also he may mean
that, on account of the incorrigibleness of the
people, the wise and the prophets would be
silent, because the more the people were rebuked, the more impatient and worse they
became. So our Lord was silent before His
judges, as had been foretold of Him; for
since they would not hear, His speaking
would only increase their condemnation[6].
If I tell you, ye will not believe; and if I also ask

you, *ye will not answer Me, nor let Me go.* So
God said by Solomon[7]: *He that reproveth a*
scorner getteth himself shame, and he that re-
buketh a wicked man getteth *himself a blot.*
And our Lord bids[8], *Give not that which is*
holy unto dogs, and cast not your pearls before
swine. They hated and rejected those who
rebuked them[9]. Since then rebuke profited
not, the prophets should hold their peace.
It is a fearful judgment, when God withholds
His warnings. In times of punishment also
the prudent keep silence. Intense affliction
is *dumb and openeth not its mouth,* owning the
hand of God. It may be too, that Amos, like
Hosea[10], expresses the uselessness of all reproof, in regard to the most of those whom
he called to repentance, even while he continued earnestly to rebuke them.

14. *Seek good and not evil,* i. e. *and seek not*
evil[11]. Amos again takes up his warning,
seek not Bethel ; seek the Lord. Now they not
only *did evil,* but they *sought*[12] it diligently;
they were diligent in doing it, and so, in
bringing it on themselves ; they sought it out
and the occasions of it. Men "[13]cannot seek
good without first putting away evil, as it is
written[14], *cease to do evil, learn to do well.*" *Ye*
cannot serve God and Mammon. He bids them
use the same diligence in seeking good which
they now used for evil. Seek it also wholly,
not seeking at one while good, at another,
evil, but wholly good, and Him Who is Good.
"He seeketh good, who believeth in Him
Who saith[15], *I am the good Shepherd.*"

That ye may live, in Him Who is *the Life ;*
and so the Lord, the God of hosts, shall be with
you, by His holy Presence, grace and protection, *as ye have spoken.* Israel looked away.
from the sins whereby he displeased God,
and looked to his half-worship of God as en-
titling him to all which God had promised
to full obedience. "[16]They gloried in the
nobleness of their birth after the flesh, not in
imitating the faith and lives of the patriarchs. So then, because they were descended
from Abraham, they thought that God must
defend them. Such were those Jews, to
whom the Saviour said[17], *If ye were Abraham's*
seed, ye would do the works of Abraham ; and
His forerunner[18], *think not to say within your-*
selves, we have Abraham for our father." They

---

[1] ii. 1, 12–15.
[2] Acts iii. 14.
[3] Num. xxxv. 22, לא תקחו כפר.
[4] 1 Sam. xii. 3.
[5] Gen. xlvii. 9.
[6] S. Luke xxii. 67, 8.
[7] Pr. ix. 7.
[8] S. Matt. vii. 6.
[9] ver. 10.
[10] iv. 4, 17.

[11] אל implying the verb.
[12] דרש
[13] S. Jer.
[14] Is. i. 16, 17.
[15] S. John x. 11.
[16] Dion.
[17] S. John viii. 39.
[18] S. Matt. iii. 9.

Before CHRIST cir. 787.

hosts, shall be with you, [t] as ye have spoken.

15 [u] Hate the evil, and love the good, and establish judgment in the gate: [x] it may be that the LORD God of hosts will be gra-

cious unto the remnant of Joseph.

Before CHRIST cir. 787.

16 Therefore the LORD, the God of hosts, the Lord, saith thus; Wailing *shall be* in all streets; and they shall say in all the high-

[t] Mic. 3. 11.
[u] Ps. 34. 14.
& 97. 10.
Rom. 12. 9.
[x] Ex. 32 30.
2 Kings 19. 4.
Joel 2. 14.

---

wished that God should abide with them, that they might [1] *abide in the land,* but they cared not to abide with God.

15. *Hate the evil and love the good.* Man will not cease wholly to *seek evil,* unless he *hate* it; nor will he *seek good,* unless he *love* it. "[2] He *hateth evil,* who not only is not overcome by pleasure, but hates its deeds; and he *loveth good,* who, not unwillingly or of necessity or from fear, doth what is good, but because it is good." "[3] Evil of sin must be hated, in and for itself; the sinner must not be hated in himself, but only the evil in him." They hated him, who reproved them; he bids them hate sin. They *set down righteousness on the ground;* he bids them, *establish,* lit. *set up firmly, judgment in the gate.* To undo, as far as any one can, the effects of past sin, is among the first-fruits of repentance.

It may be that the Lord God of Hosts will be gracious. "[3] He speaks so, in regard of the changeableness and uncertainty, not in God, but in man. There is no question but that God is gracious to all who *hate evil and love good;* but He doth not always deliver them from temporal calamity or captivity, because it is not for their salvation. Yet had Israel *hated evil and loved good,* perchance He would have delivered them from captivity, although He frequently said, they should be carried captive. For so He said to the two tribes in Jeremiah [4], *Amend your ways, and your doings, and I will cause you to dwell in this place."* But since God knew that most of them would not repent, He saith not, *will be gracious unto Israel,* but, *unto the remnant of Joseph,* i. e. [5] *the remnant, according to the election of grace;* such as had been *the seven thousand who bowed not the knee unto Baal;* those who repented, while *the rest were hardened.* He says, *Joseph,* not Ephraim, in order to recall to them the deeds of their father. Jacob's blessing on Joseph descended upon Ephraim, but was forfeited by Jeroboam's *sin wherewith he made Israel to sin.* "[6] Joseph in his deeds and sufferings was a type of Jesus Christ, in Whom the remnant is saved." A *remnant,* however only, *should be saved;* so the Prophet says;

[1] Ps. xxxvii. 3,   [2] S. Jer.   [3] Dion.   [4] vii. 3.
[5] Rom. xi. 4, 5.   [6] Rup.   [7] Is. xxiv. 21.
[8] The רחב might be a "broad" street (πλατεία)

---

16. *Therefore the Lord, the God of Hosts, the Lord.* For the third time in these three last verses Amos again reminds them, by Whose authority he speaks, His Who had revealed Himself as *I AM,* the Self-existent God, God by nature and of nature, the Creator and Ruler and Lord of all, visible or invisible, against their false gods, or fictitious substitutes for the true God. Here, over and above those titles, *HE IS,* i. e. HE Alone IS, *the God of Hosts,* God *of all things, in heaven and earth,* the heavenly bodies from whose influences the idolaters hoped for good, and the unseen evil beings [7], who seduced them, he adds the title, which men most shrink from, *Lord.* He Who so threatened, was the Same who had absolute power over His creatures, to dispose of them, as He willed. It costs men nothing to own God, as a Creator, the Cause of causes, the Orderer of all things by certain fixed laws. It satisfies certain intellects, so to own Him. What man, a sinner, shrinks from, is that the God is Lord, the absolute disposer and Master of his sinful self.

Wailing in all streets, lit. *broad places,* i. e. market-places [8]. There, where judgments were held, where were the markets, where consequently had been all the manifold oppressions through injustice in judgments and in dealings, and the wailings of the oppressed; *wailing* should come on them.

They shall say in all the highways, i. e. *streets, alas! alas!* our, *woe, woe.* It is the word so often used by our Lord; *woe unto you.* This is no imagery. Truth has a more awful, sterner, reality than any imagery. The terribleness of the prophecy lies in its truth. When war pressed without on the walls of Samaria, and within was famine and pestilence, woe, woe, woe, must have echoed in every street; for in every street was death and fear of worse. Yet imagine every sound of joy or din or hum of men, or mirth of children, hushed in the streets, and woe, woe, going up from every street of a metropolis, in one unmitigated, unchanging, ever-repeated monotony of grief. Such were the present fruits of sin. Yet what a mere shadow of the inward grief is its outward utterance!

[as] Gen. xix. 2, Jud. xix. 15, 17, 20, but, contrasted with חוצת, it is probably the "broad place" near the gate.

Before
C H R I S T
cir. 787.

ɟ Jer. 9 17.

ways, Alas! alas! and they
shall call the husbandman
to mourning, and ʸ such as
are skillful of lamentation
to wailing.

17 And in all vineyards
shall be wailing : for ᶻ I
will pass t h r o u g h thee,
saith the LORD.

18 ᵃ Woe unto you that

Before
C H R I S T
cir. 787.

ᶻ Ex. 12. 12.
Nah. 1. 12.
ᵃ Is. 5. 19.
Jer. 17. 15.
Ezek. 12. 22, 27.
2 Pet. 3. 4.

And they shall call the husbandman to mourning. To cultivate the fields would then only be to provide food for the enemy. His occupation would be gone. One universal sorrow would give one universal employment. To this, they would call those unskilled, with their deep strong voices; they would, by a public act, *proclaim wailing to* [1] *those skillful in lamentation.* It was, as it were, a dirge over the funeral of their country. As, at funerals, they employed minstrels, both men and women [2], who, by mournful anthems and the touching plaintiveness of the human voice, should stir up deeper depths of sorrow, so here, over the whole of Israel. And as at the funeral of one respected or beloved, they used exclamations of woe [3], *ah my brother!* and *ah sister, ah lord, ah his glory,* so Jeremiah bids them [4], *call and make haste and take up a wailing for us, that our eyes may run down with tears : for a voice of wailing is heard out of Zion. How are we spoiled!* " [5] In joy, men long to impart their joys to others, and exhort them to joy with them. Our Lord sanctions this, in speaking of the Good Shepherd, Who called His friends and neighbors together, *rejoice with Me, for I have found the sheep which I had lost.* Nor is it anything new, that, when we have received any great benefit from God, we call even the inanimate creation to thank and praise God. So did David ofttimes and the three children. So too in sorrow. When anything adverse has befallen us, we invite even senseless things to grieve with us, as though our own tears sufficed not for so great a sorrow." The same feeling makes the rich now clothe those of their household in mourning, which made those of old hire mourners, that all might be in harmony with their grief.

17. *And in all vineyards* shall be *wailing.* All joy should be turned into sorrow. Where aforetime was the vintage-shout in thankfulness for the ingathering, and anticipating gladness to come, there, in the source of their luxury, should be wailing, the forerunner of sorrow to come. It was a vintage, not of wine, but of woe.

For I will pass through thee. In the destruc-

tion of the firstborn in Egypt, God did not *pass through* but *passed over* them, and they kept, in memory thereof, the feast of the Passover. Now God would no longer *pass over* them and their sins. He says, *I will pass through thee,* as He then said [6], *I will pass through the land of Egypt this night, and will smite all the firstborn of the land of Egypt—and against all the gods of Egypt I will execute judgment.* As God says by Hosea [7], *I will not enter the city,* i. e. He would not make His Presence felt, or take cognizance, when to take cognizance would be to punish, so here, contrariwise, He says, *I will pass through,* taking exact and severe account, in judgment. S. Jerome further says, "so often as this word is used in Holy Scripture, in the person of God, it denotes punishment, that He would not abide among them, but would pass through and leave them. Surely, it is an image of this, that, when the Jews would have cast our Lord headlong from the brow of the hill whereon their city was built, *He passed through the midst of them* [8], so that they could not see Him nor know Him, *and so went His way.* And this, when He had just told them, that none of the widows of Israel were fed by Elias, or the lepers cleansed by Elisha, save the widow of Sarepta, and Naaman the Syrian. So should their leprosy cleave to them, and the famine of the word of God and of the oil of the Holy Spirit abide among them, while the Gentiles were washed by His laver and fed with the bread of life."

18. *Woe unto you that desire [for yourselves* [9]*] the Day of the Lord.* There were *mockers in those days* [10], as there are now, and as there shall be in the last. And as the *scoffers in the last days* [10] shall say, *Where is the promise of His coming?* so these said [11], *let Him make speed and hasten His work, that we may see it, and let the council of the Holy One of Israel draw nigh and come, that we may know it.* Jeremiah complained [12]; *they say unto me, where is the word of the Lord? let it come now!* And God says to Ezekiel [13], *Son of man, what is that proverb that ye have in the land of Israel, saying, the days are prolonged, and every*

---

[1] This is the Hebrew construction. The E. V. has followed Kimchi in assuming a transposition, which is, however, only as much as to say that the two idioms are equivalent, as they are. To "call the husbandman to mourning," or to "proclaim mourning to the husbandman" mean the same thing, though the Hebrew words can grammatically only mean the last.

[2] 2 Chr. xxxv. 25. The word *skillful* is masculine, יֹדְעֵי so in S. Matt. ix. 23.
[3] הוֹי 1 Kgs xiii. 29. Jer. xxii. 18. Amos uses a shorter form, found here only, הוֹ. [4] ix. 17-19.
[5] from Sanct. [6] Ex. xii. 12. [7] xi. 9.
[8] S. Luke iv. 30. [9] The force of לָכֶם.
[10] 2 S. Pet. iii. 3, 4, S. Jude 18. [11] Is. v. 19.
[12] xvii. 15. [13] xii. 22, 27.

Before
CHRIST
cir. 787.

desire the day of the LORD!
to what end *is* it for you?

ᵇ the day of the LORD *is*
darkness, and not light.

Before
CHRIST
cir. 787.

ᵇ Jer. 30. 7. Joel 2. 2. Zeph. 1. 15.

vision faileth? The vision that he seeth is for many days, and he prophesieth of the times far off. "They would shew their courage and strength of mind, by longing for the Day of the Lord, which the prophets foretold, in which God was to shew forth His power on the disobedient." " ¹ Let it come, what these prophets threaten till they are hoarse, let it come, let it come. It is ever held out to us, and never comes. We do not believe that it will come at all, or if it do come, it will not be so dreadful after all ; it will go as it came." It may be, however, that they who scoffed at Amos, cloked their unbelief under the form of desiring the good days, which God had promised by Joel afterward. " ² There is not," they would say, "so much of evil in the captivity, as there is of good in what the Lord has promised afterward." Amos meets the hypocrisy or the scoff, by the appeal to their consciences, *to what end is it to you?* They had nothing in common with it or with God. Whatever it had of good, was not for such as them. *The Day of the Lord is darkness, and not light.* Like the pillar of the cloud between Israel and the Egyptians, which betokened God's Presence, every day in which He shews forth His Presence, is a day of light and darkness to those of different characters. The prophets foretold both, but not to all. These scoffers either denied the Coming of that day altogether, or denied its terrors. Either way, they disbelieved God, and, disbelieving Him, would have no share in His promises. To *them,* the Day of the Lord would be unmixed darkness, distress, desolation, destruction, without one ray of gladness. The tempers of men, their belief or disbelief, are the same, as to the Great Day of the Lord, the Day of Judgment. It is all one, whether men deny it altogether or deny its terrors. In either case, they deny it, such as God has ordained it. The words of Amos condemn them too. *The Day of the Lord* had already become the name for every day of judgment, leading on to the Last Day. The principle of all God's judgments is one and the same. One and the same are the characters of those who are to be judged. In one and the same way, is each judgment looked forward to, neglected, prepared for, believed, disbelieved. In one and the same way, our Lord has taught us, will the Great Day come, as the judgments of the flood or upon Sodom, and will find men prepared or unprepared, as they were then. Words then,

which describe the character of any day of Judgment, do, according to the Mind of God the Holy Ghost, describe all, and the last also. Of this too, and that chiefly, because it is the greatest, are the words spoken, *Woe unto you, who desire,* amiss or rashly or scornfully or in misbelief, *the Day of the Lord, to what end is it for you? The Day of the Lord is darkness and not light.*

" ³ This sounds a strange woe. It had not seemed strange, had he said, 'Woe to you, who fear not the Day of the Lord.' For, ' not to fear,' belongs to bad, ungodly men. But the good may desire it, so that the Apostle says ⁴, *I desire to depart and to be with Christ.* Yet even *their* desire is not without a sort of fear. For ⁵ *who can say, I have made my heart clean?* Yet that is the fear, not of slaves, but of sons ; *nor hath* it *torment* ⁶, for it hath ⁷ *strong consolation through hope.* When then he says, *Woe unto you that desire the Day of the Lord,* he rebuketh *their* boldness, ⁸ *who trust in themselves, that they are righteous.*" "At one and the same time," says S. Jerome, "the confidence of the proud is shaken off, who, in order to appear righteous before men, are wont to long for the Day of Judgment and to say, ' Would that the Lord would come, would that we might be dissolved and be with Christ,' imitating the Pharisee, who spake in the Gospel ⁹, *God, I thank Thee, that I am not as other men are.* For the very fact, that they *desire,* and do not fear, *the Day of the Lord,* shews, that they are worthy of punishment, since no man is *without sin* ¹⁰, and *the stars are not pure in His sight* ¹¹. And He ¹² *concluded all under sin, that He might have mercy upon all.* Since, then, no one can judge concerning the Judgment of God, and we are to *give account of every idle word* ¹³, and Job *offered sacrifices* ¹⁴ daily for his sons, lest they should have thought something perversely against the Lord, what rashness it is, to long to reign alone ¹⁵ !—In troubles and distresses we are wont to say, ' would that we might depart out of the body and be freed from the miseries of this world,' not knowing that, while we are in this flesh, we have place for repentance ; but if we depart, we shall hear that of the prophet, ¹⁶ *in hell who will give Thee thanks?* That is *the sorrow of this world* ¹⁷, which worketh *death,* wherewith the Apostle would not have him sorrow who had sinned with his father's wife ; the sorrow whereby the wretched Judas too perished, who, *swallowed up with overmuch sorrow* ¹⁸, joined mur-

¹ from Lap.　　² S. Jer.
³ Rup.　⁴ Phil. i. 23.　⁵ Prov. xx. 9.
⁶ 1 S. John iv. 18.　⁷ Heb. vi. 18, Rom. v. 2.
⁸ S. Luke xviii. 9.

⁹ S. Luke xviii. 11, 12.　¹⁰ 2 Chr. vi. 36.
¹¹ Rom xxv. 5.　¹² Gal. iii. 22, Rom. xi. 32.
¹³ S. Matt. xii. 36.　¹⁴ Job i. 5.　¹⁵ 1 Cor. iv. 8.
¹⁶ Ps. vi. 5.　¹⁷ 2 Cor. vii. 10.　¹⁸ Ib. ii. 7.

Before
C H R I S T
cir. 787.

c Jer. 48. 44.

19 ᶜ As if a man did flee from a lion, and a bear met him; or went into the house, and leaned his hand on the wall, and a serpent bit him.

20 *Shall* not the day of the LORD *be* darkness, and not light? even very dark, and no brightness in it?

Before
C H R I S T
cir. 787.

d Prov. 21. 27.
Is. 1. 11–16.
Jer. 6. 20.
Hos. 8. 13.
e Lev. 26. 31.
‖ Or, *smell your holy days.*
f Is. 66. 3.
Mic. 6. 6, 7.
‖ Or, *thank offerings.*

21 ¶ ᵈ I hate, I despise your feast days, and ᵉ I will not ‖ smell in your solemn assemblies.

22 ᶠ Though ye offer me burnt offerings and your meat offerings, I will not accept *them:* neither will I regard the ‖ peace offerings of your fat beasts.

---

der[1] to his Betrayal, a murder the worst of murders, so that where he thought to find a remedy, and that death by hanging was the end of ills, there he found the lion and the bear, and the serpent, under which names I think that different punishments are intended, or else the devil himself, who is rightly called a lion or bear or serpent."

19. *As if a man did flee from a lion.* The Day of the Lord is a day of terror on every side. Before and behind, without and within, abroad under the roof of heaven, or under the shelter of his own, everywhere is terror and death. The Syrian bear is said to have been fiercer and more savage than the lion. For its fierceness and voracity[2], God made it, in Daniel's vision, a symbol of the empire of the Medes. From both lion and bear there might be escape by flight. When the man had *leaned his hand* trustfully *on the wall* of his own house, *and the serpent bit him,* there was no escape. He had fled from death to death, from peril to destruction.

20. Shall *not the Day of the Lord be darkness?* He had described that Day as a day of inevitable destruction, such as man's own conscience and guilty fears anticipate, and then appeals to their own consciences, "is it not so, as I have said?" Men's consciences are truer than their intellect. However they may employ the subtlety of their intellect to dull their conscience, they feel, in their heart of hearts, that there is a Judge, that guilt is punished, that they are guilty. The soul is a witness to its own deathlessness, its own accountableness, its own punishableness[3]. Intellect carries the question out of itself into the region of surmising and disputings. Conscience is compelled to receive it back into its own court, and to give the sentence, which it would fain withhold. Like the god of the heathen fable, who changed himself into all sorts of forms, but when he was still held fast, gave at the last,

the true answer, conscience shrinks back, twists, writhes, evades, turns away, but, in the end, it will answer truly, when it must. The Prophet then, turns quick round upon the conscience, and says, "tell me, for you know."

21. *I hate, I despise your feasts.* Israel clave to its heart's sin, the worship of the true God, under the idol-form of the calf; else, it would fain be conscientious and scrupulous. It had its *feasts of* solemn *joy*[4], and the *restraint* of its *solemn assemblies*[5], which all were constrained to keep, abstaining from all servile work. They offered *whole burnt offerings,* the token of self-sacrifice, in which the sacrificer retained nothing to himself, but gave the whole freely to God. They offered also *peace offerings,* as tokens of the willing thankfulness of souls at peace with God. What they offered, was the best of its kind, *fatted beasts.* Hymns of praise, full-toned chorus, instrumental music! What was wanting, Israel thought, to secure them the favor of God? Love and obedience. *If ye love Me, keep My commandments.* And so those things, whereby they hoped to propitiate God, were the object of His displeasure. *I hate, I despise, I will not accept* with good pleasure[6]; *I will not regard,* look toward, *I will not hear, will not smell.* The words, *I will not smell,* reminded them of that threat in the law[7], *I will make your cities waste and bring your sanctuaries unto desolation, and I will not smell the savor of your sweet odors.* In so many ways does God declare that He would not accept or endure, what they all the while were building upon, as grounds of their acceptance. And yet so secure were they, that the only sacrifice which they did *not* offer, was the sin or trespass offering. Worshiping "nature," not a holy, Personal, God, they had no sense of unholiness, for which to plead the Atoning Sacrifice to come. Truly each Day of Judgment unveils much self-deceit. How much more the Last!

---

[1] S. Matt. xxvii. 3–5.   [2] Dan. vii. 5.
[3] See Tertullian's short but remarkable treatise "of the witness of the soul," p. 132–42. Oxf. Tr.

[4] חַג.   [5] עֲצָרָה lit. restraint.
[6] אֶרְצֶה.
[7] Lev. xxvi. 31.

Before
C H R I S T
cir. 787.

23 Take thou away from me the noise of thy songs; for I will not hear the melody of thy viols.

24 [g] But let judgment [†] run down as waters, and

[e] Hos. 6. 6.
Mic. 6. 8.
† Heb. roll.

righteousness as a mighty stream.

25 [h] Have ye offered unto me sacrifices and offerings in the wilderness forty years, O house of Israel?

Before
C H R I S T
cir. 787.

[h] Deut. 32. 17.
Josh. 24. 14.
Ezek. 20. 8, 16,
24. Acts 7. 42,
43. See Is. 43.
23.

---

23. *Take thou away from Me,* lit. *from upon Me,* i. e. from being a burden to Me, a weight on Me. So God says by Isaiah [1], *your new moons and your appointed feasts My soul hateth ; they are a burden upon Me ; I am weary to bear them.* Their *songs* and hymns were but a confused, tumultuous, *noise* [2], since they had not the harmony of love. *For [And] the melody of thy viols I will not hear.* Yet the *nebel,* probably a sort of harp, was almost exclusively consecrated to the service of God, and the Psalms were God's own writing. Doubtless they sounded harmoniously in their own ears; but it reached no further. Their melody, like much Church-music, was for itself, and ended in itself. "[3] Let Christian chanters learn hence, not to set the whole devotion of Psalmody in a good voice, subtlety of modulation and rapid intonation, &c, quavering like birds, to tickle the ears of the curious, take them off to themselves and away from prayer, lest they hear from God, *I will not hear the melody of thy viols.* Let them learn that of the Apostle [4], *I will sing with the Spirit, and I will sing with the understanding also.*" "[5] If the Psalm prays, pray ; if it sorrows, sorrow ; if it is glad, rejoice ; if full of hope, hope ; if of fear, fear. For whatever is therein written, is our mirror." "[6] How many are loud in voice, dumb in heart! How many lips are silent, but their love is loud! For the ears of God are to the heart of man. As the ears of the body are to the mouth of man, so the heart of man is to the ears of God. Many are heard with closed lips, and many who cry aloud are not heard." "[7] God says, *I will not hear,* as He says [8], *praise is not seemly in the mouth of a sinner,* and [9], *to the ungodly saith God, what hast thou to do, to declare My statutes ?* and [10], *he that turneth away his ear from hearing the law, even his prayer shall be abomination.* It is not meant hereby that the wicked ought wholly to abstain from the praise of God and from prayers, but that they should be diligent to amend, and know that through such imperfect services they cannot be saved." The Prophet urges upon them the terribleness of the Day of Judgment, that they might feel and flee its terribleness, be-

fore it comes. He impresses on them the fruitlessness of their prayers, that, amending, they might so pray, that God would hear them.

24. *But [And] let judgment run down* [lit. *roll* E. M.] *like water.* The duties of either table include both ; since there is no true love for man without the love of God, nor any real love or duty to God without the love of man. Men will exchange their sins for other sins. They will not break them off unless they be converted to God. But the first outward step in conversion, is to break off sin. He bids them then *let judgment,* which had hitherto ever been perverted in its course, *roll on like a mighty tide of waters,* sweeping before it all hindrances, obstructed by no power, turned aside by no bribery, but pouring on in one perpetual flow, reaching all, refreshing all, and *righteousness like a mighty* [or ceaseless] *stream.* The word *ethan* may signify *strong* or *perennial.* Whence the seventh month, just before the early rain, was called *the month Ethanim* [11], i. e. the month of *the perennial streams,* when they alone flowed. In the meaning *perennial,* it would stand tacitly contrasted with *streams which fail* or *lie* [12]. True righteousness is not fitful, like an intermitting stream, vehement at one time, then disappearing, but continuous, unfailing.

25. *Have ye offered* [better, *Did ye offer*] *unto Me sacrifices and offerings?* Israel justified himself to himself by his half-service. This had been his way from the first. [13] *Their heart was not whole with God, neither abode they in His covenant.* He thought to be accepted by God, because he did a certain homage to Him. He acknowledged God in his own way. God sets before him another instance of this half-service and what it issued in :— the service of that generation which He brought out of Egypt, and which left their bones in the wilderness. The idolatry of the ten tribes was the revival of the idolatry of the wilderness. The ten tribes owned as the forefathers of their worship those first idolaters [14]. They identified themselves with sin which they did not commit. By approving it and copying it, they made that sin their own. As the Church of God in all

---

[1] i. 14.   [2] המון.   [3] Lap.
[4] 1 Cor. xiv. 15.
S. Aug. in Ps. xxx. Enarr. iv. [p. 263. Oxf. Tr.] L.
S. Aug. in Ps. cxix. [n. 9. T. v. p. 470. O. T.] L.

[7] Dion.   [8] Ecclus. xv. 9.   [9] Ps. l. 16.
[10] Prov. xxviii. 9.   [11] 1 Kgs viii. 2.
[12] אכזב. Jer. xv. 18, כזב. Is. lviii. 11.
[13] Ps. lxxviii. 37.   [14] See Introd. to Hos. p. 2.

26 But ye have borne || the tabernacle [1] of your

|| Or, *Siccuth your king.* [1] 1 Kings 11.33.

times is one and the same, and Hosea says of God's vision to Jacob [1], *there He spake with us,* so that great opposite camp, the city of the devil, has a continuous existence through all time. These idolaters were *filling up the measure of* their forefathers, and in the end of those forefathers, who perished in the wilderness where they sinned, they might behold their own. As God rejected the divided service of their forefathers, so He would their's.

God does not say that they did not offer sacrifice at all, but that they did not offer unto *Him.* The *unto Me* is emphatic. If God is not served wholly and alone, He is not served at all. "[2] He regardeth not the offering, but the will of the offerer." Some sacrifices were offered during the thirty-eight years and a half, after God had rejected that generation, and left them to die in the wilderness. For the rebellion of Korah and his company was a claim to exercise the priesthood, as Aaron was exercising it [3]. When atonement was to be made, the *live coals* were already on the altar [4]. These, however, were not the free-will offerings of the people, but the ordinance of God, performed by the priests. The people, in that they went after their idols, had no share in nor benefit from what was offered in their name. So Moses says [5], *they sacrificed to devils, not to God;* and Ezekiel [6], *Their heart went after their idols.* Those were the gods of their affections, whom they chose. God had taken them for His people, and had become their God, on the condition that they should not associate other gods with Him [7]. Had they loved God Who made them, they would have loved none beside Him. Since they chose other gods, these were the objects of their love. God was, at most, an object of their fear. As He said by Hosea [8], *their bread is for themselves, it shall not enter into the house of the Lord,* so here He asks, and by asking denies it, *Did ye offer unto Me?* Idolatry and heresy feign a god of their own. They do not own God as He has revealed Himself; and since they own not God as He is, the god whom they worship, is not the true God, but some creature of their own imaginings, such as they conceive God to be. Anti-Trinitarianism denies to God His essential Being, Father, Son, and Holy Ghost. Other heresies refuse to own His awful holiness and justice; others, the depth of His love and

condescension. Plainly, their god is not the one true God. So these idolaters, while they associated with God gods of cruelty and lust, and looked to them for things which God in His holiness and love refused them, did not own God, as the One Holy Creator, the Sole Disposer of all things.

26. *But ye have borne* [lit. *And ye bare*] *the tabernacle of your Moloch* [lit. *your king,* whence the idol Moloch had its name.]. He assigns the reason, why he had denied that they sacrificed to God in the wilderness. *Did ye offer sacrifices unto Me, and ye bare?* i. e. seeing that ye bare. The two were incompatible. Since they did *carry about the tabernacle of their king,* they did not really worship God. He whom they chose as "their king," was their god. The *tabernacle* or *tent* was probably a little portable shrine, such as Demetrius the silversmith and those of his craft made for the little statues of their goddess Diana [9]. Such are mentioned in Egyptian idolatry. "They carry forth," we are told [10], "the image in a small shrine of gilt wood."

Of your Moloch and Chiun. The two clauses must be read separately, *the tabernacles of Moloch* [strictly, *of your king,*] *and Chiun your images.* The two clauses, *the tabernacle of your king, and Chiun your images* [11], are altogether distinct. They correspond to one another, but they must not be read as one whole, in the sense, *the tabernacle of your king and of Chiun your images.* The rendering of the last clause is uncertain. God has so *utterly abolished the idols* [12], through whom Satan contested with Him the allegiance of His people, that we have no certain knowledge, what they were. There may be some connection between the god whom the Israelites in the wilderness worshiped as *their king,* and him whose worship Solomon, in his decay, brought into Jerusalem, the god whom the Ammonites worshiped as *the king, Hammolech,* or, as he is once called, *Molech* [13], and three times *Milchom* [14] (perhaps an abstract, as some used to speak of "*the Deity*"). He is mostly called *Hammolech,* the Ammonite way of pronouncing what the Hebrews called *Hammelech, the king.* But since the name designates the god only as *the king,* it may have been given to different gods, whom the heathen worshiped as their chief god. In Jewish idolatry, it became equivalent to Baal [15], *lord;* and to avert his displeasure, the Hebrews (as did the Carthaginians, a Phœnician people, down to

[1] xii. 4. See ab. p. 76.
[2] S. Jer.
[3] Num. xvi. 5, 9, 10.   [4] Ib. 46.   [5] Deut. xxxii. 17.
[6] xx. 16.   [7] Ex. xx. 2-5.   [8] ix. 4. see ab. p. 56.
[9] Acts xix. 24.   [10] Herod. ii. 63.

[11] את סכות מלככם

ואת כיון צלמיכם

[12] Is. ii. 18.
[13] The idol, called *Molech,* 1 Kgs xi. 7. had been called *Milchom,* Ib. 5.
[14] 1 Kgs xi. 5, 33, 2 Kgs xxiii. 13.
[15] Jer. xix. 5. xxxii. 35.

Moloch and Chiun your images, the star of your god, which ye made to yourselves,

the time of our Lord [1],) burnt their own children, *their sons and their daughters,* alive to him. Yet, even in these dreadful rites, the Carthaginian worship [2] was more cold-blooded and artificial than that of Phœnicia. But whether *the king,* whom the Israelites worshiped in the wilderness, was the same as the Ammonite Molech or no, those dreadful sacrifices were then no part of his worship; else Amos would not have spoken of the idolatry, as *the carrying about his tabernacle* only. He would have described it by its greatest offensiveness. *The king* was a title also of the Egyptian Deity, Osiris [3], who was identified with the sun, and whose worship Israel may probably have brought with them, as well as that of the calf, his symbol. Again most of the old translators have retained the Hebrew word *Chiyyun* [4], either regarding it as a proper name, or unable to translate it. Some later tradition identifies it with the planet Saturn [5], which under a different name, the Arabs propitiated as a malevolent being [6]. In S. Ephrem's time, the heathen Syrians worshiped "the child-devouring Chivan [7]." Israel however, did not learn the idolatry from the neighboring Arabs, since it is not the Arab name of that planet [8]. In Egyptian, the name of Chunsu, one of the 12 gods who severally were thought to preside over the 12 months, appears in an abridged form Chuns or Chon [9]. He was, in their mythology, held to be "the eldest son of Ammon [10];" his name is said to signify, "[11] power, might;" and he to be that ideal of might, worshiped as the Egyptian Hercules [12]. The name Chun extended into Phœnician [13] and Assyrian [14] proper names. Still Chon is not Chiyyun; and the fact that the name was re-

tained as Chon or Chun in Phœnicia (where the worship was borrowed) as well as in Assyria, is a ground for hesitating to identify with it the word of Chiyyun, which has a certain likeness only to the abridged name. S. Jerome's Hebrew teacher on the other hand knew of no such tradition, and S. Jerome renders it *image* [15]. And certainly it is most natural to render it not as a name, but as a common noun. It may probably mean, *the pedestal* [16], the *basis of your images.* The prophet had spoken of their images, as covered over with their little *shrines, the shrines of your king.* Here he may, not improbably, speak of them, as fastened to a pedestal. Such were the gods, whom they chose for the One true God, gods, *carried about,* covered over, fixed to their place, lest they should fall. The worship was certainly some form of star-worship, since there follows, *the star of your god.* It took place after the worship of the calf. For S. Stephen, after having spoken of that idolatry says [17], *Then God turned and gave them up to worship the host of heaven, as it is written in the book of the prophets.* Upon their rebellions, God at last gave them up to themselves. S. Stephen calls the god whom they worshiped, *Rephan,* quoting the then existing Greek translation, "having regard," S. Jerome says, "to the meaning rather than the words. This is to be observed in all Holy Scripture, that Apostles and Apostolic men, in citing testimonies from the Old Testament, regard, not the words, but the meaning, nor do they follow the words, step by step, provided they do not depart from the meaning."
Of the special idolatry there is no mention in Moses, in like way as the mention of the worship of the "goat [18]," a second symbol of

---

[1] "Even to the days of a Proconsul under Tiberius." Tertull. Apol. 9. pp. 20, 1. Oxf. Tr. and note k. Ges. quotes 3 Phœnician inscriptions, attesting the Punic child-sacrifices to Baal, Thes. p. 795.
[2] As described Diod. xx. 14. The Rabbins, however, speak of the sacrifices to Molech in exactly the same way, Carpzoff, Ant. 87. 484.
[3] Plutarch. Is. et Os. c. 10.
[4] The Syr. writes *Chevon; Jon. Chiun;* Aq. and Symm. in S. Jer. *Chion.* The *Rephan* of the LXX. may be only a different way of writing Chevan, the Greek translator, here as elsewhere, substituting ר for ב ; or it may be an Egyptian equivalent.
[5] In Persian, in the Dabistan, it is said, "The image of Keiwan was of black stone." Lee's Lex. v. אשרה. The Bundehesh, in enumerating the planets, places *Kivan,* the fifth, as does the Codex Nasoræus (ed. Norb. p. 54.) but all these are comparatively modern. The Copt-Arabic list of planets, which explains Rephan by the Arabic *Zochal* i. q. Saturn, may very probably have its name Rephan from the Greek.
[6] Poc spec. Hist. Arab. p. 103. 120. ed. White.
[7] Serm. 8 adv. Hær. Opp. Syr. ii. 458.
[8] The Kamoos explains the Persian *Kaivan* by the Arabic name *Zochal.*
[9] "The Coptic name Paschôns or Pachon is re-

solved into Pa-chons," "that of Chons or Chonsou; the name of the god who, according to the monuments, presided over this month." Brugsch, Eg. p. 162.
[10] Birch, from slab in the Brit. Mus. (quoted by Bunsen, Æg. Stella, i. 460.)
[11] Birch, Ib.
[12] "They say that Hercules is in Ægyptian called Chon, χῶν." Etym. M. See Sir G. Wilk. in Rawl. Herod. ii. 78. note. "The Egyptians called Hercules Chon." L. Girald [Opp. ii. 327.] from Xenophan. Antioch. Drus. but the authority given is wrong.
[13] Sanchoniathon, *Chunasun.* Movers, Phœn. i. 291.
[14] Chinzer כן־אצר, Cinneladan כון־אל־אדן in Ptol. Id. ib.
[15] Theodotion also translates it as a noun.
[16] כון from כון.   [17] Acts vii. 42.
[18] שעירים Lev. xvii. 7. rendered in the E. V. "devils;" but שעיר lit. "the hairy," is the Hebrew name of the goat, as hircus from hirtus, hirsutus. The name for "devils" in the Pentateuch is שדים Deut. xxxii. 17. Jeroboam endeavored fruitlessly to revive the worship. *He made him priests for the high places and the Seirim and 'Agalim which he had*

Before
CHRIST
cir. 787.

k 2 Kings 17. 6.

27 Therefore will I cause you to go into captivity k beyond Damascus, saith the LORD, [1] whose name is The God of hosts.

Before
CHRIST
cir. 787.

[1] ch. 4. 13.

the Pantheistic worship of Egypt [1], is contained only incidentally in the prohibition of that worship. After the final rebellion, upon which God rejected that generation, Holy Scripture takes no account of them. They had failed God; they had forfeited the distinction, for which God had created, preserved, taught them, revealed Himself to them, and had, by great miracles, rescued them from Egypt. Thenceforth that generation was cast aside unnoticed.

Which ye made to yourselves. This was the fundamental fault, that they *made it for themselves.* Instead of the tabernacle, which God, their king, appointed, they *bare about the tabernacle* of *him* whom they took for their king; and for the service which He gave, they *chose new gods* [2] for themselves. Whereas God made them for Himself, they made for themselves gods out of their own mind. All idolatry is self-will, first choosing a god, and then enslaved to it.

27. *Therefore [And]* this being so, such having been their way from the beginning until now, *will I cause you to go into captivity beyond Damascus.* Syria was the most powerful enemy by whom God had heretofore chastened them [3]. From Syria He had recently, for the time, delivered them, and had given Damascus into their hands [4]. That day of grace had been wasted, and they were still rebellious. *Now* God would bring against them a mightier enemy. Damascus, the scene of their triumph, should be their pathway to captivity. God would *cause* them *to go into captivity,* not to *Damascus,* whence they might have easily returned, but *beyond* it, as He did, *into the cities of the Medes.* But Israel had, up to the time of Amos and beyond it, no enemy, no war, *beyond Damascus.* Jehu had probably paid tribute to Shalmanubar king of Assyria, to strengthen himself [5]. The Assyrian monarch had warred against Israel's enemies, and seemingly received some check from them [6]. Against Israel he had shewn no hostility. But for the conspiracy of one yet to be born in private life, one of the captains of Israel who, by murder, became its sovereign, it might have continued on in its own land. The Assyrian monarchs needed tribute, not slaves; nor did they employ Israel as slaves. Exile was but a wholesale imprisonment of

the nation in a large but safe prison-house. Had they been still, they were more profitable to Assyria, as tributaries in their own land. There was no temptation to remove them, when Amos prophesied. The temptation came with political intrigues which had not then commenced. The then Assyrian monarch, Shamasiva, defeated their enemies the Syrians, united with and aiding the Babylonians [7]; *they* had then had no share in the opposition to Assyria, but lay safe in their mountain-fastness. It has been said, " [8] Although the 'kingdom of Israel had, through Jeroboam, recovered its old borders, yet careless insolence, luxury, unrighteousness, *must* bring the destruction of the kingdom which the Prophet foretells. The Prophet does but dimly forebode the superior power of Assyria." Solomon had declared the truth [9], *Righteousness exalteth a nation, but sin is a reproach to any people.* But there are many sorts of decay. Decay does not involve the transportation of a people. Nay, decay would not bring it, but the contrary. A mere luxurious people rots on its own soil, and would be left to rot there. It was the little remnant of energy, political caballing, warlike spirit, in Israel, which brought its ruin from man. Idolatry, "insolence, luxury, unrighteousness," bring down the displeasure of God, not of man. Yet Amos foretold, that God would bring the destruction through man. They were, too, no worse than their neighbors, nor so bad; not so bad as the Assyrians themselves, except that, God having revealed Himself to them, they had more light. The sin then, the punishment, the mode of punishment, belong to the Divine revelation. Such sins and worse have existed in Christian nations. They were in part sins directly against God. God reserves to Himself, how and when He will punish. He has annexed no such visible laws of punishment to a nation's sins that man could, of his own wisdom or observation of God's ways, foresee it. They through whom He willed to inflict it, and whom Amos pointed out, were not provoked by *those* sins. There was no connection between Israel's present sins, and Assyria's future vengeance. No Eastern despot cares for the oppressions of his subjects, so that his own tribute is collected.

made. (2 Chr. xi. 15.) *Seirim* is doubtless to be taken in its literal sense, "he goats," as *'Agalim,* with which it is joined, is of "calves."
[1] Pan, or Mendes, worshiped under the goat, was nature in one great aggregate, the oldest of their gods, according to themselves (Herod. ii. 145. add 46), as being, in fact, the principle of life, apart

from its Author. In Egyptian idolatry, the goat was accounted a special manifestation of that principle.
[2] Jud. v. 8. [3] 2 Kgs xiii. 7. [4] Ib. xiv. 25, 28.
[5] See Introd. to Hosea, p. 2. [6] See ab. on i. 3.
[7] Rawl. Herod. i. 466, from Cuneif. Inscr.
[8] De Wette, Einl. § 232. [9] Prov. xiv. 34.

Before
CHRIST
cir. 787.

CHAPTER VI.

1 *The wantonness of Israel, 7
shall be plagued with desolation, 12 and their incorrigibleness.*

W OE [a] to them *that* || *are*
at ease in Zion, and
trust in the mountain of
Samaria, *which are named*

Before
CHRIST
cir. 787.

a Luke 6. 24.
|| Or, *are secure.*

See the whole range of Mohammedan rule
now. As far too as we know, neither
Assyria nor any other power had hitherto
punished rebellious nations by transporting
them[1]; and certainly Israel had not yet rebelled, or meditated rebellion. He only Who
controls the rebellious wills of men, and
through their self-will works out His own
all-wise Will and man's punishment, could
know the future of Israel and Assyria, and
how through the pride of Assyria He would
bring down the pride of Samaria.

It has been well said by a thoughtful observer of the world's history, " Whosoever
attempts to prophesy, not being inspired, is a
fool." We English know our own sins, many
and grievous ; we know of a vast reign of violence, murder, blasphemy, theft, uncleanness, covetousness, dishonest dealing, unrighteousness, and of the breach of every
commandment of God : we know well [2] now
of an instrument in God's Hands, not far off,
like the Assyrian, but within two hours of
our coast ; armaments have been collected ;
a harbor is being formed ; our own coast
openly examined ; iron-sheeted vessels prepared ; night-signals provided ; some of our
own alienated population organized ; with a
view to our invasion. We recognize the
likelihood of the invasion, fortify our coast,
arm, not as a profession, but for security.
Our preparations testify, how wide-spread
is our expectation. No one scarcely
doubts that it will be. Yet who dare
predict the issue? Will God permit that
scourge to come? will he prevail? What
would be the extent of our sufferings or loss?
how would our commerce or our Empire be
impaired? Would it be dismembered?
Since no man can affirm anything as to this
which is close at hand, since none of us
would dare to affirm in God's Name, in regard to any one stage of all this future, that
this or that would or would not happen, then
let men have at least the modesty of the
magicians of Egypt, and seeing in God's prophets these absolute predictions of a future,
such as their own wisdom, under circumstances far more favorable, could not dare to
make, own ; [3] *This is the finger of God.* Not we
alone. We see all Europe shaken ; we see
powers of all sorts, heaving to and fro ; we
see the Turkish power ready to dissolve,
stayed up, like a dead man, only by un-Chris-

tian jealousies of Christians. Some things
we may partially guess at. But with all our
means of knowing what passes everywhere,
with all our knowledge of the internal impulses of nations, hearing, as we do, almost
every pulse which beats in the great European system, knowing the diseases which,
here and there, threaten convulsion or disso-
lution, no one dare stake his human wisdom
on any *absolute* prediction, like these of the
shepherd of Tekoa as to Damascus[1] and
Israel. To say the like in God's Name, unless inspired, we should know to be blasphemy. God Himself set the alternative before men. [4] *Let all the nations be gathered
together, and let the people be assembled ; who
among them that can declare this, and shew
former things? Let them bring forth their witnesses, that they may be justified ; or let them hear,
and say, It is truth.*

S. Stephen, in quoting this prophecy, substitutes, Babylon for Damascus, as indeed *the
cities of the Medes* were further than Babylon.
Perhaps he set the name, in order to remind
them, that as God had brought Abraham[5]
out of the land of the Chaldeans, leaving the
idols which his *fathers* had *served*[6], to serve
God only, so they, serving idols, were carried
back, whence Abraham had come, forfeiting,
with the faith of Abraham, the promises
made to Abraham ; aliens and outcasts.

Saith the Lord, the Lord of hosts, the Lord of
the heavenly hosts for whose worship they
forsook God ; the Lord of the hosts on earth,
whose ministry He employs to punish those
who rebel against Him. "[7]For He hath
many hosts to execute His judgments, the
hosts of the Assyrians, the Medes and Persians, the Greeks and Romans." All creatures in heaven and in earth are, as He says
of the holy Angels, [8] *ministers of His, that do
His pleasure.*

VI. 1. *Woe to them that are at ease.* The
word[9] always means such as are recklessly at
their ease, *the careless ones,* such as those
whom Isaiah bids, [10]*rise up, tremble, be troubled ;* for *many days and years shall ye be
troubled.* It is that luxury and ease, which
sensualize the soul, and make it dull, stupid,
hard-hearted. By one earnest, passing word,
the Prophet warns his own land, that present
sinful ease ends in future woe. [11]*Woe unto
them that laugh now: for they shall mourn and
weep.* "[7] He foretells the destruction and

1 See ab. on i. 5. pp. 160, 1.
2 Written in 1860.
4 Is. xliii. 9.
3 Ex. viii. 19.
5 Acts vii. 4.
6 Josh. xxiv. 14.
8 Ps. ciii. 21.
10 Is. xxxii. 9–11.
7 Rup.
9 שַׁאֲנַנִּים.
11 S. Luke vi. 25.

Before
CHRIST
cir. 787.

b Ex. 19. 5.
‖ Or, *firstfruits,*
c Jer. 2. 10.
d Is. 10. 9.
Taken cir. 794.

b ‖ chief of the nations, to whom the house of Israel came! 2 c Pass ye unto d Cal-

neh, and see; and from thence go ye to e Hamath the great : then go down to f Gath of the Philis-

Before
CHRIST
cir. 787.

e 2 Kings 18. 34.
f 2 Chr. 26. 6.

captivity of both Judah and Israel at once; and not only that captivity at Babylon, but that whereby they are dispersed unto this day." Luxury and deepest sins of the flesh were rife in that generation[1], which slew Him Who for our sakes became poor. *And trust in the mountain of Samaria,* not in God. Samaria was strong[2], resisted for three years, and was the last city of Israel which was taken. *The king of Assyria came up throughout all the land and went up to Samaria, and besieged it[3].* Benhadad, in that former siege, when God delivered them[4], attempted no assault, but famine only.

Which are *named the chief of the nations;* lit. *the named of the chief of the nations,* i. e. those who, in Israel, which by the distinguishing favor of God were *chief of the nations,* were themselves, marked, distinguished, *named.* The Prophet, by one word, refers them back to those first princes of the congregation, of whom Moses used that same word[5]. They were *heads of the houses of their fathers[6], renowned of the congregation, heads of thousands in Israel[7].* As, if any one were to call the Peers, "Barons of England," he would carry us back to the days of Magna Charta, although six centuries and a half ago, so this word, occurring at that time[8], here only in any Scripture since Moses, carried back the thoughts of the degenerate aristocracy of Israel to the faith and zeal of their forefathers, *what* they ought to have been, and *what* they were. As Amalek of old was *first of the nations[9]* in its enmity against the people of God[10], having, first of all, shewn that implacable hatred, which Ammon, Moab, Edom, evinced afterward, so was Israel *first of nations,* as chosen by God. It became, in an evil way, *first of nations,* i. e. distinguished above the heathen, by rejecting Him.

To whom the house of Israel came, or *have come.* They were, like those princes of old, raised above others. Israel *came* to them for judgment; and they, regardless of duty,

lived only for self-indulgence, effeminacy, and pride. S. Jerome renders in the same sense, "that enter pompously the house of Israel," lit. *enter for themselves,* as if they were lords of it, and it was made for them.

2. *Pass over to Calneh.* He bids them behold, East, North, and West, survey three neighboring kingdoms, and see whether God had not, even in the gifts of this world, dealt better with Israel. Why then so requite Him? *Calneh,* (which Isaiah calls *Calno*[11], Ezekiel, *Cannēh*[12],) was one of the four cities, built by Nimrod *in the land of Shinar*[13], *the beginning of his kingdom.* From that time, until this of Amos, no mention of it occurs. It, probably, was more than once conquered by the Assyrians[14], lying, as it did, on the Tigris, some 40 miles perhaps from Babylon. Hence it was said, under its new name Ctesiphon[15], to have been built, i. e. rebuilt, by the Macedonians[16], and again by the Parthians[17], whose "[18] kings made it their winter residence on account of its good air." It was anew destroyed by Severus[19], rebuilt by Sapor II. in the 4th Century[20]. Julian's generals held it impregnable[21], being built on a peninsula, surrounded on three sides by the Tigris[22]. It became the scene of repeated persecutions of Christianity[23]; Nestorianism was favored[24]. A centre of Persian luxury, it fell at once and for ever before Omar[25], and the Persian empire perished with it. It was replaced by the neighboring Bagdad. The history illustrates the tenacity of life in those well-chosen sites, and the character of the place, of whose conquest Sennacherib boasted, with which Amos compared the land of Israel.

Go thence to Hamath the great, originally, a Canaanite kingdom[26]. *The entrance to it* was assigned as the Northern border of Israel[27]. In David's time its king was at war with the king of Zobah[28], and made presents to David on his subdual. In Solomon's time it had fallen under the power of the king of Zobah,

[1] See S. John viii. 9, Rom. ii. 21-24, S. Luke xi. 39, 42, S. Matt. xxiii. 14, 23, 26.
[2] See ab. on iii. 9.   [3] 2 Kgs xvii. 5.
[4] Ib. vii. 6.   [5] Num. i. 17.   [6] Ib. 4.   [7] Ib. 16.
[8] The phrase of Num. i. 17. occurs only in the books of Chronicles (1 Chr. xii. 31, xvi. 41, 2 Chr. xxviii. 15, xxxi. 19) and Ezra (viii. 20) as taken from the Pentateuch. See Hengst. Auth. d. Pent. i. 97.
[9] Nu. xxiv. 20.
[10] Ex. xvii. 8-16. So Onk. S. Jer. Pseud-Jon.
[11] x. 9.   [12] xxvii. 23.   [13] Gen. x. 10.
[14] See ab. Introd. p. 149.
[15] S. Jer. here. S.Ephr. Jon.
[16] Procop. B. Pers. ii. 28.

[17] Plin. vi. 26. n. 30. It certainly existed before, Polyb. v. 46.
[18] Strabo, xvi. 1. 26, who speaks of it as existing already.
[19] Dio Cass. lxxv. Sev. 9.
[20] Mirkhond, Hist. d. Sass. in De Sacy, Men. sur la Perse, p. 316.   [21] Amm. xxiv. 7. 1.
[22] Kinneir, Geogr. Mem. of the Persian Empire, p. 252.
[23] Ass. B. O. i. 185 sqq. iii. 2. lii. sqq. Acta Mart.
[24] Ass. iii. 2. lxxxvii.
[25] Abulf. i. 233-5, Ritt. x. 172.   [26] Gen. x. 18.
[27] Num. xxxiv. 7, 8, Josh. xiii. 5.
[28] 2 Sam. viii. 9, 10.

tines: *be they* better than these kingdoms? or their

border greater than your border?

whence it was called Hamath-zobah. Solomon won it from him, incorporated it with Israel, and built towns in its territory[1]. The "Hamathites" were, under their own king, united with Benhadad, the Hittites, and the Phœnicians in their war with Shalmanubar, and defeated by him[2]. Ezekiel speaks of the *border of Damascus* and *the coast of Hamath*[3], as of places of like importance, and Zechariah[4], of their joint subdual by Alexander. To judge from the present site, it in some respects resembled Samaria. It lay in a narrow oval valley of the Orontes; its citadel on a round hill in the centre. The city rises up the steep sides of the hills which inclose it[5]. Vast water-wheels[6], some of a diameter of 67[7], 80, 90[8], feet, raise the water of the Orontes to supply, by aid of aqueducts, the upper city, or to water the neighboring gardens. "[9]The Western part of its territory is the granary of Northern Syria."[?] Even when Antiochus Epiphanes called it after himself Epiphania, its inhabitants called it after its old name[10]. Mention occurs of it in the crusades[11]. In the 13th century it had its own well-known prince[12]; and has still a population of some 30,000[13].

Gath [*Winepress*] must, from its name, have been situated in a rich country. It lay on the confines of Judea and Philistia; for Rehoboam fortified it as a border-fortress[14]. It had been contrariwise fortified by the Philistines against Judah, since, when David took it *out of the hand of the Philistines*, it had the title[15] *methegammah*, "bridle of the mother city," or metropolis. It had at that time *daughter towns*[16] dependent upon it. It must also have been Micah's birthplace, *Moresheth Gath,* i. e. Moresheth of Gath, which in S. Jerome's[17] time was "a small village near Eleutheropolis," [Bethgabrin.] Of Gath itself S. Jerome says, "[18]It is one of the five cities of Philistia, near the confines of Judea, and now too a very large village on the way from Eleutheropolis to Gaza." Eusebius says[19], "about the 5th

milestone from Eleutheropolis to Diospolis" [Lydda]. Since the Philistines carried the Ark of God from Ashdod to Gath, and thence to Ekron[20], it seems likely that Gath lay nearer to Ashdod than Ekron, although necessarily more inland than either, since it was a border-city to Judah. The Tel-es-Safiyeh corresponds with these conditions, lying at the entrance of the Shephēlah, about 5 miles from Beit-Jibrin on the road to Lydda, [Ludd]. It "[21]rises about 100 feet above the Eastern ridge which it terminates, and perhaps 200 over the plain which terminates its Western base. The ruins and subterranean reservoirs shew that it is a site of high antiquity, great strength, and importance." Gath had at this time probably been taken by Uzziah who *broke down* its *wall*[22]; and since it is not mentioned with the other four Philistine cities, whose sentence is pronounced by Amos[23] himself, Zephaniah[24], and Zechariah[25], it is probable that it never recovered.

Be they better than these kingdoms? The prophet seems purposely to say less than he might, in order that his hearers might have to supply the more. Calneh, Hamath, Gath, had not been more guilty against God than Ephraim, yet probably they had all been conquered: Gath by Judah; Hamath by Israel[26] himself; Calneh by Assyria. Both Shalmanubar and Shamasiva conquered in Babylonia[27]; and Shamasiva "[28]declares that he took above 200 towns" in Babylonia. Amos, then, upbraids Israel for their ingratitude, both as to the original gift of their good land, and its continuance. The Heathen had suffered; *they*, the guiltier, had been spared; yet still they acted no otherwise than these Heathen.

"[29]What spacious, what wide border have we, bounded as the life of God and eternity!" "[30]Our hopes and the bounds of our bliss are measured, not like those of the worldly and ungodly, by the limits of a petty time or by this dot of earth, but by the

[1] 2 Chr. viii. 3, 4,
[2] Cuneif. Inscr. in Rawl. Her. i. 463, 4.
[3] Ezek. xlvii. 16, xlviii. 1.　　[4] ix. 1, 2.
[5] Col. Squire, in Walpole Mem. 323–5.
[6] Seetzen puts them at 250. Nachlass, i. 13–15. in Ritt. xvii. 1042. Burckhardt (Syria 146.) says, "about a dozen" supply the city itself.
[7] Squire, l. c. "at least 70 feet," Burckh. l. c.
[8] Thomson, The Land, ii. 278.
[9] Burckh. 147.
[10] Jos. Ant. i. 6, 2. S. Jer. Qu. in Gen. x. 15.
[11] Ritter. 1033.　　[12] Abulfeda.　　[13] Burckhardt, Ib.
[14] 2 Chr. xi. 8.
[15] 2 Sam. viii. 1. comp. 1 Chr. xviii. 1.
[16] בְּנוֹתֶיהָ 1 Chr. Ib.　　[17] Præf. ad Mic.
[18] In Mic. i. 10.

[19] v. Γέθ (in Joshua) where he explains it to be the place where the Enakim dwelt, i. e. the Philistine Gath. Under "the Kings" v. Γεθθὰ, "whither the Philistines removed the Ark from Ashdod," he says, "there is yet a very large village called Giththa, on the road between Antipatris and Jamnia. And another, Geththaim." This which Eusebius, found probably in some other authority, would make Gath the most Northern of the Philistine towns, and near the sea, which is inconsistent with its being near Moresheth and a frontier-town of Judah.
[20] 1 Sam. v. 8, 10.　　[21] Porter, Hdb. 253, 4.
[22] 2 Chr. xxvi. 6.　　[23] i. 7, 8.　　[24] ii. 4.　　[25] ix. 5.
[26] See bel. ver. 14.
[27] Cuneif. Inscr. in Rawl. Her. i. 464.
[28] Ib. 466.　　[29] Rib.　　[30] Lap.

Before
CHRIST
cir. 787.

3 Ye that [h] put far away the [i] evil day, [k] and cause [l] the || seat of violence to come near ;

4 That lie upon beds of ivory, and || stretch them-

b Ezek. 12. 27.
i ch. 5. 18. & 9. 10.
k ch. 5. 12.
ver. 12.
l Ps. 94. 20.
|| Or, habitation.
|| Or, abound with superflui-ties.

selves upon their couches, and eat the lambs out of the flock, and the calves out of the midst of the stall;

5 [m] That || chant to the

Before
CHRIST
cir. 787.

m Is. 5. 12.
|| Or, quaver.

---

boundless space of eternity and of heaven; so that we may say confidently to the ungodly, *Is not our border wider than your border?"*
3. *Ye that put far away.* Probably *with aversion*[1]. They bade that day as it were, be gone. The Hebrew idiom expresses, how they would put it off, if they could; as far as in them lay, they *assigned a distance to it*[2], although they could not remove the day itself. The *evil day* is that same *day of the Lord,* which the scoffers or misbelievers professed to long for[3]. The thought that the Lord has a Day, in which to judge man, frets or frightens the irreligious, and they use different ways to get rid of it. The strong harden themselves against it, distort the belief in it, or disbelieve it. The weak and voluptuous shut their eyes to it, like the bird in the fable, as if what they dread would cease to be there, because they cease to see it.
And cause the seat [lit. *the session, sitting*] *of violence to come near.* They dismissed the thought of the Day of account, in order that they might sin with less fear. They put from them the judgment of God, that they might exercise violence over His creatures. Men do not put away the thought of God, except to invite His Enemy into their souls. But therewith, they *brought near* another *seat of violence,* not their own, but upon them. They brought near what they wished to put away, the day, in which, through the violence of the Assyrians, God would avenge their own.
"[4] Let *them* consider this, who put no bound to their sins. For the more they obey their own will, the more they hasten to destruction; and while they think they draw nigh to pleasures, they draw nigh to everlasting woes."
4. *That lie upon beds* (i. e. *sofas*) *of ivory,* i. e. probably inlaid with ivory. The word might, in itself, express either the bed, in which they slept by night, or the Divan, on which the Easterns lay at their meals; *and stretch them-*

selves, lit. *are poured* out[5], stretching their listless length, dissolved, unnerved, in luxury and sloth, *upon their couches,* perhaps under an awning[6]: *and eat the lambs,* probably *fatted lambs*[7], *out of the flock,* chosen, selected out of it as the best, and *calves out of the midst of the stall;* i. e. the place where they were tied up (as the word[8] means) to be fatted. They were stall-fed, as we say, and these people had the best chosen for them.
"[9] He shews how they *draw nigh the seat of violence.* They lay on beds or couches of ivory, and expended thereon the money wherewith their poor brethren were to be fed. Go now, I say not into the houses of nobles, but into any house of any rich man, see the gilded and worked couches, curtains woven of silk and gold, and walls covered with gold, while the poor of Christ are naked, shivering, shrivelled with hunger. Yet stranger is it, that while this is everywhere, scarce anywhere is there who *now* blames it. *Now* I say; for there were formerly. ' Ye array,' S. Ambrose says[10], 'walls with gold, men ye bare. The naked cries before your door and you neglect him; and are careful with what marbles you clothe your pavement. The poor seeketh money, and hath it not; man asketh for bread, and thy horse champeth gold. Thou delightest in costly ornaments, while others have not meal. What judgment thou heapest on thyself, thou man of wealth! Miserable, who hast power to keep so many souls from death, and hast not the will! The jewel of thy ring could maintain in life a whole population.' If such things are not to be blamed now, then neither were they formerly."
5. *That chant to the voice of the lyre,* accompanying *the voice of the lyre* with the human voice; giving vocal expression and utterance to what the instrumental music spoke without words. The word, which Amos alone uses in this one place, describes probably [11]a hurried flow of unmeaning, unconsidered

1 As in נָדָה from נָדַד, i. q. נָדָה. In the other place where it occurs, Is. lxvi. 5, it is united with hatred, "expelled with aversion." In 2 Kgs xxii. 21, Cheth. נָדָא is used of Jeroboam *driving* the people away from following God.
2 The force of לְ. 3 ch. v. 18. 4 Rib.
5 As in Arab. and Syr. In Heb, it is used of a vine pouring itself out, in luxuriance, Ezek. xvii. 6; of a curtain overlapping, Ezek xxiv. 12, 13; of a head-
dress hanging over, Ezek. xxiii. 15; of wisdom poured away and gone, Jer. xlix. 7.
6 צָשׁ like the Arab. 'arsh. See Judith xvi. 23.
7 As in Deut. xxxii. 14, Ps. xxxvii. 20, 1 Sam. xv. 9, Jer. li. 40.
8 מַרְבֵּק. 9 Rib. 10 de Nabuthe, c. 13.
11 The central meaning of the Arabic root is "anticipating another;" then hurry, negligence, excess, inadvertence in act, and, in speech, exaggeration

Before
CHRIST
cir. 787.

a 1 Chr. 23. 5.

sound of the viol, and invent to themselves instruments of music, [n] like David;

Before
CHRIST
cir. 787.

|| Or, in bowls of wine.

o Gen. 37. 25.

6 That drink || wine ·in bowls, and anoint themselves with the chief ointments: [o] but they

---

words, in which the rhythm of words and music was everything, the sense, nothing; much like most glees. The E. M. "quaver" has also some foundation in the root, but does not suit the idiom so well, which expresses that the act was something done *to the voice of the lyre*, accompanying the music, not altering the music itself. In fact, they would go together. An artificial, effeminate music which should relax the soul, frittering the melody, and displacing the power and majesty of divine harmony by tricks of art, and giddy, thoughtless, heartless, soulless versifying would be meet company. Debased music is a mark of a nation's decay, and promotes it. The Hebrew music seems to have been very simple ; and singing appears to have been reserved almost exclusively for solemn occasions, the Temple-service, or the greeting of victory [1]. *Singing men and singing women* were part of the state of David and Solomon [2]. Else the music at the feasts of the rich appears rather to be mentioned with blame [3]. Songs they had [4]; but the songs, for which the Hebrew exiles were celebrated, and which their Babylonian masters required them to sing, *the songs of Zion* [5], were the hymns of the temple, *the Lord's song*.

And invent to themselves instruments of music. The same pains, which David employed on music to the honor of God, they employed on their light, enervating unmeaning music, and, if they were in earnest enough, justified their inventions by the example of David. Much as people have justified our degraded, sensualizing, immodest dancing, by the religious dancing of Holy Scripture! The word can mean no other than *devised* [6]. David then did *devise* and *invent* instruments of music for the service of God. He introduced into the Temple-service the use of the stringed instruments, the *kinnor*, (the *lyre*) and the *nebel* (the *harp*) in addition to the cymbals. Whence these, in contrast with the trumpets, are called *the instruments of*

in praise, and (conj. iii.) " got the first word," "spoke precipitately, the tongue outrunning the sense." Abu'l Walid applies this last meaning, that "they, poured out words and measured out defilements." He says also that the corresponding Arabic participle is used of those "who extemporise poetry, i. e. sing extempore without thought." See the Arabic in Ges.
′1 Sam. xviii. 7.　　2 2 Sam. xix 35, Eccl. ii. 8.
3 Is. v. 12, xxiv. 9.　　4 Pr. xxv. 20.
5 Ps. cxxxvii. 3, 4.
6 It is commonly used with abstract nouns as מְזִמָּה, אָוֶן, רָעָה, מַחֲשָׁבוֹת, *devices, evil, vanity,* or with ל and the inf.; but always in the meaning of "devising," "inventing." It is used of those gifted

---

David [7]. Probably, in adapting them to the Temple-service, he, in some way, improved the existing instrument; having been, in early youth, remarkable for his skill upon the harp [8]. As *he* elevated the character and powers of the, perhaps rude, instrument which he found, and fitted it to the service of God, so these men refined it doubtless, as they thought, and fitted it for the service of luxury and sensuality. But what harm, they thought, in amending the music of their day, since so did David?

6. *That drink wine in bowls* (lit. as E. M. *drink in bowls*, lit. *sprinkling vessels, of wine*). The word is elsewhere used only of the *bowls*, out of which the blood of the sacrifice was sprinkled. Probably Amos was referring to the first offering of the Princes in the wilderness, with whom he had already tacitly contrasted these Princes [9]. *They* had shewn zeal for God in offering the massive bowls for the service of the tabernacle : the like zeal had these princes for the service of their own *god* [10], *their belly*. It may be too, (since misbelief and sensuality are necessarily irreverent) that they used for their revels vessels which had at one time been employed in sprinkling the blood of their idol-sacrifices. There was no additional desecration in it. The gold and silver vessels of the Temple were consecrated by being offered to God, by His hallowing of the Temple through His Presence, by being used in the typical sacrifices. The gold and silver, creatures of God, were desecrated by being employed in idol-worship, of which indeed sensuality was a part. Their employment in this luxury was only a continuance of their desecration, which it did but illustrate. It is nothing incredible, since among Christians, the fonts of the Church have been turned into horse-troughs by sects who disbelieved in Baptism. The vessels were, probably, large, since those offered for the tabernacle weighed 70 shekels. Private luxury vied with the ficti-

by God "to devise devices," i. e. as it is explained, *to work in gold and in silver and in brass and in setting of stones.* Ex. xxxi. 4, 5. It is used also of war-like machines, and their inventor ; as our Engineer, Engine comes from ingenium. An embroiderer, who needed continual invention, is called חוֹשֵׁב; his work, the work of an inventor (see Ex. xxvi. 1. E. M. &c.) S. Jerome's rendering, "like David, they think that they have instruments of music,' does not suit the Hebrew idioms.
7 2 Chr. xxix. 26, comp. 25. and 1 Chr. xv. 16, 19–21, 24.
8 1 Sam. xvi. 16, 18, 23.
9 Hengst. Auth. d. Pent. p. 99. See ab. p. 152.
10 Phil. iii. 19.

are not grieved for the † affliction of Joseph.

† Heb. *breach.*

tious sanctuary, which aped the sanctuary of God. Perhaps Amos would express the capacity of these vessels by saying, *that drink in bowls of wine.* Like swine in the trough, they immersed themselves in their drink, "[1] swimming in mutual swill."

All this they did, he expresses, habitually. He speaks of these their acts in a form expressing an ever-renewed present, *the putters off, the liers on couches of ivory, the out-stretched, the eating, the drinking,* men whose lives were spent in nothing else ; the voluptuaries, sensualists, " good-fellows" of Israel.

Anoint themselves with the chief ointments. Anointing the body was a sort of necessary[2] in the hot climate of the East, for bodily health. *Not* to anoint the body was the exception, as in mourning[3]. But necessaries become a vehicle for luxury. For health, olive-oil sufficed[4]. For the service of God, a rich ointment was appointed, to which odorous substances, myrrh, cinnamon, the odoriferous reed, and cassia[5] gave a scent emblematic of the fragrance of holiness. In order to separate what was sacred from ordinary uses, God forbade, on pain of death, to imitate this ointment, or *pour it on the flesh of man*[6]. Luxury vied with religion, and took to itself either the same, or ointment more costly. *They anointed themselves with the chief* [kind] *of ointments*[7]; those which held the first, highest rank among them. Nothing better or so good was left for what they thought to be the service of God, as, in times a little past, anything was thought good enough for a Church, nothing too good for a dwelling-house. Gorgeous adornments of man's house were thought splendor and good taste and fit employment of wealth ; slight adornment of the house of God was thought superstition.

But [And] they are not grieved [lit. *grieve not themselves*[8],] admit no grief[8], shut out all grief, *for the affliction* [lit. *breach*] *of Joseph.* The name of the Patriarch, Ephraim's father, recalled his suffering from his brethren. [9] His brethren cast him into a *pit without water*[10], probably an empty leaking well, (much as was that into which Jeremiah[11] was cast,) damp, fetid, and full of loathsome creatures. They[12] *saw the anguish of his soul when he besought* them, *and would not hear.* But what did they ? [13] *They sat down to eat bread.* So did these rich men deal with all their brethren, all Ephraim. They suffered not in, or with, any sufferings, present or future, of indi-

viduals or the whole. " Cast off thought," " cast off care," is the motto of sensualists and of the worldly ; " seize joyous the present hour, and leave the future," said the heathen[14]. This was the effect of their luxury and life of sense. The Prophet recounts, they stretched themselves listlessly, ate choice food, sang glees, drank deep, anointed themselves with the very best ointment, *and* grieved not themselves for any sufferings of their own flesh and blood. It followed, of necessity, from the rest. Luxury shuts out suffering, because any vivid knowledge of or dwelling upon sufferings must needs disturb its ease. Selfish wealth persuades itself that there is no suffering, lest it should be forced to think of it ; it *will* think distress either too little, so that it can relieve itself, or so great that it cannot be relieved; or it will philosophise upon distress and misery, as though it were best relieved by its own luxuries. Any how it will not know or hear of its details, it will not admit grief. "[15] Mercilessness is the own daughter of pleasure." [16] *This was the iniquity of thy sister Sodom; pride, fullness of bread, and careless ease had she and her daughters; and the hand of the poor and needy she strengthened not.* "Seest thou," says S. Chrysostom[17], " how he blames a delicate life? For in these words he accuses not covetousness, but prodigality only. And thou eatest to excess, Christ not even for need; thou various cakes, He not so much as dry bread ; thou drinkest choice wine, but on Him thou hast not bestowed so much as a cup of cold water in His thirst. Thou art on a soft, embroidered bed ; He is perishing with the cold. Be then the banquets clear from covetousness, yet they are accursed, because, while *thou* doest all beyond thy need, to Him thou givest not even His need ; and that, living in luxury on what is His ! "

And yet what was this luxury, which the Prophet so condemns? What, in us, were simplicity. What scarce any one thought of diminishing, while two millions, close by, were wasting away by famine's horrors ;— chairs or sofas inlaid, fat lamb or veal ; wine ; perfumes ; light music. The most delicate ingredient of those perfumes, cinnamon, enters into our food. " Looking at *our* times," says a writer at the close of the 16th century[18], " I marvel at the spareness of the ancients, and think that it would be well with us, if any above the poor were content with what were, of old, delicacies to kings and

---

[1] Thomson, Autumn.   [2] 2 Chr. xxviii. 15.
[3] 2 Sam. xiv. 2.   [4] Deut. xxviii. 40.
[5] Ex. xxx. 23–5.   [6] Ib. 32, 3.
[7] ראשית שמנים.

[8] לא נחלו.   [9] from Sanct.
[10] Gen. xxxvii. 24.   [11] Jer. xxxviii. 6.
[12] Gen. xlii. 21.   [13] xxxvii. 25.   [14] Hor.   [15] Lap.
[16] Ez. xvi. 49.   [17] Hom. 48. in S. Matt.   [18] Ribera.

Before CHRIST cir. 787.

7 ¶ Therefore now shall
they go captive with the
first that go captive, and
the banquet of them that
stretched themselves shall
be removed.

p Jer. 51. 14. Heb. 6. 13, 17.

8 p The Lord GOD hath
sworn by himself, saith the
LORD the God of hosts, I
abhor q the excellency of
Jacob, and hate his palaces:
therefore will I deliver up
the city with all † that is
therein.

Before CHRIST cir. 787.

q Ps. 47. 4. Ezek. 24. 21. ch. 8. 7.

† Heb. *the fulness thereof.*

nobles. Happy were these times, if they could imitate even what the prophets blame in nobles.—In the Gospel, *the King* Who *made a marriage feast for His Son said, I have prepared My dinner, My oxen and fatlings are killed, and all things are ready; come unto the marriage*[1]. When a *fatted calf* was killed for a feast, it was thought the best cheer, as when Abraham entertained Angels, or in that feast of the Father Who, when He had received back His son, said[2], *bring hither the fatted calf and kill it, and let us eat and be merry: for this My son was dead and is alive again.* So then the Prophet accuses the nobles of luxury, because they ate fat oxen and lambs. For the table of Solomon, the wealthiest of monarchs, there were brought *fat oxen, and oxen out of the pastures, sheep, besides hart and roebuck and fallow deer and fatted fowls*[3]. *Now* whatever is produced in sea or earth or sky, men think to be born to satisfy their appetites. Who could recount the manifold forms of food and condiments, which all-inventing gluttony has devised? Books had to be written; no memory sufficed. In this ocean, wealthiest patrimonies have discharged themselves and disappeared. Among the Romans, Fabius, for devouring his patrimony, was called Gurges [whirlpool]. Were this the practice now, he would have many great men surnamed from him, who, poor through gluttony, prey on the patrimonies of the poor, retain the property of the rich against their wills, and live on what is another's.—It were little to consume whole patrimonies in luxury, were it not that the virtues and nerves of the mind were also consumed and vices of all sorts crept in.—Shame to copy the luxury of Heathen, and despise their care for maintaining temperance.—We need not old examples. Such was the frugality of our Spaniards, 70 years ago, before they adopted foreign manners, that the rich had but mutton, roast and boiled, at their tables, nobles alone had poultry. Well were it then, if, in matter of food, we did only, what the Prophet in his time blamed." Spain has sunk under its luxury to a third-rate power. What can await England? What can await it, when the Prophet's blame were praise, and Dives is the pattern and ideal of the charity of most of us, and luxury, vanity, and self-indulgence are held to be the best way of ministering to the poor? Marvelous "imitation of Christ!" Once, to *forsake all* was to *follow* Christ. Now, to possess all, heap up all, to expend nothing save on self, and to *shew mercy on the poor* by allowing them to minister to our luxuries, is, according to the new philosophy of wealth, to be the counterfeit of Christian charity.

7. *Therefore now* [i. e. shortly] *shall they go captive with the first* [*at the head*] *of those who go captive.* They had sought eminence; they should have it. "[4] Ye who are first in riches, shall, the first, endure the yoke of captivity, as it is in Ezekiel[5], *begin from My sanctuary*, i. e. from the destruction of the Temple which is holy. For [6] *mighty men shall be mightily tormented;* and [7], *to whom men have committed much, of him they will ask the more.*"

And the banquet, probably, *the screech.* The root, *radsakh*, whose consonants contain most of those of our *screech*, signifies the loud sharp cry, which the mind cannot control, either in revelry or distress. Here it is probably, the drunken scream, or reckless cry of revelry, whose senseless shrillness is more piercing, in its way, than the scream of distress, of which Jeremiah[8] uses it. For it is the scream of the death of the soul. Amos seems to have purposely joined together similar harsh sibilants or guttural sounds, in order the more to express the harshness of that scream of luxurious self-indulgence. *Mirdsakh seruk-him, the screech of the outstretched.* Of this he says, *it shall depart*, and for ever. *In that very day all his thoughts perish*[9]. It shall *depart;* but by what should it be replaced to those to whom it was their god and their all? On earth, by siege, pestilence, death or captivity: after death, by hell to the unrepentant.

8. *The Lord God*, He Who alone IS and Who Alone hath power, *hath sworn by Himself*, lit. *by His soul;* as our *self* comes from the same root as *soul.* "[4] So God saith in Isaiah[10], *Your new moons and your appointed feasts My soul hateth;* not that God hath a soul, but that He speaks after the way of

[1] S. Matt. xxii. 2, 4. [2] S. Luke xv. 23, 4. [3] 1 Kgs iv. 23. [4] S. Jer. [5] ix. 6.

[6] Wisd. vi. 6. [7] S. Luke xii. 48. [8] xvi. 5. [9] Ps. cxlvi. 4. [10] i. 14.

9 And it shall come to pass, if there remain ten men in one house, t h a t they shall die.

10 And a man's uncle

shall take him up, and he that burneth him, to bring out the bones out of the house, and shall say unto him that is by the sides of

human feelings. Nor is it any marvel that He condescends to speak of Himself, as having a soul, seeing He speaks of Himself as having the other members, feet, hands, bowels, which are less precious than the soul. In God the Father, the head, hands, and the rest are not members, but by these words a diversity of powers is expressed. So also by the soul is intended not a substance, but the inward affections, and the seat of thought whereby God indicates His Will." In truth, it is one and the same condescension in Almighty God, to use of Himself any words taken from our nature, our thoughts, acts, feelings, as those taken from the members of the body. It is a yet greater condescension that God should confirm the truth of His word by an oath. For *we* call God to witness, lest, by reason of the vast reign of falsehood among men, we should be thought not to speak true. But for God to act as though He needed the assurance of an oath in order to be believed, is more condescending, than for Him to speak as though He had a soul or limbs, such as He gave to man. Yet God, [1] *willing more abundantly to shew unto the heirs of His promise the immutability of His counsel, confirmed it by an oath. He sware by Himself saying, surely blessing I will bless thee.* Now, when Israel had, by apostasy, forfeited that blessing, and a portion of it was to be withdrawn from him, God, affirms by an oath that rejection of Israel. If the words, *by His soul*, are emphatic, they relate to those attributes in God of which man's holy affections are an image. God's love, justice, righteousness, holiness, were concerned, to vindicate the oppressed and punish the oppressor. To these He appeals. Our oaths mean, " As God is true, and as He avenges untruth, this which I say is true." So God says, " As I am God, this is true." God then must cease to be God, if He did not hate oppression.

I abhor the excellency of Jacob. The word *excellency* is used of the Majesty of God Himself ; then, since man's relation to God is his only real greatness, God speaks of Himself as the *Excellency of Jacob* [2]; then of that *excellency* which God had given to *Jacob* [3]. That *excellency of their strength*, He had forwarded them in the law, that He would *break* [4].

Now that Israel took as his own what he held from God, his *excellency* became pride [5], and God says, *I abhor* it, as a thing loathsome and abominable, *and hate his palaces.* For they had been built, adorned, inhabited, filled with luxury, in the midst of, and out of, oppression and hard-hearted exaction. He calls them Jacob, perhaps as Hosea does [6], to remind them of the poverty and low estate of their forefather, out of which God had raised them, and the faithfulness of their forefather in it, in contrast with their luxury and unfaithfulness.

Therefore [And] I will deliver up ; originally, *shut up* [7], then, *shut up in the hands of* [8], so that he should have no escape. Here, where the enemy is not spoken of, it may mean, that God *shut up the city*, so that there should be no going out or coming in, in the straitness of the siege, whereupon follows the fearful description of the ravages of the pestilence. *The city* is, what was to them, above others, *the* city, the place of their luxury pride and boast, where lay their strength, Samaria.

9. *If there shall remain ten men.* He probably still denounces the punishment of the rich inhabitants of the palaces, since in these only, of old, would there be found *ten men*. They died, it seems, at once, and so probably through the plague, the common companion of the siege. The Prophet had before compared them to Sodom. It may be, that, in this mention of *ten men*, he tacitly refers to the history of that destruction. Then God promised, not to destroy the city, if there were ten righteous in it [9]. Here were *ten left*, not in one city, but in one house. Had God forgotten His loving-kindness? No! but, in Samaria, not even ten who *remained over*, and so had survived after the chastisement had begun, turned to God. All then were to be taken or destroyed. The miseries of its three years' siege by Shalmaneser may be filled up from those of its earlier siege by Benhadad [10], or from those of Jerusalem. The sufferings of a siege are in proportion to the obstinacy of the defence ; and Samaria resisted for twice the time in which Jerusalem was reduced by famine at its first captivity.

10. *And a man's uncle—and he that burneth him—*lit. *and there shall take him up his uncle*

---

[1] Heb. vi. 17, 13, 14. [2] Am. viii. 7. [3] Ps. xlvii. 4.
[4] Lev. xxvi. 19.
[5] Hence נָאוֹן is used of pride, Pr. xvi. 8. &c.

[6] xii. 12. [7] Lev. xiv. 23, xiii. 4, 5, &c.
[8] with בְיַד or (Am. i. 6, 9) לְ. [9] Gen. xviii. 32.
[10] 2 Kgs vi. 24–29.

Before
CHRIST
cir. 787.

ʳ ch. 5. 13.

the house, *Is there* yet *any* with thee? and he shall say, No. Then shall he say, ʳ Hold

thy tongue : ˢ for ‖ we may not make mention of the name of the LORD.

Before
CHRIST
cir. 787.

ˢ ch. 8. 3.
‖ Or, *they will not,or,have not.*

---

and his burner, i. e. his uncle who, as his next of kin, had the care of his interment, was himself the burner. Burial is the natural following out of the words, *dust thou art and unto dust thou shalt return.* The common burying-places (such as we find in the history of the Patriarchs) were the natural expression of the belief in the Resurrection. The bodies rested together, to be raised together. The heathen burned the bodies of Christian martyrs, and scattered their ashes in mockery of the Resurrection[1]. The heathen noticed that it was matter of piety with the Jews "[2] to bury rather than to burn bodies." The only exceptions are the history of Saul, and this place. Both were cases of emergency. The men of Jabesh-Gilead doubtless burnt the bodies of Saul and his sons[3], for fear the Philistines might disinter them, if buried, and renew their insults upon them. The Israelites still buried what would not be disturbed or could be concealed—the bones. David solemnly buried their remains in the sepulchre of Kish, Saul's father[4]. So probably here also, it is mentioned as an aggravation, that one who loved[5] them, had to burn their bodies. He does not say, why: but mentions it, as one feature of the common-suffering. Parents, brothers, all, gone, a man's uncle was his "burner." There was no other interment than this, the most alien from their affections and religion. It may have been on account of the extreme infection (the opening of a forgotten burying-place of those who died of the plague of London produced a virulent disease, though 1½ century had elapsed), or from the delay of burial, when, death reigning all round, there had been none to bury the dead.

He who is *by the sides,* i. e. the furthest part *of the house.* He was the one survivor of the ten, and he too, sick. The question, Is there *yet* any *with thee?* enquires whether there was any one, alive, to succor, or dead, to burn? There was none. All, even the bodies, had now been removed; one only remained, of all the hum, din, and throng, in that abode of luxury, one only *in the extremity* of its untenanted chambers. Probably the sick man was going to speak of God. The uncle breaks in upon his *No!* with *Hush! for we may not make mention of the*

Name of the Lord. Times of plague are, with the most, times of religious despair. They who had not feared God in their prosperity, do nothing but fear Him then. Fear, without love, turns man more away from God. He feels *then* the presence and power of God Whom he had forgotten. He owns Him as the Author of his miseries; but, not having known Him before, he knows Him now in no other relation. The words then, *for not to be mentioned is the Name of the Lord,* are very probably the voice of despair. "It is useless to name Him now. We did not name His Name in life. It is not for *us* to name it now, in death." It might be the voice of impatient aversion, which would not bear to hear of God, the Author of its woe ; or it might be the voice of superstition, which would not name God's Name, for fear of bringing fresh evil upon itself. All these grounds for not naming the Name of God and others yet worse, recur, again and again, under the pressure of a general sudden destruction. Such times bring out the soul to light, as it is. Souls, which have sinned away the grace of God and are beyond its reach, pass unobserved amid the thronging activity of ordinary life. They are arrested then. They must choose then or never. Their unchanged aversion from God, *then,* unveils what they had been before. They choose once more, deliberately, in the face of God's judgments, what they had habitually chosen before, and, by the dreadful nakedness of their choice of evil, become now unmitigatedly evil. The Prophet gives one instance of this utter misery of body and soul, because detail of misery sets the whole calamity more before men's eyes. In one picture, they see all. The words, or what the words imply, that, in extreme calamity, men mention not the Name of God, come true in different minds out of different characters of irreligion.

It has also been thought, that the brief answer, *hush!* closes the dialogue. The uncle asks, *is there yet with thee?* He answers, *None.* The other rejoins *Hush!* and the Prophet assigns the ground ; *for the Name of the Lord is not to be named.* If men have not sought God earlier, they have, when his hand is heavy upon them, no heart, nor time, nor thought, nor faith to seek Him.

---

[1] See e. g. Ep. Eccl. Vienn. et Lugd. fin. Eus. H. E. v. 1.
[2] Tac. Hist. v. 5.　　　[3] 1 Sam. end.
[4] 2 Sam. xxi. 12–14.
[5] The name of the uncle is from "love" (דוד) ;

probably, the one most loved out of the immediate household, "as חביבה, θεῖος from ἠθεῖος, amita from amata." Ges. It is not used of relationship or friendship generally, but only of the highest object of the soul's love, God. Cant. and Is. v. 1.

Before CHRIST cir. 787.	11 For, behold, ᵗthe LORD commandeth, ᵘand he will smite t h e great house with ‖ breaches, and the little house with clefts. 12 ¶ Shall horses run upon the rock? will one	plow *there* with oxen ? for ˣ ye have turned judgment into gall, and the fruit of righteousness into hemlock : 13 Ye which rejoice in a thing of nought, which say, Have we not taken	Before CHRIST cir. 787.
ᵗ Is. 55. 11. ᵘ ch. 3. 15. ‖ Or, *droppings.*			ˣ Hos. 10. 4 ch. 5. 7.

11. *The Lord commandeth and He will smite.* "¹ If He commandeth, how doth He smite? If He smiteth, how doth He command ? In that thing which He *commands* and enjoins His ministers, He Himself is seen to *smite.*— In Egypt the Lord declares that He slew the first-born, who, we read, were slain by *the destroyer*²." The *breaches* denote probably the larger, *the cleft* the smaller ruin. The greater pile was the more greatly destroyed.

12. The two images both represent a toil, which men would condemn as absurd, destructive, as well as fruitless. The horse's hoofs or his limbs would be broken; the plowing-gear would be destroyed. The Prophet gains the attention by the question. What then? they ask. The answer is implied by the *for*, which follows. Ye are they, who are so doing. As absurd is it to seek gain from injustice and oppression, to which God had annexed loss and woe, temporal and eternal. More easy to change the course of nature or the use of things of nature, than the course of God's Providence or the laws of His just retribution. They had changed the sweet laws of *justice* and equity *into the* gall of oppression, and the healthful *fruit of righteousness,* whereof they had received the seed from God, into the life-destroying poison of sin. Better to have *ploughed* the rock *with oxen* for food! For now, where they looked for prosperity, they found not barrenness, but death.

Others ³ understand the question as the taunt of unbelievers, trusting in the strength of Samaria, that when horses should run on their rocky eminence, or the oxen plough there, then might an enemy look for gain from investing the hill of Samaria. "Shall things which are against nature be done ? " "Yes," the Prophet then would answer, "for ye have done against nature yourselves. Ye have *changed justice,* the solace of the oppressed, *into wormwood,* the bitterness of oppression. Well may what ye think above the laws of physical nature be done, when ye have violated the laws of moral nature. Well may the less thing be done, your destruction, secure as by nature ye seem, when ye have done the greater, vio-

lating the laws of the God of nature." Amos, however, when he refers to the sayings of the unbelievers, distinguishes them from his own.

13. *Who rejoice* (lit. *the rejoicers !* Amos, as is his wont, speaks of them with contempt and wonder at their folly, *the rejoicers!* much as we say, the cowards! the renegades!) *in a thing of nought,* lit. *a non-thing,* (*no-whit, nought*) not merely in a thing valueless, but in a *non-thing,* that has no existence at all, as nothing has any substantial existence out of God. This *non-thing* was their power, strength, empire, which they thought they had, but which was soon to shrivel away as a scroll.

Which say, (as before, *the sayers!* they who have this saying habitually in their mouth ;) *have we not taken to ourselves horns ?* The horn is the well-known symbol of strength which repels and tosses away what opposes it, as the bull doth its assailant. Moses, in his blessing, had used this symbol, of the strength of the tribe of Joseph, and as being a blessing, he spoke of it, as the gift of God ⁴. *His glory is like the firstling of his bullock, and his horns are like the horns of buffalos ; with them he shall push the people together to the ends of the earth ; and they are the ten thousands of Ephraim, and they are the thousands of Manasseh.* To this blessing, doubtless, Zedekiah the false prophet referred ⁵, when he *made him horns of iron, and said* to Ahab, *Thus saith the Lord, with these shalt thou push the Syrians, until thou hast consumed them.* The Psalmist said, *through Thee will we push down our enemies,* as with a horn ⁶; and adds, *For I will not trust in my bow, neither shall my sword save me. For Thou hast saved us from our enemies.* Israel ascribed God's gift to himself. He had been repeatedly and greatly victorious; he had conquered every enemy, with whom he had of old been at strife ; he ascribed it to himself, and forfeited it. *By our own strength,* he said, instead of, *by the help of God ;* as if we were to ascribe our Indian victories to our generals or our armies, and to substitute self-praise for Te Deums on days of thanksgiving.

"⁷ The *sinner rejoiceth in a non-thing.* Sin is a *non-thing* 1) as being a thing of nought,

¹ S. Jer.   ² Ex. xii. 23.
³ Sanct.   ⁴ Deut. xxxiii. 17.

⁵ 1 Kgs xxii. 11. Hengst. Auth. d. Pent. i. 101. 131,
⁶ נֶגַּח Ps. xliv. 5-7.   ⁷ from Lap.

Before CHRIST cir. 787. to us horns by our own strength?

7 Jer. 5. 15. 14 But, behold, 7 I will

raise up against you a na- Before CHRIST cir. 787. tion, O house of Israel, saith the LORD the God

---

i. e. vain and valueless. 2) Its pleasure is fleeting; whence the Psalmist says [1], *all the men, whose hands are mighty, have found nothing.* 3) Sin brings the sinner to nothing, i. e. destruction and death, temporal and eternal. 4) Sin is the privation of good; but privation is a mere negative; i. e. nothing. 5) Sin deprives of God Who is All and the Creator of all. 6) Sin is nothing, because it cleaves to and joys in creatures and opposes them and prefers them to the Creator. For creatures, compared to the Creator, are shadows of things, not the very things, and so are nothing. For the Being and Name of God is, I AM that I AM [2], i. e. I Am He Who Alone have true, full, solid, eternal, infinite, Being; but creatures participate from Me a shadow of their true being; for their being is so poor, brief, fleeting, unstable, perishing, that, compared to Mine, they may rather be said, not to be, than to be. So then as creatures have no true being, so neither have they true good, but only a shadow of good.—So also as to truth, wisdom, power, justice, holiness and other attributes. These have in God their real being; in creatures a shadow of being only. Whence God is called in Scripture Alone Wise [3], Alone Mighty [4], Alone Immortal [5], Alone Lord [6], Alone Holy [7], Alone Good [8]; because He Alone has true, full, uncreated and infinite Wisdom, Power, Goodness, &c. But the sinner, in that he delights in creatures not in the Creator, delights in a shadow, a nothing, not in the true Being. But, because these shadows of creatures amid the dimness of this life appear great to man in his blindness, (as the mountains, at sunset, cast broad and deep shadows,) he admires and pursues these shadows, like the dog in the fable, who, seeing the shadow of the meat in the water, magnified in the water, snatched at it, and so lost the meat and did not attain the shadow. O Lord, dispel our darkness, lighten our eyes, that we may love and seek, not the shadows of honors, riches, and pleasures, which, like meteors, dazzle here on earth our mind's eye, but may, with fixed gaze, behold, love, and compass the real honors, riches, pleasures themselves, which Thou hast from eternity laid up and prepared in heaven for those who love Thee."

14. *But* [*For,*]—it *was* a non-thing, a non-existent thing, a phantom, whereat they rejoiced;—*for behold I raise up a nation.* God is said to *raise up,* when, by His Providence or His grace, He calls forth those who had not been called before, for the office for which He designs them. Thus, He raised up judges [9], deliverers [10], prophets [11], Nazarites [12], priests [13], kings [14], calling each separately to perform what He gave them in charge. So He is said to *raise up* even the evil ministers of His good Will, whom, in the course of His Providence, He allows to raise themselves up aloft to that eminence, so often as, in fulfilling their own bad will, they bring about, or are examples of, His righteous judgment. Thus God *raised up Hadad* as *an adversary* [15] to Solomon, and again Rezon [16]; and the Chaldees [17]. So again God says to Pharaoh, *For this have I raised thee up* [18], *to shew in thee My power.* So here He says, *I will raise up against you a nation, and they shall afflict you from the entering in of Hamath.* Israel, under Jeroboam II., had recovered a wider extent of territory, than had, in her Northern portion, belonged to her since the better days of Solomon. Jeroboam [19] *recovered Damascus and Hamath,* which belonged to *Judah, unto Israel.* He *restored,* as God promised him by Jonah, *the coast of Israel from the entering of Hamath unto the sea of the plain. The entering of Hamath* expresses the utmost Northern boundary promised to Israel [20]. But this does not in itself express whether Hamath itself was included. Hamath however, and even Damascus itself, were incorporated in the bounds of Israel. The then great scourge of Israel had become part of its strength. Southward, Ammon and even Moab, had been taken into its borders. All the country on the other side of Jordan was theirs from Hamath and Damascus to the South of the Dead Sea, a space including four degrees of Latitude, as much as from Portsmouth to Durham. Amos describes the extension of the kingdom of Israel in the self-same terms as the Book of Kings; only he names as the southern extremity, *the river of the wilderness,* instead of *the sea of the wilderness* [21]. *The sea of the wilderness,* i. e. the Dead Sea, might in itself be either its Northern or its Southern extremity. The word used by Amos, defines

1 Ps. lxxvi. 5. 2 See ab. p. 119. 3 Rom. xvi. 27.
4 1 Tim. vi. 15. 5 Ib. 16. 6 Is. xxxvii. 20.
7 Rev. xv. 4. 8 S. Luke xviii. 19.
9 Jud. ii. 16–18. 10 Ib. iii. 9–15.
11 Am. ii. 11, Jer. xxix. 15, and of the Prophet like Moses, Deut. xviii. 15.
12 Am. Ib. 13 1 Sam. ii. 35. 14 2 Sam. vii. 8.

15 1 Kgs xi. 14. 16 Ib. 23.
17 Hab. i. 6. 18 העמדתיך Ex. ix. 16.
19 2 Kgs xiv. 28, 25. 20 Num. xxxiv. 8.
21 2 Kgs מלבוא חמת עד ים הערבה
Am. מלבוא חמת עד נחל הערבה

of hosts ; and they shall afflict you from the *enter-

ing in of Hemath unto the || river of the wilderness.

---

it to be the Southern. For his use of the name, *river of the wilderness*, implies 1) that it was a well-known boundary, a boundary as well-known to Israel on the South[1], as *the entering in of Hamath* was on the North. 2) As a boundary-river, it must have been a river on the East of the Jordan, since Benjamin formed their boundary on the West of Jordan, and mountain passes, not rivers, separated them from it. 3) From its name, *river of the wilderness*, or *the Arabah*, it must, in some important part of its course, have flowed in the 'Arabah. The 'Arabah, (it is now well known,) is no other than that deep and remarkable depression, now called the Ghor, which extends from the lake of Gennesareth to the Red Sea[2]. The Dead Sea itself is called by Moses too *the sea of the Arabah*[3], lying, as it does, in the middle of that depression, and dividing it into two, the valley of the Jordan above the Dead Sea, and the Southern portion which extends uninterrupted from the Dead to the Red Sea ; and which also (although Scripture has less occasion to speak of it) Moses calls the 'Arabah[4]. A river, which fell from Moab into the Dead Sea without passing through the Arabah, would not be called "a river of the Arabah," but, at the most "a river of the sea of the Arabah." Now, besides the improbability that the name, *the river of the Arabah*, should have been substituted for the familiar names, the Arnon or the Jabbok, the Arnon does not flow into the Arabah at all, the Jabbok is no way connected with the Dead Sea, the corresponding boundary in the Book of Kings. These were both boundary-rivers, the Jabbok having been the Northern limit of what Moab and Ammon lost to the Amorite ; the Arnon being the Northern border of Moab. But there is a third boundary-river which answers all the conditions. Moab was bounded on the South by a river, which Isaiah calls *the brook of the willows*, Nahal Ha'arabim[5], across which he foretells that they should transport for safety all which they had of value. A river, now called in its upper part the Wadi-el-Ahsa, and then the Wadi-es-Safieh, which now too "[6]has more water than any South of the Yerka" [Jabbok], "divides the district of Kerek from that of Jebâl, the ancient Gebalene" (i.e. Moab from Idumæa). This river, after flow-

ing from East to West and so forming a Southern boundary to Moab, turns to the North in the Ghor or Arabah, and flows into the S. extremity of the Dead Sea[7]. This river then, answering to all the conditions, is doubtless that of which Amos spoke, and the boundary, which Jeroboam restored, included Moab also, (as in the most prosperous times of Israel,) since Moab's Southern border was now his border.

Israel, then, had no enemy, West of the Euphrates. Their strength had also, of late, been increasing steadily. Jehoash had, at the promise of Elisha, thrice defeated the Syrians, and recovered cities which had been lost, probably on the West also of Jordan, in the heart of the kingdom of Israel. What Jehoash had begun, Jeroboam II., during a reign of forty-one years, continued. Prophets had foretold and defined the successes of both kings, and so had marked them out the more to be the gift of God. Israel ascribed it to himself ; and now that the enemies, whom Israel had feared, were subdued, God says, *I will raise up an enemy, and they shall afflict thee from the entering in of Hamath unto the river of the wilderness*. The whole scene of their triumphs should be one scene of affliction and woe. This was fulfilled after some forty-five years, at the invasion of Tiglath-pileser.

VII. The visions of this chapter continue the direct prophecy of the last. That closed in the prophecy of the affliction of Israel through the Assyrian : this foretells three gradations, in which it took place. *That* spoke of a recovery of Israel after its extreme depression under Hazael ; the first of these visions exhibit it as a field shorn to the ground, shooting out anew, but threatened with a fresh destruction. The chastisements are three-fold. Two, at the intercession of Amos, stop short of utter destruction ; the 3d was final. Each also increased in severity. Such were the three invasions of the Assyrians. Pul, invited by Menahem, amid civil war, to establish him on his throne, exacted only a heavy fine. Tiglath-pileser, called in by Ahaz against Pekah, carried off the inhabitants of the East and North of Israel ; the invasion of Shalmaneser ended the empire and its idolatry.

---

[1] This altogether excludes the Kidron (which Gesenius would make it). Indeed the Kidron is 1) no border-river at all, flowing *within* Judah. 2) It does not belong to the Arabah at all, flowing from Jerusalem, mostly through deep perpendicular defiles, to the Dead Sea (see ab. p. 141). 3) It falls into the W. side of the Dead Sea, not into its Northern extremity.

[2] Burckh. Syr. 441, 2. Rob. ii. 186, 7.
[3] Deut. iii. 17, iv. 49.
[4] Ib. ii. 8, 9 (translated *plain*). See more fully Stanley, Pal. 487.
[5] Is. xv. 7.
[6] Burckh. Ib. 401.
[7] See Van de Velde's map or Kiepert's in Porter's Hdbook, or Robinson's map.

Before
CHRIST
cir. 787.

CHAPTER VII.

1 *The judgments of the grasshoppers, 4 and of the fire, are diverted by the prayer of Amos. 7 By the wall of a plumbline is signified the rejection of Israel. 10 Amaziah complaineth of Amos. 14 Amos sheweth his calling, 16 and Amaziah's judgment.*

THUS hath the Lord God shewed unto me; and, behold, he f o r m e d ‖ grasshoppers in the beginning of the shooting up

| Or, *green worms.*

of the latter growth ; and, lo, *it was* the latter growth after the king's mowings.

2 And it came to pass, *that* when they had made an end of eating the grass of the land, then I said, O Lord GOD, forgive, I beseech thee: ᵃ ‖ by whom shall Jacob arise? for he *is* small.

3 ᵇ The LORD repented for this : It shall not be, saith the LORD.

Before
CHRIST
cir. 787.

ᵃ Is. 51. 19. ver. 6.
‖ Or, *who* of (or, for,)*Jacob shall stand?*
ᵇ Deut. 32. 36.
ver. 56.
Jonah 3. 10.
James 5. 16.

---

1. *And behold He formed* (i. e. *He was forming*). The very least things then are as much in His infinite Mind, as what we count the greatest. He has not simply made "laws of nature," as men speak, to do His work, and continue the generations of the world. He Himself was still framing them, giving them being, as our Lord saith, *My Father worketh hitherto, and I work*[1]. The same power of God is seen in creating the locust, as the Universe. The creature could as little do the one as the other. But further. God was *framing* them for a special end, not of nature, but of His moral government, in the correction of man. He was *framing the locust*, that it might, at His appointed time, lay waste just those tracts which He had appointed to them. God, in this vision, opens our eyes, and lets us see Himself, framing the punishment for the deserts of the sinners, that so when hail, mildew, blight, caterpillars, or some other hitherto unknown disease, (which, because we know it not, we call by the name of the crop which it annihilates), waste our crops, we may think, not of secondary causes, but of our Judge. "[2] *Fire and hail, snow and vapors, stormy wind, fulfill His word*[3], in striking sinners as He wills. To be indignant with these, were like a dog who bit the stone wherewith it was hit, instead of the man who threw it." "[4] He who denies that he was stricken for his own fault, what does he but accuse the. justice of Him Who smiteth ?"

Grasshoppers, i. e. locusts. The name may very possibly be derived from their *creeping*[5] simultaneously, in vast multitudes, from the ground, which is the more observable in these creatures, which, when the warmth of spring hatches the eggs, creep forth at once in myriads. This first meaning of their

name must, however, have been obliterated by use (as mostly happens), since the word is also used by Nahum of a flying locust[6].

The king's mowings must have been some regalia, to meet the state-expenses. The like custom still lingers on, here and there, among us, the "first mowth" or "first vesture," that with which the fields are first clad, belonging to one person; the pasturage afterward, or "after-grass," to others. The hay-harvest probably took place some time before the corn-harvest, and the *latter grass*, "after-grass,"(lekesh) probably began to spring up at the time of the *latter rain* (malkosh). Had the grass been mown after this rain, it would not, under the burning sun of their rainless summer, have sprung up at all. At this time, then, upon which the hope of the year depended, *in the beginning of the shooting up of the latter grass*, Amos saw, in vision, God form the locust, and *the green herb of the land* (the word includes all, that which is *for the service of man* as well as for beasts,) destroyed. Striking emblem of a state, recovering after it had been mown down, and anew overrun by a numerous enemy! Yet this need but be a passing desolation. Would they abide, or would they carry their ravages elsewhere? Amos intercedes with God, in words of that first intercession of Moses, *forgive now*[7]. *By whom*, he adds, *shall Jacob arise?* lit. *Who shall Jacob arise?* i. e. who is he that he should arise, so weakened, so half-destroyed? Plainly, the destruction is more than one invasion of locusts in one year. The locusts are a symbol, (as in Joel,) in like way as the following visions are symbols.

3. *The Lord repented for this.* God is said to *repent, to have strong compassion upon* or

---

[1] S. John v. 17.   [2] Lap.   [3] Ps. cxlviii. 8.
[4] S. Greg. on Job L. xxxii. c. 4. L.

[5] from the Arab. jabaa.
[6] See Pref. to Joel, p. 150.   [7] Num. xiv. 19.

Before
CHRIST
cir. 787.

4 ¶ Thus hath the Lord God shewed unto me: and, behold, the Lord God called to contend by fire, and it devoured the great deep, and did eat up a part.

5 Then said I, O Lord God, cease I beseech thee: [c] by whom shall Jacob arise? for he *is* small.

6 The LORD repented for this: This also shall not be, saith the Lord God.

Before
CHRIST
cir. 787.

[c] ver. 2, 3.

---

over[1] evil, which He has either inflicted[2], or has said that He would inflict[3], and which, upon repentance or prayer, He suspends or checks. Here, Amos does not intercede until after the judgment had been, in part, inflicted. He prayed, when in vision the locust *had made an end of eating the grass of the land,* and when *the fire had eaten up a part.* Nor, until Israel had suffered what these visions foretold, was he *small,* either in his own or in human sight, or in relation to his general condition. The *this* then, *of which God repented* and said, *it shall not be,* is that further undefined evil, which His first infliction threatened. Evil and decay do not die out, but destroy. Oppression does not weary itself out, but increases. Visitations of God are tokens of His displeasure, and, in the order of His Justice, rest on the sinner. Pul and Tiglath-pileser, when they came with their armies on Israel, were instruments of God's chastening. According to the ways of God's Justice, or of man's ambition, the evil now begun, would have continued, but that God, at the prayer of the Prophet, said[4], *Hitherto shalt thou come, and no further.*

4. *God called to contend by fire;* i. e. He *called* His people to maintain their cause with Him *by fire,* as He says[5], *I will plead* in judgment *with him* [Gog] *with* [i. e. *by*] *pestilence and blood;* and, [6] *by fire and by His sword will the Lord plead with all flesh;* and, [7] *The Lord standeth up to plead and standeth to judge the people.* Man, by rebellion, challenges God's Omnipotence. He will have none of Him; he will find his own happiness for himself, apart from God and in defiance of Him and His laws; he plumes himself on his success, and accounts his strength or wealth or prosperity the test of the wisdom of his policy. God, sooner or later, accepts the challenge. He brings things to the issue, which man had chosen. He *enters into judgment*[8] with him. If man escapes with impunity, then he had chosen well, in rejecting God and choosing his own ways. If not, what folly and misery was his short-sighted choice; short-lived in its gain; its loss, eternal! *Fire*

stands as the symbol and summary of God's most terrible judgments. It spares nothing, leaves nothing, not even the outward form of what it destroys. Here it is plainly a symbol, since it destroys *the sea* also, which shall be destroyed only by the fire of the Day of Judgment, when [9] *the elements shall melt with fervent heat, the earth also and the works that are therein shall be burned up.* The sea is called the *great deep,* only in the most solemn language, as the history of the creation or the flood, the Psalms and poetical books. Here it is used, in order to mark the extent of the desolation represented in the vision.

And did eat up a part, rather lit. *the portion*[10], i. e. probably, *the* definite *portion* foreappointed by God to captivity and desolation. This probably our Version meant by *a part.* For although God calls Himself *the Portion* of Israel[11], and of those who are His[12], and reciprocally He calls the people *the Lord's portion*[13], and the land, *the portion*[14] of God's people; yet the land is nowhere called absolutely *the portion,* nor was the country of the ten tribes specially *the portion,* given by God. Rather God exhibits in vision to the Prophet, the ocean burned up, and *the portion* of Israel, upon which His judgments were first to fall. To this Amos points, as *the portion.* God knew *the portion,* which Tiglath-Pileser would destroy, and when he came and had carried captive the East and North of Israel, the pious in Israel would recognize the second, more desolating scourge, foretold by Amos; they would own that it was at the prayer of the Prophet that it was stayed and went no further, and would await what remained.

5. 6. As our Lord repeated the same words in the Garden, so Amos interceded with God with words, all but one[15], the same, and with the same plea, that, if God did not help, Israel was indeed helpless. Yet a second time God spared Israel. To human sight, what so strange and unexpected, as that the Assyrian and his army, having utterly destroyed the kingdom of Damascus, and carried away its people, and having devoured, like fire,

---

[1] נחם על.   [2] Deut. xxxii. 36, 1 Chr. xxi. 15.
[3] Ex. xxxii. 12, Joel ii. 13, Jon. iii. 10, Jer. xviii. 8.   [4] Job xxxviii. 11.   [5] Ezek. xxxviii. 22.
[6] Is. lxvi. 16.   [7] Ib. iii. 13.   [8] Ib. 14, &c.

[9] 2 S. Pet. iii. 10.   [10] את החלק.
[11] Deut. xxxii. 9, Jer. x. 16, Zech. ii. 12.   [12] Ps. xvi. 5, lxxiii. 26, &c. Jer. x. 16.   [13] Jer. xii. 10.
[14] Mic. ii. 4.   [15] חרל, *cease,* for סלח *forgive.*

Before
C H R I S T
cir. 787.

7 ¶ Thus he shewed me: and, behold, the Lord stood upon a wall *made* by a plumbline, with a plumbline in his hand.

8 And the LORD said unto me, Amos, what seest thou? And I said, A plumbline. Then said the Lord, Behold, ^d I will set a plumbline in the midst of my people Israel; ^e I will not again pass by them any more:

Before
C H R I S T
cir. 787.

d See 2 Kings
21. 13.
Is. 28. 17.
& 34. 11.
Lam. 2. 8.
e ch. 8. 2.
Mic. 7. 18.

more than half of Israel, rolled back like an ebb-tide, swept away to ravage other countries, and spared the capital? And who, looking at the mere outside of things, would have thought that that tide of fire was rolled back, not by anything in that day, but by the Prophet's prayer some 47 years before? Man would look doubtless for motives of human policy, which led Tiglath-pileser to accept tribute from Pekah, while he killed Rezin; and while he carried off all the Syrians of Damascus, to leave half of Israel to be removed by his successor. Humanly speaking, it was a mistake. He "scotched" his enemy only, and left him to make alliance with Egypt, his rival, who disputed with him the possession of the countries which lay between them. If we knew the details of Assyrian policy, we might know what induced him to turn aside in his conquest. There were, and always are, human motives. They do not interfere with the ground in the mind of God, Who directs and controls them. Even in human contrivances, the wheels, interlacing one another, and acting one on the other, do but transmit, the one to the other, the motion and impulse which they have received from the central force. The revolution of the earth around its own centre does not interfere with, rather it is a condition of its revolving round the centre of our system, and, amidst the alternations of night and day, brings each several portion within the influence of the sun around which it revolves. The affairs of human kingdoms have their own subordinate centres of human policy, yet even thereby they the more revolve in the circuit of God's appointment. In the history of His former people God gives us a glimpse into a hidden order of things, the secret spring and power of His wisdom, which sets in motion that intricate and complex machinery which alone we see, and in the sight of which men lose the consciousness of the unseen agency. While man strives with man, prayer, suggested by God, moves God, the Ruler of all.

7. *Stood upon* [rather *over* ¹] *a wall* made by *a plumbline*; lit. *a wall of a plumbline,* i. e. (as our's has it) *made* straight, perpendicular, by

it. The wall had been *made by a lead* or *plumbline;* by it, i. e. according to it, it should be destroyed. God had made it upright, He had given to it an undeviating rule of right, He had watched over it, to keep it, as He made it. Now *He stood over it,* fixed in His purpose, to destroy it. He marked its inequalities. Yet this too in judgment. He destroys it by that same rule of right wherewith He had built it. By that law, that right, those Providential leadings, that grace, which we have received, by the same we are judged.

8. *Amos?* "² He calls the Prophet by name, as a familiar friend, known and approved by Him, as He said to Moses³, *I know thee by name.* For ⁴ *the Lord knoweth them that are His. What seest thou?* God had twice heard the Prophet. Two judgments upon His people He had mitigated, not upon *their* repentance, but on the single intercession of the Prophet. After that, He willed to be no more entreated. And so He exhibits to Amos a symbol, whose meaning He does not explain until He had pronounced their doom. *The plumbline* was used in pulling down, as well as in building up. Whence Jeremiah says ⁵, *The Lord hath purposed to destroy the wall of the daughter of Zion; He hath stretched out a line; He hath not withdrawn His hand from destroying; therefore He made the rampart and wall to lament :* and Isaiah ⁶; *He shall stretch out upon it the line of wasteness⁷ and the stone of emptiness⁷ :* and God said of Judah⁸, *I will stretch over Jerusalem the line of Samaria and the plummet of the house of Ahab.* Accordingly God explains the vision, *Behold I will set,* i. e. shortly, [lit. *am setting*] *a plumbline in the midst of My people Israel.* The wall, then, is not the emblem of Samaria or of any one city. It is the strength and defence of the whole people, whatever held it together, and held out the enemy. As in the vision to Belshazzar, the word *Tekel, He weighed,* was explained ⁹, *Thou art weighed in the balances and art found wanting,* so God here applies the plumbline, at once to convict and to destroy upon conviction. In this Judgment, as at the Last Day, God would not condemn, without having first made clear the

1 This lies in the words נצב על.   2 Dion.
3 Ex. xxxiii. 12, 17.   4 2 Tim. ii. 19.   5 Lam. ii. 8.

6 Is. xxxiv. 11.   7 תהו בהו as in Gen. i. 2.
8 2 Kgs xxi. 13.   9 Dan. v. 27.

Before CHRIST cir. 787.

f Beer-sheba. Gen. 26. 23. & 46. 1. ch. 5. 5. & 8. 14.
g Fulfilled, 2 Kings 15. 10.

9 f And the high places of Isaac shall be desolate, and the sanctuaries of Israel shall be laid waste; and g I will rise against

the house of Jeroboam with the sword.

10 ¶ Then Amaziah h the priest of Bethel sent to i Jeroboam king of

Before CHRIST cir. 787.

h 1 Kings 12. 32.
i 2 Kings 14. 23.

---

justice of His condemnation. He sets it *in the midst of His people*, shewing that He would make trial of all, one by one, and condemn in proportion to the guilt of each. But the day of grace being past, the sentence was to be final. *I will not pass by them*, lit. *I will not pass over* [i. e. their transgressions] *to them* [1] *any more*, i. e. I will no more forgive them.

9. *The high places of Isaac.* He probably calls the ten tribes by the name of Isaac, as well as of Israel, in order to contrast their deeds with the blameless, gentle piety of Isaac, as well as the much-tried faithfulness of Israel. It has been thought too that he alludes to the first meaning of the name of Isaac. His name was given from the joyous laughter at the unheard-of promise of God, to give children to those past age; their high-places should be a laughter, but the laughter of mockery [2]. The *sanctuaries* were perhaps the two great idol-temples at Bethel and Dan, over against the one *sanctuary* of God at Jerusalem; the *high places* were the shrines of idolatry, especially where God had shewn mercy to the Patriarchs and Israel, but also all over the land. All were to be wasted, because all were idolatrous.

I will rise against the house of Jeroboam with the sword. God speaks after the manner of men, who, having been still, arise against the object of their enmity. He makes Himself so far one with the instruments of His sentence, that, what they do, He ascribes to Himself. Jeroboam II. must, from his military success, have been popular among his people. Successful valor is doubly prized, and he had both valor [3] and success. God had *saved Israel by His hand* [4]. A weak successor is often borne with for the merits of his father. There were no wars from without, which called for strong military energy or talent, and which might furnish an excuse for superseding a faineant king. Ephraim had no ambition of foreign glory, to gratify. Zechariah, Jeroboam's son, was a sensualist [5]; but many sensualists have, at all times, reigned undisturbed. Shallum who murdered Zechariah was simply a *conspirator* [6]; he represented no popular impulse, and was slain

himself a month [7] after. Yet Amos foretells absolutely that the house of Jeroboam should perish by the sword, and in the next generation his name was clean put out.

10. *Amaziah, the priest of Bethel*, was probably the high-priest, in imitation of the High Priest of the order of Aaron and of God's appointment. For the many high places around Bethel required many idol-priests; and a splendid counterfeit of the ritual at Jerusalem, which should rival it in the eyes of Israel, was part of the policy of the first Jeroboam. Amaziah was at the head of this imposture, in a position probably of wealth and dignity among his people. Like *Demetrius the silversmith* [8], he thought that the craft whereby he had his wealth was endangered. To Jeroboam, however, he says nothing of these fears. To the king he makes it an affair of state. He takes the king by what he expected to be his weak side, fear for his own power or life. *Amos hath conspired against thee.* So to Jeremiah [9] *the captain of the ward* said, *Thou fallest away to the Chaldæans.* And the princes [10]; *Let this man be put to death, for thus he weakeneth the hands of the men of war that remain in this city, and the hands of all the people, in speaking such words unto them: for this man seeketh not the welfare of this people, but the hurt.* And of our Lord they said to Pilate, [11] *If thou let this Man go, thou art not Cæsar's friend. Whosoever maketh himself a king, is an enemy to Cæsar.* And of the Apostles [12]; *these men, being Jews, do exceedingly trouble our city, and teach customs which are not lawful for us to receive, neither to observe, being Romans;* and, [13] *these that have turned the world upside down are come hither also —and these all do contrary to the decrees of Cæsar, saying that there is another king, Jesus.* And so the heathen, who were ever conspiring against the Roman Emperors, went on accusing the early Christians as disloyal to the Emperors, factious, impious, because they did not offer sacrifices for them to false gods, but prayed for them to the True God [14]. Some doubtless, moved by the words of Amos, had forsaken the state-idolatry, reformed their lives, worshiped God with the Prophet; perhaps they were called in con-

---

[1] as in viii. 2.
[2] So the LXX, and, from them, S. Cyril and Theodoret.
[3] 2 Kgs xiv. 28. נבורתו personal bravery.
[4] Ib. 27.
[5] See on Hos. vii. 7. p. 45, and Introd. p. 5.

[6] 2 Kgs xv. 10. [7] Ib. 13, 14. [8] Acts xix.
[9] Jer. xxxvii. 13. [10] Ib. xxxviii. 4.
[11] S. John xix. 12. [12] Acts xvi. 20, 1.
[13] Ib. xvii. 6, 7.
[14] Tertul. Apol. § 28–38. pp. 68–80. Oxf. Tr. ad Scap. § 2. pp. 143, 4. Ib.

Before
CHRIST
cir. 787.

Israel, saying, Amos hath conspired against thee in the midst of the house of Israel: the land is not able to bear all his words.

11 For thus Amos saith, Jeroboam shall die by the sword, and Israel shall surely be led away captive out of their own land.

12 Also Amaziah said unto Amos, O thou seer, go, flee thee away into the land of Judah, and there eat bread, and prophesy there:

Before
CHRIST
cir. 787.

---

tempt by his name, "Amosites" or "Judaizers," and were counted as *his* adherents, not as the worshipers of the one true God, *the God of their fathers*. Whence Amaziah gained the plea of a *conspiracy*, of which Amos was the head. For a *conspiracy* cannot be of one man. The word, by its force, signifies "banded [1];" the idiom, that he "banded" others "together against [2]" the king. To us Amaziah attests the power of God's word by His Prophet; *the land*, i. e. the whole people, *is not able to bear his words*, being shaken through and through.

11. *For thus Amos saith.* Amos had said, *Thus saith the Lord;* he never fails to impress on them, Whose words he is speaking. Amaziah, himself bound up in a system of falsehood and imposture, which, being a creature-worship, gave itself out as the worship of the true God, believed all besides to be fraud. Fraud always suspects fraud; the irreligious think devotion, holiness, saintliness to be hypocrisy: vice imagines virtue to be well-masked vice. The false priest, by a sort of law of corrupt nature, supposed that Amos also was false, and treats his words as the produce of his own mind.

Jeroboam shall die by the sword. Amos had not said this. The false prophet distorts the last words of Amos, which were yet in his ears, and reports to Jeroboam, as said of himself, what Amos had just said of his *house*. Amos *was* opposed to the popular religion or irreligion of which Jeroboam was the head, to the headship over which he had succeeded. Jeroboam, like the Roman Emperors, was High Priest, Pontifex Maximus, in order to get the popular worship under his control. The first Jeroboam had himself consecrated the calf-priests [2]. Amos bore also the message from God, that the reprieve, given to the house of Jehu, would not be extended, but would end. Amaziah would act on the personal fears of the king, as though there had been some present active conspiracy against him. A lie, mixed with truth, is the most deadly form of falsehood, the truth serving to gain admittance for the lie, and color it, and seeming to require explanation, and being something to fall back upon. Since thus much is certainly true, why should not the rest be so? In slander, and heresy which is slander against God, truth is used to commend the falsehood; and falsehood, to destroy the truth. The poison is received the more fearlessly because wrapt up in truth, but loses none of its deadliness.

And Israel shall surely be led away captive. This was a suppression of truth, as the other was a falsification of it. Amaziah omits both the ground of the threat, and the hope of escape urged and impressed upon them. On the one side he omits all mention of what even such a king as Jeroboam would respect, the denunciation of oppression of the poor, injustice, violence, robbery, and all their other sins against man. On the other hand, he omits the call to repentance and promises on it, *seek ye the Lord and live.* He omits too the Prophet's intercession for his people, and selects the one prophecy, which could give a mere political character to the whole. Suppression of truth is a yet subtler character of falsehood. Hence witnesses on oath are required to tell, not the truth only, but the whole truth. Yet in daily life, or in accusation of others, in detraction, or evil-speaking, men daily act, as though suppression were no lie.

12. Jeroboam apparently took no account of the false priest's message. Perhaps the memory of the true prophecies of Elisha as to the successes of his father, and of Jonah as to his own, fulfilled in his own person and still recent, inspired him with a reverence for God's prophets. To know his motive or motives, we must know his whole character, which we do not. Amaziah, failing of his purpose, uses his name as far as he dares. *Seer, go flee thee.* He probably uses the old title for a prophet, in reference to the visions which he had just related. Perhaps, he used it in irony also [3]. "Thou who seest, as thou

---

[1] קשר bound.

[2] קשר על "banded against, *conspired*." 1 Sam. xxii. 8, 13. 1 Kgs xv. 27, xvi. 9, 16, 2 Kgs

x. 9, xiv. 19, xv. 10, 15, 25, xxi. 23. So also קשר, קשורים.

[3] "Either in irony, in that he lies throughout, or because seeing, &c." (as below) S. Jer.

Before
C H R I S T
cir. 787.
k ch. 2. 12.
l 1 Kings 12. 32.
& 13. 1.
¶ Or, sanctuary.
† Heb. house of the kingdom.

13 k But prophesy not
again any more at Beth-el:
l for it *is* the king's ‖chapel
and it *is* the †king's court.

14 ¶ Then answered
Amos, and said to Amazi-
ah, I *was* no p r o p h e t,
neither *was* I m a prophet's

Before
C H R I S T
cir. 787.
m 1 Kings 20. 35.
2 Kings 2. 5.
& 4 38. & 6. 1.

deemest, what others see not, *visionary! vis-
ionist!" flee thee,* i. e. for thy good; (he acts
the patron and the counsellor;) *to the land of
Judah, and there eat bread, and there prophesy.*
Worldly men always think that those whose
profession is religious make *a gain of godliness.*
"He is paid for it," they say. "Whose
bread I eat, his song I sing." Interested
people cannot conceive of one disinterested;
nor the worldly, of one unworldly; nor the
insincere, of one sincere. Amaziah thought
then that Amos, coming out of Judah, must
be speaking in the interests of Judah; perhaps, that he was in the pay of their king.
Anyhow, prophecies, such as his against
Israel, would be acceptable there and be well
paid. The words are courteous, like so much
patronizing language now, as to God or His
revelation, His Prophets or His Apostles, or
His Divine word. The words are measured:
the meaning blasphemy. Perhaps, like the
Scribes and Pharisees afterward, *he feared the
people*[1]. "[2] Seeing that there were many
among the people who heard him gladly, he
dared not do him any open wrong, lest he
should offend them."

13. *It is the king's chapel;* better, as in the
E. M., *sanctuary*[3]. It is the name for *the
sanctuary* of God[4]. *Let them make Me a sanctuary, that I may dwell among them. Ye shall
reverence My sanctuary: I am the Lord*[5]. It
is most often spoken of as, *The sanctuary*[6];
elsewhere, but always with emphasis, of reverence, sanctity, devotion, protection, it is
called *His sanctuary; My sanctuary; Thy
sanctuary; the sanctuary of the Lord of God,
of his God*[7]; whence God Himself is called
a Sanctuary[8], as a place of refuge. In three
places only, is it called the sanctuary of
Israel; *her sanctuary.* God, in His threat to
cast them off, says[9], *I will bring your sanctuaries to desolation;* Jeremiah laments[10], *the
heathen have entered into her sanctuary;* he
says[11], *the place of our sanctuary is a glorious
high throne from the beginning,* inasmuch as
God was enthroned there. In this case too
it is *the sanctuary for* Israel, not a mere property *of* Israel. *The sanctuary of God* could
not be called the sanctuary of any man. One
man could not so appropriate *the sanctuary.*

God had ordained it for Himself. His
presence had sanctified it. Heresy, in un-
consciousness, lets out more truth than it
means. A high priest at Jerusalem could
not have said this. He knew that *the temple*
was the *sanctuary* of God, and could not have
called it *the king's sanctuary.* The sanctuary
at Bethel had no other sanction, than what
it had from the king. Jeroboam I. consecrated it and its priests[12]; and from him it
and they had their authority. Amaziah
wished to use a popular plea to rid himself
of Amos. Bethel was *the king's sanctuary and
the house,* not of God, but *of the kingdom,* i. e.
the house, which had the whole royal sanction, which with its worship was the creature
of royal authority, bound up in one with the
kingdom, and belonging to it. Or it may
be, *a royal house*[13], (not a palace, or court, for
the king's palace was at Samaria, but) a *royal
temple,* the state-Church. So the Arians betrayed their worldliness by dating one of
their Creeds from the Roman Consuls of the
year, its month and day, "[14] thereby to shew
all thinking men, that their faith dates, not
of old but now." Their faith was of yesterday. "They are wont to say," says St.
Jerome, "the Emperor communicates with
us, and, if any one resists them, forthwith
they calumniate. 'Actest thou against the
Emperor? Despisest thou the Emperor's
mandate?' And yet we may think, that
many Christian kings who have persecuted
the Church of God, and essayed to establish
the Arian impiety in the whole world, sur-
pass in guilt Jeroboam king of Israel. He
despised the message of a false priest, nor
would he make any answer to his sugges-
tions. But these, with their many Amaziah-
priests, have slain Amos the prophet and the
priest of the Lord by hunger and penury,
dungeons and exile."

14. *I was no prophet.* The order of the
words is emphatic. *No prophet I, and no prophet's son I; for a herdsman I, and dresser of
sycamores.* It may be, Amos would meet, for
the people's sake, Amaziah's taunt. He had
a living, simple indeed, yet that of the prophets was as simple. But chiefly he tells
them of the unusual character of his mission.

1 S. Matt. xxi. 26, Acts v. 26.   2 S. Jer.   3 מקדש.
4 Ex. xxv. 8.   5 Lev. xix. 30, xxvi. 2.
6 מקדש 68 times. In reference to the time
before it was built, it is called *a sanctuary,* Ex.
xxv. 8, 2 Chr. xx. 8.
7 In all, 23 times.   8 Is. viii. 14, Ezek. xi. 16.

9 Lev. xxvi. 31.   10 Lam. i. 10.   11 Jer. xvii. 12.
12 1 Kings xii. 31-3.
13 It has not the art. as בית המלכות has, Esth.
i. 9.
14 S. Ath. Counc. Arim. Sel. ₴ 3. Treat. ag. Arian. p.
76. Oxf. Tr.

Before
CHRIST
cir. 787.

n ch. 1. 1. Zech.
13. 5.
|| Or, *wild figs.*

† Heb. *from
behind.*

° Ezek. 21. 2.
Mic. 2. 6.

son; ⁿbut I *was* an herd-man, and a gatherer of || sycamore fruit:

15 And the LORD took me† as I followed the flock and the LORD said unto me, Go, prophesy unto my people Israel.

16 ¶ Now therefore hear thou the word of the LORD: Thou sayest, Prophesy not against Israel, and °drop not *thy*

word against the house of Isaac.

17 ᵖ Therefore thus saith the LORD; �q Thy wife shall be an harlot in the city, and thy sons and thy daughters shall fall by the sword, and thy land shall be divided by line; and thou shalt die in a polluted land: and Israel shall surely go into captivity forth of his land.

Before
CHRIST
cir. 787.

p See Jer. 28. 12.
& 29. 21, 25, 31,
32.
q Is. 13. 16.
Lam. 5. 11.
Hos. 4. 13.
Zech. 14. 2.

He did not belong to the order of the prophets, nor had he been educated in the schools of the prophets, nor had he any human training. He was thinking of nothing less; he was doing the works of his calling, till *God took him from following the flock,* and gave him his commission. "¹He premises humbly what he had been, what he had been made, not by merits, but by grace, that he had not assumed the prophetic office by hereditary right, nor had he begun to prophesy out of his own mind, but, being under the necessity of obeying, he had fulfilled the grace and the command of God Who inspired and sent Him." Twice he repeats, *The Lord took me; the Lord said unto me;* inculcating that, what Amaziah forbade, God bade. All was of God. *He* had but obeyed. "²As then the Apostles, when the Scribes and Pharisees forbade them to teach in the Name of Jesus, answered, ³ *We must obey God rather than man,* so Amos, when forbidden by the idol-priests to prophesy, not only prophesies, shewing that he feared God bidding, more than their forbidding, but he boldly and freely denounces the punishment of him who endeavored to forbid and hinder the word of God." "¹Heaven thundered and commanded him to prophesy; the frog croaked in answer out of his marsh, *prophesy no more."*

16. Amaziah then was in direct rebellion and contradiction against God. He was in an office forbidden by God. God's word came to him. He had his choice; and, as men do, when entangled in evil courses, he chose the more consciously amiss. He had to resign his lucrative office and to submit to God speaking to him through a shepherd, or to stand in direct opposition to God, and to confront God; and in silencing Amos, he would silence God. But, like one who would

arrest the lightning, he draws it on his own head. Amos contrasts the word of Amaziah, and the word of God; "¹ *Hear thou the word of the Lord; Thou sayest; prophesy not against Israel. Therefore thus saith the Lord.* Not only will I not cease to prophesy against Israel, but I will also prophesy to thee. Hear now thine own part of the prophecy."

Drop not. The form of expression, (not the word) is probably taken from Moses⁴. *My doctrine shall drop as the rain, my speech shall distill as the dew; as the small rain upon the tender herb, and as the showers upon the grass.* Micah speaks of the word as used by those who forbade to prophesy, as though the prophecy were a continual wearisome *dropping.* God's word comes as a gentle dew or soft rain, not beating down but refreshing; not sweeping away, like a storm, but sinking in and softening even hard ground, all but the rock; gentle, so as they can bear it. God's word was to men, such as they were toward it; dropping like the dew on those who received it; wearing, to those who hardened themselves against it. It drops in measure upon the hearts which it fertilizes, being adapted to their capacity to receive it. And so contrariwise as to the judgments with which God's prophets are charged. "² The prophets do not discharge at once the whole wrath of God, but, in their threatenings, denounce little drops of it."

17. *Thy wife shall be a harlot.* These were, and still are, among the horrors of war. His own sentence comes last, when he had seen the rest, unable to hinder it. Against his and her own will, she should suffer this. "² Great is the grief, and incredible the disgrace, when the husband, in the midst of the city and in the presence of all, cannot hinder the wrong done to his wife⁵. For

¹ Rup.   ² S. Jer.
³ Acts v. 29.   ⁴ Deut. xxxii. 2.
⁵ The recent horrors about Mount Lebanon have

renewed this description, shewing how the wrong to the Christian woman was a devilish triumph over the helpless relation.

Before
CHRIST
cir. 787.

CHAPTER VIII.

1 *By a basket of summer fruit is
shewed the propinquity of Israel's end.* 4 *Oppression is
reproved.* 11 *A famine of the
word threatened.*

THUS hath the Lord GOD
shewed unto me: and
behold a basket of summer
fruit.

2 And he said, Amos,
what seest thou? And I
said, A basket of summer

fruit. Then said the LORD
unto me, [a] The end is come
upon my people of Israel; [a] Ezek. 7. 2.
[b] I will not again pass by [b] ch. 7. 8.
them any more.

3 And [c] the songs of the [c] ch. 5. 23.
temple † shall be howlings † Heb. *shall
in that day, saith the Lord*   *howl.*
GOD: *there shall be* many
dead bodies in every place;
[d] they shall cast them forth [d] ch. 6. 9. 10.
† with silence.   † Heb. *be silent.*

Before
CHRIST
cir. 787.

---

the husband had rather hear that his wife
had been slain, than defiled." What he
adds, *thy daughters* (as well as his *sons*) *shall
fall by the sword,* is an unwonted barbarity,
and not part of the Assyrian customs, who
carried off women in great numbers, as wives
for their soldiery[1]. Perhaps Amos mentions the unwonted cruelty, that the event
might bring home the more to the minds of
the people the prophecies which relate to
themselves. When this had been fulfilled
before his eyes, "[2] Amaziah himself, who
now gloried in the authority of the priesthood, was to be led into captivity, die in a
land polluted by idols, yet not before he saw
the people whom he had deceived, enslaved
and captive." Amos closes by repeating emphatically the exact words, which Amaziah
had alleged in his message to Jeroboam; *and
Israel shall surely go into captivity forth of his
land.* He had not said it before in these
precise words. Now he says it, without reserve of their repentance, as though he would
say, "Thou hast pronounced thine own sentence; thou hast hardened thyself against
the word of God; thou hardenest thy people against the word of God; it remains then
that it should fall on thee and thy people."
"[3] How and when the prophecy against
Amaziah was fulfilled, Scripture does not
relate. He lies hid amid the mass of
miseries[4]." Scripture hath no leisure to
relate all which befalls those of the viler
sort. "The majesty of Holy Scripture does
not lower itself to linger on baser persons,"
whom God had rejected.

VIII. 1. *Thus hath the Lord God shewed
me.* The sentence of Amaziah pronounced,
Amos resumes just where he left off, before
Amaziah broke in upon him. His vehement
interruption is like a stone cast into the
deep waters. They close over it, and it
leaves no trace. Amos had authenticated

the third vision; *Thus hath the Lord God
shewed me.* He resumes in the self-same
calm words. The last vision declared that
the end was certain; this, that it was at
hand.

A basket of summer fruit. The fruit was
the latest harvest in Palestine. When *it*
was gathered, the circle of husbandry was
come to its close. The sight gives an idea
of completeness. The symbol, and the word
expressing it, coincide. The fruit-gathering
(*kaits*), like our "crop," was called from
"cutting." So was the word, *end,* "cutting-
off," in *kets.* At harvest-time there is no
more to be done for that crop. Good or bad,
it has reached its end, and is cut down. So
the harvest of Israel was come. The whole
course of God's providences, mercies, chastenings, visitations, instructions, warnings, inspirations, were completed. *What could have
been done more to My vineyard,* God asks[5],
that I have not done in it? "To the works of
sin, as of holiness, there is a beginning, progress, completion;" a "sowing of wild oats,"
as men speak, and a ripening in wickedness;
a maturity of men's plans, as they deem; a
maturity for destruction, in the sight of God.
There was no more to be done. Heavenly
influences can but injure the ripened sinner,
as dew, rain, sun, but injure the ripened fruit.
Israel was ripe, but for destruction.

3. *The songs of the temple shall be howlings,*
lit. *shall howl*[6]. It shall be, as when mirthful
music is suddenly broken in upon, and,
through the sudden agony of the singer, ends
in a shriek or yell of misery. When sounds
of joy are turned into wailing, all must be
complete sorrow. They are not hushed only,
but are turned into their opposite. Since
Amos is speaking to, and of, Israel, *the temple*
is, doubtless, here the great idol-temple at
Bethel, and *the songs* were the choral music,
with which they counterfeited the temple-

---

[1] Fox Talbot, Ass. texts.   [2] S. Jer.

[3] Rup.   [4] See above, Introd. p. 153.

[5] Is. v. 4.

[6] היליל our "yell" or "howl," "ululo."

Before
CHRIST
cir. 787.

ᵉ Ps. 14. 4.
Prov. 30. 14.

‖ Or, *month.*

4 ¶ Hear this, O ye that
ᵉ swallow up the needy, even
to make the poor of the
land to fail,

5 Saying, When will the
‖ new moon be gone, that

we may sell corn? and ʳthe
sabbath, that we may † set
forth wheat, ᵍ making the
ephah small, and the shekel
great, and † falsifying the
balances by deceit?

Before
CHRIST
cir. 787.

ʳNeh. 13. 15, 16.
† Heb. *open.*
ᵍ Mic. 6. 10, 11.
† Heb. *pervert-
ing the balances
of deceit,* Hos.
12. 7.

music, as arranged by David, praising (they
could not make up their minds which,) Nature or "the God of nature," but, in truth,
worshiping the creature. The temple was
often strongly built and on a height, and,
whether from a vague hope of help from God,
(as in the siege of Jerusalem by the Romans,) or from some human trust, that the
temple might be respected, or from confidence
in its strength, or from all together, was the
last refuge of the all-but-captive people.
Their last retreat was often the scene of the
last reeling strife, the battle-cry of the assailants, the shrieks of the defenceless, the groans
of the wounded, the agonized cry of unyield-
ing despair. Some such scene the Prophet
probably had before his mind's eye; for he
adds;

There shall be *many dead bodies,* lit. *Many
the corpse in every place.* He sees it, not as
future, but before him. The whole city, now
so thronged with life, "the oppressor's wrong,
the proud man's contumely," lies before him
as one scene of death; every place thronged
with corpses; none exempt; at home, abroad,
or, which he had just spoken of, the temple;
no time, no place for honorable burial. *They,*
lit. *he casts forth, hush!* Each casts forth those
dear to him, as [1] *dung on the face of the earth.*
Grief is too strong for words. Living and
dead are hushed as the grave. "Large cities
are large solitudes," for want of mutual love;
in God's retribution, all their din and hum
becomes anew a solitude.

4. *Here ye this, ye that swallow* (or, better in
the same sense, *that pant for) the needy;* as
Job says [2], *the hireling panteth for the evening.*
They *panted for the poor,* as the wild beast for
its prey; and *that to make the poor* or (better,
as the Hebrew text,) *the meek* [3], those not poor
only, but who, through poverty and affliction,
are *poor in spirit* also, *to fail.* The land being divided among all the inhabitants, they,
in order *to lay field to field* [4], had to rid themselves of the poor. They did rid themselves
of them by oppression of all sorts.

5. *When will the new moon be gone?* They
kept their festivals, though weary and impatient for their close. They kept sabbath
and festival with their bodies, not with their
minds. The Psalmist said [5], *When shall I*

come to appear before the presence of God?
These said, perhaps in their hearts only
which God reads to them, "when will this
service be over, that we may be our own
masters again?" They loathed the rest of
the sabbath, because they had, thereon, to
rest from their frauds. He instances *the new
moons* and *sabbaths,* because these, recurring
weekly or monthly, were a regular hindrance
to their covetousness.

The *ephah* was a measure containing 72
Roman pints or nearly $1\frac{1}{10}$ English Bushel;
the shekel was a fixed weight, by which, up
to the time of the Captivity [6], money was
still weighed; and that, for the price of bread
also [7]. They increased the price both ways,
dishonestly and in hypocrisy, paring down
the quantity which they sold, and obtaining
more silver by fictitious weights; and weighing in uneven balances. All such dealings
had been expressly forbidden by God; and
that, as the condition of their remaining in the
land which God had given them [8]. *Thou
shalt not have in thy bag divers weights, a great
and a small. Thou shalt not have in thy house
divers measures, a great and a small. But thou
shalt have a perfect and just weight; a perfect
and just measure shalt thou have, that thy days
may be lengthened in the land which the Lord thy
God giveth thee.* Sin in wrong measures, once
begun is unbroken. All sin perpetuates itself. It is done again, because it has been
done before. But sins of a man's daily occupation are continued of necessity, beyond the
simple force of habit and the ever-increasing
dropsy of covetousness. To interrupt sin is
to risk detection. But then how countless
the sins, which their poor slaves must needs
commit hourly, whenever the occasion comes!
And yet, although among us human law re-
cognizes the Divine law and annexes punishment to its breach, covetousness sets both at
nought. When human law was enforced in
a city after a time of negligence, scarcely a
weight was found to be honest. Prayer went
up to God on *the sabbath,* and fraud on the
poor went up to God in every transaction on
the other six days. We admire the denunciations of Amos, and condemn the make-
believe service of God. Amos denounces us,
and we condemn ourselves. Righteous deal-

---

[1] Jer. viii. 2, &c.   [2] vii. 2.
[3] The E. V. has followed the correction of the
Kri. The textual reading is almost always the best.

[4] Is. v. 8.   [5] Ps. xli. 2.
[6] 2 Sam. xviii. 12, 1 Kings xx. 39, Jer. xxxii. 9.
[7] Is. lv. 2.   [8] Deut. xxv. 13-15.

Before CHRIST cir. 787.

6 That we may buy the poor for ʰsilver, and the needy for a pair of shoes; *yea*, and sell the refuse of the wheat?

7 The LORD hath sworn by ⁱthe excellency of Jacob, Surely ᵏI will never forget any of their works.

8 ¹Shall not the land tremble for this, and every one mourn that dwelleth therein? and it shall rise up wholly as a flood; and it shall be cast out and drowned, ᵐas *by* the flood of Egypt.

9 And it shall come to

ʰ ch. 2. 6.

ⁱ ch. 6. 8.

ᵏ Hos. 8. 13. & 9. 9.

Before CHRIST cir. 787.

¹ Hos. 4. 3.

ᵐ ch. 9. 5.

791.

ing in weights and measures was one of the conditions of the existence of God's former people. What must then be our national condition before God, when, from this one sin, so many thousand, thousand sins go up daily to plead against us to God?

6. *That we may buy*, or, indignantly, *To buy the poor!* lit. *the afflicted*, those in *low* estate. First, by dishonesty and oppression they gained their lands and goods. Then the poor were obliged to sell themselves. The slight price, for which a man was sold, shewed the more contempt for *the image of God*. Before[1], he said, *the needy* were *sold for a pair of sandals;* here, that they were bought for them. It seems then the more likely that such was a real price for man.

And sell the refuse [lit. the *falling*] *of wheat*, i. e. what fell through the sieve, either the bran, or the thin, unfilled, grains which had no meal in them. This they mixed up largely with the meal, making a gain of that which they had once sifted out as worthless; or else, in a time of dearth, they sold to men what was the food of animals, and made a profit on it. Infancy and inexperience of cupidity, which adulterated its bread only with bran, or sold to the poor only what, although unnourishing, was wholesome! But then, with the multiplied hard-dealing, what manifoldness of the *woe!*

7. *By the excellency of Jacob*, i. e. by Himself Who was its Glory, as Samuel calls Him ²*the Strength* or the Glory of Israel. Amos had before said, *God sware by His Holiness*, and *by Himself* or *His soul*. Now, in like way, He pledges that Glory wherewith He was become the Glory of His people. He reminds them, *Who* was the sole Source of their glory; not their calves, but Himself, their Creator; and that He would not forget their deeds. *I will not forget any*, lit. *all;* as David and S. Paul say, *all flesh*, all living men, *shall not be justified*, i. e. none, no one, neither the whole nor any of its parts. Amos brings before the mind *all* their doings, and

then says of all and each, the Lord will not forget them. God must cease to be God, if He did not do what He sware to do, punish the oppressors and defrauders of the poor.

8. *Shall not the land tremble for this?* "[3] For the greater impressiveness, he ascribes to the insensate earth sense, indignation, horror, trembling. For all creation feels the will of its Creator." *It shall rise up wholly as a flood*, lit. *like the river*. It is the Egyptian name for *river*[4], which Israel brought with it out of Egypt, and is used either for the Nile, or for one of the artificial *trenches*, derived from it. *And it shall be cast out and drowned*, lit. *shall toss to and fro* as the sea, *and sink* [5] *as the river of Egypt*. The Prophet represents the land as heaving like the troubled sea. As the Nile rose, and its currents met and drove one against the other, covered and drowned the whole land like one vast sea, and then sank again, so the earth should rise, lift up itself, and heave and quake, shaking off the burden of man's oppressions, and sink again. It may be, he would describe the heaving, the rising and falling, of an earthquake. Perhaps, he means that as a man forgat all the moral laws of nature, so inanimate nature should be freed from its wonted laws, and shake out its inhabitants or overwhelm them by an earthquake, as in one grave.

9. *I will cause the sun to go down.* Darkness is heaviest and blackest in contrast with the brightest light; sorrow is saddest, when it comes upon fearless joy. God commonly, in His mercy, sends heralds of coming sorrow; very few burst suddenly on man. Now, in the meridian brightness of the day of Israel, the blackness of night should fall at once upon him. Not only was light to be displaced by darkness, but *then*, when it was most opposite to the course of nature. Not by gradual decay, but by a sudden unlooked-for crash, was Israel to perish. Pekah was a military chief; he had reigned more than seventeen years over Israel in peace, when, together with Rezin king of Damascus, he attempted

¹ ii. 6. ² 1 Sam. xv. 29. ³ Lap.
⁴ יְאֹר, the same as the Memph. *iaro*, כָּאוּר i. q. כִּיאֹר is the old reading, as appeared from Ecclus. xxiv. 27.

⁵ The kethib נָשְׁקָה is probably a 2d peculiarity as to a guttural in Amos (See ab. p. 152), as a different pronunciation of what stands in the kri, נָשְׁקְעָה.

Before
CHRIST
cir. 787.

ª Job. 5. 14.
Is. 13. 10.
& 59. 9, 10. Jer. 15. 9. Micah. 3. 6.

pass in that day, saith the Lord God, ª that I will cause the sun to go down at noon, and I will darken the earth in the clear day :

Before
CHRIST
cir. 787.

to extirpate the line of David, and to set a Syrian, one *son of Tabeal*[1], on his throne. Ahaz was weak, with no human power to resist; his *heart was moved, and the heart of his people, as the trees of the forest are moved with the wind*[2]. Tiglath-pileser came upon Pekah and carried off the tribes beyond Jordan[3]. Pekah's sun set, and all was night with no dawn. Shortly after, Pekah himself was murdered by Hoshea[4], as he had himself murdered Pekahiah. After an anarchy of nine years, Hoshea established himself on the throne ; the nine remaining years were spent in the last convulsive efforts of an expiring monarchy, subdual to Shalmaneser, rebellious alliance with So, king of Egypt, a three years' siege, and the lamp went out[5].

And I will darken the earth at noon-day. To the mourner "all nature seems to mourn." "Not the ground only, " says S. Chrysostom in the troubles at Antioch[6], "but the very substance of the air, and the orb of the solar rays itself seems to me now in a manner to mourn and to shew a duller light. Not that the elements change their nature, but that our eyes, confused by a cloud of sorrow, cannot receive the light from it's rays purely, nor are they alike impressible. This is what the Prophet of old said mourning, *Their sun shall set to them at noon, and the day shall be darkened.* Not that the sun was hidden, or the day disappeared, but that the mourners could see no light even in midday, for the darkness of their grief." No eclipse of the sun, in which the sun might seem to be shrouded in darkness at midday, has been calculated which should have suggested this image to the Prophet's mind. It had been thought, however, that there might be reference to an eclipse of the sun which took place a few years after this prophecy, viz. Feb. 9. 784, B. C. the year of the death of Jeroboam II[7]. This eclipse did reach its height at Jerusalem a little before mid-day, at 11 ʰ 24 ᵐ A. M.[8]. An accurate calculation, however, shews that, although total in Southern latitudes, the line of totality was, at the longitude of Jerusalem or Samaria, about 11 degrees South Latitude, and so above 43 degrees South of Samaria, and that it did not reach the same latitude as Samaria until near the close of the eclipse, about 64 degrees West of Samaria in the Easternmost part of Thibet[9]. "[10]The central eclipse commenced in the Southern Atlantic Ocean, passed nearly exactly over St. Helena[11], reached the continent of Africa in Lower Guinea, traversed the interior of Africa, and left it near Zanzibar, went through the Indian Ocean and entered India in the Gulf of Gambay, passed between Agra and Allahabad into Thibet and reached its end on the frontiers of China." The Eclipse then would hardly have been noticeable at Samaria, certainly very far indeed from being an eclipse of such magnitude, as could in any degree correspond with the expression, *I will cause the sun to go down at noon.*

Archbishop Ussher suggests, if true, a different coincidence. "[12]There was an eclipse of the sun of about 10 digits in the

[1] Is. vii. 6.　[2] Ib. 2.　[3] 2 Kgs xv. 29.　[4] Ib. 30.
[5] Ib. xvii. 1-9.　[6] Hom. 2 on the Statues, § 2.
[7] Hitzig says, "Since the sun was to set at noon-day, and since, just before, mention was made of the death of Jeroboam" [rather of the destruction of the house of Jeroboam, vii. 9, the mention of his own death being merely a distortion of Amaziah], " we have to think of the total Eclipse which took place in the year of his death, Feb. 9. 784, which reached its centre at Jerusalem about 1."
[8] "9 A. M. Greenwich time, or at 11ʰ.24ᵐ A. M. Jerusalem time." Letter of the Rev. Robert Main, Radcliffe Observer and President of the Royal Astron. Soc. Upon my enquiring as to the facts of this eclipse to which Hitzig had drawn attention, Mr. Main kindly directed Mr. Quirling his First Assistant to compute under his own superintendence the circumstances of the Eclipse of 784, B. C. Feb. 9. which had "originally been calculated by Pingré (Mém. de l'Acad. des. Inscr. vol. 52 in which the year is given 783 B. C. In l'Art de vérifier les Dates, T. i. the years are all altered by one unit, to make them agree with the mode of reckoning in ordinary chronology). Mr. Quirling, employing Hansen's lunar tables and Hansen's and Olufsen's solar tables, found, that on the given day, there was an eclipse, which would however be very small for Palestine, and that the apparent diameters of the sun and moon were so nearly equal that at no place could the totality be of more than 40ˢ duration. The general conjunction was at 9ʰ. A. M. (Greenwich time, i. e. 11ʰ. 24ᵐ. Jerusalem time), of Feb. 9. and the Geo-centric Semi-diameters of the Sun and Moon were 16′ 17″. 25. and 16′ 0″. 88. at Greenwich noon." "Pingré's calculation must have been tolerably accurate; for he gives 11¼ A. M. Paris time."
[9] Mr. Main has kindly furnished me with a detailed account of the path of the central eclipse from which the following statements are taken. "It began—10° 13′ lat. 347° 49′ long. at 19ʰ 1ᵐ (7ʰ 1ᵐ A. M.) Greenwich Time, and ended at, + 32° 35′ lat. 100° 42′ long. at 22ʰ 32ᵐ (10ʰ 32ᵐ) Gr. Time." Samaria is 32° 15′ lat. 35° 14′ long. "The path of the central eclipse was—14 lat. 30° 6′ long. ;—10 lat. 38° 14′ long."
[10] Mr. Main's letter.
[11] Every place here mentioned was "rigorously computed" by Mr. Quirling.
[12] Usserii Annales, A. M. 3213. p. 45. fol. [Prof. Donkin has verified Ussher's statement as to the eclipse Nov. 8. 771 B. C., and calculated that it was visible in Palestine at 12.55. P. M. Dr. Stanley, (J. Ch. ii. 363.) who reports this, supposes, in the way of his school, that Amos might be alluding to a past event, contrary to the date Am. i. 1, according to which he prophesied not later than 784 B. C. Ed. 2.]

Before
CHRIST
cir. 787.

10 And I will turn your feasts into mourning, and all your songs into lamentation; ° and I will bring up sackcloth upon all

° Is. 15. 2, 3.
Jer. 48. 37.
Ezek. 7. 18.
& 27. 31.

loins, and baldness upon every head; ᵖ and I will make it as the mourning of an only *son*, and the end thereof as a bitter day.

Before
CHRIST
cir. 787.

ᵖ Jer. 6. 26.
Zech. 12. 10.

Julian year 3923 (B. C. 791,) June 24, in the Feast of Pentecost; another, of about 12 digits, 20 years afterward, 3943, B. C. 771, Nov. 8, on the Day of the Feast of Tabernacles; and a third of more than 11 digits, on the following year 3944, May 5, on the Feast of the Passover. Consider whether that prophecy of Amos does not relate to it, *I will cause the sun to go down at noon, and I will darken the earth in the clear day, and I will turn your feasts into mourning.* Which, as the Christian Fathers have adapted in an allegorical sense to the darkness at the time of our Lord's Passion in the feast of the Passover, so it may have been fulfilled, in the letter, in these three great eclipses, which darkened the day of the three festivals in which all the males were bound to appear before the Lord. So that as, among the Greeks, Thales, first, by astronomical science, predicted eclipses of the sun [1], so, among the Hebrews, Amos first seems to have foretold them by inspiration of the Holy Spirit." The eclipses, pointed out by Ussher, must have been the one total, the others very considerable [2]. Beforehand, one should not have expected that an eclipse of the sun, being itself a regular natural phænomenon, and having no connection with the moral government of God, should have been the subject of the Prophet's prediction. Still it had a religious impressiveness then, above what it has now, on account of that wide-prevailing idolatry of the sun. It exhibited the object of their false worship, shorn of its light and passive. If Archbishop Ussher is right as to the magnitude of those eclipses in the latitude of Jerusalem, and as to the correspondence of the days of the solar year, June 24, Nov. 8, May 5, in those years, with the days of the lunar year upon which the respective feasts fell, it would be a remarkable correspondence. Still the years are somewhat arbitrarily chosen, the second only B. C. 771, (on which the house of Jehu came to an end through the murder of the weak and sottish Zechariah,) corresponding with any marked event in the kingdom of Israel. On the other

hand, it is the more likely that the words, *I will cause the sun to go down at noon,* are an image of a sudden reverse, in that Micah also uses the words as an image [3], *the sun shall go down upon the prophets and the day shall be dark upon* [or, *over*] *them.*

10. *I will turn your feasts into mourning.* He recurs to the sentence which he had pronounced [4], before he described the avarice and oppression which brought it down. Hosea too had foretold [5], *I will cause all her mirth to cease, her feast-days, &c.* So Jeremiah describes [6], *the joy of our heart is ceased; our dance is turned into mourning.* The book of Tobit bears witness how these sayings of Amos lived in the hearts of the captive Israelites. The word of God seems oftentimes to fail, yet it finds those who are His. *I remembered,* he said [7], *that prophecy of Amos, your feasts shall be turned into mourning.*

The correspondence of these words with the miracle at our Blessed Lord's Passion, in that *the earth was darkened in the clear day, at noon-day,* was noticed by the earliest Fathers [8], and that the more, since it took place at the Feast of the Passover, and, in punishment for that sin, their *feasts were turned into mourning,* in the desolation of their country and the cessation of their worship.

I will bring up sackcloth (i. e. the rough coarse haircloth, which, being fastened with the girdle tight over the loins [9], was wearing to the frame) *and baldness upon every head.* The mourning of the Jews was no half-mourning, no painless change of one color of becoming dress for another. For the time, they were dead to the world or to enjoyment. As the clothing was coarse, uncomely, distressing, so they laid aside every ornament, the ornament of their hair also (as English widows used, on the same principle, to cover it). They shore it off; each sex, what was the pride of their sex; the men, their beards; the women, their long hair. The strong words, *baldness, is balded* [10], *shear* [11], *hew off* [12], *enlarge thy baldness* [13], are used to shew the completeness of this expression of sorrow.

---

[1] See Rawl. on Herod. i. 74. T. i. p. 212.
[2] Mr. Main tells me that, in the old mode of marking eclipses, the whole was divided into 12 digits, so that eclipses of 12 digits were total; those of 11 and 10, large.
[3] Mic. ii. 6. Am. השמש ובאה השמש על הנביאים
והבאתי.
[4] ver. 3.   [5] ii. 11.   [6] Lam. v. 15.   [7] Tob. ii. 6.

[8] S. Iren. iv. 33. 12. Tert. in Marc. iv. 42. S. Cypr. Test. ii. 23. p. 58. Oxf. Tr. S. Cyril, Cat. xiii. 25. Eus. Dem. Ev. x. 6.
[9] See ab. Joel i. 8, 13. pp. 107, 109.   [10] Jer. xvi. 6.
[11] נזז Mic. i. 16, Jer. vii. 29.
[12] גרע (Is. xv. 2, Jer. xlviii. 37) although less strong than גרד, is harsher than the ordinary גלח.   [13] Mic. 1. c.

Before
CHRIST
cir. 787.

11 ¶ Behold, the days come, saith the Lord GOD, that I will send a famine in the land, not a famine of bread, nor a thirst for water, but [q] of hearing the words of the LORD.

[q] 1 Sam. 3. 1.
Ps. 74. 9.
Ezek. 7. 26.

Before
CHRIST
cir. 787.

12 And they shall wander from sea to sea, and from the north even to the east, they shall run to and fro to seek the word of the LORD, and shall not find *it*.

13 In that day shall the

None exempted themselves in the universal sorrow; *on every head* came up *baldness*.

And I will make it (probably, the whole state and condition of things, everything, as we use our *it) as the mourning of an only son*. As, when God delivered Israel from Egypt, *there was not*, among the Egyptians, *a house where there was not one dead* [1], and one universal cry arose from end to end of the land, so now too in apostate Israel. The whole mourning should be the one most grievous mourning of parents, over the one child in whom they themselves seemed anew to live.

And the end thereof as a bitter day. Most griefs have a rest or pause, or wear themselves out. *The end* of this should be like the beginning, nay, one concentrated grief, a whole day of bitter grief summed up in its close. It was to be no passing trouble, but one which should end in bitterness, an unending sorrow and destruction; image of the undying death in hell.

11. *Not a famine for bread.* He does not deny that there should be bodily famine too; but this, grievous as it is, would be less grievous than the famine of which he speaks, *the famine of the word of the Lord.* In distress we all go to God. "[2] They who now cast out and despise the prophets, when they shall see themselves besieged by the enemy, shall be tormented with a great hunger of hearing the word of the Lord from the mouths of the prophets, and shall find no one to lighten their distresses. This was most sad to the people of God; [3] *we see not our tokens; there is not one prophet more; there is not one with us who understandeth, how long!*" Even the profane, when they see no help, will have recourse to God. Saul, in his extremity, [4] *enquired of the Lord* and *He answered him not, neither by dreams, nor by Urim, nor by prophets.* Jeroboam sent his wife to enquire of the prophet Ahijah about his son's health [5]. They sought for temporal relief only, and therefore found it not.

12 *They shall wander*, lit. *reel.* The word is used of the reeling of drunkards, of the swaying to and fro of trees in the wind, of the quivering of the lips of one agitated, and

then of the unsteady seeking of persons bewildered, looking for what they know not where to find. *From sea to sea,* from the sea of Galilee to the Mediterranean, i. e. from East to West, *and from the North even to the sunrising,* round again to the East, whence their search had begun, where light should be, and was not. It may be, that Amos refers to the description of the land by Moses, adapting it to the then separate condition of Ephraim, [6] *your South border shall be from the extremity of the Salt sea* (Dead sea) *Eastward—and the goings out of it shall be at the sea, and for the Western border ye shall have the great sea for a border. And this shall be your North border—and the border shall descend and shall reach to the side of the sea of Chinnereth Eastward.* Amos does not mention *the South,* because *there* alone, where they might have found, where the true worship of God was, they did not seek. Had they sought God in Judah, instead of seeking to aggrandize themselves by its subdual, Tiglath-pileser would probably never have come against them. One expedition only in the seventeen years of his reign was directed Westward [7], and that was at the petition of Ahaz.

The principle of God's dealings, that, in certain conditions of a sinful people, He will withdraw His word, is instanced in Israel, not limited to it. God says to Ezekiel [8], *I will make thy tongue cleave to the roof of thy mouth, and thou shalt be dumb; and shalt not be to them a reprover; for it is a rebellious house;* and Ezekiel says [9], *Destruction shall come upon destruction, and rumor shall be upon rumor, and they shall seek a vision from the prophet, and the law shall perish from the priest and counsel from the ancients.* "[10] God turns away from them, and checks the grace of prophecy. For since they neglected His law, He on His side, stays the prophetic gift. *And the word was precious in those days, there was no open vision,* i. e. God did not speak to them through the prophets; He breathed not upon them the Spirit through which they spake. He did not appear to them, but is silent and hidden. There was silence, enmity between God and man."

13. In this hopelessness as to all relief,

---

[1] Ex. xii. 30.　　　　[2] Rib.
[3] Ps. lxxiv. 9.　　　　[4] 1 Sam. xxviii. 6.
[5] 1 Kings xiv. 2, 3.　　[6] Num. xxxiv. 3-12.

[7] Rawl. Herod. i. 470.
[8] Ezek. iii. 26.　　　　[9] vii. 26.
[10] from S. Chrys. in Is. vi. 1. Hom. 4. T. vi. p. 130.

Before
CHRIST
cir. 787.

r Hos. 4. 15.
s Deut. 9. 21.

† Heb. way:
See Acts 9. 2.
& 18. 25. & 19.
9, 23. & 24. 14.

t ch. 5. 5.

fair virgins and young men
faint for thirst.

14 They that ʳ swear by
ˢ the sin of Samaria, and
say, Thy God, O Dan,
liveth; and, The † manner
ᵗ of Beer-sheba liveth; even
they shall fall, and never
rise up again.

1 *The certainty of the desolation.*
11 *The restoring of the taber-*
nacle of David.

I SAW the Lord standing
upon the altar : and he
said, Smite the ‖ lintel of
the door, that the posts
may shake: and ‖ ª cut

Before
CHRIST
cir. 787.

‖ Or, *chapiter*, or,
knop.
‖ Or, *wound*
them.
ª Ps. 68. 21.
Hab. 3. 13.

those too shall fail and sink under their
sufferings, in whom life is freshest and
strongest and hope most buoyant. Hope
mitigates any sufferings. When hope is gone,
the powers of life, which it sustains, give
way. *They shall faint for thirst,* lit. "shall be
mantled over, covered[1]," as, in fact, one
fainting seems to feel as if a veil came over
his brow and eyes. *Thirst,* as it is an in-
tenser suffering than bodily hunger, includes
sufferings of body and mind. If even over
those, whose life was firmest, a veil came, and
they fainted for thirst, what of the rest?

14. *Who swear,* lit. *the swearing,* they who
habitually swear. He assigns, at the end,
the ground of all this misery, the forsaking
of God. God had commanded that all
appeals by oath should be made to Himself,
Who alone governs the world, to Whom
alone His creatures owe obedience, Who
alone revenges. [2] *Thou shalt fear the Lord
thy God and serve Him and swear by His
Name.* On the other hand Joshua warned
them[3], *Neither make mention of the name of
their gods nor cause to swear by them nor serve
them.* But these *sware by the sin of Samaria,*
probably *the calf at Bethel,* which was nigh to
Samaria and the centre of their idolatry,
whence Hosea calls it *thy calf*[4]. *Thy calf, O
Samaria, hath cast thee off. The calf of Samaria
shall be broken in pieces.* He calls it *the guilt
of Samaria,* as the source of all their guilt, as
it is said of the princes of Judah using this
same word[5], *they left the house of the Lord God
of their fathers, and served idols, and wrath came
upon Judah and Jerusalem for this their trespass.
And say, thy god, O Dan! liveth,* i. e. as surely
as thy god liveth! by the life of thy god!
as they who worshiped God said, *as the Lord
liveth!* It was a direct substitution of the
creature for the Creator, an ascribing to it
the attribute of God; *as the Father hath life
in Himself*[6]. It was an appeal to it, as the
Avenger of false-swearing, as though it were
the moral Governor of the world.

The manner of Beersheba liveth! lit. *the way.*

This may be, either the religion and worship
of the idol there, as S. Paul says, *I persecuted
this way unto the death*[7], whence Mohammed
learnt to speak of his imposture, as "the
way of God." Or it might mean the actual
way to Beersheba, and may signify all the
idolatrous places of worship in the way
thither. They seem to have made the way
thither one long avenue of idols, culminating
in it. For Josiah, in his great destruction of
idolatry[8], *gathered all the priests from the cities
of Judah, and defiled the high-places, where the
priests sacrificed from Gebah to Beersheba:*
only, this may perhaps simply describe the
whole territory of Judah from North to
South. Anyhow, Beersheba stands for the
god worshiped there, as, *whoso sware by the
Temple, sware,* our Lord tells us[9], *by it and by
Him that dwelleth therein.*

IX. 1. *I saw the Lord.* He saw God in
vision; yet God no more, as before, asked
him what he saw. God no longer shews him
emblems of the destruction, but the destruction itself. Since Amos had just been speaking of the idolatry of Samaria, as the ground
of its utter destruction, doubtless this vision
of such utter destruction of the place of worship, with and upon the worshipers, relates
to those same idolaters and idolatries[10]. True,
the condemnation of Israel would become
the condemnation of Judah, when Judah's
sins, like Israel's, should become complete.
But directly, it can hardly relate to any other
than those spoken of before and after, Israel.
The altar, then, *over*[11] which Amos sees God
stand, is doubtless the altar on which Jeroboam sacrificed, *the altar* which he set up
over-against the altar at Jerusalem, the centre of the calf-worship, whose destruction
the man of God foretold on the day of its
dedication. There where, in counterfeit of
the sacrifices which God had appointed, they
offered would-be-atoning sacrifices and sinned
in them, God appeared, standing, to behold,
to judge, to condemn. *And He said, smite
the lintel,* lit. *the chapter,* or *capital,* probably so

[1] The metaphor occurs both in Heb. and Arab.
[2] Deut. vi. 13, x. 20.   [3] Josh. xxiii. 7.
[4] Hos. viii. 5, 6.   [5] 2 Chr. xxiv. 18.
[6] S. John v. 26.

[7] Acts xxii. 4, add ix. 2, xix. 9, 23.
[8] 2 Kings xxiii. 8.   [9] S. Matt. xxiii. 21.
[10] S. Jer. Theod. understand it of "*the* altar" at
Jerusalem.   [11] not, *upon.*

Before
C H R I S T
cir. 787.

them in the head, all of them ; and I will slay the last of them with the sword : [b] he that fleeth of them shall not flee away, and he that escapeth of them shall not be delivered.

2 [c] Though they dig into hell, thence shall mine

[b] ch. 2. 14.

[c] Ps. 139. 8. &c.

hand take them ; [d] though they climb up to heaven, thence will I bring them down ;

3 And though they hide themselves in the top of Carmel, I will search and take them out thence ; and though they be hid from my sight in the bottom of

Before
C H R I S T
cir. 787.

[d] Job 20. 6.
Jer. 51. 53.
Obad. 4.

called from *crowning* the pillar with a globular form, like a pomegranate. This, the spurious outward imitation of the true sanctuary, God commands to be stricken, *that the posts,* or probably *the thresholds, may shake.* The building was struck from above, and reeled to its base. It does not matter, whether any blow on the capital of a pillar would make the whole fabric to shake. For the blow was no blow of man. God gives the command probably to the Angel of the Lord, as, in Ezekiel's vision of the destruction of Jerusalem, the charge to destroy was given to six men[1]. So the first-born of Egypt, the army of Sennacherib, were destroyed by an Angel[2]. An Angel stood with his sword over Jerusalem[3], when God punished David's presumption in numbering the people. At one blow of the heavenly Agent the whole building shook, staggered, fell.

And cut them in the head, all of them[4]. This may be either by the direct agency of the Angel, or the temple itself may be represented as falling on the heads of the worshipers. As God, through Jehu, destroyed all the worshipers of Baal in the house of Baal, so here He foretells, under a like image, the destruction of all the idolaters of Israel. He had said, *they that swear by the sin of Samaria— shall fall and never rise up again.* Here he represents the place of that worship, the idolaters, as it seems, crowded there, and the command given to destroy them all. All Israel was not to be destroyed. *Not the least grain* was to *fall upon the earth*[5]. Those then here represented as destroyed to the last man, must be a distinct class. Those destroyed in the temple must be the worshipers in the temple. In the Temple of God at Jerusalem, none entered except the priests. Even the space *between the porch and the altar* was set apart for the priests. But heresy is necessarily irreverent, because, not worshiping

the One God, it had no Object of reverence. Hence the temple of Baal was full *from end to end*[6], and the worshipers of the sun at Jerusalem turned *their backs toward the Temple,* and *worshiped the sun toward the East, at the door of the Temple, between the porch and the altar*[7]. The worshipers of the calves were commanded to *kiss*[8] them, and so must have filled the temple, where they were.

And I will slay the last of them. The Angel is bidden to destroy those gathered in open idolatry in one place. God, by His Omniscience, reserved the rest for His own judgment. All creatures, animate or inanimate, rational or irrational, stand at His command to fulfill His will. The mass of idolaters having perished in their idolatry, the rest, not crushed in the fall of the temple, would fain flee away, but *he that fleeth shall not flee,* God says, to any good *to themselves*[9]; yea, although they should do what for man is impossible, they should not escape God.

2. Height or depth are alike open to the Omnipresent God. The grave is not so awful as God. The sinner would gladly *dig through* into hell, bury himself, the living among the dead, if so he could escape the sight of God. But *thence,* God says, *My hand shall take them,* to place them in His presence, to receive their sentence. Or if, like the rebel angels, they could *place* their *throne amid the stars*[10] *of* God, *thence will I bring them down,* humbling, judging, condemning.

3. He had contrasted heaven and hell, as places impossible for man to reach ; as David says, [11] *If I ascend into heaven, Thou art there : If I make my bed in hell, behold Thee.* Now, of places in a manner accessible, he contrasts Mount Carmel, which rises abruptly out of the sea, with depths of that ocean which it overhangs. Carmel was in two ways a hiding place. 1) Through its caves (some say

[1] Ezek. ix. 2.   [2] Ex. xii. 23, 2 Kgs xix. 34, 5.
[3] 2 Sam. xxiv. 1, 15, 16.
[4] Others render, *break them,* i. e. the capitals, *in pieces on the head of all of them;* but יִצֵּעַ signifies *cut, wound,* rather than *break;* and the plural םָ is

more naturally referred to the same objects as כַּפְתּוֹר, than to the singular כֶּלֶם.
[5] ix. 9.   [6] 2 Kings x. 21.   [7] Ezek. viii. 16, xi. 1.
[8] Hos. xiii. 2.   [9] the force of לָהֶם.
[10] Is. xiv. 12–14.   [11] Ps. cxxxix. 8.

Before CHRIST cir. 787.	the sea, thence will I command the serpent, and he shall bite them :
	4 And though they go

into captivity before their enemies, [e] thence will I command the sword, and it shall slay them: and [f] I	Before CHRIST cir. 787. [e] Lev. 26, 33. Deut. 28. 65. Ezek. 5. 12. [f] Lev. 17. 10. Jer. 44. 11.

1000 [1], some 2000) with which it is perforated, whose entrance sometimes scarcely admits a single man; so close to each other, that a pursuer would not discern into which the fugitive had vanished; so serpentine within, that, "10 steps apart," says a traveler [2], "we could hear each others' voices, but could not see each other." "[3] Carmel is perforated by hundredfold greater or lesser clefts. Even in the garb of loveliness and richness, the majestic Mount, by its clefts, caves, and rocky battlements, excites in the wanderer who sees them for the first time, a feeling of mingled wonder and fear.—A whole army of enemies, as of nature's terrors, could hide themselves in these rock-clefts." 2) Its summit, about 1800 feet above the sea [4], "is covered with pines and oaks, and lower down with olive and laurel trees [5]." These forests furnished hiding places to robberhordes [6] at the time of our Lord. In those caves, Elijah probably at times was hidden from the persecution of Ahab and Jezebel. It seems to be spoken of as his abode [7], as also one resort of Elisha [8]. Carmel, as the Western extremity of the land, projecting into the sea, was the last place which a fugitive would reach. If he found no safety there, there was none in his whole land. Nor was there by sea;

And though they be hid [rather, *hide themselves*] *from My sight in the bottom of the sea,*

thence will I command the serpent. The sea too has its deadly serpents. Their classes are few; the individuals in those classes are much more numerous than those of the land-serpents [9]. Their shoals have furnished to sailors tokens of approaching land [9]. Their chief abode, as traced in modern times, is between the Tropics [10]. The ancients knew of them perhaps in the Persian gulf or perhaps the Red Sea [11]. All are "[12] highly venomous" and "[13] very ferocious." "[14] The virulence of their venom is equal to that of the *most* pernicious land-serpents." All things, with their will or without it through animal instinct, as the serpent, or their savage passions, as the Assyrian, fulfill the will of God. As, at His command, the fish whom He had prepared, swallowed Jonah, for his preservation, so, at His *command, the serpent* should come forth from the recesses of the sea to the sinner's greater suffering.

4. *Captivity,* at least, seemed safe. The horrors of war are over. Men enslave, but do not commonly destroy those whom they have once been at the pains to carry captive. Amos describes them in their misery, as *going willingly, gladly, into captivity before their enemies,* like a flock of sheep. Yet *thence* too, out of *the captivity,* God would command the sword, and it should slay them. So God had forewarned them by Moses, that captivity should be an occasion, not an end, of

---

[1] "The caves in Carmel are exceeding many, especially on the W. It is said above 1000. In one part, there are 400 close together." v. Richter, 65. "more than 2000," Mislin, Les Saints Lieux, ii. 46. in Smith's Bibl. Dict.
[2] Schulz, Leit. d. Hochstens, v. 186. Paulus, Reisen, vii. 43.
[3] v. Schubert, iii. 205.
[4] V. de Velde, Mem. 177.   [5] Richter, 66.
[6] Strab. 16. 2. 28.   [7] 1 Kings xviii. 19.
[8] 2 Kings ii. 25, iv. 25.
[9] Cantor, in Zoolog. Trans. T. ii. n. xxi. p. 306.
[10] "Intertropical, or near the tropics, between 90 and 230 degree long. meridian of Ferro." Schlegel, Essai sur la physion. d. serpens, p. 491. Cantor, ib. Orr; "The Hydrophidæ are found exclusively in the seas of the warmer parts of the Eastern Hemisphere, on the coasts of the Indian and Pacific Oceans. Some of them occur as far South as the coasts of N. Zealand and Australia. A few are found occasionally in salt-water tanks and canals, but they usually confine themselves to the Ocean, and rarely ascend beyond the mouths of rivers.— They are exceedingly venomous and are regarded with great dread by the fishermen in whose nets they are not unfrequently caught." Circle of the Sciences, T. iii. p. 111. Dr. Rolleston (Linacre Professor at Oxford) who kindly supplied me with these facts informs me that up to this time the hydrophidæ have only been found "in the Indian and the Pacific and the seas which are their de-

pendencies;" but he drew my attention to the extreme warmth of the Red Sea and the causes of that warmth.
[11] "It is in great measure from the statements of the Ancients, that the presence of the Hydrophidæ in the Red Sea and the Persian Gulf has been asserted; which may well be, although their observations need confirmation from further researches." Schlegel, p. 490. The accuracy of Pliny's statement as to their venom, which modern enquiry has confirmed, (Schlegel, p. 488. Duméril, Erpétologie vii. 1316–18. Cantor. p. 303, 6, 9, 10, 11. Orr, above) shews that he must have known the creature. "The most beautiful kind of snake in the world is that which lives in the waters too; they are called hydri; *inferior in venom to none of the serpents.*" N. H. xxix. 4. 22. More than half of the Red Sea is within the tropics, and it is, from its narrowness perhaps and the hot winds which blow over it from the deserts, one of the warmest seas; but it has been very little examined. Burckhardt says (Syria, 449) of the Gulf of Akaba, "the sands on the shore everywhere bore the impression of the passage of serpents, crossing each other in many directions. Ayd [an Arab fisher] told me that serpents were very common in these parts, that the fishermen were very much afraid of them." But these must have been land serpents. It is possible that both the Hebrews and Pliny knew of them through the commerce with India.
[12] Cantor, p. 303.   [13] Id. 307.   [14] Id. 309.

will set mine eyes upon
them for evil, and not for
good.

5 And the Lord GOD of
hosts *is* he that toucheth
ᵍ Mic. 1. 4.   the land, and it shall ᵍ melt,
ʰ ch. 8. 8.   ʰ and all that dwell therein
shall mourn : and it shall

rise up wholly like a flood;
and shall be drowned, as
by the flood of Egypt.

6 *It is* he that buildeth
his || †ⁱstories in the
heaven, and hath founded
his || troop in the earth;
he that ᵏcalleth for the

|| Or, *spheres.*
† Heb. *ascen-*
sions.
ⁱ Ps. 104. 3, 13.
|| Or, *bundle.*
ᵏ ch. 5. 8.

---

slaughter. ¹ *I will scatter you among the
heathen, and will draw out a sword after you.*
² *And among these nations shalt thou find no
ease—and thy life shall hang in doubt before thee,
and thou shalt fear day and night, and shalt have
none assurance of thy life.* The book of Esther
shews how cheaply the life of a whole nation
was held by Eastern conquerors; and the
book of Tobit records, how habitually Jews
were slain and cast out unburied ³. The account also that Sennacherib ⁴ avenged the
loss of his army, and *in his wrath killed many,*
is altogether in the character of Assyrian
conquerors. Unwittingly he fulfilled the
command of God, *I will command the sword and
it shall slay them.*
I will set mine eyes upon them for evil. So
David says, ⁵ *The eyes of the Lord are over the
righteous, and His ears are open to their prayers.
The Face of the Lord is against them that do
evil, to root out the remembrance of them from off
the earth.* The Eye of God rests on each
creature which He hath made, as entirely as
if He had created it alone. Every moment
is passed in His unvarying sight. But, as
man *sets his eye* on man, watching him and
with purpose of evil, so God's Eye is felt to
be on man in displeasure, when sorrow and
calamity track him and overtake him, coming he knows not how, in unlooked-for ways
and strange events. The Eye of God upon
us is our whole hope and stay and life. It is
on the Confessor in prison, the Martyr on the
rack, the poor in their sufferings, the mourner
in the chamber of death, for good. What
when everywhere that Eye, the Source of
all good, rests on His creature only for
evil! *and not for good,* he adds; *not,* as is the
wont and the Nature of God; *not,* as He had
promised, if they were faithful; *not,* as perhaps they thought, *for good.* He utterly
shuts out all hope of good. It shall be all
evil, and no good, such as is hell.
5. And Who is He Who should do this?
God, at Whose command are all creatures.
This is the hope of His servants; whence

Hezekiah begins his prayer, *Lord of hosts,
God of Israel* ⁶. This is the hopelessness of
His enemies. *That toucheth the land* or *earth,
and it shall melt,* rather, *hath melted.* His
Will and its fulfillment are one. ⁷ *He spake,
and it was; He commanded and it stood fast.*
His Will is first, as the cause of what is done;
in time they co-exist. He hath no need to
put forth His strength; a touch, the slightest
indication of His Will, sufficeth. If the solid
earth, how much more its inhabitants! So
the Psalmist says, ⁸ *The heathen raged, the
kingdoms were moved; He uttered His voice, the
earth melted.* The hearts of men melt when
they are afraid of His Presence; human
armies melt away, dispersed; the great globe
itself shall dissolve into its ancient chaos at
His Will.
6. *He that buildeth His stories.* The word
commonly means *steps,* nor is there any reason
to alter it. We read of *the third heaven* ⁹, *the
heavens of heavens* ¹⁰; i. e. heavens to which
this heaven is as earth. They are different
ways of expressing the vast unseen space
which God has created, divided, as we know,
through the distance of the fixed stars, into
countless portions, of which the lower, or
further removed, are but as *steps* to the Presence of the Great King, where, *above all
heavens* ¹¹, Christ sitteth at the Right Hand of
God. It comes to the same, if we suppose
the word to mean *upper chambers* ¹². The metaphor would still signify heavens above our
heavens.
And hath founded His troop [lit. *band* ¹³] *in
the earth;* probably, *founded His arch upon the
earth,* i. e. His visible heaven, which seems,
like an arch, to span the earth. The whole
then describes " all things visible and invisible ; " all of this our solar system, and all
beyond it, the many gradations to the Throne
of God. " ¹⁴ He daily *buildeth His stories in
the heavens,* when He raiseth up His saints
from things below to heavenly places, presid-
ing over them, ascending in them. In devout
wayfarers too, whose *conversation is in Heaven* ¹⁵,

¹ Lev. xxvi. 33.   ² Deut. xxviii. 65, 6.
³ Tob. i. 17, ii. 3. ⁴ Ib. i. 18. ⁵ Ps. xxxiv. 15, 16.
⁶ Is. xxxvii. 16. ⁷ Ps. xxxiii. 9. ⁸ Ps. xlvi. 6.
⁹ 2 Cor. xii. 2.
¹⁰ Deut. x. 14, 1 Kings viii. 27, Ps. cxlviii. 4.
¹¹ Eph. iv. 10

¹² as if מִעֲלוֹת were the same as עֲלִיוֹת.
¹³ It is used of "a bunch of hyssop" (Ex. xii. 22);
"*bands* of a yoke" (Is. lviii. 6); "a band of men"
(2 Sam. ii. 25); hence in Arab. Ijâd signifies an arch,
as firmly held together, as our *apse* is from the
Greek ἅπτω.   ¹⁴ Dion.   ¹⁵ Phil. iii. 20.

waters of the sea, and poureth them out upon the

face of the earth : [1] The LORD is his name.

7 *Are* ye not as children

of the Ethiopians unto me, O children of Israel? saith the LORD. Have not I brought up Israel out of the land of Egypt? and

---

He ascendeth, sublimely and mercifully indwelling their hearts. In those who have the fruition of Himself in those Heavens, He ascendeth by the glory of beatitude and the loftiest contemplation, as He walketh in those who walk, and resteth in those who rest in Him."

To this description of His power, Amos, as before [1], adds that signal instance of its exercise on the ungodly, the flood, the pattern and type of judgments which no sinner escapes. God then hath the power to do this. Why should He not?

Are ye not as children of the Ethiopians unto Me, O children of Israel! Their boast and confidence was that they were children of the Patriarch, to whom God made the promises. But they, not following the faith nor doing the deeds of Israel, who was *a prince with God,* or of Abraham, the father of the faithful, had, for *Bene Israel,* children of Israel, become as *Bene Cushiim, children of the Ethiopians,* descendants of Ham, furthest off from the knowledge and grace of God, the unchangeableness of whose color was an emblem of unchangeableness in evil [2]. *Can the Ethiopian change his skin, or the leopard his spots? then may ye also do good, that are accustomed to do evil.*

Have I not brought up [Did I not bring up] Israel out of the land of Egypt? Amos blends in one their plea and God's answer. God, by bringing them up out of Egypt, had pledged His truth to them to be their God, to protect and preserve them. True! so long as they retained God as their God, and kept His laws. God chose them, that they might choose Him. By casting Him off, as their Lord and God, they cast themselves off and out of God's protection. By estranging themselves from God, they became as strangers in His sight. His act in bringing them up from Egypt had lost its meaning for them. It became no more than any other event in His Providence, by which He brought up *the Philistines from Caphtor,* who yet were aliens from Him, and *the Syrians from Kir,* who, He had foretold, should be carried back thither.

This immigration of the Philistines from Caphtor must have taken place before the return of Israel from Egypt. For Moses says [3], *The Caphtorim, who came forth from*

Caphtor, had at this time *destroyed the Avvim who dwelt in villages unto Gazah, and dwelt in their stead.* An entire change in their affairs had also taken place in the four centuries and a half since the days of Isaac. In the time of Abraham and Isaac, Philistia was a kingdom ; its capital, Gerar. Its king had a standing army, Phichol being *the captain of the host* [4]: he had also a privy councillor, Ahuzzath [5]. From the time after the Exodus, Philistia had ceased to be a kingdom, Gerar disappears from history ; the power of Philistia is concentrated in five new towns, Gaza, Ashdod, Askelon, Gath, Ekron, with five heads, who consult and act as one [6]. The Caphtorim are in some sense also distinct from the old Philistines. They occupy a district not co-extensive with either the old or the new land of the Philistines. In the time of Saul, another Philistine clan is mentioned, the Cherethite. The Amalekites made a marauding inroad into the South country of the Cherethites [7]; which immediately afterward is called [8] *the land of the Philistines.* Probably then, there were different immigrations of the same tribe into Palestine, as there were different immigrations of Danes or Saxons into England, or as there have been and are from the old world into the new, America and Australia. They were then all merged in one common name, as English, Scotch, Irish, are in the United States. The first immigration may have been that from the Casluhim, *out of whom came Philistim* [9]; a second, from the Caphtorim, a kindred people, since they are named next to the Casluhim [10], as descendants of Mizraim. Yet a third were doubtless the Cherethim. But all were united under the one name of Philistines, as Britons, Danes, Saxons, Normans, are united under the one name of English. Of these immigrations, that from Caphtor, even if (as seems probable) second in time, was the chief; which agrees with the great accession of strength, which the Philistines had received at the time of the Exodus; whence the Mediterranean had come to be called by their name, *the sea of the Philistines* [11]; and, in Moses' song of thanksgiving, *the inhabitants of Philistia* are named on a level with *all the inhabitants of Canaan* [12]; and God led His people by the way of Mount Sinai, in order not to expose them at once to

Before CHRIST cir. 787.

the [m] Philistines from [n] Caphtor, and the Syrians from [o] Kir?

8 Behold, [p] the eyes of the Lord God *are* upon the sinful kingdom, and I [q] will destroy it from off the face of the earth; saving that I will not utterly destroy the house of Jacob, saith the LORD.

9 For, lo, I will command, and I will † sift the house of Israel among all nations, like as *corn* is sifted in a sieve, yet shall not the least † grain fall upon the earth.

m Jer. 47. 4.
n Deut. 2. 23. Jer. 47. 4.
o ch. 1. 5.
p ver. 4.
q Jer. 30. 11. & 31. 35, 36. Obad. 16, 17.

† Heb. *cause to move.*
† Heb. *stone.*

so powerful an enemy[1]. A third immigration of Cherethim, in the latter part of the period of the Judges, would account for the sudden increase of strength, which they seem then to have received. For whereas heretofore those whom God employed to chasten Israel in their idolatries, were kings of Mesopotamia, Moab, Hazor, Midian, Amalek, and the children of the East[2], and Philistia had, at the beginning of the period, lost Gaza, Ashkelon, and Ekron[3], to Israel, and was repulsed by Shamgar, thenceforth, to the time of David, they became the great scourge of Israel on the West of Jordan, as Ammon was on the East.

The Jewish traditions in the LXX, the Vulgate, and three Targums, agree that Caphtor was Cappadocia, which, in that it extended to the Black Sea, might be called *I, sea-coast*, lit. "habitable land[4]," as contrasted with the sea which washed it, whether it surrounded it or no. The Cherethites may have come from Crete, as an intermediate resting-place in their migrations.

8. *Behold the eyes of the Lord* are *upon the sinful kingdom. The sinful kingdom* may mean each *sinful kingdom*, as St. Paul says[5], God *will render unto every man according to his deeds,—unto them who do not obey the truth but obey unrighteousness, tribulation and anguish upon every soul of man that doeth evil, of the Jew first, and also of the Gentile.* His *Eyes* are *on the sinful kingdom*, whatsoever or wheresoever it be, and so on Israel also: *and I will destroy it from off the face of the earth.* In this case, the emphasis would be on the, "I will not *utterly* destroy." God would destroy sinful kingdoms, yet Israel, although sinful, He would not *utterly* destroy, but would leave a remnant, as He had so often promised. Yet perhaps, and more probably, the contrast is between *the kingdom* and *the house of Israel. The kingdom*, being founded in sin, bound up inseparably with sin, God says, *I will destroy from off the face of the earth*, and it ceased for ever. Only, with the kingdom, He says, *I will not utterly destroy the house of Jacob*, to whom were the promises, and to whose seed, whosoever were the true Israel, those promises should be kept. So He explains;

9. *For lo! I will command!* lit. *lo! see, I am commanding.* He draws their attention to it, as something which shall shortly be; and inculcates that He is the secret disposer of all which shall befall them. *And I will sift the house of Israel among all nations.* Amos enlarges the prophecy of Hosea, *they shall be wanderers among the nations.* He adds two thoughts; the violence with which they shall be shaken, and that this their unsettled life, to and fro, shall be not *among the nations* only, but *in all* nations. In every quarter of the world, and in well-nigh every nation in every quarter, Jews have been found. The whole earth is, as it were, one vast sieve in the Hands of God, in which Israel is shaken from one end to the other. There has been one ceaseless tossing to and fro, as the corn in the sieve is tossed from side to side, and rests nowhere, till all is sifted. Each nation in whom they have been found has been an instrument of their being shaken, sifted, severed, the grain from the dirt and chaff. And yet in their whole compass, *not the least grain*, no solid corn, not one grain, should *fall to the earth.* The chaff and dust would be blown away by the air; the dirt which clave to it would fall through; but *no one grain.* God, in all these centuries, has had an eye on each soul of His people in their dispersion throughout all lands. The righteous too have been shaken up and down, through and through; yet not one soul has been lost, which, by the help of God's Holy Spirit, willed truly and earnestly to be saved. Before Christ came, they who were His, believed in Him Who should come; when He came, they who were His were converted to Him; as S. Paul saith[6], *Hath God cast away His people? God forbid! For I also am an Israelite, of the seed of Abraham, of the tribe of Benjamin—God hath not cast away His people which He foreknew—At this present time also there is a remnant, according to the election of grace.*

"[7] What is here said of all, God doth daily in each of the elect. For they are *the*

[1] Ex. xiii. 17.
[2] Judg. iii.—x. 5.
[3] Ib. i. 18.
[4] אִי from אוי.
[5] Rom. ii. 6-9.
[6] Rom. xi. 1, 2, 5.
[7] Rib.

Before CHRIST cir. 787.	10 All the sinners of my people s h a l l die by the sword, ʳwhich say, The	evil shall not overtake nor prevent us.	Before CHRIST cir. 787.
ʳ ch. 6. 3.		11 ¶ ˢ In that day will	ˢ Acts 15. 16, 17.

wheat of God, which, in order to be *laid up in the heavenly garner*, must be pure from chaff and dust. To this end He sifts them by afflictions and troubles, in youth, manhood, old age, wheresoever they are, in whatsoever occupied, and proves them again and again. At one time the elect enjoyeth tranquillity of mind, is bedewed by heavenly refreshments, prayeth as he wills, loveth, gloweth, hath no taste for ought except God. Then again he is dry, experienceth the heaven to be as brass, his prayer is hindered by distracting thoughts, his feet are as lead to deeds of virtue, his *hands hang down*, his *knees* are *feeble*[1], he dreads death; he sticks fast, languishes. He is shaken in a sieve, that he may mistrust self, place his hope in God, and the dust of vain-glory may be shaken off. He is proved, that it may appear whether he cleave to God for the reward of present enjoyment, or for the hope of future, for longing for the glory of God and for love of Himself. God suffereth him also to be sifted by the devil through various temptations to sin, as he said to the Apostle, *Simon, lo! Satan hath desired you, to sift you as wheat*[2]. But this is the power of God, this His grace to the elect, this the devil attaineth by his sifting, that the dust of immoderate self-love, of vain confidence, of love of the world, should fall off: *this* Satan effecteth not, that the least deed which appertaineth to the inward house and the dwelling which they prepare in their souls for God, should perish. Rather, as we see in holy Job, virtues will increase, grow, be strengthened."

10. *All the sinners of My people shall perish.* At the last, when the longsuffering of God has been despised to the uttermost, His Providence is exact in His justice, as in His love. As not *one grain should fall to the earth*, so not one sinner should escape. "[3] Not because they sinned aforetime, but because they persevered in sin until death. The Æthiopians are changed into sons of God, if they repent; and the sons of God pass away into Æthiopians, if they fall into the depth of sin."

Which say, The evil shall not overtake nor prevent us. Their security was the cause of their destruction. They perished the more miserably, being buoyed up by the false confidence that they should not perish. So it was in both destructions of Jerusalem. Of the first, Jeremiah says to the false prophet Hananiah[4], *Thus saith the Lord, Thou hast broken the yokes of wood; but thou shalt make for them*

yokes of iron; and to Zedekiah[5], *Obey, I beseech thee, the voice of the Lord, which I speak unto thee; so shall it be well unto thee, and thy soul shall live. But if thou refuse to go forth—thou shalt not escape out of their hand, but shalt be taken by the hand of the king of Babylon, and thou shalt burn this city with fire.* At the second, while the Christians (mindful of our Lord's words) fled to Pella, the Jews were, to the last, encouraged by their false prophets to resist. "The cause of this destruction," at the burning of the temple, says their own historian[6], "was a false prophet, who on that day proclaimed to those in the city, ' God commands to go up to the temple, to receive the signs of deliverance.' There were too, at that time, among the people many prophets suborned by the tyrants, bidding them await the help from God, that they might not desert, and that hope might prevail with those, who were above fear and restraint. Man is soon persuaded in calamity. And when the deceiver promises release from the evils which are upon him, the sufferer gives himself wholly up to hope. These deceivers then and liars against God at this time mispersuaded the wretched people, so that they neither regarded, nor believed, the plain evident prodigies, which foretokened the coming desolation, but, like men stupefied, who had neither eyes nor mind, disobeyed the warnings of God."—Then, having related some of the prodigies which occurred, he adds[7];—"But of these signs, some they interpreted after their own will, some they despised, until they were convicted of folly by the capture of their country and their own destruction." So too now, none are so likely to perish forever, as they *who say, The evil shall not overtake us.* "I will repent hereafter." "I will make my peace with God before I die." "There is time enough yet." "Youth is for pleasure, age for repentance." "God will forgive the errors of youth, and the heat of our passions." "Any time will do for repentance; health and strength promise long life;" "I cannot do without this or that now." "I will turn to God, only not yet." "God is merciful and full of compassion." Because Satan thus deludes thousands upon thousands to their destruction, God cuts away all such vain hopes with His word, *All the sinners of My people shall die which say, the evil shall not overtake nor come upon us.*

11. *In that day I will raise up.* Amos, as the prophets were taught to do, sums up his

---

[1] Heb. xii. 12.
[3] S. Jer.
[2] S. Luke xxii. 31.
[4] Jer. xxviii. 13.
[5] Ib. xxxviii. 20, 23; add xxvii. 9, 10, 19.
[6] Joseph. B. J. 6. 5. § 2. 3.
[7] Ib. § 4.

I raise up the tabernacle of David that is fallen, and † close up the b r e a c h e s

thereof; and I will raise up his ruins, and I will build it as in the days of old:

prophecy of woe with this one full promise of overflowing good. For the ten tribes, in their separate condition, there was no hope, no future. He had pronounced the entire destruction of the *kingdom* of Israel. The ten tribes were, thenceforth, only an aggregate of individuals, good or bad. They had no separate corporate existence. In their spiritual existence, they still belonged to the one family of Israel; and, belonging to it, were heirs of the promises made to it. When no longer separate, individuals out of its tribes were to become Apostles to their whole people and to the Gentiles. Of individuals in it, God had declared His judgment, anticipating the complete exactness of the Judgment of the Great Day. *All the sinners of* His *people* should *die* an untimely death *by the sword;* not one of those who were the true grain should perish with the chaff.

He now foretells, how that salvation, of those indeed His own, should be effected through the house of David, in whose line Christ was to come. He speaks of the house of David, not in any terms of royal greatness; he tells, not of its palaces, but of its ruins. Under the word *tabernacle*, he probably blends the ideas, that it should be in a poor condition, and yet that it should be the means whereby God should protect His people. The *succah*, tabernacle, (translated *booth* in Jonah[1]), was originally a rude hut, formed of *intertwined*[2] branches. It is used of the cattle-shed[3], and of the rough tents used by soldiers in war[4] or by the watchman in the vineyard[5], and of those wherein God *made the children of Israel to dwell, when He brought them out of the land of Egypt*[6]. The name of the feast of *Tabernacles, Succoth,* as well as the rude temporary huts[7] in which they were commanded to dwell, associated the name with a state of outward poverty under God's protection. Hence, perhaps, the word is employed also of the secret place of the Presence of God[8]. Isaiah, as well as Amos, seems, in the use of the same word[9], to hint that what is poor and mean in man's sight would be, in the Hands of God, an effectual protection. This *hut of David* was also at that time to be *fallen.* When Amos prophesied, it had been weakened by the schism of the ten tribes, but Azariah, its king, was mighty[10]. Amos had already foretold the destruction of the *palaces of Jerusalem*

by fire[11]. Now he adds, that the abiding condition of the house of David should be a state of decay and weakness, and that from that state, not human strength, but God Himself should *raise* it. *I will raise up the hut of David, the fallen.* He does not say, of *that* time, "the hut that *is* fallen," as if it were already fallen, but *the hut, the fallen*[12], i. e. the hut of which the character should then be its falling, its caducity. So, under a different figure, Isaiah prophesied, *There shall come forth a rod out of the stump*[13] *of Jesse, and a Branch shall put forth from its roots.* When the trunk was hewn down even with the ground, and the rank grass had covered the *stump,* that *rod* and *Branch* should come forth which should rule the earth, and *to* which *the Gentiles should seek*[14]. From these words of Amos, "the Son of the fallen," became, among the Jews, one of the titles of the Christ. Both in the legal and mystical schools the words of Amos are alleged, in proof of the fallen condition of the house of David, when the Christ should come. "Who would expect," asks one[15], "that God would raise up the fallen tabernacle of David? and yet it is said, *I will raise up the tabernacle of David which is fallen down.* And who would hope that the whole world should become one band? as it is written[16], *Then I will turn to the people a pure language, that they may all call upon the name of the Lord, to serve him with one shoulder.* This is no other than the king Messiah." And in the Talmud[17]; "R. Nachman said to R. Isaac; Hast thou heard when 'the Son of the fallen' shall come? He answered, Who is he? R. Nachman; The Messiah. R. Isaac; Is the Messiah so called? R. Nachman; Yes; *In that day will I raise up the tabernacle of David which is fallen down.*"

And close up, lit. *wall up, the breaches thereof.* The house of David had at this time sustained breaches. It had yet more serious breaches to sustain thereafter. The first great breach was the rending off of the ten tribes. It sustained breaches, through the Assyrians; and yet more when itself was carried away captive to Babylon, and so many of its residue fled into Egypt. Breaches are repaired by new stones; the losses of the house of David were to be filled up by accessions from the Gentiles. God Himself should *close up the breaches;* so should they remain closed; and

[1] Jon. iv. 5, Gen. xxxiii. 17.　　[2] from סכך i. q. שׂוּךְ.
[3] Gen. xxxiii. 17.　　　　　　[4] 2 Sam. xi. 11.
[5] Is. i. 8, Job xxvii. 18.　　　　[6] Lev. xxiii. 43.
[7] Ib. 40, see on Hos. xii. 9. p. 79.
[8] Ps. xviii. 11, Job xxxvi. 29.　　　[9] Is. iv. 6.

[10] 2 Chr. xxvi. 6-15.　　[11] ii. 5.　　[12] הַנֹּפֶלֶת.
[13] גֶּזַע Is. xi. 1.　　　　　　　[14] Ib. 10.
[15] Bereshith Rabba S. 88. fin. quoted by Schoettg.
loc. gen. n. 18. p. 70.　　　　　[16] Zeph. iii. 9.
[17] Sanhedr. f. 96. 2. Schoettg. de Mess. p. 16.

Before
C H R I S T
cir. 787.

t Obad. 19.
u Num. 24. 18.

12 [t]That they may possess the remnant of [u]Edom, and of all the heathen, [†]which are called by my name, saith the LORD that doeth this.

Before
C H R I S T
cir. 787.

† Heb. *upon whom my name is called.*

the gates of hell should not prevail against the Church which He builded. Amos heaps on one another the words implying destruction. A *hut* and that *falling ; breaches ; ruins ;* (lit. *his ruinated, his destructions*). But he also speaks of it in a way which excludes the idea of *the hut of David,* being "the royal Dynasty " or "the kingdom of Judah." For he speaks of it, not as an abstract thing, such as a kingdom is, but as a whole, consisting of individuals. He speaks not only of *the hut of David,* but of " *their (fem.)* breaches," " *his* ruins," that God would " build *her* up," "that *they* (masc.) may inherit;" using apparently this variety of numbers and genders [1], in order to shew that he is speaking of one living whole, the Jewish Church, now rent in two by the great schism of Jeroboam, but which should be reunited into one body, members of which should win the Heathen to the true faith in God. " I will raise up," he says, "the tabernacle of David, the fallen, and will wall up *their* breaches, " [the breaches of the two portions into which it had been rent] and I will raise up *his* ruins [the "ruinated places" of David] and I will build *her* [as one whole] as in the days of old, [before the rent of the ten tribes, when all worshiped as one], that *they,* (masc.) i. e. individuals who should go forth out of her, " may inherit, &c."

12. *That they may possess,* rather, *inherit, the remnant of Edom.* The restoration was not to be for themselves alone. No gifts of God end in the immediate object of His bounty and love. They were restored, in order that they, the first objects of God's mercies, might win others to God; not Edom only, *but all nations, upon whom,* God says, *My Name is called.* Plainly then, it is no temporal subjugation, nor any earthly kingdom. The words, *upon whom the name is called,* involve, in any case, belonging to, and being owned by, him whose name is called upon them. It is said of the wife bearing the name of the husband and becoming his, *let thy name be called upon us* [2]. When Jacob specially adopts Ephraim and Manasseh as his own, he says, *let my name be named upon them, and the name of My fathers, Abraham and Isaac* [3]. In relation to God, the words are used of persons and of places especially appropriated to God ; as the whole Jewish Church and

people, His Temple [4], His Prophets [5], the city of Jerusalem [6] by virtue of the Temple built there. Contrariwise, Isaiah pleads to God, that the Heathen *were never called by Thy Name* [7]. This relation of being *called* by the *Name* of God, was not outward only, nor was it ineffective. Its characteristics were holiness imparted by God to man, and protection by God. Thus Moses, in his blessing on Israel if obedient, says [8], *The Lord shall establish thee an holy people unto Himself, as He hath sworn to thee, if thou shalt keep the commandments of the Lord thy God, and walk in His ways ; and all the people of the earth shall see that the Name of the Lord thy God is called upon thee, and they shall fear thee.* And Jeremiah says to God [9], *Thy word was unto me the joy and rejoicing of my heart ; for Thy name was called upon me, O Lord God of Hosts.*

Israel then, or the Jewish Church, was to inherit, or take into itself, not Edom only, but all nations, and that, by their belonging to God. Edom, as the brother of Israel and yet his implacable enemy, stands as a symbol of all who were alien from God, over against His people. He says, the *residue of Edom,* because he had foretold the destruction which was first to come upon Edom [10] ; and Holy Scripture everywhere speaks of those who should be converted, as a *remnant* only. The Jews themselves are the keepers and witnesses of these words. Was it not foretold? It stands written. Is it not fulfilled? The whole world from this country to China, and from China round again to us, as far as it is Christian, and as, year by year, more are gathered into the fold of Christ, are the inheritance of those who were the seed of Abraham, Isaac and Jacob.

S. James quoted these words in the Council of Jerusalem, to show how the words of the Prophet were in harmony with what S. Peter had related, how [11] *God at the first did visit the Gentiles, to take out of them a people for His Name.* He quotes the words as they stood in the version which was understood by the Gentiles who came from Antioch. In it the words are paraphrased, but the meaning remains the same. The Greek translators took away the metaphor, in order, probably, to make the meaning more intelligible to Greeks, and paraphrased the Hebrew words, imagining other words, as like as might he

[1] Hengstenberg, Christologie, i. 447, 8 ed. 2.
[2] Is. iv. 1.   [3] Gen. xlviii. 16.
[4] 1 Kings viii. 43, Jer. vii. 10, 11, 14, 30, xxxiv. 15.

[5] Jer. xv. 16.   [6] Dan. ix. 18, 19.   [7] Is. lxiii. 19.
[8] Deut. xxviii. 9, 10.   [9] l. c.   [10] See ab. 106.
[11] Acts xv. 14.

Before
CHRIST
cir. 787.

x Lev. 26. 5.

13 Behold, [x]the days come, saith the LORD, that the plowman shall over-

take the reaper, and the treader of grapes him that [†]soweth seed; [y]and the

Before
CHRIST
cir. 787.

† Heb. *draweth forth.*
y Joel 3. 18.

to the Hebrew[1]. They render, "that the residue of men may seek, and all the nations upon whom My name is called." The force of the prophecy lies in these last words, that "the Name of God should be called upon all nations." S. James, then, quoted the words as they were familiar to his hearers, not correcting those which did not impair the meaning. The so doing, he shews us incidentally, that even imperfection of translation does not empty the fullness of God's word. The words, "shall seek the Lord," although not representing anything expressed here in the original, occur in the corresponding prophecy of Isaiah as to the root of Jesse[2], *In that day there shall be a root* (i. e. a sucker from the root) *of Jesse, which shall stand for an ensign of the people, and to it shall the Gentiles seek.* It may be, that S. James purposely uses the plural, *the words of the prophets,* in order to include, together with the Prophet Amos, other prophets who had foretold the same thing. The statements, that the Jewish Church should inherit the Gentiles, that the Name of God should be called upon the Gentiles, and that the Gentiles should seek the Lord, are parts of one whole ; that they should be called, that they should obey the call, and, obeying, he enrolled in the one family of God.

13. *Behold the days are coming.* The Day of the Lord is ever coming on : every act, good or bad, is drawing it on : everything which fills up the measure of iniquity or which "hastens the accomplishment of the number of the elect ;" all time hastens it by. *The ploughman shall overtake the reaper and the treader of grapes him that soweth seed.* The image is taken from God's promise in the law[3] ; *Your threshing shall reach unto the vintage, and the vintage shall reach unto the sowing time ;* which is the order of agriculture. The harvest should be so copious that it should not be threshed out until the vintage : the vintage so large, that, instead of ending, as usual, in the middle of the 7th month, it should continue on to the seed-time in November. Amos appears purposely to have altered this. He describes what is wholly beyond nature, in order that it might the more appear that he was speaking of no mere gifts of nature, but, under natural emblems, of the abundance of gifts of grace. *The ploughman,* who breaks up the fallow ground, *shall overtake,* or *throng, the reaper.*

The *ploughman* might *throng,* or *join on* to *the reaper,* either following upon him, or being followed by him ; either preparing the soil for the harvest which the reaper gathers in, or breaking it up anew for a fresh harvest after the in-gathering. But the vintage falls between the harvest and the seed-time. If then by the *ploughmen thronging on the reaper,* we understand that the harvest should, for its abundance, not be over before the fresh seed-time, then, since the vintage is much nearer to the seed-time than the harvest had been, the words, *he that treadeth out the grapes, him that soweth the seed,* would only say the same less forcibly. In the other way, it is one continuous whole. So vast would be the soil to be cultivated, so beyond all the powers of the cultivator, and yet so rapid and unceasing the growth, that seed-time and harvest would be but one. So our Lord says[4], *Say not ye, There are yet four months, and then cometh harvest ? Behold, I say unto you, Lift up your eyes, and look on the fields ; for they are white already to harvest. Four months* ordinarily intervened between seed-time and harvest. Among these Samaritans, seed-time and harvest were one. They had not, like the Jews, had teachers from God ; yet, as soon as our Lord taught them, they believed. But, as seed time and harvest should be one, so should the vintage be continuous with the following seed-time. *The treader of grapes,* the last crowning act of the year of cultivation, should join on to *him that soweth* (lit. *draweth* forth, soweth broadcast, scattereth far and wide the) *seed.* All this is beyond nature, and so, the more in harmony with what went before, the establishment of a kingdom of grace, in which *the Heathen* should have *the Name of God called upon* them. He had foretold[5] to them, how God would *send famine on the land, not a famine of bread, nor a thirst for water, but of hearing the words of the Lord.* Now, under the same image, he declares the repeal of that sentence. He foretells, not the fullness only of God's gifts, but their unbroken continuance. "[6] All shall succeed one another, so that no day should be void of corn, wine, and gladness." And they shall not follow only on one another, but shall all go on together in one perpetual round of toil and fruitfulness. There shall be one unceasing inpouring of riches ; no break in the heavenly husbandry ; labor shall at once yield fruit ; the harvest shall

[1] As though there had stood אדם for אדום ; and ירשו יד for יירש, the difference in each case lying in one letter.

[2] Is. xi. 10.
[4] S. John iv. 35.
[6] S. Jer.

[3] Lev. xxvi. 5.
[5] viii. 11.

Before CHRIST cir. 787.	

mountains shall drop ‖ sweet wine, and all the hills shall melt.

¶ Or, *new wine.*

ˣ Jer. 30. 3.

14 ˣ And I will bring again the captivity of my people of Israel, and ᵃ they shall build the waste cities,

ᵃ Is. 61. 4. & 65. 21.
Ezek. 36. 33-36.

and inhabit *them;* and they shall plant vineyards, and drink the wine thereof; they shall also make gardens, and eat the fruit of them.

15 And I will plant

Before CHRIST cir. 787.	

---

but encourage fresh labor. The end shall come swiftly on the beginning; the end shall not close the past only, but issue forth anew. Such is the character of the toils of the Gospel. All the works of grace go on in harmony together; each helps on the other; in one, the fallow-ground of the heart is broken up; in another, seed is sown, the beginning of a holy conversation; in another, is the full richness of the ripened fruit, in advanced holiness or the blood of Martyrs. And so, also, of the ministers of Christ, some are adapted especially to one office, some to another; yet all together carry on His one work. All, too, Patriarchs, Prophets, Apostles, shall meet together in one; they who, before Christ's Coming, "[1] sowed the seed, the promises of the Blessed Seed to come," and they who *entered into their labors,* not to displace, but to complete them; all shall rejoice together in that Seed which is Christ.

And the mountains shall drop sweet wine and all the hills shall melt. Amos takes the words of Joel, in order to identify their prophecies [2], yet strengthens the image. For instead of saying, *the hills shall flow with milk,* he says, *they shall melt, dissolve themselves* [3]. Such shall be the abundance and super-abundance of blessing, that it shall be as though the hills dissolved themselves in the rich streams which they poured down. The mountains and hills may be symbols, in regard either to their height,'or their natural barrenness or their difficulty of cultivation. In past times they were scenes of idolatry [4]. In the time of the Gospel, all should be changed; all should be above nature. All should be obedient to God; all, full of the graces and gifts of God. What was exalted, like the Apostles, should be exalted not for itself, but in order to pour out the streams of life-giving doctrine and truth, which would refresh and gladden the faithful. And the lesser heights, *the hills,* should, in their degree, pour out the same streams. Everything, heretofore barren and unfruitful, should overflow with spiritual blessing. The mountains and hills of Judæa, with their terraced sides clad with the vine were a natural symbol fruitfulness to the Jews, but they themselves could not

think that natural fruitfulness was meant under this imagery. It would have been a hyperbole as to things of nature; but what, in natural things, is a hyperbole, is but a faint shadow of the joys and rich delights and glad fruitfulness of grace.

14. *And I will bring again the captivity of My people.* Where all around is spiritual, there is no reason to take this alone as earthly. An earthly restoration to Canaan had no value, except as introductory to the spiritual. The two tribes were, in a great measure, restored to their own land, when Zachariah, being [5] *filled with the Holy Ghost, prophesied,* as then about to be accomplished, that *God hath visited and redeemed His people, and hath raised up a horn of salvation to us in the house of His servant David, as He spake by the mouth of His holy prophets—that we, being delivered from the hands of our enemies, might serve Him without fear, in holiness and righteousness before Him.* So our Lord said [6]; *ye shall know the truth, and the truth shall make you free.— Whosoever committeth sin, is the servant of sin.—If the Son shall make you free, ye shall be free indeed.* And Saint Paul [7], *The law of the Spirit of life in Christ Jesus has made me free from the law of sin and death.*

And they shall build the waste [rather *shall build waste* [8]] *cities.* "As they who are freed from captivity and are no longer in fear of the enemy, *build cities and plant vineyards* and gardens," so shall these unto God. "This," says one of old [1], "needs no exposition, since, throughout the world, amid the desert of Heathendom, which was before deserted by God, Churches of Christ have arisen, which, for the firmness of faith, may be called *cities,* and, for the gladness of *hope which maketh not ashamed, vineyards,* and for the sweetness of charity, gardens; wherein they dwell, who have builded them through the word; whence they drink the wine of gladness, who formed them by precepts; whence they eat fruits, who advanced them by counsels, because, as *he who reapeth,* so he too who *buildeth* such *cities,* and he who *planteth* such *vineyards,* and he who *maketh* such *gardens, receiveth wages and gathereth fruit unto life eternal* [9]."

15. *And I will plant them upon their own*

---

[1] Rup. [2] See ab. p. 94, 5, 149. [3] התמוגגנה.
[4] See above, p. 30. [5] S. Luke i. 68–70, 4, 5.

[6] S. John viii. 32, 4, 6. [7] Rom. viii. 2.
[8] There is no article. [9] S. John iv. 36.

Before
CHRIST
cir. 787. them upon their land, and ‖ [b] they shall no more be Before
CHRIST
cir. 787.

[b] Is. 60. 21. Jer. 32. 41. Ezek. 34. 28.
Joel 3. 20.

land. The promises and threatenings of God
are, to individuals, conditional upon their
continuing to be of that character, to which
God annexes those promises or threats.
"[1] The God of all often promises, when those
who receive the promises, by joying in iniquity hinder those promises from taking
effect. At times also he threatens heavy
things, and they who for their offences were
the objects of those threats, being, through
fear of them, converted, do not in act experience them." The two tribes received some
little shadow of fulfillment of these promises
on the return from Babylon. *They were
planted in their own land.* The non-fulfillment
of the rest, as well as the evident symbolic
character of part of it, must have shewn them
that such fulfillment was the beginning, not
the end. Their land was *the Lord's land;*
banishment from it was banishment from the
special presence of God, from the palce where
He manifested Himself, where alone the
typical sacrifices, the appointed means of
reconciliation, could be offered. Restoration
to their own land was the outward symbol
of restoration to God's favor, of which it was
the fruit. It was a condition of the fulfillment of those other promises, the Coming of
Him in Whom the promises were laid up,
the Christ. He was not simply to be of
David's seed, according to the flesh. Prophecy, as time went on, declared His birth at
Bethlehem, His revelation in Galilee, His
Coming to His Temple, His sending forth
His law from Jerusalem. Without some
restoration to their own land, these things
could not be. Israel was restored in the
flesh, that, after the flesh, the Christ might
be born of them, where God foretold that He
should be born. But the temporal fulfillment
ended with that Event in time in which
they were to issue, for whose sake they were;
His Coming. They were but the vestibule to
the spiritual. As shadows, they ceased when the
Sun arose. As means, they ended, when the
end, whereto they served, came. There was no
need of a temporal Zion, when He Who was
to send forth His law thence, had come and
sent it forth. No need of a Temple when
He Who was to be its Glory, had come, illumined it, and was gone. No need of one of
royal birth in Bethlehem, when *the Virgin*
had *conceived and borne a Son,* and *God* had
been *with us.* And so as to other prophecies.
'All which were bound to the land of Judah,
were accomplished. As the true Israel expanded and embraced all nations, the whole
earth became *the land* of God's people. Pal-

estine had had its prerogatives, because God
manifested Himself there, was worshiped
there. When God's people was enlarged, so
as *to inherit the heathen,* and God was worshiped everywhere, His land too was everywhere. His promises accompanied His people, and these were in all lands. His words
then, *I will plant them upon their own land, and
they shall no more be pulled up out of their land
which I have given them,* expanded with their
expansion. It is a promise of perpetu-
ity, like that of our Lord; *Lo! I am with
you alway, even to the end of the world. The
gates of hell shall not prevail against* the Church,
the people of God. The world may gnash
its teeth; kings may oppress; persecutors
may harass; popular rage may trample on
her; philosophy may scoff at her; unbelief
may deny the promises made to her; the
powers of darkness may rage around her;
her own children may turn against her. In
vain! "[2] She may be shaken by persecutions, she cannot be uprooted; she may be
tempted, she cannot be overcome. For the
Lord God Almighty, the Lord her God,
hath promised that He will do it, Whose
promise is the law to nature."
Saith the Lord thy God. "[3] O Israel of
God, O Catholic Church, to be gathered out
of Jews and Gentiles, doubt not, he would
say, thy promised happiness. For thy God
Who loveth thee and Who from eternity hath
chosen thee, hath commanded me to say this
to thee in His Name." "[4] He turneth too
to the ear of each of us, giving us joy, in His
word, *saith the Lord thy God."* "[3] They too
who are plants which God hath planted, and
who have so profited, that through them
many daily profit, *shall be planted upon their
own ground,* i. e. each, in his order and in
that kind of life which he has chosen, shall
strike deep roots in true piety, and they shall
be so preserved by God, that by no force of
temptations shall they be uprooted, but each
shall say with the holy prophet[5], *I* am *like a
green olive tree in the house of God; I trust in
the mercy of God forever and ever.* Not that
every tree, planted in the ground of the
Church militant, is so firm that it cannot be
plucked up, but many there are, which are
not plucked up, being protected by the Hand
of Almighty God. O blessed that land,
where no tree is plucked up, none is injured
by any worm, or decays through any age.
How many great, fruit-bearing, trees do we
see plucked up in this land of calamity and
misery! Blessed day, when we shall be
there, where we need fear no storm!" Yet

[1] Theod.
[2] S. Jer.

[3] Rib.　　[4] Rup.
[5] Ps. lii. 9.

Before
CHRIST
cir. 787.
pulled up out of their land which I have given

them, saith the LORD thy God.
Before
CHRIST
cir. 787.

this too abideth true ; *none shall be plucked up.* Without our own will, neither passions within, nor temptations without, nor the malice or wiles of Satan, can *pluck us up.* None can *be plucked up*, who doth not himself loose his hold, whose root is twisted round the Rock, which is Thou, O Blessed Jesu. For Thou hast said [1], *they shall never perish, neither shall any pluck them out of My Hand.*

[1] S. John x. 28.

INTRODUCTION

TO

THE PROPHET

OBADIAH.

THE silence of Holy Scripture as to the Prophet Obadiah stands in remarkable contrast with the anxiety of men to know something of him. It were even waste labor to examine the combinations, by which, of old, the human mind tried to justify its longing to know more of him, than God had willed to be preserved. Men go over them with the view of triumphing in the superior sagacity of later days, and slaying the slain. It was a good and pious feeling which longed to know more of the men of God, whose prophecies He has preserved to us, and, with this view, looked about whether they could not identify their benefactor (such as each Prophet is) with some one of whom more details are recorded. Hence they hoped that Obadiah might prove to have been the faithful protector of the prophets under Ahab, or the son of the Shunamite, whom Elijah recalled to life, or the Obadiah whom Jehoshaphat sent to teach in the cities of Judah [a] or the Levite who was selected, with one other, to be the overseer set over the repair of the temple in the reign of Josiah [b]. Fruitless guesses at what God has hidden! God has willed that his name alone and this brief prophecy should be known in this world. Here, he is known only as Obadiah, "worshiper of God [c]."

Yet these guesses of pious minds illustrate this point, that the arranger of the Canon had some other ground upon which he assigned to Obadiah his place in it, than any identification of the Prophet with any other person mentioned in Holy Scripture. For whereas, of the Obadiahs, of whom Holy Scripture mentions more than the name, two lived in the reign of Ahab, one after the captivity of the ten tribes, the Prophet is, by the framer of the Canon, placed in the time of Uzziah and Jeroboam II., in which those placed before and after him, flourished. Moderns, having slighted these pious longings, are still more at fault in *their* way. German critics have assigned to the Prophet dates, removed from each other by above 600 years; just as if men doubted, *from internal evidence*, whether a work were written in the time of William the Conqueror, or in that of Cromwell; of S. Louis, or Louis XVIII.; or whether Hesiod was a contemporary of Callimachus, and Ennius of Claudian; or the author of the Nibelungen Lied lived with Schiller. Such difference, which seems grotesque, as soon as it is applied to any other case, was the fruit of unbelief. Two or rather three great facts are spoken of in the prophecy, the capture of Jerusalem, and a two-fold punishment of Edom consequent on his malicious triumph over his brother's fall; the one through Heathen, the other through the restored Jews. The punishment of Edom the Prophet clearly foretells, as yet to come; the destruction of Jerusalem, which, according to our version is spoken of as past, is in reality foretold also. Unbelief denies all prophecy. Strange, that unbelief, denying the existence of the jewel—God's authentic and authenticated voice to man—should trouble itself about the age of the casket. Yet so it was. The prophets of Israel used a fascinating power over those who denied their inspiration. They denied

---

[a] 2 Chr. xvii. 7.
[b] Ib. xxxiv. 12.

[c] Obadiah is "worshiper of the Lord;" Abdi, or Abdiah, "the servant of the Lord."

prophecy, but employed themselves about the Prophets. Unbelief, denying prophecy, had to find out two events in history, which should correspond with these events in the Prophet, a capture of Jerusalem, and a subsequent,—*it* could not say, consequent,—suffering on the part of Edom. And since Jerusalem was first taken under Shishak king of Egypt, in the 5th year of Rehoboam, B.C. 970, and Josephus relates[d], that B.C. 301, Ptolemy Lagus treacherously got possession of it under plea of offering sacrifice, treated it harshly, took many captive from the mountainous part of Judæa and the places round Jerusalem, from Samaritis, Gerizim, and settled them all in Egypt; unbelieving criticism had a wide range, in which to vacillate. And so it reeled to and fro between the first and last of these periods, agreeing that Obadiah did not prophesy, and disagreeing as to all besides. Eichhorn[e], avowedly on his principle of unbelief, that God's prophets, when they spoke of detailed events, as future, were really describing the past, assumed that the last five verses were written in the time of Alexander Janneus, two centuries later than the latest, about B.C. 82[f]. As though a Hebrew prophet would speak of one, detestable for his wanton cruelty[g], as a Saviour!

The real question as to the age of Obadiah turns upon two points, the one external, the other internal. The external is, whether in regard to those verses which he has in common with Jeremiah, Obadiah gathered into one, verses which lie scattered in Jeremiah, or whether Jeremiah, in renewing the prophecies against Edom, incorporated verses of Obadiah. The question, internal to Obadiah, is, whether he speaks of the capture of Jerusalem in the prophetic or the real past, and (as determining this), whether he reproves Edom for past malice at the capture of Jerusalem, or warns him against it in the future.

The English version in the text supposes that Obadiah reproves for past sin. For it renders; *Thou shouldest not have looked on the day of thy brother, in the day when he became a stranger; neither shouldest thou have rejoiced over the children of Judah in the day of their destruction; neither shouldest thou have spoken proudly in the day of their distress*[h]. The English margin gives the other, as a probable rendering, *do not behold, &c.* But it is absolutely certain that *al* with the future forbids or deprecates a thing future. In all the passages, in which *al* occurs in the Hebrew Bible[i], it signifies "do not." We might as well say that "do not steal" means "thou shouldest not have stolen," as say that *veal*

tēreh, and do not look, means "thou shouldest not have looked." It is true that in a vivid form of question, belonging to strong feeling, the soul going back in thought to the time before a thing happened, can speak of the past as yet future. Thus David says[k], *The death of fools shall Abner die?* while mourning over his bier; or Job, having said to God, *why didst Thou bring me forth from the womb?* places himself as at that time and says[l] (literally), *I shall expire, and eye shall not see me; as if I had not been, I shall be; from the womb to the grave I shall be carried.* He contemplates the future, as it would have been, had he died in the birth. It was a relative future. We could almost, under strong emotion, use our "is to" in the same way. We could render, *Is Abner to die the death of fools?* But these cases have nothing to do with the uniform idiom; "do not." We must not, on any principle of interpretation, in a single instance, ascribe to a comon idiom, a meaning which it has not, because the meaning which it has, does not suit us. There *is* an idiom to express this. It is the future with *lo,* not with *al.*

It agrees with this, that just before[m], where our version renders, *thou wert as one of them,* the Hebrew (as, in our Bibles, is marked by the Italics) has only, *thou as one of them!* not expressing any time. The whole verse expresses no time as to Edom. *In the day of thy standing on the other side, in the day of strangers carrying captive his might, and strangers entered his gates and cast lots on Jerusalem, thou too as one of them.*

This too is a question not of rhetoric, but of morals. We cannot imagine that Almighty God, Who warns that he may not strike, would eight times repeat the exhortation,—a repetition which in itself has so much earnestness, "do not," "do not," "do not," in regard to sin which had been already ended. As to past sin, God exhorts to repent, to break it off, not to renew it. He does not exhort to that which would be a contradiction even to His own Omnipotence, not to do what had been already done.

According to the only meaning, then, which the words bear, Edom had not yet committed the sin against which Obadiah warns him, and so Jerusalem was not yet destroyed, when the Prophet wrote. For the sevenfold[n], *the day of thy brother,* (which is explained to be *the day of his calamity*), *the day of their destruction, the day of distress,* the mention whereof had just preceded, can be no other than *the day when strangers carried away his strength, and foreigners entered his gates, and cast lots on Jerusalem.* But no day was the day of utter destruction to Jerusa-

---

[d] Ant. xii. 1. 1.   [e] Einl. ins. A. T. iv. § 570.
[f] i. e. three years before his death. Jos. Ant. xiii. 15. 4.
[g] See Jos. Ib. xiii. 14. and 15.

[h] ver. 12, and so in ver. 13, 14.
[i] Calasio's Concordance furnishes 207 instances.
[k] 2 Sam. iii. 33.   [l] Job x. 18. 19.
[m] ver. 11.   [n] ver. 12–14.

lem, except that of its capture by Nebuchadnezzar. Its capture by Shishak[o], or by the Chaldees under[p] Jehoiakim and Jehoiachin[q], left it uninjured; Jehoash, when he had defeated Amaziah, broke down a part of its walls only[r].

The relation of Obadiah to Jeremiah agrees with this. This argument in proof of that relation has been so carefully drawn out by Caspari[s], that little is needed except clearly to exhibit it. Few indeed, I should think, (unless under some strong contrary bias), could read the five first verses of Obadiah in the book of the Prophet himself, and, as they occur, scattered in the 49th chapter of Jeremiah, and not be convinced that Jeremiah reset the words of Obadiah in his own prophecy.

This is, in itself, probable, because Jeremiah certainly incorporated eight verses of Isaiah in his prophecy against Moab[t], and four of the same Prophet in his prophecy against Babylon[u], in addition to several allusions to his prophecies contained in a word or idiom, or mode of expression[v]. In like way, he closes his prophecy against Damascus, with a verse from the prophecy of Amos against it[x]; and he inserts a verse of Amos against Ammon in his own prophecy against that people[y]. This is the more remarkable, because the prophecy of Amos against each people consists of three verses only. This, of course, was done designedly. Probably in renewing the prophecies against those nations, Jeremiah wished to point out that those former prophecies were still in force; that they had not yet been exhausted; that the threatenings of God were not the less certain, because they were delayed; that His word would not the less come true, because He was long-suffering. The insertion of these former prophecies, longer or shorter, are a characteristic of Jeremiah's prophecies against the nations, occurring, as they do, in those against Babylon, Damascus, Moab, Ammon, and therefore probably in that also against Edom.

The eight verses, moreover, common to Obadiah and Jeremiah form one whole in Obadiah; in Jeremiah they are scattered amid other verses of his own, in precisely the same way as we know that he introduced verses of Isaiah against Moab. But beside this analogy of the relation of the prophecy of Jeremiah to that of Isaiah, it is plainly

more natural to suppose that Jeremiah enlarged an existing prophecy, adding to it words which God gave him, than that Obadiah put together scattered sayings of Jeremiah, and yet that these sayings, thus severed from their context, should still have formed as they do, one compact, connected whole.

Yet this *is* the case as to these verses of Obadiah. Apart, for the time, from the poetic imagery, the connection of thought in Obadiah's prophecy is this; 1) God had commanded nations to come against Edom, 2) determining to lower it; 3) it had trusted proudly in its strong position; 4) yet God would bring it down; and that, 5) through no ordinary spoiler, but 6) by one who should search out its most hidden treasures; 7) its friends should be its destroyers; 8) its wisdom, and 9) might should fail it, and 10) it should perish, for its malice to its brother Jacob; the crowning act of which would be at the capture of Jerusalem; (11–14) but God's day was at hand, the heathen should be requited; (15, 16) the remnant of Zion, being delivered, would dispossess their dispossessors, would spread far and wide; (17–20) a Saviour should arise out of Zion, and the kingdom should be the Lord's. (21)

Thus, not the eight verses only of Obadiah, five of which recur in Jeremiah, and three others, to which he alludes, stand in close connection in Obadiah, but they form a part of one well-arranged whole. The connection is sometimes very close indeed; as when, to the proud question of Esau, *mi yorideni arets*[a], *who will bring me down to the ground?* God answers, *though thou place thy nest among the stars, mishsham orideca*[b], *thence will I bring thee down*.

Jeremiah, on the contrary, the mourner among the prophets, is plaintive, even in his prophecies against the enemies of God's people. Even in this prophecy he mingles words of tenderness[c]; *Leave thy fatherless children, I will preserve them alive; and let thy widows trust in Me.* Jeremiah, accordingly, has a succession of striking pictures; but the connection in him is rather one of oratory than of thought. His object is to impress; he *does* impress, by an accumulation of images of terror or desolation. Closeness of thought would not aid his object, and he neglects it, except when he retains the order of Obadiah. But plainly it is most probable,

[o] 1 Kings xiv. 25-27.
[p] 2 Kings xxiv. 2 Chr. xxxvi. 6, 7.
[q] 2 Chr. xxxvi. 10.   [r] 2 Kings xiv. 13.
[s] Der Prophet Obadia, pp. 4. sqq.
[t] Jer. xlviii. 29, 30, from Is. xvi. 6; Jer. xlviii. 31, from Is. xv. 5, xvi. 7, 11; Jer. xlviii. 32, from Is. xvi. 8, 9. 10; Jer. xlviii. 34, from Is. xv. 4-6; Jer. xlviii. 36, from Is. xvi. 11, xv. 7; Jer. xlviii. 37, from Is. xv. 2, 3; also Jer. xlviii. 43, 44, from Is. xxiv. 17, 18.
[u] Jer. l. 16, from Is. xiii. 14; Jer. l. 39; from Is. xiii. 21. 20; and Jer. l. 40, from Is. xiii. 9.

[v] Jer. l. 2. refers to Is. xlvi. 1; Jer. l. 8, to Is. xlviii. 20; Jer. l. 23, to Is. xiv. 6, 4; Jer. l. 25, to Is. xiii. 5; Jer. l. 34, to Is. xlvii. 4; Jer. l. 38, to Is. xliv. 27; Jer. li. 11, to Is. xiii. 17.
[x] Jer. xlix. 27. from Am. i. 4.
[y] Am. i. 15, in Jer. xlix. 3, besides the allusion in ver. 2. כאשׁ תצתנה, and תרועת מלחמה.
משם אורידך[b] ver. 3.   מי יורידני ארץ[a] ver. 4.
[c] xlix. 11.

that *that* is the original form of the prophecy, where the order is the sequence of thought. That sequence is a characteristic, not of these verses only of Obadiah, but of the whole. The whole twenty-one verses of the Prophet pursue one connected train of thought, from the beginning to the end. No one verse could be displaced, without injuring that order. Thoughts flow on, the one out of the other. But nothing is more improbable than to suppose that this connected train of thought was produced by putting together thoughts, which originally stood unconnected.

The slight variations also in these verses, as they stand in the two prophets, are characteristic. Wherever the two prophets in any degree vary, Obadiah is the more concise, or abrupt; Jeremiah, as belongs to his pathetic character, the more flowing. Thus Obadiah begins, *Thus saith the Lord God, of Edom. A report we have heard from the Lord, and a messenger among the heathen is sent; Arise and let us arise against her to battle.* The words, *Thus saith the Lord God, of Edom,* declare that the whole prophecy which follows came from God; then Obadiah bursts forth with what he had heard from God, *A report we have heard from the Lord.* The words are joined in meaning; the grammatical connection, if regarded, would be incorrect. Again, in the words, *we have heard,* the Prophet joins his people with himself. Jeremiah substitutes the more precise, *I have heard,* transposes the words to a later part of the prophecy, and so obviates the difficulty of the connection: then he substitutes the regular form, *shaluach,* for the irregular, *shullāch;* and for the one abrupt sentence, *Arise, and arise we against her to battle,* he substitutes the Hebrew parallelism, *Gather ye yourselves and come against her; and arise to battle.* Next, Obadiah has, *Behold! small have I made thee among the nations; despised art thou exceedingly.* Jeremiah connects the verse with the preceding by the addition of the particle *for,* and makes the whole flow on, depending on the word, *I have made. For behold! small have I made thee among the heathen, despised among men.* Obadiah, disregarding rules of parallelism, says; *The pride of thy heart hath deceived thee, dweller in rock-clefts, his lofty seat; who says in his heart, who will bring me down to the earth?* Jeremiah with a softer flow; *Thy alarmingness hath deceived thee, the pride of thy heart; dweller in the clefts of the rock, holding the height of a hill.* Obadiah has very boldly;

[d] xlix. 7, comp. ii. 14, viii. 19, xiv. 19, xviii. 14, 20, xxii. 28, xxx. 6, xxxi. 20, xlix. 1.
[e] xlix. 8, comp. xlix. 30, xlviii. 6.
[f] xlix. 13, comp. xxiv. 9, xxv. 9, 18, xxix. 18, xlii. 18, xliv. 12, 22, besides other accumulations as in vii. 34, xxii. 5. or lesser degrees of accumulation, fullness of language being a characteristic of Jeremiah.
[g] xlix. 17, comp. xviii. 16, xix. 8, l. 13, Lam. ii. 15.

Though thou exalt as the eagle, and though amid stars set thy nest, thence will I bring thee down, saith the Lord. Jeremiah contracts this, omits an idiom, for boldness, almost alone in Hebrew, *veim bein cocabim sim, and though amid stars set,* and has only, *when thou exaltest, as an eagle, thy nest, thence will I bring thee down, saith the Lord,* where also, through the omission of the words "amid stars," the word "thence" has, in Jeremiah, no exact antecedent. In like way Jeremiah smooths down the abrupt appeal, *If thieves had come to thee, if spoilers of the night (how art thou cut off!) will they not steal their enough? If grape-gatherers had come to thee, will they not leave gleanings?* Jeremiah changes it into two even half-verses; *If grape-gatherers had come to thee, will they not leave gleanings? If thieves by night, they had spoiled their enough.* Again, for the 5 bold words of Obadiah, *eik nechphesu Esau, nib'u matsmunaiv,* lit. *how are Esau outsearched, sought out his hidden places,* Jeremiah substitutes, *For I have laid bare Esau; I have discovered his hidden places, and he cannot be hid.*

Again, even an English reader of Jeremiah will have noticed that Jeremiah has many idioms or phrases or images, which he has pleasure in repeating. They are characteristic of his style. Now, in these verses which Obadiah and Jeremiah have in common, there is no one idiom which occurs elsewhere in Jeremiah; whereas, in the other verses of the prophecy of Jeremiah against Edom, in which they are, as it were, inlaid, there are several such, so to say, favorite turns of expressions. As such, there have been noticed, the short abrupt questions with which Jeremiah opens his prophecy against Edom[d]; *Is wisdom no more in Teman?* the hurried imperatives accumulated on one another[e], *Flee, turn, dwell deep;* the accumulation of words expressive of desolation[f]; *Bozrah shall become a desolation, a reproach, a waste and a curse; and all her cities, perpetual wastes;* the combination of the two strong words, *shall be stupefied, shall hiss,* in amazement at her overthrow; [g] *Every one who goeth by her shall be stupefied* [we say "struck dumb"] *and shall hiss at all her plagues.* Such again are the comparison to the overthrow of Sodom and Gomorrah[h]; the image of "the lion coming up from the pride of Jordan[i];" the burden of these prophecies, [k] *the day of the destruction of Edom and time of his visitation.* [l] *Wherefore hear ye the counsel of the Lord against Edom and His purposes which He has purposed toward Teman.* Then

from the vision, 1 Kings ix. 8, also Ezek. xxvii. 36, Zeph. ii. 15.
[h] xlix. 18, comp. l. 40. [i] xlix. 19, comp. i. 44.
[k] xlix. 8, comp. xlvi. 21, l. 27, 31, xlviii. 44, vi. 15, x. 15.
[l] xlix. 20 repeated l. 45. חשב מַחֲשָׁבוֹת occurs more in Jeremiah than in any other Book; xi. 19, xviii. 11, 18, xxix. 11, xlix. 30.

also, whole verses are repeated in these prophecies[m].

Out of 16 verses of which the prophecy of Jeremiah against Edom consists, four are identical with those of Obadiah; a fifth embodies a verse of Obadiah's; of the eleven which remain, ten have some turns of expression or idioms, more or fewer, which recur in Jeremiah, either in these prophecies against foreign nations, or in his prophecies generally. Now it would be wholly improbable that a prophet, selecting verses out of the prophecy of Jeremiah, should have selected precisely those which contain none of Jeremiah's characteristic expressions; whereas it perfectly fits in with the supposition that Jeremiah interwove verses of Obadiah with his own prophecy, that in verses so interwoven there is not one expression which occurs elsewhere in Jeremiah.

One expression, which has been cited as an exception, if it is more than an accidental coincidence, the rather confirms this. Obadiah, in one of the earlier verses which Jeremiah has not here employed, says, *To the border have sent thee forth the men of thy covenant; the men of thy peace have deceived thee, have prevailed against thee; thy bread* [i. e. the men of thy bread, they who ate bread with thee] *have laid a snare under thee.* In the middle of this threefold retribution for their misdealing to their brother Judah, there occur the words, *the men of thy peace,* which are probably taken from a Psalm of David[n]. But the word *hishshiucha,* "*have deceived thee,*" corresponds to the word *hishshiecha*[o] in v. 3. "*deceived thee* hath the pride of thy heart." The deceit on the part of their allies was the fruit and consequence of their self-deceit through the pride of their own heart. The verse in Obadiah then stands in connection with the preceding, and it is characteristic of Obadiah to make one part of his prophecy bear upon another, to shew the connection of thoughts and events by the connection of words. The taunting words against Zedekiah, which Jeremiah puts into the mouth of the women left in the house, when they should be brought before the king of Babylon's princes, *Thy friends, lit. the men of thy peace, have set thee on, hissithuca*[p], *and have prevailed against thee,* may very probaby be a reminiscence of the words of Obadiah (although only the words, *men of thy peace,* are the same) : but they stand in no connection with any other words in Jeremiah, as those of Obadiah do with the previous words.

The prophecy of Jeremiah in which he incorporated these words of Obadiah, itself also speaks of the destruction of Jerusalem as still future. For he says to Edom[q], *Lo ! they whose judgment was not to drink the cup, shall indeed drink it; and shalt thou be unpunished? Thou shalt not be unpunished; for thou shalt indeed drink it.* It is plainly wrong (as even our own Version has done) to render the self-same expression *shatho yishtu* as past, in the first place, *have assuredly drunken,* and as future in the second, *ki shatho tishteh*[r], *for thou shalt surely drink of it.* Since they must be future in the second place, so must they also in the first. Jeremiah too elsewhere contrasts, as future, God's dealings with His own people and with the nations, in this self-same form of words. [s] *Thus saith the Lord of hosts, Ye shall certainly drink; for lo ! I begin to bring evil on the city which is called by My Name, and shall ye be utterly unpunished? Ye shall not be unpunished; for I will call for a sword upon all the inhabitants of the earth, saith the Lord of hosts.* The form of words, [t] *hinneh bair anochi mechel leharea',* in itself requires, at least a proximate future, (for *hinneh* with a participle always denotes a future, nearer or further) and the words themselves were spoken in the fourth year of Jehoiakim.

In that same fourth year of Jehoiakim, Jeremiah received from God the command to write in that roll which Jehoiakim burnt when a little of it had been read to him[u], *all the words that I have spoken unto thee against Israel and against Judah and against all the nations, from the day I spake unto thee, from the days of Josiah even unto this day.* After Jehoiakim had burnt the roll, that same collection was renewed, at God's command, *with many like words*[v]. Now immediately upon this, follows, in the book of Jeremiah, the collection of prophecies against the foreign nations, and in this collection three contain some notice that they were written in that 4th year of Jehoiakim, and only the two last, those against Elam and Babylon, which may have been added to the collection, bear any later date. The prophecy against Babylon is at its close marked as wholly by itself[w]. For Seraiah is bidden, when he had come to Babylon, and had *made an end of reading the book,* to *bind a stone* upon it, and *cast it into the Euphrates,* and say, *Thus shall Babylon sink, and shall not rise again from the evil which I bring upon her.* These chapters then as to Babylon, although connected with the preceding in that they are prophecies against enemies of God's people, are marked as in one way detached from them, *a book*[x] by themselves. And in conformity with this, they are stated, in the beginning, to have been written in the 4th year of Zedekiah. In like way, the prophecy against Elam,

[m] xlix. 18 repeated xlix. 33, l. 40, li. 43; and xlix. 22 in xlviii. 40, l.
[n] Ps. xli. 10. [o] הִשִּׁיאוּךְ, הִשִּׁיאֶךָ.
[p] הִסִּיתוּךְ Jer. xxxviii. 22. [q] xlix. 12.

[r] כִּי שָׁתוֹ תִשְׁתֶּה, שָׁתוֹ יִשְׁתּוּ: [s] xxv. 28, 29.
הִנֵּה בָעִיר אָנֹכִי מֵחֵל לְהָרֵעַ: [u] xxv. 1.
[v] xxxvi. 1, 2. [w] Jer. li. 60-4. [x] Ib. 60, 63.

which was uttered in the beginning of the reign of Zedekiah, was occasioned probably by misdeeds of that then savage people, serving, as they did, in the army of the Chaldees [y] against Jerusalem, when Nebuchadnezzar took Jehoiakim captive to Babylon. It is distinguished from the earlier prophecies, in that Elam was no inveterate enemy of God's people, and the instrument of his chastisement was not to be Babylon.

Those earlier prophecies (ch. xlvi–xlix. 33.) against Egypt, Philistia (including Tyre and Zidon), Moab, Ammon, Edom, Damascus, Kedar and the kingdoms of Hazor, all have this in common; 1) that they are directed against old and inveterate enemies of God's people; 2) they all threaten destruction from one source, the North [z], or Nebuchadnezzar himself, either naming [a] or describing him [b]. They are then probably one whole, a book of the visitations of God upon His enemies through Nebuchadnezzar. But the first of the two prophecies against Egypt relates to the expedition of Pharaoh Necho against Assyria, the utter overthrow of whose vast army at the Euphrates he foretells. That overthrow took place at Carchemish in the fourth year of Jehoiakim [c]. The next prophecy against Egypt relates to the expedition of Nebuchadnezzar against it, which followed immediately on the defeat of Pharaoh [d]. The third prophecy against Philistia was, before Pharoah smote Gaza [e]; but this was probably on his march against Assyria in that same fourth year of Jehoiakim, before his own power was broken for ever.

But since the prophecy of Obadiah was anterior to that of Jeremiah, it was probably long anterior to it. For Jeremiah probably incorporated it, in order to shew that there was yet a fulfillment in store for it. And with this it agrees, that Obadiah does employ in his prophecy language of Balaam, of a Psalm of David, of Joel and Amos, and of no later prophet. This could not have been otherwise, if he lived at the time, when he is placed in the series of the Minor Prophets. Had he lived later, it is inconceivable that, using of set purpose, as he does, language of Joel and Amos, his prophecy should exhibit no trace of any other later writing. The expressions taken from the book of Joel are remarkable, considering the small extent of both books. Such are undoubtedly the phrases; it, Jerusalem, shall be

holiness, kodesh [f]; In mount Zion there shall be a remnant [g]; For near is the Day of the Lord [h]; I will return thy recompense upon thy head [i], the phrase yaddu goral [k] for "cast lots." These are not chance idioms. They are not language of imagery. They are distinguished in no poetical or rhetorical manner from idioms which are not used. They are not employed, because they strike the senses or the imagination. One prophet does not borrow the imagery of another. They are part of the religious language of prophecy, in which when religious truth had once been embodied, the prophets handed it on from one generation to another. These words were like some notes of a loved and familiar melody, which brought back to the soul the whole strain, of which they were a part. The Day of the Lord having been described in such awful majesty by Joel, thenceforth the saying, near is the Day of the Lord, repeated in his own simple words, conveyed to the mind all those circumstances of awe, with which it was invested. In like way the two words, it shall be holiness, suggested all that fullness of the outpouring of God's Spirit, the sole Source of holiness, with which the words were associated in Joel; they are full of the Gospel promise, that the Church should be not holy only, but the depository of holiness, the appointed instrument through which God would diffuse it. Equally characteristic is that other expression; In Mount Sion shall be a remnant. It gives prominence to that truth, so contrary to flesh and blood, which S. Paul had to develop, that all were not Israel who were of Israel [l]. It presented at once the positive and negative side of God's mercies, that there would be salvation in Mount Zion, but of a remnant only. So, on the other side, the use of the idiom mechamas achica Yaakob, repeated but intensified from that of Joel, mēchamas benĕ Yehudah, continued on the witness against that abiding sin for which Joel had foretold the desolation of Edom, his violence toward his brother Jacob.

The promise in Amos of the expansion of Jacob, that they may inherit the residue of Edom, and all nations upon whom My Name is called, is, in like way, the basis of the detailed promise of its expansion in all directions, E. W. N. S. which Obadiah, like Amos, begins with the promise, that the people of God should inherit Edom: And the South shall inherit Mount Esau, and the plain

---

[y] Is. xxii. 6, Ezek. xxxii. 24.

[z] Jer. xlvi. 10, 20, 24, xlvii. 2.

[a] Jer. xlvi. 2, 13, 26, xlix. 28, 30.

[b] Jer. xlviii. 40, xlix. 22.

[c] Jer. xlvi. 2.

[d] Ib. 13.

[e] xlvii. 1.

[f] והיתה ירושלם קדש Ob. 17. והיה קדש Joel iv. 17.

[g] כי בהר ציון ובהר ציון תהיה פלטה Ob. 17. ובירושלם תהיה פלטה Joel iii. 5.

[h] כי קרוב Ob. 15. כי קרוב יום יי על כל הגוים
יום יי בעמק החרוץ Joel i. 15.

[i] אשיב גמלכם Ob. 15. גמלך ישוב בראשך
והשבתי גמלכם בראשכם Joel iv. 4. בראשכם iv. 7.

[k] ידו גורל Ob. 11, Joel iv. 3; else only in Nah. iii. 10. Elsewhere with גורל there are united גורל ,ידה, השליך ,הפיל, נתן, הטיל not ידד.

[l] Rom. ix. 6.

the Philistines. Amos, taking Edom as a specimen and type of those who hated God and His people, promises that they and all nations should become the inheritance of the Church. Obadiah, on the same ground, having declared God's sentence on Edom, describes how each portion of the people of God should be enlarged and overspread beyond itself.

While thus alluding to the words of Amos, Obadiah further embodies an expression of Balaam, to which Amos also refers. Balaam says, *Edom shall be an heritage* (yereshah), *Seir also shall be an heritage to his enemies; and Jacob shall do valiantly; and one out of Jacob shall have dominion, and shall destroy the remnant* (sarid) *out of the city.* The union of these two declarations of Balaam (one only of which had been employed by Amos) cannot be accidental. They lie in the two adjacent verses in each. *The house of Jacob shall be a fire, and the house of Joseph a flame, and the house of Esau stubble, and they shall burn them, and devour them; and there shall be no remnant* (sarid) *to the house of Esau; for the Lord hath spoken it; and the south shall inherit* (yereshu) *the mount of Esau.* In the fourth verse, also, Obadiah has an idiom from the prophecy of Balaam, which occurs nowhere besides; *strong is thy dwelling, and place* (vesim kinnecha) *in the rock thy nest.*[m] This infinitive here is a very vivid but anomalous construction. It cannot be by accident, that this idiom occurs in these two places alone in the Hebrew Scriptures.

This employment of prophetic language of earlier prophets is the more remarkable, from the originality and freshness of Obadiah's own diction. In his 21 verses he has several words which occur nowhere else[n]. They are mostly simple words and inflections of words in use. Still they were probably framed by the Prophet himself. One, who himself adds to the store of words in a language, has no occasion to borrow them of another. Obadiah adopts that other prophetic language, not as needing it to express his own meaning, but in order to give to it a fresh force and bearing.

But on the same ground, on which Obadiah employs the language of prophets who lived before him, he would have used the words of later prophets, had he lived later.

The framing of single words or forms is the least part of the originality of Obadiah's style. Vividness, connectedness, power, are characteristics of it. As it begins, so it continues and ends. It has no breaks, nor interruptions. Thought follows on thought, as wave rolls upon wave, but all marshalled to one end, marching on, column after column,

to the goal which God hath appointed for them. Each verse grows out of that which was before it, and carries on its thought. The cadence of the words in the original is a singular blending of pathos and strength. The pathos of the cadence consists in a somewhat long sustained measure, in which the Prophet dwells on the one thought which he wishes to impress; the force, in the few brief words in which he sums up some sentence. That lengthened flow will have struck even an English reader; the conciseness can only be seen in Hebrew. Those 5 words, *how are Esau outsearched! outsought his secret places!* have been already alluded to. Other such instances are, *Ein tebunah bo* with which v. 7. closes; *gam attah ceachad mehem,* "thou too as one of them," v. 11; *caasher 'asitha, ye'aseh lac* after the long exhortation in v. 12–14. or the 3 words *vehaiu celo haiu,* which close the description in v. 16, 17. or those three which so wonderfully sum up the whole prophecy, *vehayethah ladonai hammeluchah, and the kingdom shall be the Lord's.* Even the repetition which occurs in the Prophet, adds to the same effect, as in the two brief words, *beyom nochro, beyom obdam, beyom zarah, beyom eidam, beyom eido,* with which he closes each clause of the exhortation against malicious joy in the calamity of their brother. The characteristic, vivid detail in description, and, in the midst of it, great conciseness without sameness, occurs throughout Obadiah.

It would then be the more strange, that a prophecy so brief and so connected as that of Obadiah should have been severed into two (one part of which is to belong to some earlier prophet, the other is to have been written after the destruction of Jerusalem), but that the motive of this disruption of the prophecy is apparent. "The oracle on Edom preserved under the name of Obadiah *can,*" says one[o], "in its present form, be of no earlier date than the Babylonish Captivity. The destruction and entire desolation of Jerusalem is here described; the prophet himself wrote among the exiles." It *cannot* be of any earlier date, according to this writer, because, in his belief, there *cannot* be any certain prediction of details of the future, or any knowledge of that future, beyond those dim anticipations which man's own conscience and the survey of God's ordinary Providence may suggest; a *cannot,* which presupposes another *cannot,* that God *cannot* reveal Himself to His creatures.

But then this writer also could not altogether escape the impression, that great part of this prophecy must belong to a period long before the captivity. The only way

---

[m] Num. xxiv. 21, Ob. 4.

[n] פֶּרֶק, our "fork," where two ways part, v. 14, נִבְעוּ, v. 16, לְעוּ v. 7, מֵזוּר v. 9, קָטֹל v. 6, מִצְפּוּנֶיךָ

searched out, v. 6, are words peculiar in this sense to Obadiah: חֲגוי סֶלַע v. 3 occurs only in Cant. ii. 14.

[o] Ewald Proph. i. 398.

of reconciling these contradictions, this *must* of external evidence, and this *cannot* of anti-doctrinal prejudice, was to divide in twain this living whole, and to assign to the earlier period such portions relating to Edom, as contained no allusion to the destruction of Jerusalem. This then is done. " Further investigation," the writer proceeds, " shews, that the later prophet employed a fragment of an earlier prophet as to Edom. More than half of what is now extant, i. e. v. 1–10. half of v. 17. and v. 18. by their contents, language, and coloring, indicate very clearly such an earlier prophet; and moreover, about the same time Jeremiah employed the earlier fragment, in that very much out of verses 1-9. recurs in Jeremiah, but nothing of the words which belong most visibly to the later prophet, 11–16, 19–21."

i. Now, plainly, as Jeremiah is not here to tell us, why he did incorporate in his pro-phecy certain verses, and did not refer to certain other verses of Obabiah, it is, in the last degree, rash to make a positive inference from the mere fact of his not employing those verses, that he had them not to employ. He does embody in his prophecy the five first verses of Obadiah, and there the correspon-dence between the two Prophets almost ceases. The *thought* of ver. 6, but not one word of it recurs in Jeremiah [p]; to ver. 7. there is no allusion whatever; of ver. 8. again, the thought is retained, but only *one word,* and that, in a form altogether different [q]. This eighth verse is the last in Obadiah, to which Jeremiah refers. Ewald has to manufacture his " earlier prophet" out of those five first verses, which Jeremiah does embody; of other two, of which the thought only recurs in Jeremiah ; and five more [r], to which there is, in Jeremiah, no allusion whatever ; and having culled these ad libitum out of the whole chapter, he argues against the non-existence of the rest on the ground that Jeremiah does not employ them, whereas Jeremiah equally does not employ five of those, the existence of which at that same time Ewald acknowledges, and to two others Jeremiah alludes but very distantly. Since Jeremiah's not alluding to five of these verses, does not prove, according to Ewald, that they did not then exist, neither does his not em-ploying the remainder prove it as to them.

ii. Jeremiah assigns no ground for the punishment of Edom, except his pride; nor does he, in any of those prophecies as to those lesser nations, foretell anything as to the future of Judah. This was not assigned to him, as his subject here. He does in the prophecies against Egypt and Babylon ; for

those were the great dynasties, on whom, in human eyes, the existence of Judah depended. There he fortells, that God would *make a full end of* all *the nations whither* He had *driven* them, but not *of Jacob His servant* [s]. The future lot of Judah, as a whole, did not depend on those little nations. It may be on this ground, that Jeremiah foretells *their* destruction and the restoration of Moab and Ammon [t], and is silent as to Judah. Again, the immediate punishment of all these petty nations through Nebuchadnezzar was the subject of Jeremiah's prophecy, not ulterior suffering at the hands of Judah. Now these subjects, the *violence* of Esau against his *brother Jacob,* as the ground of Edom's punish-ment [u], the future enlargement of Jacob [v], and an ulterior retribution on Edom [w] through Judah, occupy most of those verses of Obadiah, to which there is no allusion in Jeremiah. This accounts (if there were any need to account for it) for the absence of allu-sion to almost all of Obadiah to which Jeremiah does not allude, both as to the part which Ewald accounts for in *his* way, and as to most of that part which he leaves unaccounted for.

But altogether, it must be said, that God's Prophets employ freely, as God taught them, what they do employ of the former Prophets. They do not copy them in a mechanical way, as if they were simply re-writing a work which lay before them, so that we should have to account for anything which they did not think good to repeat. In making the like use of Isaiah's prophecy as to Moab, Jeremiah makes no reference to the five first verses.

iii. So far from " writing among the exiles," Obadiah implies that the Captivity had not yet commenced. He speaks of Judah and Benjamin, as in their own land, and foretells that they shall enlarge themselves on all sides. Hosea and Amos had, at that time, prophesied the final destruction of the *kingdom* [x] of Israel and the dispersion [y] of the ten tribes. In conformity with this, Obadiah foretells to the two tribes, that they should occupy the vacated places of the land of promise. In contrast with this enlarge-ment of Judah and Benjamin, he speaks of those already in captivity, and prophesies their restoration. He speaks of two bodies of present exiles, " the captivity of *this* host of the children of Israel," " the captivity of Jerusalem which is at Sepharad." Of these he probably says [z], *The captivity of this host of the children of Israel which* are among *the Canaanites as far as Zarephath, and the captivity of Jerusalem which is in Sepharad, shall possess*

[p] Jer. xlix. 10.
[q] *Shall I not destroy* (הַאֲבַדְתִּי) *the wise?* Ob. 8; *Is wisdom perished?* אָבְדָה Jer. xlix. 7.
[r] 7–9, 10, 17, 18.
[s] Jer. xlvi. 27, 8; see also l. 4–8, 19, 20, 28, 33, 4, li. 5, 6, 10, 45.   [t] xlviii. 47, xlix. 6.

[u] 10–14. In 15, 16, Obadiah, having rehearsed the offence, repeats the sentence.
[v] 17–21.   [w] 18.
[x] Hos. i. 4, Am. v. 27. ab. p. 201, vi. 7, ix. 9.
[y] Hos. ix. 17. ab. pp. 61. 2; Am. ix. 9.
[z] ver. 20.

the cities of the South. Both these sets of captives must have been limited in number. Those *of Jerusalem at Sepharad* or Sardis [a], the capital of the Lydian empire, could only have been such as were exported by means of the slave trade. The only public settlement of Jews there, was in times long subsequent, about B. C. 200, when Antiochus the Great, in order to check the seditions in Lydia and Phrygia, "[b] removed thither at much cost 2000 Jewish families out of Mesopotamia and Babylonia, with their goods," on account of their tried faithfulness and zealous service to his forefathers. This removal, accompanied with grants of land, exemption from tribute for ten years, personal and religious protection, *was* a continuation of the commenced *dispersion;* it was not a *captivity.* They were the descendants of those who might have returned to their country, if they would. They were in the enjoyment of all the temporal benefits, for which their forefathers had bartered their portion in their own land. There was nothing peculiar why they should be singled out as the objects of God's promise. Jews were then dispersing everywhere, to be the future disciples or persecutors of the Gospel in all lands. Seleucus Nicator, a century before, had found Jews in Asia and Lower Syria, and had given them like privileges with the Macedonians and Greeks whom he settled there. Jews had shared his wars. Alexander had, at Alexandria, bestowed like privileges on the Egyptian Jews [c]. In such times, then, there was no *captivity at Sepharad;* no Lydian empire; nothing to distinguish the Jews there, from any others who remained willingly expatriated.

On the other side, the place which the Prophet assigns to those captives on their return is but a portion of Judah, *the cities of the South,* which he does not represent as unpeopled. In like way, whether the words as to Israel are rendered, "*which* are among *the Canaanites as far as Zarephath,*" or, "shall possess *the Canaanites as far as Zarephath,*" in either case the Prophet must be speaking of a very limited number. Had he been speaking in reference to the ten tribes or their restoration, he would not have assigned their territory, "Ephraim, Samaria, Gilead," to the two tribes, nor would he have assigned to them so small a tract. This limited number of captives exactly agrees with the state of things, supposing Obadiah to have lived,

when, according to his place in the Canon, he did live, near the time of Joel. For Joel denounces God's judgments on Tyre, Zidon and Philistia for selling unto the Grecians the children of Judah and Jerusalem. These captives, of whom Obadiah speaks, were some probably yet unsold, at Sarepta, and some at Sepharad or Sardis among the Grecians. On the other hand, it is inconceivable that Obadiah would have contrasted the present captivity, "*this* captivity of the children of Israel," "the captivity of Jerusalem which is in Sepharad," with Judah and Benjamin in their ancient possessions, had Judah and Benjamin been, when he wrote, themselves in captivity in Babylon, or that he would have prophesied concerning some little fragment of Israel, that it should be restored, and would have passed over the whole body of the ten tribes, if, when he prophesied, it had been in captivity. Nor is there again any likelihood, that by "this captivity of Jerusalem in Sepharad," Obadiah means any captives, among whom he himself was, (which is the whole ground-work of this theory of Ewald) for, in that case, he would probably have addressed the consolation and the promise of return *to* them (as do the other prophets) and not have spoken *of* them only.

A few years hence, and this theory will be among the things which have been. The connection of thought in Obadiah is too close, the characteristics of his style occur too uniformly throughout his brief prophecy, to admit of its being thus dislocated. Nowhere, throughout his prophecy, can one word or form be alleged, of which it can even be said, that it was used more frequently in later Hebrew. All is one original, uniform, united whole.

"Obadiah," says Hugh of S. Victor, "is simple in language, manifold in meaning; few in words, abundant in thoughts, according to that, 'the wise man is known by the fewness of his words.' He directeth his prophecy, according to the letter, against Edom; allegorically, he inveighs against the world; morally, against the flesh. Bearing an image of the Saviour, he hinteth at His Coming Through Whom the world is destroyed, through Whom the flesh is subdued, through Whom freedom is restored." "Among all the prophets," says another [d], "he is the briefest in number of words; in the grace of mysteries he is their equal."

[a] "CPaRaD occurs three times in Cuneiform Inscriptions in a list of Asiatic nations after ARMIN between KaTaPaTUK (Cappadocia) and IaUNA (Ionia), Niebuhr Reiseb. T. ii. Tab. xxxi. l. 12. p. 152, in the Epitaph of Darius at Nakshi Rustam l. 28. before Ionia, in Col. 1 of the Inscription of Bisutun, l. 15." After it had been decyphered, De Sacy identified the CPRD of the Inscriptions with the "Sepharad" of Obadiah. (Burnouf, Mémoire sur deux Inscriptions Cunéiformes, 1836. p. 147.) Then Lassen (Hall. Encyclop. v. Persepolis, S. iii. Vol. 17. p. 36.) identified CRPD with SaRDis, the

Greeks omitting the v or *ph,* and adding, according to their wont, their termination to the Asiatic name. S. Jerome's Hebrew instructor told him that it meant the "Bosphorus:" but this *may* have been his own conjecture, the letters "sphr" occurring in both; and if he took in the Prepos. ב, he had "bsphr" as the ground of his conjecture, taking in the ב which he ought not, and leaving out the ר which he ought to have accounted for.
[b] Jos. Ant. xii. 3. 4.
[c] Josephus (Ant. xii. 3. 1.) contrasts them with the ἐνοικισθεῖσιν. [d] Isid. lib. alleg. S. Scr.

OBADIAH.

1 *The destruction of Edom,* 3 *for their pride,* 10 *and for their wrong unto Jacob.* 17 *The salvation and victory of Jacob.*

THE vision of Obadiah. Thus saith the Lord

GOD [a] concerning Edom; [b] We have heard a rumor from the LORD, and an ambassador is sent among the heathen, Arise ye, and let us rise up against her in battle.

[a] Isai. 21. 11. & 34. 5. Ezek. 25. 12, 13, 14. Joel 3. 19. Mal. 1. 3.
[b] Jer. 49. 14, &c.

VER. 1. *The vision of Obadiah,* i. e. *of the worshiper of God.* The Prophet would be known only by that which his name imports, that he worshiped God. He tells us in this double title, through whom the prophecy came, and from Whom it came. His name authenticated the prophecy to the Jewish Church. Thenceforth he chose to remain wholly hidden. He entitles it *a vision,* as the prophets were called *seers* [1], although he relates, not the vision which he saw, but its substance and meaning. Probably the future was unfolded to him in the form of sights spread out before his mind, of which he spoke in words given to him by God. His language consists of a succession of pictures, which he may have seen, and, in his picture-language, described. "[2] As prophecy is called *the word,* because God spake to the prophets within, so it is called *vision,* because the prophet saw, with the eyes of the mind and by the light wherewith they are illumined, what God willeth to be known to them." The name expresses also the certainty of their knowledge. "[3] Among the organs of our senses, sight has the most evident knowledge of those things which are the object of our senses. Hence the contemplation of the things which are true is called *vision,* on account of the evidence and assured certainty. On that ground the prophet was called *seer.*"

Thus saith the Lord God concerning Edom. This second title states, that the whole which follows is from God. What immediately follows is said in Obadiah's own person; but all, whether so spoken or directly in the Person of God, was alike the word of God. God spake in or by the prophets, in both ways, since [4] *prophecy came not by the will of man, but holy men of God spake* as they were *moved by the Holy Ghost.* Obadiah, in that he uses, in regard to his whole prophecy, words which other prophets use in delivering a direct message from God, ascribes the whole of his prophecy to God, as immediately as other prophets did any words which God commanded them to speak. The words are a rule for all prophecy, that all comes directly from God.

We have heard a rumor, rather, *a report;* lit. *a hearing, a thing heard,* as Isaiah says [5], *Who hath believed our report?* A report is certain or uncertain, according to the authority from whom it comes. This *report* was certainly true, since it was *from the Lord.* By the plural, *we,* Obadiah may have associated with himself, either other prophets of his own day as Joel and Amos, who, with those yet earlier, as Balaam and David, had prophesied against Edom, or the people, for whose sakes God made it known to them. In either case, the Prophet does not stand alone for himself. He hears with "the goodly company of the Prophets;" and the people of God hear in him, as Isaiah says again [6], *that which I have heard from the Lord of hosts, the God of Israel, have I declared unto you.*

And an ambassador is sent among the heathen. The *ambassador* is any agent, visible or invisible, sent by God. Human powers, who wish to stir up war, send human messengers. All things stand at God's command, and whatever or whomsoever He employs, is *a messenger* from Him. He uses our language to us. He may have employed an angel, as He says [7], *He sent evil angels among them,* and as, through the permission given to *a lying spirit* [8], He executed His judgments on Ahab, of his own free will believing the evil spirit, and disbelieving Himself. So [9] *God sent an evil spirit between Abimelech and the men of Shechem,* allowing His rebellious spirit to bring about the punishment of evil men, by inflaming yet more the evil passions, of which they were slaves. Evil spirits, in their malice and rebellion, while stirring up the lust of conquest, are still God's *messengers,* in that He overrules them; as, to St. Paul [10], *the thorn in the flesh, the messenger of Satan to buffet him,* was still the gift of God. *It was given me,* he says.

Arise ye and let us rise. He who rouseth them, says, *Arise ye,* and they quickly echo the words, *and let us arise.* The will of God is fulfilled at once. While eager to accomplish their own ends, they fulfill, the more, the purpose of God. Whether the first agent be man's own passions, or the evil spirit who

---

[1] 1 Sam. ix. 9.
[2] Rib,
[3] Comm. in Is. § 8. ap. S. Basil. i. 383.
[4] 2 S. Pet. i. 21.
[5] liii. 1.

[6] xxi. 10.
[7] Ps. lxxviii. 49.
[8] 1 Kings xxii. 21-23.
[9] Jud. ix. 23.
[10] 2 Cor. xii. 7.

Before CHRIST cir. 587.

2 Behold, I have made thee small among the heathen: thou art greatly despised.

3 ¶ The pride of thine heart hath deceived thee, thou that dwellest in the clefts ᵉof the rock, whose

Before CHRIST cir. 587.

ᵉ 2 Kings 14. 7.

stirs them, the impulse spreads from the one or the few to the many. But all catch the spark, cast in among them. The summons finds a ready response. *Arise,* is the command of God, however given; *let us arise,* is the eager response of man's avarice or pride or ambition, fulfilling impetuously the secret will of God; as a tiger, let loose upon man by man, fulfills the will of its owner, while sating its own thirst for blood. So Isaiah hears[1] *the noise of a multitude in the mountains, like as of a great people, a tumultuous noise of the kingdoms of nations gathered together.* The Medes and Persians thought at that time of nothing less, than that they were instruments of the One God, Whom they knew not. But Isaiah continues; *The Lord of hosts mustereth the host of the battle;* and, when it was fulfilled, Cyrus saw and owned it[2].

2. *Behold, I have made thee small.* God, having declared His future judgments on Edom, assigns the first ground of those judgments. Pride was the root of Edom's sin, then envy; then followed exultation at his brother's fall, hard-heartedness and bloodshed. All this was against the disposition of God's Providence for him. God had *made* him *small,* in numbers, in honor, in territory. Edom was a wild mountain people. It was strongly guarded in the rock-girt dwelling, which God had assigned it. Like the Swiss or the Tyrolese of old, or the inhabitants of Mount Caucasus now, it had strength for resistance through the advantages of its situation, not for aggression, unless it were that of a robber-horde. But lowness, as men use it, is the mother either of lowliness or pride. A low estate, acquiesced in by the grace of God, is the parent of lowliness; when rebelled against, it generates a greater intensity of pride than greatness, because that pride is against nature itself and God's appointment. The pride of human greatness, sinful as it is, is allied to a natural nobility of character. Copying pervertedly the greatness of God, the soul, when it receives the Spirit of God, casts off the slough, and

retains its nobility transfigured by grace. The conceit of littleness has the hideousness of those monstrous combinations, the more hideous, because unnatural, not a corruption only but a distortion of nature. Edom never attempted anything of moment by itself. *Thou art greatly despised.* Weakness, in itself, is neither despicable nor *despised.* It is despised only, when it vaunts itself to be, what it is not. God tells Edom what, amid its pride, it was in itself, *despicable;* what it would thereafter be, *despised*[3].

3. *The pride of thy heart hath deceived thee.* Not the strength of its mountain-fastnesses, strong though they were, deceived Edom, but *the pride of his heart.* That strength was but the occasion which called forth the *pride.* Yet it was strong in its abode. God, as it were, admits it to them. *Dweller in the clefts of the rocks, the loftiness of his habitation.* "The whole Southern country of the Edomites," says S. Jerome, "from Eleutheropolis to Petra and Selah (which are the possessions of Esau), hath minute dwellings[4] in caves; and on account of the oppressive heat of the sun, as being a southern province, hath underground cottages." Its inhabitants, whom Edom expelled[5], were hence called Horites, i. e. dwellers in caves. Its chief city was called Selah or Petra, "rock." It was a city single of its kind amid the works of man. "[6] *The eagles* placed their nests in the rocky caves at a height of several hundred feet above the level of the valley." "[6] The power of the conception which would frame a range of mountain-rocks into a memorial of the human name, which, once of noble name and high bepraised, sought, through might of its own, to clothe itself with the imperishableness of the eternal Word, is here the same as in the contemporary monuments of the temple-rocks of Elephantine or at least those of the Egyptian Thebes." The ornamental buildings, so often admired by travelers, belong to a later date. Those nests in the rocks, piled over one another, meeting you in every recess, lining each fresh winding of the valleys, as each opened on the discoverer[7],

[1] Is. xiii. 4.   [2] Ezr. i. 1, 2.
[3] יִבְזֶה is at once a passive participle and an adjective.
[4] habitatiunculas.   [5] Deut. ii. 12.
[6] Schubert, Reise, ii. 428. ed. 2.
[7] "The most striking feature of the place consists, not in the fact that there are occasional excavations and sculptures, like those above described, but in the innumerable multitude of such excavations along the whole coast of perpendicular rocks, adjacent to the main area, and in all the lateral

vallies and chasms." Rob. ii. 139. "What remains are the mere débris of what the precipices once presented to view.—Many of the excavations are so difficult to reach and some are such mere wall or surface, that it appears as if the whole front of the rock, to a considerable depth, had fallen. The conduits, cisterns, flights of steps scattered over the rocks and among the precipices, indicate a larger number of rock-dwellings than remain now, very great as that number is.—As he pointed up two or three ravines, counting the holes in a single

Before CHRIST cir. 587. habitation *is* high; [d] that saith in his heart, Who

[d] Isai. 14. 13, 14, 15. Rev. 18. 7.

shall bring me down to the ground? Before CHRIST cir. 587.

often at heights, where (now that the face of the rock and its approach, probably hewn in it, have crumbled away[1]) you can scarcely imagine how human foot ever climbed[2], must have been the work of the first hardy mountaineers, whose feet were like the chamois. Such habitations imply, not an uncivilized, only a hardy, active, people. In those narrow valleys, so scorched by a southern sun, they were at once the coolest summer dwellings, and, amid the dearth of fire-wood, the warmest in winter. The dwellings of the living and the sepulchres of the dead were, apparently, hewn out in the same soft red sandstone-rock, and perhaps some of the dwellings of the earlier rock-dwellers were converted into graves by the Nabatæans and their successors who lived in the valley. The central space has traces of other human habitations. "[3] The ground is covered with heaps of hewn stones, foundations of buildings and vestiges of paved streets, all clearly indicating that a large city once existed here." "[4] They occupy two miles in circumference, affording room in an oriental city for 30, or 40,000 inhabitants." Its theatre held "[5] above 3000." Probably this city belonged

altogether to the later, Nabatæan, Roman, or Christian times. Its existence illustrates the extent of the ancient city of the rock. The whole space, rocks and valleys, imbedded in the mountains which girt it in, lay invisible even from the summit of Mount Hor[6]. So nestled was it in its rocks, that an enemy could only know of its existence, an army could only approach it, through treachery. Two known approaches[7] only, from E. and W., enter into it. The least remarkable is described as lying amid "[8] wild fantastic mountains," "rocks in towering masses," "over steep and slippery passes," or "winding in recesses below." Six[9] hours of such passes led to the Western side of Petra. The Greeks spoke of it as two days' journey from their "world[10]." Approach how you would, the road lay through defiles[11]. The Greeks knew but of "[12] one ascent to it, and that," (as they deemed) "made by hand;" [that from the E.] The Mohammedans now think the Sik or chasm, the two miles of ravine by which it is approached, supernatural, made by the rod of Moses when he struck the rock[13]. Demetrius, "the Besieger[14]," at the head of 8000 men, (the 4000 infantry selected

[1] rock-face, and reminded me, how small a proportion these bore to the whole, I was indeed astonished." Miss Mart. Eastern Life, iii. 2, 3. "I do not doubt that by calculation of all in the outlying ravines, you might count up thousands, but in the most populous part that I could select, I could not number in one view more than fifty, and generally much fewer. It is these immense ramifications, rather than their concentrated effect, that is remarkable; and this, of course, can no more be seen in one view, than all the streets of London." Stanley, 88.

[1] Martin. ab. note 5. She speaks also of "short and odd staircases, twisting hither and thither among the rocks," iii. 19. "little flights of steps scattered over the slopes." ii. 319. "Wherever your eyes turn along the excavated sides of the rocks, you see steps often leading to nothing, or to something which has crumbled away; often with their first steps worn away, so that they are now inaccessible," Stanley, 91. "the thousand excavations" beyond, Ib. 90. "There [in the Sik] they are most numerous, the rock is honey-combed with cavities of all shapes and sizes." Ib. 91.

[2] "Had the ancient builders of these rockworks wings like the eagle, with which they raised themselves to those perpendicular precipices?" "Who now, even with the feet of the chamois, could climb after them?" V. Schubert, ii. 429. Miss Martineau uses the same image of wings, Eastern Life, ii. 320, iii. 20.

[3] Burckhardt, Syr. p. 427. "On the left side of the river," he adds, "is a rising ground extending westward for nearly ¼ of an hour, entirely covered with similar remains. In the right bank, where the ground is more elevated, ruins of the same description are also seen."

[4] Robins. ii. 136.

[5] 3000. Burckhardt, Ib. "more than 3000." Rob. ii. 134.

[6] Stanley, 87. "Petra itself is entirely shut out by the intervening rocks.—The great feature of the

mountains of Edom is the mass of red bald-headed sandstone rocks, intersected, not by valleys but by deep seams. In the heart of these rocks, itself invisible, lies Petra." See Woodcut.

[7] In regard to the brook of Wadi Musa, Robinson says, "no one could tell in what direction the waters, when swollen, find their way through the cliffs. This only is certain that the Wady does not, as Wady Musa, extend down to the Arabah." ii. 137. Dr. Wilson (1847) says, "the water found a subterraneous exit by the passage through the rocks on the W. side of-the valley, through which they now flow." Lands, &c. i. 306. Any way, it was a passage impassable by man.

[8] Martineau, ii. 317, 8. She continues, "A little further on we stopped in a hollow of the hills.— Our path, our very narrow path, lay over these whitish hills, now up, now down, and then and then again we were slipping and jerking down slopes of gaudy rock. For nearly an hour longer we were descending the pass, down we went and still down, at length we came upon the platform above the bed of the torrent; near which stands the only edifice in Petra." Ib. 319, 20.

[9] Ib. ii. 316–19.

[10] τῆς οἰκουμένης. "The place was strong in the extreme, but unwalled, and two days journey, &c." Diod. Sic. xix. 95.

[11] See the accounts in Burckhardt, Syria, 421. Laborde, c. 8–10. Eng. Tr. Lindsay, pp. 220–30. Irby and M. c. 8. Rob. ii. 107. Stanley, 87, 98.

[12] Diod. Sic. xix. 97. "The corrosion of the surface of the rock by time and weather has so much the appearance of architectural intention, that it is at first difficult in Petra itself to distinguish the worn from the chiselled face of the precipices." Mart. ii. 317. "One striking feature of the whole scenery is, that not merely the excavations and buildings, but the rocks themselves are in a constant state of mouldering decay. You can scarcely tell where excavation begins or decay ends." Stanley, 88. [13] Stanley, 89. [14] Poliorcetes.

Before
CHRIST
cir. 587.

e Job 20. 6.
Jer. 49. 16.
& 51. 53. Amos 9. 2.   f Hab. 2. 9.

4 e Though thou exalt *thyself* as the eagle, and though thou f set thy nest among the stars, thence will I bring thee down, saith the LORD.

for their swiftness of foot from the whole army [1]) made repeated assaults on the place, but "[2] those within had an easy victory from its commanding height." "[3] A few hundred men might defend the entrance against a large army." Its width is described as from 10 to 30 feet [4], "[5] a rent in a mountain-wall, a magnificent gorge, a mile and a half long, winding like the most flexible of rivers, between rocks almost precipitous, but that they overlap and crumble and crack, as if they would crash over you. The blue sky only just visible above. The valley opens, but contracts again. Then it is honey-combed with cavities of all shapes and sizes. Closing once more, it opens in the area of Petra itself, the torrent-bed passing now through absolute desolation and silence, though strewn with the fragments which shew that you once entered on a splendid and busy city, gathered along in the rocky banks, as along the quays of some great Northern river." Beyond this immediate rampart of rocks, there lay between it and the Eastern Empires that vast plateau, almost unapproachable by an enemy who knew not its hidden artificial reservoirs of waters. But even the entrance gained, what gain beside, unless the people and its wealth were betrayed to a surprise? Striking as the rock-girt Petra was, a gem in its mountain-setting, far more marvelous was it, when, as in the Prophet's time, the rock itself was Petra. Inside the defile, an invader would be outside the city yet. He might himself become the besieged, rather than the besieger. In which of these eyries along all those ravines were the eagles to be found? From which of those lairs might not Edom's lion-sons burst out upon them? Multitudes gave the invaders no advantage in scaling those mountain-sides, where, observed themselves by an unseen enemy, they would at last have to fight man to man. What a bivouac were it, in that narrow spot, themselves encircled by an enemy everywhere, anywhere, and visibly nowhere, among those thousand caves, each larger cave, may be, an ambuscade! In man's sight Edom's boast was well-founded; but what before God?

That saith in his heart. The heart has its own language, as distinct and as definite as that formed by the lips, mostly deeper, often truer. It needeth not the language of the lips, to offend God. As He answers the heart which seeks Him,so also He replies in displeasure to the heart which despises Him. *Who shall bring me down to the earth?* Such is the language of all self-sufficient security. "Can Alexander fly?" answered the Bactrian chief from another Petra. On the second night he was prisoner or slain [6]. Edom probably, under his Who? included God Himself, Who to him was the God of the Jews only. Yet men now too include God in their defiance, and scarcely veil it from themselves by speaking of "fortune" rather than God; or, if of a coarser sort, they do not even veil it, as in that common terrible saying, "He fears neither God nor devil." God answers his thought;

4. *Though thou exalt* thyself [or, thy nest] *like the eagle.* The eagle builds its nest in places well-nigh inaccessible to man. The Edomites were a race of eagles [7]. It is not the language of poetry or exaggeration; but is poetic, because so true. *And though thou set thy nest in the stars.* This is men's language, strange as it is. "[8] I shall touch the stars with my crown;" "I shall strike the stars with my lofty crown;" "since I have touched heaven with my lance." As Job says [9], *Though his excellency mount up to the heavens and his head reacheth unto the clouds, yet he shall perish forever, like his own dung.* And Isaiah to the king of Babylon, the type of Anti-Christ and of the Evil one [10], *Thou hast said in thy heart, I will exalt my throne above the stars of God ; thy pomp is brought down to the grave, the worm is spread under thee, and the worms cover thee.* "[11] The heathen saw this. Æsop, when asked, what doeth God? said, 'He humbles the proud and exalts the humble.' And another [12], 'Whom morning's dawn beholdeth proud, The setting sun beholdeth bowed.'"

"[13] They who boast of being Christians, and are on that ground self-satisfied, promising themselves eternal life, and thinking that they need not fear Hell, because they are Christians and hold the faith of the Apostles, while their lives are altogether alien from

[1] Diod. Ib. 96.
[2] Schubert, Reise, ii. 428. ed. 2.
[3] Burckhardt, 434. "The footing is extremely bad, and the passage so completely commanded from the sides, and so obstructed by huge masses of sandstone that had rolled down from above, that it was obvious a very small force would be capable of holding it against a great superiority of numbers." Captains Irby and M. c. 8.
[4] Mart. iii. 11. "The width is not more than just

sufficient for the passage of two horsemen abreast, the sides are in all parts perpendicular." I. & M. p. 127.
[5] Stanley, 89–91.
[6] Q. Curt. vii. 41. 2. L. Arr. iv. 18. 19.
[7] See p. 235.
[8] Ovid, Horace, Lysimachus in Plutarch de fort. Alex. L. ii. Lap.
[9] xx. 6, 7.   [10] xiv. 13, 11.   [11] Lap.
[12] Sen. Herc. fur. Ib.   [13] Rib.

Before
C H R I S T
cir. 587.

g Jer. 49. 9.

5 If ^gthieves came to thee, if robbers by night, (how art thou cut off!) would they not have stolen till they had enough? if the grape-gatherers came

to thee, ^hwould they not leave || *some* grapes?

6 How are *the things of* Esau searched out! *how* are his h i d d e n things sought up!

Before
C H R I S T
cir. 587.

h Deut. 24. 21.
Is. 17. 6.
& 24. 13.
|| Or, *gleanings* ?

Christianity, are such Edomites, priding themselves because they dwell in clefts of the rocks. For it sufficeth not to believe what Christ and the Apostles taught, unless thou do what they commanded.—These spiritual Edomites, from a certain love or some fear of future torments, are moved by grief for sin, and give themselves to repentance, fastings, almsgiving, which is no other than to enter the clefts of the rocks; because they imitate the works of Christ and the holy Apostles who are called rocks, like those to whom John said [1], *O ye generation of vipers, who hath warned you to flee from the wrath to come?* But, since they have no humility, they become thereby the more inflated with pride, and the more of such works they do, the more pleasures they allow themselves, and become daily the prouder and the wickeder. *The pride* then *of their heart deceiveth* them, because they seem in many things to follow the deeds of the holy, and they fear no enemies, as though they *dwelt in clefts of the rocks.* They exalt their throne, in that, through the shadow of lofty deeds, they seem to have many below them, mount as high as they can, and place themselves, where they think they need fear no peril. But to them the Lord saith, *Though thou exalt thyself as the eagle,— thence will I bring thee down.* For, however exalted they be, and however they seem good and great, they are *brought down to the ground* and out from the caverns of the rocks, wherein they deemed that they dwelt securely, in that they lapse into overt shameful sin; whence all perceive, what they were then too, when they were thought to be righteous. And striking is it, that they are compared to *eagles.* For although the eagle fly aloft, yet thence it looks to the earth and the carcases and animals which it would devour, as Job writes of it [2], *She dwelleth and abideth upon the rock, upon the crag of the rock, and the strong place. From thence she seeketh the prey; her eyes behold afar off; her young ones also suck up blood, and where the slain are, there is she.* So these, while they pretend perfection, never turn their eyes away from earthly goods, always casting them on honors, or wealth, or pleasure, without which they count life to be no life. Well too is it called their *nest.* For, toil how they may, in seeking an assured,

restful, security of life, yet what they build, is a nest made of hay and stubble, constructed with great toil, but lightly destroyed. This security of rest they lose, when they are permitted, by the just judgment of God, to fall into uncleanness, ambition or foulest sins, and are deprived of the glory which they unjustly gained, and *their folly becomes manifest to all.* Of such, among the Apostles, was the traitor Judas.—But the rich too and the mighty of this world, although they think that their possessions and what, with great toil, they have gained, when they have raised themselves above others, are most firm, it is but that nest which they have placed among the stars, soon to be dissipated by wind and rain."

5. *If thieves came to thee.* The Prophet describes their future punishment, by contrast with that which, as a marauding people, they well knew. Thieves and robbers spoil only for their petty end. They take what comes to hand; what they can, they carry off. Shortness of time, difficulty of transport, necessity of providing for a retreat, limit their plunder. When they have gorged themselves, they depart. *Their* plunder is limited. The *grape-gatherer* leaves gleanings. God promises to His own people, under the same image, that they should have a remnant left [3]. *Gleaning grapes shall be left in it.* It shall be, *as gleaning grapes, when the vintage is done.* The Prophet anticipates the contrast by a burst of sympathy. In the name of God, he mourns over the destruction which he fore-announces. He laments over the destruction, even of the deadly enemy of his people. *How art thou destroyed!* So the men of God are wont to express their amazement at the greatness of the destruction of the ungodly. [4] *How are they* brought *into desolation as in a moment!* [5] *How hath the oppressor ceased! How art thou fallen from heaven, O Lucifer son of the morning!* [6] *How is the hammer of the whole earth cut asunder and broken! how is Babylon become a desolation among the nations!* [7] *How is Sheshach taken! How is the praise of the whole earth surprised.*

6. *How are the things of Esau searched out!* lit. *How are Esau outsearched!* i. e. Esau, as a whole and in all its parts and in all its belongings, all its people and all its property,

[1] St. Matt. iii. 7.   [2] Job xxxix. 28–30.
[3] Is. xvii. 6, xxiv. 13.

[4] Ps. lxxiii. 19.   [5] Is. xiv. 4, 12.
[6] Jer. 1. 23.   [7] Ib. li. 41.

Before
CHRIST
cir. 587.

† Heb. the men
of thy peace.
¹ Jer. 38. 22.

7 All the men of thy confederacy have brought thee *even* to the border : † ¹ the men that were at

peace with thee have deceived thee, *and* prevailed against thee ; † *they that eat* thy bread have laid a

Before
CHRIST
cir. 587.

† Heb. the men
thy bread.

one and all. The name *Esau* speaks of them as a whole ; the plural verb, *are outsearched*, represents all its parts. The word signifies a diligent search and tracking out, as in Zephaniah ¹, *I will search out Jerusalem with candles*, as a man holdeth a light in every dark corner, in seeking diligently some small thing which has been lost. *The hidden things*, i. e. his hidden treasures, *are sought up.* The enemy who should come upon him, should make no passing foray, but should abide there, seeking out of their holes in the rocks, themselves and their treasures. Petra, through its rocky ramparts, was well suited, as Nineveh in the huge circuit of its massive walls was well built, to be the receptacle of rapine. And now it was gathered, as all rapine is, first or last, for the spoiler. It was safe stored up there, to be had for the seeking. No exit, no way of escape. Edom, lately so full of malicious energy, so proud, should lie at the proud foot of its conqueror, as passive as the sheep in this large shamble, or as the inanimate hoards which they had laid up and which were now *tracked out.* Soon after Obadiah's prophecy, Judah, under Ahaz, lost again to Syria, Elath ², which it had now under Uzziah recovered ³. The Jews were replaced, it is uncertain whether by Edomites or by some tribe of Syrians ⁴. If Syrians they were then friendly ; if Edomites, Elath itself must, on the proximate captivity of Syria, have become the absolute possession of Edom. Either way, commerce again poured its wealth into Edom. To what end ? to be possessed and to aggrandize Edom, thought her wealthy and her wise men ; to be searched out and plundered, said the word of God. And it was so.

7. *All the men of thy confederacy have brought thee even to the border.* Destruction is more bitter, when friends aid in it. Edom had all along with unnatural hatred persecuted his *brother*, Jacob. So, in God's just judgment, its friends should be among its destroyers. Those *confederates* were probably Moab and Ammon, Tyre and Zidon, with whom they united to resist Nebuchadnezzar ⁵, and seduced Zedekiah to rebel, although Moab, Ammon, and Edom turned against him ⁶.

These then, he says, sent them *to the border.* " ⁷ So will they take the adversary's part, that, with him, they will drive thee forth from the borders, thrusting thee into captivity, to gain favor with the enemy." This they would do, he adds, through mingled treachery and violence. *The men of thy peace have deceived, have prevailed against thee.* As Edom turned peace with Judah into war, so those at peace with Edom should use deceit and violence against them, being admitted, perhaps, as allies within their borders, and then betraying the secret of their fastnesses to the enemy, as the Thessalians dealt toward the Greeks at Thermopylæ. It was to be no common deceit, no mere failure to help them. The men of *thy bread have laid a wound* (better, *a snare* ⁸) *under thee.* Perhaps Obadiah thought of David's words ⁹, *mine own familiar friend, in whom I trusted, who did eat of my bread, hath lifted up his heel against me.* As they had done, so should it be done to them. *They that take the sword*, our Lord says ¹⁰, *shall perish by the sword ;* so they who shew bad faith, are the objects of bad faith, as Isaiah says ¹¹. The proverb which says, " there is honor among thieves," attests how limited such mutual faith is. It lasts, while it seems useful. Obadiah's description relates to one and the same class, the allies of Edom ; but it heightens as it goes on ; not confederates only, but those confederates, friends ; not friends only, but friends indebted to them, familiar friends ; those joined to them through that tie, so respected in the East, in that they had eaten of their bread. Those banded with them should, with signs of friendship, conduct them to their border, in order to expel them ; those at peace should prevail against them in war ; those who ate their bread should requite them with a snare.

There is none understanding in him. The brief words comprise both cause and effect. Had Edom not been without understanding, he had not been thus betrayed ; and when betrayed in his security, he was as one stupefied. Pride and self-confidence betray man to his fall ; when he is fallen, self-confidence betrayed passes readily into despair. In the sudden shock, the mind collapses. Men do

¹ i. 12.   ² 2 Kings xiv. 6.   ³ Ib. xiv. 22.
⁴ The Hebrew text has אֲרוֹמִים, which the E. V. renders Syrians, but which is not the plural of אֲרָם. The Kri corrects אֲרוֹמִים, which would indeed be the plural of אֲדוֹם, but which is nowhere used for Edomites. It might have the meaning, however, that single "Edomites" (not, "the children of Edom" nationally) settled there. The Kri is, however, but a conjectural correction ; the reading of

the text has, in its favor, the general presumption everywhere in favor of the textual and harder reading. The LXX and Vulg. render " Edomites."

⁵ Jer. xxvii. 3.   ⁶ Zeph. ii. 8, Ezek. xxv.
⁷ Theod.
⁸ זוּר from מָזוֹר (a softer form probably of צוּר in a like meaning).
⁹ Ps. xli. 9.   ¹⁰ S. Matt. xxvi. 52.
¹¹ Is. xxxiii. 1. See ab. p. 182.

Before
CHRIST
cir. 587.

wound under thee : [k] *there
is* none understanding ‖ in
him.

[k] Is. 19. 11, 12.
[l] Or. *of it.*
[l] Job 5. 12, 13.
Is. 29. 14.
Jer. 49. 7.

8 [1]Shall I not in that
day, saith the LORD, even
destroy the wise *men* out

of Edom, and understand-
ing out of the mount of
Esau?

9 And thy mighty
[m] *men;* O [n] Teman, shall be
dismayed, to the end that

Before
CHRIST
cir. 587.

[m] Ps. 76. 5.
Amos 2. 16.
[n] Jer. 49. 7.

not use the resources which they yet have,
because what they had overvalued, fails them.
Undue confidence is the parent of undue
fear. The Jewish historian relates, how, in
the last dreadful siege, when the outer wall
began to give way, "[l] fear fell on the tyrants,
more vehement than the occasion called for.
For, before the enemy had mounted, they
were paralyzed, and ready to flee. You
might see men, aforetime stouthearted and
insolent in their impiety, crouching and
trembling, so that, wicked as they were, the
change was pitiable in the extreme.—Here
especially one might learn the power of God
upon the ungodly. For the tyrants bared
themselves of all security, and, of their own
accord, came down from the towers, where
no force, but famine alone, could have taken
them: For those three towers were stronger
than any engines."

8. *Shall I not in that day even destroy the
wise out of Edom?* It was then no common,
no recoverable, loss of wisdom ; for God, the
Author of wisdom, had destroyed it. The
heathen had a proverb, "whom God willeth
to destroy, he first dements." So Isaiah foretells of Judah [2], *The wisdom of their wise shall
perish, and the understanding of their prudent
shall be hid.* Edom was celebrated of old for
its wisdom. Eliphaz, the chief of Job's
friends, the representative of human wisdom,
was a Temanite [3]. A vestige of the name of
the Shuhites, whence came another of his
friends, probably still lingers among the
mountains of Edom [4]. Edom is doubtless included among the *sons of the East* [5], whose
wisdom is set as a counterpart to that of
Egypt, the highest human wisdom of that
period, by which that of Solomon would be
measured. *Solomon's wisdom excelled the wisdom
of all the children of the East country and all the
wisdom of Egypt.* In Baruch, they are still
mentioned among the chief types of human
wisdom. [6] *It* (wisdom) *hath not been heard of
in Chanaan, neither hath it been seen in Theman.
The Agarenes that seek wisdom upon earth, the
merchants of Meran and of Theman, the authors
of fables and searchers-out of understanding, none
of these have known the way of wisdom, or remember her paths.* Whence Jeremiah [7], in using
these words of Obadiah, says, *Is wisdom no*

*more in Teman? is counsel perished from the
prudent? is their wisdom vanished?* He speaks,
as though Edom were a known abode of
human wisdom, so that it was strange that it
was found there no more. He speaks of the
Edomites *as prudent*, discriminating [8], full of
judgment, and wonders that counsel should
have *perished* from them. They had it eminently then, before it *perished*. They thought
themselves wise ; they were thought so; but
God took it away at their utmost need. So
He says of Egypt, [9]*I will destroy the counsel
thereof. The counsel of the wise counsellors of
Pharaoh is become brutish. How say ye unto
Pharaoh, I am the son of the wise, the son of
ancient kings? Where are they? who are thy
wise? and let them tell thee now, and let them
know, what the Lord of hosts hath purposed upon
Egypt.* And of Judah, [10]*I will make void the
counsel of Judah and Jerusalem in this place.*
The men of the world think that they hold
their wisdom and all God's natural gifts, in-
dependently of the Giver. God, by the
events of His natural Providence, as here by
His word, shews, through some sudden withdrawal of their wisdom, that it is His, not
their's. Men wonder at the sudden failure,
the flaw in the well-arranged plan, the one
over-confident act which ruins the whole
scheme, the over-shrewdness which betrays
itself, or the unaccountable oversight. They
are amazed that one so shrewd should overlook this or that, and think not that He, in
Whose Hands are our powers of thought,
supplied not just that insight, whereon the
whole depended.

9. *And thy mighty, O Teman, shall be dismayed.* The heathen, more religiously than
we, ascribed panic to the immediate action
of one of their gods, or to Nature deified,
Pan, i. e. the Universe: wrong as to the
being whom they *ignorantly worshiped ;* right,
in ascribing it to what they thought a Divine
agency. Holy Scripture at times discovers
the hidden agency, that we may acknowledge
God's Hand in those terrors which we cannot
account for. So it relates, on occasion of
Jonathan's slaughter of the Philistine garrison, [11]*there was a trembling in the host and in
the field, and among all the people: the garrison
and the spoilers, they also trembled, and the earth*

[1] Jos. B. J. vi. 8. 4.   [2] xxix. 14.   [3] Job iv. 1.
[4] "Ssihhan, a ruined place in the S. mountains of
the Ghoeyr." Burckh. Syr. p. 414.

[5] 1 Kings iv. 30.   [6] Bar. iii. 22, 3.   [7] xlix. 7.
[8] בני   [9] Is. xix. 3, 11, 12.
[10] Jer. xix. 7.   [11] 1 Sam. xiv. 15.

Before
CHRIST
cir. 587.

o Gen. 27. 41.
Ps. 137. 7.
Ezek. 25. 12.
& 35. 5.
Amos 1. 11.

every one of the mount of
Esau may be cut off by
slaughter.

10 ¶ For *thy*° violence
against thy brother Jacob

shame shall cover thee,
and ᴾ thou shalt be cut off
for ever.

11 In the day that thou
stoodest on the other side,

Before
CHRIST
cir. 587.

ᴾ Ezek. 25. 9.
Mal. 1. 4.

quaked, so it became a trembling from God, or
(in our common word,) a panic from God.
All then failed Edom. Their allies and
friends betrayed them; God took away their
wisdom. Wisdom was turned into witless-
ness, and courage into cowardice; *to the end
that every one from mount Esau may be cut off by
slaughter.* The Prophet sums up briefly God's
end in all this. The immediate means were
man's treachery, man's violence, the failure
of wisdom in the wise, and of courage in the
brave. The end of all, in God's Will, was
their destruction. [1] *All things work together to
good to those who love God*, and to evil to those
who hate Him.

By slaughter, lit. *from slaughter*, may mean
either the immediate or the distant cause of
their being *cut off*, either the means which
God employed [2], that Edom was cut off by
one great slaughter by the enemy; or that
which moved God to give them over to destruction, their own *slaughter* of their brethren, the Jews, as it follows;

10. *For thy violence against thy brother
Jacob.* To Israel God had commanded [3],
*Thou shalt not abhor an Edomite ; for he is thy
brother.—The children that are begotten of them
shall enter into the congregation of the Lord in
their third generation.* Edom did the contrary
to all this. *Violence* includes all sorts of ill-
treatment, from one with whom "might is
right," *because it is in the power of their hand* [4]
to do it. This they had done to the descendants of their brother, and him, their twin-
brother, Jacob. They helped the Chaldæans
in his overthrow, rejoiced ·in his calamity,
thought that, by this co-operation, they had
secured themselves. What, when from those
same Chaldees, those same calamities, which
they had aided to inflict on their brother,
came on themselves, when, as they had betrayed him, they were themselves betrayed;
as they had exulted in his overthrow, so their
allies exulted in their's! The *shame* of which
the Prophet spake, is not the healthful distress at the evil of sin, but at its evils and
disappointments. Shame at the evil which
sin is, works repentance and turns aside the
anger of God. Shame at the evils which sin
brings, in itself leads to further sins, and endless, fruitless, shame. Edom had laid his
plans, had succeeded; the wheel, in God's
Providence, turned round and he was crushed.

[1] Rom. viii. 23.
[2] as in Gen. ix. 11, *all flesh shall no more be cut
off by* מ יכרת *the waters of the flood.*

So Hosea said [5], *they shall be ashamed through
their own counsels;* and Jeremiah [6], *we lie down
in our shame and our confusion covereth us;* and
David [7], *let mine adversaries be clothed with
shame, and let them cover themselves with their
own confusion as with a mantle.* As one, covered
and involved in a cloak, can find no way to
emerge; as one, whom the waters cover [8], is
buried under them inextricably, so, wherever
they went, whatever they did, shame covered
them. So the lost shall *rise to shame and
everlasting contempt* [9].

Thou shalt be cut off for ever. One word expressed the sin, *violence ;* four words, over
against it, express the sentence; shame encompassing, everlasting excision. God's
sentences are not completed at once in this
life. The branches are lopped off; the tree
decays; the axe is laid to the root; at last it
is cut down. As the sentence on Adam, *in
the day that thou eatest thereof thou shalt surely
die*, was fulfilled, although Adam did not die,
until he had completed 930 years [10], so was
this on Edom, although fulfilled in stages
and by degrees. Adam bore the sentence of
death about him. The 930 years wore out
at last that frame, which, but for sin, had
been immortal. So Edom received this
sentence of excision, which was, on his final
impenitence, completed, although centuries
witnessed the first earnest only of its execution. Judah and Edom stood over against
each other, Edom ever bent on the extirpation of Judah. At that first destruction of
Jerusalem, Edom triumphed, *Raze her, raze
her, even to the ground.* Yet, though it tarried
long, the sentence was fulfilled. Judah, the
banished, survived; Edom, the triumphant,
was, in God's time and after repeated trials,
cut off for ever. Do we marvel at the slowness
of God's sentence? Rather marvel we, with
wondering thankfulness, that His sentences,
on nations or individuals, are slow, yet stand
we in awe, because, if unrepealed, they are
sure. Centuries, to Edom, abated not their
force or certainty; length of life changes not
the sinner's doom.

11. *In the day that thou stoodest on the other
side.* The time when they so stood, is not
defined in itself, as a past or future. It is
literally; *In the day of thy standing over
against*, i. e. to gaze on the calamities of God's
people; *in the day of strangers carrying away*

[3] Deut. xxiii. 7, 8. [8, 9 Heb.]
[4] Mic. ii. 2.
[5] x. 6.　[6] iii. 25.　[7] Ps. cix. 29.
[8] Ex. xv. 10.
[9] Dan. xii. 2.
[10] Gen. v. 5.

Before CHRIST cir. 587.

‖ Or, *carried away his substance.*
q Joel. 3. 3.
Nah. 3. 10.
‖ Or, *do not behold, &c.*
r Ps. 22. 17.
& 54. 7.
& 59. 10.
Mic. 4. 11.
& 7. 10.
s Ps. 37. 13.
& 137. 7.

t Job 31. 29.
Prov. 17. 5.
& 24. 17, 18.
Mic. 7. 8.

in the day that the strangers ‖ carried away captive his forces, and foreigners entered into his gates, and q cast lots upon Jerusalem, even thou *wast* as one of them.

12 But ‖ thou shouldest not have r looked on s the day of thy brother in the day that he b e c a m e a stranger; neither shouldest thou h a v e t rejoiced over the children of Judah in

the day of their destruction; neither s h o u l d e s t thou have † spoken proudly in the day of distress.

13 Thou shouldest not have entered into the gate of my people in the day of their calamity; yea, thou shouldest not have looked on their affliction in the day of their calamity, nor have laid *hands* on their ‖ substance in the day of their calamity.

Before CHRIST cir. 587.

† Heb. *magnified thy mouth.*

‖ Or, *forces.*

---

his strength, i. e. *the strength of thy brother Jacob,* of whom he had just spoken, *and foreigners entered into his gates, and cast lots on Jerusalem, thou too as one of them.* One of them they were not. Edom was no stranger, no alien, no part of the invading army; he whose strength they carried away, was, he had just said, his *brother Jacob.* Edom burst the bonds of nature, to become what he was not, *as one of them.* He purposely does not say, *thou too wast* (hayitha) *as of them;* as he would have said, had he wished to express what was past. Obadiah seeing, in prophetic vision, the destruction of Jerusalem, and the share which the Edomites took thereat, describes it as it is before his eyes, as past. We see before us, the enemy carrying off all in which the human strength of Judah lay, his forces and his substance, and casting lots on Jerusalem, its people and its possessions. He describes it as past, yet not more so, than the visitation itself which was to follow, some centuries afterward. Of both, he speaks alike as past; of both, as future. He speaks of them as past, as being so beheld in *His* mind in Whose Name he speaks. God's certain knowledge does not interfere with our free agency. "[1] God compelleth no one to sin; yet foreseeth all who shall sin of their own will. How then should He not justly avenge what, foreknowing, He does not compel them to do? For as no one, by his memory, compelleth to be done things which pass, so God, by His foreknowledge, doth not compel to be done things which will be. And as man remembereth some things which he hath done, and yet hath not done all which he remembereth; so God foreknoweth all things

whereof He is Himself the Author, and yet is not Himself the Author of all which He foreknoweth. Of those things then, of which He is no evil Author, He is the just Avenger.

12–14. *But thou shouldest not,* rather it means, and can only mean [2], (as in the E. M.) *And look not* (i. e. gaze not with pleasure [3]) *on the day of thy brother in the day of his becoming a stranger* [4]; *and rejoice not over the children of Judah in the day of their destruction; and enlarge not thy mouth in the day of distress. Enter not into the gate of My people in the day of their calamity; look not, thou too, on his affliction in the day of his calamity; and lay not hands on his substance in the day of his calamity; And stand not on the crossway, to cut off his fugitives; and shut not up his remnants in the day of distress.* Throughout these three verses, Obadiah uses the future only. It is the voice of earnest, emphatic, dehortation and entreaty, not to do what would displease God, and what, if done, would be punished. He dehorts them from malicious rejoicing at their brother's fall, first in look, then in word, then in act, in covetous participation of the spoil, and lastly in murder. Malicious gazing on human calamity, forgetful of man's common origin and common liability to ill, is the worst form of human hate. It was one of the contumelies of the Cross, *they gaze, they look* with joy *upon Me* [5]. The *rejoicing over* them was doubtless, as among savages, accompanied with grimaces [6]. Then follow words of insult. The *enlarging the mouth* is uttering a tide of large words, here against the people of God; in Ezekiel, against Himself [7]: *Thus with your mouth ye have en-*

---

[1] S. Aug. de lib. arb. iii. 4.
[2] See Introd. to Obad. p. 228. [3] as in Mic. vii. 10.
[4] Others, *of his strange unheard of calamity.* Others *of his* being rejected *as a stranger* by God, as 1 Sam. xxiii. 7; *estranged* as Jer. xix. 4. Either of

these meanings suits the word נכר Job xxxi. 3, *rejection, reprobation,* or, as ours, *strange calamity.* Anyhow it is not *mere* calamity, as neither is it in Arabic. [5] Ps. xxii. 17.
[6] as in Ps. xxxv. 19, xxxviii. 16. [7] Ez. xxxv. 13.

Page 362 — OBADIAH

362 — OBADIAH.

(Before CHRIST cir. 587.)

14 Neither shouldest thou have stood in the crossway, to cut off those of his that did escape; neither shouldest thou have ‖ delivered up those of his that did remain in the day of distress.

‖ Or, shut up, Ps. 31. 8.

15 " For the day of the LORD is near upon all the heathen: * as thou hast done, it shall be done unto thee: thy reward shall return upon thine own head.

16 ʸ For as ye have drunk upon my holy

u Ezek. 30. 3. Joel 3. 14.
x Ezek. 35. 15. Hab. 2. 8. cir. 585.
y Jer. 25. 28, 29. & 49, 12. Joel 3. 17. 1 Pet. 4. 17.

larged against Me and have multiplied your words against Me. I have heard. Thereon follows Edom's coming yet closer, entering *the gate of God's people* to share the conqueror's triumphant gaze on his calamity. Then, the violent, busy, laying the hands on the spoil, while others of them stood in cold blood, taking the *fork* where the ways parted, in order to intercept the fugitives before they were dispersed, or to shut them up with the enemy, driving them back on their pursuers. The Prophet beholds the whole course of sin and persecution, and warns them against it, in the order, in which, if committed, they would commit it. Who would keep clear from the worst, must stop at the beginning. Still God's warnings accompany him step by step. At each step, some might stop. The warning, although thrown away on the most part, might arrest the few. At the worst, when the guilt had been contracted and the punishment had ensued, it was a warning for their posterity and for all thereafter. Some of these things Edom certainly did, as the Psalmist prays [1], *Remember, O Lord, to the children of Edom the day of Jerusalem, who said, Lay bare, lay bare, even to the foundation in her.* And Ezekiel [2] alluding to this language of Obadiah [3], *because thou hast had a perpetual hatred, and hast shed the blood of the children of Israel by the force of the sword in the time of their calamity, in the time that their iniquity had an end, therefore, as I live, saith the Lord God, I will prepare thee unto blood, and blood shall pursue thee; sith thou hast not hated blood, even blood shall pursue thee.* Violence, bloodshed, unrelenting, deadly hatred against the whole people, a longing for their extermination, had been inveterate characteristics of Esau. Joel and Amos had already denounced God's judgments against them for two forms of this hatred, the murder of settlers in their own land or of those who were sold to them [4]. Obadiah warns them against yet a third, intercepting their fugitives in their escape from the more powerful enemy. *Stand not in the crossway.* Whoso puts himself in the situation to commit an old sin, does, in fact, will

to renew it, and will, unless hindered from without, certainly do it. Probably he will, through sin's inherent power of growth, do worse. Having anew tasted blood, Ezekiel says, that they sought to displace God's people and remove God Himself [5]. *Because thou hast said, these two nations and these two countries shall be mine, and we will possess it, whereas the Lord was there, therefore, as I live, saith the Lord God, I will even do according to thine anger, and according to thine envy, which thou hast used out of thy hatred against them.*

15. *For the day of the Lord is near upon all the heathen.* The Prophet once more enforces his warning by preaching judgment to come. *The day of the Lord* was already known [6], as a day of judgment upon *all nations*, in which God would *judge all the heathen*, especially for their outrages against His people. Edom might hope to escape, were it alone threatened. The Prophet announces one great law of God's retribution, one rule of His righteous judgment. *As thou hast done, it shall be done unto thee.* Heathen justice owned this to be just, and placed it in the mouth of their ideal of justice [7]. *Blessed he,* says the Psalmist [8], *that recompenses unto thee the deed which thou didst to us. Blessed,* because he was the instrument of God. Having laid down the rule of God's judgment, he resumes his sentence to Edom, and speaks to all in him. In the day of Judah's calamity Edom made itself as *one of them.* It, Jacob's brother, had ranked itself among the enemies of God's people. It then too should be swept away in one universal destruction. It takes its place with them, undistinguished in its doom as in its guilt, or it stands out as their representative, having the greater guilt, because it had the greater light. Obadiah, in adopting Joel's words [9], *thy reward shall return upon thine own head,* pronounces therewith on Edom all those terrible judgments contained in the sentence of retribution as they had been expanded by Joel.

16. *For as ye have drunk.* Revelry always followed heathen victory; often, desecration. The Romans bore in triumph the vessels of

[1] Ps. cxxxvii. 7.
[2] xxxv. 5. 6.
[3] בְעֵת אֵידָם ver. 5. referring to the thrice repeated בְיוֹם אֵידָם, בְיוֹם אֵידוֹ. Ob. 13.
[4] Joel iii. 19. Am. i. 6, 9, 11.
[5] Ez. xxxv. 10, 11.
[6] Joel i. 15, ii. 1, 31.
[7] Rhadamanthus Aris. Eth. v. 5.
[8] Ps. cxxxvii. 8.
[9] iii. 7.

mountain, *so* shall all the ‖ heathen drink continually,

the second temple, Nebuchadnezzar carried away the sacred vessels of the first. Edom, in its hatred of God's people, doubtless regarded the destruction of Jerusalem, as a victory of polytheism (the gods of the Babylonians, and their own god Coze), over God, as Hyrcanus, in his turn, required them, when conquered, to be circumcised. God's *holy mountain* is *the hill of Zion*, including mount Moriah on which the temple stood. This they desecrated by idolatrous revelry, as, in contrast, it is said that, when the heathen enemy had been destroyed, *mount Zion* should *be holiness*[1]. Brutal, unfeeling, excess had been one of the sins on which Joel had declared God's sentence, [2] *they cast lots on My people; they sold a girl for wine, that they might drink.* Heathen tempers remain the same; under like circumstances, they repeat the same circle of sins, ambition, jealousy, cruelty, bloodshed, and, when their work is done, excess, ribaldry, profaneness. The completion of sin is the commencement of punishment. *As ye,* he says, heathen yourselves and *as one of* the heathen, *have drunk* in profane revelry, on the day of your brother's calamity, *upon My holy mountain,* defiling it, *so shall all the heathen drink* continually. But what draught? a draught which shall never cease, *continually; yea, they shall drink* on, *and shall swallow down,* a full, large, maddening draught, whereby they shall reel and perish, *and they shall be as though they had never been.* "[3] For whoso cleaveth not to Him Who saith, I AM, is not." The two cups of excess and of God's wrath are not altogether distinct. They are joined, as cause and effect, as beginning and end. Whoso drinketh the draught of sinful pleasure, whether excess or other, drinketh therewith the cup of God's anger, consuming him. It is said of the Babylon of the world, in words very like to these[4]; *All nations have drank of the wine of her fornications—reward her as she has rewarded you; in the cup which she hath filled, fill to her double. All nations* are, in the first instance, all who had been leagued against God's people; but the wide term, *all nations,* comprehends all, who, in time, become like them. It is a rule of God's justice for all times. At each and at all times, God requites them to the uttermost. The continuous drinking is fulfilled in each. Each drinketh the cup of God's anger, till death and in death. God employs each nation in turn to give that cup to the other. So Edom drank it at the hand of Babylon, and Babylon from the Medes, and the Medes and Persians from the Macedonians, and the Macedonians

from the Romans, and they from the Barbarians. But each in turn drank continuously, until it became as though it had never been. To swallow up, and be swallowed up in turn, is the world's history.

The details of the first stage of the excision of Edom are not given. Jeremiah distinctly says that Edom should be subjected to Nebuchadnezzar[5]. *Thus saith the Lord; make thee bonds and yokes, and put them upon thy neck, and send them to the king of Edom, and to the king of Moab, and to the king of the Ammonites, and to the king of Tyrus, and to the king of Zidon, by the hands of the messengers which come to Jerusalem unto Zedekiah king of Judah, and command them to say to their masters,—I have given all these lands into the hand of Nebuchadnezzar king of Babylon, My servant.* Holy Scripture gives us both prophecy and history; but God is at no pains to clear, either the likelihood of His history, or the fulfillment of His prophecies. The sending of messengers from these petty kings to Zedekiah looks as if there had been, at that time, a plan to free themselves jointly, probably by aid of Egypt, from the tribute to Nebuchadnezzar. It may be that Nebuchadnezzar knew of this league, and punished it afterward. Of these six kings, we know that he subdued Zedekiah, the kings of Tyre, Moab and Ammon. Zion doubtless submitted to him, as it had aforetime to Shalmaneser[6]. But since Nebuchadnezzar certainly punished four out of these six kings, it is probable that they were punished for some common cause, in which Edom also was implicated. In any case, we know that Edom was desolated at that time. Malachi, after the captivity, when upbraiding Israel for his unthankfulness to God, bears witness that Edom had been made utterly desolate[7]. *I have loved Jacob, and Esau I have hated, and laid his mountains and his heritage waste for the jackals of the wilderness.* The occasion of this desolation was doubtless the march of Nebuchadnezzar against Egypt, when, Josephus relates, he subdued Moab and Ammon[8]. Edom lay in his way from Moab to Egypt. It is probable, anyhow, that he then found occasion (if he had it not) against the petty state, whose submission was needed to give him free passage between the Dead Sea and the Gulf of Akaba, the important access which Edom had refused to Israel, as he came out of Egypt. There Edom was *sent forth to its borders,* i. e. misled to abandon its strong fastnesses, and so, falling into the hands of Nebuchadnezzar, it met with the usual lot of the conquered, plunder, death,

---

[1] ver. 17.   [2] iii. 3.
[3] Gloss.   [4] Rev. xviii. 3, 6.   [5] xxvii. 2–4, 6.

[6] Menander in Jos. Ant. ix. 14. 2.
[7] Mal. i. 2, 3.   [8] Ant. x. 9. 7.

yea, they shall drink, and they shall ‖ swallow

‖ Or, *sup up.*

captivity. Malachi does not verbally allude to the prophecy of Obadiah; for his office related to the restored people of God, not to Edom. But whereas Obadiah had prophesied the slaughter of Edom and the searching out of his treasures, Malachi appeals to all the Jews, their immediate neighbors, that, whereas Jacob was in great degree restored through the love of God, Edom lay under His enduring displeasure; his mountains were, and were to continue to be[1], a waste; he was *impoverished;* his places were desolate. Malachi, prophesying toward[2] 415 B. C., foretold a further desolation. A century later, we find the Nabathæans in tranquil and established possession of Petra, having there deposited the wealth of their merchandise, attending fairs at a distance, avenging themselves on the General of Antigonus, who took advantage of their absence to surprise their retreat, holding their own against the conqueror of Ptolemy who had recovered Syria and Palestine; in possession of all the mountains around them, whence, when Antigonus, despairing of violence, tried by falsehood to lull them into security, they trans-

mitted to Petra by fiery beacons the tidings of the approach of his army[3]. How they came to replace Edom, we know not. They were of a race, wholly distinct; active friends of the Maccabees[4], while the Idumæans were their deadly enemies. Strabo relates[5], that the Edomites " were expelled from the country of the Nabathæans in a sedition, and so joined themselves to the Jews and shared their customs." Since the alleged incorporation among the Jews is true, although at a later period, so may also the expulsion by the Nabathæans be, although not the cause of their incorporation. It would be another instance of requital by God, that " *the men of their confederacy brought* them *to their border, the men of their peace prevailed against* them." A mass of very varied evidence establishes as an historical certainty, that the Nabathæans were of Aramaic[6], not of Arabic, origin. They were inhabitants of Southern Mesopotamia, and, according to the oldest evidence short of Holy Scripture, were the earliest inhabitants, before the invasion of the Chaldæans[7]. Their country, Irak, "extended lengthways[8] from Mosul or Nineveh to Aba-

---

[1] Mal. i. 4.   [2] See Introd. to Malachi.   [3] Diod. Sic. xix. 94–8.   [4] See 1 Macc. v. 24–27, ix. 35. Jos. Ant. xii. 8. 3. xiii. 1. 2.   Aretas of Petra aided the Romans 3, B. C. against Jews and Idumæans. Ib. xvii. 10. 9.

[5] Strabo's words are, " The Idumæans are Nabatæans, but in a sedition having been expelled thence," [i. e. from the country of the Nabatæans,] " they, &c." The identifying of the Edomites and Nabathæans is a slight error in a Greek.

[6] The Arabian historians assert that the Nabathæans were Syrians; the Syrian writers equally claiming them as Syrians. This was first established out of the original unpublished writers by Quatremère (Nouveau Journal Asiatique, 1835. T. xv. reprinted, Mémoire sur les Nabatéens,) followed and illustrated by Larsow (de Dialect. ling. Syriac. reliquiis, Berlin, 1841.) and supplemented by Chwolson (die Ssabier, ii. 1. T. i. p. 697–711. and T. ii. 163. 844.) Their descendants who, according to the Arabic lexicographers, continued to live in "the marshes between the two Iraks," (Djauh. and Kam. in Quatr. p. 54, remained heathen (See Chwols. i. 821, 2. ii. 629, 664, 6). Whence the Syrians used the name Armoio, (as distinct from Oromoio) "Aramæon," to signify "Nabathæan," and "heathen." (Bar Ali, Lex, MS. sub v. See Larsow, p. 9–16.) Blau (in Zeitschr. d. Deutsch. Morg. Ges. 1855, pp. 235, 6.) contends that the Nabathæans of Petra were Arabs, on the following grounds; 1) the statements of Diodorus (xix. 94), Strabo (xvi. 2. 34. Ib. 4. 2 & 21), Josephus (Ant. i. 12, 4.), S. Jerome and some later writers. 2) The statement of Suidas (A. D. 980.) that Dusares, an Arab idol, was worshiped there. 3) The Arabic name of Aretas, king of Petra. 4) Arabic names of places, near Petra. Four such are alleged; *Arindela* (*if* the same as *this* Ghurundel) 18 hours from Petra (Porter, Handb. p. 58); *Negla,* (site unknown); *Auara,* a degree North, (Ptol. in Reland, 463); *Elji,* close to Petra. But as to 1) Diodorus, who calls the Nabathæans Arabs, says that they wrote *Syriac;* Strabo calls the *Edomites* Nabathæans, and the inhabitants of Galilee, Jericho, Philadelphia and Samaria, "a mixed race of Egyptians, Arabians, and Phœnicians" (§ 34), and

speaks of "Nabathæan Arabia" as a distinct country (xvii. l. 21)   Josephus, and S. Jerome (Qu. in Gen. 25. 13) following him, include the whole country from the Euphrates to Egypt, and so some whose language was Aramaic. As to 2) Dusares, though at first an Arab idol, was worshiped far and wide, in Galatia, Bostra, even Italy (See coins in Eckhel, Tanini, in Zoega de Obelisc. pp. 205–7, and Zoega himself, p. 205). As to 3) the kings named by Josephus, (see the list in Vincent's Commerce, ii. 273-6) Arethas, Malchus, Obodas, may be equally Aramaic, and Obodas has a more Aramaic sound. Anyhow the Nabathæans, if placed in Petra by Nebuchadnezzar, were not conquerors, and may have received an Arab king in the four centuries between Nebuchadnezzar and the first Aretas known at Petra. What changes those settled in Samaria underwent! As to 4) the names of places are not altered by a garrison in a capital. Our English names were not changed even by the Norman conquest; nor those of Samaria by the Assyrian. How many live on till now! Then of the four names, none occurs until after the Christian era. There is nothing to connect them with the Nabathæans. They may have been given before or long after them.

[7] " The Nabathæans, who were inhabitants of the country of Babel before the Chaldæans." Babylonian Agric. quoted by Makrizi. Quatremère, p. 61. Chwolson, ii. 606.

[8] Yacut in Notices et Extraits, ii. 446.   "Masudi says: The inhabitants of Nineveh formed a part of those whom we call Nabits or Syrians, who form one people and speak one language. That of the Nabits differs only in a few letters, but the basis of the language is the same " (Quatr. p. 59).   " The Chaldees " [he means Nabathæans] " are an ancient people who dwelt in Irak and Mesopotamia; of them were the Nimrods, kings of the earth after the deluge; and of them was Bakhtnasr (Nebuchadnezzar) and their tongue was Syriac, and they did not disuse it, until the Persians came upon them and subdued their kingdom." (Hajji. Khal. pp. 70, 1.)

down, and they shall be as though they had not been.

dan, and in breadth from Cadesia to Hulvan." Syrian writers claimed that their's was the primæval language [1]; Mohammedan writers, who deny this, admit that their language was Syriac [2]. A learned Syriac writer [3] calls the three Chaldee names in Daniel, Shadrach, Meshach, Abednego, Nabathæan. The surviving words of their language are mostly Syriac [4]. Mohammedan writers suppose them to be descended from Aram son of Shem [5]. Once they were a powerful nation, with a highly cultivated language [6]. One of their books, written before the destruction of Nineveh and Babylon [7], itself mentions an ancient literature, specifically on agriculture,

medicine, botany, and, that favorite study of the Chaldæans, astrology, "the mysteries," star-worship and a very extensive, elaborate, system of symbolical representation [8]. But the Chaldees conquered them; they were subjects of Nebuchadnezzar, and it is in harmony with the later policy of the Eastern Monarchies, to suppose that Nebuchadnezzar placed them in Petra, to hold in check the revolted Idumæans [9]. Diodorus [10] relates that the Nabathæans there "wrote in Syriac" a letter of remonstrance to Antigonus. "A tribe of Babylonians" were still, in the 6th century, "at Karak-Moab [11]," 60 geographical miles from Petra. Anyhow, B. C. 312,

[1] The Syrian Theodorus, quoted in the Alfehrest, says that "it was in this language that God spake to Adam." "Adam and his children spoke Syriac; some say, Nabathæan." (Ikhwan-alsafa, Quatr. 91.) "The primitive language which Adam spoke was that now used by the Chaldees; for Abraham was Chaldee by birth, and the language which he learnt of his fathers is that still used among us Syro-Chaldees." (Patriarch Michael, Chron. Ib. 91, 2.)

[2] "The Syriac writing is that of the Nabathæans and Chaldees. Ignorant men maintain that it is the primitive writing, on account of its great antiquity, and that it is used by the most ancient people; but it is an error." Ibn. Khaldun, Ib. 92.

[3] Abulfaraj, p. 74. "Nebuchadnezzar gave Hananiah, Mishael, and Azariah, Nabathæan names, Shadrach, &c.

[4] Words of the Nabathæan dialect are preserved both in Syriac and Arabic Lexica. On those in Syriac see Quatr. 104 sqq, Larsow, p. 15–26. The Arabic are given by Golius and Freytag.

[5] Masudi, (from Quatr. translation, p. 56.) "Among the sons of Mash, son of Aram, son of Shem, son of Noah, is Nabit, from whom are sprung all the Nabathæans and their kings." "Nabit, son of Mash, having fixed his residence at Babel, his descendants seized all Irak. These Nabathæans gave kings to Babel, who covered the land with cities, introduced civilization, and reigned with unequaled glory. Time has taken away their greatness and empire; and their descendants, in a state of dependence and humiliation, are now dispersed in Irak and other provinces." "After the deluge, men settled in different countries, as the Nabathæans who founded Babel, and the sons of Ham who settled in the same country under Nimrod." "The Chaldæans are the same as the Syrians, formerly called Nabathæans" (Ib. p. 59). "The Nimrods were the kings of the Syrians, whom the Arabs call Nabathæans." "The Nabathæans say that Iran was theirs, that the country belonged to them, and that they once possessed it, that their kings were the Nimrods, of whom was the Nimrod in the time of Abraham, and that Nimrod was the name of their kings" (Ib. 58); that Iran was named from them, Arian-shehr, land of lions, ariam (plur. of aria) "signifying in Nabathæan, lion." Ib. "The last king who fell before Ardeshir (Alexander) was a king of the Nabathæans, who lived in the towns of Irak." Ib. 60.

[6] In the 13th century, there were still three chief dialects of Syriac, 1) Aramæan, the dialect of Edessa, Haran, and Mesopotamia. 2) Palestine, that of Damascus, Lebanon, and the rest of inner (i. e. proper) Syria. 3) The Chaldee-Nabathæan, that of the mountaineers of Assyria, and the villages of Irak. (Abulfaraj, Hist. Arab. p. 70.) Of these the Nabathæan was once the purest; afterward, it appears to

have been corrupted by contact with the proper Chaldæans, and (as is the wont in mountainous districts and among peasants) was debased among an uneducated people. Theodorus the Syrian says, "This language is the most elegant of the Syriac dialects—The inhabitants of Babel spoke it. When God confounded the languages, and men dispersed in different countries, the language of the inhabitants of Babel remained unchanged. As for the Nabathæan spoken in villages, it is a corrupt Syriac and full of vicious idioms." (in Arab. Hist. Quatr. 95.) Barhebræus says, "Syriac, more than any other language, being spread over countries far apart, underwent changes so great, that those who speak different dialects of it do not understand each other, but require an interpreter, as if they spoke foreign languages. The dialects are three, that of Syria, that of Palestine, and that of the Easterns. This, more than the rest, has adopted very anomalous forms, and assimilated itself to the Chaldee. The Syriac is spoken at Edessa, Melitene, Marde; of those who use the Eastern, the Nestorian Christians are conspicuous." (Gramm. Syr. Quatr. 97.)

"In the Fehrest (A. D. 987) it is said that Nabathæan was purer than Syriac, and that the people of Babylon spoke it, but that the Nabathæan spoken in villages was inelegant Syriac." H. Khal. p. 71. ed. Flüg. "The people of Suwad [Babylonia] spoke Syriac, and letters were written in a peculiar dialect, Syro-Persic." (Ibn Mocanna, Ib. 70.)

[7] Quatr. 45, 6. "The temples of Babylon were still standing." Id. Ibn Wahshiyyah the Chaldæan, who states that he translated the "Nabathæan Agriculture into Arabic from Chaldee," ascribed to it a fabulous antiquity. (ap. Makrizi in Chwols. i. 699.) Ibn Awwam, who used it largely, says that it was "built on the words of the greatest wise, and mentions their names and numbers." (p. 8, 9. Chw. i. 706.) "It was adapted to the climate of Babylon especially, and to countries with a similar climate." Ssagrit, its original author ap. Abn Awwam, i. p. 82. (Chw. i. 699.)

[8] Quatremère, p. 108 sqq. Chwols. i. 107. "The Chaldæans, before them the Syrians, and in their time the Nabathæans, gave themselves eagerly to the study of magic, astrology, and talismans." Ibn Khald. in Quatr. 61. "Chwolson states that he has found in the fragments of these different writings, very lofty speculations on philosophy and natural history, and a very remarkable political and social legislation. Libraries are mentioned; all the branches of religious and profane literature, history, biography, &c. appear there very developed." Renan, Hist. d. Langues Semit. iii. 2. T. i. p. 239.

[9] I find this same conjecture in Quatremère.

[10] xix. 96.

[11] Steph. Byz. v. 'Αδαρούπολις. quoted by Quatremère, p. 87.

Before
CHRIST
cir. 587.

* Joel 2. 32.
ª Amos 9. 8.
‖ Or, *they that
escape.*
‖ Or, *it shall be
holy,*
Joel 3. 17.

17 ¶ * But upon mount Zion ª shall be ‖ deliverance, ‖ and there shall be holiness; and the house of Jacob shall possess their possessions.

18 And the house of Jacob ᵇ shall be a fire, and the house of Joseph a flame, and the house of Esau for stubble, and they shall kindle in them, and devour

Before
CHRIST
cir. 587.

ᵇ Is. 10. 17.
Zech. 12. 6.

Edom had long been expelled from his native mountains. He was not there about B. C. 420, the age of Malachi. Probably then, after the expulsion foretold by Obadiah, he never recovered his former possessions, but continued his robber-life along the Southern borders of Judah, unchanged by God's punishment, the same deadly enemy of Judah.

17. *But* [*And*] *upon* [*in*] *Mount Zion shall be deliverance,* or, *an escaped remnant, and there* [*and it*] *shall be holiness.* The sifting times of the Church are the triumph of the world; the judgment of the world is the restoration of the Church. In the triumph of the world, the lot was cast on Jerusalem, her sons were carried captive and slain, her holy places were desecrated. On the destruction of the nations, Mount Zion rises in calm majesty, as before; *a remnant* is replaced there, after its sifting; it is again *holiness;* not holy only, but a channel of holiness; *and the house of Jacob shall possess their possessions;* (lit. *inherit their inheritances,*) either their own former possessions, receiving and *inheriting* from the enemy, what they had lost; or the *inheritances* of the nations. For the whole world is the inheritance of the Church, as Jesus said to the Apostles, sons of Zion, ¹ *Go ye and teach all nations, baptizing them in the Name of the Father and of the Son and of the Holy Ghost.* ² *Go ye into all the world and preach the Gospel to every creature.* Holiness is its title-deeds to the inheritance of the world, that holiness, which was in *the upper chamber in Mount Zion,* the presence of God the Holy Ghost, issuing in holy teaching, holy Scriptures, holy institutions, holy Sacraments, holy lives.

18. Having given, in summary, the restoration and expansion of Judah, Obadiah, in more detail, first mentions a further chastisement of Edom, quite distinct from the former. In the first, for which God summoned the heathen, there is no mention of Judah, the desolation of whose holy City, Jerusalem, for the time, and their own captivity is presupposed. In the second, which follows on the restoration of its remnant, there is no mention of heathen. Obadiah, whose mission was to Judah, gives to it the name of the whole, *the house of Jacob.* It alone had the true worship of God, and His promises. Apart from it, there was no one-

ness with the faith of the fathers, no foreshadowing sacrifice for sin. Does the *house of Joseph* express the same in other words? or does it mean, that, after that first destruction of Jerusalem, Ephraim should be again united with Judah? Asaph unites, as one, *the sons of Jacob and Joseph* ³, Israel and Joseph ⁴; Israel, Jacob, Joseph ⁵. Zechariah ⁶ after the captivity, speaks of *the house of Judah* and *the house of Joseph,* as together forming one whole. Amos, about this same time, twice speaks of Ephraim ⁷ under the name of Joseph. And although Asaph uses the name of Joseph, as Obadiah does, to designate Israel, including Ephraim, it does not seem likely that it should be used of Israel, excluding those whose special name it was. While then Hosea and Amos foretold the entire destruction of the *kingdom* of Israel, Obadiah foretells that some should be there, after the destruction of Jerusalem also, united with them. And after the destruction of Samaria, there did remain in Israel, of the poor people, many who returned to the worship of God. Hezekiah invited Ephraim and Manasseh to the passover ⁸, from Beersheba to Dan ⁹, addressing them as *the remnant, that are escaped out of the hands of the kings of Assyria* ¹⁰. The more part mocked ¹¹; yet *divers of Asher, Manasseh and Zabulon* ¹², came from the first, and afterward *many of Ephraim and Issachar as well as Manasseh and Zabulon* ¹³. Josiah destroyed all the places of idolatry in Bethel ¹⁴ and *the cities of Samaria* ¹⁵, *of Manasseh and Ephraim and Simeon even unto Naphtali* ¹⁶. *Manasseh, Ephraim, and all the remnant of Israel* gave money for the repair of the temple, and this was *gathered by the Levites who kept the doors* ¹⁷. After the renewal of the covenant to keep the law, *Josiah removed all the abominations out of all the countries, that* pertained *to the children of Israel and made all found in Israel to serve the Lord their God* ¹⁸.

The heathen colonists were placed *by the king of Assyria in Samaria and the cities thereof* ¹⁹, probably to hold the people in the country in check. The remnant of *the house of Joseph* dwelt in the open country and the villages.

And the house of Esau for stubble. At some time after the first desolation by Nebuchad-

---

¹ S. Matt. xxviii. 19.   ² S. Mark xvi. 15.
³ Ps. lxxvii. 15.   ⁴ Ps. lxxx. 1.   ⁵ Ps. lxxxi. 4, 5.
⁶ x. 6.   ⁷ v. 15, vi. 6.   ⁸ 2 Chr. xxx. 1.

⁹ Ib. 5.   ¹⁰ Ib. 6.   ¹¹ Ib. 10.   ¹² Ib. 11.   ¹³ Ib. 18.
¹⁴ 2 Kings xxiii. 15.   ¹⁵ Ib. 19.   ¹⁶ 2 Chr. xxxiv. 6.
¹⁷ Ib. 9.   ¹⁸ Ib. 33.   ¹⁹ 2 Kings xvii. 24.

Before CHRIST cir. 587. them; and there shall not be *any* remaining of the house of Esau; for the LORD hath spoken *it*.

19 And *they of* the south ᵇ Amos 9. 12. ᶜ shall possess the mount of

Esau; ᵈ and *they of* the plain the Philistines: and they shall possess the fields of Ephraim, and the fields of Samaria: and Benjamin *shall possess* Gilead.

Before CHRIST cir. 587.

ᵈ Zeph. 2. 7.

nezzar, Esau fulfilled the boast which Malachi records, *we will return and build up the desolate places* [1]. Probably during the oppression of Judah by Antiochus Epiphanes, they possessed themselves of the South of Judah, bordering on their own country, and of Hebron [2], 22 miles from Jerusalem [3], where Judah had dwelt in the time of Nehemiah [4]. Judas Maccabæus was reduced to [5] *fortify Bethzur*, lit. *house of the rock*, (20 miles only from Jerusalem [6]) *that the people might have a defence against Idumæa*. Maresha and Adoraim, 25 miles S. W. of Jerusalem, near the road to Gaza, were cities of Idumæa [7]. The whole of Simeon was absorbed in it [8]. Edom was still on the aggressive, when Judas Maccabæus smote them at Arrabatene. It was "[9] because they beset Israel round about," that "Judas fought against the children of Esau in Idumea at Arrabatene and gave them a great overthrow." His second battle against them was in Judæa itself. He "[10] fought against the children of Esau in the land toward the South, where he smote Hebron and her daughters, and pulled down its fortress and burned the towns thereof round about." About 20 years afterward, Simon had again to recover Bethzur [11], and again to fortify it, as still lying on the borders of Judah [12]. Twenty years later, John Hyrcanus, son of Simon [13], "[14] subdued all the Edomites, and permitted them to remain in the country, on condition that they would receive circumcision, and adopt the laws of the Jews." This they did, continues Josephus; "and henceforth became Jews." Outwardly they appear to have given up their idolatry. For although Josephus says, "[15] the Edomites *account* [not, accounted] Koze a god," he relates that, after this forced adoption of Jewish customs, Herod made Costobar, of the sacerdotal family, prefect of Idumæa and Gaza [15]. Their character remained unchanged. The Jewish historian, who knew them well, describes them as "[16] a tumultuous disorderly race, ever alive to commotions, delighting in change, who went to engagements as to a

feast:" "[17] by nature most savage for slaughter." 3, B. C. they took part in the sedition against the Romans [18], using, as a pretext probably, the Feast of Pentecost, to which they went up with those of Galilee, Jericho, the country beyond Jordan, and "the Jews themselves." Just before the last siege of Jerusalem, the Zealots sent for them, on pretext that the city was betrayed to the Romans. "All took arms, as if in defence of their metropolis, and, 20,000 in number, went to Jerusalem [19]." After massacres, of which, when told that they had been deceived, they themselves repented, they returned; and were, in turn, wasted by Simon the Gerasene. "[20] He not only destroyed cities and villages, but wasted the whole country. For as you may see wood wholly bared by locusts, so the army of Simon left the country behind them, a desert. Some things they burnt, others they razed." After a short space, "he returned to the remnant of Edom, and, chasing the people on all sides, constrained the many to flee to Jerusalem [21]." There they took part against the Zealots [22], "were a great part of the war [23]" against the Romans, and perished, "[24] rivals in phrensy" with the worst Jews in the time of that extreme, superhuman, wickedness. Thenceforth their name disappears from history. The "greater part" of the remnant of the nation had perished in that dreadful exterminating siege; if any still survived, they retained no known national existence. Arabian tradition preserves the memory of three Jewish Arab tribes, none of the Edomites.

19. *And they of the South shall possess the mount of Esau.* The Church was now hemmed in within Judah and Benjamin. They too were to go into captivity. The Prophet looks beyond the captivity and the return, and tells how that original promise to Jacob [25] should be fulfilled; *Thy seed shall be as the dust of the earth, and thou shalt break forth to the West, and to the East, and to the North, and to the South; and in thee and in thy seed shall all the families of the earth be blessed.*

number. "The princes of the Idumæans sped like madmen round the nation, and proclaimed the expedition throughout. *The* multitude was assembled, earlier than was commanded, and *all* took arms," &c.

[20] Ib. iv. 9. 7. The Edomites were again in possession of Hebron. Simon took it.
[21] Ib. 10. [22] Ib. 11. [23] Ib. vi. 8. 2. [24] Ib. vii. 8. 1.
[25] Gen. xxviii. 14.

[1] Mal. i. 4. [2] 1 Macc. v. 65. [3] Eus. V. Ἀρκώ. [4] Neh. xi. 25. [5] 1 Macc. iv. 61. [6] Eus. [7] Jos. Ant. xiii. 15. 4. [8] Ib. v. 1. 22. [9] 1 Macc. v. 3. [10] Ib. 65. [11] Ib. xi. 65, 6. [12] Ib. xiv. 33. [13] Ib. xiii. 53. [14] Ant. xiii. 9, 1. [15] Ib. xv. 7, 9. [16] Id. B. J. iv. 4. 1. [17] Ib. iv. 5. 1. [18] Ant. xvii. 10. 2. [19] B. J. iv. 4. 2. It would seem from Josephus that their fighting men were already reduced to this

Before
CHRIST
cir. 587.

•1 Kings 17.
9, 10.

20 And the captivity of
this host of the children of
Israel *shall possess* that of
the Canaanites *even* °unto
Zarephath; and the cap-

tivity of Jerusalem,
|| which *is* in Sepharad,
ʳ shall possess the cities of
the south.
21 And ᵍ saviours shall

Before
CHRIST
cir. 587.

|| Or, shall
possess *that
which is in
Sepharad.*
ʳ Jer. 32. 44.
ᵍ 1 Tim. 4. 16.
Jam. 5. 20.

Hosea and Amos had, at this time, prophesied the final destruction of the kingdom of Israel. Obadiah describes Judah, as expanded to its former bounds including Edom and Philistia, and occupying the territory of the ten tribes. *The South*[1], i. e. they of the *hot* and *dry* country to the South of Judah bordering on Edom, *shall possess the mountains of Esau,* i. e. his mountain country, on which they bordered. And *the plain,* they on the West, in the great maritime plain, the *shephēlah,* should spread over the country of the Philistines, so that the sea should be their boundary; and on the North, over the country of the ten tribes, *the fields of Ephraim and the fields of Samaria.* The territory of *Benjamin* being thus included in Judah, to it is assigned the country on the other side Jordan; *and Benjamin, Gilead.*

20. *And the captivity of this host of the children of Israel,* [it must, I believe, be rendered[2],] *which are among the Canaanites, as far as Zarephath, and the captivity of Jerusalem which is in Sepharad, shall possess the cities of the South.* Obadiah had described how the two tribes, whose were the promises to the house of David, should spread abroad on all sides. Here he represents how Judah should, in its turn, receive into its bosom those now carried away from them; so should all again be one fold.

Zarephath (probably "smelting-house," and so a place of slave-labor, pronounced Sarepta in S. Luke[3]) belonged to Sidon[4], lying on the sea[5] about half-way[6] between it and Tyre[7]. These were then, probably, captives, placed by Tyrians for the time in safe keeping in the narrow plain[8] between Lebanon and the sea, intercepted by Tyre itself[9] from

their home, and awaiting to be transported to a more distant slavery. These, with those already sold to the Grecians and in slavery at Sardis, formed one whole. They stand as representatives of all who, whatever their lot, had been rent off from the Lord's land, and had been outwardly severed from His heritage.

21. *And saviours shall ascend on Mount Zion.* The body should not be without its head; saviours there should be, and those, successively. The title was familiar to them of old. [10] *The children of Israel cried unto the Lord, Who raised them up a saviour, and he saved them.* And the Lord gave unto Israel a saviour[11], in the time of Jehoahaz. Nehemiah says to God[12], *According to Thy manifold mercies, Thou gavest them saviours, who should save them from the hands of their enemies.* So there should be thereafter. Such were Judas Maccabæus and his brothers, and Hyrcanus, Alexander, Aristobulus. They are said to *ascend* as to a place of dignity, to *ascend on Mount Zion;* not to go up thither*ward,* but to dwell and abide *in*[13] it, which aforetime was defiled, which now was to be holy. He ends, as he began, with Mount Zion, the *holy hill,* where God was pleased to dwell[14], to reveal Himself. In both, is the judgment of Esau. Mount Zion stands over against Mount Esau, God's holy mount against the mountains of human pride, the Church against the world. And with this agrees the office assigned, which is almost more than that of man. He began his prophecy of the deliverance of God's people, *In Mount Zion shall be an escaped remnant;* he ends, *saviours shall ascend on Mount Zion:* he began, *it shall be*

the previous clauses. Hence the Chaldee has supplied ב before כנענים, from the corresponding בספרד, and renders, "which are in the land of the Canaanites." [3] iv. 26. [4] 1 Kings xvii. 9.
[5] Phocas, Loc. Sanct. in Reland, 985.
[6] Russegger, Reisen, iv 145. note. "Sarafend," in which the old name is nearly preserved, (Reland, ib.) is a little inland. It is 4½ hours both from Tyre and Sidon. (Russ. 145, 6.) The maps are wrong Id. [7] Jos. Ant. viii. 13. 2.
[8] "Its breadth is nowhere more than ½ an hour, except around Tyre and Sidon, where the mountains retreat somewhat further. In some places they approach quite near to the shore." Rob. ii. 473.
[9] In the term, "the Canaanites as far as Zarephath," the starting-point is naturally the confines of Canaan and Israel, and so Zarephath is the furthest point N. of Judah.
[10] Judg. iii. 9, 15. [11] 2 Kings xiii. 5.
[12] Neh ix. 27. [13] not אל nor על but ב.
[14] Ps ii. 6, lxviii 16.

[1] נגב
[2] The difficulty arises from the necessity of supplying something to fill up the construction of אשר כנענים lit. *which the Canaanites.* Our translation, following the Latin, has, *shall possess that of the Canaanites.* In this sense, we should have expected את אשר לכנענים, *that which belongs to the Canaanites,* the object having, in all the preceding instances, been marked by the את and אשר כנענים not being the Hebrew for "that which belongs to." On the other hand, the Hebrew accent, the parallelism, and the uniform use of the accusative here, point to the rendering, "*which* are among the *Canaanites,*" which is that of the Chaldee, while the construction is that of the LXX. and Syr ונלת החל הזה לבני ישראל corresponds with ונלת אשר עד צרפת כנענים; the ;ירושלם with בספרד; and then the remainder, "shall inherit the cities of the South," ירשו את ערי הנגב, is the predicate of both, in exact correspondence with

Before
CHRIST
cir. 587. come up on mount Zion to judge the mount of Esau ;

and the [b] kingdom shall be the LORD'S. Before
CHRIST
cir. 587.

[b] Ps. 22. 28. Dan. 2. 44. & 7. 14, 27. Zech. 14. 9. Luke 1. 33. Rev. 11. 15. & 19. 6.

---

holiness; he closes, *and the kingdom shall be the Lord's. To judge the mount of Esau.* Judges, appointed by God, judge His people; saviours, raised up by God, deliver them. But once only does Ezekiel speak of man's judging another nation, as the instrument of God. [1] *I, the Lord, have spoken it—and I will do it; I will not go back, neither will I spare, neither will I repent; according to thy ways and according to thy doings shall they judge thee, saith the Lord God.* But it is the prerogative of God. And so, while the word *saviours* includes those who, before and afterward, were the instruments of God in saving His Church and people, yet all saviours shadowed forth or back the one Saviour, Who alone has the office of Judge, in Whose kingdom, and associated by Him with Him, [2] *the saints shall judge the world,* as He said to His Apostles [3], *ye which have followed Me, in the regeneration when the Son of man shall sit in the throne of His glory, ye also shall sit upon twelve thrones, judging the twelve tribes of Israel.* And the last words must at all times have recalled that great prophecy of the Passion, and of its fruits in the conversion of the Heathen, from which it is taken, the twenty-second Psalm. The outward incorporation of Edom in Judah through Hyrcanus was but a shadow of that inward union, when the kingdom of God was established upon earth, and Edom was enfolded in the one kingdom of Christ, and its cities, whence had issued the wasters and deadly foes of Judah, became the sees of Christian Bishops. And in this way too Edom was but the representative of others, aliens from and enemies to God, to whom His kingdom came, in whom He reigns and will reign, glorified for ever in His Saints, whom He has redeemed with His most precious Blood.

And the kingdom shall be the Lord's. Majestic, comprehensive simplicity of prophecy! All time and eternity, the struggles of time and the rest of eternity, are summed up in those three words [4]; Zion and Edom retire from sight; both are comprehended in that one kingdom, and God is *all in all.* [5] The strife is ended ; not that ancient strife only between the evil and the good, the oppressor and the oppressed, the subduer and the subdued ; but the whole strife and disobedience of the creature toward the Creator, man against his God. Outward prosperity had passed away, since David had said the great words [6], *the kingdom is the Lord's.* Dark days had come. Obadiah saw on and beyond to darker yet,

but knits up all his prophecy in this; *the kingdom shall be the Lord's.* Daniel saw what Obadiah foresaw, the kingdom of Judah also broken ; yet, as a captive, he repeated the same to the then monarch of the world, [7] *the hammer of the whole earth,* which had broken in pieces the petty kingdom of Judah, and carried captive its people [8]; *the God of heaven shall set up a kingdom, which shall never be destroyed.* Zechariah saw the poor fragments which returned from the captivity and their poor estate, yet said the same [9]; *The Lord shall be king over all the earth.* All at once that kingdom came ; the fishermen, the tax-gatherer and the tentmaker were its captains; the scourge, the claw, thongs, rack, hooks, sword, fire, torture, the red-hot iron seat, the cross, the wild-beast, not employed, but endured, were its arms ; the dungeon and the mine, its palaces; fiery words of truth, its [10] *sharp arrows in the hearts of the King's enemies;* for One spake by them, Whose *Word is with power.* The strong sense of the Roman, the acuteness of the Greek, and the simplicity of the Barbarian, cast away their unbelief or their misbelief, and joined in the one song [11], *The Lord God Omnipotent reigneth.* The imposture of Mohammed, however awfully it rent off countless numbers from the faith of Christ, still was forced to spread the worship of the One God, Who, when the Prophets spake, seemed to be the God of the Jews only. Who could foretell such a kingdom, but He Who Alone could found it, Who alone has for these eighteen centuries preserved, and now is anew enlarging it, God Omnipotent and Omniscient, Who waked the hearts which He had made, to believe in Him and to love Him ? [12] Blessed peaceful kingdom even here, in this valley of tears and of strife, where God rules the soul, freeing it from the tyranny of the world and Satan and its own passions, inspiring it to know Himself, the Highest Truth, and to love Him Who is Love, and to adore Him Who is Infinite Majesty ! Blessed kingdom, in which God reigns in us by grace, that He may bring us to His heavenly kingdom, where is the manifest vision of Himself, and perfect love of Him, blissful society, eternal fruition of Himself; "[13] where is supreme and certain security, secure tranquillity, tranquil security, joyous happiness, happy eternity, eternal blessedness, blessed vision of God for ever, where is perfect love, fear none, eternal day and One Spirit in all ! "

---

[1] Ezek. xxiv. 14.   [2] 1 Cor. vi. 2.

[3] S. Matt. xix. 28.   וְהָיְתָה לַיהוָה הַמְּלוּכָה [4]

[5] 1 Cor. xv. 28.   [6] Ps. xxii. 28.   [7] Jer. l. 23.

24

[8] Dan. ii. 44, add vii. 14, 27.   [9] Zech. xiv. 9.

[10] Ps. xlv. 5.   [11] Rev. xix. 6.   [12] from Lap.

[13] Medit. c. 37. ap. S. Aug. vi. p. 125. App.

INTRODUCTION

TO

THE PROPHET

JONAH.

THE Prophet Jonah, who was at once the author and in part the subject of the book which bears his name, is, beyond question, the same who is related in the book of Kings [a] to have been God's messenger of comfort to Israel, in the reign of Jeroboam II. For his own name, in English "Dove," as well as that of his father, Amittai, "The Truth of God," occurs nowhere else in the Old Testament; and it is wholly improbable that there should have been two prophets of the same name, sons of fathers of the same name, when the names of both son and father were so rare as not to occur elsewhere in the Old Testament. The place which the Prophet occupies among the twelve agrees therewith. For Hosea and Amos, prophets who are known to have prophesied in the time of Jeroboam, and Joel, who prophesied before Amos, are placed before him; Micah, who prophesied after the death of Jeroboam and Uzziah, is placed after him.

A remarkable and much-misunderstood

[a] 2 Kings xiv. 25.
[b] Davidson, in Horne's Introd. ii. 958.
[c] Ps. cxxxix. 7.

[d] It is מלפני, not מפני. But לפני יהוה and מלפני יהוה, which correspond to one another, have very definite meanings. לפני יהוה is "before the Lord;" מלפני יהוה is "from being before the Lord." לפני יהוה is used in a variety of ways, of the place where God specially manifests Himself the tabernacle, or the temple. With verbs, it is used of passing actions, as sacrificing (with different verbs, Ex. xxix. 23, Lev. vii. 1-7, 2 Chr. vii. 4); of sprinkling the blood (Lev. iv. 16, &c. often); entering His Presence (Ex. xxxiv. 34, Lev. xv. 14); drawing near (Ex. xvi. 9); rejoicing in His Presence (2 Sam. vi. 5, 21, &c.); weeping before Him (Judg. xx. 23); or of abiding conditions, as walking habitually (Ps. lv. 14); dwelling (Is. xxiii. 18); or standing,

expression of the Prophet shews that this mission fell in the later part of his life, at least after he had already exercised the prophetic office. Our translation has, *Jonah rose up to flee from the presence of the Lord.* It has been asked [b], "How could a *Prophet* imagine that he could flee from the presence of God?" Plainly he could not. Jonah, so conversant with the Psalms, doubtless knew well the Psalm of David [c], *Whither shall I go from Thy Spirit, and whither shall I flee from Thy presence?* He could not but know, what every instructed Israelite knew. And so critics should have known that such could *not* be the meaning. The words are used, as we say, "he went out of the king's presence," or the like. It is literally, *he rose to flee from being in the Presence of the Lord,* i. e. from standing in His Presence as His Servant and Minister [d]. Then he must have so stood before; he must have had the office, which he sought to abandon.

He was then a prophet of Israel, born at

as His habitual Minister, as the Levites (Deut. x. 8, 2 Chr. xxix. 11, Ezek. xliv. 15); or a prophet (1 Kings xvii. 1, Jer. xvi. 19); or the priest or the Nazarite (see ab. p. 176. col. 1). In correspondence with this, מלפני יהוה signifies "from before the Lord." It is used in special reference to the tabernacle, as of the fire which went forth from the Presence of God there (Lev. ix. 24, x. 2); the plague (Num. xvii. 11 Heb. [xvi. 46 Eng.]); the rods brought out (Num. xvii. 24 Heb. [10 Eng.]); or the shew bread removed thence (1 Sam. xxi. 6). And so it signifies, not that one fled *from* God, but that he removed from standing in His Presence. So *Cain went out from* the Presence of God (מלפני), Gen. iv. 16); and of an earthly ruler it is said, a man "went forth out of his presence" [Gen. xli. 46, xlvii. 10 &c.]; and to David God promises, "there shall not be cut off to thee a man from before Me," i. e., "from standing before Me," (מלפני) 1 Kings viii. 25, 2 Chr.

371

Gath-hepher, "a small village" of Zabulon [e], which lies, S. Jerome says, "two miles from Sepphorim which is now called Diocæsarea, in the way to Tiberias, where his tomb also is pointed out." His tomb was still shewn in the hills near Sipphorim in the 12th century, as Benjamin of Tudela [f] relates; at the same place, " [g] on a rocky hill 2 miles East of Sepphuriah," is still pointed out the tomb of the Prophet, and "Moslems and the Christians of Nazareth alike regard the village (el-Meshhad) as his native village." The tomb is even now venerated by the Moslem inhabitants.

But although a prophet of Israel, he, like Daniel afterward or his great predecessor Elisha, had his mission also beyond the bounds of Israel. Whenever God brought His people into any relation with other people, He made Himself known to them. The mode of His manifestation varied; the fact remained uniform. So He made Himself known to Egypt through Joseph and Moses; to the Philistines at the capture of the ark; to the Syrians by Elisha; to Nebuchadnezzar and Belshazzar by Daniel, as again to Darius and Cyrus. The hindrances interposed to the edict of Darius perpetuated that knowledge among his successors. Yet further on, the High Priest Jaddua shewed to Alexander the prophecy of Daniel " [h] that a Greek should destroy the Persian Empire." For there is no ground to question the account of Josephus. The mission then of Jonah to Nineveh is in harmony with God's other dealings with heathen nations, although, in God's manifold wisdom, not identical with any.

To Israel the history of that mission revealed that same fact which was more fully declared by S. Peter [i] ; *I perceive that God is no respecter of persons ; but in every nation he that feareth Him and worketh righteousness, is accepted with Him.* This righteous judgment of God stands out the more, alike in the

history of the mariners and of the Ninevites, in that the character of both is exhibited advantageously, in comparison with that of the Prophet. The Prophet brings out the awe, the humanity, the earnestness of the natural religion, and the final conversion of the sailors, and the zealous repentance of the Ninevites, while he neglects to explain his own character, or, in the least, to soften its hard angles. Rather, with a holy indifference, he has left his character to be hardly and unjustly judged by those who, themselves sharing his infirmities, share not his excellences. Disobedient once, he cares only to teach us what God taught him for us. The mariners were spared, the Hebrew Prophet was cast forth as guilty. The Ninevites were forgiven: the Prophet, rebuked.

That other moral, which our Lord inculcated, that the heathen believed and repented with less light, the Jews, amid so much greater light, repented not, also lay there, to be drawn out by men's own consciences. "To the condemnation of Israel," says S. Jerome [k], "Jonah is sent to the Gentiles, because, whereas Nineveh repented, Israel persevered in his iniquity." But this is only a secondary result of his prophecy, as all Divine history must be full of teaching, because the facts themselves are instructive. Its instructiveness in this respect depends wholly upon the truth of the facts. It is the real repentance of the Ninevites, which becomes the reproach of the impenitent Jew or Christian.

Even among the Jews, a large school, the Cabbalists, (although amid other error,) interpreted the history of Jonah as teaching the resurrection of the dead, and (with that remarkable correctness of combination of different passages of Holy Scripture which we often find) in union with the prophecy of Hosea. " [l] The fish's belly, where Jonah was enclosed, signifies the tomb, where the body is covered and laid up. But as Jonah was given back on the third day, so shall we

---

vi. 16; comp. Is. xlviii. 19, Jer. xxxiii. 18. of Israel) and David prays, "Cast me not away from Thy presence," lit. "from before Thee" (Ps. li. 11). Aben Ezra noticed the distinction in part, "And as I have searched in all Scripture, and I have not found the word בֶּרֶךְ used otherwise than united with the word מִפְּנֵי, as in Ps. cxxxix. 7 and Judg. xi. 3, and in the prophecy of Jonah I have not found that he fled מִפְּנֵי, 'from the face of the Lord' but מִלְפְּנֵי, 'from before the Presence of the Lord;' and it is written, 'As the Lord liveth, *before Whom* I stand' (לְפָנַי). And so, on the other hand, it is always מִלְפְּנֵי. And so it is, 'And Cain went out מִלְפְּנֵי from before the presence of God'—And it is written ' to go into the clefts of the rocks and into the fissures of the cliff from the fear (לָבוֹא-מִפְּנֵי פַּחַד) of the Lord' (Is. ii. 21), and (in Jonah) it is written, to go with them from the Presence לָבוֹא-מִלְפְּנֵי of the Lord (Jon. i. 3), and the wise will understand." In one place (1 Chr. xix. 18) מִלְפְּנֵי is used, not with בֶּרֶךְ (of

which alone Aben Ezra speaks) but with נוּס. The idiom also is different, 1) since the two armies had been engaged face to face, (as Amaziah said, 'Let us look one another in the face,' 2 Kings xiv. 8, and the like idioms,) but 2) chiefly, in that מִלְפְּנֵי יהוה is, by the force of the term, contrasted with the other idiom לְפְּנֵי יהוה, and therefore cannot be a mere substitute for מִפְּנֵי.

[e] Josh. xix. 13.   [f] p. 44. 2. ed. Asher.
[g] Porter, in Smith, Bibl. Dict. p. 656. v. Gath-hepher. A Jewish traveller, A.D. 1637, places the tomb at Caphar Kena (קֵינָא.) "There is buried Jonah son of Amittai, on the top of a hill in a beautiful Church of the Gentiles," in Hottinger Cippi Hebr. pp. 74, 5.
[h] Ant. xi. 8. 5. Justin alludes to the meeting, xi. 10.
[i] Acts x. 34, 5.
[k] in Jon. i. 1.
[l] Menasseh B. Israel de resurr. mort. c. 5. p. 36. from "the divine Cabbalists who, from the history of Jonah, prove, by way of allegory, the resurrection of the dead." Ib. p. 34.

also on the third day rise again and be restored to life. As Hosea says [m], *On the third day He will raise us up, and we shall live in His sight.*" Talmudic Jews [n] identified Jonah with their Messiah ben Joseph, whom they expected to die and rise again. The deeper meaning then of the history was not, at least in later times, unknown to them, a meaning which entirely depended on its truth.

The history of his mission, Jonah doubtless himself wrote. Such has been the uniform tradition of the Jews, and on this principle alone was his book placed among the prophets. For no books were admitted among the prophets but those which the arranger of the Canon *believed* (if this was the work of the great synagogue) or (if it was the work of Ezra) *knew*, to have been written by persons called to the prophetic office. Hence the Psalms of David, (although many are prophetic, and our Lord declares him to have been inspired by the Holy Ghost [o],) and the book of Daniel, were placed in a separate class, because their authors, although eminently endowed with prophetic gifts, did not exercise the pastoral office of the Prophet. Histories of the Prophets, as Elijah and Elisha, stand, not under their own names, but in the books of the prophets who wrote them. Nor is the book of Jonah a history of the Prophet, but of that one mission to Nineveh. Every notice of the Prophet is omitted, except what bears on that mission. The book also begins with just that same authentication, with which all other prophetic books begin. As Hosea and Joel and Micah and Zephaniah open, *The word of the Lord that came unto Hosea, Joel, Micah, Zephaniah,* and other prophets in other ways ascribe their books not to themselves, but to God, so Jonah opens, *And the word of the Lord came unto Jonah, the son of Amittai, saying.* This inscription is an integral part of the book; as is marked by the word, *saying.* As the historical books are joined on the sacred writings before them, so as to form one continuous stream of history, by the *and*, with which they begin, so the book of Jonah is tacitly joined on to other books of other prophets by the word, *and*, with which it commences [p]. The words, *The word of the Lord came to*, are the acknowledged form [q] in which the commission of God to prophesy is recorded. It is used of the commission to deliver a single prophecy, or it describes the whole collection of prophecies, with which any prophet was entrusted [r]; *The word of the Lord which came to Micah* or *Zephaniah.* But the whole history of the

prophecy is bound up with, and a sequel of those words.

Nor is there anything in the style of the Prophet at variance with this.

It is strange that, at any time beyond the babyhood of criticism, any argument should be drawn from the fact that the Prophet writes of himself in the third person. Manly criticism has been ashamed to use the argument, as to the commentaries of Cæsar or the Anabasis of Xenophon [s]. However the genuineness of those works may have been at times questioned, here we were on the ground of genuine criticism, and no one ventured to use an argument so palpably idle. It has been pointed out that minds so different, as Barhebræus, the great Jacobite historian of the East [t], and Frederick the Great wrote of themselves in the third person; as did also Thucydides and Josephus [v], even after they had attested that the history, in which they so speak, was written by themselves.

But the real ground lies much deeper. It is the *exception*, when any sacred writer speaks of himself in the first person. Ezra and Nehemiah do so; for they are giving an account, not of God's dealings with His people, but of their own discharge of a definite office, allotted to them by man. Solomon does so in Ecclesiastes, because he is giving the history of his own experience; and the vanity of all human things, in themselves, could be attested so impressively by no one, as by one, who had all which man's mind could imagine.

On the contrary, the Prophets, unless they speak of God's revelations to them, speak of themselves in the third person. Thus Amos relates in the first person, what God shewed him in vision [w]; for God spoke to him, and he answered and pleaded with God. In relating his persecution by Amaziah, he passes at once to the third; [x] *Amaziah said to Amos; Then answered Amos and said to Amaziah.* In like way, Isaiah speaks of himself in the third person, when relating how God sent him to meet Ahaz [y]; commanded him to walk three years, naked and barefoot [z], Hezekiah's message to him, to pray for his people, and his own prophetic answer; his visit to Hezekiah in the king's sickness, his warning to him, his prophecy of his recovery, the sign which at God's command Isaiah gave him, and the means of healing he appointed [a]. Jeremiah, the mourner over his people more than any other prophet, speaks and complains to his God in the midst of his prophecy. In no other prophet do we see so much the workings of his inmost soul.

---

[m] vi. 2. (Eng.) see ab. p. 38.
[n] See in Eisenmenger, Entdecktes Judenthum, ii. 725.
[o] S. Matt. xxii. 43, S. Mark xii. 36.
[p] See more on Jon. i. 1.
[q] Gesenius, Thes. v. רבד. [r] Mic. i. 1, Zeph. i. 1.

[s] See Hengstenb. Auth. d. Pent. ii. 167-9.
[t] Hengst. ii. 170, from Ass. B. O. ii. 248 sqq.
[v] B. J, ii. 20. 4, 21, iii. 4, 6, 7, & 8.
[w] Am. vii. 1-8, viii. 1, 2, ix. 1.
[x] Ib. vii. 12, 14. [y] Is. vii. 3. [z] Ib. xx. 2, 3.
[a] Is. xxxvii, 2, 5, 6, 21, xxxviii. 1, 4, 21.

Such souls would most use the first person; for it is in the use of the first person that the soul pours itself forth. In relating of himself in the third person, the Prophet restrains himself, speaks of the event only. Yet it is thus that Jeremiah relates almost all which befell him; Pashur's smiting him and putting him in the stocks [b]; the gathering of the people against him to put him to death, his hearing before the princes of Judah and his deliverance [c]; the contest with Hananiah, when Hananiah broke off the symbolic yoke from his neck and prophesied lies in the name of God, and Jeremiah foretold his death [d], which followed; the letters of Shemaiah against him, and his own prophecy against Shemaiah [e]; his trial of the Rechabites and his prophecy to them [f]; the writing the roll, which he sent Baruch to read in God's house, and its renewal when Jehoiakim had burnt it, and God's concealing him and Baruch from the king's emissaries [g]; his purpose to leave Jerusalem when the interval of the last siege gave him liberty [h]; the false accusations against him, the designs of the princes to put him to death, their plunging him in the yet deeper pit, where was no water but mire, the milder treatment through the intercession of Ebed-melech; Zedekiah's intercourse with him [i]; his liberation by Nebuzaradan, his choice to abide in the land, his residence with Gedaliah [k]; Johanan's hypocritical enquiring of God by him and disobedience [l], his being carried into Egypt [m], the insolent answer of the Jews in Egypt to him and his denunciation upon them [n]. All this, the account of which occupies a space, many times larger than the book of Jonah, Jeremiah relates as if it were the history of some other man. So did God teach His prophets to forget themselves. Haggai, whose prophecy consists of exhortations which God directed him to address to the people, speaks of himself, solely in the third person. He even relates the questions which he puts to the priests and their answers still in the third person [o]; "then said Haggai;" "then answered Haggai." Daniel relates in the third person, the whole which he does give of his history; how when young he obtained exemption from the use of the royal luxuries and from food unlawful to him; the favor and wisdom which God gave him [p]; how God saved him from death, revealing to him, on his prayer, the dream of Nebuchadnezzar and its meaning; how Nebuchadnezzar made him ruler over the whole

province of Babylon [q]; how he was brought into Belshazzar's great impious feast, and interpreted the writing on the wall; and was honored [r]; how, under Darius, he persevered in his wonted prayer against the king's command, was cast into the den of lions, was delivered, and *prospered in the reign of Darius and in the reign of Cyrus the Persian* [s]. When Daniel passes from history to relate visions vouchsafed to himself, he authenticated them with his own name, *I Daniel* [t]. It is no longer his own history. It is the revelation of God by him. In like way, S. John, when referring to himself in the history of his Lord, calls himself *the disciple whom Jesus loved.* In the Revelations, he authenticates his visions by his own name; [u] *I John.* Moses relates how God commanded him to write things which he wrote, in the third person. S. Paul, when he has to speak of his overpowering revelations, says [v], *I knew a man in Christ.* It seems as if he could not speak of them as vouchsafed to himself. He lets us see that it was himself, when he speaks of the humiliations [w], which God saw to be necessary for him. To ordinary men it would be conceit or hypocrisy to write of themselves in the third person. They would have the appearance of writing impartially of themselves, of abstracting themselves from themselves, when, in reality, they were ever present to themselves. The men of God were writing of the things of God. They had a God-given indifference how they themselves would be thought of by man. They related, with the same holy unconcern, their praise or their blame. Jonah has exhibited himself in his infirmities, such as no other but himself would have drawn a Prophet of God. He has left his character, unexplained, unsoftened; he has left himself lying under God's reproof; and told us nothing of all that which God loved in him, and which made him too a chosen instrument of God. Men, while they measure Divine things, or characters formed by God, by what would be natural to themselves, measure by a crooked rule. [x] *It is a very small thing,* says S. Paul, *that I should be judged of you, or of man's judgment.* Nature does not measure grace; nor the human spirit, the Divine.

As for the few words, which persons who disbelieved in miracles selected out of the book of Jonah as a plea for removing it far down beyond the period when those miracles took place [y], they rather indicate the contrary. They are all genuine Hebrew words

[b] Jer. xx 1, 3.   [c] Ib. xxvi. 7, 8, 12, 24.
[d] xxviii. 5, 6, 10, 12, 15   [e] xxix. 27, 29, 30.
[f] xxxv   [g] xxxvi. 1, 4, 5, 26, 27, 32.
[h] xxxvii. 2–6, 12–21.
[i] xxxviii 1, 6, 12–28, xxxii. 2–5.   [k] xl. 2–6
[l] xlii.   [m] xliii.   [n] xliv 15, 20, 24.
[o] Hagg i 1, 3, 12, 13, ii. 1, 10, 13, 14, 20.
[p] Dan. i 6–end   [q] ii. 13–27, 46, 47, 49.
[r] v. 12, 13, 17, 29.   [s] ch. vi.

[t] vii. 15, 28, viii. 1, 15, 27, ix. 2, x. 2, 7, xii. 5.
[u] Rev. i. 9, xxi. 2, xxii. 8.   [v] 2 Cor. xii. 2–4.
[w] Ib. 7.   [x] 1 Cor. iv. 3.
[y] "We heed not," says Rosenmuller, Præf. c. 7. "the opinion of those who think that Jonah himself committed to writing in this book what befel himself, *since we do not admit* that any real history is contained in it." "Formerly, when people saw in the book of Jonah pure history, no one doubted

or forms, except the one Aramaic name for the decree of the king of Nineveh, which Jonah naturally heard in Nineveh itself.

A writer [z], equally unbelieving, who got rid of the miracles by assuming that the book of Jonah was meant only for a moralizing fiction, found no counter-evidence in the language, but ascribed it unhesitatingly to the Jonah, son of Amittai, who prophesied in the reign of Jeroboam II. He saw the nothingness of the so-called proof, which he had no longer any interest in maintaining.

The examination of these words will require a little detail, yet it may serve as a specimen (it is no worse than its neighbors) of the way in which the disbelieving school picked out a few words of a Hebrew Prophet or section of a Prophet, in order to disparage the genuineness of what they did not believe.

The words are these:

1) The word *sephinah*, lit. "a decked vessel," is a genuine Hebrew word from *saphan*, "covered, ceiled [a]." The word was borrowed from the Hebrew, not by Syrians or Chaldees only but by the Arabians, in none of which dialects is it an original word. A word plainly is original in that language in which it stands connected with other meanings of the same root, and not in that in which it stands isolated. Naturally too, the term for a *decked* vessel would be borrowed by inland people, as the Syrians, from a notion living on the sea shore, not conversely. This is the first occasion for mentioning a *decked* vessel. It is related that Jonah went in fact "below deck," *was gone down into the sides of the decked vessel*. Three times in those verses [b], when Jonah did not wish to express that the vessel was decked, he uses the common Hebrew word, *oniyyah*. It was then of set purpose that he, in the same verse, used the two words, *oniyyah* and *sephinah*.

2) *Mallach* is also a genuine Heb. word from *melach, salt* sea, as ἁλιεύς from ἅλς "salt," then (masc.) in poetry "brine." It is formed strictly, as other Hebrew words denoting an occupation [c]. It does not occur in earlier books, because "seamen" are not mentioned earlier.

3) *Rab hachobel*, "chief of the sailors," "captain." *Rab* is Phœnician also, and this was a Phœnician vessel. It does not occur earlier, because "the captain of a vessel" is not mentioned earlier. One says " [d] it is the

same as *sar, chiefly* in later Hebrew." It occurs, in *all*, only four times, and in all cases, as here, of persons not Hebrew; Nebuzaradan, *rab Tabbachim* [e], *captain* of the guard;" *rab Sarisim* [f], "chief of the eunuchs;" col *rab baitho* [g], "every officer of his house." *Sar*, on the other hand, is never used except of an *office* of authority, of one who had a place of authority given by one higher. It occurs as much in the later as in the earlier books, but is not used in the singular of an inferior office. It is used of military, but not of any inferior secular command. It would probably have been a solecism to have said *sar hachobel*, as much as if we were to say "prince of sailors." Chobel, which is joined with it, is a Hebrew not Aramaic word.

4) *Ribbo*, "ten thousand," they say, "is a word of later Hebrew." Certainly neither it, nor any inflection of it occurs in the Pentateuch, Judges, Samuel, Canticles, in all which we have the word *rebabah*. It is true also that the form *ribbo* or derivative forms occur in books of the date of the Captivity, as Daniel, Chronicles, Ezra, and Nehemiah [h]. But it also occurs in a Psalm of David [i], and in Hosea [k] who is acknowledged to have prophesied in the days of Jeroboam, and so was a contemporary of Jonah. It might have been, accordingly, a form used in Northern Palestine, but that its use by David does not justify such limitation.

5) *Yith' ashshath*, "thought, purposed," is also an old Hebrew word, as appears from its use in the number *eleven* [l], as the first number which is conceived in *thought*, the ten being numbered on the fingers. The root occurs also in Job, a Psalm [m], and the Canticles. In the Syriac, it does not occur; nor, in the extant Chaldee, in the sense in which it is used in Jonah. For in Jonah it is used of the merciful *thoughts* of God; in Chaldee, of the evil thoughts of man. Beside, it is used in Jonah not by the Prophet himself, but by the shipmaster, whose words he relates.

6) The use of the abridged forms of the relative *she* for *asher*, twice in composite words *beshellemi* [n], *beshelli* [o], (the fuller form, *baasher lemi* [p], also occurring) and once in union with a noun *shebbin* [q].

There is absolutely no plea whatever for making this an indication of a later style, and yet it occurs in every string of words, which have been assumed to be indications of such style. It is not Aramaic at all, but Phœnician [r]

---

that the Prophet Jonah himself wrote his wondrous lot." Bertholdt, Einl. § 564.

[z] Paulus, Memorabil. St. 6. p. 69.

[a] סְפַן "cover" occurs in Talmudic (as derived from the Hebrew) not in Chald. In Arabic it means "planed," smoothed, swept the earth, not "ceiled." So our deck is from the Dutch dekken, to cover.

[b] i. 3, 4, 5.   מַלָּח.   [d] See Gesen. 1254.

[e] 2 Kings xxv. 8.   [f] Dan. i. 3.   [g] Esth. i. 8.

[h] In 1 Chron. xxix. 7. twice, Daniel once, Ezra twice; Nehemiah thrice.

[i] רְבֹתִים Ps. lxviii. 18.   [k] viii. 12 Ch.

עִשְׁתֵּי עָשָׂר So A. E. Kim.   [m] Ps. cxlvi. 4.

[n] i. 7.   [o] i. 12.   [p] i. 8.   [q] iv. 10. (2).

[r] Ges. Thes. p. 1845. after Quatremère, Journ. Asiat. 1828. pp. 15. sqq. Journ. d. Savans, 1838. Oct.

In Aramaic it is דְ, דִי, דִיל. "Every one skilled herein knows now, that in Punic אֲשׁ is the relative pronoun." Roed. Ib. Add. Em. 113.

and old Hebrew. In Phœnician, *esh* is the relative, which corresponds the more with the Hebrew in that the following letter was doubled, as in the Punic words in Plautus, *syllohom, siddoberim* [s], it enters into two Proper names, both of which occur in the Pentateuch, and one, only there, *Methushael* [t], "a man of God," and *Mishael* [u], the same as Michael, "who is like God?" lit. "Who is what God is?" Probably, it occurs also in the Pentateuch in the ordinary language [v]. Perhaps it was used more in the dialect of North Palestine [w]. Probably it was also the spoken language [x], in which abridged forms are used in all languages. Hence perhaps its frequent use in the Song of Solomon [y], which is all dialogue, and in which it is employed to the entire exclusion of the fuller form ; and that, so frequently, that the instances in the Canticles are nearly ¼ of those in the whole Old Testament [z]. In addition to this, half of the whole number of instances, in which it occurs in the Bible, are found in another short book, Ecclesiastes. In a book, containing only 222 verses, it occurs 66 times [a]. This, in itself, requires some ground for its use, beyond that of mere date. Of books which are really later, it does *not* occur in Jeremiah's prophecies, Ezekiel, Daniel, or any of the 6 later of the Minor Prophets, nor in Nehemiah or Esther. It occurs once only in Ezra [b], and twice in the first book of Chronicles [c], whereas it occurs four times in the Judges [d], and once in the Kings [e], and once probably in Job [f]. Its use belongs to that wide principle of condensation in Hebrew, blending in one, in different ways, what we express by separate words. The relative pronoun is confessedly, on this ground, very often omitted in Hebrew poetry, when it would be used in prose. In the Canticles Solomon does not once use the ordinary separate relative, *asher*. Of the 19 instances in the Psalms, almost half, 9, occur in those Psalms of peculiar rhythm, the gradual Psalms [g] ; four more occur in two other Psalms [h], which belong to one another, the latter of which has that remarkable burden, *for His mercy endureth for-ever*. Three are condensed into a solemn

denunciation of Babylon in another Psalm [i]. Of the ten Psalms, in which it occurs, four are ascribed to David, and one only, the 137th, has any token of belonging to a later date. In the two passages in the Chronicles, it occurs in words doubly compounded [c]. The principle of rhythm would account for its occurring four times in the five chapters of the Lamentations [k] of Jeremiah, while in the 52 chapters of his prophecies it does not occur once. In Job also, it is in a solemn pause [l]. Altogether, there is no proof whatever that the use of *she* for *asher* is any test of the date of any Hebrew book, since 1) it is not Aramaic, 2) it occurs in the earliest, and 3) not in the latest books : 4) its use is idiomatic, and nowhere except in the Canticles and Ecclesiastes does it pervade any book. Had it belonged to the ordinary idiom at the date of Ezra, it would not have been so entirely insulated as it is, in the three instances in the Chronicles and Ezra. It would not have occurred in the earlier books in which it does occur, and would have occurred in later books in which it does not. In Jonah, its use in two places is peculiar to himself, occurring nowhere else in the Hebrew Scriptures. In the first, its Phœnician form is used by the Phœnician mariners ; in the 2d it is an instance of the spoken language in the mouth of the Prophet, a native of North Palestine, and in answer to Phœnicians. In the third instance, (where it is the simple relative) its use is evidently for condensation. Its use in any case would agree with the exact circumstances of Jonah, as a native of North Palestine, conversing with the Phœnician mariners. The only plea of argument has been gained by arguing in a circle, assuming without any even plausible ground that the Song of Solomon or Psalms of David were late, because they had this form, and then using it as a test of another book being late ; ignoring alike the earlier books which have it and the later books which have it not, and its exceptional use (except in the Canticles and Ecclesiastes,) in the books which have it.

7) It is difficult to know to what end the use of *manah*, "appoint [1]" or "prepare," is

---

[s] Plaut. Pœnul. v. 1. 4. 6. See Ges.

[t] Gen. iv. 18.

[u] Ex. vi. 22, Lev. x. 4; also in Daniel and Nehemiah.

[v] Gen. vi. 3.

[w] Hence perhaps in the song of Deborah, Judg. v. 7.

[x] Judg. vi. 17, 2 Kings vi. 11. Two of the instances in the Lamentations are words in the mouth of the heathen, Lam. ii. 15, 16.

[y] i. 6 (2), 7 (2), ii. 7, 17, iii. 1, 2, 3, 4 (4), 5, 7, iv. 1, 2 (2), 6, v. 2, 8, 9, vi. 5 (2), 6 (2), viii. 4. 8, 12.

[z] It occurs in all, I believe, 132 times, apart from its use as entering into the two proper names. Of these 29 are in the Canticles, 66 in Ecclesiastes, 19 in the Psalms, 1 in Genesis, 1 in Job, 4 in Judges, 1 in Kings, 4 in Lamentations, 1 in Ezra, 2 in Chronicles.

[a] Eccl. i. 3, 7, ט (4), 10, 11 (2), 14, 17, ii. 9, 11 (2), 12,

13, 14, 15, 16, 17, 18 (3), 19 (2), 20, 21 (2), 22, 24, 26, iii. 13, 14, 15, 18, 22, iv. 2, 10, v. 4, 14 (2), 15 (2), 17, vi. 3, 10 (2), vii. 10, 14, 24, viii. 7, 14, 17 ix. 5, 12 (2), x. 3, 5, 14, 16, 17, xi. 3, 8, xii. 3, 7, 9.

[b] viii. 20.

[c] 1 Chr. v. 20. שֶׁעֲמָהֶם, xxvii. 27. שֶׁבַכְרִמִים.

[d] v. 7, vi. 17, vii. 12, viii. 26.

[e] 2 Kings vi. 11. מִשֶּׁלָנוּ.

[f] xix. 29, ending with שַׁדִּין.

[g] Ps. cxxii. 3, 4, cxxiii. 2, cxxiv 1, 6, cxxix. 6, 7, cxxxiii. 2, 3.

[h] cxxv. 2, 8, 10, cxxxvi. 23.

[i] cxxxvii. 8 (2), 9. The remaining are Ps. cxliv. 15. שֶׁכַכ and cxlvi. 3, 5.

[k] ii. 15, 16, iv. 19, v. 18.

[l] The word occurs in Arabic also in this sense, which is a primary meaning of the root, and allied to its use in the transposed Greek form, νέμω.

alleged, since it occurs in a Psalm of David[m]. Jonah uses it in a special way as to acts of God's Providence, "preparing" before, what He wills to employ. Jonah uses the word of the "preparing" of the fish, the palm-christ, the worm which should destroy it, the East wind. He evidently used it with a set purpose, to express what no other word expressed equally to his mind, how God prepared by His Providence the instruments which He willed to employ.

8) There remains only the word used for the decree of the king of Nineveh, taam. This is a Syriac word; and accordingly, since it has now been ascertained beyond all question, that the language of Nineveh was a dialect of Syriac, it was, with a Hebrew pronunciation[n], the very word used of this decree at Nineveh. The employment of the special word is a part of the same accuracy with which Jonah relates that the decree used was issued not from the king only, but from the king and his nobles, one of those minute touches, which occur in the writings of those who describe what they have seen, but supplying a fact as to the Assyrian polity, which we should not otherwise have known, that the nobles were in some way associated in the decrees of the king.

Out of these eight words or forms, three are naval terms, and, since Israel was no seafaring people, it is in harmony with the history, that these terms should first occur in the first prophet who left the land of his mission by sea. So it is also, that an Assyrian technical term should first occur in a prophet who had been sent to Nineveh. A fifth word occurs in Hosea, a contemporary of Jonah, and in a Psalm of David. The abridged grammatical form was Phœnician, not Aramaic, was used in conversation, occurs in the oldest proper names, and in the Northern tribes. The 7th and 8th do not occur in Aramaic in the meaning in which they are used by Jonah.

In truth, often as these false criticisms have been repeated from one to the other, they would not have been thought of at all, but for the miracles related by Jonah, which the devisers of these criticisms did not believe. A history of miracles, such as those in Jonah, would not be published at the time, unless they were true. Those then who did not believe that God worked any

miracles, were forced to have some plea for saying that the book was not written in the time of Jonah. Prejudices against faith have, sometimes openly, sometimes tacitly, been the ruling principle on which earlier portions of Holy Scripture have been classed among the latter by critics who disbelieved what those books or passages related. Obviously no weight can be given to the opinions of critics, whose criticisms are founded, not on the study of the language, but on unbelief. It has recently been said, "[o] the joint decision of Gesenius, De Wette and Hitzig ought to be final." A joint decision certainly it is not. For De Wette places the book of Jonah before the captivity[p]; Gesenius[q] and Ewald[r], when prophecy had long ceased; Ewald, partly on account of its miracles, in the 5th century, B.C.; and Hitzig, with his wonted wilfulness and insulatedness of criticism, built a theory that the book is of Egyptian origin on his own mistake that the kikaion grew only in Egypt, and placed it in the 2d century, B.C., the times of the Maccabees[s]. The interval is also filled up. Every sort of date and contradictory grounds for those dates have been assigned. So then one places the book of Jonah in the time of Sennacherib[t], i.e. of Hezekiah; another under Josiah[u]; another before the Captivity[v]; another toward the end of the Captivity, after the destruction of Nineveh by Cyaxares[w]; a fifth lays chief stress on the argument that the destruction of Nineveh is not mentioned in it[x]; a sixth[y] prefers the time after the return from the Captivity to its close; a seventh doubted not, "from its argument and purpose, that it was written before the order of prophets ceased[z]," others of the same school are as positive from its arguments and contents, that it must have been written after that order was closed[a].

The style of the book of Jonah is, in fact pure and simple Hebrew, corresponding to the simplicity of the narrative and of the Prophet's character. Although written in prose, it has poetic language, not in the thanksgiving only, but whenever it suits the subject. These expressions are peculiar to Jonah. Such are, in the account of the storm, "the Lord cast[b] a strong wind," "the vessel thought[c] to be broken," "the sea shall be silent[d]" (hushed, as we say) i.e. calm; "the wind was advancing and storming[e],"

---

[m] Ps. lxi. 8.   [n] טַעַם for טְעֵם.

[o] Mr. G. Vance Smith, Prophecies concerning Nineveh p. 257, who however (p. 294,) rightly rejects their grounds, the occurrence of the words discussed above, as inadequate. The only other ground is their unbelief.

[p] Einl. § 237.   [q] Hall. A. L. Z. 1813. n. 23. p. 180.

[r] Propheten, p. 559.   [s] Kl. Proph. Jonah, § 6.

[t] Goldhorn, Excurse zum B. Jonah, pp. 16 sqq.

[u] Rosenmüller, Prol. in Jon. § 7.   [v] De Wette.

[w] Müller, in Memorabilien, P. vi. pp. 146 sqq.

[x] Bertholdt, § 564.   [y] Jahn, Einl. § 129.

[z] Maurer, Præf. in Jon. p. 426.

[a] Ges. and Ew. above, Umbreit tacitly drops it out of "the twelve."

[b] הֵטִיל i. 4; the word describing how the wind "swept along," as we say; Jonah also uses it of casting out, along, from the vessel, i. 5, 12, 15.

[c] חִשְּׁבָה i. 4, the only place where it is used of lifeless things.

[d] שָׁתַק i. 11, 12. used of the men in the vessel, Ps. cvii. 30; of ceasing of strife, Prov. xxvi. 20.

[e] הוֹלֵךְ וְסֹעֵר i. 11, 13.

as with a whirlwind; [the word is used as to the sea by Jonah only,] "the men ploughed" or "dug f" [in rowing] "the sea stood g from its raging." Also "let man and beast *clothe themselves* h with sackcloth," and that touching expression, "son of a night i, it [the palma Christi] came to being, and son of a night [i.e. in a night] it perished." It is in harmony with his simplicity of character, that he is fond of the old idiom, by which the thought of the verb is carried on by a noun formed from it. "The men *feared* a great *fear* k," "It *displeased* Jonah a great *displeasure* l," "Jonah *joyed* a great *joy* m." Another idiom n has been observed, which occurs in no writer later than the judges.

But in the history every phrase is vivid and graphic. There is not a word which does not advance the history. There is no reflection. All hastens on to the completion, and when God has given the key to the whole, the book closes with His words of exceeding tenderness, lingering in our ears. The Prophet, with the same simplicity and beginning with the same words, says he did not, and he did, obey God. The book opens, after the first authenticating words, *Arise, go to Nineveh, that great city, and cry against it; for the wickedness is come up before Me.* God had bidden him arise o; the narrative simply repeats the word, *And Jonah arose* p,—but for what? to flee in the very opposite direction *from being before the Lord* q, i. e. from standing in His Presence, as His servant and minister. He lost no time, to do the contrary. After the miracles, by which he had been both punished and delivered, the history is resumed with the same simple dignity as before, in the same words ; the disobedience being noticed only in the word, *a second time. And the word of the Lord came to Jonah a second time, saying, Arise, go to Nineveh, that great city, and cry unto it that cry which I say unto thee.* This time it follows, *And Jonah arose and went to Nineveh.*

Then in the history itself we follow the Prophet step by step. He arose to flee to Tarshish, went down to Joppa, a perilous, yet the only sea-port for Judæa r. He finds the ship, *pays its fare,* (one of those little touches of a true narrative); God sends the storm, man does all he can; and all in vain. The character of the heathen is brought out in contrast with the then sleeping conscience and despondency of the Prophet. But it is all in act. They are all activity; he, sim-

ply passive. They pray, (as they can) each man to his gods; he is asleep : they do all they can, lighten the ship, the ship-master rouses him, to pray to his God, since their own prayers avail not; they propose the lots, cast them ; the lot falls on Jonah. Then follow their brief accumulated enquiries ; Jonah's calm answer, increasing their fear ; their enquiry of the Prophet himself, what they are to do to him ; his knowledge that he must be cast over; the unwillingness of the Heathen ; one more fruitless effort to save both themselves and the Prophet; the increasing violence of the storm ; the prayer to the Prophet's God, not to lay innocent blood to them, who obeyed His Prophet; the casting him forth ; the instant hush and silence of the sea; their conversion and sacrifice to the true God—the whole stands before us, as if we saw it with our own eyes.

And yet, amid, or perhaps as a part of, that vividness, there is that characteristic of Scripture-narratives, that some things even seem improbable, until, on thought, we discover the reason. It is not on a first reading, that most perceive the naturalness either of Jonah's deep sleep, or of the increase of the mariner's fear, on his account of himself. Yet that deep sleep harmonizes at least with his long hurried flight to Joppa, and that mood with which men who have taken a wrong step, try to forget themselves. He relates that he *was gone down* s, i. e. before the storm began. The sailors' increased fear surprises us the more, since it is added, "they knew that he had fled from before the presence of God, *because he had told them.*" One word explained it. He had told them, from Whose service he had fled, but not that He, against Whom he had sinned, and Who, they would think, was pursuing His fugitive, was "the Maker of the sea," whose raging was threatening their lives.

Again, the history mentions only, that Jonah was cast over; that God prepared a fish to swallow him; that he was in the belly of the fish three days and three nights; that he, at the end of that time, prayed to God out of the fish's belly, and at the close of the prayer was delivered. The word "prayed" obviously includes "thanksgiving" as the act of adoring love from the creature to the Creator. It is said that *Hannah prayed* t; but her hymn, as well as Jonah's does not contain one petition. Both are the outpouring

---

f חתר, "Æquor arare." Virg. Æn. ii. 780. Ov. Trist. i. 2, 76.

g יעמד־מזעפו i. 15.   h יתכסו iii. 8.

i בן־לילה iv. 10.   k i. 10, 16. יראה יראו.

l iv. 1. ירע רעה.   m Ib. 6. ישמח שמחה.

n עד with the inf. (for בעוד) iv. 2. coll. Jud. iii. 26. (Delitzsch in Zeitschr. f. Luth. Theol. 1840. p. 118.) But two passages do not furnish an induction.

הרבה for יותר iv. 11. (mentioned ib.) cannot prove anything, since it occurs, 2 Chr. xxv. 9.   o קום.

p ויקם, more expressive in the original, as being the first word in the clause; "The Lord said, *Arise; And arose* Jonah," to do the contrary.

q See ab. p. 371.

r 1 Kings v. 9, 2 Chron. ii. 16, and after the captivity, Ezr. iii. 7.

s i. 5.   t 1 Sam. ii. 1.

of thanksgiving from the soul, to which God had given what it *had* prayed for. As, before, it was not said, whether he prayed, on the ship-master's upbraiding, or no, so here nothing is said in the history, except as to the last moment, on which he was cast out on the dry ground. The prayer incidentally supplies the rest. *It* is a simple thanksgiving of one who *had* prayed, and *had* been delivered. [u] *I cried unto the Lord, and He heard me.* In the first mercy, he saw the earnest of the rest. He asks for nothing, he only thanks. But that for which he thanks is the deliverance from the perils of the *sea.* The thanksgiving corresponds with the plain words, that he *prayed out of the fish's belly.* They are suited to one so praying, who looked on in full faith to the future completion of his deliverance, although *our* minds might rather have been fixed on the actual peril. It is a thanksgiving of faith, but of stronger faith than many moderns have been able to conceive [v].

The hymn itself is a remarkable blending of old and new, as our Lord says [w]; *Therefore is the kingdom of heaven like a householder, who bringeth out of his treasure new and old.* The Prophet teaches us to use the Psalms, as well as how the holy men of old used them. In that great moment of religious life, the well-remembered Psalms, such as he had often used them, were brought to his mind. What had been figures to David or the sons of Korah, as [x], *the waters are come in even unto my soul;* [y] *all Thy billows and Thy waves passed over me,* were strict realities to him. Yet only in this last sentence and in one other sentence which doubtless had become a proverb of accepted prayer, [z] *I cried out of my trouble unto the Lord and He heard me,* does Jonah use exactly the words of earlier Psalms. Elsewhere he varies or amplifies them according to his own special circumstances. Thus, where David said, "the waters are *come in,* even unto my soul," Jonah substitutes the word which described best the condition from which God had delivered *him,* "The water *compassed me about,* even to the soul." Where David said [a], "*I am cut off* from before Thine eyes," expressing an abiding condition, Jonah, who had for disobedience been cast into the sea, uses the strong word, "[b] *I am cast out* from before Thine eyes." David says, "I said in my haste;"

Jonah simply, "I said;" for he had deserved it. David said [c], "when my spirit was overwhelmed" or "fainted within me," "*Thou knewest my path;*" Jonah substitutes, "When my soul fainted within me, *I remembered the Lord* [d];" for when he rebelled, he forgat Him. David said, "[e] *I hate* them that observe lying vanities;" Jonah, who had himself disobeyed God, says mournfully, "[f] They that observe lying vanities, *forsake their own mercy,*" i. e. their God, Who is Mercy.

Altogether, Jonah's thanksgiving is that of one whose mind was stored with the Psalms which were part of the public worship, but it is the language of one who uses and re-casts them freely, as he was taught of God, not of one who copies. No one verse is taken entirely from any Psalm. There are original expressions everywhere [g]. The words, "I went down to the cuttings-off of the mountains," "the sea-weed bound around my head;" "the earth, its bars around me for ever;" perhaps the coral reefs which run along all that shore [h], vividly exhibit him, sinking, entangled, imprisoned, as it seems, inextricably; he goes on; we should expect some further description of his state; but he adds, in five simple words [i], *Thou broughtest up my life from corruption, O Lord My God.* Words, somewhat like these last, occur elsewhere [j] *thou hast brought up my soul from hell,* agreeing in the one word "brought up." But the majesty of the Prophet's conception is in the connection of the thought; the sea-weed was bound round his head as his grave-clothes; the solid bars of the deep-rooted earth, were around him, and—God brought him up. At the close of the thanksgiving, *Salvation is the Lord's,* deliverance is completed, as though God had only waited for this act of complete faith.

So could no one have written, who had not himself been delivered from such an extreme peril of drowning, as man could not, of himself, escape from. True, that no image so well expresses the overwhelmedness under affliction or temptation, as the pressure of storm by land, or being overflooded by the waves of the sea. Human poetry knows of "a sea of troubles," or "the triple wave of evils." It expresses how we are simply passive and powerless under a trouble, which leaves us neither breath nor power of motion; under which we can be but still, till, by

---

[u] ii. 3.

[v] "In the fish's belly, he prays as tranquilly as if on land," says even Jahn, as an objection. Einl. § 126.

[w] S. Matt. xiii. 52.   [x] Jon. ii. 5, Ps. lxix. 2.

[y] Jon. ii. 3, Ps. xlii. 8.

[z] Jon. ii. 2, Ps. cxx. 1.

[a] Ps. xxxi. 22. נִגְזַרְתִּי.

[b] Jon. ii. 4. [5] נִגְרַשְׁתִּי.

[c] Ps. cxlii. 8.   [d] ii. 7. (8).

[e] Ps. xxxi. 7.   [f] ii. 9.

[g] מִבֶּטֶן שְׁאוֹל ii. 3; נהר of the currents of the

---

sea, 4; קַצְבֵי הָרִים [7]; סוּף חָבוּשׁ לְרֹאשׁ, 6; הָאָרֶץ

8, חֲסָרִים יְזֻבּוּ, 1b. בְּרִיחֶיהָ בַעֲדִי לְעוֹלָם

[h] "Considerable quantities of coral are found in the adjacent sea." W. G. Browne, writing of Jaffa, Travels, p. 360. "Coral-reefs run along the coast as far as Gaza, which cut the cables in two, and leave the ships at the mercy of the storms. None lie here on the coast, which is fuller of strong surfs (brandings,) and unprotected against the frequent West winds." Ritter, ii. 399. ed. 1.

וַתַּעַל מִשַּׁחַת חַיַּי יְהוָה אֱלֹהַי.   [j] Ps. xxx. 3.

God's mercy it passes. "We are sunk, over-head, deep down in temptations, and the masterful current is sweeping in eddies over us." Of this sort are those images which Jonah took from the Psalms. But a description so minute as the whole of Jonah's would be allegory, not metaphor. What, in it, is most descriptive of Jonah's situation [k], as "binding of the sea-weed around the head, the sinking down to the roots of the mountains, the bars of the earth around him," are peculiar to this thanksgiving of Jonah ; they do not occur elsewhere ; for, except through miracle, they would be images not of peril but of death.

The same vividness, and the same steady directions to its end, characterizes the rest of the book. Critics have wondered [l], why Jonah does not say, on what shore he was cast forth, why he does not describe his long journey to Nineveh, or tell us the name of the Assyrian king, or what he himself did, when his mission was closed. Jonah speaks of himself, only as relates to his mission, and God's teaching through him ; he tells us not the king's name, but his deeds. The description of the size of Nineveh remarkably corresponds alike with the ancient accounts and modern investigations. Jonah describes it as "a city of three days' journey." This obviously means its circumference ; for, unless the city were a circle, (as no cities are,) it would have no one diameter. A person might describe the average length *and* breadth of a city, but no one who gave any one measure, by days or miles or any other measure, would mean anything else than its circumference. Diodorus (probably on the authority of Ctesias) states that "[m] it was well-walled, of unequal lengths. Each of the longer sides was 150 furlongs; each of the shorter, 90. The whole circuit then being 480 furlongs [60 miles] the hope of the founder was not disappointed. For no one afterward built a city of such compass, and with walls so magnificent." To Babylon "Clitarchus and the companions of Alexander in their writings, assigned a circuit of 365 furlongs, adding that the number of furlongs was conformed to the number of days in the year [n]." Ctesias, in round numbers, calls them 360 [o]; Strabo, 385 [p]. All these accounts agree with the statement of Strabo, "Nineveh was much larger than Babylon [q]." The 60 miles of Diodorus exactly correspond

with the three days' journey of Jonah. A traveler of our own at the beginning of the 17th century, J. Cartwright, states that with his own eyes he traced out the ruinous foundations, and gives their dimensions. "[r] It seems by the ruinous foundation (*which I thoroughly viewed*) that it was built with four sides, but not equal or square. For the two longer sides had each of them (as we guess) 150 furlongs, the two shorter sides ninety furlongs, which amounteth to four hundred and eighty furlongs of ground, which makes the threescore miles, accounting eight furlongs to an Italian mile." No one of the four great mounds, which lie around the site of ancient Nineveh, Nimrud, Kouyunjik, Khorsabad, Karamless, is of sufficient moment or extent to be identified with the old Nineveh. But they are connected together by the sameness of their remains. Together they form a parallelogram, and this of exactly the dimensions assigned by Jonah. "[s] From the Northern extremity of Kouyunjik to Nimrud, is about 18 miles, the distance from Nimrud to Karamless, about 12 ; the opposite sides, the same." "A recent trigonometrical survey of the country by Captain Jones proves, I am informed," says Layard [t], "that the great ruins of Kouyunjik, Nimrud, Karamless, and Khorsabad form very nearly a perfect parallelogram."

This is perhaps also the explanation, how, seeing its circumference was three days' journey, Jonah entered a day's journey *in* the city and, at the close of the period, we find him at the East side of the city, the opposite to that at which he had entered.

His preaching seems to have lasted only this one day. He *went*, we are told, *one day's journey in the city.* The 150 stadia are nearly 19 miles, a day's journey, so that Jonah walked through it from end to end, repeating that one cry, which God had commanded him to cry. We seem to see the solitary figure of the Prophet, clothed (as was the prophet's dress) in that one rough garment of hair cloth, uttering the cry which we almost hear, echoing in street after street, "ōd arbaim yom venineveh nehpācheth," "yet forty days and Nineveh overthrown." The words which he says he cried and said, belong to that one day only. For on that one day only, was there still a respite of *forty days*. In one day, the grace of God prevailed. The conversion of a whole people upon one

---

[k] See below on ii. 5, 6.

[l] Hitzig. Jona, § 3. Jahn added, as the current objections, the omissions, "what vices prevailed in Nineveh," [it is incidentally said, "violence," iii. 8] how Jonah brought home to the inhabitants the sense of their guilt; by what calamity, earthquake, inundation or war, the city was to perish ; whether, in the general repentance, idolatry was abolished." § 126. 4. All mere by-questions, not affecting the main issue, God's pardoning mercy to the penitent heathen !

[m] ii. 3. So too Q. Curtius v. 4.   [n] Diod. ii. 7.
[o] in Diod. l. c.   [p] xvi. 1. 5.   [q] Ib. 3.
[r] Mr. John Cartwright, The Preacher's Travels, Nineveh, c. 4. Lord Oxford's Collection, i. 745. London, 1745, abridged in Purchas, T. ii. p. 1435.
[s] Layard, Nineveh, P. 2. c. 2. T. ii. 247 note.
[t] Ninev. and Bab. p. 640. Capt. Jones, although treating Ctesias' account as fabulous, states "the entire circuit is but 61½ English miles." Topography of Nineveh, Journ. As. Soc. T. xv. p. 303. See Plan, p. 254.

day's preaching of a single stranger, stands in contrast with the many years during which, God says [u], *since the day that your fathers came forth out of the land of Egypt unto this day, I have sent unto you all My servants the prophets, daily rising up early and sending them, yet they hearkened not unto Me.* Many of us have wondered what the Prophet did on the other thirty-nine days; people have imagined the Prophet preaching as moderns would, or telling them his own wondrous story of his desertion of God, his miraculous punishment, and, on his repentance, his miraculous deliverance. Jonah says nothing of this. The one point he brought out was the conversion of the Ninevites. This he dwells on in circumstantial details. His own part he suppresses; he would be, like S. John Baptist, but the voice of one crying in the wild waste of a city of violence.

This simple message of Jonah bears an analogy to what we find elsewhere in Holy Scripture. The great preacher of repentance, S. John Baptist, repeated doubtless oftentimes that one cry [x], *Repent ye, for the kingdom of heaven is at hand.* Our Lord vouchsafed to begin His own office with those self-same words [y]. And probably, among the civilized but savage inhabitants of Nineveh, that one cry was more impressive than any other would have been. Simplicity is always impressive. They were four words which God caused to be written on the wall amid Belshazzar's impious revelry [z]; *Mene, mene, tekel, upharsin.* We all remember the touching history of Jesus the son of Anan, an unlettered rustic, who, "[a] four years before the war, when Jerusalem was in complete peace and affluence," burst in on the people at the feast of tabernacles with one oft-repeated cry, "A voice from the East, a voice from the West, a voice from the four winds, a voice on Jerusalem and the temple, a voice on the bridegrooms and the brides, a voice on the whole people;" how he went about through all the lanes of the city, repeating, day and night, this one cry; and when scourged until his bones were laid bare, echoed every lash with "woe, woe, to Jerusalem," and continued as his daily dirge and his one response to daily good or ill-treatment, "woe, woe, to Jerusalem." The magistrates and even the cold Josephus thought that there was something in it above nature.

In Jerusalem, no effect was produced, because they had filled up the measure of their sins and God had abandoned them. All conversion is the work of the grace of God. That of Nineveh remains, in the history of mankind, an insulated instance of God's overpowering grace. All which can be pointed out as to the book of Jonah, is the latent suitableness of the instruments employed. We know from the Cuneiform Inscriptions that Assyria had been for successive generations at war [b] with Syria. Not until the time of Ivalush or Pul [c], the Assyrian monarch, probably, at the time of Jonah's mission, do we find them tributary to Assyria. They were hereditary enemies of Assyria, and probably their chief opponents on the North East. The breaking of their power then, under Jeroboam, which Jonah had foretold, had an interest for the Assyrians; and Jonah's prophecy and the fact of its fulfillment may have reached them. The history of his own deliverance, we know from our Lord's own words, did reach them. He was a sign [d] *unto the Ninevites.* The word, under which he threatened their destruction, pointed to a miraculous overthrow. It was a turning upside down [e], like the overthrow of the five cities of the plain which are known throughout the Old Testament [f], and still throughout the Mohammedan East, by the same name, "almoutaphikat [g], the overthrown."

The Assyrians also, amidst their cruelties, had a great reverence for their gods, and (as appears from the inscriptions, ascribed to them their national greatness [h]. The variety of ways in which this is expressed, implies a far more personal belief, than the statements which we find among the Romans, and would put to shame almost every English manifesto, or the speeches put into the mouth of the Queen. They may have been, then, the more prepared to fear the prophecy of their destruction from the true God. Layard relates that he has "known a Christian priest frighten a whole Mussulman town to repentance, by proclaiming that he had a Divine mission to announce a coming earthquake or plague [i]."

These may have been predisposing causes. But the completeness of the repentance, not outward only, but inward, "turning from their evil way," is, in its extent, unexampled.

---

[u] Jer. vii. 25, add 13, xi. 7, xxv. 3, 4, xxvi. 5, xxix. 19, xxxii. 33, xxxv. 14, 15, xliv. 4.
[x] S. Matt. iii. 2.   [y] Ib. iv. 17, S. Mark i. 15.
[z] Dan. v. 25.   [a] Jos. de B. J. vi. 5. 3.
[b] See above on Am. i. 3. p. 157.
[c] Rawl. Herod. i. 466, 7.   [d] S. Luke xi. 30.
[e] as Judg. vii. 13, Job ix. 5, xxviii. 9.
[f] Gen. xix. 21, 25, Deut. xxix. 23, Am. iv. 11, Jer. xx. 16, Lam. iv. 6.
[g] from Cor. ix. 71, liii. 53, lxix. 9.
[h] Thus in one inscripton, "Ashur, the giver of sceptres and crowns, the appointer of sovereignty;" "the gods, the guardians of the kingdom of Tig-

lath-pileser, gave government and laws to my dominions, and ordered an enlarged frontier to my territory;" "they withheld the tribute due to Ashur my Lord;" "the exceeding fear of the power of Ashur, my Lord, overwhelmed them; my valiant servants (or powerful arms) to which Ashur the Lord gave strength." "In the service of my Lord Ashur;" "whom Ashur and Ninep have exalted to the utmost wishes of his heart;" "the great gods, guardians of my steps," &c. Journ. Asiat. Soc. 1860. xviii. pp. 1(4, 8, 170, 4, 6, (and others 172, 8, 180, 4) 192, 8, 206, 10, 14, and Rawl. Herod. i. 457, 587, and note 7.   [i] Ninev. and Babyl. p. 632 note.

The fact rests on the authority of *One greater than Jonah*. Our Lord relates it as a fact. He contrasts people with people, the penitent heathen with the impenitent Jews, the inferior messenger who prevailed, with Himself, Whom His own received not. [k] *The men of Nineveh shall raise up with this generation and shall condemn it, because they repented at the preaching of Jonas, and behold, a greater than Jonas is here.*

The chief subject of the repentance of the Ninevites agrees also remarkably with their character. It is mentioned in the proclamation of the king and his nobles, "let them turn every one from his evil way *and from the violence* that is in their hands." Out of the whole catalogue of their sins, conscience singled out *violence*. This incidental notice, contained in the one word, exactly corresponds in substance with the fuller description in the Prophet Nahum, "[l] Woe to the bloody city; it is all full of lies and *robbery*; the *prey* departeth not." "[m] The lion did tear in pieces enough for his whelps, and strangled for his lionesses, and filled his holes with *prey* and his dens with *ravin*." "[n] Upon whom hath not thy wickedness [ill-doing] passed continually?" "The Assyrian records," says Layard [o], "are nothing but a dry register of military campaigns, spoilations and cruelties."

The direction, that the animals also should be included in the common mourning, was according to the analogy of Eastern custom. When the Persian general Masistius fell at the battle of Platæa [p], the "whole army and Mardonius above all, made a mourning, *shaving themselves, and the horses, and the beasts of burden*, amid surpassing wailing—Thus the Barbarians after their manner honored Masistius on his death." Alexander imitated apparently the Persian custom in his mourning for Hephæstion [q]. The characteristic of the mourning in each case is, that they include the animals in that same mourning which they made themselves. The Ninevites had a right feeling, (as God Himself says) that the mercies of God were over man and beast [r]; and so they joined the beasts with themselves, hoping that the Creator of all would the rather have mercy on their common distress. [s] *His tender mercies are over all His works:* [t] *Thou, Lord, shalt save both man and beast.*

The name of the king cannot yet be ascertained. But since this mission of Jonah fell in the latter part of his prophetic office, and so probably in the latter part of the reign of Jeroboam or even later, the Assyrian king was probably Ivalush III. or the Pul of Holy Scripture. Jonah's human fears would, in that case, have been soon fulfilled. For Pul was the first Assyrian Monarch through whom Israel was weakened; and God had foreshewn by Amos that through the third it would be destroyed. Characteristic, on account of the earnestness which it implies, is the account that the men of Nineveh proclaimed the fast, before tidings reached the king himself. This is the plain meaning of the words; yet on account of the obvious difficulty they have been rendered, *and word had come to the king* [u]. The account is in harmony with that vast extent of the city, as of Babylon, of which "[x] the residents related that, after the outer portions of the city were taken, the inhabitants of the central part did not know that they were taken." It could scarcely have occurred to one who did not know the fact.

The history of Jonah, after God had spared Nineveh, has the same characteristic touches. He leaves his own character unexplained, its severity rebuked by God, unexcused and unpalliated. He had some special repugnance to be the messenger of mercy to the Ninevites. *For this cause*, he says to God, *I fled before to Tarshish; for I knew that Thou art a merciful God, and repentest Thee of the evil.* The circumstances of his time explain that repugnance. He had already been employed to prophesy the partial restoration of the boundaries of Israel. He was the contemporary of Hosea who foretold of his people, the ten tribes [y], *they shall not dwell in the Lord's land, they shall eat unclean things in Assyria.* God, in giving him his commission to go to Nineveh, the capital of Assyria, and *cry against it*, assigned as the reason, *for its wickedness is come up before Me;* words which to Jonah would suggest the memory of the wickedness of Sodom and its destruction. Jonah was a Prophet, but he was also an Israelite. He was commanded by God to call to repentance the capital of the country by which his own people, nay the people of his God, were to be carried captive. And he rebelled. *We* know more of the love of God than Jonah, for we have known the love of the Incarnation and the Redemption. And yet, were it made known to us, that some European or Asiatic people were to carry our own people captive out of our land, more than would be willing to confess it of themselves, (whatever sense they might have of the awfulness of God's judgments, and what-

---

[k] S. Matt. xii. 41.   [l] iii. 1.
[m] ii. 12.   [n] iii. 19.
[o] Nineveh and Bab. p. 631.
[p] Herod. ix. 24. Plutarch Aristid. c. 14; see Rawlinson's note on Her. T. iv. p. 401.
[q] Plutarch Alex. c. 72. "he commanded to shave all the horses and mules, as mourning."

[r] See on Joel i. 20. p. 111.   [s] Ps. cxlv. 9.
[t] Ib. xxxvi. 7.
[u] The Vulg. has rightly, "et pervenit." Lapide explains this wrongly, "id est, quia pervenerat." The E. V. smooths the difficulty wrongly by rendering, "For word came."
[x] Herod. i. 191.   [y] ix. 3.

ever feelings belonging to our common humanity,) would still inwardly rejoice to hear, that such a calamity as the earthquake at Lisbon befell its capital. It is the instinct of self-preservation and the implanted love of country. Jonah's murmuring related solely to God's mercy shewn to them as to this world. For the Ninevites had repented, and so were in the grace of God. The older of us remember what awful joy was felt when that three days' mortal strife at Leipzig at length was won, in which 107,000 were killed or wounded [z]; or when out of 647,000 men who swept across Europe (a mass larger than the whole population of Nineveh) only "85,000 escaped; 125,000 were slain in battle, 132,000 perished by cold, fatigue and famine [a]." A few years ago, how were Sebastopol and the Krimea in men's mouths, although that war is reputed to have cost the five nations involved in it 700,000 lives, more, probably, than all the inhabitants of Nineveh. Men forget or abstract themselves from all the individual sufferings, and think only of the result of the whole. A humane historian says of the battle of Leipzig [b], "a prodigious sacrifice, but one which, great as it was, humanity has no cause to regret, for it delivered Europe from French bondage, and the world from revolutionary aggression." He says on the Russian campaign of Napoleon I.[c], "the faithful throughout Europe repeated the words of the Psalm, Efflavit Deus et dissipantur."

Look at Dr. Arnold's description of the issue of the Russian campaign. "[d] Still the flood of the tide rose higher and higher, and every successive wave of its advance swept away a kingdom. Earthly state has never reached a prouder pinnacle, than when Napoleon in June, 1812, gathered his army at Dresden, that mighty host, unequalled in all time, of 450,000, not men merely but, effective soldiers, and there received the homage of subject kings. And now, what was the principal adversary of this tremendous power? by whom was it checked, resisted, and put down? By none, and by nothing but the direct and manifest interposition of God. I know no language so well fitted to describe the victorious advance to Moscow, and the utter humiliation of the retreat, as the language of the prophet with respect to the advance and subsequent destruction of the host of Sennacherib. *When they arose early in the morning, behold they were all dead corpses,* applied almost literally to that memorable night of frost in which 20,000 horses perished, and the strength of the French army was utterly broken. Human instruments no doubt were employed in the

remainder of the work, nor would I deny to Germany and to Russia the glories of that great year 1813, nor to England the honor of her victories in Spain or of the crowning victory of Waterloo. But at the distance of thirty years those who lived in the time of danger and remember its magnitude, and now calmly review what there was in human strength to avert it, must acknowledge, I think, beyond all controversy, that the deliverance of Europe from the dominion of Napoleon was effected neither by Russia nor by Germany nor by England, but by the hand of God alone." Jonah probably pictured to himself some sudden and almost painless destruction, which the word, *overthrown,* suggested, in which the whole city would be engulfed in an instant and the power which threatened his people, the people of God, broken at once. God reproved Jonah; but, before man condemns him, it were well to think, what is the prevailing feeling in Christian nations, at any signal calamity which befalls any people who threaten their own power or honor;—we cannot, in Christian times, say, their existence. "Jonah," runs an old traditional saying among the Jews [e], "sought the honor of the son [Israel], and sought not the honor of the Father."

An uninspired writer would doubtless at least have brought out the relieving points of Jonah's character, and not have left him under the unmitigated censure of God. Jonah tells the plain truth of himself, as S. Matthew relates his own desertion of his Lord among the Apostles, or S. Mark, under the guidance of S. Peter, relates the great fall of the great Apostle.

Amid this, Jonah remains the same throughout. It is one strong impetuous will, bent on having no share in that which was to bring destruction on his people, fearless of death and ready to give up his life. In the same mind he gives himself to death amid the storm, and, when his mission was accomplished, asks for death in the words of his great predecessor Elijah, when he fled from Jezebel. He probably justified his impatience to himself by the precedent of so great a prophet. But although he complains, he complains to God of Himself. Having complained, Jonah waits. It may be that he thought, although God did not execute His judgments on the 40th day, He might still fulfill them. He had been accustomed to the thought of the long-suffering of God, delaying even when He struck at last. "Considering with himself," says Theodorus, "the greatness of the threat, he imagined that something might perchance still happen even

---

[z] Alison, Hist. of Europe, c. 81. T. xii. p. 255.
[a] Ib. c. 73. T. xi. 199; c. 74. ib. 229.
[b] Alison, l. c.

[c] Alis. xi. 213.　[d] Lecture iii. pp. 177-9.
[e] "Words of the Rabbies of blessed memory." Kim. on Jon. i.

after this." The patience of God amid the
Prophet's impatience, the still, gentle inquiry,
(such as He often puts to the conscience now,)
Doest thou well to be angry? and his final
conviction of the Prophet out of his own
feelings towards one of God's inanimate
creatures, none would have ventured to
picture, who had not known or experienced it.

In regard to the miracles in Jonah's history, over and above the fact, that they occur
in Holy Scripture, we have our Lord's own
word for their truth. He has set His seal on
the whole of the Old Testament [f]; He has
directly authenticated by His own Divine
authority the physical miracle of Jonah's
preservation for three days and nights in the
belly of the fish [g], and the yet greater moral
miracle of the conversion of the Ninevites [h].
He speaks of them both, as facts, and of the
stay of Jonah in the fish's belly, as a type of
His own stay in the heart of the earth.
He speaks of it also as a miraculous sign [i].

The Scribes and Pharisees, unable to
answer His refutation of their blasphemy,
imputing His miracles to Beelzebub, asked
of Him a miraculous sign [k] from Heaven.
Probably, they meant to ask that one sign,
for which they were always craving. Con-
founding His first Coming with His second,
and interpreting, according to their wishes,
of His first Coming all which the prophets
foretold of the Second, they were ever looking out for that His Coming in glory *with the
clouds of heaven* [l], to humble, as they thought,
their own as well as His enemies. Our Lord
answers, that this their craving for a sign
was part of their faithlessness. *An evil and
adulterous generation seeketh after a sign: and
there shall no sign be given them, but the sign of
the Prophet Jonas.* He uses three times their
own word *sign.* He speaks of a miraculous
sign, *the sign of Jonas,* a miracle which was
the sign of something beyond itself. [h] *For as
Jonas was three days and three nights in the
whale's belly, so shall the Son of Man be three
days and three nights in the heart of the earth.*
He gave them the sign from earth, not from
Heaven; a miracle of humility, not of glory;
of deliverance from death, and, as it were, a
resurrection. A *sign,* such as Holy Scripture
speaks of, need not at all times be a miraculous, but it is always a real *sign.* Isaiah and
his sons, by real names, given to them by
God, or the prophet by his walking barefoot,
or Ezekiel by symbolic acts, were signs; not
by miraculous but still by real acts. In *this*
case, the Jews asked for a miraculous sign;
our Lord promises them a miraculous sign,
although not one such as they wished for, or
which would satisfy *them;* a miraculous sign,

of which the miraculous preservation of
Jonah was a type. Our Lord says, " [h] Jonah
was three days and three nights in the
whale's belly," and no one who really believes
in Him, dare think that he was not.

It is perhaps a part of the simplicity of
Jonah's narrative, that he relates these great
miracles, as naturally as he does the most
ordinary events. To God nothing is great
or small; and the Prophet, deeply as he feels
God's mercy, relates the means which God
employed, as if it had been one of those every
day miracles of His power and love, of which
men think so little because God worketh them
every day.

God prepared a great fish, he says, *God prepared a palmchrist; God prepared a worm;
God prepared a vehement East wind.* Whether
Jonah relates God's ordinary or His extraordinary workings, His workings in the way
in which He upholdeth in being the creatures
of His Will, or in a way which involves a
miracle, i. e. God's acting in some unusual
way, Jonah relates it in the same way, with
the same simplicity of truth. His mind is
fixed on God's Providence, and he relates
God's acts, as they bore upon God's Providential dealings with him. He tells of God's
preparing the East Wind which smote the
palmchrist, in the same way in which he
speaks of the supernatural growth of the
palmchrist, or of God's Providence, in ap-
pointing that the fish should swallow him.
He mentions this, which was in the order of
God's Providence; he nowhere stops to tell
us the "how." How God converted the
Ninevites, how He sustained his life in the
fish's belly, he tells not. He mentions only
the great facts themselves, and leaves them
in their mysterious greatness.

It is not strange, the heathen scoffers fixed
upon the physical miracles in the history of
Jonah for their scorn. They could have no
appreciation of the great moral miracle of
the conversion of a whole Heathen city at
the voice of a single unknown Prophet.
Such a conversion is unexampled in the
whole revelation of God to man, greater in
its immediate effects than the miracle of the
Day of Pentecost. Before this stupendous
power of God's grace over the unruly will of
savage, yet educated, men, the physical miracles, great as they are, shrink into nothing.
The wielding and swaying of half a million
of human wills, and turning them from Satan
to God, is a power of grace, as much above
and beyond all changes of the unresisting
physical creation, as the spirits and intelli-
gences which God has created are higher
than insentient matter. Physical miracles
are a new exercise of the creative power of

---

[f] S. Luke xxiv. 24.   [g] S. Matt. xii. 40.
[h] Ib. 41, S. Luke xi. 32.
[i] S. Matt. xii. 38–40, S. Luke xi. 16, 29, 30.

[k] σημεῖον.
[l] Dan. vii. 13, 14, S. Matt. xvi. 27, xxiv. 30, xxvi.
64, S. Luke xxi. 27, 1 Thess. iv. 16, Rev. i. 7.

God : the moral miracles were a sort of first-fruit of the re-creation of the Gentile world. Physical miracles were the simple exercise of the Will of God; the moral miracles were, in these hundreds of thousands, His overpowering grace, pouring itself into the heart of rebellious man and re-creating it. As many souls as there were, so many miracles were there, greater even than the creation of man. The miracles too are in harmony with the nature around. The Hebrews, who were, at this time, not a maritime people, scarcely knew probably of those vast monsters, which our manifold researches into God's animal kingdom have laid open to us. Jonah speaks only of *a great fish.* The Greek word[m], by which the LXX translated it, and which our Lord used, is, (like our "*cetacea*" which is taken from it,) the name of a genus, not of any individual fish. It is the equivalent of the *great fish* of Jonah. The Greeks use the adjective[n], as we do, but they also use the substantive which occurs in S. Matthew. This designates a class which *includes* the whale, but is never used to designate the whale. In Homer[o], it includes "dolphins and the dog." In the natural historians, (as Aristotle[p],) it designates the whole class of sea-creatures which are viviparous, "as the dolphin, the seal, the whale;" Galen[q] adds the Zygæna (a shark) and large tunnies; Photius says that "the Carcharias," or white shark, "is a species of it[r]." Oppian[s] recounts, as belonging to the Cete, several species of sharks[t] and whales[u], some with names of land animals[x], and also the black tunnies[y]. Ælian enumerates most of these under the same head[z]. Our Lord's words then would be rendered more literally, in *the fish's belly*[a], than *in the whale's belly.* Infidels seized eagerly on the fact of the narrowness of the whale's throat; their cavil applied only to an incorrect rendering of modern versions. Fish, of such size that they can swallow a man whole, and which are so formed as naturally to swallow their prey whole, have been found in the Mediterranean. The white shark, having teeth merely incisive, has no choice, except between swallowing its prey whole, or cutting off a portion of it. It cannot *hold* its prey, or swallow it piecemeal. Its voracity leads it to swallow at once all which it can[b]. Hence Otto Fabricius relates[c], "its wont is to swallow down dead

and, sometimes also, living men, which it finds in the sea."

A natural historian of repute relates[d], "In 1758 in stormy weather a sailor fell overboard from a frigate in the Mediterranean. A shark was close by, which, as he was swimming and crying for help, took him in his wide throat, so that he forthwith disappeared. Other sailors had leapt into the sloop, to help their comrade, while yet swimming; the captain had a gun which stood on the deck discharged at the fish, which struck it so, that it cast out the sailor which it had in its throat, who was taken up, alive and little injured, by the sloop which had now come up. The fish was harpooned, taken up on the frigate, and dried. The captain made a present of the fish to the sailor who, by God's Providence, had been so wonderfully preserved. The sailor went round Europe exhibiting it. He came to Franconia, and it was publicly exhibited here in Erlangen, as also at Nurnberg and other places. The dried fish was delineated. It was 20 feet long, and, with expanded fins, nine feet wide, and weighed 3924 pounds. From all this, it is probable that this was the fish of Jonah." This is by no means an insulated account of the size of this fish. Blumenbach[e] states, "the white shark, or Canis carcharias, is found of the size of 10,000 lbs, and horses have been found whole in its stomach." A writer of the 16th century on "the fish of Marseilles[f]" says, "they of Nice attested to me, that they had taken a fish of this sort, approaching to 4000 lbs weight, in whose body they had found a man whole. Those of Marseilles told something similar, that they had once taken a Lamia (so they still popularly call the Carcharias) and found in it a man in a coat of mail [loricatus.]" Rondelet says, "[g] sometimes it grows to such size, that, placed on a carriage, it can hardly be drawn by two horses. I have seen one of moderate size, which weighed 1000 lbs, and, when disembowelled and cut to pieces, it had to be put on two carriages." "I have seen on the shore of Saintonge a Lamia, whose mouth and throat were of such vast size, that it would easily swallow a large man."

Richardson[h], speaking of the white shark in N. America, says that they attain the length of 30 feet, i. e. a 3d larger than that

[m] κῆτος. [n] κητώδη.
[o] δελφῖνάς τε κύνας τε καὶ εἴποτε μεῖζον ἔληται κῆτος. Od. xii. 37.
[p] Hist. Anim. iii. 20. T. ii. 258.
[q] de alim. fac. iii. 37. T. iv. 349. Sostratus in Athen. vii. 66. says that "the Pelamus (a tunny) when exceeding large is called κῆτος."
[r] Lex. V. καρχαρίας. [s] Halieut. i. 360-382.
[t] The ζύγαινα, λάμνη or λάμια (our "lamia") κεντρίνης, γαλεός, ἀκανθίας, λεῖος, ῥίνη, and probably the πάρδαλις.
[u] The φύσαλοι, (i. q. physeter Linn.) and πρῆστις.
[x] λέων, πάρδαλις, κριὸς, ὕαινα, γαλεός, σκύμνος.

[y] μελανθύνων. [z] de animal. ix. 49.
[a] S. Matt. xii. 40.
[b] "It swallows everything without chewing." P. du Tertre, Hist. des. Antilles, ii. 203.
[c] Fauna Gronlandica, p. 129.
[d] Müller, Vollstandige Natursystem des Ritters Karl von Linné. Th. iii. p. 268, quoted by Eichhorn, Einl. T. iv. §574.
[e] Naturgesch. v. Squalus, Carcharias.
[f] P. Gyll. de Gall. et Lat. nom. pisc. Massil. c. 99. A. D. 1535.
[g] de piscib. xiii. 12, referred to by Bochart.
[h] Fauna Boreali-Americana, p. 289.

25

which swallowed the sailor whole. Lacepède speaks of fish of this kind as "more than 30 feet long[i]." "The contour," he adds[k], "of the upper jaw of a requin of 30 feet, is about 6 feet long; its swallow is of a diameter proportionate."

"[l] In all modern works on Zoology, we find 30 feet given as a common length for a shark's body. Now a shark's body is usually only about eleven times the length of the half of its lower jaw. Consequently a shark of 30 feet would have a lower jaw of nearly six feet in its semicircular extent. Even if such a jaw as this was of hard bony consistence instead of a yielding cartilaginous nature, it would qualify its possessor for engulfing one of our own species most easily. The power which it has, by virtue of its cartilaginous skeleton, of stretching, bending and yielding, enables us to understand how the shark can swallow entire animals as large or larger than ourselves. Such an incident is related to have occurred A. D. 1802, on the authority of a Captain Brown, who found the body of a woman entire with the exception of the head within the stomach of a shark killed by him at Surinam[m]."

In the Mediterranean there are traces of a yet larger race, now extinct[n]. "[o] However large or dangerous the existing race may be, yet from the magnitude of the fossil teeth found in Malta and elsewhere, some of which measure 4½ inches from the point to the base, and 6 inches from the point to the angle, the animal, to which they belonged, must have much exceeded the present species in size." "The mouth of a fish of this sort," says Bloch[p], "is armed with 400 teeth of this kind. In the Isle of Malta and in Sicily, their teeth are found in great numbers on the shore. Naturalists of old took them for tongues of serpents. They are so compact that, after having remained for many centuries in the earth, they are not yet decayed. The quantity and size of those which are found proves that these creatures existed formerly in great numbers, and that some

were of extraordinary size. If one were to calculate from them what should, in proportion, be the size of the throat which should hold such a number of such teeth, it ought to be at least 8 or 10 feet wide. In truth, these fish are found to this day of a terrific size.—This fish, celebrated for its voracity and courage, is found in the Mediterranean and in almost every Ocean. It generally keeps at the bottom, and rises only to satisfy its hunger. It is not seen near shore, except when it pursues its prey, or is pursued by the mular[q], which it does not venture to approach, even when dead. It swallows all sorts of aquatic animals, alive or dead, and pursues especially the sea-calf and the tunny. In its pursuit of the tunny, it sometimes falls into nets, and some have been thus taken in Sardinia, which weighed 400 lbs and in which 8 or 10 tunnies were found still undigested. It attacks men wherever it can find them, whence the Germans call it 'menschenfresser' (men-eater.) Gunner[r] speaks of a sea-calf 'of the size of an ox, which has also been found in one of these animals; and in another a reindeer without horns, which had fallen from a rock.' This fish attains a length of 25–30 feet. Müller[s] says that one was taken near the Island of St. Marguerite which weighed 1500 lbs. On opening it, they found in it a horse, quite whole: which had apparently been thrown overboard. M. Brünniche says[t] that during his residence at Marseilles, one was taken near that city, 15 feet long, and that two years before, two, much larger, had been taken, in one of which had been found two tunnies and a man quite dressed. The fish were injured, the man not at all. In 1760 there was exhibited at Berlin a requin stuffed, 20 feet long, and 9 in circumference, where it was thickest. It had been taken in the Mediterranean. Its voracity is so great, that it does not spare its own species. Leem[u] relates, that a Laplander, who had taken a requin, fastened it to his canoe; soon after, he missed it. Some time after, having taken a larger, he found in its stomach the

[i] Lacep. Hist. des. Poissons, i. p. 189.
[k] Ib. 191. "We have ascertained, from several comparisons, that the contour of one side of the upper jaw, measured from the angle of the two jaws to the summit of the upper jaw nearly equals one-eleventh of the animal. One ought not then to be surprised, to read in Rondelet and other authors, that large requins can swallow a man whole."
[l] MS. statement furnished me by Dr. Rolleston, Linacre Prof. Oxford.
[m] Buffon, ed. C. Sonnini, Poissons, iii. p. 344. Ed. 1803.
[n] This appears from the following statement with which Prof. Phillips has kindly furnished me. "The earliest notice of them which has met my eye is in Scilla's very curious work, La vana Speculazione disingannata. Napoli, 1670. Tav. iii. fig. 1. gives a fair view of some of their teeth, which are stated to have been found in 'un Sasso di Malta'; he rightly enough calls them teeth of Lamia (i. e. Shark) petrified. Mr. Bowerbank, in Reports of the Brit. Association, 1851, gives measures of these

teeth, and estimates of the size of the animal to which they belonged. His specimens are from Suffolk, from the Red Crag, where sharks' teeth, of several sorts, and a vast variety of shells, corals, &c. are mixed with some remains of mostly extinct mammalia. The marine races are also for the most part of extinct kinds. These deposits in Suffolk and Malta are of the later Tertiary period; specimens derived from them may be found on the shores no doubt, but there is also no doubt of their original situation being in the stratified earth-crust. The living sharks to which the fossil animal may have most nearly approached are included in the genus Carcharias, the teeth being beautifully serrated on the edges."
[o] Stark, Animal kingdom, p. 305.
[p] Hist. des Poissons, iv. 31. ⅔ xi.
[q] Physeter Macrocephalus, Linn. The Spermaceti whale.
[r] Dict. des Anim. iii. p. 683. Schrift. der Dront. Gesellch. T. ii. p. 299.   [s] L. S. T. iii. p. 267.
[t] Pisc. Mass. p. 6.   [u] Lappl. p. 150.

requin which he had lost." " ˣ The large Australian shark (Carcharias glaucus), which has been measured after death 37 feet long, has teeth about 2⅜ inches long."

Such facts ought to shame those who speak of the miracle of Jonah's preservation through the fish, as a thing less credible than any other of God's miraculous doings. There is no greater or less to Omnipotence. The creation of the Universe, the whole stellar system, or of a fly, are alike to Him, simple acts of His Divine Will. *He spake, and it was* ʸ. What to men seem the greatest miracles or the least, are alike to Him, the mere *Let it be* of His All-Holy Will, acting in a different way for one and the same end, the instruction of the intelligent creatures which He has made. Each and all subserve, in their several places and occasions, the same end of the manifold Wisdom of God. Each and all of these, which to us seem interruptions of His ordinary workings in nature, were from the beginning, before He had created anything, as much a part of His Divine purpose, as the creation of the Universe. They are not disturbances of His laws. Night does not disturb day which it closes, nor day night. No more does any work which God, before the creation of the world, willed to do, (for, ᶻ *known unto God are all His ways from the beginning of the world,*) interfere with any other of His workings. His workings in nature, and His workings above nature, form one harmonious whole. Each are a part of His ways; each is essential to the manifestation of God to us. That wonderful order and symmetry of God's creation exhibits to us some effluences of the Divine Wisdom and Beauty and Power and Goodness; that regularity itself sets forth those other foreknown operations of God, whereby He worketh in a way different from His ordinary mode of working in nature. "They who know not God, will ask," says S. Cyril ª, "how was Jonah preserved in the fish? how was he not consumed? how did he endure that natural heat, and live, surrounded by such moisture, and was not rather digested? For this poor body is very weak and perishable. Truly wonderful was it, surpassing reason and wontedness. But if God be declared its Author, who would any more disbelieve? For God is All-powerful, and transmouldeth easily the nature of things which are, to what He willeth, and nothing resisteth His ineffable Will. For that which is perishable can at His Will easily become superior to corruption; and what is firm and unshaken and undecaying is easily subjected thereto. For nature, I deem, to the things which be, is, what seemeth good to the Creator." S. Au-

gustine well points out the inconsistency, so common now, of excepting to the one or the other miracle, upon grounds which would in truth apply to many or to all. " ᵇ The answer" to the mockery of the Pagans, "is that either all Divine miracles are to be disbelieved, or there is no reason why *this* should not be believed. For we should not believe in Christ Himself that He rose on the third day, if the faith of the Christians shrank from the mockery of Pagans. Since our friend does not put the question, Is it to be believed that Lazarus rose on the 4th day, or Christ Himself on the third day, I much marvel that he put this as to Jonah as a thing incredible, unless he think it easier for one dead to be raised from the tomb, than to be preserved alive in that vast belly of the fish. Not to mention how vast the size of marine creatures is said to be by those who have witnessed it, who could not conceive what numbers of men that stomach could contain which was fenced by those ribs, well known to the people at Carthage, where they were set up in public?—how vast must have been the opening of that mouth, the door, as it were, to that cave." "But, troth, they have found in a Divine miracle something which they need not believe; viz. that the gastric juice whereby food is digested could be so tempered as not to injure the life of man. How still less credible would they deem it, that those three men, cast into the furnace of the impious king, walked up and down in the midst of the fire! If then they refuse to believe *any* miracles of God, they must be answered in another way. But they ought not to question any *one*, as though *it* were incredible, but at once all which are as, or even more, marvelous. He who proposed these questions, let him be a Christian now, lest, while he waits first to finish the questions on the sacred books, he come to the end of his life, before he have passed from death to life.—Let him, if he will, first ask questions such as he asked concerning Christ, and those few great questions to which the rest are subordinate. But if he think to finish all such questions as this of Jonah, before he becomes a Christian, he little appreciates human mortality or his own. For they are countless; not to be finished before accepting the faith, lest life be finished without faith. But, retaining the faith, they are subjects for the diligent study of the faithful; and what in them becomes clear is to be communicated without arrogance, what still lies hid, to be borne without risk to salvation."

The other physical miracle of the rapid production of the Palma Christi, which God created to overshadow Jonah, was plainly

---

Prof. Phillips, MS. letter. He adds, "but our fossil shark's teeth are 4½ to even 5 inches long. Its length has been inferred to have reached 65 feet."

ʸ Ps. xxxiii. 9.   ᶻ Acts xv. 18.
ª on Jon. c. 2. beg.
ᵇ Ep. 102. q. 6. §31.

supernatural in that extreme rapidity of growth, else in conformity with the ordinary character of that plant. "The kikaion, as we read in the Hebrew, called kikeia [or, Elkeroa[c],] in Syriac and Punic," says S. Jerome[d], "is a shrub with broad leaves like vine-leaves. It gives a very dense shade, supports itself on its own stem. It grows most abundantly in Palestine, especially in sandy spots. If you cast the seed into the ground, it is soon quickened, rises marvelously into a tree, and a few days what you had beheld an herb, you look up to, a shrub.— The kikaion, a miracle in its instantaneous existence, and an instance of the power of God in the protection given by this living shade, followed the course of its own nature." It is a native of all North Africa, Arabia, Syria, India. In the valley of the Jordan it still grows to a "large size, and has the character," an eyewitness writes[e], "of a perennial tree, although usually described as a biennial plant." "[f] It is of the size of a small fig tree. It has leaves like a plane, only larger, smoother, and darker." The name of the plant is of Egyptian origin, kiki; which Dioscorides and Galen identify with the croton[g]; Herodotus with the Silicyprion[h], which, in the form seselicyprion, Dioscorides mentions as a name given to the kiki or kroton[f]; Pliny[i] with the Ricinus also (the Latin name for the croton), our Palma Christi; Hebrews[k] with the Arabic Elkeroa, which again is known to be the Ricinus. The growth and occasional perishing of the Palma Christi have both something analogous to the growth and decay related in Jonah. Its rapidity of growth is remarked by S. Jerome and Pliny, who says, "[l] in Spain it shoots up rapidly, of the height of an olive, with hollow stem," and branches[f].

"[l] All the species of the Ricinus shoot up quickly, and yield fruit within three months, and are so multipled from the seed shed, that, if left to themselves, they would occupy in short space the whole country." In Jamaica, "[m] it grows with surprising rapidity to the height of 15 or 16 feet." Niebuhr says[n], "it has the appearance of a tree. Each branch of the kheroa has only one leaf, with 6, 7, or 8 indentures. This plant was near a stream which watered it adequately. At the end of Oct. 1765, it had, in 5 months, grown about 8 feet, and bore, at once, flowers and fruit, green and ripe." This rapidity of growth has only a sort of likeness to the miracle, which quickened in a way far above nature the powers implanted in nature. The destruction may have been altogether in the way of nature, except that it happened at that precise moment, when it was to be a lesson to Jonah. "[o] On warm days, when a small rain falls, black caterpillars are generated in great numbers on this plant, which, in one night, so often and so suddenly cut off its leaves, that only their bare ribs remain, which I have often observed with much wonder, as though it were a copy of that destruction of old at Nineveh." The Ricinus of India and Assyria furnishes food to a different caterpillar from that of Amboyna[p], but the account illustrates the rapidity of the destruction. The word "worm" is elsewhere also used collectively, not of a single worm only[q], and of creatures which, in God's appointment, devour the vine[r]. There is nothing in the text, implying that the creature was one which gnawed the stem rather than the leaves. The peculiar word, smote[s], is probably used, to correspond with the mention of the sun smiting[t] on the head of Jonah.

These were miracles, like all the other miracles of Scripture, ways, in which God made Himself and His power known to us, shewing Himself the Lord of that nature which men worshiped and worship, for the

---

[c] Elkeroa is the reading of Erasmus and Victorius, who used MSS. and do not mention any conjecture. The Benedictines substituted kikeion, their MSS. having Siceia. In S. Jerome, Ep. ad Aug. Ep. 112. n. 22. their MSS. had ciceiam or κηκηαμ. If this is right, S. Jerome must have meant Chaldee by Syriac, the word being retained in Jonathan. Only if S. Jerome had meant that the "Syriac" word was the same, one should have thought that he would have said so. The Peshito has probably been corrupted out of the LXX.
[d] on Jon. iv. 6.   [e] Robinson, i. 553.
[f] Dioscor. iv. 164.
[g] Diosc. ib. Galen Lex. Hipp. p. 82; also Paul. Ægin. vii. 297.
[h] Herod. ii. 94.   [i] xv. 7.
[k] Samuel B. Hophni, A. D. 1054, ap. Kim. Resh Lachish (2d cent. Wolf, Bibl. H. ii. 881, 2 coll. 844.) says that "the oil of Kik" (forbidden in the Mishnah Shabbath, c. 2. to be used for lights on the sabbath) is the kikaion of Jonah, (Kim.) "The oil of Kik" is the ἔλαιον κίκινον of Galen (Lex. Hipp. p. 58) the "oleum cicinum" of Pliny (xxiii. 4). Resh Lachish identified the kikaion with the Alekeroa' (Boch. Ep. ad Morin. Geogr. S. p. 918) which Ibn Baithar uses to translate the kiki, κροτών (Boch. Hieroz. ii. 24). R. Nathan, Maimonides on Tr. Shab-

bath, c. 2. n. l, and "some" in Bartenora, (Ib.) also explain it of the keroa. R. Bar Bar Channach, (early 3d cent. Wolf, ib. 880. coll. 879) identifies it with the Zelulibah (Kim.) which again is explained to be the Elkeroa' (respons. Geonim in Boch. Hieroz. ii. 24. p. 42. ed. Leipz.) and whose oil is called "oil of keroa" i. e. the castor or croton oil (Buxt. Lex. Talm. v. צלוליבא.)
[1] Rumph. Herb. Amboin. vi. 46. T. iv. p. 92.
[m] Long's Jamaica, T. iii. p. 712.
[n] Descr. de l' Arab. p. 130.
[o] Rumph. Ib. p. 94.
[p] Sir W. Hooker kindly pointed this out to me, referring to a description and picture of the caterpillar, or silk-worm, the Phalæna Cynthia or the Arrindy silk-worm, in the Linn. Trans. T. iii. p. 42. He also kindly pointed out to me the drawing of the Ricinus in the Flora Græca, T. ix. Tab. 952, given on a reduced scale on the opposite page, as the best representation of the Palma Christi.
[q] התולעת, as we say, "the worm" which preys on the dead body, Is. xiv. 11 (and thence the worm which dieth not. Ib. lxvi. 24). תולעת שני, "the cochineal grub," kermez.   [r] Deut. xxviii. 39.
[s] וַתַּךְ Jon. iv. 7.   [t] Ib. 8.

present conversion of a great people, for the conviction of Israel, a hidden prophecy of the future conversion of the heathen, and an example of repentance and its fruits to the end of time. They have no difficulty except to the rebelliousness of unbelief.

Other difficulties people have made for themselves. In a planked-roof booth such as ours, Jonah would not have needed the shadow of a plant. Obviously then, Jonah's booth, even if we knew not what it was, was not like our's. A German critic has chosen to treat this as an absurdity. "[u] Although Jonah makes himself a shady booth, he still further needs the overshadowing kikaion." Jonah however, being an Israelite, made booths, such as Israel made them. Now we happen to know that the Jewish succah, or booth, being formed of the interlaced branches of trees, did not exclude the sun. We know this from the rules in the Talmud as to the construction of the Succah or "tabernacle" for the feast of Tabernacles. It lays down,[v] "A Succah whose height is not ten palms, and which has not three sides, and which has more sun than shade [i. e. more of whose floor is penetrated by light through the top of the Succah, than is left in shade], is profane." And again [w], "Whoso spreadeth a linen cloth over the Succah, to protect him from the sun, it is profane." "[x] Whoso raiseth above it the vine or gourd or ivy, and so covers it, it is profane; but if the roof be larger than they, or if one cut them, they are lawful." "[y] With bundles of straw, and bundles of wood, and bundles of faggots, they do not cover it; and all these, if undone, are lawful." "[z] They cover it with planks according to R. Jonah; and R. Meir forbids; whoso putteth upon it one plank of four palms' breadth it is lawful, only he must not sleep under it." Yet all held [a] that a plank thus broad was to overlap the booth, in which case it would not cover it. The principle of all these rules is, that the rude hut, in which they dwelt during the feast of Tabernacles, was to be a shade, symbolizing God's overshadowing them in the wilderness; the Succah itself, not anything adscititious, was to be their shade; yet it was but an imperfect protection, and was indeed intended so to be, in order to symbolize their pilgrim-state. Hence the contrivances among those who wished to be at ease, to protect themselves; and hence the inconvenience which God turned into an instruction to Jonah. Even "the Arabs," Layard tells us [b] in a Nineveh summer, "struck their black tents and lived in sheds, constructed of reeds and grass along the banks of the river." "The heats of sum-

mer made it impossible to live in a white tent." Layard's resource of a "recess, cut into the bank of the river where it rose perpendicularly from the water's edge, screening the front with reeds and boughs of trees, and covering the whole with similar materials," corresponds with the hut of Jonah, covered by the Kikaion.

No heathen scoffer, as far as we know, when he became acquainted with the history of Jonah, likened it to any heathen fable. This was reserved for so-called Christians. Some heathen mocked at it, as the philosophers of Mars'-hill mocked at the resurrection of Christ [c]. "This sort of question" [about Jonah], said a heathen, who professed to be an enquirer, "I have observed to be met with broad mockery by the pagans [d]." They mocked, but they did not insult the history by likening it to any fable of their own. S. Jerome, who mentions incidentally that "[e] Joppa is the place in which, to this day, rocks are pointed out in the shore, where Andromeda, being bound, was once on a time freed by the help of Perseus," does not seem aware that the fable could be brought into any connection with the history of Jonah. He urges on the heathen the inconsistency of believing their own fables, which besides their marvelousness were often immoral, and refusing to believe the miracles of Scripture histories; but the fable of Andromeda or of Hesione do not even occur to him in this respect. "[f] I am not ignorant that to some it will seem incredible that a man could be preserved alive 3 days and nights in the fish's belly. These must be either believers or unbelievers. If believers, they must needs believe much greater things, how the three youths, cast into the burning fiery furnace, were in such sort unharmed, that not even the smell of fire touched their dress; how the sea retired, and stood on either side rigid like walls, to make a way for the people passing over; how the rage of lions, aggravated by hunger, looked, awestricken, on its prey, and touched it not, and many like things. Or if they be unbelievers, let them read the 15 books of Ovid's metamorphoses, and all Greek and Latin story, and there they will see—where the foulness of the fables precludes the holiness of a divine origin. *These things they believe*, and that to God all things are possible. Believing foul things, and defending them by alleging the unlimited power of God, they do not admit the same power as to things moral." In Alexandria and in the time of S. Cyril, the old heathen fables were tricked up again. He alludes then to Lycophron's version of

[u] Hitzig, Kl. Proph. p. 160.
[v] Massecheth Succa, i. 1. Dachs Succa, p. 1.
[w] Ib. § 3. p. 30.   [x] § 4. p. 29.   [y] § 5. p. 49.
[z] § 6. p. 51.

[a] Yom tob and Rashi on Gem. Succah, f. 14. 2.
[b] Ninev. i. 123.   [c] Acts xvii. 32.
[d] in S. Aug. Ep. 102. See ab. p. 259.
[e] on Jon. i. 3.   [f] on Jon. ii. 2.

the story of Hercules[g], in order, like S.
Jerome, to point out the inconsistency of believing heathen fables and rejecting Divine
truth. "We," he says, "do not use their
fables to confirm things Divine, but we mention them to a good end, in answer to unbelievers, that *their* received histories too do
not reject such relations." The philosophers
wished at once to defend their own fables and
to attack the Gospel. Yet it was an unhappy
argumentum ad hominem. Modern infidelity
would find a likeness, where there is no
shadow of it. The two heathen fables had
this in common; that, in order to avert the
anger of the gods, a virgin was exposed to be
devoured by a sea-monster, and delivered
from death by a hero, who slew the monster
and married the princess whom he delivered.
This, as given by S. Cyril, was a form of the
fable, long subsequent to Jonah. The original simple form of the story was this,
"[h] Apollo and Poseidon, wishing to make
trial of the insolence of Laomedon, appearing in the likeness of men, promised for a
consideration to fortify Pergamus. When
they had fortified it, he did not pay them
their hire. Wherefore Apollo sent a pestilence, and Poseidon a sea-monster, cast on
shore by the flood-tide, who made havoc of
the men that were in the plain. The oracle
said that they should be freed from these
misfortunes, if Laomedon would set his
daughter Hesione as food for the monster; he
did so set her, binding her to the rocks near
to the plain; Hercules, seeing her thus exposed, promised to save her, if he might have
from Laomedon the horses, which Zeus had
given in compensation for the rape of Gany-
mede. Laomedon saying that he would give
them, he slew the monster and set Hesione
free."
This simple story is repeated, with unim-
portant variations, by Diodorus Siculus[i],
Hyginus[k], Ovid[l], Valerius Flaccus[m]. Even
later, the younger Philostratus, depicting the
story, has no other facts[n]. An old icon represents the conflict in a way inconsistent with
the later form of the story[o].
The story of Andromeda is told by Apollodorus[p], in part in the very same words.
The Nereids were angered by Cassiope the
mother of Andromeda, for boasting herself
more beautiful than they. Then follows the
same history, Poseidon sending a flood-tide
and a sea-monster; the same advice of the

oracle; the setting Andromeda in chains, as
food for the sea-monster; Perseus' arrival,
bargain with the father, the killing of the
sea-monster, the deliverance of Andromeda.
Fable as all this is, it does not seem to have
been meant to be fable. Pliny relates, "[q] M.
Scaurus, when Ædile, exhibited at Rome,
among other marvels, the bones of the monster to which Andromeda was said to have
been exposed, which bones were brought from
Joppa, a city of Judæa, being 40 feet long, in
height greater than the ribs of the Indian
elephant, and the vertebræ a foot and a half
thick." He describes Joppa as "seated on a
hill, with a projecting rock, in which they
shew the traces of the chains of Andromeda[r]."
Josephus says the same[s]. Pausanias relates,
"[t] the country of the Hebrews near Joppa
supplies water blood-red, very near the sea.
The natives tell, that Perseus, when he had
slain the monster to which the daughter of
Cepheus was exposed, washed off the blood
there." Mela, following perhaps his Greek
authority[u], speaks in the present[v], "an
illustrious trace of the preservation of Andromeda by Perseus, they *shew* vast bones of
a sea-monster."
But, whether the authors of these fables
meant them for matters of fact, or whether
the fables had any symbolical meaning, they
have not, in any form which they received
until long after the time of Jonah, any connection with the book of Jonah.
The history of Andromeda has in common
with the book of Jonah, this only, that,
whereas Apollodorus and the ancients[w]
placed the scene of her history in Æthiopia,
writers who lived some centuries after the
time of Jonah removed it to Joppa, the seaport
whence Jonah took ship. "There are some,"
says Strabo[x], speaking of his own day, "who
transfer Æthiopia to our Phœnicia, and say
that the matters of Andromeda took place at
Joppa; and this, not out of ignorance of
places, but rather in the form of a myth."
The transfer, doubtless, took place in the 800
years which elapsed between Jonah and
Strabo, and was occasioned perhaps by the
peculiar idolatry of the coast, the worship of
Atargatis or Derceto. Pliny, at least, immediately after that statement about the chains
of Andromeda at Joppa, subjoins, "[y] The
fabulous Ceto is worshiped there." Ceto is
doubtless the same as "Derceto," of which
Pliny uses the same epithet a little after-

---

[g] on Jon. ii. beg. T. iii. p. 376.
[h] Apollodorus, iii. 4. 1.   [i] iv. 42.   [k] Fab. 89.
[l] Metam. iv. 202-15.   [m] Argon. ii. 451-546.
[n] Imag. 12.
[o] in Chosil. and in Beyer, Spicil. Antiq. p. 154. It
represents Hercules laurel-crowned and bene coma-
tus. Fabric. ad Sext. Empiric. p. 270.
[p] ii. 43.   [q] N. H. ix. 5.
[r] Ib. v. 13.   [s] B. J. iii. 9. 3.
[t] iv. 35.   [u] So Voss conjectures.
[v] i. 11.

[w] Euripides (in Plutarch de aud. poet.) speaks of
the animal as "rushing from the Atlantic sea."
(Fragm. Androm. T. ix. p. 45. ed. Matth.). Tacitus,
in giving the heathen notions of the origin of the
Jews, says, "*most* think that they are offspring of
Æthiopians, whom, *when Cepheus was* king (of Æthiopia) fear and hatred compelled to change their
abode." (Hist. v. 2.) Ovid still placed the scene in
Æthiopia, (Met. iv. 668.) and ascribed the Oracle to
Ammon. (670.)
[x] i. 2. 35. ed. Kr.   [y] v. 13.

ward [z]. "There," at Hierapolis, "is worshiped the prodigious Atargatis, which the Greeks call Derceto." The Greeks appear (as their way was), on occasion of this worship of Ceto, to have transferred here their own story of Andromeda and the Cetos.

Ceto, i. e. Derceto, and Dagon were the corresponding male and female deities, under whose names the Philistines worshiped the power which God has implanted in nature to reproduce itself. Both were fish-forms, with human hands and face. Derceto or Atargatis was the Syriac Ter'to, whose worship at Hierapolis or Mabug had a far-known infamy, the same altogether as that of Rhea or Cybele [a]. The maritime situation of Philistia probably led them to adopt the fish as the symbol of prolific reproduction. In Holy Scripture we find chiefly the worship of the male god Dagon, lit. "great fish." He had temples at Gaza [b], and Ashdod [c], whither all the lords of the Philistines assembled. Five other places are named from his worship, four near the sea coast, and one close to Joppa itself [d]. But in later times the name of the goddess became more prominent, and, among the Greeks, exclusive. Atargatis or Derceto had, in the time of the Maccabees, a celebrated temple at Carnion [e], i. e. Ashteroth Carnaim in Gilead, and, according to Pliny, at Joppa itself. This furnished an easy occasion to the Greeks to transfer thither their story of the Cetos. The Greeks had peopled Joppa [f], before Simon retook it from Antiochus. In Jonah's time, it was Phœnician. It was not colonized by Greeks until 5 centuries later. Since then Andromeda is a Greek story which they transferred to Joppa with themselves, the existence of the Greek story, at a later date, can be no evidence for "a Phœnician legend," of which the rationalists have dreamed, nor can it have any connection with Jonah who lived half a millen-

nium before the Greeks came, eight hundred years before the story is mentioned in connection with Joppa.

With regard to the fables of Hercules, Diodorus Siculus thought that there was a basis of truth in them. The story of Hercules and Hesione, as alluded to by Homer and told by Apollodorus, looks like an account of the sea breaking in upon the land and wasting it; a human sacrifice on the point of being offered, and prevented by the removal of the evil through the building of a sea-wall. Gigantic works were commonly attributed to superior agency, good or evil. In Homer, the mention of the sea-wall is prominent. "[g] He led the way to the lofty wall of mounded earth of the divine Hercules, which the Trojans and Minerva made for him, that, eluding the sea-monster, he might escape, when he rushed at him from the beach toward the plain." In any case a monster, which came up from the sea and wasted the land, is no fish; nor has the story of one who *destroyed* such a monster, any bearing on that of one whose life God *preserved* by a fish. Nor is the likeness really mended by the later version of the story, originating in an Alexandrian [h], after the book of Jonah had been translated into Greek at Alexandria. The writer of the Cassandra, who lived at least five centuries after Jonah, represents Hercules as "a lion, the offspring of three nights, which aforetime the jagged-toothed dog of Triton lapped up in his jaws; and he, a living carver of his entrails, scorched by the steam of a cauldron on the fireless hearths, shed the bristles of his head upon the ground, the infanticide waster of my country." In that form the story re-appears in a heathen philosopher [i] and an Alexandrian father [k], but, in both, as borrowed from the Alexandrian poet. Others, who were unacquainted with Lycophron, heathen [l]

---

[z] v. 19.

[a] Lucian, de dea Syra, attests the celebrity of this dreadful worship; among the Syrians S. James of Sarug attests its prevalence in Haran (Ass. B. O. i. 328.) and Bardesanes, in Syria generally with its special enormities. (in Cureton, Spicil. Syr. p. 32 Syr. p. 20 Gr.) Diodorus Sic. [ii. 4.] mentions the woman's face and fish-body of Derceto.

[b] Judg. xvi. 23.

[c] 1 Sam. v. 1. 1 Macc. x. 83, xi. 4.

[d] 1) *Bethdagon* ("temple of Dagon") in the S. W. of Judah (Josh. xv. 41.) and so, near Philistia; 2) Another, in Asher also near the sea; 3) *Caphar Dagon* ("village of D.") "a very large village between Jamnia and Diospolis." (Euseb. Onom. sub v.) 4) *Beit Dejan* [Beth Dagon] about 6 miles N. W. of Ramlah (Robinson, Bibl. R. ii. 232; see map) accordingly distinct from *Caphar Dagon*, and 4½ hours from Joppa; 5) Another *Beit Dejan*, E. of Nablus. (Ib. 282.)

[e] 2 Macc. xii. 26. [f] 1 Macc. x. 75, xiv. 34.

[g] Il. xx. 144-8.

[h] "Lycophron the obscure," if it was his work, lived under Ptolemy Philadelphus, B. C. 283-247. Niebuhr, following and justifying an old Scholiast, (Kl. hist. Schrift. i. 438-50) places the writer of the Cassandra not earlier than 190, B. C. on the ground

of allusions to Roman greatness (1226-82. 1446-51.) which he thinks inconsistent in a friend of Ptolemy's. Welcker (die Griech. Trag. p. 1259-62) thinks both passages interpolated.

[i] Sextus Empiricus, (about 3d century) adv. Gramm. i. 12. p. 255.

[k] S. Cyril Al. quoting Lycophron. Later Greek writers, as Isaac Comnenus (A. D. 1057,) add to Homer's fable, that Hercules leapt armed into the jaws of the monster, and so cut him up (de præterm. ab Hom. in Allat. Excerpta Var. p. 274.). The Empress Eudocia (A. D. 1067, &c.) adds the new and false interpretation of τριέσπερος (Violet. in Villoison, Anecd. i. 344), but also the old explanation (Ib. p. 211). These, as also Theophylact (A. D. 1077,) and Sextus, show by their relation their acquaintance with Lycophron.

[l] See p. 262. 1. A scholiast on Homer (Il. xx. 245) having given the story, adds "The history is in Hellanicus." But 1) had this history been in Hellanicus, it would have been known to writers (as Apollodorus &c.) who used Hellanicus. 2) It is only a general statement, that the history in the main was in Hellanicus, not extending to details. 3) "Such statements as, 'thus relates Pherecydes,' 'The history is in Acusilaus,' do not always exhibit the account of the writers whom he quotes, but he

and Christian [m] alike, knew nothing of it. One Christian writer, at the end of the 5th century [n], a Platonic philosopher, gives an account, distinct from any other, heathen or Christian, probably confused from both. In speaking of marvelous deliverances, he says; "[o]As Hercules too is sung" [i. e. in Greek poetry], "when his ship was broken, to have been swallowed up by a ketos, and, having come within, was preserved." In the midst of the 11th century after our Lord, some writers on Greek fable, in order to get rid of the very offensive story of the conception of Hercules, interpreted the word of Lycophron which alludes to it, of his employing, in the destruction of the monster, three periods of 24 hours, called "nights" from the darkness in which he was enveloped. Truly, full often have those words of God been fulfilled, that [p] *men shall turn away their ears from the truth, and shall be turned unto fables.* Men, who refused to believe the history of Jonah, although attested by our Lord, considered Æneas Gazæus, who lived about 13 centuries after Jonah, to be an authentic witness of an imaginary Phœnician tradition [q], 13 centuries before his own time; and that, simply on the ground that he has his name from Gaza; whereas he expressly refers, not to Phœnician tradition but to Greek poetry.

Such are the stories, which became a traditional argument among unbelieving critics [r] to justify their disbelief in miracles accredited by our Lord. Flimsy spider-webs, which a critic of the same school brushes away [s], as soon as he has found some other expedient, as flimsy, to serve his purpose! The majestic simplicity of Holy Scripture and its moral greatness stand out the more, in contrast with the unmeaning fables, with which men

have dared, amid much self-applause, to compare it. A more earnest, but misled, mind, even while unhappily disbelieving the miracle of Jonah, held the comparison, on ground of "reason, ludicrous; but not the less frivolous and irreverent, as applied to Holy Scripture [t]."

It was assumed by those who first wrote against the book of Jonah, that the thanksgiving in it was later than Jonah, "a cento from the Psalms." They objected that it did not allude to the history of Jonah. One critic repeated after the other [u], that the Psalm was a "mere cento" of Psalms. However untrue, nothing was less doubted. A later critic felt that the Psalm must have been the thanksgiving of one delivered from great peril of life in the sea. "The images," he says [v], "are too definite, they relate too exclusively to such a situation, to admit of being understood vaguely of any great peril to life, as may Psalms 18 and 42, (which the writer may have had in his mind) or Psalm 124." Another, to whom attention has been recently drawn, maintained the early date of the thanksgiving, and held that it contained so much of the first part of Jonah's history, that that history might be founded on the thanksgiving [w]. This was one step backward toward the truth. It is admitted that the thanksgiving is genuine, is Jonah's, and relates to a real deliverance of the real Prophet. But the thanksgiving would not suggest the history [x]. Jonah thanks God for his deliverance from the depths of the sea, from which no man could be delivered, except by miracle. He describes himself, not as struggling with the waves, but as sunk beneath them to the bottom of the sea, whence no other ever rose [y]. Jonah does not tell God, how He had

---

frequently interweaves a history out of many authors, and inserts what he had read elsewhere. See Sturz, Hellanici Fragm. n. xxvi. ed. Cant. Forbiger de Lycophr. 1827. p. 16. Porphyry speaks of the "Barbarian customs of Hellanicus," as, "a mere compound of the works of Herodotus and Damasus;" in Eus. Præp. Ev. x. 3.

[m] Not Theodorus or Theodoret, or S. Jerome (fond as he is of such allusions), nor the early author of the Orat. ad Græcos in S. Justin, although referring to the fables on Hercules.

[n] Æneas Gazæus. See Gall. T. x. Proleg. c. 12.

[o] Gall. x. 645. or p. 37. ed. Boiss. [p] 2 Tim. iv. 4.

[q] Friederichsen, Jonas, p. 311. 2, &c.

[r] Bauer, Rosenmüller, Gesenius, De Wette, Bertholdt, Gramberg (Religions-Id. ii. 510), Knobel, (Prophetismus, ii. 372.) Goldhorn. Friederichsen, Forbiger, &c.

[s] "What has the myth of Perseus, rightly understood, and with no foreign ingredients, in common with the history of Jonah, but the one circumstance, that a sea-creature is mentioned in each? And how different the meaning! Neither the myth of Perseus and Andromeda, nor the fully corresponding myth of Hercules and Hesione, can serve either to confirm the truth of the miracles in the book of Jonah" [as though the truth needed support from a fable], "nor to explain it as a popular heathen tradition, inasmuch as the analogy is too distant and indefinite to explain the whole. Unsatisfactory as such parallels are as soon as we

look, not merely at incidental and secondary points, but at the central point to be compared," &c. Baur (in Illgen Zeitschr. 1837 p. 101.) followed by Hitzig. Winer also rejects it.

[t] "In classical philology we should simply add, 'to think this in earnest were ludicrous;' 'but not the less frivolous and irreverent,' we may well add in the criticism of Scripture." Bunsen, Gott. in d. Gesch. i. 354. Eichhorn would not decide which was taken from the other. Einl. 577. ed. 1.

[u] Eichhorn, De Wette, Rosenmuller, Bertholdt, Hitzig, Maurer, &c. (Eichhorn admits the beauty of the Psalms employed.)

[v] Ewald Poet. Büch. d. A. Test. i. 122.

[w] Bunsen, Ib. i. 359 sqq.

[x] The heathen ode in praise of the god of the waters which appears in Ælian (Hist. Anim. xii. 45) about 220, A. D. (Fabr. Bibl. Gr. iv. 21. 1.) contains the whole fable about Arion (B. C. 625, or 615,) being thrown overboard treacherously and borne to shore on the backs of dolphins. The ode then did not suggest the fable (as Bunsen makes it); for it contains it. The Dolphin, playing as it does about vessels, was a Greek symbol of the sea; and the human figure upon it a votive offering for a safe arrival. Welcker gives 6 fables of persons, dead or alive, brought ashore by Dolphins. (Welcker, Kl. Schrift, i. 90 1.) The symbol was turned by the fertile Greek into the myth.

[y] Bunsen, in his Epitome of the thanksgiving, omitted the characteristic part of it, p. 364.

delivered him. Who does? He rehearses to God the hopeless peril, out of which He had delivered him. On this the soul dwells; for this is the ground of its thankfulness. The delivered soul loves to describe to God the death out of which it had been delivered. Jonah thanks God for one miracle; he gives no hint of the other, which, when he uttered the thanksgiving, was not yet completed. The thanksgiving bears witness to a miracle; but does not suggest its nature. The history supplies it.

It is instructive that the writer who, disbelieving the miracles in the book of Jonah, "*restores* his history [z]" by effacing them, has also to "*restore* the history [a][v] of the Saviour of the world, by omitting His testimony to them. But this is to subject the revelation of God to the variations of the mind of His creatures, believing what they like, disbelieving what they dislike.

Our Lord Himself attested that this miracle on Jonah was an image of His own entombment and Resurrection. He has compared the preaching of Jonah with His own. He compares it as a real history, as He does the coming of the Queen of Sheba to hear the wisdom of Solomon. Modern writers have lost sight of the principle, that men, as individuals, amid their infirmities and sins, are but types of man; in their history alone, their office, their sufferings, can they be images of their Redeemer. God portrayed doctrines of the Gospel in the ritual of the law. Of the offices of Christ and, at times, His history, He gave some faint outline in offices which He instituted, or persons whose history He guided. But they are types only, in that which is of God. Even that which was good in any was no type of His goodness; nay, the more what is human is recorded of them, the less they are types of Him. Abraham who acted much, is a type, not of Christ, but of the faithful. Isaac, of whom little is recorded, except his sacrifice, becomes the type of Christ. Melchisedek, who comes forth once in that great loneliness, a King of Righteousness and of peace, a Priest of God, refreshing the father of the faithful with the sacrificial bread and wine, is a type, the more, of Christ's everlasting priesthood, in that he stands alone, without father, without known descent, without known beginning or end, majestic in his one office, and then disappearing from our sight. Joseph was a type of our Lord, not in his chastity or his personal virtues but in his history; in that he was rejected by his brethren, sold at the price of a slave, yet, with kingly authority, received, supported, pardoned, gladdened, feasted, his brethren who had sold him. Even so the history of Jonah had two aspects. It is, at once, the history of his mission and of his own personal conduct in

it. These are quite distinct. The one is the history of God's doings in him and through him; the other is the account of his own soul, its rebellions, struggles, conviction. As a man, he is himself the penitent; as a Prophet, he is the preacher of repentance. In what was human infirmity in him, he was a picture of his people, whose cause he espoused with too narrow a zeal. Zealous too for the honor of God, although not with God's all-enfolding love, willing that that honor should be vindicated in his own way, unwilling to be God's instrument on God's terms, yet silenced and subdued at last, he was the image and lesson to those who murmured at S. Peter's mission to Cornelius, and who, only when they heard how God the Holy Ghost had come down upon Cornelius' household, *held their peace and glorified God, saying, then hath God to the Gentiles also granted repentance unto life* [b]. What coinciding visions to Cornelius and S. Peter, what evident miracles of power and of grace, were needed after the Resurrection to convince the Jewish converts of that same truth, which God made known to and through Jonah! The conversion of the Gentiles and the saving of a remnant only of the Jews are so bound together in the prophets, that it may be that the repugnance of the Jewish converts was founded on an instinctive dread of the same sort which so moved Jonah. It was a superhuman love, through which S. Paul contemplated *their fall as the riches of the Gentiles* [c].

On the other hand, that, in which Jonah was an image of our Lord, was very simple and distinct. It was where Jonah was passive, where nothing of his own was mingled. The storm, the casting over of Jonah, were the works of God's Providence; his preservation through the fish was a miracle of God's power; the conversion of the Ninevites was a manifold miracle of His grace. It might have pleased God to send to convert a heathen people one whom He had not so delivered; or to have subdued the will of the Prophet whom He sent on some other mission. But now sign answers to sign, and mission shadows out mission. Jonah was first delivered from his three days' burial in that living tomb by a sort of resurrection, and then, whereas he had previously been a Prophet to Israel, he thenceforth became a Prophet to the heathen, whom, and not Israel, he converted, and, in their conversion, his, as it were, resurrection was operative. The correspondence is there. We may lawfully dwell on subordinate details, how man was tempest-tost and buffeted by the angry waves of this perilous and bitter world; Christ, as one of us, gave His life for our lives, the storm at once was hushed, there is a deep calm of inward peace, and our haven was secured. But the great

[a] Bunsen, ib. 372.   [a] Ib. 379.   [b] Acts xi. 18.   [c] Rom. xi. 12.

outstanding facts, which our Lord Himself has pointed out, are, that he who had heretofore been the Prophet of Israel only, was, after a three days' burial, restored through miracle to life, and then the heathen were converted. Our Lord has set His seal upon the facts. They were to Israel a sacred enigma, a hidden prophecy, waiting for their explanation. They were a warning, how those on whom God then seemed not to have pity, might become the object of His pity, while they themselves were cast out. Now the marvelous correspondence is, even on the surface, a witness to the miracle. Centuries before our Lord came, there was the history of life preserved by miracle in death and out of death; and thereupon the history of heathen converted to God and accepted by Him. Is this, even a doubting mind might ask, accidental coincidence? or are it and the other like resemblances, the tracing of *the finger of God*, from whom is all harmony, Who blends in one all the gradations of His creation, all the lineaments of history, His natural and His moral world, the shadow of the law with the realities of the Gospel? How should such harmony exist, but for that harmonizing Hand, Who "binds and blends in one" the morning and evening of His creation.

JONAH.

CHAPTER I.

1 *Jonah, sent to Nineveh, fleeth
to Tarshish.* 4 *He is bewrayed
by a tempest,* 11 *thrown into the
sea,* 17 *and swallowed by a fish.*

NOW the word of the
LORD came unto [a]
‖ Jonah the son of Amit-
tai saying,

Before
CHRIST
cir. 780.
[a] 2 Kings 14. 25.
‖ Called.
Matt. 12. 39.
Jonas.

CHAP. I. ver. 1. *Now the word of the Lord,* lit. *And, &c.* This is the way in which the several inspired writers of the Old Testament mark that what it was given them to write, was united on to those sacred books which God had given to others to write, and formed with them one continuous whole. The word, *And,* implies this. It would do so in any language, and it does so in Hebrew as much as in any other. As neither we, nor any other people, would, without any meaning, use the word, *And,* so neither did the Hebrews. It joins the four first books of Moses together; it carries on the history through Joshua, Judges, the books of Samuel and the Kings. After the captivity, Ezra and Nehemiah begin again where the histories before left off; the break of the captivity is bridged over; and Ezra, going back in mind to the history of God's people before the captivity, resumes the history, as if it had been of yesterday, *And in the first year of Cyrus.* It joins in the story of the book of Ruth before the captivity, and that of Esther afterward. At times, even prophets employ it, in using the narrative form of themselves, as Ezekiel, *And it was in the thirtieth year, in the fourth month, in the fifth day of the month, and I was in the captivity by the river of Chebar, the heavens opened and I saw.* If a prophet or historian wishes to detach his prophecy or his history, he does so; as Ezra probably began the book of Chronicles anew from Adam, or as Daniel makes his prophecy a whole by itself. But then it is the more obvious that a Hebrew prophet or historian, when he does begin with the word, *And,* has an object in so beginning; he uses an universal word of all languages in its uniform meaning in all language, to join things together.

And yet more precisely; this form, *And the word of the Lord came to—saying,* occurs over and over again, stringing together the pearls of great price of God's revelations, and uniting this new revelation to all those which had preceded it. The word, *And,* then joins on histories with histories, revelations with revelations, uniting in one the histories of God's works and words, and blending the books of Holy Scripture into one Divine book.

But the form of words must have suggested to the Jews another thought, which is part of our thankfulness and of our being, [1] *then to*

the Gentiles also hath God given repentance unto life. The words are the self-same familiar words with which some fresh revelation of God's Will to His people had so often been announced. Now they are prefixed to God's message to the heathen, and so as to join on that message to all the other messages to Israel. Would then God deal thenceforth with the heathen as with the Jews? Would they have their prophets? Would they be included in the one family of God? The mission of Jonah in itself was an earnest that they would; for God, Who does nothing fitfully or capriciously, in that He had begun, gave an earnest that He would carry on what He had begun. And so thereafter, the great prophets, Isaiah, Jeremiah, Ezekiel, were prophets to the nations also; Daniel was a prophet among them, to them as well as to their captives. But the mission of Jonah might, so far, have been something exceptional. The enrolling his book, as an integral part of the scriptures, joining on that prophecy to the other prophecies to Israel, was an earnest that they were to be parts of one system. But then it would be significant also, that the records of God's prophecies to the Jews, all embodied the accounts of their impenitence. Here is inserted among them an account of God's revelation to the heathen, and their repentance. "[2] So many prophets had been sent, so many miracles wrought, so often had captivity been foreannounced to them for the multitude of their sins, and they never repented. Not for the reign of one king did they cease from the worship of the calves; not one of the kings of the ten tribes departed from the sins of Jeroboam? Elijah, sent in the Word and Spirit of the Lord, had done many miracles, yet obtained no abandonment of the calves. His miracles effected this only, that the people knew that Baal was no god, and cried out, *the Lord He is the God.* Elisha his disciple followed him, who asked for a double portion of the Spirit of Elijah, that he might work more miracles, to bring back the people.—He died, and, after his death as before it, the worship of the calves continued in Israel. The Lord marvelled and was weary of Israel, knowing that if He sent to the heathen they would hear, as he saith to Ezekiel. To make trial of this, Jonah was chosen, of whom it is recorded in the book of Kings that he prophesied the

---

[1] Acts xi. 18. [2] Rup.

2 Arise, go to Nineveh, that [b]great city and cry

[b] Gen. 10. 11, 12. ch. 3. 2, 3. & 4. 11.

against it; for [c]their wickedness is come up before me.

[c] Gen. 18. 20, 21. Ezra 9. 6. Jam. 5. 4. Rev. 18. 5.

restoration of the border of Israel. When then he begins by saying, *And the word of the Lord came to Jonah,* prefixing the word *And,* he refers us back to those former things, in this meaning. The children have not hearkened to what the Lord commanded, sending to them by His servants the prophets, but have hardened their necks and given themselves up to do evil before the Lord and provoke Him to anger; *and* therefore *the word of the Lord came to Jonah, saying, Arise and go to Nineveh that great city, and preach unto her,* that so Israel may be shewn, in comparison with the heathen, to be the more guilty, when the Ninevites should repent, the children of Israel persevered in unrepentance."

Jonah the son of Amittai. Both names occur here only in the Old Testament, Jonah signifies "Dove," Amittai, "the truth of God." Some of the names of the Hebrew prophets so suit in with their times, that they must either have been given them prophetically, or assumed by themselves, as a sort of watchword, analogous to the prophetic names, given to the sons of Hosea and Isaiah. Such were the names of Elijah and Elisha, "The Lord is my God," "my God is salvation." Such too seems to be that of Jonah. The "dove" is everywhere the symbol of "mourning love." The side of his character which Jonah records is that of his defect, his want of trust in God, and so his unloving zeal against those, who were to be the instruments of God against his people. His name perhaps preserves that character by which he willed to be known among his people, one who moaned or mourned over them.

2. *Arise, go to Nineveh, that great city.* The Assyrian history, as far as it has yet been discovered, is very bare of events in regard to this period. We have as yet the names of three kings only for 150 years. But Assyria, as far as we know its history, was in its meridian. Just before the time of Jonah, perhaps ending in it, were the victorious reigns of Shalmanubar and Shamasiva; after him was that of Ivalush or Pul, the first aggressor upon Israel. It is clear that this was a time of Assyrian greatness: since God calls it *that great city,* not in relation to its extent only, but its power. A large weak city would not have been called *a great city unto God* [1].

And cry against it. The substance of that *cry* is recorded afterward, but God told to Jonah now, what message he was to *cry* aloud

[1] Jon. iii. 3. [2] Ex. xxxii. 32. [3] Rom. ix. 3.
[4] Nah. ii. 11, 12. [5] Gen. iv. 10.
[6] xviii. 20, 21.

to it. For Jonah relates afterward, how he expostulated now with God, and that his expostulation was founded on this, that God was so merciful that He would not fulfill the judgment which He threatened. Faith was strong in Jonah, while, like Apostles "the sons of thunder," before the Day of Pentecost, he knew not "what spirit *he* was of." Zeal for the people and, as he doubtless thought, for the glory of God, narrowed love in him. He did not, like Moses, pray [2], or else blot me also out of Thy book, or like St. Paul, desire even to be *an anathema from Christ* [3] for his people's sake, so that there might be more to love his Lord. His zeal was directed, like that of the rebuked Apostles, against others, and so it too was rebuked. But his faith was strong. He shrank back from the office, as believing, not as doubting, the might of God. He thought nothing of preaching, amid that multitude of wild warriors, the stern message of God. He was willing, alone, to confront the violence of a city of 600,000, whose characteristic was violence. He was ready, at God's bidding, to enter what Nahum speaks of as a den of lions; [4] *The dwelling of the lions and the feeding-place of the young lions, where the lion did tear in pieces enough for his whelps, and strangled for his lionesses.* He feared not the fierceness of their lion-nature, but God's tenderness, and lest that tenderness should be the destruction of his own people.

Their wickedness is come up before Me. So God said to Cain, [5] *The voice of thy brother's blood crieth unto Me from the ground:* and of Sodom [6], *The cry of Sodom and Gomorrah is great, because their sin is very grievous; the cry of it is come up unto Me.* The *wickedness* is not the mere mass of human sin, of which it is said [7], *the whole world lieth in wickedness,* but evil-doing [8] toward others. This was the cause of the final sentence on Nineveh, with which Nahum closes his prophecy, *upon whom hath not thy wickedness passed continually?* It had been assigned as the ground of the judgment on Israel through Nineveh. [9] *So shall Bethel do unto you, on account of the wickedness of your wickedness.* It was the ground of the destruction by the flood. [10] *God saw that the wickedness of man* was *great upon the earth.* God represents Himself, the Great Judge, as sitting on His Throne in heaven, Unseen but All-seeing, to Whom the wickedness and oppressiveness of man against man *goes up,* appealing for His sentence against the oppressor.

[7] I S. John v. 19.
[8] רעה is almost always evil, suffered or afflicted.
[9] Hos. x. 14, 15. [10] Gen. vi. 5.

Before
CHRIST
cir. 780.
_____

d ch. 4. 2.

3 But ^d Jonah rose up to flee unto Tarshish from the presence of the LORD, and went down to ^e Joppa;

Before
CHRIST
cir. 780.
_____

^e Josh. 19. 46. 2 Chr. 2. 16. Acts 9. 36.

The cause seems ofttimes long in pleading. God is long-suffering with the oppressor too, that if so be, he may repent. So would a greater good come to the oppressed also, if the wolf became a lamb. But meanwhile, "[1]every iniquity has its own voice at the hidden judgment seat of God." Mercy itself calls for vengeance on the unmerciful.

3. *But [And] Jonah rose up to flee—from the presence of the Lord;* lit. *from being before the Lord*[2]. Jonah knew well, that man could not escape from the Presence of God, Whom he knew as the Self-existing, He Who alone IS, the Maker of heaven, earth and sea. He did not *flee* then *from His presence,* knowing well what David said, [3]*whither shall I go from Thy Spirit, or whither shall I flee from Thy presence ? If I take the wings of the morning,* and *dwell in the uttermost parts of the sea, even there shall Thy hand lead me and Thy right hand shall hold me.* Jonah fled, not from God's Presence, but from standing before him, as His servant and minister. He refused God's service, because, as he himself tells God afterward[4], he knew what it would end in, and he misliked it. So he acted, as men often do, who mislike God's commands. He set about removing himself as far as possible from being under the influence of God, and from the place where he *could* fulfill them. God bid him go to Nineveh, which lay North-East from his home; and he instantly set himself to flee to the then furthermost West. Holy Scripture sets the rebellion before us in its full nakedness. *The word of the Lord came unto Jonah, go to Nineveh, and Jonah rose up ;* he did something instantly, as the consequence of God's command. He *rose up,* not as other prophets, to obey, but to disobey ; and that, not slowly nor irresolutely, but *to flee, from* standing *before the Lord.* He renounced his office. So when our Lord came in the Flesh, those who found what He said to be *hard sayings,* went away from Him, *and walked no more with Him*[5]. So the rich *young man went away sorrowful,* [6]*for he had great possessions.* They were perhaps afraid of trusting themselves in His Presence ; or they were ashamed of staying there, and not doing what He said. So men, when God secretly calls them to prayer, go and immerse themselves in business; when, in solitude, He says to their souls something which they like not, they escape His Voice in a throng. If He calls them to make sacrifices for His poor, they order themselves a new dress or

some fresh sumptuousness or self-indulgence ; if to celibacy, they engage themselves to marry forthwith ; or, contrariwise, if He calls them not to do a thing, they do it at once, to make an end of their struggle and their obedience ; to put obedience out of their power ; to enter themselves on a course of disobedience. Jonah, then, in this part of his history, is the image of those who, when God calls them, disobey His call, and how He deals with them, when he does not abandon them. He lets them have their way for a time, encompasses them with difficulties, so that they shall "[7]flee back from God displeased to God appeased."

"[8]The whole wisdom, the whole bliss, the whole of man lies in this, to learn what God wills him to do, in what state of life, calling, duties, profession, employment, He wills him to serve Him." God sent each one of us into the world, to fulfill his own definite duties, and, through His grace, to attain to our own perfection in and through fulfilling them. He did not create us at random, to pass through the world, doing whatever self-will or our own pleasure leads us to, but to fulfill His Will. This Will of His, if we obey His earlier calls, and seek Him by prayer, in obedience, self-subdual, humility, thoughtfulness, He makes known to each by His own secret drawings, and, in absence of these, at times by His Providence or human means. And then, "[9]to follow Him is a token of predestination." It is to place ourselves in that order of things, that pathway to our eternal mansion, for which God created us, and which God created for us. So Jesus says[10], *My sheep hear My voice and I know them, and they follow Me, and I give unto them eternal life, and they shall never perish, neither shall any man pluck them out of My Hand.* In these ways, God has foreordained for us all the graces which we need ; in these, we shall be free from all temptations which might be too hard for us, in which our own special weakness would be most exposed. Those ways, which men choose out of mere natural taste or fancy, are mostly those which expose them to the greatest peril of sin and damnation. For they choose them, just because such pursuits flatter most their own inclinations, and give scope to their natural strength and their moral weakness. So Jonah, misliking a duty, which God gave him to fulfill, separated himself from His service, forfeited his past calling,

---

[1] S. Greg. Mor. v. 20.
[2] Not יי מפני but מלפני ; see Introd. p. 247.
[3] Ps. cxxxix. 7, 9, 10.
[4] iv. 2.

[5] S. John vi. 66.
[7] S. Aug. in Ps. lxx.
[9] Bourdaloue.

[6] S. Matt. xix. 22.
[8] from Lap.
[10] S. John x. 27, 28.

and he found a ship going to Tarshish : so he paid | the fare thereof, and went down into it, to go with

lost, as far as in him lay, his place among "the goodly fellowship of the prophets," and, but for God's overtaking grace, would have ended his days among the disobedient. As in Holy Scripture, David stands alone of saints, who had been after their calling, bloodstained ; as the penitent Robber stands alone converted in death ; as S. Peter stands singly, recalled after denying his Lord ; so Jonah stands, the one Prophet, who, having obeyed and then rebelled, was constrained by the overpowering Providence and love of God, to return and serve Him.

"[1] Being a Prophet, Jonah could not be ignorant of the mind of God, that, according to His great Wisdom and His unsearchable judgments and His untraceable and incomprehensible ways, He, through the threat, was providing for the Ninevites that they should not suffer the things threatened. To think that Jonah hoped to hide himself in the sea and elude by flight the great Eye of God, were altogether absurd and ignorant, which should not be believed, I say not of a prophet, but of no other sensible person who had any moderate knowledge of God and His supreme power. Jonah knew all this better than any one, that, planning his flight, he changed his place, but did not flee God. For this could no man do, either by hiding himself in the bosom of the earth or depths of the sea or ascending (if possible) with wings into the air, or entering the lowest hell, or encircled with thick clouds, or taking any other counsel to secure his flight. This, above all things and alone, can neither be escaped nor resisted, God. When He willeth to hold and grasp in His Hand, He overtaketh the swift, baffleth the intelligent, overthroweth the strong, boweth the lofty, tameth rashness, subdueth might. He who threatened to others the mighty Hand of God, was not himself ignorant of nor thought to flee, God. Let us not believe this. But since he saw the fall of Israel and perceived that the prophetic grace would pass over to the Gentiles, he withdrew himself from the office of preaching, and put off the command." "[2] The Prophet knoweth, the Holy Spirit teaching him, that the repentance of the Gentiles is the ruin of the Jews. A lover then of his country, he does not so much envy the deliverance of Nineveh, as will that his own country should not perish.—Seeing too that his fellow-prophets are

sent to the lost sheep of the house of Israel, to excite the people to repentance, and that Balaam the soothsayer too prophesied of the salvation of Israel, he grieveth that he alone is chosen to be sent to the Assyrians, the enemies of Israel, and to that greatest city of the enemies where was idolatry and ignorance of God. Yet more he feared lest they, on occasion of his preaching, being converted to repentance, Israel should be wholly forsaken. For he knew by the same Spirit whereby the preaching to the Gentiles was entrusted to him, that the house of Israel would then perish ; and he feared that what was at one time to be, should take place in his own time." "[3] The flight of the Prophet may also be referred to that of man in general who, despising the commands of God, departed from Him and gave himself to the world, where subsequently, through the storms of ill and the wreck of the whole world raging against him, he was compelled to feel the Presence of God, and to return to Him Whom he had fled. Whence we understand, that those things also which men think for their good, when against the Will of God, are turned to destruction; and help not only does not benefit those to whom it is given, but those too who give it, are alike crushed. As we read that Egypt was conquered by the Assyrians, because it helped Israel against the Will of God. The ship is emperilled which had received the emperilled ; a tempest arises in a calm ; nothing is secure, when God is against us."

Tarshish, named after one of the sons of Javan [4], was an ancient merchant-city of Spain, once proverbial for its wealth [5], which supplied Judæa with silver [6], Tyre with *all manner of riches*, with iron also, tin, lead [7]. It was known to the Greeks and Romans, as (with a harder pronunciation) Tartessus; but in our first century, it had either ceased to be, or was known under some other name [8]. Ships destined for a voyage, at that time, so long, and built for carrying merchandise, were naturally among the largest then constructed. *Ships of Tarshish* corresponded to the " East-Indiamen " which some of us remember. The breaking of *ships of Tarshish by the East Wind* [9] is, on account of their size and general safety, instanced as a special token of the interposition of God.

And went down to Joppa. Joppa, now Jaffa, was the one well-known port of Israel on the

[1] S. Greg. Naz. Apol. pro fuga, prope fin.
[2] S. Jer. on Jon. i. 3.
[3] Id. on i. 4.   [4] Gen. x. 4.
[5] Ps. lxxii. 10. Strabo iii. 2. 14.   [6] Jer. x. 9.
[7] Ezek. xxvii. 12, 25.

[8] Pliny (iii. 3) speaks of Carteia as so called by the Greeks; in iv. 36, he identifies Gades, the Carthaginian Gadir, with the Roman Tartessus. Strabo says, "some call the present Karteia, Tartessus." (l. c.)   [9] Ps. xlviii. 7.

Before CHRIST cir. 780.

them unto Tarshish [f] from the presence of the LORD.

[f] Gen. 4. 16. Job 1. 12. & 2. 7.

4 ¶ But [g] the LORD † sent out a great wind

Before CHRIST cir. 780.

[g] Ps 107. 25. † Heb. cast forth.

Mediterranean. Thither the cedars were brought from Lebanon for both the first and second temple[1]. Simon the Maccabee " [2] took it again for a haven, and made an entrance to the isles of the sea." It was subsequently destroyed by the Romans, as a pirate-haven[3]. At a later time, all describe it as an unsafe haven. Perhaps the shore changed, since the rings, to which Andromeda was fabled to have been fastened, and which probably were once used to moor vessels, were high above the sea. Perhaps, like the Channel Islands, the navigation was safe to those who knew the coast, unsafe to others. To this port Jonah *went down* from his native country, the mountain district of Zabulon. Perhaps it was not at this time in the hands of Israel. At least, the sailors were heathen. He *went down*, as the man who fell among the thieves, is said to have *gone down from Jerusalem to Jericho*[4]. He *went down* from the place which God honored by His Presence and protection.

And he paid the fare thereof. Jonah describes circumstantially, how he took every step to his end. He went down, found a strong-built ship going whither he wished, paid his fare, embarked. He seemed now to have done all. He had severed himself from the country where his office lay. He had no further step to take. Winds and waves would do the rest. He had but to be still. He went, only to be brought back again.

" [5] Sin brings our soul into much senselessness. For as those overtaken by heaviness of head and drunkenness, are borne on simply and at random, and, be there pit or precipice or whatever else below them, they fall into it unawares; so too, they who fall into sin, intoxicated by their desire of the object, know not what they do, see nothing before them, present or future. Tell me, Fleest thou the Lord? Wait then a little, and thou shalt learn from the event, that thou canst not escape the hands of His servant, the sea. For as soon as he embarked, it too roused its waves and raised them up on high; and as a faithful servant, finding her fellow-slave stealing some of his master's property, ceases not from giving endless trouble to those who take him in, until she recover him, so too the sea, finding and recognizing her fellow-servant, harasses the sailors unceasingly, raging, roaring, not dragging them to a tribunal but threatening to sink the vessel with all its men, unless they restore to her, her fellow-servant."

[1] 2 Chr. iii. 16, Ezr. ii. 7.
[2] 1 Macc. xiv. 5.
[3] Jos. B. J. iii. 9. 3, and Strabo xvi. 2. 28.

" [6] The sinner *arises*, because, will he, nill he, toil he must. If he shrinks from the way of God, because it is hard, he may not yet be idle. There is the way of ambition, of covetousness, of pleasure, to be trodden, which certainly are far harder. 'We wearied ourselves[7],' say the wicked, 'in the way of wickedness and destruction, yea, we have gone through deserts where there lay no way; but the way of the Lord we have not known.' Jonah would not arise, to go to Nineveh at God's command; yet he must needs arise, to flee to Tarshish from before the Presence of God. What good can he have who fleeth the Good? what light, who willingly forsaketh the Light? *He goes down to Joppa.* Wherever thou turnest, if thou depart from the Will of God, thou goest down.—Whatever glory, riches, power, honors, thou gainest, thou risest not a whit; the more thou advancest, while turned from God, the deeper and deeper thou goest down.— Yet all these things are not had, without paying the price. At a price and with toil, he obtains what he desires; he receives nothing gratis, but, at great price purchases to himself storms, griefs, peril. There arises a great tempest in the sea, when various contradictory passions arise in the heart of the sinner, which take from him all tranquillity and joy. There is a tempest in the sea, when God sends strong and dangerous disease, whereby the frame is in peril of being broken. There is a tempest in the sea, when, thro' rivals or competitors for the same pleasures, or the injured, or the civil magistrate, his guilt is discovered, he is laden with infamy and odium, punished, withheld from his wonted pleasures. [8] *They who go down to the sea* of this world, *and do business in mighty waters—their soul melteth away because of trouble ; they reel to and fro and stagger like a drunken man, and all their wisdom is swallowed up.*"

4. *But [And] the Lord sent out* [lit. *cast along*]. Jonah had done his all. Now God's part began. This He expresses by the word, *And.* Jonah took *his* measures, *and* now God takes *His.* He had let him have his way, as He often deals with those who rebel against Him. He lets them have their way up to a certain point. He waits, in the tranquillity of His Almightiness, until they have completed their preparations ; and then, when man has ended, He begins, that man may see the more that it is His doing. " [9] He

[4] S. Luke x. 30.
[5] S. Chrys. Hom. 5. de Pœnit. n. 3. T. ii. p. 312.
[6] Rib. [7] Wisd. v. 7. [8] Ps. cvii. 23-7. [9] Lap.

Before
C H R I S T
cir. 780.
into the sea, and there was
a mighty tempest in the
sea, so that the ship was
† like to be broken.

† Heb. *thought to be broken.*

5 Then the m a r i n e r s
were a f r a i d, and cried
every man unto his god,

Before
C H R I S T
cir. 780.

h So Acts 27.
18, 19, 38.

i 1 Sam. 24. 3.
h and cast forth the wares
that *were* in the ship into
the sea, to lighten *it* of
them. But J o n a h was
gone down ¹ into the sides
of the ship; and he lay,
and was fast asleep.

---

takes those who flee from Him in their flight,
the wise in their counsels, sinners in their
conceits and sins, and draws them back to
Himself and compels them to return. Jonah
thought to find rest in the sea, and lo! a
tempest." Probably, God summoned back
Jonah, as soon as he had completed all on
his part, and sent the tempest, soon after he
left the shore. At least, such tempests often
swept along that shore, and were known by
their own special name, like the Euroclydon
off Crete. Jonah too alone had gone down
below deck to sleep, and, when the storm
came, the mariners thought it possible to put
back. Josephus says of that shore, "¹ Joppa
having by nature no haven, for it ends in a
rough shore, mostly abrupt, but for a short
space having projections, i. e. deep rocks and
cliffs advancing into the sea, inclining on
either side toward each other (where the traces
of the chains of Andromeda yet shewn accredit
the antiquity of the fable,) and the North wind
beating right on the shore, and dashing the
high waves against the rocks which receive
them, makes the station there a harborless
sea. As those from Joppa were tossing here,
a strong wind (called by those who sail here,
the black North wind) falls upon them at
daybreak, dashing straightway some of the
ships against each other, some against the
rocks, and some, forcing their way against the
waves to the open sea, (for they fear the
rocky shore—) the breakers towering above
them, sank."

The ship was like [lit. *thought*] *to be broken.*
Perhaps Jonah means by this very vivid
image to exhibit the more his own dullness.
He ascribes, as it were, to the ship a sense of
its own danger, as she heaved and rolled and
creaked and quivered under the weight of
the storm which lay on her, and her masts
groaned, and her yard-arms shivered. To
the awakened conscience everything seems to
have been alive to God's displeasure, except
itself.

5. *And cried, every man unto his God.*
They did what they could. "² Not knowing the truth, they yet know of a Providence,

and, amid religious error, know that there is
an Object of reverence." In ignorance
they had received one who offended God.
And now God, *Whom they ignorantly wor-
shiped³,* while they cried to the gods, who,
they thought, disposed of them, heard them.
They escaped with the loss of their wares,
but God saved their lives and revealed Himself to them. God hears ignorant prayer,
when ignorance is not wilful and sin.

To lighten it of them, lit. *to lighten from
against them, to lighten* what was so much *against
them,* what so oppressed them. "²They
thought that the ship was weighed down by
its wonted lading, and they knew not that
the whole weight was that of the fugitive
Prophet." "⁴ *The sailors cast forth their wares,*
but the ship was not lightened. For the
whole weight still remained, the body of the
Prophet, that heavy burden, not from the
nature of the body, but from the burden of sin. For nothing is so onerous and
heavy as sin and disobedience. Whence
also Zechariah ⁵ represented it under the
image of lead. And David, describing its
nature, said ⁶, *my wickednesses are gone over my
head; as a heavy burden they are too heavy for
me.* And Christ cried aloud to those who
lived in many sins⁷, *Come unto Me, all ye that
labor and are heavy-laden, and I will refresh
you.*"

Jonah was gone down, probably before the
beginning of the storm, not simply before the
lightening of the vessel. He could hardly
have fallen asleep *then.* A heathen ship was
a strange place for a prophet of God, not *as a*
prophet, but as a fugitive; and so, probably,
ashamed of what he had completed, he had
withdrawn from sight and notice. He did
not embolden himself in his sin, but shrank
into himself. The conscience most commonly
awakes, when the sin is done. It stands aghast
at itself; but Satan, if he can, cuts off its retreat. Jonah had no retreat now, unless God
had made one.

And was fast asleep. The journey to Joppa
had been long and hurried; he had *fled.*
Sorrow and remorse completed what fatigue

---

¹ B. J. iii. 9. 3. In the Ant. xv. 9. 6. he says that
Herod made the port of Cæsarea, "between Dora
[in Manasseh] and Joppa, small towns on the sea-
shore, with bad harborage, on account of the strong
blasts from the South-West, which, accumulating

the sea-sand on the shore, admit of no quiet moor-
age, but merchants must mostly ride at anchor out
at sea."   ² S. Jer.   ³ Acts xvii. 23.
⁴ S. Chrys. Ib.   ⁵ v. 7.
⁶ Ps. xxxviii. 4.   ⁷ S. Matt. xi. 28.

Before CHRIST cir. 780.	6 So the shipmaster came to him, and said unto him, What meanest thou, O sleeper? arise, [k] call upon thy God, [l] if so be

k Ps. 107. 28.

l Joel 2. 14.

that God will think upon us, that we perish not.

7 And they said every one to his fellow, Come, and let us [m] cast lots, that

Before CHRIST cir. 780.

m Josh. 7. 14, 16.
1 Sam. 10. 20,
21. & 14. 41, 42.
Prov. 16. 33.
Acts 1. 26.

began. Perhaps he had given himself up to sleep, to dull his conscience. For it is said, *he lay down and was fast asleep.* Grief produces sleep; whence it is said of the Apostles in the night before the Lord's Passion, when Jesus *rose up from prayer and was come to His disciples, He found them sleeping for sorrow* [1]. " [2] Jonah slept heavily. Deep was the sleep, but it was not of pleasure but of grief; not of heartlessness, but of heavy-heartedness. For well-disposed servants soon feel their sins, as did he. For when the sin has been done, then he knows its frightfulness. For such is sin. When born, it awakens pangs in the soul which bare it, contrary to the law of our nature. For so soon as *we* are born, we end the travail-pangs; but sin, so soon as born, rends with pangs the thoughts which conceived it." Jonah was in a deep sleep, a sleep by which he was fast held and bound [3]; a sleep as deep as that from which Sisera never woke [4]. Had God allowed the ship to sink, the memory of Jonah would have been that of the fugitive prophet. As it is, his deep sleep stands as an image of the lethargy of sin. " [5] This most deep sleep of Jonah signifies a man torpid and slumbering in error, to whom it sufficed not to flee from the face of God, but his mind, drowned in a stupor and not knowing the displeasure of God, lies asleep, steeped in security."

6. *What meanest thou?* or rather, *what aileth thee?* [lit. *what is to thee?*] The shipmaster speaks of it (as it was) as a sort of disease, that he should be thus asleep in the common peril. *The shipmaster,* charged, as he by office was, with the common weal of those on board, would, in the common peril, have one common prayer. It was the Prophet's office to call the heathen to prayers and to calling upon God. God reproved the Scribes and Pharisees by the mouth of the children who *cried Hosanna* [6]; Jonah by the shipmaster; David by Abigail [7]; Naaman by his servants. Now too he reproves worldly priests by the devotion of laymen, sceptic intellect by the simplicity of faith.

If so be that God will think upon us, [lit. *for us*] i. e. for good; as David says [8], *I am poor and needy, the Lord thinketh upon* [lit. *for*] *me.* Their calling upon their own gods had failed them. Perhaps the shipmaster had seen

something special about Jonah, his manner, or his prophet's garb. He does not only call Jonah's God, *thy God,* as Darius says to Daniel *thy God* [9], but also *the God,* acknowledging the God Whom Jonah worshiped, to be *the God.* It is not any heathen prayer which he asks Jonah to offer. It is the prayer of the creature in its need to God Who can help; but knowing its own ill-desert, and the separation between itself and God, it knows not whether He will help it. So David says [10], *Remember not the sins of my youth nor my transgressions; according to Thy mercy remember Thou me for Thy goodness' sake, O Lord.*

" [2] The shipmaster knew from experience, that it was no common storm, that the surges were an infliction borne down from God, and above human skill, and that there was no good in the master's skill. For the state of things needed another Master Who ordereth the heavens, and craved the guidance from on high. So then they too left oars, sails, cables, gave their hands rest from rowing, and stretched them to heaven and called on God."

7. *Come, and let us cast lots.* Jonah too had probably prayed, and his prayers too were not heard. Probably, too, the storm had some unusual character about it, the suddenness with which it burst upon them, its violence, the quarter whence it came, its whirlwind force. " [5] They knew the nature of the sea, and, as experienced sailors, were acquainted with the character of wind and storm, and had these waves been such as they had known before, they would never have sought by lot for the author of the threatened wreck, or, by a thing uncertain, sought to escape certain peril." God, Who sent the storm to arrest Jonah and to cause him to be cast into the sea, provided that its character should set the mariners on divining, why it came. Even when working great miracles, God brings about, through man, all the fore-running events, all but the last act, in which He puts forth His might. As, in His people, he directed the lot to fall on Achan or on Jonathan, so here He overruled the lots of the heathen sailors to accomplish His end. " [5] We must not, on this precedent, forthwith trust in lots, or unite with this testimony that from the Acts of the Apostles, when Matthias

---

[1] S. Luke xxii. 45.   [2] S. Chrys. Ib.
[3] The Hebrew form is passive, נרדם.
[4] The same word is used Judg. iv. 21.   [5] S. Jer.

[6] S. Matt. xxi. 15.   [7] 1 Sam. xxv. 32-34.
[8] Ps. xl. 17.
[9] Dan. vi. 20.   [10] Ps. xxv. 7.

26

Before
CHRIST
cir. 780.
we may know for whose
cause this evil *is* upon us.
So they cast lots, and the
lot fell upon Jonah.

8 Then said they unto

ⁿ Josh. 7. 19.
1 Sam. 14. 43.
him, ⁿTell us, we pray

thee, for whose cause this
evil *is* upon us; What *is*
thine o c c u p a t i o n? and
whence comest thou? what
is thy country? a n d of
what people *art* thou?

Before
CHRIST
cir. 780.

was by lot elected to the Apostolate, since the privileges of individuals cannot form a common law." "Lots," according to the ends for which they were cast, were[1] for i) dividing; ii) consulting; iii) divining. i.) The lot for dividing is not wrong if not used, 1) "[2] without any necessity; for this would be to tempt God:" 2) "if[2] in case of necessity, not without reverence of God, as if Holy Scripture were used for an earthly end," as in determining any secular matter by opening the Bible[3]: 3) for objects which ought to be decided otherwise, (as, an office ought to be given to the fittest:) 4) in dependence upon any other than God. ' *The lot is cast into the lap, but the whole disposing of it is the Lord's.* So then they are lawful "[5] in secular things which cannot otherwise be conveniently distributed," or "[6] when there is no apparent reason why, in any advantage or disadvantage, one should be preferred to another." S. Augustine even allows[7] that, in a time of plague or persecution, the lot might be cast to decide who should remain to administer the Sacraments to the people, lest, on the one side, all should be taken away, or, on the other, the Church be deserted. ii. The lot for consulting, i. e. to decide what one should do, is wrong, unless in a matter of mere indifference, or under inspiration of God, or in some extreme necessity where all human means fail. iii. The lot for divining, i. e. to learn truth, whether of things present or future, of which we can have no human knowledge, is wrong, except by direct inspiration of God. For it is either to tempt God Who has not promised so to reveal things, or, against God, to seek superhuman knowledge by ways unsanctioned by Him. Satan may readily mix himself unknown in such enquiries, as in mesmerism. Forbidden ground is his own province.

God overruled the lot in the case of Jonah, as He did the sign which the Philistines sought. "[8] He made the heifers take the way to Bethshemesh, that the Philistines might know that the plague came to them, not by chance, but from Himself." "[9] The

fugitive (Jonah) was taken by lot, not by any virtue of the lots, especially the lots of heathen, but by the Will of Him Who guided the uncertain lots." "[10] The lot betrayed the culprit. Yet not even thus did they cast him over; but, even while such a tumult and storm lay on them, they held, as it were, a court in the vessel, as though in entire peace, and allowed him a hearing and defence, and sifted everything accurately, as men who were to give account of their judgment. Hear them sifting all as in a court.—The roaring sea accused him; the lot convicted and witnessed against him, yet not even thus did they pronounce against him—until the accused should be the accuser of his own sin. The sailors, uneducated, untaught, imitated the good order of courts. When the sea scarce allowed them to breathe, whence such forethought about the Prophet? By the disposal of God. For God by all this instructed the Prophet to be humane and mild, all but saying aloud to him; 'Imitate these uninstructed sailors. They think not lightly of one soul, nor are unsparing as to one body, thine own. But thou, for thy part, gavest up a whole city with so many myriads. They, discovering thee to be the cause of the evils which befell them, did not even thus hurry to condemn thee. Thou, having nothing whereof to accuse the Ninevites, didst sink and destroy them. Thou, when I bade thee go and by thy preaching call them to repentance, obeyedst not; these, untaught, do all, compass all, in order to recover thee, already condemned, from punishment.' "

8. *Tell us, for whose cause* [lit. *for what to whom.*] It may be that they thought that Jonah had been guilty toward some other. The lot had pointed him out. The mariners, still fearing to do wrong, ask him thronged questions, to know why the anger of God followed him; *what hast thou done to whom? what thine occupation?* i. e. either his ordinary occupation, whether it was displeasing to God? or this particular *business* in which he was engaged, and for which he was come on board. Questions so thronged have been ad-

[1] Aquin. 2. 2. q. 95. art. 8.　　[2] Aquin. l. c.
[3] From S. Aug. Ep. 55. ad inquis. Januar.
[4] Prov. xvi. 33.
[5] Less. de justit. &c. ii. 43. Dub. 9. L.
[6] Id. quoting S. Aug. de doctr. Xt. i. 28. "If any have a superfluity which ought to be given to such as have not, and cannot be given to two, and two

come to you, of whom neither is to be preferred to the other from want or any urgent necessity, you cannot do anything more just than choose by lot, to which that should be given which cannot be given to both." also in Aquin. l. c.
[7] Ep. 228. ad Honorat. n. 12.　　[8] Lap.
[9] S. Jer.　　　　　[10] S. Chrys. Ib. p. 313.

Before
CHRIST
cir. 780.

‖ Or,
JEHOVAH.
° Ps. 146. 6.
Acts. 17. 24.

9 And he said unto them, I *am* an Hebrew; and I fear ‖ the LORD, the God of heaven, ° which hath made the sea and the dry *land.*

10 Then were the men

† exceedingly afraid, and said unto him, Why hast thou done this? For the men knew that he fled from the presence of the LORD, because he had told them.

Before
CHRIST
cir. 780.

† Heb. *with
great fear.*

mired in human poetry, S. Jerome says. For it is true to nature. They think that some one of them will draw forth the answer which they wish. It may be that they thought that his country, or people, or parents, were under the displeasure of God. But perhaps, more naturally, they wished to " know all about him," as men say. These questions must have gone home to Jonah's conscience. *What is thy business?* The office of Prophet which he had left. *Whence comest thou?* From standing before God, as His minister. *What thy country? of what people art thou?* The people of God, whom he had quitted for heathen; not to win them to God, as He commanded; but, not knowing what they did, to abet him in his flight.

What is thine occupation? They should ask themselves, who have Jonah's office to speak in the name of God, and preach repentance. " [1] What should be thy business, who hast consecrated thyself wholly to God, whom God has loaded with daily benefits? who approachest to Him as to a Friend? *What is thy business?* To live for God, to despise the things of earth, to behold the things of Heaven," to lead others heavenward.

Jonah answers simply the central point to which all these questions tended;

9. *I am an Hebrew.* This was the name by which Israel was known to foreigners. It is used in the Old Testament, only when they are spoken of by foreigners, or speak of themselves to foreigners, or when the sacred writers mention them in contrast with foreigners [2]. So Joseph spoke of his land [3], and the Hebrew midwives [4], and Moses' sister [5], and God in His commission to Moses [6] as to Pharaoh, and Moses in fulfilling it [7]. They had the name, as having passed the river Euphrates, " emigrants." The title might serve to remind themselves, that they were *strangers and pilgrims* [8], whose fathers had left their home at God's command and for God, " [9] *passers by*, through this world to death, and through death to immortality."

And I fear the Lord, i. e. I am a worshiper

of Him, most commonly, one who habitually stands in awe of Him, and so one who stands in awe of sin too. For none really fear God, none fear Him as sons, who do not fear Him in act. To be afraid of God is not to fear Him. To be afraid of God keeps men away from God; to fear God draws them to Him. Here, however, Jonah probably meant to tell them, that the Object of his fear and worship was the One Self-existing God, He Who alone IS, Who made all things, in Whose hands are all things. He had told them before, that he had fled *from being before the* LORD. They had not thought anything of this, for they thought of the LORD, only as the God of the Jews. Now he adds, that He, Whose service he had thus forsaken, was *the God of heaven, Who made the sea and dry land*, that sea, whose raging terrified them and threatened their lives. The title, *the God of heaven*, asserts the doctrine of the creation of the heavens by God, and His supremacy. Hence Abraham uses it to his servant [10], and Jonah to the heathen mariners, and Daniel to Nebuchadnezzar [11]; and Cyrus in acknowledging God in his proclamation [12]. After his example, it is used in the decrees of Darius [13] and Artaxerxes [14], and the returned exiles use it in giving account of their building the temple to the Governor [15]. Perhaps, from the habit of intercourse with the heathen, it is used once by Daniel [16] and by Nehemiah [17]. Melchisedek, not perhaps being acquainted with the special name, the LORD, blessed Abraham in the Name of *God, the Possessor* or *Creator of heaven and earth* [18], i. e. of all that is. Jonah, by using it, at once taught the sailors that there is One Lord of all, and why this evil had fallen on them, because they had with them himself, the renegade servant of God. " [19] When Jonah said this, he indeed feared God and repented of his sin. If he lost filial fear by fleeing and disobeying, he recovered it by repentance."

10. *Then were the men exceedingly afraid.* Before, they had feared the tempest and the loss of their lives. Now they feared God. They feared, not the creature but the Creator. They knew that what they had feared

[1] Sanch.   [2] In all 32 times in the O. T.
[3] Gen. xl. 15.   [4] Ex. i. 19.
[5] Ib. ii. 7.   [6] Ib. iii. 18, vii. 16. ix. 1.
[7] Ib. v. 3.   [8] Heb. xi. 13.   [9] Lap.

[10] Gen. xxiv. 7.   [11] Dan. ii. 37, 44.
[12] 2 Chr. xxxvi. 23, Ezr. i. 2.   [13] Ezr. vi. 9. 10.
[14] Ib. vii. 12, 21, 23.   [15] Ib. v. 11, 12.   [16] ii. 18.
[17] i. 4, 5, ii. 4, 20.   [18] Gen. xiv. 19.   [19] Dion.

Before
CHRIST
cir. 780.

11 ¶ Then said they unto him, What shall we do unto thee that the sea † may be calm unto us? for the sea ‖ † w r o u g h t, and was tempestuous.

12 And he said unto

† Heb. *may be silent from us.*
‖ Or, *grew more and more tempestuous.*
† Heb. *went.*

them, ᴾ Take me up, and cast me forth into the sea, so shall the sea be calm unto you: for I know that for my sake this great tempest *is* upon you.

Before
CHRIST
cir. 780.

ᴾ John 11. 50.

---

was the doing of His Almightiness. They felt how awful a thing it was to be in His Hands. Such fear is the beginning of conversion, when men turn from dwelling on the distresses which surround them, to God Who sent them.

Why hast thou done this? They are words of amazement and wonder. Why hast thou not obeyed so great a God, and how thoughtest thou to escape the hand of the Creator? "[1] What is the mystery of thy flight? Why did one, who feared God and had revelations from God, flee, sooner than go to fulfill them? Why did the worshiper of the One true God depart from his God?" "[2] A servant flee from his Lord, a son from his father, man from his God!" The inconsistency of believers is the marvel of the young Christian, the repulsion of those without, the hardening of the unbeliever. If men really believed in eternity, how could they be thus immersed in things of time? If they believed in hell, how could they so hurry thither? If they believed that God died for them, how could they so requite Him? Faith without love, knowledge without obedience, conscious dependence and rebellion, to be favored by God yet to despise His favor, are the strangest marvels of this mysterious world. All nature seems to cry out to and against the unfaithful Christian, *why hast thou done this?* And what a *why* it is! A scoffer has lately said truly, "[3] Avowed scepticism cannot do a tenth part of the injury to practical faith, that the constant spectacle of the huge mass of worldly unreal belief does." It is nothing strange, that the world or unsanctified intellect should reject the Gospel. It is a thing of course, unless it be converted. But, to know, to believe, and to disobey! To disobey God, in the name of God. To propose to halve the living Gospel, as the woman who had killed her child[4], and to think that the poor quivering remnants would be the living Gospel any more! As though the Will of God might, like those lower forms of His animal creation, be divided endlessly, and, keep what fragments we will, it would still be a living whole, a vessel of His Spirit! Such unrealities and inconsistencies would be a sore trial of faith, had not Jesus, Who

[1] Dion.
[2] S. Jer.
[3] In the Times.
[4] 1 Kings iii. 26.

[5] *knew what is in man,* forewarned us that it should be so. The scandals against the Gospel, so contrary to all human opinion, are but a testimony the more to the Divine knowledge of the Redeemer.

11. *What shall we do unto thee?* They knew him to be a prophet; they ask him the mind of his God. The lots had marked out Jonah as the cause of the storm; Jonah had himself admitted it, and that the storm was for *his* cause, and came from *his* God. "[2] Great was he who fled, greater He Who required him. They dare not give him up; they cannot conceal him. They blame the fault; they confess their fear; they ask *him* the remedy, who was the author of the sin. If it was faulty to receive thee, what can we do, that God should not be angered? It is thine to direct; ours, to obey."

The sea wrought and was tempestuous, lit. *was going and whirling.* It was not only increasingly tempestuous, but, like a thing alive and obeying its Master's Will, it was holding on its course, its wild waves tossing themselves, and marching on like battalions, marshalled, arrayed for the end for which they were sent, pursuing and demanding the runaway slave of God. "[2] It was going, as it was bidden; *it was going* to avenge its Lord; *it was going,* pursuing the fugitive Prophet. It was swelling every moment, and, as though the sailors were too tardy, was rising in yet greater surges, shewing that the vengeance of the Creator admitted not of delay."

12. *Take me up, and cast me into the sea.* Neither might Jonah have said this, nor might the sailors have obeyed it, without the command of God. Jonah might will alone to perish, who had alone offended; but, without the command of God, the Giver of life, neither Jonah nor the sailors might dispose of the life of Jonah. But God willed that Jonah should be cast into the sea, whither he had gone for refuge, that[6] *wherewithal* he had *sinned, by the same also he might be punished* as a man; and, as a Prophet, that he might, in his three days' burial, prefigure Him Who, after His Resurrection, should convert, not Nineveh, but the world, the cry of whose wickedness went up to God.

For I know that for my sake. "[7] In that he

[5] S. John ii. 25
[6] Wisd. xi. 16.
[7] Alb. M.

13 Nevertheless the men † rowed hard to bring *it* to the land ; q but they could not : for the sea wrought, and was t e m p e s t u o u s against them.

14 Wherefore they cried unto the LORD, and said, We beseech thee, O LORD, we beseech thee, let us not perish for this man's life, and r lay not upon us in-

says, *I know,* he marks that he had a revelation ; in that he says, *this great storm,* he marks the need which lay on those who cast him into the sea."

13. *The men rowed hard,* lit. *dug.* The word, like our "ploughed the main," describes the great efforts which they made. Amid the violence of the storm, they had furled their sails. These were worse than useless. The wind was off shore, since by rowing alone they hoped to get back to it. They put their oars well and firmly in the sea, and turned up the water, as men turn up earth by digging. But in vain! God willed it not. The sea went on its way, as before. In the description of the deluge, it is repeated, [1] *the waters increased and bare up the ark, and it was lifted up above the earth; the waters increased greatly upon the earth ; and the ark went upon the face of the waters.* The waters raged and swelled, drowned the whole world, yet only bore up the ark, as a steed bears its rider : man was still, the waters obeyed. In *this* tempest, on the contrary, man strove, but, instead of the peace of the ark, the burden is, the violence of the tempest ; *the sea wrought and was tempestuous against them.* "[2] The Prophet had pronounced sentence against himself, but they would not lay hands upon him, striving hard to get back to land, and escape the risk of bloodshed, willing to lose life rather than cause its loss. O what a change was there. The people who had served God, said, Crucify Him, Crucify Him ! These are bidden to put to death ; the sea rageth ; the tempest commandeth ; and they are careless as to their own safety, while anxious about another's."

14. *Wherefore [And] they cried unto the Lord.* They cried no more each man to his *god,* but to the one God, Whom Jonah had made known to them ; and to Him they cried with an earnest, submissive, cry, repeating the words of beseeching, as men, do in great earnestness ; *we beseech Thee, O Lord, let us not, we beseech Thee, perish for the life of this man* (i. e. as a penalty for taking it, as it is said, [3] *we will slay him for the life of his brother,* and, [4] *life for life.*) They seem to have known what is said, [5] *your blood of your lives will I*

require; *at the hand of every beast will I require it and at the hand of man ; at the hand of every man's brother will I require the life of man. Whoso sheddeth man's blood, by man shall his blood be shed ; for in the image of God made He man.* "[2] Do not these words of the sailors seem to us to be the confession of Pilate, who washed his hands, and said, *I am clean from the blood of this Man ?* The Gentiles would not that Christ should perish ; they protest that His Blood is innocent."

And lay not upon us innocent blood ; innocent as to them, although, as to this thing, guilty before God, and yet, as to God also, more innocent, they would think, than they. For, strange as was this one disobedience, *their* whole life, they now knew, was disobedience to God ; *his,* but one act in a life of obedience. If God so punishes one sin of the holy, [6] *where shall the ungodly and sinner appear ?* Terrible to the awakened conscience are God's chastenings on some (as it seems) single offence of those whom He loves.

For Thou, Lord, [Who knowest the hearts of all men,] hast done, as it pleased Thee. Wonderful, concise, confession of faith in these new converts ! Psalmists said it [7], *Whatsoever God willeth, that doeth He in heaven and in earth, in the sea and in all deep places.* But these had but just known God, and they resolve the whole mystery of man's agency and God's Providence into the three simple words [8], *as* [Thou] *willedst* [Thou] *didst.* "[2] That we took him aboard, that the storm ariseth, that the winds rage, that the billows lift themselves, that the fugitive is betrayed by the lot, that he points out what is to be done, it is of Thy Will, O Lord." "[2] The tempest itself speaketh, that *Thou, Lord, hast done as Thou willedst.* Thy Will is fulfilled by our hands." "[9] Observe the counsel of God, that, of his own will, not by violence or by necessity, should he be cast into the sea. For the casting of Jonah into the sea signified the entrance of Christ into the bitterness of the Passion, which He took upon Himself of His own Will, not of necessity. [10] *He was offered up, and He willingly submitted Himself.* And as those who sailed with Jonah were delivered, so the faithful in the Passion of Christ. [11] *If ye seek Me, let these go their way, that the saying might be fulfilled which*

[1] Gen. vii. 17, 18.   [2] S. Jer.
[3] 2 Sam. xiv. 7.   [4] Deut. xix. 21.
    [5] Gen. ix. 5, 6.

[6] 1 S. Pet. iv. 18.   [7] Ps. cxxxv. 6, cxv. 3.
[8] כַּאֲשֶׁר חָפֵץ עָשִׂית.   [9] Alb. M.
[10] Is. liii. 7.   [11] S. John xviii. 8, 9.

Before
CHRIST
cir. 780.

ª Ps. 115. 3.

ᵗ Ps. 89. 9.
Luke 8. 24.
†Heb. stood.

ᵘ Mark 4. 41.
Acts 5. 11.

nocent blood: for thou, O
LORD, ª hast done as it
pleased thee.

15 So they took up Jo-
nah, and cast him forth
into the sea: ᵗand the sea
† ceased from her raging.

16 Then the men ᵘfeared
the LORD exceedingly, and

† offered a sacrifice unto
the LORD, and made
vows.

17 ¶ Now the LORD
had prepared a great fish
to swallow up Jonah. And
ˣ Jonah was in the † belly
of the fish three days and
three nights.

Before
CHRIST
cir. 780.

† Heb. sacrificed
a sacrifice unto
the LORD, and
vowed vows.

ˣ Matt. 12. 40.
& 16. 4.
Luke 11. 30.
† Heb. bowels.

Jesus spake, Of them which Thou gavest Me, I have lost none."

15. They took up Jonah. "¹ He does not say, 'laid hold on him', nor 'came upon him' but lifted him; as it were, bearing him with respect and honor, they cast him into the sea, not resisting, but yielding himself to their will."

The sea ceased [lit. stood] from his raging. Ordinarily, the waves still swell, when the wind has ceased. The sea, when it had received Jonah, was hushed at once, to shew that God alone raised and quelled it. It stood still, like a servant, when it had accomplished its mission. God, Who at all times saith to it, ² Hitherto shalt thou come and no further, and here shall thy proud waves be stayed, now unseen, as afterwards in the Flesh, ³ rebuked the winds and the sea, and there was a great calm. "¹ If we consider the errors of the world before the Passion of Christ, and the conflicting blasts of divers doctrines, and the vessel, and the whole race of man, i. e. the creature of the Lord, imperilled, and, after His Passion, the tranquillity of faith and the peace of the world and the security of all things and the conversion to God, we shall see how, after Jonah was cast in, the sea stood from its raging." "¹ Jonah, in the sea, a fugitive, shipwrecked, dead, saveth the tempest-tost vessel; he saveth the heathen, aforetime tossed to and fro by the error of the world into divers opinions. And Hosea, Amos, Isaiah, Joel, who prophesied at the same time, could not amend the people in Judæa; whence it appeared that the breakers could not be calmed, save by the death of [Him typified by] the fugitive."

16. And the men feared the Lord with a great fear; because, from the tranquillity of the sea and the ceasing of the tempest, they saw that the Prophet's words were true. This great miracle completed the conversion of the mariners. God had removed all human cause of fear; and yet, in the same words as before, he says, they feared a great fear; but he adds, the Lord. It was the great fear, with which even the disciples of Jesus feared,

when they saw the miracles which He did, which made even Peter say, ⁴ Depart from me, for I am a sinful man, O Lord. Events full of wonder had thronged upon them; things beyond nature, and contrary to nature; things which betokened His Presence, Who had all things in His hands. They had seen wind and storm fulfilling His word ⁵, and, forerunners of the fishermen of Galilee, knowing full well from their own experience that this was above nature, they felt a great awe of God. So He commanded His people, Thou shalt fear the Lord thy God ⁶, for thy good always ⁷.

And offered a sacrifice. Doubtless, as it was a large decked vessel and bound on a long voyage, they had live creatures on board, which they could offer in sacrifice. But this was not enough for their thankfulness; they vowed vows. They promised that they would do thereafter what they could not do then; "¹ that they would never depart from Him Whom they had begun to worship." This was true love, not to be content with aught which they could do, but to stretch forward in thought to an abiding and enlarged obedience, as God should enable them. And so they were doubtless enrolled among the people of God, first-fruits from among the heathen, won to God Who overrules all things, through the disobedience and repentance of His Prophet. Perhaps, they were the first preachers among the heathen, and their account of their own wonderful deliverance prepared the way for Jonah's mission to Nineveh.

17. Now the Lord had [lit. And the Lord] prepared. Jonah (as appears from his thanksgiving) was not swallowed up at once, but sank to the bottom of the sea, God preserving him in life there by miracle, as He did in the fish's belly. Then, when the sea-weed was twined around his head, and he seemed to be already buried till the sea should give up her dead, God prepared the fish to swallow Jonah. "⁸God could as easily have kept Jonah alive in the sea as in the fish's belly, but, in order to prefigure the burial of the Lord, He willed him to be within the fish whose

¹ S. Jer.   ² Job xxxviii. 11.
³ S. Matt. viii. 26.   ⁴ S. Luke v. 8.
⁵ Ps. cxlviii. 8.   ⁶ Deut. vi. 13.
⁷ Ib. 24.   ⁸ Dion.

CHAPTER II.

1 *The prayer of Jonah.* 10 *He is delivered from the fish.*

THEN Jonah prayed unto the LORD his God out of the fish's belly,

belly was as a grave." Jonah, does not say what fish it was; and our Lord too used a name, signifying only one of the very largest fish[1]. Yet it were no greater miracle to create a fish which should swallow Jonah, than to preserve him alive when swallowed. "[2] The infant is buried, as it were, in the womb of its mother; it cannot breathe, and yet, thus too, it liveth and is preserved, wonderfully nurtured by the will of God." He Who preserves the embryo in its living grave can maintain the life of man as easily without the outward air as with it. The same Divine Will preserves in being the whole creation, or creates it. The same Will of God keeps us in life by breathing this outward air, Which preserved Jonah without it. How long will men think of God, as if He were man, of the Creator as if He were a creature, as though creation were but one intricate piece of machinery, which is to go on, ringing its regular changes until it shall be worn out, and God were shut up, as a sort of mainspring within it, Who might be allowed to be a primal Force, to set it in motion, but must not be allowed to vary what He has once made? "We must admit of the agency of God," say these men[3] when they would not in name be Atheists, "once in the beginning of things, but must allow of His interference as sparingly as may be." Most wise arrangement of the creature, if it were indeed the god of its God! Most considerate provision for the non-interference of its Maker, if it could but secure that He would not interfere with it for ever! Acute physical philosophy, which, by its omnipotent word, would undo the Acts of God! Heartless, senseless, sightless, world, which exists in God, is upheld by God, whose every breath is an effluence of God's love, and which yet sees Him not, thanks Him not, thinks it a greater thing to hold its own frail existence from some imagined law, than to be the object of the tender personal care of the Infinite God, Who is Love! Poor hoodwinked souls, which would extinguish for themselves the Light of the world, in order that it may not eclipse the rushlight of their own theory!

And Jonah was in the belly of the fish. The time that Jonah was in the fish's belly was a hidden prophecy. Jonah does not explain nor point it. He tells the fact, as Scripture is wont. Then he singles out one, the turning point in it. Doubtless in those three days and nights of darkness, Jonah, (like him who

after his conversion became S. Paul,) meditated much, repented much, sorrowed much, for the love of God, that he had ever offended God, purposed future obedience, adored God with wondering awe for His judgment and mercy. It was a narrow home, in which Jonah, by miracle, was not consumed; by miracle, breathed; by miracle, retained his senses in that fetid place. Jonah doubtless, repented, marvelled, adored, loved God. But, of all, God has singled out this one point, how, out of such a place, Jonah thanked God. As He delivered Paul and Silas from the prison, when they prayed with a loud voice to Him, so when Jonah, by inspiration of His Spirit, thanked Him, He delivered him. To thank God, only in order to obtain fresh gifts from Him, would be but a refined, hypocritical form of selfishness. Such a formal act would not be thanks at all. We thank God, because we love Him, because He is so infinitely Good, and so good to us, unworthy. Thanklessness shuts the door to His personal mercies to us, because it makes them the occasion of fresh sins of our's. Thankfulness sets God's essential Goodness free (so to speak) to be good to us. He can do what He delights in doing, be good to us, without our making His Goodness a source of harm to us. Thanking Him through His grace, we become fit vessels for larger graces. "[4] Blessed he who, at every gift of grace, returns to Him in Whom is all fullness of graces; to Whom when we shew ourselves not ungrateful for gifts received, we make room in ourselves for grace, and become meet for receiving yet more." But Jonah's was that special character of thankfulness, which thanks God in the midst of calamities from which there was no human exit; and God set His seal on this sort of thankfulness, by annexing this deliverance, which has consecrated Jonah as an image of our Lord, to his wonderful act of thanksgiving.

II. 1. *Then [And] Jonah prayed,* i. e. when the three days and nights were passed, he uttered this devotion. The word *prayed* includes thanksgiving, not petition only. It is said of Hannah that she *prayed*[5]; but her canticle is all one thanksgiving without a single petition. In this thanksgiving Jonah says how his prayers had been heard, but prays no more. God had delivered him from the sea, and he thanks God, in the fish's belly, as undisturbed as in a Church or an oratory, secure that God, Who had done so

---

[1] See ab. Introd. p. 257.   [2] S. Cyr.
[3] Westminster Review.

[4] S. Bern. Serm. 27. c. pessim. vit. in gratitud. i. 1142.   [5] 1 Sam. ii. 1.

Before
CHRIST
cir. 780.
ᵃ Ps. 120. 1.
& 130. 1.
& 142. 1.
Lam. 3. 55, 56.
‖ Or, *out of mine
affliction.*
ᵇ Ps. 65. 2.
‖ Or, *the grave.*
Is. 14. 9.

2 And said, I ᵃcried ‖ by reason of mine affliction unto the LORD, ᵇ and he heard me; out of the belly of ‖ hell cried I, *and* thou heardest my voice.

3 ᶜFor thou hadst cast me into the deep, in the †midst of the seas; and the floods compassed me about: ᵈ all thy billows and thy waves passed over me.

Before
CHRIST
cir. 780.
ᶜ Ps. 88. 6.
† Heb. *heart.*
ᵈ Ps. 42. 7.

much, would fulfill the rest. He called God, *his God,* Who had in so many ways shewn Himself his, by His revelations, by His inspirations, by His chastisements, and now by His mercy. "¹ From these words, *Jonah prayed unto the Lord his God out of the fish's belly,* we perceive that, after he felt himself safe in the fish's belly, he despaired not of God's mercy."

2. *I cried by reason of mine affliction,* or, *out of affliction* which came *to me.* So the Psalmist thanked God in the same words, though in a different order²; *To the Lord in trouble to me I called, and He heard me.* He *called,* and God heard and answered. "¹ He does not say, *I call,* but *I called;* he does not pray for the future, but gives thanks for the past." Strange cause of thankfulness this would seem to most faith, to be alive in such a grave; to abide there hour after hour, and day after day, in one unchanging darkness, carried to and fro helplessly, with no known escape from his fetid prison, except to death! Yet spiritual light shone on that depth of darkness. The voracious creature, which never opened his mouth save to destroy life, had swallowed him, to save it. "¹ What looked like death, became safe-keeping," and so the Prophet who had fled to avoid doing the Will of God and to do his own, now willed to be borne about, he knew not whither, at the will, as it seemed, of the huge animal in which he lay, but in truth, whither God directed it, and he gave thanks. God had heard him. The first token of God's mercy was the earnest of the whole. God was dealing with him, was looking on him. It was enough.

Out of the belly of hell cried I. The deep waters were as a grave, and he was counted *among the dead*³. Death seemed so certain that it was all one as if he were in the womb of hell, not to be re-born to life until the last Day. So David said⁴, *The bands of death compassed me round about;* and, ⁵ *Thou hast drawn my life out of hell.* The waters choked his speech; but he cried with a loud cry to God Who knew the heart. *I cried; Thou heardest.* The words vary only by a kindred letter⁶, *Shivva'ti, Shama'ta.* The real heart's-

cry to God according to the mind of God and His hearing are one, whether, for man's good, He seem at the time to hear or no.

"⁷ Not of the voice but of the heart is God the Hearer, as He is the Seer.—Do the ears of God wait for sound? How then could the prayer of Jonah from the inmost belly of the whale, through the bowels of so great a creature, out of the very bottomless depths, through so great a mass of waters, make its way to Heaven?" "⁸ Loud crying to God is not with the voice but with the heart. Many, silent with their lips, have cried aloud with their heart; many, noisy with their lips, could, with heart turned away, obtain nothing. If then thou criest, cry within, where God heareth." "⁹ Jonah cried aloud to God out of the fish's belly, out of the deep of the sea, out of the depths of disobedience; and his prayer reached to God, Who rescued him from the waves, brought him forth out of the vast creature, absolved him from the guilt. Let the sinner too cry aloud, whom, departing from God, the storm of desires overwhelmed, the malignant Enemy devoured, the waves of this present world sucked-under! Let him own that he is in the depth, that so his prayer may reach to God."

3. *For Thou hadst [didst] cast me into the deep.* Jonah continues to describe the extremity of peril, from which God had already delivered him. Sweet is the memory of perils past. For they speak of God's Fatherly care. Sweet is it to the Prophet to tell God of His mercies; but this is sweet only to the holy; for God's mercy convicts the careless of ingratitude. Jonah then tells God, how He had cast him vehemently forth into the *eddying*¹⁰ *depth,* where, when Pharaoh's army *sank like a stone*¹¹, they never rose, and that, *in the heart* or *centre of the seas,* whence no strong swimmer could escape to shore. *The floods* or *flood,* [lit. *river,*] the sea with its currents, *surrounded* him, encompassing him on all sides; and, above, tossed its multitudinous waves, passing over him, like an army trampling one prostrate under foot. Jonah remembered well the temple-psalms, and, using their words, united himself with those other worshipers who sang them, and

¹ S. Jer.　　　　　　　　² See Introd. p. 252.
³ Ps. lxxxviii. 4.　⁴ Ib. xviii. 5.　⁵ Ib. xxx. 3.
⁶ שִׁוַּעְתִּי שָׁמַעְתָּ.
⁷ Tert. de Orat. § 17. p. 311. Oxf. Tr.

⁸ S. Aug. in Ps. 30. Enarr. 4. § 10: see others referred to on Tert. l. c. p. 310. n. v.
⁹ S. Greg. in Ps. 6. Pœnit. L.　　　¹⁰ מְצוּלָה.
¹¹ Ex. xv. 5, add 10.

Before
CHRIST
cir. 780.

e Ps. 31. 22.
f 1 Kings 8. 38.

g Ps. 69. 1.
Lam. 3. 54.

4 e Then I said, I am cast out of thy sight, yet I will look again f toward thy holy temple.

5 The g waters compassed me about, even to the soul: the depth closed me round

about, the weeds were wrapped about my head.

6 I went down to the † bottoms of the mountains; the earth with her bars was about me for ever: yet hast thou

Before
CHRIST
cir. 780.

† Heb. cuttings
off.

taught us how to speak them to God. The sons of Korah[1] had poured out to God in these self-same words the sorrows which oppressed them. The rolling billows[2] and the breakers[3], which, as they burst upon the rocks, shiver the vessel and crush man, are, he says to God, Thine, fulfilling Thy Will on me.

4. I am cast out of Thy sight, lit. from before Thine eyes. Jonah had wilfully withdrawn from standing in God's presence. Now God had taken him at his word, and, as it seemed, cast him out of it. David had said in his haste, I am cut off. Jonah substitutes the stronger word, I am cast forth[4], driven forth, expelled, like the mire and dirt[5] which the waves drive along, or like the waves themselves in their restless motion[6], or the heathen (the word is the same) whom God had driven out before Israel[7], or as Adam from Paradise[8].

Yet [Only] I will look again. He was, as it were, a castaway, cast out of God's sight, unheeded by Him, his prayers unheard; the storm unabated, until he was cast forth. He could no longer look with the bodily eye even toward the land where God shewed the marvels of His mercy, and the temple where God was worshiped continually. Yet what he could not do in the body, he would do in his soul. This was his only resource. "If I be cast away, this one thing will I do, I will still look to God." Magnificent faith! Humanly speaking, all hope was gone, for, when that huge vessel could scarcely live in the sea, how should a man? when God had given it no rest, while it contained Jonah, how should He will that Jonah should escape? Nay, God had hidden His Face from him; yet he did this one, this only thing; only this, "once more, still I will add to look to God." Thitherward would he look, so long as his mind yet remained in him. If his soul parted from him, it should go forth from him in that gaze. God gave him no hope, save that He preserved him alive. For he seemed to himself forsaken of God. Won-

derful pattern of faith which gains strength even from God's seeming desertion! "I am cast vehemently forth from before Thine eyes; yet this one thing will I do; mine eyes shall be unto Thee, O Lord." The Israelites, as we see from Solomon's dedication-prayer, prayed toward the temple[9], where God had set His Name and shewn His glory, where were the sacrifices which foreshadowed the Great Atonement. Thitherward they looked in prayer, as Christians, of old, prayed toward the East, the seat of our ancient Paradise, where our Lord shall appear unto them that look for Him, a second time unto salvation[10]. Toward that Temple then he would yet look with fixed eye[11] for help, where God, Who fills heaven and earth, shewed Himself to sinners reconciled.

5. The waters compassed me about even to the soul. Words which to others were figures of distress, [12] the waters have come even to the soul, were to Jonah realities. Sunk in the deep seas, the water strove to penetrate at every opening. To draw breath, which sustains life, to him would have been death. There was but a breath between him and death. The deep encompassed me, encircling, meeting him whithersoever he turned, holding him imprisoned on every side, so that there was no escape, and, if there otherwise had been, he was bound motionless, the weed was wrapped around my head, like a grave-band. The weed was the well-known sea-weed, which, even near the surface of the sea where man can struggle, twines round him, a peril even to the strong swimmer, entangling him often the more, the more he struggles to extricate himself from it. But to one below, powerless to struggle, it was as his winding-sheet.

6. I went down to the bottoms, [lit. the cuttings off] of the mountains, the "roots" as the Chaldee[13] and we call them, the hidden rocks, which the mountains push out, as it were, into the sea, and in which they end. Such hidden rocks extend along the whole length of that coast[14]. These were his dun-

1 Ps. xlii. 7. 2 גִּילְךְ.
3 מִשְׁבָּרֶיךָ. 4 See Introd. p. 252. 5 Is. lvii. 20.
6 Ib. 7 Ex. xxxiv. 11. and Piel often.
8 Gen. iii. 24. 10 Heb. ix. 28.
9 1 Kings viii. 29, 30, 35, &c.
11 הַבִּיט אֶל is, "look intently towards," as Moses at the bush, Ex. iii. 6.

12 Ps. lxix. 2. See ab. Introd. p. 252.
13 Jon. here.
14 "The road is very dangerous; for the bottom is a mere bank of rocks, which extend the whole length of the coast. It is thought that the sharp rocks which pierce to the surface of the sea are the remains of the Isle Paria, mentioned by Pliny v. 31." Mislin, Les Saints Lieux, ii. 137.

Before CHRIST cir. 780.

h Ps. 16. 10.
|| Or, *the pit.*

i Ps. 18. 6.

brought up my life ^h from
|| corruption, O Lord my
God.

7 When my soul fainted
within me I remem-
bered the Lord: ⁱ and

my prayer came in
unto thee, into thine holy
temple.

8 They that observe
^k lying vanities forsake
their own mercy.

Before CHRIST cir. 780.

k 2 Kings 17. 15.
Ps. 31. 6.
Jer. 10. 8.
& 16. 19.

---

geon-walls; *the earth, her bars,* those long sub-
marine reefs of rock, his prison-bars, *were
around* him *for ever:* the sea-weeds were his
chains: and, even thus, when things were at
their uttermost, *Thou hast brought up my life
from corruption,* to which his body would have
fallen a prey, had not God sent the fish to
deliver him. The deliverance for which he
thanks God is altogether past: *Thou broughtest me up.* He calls *the* Lord, *my* God, because, being the God of all, He was especially
his God, for whom He had done things of such
marvellous love. God loves each soul which
He has made with the same infinite love with
which He loves all. Whence S. Paul says of
Jesus¹, *Who loved me and gave Himself for me.*
He loves each, with the same undivided love,
as if He had created none besides; and He allows each to say, *My God,* as if the Infinite
God belonged wholly to each. So would He
teach us the oneness of Union between the
soul which God loves and which admits His
love, and Himself.

7. *When my soul fainted,* lit. *was covered,
within me,* was dizzied, overwhelmed. The
word is used of actual faintness from heat²,
thirst³, exhaustion⁴, when a film comes over
the eyes, and the brain is, as it were, man-
tled over. The soul of the pious never is so
full of God, as when all things else fade from
him. Jonah could not but have remembered
God in the tempest; when the lots were cast;
when he adjudged himself to be cast forth.
But when it came to the utmost, then he
says, *I remembered the Lord,* as though, in the
intense thought of God then, all his former
thought of God had been forgetfulness. So
it is in every strong act of faith, of love, of
prayer; its former state seems unworthy of the
name of faith, love, prayer. It believes, loves,
prays, as though all before had been forgetfulness.

And my prayer came in unto Thee. No
sooner had he so prayed, than God heard.
Jonah had thought himself cast out of His
sight; but his prayer entered in thither.
His *holy temple* is doubtless His actual Temple,
whitherward he prayed. God, Who is
wholly everywhere but the whole of Him
nowhere, was as much in the Temple as
in heaven; and had manifested Himself
to Israel in their degree in the Temple,

as to the blessed saints and angels in
heaven.

8 *They that observe lying vanities,* i. e. (by
the force of the Hebrew form⁵,) that diligently watch, pay deference to, court, sue,
vanities of vanities, vain things, which prove
themselves vain at last, failing the hopes
which trust in them. Such were actual
idols, in which men openly professed that
they trusted Such are all things in
which men trust, out of God. One is not
more vain than another. All have this
common principle of vanity, that men look,
out of God, to that which has its only existence or permanence from God. It is then
one general maxim, including all men's idols,
idols of the flesh, idols of intellect, idols of
ambition, idols of pride, idols of self and self-
will. Men *observe* them, as gods, watch them,
hang upon them, never lose sight of them,
guard them as though they could keep them.
But what are they? *lying vanities,* breath and
wind, which none can grasp or detain, van-
ishing like air into air. And what do they
who so *observe* them? All alike *forsake their
own mercy;* i. e. God, "Whose property is,
always to have mercy," and Who would be
Mercy to them, if they would. So David
calls God, *my Mercy⁶*. Abraham's servant
and Naomi praise God, that He *hath not forsaken His mercy⁷.* Jonah does not, in this,
exclude himself. His own idol had been his
false love for his country, that he would not
have his people go into captivity, when God
would; would not have Nineveh preserved,
the enemy of his country; and by leaving
his office, he left his God, *forsook* his *own
Mercy.* See how God speaks of Himself, as
wholly belonging to them, who are His. He
calls Himself *their own Mercy.* "⁸ He saith
not, *they who* do vanities, (for ⁹ *vanity of vanities,
and all things* are *vanity*) lest he should seem
to condemn all, and to deny mercy to the
whole human race; but *they who observe,
guard vanities,* or lies; *they,* into the affections
of whose hearts those *vanities* have entered;
who not only *do vanities,* but who *guard* them,
as loving them, deeming that they have
found a treasure—These *forsake their own
Mercy.* Although *mercy* be offended, (and
under Mercy we may understand God Him-
self, for God is ¹⁰ *gracious and full of compassion;*

---

¹ Gal. ii. 20.   ² Jon. iv. 8.   ³ Am. viii. 13.
⁴ Is. li. 20.   ⁵ שמרים.

⁶ Ps. cxliv 2.   ⁷ Gen. xxiv. 27, Ruth ii. 20.
⁸ S. Jer.   ⁹ Eccl. i. 2.   ¹⁰ Ps. cxlv. 8.

Before
CHRIST
cir. 780.

[1] Ps. 50. 14, 23.
& 116. 17. 18.
Hos. 14. 2.
Heb. 13. 15.
[m] Ps. 3. 8.

9 But I will [1]sacrifice unto thee with the voice of thanksgiving; I will pay *that* that I have vowed. [m]Salvation *is* of the LORD.

10 ¶ And the LORD spake unto the fish, and it vomited out Jonah upon the dry land.

Before
CHRIST
cir. 780.

---

slow to anger and of great mercy,) yet he doth not *forsake*, doth not abhor, *those who guard vanities*, but awaiteth that they should return: these contrariwise, of their own will, *forsake Mercy* standing and offering Itself."

9. *But [And] with the voice of thanksgiving will I [would I fain] sacrifice unto Thee; what I have vowed, I would pay.* He does not say, *I will;* for it did not depend upon him. Without a further miracle of God, he could do nothing. But he says, that he would nevermore forsake God. The law appointed sacrifices of thanksgiving[1]; these he would offer, not in act only, but with words of praise. He would *pay what he had vowed*, and chiefly himself, his life which God had given back to him, the obedience of his remaining life, in all things. For [2] *he that keepeth the law bringeth offerings enough; he that taketh heed to the commandments offereth a peace-offering.* Jonah neglects neither the outward nor the inward part, neither the body nor the soul of the commandment.

Salvation is of [lit. *to*] *the Lord.* It is wholly His; all belongs to Him, so that none can share in bestowing it; none can have any hope, save from Him. He uses an intensive form, as though he would say, strong *mighty salvation*[3]. God seems often to wait for the full resignation of the soul, all its powers and will to Him. Then He can shew mercy healthfully, when the soul is wholly surrendered to Him. So, on this full confession, Jonah is restored. The Prophet's prayer ends almost in promising the same as the mariners. They *made vows;* Jonah says, *I will pay that I have vowed.* Devoted service in the creature is one and the same, although diverse in degree; and so, that Israel might not despise the heathen, he tacitly likens the act of the new heathen converts and that of the Prophet.

10. *And the Lord spake unto the fish.* [4] *Wind and storm fulfill His word.* The irrational creatures have wills. God had commanded the Prophet, and he disobeyed. God, in some way, commanded the fish. He laid His will upon it, and the fish forthwith obeyed; a pattern to the Prophet when He released him. "[5] God's Will, that anything should be completed, is law and fulfillment and hath the power of law. Not that Almighty God commanded the fish, as He doth us or the Holy Angels, uttering in its mind

what is to be done, or inserting into the heart the knowledge of what He chooseth. But if He be said to command irrational animals or elements or any part of the creation, this signifieth the law and command of His Will. For all things yield to His Will, and the mode of their obedience is to us altogether ineffable, but known to Him." "Jonah," says S. Chrysostom, "[6] fled the land, and fled not the displeasure of God. He fled the land, and brought a tempest on the sea: and not only himself gained no good from flight, but brought into extreme peril those also who took him on board. When he sailed, seated in the vessel, with sailors and pilot and all the tackling, he was in the extremest peril: when, sunk in the sea, the sin punished and laid aside, he entered that vast vessel, the fish's belly, he enjoyed great fearlessness; that thou mayest learn that, as no ship availeth to one living in sin, so when freed from sin, neither sea destroyeth, nor beasts consume. The waves received him, and choked him not; the vast fish received him and destroyed him not; but both the huge animal and the element gave back their deposit safe to God, and by all things the Prophet learnt to be mild and tender, not to be more cruel than the untaught mariners or wild waves or animals. For the sailors did not give him up at first, but after manifold constraint; and the sea and the wild animal guarded him with much benevolence, God disposing all these things. He returned then, preached, threatened, persuaded, saved, awed, amended, stablished, through that one first preaching. For he needed not many days, nor continuous exhortation; but, speaking those words he brought all to repentance. Wherefore God did not lead him straight from the vessel to the city; but the sailors gave him over to the sea, the sea to the vast fish, the fish to God, God to the Ninevites, and through this long circuit brought back the fugitive; that He might instruct all, that it is impossible to escape the Hands of God. For come where a man may, dragging sin after him, he will undergo countless troubles. Though man be not there, nature itself on all sides will oppose him with great vehemence."

"[7] Since the elect too at times strive to be sharp-witted, it is well to bring forward another wise man, and shew how the craft of mortal man is comprehended in the Inward

[1] Lev. vii. 12–15.   [2] Ecclus. xxxv. 1.   [3] יְשׁוּעָתָה׃
[4] Ps. cxlviii. 8.   [5] S. Cyr. on Jon. ii. init.

[6] Hom. on the Statues, v. 6.
[7] S. Greg. Mor. vi. 31.

CHAPTER III.

1 *Jonah, sent again, preacheth to
the Ninevites.* 5 *Upon their
repentance,* 10 *God repenteth.*

A ND the word of the
LORD came unto Jo-
nah the second time, say-
ing,

Counsels. For Jonah wished to exercise a prudent sharpness of wit, when, being sent to preach repentance to the Ninevites, in that he feared that, if the Gentiles were chosen, Judæa would be forsaken, he refused to discharge the office of preaching. He sought a ship, chose to flee to Tarshish ; but forthwith a tempest arises, the lot is cast, to know for whose fault the sea was troubled. Jonah is taken in his fault, plunged in the deep, swallowed by the fish, and carried by the vast beast thither whither he set at naught the command to go. See how the tempest found God's runaway, the lot binds him, the sea receives him, the beast encloses him, and, because he sets himself against obeying his Maker, he is carried a culprit by his prison-house to the place whither he had been sent. When God commanded, man would not minister the prophecy ; when God enjoined, the beast cast forth the Prophet. The Lord then *taketh the wise in their own craftiness,* when He bringeth back to the service of His own Will, that whereby man's will contradicts Him." "[1] Jonah, fleeing from the perils of preaching and salvation of souls, fell into peril of his own life. When, in the ship, he took on himself the peril of all, he saved both himself and the ship. ' He fled as a man ; he exposed himself to peril, as a prophet." "[2] Let them think so, who are sent by God or by a superior to preach to heretics or to heathen. When God calleth to an office or condition whose object it is to live for the salvation of others, He gives grace and means necessary or expedient to this end. For so the sweet and careful ordering of His Providence requireth.—Greater peril awaiteth us from God our Judge, if we flee His calling as did Jonah, if we use not the talents entrusted to us to do His Will and to His glory. We know the parable of the servant who buried the talent, and was condemned by the Lord."

And it vomited out Jonah. Unwilling, but constrained, it cast him forth, as a burden to it. "[3] From the lowest depths of death, Life came forth victorious." "[4] He is swallowed by the fish, but is not consumed ; and then calls upon God, and (marvel !) on the third· day is given back with Christ." "[5] What it prefigured, that that vast animal on the third day gave back alive the Prophet which it had swallowed, no need to ask of us, since Christ explained it. As then Jonah passed from the ship into the fish's

belly, so Christ from the wood into the tomb or the depth of death. And as he for those imperilled in the tempest, so Christ for those tempest-tossed in this world. And as Jonah was first enjoined to preach to the Ninevites, but the preaching of Jonah did not reach them before the fish cast him forth, so prophecy was sent beforehand to the Gentiles, but did not reach them until after the resurrection of Christ." "[6] Jonah prophesied of Christ, not so much in words as by a suffering of his own ; yet more openly than if he had proclaimed by speech His Death and Resurrection. For why was he received into the fish's belly, and given back the third day, except to signify that Christ would on the third day return from the deep of hell ? "

S. Irenæus looks on the history of Jonah as the imaging of man's own history. "[7] As He allowed Jonah to be swallowed by the whale, not that he should perish altogether, but that, being vomited forth, he might the more be subdued to God, and the more glorify God Who had given him such unlooked-for deliverance, and bring those Ninevites to solid repentance, converting them to the Lord Who would free them from death, terrified by that sign which befell Jonah (as Scripture says of them, *They turned every man from his evil way, &c.* . . . . .) so from the beginning, God allowed man to be swallowed up by that vast Cetos who was the author of the transgression, not that he should altogether perish, but preparing a way of salvation, which, as foresignified by the word in Jonah, was formed for those who had the like faith as to the Lord as Jonah, and with him confessed, *I fear the Lord, &c.* that so man, receiving from God unlooked-for salvation, might rise from the dead and glorify God, &c. . . . . . This was the long-suffering of God, that man might pass through all, and acknowledge his ways ; then, coming to the resurrection and knowing by trial from what he had been delivered, might be for ever thankful to God, and, having received from Him the gift of incorruption, might love Him more (for he to whom much is forgiven, loveth much) and know himself, that he is mortal and weak, and understand the Lord, that He is in such wise Mighty and Immortal, that to the mortal He can give immortality and to the things of time eternity."

III. 1. *And the word of the Lord came a*

---

[1] Lap. from S. Chrys.   [2] from Lap.   [3] S. Jer.
[4] S. Greg. Naz l. c.   [5] S. Aug. Ep. 102. q. 6. n. 34.

[6] de Civ. Dei, xviii. 30. 2.
[7] iii. 20. p. 213. ed. Mass L.

Before
CHRIST
cir. 780.

2 Arise, go unto Nineveh, that great city, and preach unto it the preaching that I bid thee.

3 So Jonah arose, and went unto Nineveh, according to the word of the LORD. Now Nineveh was an † exceeding great city of three days' journey.

Before
CHRIST
cir. 780.

† Heb. of God.
So Gen. 30. 8.
Ps. 36. 6.
& 80. 10.

second time to Jonah. "[1] Jonah, delivered from the whale, doubtless went up to Jerusalem to pay his vows and thank God there. Perhaps he hoped that God would be content with this his punishment and repentance, and that He would not again send him to Nineveh." Anyhow he was in some settled home, perhaps again at Gathhepher. For God bids him, *Arise, go.* "[2] But one who is on his way, is not bidden to *arise* and go." God may have allowed an interval to elapse, in order that the tidings of so great a miracle might spread far and wide. But Jonah does not supply any of these incidents[3]. He does not speak of himself[3], but of his mission only, as God taught him.

2. *Arise, go to Nineveh that great city, and preach* [or *cry*] *unto it.* God says to Jonah the self-same words which He had said before; only perhaps He gives him an intimation of His purpose of mercy, in that he says no more, *cry against her,* but *cry unto her.* He might *cry against* one doomed to destruction; to *cry unto her,* seems to imply that she had some interest in, and so some hope from, this cry. *The preaching that I bid thee.* This is the only notice which Jonah relates that God took of his disobedience, in that He charged him to obey exactly what He commanded. "[4] He does not say to him, why didst thou not what I commanded?" He had rebuked him in deed; He amended him and upbraided him not. "[4] The rebuke of that shipwreck and the swallowing by the fish sufficed, so that he who had not felt the Lord commanding, might understand Him, delivering." Jonah might have seemed unworthy to be again inspired by God. But *whom the Lord loveth, He chasteneth;* whom He chasteneth, He loveth. "[5] The hard discipline, the severity and length of the scourge, were the earnests of a great trust and a high destination." He knew him to be changed into another man, and, by one of His most special favors, gives him that same trust which he had before deserted. "[2] As Christ, when risen, commended His sheep to Peter, wiser now and more fervent, so to Jonah risen He commends the conversion of Nineveh. For so did Christ risen bring about the conversion of the heathen, by sending His Apostles, each into large provinces, as Jonah was sent alone to a large city." "[6] He bids him declare not only the sentence of God,

but in the self-same words; not to consider his own estimation or the ears of his hearers, nor to mingle soothing with severe words, and convey the message ingeniously, but with all freedom and severity to declare openly what was commanded him. This plainness, though, may be, less acceptable to people or princes, is ofttimes more useful, always more approved by God. Nothing should be more sacred to the preacher of God's word, than truth and simplicity and inviolable sanctity in delivering it. Now alas, all this is changed into vain show at the will of the multitude and the breath of popular favor."

3. *And Jonah arose and went unto Nineveh,* as ready to obey, as before to disobey. Before, when God said those same words, *he arose and fled;* now, *he arose and went.* True conversion shews the same energy in serving God, as the unconverted had before shewn in serving self or error. Saul's spirit of fire, which persecuted Christ, gleamed in S. Paul like lightning through the world, to win souls to Him.

Nineveh was an exceeding great city; lit. *great to God,* i. e. what would not only appear great to man who admires things of no account, but what, being really great, is so in the judgment of God Who cannot be deceived. God *did* account it great, Who says to Jonah, *Should not I spare Nineveh that great city, which hath more than six score thousand that cannot discern between their right hand and their left?* It is a different idiom from that, when Scripture speaks of *the mountains of God, the cedars of God.* For of these it speaks, as having their firmness or their beauty from God as their Author.

Of three days' journey, i. e. sixty miles in circumference. It *was* a great city. Jonah speaks of its greatness, under a name which he would only have used of real greatness. Varied accounts agree in ascribing this size to Nineveh[7]. An Eastern city enclosing often, as did Babylon, ground under tillage, the only marvel is, that such a space was enclosed by walls. Yet this too is no marvel, when we know from inscriptions, what masses of human strength the great empires of old had at their command, or of the more than threescore pyramids of Egypt[8]. In population it was far inferior to our metropolis, of which, as of the suburbs of Rome of old, "[9] one would hesitate to say,

[1] Lap.   [2] Castr.   [3] See Introd. p. 253   [4] S. Jer.   [5] from Sanch.   [6] Mont.

[7] See ab. Introd. pp. 253, 4.   [8] 67. Lepsius.   [9] Dionys. Hal. T. i. p. 219. L.

Before
CHRIST
cir. 780.

a See Deut.
18. 22.

4 And Jonah began to
enter into the city a day's
journey, and [a] he cried, and
said, Yet forty days, and

Nineveh shall be over-
thrown.

5 ¶ So the people of
Nineveh [b] believed God,

Before
CHRIST
cir. 780.

b Matt. 12. 41.
Luke 11. 32.

where the city ended, where it began. The
suburban parts are so joined on to the city
itself, and give the spectator the idea of
boundless length." An Eastern would the
more naturally think of the circumference of
a city, because of the broad places, similar to
the boulevards of Paris, which encircled it,
so that men could walk around it, within it.
"[1] The buildings," it is related of Babylon,
"are not brought close to the walls, but are
at about the distance of an acre from them.
And not even the whole city did they occupy
with houses; 80 furlongs are inhabited, and
not even all these continuously, I suppose
because it seemed safer to live scattered in
several places. The rest they sow and till,
that, if any foreign force threaten them, the
besieged may be supplied with food from
the soil of the city itself." Not Babylon
alone was spoken of, of old, as "[2] having the circumference of a nation rather than of a city."

4. *And Jonah began to enter the city a day's
journey.* Perhaps the day's journey enabled
him to traverse the city from end to end, with
his one brief, deep cry of woe; *Yet forty
days and Nineveh overthrown*[3]. He prophesied
an utter overthrow, a turning it upside
down[4]. He does not speak of it as to happen
at a time beyond those days. The close of
the forty days and the destruction were to be
one. He does not say strictly, *Yet forty days
and Nineveh shall be overthrown*, but, *Yet forty
days and Nineveh overthrown*. The last of
those forty days was, ere its sun was set, to
see Nineveh as *a thing overthrown*. Jonah
knew from the first God's purpose of mercy
to Nineveh; he had a further hint of it in
the altered commission which he had received. It is perhaps hinted in the word
Yet. "[5] If God had meant unconditionally
to overthrow them, He would have overthrown them without notice. *Yet*, always
denotes some long-suffering of God." But,
taught by that severe discipline, he discharges
his office strictly. He cries, what God had
bidden him to cry, without reserve or exception. The sentence, as are all God's threatenings until the last, was conditional. But
God does not say this. That sentence was
now within forty days of its completion; yet
even thus it was remitted. Wonderful encouragement, when one Lent sufficed to save

some six hundred thousand souls from perishing! Yet the first visitation of the Cholera
was checked in its progress in England,
upon one day's national fast and humiliation;
and we have seen how general prayer has
often-times at once opened or closed the
heavens as we needed. "A few years ago,"
relates S. Augustine[6], "when Arcadius was
Emperor at Constantinople (what I say, some
have heard, some of our people were present
there,) did not God, willing to terrify the
city, and, by terrifying, to amend, convert,
cleanse, change it, reveal to a faithful servant
of His (a soldier, it is said), that the city
should perish by fire from heaven, and
warned him to tell the Bishop! It was told.
The Bishop despised it not, but addressed the
people. The city turned to the mourning of
penitence, as that Nineveh of old. Yet lest
men should think that he who said this,
deceived or was deceived, the day which
God had threatened, came. When all were
intently expecting the issue with great fears,
at the beginning of night as the world was
being darkened, a fiery cloud was seen from
the East, small at first, then, as it approached
the city, gradually enlarging, until it hung
terribly over the whole city. All fled to the
Church; the place did not hold the people.
—But after that great tribulation, when God
had accredited His word, the cloud began to
diminish and at last disappeared. The people, freed from fear for a while, again heard
that they must migrate, because the whole city
should be destroyed on the next sabbath.
The whole people left the city with the
Emperor; no one remained in his house.—
That multitude, having gone some miles,
when gathered in one spot to pour forth
prayer to God, suddenly saw a great smoke,
and sent forth a loud cry to God." The city
was saved. "What shall we say?" adds S.
Augustine. "Was this the anger of God, or
rather His mercy? Who doubts that the
most merciful Father willed by terrifying to
convert, not to punish by destroying? As
the hand is lifted up to strike, and is recalled
in pity, when he who was to be struck is terrified, so was it done to that city." Will any
of God's warnings *now* move our great Babylon to repentance, that it be not ruined?

5. *And the people of Nineveh believed God;*

a nation rather than of a city, at the taking of
which they say that some parts of the city did not
hear of it for three days."
[3] Introd. p. 253.
[4] Ib. p. 255.   [5] Castr.
[6] de excid. urb. c. 6. (L.) add Paul. Diac. L. 13.

[1] Q. Curt. v. 4.
[2] Aristot. Polit. iii. 2. "You cannot judge whether
a city is one or no by there being walls. For it
would be possible to carry one wall round Pelopon-
nesus; and perhaps Babylon is something of this
sort, and *every city* which had the circumference of

and proclaimed a fast, and put on sackcloth, from the greatest of them even to the least of them.

6 For word came unto the king of Nineveh, and he arose from his throne, and he laid his robe from

strictly, *believed in God.* To *believe in God* expresses more heart-belief, than to *believe God* in itself need convey. To *believe God* is to believe what God says, to be true ; *to believe in* or *on God* expresses not belief only, but that belief resting in God, trusting itself and all its concerns with Him. It combines hope and trust with faith, and love too, since, without love, there cannot be trust. They believed then the preaching of Jonah, and that He, in Whose Name Jonah spake, had all power in heaven and earth. But they believed further in His unknown mercies; they cast themselves upon the goodness of the hitherto *unknown God.* Yet they believed in Him, as the Supreme God, *the* object of awe, *the* God (Elohim [1], Haelohim [2]), although they knew Him not, as He Is [3], the Self-Existent. Jonah does not say how they were thus persuaded. God the Holy Ghost relates the wonders of God's Omnipotence as common every-day things. They are no marvels to Him Who wrought them. *He commanded and they were done.* He spake with power to the hearts which He had made, and they were turned to Him. Any human means are secondary, utterly powerless, except in *His* hands Who Alone doth all things through whomsoever He doth them. Our Lord tells us that *Jonah himself was a sign unto the Ninevites* [4]. Whether then the mariners spread the history [5], or howsoever the Ninevites knew the personal history of Jonah, he, in his own person and in what befell him, was a *sign* to them. They believed that God, Who avenged *his* disobedience, would avenge their's. They believed perhaps, that God must have some great mercy in store for them, Who not only sent His Prophet so far from his own land to *them* who had never owned, never worshiped Him, but had done such mighty wonders to subdue His Prophet's resistance and to make him go to them.

And proclaimed a fast and put on sackcloth. It was not then a repentance in word only, but in deed. A fast was at that time entire abstinence from all food till evening ; the haircloth was a harsh garment, irritating and afflictive to the body. They who did so, were (as we may still see from the Assyrian sculptures) men of pampered and luxurious habits, uniting sensuality and fierceness. Yet

this they did at once, and as it seems, for the 40 days. They *proclaimed a fast.* They did not wait for the supreme authority. Time was urgent, and they would lose none of it. In this imminent peril of God's displeasure, they acted as men would in a conflagration. Men do not wait for orders to put out a fire, if they can, or to prevent it from spreading. Whoever they were who proclaimed it, whether those in inferior authority, each in his neighborhood, or whether it spread from man to man, as the tidings spread, it was done at once. It seems to have been done by acclamation, as it were, one common cry out of the one common terror. For it is said of them, as one succession of acts, *the men of Nineveh believed in God, and proclaimed a fast, and put on sackcloth from their great to their little,* every age, sex, condition. " [6] Worthy of admiration is that exceeding celerity and diligence in taking counsel, which, although in the same city with the king, perceived that they must provide for the common and imminent calamity, not waiting to ascertain laboriously the king's pleasure." In a city, 60 miles in circumference, some time must needs be lost, before the king could be approached ; and we know, in some measure, the forms required in approaching Eastern monarchs of old.

6. *For word came,* rather, *And the matter* [7] *came,* i. e. the " whole *account*," as we say. *The word, word,* throughout Holy Scripture, as in so many languages, stands for that which is reported of [8]. *The* whole *account,* viz. how this stranger, in strange austere attire, had come, what had happened to him before he came, how he preached, how the people had believed him, what they had done, as had just been related, *came to the king.* The form of words implies that what Jonah relates in this verse took place after what had been mentioned before. People are slow to carry to sovereigns matters of distress, in which they cannot help. This was no matter of peril from man, in which the counsel or energy of the king could be of use. Anyhow it came to him last. But when it came to him, he disdained not to follow the example of those below him. He was not jealous of his prerogative, or that his advice had not been had ; but, in the common peril, acted as his subjects had, and humbled him-

[1] iii. 5, 8.   [2] Ib. 9.
[3] יהוה occurs once only in this chapter, of God speaking to Jonah, iii. 1.
[4] See ab. pp. 256, 7.
[5] Dion. suggests this as a conjecture. Aben Ezra

quotes the same from R. Jesua. Kimchi says the same.   [6] Mont.   [7] It is, *the word,* הדבר.
[8] See Lex. of the Old or New Testament v. דבר, ἔπος, ῥῆμα. So in Arab. Aram. Æthiop. Ges. adds Pers. and Germ. "Sache" from "sagen," "Ding."

c Job 2. 8.

d 2 Chr. 20. 3.
Joel 2. 15.

† Heb. *said.*

him, and covered *him* with sackcloth, c and sat in ashes.

7 d And he caused *it* to be proclaimed and † published through Nineveh by

the decree of the king and his † nobles, saying, Let neither man nor beast, herd nor flock, taste any thing: let them not feed, nor drink water:

† Heb. *great men.*

---

self as they did. Yet this king was the king of Nineveh, the king, whose name was dreaded far and wide, whose will none who disputed, prospered. "[1] He who was accounted and was the greatest of the kings of the earth, was not held back by any thought of his own splendor, greatness or dignity, from fleeing as a suppliant to the mercy of God, and inciting others by his example to the same earnestness." The kings of Assyria were religious, according to their light. They ascribed all their victories to their god, Asshur [2]. When the king came to hear of One Who had a might, such as he had not seen, he believed in Him.

And he arose from his throne. He lost no time; he heard, *and he arose.* "[1] It denotes great earnestness, haste, diligence." *And he laid his robe from him.* This was the large costly upper garment, so called from its amplitude [3]. It is the name of the goodly Babylonian garment [4] which Achan coveted. As worn by kings, it was the most magnificent part of their dress, and a special part of their state. Kings were buried as they lived, in splendid apparel [5]; and rich adornments were buried with them [6]. The king of Nineveh dreads no charge of precipitancy nor man's judgment. "[1] He exchanges purple, gold, gems for the simple rough and sordid sackcloth, and his throne for the most abject ashes, the humblest thing he could do, fulfilling a deeper degree of humility than is related of the people." Strange credulity, had Jonah's message not been true; strange madness of unbelief which does not repent when a Greater than Jonah cries [7], *Repent ye, for the kingdom of heaven is at hand.* Strange garb for the king, in the eyes of a luxurious age; acceptable in His Who said [8], *if the mighty works which have been done in you had been done in Tyre and Sidon, they would have repented long ago in sackcloth and ashes.* "[9] Many wish to repent, yet so as not to part with their luxuries or the vanity of their dress, like the Greek who said he would 'like to be a philosopher, yet in a few things, not altogether.' To whom we may answer, 'delicate food and costly dress agree not with

penitence; and that is no great grief which never comes to light.'" "[10] It was a marvelous thing, that purple was outvied by sackcloth. Sackcloth availed, what the purple robe availed not. What the diadem accomplished not, the ashes accomplished. Seest thou, I said not groundlessly that we should fear, not fasting but drunkenness and satiety? For drunkenness and satiety shook the city through and through, and were about to overthrow it; when it was reeling and about to fall, fasting stablished it." "[11] The king had conquered enemies by valor; he conquered God by humility. Wise king, who, for the saving of his people, owns himself a sinner rather than a king. He forgets that he is a king, fearing God, the King of all; he remembereth not his own power, coming to own the power of the Godhead. Marvelous! While he remembereth not that he is a king of men, he beginneth to be a king of righteousness. The prince, becoming religious, lost not his empire but changed it. Before, he held the princedom of military discipline; now, he obtained the princedom in heavenly disciplines."

7. *And he caused it to be proclaimed and published through Nineveh;* lit. *And he cried and said, &c.* The cry or proclamation of the king corresponded with the cry of Jonah. Where the Prophet's cry, calling to repentance, had reached, the proclamation of the king followed, obeying. *By the decree of the king and his nobles.* This is a hint of the political state of Nineveh, beyond what we have elsewhere. It was not then an absolute monarchy. At least, the king strengthened his command by that of his nobles, as Darius the Mede sealed the den of lions, into which Daniel was cast, with the signet of his lords as well as his own [12], *that the purpose might not be changed concerning him.*

Let neither man nor beast, &c. "[13] Are brutes too then to fast, horses and mules to be clothed with sackcloth? Yes, he says. For as, when a rich man dies, his relatives clothe not only the men and maidservants, but the horses too with sackcloth, and, giving them to the grooms, bid that they should follow to the tomb, in token of the greatness of the

---

[1] Mont.

[2] Cuneiform Inscriptions. See ab. p. 255. n. h.

[3] אַדֶּרֶת. It expresses size, not magnificence, since a wide garment of hair, such as the prophets afterwards wore, (Zech. xiii. 4, 2 Kings ii. 13, 14) was so called, Gen. xxv. 25.

[4] Josh. vii. 21.

[5] Jos. Ant. xvii. 8. 3.

[6] Id. xv. 3. 4. xvi. 7. 1.

[7] S. Matt. iv. 17.

[8] S. Matt. xi. 21.

[9] Rib.

[10] S. Chrys. Hom. v. de Pœnit. n. 4. ii. 314.

[11] S. Maximus in Jon. Bibl. Patr. T. vi. f. 28.

[12] Dan. vi. 17.

[13] S. Chrys. on the Statues, Hom. iii. 4.

8 But let man and beast be covered with sackcloth,

and cry mightily unto God: yea, ᵉ let them turn every
ᵉ Is. 58. 6.

calamity and inviting all to sympathy, so also when that city was about to perish, they clad the brute natures in sackcloth, and put them under the yoke of fasting. The irrational animals cannot, through words, learn the anger of God; let them learn through hunger, that the infliction is from God: for if, he says, the city should be overthrown, it would be one grave of us the inhabitants and of them also." It was no arbitrary nor wanton nor careless act of the king of Nineveh to make the dumb animals share in the common fast. It proceeded probably from an indistinct consciousness that God cared for them also, and, that *they* were not guilty. So the Psalmist looked on God's care of His creatures as a fresh ground for man's trust in Him[1], *O Lord, Thou preservest man and beast: How excellent is Thy loving-kindness, O Lord, therefore the children of men put their trust under the shadow of Thy wings.* As our Lord teaches that God's care of the sparrows is a pledge to man of God's minute unceasing care for him, so the Ninevites felt truly that the cry of the poor brutes would be heard by God. And God confirmed that judgment, when He told Jonah of the *much cattle*[2], as a ground for having pity on Nineveh. The moanings and lowings of the animals, their voices of distress, pierce man's heart too, and must have added to his sense of the common misery. Ignorance or pride of human nature alone could think that man's sorrow is not aided by these objects of sense. Nature was truer in the king of Nineveh.

8. *Let man and beast be covered with sackcloth.* The gorgeous caparisons of horses, mules and camels was part of Eastern magnificence. Who knows not how man's pride is fed by the sleekness of his stud, their "well-appointed" trappings? Man, in his luxury and pride, would have everything reflect his glory, and minister to pomp. Self-humiliation would have everything reflect its lowliness. Sorrow would have everything answer to its sorrow. Men think it strange that the horses at Nineveh were covered with sackcloth, and forget how, at the funerals of the rich, black horses are chosen and are clothed with black velvet.

And cry unto God mightily, "with might which conquereth judgment." A faint prayer does not express a strong desire, nor obtain what it does not strongly ask for, as having only half a heart.

And let them turn, every man from his evil way. "⁶ See what removed that inevitable wrath. Did fasting and sackcloth alone? No, but the

change of the whole life. How does this appear? From the Prophet's word itself. For he who spake of the wrath of God and of their fast, himself mentions the reconciliation and its cause. *And God saw their works.* What works? that they fasted? that they put on sackcloth? He passes by these, and says, *that every one turned from his evil ways, and God repented of the evil which He had said that He would do unto them.* Seest thou, that not the fast plucked them from the peril, but the change of life made God propitious to these heathen. I say this, not that we should dishonor, but that we may honor fasting. For the honor of a fast is not in abstinence from food, but in avoidance of sin. So that he who limiteth fasting to the abstinence from food only, he it is, who above all dishonoreth it. Fastest thou? Shew it me by its works. 'What works?' askest thou? If you see a poor man, have mercy; if an enemy, be reconciled; if a friend doing well, envy him not; if a beautiful woman, pass on. Let not the mouth alone fast; let eyes too, and hearing and feet, and hands, and all the members of our bodies. Let the hands fast, clean from rapine and avarice! let the feet fast, holding back from going to unlawful sights! let the eyes fast, learning never to thrust themselves on beautiful objects, nor to look curiously on others' beauty; for the food of the eye is gazing.—Let the ear too fast; for the fast of the ears is not to hear detractions and calumnies. Let the mouth too fast from foul words and reproaches. For what boots it, to abstain from birds and fish, while we bite and devour our brethren? The detractor preys on his brother's flesh."

He says, *each from his evil way,* because, in the general mass of corruption, each man has his own special heart's-sin. All were to return, but by forsaking, each, one by one, his own habitual, favorite sin.

And from the violence. Violence is singled out as the special sin of Nineveh, out *of all their evil way;* as the Angel saith[3], *tell His disciples and Peter.* This was the giant, Goliath-sin. When this should be effaced, the rest would give way, as the Philistines fled, when their champion was fallen to the earth dead. *That is in their hands,* lit. *in their palms*[4], the hollow of their hand. The hands being the instruments alike of using violence and of grasping its fruits, the violence cleaves to them in both ways, in its guilt and in its gains. So Job and David say[5], *while there was no violence in my hands;* and Isaiah[6], *the*

[1] Ps. xxxvi. 6, 7.   [2] iv. ult.
[3] S. Mark xvi. 7.   [4] בְּכַפֵּיהֶם.
[5] Job xvi. 17, 1 Chr. xii. 17.
[6] Is. lix. 6.

27

Before
CHRIST
cir. 780.

[f] Is. 59. 6. one from his evil way, and from [f] the violence that is in their hands.

9 [s] Who can tell *if* God will turn and repent, and turn away from his fierce Before
CHRIST
cir. 780.

[s] 2 Sam. 12. 22.
Joel 2. 14.

work of wickedness is in their hands. Repentance and restitution clear the hands from the guilt of the violence: restitution, which gives back what was wronged; repentance, which, for love of God, hates and quits the sins, of which it repents. "Keep the winning, keep the sinning." The fruits of sin are temporal gain, eternal loss. We cannot keep the gain and escape the loss. Whoso keeps the gain of sin, loves it in its fruits, and will have them, all of them. The Hebrews had a saying, "[1] Whoso hath stolen a beam, and used it in building a great tower, must pull down the whole tower and restore the beam to its owner," i. e. restitution must be made at any cost. "He," they say [2], "who confesses a sin and does not restore the thing stolen, is like one who holds a reptile in his hands, who, if he were washed with all the water in the world, would never be purified, till he cast it out of his hands; when he has done this, the first sprinkling cleanses him."

9. *Who can tell* if *God will turn and repent?* The Ninevites use the same form of words, which God suggested by Joel to Judah. Perhaps He would thereby indicate that He had Himself put it into their mouths. "[3] In uncertainty they repented, and obtained certain mercy." "[4] It is therefore left uncertain, that men, being doubtful of their salvation, may repent the more vehemently and the more draw down on themselves the mercy of God." "[5] Most certain are the promises of God, whereby He has promised pardon to the penitent. And yet the sinner may well be uncertain whether he have obtained that penitence which makes him the object of those promises, not a servile repentance for fear of punishment, but true contrition out of the love of God." And so by this uncertainty, while, with the fear of hell, there is mingled the fear of the loss of God, the fear of that loss, which in itself involves some love, is, by His grace, turned into a contrite love, as the terrified soul thinks *Who* He is, Whom it had all but lost, Whom, it knows not whether it may not lose. In the case of the Ninevites, the remission of the temporal and eternal punishment was bound up in one, since the only punishment which God had threatened was temporal, and if this was forgiven, that forgiveness was a token that His displeasure had ceased.

"[6] They know not the issue, yet they neglect not repentance. They are unacquainted with the method of the loving-kindness of God, and they are changed amid uncertainty. They had no other Ninevites to look to, who had repented and been saved. They had not read the Prophets nor heard the Patriarchs, nor benefited by counsel, nor partaken of instruction, nor had they persuaded themselves that they should altogether propitiate God by repentance. For the threat did not contain this. But they doubted and hesitated about this, and yet repented with all carefulness. What account then shall we give, when these, who had no good hopes held out to them as to the issue, gave evidence of such a change, and thou, who mayest be of good cheer as to God's love for men, and hast many times received many pledges of His care, and hast heard the Prophets and Apostles, and hast been instructed by the events themselves, strivest not to attain the same measure of virtue as they? Great then was the virtue too of these men, but much greater the loving-kindness of God; and this you may see from the very greatness of the threat. For on this ground did He not add to the sentence, 'but if ye repent, I will spare,' that, casting among them the sentence unconditioned, He might increase the fear, and, increasing the fear, might impel them the more speedily to repentance." "[7] That fear was the parent of salvation; the threat removed the peril; the sentence of overthrow stayed the overthrow. New and marvelous issue! The sentence threatening death was the parent of life. Contrary to secular judgment, the sentence lost its force, when passed. In secular courts, the passing of the sentence gives it validity. Contrariwise with God, the pronouncing of the sentence made it invalid. For had it not been pronounced, the sinners had not heard it: had they not heard it, they would not have repented, would not have averted the chastisement, would not have enjoyed that marvelous deliverance. They fled not the city, as we do now [from the earthquake], but, remaining, established it. It was a snare, and they made it a wall; a quicksand and precipice, and they made it a tower of safety."

"[7] Was Nineveh destroyed? Quite the contrary. It arose and became more glorious, and all this intervening time has not effaced its glory, and we all yet celebrate it and marvel at it, that thenceforth it has become a most safe harbor to all who sin, not allowing them to sink into despair, but calling all to repentance, both by what it did and by what

[1] in Kimchi.　　　　　　[2] in Merc.
[3] S. Aug. in Ps. 50. L.　　[4] S. Jer.　　[5] in Lap.

[5] S. Chrys. on Statues, Hom. v. n. 6.
[7] Ib. n. 5.

anger, that we perish not?

10 ¶ [h] And God saw their works, that they

[h] Jer. 18. 8. Amos 7. 3, 6.

it gained from the Providence of God, persuading us never to despair of our salvation, but living the best we can, and setting before us a good hope, to be of good cheer that the end will anyhow be good." "[1] What *was* Nineveh? *They ate, they drank; they bought, they sold; they planted, they builded;* they gave themselves up to perjuries, lies, drunkenness, enormities, corruptions. This *was* Nineveh. Look at Nineveh now. They mourn, they grieve, are saddened, in sackcloth and ashes, in fastings and prayers. Where is that Nineveh? It is overthrown."

10. *And God saw their works.* "[2] He did not then first see them; He did not then first see their sackcloth when they covered themselves with it. He had seen them long before He sent the Prophet thither, while Israel was slaying the prophets who announced to them the captivity which hung over them. He knew certainly, that if He were to send the prophets far off to the Gentiles with such an announcement, they would hear and repent." God saw them, looked upon them, approved them, accepted the Ninevites not for time only, but, as many as persevered, for eternity. It was no common repentance. It was the penitence, which our Lord sets forth as *the* pattern of true repentance before His Coming. [3] *The men of Nineveh shall rise in judgment with this generation and shall condemn it, because they repented at the preaching of Jonah, and behold a greater than Jonah is here.* They believed in the One God, before unknown to them; they humbled themselves; they were not ashamed to repent publicly; they used great strictness with themselves; but, what Scripture chiefly dwells upon, their repentance was not only in profession, in belief, in outward act, but in the fruit of genuine works of repentance, a changed life out of a changed heart. *God saw their works, that they turned from their evil way.* Their whole way and course of life was evil; they broke off, not the one or other sin only, but all *their* whole *evil way.* "[4] The Ninevites, when about to perish, appoint them a fast; in their bodies they chasten their souls with the scourge of humility; they put on haircloth for raiment; for ointment they sprinkle themselves with ashes; and, prostrate on the ground, they lick the dust.—They publish their guilt with groans and lay open their secret misdeeds. Every age and sex alike applies itself to offices of mourning; all ornament was laid aside; food was refused to

the suckling, and the age, as yet unstained by sins of its own, bare the weight of those of others; the dumb animals lacked their own food. One cry of unlike natures was heard along the city-walls; along all the houses echoed the piteous lament of the mourners; the earth bore the groans of the penitents; heaven itself echoed with their voice. That was fulfilled; [5] *The prayer of the humble pierceth the clouds.*" "[6] The Ninevites were converted to the fear of God, and laying aside the evil of their former life, betook themselves through repentance to virtue and righteousness, with a course of penitence so faithful, that they changed the sentence already pronounced on them by God." "[7] As soon as prayer took possession of them, it both made them righteous, and forthwith corrected the city which had been habituated to live with profligacy and wickedness and lawlessness. More powerful was prayer than the long usage of sin. It filled that city with heavenly laws, and brought along with it temperance, loving kindness, gentleness and care of the poor. For without these it cannot abide to dwell in the soul. Had any then entered Nineveh, who knew it well before, he would not have known the city; so suddenly had it sprung back from life most foul to godliness."

And God repented of the evil. This was no real change in God; rather, the object of His threatening was, that He might not do what He threatened. God's threatenings are conditional, "unless they repent," as are His promises, "if they *endure to the end*[8]." God said afterward by Jeremiah[9], At what *instant I shall speak concerning a nation and concerning a kingdom, to pluck up and to pull down and to destroy* it, *if that nation, against whom I had pronounced, turn from their evil, I will repent of the evil that I thought to do unto them.* "[10] As God is unchangeable in nature, so is He unchangeable in Will. For no one can turn back His thoughts. For though some seem to have turned back His thoughts by their deprecations, yet this was His inward thought, that they should be able by their deprecations to turn back His sentence, and that they should receive from Him whereby to avail with Him.—When then outwardly His sentence seemeth to be changed, inwardly His counsel is unchanged, because He inwardly ordereth each thing unchangeably, whatsoever is done outwardly with change." "[11] It is said that He *repented,* because He

[1] S. Aug. Serm. 361. de res. n. 20.   [2] Rup.
[3] S. Matt. xii. 41.
[4] S. Amb. de Pœnit. c. 6. L.   [5] Ecclus. xxxv. 17.
[6] S. Chrys. Hom. quod nemo læditur nisi a seipso.

[7] de precat. i. inter dub. S. Chrys. T. ii. 781.
[8] S. Matt. x. 22.   [9] xviii. 7, 8.
[10] S. Greg. Mor. xvi. n. 46.
[11] S. Aug. in Ps. cv. n. 35.

turned from their evil way; and God repented of the evil, that he had said
that he would do unto them; and he did *it* not.

changed that which He seemed about to do, to destroy them. In God all things are disposed and fixed, nor doth He anything out of any sudden counsel, which He knew not in all eternity that He should do; but, amid the movements of His creature in time, which He governeth marvelously, He, not moved in time, as by a sudden will, is said to do what He disposed by well-ordered causes in the immutability of His most secret counsel whereby things which come to knowledge, each in its time, He both doth when they are present, and already did when they were future." "[1] God is subject to no dolor of repentance, nor is He deceived in anything, so as to wish to correct wherein He erred. But as man, when he repenteth willeth to change what he has done, so when thou hearest that God repenteth, look for the change. God, although He calleth it 'repenting,' doth it otherwise than thou. Thou doest it, because thou hast erred; He, because He avengeth or freeth. He changed the kingdom of Saul when He *repented*. And in the very place, where Scripture saith, *He repenteth*, it is said a little after, *He is not a man that He should repent.* When then He changes His works through His unchangeable counsels, He is said to repent, on account of the change, not of the counsel, but of the act." S. Augustine thinks that God, by using this language of Himself, which all would feel to be inadequate to His Majesty, meant to teach us that all language is inadequate to His Excellences. "[2] We say these things of God, because we do not find anything better to say. I say, 'God is just,' because in man's words I find nothing better; for He is beyond justice. It is said in Scripture, *God is just and loveth justice*. But in Scripture it is said, that *God repenteth,* 'God is ignorant.' Who would not start back at this? Yet to that end Scripture condescendeth healthfully to those words from which thou shrinkest, that thou shouldest not think that what thou deemest great is said worthily of Him. If thou ask, 'what then is said worthily of God?' one may perhaps answer, that 'He is just.' Another more gifted would say, that this word too is surpassed by His Excellence, and that this too is said, not worthily of Him, although suitably according to man's capacity: so that, when he would prove out of Scripture that it is written, *God is just,* he may be answered rightly, that the same Scriptures say that *God repenteth;* so, that, as

he does not take that in its ordinary meaning, as men are wont to repent, so also when He is said to be just, this does not correspond to His supereminence, although Scripture said this also well, that, through these words such as they are, we may be brought to that which is unutterable." "Why predictest Thou," asks S. Chrysostom[3], "the terrible things which Thou art about to do? That I may not do what I predict. Wherefore also He threatened hell, that He may not bring to hell. Let words terrify you that ye may be freed from the anguish of deeds." "[4] Men threaten punishment and inflict it. Not so God; but contrariwise, He both predicts and delays, and terrifies with words, and leaves nothing undone, that He may not bring what He threatens. So He did with the Ninevites. He bends His bow, and brandishes His sword, and prepares His spear, and inflicts not the blow. Were not the Prophet's words bow and spear and sharp sword, when he said, *yet forty days and Nineveh shall be destroyed?* But He discharged not the shaft; for it was prepared, not to be shot, but to be laid up."

"[5] When we read in the Scriptures or hear in Churches the word of God, what do we hear but Christ? *And behold a greater than Jonas is here.* If they repented at the cry of one unknown servant, of what punishment shall not we be worthy, if, when the Lord preacheth, Whom we have known through so many benefits heaped upon us, we repent not? To them one day sufficed; to us shall so many months and years not suffice? To them the overthrow of the city was preached, and 40 days were granted for repentance: to us eternal torments are threatened, and we have not half an hour's life certain."

And He did it *not.* God willed rather that His prophecy should seem to fail, than that repentance should fail of its fruit. But it did not indeed fail, for the condition lay expressed in the threat. "Prophecy," says Aquinas[6] in reference to these cases, "cannot contain anything untrue." For "prophecy is a certain knowledge impressed on the understanding of the Prophets by revelation of God, by means of certain teaching. But truth of knowledge is the same in the Teacher and the taught, because the knowledge of the learner is a likeness of the knowledge of the Teacher. And in this way, Jerome saith that 'prophecy is a sort of sign of Divine foreknowledge.' The truth then of

---

[1] S Aug. in Ps. cxxxi. n. 18.
[2] Id. Serm. 341. n. 9.

[3] De pœnit. Hom. v. n. 2. T. ii. p. 311 L.
[4] Id. in Ps. vii.   [5] Rib.   [6] 2. 2. q. 171. art. 6.

CHAPTER IV.

1 *Jonah, repining at God's mercy,* 4 *is reproved by the type of a gourd.*

the prophetic knowledge and utterance must be the same as that of the Divine knowledge, in which there can be no error.—But although in the Divine Intellect, the two-fold knowledge [of things as they are in themselves, and as they are in their causes,] is always united, it is not always united in the prophetic revelation, because the impression made by the Agent is not always adequate to His power. Whence, sometimes, the prophetic revelation is a sort of impressed likeness of the Divine Foreknowledge, as it beholds the future contingent things in themselves, and these always take place as they are prophesied : as, *Behold, a virgin shall conceive.* But sometimes the prophetic revelation is an impressed likeness of Divine Foreknowledge, as it knows the order of causes to effects; and then at times the event is other than is foretold, and yet there is nothing untrue in the prophecy. For the meaning of the prophecy is, that the disposition of the inferior causes, whether in nature or in human acts, is such, that such an effect would follow" (as in regard to Hezekiah and Nineveh), "[1] which order of the cause to the effect is sometimes hindered by other things supervening." "The Will of God," he says again [2], "being the first, universal Cause, does not exclude intermediate causes, by virtue of which certain effects are produced. And since all intermediate causes are not adequate to the power of the First Cause, there are many things in the Power, Knowledge, and Will of God, which are not contained in the order of the inferior causes, as the resurrection of Lazarus. Whence one, looking to the inferior causes, might say, ' Lazarus will not rise again : ' whereas, looking to the First Divine Cause, he could say, ' Lazarus will rise again.' And each of these God willeth, viz. that a thing should take place according to the inferior cause : which shall not take place, according to the superior cause, and conversely. So that God sometimes pronounces that a thing shall be, as far as it is contained in the order of inferior causes (as according to the disposition of nature or deserts), which yet doth not take place, because it is otherwise in the superior Divine cause. As when He foretold Hezekiah, [3] *Set thy house in order, for thou shalt die and not live ;* which yet did not take place, because from eternity it was otherwise in the Knowledge and Will of God which is unchangeable. Whence Gregory saith [4], ' though God changeth the

thing, His counsel He doth not change.' When then He saith, *I will repent* [5], it is understood as said metaphorically; for men, when they fulfil not what they threatened, seem to repent."

IV. 1. *And Jonah was displeased exceedingly.* It was an untempered zeal. The Prophet himself records it as such, and how he was reproved for it. He would, like many of us, govern God's world better than God Himself. Short-sighted and presumptuous! Yet not more short-sighted than those who, in fact, quarrel with God's Providence, the existence of evil, the baffling of good, " the prison-walls of obstacles and trials," in what we would do for God's glory. What is all discontent, but anger with God ? The marvel is that the rebel was a prophet! " [6] What he desired was not unjust in itself, that the Ninevites should be punished for their past sins, and that the sentence of God pronounced against them should not be recalled, although they repented. For so the judge hangs the robber for theft, however he repent." He sinned, in that he disputed with God. Let *him* cast the first stone, who never rejoiced at any overthrow of the enemies of his country, nor was glad, in a common warfare, that they lost as many soldiers as we. As if God had not instruments enough at His Will! Or as if He needed the Assyrians to punish Israel, or the one nation, whose armies are the terror of Europe, to punish us, so that if they should perish, Israel should therefore have escaped, though it persevered in sin, or we!

And he was very angry, or, it may be, *very grieved.* The word expresses also the emotion of burning grief, as when Samuel was grieved at the rejection of Saul, or David at *the breach upon Uzzah* [7]. Either way, he was displeased with what God did. Yet so Samuel and David took God's doings to heart; but Samuel and David were grieved at God's judgments ; Jonah, at what to the Ninevites was mercy, only in regard to his own people it seemed to involve judgment. Scripture says that he was displeased, because the Ninevites were spared ; but not, why this displeased him. It has been thought, that it was jealousy for God's glory among the heathen, as though the Ninevites would think that God in Whose Name he spake had no certain knowledge of things to come ; and so that his fault was mistrust in God's Wisdom or Power to vindicate His own honor.

B. UT it displeased Jonah exceedingly, and he was very angry.

---

[1] 2. 2. q. 174. art. 1.   [2] P. q. 19. art. 7. concl.
[3] Is. xxxviii. 1.   [4] Mor. xx. 32. n. 63.

[5] Jer. xviii. 8.   [6] Lap.
[7] 2 Sam. vi. 8, 1 Chr. xiii. 11.

Before
CHRIST
cir. 780.

2 And he prayed unto the LORD, and said, I pray thee, O LORD, *was* not this my saying, when I was yet in my country? Therefore I ^afled before unto Tarshish: for I knew that thou *art* a ^bgracious God, and merciful, slow to anger, and

ᵃ ch. 1. 3.

ᵇ Ex. 34. 6.
Ps. 86. 5.
Joel 2. 13.

of great kindness, and repentest thee of the evil.

3 ^cTherefore now, O LORD, take, I beseech thee, my life from me; for ^d*it is* better for me to die than to live.

4 ¶ Then said the Lord, || Doest thou well to be angry?

Before
CHRIST
cir. 780.

ᶜ 1 Kings 19. 4.

ᵈ ver. 8.

|| Or, *Art thou greatly angry ?*

But it seems more likely, that it was a mistaken patriotism, which idolized the wellbeing of his own and God's people, and desired that its enemy, the appointed instrument of its chastisement, should be itself destroyed. Scripture being silent about it, we cannot know certainly. Jonah, under God's inspiration, relates that God pronounced him wrong. Having incurred God's reproof, he was careless about men's judgment, and left his own character open to the harsh judgments of men; teaching us a holy indifference to man's opinion, and, in our ignorance, carefulness not to judge unkindly.

2. *And he prayed unto the Lord.* Jonah, at least, did not murmur or complain of God. He complained to God of Himself. He expostulates with Him. Shortsighted indeed and too wedded to his own will! Yet his will was the well-being of the people whose Prophet God had made him. He tells God, that this it was, which he had all along dreaded. He softens it, as well as he can, by his word, *I pray Thee,* which expresses deprecation and submissiveness. Still he does not hesitate to tell God that this was the cause of his first rebellion! Perilous to the soul, to speak without penitence of former sin; yet it is to God that he speaks, and so God, in His wonderful condescension, makes him teach himself.

I knew that Thou art *a gracious God.* He repeats to God to the letter His own words by Joel [1]. God had so revealed Himself anew to Judah. He had, doubtless, on some repentance which Judah had shewn, turned away the evil from them. And now by sending him as a preacher of repentance, He implied that He would do the same to the enemies of his country. God confirms this by the whole sequel. Thenceforth then Israel knew, that to the heathen also God was intensely, infinitely full of gracious and yearning love [2], nay (as the form rather implies [3]) mastered (so to speak) by the might

and intensity of His gracious love, *slow to anger* and delaying it, *great in loving-tenderness,* and abounding in it; and that toward them also, when the evil is about to be inflicted, or has been partially or wholly inflicted, He will repent of it and replace it with good, on the first turning of the soul or the nation to God.

3. *Therefore now, O Lord, take I beseech Thee my life from me.* He had rather die, than see the evil which was to come upon his country. Impatient though he was, he still cast himself upon God. By asking of God to end his life, he, at least, committed himself to the sovereign disposal of God. "[4] Seeing that the Gentiles are, in a manner, entering in, and that those words are being fulfilled, [5] *They have moved Me to jealousy with* that which is *not God, and I will move them to jealousy with* those which are *not a people, I will provoke them to anger with a foolish nation,* he despairs of the salvation of Israel, and is convulsed with great sorrow, which bursts out into words and sets forth the causes of grief, saying in a manner, ' Am I alone chosen out of so many prophets, to announce destruction to my people through the salvation of others?' He grieved not, as some think, that the multitude of nations is saved, but that Israel perishes. Whence our Lord also wept over Jerusalem. The Apostles first preached to Israel. Paul wishes to become an anathema for his [6] *brethren who are Israelites, whose is the adoption and the glory and the covenant, and the giving of the law and the service of God, and the promises, whose are the fathers, and of whom, as concerning the flesh, Christ came.*" Jonah had discharged his office faithfully now. He had done what God commanded; God had done by him what He willed. Now, then, he prayed to be discharged. So S. Augustine in his last illness prayed that he might die, before the Vandals brought suffering and devastation on his country [7].

4. *And the Lord said, Doest thou well [8] to be angry?* God, being appealed to, answers the

¹ ii. 13.
² רחום חנון, both intensives. See on Joel ii. 13.
³ In that both words, רחום ,חנון, although adjectives, partake of the passive form.

⁴ S. Jer.   ⁵ Deut. xxxii. 21.   ⁶ Rom. ix. 3-5.
⁷ Posid. vit. S. Aug.
⁸ היטיב, *do well,* is used almost adverbially of "*doing* a thing very perfectly," and by a deep irony in one place of doing evil very perfectly (see bel.

Before
CHRIST
cir. 780.
5 So Jonah went out of the city, and sat on the east side of the city, and there made him a booth, and sat under it in the shadow, till he might see what would become of the city.

6 And the Lord God prepared a || † gourd, and made *it* to come up over Jonah, that it might be a shadow over his head, to deliver him from his grief. So Jonah † was exceeding glad of the gourd.

Before
CHRIST
cir. 780.

|| Or, *palmchrist.*
† Heb. *Kikajon.*

† Heb. *rejoiced with great joy.*

---

appeal. So does He often in prayer, by some secret voice, answer the enquirer. There is right anger against the sin. Moses' anger was right, when he broke the tables[1]. God secretly suggests to Jonah that *his* anger was not right, as our Lord instructed [2] S. James and S. John that *theirs* was not. The question relates to the quality, not to the greatness of his anger. It was not the vehemence of his passionate desire for Israel, which God reproves, but that it was turned *against* the Ninevites. "[3] What the Lord says to Jonah, he says to all, who in their office of the cure of souls are angry. They must, as to this same anger, be recalled into themselves, to regard the cause or object of their anger, and weigh warily and attentively whether they *do well to be angry.* For if they are angry, not with men but with the sins of men, if they hate and persecute, not men, but the vices of men, they are rightly angry, their zeal is good. But if they are angry, not with sins but with men, if they hate, not vices but men, they are angered amiss, their zeal is bad. This then which was said to one, is to be watchfully looked to and decided by all, *Doest thou well to be angry ?* "

5. *So Jonah went out of the city*[4]. The form of the words implies (as in the Eng. V.), that this took place after Jonah was convinced that God would spare Nineveh; and since there is no intimation that he knew it by revelation, then it was probably after the 40 days. "[5] The days being now past, after which it was time that the things foretold should be accomplished, and His anger as yet taking no effect, Jonah understood that God had pity on Nineveh. Still he does not give up all hope, and thinks that a respite of the evil has been granted them on their willingness to repent, but that some effect of His displeasure would come, since the pains of their repentance had not equalled their offences. So thinking in himself apparently, he departs from the city, and waits to see what will become of them." "He expected" apparently "that it

would either fall by an earthquake, or be burned with fire, life Sodom." "[6] Jonah, in that he built him a tabernale and sat over against Nineveh, awaiting what should happen to it, wore a different, foresignifying character. For he prefigured the carnal people of Israel. For these too were sad at the salvation of the Ninevites, i. e. the redemption and deliverance of the Gentiles. Whence Christ came to call, not the righteous but sinners to repentance. But the overshadowing gourd over his head was the promises of the Old Testament or those offices in which, as the Apostle says, there was *a shadow of good things to come,* protecting them in the land of promise from temporal evils ; —all which are now emptied and faded. And now that people, having lost the temple at Jerusalem and the priesthood and sacrifice (all which was a shadow of that which was to come) in its captive dispersion, is scorched by a vehement heat of tribulation, as Jonah by the heat of the sun, and grieves greatly ; and yet the salvation of the heathen and the penitent is accounted of more moment than its grief, and the shadow which it loved."

6. *And the Lord God prepared a gourd,* [*a palmchrist,* E. M. rightly.] "[7] God again commanded the gourd, as he did the whale, willing only that this should be. Forthwith it springs up beautiful and full of flower, and straightway was a roof to the whole booth, and anoints him so to speak with joy, with its deep shade. The Prophet rejoices at it exceedingly, as being a great and thankworthy thing. See now herein too the simplicity of his mind. For he was grieved exceedingly, because what he had prophesied came not to pass ; he rejoiced exceedingly for a plant. A blameless mind is lightly moved to gladness or sorrow. You will see this in children.—For as people who are not strong, easily fall, if some one gives them no very strong push, but touches them as it were with a lighter hand, so too the guileless mind is easily carried away by anything which delights or grieves it." Little as the

---

[1] Ex. xxxii. 19.   [2] S. Luke ix. 55.   [3] Rup.
[4] Some render, contrary to grammar, "And Jonah had gone, &c."
[5] S. Cyr.
[6] S. Aug. Ep. 102. q. 6. n. 35.   [7] S. Cyr.

Mic. vii. 3), but it is nowhere used, of a passion or quality *existing* (passively) in a strong degree. The E. V. then is right. The E. M. *art thou greatly angry?* (the rendering of the LXX) is against the language.

7 But God prepared a worm when the morning rose the next day, and it smote the gourd that it withered.

8 And it came to pass, when the sun did arise, that God prepared a ‖ vehement east wind; and the sun beat upon the head of Jonah, that he fainted, and wished in himself to die, and said, ᵉ *It is* better for me to die than to live.

‖ Or, *silent.*

ᵉ ver. 3.

---

shelter of the palm-christ was in itself, Jonah must have looked upon its sudden growth, as a fruit of God's goodness toward him, (as it was) and then perhaps went on to think (as people do) that this favor of God shewed that He meant, in the end, to grant him what his heart was set upon. Those of impulsive temperaments are ever interpreting the acts of God's Providence, as bearing on what they strongly desire. Or again, they argue, ' God throws this or that in our way; therefore He means us not to relinquish it for His sake, but to have it.' By this sudden miraculous shelter against the burning Assyrian sun, which God provided for Jonah, He favored his waiting on there. So Jonah may have thought, interpreting rightly that God willed him to stay; wrongly, why He so willed. Jonah was to wait, not to see what he desired, but to receive, and be the channel of the instruction which God meant to convey to him and through him.

7. *When the morning rose,* i. e. in the earliest dawn, before the actual sunrise. For one day Jonah enjoyed the refreshment of the palm-christ. In early dawn, it still promised the shadow; just ere it was most needed, at God's command, it withered.

8. *God prepared a vehement*[1] [E. M. following the Chaldee, *silent,* i. e. sultry] *East wind.* The winds in the East, blowing over the sand-deserts, intensely increase the distress of the heat. A sojourner describes on two occasions an Assyrian summer. "[2] The change to summer had been as rapid as that which ushered in the spring. The verdure of the plain had perished almost in a day. Hot winds, coming from the desert, had burnt up and carried away the shrubs.—The heat was now almost intolerable. Violent whirlwinds occasionally swept over the face of the country." "[3] The spring was now fast passing away; the heat became daily greater; the corn was cut; and the plains and hills put on their summer-clothing of dull parched yellow. *The pasture is withered, the herbage faileth; the green grass is not.* It was the season too of the Sherghis, or burning winds from the South, which occasionally swept over the face of the country, driving in their short-lived fury everything before them.—We all went below [ground] soon after the sun had risen, and remained there [in the tunnels] without again seeking the open air until it was far down in the Western horizon." The "Sherghi" must be rather the East-wind, Sherki, whence Sirocco. At Sulimania in Koordistan (about 2⅓ degrees E. of Nineveh, and ¾ of a degree South)"[4] the so much dreaded Sherki seems to blow from any quarter, from E. to N. E.—It is greatly feared for its violence and relaxing qualities," "[5] hot, stormy and singularly relaxing and dispiriting." Suffocating heat is a characteristic of these vehement winds. Morier relates at Bushire; "[6] A gale of wind blew from the Southward

---

[1] The root חָרַשׁ signifying to *cut,* then to *cut into,* "plough," then, passive, to be *cut off* from hearing or intercourse, "deaf," "dumb," (as in the Arab. and κωφὸς from κόπτω) and thence " silent," (as we speak of one voluntarily "dumb," i. e. silent), the meaning *silent* has been derived from this last sense; that of *vehement* comes either directly from the root, (as we speak of a "cutting" wind, although our cutting winds are cold), or from "deafening" (Kim.), as we speak of "a deafening noise," and as strong winds do hinder hearing; or, as matter of fact, from the strong dry winds in Autumn, in which way חָרִישׁ is derived directly from חָרַשׁ *earing* (i. e. ploughing) *time,* Ex. xxxiv. 21. The English Version "vehement," lies more in the direct meaning of the root, than "silent," and agrees with the description, although not what one, unacquainted with Eastern nature, would expect. Next to this, the harvest or autumn wind seems perhaps the most probable.

[2] Layard, Nineveh, (1846) c. 5. i. 123.
[3] Nin. and Bab. [1850] pp. 364, 5.
[4] Rich's Koordistan, i. 125, add 133. " Just as the moon rose about 10, an intolerable puff of wind came from the N. E. All were immediately silent

as if they had felt an earthquake, and then exclaimed in a dismal tone, 'the Sherki is come.' This was indeed the so much dreaded Sherki, and it has continued blowing ever since with great violence from the E. and N E. the wind being heated like our Bagdad Saum, but I think softer and more relaxing. This wind is the terror of these parts." Ib. 165. " The extraordinary prevalence of the Sherki or Easterly wind this year, renders this season intolerably hot and relaxing. They had not had 3 days together free from this wind since the beginning of the summer." Ib. 271. " In the summer the climate is pleasant, except when the Easterly wind blows, which it does with prodigious violence sometimes for 8 or 10 days successively. The wind is hot and relaxing in summer, and what is very curious, is it not felt at the distance of 2 or 3 hours." Ib. 113. "This is asserted by every one in the country." Ib. 125.
[5] Ib. ii. 35.

[6] 2d journey, p. 43. He continues, " Again from the 23d to the 25th, the wind blew violently from the S. E. accompanied by a most suffocating heat, and continued to blow with the same strength until the next day at noon, when it suddenly veered

9 And God said to Jonah, ‖ Doest thou well to be angry for the gourd?

And he said, ‖ I do well to be angry, *even* unto death.

and Eastward with such violence, that three of our largest tents were leveled with the ground. The wind brought with it such hot currents of air, that we thought it might be the precursor of the *Samoun* described by Chardin, but upon enquiry, we found that the autumn was generally the season for that wind. The *Sam* wind commits great ravages in this district. It blows at night from about midnight to suurise, comes in a hot blast, and is afterward succeeded by a cold one. About 6 years ago, there was a *sam* during the summer months which so totally burnt up all the corn, then near its maturity, that no animal would eat a blade of it, nor touch any of its grain."

The sun beat upon the head of Jonah. "[1] Few European travelers can brave the perpendicular rays of an Assyrian sun. Even the well-seasoned Arab seeks the shade during the day, and journeys by night, unless driven forth at noontide by necessity, or the love of war."

He wished in himself to die. [lit. *he asked as to his soul, to die*]. He prayed for death. It was still the same dependence upon God, even in his self-will. He did not murmur, but prayed God to end his life here. When men are already vexed in soul by deep inward griefs, a little thing often oversets patience. Jonah's hopes had been revived by the mercy of the palmchrist; they perished with it. Perhaps he had before him the thought of his great predecessor, Elijah, how he too wished to die, when it seemed that his mission was fruitless. They differed in love. Elijah's preaching, miracles, toil, sufferings, seemed to him, not only to be in vain, but (as they must, if in vain), to add to the guilt of his people. God corrected him too, by showing him his own short-sightedness, that he knew not of *the seven thousand who had not bowed their knees unto Baal,* who were, in part, doubtless, *the travail of his soul.* Jonah's mission to his people seemed also to be fruit-

less; his hopes for their well-being were at an end; the temporal mercies of which he had been the Prophet, were exhausted; Nineveh was spared; his last hope was gone; the future scourge of his people was maintained in might. The soul shrinks into itself at the sight of the impending visitation of its country. But Elijah's zeal was *for* his people only and the glory of God in it, and so it was pure love. Jonah's was directed *against* the Ninevites, and so had to be purified.

9. *Doest thou well to be angry?* "[2] See again how Almighty God, out of His boundless loving-kindness, with the yearning tenderness of a father, almost disporteth with the guileless souls of the saints! The palmchrist shades him: the Prophet rejoices in it exceedingly. Then, in God's Providence, the caterpillar attacks it, the burning East-wind smites it, shewing at the same time how very necessary the relief of its shade, that the Prophet might be the more grieved, when deprived of such a good.—He asketh him skillfully, was he very grieved? and that for a shrub? He confesseth, and this becometh the defence for God, the Lover of mankind."

I do well to be angry, unto death. "[3] Vehement anger leadeth men to long and love to die, especially if thwarted and unable to remove the hindrance which angers them. For then vehement anger begetteth vehement sorrow, grief, despondency." We have each, his own palmchrist; and our palmchrist has its own worm. "[4] In Jonah, who mourned when he had discharged his office, we see those who, in what they seem to do for God, either do not seek the glory of God, but some end of their own, or at least, think that glory to lie where it does not. For he who seeketh the glory of God, and not *his own* [5] things, but those of Jesus Christ, ought to will what God hath willed and done. If he wills aught else, he declares plainly that he sought himself, not God, or himself more

round to the N. W. with a violence equal to what it had blown from the opposite point." And again (p. 97) "When there was a perfect calm, partial and strong currents of air would arise and form whirlwinds,which produced high columns of sand all over the plain. They are looked upon as the sign of great heat. Their strength was very various. Frequently they threw down our tents." Burckhardt, when professedly lessening the general impression as to these winds, says, "The worst effect [of the Semoum "a violent S. E. wind"] is that it dries up the water in the skins, and so far endangers the traveler's safety.—In one morning ⅓ of the contents of a full water-skin was evaporated. I always observed the whole atmosphere appear as if in a state of combustion; the dust and sand are carried high into the air, which assumes a reddish

or blueish or yellowish tint, according to the nature and color of the ground, from which the dust arises. The Semoum is not always accompanied by whirlwinds: in its less violent degree it will blow for hours with little force, although with oppressive heat; when the whirlwind raises the dust, it then increases several degrees in heat. In the Semoum at Esne, the thermometer mounted to 121° in the shade, but the air seldom remains longer than a quarter of an hour in that state, or longer than the whirlwind lasts. The most disagreeable effect of the Semoum on man is, that it stops perspiration, dries up the palate, and produces great restlessness." Travels in Nubia, pp. 204, 5.
[1] Layard, Nin. and Bab 366.
[2] S. Cyr.
[3] Lap.
[4] Rib.
[5] Phil. ii. 21.

10 Then said the LORD, Thou hast || had pity on

|| Or, *spared.*

the gourd, for the which thou hast not labored, neither madest it grow;

which † came up in a night, and perished in a night:

11 And should not I spare Nineveh, ᶠthat great

† Heb. *was the son of the night.*

ᶠch. 1. 2. & 3. 2, 3.

than God.—Jonah sought the glory of God wherein it was not, in the fulfillment of a prophecy of woe. And choosing to be led by his own judgment, not by God's, whereas he ought to have joyed exceedingly, that so many thousands, being *dead, were alive again,* being *lost, were found,* he, when *there was joy in heaven among the angels of God over* so many repenting sinners, was *afflicted with a great affliction* and was angry. This ever befalls those who wish *that* to take place, not what is best and most pleasing to God, but what they think most useful to themselves. Whence we see our very great and common error, who think our peace and tranquillity to lie in the fulfillment of our own will, whereas this will and judgment of our own is the cause of all our trouble. So then Jonah prays and tacitly blames God, and would not so much excuse as approve that, his former flight, to *Him Whose eyes are too pure to behold iniquity.*— And since all inordinate affection is a punishment to itself, and he who departeth from the order of God hath no stability, he is in such anguish, because what he wills, will not be, that he longs to die. For it cannot but be that *his* life, who measures everything by his own will and mind, and who followeth not God as his Guide but rather willeth to be the guide of the Divine Will, should be from time to time troubled with great sorrow. But since *the merciful and gracious Lord* hath pity on our infirmity and gently admonisheth us within, when He sees us at variance with Him, He forsakes not Jonah in that hot grief, but lovingly blames him.— How restless such men are, we see from Jonah. The *palmchrist* grows over his head, and *he was exceeding glad of the palmchrist.* Any labor or discomfort they bear very ill, and being accustomed to endure nothing and follow their own will, they are tormented and cannot bear it, as Jonah did not the sun. If anything, however slight, happen to lighten their grief, they are immoderately glad. Soon gladdened, soon grieved, like children. They have not learned to bear anything moderately. What marvel then that their joy is soon turned into sorrow? They are joyed over a palmchrist, which soon greeneth, soon drieth, quickly falls to the ground and is trampled upon.—Such are the things of this world, which, while possessed, seem great and lasting; when suddenly lost, men see how vain and passing

¹ Rup.

they are, and that hope is to be placed, not in them but in their Creator, Who is Unchangeable. It is then a great dispensation of God toward us, when those things in which we took especial pleasure are taken away. Nothing can man have so pleasing, green, and, in appearance, so lasting, which has not its own worm prepared by God, whereby, in the dawn, it may be smitten and die. The change of human will or envy disturbs courtfavor; manifold accidents, wealth; the varying opinion of the people or of the great, honors; disease, danger, poverty, infamy, pleasure. Jonah's palmchrist had one worm; our's, many; if other were wanting, there is the restlessness of man's own thoughts, whose food is restlessness."

10. *Thou hadst pity on the palmchrist.* In the feeling of our common mortality, the soul cannot but yearn over decay. Even a drooping flower is sad to look on, so beautiful, so frail. It belongs to this passing world, where nothing lovely abides, all things beautiful hasten to cease to be. The natural God-implanted feeling is the germ of the spiritual.

11. *Should I not spare?* lit. *have pity* and so *spare.* God waives for the time the fact of the repentance of Nineveh, and speaks of those on whom man must have pity, those who never had any share in its guilt, the 120,000 children of Nineveh, "¹ who, in the weakness of infancy, knew not which hand, *the right* or *the left,* is the stronger and fitter for every use." He Who would have spared Sodom *for ten's sake,* might well be thought to spare Nineveh for the 120,000's sake, in whom the inborn corruption had not developed into the malice of wilful sin. If these 120,000 were the children under three years old, they were ⅕ (as is calculated) of the whole population of Nineveh. If of the 600,000 of Nineveh all were guilty, who by reason of age could be, above ⅕ were innocent of actual sin.

To Jonah, whose eye was evil to Nineveh for his people's sake, God says, as it were, "¹ Let the *spirit* which *is willing* say to the *flesh* which *is weak,* ' Thou grievest for the palmchrist, that is, thine own kindred, the Jewish people; and *shall not I spare Nineveh that great city,* shall not I provide for the salvation of the Gentiles in the whole world, who are in ignorance and error? For there are many thousands among the Gentiles, who go after ² *dumb idols even as they are led,* not out of

²1 Cor. xii. 2.

Before
CHRIST
cir. 780.

ᶠ Deut. 1. 39.

city, wherein are more than sixscore thousand persons ᵍ that cannot discern be-

tween their right hand and their left hand; and *also* much ʰ cattle?

Before
CHRIST
cir. 780.

ʰ Ps. 36. 6.
& 145. 9.

malice but out of ignorance, who would without doubt correct their ways, if they had the knowledge of the truth, if they were shewn the difference *between their right hand and their left*, i. e. between the truth of God and the lie of men.'" But, beyond the immediate teaching to Jonah, God lays down a principle of His dealings at all times, that, in His visitations of nations, He, [1] *the Father of the fatherless and judge of the widows*, takes especial account of those who are of no account in man's sight, and defers the impending judgment, not for the sake of the wisdom of the wise or the courage of the brave, but for the helpless, weak, and, as yet, innocent as to actual sin. How much more may we think that He regards those with pity who have on them not only the recent uneffaced traces of their Maker's Hands, but have been reborn in the Image of Christ His Only-Begotten Son! The infants clothed with Christ [2] must be a special treasure of the Church in the Eyes of God.

"[3] How much greater the mercy of God than that even of a holy man; how far better to flee to the judgment-seat of God than to the tribunal of man. Had Jonah been judge in the cause of the Ninevites, he would have passed on them all, although penitent, the sentence of death for their past guilt, because God had passed it before their repentance. So David said to God; [4] *Let us fall now into the hand of the Lord; for His mercies are great; and let me not fall into the hand of man.* Whence the Church professes to God, that mercy is the characteristic of His power; '[5] O God, who shewest Thy Almighty power most chiefly in shewing mercy and pity, mercifully grant unto us

[1] Ps. lxviii. 5.
[2] Gal. iii. 27.   [3] Lap.

such a measure of Thy grace, that we, running the way of Thy commandments, may obtain Thy gracious promises, and be made partakers of Thy heavenly treasure.'"

"Again, God here teaches Jonah and us all to conform ourselves in all things to the Divine Will, we should forthwith begin and continue it with alacrity and courage; when He bids us cease from it, or deprives it of its fruit and effect, we should forthwith tranquilly cease, and patiently allow our work and toil to lack its end and fruit. For what is our aim, save to do the Will of God, and in all things to confirm ourselves to it? But now the Will of God is, that thou shouldest resign, yea destroy, the work thou hast begun. Acquiesce then in it. Else thou servest not the Will of God, but thine own fancy and cupidity. And herein consists the perfection of the holy soul, that, in all acts and events, adverse or prosperous, it should with full resignation resign itself most humbly and entirely to God, and acquiesce, happen what will, yea, and rejoice that the Will of God is fulfilled in this thing, and say with holy Job, *The Lord gave, The Lord hath taken away; blessed be the Name of the Lord*—S. Ignatius had so transferred his own will into the Will of God, that he said, ' If perchance the society, which I have begun and furthered with such toil, should be dissolved or perish, after passing half an hour in prayer, I should, by God's help, have no trouble from this thing, than which none sadder could befall me.' The saints let themselves be turned this way and that, round and round, by the Will of God, as a horse by its rider."

[4] 2 Sam. xxiv. 14.
[5] Collect for the eleventh Sunday after Trinity.

END OF VOL. I.